West Sales Associates are ready to answer your questions and help you get additional copies fast.
1-800-328-9352

Handle trusts, wills and estates more quickly and accurately—while you increase your income and expand your practice!

Providing estate planning documents not only generates revenue, but also offers you a chance to provide a relationship-building service for existing and new clients.

Now, with disk products from *West's® Desktop Practice Systems®*, you can use the power of your personal computer to handle more trusts and wills—more efficiently and profitably!

CREATE THESE ESTATE PLANNING DOCUMENTS WITH PUSH-BUTTON EASE AND SPEED

- simple and complex wills
- living wills
- revocable and irrevocable trusts
- anatomical gifts
- codicils and trust amendments
- disclaimers
- powers of attorney
- and many more

CHOOSE DOCUMENT ASSEMBLY OR \FAST™ SOFTWARE.

ILLINOIS TRUSTS AND WILLS DOCUMENT ASSEMBLY

by Lawrence A. Jegen and William M. McGovern

Document assembly software makes it push-button easy to assemble each document, reducing typing time and errors. Just select the document and clauses you need, then fill in the blanks for a completed document. The information you enter automatically ripples through that document and any other documents you assemble for that client.

ILLINOIS TRUSTS AND WILLS PRACTICE FORMS\FAST™

by Lawrence A. Jegen and William M. McGovern

Create complete, accurate documents that comply with all applicable Illinois laws. Quickly word-search from among hundreds of model documents and clauses. Then, "cut and paste" selected material into your DOS or Windows™ word processor for final formatting.

CALL TODAY
1-800-328-9352.

West Publishing
More ways to win

© 1995 West Publishing   West. An American company serving the legal world.   5-9196-2/1-95   440987

COORDINATED RESEARCH IN ILLINOIS FROM WEST

Illinois Practice of Family Law
Muller Davis

ILLINOIS PRACTICE SERIES

Illinois Uniform Commercial Code Forms Annotated
William B. Davenport and Ray D. Henson

Illinois Civil Procedure Before Trial
Richard A. Michael

Illinois Criminal Practice and Procedure
Linda S. Pieczynski

JURY INSTRUCTIONS

Illinois Pattern Jury Instructions [IPI]—Criminal
Illinois Supreme Court Committee on Pattern Jury Instructions in Criminal Cases

Illinois Pattern Jury Instructions [IPI]—Civil
Illinois Supreme Court Committee on Pattern Jury Instructions in Civil Cases

WEST'S ILLINOIS FORMS
Ray E. Poplett

Civil Practice—Forms

Domestic Relations—Forms

Wills and Trusts—Forms

Probate and Administration of Estates—Forms

Real Estate Transactions—Forms

Debtor–Creditor Relations—Forms

West's Smith-Hurd Illinois Compiled Statutes Annotated

Illinois Compiled Statutes (State Bar Association Edition)

Illinois Code of Civil Procedure and Court Rules Pamphlet

COORDINATED RESEARCH FROM WEST

Illinois Criminal Law and Procedure Pamphlet

Illinois Insurance Laws Pamphlet

Illinois Family Law and Court Rules Pamphlet

Illinois Probate Act and Related Laws Pamphlet

Illinois Vehicle Code Pamphlet

Illinois Digest

Illinois Law Finder

Illinois Law and Practice

Illinois Decisions

West's Illinois Decisions

West CD–ROM Libraries™

WESTLAW®

WEST*Check*® and WESTMATE®

WIN®

WEST*fax*®

West Books, CD–ROM Libraries, Disk Products and WESTLAW
The Ultimate Research System

For more information about any of these Illinois practice resources, please call your West Representative or 1–800–328–9352.

February, 1995

ILLINOIS PRACTICE
OF FAMILY LAW

1995 Edition

By

MULLER DAVIS
of the Illinois Bar

ST. PAUL, MINN.
WEST PUBLISHING CO.
1995

COPYRIGHT © 1995

By

WEST PUBLISHING CO.

ISBN 0–314–05967–9

Library of Congress CAtalog Card Number: 95–060038

To all of the lawyers and judges with whom I have worked, but, most of all, to Benjamin B. Davis, primus, not primus inter pares.

*

INTRODUCTION

Representing a child who may or may not become a complete adult, a husband who is also a father, or a wife who is also a mother, is not a transaction of the marketplace. The family lawyer is held to a higher standard. His representation is a trusteeship. His mind is bent to fairness. He steadfastly advances the cause of his client while exercising care not to destroy the other participants. He works as a craftsman whose product governs fragile relationships for substantial periods of time. The lawyer's own concerns have no place until the case is completed. A family is at stake, and, projected from there, so is society.

*

ABOUT THE AUTHOR

Muller Davis has been practicing law in Illinois for 34 years and has specialized in family law for 27 of those years. Mr. Davis graduated with honors from Phillips Exeter Academy in 1953; he received a B.A. degree, Magna Cum Laude, from Yale University in 1957 and a J.D. degree from Harvard Law School in 1960. He appears in the Family Law Section of *Best Lawyers in America*, and in many other reference works. Upon release from the military in 1961, Mr. Davis joined the Chicago litigation firm of Jenner & Block as an associate. In 1967, he became a partner of the predecessor firm of Davis, Friedman, Zavett, Kane & MacRae, and has remained a partner of that firm since 1967. The firm has always specialized in family law. Mr. Davis is a Fellow of the American Academy of Matrimonial Lawyers and the American Bar Foundation, and is a member of many bar associations. From 1981 to 1982, he was chairman of the Civil Practice Committee of the Chicago Bar Associa-tion. Mr. Davis has spent almost his entire career handling and litigating important family law cases and has written and lectured extensively on family law matters.

*

PREFACE

The objective of The Illinois Practice of Family Law book is to provide a comprehensive one volume reference to all aspects of family law for lawyers and judges. The book draws together under one cover: substantive Illinois and Federal family law; Federal and State tax ramifications of family law transactions; applicable litigation procedural law from the Illinois Code of Civil Procedure and Supreme Court Rules; detailed explanatory Author's Notes; case law; and discovery, settlement, and litigation forms. A lawyer or judge can obtain from The Illinois Practice of Family Law book, for example, the discovery form with which to gather income information, the statutory and case law criteria for establishing maintenance, model maintenance agreement and judgment forms, the Federal and State tax law of maintenance, and a table to calculate the true net incomes of each party after the payment of maintenance. From the same book, the lawyer can use the cases and forms in the Author's Notes to the Illinois Marriage and Dissolution of Marriage Act and the Injunction Act to maintain the financial status quo, refer to the Illinois Domestic Violence Act for a remedy, and even consult The Hague Convention to recover an abducted child. The book is designed to be of assistance to the lawyer or judge specialist who knows the law but needs a quick case, form, statutory reference, or tax explanation, as well as to the lawyer who has only an occasional family law client, or maybe just an adoption, who requires information from start to finish. The purpose of the book is to be of use. Criticisms and suggestions, whether of omission or commission, will be gratefully accepted, and are hereby actively solicited, for consideration in subsequent editions.

*

ACKNOWLEDGMENTS

This book would not have been possible without the contributions made by the able persons here gratefully acknowledged.

Jody Yazici was the research assistant and an editor of the text for the entire book from its beginning. She well managed that large undertaking while also a student at Cornell Law School, a summer intern, and finally an associate of our law firm.

Muriel Kuhs, an associate of our law firm, was responsible for the Author's Notes for the Uniform Child Custody Jurisdiction Act, Adoption Act, Abused and Neglected Child Reporting Act, Section 506 of the Illinois Marriage and Dissolution of Marriage Act, and the Mental Health and Developmental Disabilities Confidentiality Act. She provided other on the spot invaluable help as well.

Susie Allen produced the complete book on her word processor, kept our style consistent, did not tire of draft after draft, and provided strength through organization. She was the wizard behind all of our efforts.

Karin Stein O'Boyle, our editor at West Publishing Company, not only edited the book and gave to us the benefit of her experience from similar books, but she also was a never flagging source of encouragement and support, even after we had missed many deadlines.

Others who willingly answered questions, made suggestions, or provided information where it was needed include: Roderick E. MacRae, Nathan M. Grossman, Marta Coblitz, Sharon M. Shapiro, George Sullivan, Norah M. Plante, Colleen Crean Wolfe, Jeffrey Garfinkel, Kay Zelkin, Megan Stark, and my partners and associates at Davis, Friedman, Zavett, Kane & MacRae in addition to those specifically mentioned.

My wife, Jane Davis, supported and encouraged me in this time consuming project, as she has in every other endeavor for the past 31 years.

To all of the above, and to others, your contributions are a major part of whatever merit this book may have.

*

NOTE

This book is for men and women lawyers and judges, and it is about family issues involving men and women. The text sometimes refers to "he" and sometimes to "she." Petitioners and Respondents may be male or female. The pronouns and the parties are meant to be interchangeable and at almost all times to represent either women or men.

*

WESTLAW® ELECTRONIC RESEARCH GUIDE

Coordinating Legal Research With WESTLAW

The *Illinois Practice of Family Law* book is an essential aid to legal research on Illinois Family Law. WESTLAW provides additional resources. This guide will assist your use of WESTLAW to supplement research begun in this publication.

Databases

A database is a collection of documents with some features in common. It may contain statutes, court decisions, administrative materials, commentaries, news or other information. Each database has a unique identifier, used in many WESTLAW commands to select a database of interest. For example, the database containing Illinois cases has the identifier IL-CS.

The WESTLAW Directory is a comprehensive list of databases with information about each database, including the types of documents each contains. The first page of a standard or customized WESTLAW Directory is displayed upon signing on to WESTLAW, except when prior, saved research is resumed. To access the WESTLAW Directory at any time, enter DB.

A special subdirectory, accessible from the main WESTLAW Directory, lists databases applicable to Family Law research.

Databases of potential interest in connection with your research include:

ILFL-CS	Illinois Family Law Cases
FFL-CS	Federal Cases - Family Law
FFL-USCA	U.S. Code Sections - Family Law
FL-TP	Law Reviews, Texts & Journals - Family Law
WLD-FAM	West's Legal Directory - Family
FAM-RES	Family Resources (DIALOG)

For information as to currentness and search tips regarding any WESTLAW database, enter the SCOPE command SC followed by the database identifier (e.g., SC IL-CS). It is not necessary to include the identifier to obtain scope information about the currently selected database.

WESTLAW Highlights

Use of this publication may be supplemented through the WESTLAW Bulletin (WLB), the WESTLAW Illinois State Bulletin (WSB-IL) and various Topical Highlights, including Family Law Highlights (WTH-FL). Highlights databases contain summaries of significant judicial, legislative and administrative developments and are updated daily; they are searchable both from an automatic list of recent documents and using general WESTLAW search methods for documents accumulated over time. The full text of any judicial decision may be retrieved by entering FIND.

WESTLAW ELECTRONIC RESEARCH GUIDE

Consult the WESTLAW Directory (enter DB) for a complete, current listing of highlights databases.

Retrieving a Specific Case

The FIND command can be used to quickly retrieve a case whose citation is known. For example:

FI 620 N.E.2d 1368

Updating Caselaw Research

There are a variety of citator services on WESTLAW for use in updating research.

Insta-Cite® may be used to verify citations, find parallel citations, ascertain the history of a case, and see whether it remains valid law. References are also provided to secondary sources, such as Corpus Juris Secundum®, that cite the case. To view the Insta-Cite history of a displayed case, simply enter the command IC. To view the Insta-Cite history of a selected case, enter a command in this form:

IC 618 N.E.2d 566

Shepard's® Citations provides a comprehensive list of cases and publications that have cited a particular case, with explanatory analysis to indicate how the citing cases have treated the case, e.g., "followed," "explained." To view the Shepard's Citations about a displayed case, enter the command SH. Add a case citation, if necessary, as in the prior Insta-Cite example.

For the latest citing references, not yet incorporated in Shepard's Citations, use Shepard's PreView® (SP command) and QuickCite™ (QC command), in the same way.

To see a complete list of publications covered by any of the citator services, enter its service abbreviation (IC, SH, SP or QC) followed by PUBS. To ascertain the scope of coverage for any of the services, enter the SCOPE command (SC) followed by the appropriate service abbreviation. For the complete list of commands available in a citator service, enter its service abbreviation (IC, SH, SP or QC) followed by CMDS.

Retrieving Statutes, Court Rules and Regulations

Annotated and unannotated versions of the Illinois statutes are searchable on WESTLAW (identifiers IL-ST-ANN and IL-ST), as are Illinois court rules (IL-RULES).

The United States Code and United States Code - Annotated are searchable databases on WESTLAW (identifiers USC and USCA, respectively), as are federal court rules (US-RULES) and regulations (CFR).

In addition, the FIND command may be used to retrieve specific provisions by citation, obviating the need for database selection or search. To FIND

WESTLAW ELECTRONIC RESEARCH GUIDE

a desired document, enter FI, followed by the citation of the desired document, using the full name of the publication, or one of the abbreviated styles recognized by WESTLAW.

If WESTLAW does not recognize the style you enter, you may enter one of the following, using US, IL, or any other state code in place of XX:

FI XX-ST	Displays templates for codified statutes
FI XX-LEGIS	Displays templates for legislation
FI XX-RULES	Displays templates for rules
FI XX-ORDERS	Displays templates for court orders

Alternatively, entering FI followed by the publication's full name or an accepted abbreviation will normally display templates, useful jump possibilities, or helpful information necessary to complete the FIND process. For example:

FI USCA	Displays templates for United States Code - Annotated
FI FRAP	Displays templates for Federal Rules of Appellate Procedure
FI FRCP	Displays templates for Federal Rules of Civil Procedure
FI FRCRP	Displays templates for Federal Rules of Criminal Procedure
FI FRE	Displays templates for Federal Rules of Evidence
FI CFR	Displays templates for Code of Federal Regulations
FI FR	Displays templates for Federal Register

To view the complete list of FINDable documents and associated prescribed forms, enter FI PUBS.

Updating Research in re Statutes, Rules and Regulations

When viewing a statute, rule or regulation on WESTLAW after a search or FIND command, it is easy to update your research. A message will appear on the screen if relevant amendments, repeals or other new material are available through the UPDATE feature. Entering the UPDATE command will display such material.

Documents used to update Illinois statutes are also searchable in Illinois Legislative Service (IL-LEGIS). Those used to update rules are searchable in Illinois Orders (IL-ORDERS).

Documents used to update federal statutes, rules, and regulations are searchable in the United States Public Laws (US-PL), Federal Orders (US-ORDERS) and Federal Register (FR) databases, respectively.

When documents citing a statute, rule or regulation are of interest, Shepard's Citations on WESTLAW may be of assistance. That service covers federal constitutional provisions, statutes and administrative provisions, and corresponding materials from many states. The command SH PUBS displays a directory of publications which may be Shepardized on WESTLAW. Consult the WESTLAW manual for more information about citator services.

A citation to Illinois Revised Statutes of 1991 or Smith-Hurd Illinois Annotated Statutes may be converted to corresponding citations to Illinois Compiled Statutes or West's Smith-Hurd Illinois Compiled Statutes Annotated, by consulting the tables volume in West's Smith-Hurd Illinois Compiled Statutes Annotated. Alternatively, sign on to the IL-ST or IL-ST-ANN database, and search for the former citation in the Credit (CR) field. The following query, for example, will retrieve S.H.A. 705 ILCS 50/2, the current section corresponding to Ill.Rev.Stat.1991, Ch. 37, P. 902:

CR(Formerly /s 37 +7 902)

Using WESTLAW as a Citator

For research beyond the coverage of any citator service, go directly to the databases (cases, for example) containing citing documents and use standard WESTLAW search techniques to retrieve documents citing specific constitutional provisions, statutes, standard jury instructions or other authorities.

Fortunately, the specific portion of a citation is often reasonably distinctive, such as 22:636.1, 301.65, 401(k), 12-21-5, 12052. When it is, a search on that specific portion alone may retrieve applicable documents without any substantial number of inapplicable ones (unless the number happens to be coincidentally popular in another context). Illinois statutes fall into this category.

Similarly, if the citation involves more than one number, such as 42 U.S.C.A. 1201, a search containing both numbers (e.g., 42 +5 1201) is likely to produce mostly desired information, even though the component numbers are common.

If necessary, the search may be limited in several ways:

A. Switch from a general database to one containing mostly cases within the subject area of the cite being researched;

B. Use a connector (&, /S, /P, etc.) to narrow the search to documents including terms which are highly likely to accompany the correct citation in the context of the issue being researched;

C. Include other citation information in the query. Because of the variety of citation formats used in documents, this option should be used primarily where other options prove insufficient. Below are illustrative queries for any database containing Illinois cases:

S.H.A.Const! Ill.Const! Const.! Constitution /s 5 V +3 15

will retrieve cases citing Illinois Constitution, Article V, Section 15; and

Sup.Ct.! (Supreme /7 Rule) /7 341

will retrieve cases citing Supreme Court Rule 341.

Reminder: When searching for cases citing Illinois statutes, cites to either the current or former cites may be obtained by a single query, as follows:

(705 +7 50/2) (37 +7 902)

WESTLAW ELECTRONIC RESEARCH GUIDE

Alternative Retrieval Methods

WIN® (WESTLAW Is Natural™) allows you to frame your issue in plain English to retrieve documents:

> Right to counsel in contempt proceeding for failure to make child support payment.

Alternatively, retrieval may be focused by use of the Terms and Connectors method:

> DI(CONTEMPT /P CHILD! /P SUPPORT! PAY! PAID /P ATTORNEY LAWYER COUNSEL)

In databases with Key Numbers, either of the above examples will identify Divorce ⟐311(2) and Parent and Child ⟐3.3(9) as Key Numbers collecting headnotes relevant to this issue if there are pertinent cases.

Since the Key Numbers are affixed to points of law by trained specialists based on conceptual understanding of the case, relevant cases that were not retrieved by either of the language-dependent methods will often be found at a Key Number.

Similarly, citations in retrieved documents (to cases, statutes, rules, etc.) may suggest additional, fruitful research using other WESTLAW databases (e.g., annotated statutes, rules) or services (e.g., citator services).

Key Number Search

Frequently, caselaw research rapidly converges on a few topics, headings and Key Numbers within West's Key Number System that are likely to contain relevant cases. These may be discovered from known, relevant reported cases from any jurisdiction; Library References in West publications; browsing in a digest; or browsing the Key Number System on WESTLAW using the JUMP feature or the KEY command.

Once discovered, topics, subheadings or Key Numbers are useful as search terms (in databases containing reported cases) alone or with other search terms, to focus the search within a narrow range of potentially relevant material.

For example, to retrieve cases with at least one headnote classified to Parent and Child ⟐3.3(9), sign on to a caselaw database and enter

> 285k3.3(9)   [use with other search terms, if desired]

The topic name (Parent and Child) is replaced by its numerical equivalent (285) and the ⟐ by the letter k. A list of topics and their numerical equivalents is in the WESTLAW Reference Manual and is displayed in WESTLAW when the KEY command is entered.

Other topics of special interest are listed below.

Abortion and Birth Control (4)
Adoption (17)
Children Out-of-Wedlock (76H)
Divorce (134)

Husband and Wife (205)
Incest (207)
Infants (211)
Marriage (253)

WESTLAW ELECTRONIC RESEARCH GUIDE

Using JUMP

WESTLAW's JUMP feature allows you to move from one document to another or from one part of a document to another, then easily return to your original place, without losing your original result. Opportunities to move in this manner are marked in the text with a JUMP symbol (▶). Whenever you see the JUMP symbol, you may move to the place designated by the adjacent reference by using the Tab, arrow keys or mouse click to position the cursor on the JUMP symbol, then pressing Enter or clicking again with the mouse.

Within the text of a court opinion, JUMP arrows are adjacent to case cites and federal statute cites, and adjacent to parenthesized numbers marking discussions corresponding to headnotes.

On a screen containing the text of a headnote, the JUMP arrows allow movement to the corresponding discussion in the text of the opinion,

▶ (3)

and allow browsing West's Key Number System beginning at various heading levels:

▶ 285   PARENT AND CHILD
▶ 285k3   Support and Education of Child
▶ 285k3.3   Actions to Compel Support or Payment for Necessaries
▶ 285k3.3(9) k. Enforcement of decree.

To return from a JUMP, enter GB (except for JUMPs between a headnote and the corresponding discussion in opinion, for which there is a matching number in parenthesis in both headnote and opinion). Returns from successive JUMPs (e.g., from case to cited case to case cited by cited case) without intervening returns may be accomplished by repeated entry of GB or by using the MAP command.

General Information

The information provided above illustrates some of the ways WESTLAW can complement research using this publication. However, this brief overview illustrates only some of the power of WESTLAW. The full range of WESTLAW search techniques is available to support your research.

Please consult the WESTLAW Reference Manual for additional information or assistance or call West's Reference Attorneys at 1–800–REF–ATTY (1–800–733–2889).

For information about subscribing to WESTLAW, please call 1–800–328–0109.

SUMMARY OF CONTENTS

	Page
TABLE OF FORMS	XLV

DIVISION A. FAMILIES

Chapter 750. Families 1
Act
- 5. Illinois Marriage and Dissolution of Marriage Act 1
- 10. Illinois Uniform Premarital Agreement Act 281
- 15. Non-Support of Spouse and Children Act 304
- 20. Revised Uniform Reciprocal Enforcement of Support Act 321
- 22. Uniform Interstate Family Support Act 349
- 25. Expedited Child Support Act of 1990 373
- 30. Emancipation of Mature Minors Act 384
- 35. Uniform Child Custody Jurisdiction Act 388
- 40. Illinois Parentage Act 407
- 45. Illinois Parentage Act of 1984 408
- 50. The Adoption Act 434
- 55. Contest of Adoptions Act 487
- 60. Illinois Domestic Violence Act of 1986 488
- 65. Rights of Married Persons Act 549

Chapter 325. Children 557
Act
- 5. Abused and Neglected Child Reporting Act 557

Chapter 720. Criminal Offenses 583
Act
- 5. Criminal Code of 1961 (Selected Provisions) 583
- 525. Adoption Compensation Prohibition Act (Selected Provisions) .. 588

DIVISION B. CIVIL LIABILITIES

Chapter 740. Civil Liabilities 591
Act
- 5. Alienation of Affections Act 591
- 15. Breach of Promise Act 593
- 110. Mental Health and Developmental Disabilities Confidentiality Act (Selected Provisions) 596
- 115. Parental Responsibility Law 617

DIVISION C. PROBATE

Chapter 755. Estates 619
Act
- 5. Probate Act of 1975 (Selected Provisions) 619

SUMMARY OF CONTENTS

DIVISION D. PROCEDURE

	Page
Chapter 735. Civil Procedure	627
Act	
5. Code of Civil Procedure (Selected Provisions)	627
Illinois Supreme Court Rules (Selected Rules)	668

DIVISION E. FEDERAL LAWS

Internal Revenue Code (26 U.S.C.A. Selected Provisions)	821
Employee Retirement Income Security Program (29 U.S.C.A. § 1169)	897
United States Bankruptcy Code (11 U.S.C.A. Selected Provisions)	905
The International Child Abduction Remedies Act (The Hague Convention) (42 U.S.C.A. §§ 11601 et seq.)	908

DIVISION F. SELECTED NOTES AND STATUTES

Hearsay	941
Objection: Not Responsive	944
Offers of Proof	944
State and Federal Eavesdropping Statutes (720 ILCS 5/14-1 et seq.; 18 U.S.C.A. § 2510 et seq.)	945
Federal and State Constitutional Right Against Self-Incrimination (U.S. Const. amend. V; Ill. Const. art. I, § 10)	961
Perjury	963
Conflicts of Interest	963
Table of Cases	967
Table of Statutes	987
Table of Rules and Revenue Rulings	1005
Table of Authorities	1009
Index	1011

TABLE OF CONTENTS

                                                                                                      Page

TABLE OF FORMS XLV

DIVISION A. FAMILIES

CHAPTER 750. FAMILIES (p. 1)

Act 5. Illinois Marriage and Dissolution of Marriage Act. (p. 1)

PART I. GENERAL PROVISIONS (p. 1)

Section
- 101. Short title.
- 102. Purposes—Rules of construction.
- 103. Trial by jury.
- 104. Venue.
- 105. Application of civil practice law.
- 106. Employment of administrative aides.
- 107. Order of protection; Status.

PART II. MARRIAGE (p. 4)

- 201. Formalities.
- 202. Marriage license and marriage certificate.
- 203. License to marry.
- 204. Medical information brochure.
- 205. Exceptions.
- 206. Records.
- 207. Effective date of license.
- 208. Judicial approval of underage marriages.
- 209. Solemnization and registration.
- 210. Registration of marriage certificate.
- 211. Reporting.
- 212. Prohibited marriages.
- 213. Validity.
- 214. Invalidity of common law marriages.
- 215. Penalty.
- 216. Prohibited marriages void if contracted in another state.
- 217. Marriage by non-residents—When void.
- 218. Duty of officer issuing license.
- 219. Offenses.

PART III. DECLARATION OF VALIDITY OF MARRIAGE (p. 11)

- 301. Declaration of invalidity—Grounds.
- 302. Time of commencement.
- 303. Legitimacy of children.
- 304. Retroactivity.
- 305. Putative spouse.
- 306. Commencement of action.

TABLE OF CONTENTS

Act 5. Illinois Marriage and Dissolution of Marriage Act—Continued

PART IV. DISSOLUTION AND LEGAL SEPARATION (p. 14)

Section
- 401. Dissolution of marriage.
- 402. Legal separation.
- 403. Pleadings—Commencement—Abolition of existing defenses—Procedure.
- 404. Conciliation.
- 404.1 Educational program—Effects of dissolution of marriage on the children.
- 405. Hearing on default—Notice.
- 406. Fault or conduct of petitioner.
- 407. Admission of respondent.
- 408. Collusion—Assent or consent of petitioner.
- 409. Proof of foreign marriage.
- 410. Process—Practice—Proceedings—Publication.
- 411. Commencement of action.
- 412. Filing of petition—Cases requiring service by publication.
- 413. Judgment.

PART IV-A. JOINT SIMPLIFIED DISSOLUTION PROCEDURE (p. 49)

- 451. Applicability.
- 452. Petition.
- 453. Procedure; Judgment.
- 454. Affidavit.
- 455. Copies of judgment.
- 456. Forms.
- 457. Brochure to describe proceedings.

PART V. PROPERTY, SUPPORT, AND ATTORNEY FEES (p. 59)

- 501. Temporary relief.
- 501.1 Dissolution action stay.
- 502. Agreement.
- 503. Disposition of property.
- 504. Maintenance.
- 505. Child support; Contempt; Penalties.
- 505.1 Unemployed persons owing duty of support.
- 505.2 Health insurance.
- 506. Representation of child.
- 507. Payment of maintenance or support to court.
- 508. Attorney's fees.
- 509. Independence of provisions of judgment or temporary order.
- 510. Modification and termination of provisions for maintenance, support, educational expenses, and property disposition.
- 511. Procedure.
- 512. Post-judgment venue.
- 513. Support for non-minor children and educational expenses.
- 514. Partition of real estate.
- 515. Partition to be filed in counties where real estate located.
- 516. Public Aid collection fee.

TABLE OF CONTENTS

Act 5. Illinois Marriage and Dissolution of Marriage Act—Continued

PART VI. CUSTODY (p. 221)

Section
- 601. Jurisdiction—Commencement of proceeding.
- 602. Best interest of child.
- 602.1 Parental powers—Joint custody—Criteria.
- 603. Temporary orders.
- 604. Interviews.
- 605. Investigations and reports.
- 606. Hearings.
- 607. Visitation.
- 607.1 Enforcement of visitation orders; Visitation abuse.
- 608. Judicial supervision.
- 609. Leave to remove children.
- 610. Modification.
- 611. Enforcement of custody order or order prohibiting removal of child from the jurisdiction of the court.

PART VII. MISCELLANEOUS (p. 251)

- 701. Marital residence—Order granting possession to spouse.
- 702. Maintenance in case of bigamy.
- 703. Lien of judgment—Sales.
- 704. Public Aid provisions.
- 705. Support payments—Receiving and disbursing agents.
- 706.1 Withholding of income to secure payment of support.
- 706.2 Posting security, bond or guarantee to secure payment.
- 707. Certificate of dissolution or invalidity of marriage—Filing with Department of Public Health.
- 708. Disclosure of address.
- 709. Mandatory child support payments to clerk.
- 710. Enforcement; Penalties.
- 711. Fees.
- 712. Child support enforcement program—Certification—Child and Spouse Support Unit in Department of Public Aid—Powers and duties—Financial assistance in counties.
- 713. Attachment of the body.

PART VIII. APPLICATION AND SEVERABILITY (p. 280)

- 801. Application.
- 802. Court rules.

Act 10. Illinois Uniform Premarital Agreement Act. (p. 281)

Section
- 1. Short title.
- 2. Definitions.
- 3. Formalities.
- 4. Content.
- 5. Effect of marriage.
- 6. Amendment, revocation.
- 7. Enforcement.

TABLE OF CONTENTS

Act 10. Illinois Uniform Premarital Agreement Act—Continued

Section
- 8. Enforcement: Void marriage.
- 9. Limitation of actions.
- 10. Application and construction.
- 11. Time of taking effect.

Act 15. Non-support of Spouse and Children Act. (p. 304)

Section
- 1. Neglect to support wife or child; Punishment; Civil action.
- 1a. Citation of Act.
- 1b. Prosecutions by Attorney General.
- 2. Proceedings.
- 2.1 Support money; Receiving and disbursement agents.
- 3. Temporary order for support.
- 4. Fine; Release of defendant on probation; Orders to be series of judgments.
- 4.1 Withholding of income to secure payment of support.
- 5. Violation of order; Forfeiture or recognizance.
- 6. Evidence.
- 7. Husband or wife as competent witness.
- 8. Actions may be prosecuted during existence of marriage relations.
- 9. Prosecutions; Age of children.
- 10. Offenses, how construed.
- 11. Public Aid collection fee.
- 12. Unemployed persons owing duty of support.
- 12.1 Order of protection; Status.

Act 20. Revised Uniform Reciprocal Enforcement of Support Act. (p. 321)

PART I. GENERAL PROVISIONS (p. 321)

Section
- 1. Short title; Purposes.
- 2. Definitions.
- 3. Remedies additional to those now existing.
- 4. Extent of duties of support.
- 4.1 Convention Country.

PART II. CRIMINAL ENFORCEMENT (p. 324)

- 5. Interstate rendition.
- 6. Conditions of interstate rendition.

PART III. CIVIL ENFORCEMENT (p. 325)

- 7. Choice of law.
- 8. Remedies of state or political subdivision furnishing support.
- 9. How duties of support enforced.
- 10. Jurisdiction.
- 11. Contents and filing of petition for support; Venue.
- 12. Officials to represent obligee.
- 13. Petition for a minor.

TABLE OF CONTENTS

Act 20. Revised Uniform Reciprocal Enforcement of Support Act—Continued

Section
- 14. Duty of initiating court.
- 15. Costs and fees.
- 15a. Public Aid collection fee.
- 16. Jurisdiction by arrest.
- 17. State information agency.
- 18. Duty of the court and officials of this state as responding state.
- 19. Further duties of court and officials in the responding state.
- 20. Hearing and continuance.
- 21. Immunity from criminal prosecution.
- 22. Evidence of husband and wife.
- 23. Rules of evidence.
- 24. Order of support.
- 24.1 Unemployed persons owing duty of support.
- 25. Responding court to transmit copies to initiating court.
- 26. Additional powers of responding court.
- 26.1 Withholding of income to secure payment of support.
- 27. Paternity.
- 28. Additional duties of responding court.
- 29. Additional duty of initiating court.
- 29A. Notice to clerk of initiating or responding circuit court of payment received by Illinois Department of Public Aid for recording.
- 29B. Time of payment transmittal by circuit court to Department of Public Aid.
- 30. Proceedings not to be stayed.
- 31. Application of payments.
- 32. Effect of participation in proceeding.
- 33. Intrastate application.
- 34. Appeals.

PART IV. REGISTRATION OF FOREIGN SUPPORT ORDERS (p. 347)

- 35. Additional remedies.
- 36. Registration.
- 37. Registry of Foreign Support Orders.
- 38. Official to represent obligee.
- 39. Registration procedure; Notice.
- 40. Effect of registration; Enforcement procedure.
- 41. Uniformity of interpretation.
- 42. Severability.

Act 22. Uniform Interstate Family Support Act. (p. 349)

ARTICLE I. GENERAL PROVISIONS (p. 349)

Section
- 100. Short title.
- 101. Definitions.
- 102. Tribunal of this State.
- 103. Remedies cumulative.

TABLE OF CONTENTS

Act 22. Uniform Interstate Family Support Act—Continued

ARTICLE II. JURISDICTION (p. 352)

PART A. EXTENDED PERSONAL JURISDICTION (p. 352)

Section
201. Bases for jurisdiction over nonresident.
202. Procedure when exercising jurisdiction over nonresident.

PART B. PROCEEDINGS INVOLVING TWO OR MORE STATES (p. 353)

203. Initiating and responding tribunal of this State.
204. Simultaneous proceedings in another state.
205. Continuing, exclusive jurisdiction.
206. Enforcement and modification of support order by tribunal having continuing jurisdiction.

PART C. RECONCILIATION WITH ORDERS OF OTHER STATES (p. 355)

207. Recognition of child support orders.
208. Multiple child support orders for two or more obligees.
209. Credit for payments.

ARTICLE III. CIVIL PROVISIONS OF GENERAL APPLICATION (p. 356)

301. Proceedings under this Act.
302. Action of minor parent.
303. Application of law of this State.
304. Duties of initiating tribunal.
305. Duties and powers of responding tribunal.
306. Inappropriate tribunal.
307. Duties of support enforcement agency.
308. Duty of Attorney General.
309. Private Counsel.
310. Duties of the Illinois Department of Public Aid.
311. Pleadings and accompanying documents.
312. Nondisclosure of information in exceptional circumstances.
313. Costs and fees.
314. Limited immunity of obligee.
315. Nonparentage as defense.
316. Special rules of evidence and procedure.
317. Communications between tribunals.
318. Assistance with discovery.
319. Receipt and disbursement of payments.

ARTICLE IV. ESTABLISHMENT OF SUPPORT ORDER (p. 363)

401. Petition to establish support order.

ARTICLE V. DIRECT ENFORCEMENT OF ORDER OF ANOTHER STATE WITHOUT REGISTRATION (p. 364)

501. Recognition of income-withholding order of another state.
502. Administrative enforcement of orders.

TABLE OF CONTENTS

Act 22. Uniform Interstate Family Support Act—Continued

ARTICLE VI. ENFORCEMENT AND MODIFICATION OF SUPPORT ORDER AFTER REGISTRATION (p. 365)

PART A. REGISTRATION AND ENFORCEMENT OF SUPPORT ORDER (p. 366)

Section
601. Registration of order for enforcement.
602. Procedure to register order for enforcement.
603. Effect of registration for enforcement.
604. Choice of law.

PART B. CONTEST OF VALIDITY OR ENFORCEMENT (p. 367)

605. Notice of registration of order.
606. Procedure of contest validity or enforcement of registered order.
607. Contest of registration or enforcement.
608. Confirmed order.

PART C. REGISTRATION AND MODIFICATION OF CHILD SUPPORT ORDER (p. 369)

609. Procedure to register child support order of another state for modification.
610. Effect of registration for modification.
611. Modification of child support order of another state.
612. Recognition of order modified in another state.

ARTICLE VII. DETERMINATION OF PARENTAGE (p. 370)

701. Proceeding to determine parentage.

ARTICLE VIII. INTERSTATE RENDITION (p. 371)

801. Grounds for rendition.
802. Conditions of rendition.

ARTICLE IX. MISCELLANEOUS PROVISIONS (p. 372)

901. Uniformity of application and construction.
902. Short title.
903. Severability clause.
904. Effective date.
905. Repeal.
910. Conflict.
999. Effective date.

Act 25. Expedited Child Support Act of 1990. (p. 373)

Section
1. Short title.
2. Purpose.
3. Definitions.
4. Establishment of the Expedited Child Support System.
5. Actions subject to expedited child support hearings.
6. Authority of hearing officers.
7. Expedited child support hearings.

TABLE OF CONTENTS

Act 25. Expedited Child Support Act of 1990—Continued
Section
- 8. Authority retained by the court.
- 9. Judicial hearings.
- 10. Failure to appear.

Act 30. Emancipation of Mature Minors Act. (p. 384)
Section
- 1. Short title.
- 2. Purpose and policy.
- 3. Definitions.
- 3–1. Minor.
- 3–2. Mature minor.
- 3–3. Parents.
- 3–4. Guardian.
- 3–5. Petition.
- 4. Jurisdiction.
- 5. Rights and responsibilities of an emancipated minor.
- 6. Duration of emancipation and discharge of proceedings.
- 7. Petition.
- 8. Notice.
- 9. Hearing.
- 10. Joinder, juvenile court proceedings.
- 11. Appeal.

Act 35. Uniform Child Custody Jurisdiction Act. (p. 388)
Section
- 1. Short title.
- 2. Purposes of Act; Construction of provisions.
- 3. Definitions.
- 4. Jurisdiction.
- 5. Notice and opportunity to be heard.
- 6. Process and notice to persons outside this State.
- 7. Simultaneous proceedings in other states.
- 8. Inconvenient forum.
- 9. Jurisdiction declined by reason of conduct.
- 10. Information under oath to be submitted to the court.
- 11. Additional parties.
- 12. Appearance of parties and the child.
- 13. Binding force and res judicata effect of custody judgment.
- 14. Recognition of out-of-state custody judgments.
- 15. Modification of custody judgment of another state.
- 16. Filing and enforcement of custody judgment of another state.
- 17. Registry of out-of-state custody judgments and proceedings.
- 18. Certified copies of custody judgment.
- 19. Testimony by deposition in another state.
- 20. Hearings and studies in another state.
- 21. Assistance to courts of other states.
- 22. Preservation of documents for use in other states.
- 23. Request for court records of another state.
- 24. International application.

TABLE OF CONTENTS

Act 35. Uniform Child Custody Jurisdiction Act—Continued
Section
- 25. Priority.
- 26. Severability.

Act 40. Illinois Parentage Act. (p. 407)
Section
- 1. Short title.
- 2. Child born as result of artificial insemination; Treatment as naturally conceived legitimate child.
- 3. Husband of wife artificially inseminated; Treatment as natural father.

Act 45. Illinois Parentage Act of 1984. (p. 408)
Section
- 1. Short title.
- 1.1 Public policy.
- 2. Parent and child relationship defined.
- 3. Relationship and support not dependent on marriage.
- 3.1 Minor parent obligation.
- 4. How parent and child relationship established.
- 5. Presumption of paternity.
- 6. Establishment of parent and child relationship by consent of the parties.
- 7. Determination of father and child relationship; Who may bring action; Parties.
- 8. Statute of limitations.
- 9. Jurisdiction; Venue.
- 9.1 Notice to presumed father.
- 10. Pre-trial proceedings.
- 11. Blood tests.
- 12. Pre-trial recommendations.
- 12.1 Settlement orders.
- 13. Civil action; Jury.
- 14. Judgment.
- 15. Enforcement of judgment or order.
- 15.1 Unemployed persons owing duty of support.
- 15.2 Order of protection; Status.
- 16. Modification of judgment.
- 17. Costs.
- 18. Right to counsel; Free transcript on appeal.
- 19. Action to declare mother and child relationship.
- 20. Withholding of income to secure payment of support.
- 21. Support payments—Duties of person or agencies receiving or disbursing support monies.
- 22. Public Aid collection fee.
- 23. Notice to clerk of circuit court of payment received by Illinois Department of Public Aid for recording.
- 25. Savings clause.
- 26. Severability.

TABLE OF CONTENTS

Act 50. The Adoption Act. (p. 434)

Section

0.01 Short title.
1. Definitions.
2. Who may adopt a child.
2.1 Construction of Act.
3. Who may be adopted.
4. Jurisdiction and venue.
4.1 Placements—Compliance with law—Rules.
5. Petition, contents, verification, filing.
6. Investigation.
7. Process.
8. Consents to adoption and surrenders for purposes of adoption.
9. Time for taking a consent or surrender.
10. Forms of consent and surrender; Execution and acknowledgment thereof.
11. Consents, surrenders, irrevocability.
12. Consent of child or adult.
12.1 Putative Father Registry.
12a. Notice to putative father.
13. Interim order.
14. Judgment.
14a. Death of child prior to final judgment.
15. Welfare of child—Same religious belief.
15.1 Licensed foster parent.
16. Entry of judgment.
17. Effect of order terminating parental rights or judgment of adoption.
18. Records confidential.
18.1 Procedure for the disclosure of identifying information—Confidentiality.
18.2 Forms.
18.3 Biological parents—Written statement—Identifying information—Disclosure of information.
18.3a Confidential intermediary.
18.4 Information given to adoptive parents.
18.4a Medical and mental health histories—Contents—Release.
18.5 Exemption from liability.
18.6 Fees and charges.
19. Registration new birth certificate.
20. Practice.
20a. Construction of Act.
20b. Time limit for relief from final judgment or order.
21. Compensation for placing of children prohibited.
22. Partial invalidity.
23. Repeal—Saving.
24. Effective date.

Act 55. Contest of Adoptions Act. (p. 487)

Section

0.01. Short title.
1. Notice—Attack on proceedings for failure to give.

TABLE OF CONTENTS

Act 60. Illinois Domestic Violence Act of 1986. (p. 488)

ARTICLE I. GENERAL PROVISIONS (p. 488)

Section
- 101. Short title.
- 102. Purposes; Rules of construction.
- 103. Definitions.

ARTICLE II. ORDERS OF PROTECTION (p. 492)

- 201. Persons protected by this Act.
- 201.1 Access of high-risk adults.
- 202. Commencement of action; Filing fees; Dismissal.
- 203. Pleading; Non-disclosure of address.
- 204. Petitions of indigent persons.
- 205. Application of rules of civil procedure; Domestic abuse advocates.
- 206. Trial by jury.
- 207. Subject matter jurisdiction.
- 208. Jurisdiction over persons.
- 209. Venue.
- 210. Process.
- 210.1 Service of notice in conjunction with a pending civil case.
- 211. Service of notice of hearings.
- 212. Hearings.
- 213. Continuances.
- 213.1 Hearsay exception.
- 213.2 Waiver of privilege.
- 213.3 Independent counsel; Temporary substitute guardian.
- 214. Order of protection; Remedies.
- 215. Mutual orders of protection; Correlative separate orders.
- 216. Accountability for actions of others.
- 217. Emergency order of protection.
- 218. 30–Day interim order of protection.
- 219. Plenary order of protection.
- 220. Duration and extension of orders.
- 221. Contents of orders.
- 222. Notice of orders.
- 223. Enforcement of orders of protection.
- 223.1 Order of protection; status.
- 224. Modification and re-opening of orders.
- 225. Immunity from prosecution.
- 226. Untrue statements.
- 227. Privileged communications between domestic violence counselors and victims.
- 227.1 Other privileged information.

ARTICLE III. LAW ENFORCEMENT RESPONSIBILITIES (p. 544)

- 301. Arrest without warrant.
- 301.1 Law enforcement policies.
- 302. Data maintenance by law enforcement agencies.
- 303. Reports by law enforcement officers.
- 304. Assistance by law enforcement officers.

TABLE OF CONTENTS

Act 60. Illinois Domestic Violence Act of 1986—Continued

Section
- 305. Limited law enforcement liability.
- 306. Domestic Violence Training and Curriculum Task Force.

ARTICLE IV. HEALTH CARE SERVICES (p. 549)

- 401. Health care services—Liability.

Act 65. Rights of Married Persons Act. (p. 549)

Section
- 0.01 Short title.
- 1. Rights to sue and be sued.
- 2. Defending in own right or for other.
- 3. Desertion by one spouse; Other may use deserter's name.
- 4. Recovery of damages.
- 5. Not liable for each other's debts.
- 6. Contracts.
- 7. Earnings.
- 8. Repealed.
- 9. Property.
- 10. Suit for property unlawfully obtained.
- 11. Abandonment by one spouse; Proceedings to sell property by other.
- 12. Acts binding on both spouses.
- 13. When order may be set aside.
- 14. Attorney in fact.
- 15. Expenses of family.
- 16. Removal from homestead; Custody of children.
- 17. Legal disability; Conveyances; Petitioner.
- 18. Oath; Notice; Proceedings.
- 19. Judgment.
- 20. Mentally ill person's rights secured.
- 21. Effect of conveyances.
- 22. Devise, conveyance, assignment or other transfer of homestead; Tenancy by the entirety.

CHAPTER 325. CHILDREN (p. 557)

Act 5. Abused and Neglected Child Reporting Act. (p. 557)

Section
- 1. Short title.
- 2. Protective services; Application of Act.
- 2.1 Persons eligible to use services and facilities; Referral.
- 3. Definitions.
- 4. Persons required to report; Medical personnel; Privileged communications; Transmitting false report.
- 4.02 Failure to report suspected abuse or neglect.
- 4.1 Death caused by abuse or neglect; Reports.
- 5. Temporary protective custody.
- 6. Photographs and x-rays of child; Photographs of environment.
- 7. Time and manner of making report; Confirmation of report.
- 7.1 Cooperation of agencies; Multi-disciplinary teams.
- 7.2 Child protective service unit; Establishment.

TABLE OF CONTENTS

Act 5. Abused and Neglected Child Reporting Act—Continued

Section

- 7.3 Investigations; Responsibilities of department.
- 7.3a Perinatal coordinator; Appointment; Duties.
- 7.3b Referral of addicted pregnant persons; Services.
- 7.4 Time and manner of making investigations; Emergency services.
- 7.5 Access to child for examination or interview; Intervention of law enforcement agencies; Court orders.
- 7.6 Toll-free telephone number; Posted notice of criminal offense.
- 7.7 Register of reported cases.
- 7.8 Notification of previous reports to child protective service units.
- 7.9 Form and contents of reports.
- 7.10 Copies of reports; Transmission to central register; Contents of preliminary reports.
- 7.12 Determination of classification of report.
- 7.13 Additional information; Reports.
- 7.14 Categories of classification; Reports.
- 7.15 Contents of central register; Additional information; Expungement of records.
- 7.16 Application of expungement; Hearing; Review under Administrative Review Law.
- 7.17 Notice of amendment on expungement; Local records.
- 7.18 Amendment of reports.
- 7.19 Copies of report to subject.
- 8.1 Disposition by Child Protective Service Unit.
- 8.2 Service plan.
- 8.3 Court proceedings; Assistance of Child Protective Services Unit.
- 8.4 Rehabilitative services; Monitoring.
- 8.5 Local child abuse and neglect index.
- 9. Immunity from liability; Presumption.
- 9.1 Employer discrimination.
- 10. Testimony by person making report.
- 11. Confidentiality of records; Violations.
- 11.1 Access to records.
- 11.2 Disclosure to mandated reporting sources.
- 11.3 Publicizing disclosed information; Court actions; Violations.
- 11.4 Court and criminal records; Effect of Act.
- 11.5 Continuing education program.
- 11.6 Review under Administrative Review Law.
- 11.7 State-wide citizens committee on child abuse and neglect.

CHAPTER 720. CRIMINAL OFFENSES (p. 583)

Act 5. Criminal Code of 1961. (Selected Provisions) (p. 583)

ARTICLE X. KIDNAPPING AND RELATED OFFENSES (p. 583)

Section

- 10–5. Child abduction.
- 10–5.5 Unlawful visitation interference.
- 10–6. Harboring a runaway.
- 10–7. Aiding and abetting child abduction.

TABLE OF CONTENTS

Act 525. Adoption Compensation Prohibition Act. (Selected Provisions) (p. 588)

Section
- 0.01 Short title.
- 1. Receipt of compensation for placing out prohibited; Exception.
- 2. Payment of compensation for placing out prohibited; Exception.
- 3. "Placing out" defined.
- 4. Certain payments of salaries and medical expenses not prevented.
- 5. Violations.

DIVISION B. CIVIL LIABILITIES

CHAPTER 740. CIVIL LIABILITIES (p. 591)

Act 5. Alienation of Affections Act. (p. 591)

Section
- 0.01 Short title.
- 1. Declaration of public policy.
- 2. Actual damages, only, recoverable.
- 3. Punitive, exemplary, vindictive or aggravated damages not recoverable.
- 4. Elements not to be considered in determining damages.
- 5. Application of Act.
- 6. Criminal laws not affected.
- 7. Liberal construction; Partial invalidity.

Act 15. Breach of Promise Act. (p. 593)

Section
- 0.01 Short title.
- 1. Legislative declaration of necessity.
- 2. Actual damages only recoverable.
- 3. Punitive, exemplary, vindictive or aggravated damages not recoverable.
- 4. Notice required before bringing action for breach of promise.
- 5. Action barred unless notice is given.
- 6. Limitations.
- 7. Retroactive effect.
- 8. Criminal laws not affected.
- 9. Liberal construction; Partial invalidity.
- 10. Effective date.

Act 110. Mental Health and Developmental Disabilities Confidentiality Act. (Selected Provisions) (p. 596)

Section
- 1. Short title.
- 2. Definitions.
- 3. Records and communications—Personal notes of therapist—Psychological test material.
- 4. Persons entitled to inspect and copy recipient's record.
- 5. Written consent for disclosure of records and communications.
- 6. Information used in application for benefits—Disclosure without consent.
- 7. Review of therapist or agency; Use of recipient's record.
- 7.1 Interagency disclosures.
- 8. Regional human rights authority—Consent to inspect or copy recipient's records during investigations.

TABLE OF CONTENTS

Act 110. Mental Health and Developmental Disabilities Confidentiality Act (Selected Provisions)—Continued

Section
- 8.1   Access to records of developmentally disabled residing in facilities.
- 9.   Disclosure by therapist without consent.
- 9.1   Disclosure without consent.
- 9.2.   Interagency disclosure of recipient information.
- 10.   Civil, criminal, administrative, or legislative proceedings.
- 11.   Disclosure of records and communications.
- 12.   Information to be furnished to United States Secret Service and Department of State Police.
- 12.1.   Report of violation or incident—Investigation.
- 12.2   Recipients on unauthorized absence—Disclosure of identifying information.
- 12.3   Notice of discharge.
- 13.   Disclosure without consent.
- 14.   Agreement to waive Act—Void.
- 15.   Actions by aggrieved parties for violation of Act—Fees and costs.
- 16.   Violations—Penalty.
- 17.   Rules and regulations.

Act 115. Parental Responsibility Law. (p. 617)

Section
- 1.   Short title and citation.
- 2.   Definitions.
- 3.   Parent or legal guardian; Liability; Willful or malicious acts of minor.
- 4.   Persons or entities entitled to enforce Act.
- 5.   Limitation on damages; Damages allowable.
- 6.   Common law damages.
- 7.   Judgments; Applicability of other Act.

DIVISION C. PROBATE

CHAPTER 755. ESTATES (p. 619)

Act 5. Probate Act of 1975. (Selected Provisions) (p. 619)

ARTICLE IV. WILLS (p. 619)

Section
- 4–7.   Revocation—Revival.

ARTICLE XI. MINORS (p. 620)

- 11–1.   Minor defined.
- 11–3.   Who may act as guardian.
- 11–5.   Appointment of guardian.
- 11–6.   Venue.
- 11–7.   Parental right to custody.
- 11–7.1   Visitation rights.
- 11–8.   Petition for guardian of minor.
- 11–9.   Domestic violence: Order of protection.
- 11–10.1   Procedure for appointment of a guardian of a minor.

TABLE OF CONTENTS

Act 5. Probate Act of 1975 (Selected Provisions)—Continued

Section
- 11–11. Costs in certain cases.
- 11–13. Duties of guardian of a minor.
- 11–14.1 Revocation of letters.
- 11–18. Successor guardian.

DIVISION D. PROCEDURE

CHAPTER 735. CIVIL PROCEDURE (p. 627)

Act 5. Code of Civil Procedure. (Selected Provisions) (p. 627)

ARTICLE I. GENERAL PROVISIONS (p. 627)

Section
- 1–109. Verification by certification.

ARTICLE II. CIVIL PRACTICE (p. 628)

- 2–104. Wrong venue—Waiver—Motion to transfer.
- 2–106. Transfer.
- 2–107. Costs and expenses of transfer.
- 2–202. Persons authorized to serve process; Place of service; Failure to make return.
- 2–203. Service on individuals.
- 2–203.1 Service by special order of court.
- 2–206. Service by publication—Affidavit—Mailing—Certificate.
- 2–207. Period of publication—Default.
- 2–208. Personal service outside State.
- 2–209. Act submitting to jurisdiction—Process.
- 2–620. Practice on motions.
- 2–701. Declaratory judgments.
- 2–1001. Substitution of judge.
- 2–1001.5 Change of Venue.
- 2–1102. Examination of adverse party or agent.
- 2–1203. Motions after judgment in non-jury cases.
- 2–1301. Judgments—Default—Confession.
- 2–1302. Notice of entry of default order.
- 2–1303. Interest on judgment.
- 2–1401. Relief from judgments.
- 2–1501. Writs abolished.
- 2–1901. Lis pendens—Operative date of notice.
- 84. Torrens Act Notice.

ARTICLE VIII. EVIDENCE (p. 655)

- 8–801. Privileged communications, husband and wife.
- 8–2601. Admissibility of evidence; Out of court statements; Child abuse.

ARTICLE XI. INJUNCTION (p. 656)

- 11–101. Temporary restraining order.
- 11–102. Preliminary injunction.
- 11–103. Bond.
- 11–104. Bond before court or clerk.

TABLE OF CONTENTS

Act 5. Code of Civil Procedure (Selected Provisions)—Continued

Section

11–105.	Filing of bond.
11–106.	Injunctive relief on Saturday, Sunday or legal holiday.
11–107.	Seeking wrong remedy not fatal.
11–107.1	Injunctive relief for the father of an unborn child in an abortion related decision by the mother.
11–108.	Motion to dissolve.
11–109.	Affidavits in support of motion to dissolve.
11–110.	Assessing damages.

ARTICLE XII. JUDGMENTS—ENFORCEMENT (p. 661)

12–650.	Short title.
12–651.	Definition.
12–652.	Filing and status of foreign judgments.
12–653.	Notice of filing.
12–654.	Stay.
12–655.	Fees.
12–656.	Optional procedure.
12–657.	Uniformity of interpretation.

ARTICLE XXI. CHANGE OF NAME (p. 663)

21–101.	Change of name; Proceedings; Parties.
21–102.	Petition.
21–103.	Notice by publication.
21–104.	Process and notice to persons outside this State.

ILLINOIS SUPREME COURT RULES (Selected Rules) (p. 669)

Rule

11.	Manner of serving papers other than process and complaint on parties not in default in the trial and reviewing courts.
12.	Proof of service in the trial and reviewing courts; Effective date of service.
13.	Appearances—Time to plead—Withdrawal.
100.1	Expedited child support rules. Implementation of Expedited Child Support System.
100.2	Appointment, qualification and compensation of administrative hearing officers.
100.3	Actions subject to expedited child support hearings.
100.4	Authority of administrative hearing officers.
100.5	Blood tests.
100.6	Scheduling of the hearings.
100.7	Conduct of the hearing.
100.8	Absence of party at hearing.
100.9	Transfers for judicial hearings.
100.10	Submission of recommendations to the court.
100.11	Authority retained by the court.
100.12	Judicial hearings.
100.13	Definitions.
101.	Summons and original process—Form and issuance.
102.	Service of summons and complaint—Return.

TABLE OF CONTENTS

ILLINOIS SUPREME COURT RULES (Selected Rules)—Continued

Rule
104.	Service of pleadings and other papers—Filing.
105.	Additional relief against parties in default—Notice.
106.	Notice of petitions filed for relief from, or revival of, judgments.
137.	Signing of pleadings, motions and other papers—Sanctions.
201.	General discovery provisions.
202.	Purposes for which depositions may be taken in pending action.
203.	Where depositions may be taken.
204.	Compelling appearance of deponent.
206.	Method of taking depositions on oral examination.
207.	Signing and filing depositions.
208.	Fees and charges—Copies.
209.	Failure to attend or serve subpoena—Expenses.
210.	Depositions on written questions.
211.	Effect of errors and irregularities in depositions—Objections.
212.	Use of depositions.
213.	Written interrogatories to parties.
214.	Discovery of documents, objects, and tangible things—Inspection of real estate.
215.	Physical and mental examination of parties and other persons.
216.	Admission of fact or of genuineness of documents.
218.	Pretrial procedure.
219.	Consequences of refusal to comply with rules or order relating to discovery or pretrial conferences.
220.	Expert witnesses.
231.	Motions for continuance.
236.	Admission of business records in evidence.
237.	Compelling appearance of witnesses at trial.
238.	Impeachment of witnesses—Hostile witnesses.
272.	When judgment is entered.
296.	Enforcement of order for support.
301.	Method of review.
303.	Appeals from final judgments of the circuit courts in civil cases.
304.	Appeals from final judgments that do not dispose of an entire proceeding.
305.	Stay of judgments pending appeal.
306.	Appeals from orders of the circuit court granting new trials and granting or denying certain motions.
307.	Interlocutory appeals as of right.
308.	Interlocutory appeals by permission.
311.	Accelerated docket.
312.	Docketing statement.
366.	Powers of reviewing court—Scope of review and procedure—Lien of judgment.

DIVISION E. FEDERAL LAWS

26 U.S.C.A. INTERNAL REVENUE CODE (Selected Provisions) (p. 821)

Section
71.	Alimony and separate maintenance payment.
215.	Alimony, etc., payments.

TABLE OF CONTENTS

26 U.S.C.A. INTERNAL REVENUE CODE (Selected Provisions)—Continued

Section

414(p).	Qualified Domestic Relations Order defined.
408(d)(6).	Transfer of account incident to divorce.
3405(c).	Eligible rollover distributions.
682.	Income of an estate or trust in case of divorce, etc.
1041.	Transfers of property between spouses or incident to divorce.
1034.	Rollover of gain on sale of principal residence.
121.	One-time exclusion of gain from sale of principal residence by individual who has attained age 55.
151.	Allowance of deductions for personal exemptions.
152.	Dependent defined.
262.	Personal, living, and family expenses.
2(b).	Definitions and special rules.
7703.	Determination of marital status.
6013.	Joint returns of income tax by husband and wife.

29 U.S.C.A. EMPLOYEE RETIREMENT INCOME SECURITY PROGRAM (Selected Provisions) (p. 897)

Section

1169.	Additional standards for group health plans.

11 U.S.C.A. UNITED STATES BANKRUPTCY CODE (Selected Provisions) (p. 905)

Section

523.	Exceptions to discharge.

42 U.S.C.A. THE INTERNATIONAL CHILD ABDUCTION REMEDIES ACT (THE HAGUE CONVENTION) (p. 908)

Section

11601.	Findings and declarations.
11602.	Definitions.
11603.	Judicial remedies.
11604.	Provisional remedies.
11605.	Admissibility of documents.
11606.	United States Central Authority.
11607.	Costs and fees.
11608.	Collection, maintenance, and dissemination of information.
11609.	Interagency coordinating group.
11610.	Authorization of appropriations.

Text of Hague Convention.
State Department Analysis of Hague Convention.

DIVISION F. SELECTED NOTES AND STATUTES

Hearsay. (p. 941)

Objection: Not responsive. (p. 944)

Offers of proof. (p. 944)

State and Federal Eavesdropping Statutes (720 ILCS 5/14–1 et seq.; 18 U.S.C.A. § 2510 et seq.) (p. 945)

Federal and State Constitutional Right Against Self–Incrimination. (U.S. Const. amend. V; Ill. Const. art. I, § 10) (p. 961)

Perjury. (p. 963)

Conflicts of Interest. (p. 963)

TABLE OF CONTENTS

	Page
Table of Cases	967
Table of Statutes	987
Table of Rules and Revenue Rulings	1005
Table of Authorities	1009
Index	1011

TABLE OF FORMS

	Page
Affidavit and Stipulation (waiving two years separation)	18
Petition for Dissolution of Marriage	24
Praecipe	33
Judgment for Dissolution of Marriage	36
Certification and Agreement by Counsel (uncontested prove-up)	43
Family Support Affidavit	44
Release of Errors by the Respondent; Release of Errors by the Petitioner	46
Partial Release (Satisfaction) of Judgment	49
Joint Petition for Simplified Dissolution of Marriage	53
Agreement—Joint Petition for Simplified Dissolution of Marriage	55
Affidavit in Support of Joint Petition for Simplified Dissolution of Marriage	56
Judgment for Joint Simplified Dissolution of Marriage	57
Petition for Temporary Support	62
Income and Expense Affidavit	64
Petition for an Injunction	71
Affidavit (injunction)	73
Temporary Restraining Order	75
Settlement Agreement	85
Insurance Trust	111
Order Appointing Attorney for Minor Child(ren) and/or Guardian Ad Litem	177
Petition for Temporary Attorney's Fees	185
Amendment to Judgment	198
Petition for Rule to Show Cause	209
Order (rule to show cause)	211
Attachment Order	212
Petition for the Partition of Real Estate	218
Joint Parenting Agreement	231
Order for Withholding	268
Petition to Stay Service of Order for Withholding and Notice of Delinquency	270
Certificate of Dissolution, Invalidity of Marriage or Legal Separation	272
Premarital Agreement	290
Petition for Order of Protection	497
Order (extension of order of protection)	526
Emergency Order of Protection	529
Order of Protection (interim or plenary)	533
Motion for Appointment of Special Process Server	631
Letter and Affidavit (service outside of state)	635
Notice of Motion	639
Notice of Filing	640
Lis Pendens Notice	653
Substitution of Attorneys Stipulation	672

TABLE OF FORMS

	Page
Order (substitution of attorneys)	673
Summons	699
Protective Order (confidentiality)	707
Notice of Subpoena for Deposition	710
Subpoena for Deposition	711
Subpoena for Deposition (Records Only)	712
Notice of Deposition (records rider)	714
Motion (out-of-state deposition)	723
Order (out-of-state deposition)	725
Notice of Deposition (out-of-state deposition)	726
Interrogatories (seeking identity of persons having knowledge of relevant facts)	738
Interrogatories (regarding non-marital property)	739
Notice to Produce (documents)	745
215 Motion (examination)	749
Requests for the Admission of Facts and the Genuineness of Documents	752
Pre-trial Memorandum	755
Motion for Sanctions for Failure to Comply with Discovery	775
Interrogatories Pursuant to Supreme Court Rule 220 (experts)	781
Rule 220 Disclosure Statement (experts)	783
Motion to Allow Testimony of Experts, or, in Alternative, to Set Discovery Schedule, or to Continue Trial	786
Subpoena (trial witness)	793
Notice to Appear and Produce (trial)	794
Qualified Domestic Relations Order	861
Release of Claim to Exemption for Child of Divorced or Separated Parents	885
Joint Tax Return Indemnity	897
Qualified Medical Child Support Order	902
Request for Return (Hague Convention)	940
Consent to Waive Conflict of Interest	964

DIVISION A. FAMILIES

CHAPTER 750
FAMILIES

ACT 5. ILLINOIS MARRIAGE AND DISSOLUTION OF MARRIAGE ACT

PART I. GENERAL PROVISIONS

Analysis

Sec.
101. Short title.
102. Purposes—Rules of construction.
103. Trial by jury.
104. Venue.
105. Application of civil practice law.
106. Employment of administrative aides.
107. Order of protection; Status.

WESTLAW Electronic Research
See WESTLAW Electronic Research Guide preceding the Summary of Contents.

---

750 ILCS 5/101

§ 101. Short title

This Act may be cited as the "Illinois Marriage and Dissolution of Marriage Act."

Author's Notes

(1) **Citation.** The Illinois Marriage and Dissolution of Marriage Act is sometimes cited herein by its acronym "IMDMA."

750 ILCS 5/102

§ 102. Purposes—Rules of construction

This Act shall be liberally construed and applied to promote its underlying purposes, which are to:

(1) provide adequate procedures for the solemnization and registration of marriage;

(2) strengthen and preserve the integrity of marriage and safeguard family relationships;

(3) promote the amicable settlement of disputes that have arisen between parties to a marriage;

(4) mitigate the potential harm to the spouses and their children caused by the process of legal dissolution of marriage;

(5) make reasonable provision for spouses and minor children during and after litigation;

(6) eliminate the consideration of marital misconduct in the adjudication of rights and duties incident to the legal dissolution of marriage, legal separation and declaration of invalidity of marriage;

(7) secure the maximum involvement and cooperation of both parents regarding the physical, mental, moral and emotional well-being of the children during and after the litigation; and

(8) make provision for the preservation and conservation of assets during the litigation.

Author's Notes

(1) **Consideration of marital misconduct.** Although IMDMA § 102(6) states that one of the purposes of the statute is to eliminate consideration of marital misconduct, evidence of such behavior continues to enter the proceedings in both the adjudication of maintenance and property distribution. Both the property provisions, IMDMA § 503(d)(1), and the maintenance provisions, IMDMA § 504(a)(10), consider "contribution," which can encompass negative contribution or misconduct as well as affirmative contribution. See IMDMA §§ 503(d)(1) and 504(a)(10) and accompanying Author's Notes. Fault is also expressly in the statute in the retention of the traditional fault grounds for divorce and as a bar to a claim for support in legal separation actions. See IMDMA §§ 401(a)(1) and 402(a) and accompanying Author's Notes.

750 ILCS 5/103

§ 103. Trial by jury

There shall be no trial by jury under this Act.

750 ILCS 5/104

§ 104. Venue

The proceedings shall be had in the county where the plaintiff or defendant resides, except as otherwise provided herein, but process may be directed to any county in the State. Objection to venue is barred if not made within such time as the defendant's response is due. In no event shall venue be deemed jurisdictional.

Author's Notes

Analysis

1. Venue cross references.

2. Convenient venue.
3. Residence.

(1) **Venue cross references.** IMDMA § 104 directs the proper county for the filing of dissolution and declaration of invalidity actions, and provides limits for objections to improper venue. Venue is also treated in the following relevant statutory sections: IMDMA § 402(b), legal separation actions; IMDMA § 512, post judgment venue; IMDMA § 601(b), independent custody actions; Illinois Code of Civil Procedure: 735 ILCS 5/2-104–107, limits for objections to improper venue and method of transfer; 735 ILCS 5/2-1001, motions for change of judge because of perceived prejudice; and 735 ILCS 5/2-1001.5, motion for change of county because of perceived prejudice. See those Sections and accompanying Author's Notes.

(2) **Convenient venue.** In re Marriage of Jones, 104 Ill.App.3d 490, 60 Ill.Dec. 214, 432 N.E.2d 1113 (1st Dist.1982), *appeal after remand*, 187 Ill.App.3d 206, 134 Ill.Dec. 836, 543 N.E.2d 119 (1st Dist.1989), purportedly eliminated the opportunity for a lawyer to choose a venue where neither party resides, for her convenience. The parties in *Jones* filed in a county in which neither resided, and argued that venue was proper under IMDMA § 104 unless one of the parties objected. The appellate court, however, interpreted the statute more narrowly; holding that if neither party resided in the county where the case was filed, the parties should have timely advised the court that the venue was not proper, and attempted to obtain a court order allowing the filing in the improper venue. The mandate of *Jones* therefore seems to be a requirement to disclose improper venue to the court and attempt to obtain an order permitting the proceedings in the improper venue. Since *Jones* itself disposed of the case on an issue other than venue, and since IMDMA § 104 states that an objection to venue is barred if not made within such time as defendant's response is due, it is unclear what the sanction is for failure to disclose the improper venue to the court. See also the Illinois Code of Civil Procedure, 735 ILCS 5/2-104.

(3) **Residence.** "Residence" means the permanent abode of one of the parties. See IMDMA § 401(a) and accompanying Author's Notes. Venue is not jurisdictional. In re Marriage of Heady, 115 Ill.App.3d 126, 71 Ill.Dec. 27, 450 N.E.2d 462 (5th Dist.1983). But residence in Illinois for the requisite time pursuant to IMDMA § 401(a) is jurisdictional. Riordan v. Riordan, 47 Ill.App.3d 1019, 8 Ill.Dec. 254, 365 N.E.2d 492 (1st Dist.1977).

750 ILCS 5/105

§ 105. Application of civil practice law

(a) The provisions of the Civil Practice Law shall apply to all proceedings under this Act, except as otherwise provided in this Act.

(b) A proceeding for dissolution of marriage, legal separation or declaration of invalidity of marriage shall be entitled "In re the Marriage of ... and ...". A custody or support proceeding shall be entitled "In re the (Custody) (Support) of ...".

(c) The initial pleading in all proceedings under this Act shall be denominated a petition. A responsive pleading shall be denominated a response. All other pleadings under this Act shall be denominated as provided in the Civil Practice Law.

750 ILCS 5/106

§ 106. Employment of administrative aides

The employment of qualified administrative aides to assist the court of any county in the administration of proceedings hereunder may be provided for by such county as the case may be. All such aides shall be appointed by the authority which provided for them, subject to the approval of a majority of the judges of each court involved, and shall serve for such terms and shall receive such compensation as provided by ordinance.

(a) The administrative aides shall perform such nonjudicial duties with respect to proceedings hereunder and matters ancillary thereto as the court shall direct.

(b) Any county may make such appropriations as may be necessary to provide for the expense and compensation of the administrative aides.

750 ILCS 5/107

§ 107. Order of protection; Status

Whenever relief is sought under Part V, Part VI or Part VII of this Act, the court, before granting relief, shall determine whether any order of protection has previously been entered in the instant proceeding or any other proceeding in which any party, or a child of any party, or both, if relevant, has been designated as either a respondent or a protected person.

PART II. MARRIAGE

Analysis

Sec.
201. Formalities.
202. Marriage license and marriage certificate.
203. License to marry.
204. Medical information brochure.
205. Exceptions.
206. Records.
207. Effective date of license.
208. Judicial approval of underage marriages.
209. Solemnization and registration.
210. Registration of marriage certificate.
211. Reporting.
212. Prohibited marriages.
213. Validity.
214. Invalidity of common law marriages.
215. Penalty.
216. Prohibited marriages void if contracted in another state.
217. Marriage by non-residents—When void.
218. Duty of officer issuing license.
219. Offenses.

WESTLAW Electronic Research

See WESTLAW Electronic Research Guide preceding the Summary of Contents.

750 ILCS 5/201

§ 201. Formalities

A marriage between a man and a woman licensed, solemnized and registered as provided in this Act is valid in this State.

750 ILCS 5/202

§ 202. Marriage license and marriage certificate

(a) The Director of Public Health shall prescribe the form for an application for a marriage license, which shall include the following information:

(1) name, sex, occupation, address, social security number, date and place of birth of each party to the proposed marriage;

(2) if either party was previously married, his name, and the date, place and court in which the marriage was dissolved or declared invalid or the date and place of death of the former spouse;

(3) name and address of the parents or guardian of each party; and

(4) whether the parties are related to each other and, if so, their relationship.

(b) The Director of Public Health shall prescribe the forms for the marriage license, the marriage certificate and, when necessary, the consent to marriage.

750 ILCS 5/203

§ 203. License to marry

When a marriage application has been completed and signed by both parties to a prospective marriage and both parties have appeared before the county clerk and the marriage license fee has been paid, the county clerk shall issue a license to marry and a marriage certificate form upon being furnished:

(1) satisfactory proof that each party to the marriage will have attained the age of 18 years at the time the marriage license is effective or will have attained the age of 16 years and has either the consent to the marriage of both parents or his guardian or judicial approval; provided, if one parent cannot be located in order to obtain such consent and diligent efforts have been made to locate that parent by the consenting parent, then the consent of one parent plus a signed affidavit by the consenting parent which (i) names the absent parent and states that he or she cannot be located, and (ii) states what diligent efforts have been made to locate the absent parent, shall have the effect of both parents' consent for purposes of this Section;

(2) satisfactory proof that the marriage is not prohibited; and

(3) an affidavit or record as prescribed in subparagraph (1) of Section 205 or a court order as prescribed in subparagraph (2) of Section 205, if applicable.

750 ILCS 5/203 **FAMILIES**

With each marriage license, the county clerk shall provide a pamphlet describing the causes and effects of fetal alcohol syndrome.

750 ILCS 5/204

§ 204. Medical information brochure

The county clerk shall distribute free of charge, to all persons applying for a marriage license, a brochure prepared by the Department of Public Health concerning sexually transmitted diseases and inherited metabolic diseases.

750 ILCS 5/205

§ 205. Exceptions

(1) Irrespective of the results of laboratory tests and clinical examination relative to venereal diseases, the clerks of the respective counties shall issue a marriage license to parties to a proposed marriage (a) when a woman is pregnant at the time of such application, or (b) when a woman has, prior to the time of application, given birth to an illegitimate child which is living at the time of such application and the man making such application makes affidavit that he is the father of such illegitimate child. The county clerk shall, in lieu of the health certificate required hereunder, accept, as the case may be, either an affidavit on a form prescribed by the State Department of Public Health, signed by a physician duly licensed in this State, stating that the woman is pregnant, or a copy of the birth record of the illegitimate child, if one is available in this State, or if such birth record is not available, an affidavit signed by the woman that she is the mother of such child.

(2) Any judge of the circuit court within the county in which the license is to be issued is authorized and empowered on joint application by both applicants for a marriage license to waive the requirements as to medical examination, laboratory tests, and certificates, except the requirements of paragraph (4) of subsection (a) of Section 212 of this Act which shall not be waived; and to authorize the county clerk to issue the license if all other requirements of law have been complied with and the judge is satisfied, by affidavit, or other proof, that the examination or tests are contrary to the tenets or practices of the religious creed of which the applicant is an adherent, and that the public health and welfare will not be injuriously affected thereby.

750 ILCS 5/206

§ 206. Records

Any health certificate filed with the county clerk, or any certificate, affidavit, or record accepted in lieu thereof, shall be retained in the files of the office for one year after the license is issued and shall thereafter be destroyed by the county clerk.

750 ILCS 5/207
§ 207. Effective date of license

A license to marry becomes effective in the county where it was issued one day after the date of issuance, unless the court orders that the license is effective when issued, and expires 60 days after it becomes effective.

750 ILCS 5/208
§ 208. Judicial approval of underage marriages

(a) The court, after a reasonable effort has been made to notify the parents or guardian of each underaged party, may order the county clerk to issue a marriage license and a marriage certificate form to a party aged 16 or 17 years who has no parent capable of consenting to his marriage or whose parent or guardian has not consented to his marriage.

(b) A marriage license and a marriage certificate form may be issued under this Section only if the court finds that the underaged party is capable of assuming the responsibilities of marriage and the marriage will serve his best interest. Pregnancy alone does not establish that the best interest of the party will be served.

750 ILCS 5/209
§ 209. Solemnization and registration

(a) A marriage may be solemnized by a judge of a court of record, or a retired judge of a court of record, unless the retired judge was removed from office by the Judicial Inquiry Board, except that a retired judge shall not receive any compensation from the State, a county or any unit of local government in return for the solemnization of a marriage and there shall be no effect upon any pension benefits conferred by the Judges Retirement System of Illinois, by a county clerk in counties having 2,000,000 or more inhabitants, by a public official whose powers include solemnization of marriages, or in accordance with the prescriptions of any religious denomination, Indian Nation or Tribe or Native Group, provided that when such prescriptions require an officiant, the officiant be in good standing with his religious denomination, Indian Nation or Tribe or Native Group. Either the person solemnizing the marriage, or, if no individual acting alone solemnized the marriage, both parties to the marriage, shall complete the marriage certificate form and forward it to the county clerk within 10 days after such marriage is solemnized.

(b) The solemnization of the marriage is not invalidated by the fact that the person solemnizing the marriage was not legally qualified to solemnize it, if either party to the marriage believed him to be so qualified.

750 ILCS 5/210
§ 210. Registration of marriage certificate

Upon receipt of the marriage certificate, the county clerk shall register the marriage. Within 45 days after the close of the month in which a

750 ILCS 5/210

marriage is registered, the county clerk shall make to the Department of Public Health a return of such marriage. Such return shall be made on a form furnished by the Department of Public Health and shall substantially consist of the following items:

(1) A copy of the marriage license application signed and attested to by the applicants, except that in any county in which the information provided in a marriage license application is entered into a computer, the county clerk may submit a computer copy of such information without the signatures and attestations of the applicants.

(2) The date and place of marriage.

(3) The marriage license number.

750 ILCS 5/211

§ 211. Reporting

In transmitting the required returns, the county clerk shall make a report to the Department of Public Health stating the total number of marriage licenses issued during the month for which returns are made, and the number of marriage certificates registered during the month.

750 ILCS 5/212

§ 212. Prohibited marriages

(a) The following marriages are prohibited:

(1) a marriage entered into prior to the dissolution of an earlier marriage of one of the parties;

(2) a marriage between an ancestor and a descendant or between a brother and a sister, whether the relationship is by the half or the whole blood or by adoption;

(3) a marriage between an uncle and a niece or between an aunt and a nephew, whether the relationship is by the half or the whole blood;

(4) a marriage between cousins of the first degree; however, a marriage between first cousins is not prohibited if:

(i) both parties are 50 years of age or older; or

(ii) either party, at the time of application for a marriage license, presents for filing with the county clerk of the county in which the marriage is to be solemnized, a certificate signed by a licensed physician stating that the party to the proposed marriage is permanently and irreversibly sterile.

(b) Parties to a marriage prohibited under subsection (a) of this Section who cohabit after removal of the impediment are lawfully married as of the date of the removal of the impediment.

(c) Children born or adopted of a prohibited or common law marriage are legitimate.

750 ILCS 5/213

§ 213. Validity

All marriages contracted within this State, prior to the effective date of this Act, or outside this State, that were valid at the time of the contract or subsequently validated by the laws of the place in which they were contracted or by the domicile of the parties, are valid in this State, except where contrary to the public policy of this State.

750 ILCS 5/214

§ 214. Invalidity of common law marriages

Common law marriages contracted in this State after June 30, 1905 are invalid.

Author's Notes

Analysis

1. Legal marriage required.
2. Contracts.
3. Other states.

(1) **Legal marriage required.** The state of Illinois does not recognize common law marriages. Few states currently recognize common law marriages, and they are disfavored even in such states. Hewitt v. Hewitt, 77 Ill.2d 49, 64–65, 31 Ill.Dec. 827, 833–34, 394 N.E.2d 1204, 1211 (1979). The IMDMA generally applies to legally married couples only. But see IMDMA § 212(c) concerning the legitimacy of children of common law marriages. Maintenance pursuant to IMDMA § 504 cannot be sought by one unmarried party from his or her partner, even though the parties have cohabited. Similarly, property allocations pursuant to IMDMA § 503 are also unavailable to unmarried couples. Hewitt v. Hewitt, 77 Ill.2d 49, 31 Ill.Dec. 827, 394 N.E.2d 1204 (1979). Child support, however, can be obtained for children born to unmarried couples. Child support can be obtained under IMDMA §§ 505(a) and 601(b) in the absence of marriage, under the Illinois Parentage Act of 1984, 750 ILCS 45/1 et seq., and under the Non-Support of Spouse and Children's Act, 750 ILCS 15/1 et seq.

Maintenance awarded after the dissolution of a valid marriage, unless otherwise agreed, terminates by statute if the recipient cohabits on a resident, continuing conjugal basis, even though not legally married. See IMDMA § 510(c) and accompanying Author's Notes.

(2) **Contracts.** Even though Illinois does not recognize common law marriage, unmarried cohabiting parties can regulate their property and support rights by means of contracts, which are enforceable if the requirements for a valid contract have been satisfied. See, e.g., *Hewitt*, 77 Ill.2d at 59, 31 Ill.Dec. at 831 ("cohabitation by the parties may not prevent them from forming valid contracts about independent matters, for which ... sexual relations do not form part of the consideration").

(3) **Other states.** Illinois will recognize the validity of a common law marriage when a couple "resides" in another state that recognizes their common law marriage, and the couple moves to Illinois. In re Marriage of Mosher, 243 Ill.App.3d 97, 183 Ill.Dec. 911, 612 N.E.2d 838 (3d Dist.1993). If the couple is "domiciled" in Illinois and

750 ILCS 5/214 — FAMILIES

moves to another state that recognizes common law marriage with the intention to return to Illinois, however, Illinois will not recognize their common law marriage. See Peirce v. Peirce, 379 Ill. 185, 191, 39 N.E.2d 990, 993 (1942).

750 ILCS 5/215

§ 215. Penalty

Unless otherwise provided by law, any person who violates any provision of Part II of this Act is guilty of a Class B misdemeanor.

750 ILCS 5/216

§ 216. Prohibited marriages void if contracted in another state

That if any person residing and intending to continue to reside in this state and who is disabled or prohibited from contracting marriage under the laws of this state, shall go into another state or country and there contract a marriage prohibited and declared void by the laws of this state, such marriage shall be null and void for all purposes in this state with the same effect as though such prohibited marriage had been entered into in this state.

750 ILCS 5/217

§ 217. Marriage by non-residents—When void

No marriage shall be contracted in this state by a party residing and intending to continue to reside in another state or jurisdiction if such marriage would be void if contracted in such other state or jurisdiction and every marriage celebrated in this state in violation of this provision shall be null and void.

750 ILCS 5/218

§ 218. Duty of officer issuing license

Before issuing a license to marry a person who resides and intends to continue to reside in another state, the officer having authority to issue the license shall satisfy himself by requiring affidavits or otherwise that such person is not prohibited from intermarrying by the laws of the jurisdiction where he or she resides.

750 ILCS 5/219

§ 219. Offenses

Any official issuing a license with knowledge that the parties are thus prohibited from intermarrying and any person authorized to celebrate marriage who shall knowingly celebrate such a marriage shall be guilty of a petty offense.

PART III. DECLARATION OF INVALIDITY OF MARRIAGE

Analysis

Sec.
301. Declaration of invalidity—Grounds.
302. Time of commencement.
303. Legitimacy of children.
304. Retroactivity.
305. Putative spouse.
306. Commencement of action.

WESTLAW Electronic Research

See WESTLAW Electronic Research Guide preceding the Summary of Contents.

---

750 ILCS 5/301

§ 301. Declaration of invalidity—Grounds

The court shall enter its judgment declaring the invalidity of a marriage (formerly known as annulment) entered into under the following circumstances:

(1) a party lacked capacity to consent to the marriage at the time the marriage was solemnized, either because of mental incapacity or infirmity or because of the influence of alcohol, drugs or other incapacitating substances, or a party was induced to enter into a marriage by force or duress or by fraud involving the essentials of marriage;

(2) a party lacks the physical capacity to consummate the marriage by sexual intercourse and at the time the marriage was solemnized the other party did not know of the incapacity;

(3) a party was aged 16 or 17 years and did not have the consent of his parents or guardian or judicial approval; or

(4) the marriage is prohibited.

Author's Notes

Analysis

1. Infrequently used remedy.
2. Fraud.
3. Prohibited marriages.

(1) **Infrequently used remedy.** The remedy of declaration of invalidity of a marriage is seldom employed, because the grounds for invalidity of a marriage are generally more difficult to prove than is the no-fault ground of separation and irretrievable breakdown for dissolution of marriage. There are some cases where grounds for declaration of invalidity obviously exist, and the remedy is employed when it is important to one or both of the parties not to have a divorce in their history.

750 ILCS 5/301 FAMILIES

(2) **Fraud.** The ground of fraud involving the essentials of the marriage for a declaration of invalidity has generally been strictly construed by the Illinois Courts. See, e.g., Bielby v. Bielby, 333 Ill. 478, 484, 165 N.E. 231 (1929):

> False representations as to fortune, character and social standing are not essential elements of the marriage, and it is contrary to public policy to annul a marriage for fraud or misrepresentations as to personal qualities. The fraudulent representations for which a marriage may be annulled must be of something essential to the marriage relation—of something making impossible the performance of the duties and obligations of that relation or rendering its assumption and continuance dangerous to health or life.

On the other hand, a misrepresentation by a party concerning his capacity for sexual intercourse would be fraud involving the essentials of the marriage, and would constitute a sufficient ground for a declaration of invalidity. See, e.g., In re Marriage of Naguit, 104 Ill.App.3d 709, 60 Ill.Dec. 499, 433 N.E.2d 296 (5th Dist.1982); Louis v. Louis, 124 Ill.App.2d 325, 260 N.E.3d 469 (1st Dist.1970).

(3) **Prohibited marriages.** See IMDMA § 212 for prohibited marriages.

750 ILCS 5/302

§ 302. Time of commencement

(a) A declaration of invalidity under paragraphs (1) through (3) of Section 301 may be sought by any of the following persons and must be commenced within the times specified:

(1) for any of the reasons set forth in paragraph (1) of Section 301, by either party or by the legal representative of the party who lacked capacity to consent, no later than 90 days after the petitioner obtained knowledge of the described condition;

(2) for the reason set forth in paragraph (2) of Section 301, by either party, no later than one year after the petitioner obtained knowledge of the described condition;

(3) for the reason set forth in paragraph (3) of Section 301, by the underaged party, his parent or guardian, prior to the time the underaged party reaches the age at which he could have married without needing to satisfy the omitted requirement.

(b) In no event may a declaration of invalidity of marriage be sought after the death of either party to the marriage under subsections (1), (2) and (3) of Section 301.

(c) A declaration of invalidity for the reason set forth in paragraph (4) of Section 301 may be sought by either party, the legal spouse in case of a bigamous marriage, the State's Attorney or a child of either party, at any time not to exceed 3 years following the death of the first party to die.

750 ILCS 5/303

§ 303. Legitimacy of children

Children born or adopted of a marriage declared invalid are legitimate. Children whose parents marry after their birth are legitimate.

750 ILCS 5/304

§ 304. Retroactivity

Unless the court finds, after a consideration of all relevant circumstances, including the effect of a retroactive judgment on third parties, that the interests of justice would be served by making the judgment not retroactive, it shall declare the marriage invalid as of the date of the marriage. The provisions of this Act relating to property rights of the spouses, maintenance, support and custody of children on dissolution of marriage are applicable to non-retroactive judgments of invalidity of marriage only.

Author's Notes

Analysis

1. Retroactivity.
2. Custody and support.
3. Maintenance.

(1) **Retroactivity.** Ordinarily when the court enters a Judgment of Declaration of Invalidity of Marriage, the annulment of the marriage dates back to the time of the marriage, and therefore the court has no authority to adjudicate support, property rights, or the custody of children under IMDMA, inasmuch as the court is declaring the marriage invalid *ab initio*. Section 304, however, allows the court to make the judgment not retroactive, in which case the court pursuant to § 304 has the authority to adjudicate support, property, and the custody of children as in a dissolution of marriage proceeding. In re Marriage of Plymale, 172 Ill.App.3d 455, 122 Ill.Dec. 489, 526 N.E.2d 882 (2d Dist.), *appeal denied* 123 Ill.2d 566, 128 Ill.Dec. 898, 535 N.E.2d 409 (1988) (trial court did not intend that the judgment of invalidity of marriage be retroactive despite use of the term "void *ab initio*;" property and child support awards proper).

(2) **Custody and support.** In cases where the invalidity is retroactive to the date of the marriage, custody, visitation, and child support can be obtained under the Illinois Parentage Act of 1984, 750 ILCS 45/1 et seq. and, for child support, also the Non–Support of Spouse and Children's Act, 750 ILCS 15/1 et seq. An action for custody and support pursuant to IMDMA §§ 505(a) and 601(b) is probably also not barred by § 304.

(3) **Maintenance.** For maintenance in cases of bigamy, see IMDMA § 702.

750 ILCS 5/305

§ 305. Putative spouse

Any person, having gone through a marriage ceremony, who has cohabited with another to whom he is not legally married in the good faith belief that he was married to that person is a putative spouse until knowledge of the fact that he is not legally married terminates his status and prevents acquisition of further rights. A putative spouse acquires the rights conferred upon a legal spouse, including the right to maintenance following termination of his status, whether or not the marriage is prohibited, under Section 212, or declared invalid, under Section 301. If there is a legal spouse or other

750 ILCS 5/305

putative spouse, rights acquired by a putative spouse do not supersede the rights of the legal spouse or those acquired by other putative spouses, but the court shall apportion property, maintenance and support rights among the claimants as appropriate in the circumstances and in the interests of justice. This Section shall not apply to common law marriages contracted in the State after June 30, 1905.

750 ILCS 5/306

§ 306. Commencement of action

Actions for declaration of invalidity of marriage shall be commenced as in other civil cases.

PART IV. DISSOLUTION AND LEGAL SEPARATION

Analysis

Sec.
- 401. Dissolution of marriage.
- 402. Legal separation.
- 403. Pleadings—Commencement—Abolition of existing defenses—Procedure.
- 404. Conciliation.
- 404.1 Educational program—Effects of dissolution of marriage on the children.
- 405. Hearing on default—Notice.
- 406. Fault or conduct of petitioner.
- 407. Admission of respondent.
- 408. Collusion—Assent or consent of petitioner.
- 409. Proof of foreign marriage.
- 410. Process—Practice—Proceedings—Publication.
- 411. Commencement of action.
- 412. Filing of petition—Cases requiring service by publication.
- 413. Judgment.

WESTLAW Electronic Research

See WESTLAW Electronic Research Guide preceding the Summary of Contents.

---

750 ILCS 5/401

§ 401. Dissolution of marriage

(a) The court shall enter a judgment of dissolution of marriage if at the time the action was commenced one of the spouses was a resident of this State or was stationed in this State while a member of the armed services, and the residence or military presence had been maintained for 90 days next preceding the commencement of the action or the making of the finding; provided, however, that a finding of residence of a party in any judgment entered under this Act from January 1, 1982 through June 30, 1982 shall satisfy the former domicile requirements of this Act; and if one of the following grounds for dissolution has been proved:

(1) That, without cause or provocation by the petitioner: the respondent was at the time of such marriage, and continues to be naturally impotent; the respondent had a wife or husband living at the time of the marriage; the respondent had committed adultery subsequent to the marriage; the respondent has wilfully deserted or absented himself or herself from the petitioner for the space of one year, including any period during which litigation may have pended between the spouses for dissolution of marriage or legal separation; the respondent has been guilty of habitual drunkenness for the space of 2 years; the respondent has been guilty of gross and confirmed habits caused by the excessive use of addictive drugs for the space of 2 years, or has attempted the life of the other by poison or other means showing malice, or has been guilty of extreme and repeated physical or mental cruelty, or has been convicted of a felony or other infamous crime; or the respondent has infected the other with a communicable venereal disease. "Excessive use of addictive drugs", as used in this Section, refers to use of an addictive drug by a person when using the drug becomes a controlling or a dominant purpose of his life; or

(2) That the spouses have lived separate and apart for a continuous period in excess of 2 years and irreconcilable differences have caused the irretrievable breakdown of the marriage and the court determines that efforts at reconciliation have failed or that future attempts at reconciliation would be impracticable and not in the best interests of the family. If the spouses have lived separate and apart for a continuous period of not less than 6 months next preceding the entry of the judgment dissolving the marriage, as evidenced by testimony or affidavits of the spouses, the requirement of living separate and apart for a continuous period in excess of 2 years may be waived upon written stipulation of both spouses filed with the court. At any time after the parties cease to cohabit, the following periods shall be included in the period of separation:

(A) any period of cohabitation during which the parties attempted in good faith to reconcile and participated in marriage counseling under the guidance of any of the following: a psychiatrist, a clinical psychologist, a clinical social worker, a marriage and family therapist, a person authorized to provide counseling in accordance with the prescriptions of any religious denomination, or a person regularly engaged in providing family or marriage counseling; and

(B) any period of cohabitation under written agreement of the parties to attempt to reconcile.

In computing the period during which the spouses have lived separate and apart for purposes of this Section, periods during which the spouses were living separate and apart prior to July 1, 1984 are included.

(b) Judgment shall not be entered unless, to the extent it has jurisdiction to do so, the court has considered, approved, reserved or made provision for

750 ILCS 5/401   FAMILIES

child custody, the support of any child of the marriage entitled to support, the maintenance of either spouse and the disposition of property. The court may enter a judgment for dissolution that reserves any of these issues either upon (i) agreement of the parties; or (ii) motion of either party and a finding by the court that appropriate circumstances exist.

The death of a party subsequent to entry of a judgment for dissolution but before judgment on reserved issues shall not abate the proceedings.

If any provision of this Section or its application shall be adjudged unconstitutional or invalid for any reason by any court of competent jurisdiction, that judgment shall not impair, affect or invalidate any other provision or application of this Section, which shall remain in full force and effect.

Author's Notes

Analysis

1. Residence.
2. Duration of residence requirements.
3. Grounds for dissolution.
4. No-fault grounds: Finding of irreconcilable differences.
5. No-fault grounds: Time requirements.
6. No-fault grounds: Same house.
7. Affidavit and Stipulation—Form.
8. Cross reference.
9. Fault grounds.
10. Bifurcated divorce.
11. Death of a party.

(1) **Residence.** The court has the power to enter a judgment of dissolution of marriage if: 90 days prior to the commencement of the action or 90 days prior to the making of a finding of residence, one of the parties either was a resident of Illinois or was stationed in the State as a member of the armed forces. Residence is defined as a person's "permanent abode"; the "place one considers 'home.'" Garrison v. Garrison, 107 Ill.App.2d 311, 246 N.E.2d 9 (2d Dist.1969). Domicile, in contrast, is merely the place where a person lives. The two may, but need not, be identical.

The paramount factor in determining residence is the person's intent to live there as her permanent home. Garrison v. Garrison, 107 Ill.App.2d 311, 314, 246 N.E.2d 9, 11 (2d Dist.1969). Intent is determined primarily from the acts of the person, because acts and conduct may negate declarations of intent. Garrison v. Garrison, 107 Ill.App.2d 311, 314, 246 N.E.2d 9, 11 (2d Dist.1969) (Residence established when defendant was president of an Illinois company and maintained a home in Illinois, although spouse and children lived in a jointly-owned house in Florida); Rosenshine v. Rosenshine, 60 Ill.App.3d 514, 17 Ill.Dec. 942, 377 N.E.2d 132 (1st Dist.1978) (Plaintiff's actions were sufficient to demonstrate that she intended to abandon residence in Illinois and establish permanent residence in Israel).

(2) **Duration of residence requirements.** Either the Petitioner or the Respondent must maintain residence in Illinois for the 90 days immediately preceding either the commencement of the action or the finding by the court of residency. A party therefore may initiate a cause of action, and obtain temporary relief, even

though neither party is an Illinois resident at the time of the commencement of the action. See, e.g., In re Marriage of Weiss, 87 Ill.App.3d 643, 649, 42 Ill.Dec. 714, 719, 409 N.E.2d 329, 334 (1st Dist.1980). In that instance, however, the court will not enter a judgment for dissolution unless one of the parties has been an Illinois resident for 90 days prior to the time of the court's finding of residency, which generally occurs at the time of the entry of the judgment.

(3) **Grounds for dissolution.** The current statute retains traditional fault grounds for dissolution of marriage, see e.g., Graham v. Graham, 44 Ill.App.3d 519, 527, 3 Ill.Dec. 141, 146, 358 N.E.2d 308, 313 (5th Dist.1976) ("That the divorce statute is to be strictly construed, and a divorce to be granted only for one of the causes enumerated therein, are propositions that require no citation of authority"), and adopts no-fault grounds. The addition of no-fault dissolution reflects the theory that the State's interest in preserving a marriage is no longer served when the parties do not share that interest. In re Marriage of Smoller, 218 Ill.App.3d 340, 345, 161 Ill.Dec. 129, 132, 578 N.E.2d 256, 259 (1st Dist.1991). Also, no-fault grounds are intended to reduce the acrimony attendant to dissolutions of marriage, and the amount of dissolution litigation crowding the courts. In re Marriage of Van Zuidam, 162 Ill.App.3d 942, 945, 114 Ill.Dec. 176, 178, 516 N.E.2d 331, 333 (1st Dist.1987), *appeal denied*, 118 Ill.2d 552, 117 Ill.Dec. 232, 520 N.E.2d 393 (1988).

(4) **No-fault grounds: Finding of irreconcilable differences.** The statute requires a showing that irreconcilable differences have caused an irretrievable breakdown of the marriage, and that attempts at reconciliation would be impracticable and not in the best interests of the family. The Illinois courts have looked to other states to define irreconcilable differences. In re Marriage of Bates, 141 Ill.App.3d 566, 570, 95 Ill.Dec. 922, 924, 490 N.E.2d 1014, 1016 (1986), cites courts in California, In re Marriage of Walton, 28 Cal.App.3d 108, 116, 104 Cal.Rptr. 472, 479 (1972) ("the existence of marital problems which have so impaired the marriage relationship that the legitimate objects of matrimony have been destroyed"), and Georgia, Harwell v. Harwell, 233 Ga. 89, 90, 209 S.E.2d 625, 627 (1974) ("where either or both parties are unable or refuse to cohabit and there are no prospects for a reconciliation"). See also In re Marriage of Smoller, 218 Ill.App.3d 340, 344, 161 Ill.Dec. 129, 132, 578 N.E.2d 256, 259 (1st Dist.1991). As a practical matter, where one spouse is determined to obtain a divorce, and the time requirements have been satisfied, he will be able to obtain a no fault dissolution of his marriage in Illinois.

(5) **No-fault grounds: Time requirements.** The parties must live separate and apart for two years in order to obtain a dissolution of marriage on the no-fault ground of irreconcilable differences. However, if the parties agree by written stipulation to waive the two year requirement, they may obtain a dissolution after living separate and apart for six months. Oral waiver of the two-year waiting period is insufficient. In re Marriage of Robinson, 225 Ill.App.3d 1037, 167 Ill.Dec. 1113, 588 N.E.2d 1243 (3d Dist.1992). Frequently the two year waiver is signed by the parties if and after the disputed custody and financial issues are settled prior to the expiration of the two years.

The period of separation includes time spent in cohabitation when the parties are attempting to reconcile and participating in marriage counselling, or where they are cohabiting under a written agreement to attempt to reconcile.

(6) **No-fault grounds: Same house.** The courts generally agree that the "separate and apart" requirement is satisfied when the spouses have not cohabited for the requisite period of time, even though they have continued to live in the same

house. In re Marriage of Kenik, 181 Ill.App.3d 266, 129 Ill.Dec. 932, 536 N.E.2d 982 (1st Dist.), *appeal denied*, 127 Ill.2d 618, 136 Ill.Dec. 587, 545 N.E.2d 111 (1989) (irreconcilable differences can be established without physical distance between the parties); In re Marriage of Dowd, 214 Ill.App.3d 156, 157 Ill.Dec. 894, 573 N.E.2d 312 (2d Dist.), *appeal denied*, 141 Ill.2d 538, 162 Ill.Dec. 485, 580 N.E.2d 111 (1991) (spouses using separate bedrooms, with no meaningful communication but sharing fundamental financial obligations, were living separate and apart in the same home). Note, however, that not all the districts have ruled on the issue.

(7) **Affidavit and Stipulation—Form.** There follows a model affidavit and stipulation waiving the two-year period of living separate and apart in favor of the six-month period.

Firm #_____

IN THE CIRCUIT COURT OF COOK COUNTY, ILLINOIS
COUNTY DEPARTMENT, DOMESTIC RELATIONS DIVISION

IN RE THE MARRIAGE OF)
)
ELLEN JARNDYCE,[1])
)
    Petitioner,)
)
and) No. ____ D _____
)
JOHN JARNDYCE,)
)
    Respondent.)

AFFIDAVIT AND STIPULATION

ELLEN JARNDYCE ("ELLEN") and JOHN JARNDYCE ("JOHN") on oath state:

1. ELLEN and JOHN have lived separate and apart for a continuous period of more than six months next preceding the entry of the Judgment herein, having separated on _____, 199__.

2. ELLEN and JOHN do hereby waive the requirement of living separate and apart for a continuous period in excess of two years pursuant to Section 401(a)(2) of the Illinois Marriage and Dissolution of Marriage Act in order to proceed to the dissolution of their marriage on the grounds of irreconcilable differences.

3. If called upon to testify, ELLEN and JOHN would testify as aforesaid.

---

1. The parties in the pleadings and elsewhere in the Practice Book are based upon the marvelous characters in Charles Dickens's *Bleak House*. See Alex J. Philip & Lawrence Gadd, *Who's Who in Dickens*, (1992); Charles Dickens, *Bleak House*, (1852–53); and Charles Dickens, *Bleak House, A Norton Critical Edition*, (George Ford & Sylvere Monod, eds., 1977).

ELLEN JARNDYCE	JOHN JARNDYCE
Subscribed and Sworn to before me this ___ day of _____, 199_.	Subscribed and Sworn to before me this ___ day of _____, 199_.
Notary Public	Notary Public

Frederick Tulkinghorn
Attorney for ELLEN JARNDYCE
Address
Telephone number

(8) **Cross reference.** See IMDMA § 403 Author's Note (6) for a model petition for dissolution of marriage.

(9) **Fault grounds.** The courts do not favor fault grounds, and attorneys therefore use them infrequently in contested matters or uncontested prove ups. Where the separation prior to the prove up or trial is more than six months but less than two years, the parties generally give the court a waiver. The fault grounds are frequently pleaded when the two years of separation necessary to obtain a no-fault divorce have not elapsed at the time of filing of the petition for dissolution of marriage. A fault ground, such as mental cruelty, is often included in an initial pleading in the alternative with a no-fault allegation, in order to preserve the petition against a motion to dismiss. Where only a fault ground is alleged, the courts liberally allow amendment to no-fault grounds when the requisite time period has elapsed at the time of the prove up or trial. A fault ground may be relied upon when the case is before the court prior to the expiration of six months of separation.

(10) **Bifurcated divorce.** Subsection 401(b) addresses the circumstances when the court can enter a judgment of dissolution of marriage and reserve the custody and financial issues for later determination. This is known as a bifurcated divorce. The court has the power to enter a bifurcated divorce upon the agreement of the parties, or upon a motion of either party and a finding by the court that appropriate circumstances exist.

Courts are reluctant to grant bifurcated divorces when they have jurisdiction over both spouses. Potential problems that can arise when a divorce is granted without a comprehensive agreement or adjudication include: loss of medical insurance coverage, the inability to file joint income tax returns, the possibility of an intervening death of one of the parties, and the entanglements of rights of third parties (including subsequent spouses). In re Marriage of Kenik, 181 Ill.App.3d 266, 129 Ill.Dec. 932, 536 N.E.2d 982 (1st Dist.), *appeal denied*, 127 Ill.2d 618, 136 Ill.Dec. 587, 545 N.E.2d 111 (1989).

Unless by agreement, courts rarely enter bifurcated divorces when both parties are before the court, and "appropriate circumstances" may be difficult to prove. Acceptable circumstances include, but are not limited to, instances in which the court cannot exercise in personam jurisdiction over the respondent, a party would be unable to pay maintenance or child support if so ordered, or the child does not live with either parent. In re the Marriage of Cohn, 94 Ill.App.3d 732, 739, 50 Ill.Dec. 621, 419 N.E.2d

729, 735 (2d Dist.1981), *judgment aff'd*, 93 Ill.2d 190, 66 Ill.Dec. 615, 443 N.E.2d 541 (1982) (no appropriate circumstances to warrant bifurcation); In re Marriage of Kenik, 181 Ill.App.3d 266, 129 Ill.Dec. 932, 536 N.E.2d 982 (1st Dist.), *appeal denied*, 127 Ill.2d 618, 136 Ill.Dec. 587, 545 N.E.2d 111 (1989) (bifurcation allowed when there was a relative lack of "complications" and "entanglements," and where respondent was pregnant and planning to marry the father of her child, and the father of the child could provide health insurance for the child that the husband could not). Parties rarely make agreements for bifurcation, because of the problems that have been described, and also because one spouse usually does not want to consent to a divorce until there is a settlement or adjudication of the issues outstanding between the parties. See also 735 ILCS 5/2–209 Author's Note (1) for bifurcated divorce when court does not have jurisdiction of the respondent.

Bifurcated judgments are not final and appealable until the court has decided all claims in the dissolution proceeding. The interdependence of issues involved in a dissolution of marriage necessitates concurrent resolution. In re Marriage of Leopando, 96 Ill.2d 114, 70 Ill.Dec. 263, 449 N.E.2d 137 (1983). See, e.g., In re Marriage of Rosenow, 123 Ill.App.3d 546, 78 Ill.Dec. 933, 462 N.E.2d 1287 (4th Dist.1984) (judgment in dissolution reserving apportionment of pension benefits not appealable), but see In re Marriage of Britton, 141 Ill.App.3d 588, 592, 96 Ill.Dec. 43, 45, 490 N.E.2d 1079, 1081 (5th Dist.1986) ("Such a result is unacceptable because it means a judgment might not be appealable for many years if the court decides to reserve the issue until the employee spouse retires."); In re Marriage of Derning, 117 Ill.App.3d 620, 72 Ill.Dec. 785, 453 N.E.2d 90 (2d Dist.1983) (judgment reserving question of attorney's fees not appealable); In re Marriage of Koch, 119 Ill.App.3d 388, 74 Ill.Dec. 923, 456 N.E.2d 644 (2d Dist.1983) (judgment failing to resolve support and maintenance, property distribution and attorney's fees issues not appealable).

(11) **Death of a party.** The death of a party prior to the entry of a judgment for dissolution generally abates the proceedings. See, e.g., Brandon v. Caisse, 172 Ill. App.3d 841, 844, 122 Ill.Dec. 746, 748, 527 N.E.2d 118, 120 (2d Dist.1988); In re Marriage of Black, 155 Ill.App.3d 52, 53, 107 Ill.Dec. 790, 791, 507 N.E.2d 943, 944 (3d Dist.1987) ("The rationale for the rule is that the death of one of the parties to a marriage extinguishes the subject matter of the dissolution action."). For example, a wife could not press her dissolution claims for support and property against the estate of her deceased husband who has died in the middle of divorce litigation but prior to the entry of a judgment for dissolution. On the other hand, a death after a judgment of dissolution in a bifurcated proceeding but before judgment on reserved issues does not abate the proceedings. Therefore, the same wife after entry of a bifurcated judgment of dissolution could continue to seek a property division against the estate of her deceased ex-husband. In re Marriage of Garlinski, 99 Ill.App.3d 107, 54 Ill.Dec. 510, 425 N.E.2d 22 (1981) (Proceedings on property rights did not abate on husband's death subsequent to order of dissolution but prior to termination of property rights). See also In re Marriage of Black, 155 Ill.App.3d 52, 107 Ill.Dec. 790, 507 N.E.2d 943 (3d Dist.1987). The substantive rationale, if any, for this peculiar dichotomy is presumably that before a divorce a wife possesses rights to her husband's estate that she would lose after a divorce. The spouse's statutory elective share against her deceased spouse's estate, however, can be much smaller than the potential for property and maintenance recovery in many dissolution actions. This disparity, coupled with the difficulty of obtaining a bifurcated divorce, can cause injustice to a party whose estranged spouse dies prior to the entry of a dissolution of their marriage. Conversely, a death of a spouse prior to the entry of a dissolution judgment when the deceased

spouse has a large estate of non-marital property could work to the surviving spouse's advantage, if the statutory share attaches against the non-marital property.

750 ILCS 5/402

§ 402. Legal separation

(a) Any person living separate and apart from his or her spouse without fault may have a remedy for reasonable support and maintenance while they so live apart.

(b) Such action shall be brought in the circuit court of the county in which the respondent resides or in which the parties last resided together as husband and wife. In the event the respondent cannot be found within the State, the action may be brought in the circuit court of the county in which the petitioner resides. Commencement of the action, temporary relief and trials shall be the same as in actions for dissolution of marriage.

(c) A proceeding or judgment for legal separation shall not bar either party from instituting an action for dissolution of marriage, and if the party so moving has met the requirements of Section 401, a judgment for dissolution shall be granted.

Author's Notes

Analysis

1. Living separate and apart without fault.
2. Where actions may be brought.
3. Infrequent use of § 402.
4. Distribution of property during legal separation.

(1) **Living separate and apart without fault.** Section 402 allows a person living separate and apart from his or her spouse without fault to bring a support action against the other spouse. "Fault" is defined as either voluntary consent to a separation, or failure of duty or misconduct materially contributing to a disruption of the marital relationship. Graham v. Graham, 44 Ill.App.3d 519, 525, 3 Ill.Dec. 141, 145, 358 N.E.2d 308, 312 (5th Dist.1976) (Plaintiff consented to the separation; is not without fault within the meaning of the statute). However, the statute does not require that the plaintiff be wholly blameless. *Id.*

A 1982 amendment deleted the explicit requirement in the statute that the petitioner reside in a separate abode continuously since the separation. P.A. 82–716 § 1, eff. July 1, 1982.

(2) **Where actions may be brought.** Section 402(b) sets out the counties in which the proceeding may be brought. See IMDMA § 104 and Illinois Code of Civil Procedure, 735 ILCS 5/2-104, and accompanying Author's Notes for motions for change of venue.

(3) **Infrequent use of § 402.** Actions for legal separation are uncommon. Although an action for legal separation engages attorneys and expense, it does not conclude the matter with either a dissolution of the marriage or a reconciliation. A legal separation judgment leaves the parties in the limbo of being married but not living together, and is therefore almost always temporary in nature. Alternatives to

legal separation actions for establishing temporary support are available. Support arrangements in trial separations can often be accomplished informally by agreement, making legal separation actions unnecessary. Temporary support in contested matters is commonly accomplished in a dissolution action by a motion for temporary support. Temporary support motions in dissolution actions also are not barred by the anomalous "without fault" requirement that can bar recovery in actions for legal separation. See IMDMA § 501(a)(1) and accompanying Author's Notes.

A legal separation decree can be useful: (a) in the unusual contested case where a spouse wants support, but not a divorce; (b) during a prolonged separation in order to gain tax deductibility for support (see Internal Revenue Code §§ 71 and 215); and (c) in order to terminate the accrual of marital property. (See Illinois Marriage and Dissolution of Marriage Act § 503(a)(3), which provides that one of the criteria for determining non-marital property is property acquired by a spouse after a judgment of legal separation.)

(4) **Distribution of property during legal separation.** The court in a proceeding for legal separation generally does not have jurisdiction to distribute marital and non-marital property. However, the court may acquire jurisdiction to adjudicate property rights when parties, by their conduct, submit the property issues to the court. See In re Marriage of O'Brien, 235 Ill.App.3d 520, 176 Ill.Dec. 529, 601 N.E.2d 1227 (1st Dist.1992); In re Marriage of Lipkin, 163 Ill.App.3d 1033, 115 Ill.Dec. 76, 517 N.E.2d 41 (4th Dist.1987); In re Marriage of Leff, 148 Ill.App.3d 792, 102 Ill.Dec. 262, 499 N.E.2d 1042 (2d Dist.1986), *appeal denied*, 113 Ill.2d 576, 106 Ill.Dec. 48, 505 N.E.2d 354 (1987).

750 ILCS 5/403

§ 403. Pleadings—Commencement—Abolition of existing defenses—Procedure

(a) The petition for dissolution of marriage or legal separation shall be verified and shall minimally set forth:

(1) the age, occupation and residence of each party and his length of residence in this State;

(2) the date of the marriage and the place at which it was registered;

(3) that the jurisdictional requirements of subsection (a) of Section 401 have been met and that there exist grounds for dissolution of marriage or legal separation. The petitioner need only allege the name of the particular grounds relied upon, which shall constitute a legally sufficient allegation of the grounds; and the respondent shall be entitled to demand a bill of particulars prior to trial setting forth the facts constituting the grounds, if he so chooses. The petition must also contain:

(4) the names, ages and addresses of all living children of the marriage and whether the wife is pregnant;

(5) any arrangements as to support, custody and visitation of the children and maintenance of a spouse; and

(6) the relief sought.

(b) Either or both parties to the marriage may initiate the proceeding.

(c) The previously existing defense of recrimination is abolished. The defense of condonation is abolished only as to condonations occurring after a proceeding is filed under this Act and after the court has acquired jurisdiction over the respondent.

(d) The court may join additional parties necessary and proper for the exercise of its authority under this Act.

(e) Contested trials shall be on a bifurcated basis with the grounds being tried first. Upon the court determining that the grounds exist, the court may allow additional time for the parties to settle amicably the remaining issues before resuming the trial, or may proceed immediately to trial on the remaining issues. In cases where the grounds are uncontested and proved as in cases of default, the trial on all other remaining issues shall proceed immediately, if so ordered by the court or if the parties so stipulate, issue on the pleadings notwithstanding.

(f) Even if no bill of particulars shall have been filed demanding the specification of the particular facts underlying the allegation of the grounds, the court shall nonetheless require proper and sufficient proof of the existence of the grounds.

Author's Notes

Analysis

1. Petition requirements.
2. Recrimination.
3. Condonation.
4. Bifurcation.
5. Proof of grounds for dissolution.
6. Petition for Dissolution of Marriage—Form.
7. Plead dissipation and house sales.

(1) **Petition requirements.** Section 403 establishes the minimum requirements for petitions for dissolution of marriage or legal separation. The pleadings must be verified. See Illinois Code of Civil Procedure, 735 ILCS 5/1–109. The statute allows notice pleading of the grounds for dissolution, but entitles the respondent to a bill of particulars prior to trial.

(2) **Recrimination.** Under the doctrine of recrimination, if both parties were guilty of a ground for divorce, a divorce could not be granted. See, e.g., Haring v. Haring, 125 Ill.App.2d 116, 260 N.E.2d 396 (5th Dist.1970) (defendant's defense of recrimination, if proven, would bar plaintiff's divorce on grounds of cruelty); Levy v. Levy, 388 Ill. 179, 57 N.E.2d 366 (1944) (divorce is a remedy provided for an innocent party; when both have committed cause for divorce, neither may complain); Martin v. Martin, 327 Ill.App. 552, 64 N.E.2d 379 (1st Dist.1946) (parties who are in *pari delicto* may not obtain a divorce). The statute abolishes the defense of recrimination.

(3) **Condonation.** Condonation is the forgiveness of a ground for divorce. Pope v. Pope, 12 Ill.App.3d 800, 299 N.E.2d 161 (1st Dist.1973) (condonation is defined as "forgiveness of an antecedent matrimonial offense on the condition that it not be

repeated and that the forgiving party shall thereafter be treated with conjugal kindness by the offender"); McGaughy v. McGaughy, 410 Ill. 596, 102 N.E.2d 806 (1952) (condonation is "the free, voluntary, and full forgiveness and remission of a matrimonial offense"). The statute abolishes condonation as a defense only as to condonations occurring after an action for dissolution or legal separation has been filed and the court has acquired jurisdiction over the respondent.

Attempted reconciliation may constitute condonation, particularly when accompanied by cohabitation. Pope v. Pope, 12 Ill.App.3d 800, 299 N.E.2d 161 (1st Dist.1973); Rasgaitis v. Rasgaitis, 347 Ill.App. 477, 107 N.E.2d 273 (1st Dist.1952). Therefore, § 403(c) was thought to be useful to preserve a cause of action when the parties want to attempt a reconciliation without relinquishing their rights. Since condonation is only a defense to the fault grounds, however, the advent of no fault divorce made condonation either before or after filing a suit almost irrelevant.

(4) **Bifurcation.** Subsection 403(e) provides for bifurcated trials in contested dissolutions. Judgments, however, are seldom entered on a bifurcated basis. See IMDMA § 401(b) and accompanying Author's Note (10).

(5) **Proof of grounds for dissolution.** The act requires that the parties prove the existence of the grounds for divorce to the court, even if the respondent does not request a bill of particulars. A party must provide proof of the grounds for dissolution even where one party is in default. See IMDMA § 405 and accompanying Author's Notes.

(6) **Petition for Dissolution of Marriage—Form.** There follows a model petition for dissolution of marriage.

FIRM #_____

IN THE CIRCUIT COURT OF COOK COUNTY, ILLINOIS
COUNTY DEPARTMENT—DOMESTIC RELATIONS DIVISION

IN RE THE MARRIAGE OF	)
	)
ELLEN JARNDYCE,	)
	)
Petitioner,	)
	)
and	) No. ___ D _____
	)
JOHN JARNDYCE,	)
	)
Respondent.	)

PETITION FOR DISSOLUTION OF MARRIAGE

Petitioner, ELLEN JARNDYCE, brings the following Petition for Dissolution of Marriage against Respondent, JOHN JARNDYCE:

1. Petitioner is _____ years of age, resides at _____, _____, Illinois 60_____, and has been a resident of the State of Illinois for _____ years. Petitioner is a part-time real estate broker.

2. Respondent is _____ years of age, resides at _____, _____, Illinois 60_____, and has been a resident of the State of Illinois for _____ years. Respondent is a business executive.

3. Petitioner and Respondent were married on _____, 19__, in _____, _____ and the marriage was registered in _____ County, _____. Petitioner and Respondent lived together as husband and wife from the time of the marriage until _____, 19__.

4. Petitioner and Respondent *(or either one of them)* are residents of the State of Illinois, and have been residents of the State of Illinois for more than ninety (90) days next preceding the commencement of this action. Petitioner resides in Cook County, Illinois. The jurisdictional requirements of the Illinois Marriage and Dissolution of Marriage Act therefore exist, and there exist grounds for the dissolution of the marriage of the parties.

5. Three children were born to the parties as the issue of the marriage, whose names, ages, and addresses are: _____, __ years of age, who resides at _____, _____, Illinois 60__; _____, __ years of age, who resides at _____, _____, Illinois 60__; _____, __ years of age, who resides at _____, _____, Illinois 60__. No children were adopted by the parties, and Petitioner is not pregnant.

6. Petitioner is a fit and proper person and Petitioner should have the sole care, custody, and control of the minor children of the parties *(or both parties are fit and proper persons and should have the joint care, custody and control of the minor children)*.

7. The spouses have lived separate and apart for a continuous period in excess of two years, and irreconcilable differences have caused an irretrievable breakdown of the marriage. Efforts at reconciliation have failed, and future efforts at reconciliation would be impracticable and not in the best interests of the family.

8. Respondent, during the marriage, has been guilty of extreme and repeated mental cruelty toward the Petitioner, without cause or provocation by the Petitioner. *(Mental cruelty is commonly alleged with irreconcilable differences if the separation period is less than 2 years.)*

9. There are not presently any arrangements between the parties concerning the support, custody, education, and visitation of the minor children of the parties, nor concerning the maintenance of the Petitioner, nor concerning the allocation of the property held by the parties.

10. The parties, during the marriage, have acquired substantial marital property, including, but not limited to, the marital home of the parties located at _____, _____, Illinois, pensions, investments, corporate benefits, and other assets, the details of which are unknown to Petitioner, but which are well known to Respondent. Petitioner is entitled to a disproportionately larger share of the marital property than is the Respondent, because of Petitioner's contributions to the marriage, and because Respondent enjoys a

750 ILCS 5/403   **FAMILIES**

substantial earning power and the ability to accumulate assets, whereas Petitioner has only negligible earning power, and no ability to acquire assets.

11. Respondent is an executive of _____ Corporation, and last year earned in excess of $_____. Petitioner earns only a nominal income, and is completely dependent for her support and that of the three minor children of the parties upon Respondent, who is well able to provide for them.

12. Petitioner owns a small amount of inherited non-marital property, which should be assigned to Petitioner.

WHEREFORE, Petitioner, ELLEN JARNDYCE, prays as follows:

1. A Judgment for the dissolution of the marriage of the parties be entered in accordance with the statute.

2. Petitioner be awarded the sole care, custody, and control of the three minor children of the parties. *(Or Petitioner and Respondent be awarded the joint care, etc.)*

3. Respondent be ordered to make suitable and proper provision for the support and maintenance of the Petitioner and the minor children of the parties, both during the pendency of this cause and permanently thereafter, and Respondent be further ordered to advance on behalf of Petitioner reasonable sums of money on account of attorney's fees, court costs, and suit money.

4. Petitioner be awarded a disproportionately larger share of the marital property of the parties than that which is allocated to Respondent.

5. Petitioner's non-marital property be assigned to Petitioner.

6. Petitioner be granted such other and further relief as may be appropriate under the evidence and circumstances.

                                           _____
                                                   ELLEN JARNDYCE

_____
FREDERICK TULKINGHORN, One
of the
Attorneys for Petitioner,
ELLEN JARNDYCE

                         VERIFICATION BY CERTIFICATION

Under penalties of perjury as provided by law pursuant to Section 1–109 of the Code of Civil Procedure, the undersigned certifies that the statements set forth in this instrument are true and correct, except as to matters therein stated to be on information and belief and, as to such matters, the undersigned certifies as aforesaid that I verily believe the same to be true.

DATED: _____   _____
                                                     ELLEN JARNDYCE

Frederick Tulkinghorn
Address
Telephone number

(7) **Plead dissipation and house sales.** Where there is a claim of dissipation or where a party seeks to have the marital home sold, those claims should be specifically pleaded so as not to risk waiver. See 750 ILCS 5/503(d)(2) Author's Note (21) (dissipation), and 750 ILCS 5/514 Author's Note (3) (sale).

750 ILCS 5/404

§ 404. Conciliation

(a) If the court concludes that there is a prospect of reconciliation, the court, at the request of either party, or on its own motion, may order a conciliation conference. The conciliation conference and counseling shall take place at the established court conciliation service of that judicial district or at any similar service or facility where no court conciliation service has been established.

(b) The facts adduced at any conciliation conference resulting from a referral hereunder, shall not be considered in the adjudication of a pending or subsequent action, nor shall any report resulting from such conference become part of the record of the case unless the parties have stipulated in writing to the contrary.

(c) The court, upon good cause shown, may prohibit conciliation, mediation, or other process that requires the parties meet and confer without counsel.

Author's Notes

(1) **Privileged status of conciliation conferences.** This Section provides that the facts adduced at any court-ordered conciliation conference will remain privileged. But it is unlikely that courts will permit litigants to secrete facts by telling them to conciliators. *Cf.* Johnson v. Frontier Ford, Inc., 68 Ill.App.3d 315, 319–321, 24 Ill.Dec. 908, 911–912, 386 N.E.2d 112, 115–116 (2d Dist.1979).

750 ILCS 5/404.1

§ 404.1 Educational program—Effects of dissolution of marriage on the children

(a) In an action for dissolution of marriage involving minor children, or in a post-judgment proceeding involving minor children, the court may on its own motion order the parties, excluding the minor children, to attend an educational program concerning the effects of dissolution of marriage on the children, if the court finds that it would be in the best interests of the minor children. The program may be divided into sessions, which in the aggregate shall not exceed 4 hours in duration. The program shall be educational in nature and not designed for individual therapy.

750 ILCS 5/404.1   FAMILIES

(b) The facts adduced at any educational session resulting from a referral under this Section shall not be considered in the adjudication of a pending or subsequent action, nor shall any report resulting from such educational session become part of the record of the case unless the parties have stipulated in writing to the contrary.

(c) The fees or costs of educational sessions under this Section shall be borne by the parties and may be assessed by the court as it deems equitable.

Author's Notes

Analysis

1. Privileged status of educational sessions.
2. Actual implementation of parental educational sessions.
3. Cook County Rule.

(1) **Privileged status of educational sessions.** Section 404.1 establishes the same privilege as that contained in § 404. See IMDMA § 404 Author's Note (1).

(2) **Actual implementation of parental educational sessions.** Courts are only just beginning to implement programs of the type envisioned by § 404.1. Effective April 18, 1994, Cook County has established a "Focus on Children" program. DuPage and Lake Counties also have parenting education programs.

(3) **Cook County Rule.** Cook County Rule 13.9 establishing the "Focus on Children" program follows. The rule has been successfully challenged in the trial court. *Chicago Law Bulletin*, August 17, 1994, p. 1.

13.9 Parenting Education

(a) A Parenting Education program is established for the Domestic Relations Division as provided by 750 ILCS 5/404.1 (1993). The program shall be called FOCUS ON CHILDREN.

(b) The program may be divided into sessions, which in the aggregate shall not exceed four (4) hours in duration. A certificate shall be issued in the name of the attendee upon completion and shall be filed.

(c) The program shall be educational in nature and not designed for individual therapy.

(d) All parents of minor children who have appeared or who have otherwise personally submitted to the jurisdiction of this Court in any dissolution of marriage or custody proceeding shall attend the Parenting Education program, FOCUS ON CHILDREN, before judgment is entered. In the event contested issues of custody or visitation are presented to the Court, the Parenting Education program must be completed by both parents before mediation commences.

(e) In addition, parents of minor children who have appeared in dissolution of marriage and custody proceedings filed before the effective date of this Rule or in post-judgment proceedings may be referred to FOCUS ON CHILDREN on an individual basis by the Judge to whom the case is assigned.

(f) Where a parent resides outside the State of Illinois, the Court may accept evidence of attendance at a similar Parenting Education program offered by any court of competent jurisdiction in that state, in lieu of his/her attendance at the FOCUS ON CHILDREN program.

(g) Each person shall pay a fee before registering for the educational session. The standard fee shall be TWENTY FIVE DOLLARS ($25.00) and shall be paid to the Clerk of Court upon Court order. The fee shall be waived for parties represented by civil legal service providers in accordance with 735 ILCS 5/5–105.5 (1993).

(h) The standard fee also may be reduced or waived for persons whose income from all sources is 125 percent or less of the current official federal poverty income guidelines. All persons requesting such relief shall apply to the Judge to whom the case is assigned or to the Presiding Judge before assignment and shall execute the appropriate form provided by the Clerk of the Court.

(i) Persons registered for a session who do not attend or complete that session and who do not cancel their registration at least twenty-four (24) hours in advance shall be required to re-register and pay an additional full fee.

(j) It is in the best interests of the minor child/children that this be done.

(Adopted, Mar. 29, 1994; effective Apr. 18, 1994.)

750 ILCS 5/405

§ 405. Hearing on default—Notice

If the respondent is in default, the court shall proceed to hear the cause upon testimony of petitioner taken in open court, and in no case of default shall the court grant a dissolution of marriage or legal separation or declaration of invalidity of marriage, unless the judge is satisfied that all proper means have been taken to notify the respondent of the pendency of the suit. Whenever the judge is satisfied that the interests of the respondent require it, the court may order such additional notice as may be required.

Author's Notes

Analysis

1. Adequate notice.
2. Vacation of a default judgment.
3. Defaulting pro se parties.

(1) **Adequate notice.** Adequate notice apprises the respondent of the claims to be defended against, and allows the party to anticipate the possible effects of a proceeding. Additional notice is required only if the trial court is not satisfied that the respondent received notice of the action. In re Marriage of Sheber, 121 Ill.App.3d 328, 337, 76 Ill.Dec. 921, 928, 459 N.E.2d 1056, 1063 (1st Dist.1984). Therefore, the *Sheber* court rejected the respondent's claim for additional notice when he admitted to having notice of the date of the final hearing on grounds for dissolution, custody, and property issues. See also In re Marriage of Kopec, 106 Ill.App.3d 1060, 62 Ill.Dec. 658, 436 N.E.2d 684 (1st Dist.1982) (No additional notice required prior to entry of final order granting petitioner the value of her equity in a jointly owned marital residence; respondent had a duty to follow the progress of the case after learning that his attorney had withdrawn, and after respondent had been afforded a hearing on his motion to vacate a default order before the entry of a final judgment of dissolution.)

(2) **Vacation of a default judgment.** The standard for vacating a default judgment has two prongs. The first consideration is whether substantial justice is being done between the litigants. The second factor is whether, under the circumstances of the case, it is reasonable to compel the other party to go to trial on the merits. In re Marriage of Kopec, 106 Ill.App.3d 1060, 62 Ill.Dec. 658, 436 N.E.2d 684 (1st Dist.1982).

(3) **Defaulting pro se parties.** In default cases, where the party in default is not represented by counsel, it is good practice to give the party in default notice of every court appearance, and to serve the party in default with a copy of the proposed judgment, before entry.

750 ILCS 5/406

§ 406. Fault or conduct of petitioner

In every action for a dissolution of marriage or legal separation, or declaration of invalidity of marriage, the conduct of the petitioner, unless raised by the pleadings, is not a bar to the action nor a proper basis for the refusal of a judgment of dissolution of marriage or legal separation or declaration of invalidity of marriage. Defenses which may be raised by the pleadings, however, shall not include the defenses abolished under Section 403(c).

Author's Notes

(1) **Defenses.** A respondent must specifically plead any defense based on the conduct of the petitioner that seeks to bar the dissolution or separation action. Because IMDMA § 403(c) abolishes the defenses of recrimination, and condonation after the existence of a suit with jurisdiction over the respondent, they are not available as affirmative defenses under IMDMA § 406. Available defenses that must be pled include: cause or provocation by petitioner (IMDMA § 401(a)(1)), the fault of a petitioner in a legal separation action (IMDMA § 402(a)), and condonation before the existence of a suit with jurisdiction over the respondent (IMDMA § 403(c)). Because of no fault divorce, IMDMA § 406 is seldom a factor.

750 ILCS 5/407

§ 407. Admission of respondent

No admission of the respondent shall be taken as evidence unless the court shall be satisfied that such admission was made in sincerity and without fraud or collusion to enable the petitioner to obtain a dissolution of marriage or legal separation or declaration of invalidity of marriage.

Author's Notes

(1) **Cross reference.** See Author's Notes IMDMA § 408.

750 ILCS 5/408

§ 408. Collusion—Assent or consent of petitioner

If it appears, to the satisfaction of the court, that the injury complained of was occasioned by collusion of the parties, or done with the assent of the petitioner for the purpose of obtaining a dissolution of marriage or legal separation or declaration of invalidity of marriage, or that the petitioner was consenting thereto, then no dissolution of marriage or legal separation or declaration of invalidity of marriage may be adjudged.

Author's Notes

(1) **Disuse of §§ 407, 408.** Sections 407 and 408 are almost irrelevant today, because divorces can be obtained by *de facto* agreement under the no-fault irreconcilable differences provisions of IMDMA § 401(a)(2). An express agreement of the parties is required to proceed if the separation period is more than six months but less than two years. See Affidavit and Stipulation at IMDMA § 401 Author's Note (7). An express agreement by the parties to divorce is also taken to hear matters as uncontested cases. See Stipulation and Request to Hear Uncontested Cause section of Certification and Agreement by Counsel at IMDMA § 413 Author's Note (9). Sections 407 and 408 are relics from the era of fault-oriented divorce.

750 ILCS 5/409

§ 409. Proof of foreign marriage

A marriage which may have been celebrated or had in any foreign state or country, may be proved by the acknowledgment of the parties, their cohabitation, and other circumstantial testimony.

750 ILCS 5/410

§ 410. Process—Practice—Proceedings—Publication

The process, practice and proceedings under this Act shall be the same as in other civil cases, except as otherwise provided by this Act, or by any law or rule of court, and except that when the parties resided in a municipality, in a county with a population under 2,000,000, at the time the cause of action arose, and if service by publication is necessary, publication shall be in a newspaper published in such municipality if there is one.

750 ILCS 5/411

§ 411. Commencement of action

(a) Actions for dissolution of marriage or legal separation shall be commenced as in other civil cases or, at the option of petitioner, by filing a praecipe for summons with the clerk of the court and paying the regular filing fees, in which latter case, a petition shall be filed within 6 months thereafter.

(b) When a praecipe for summons is filed without the petition, the summons shall recite that petitioner has commenced suit for dissolution of marriage or legal separation and shall require the respondent to file his or her appearance not later than 30 days from the day the summons is served and to plead to the petitioner's petition within 30 days from the day the petition is filed.

750 ILCS 5/411   **FAMILIES**

Until a petition has been filed, the court, pursuant to subsections (c) and (d) herein, may dismiss the suit, order the filing of a petition, or grant leave to the respondent to file a petition in the nature of a counter petition.

After the filing of the petition, the party filing the same shall, within 2 days, serve a copy thereof upon the other party, in the manner provided by rule of the Supreme Court for service of notices in other civil cases.

(c) Unless a respondent voluntarily files an appearance, a praecipe for summons filed without the petition shall be served on the respondent not later than 30 days after its issuance, and upon failure to obtain service upon the respondent within the 30 day period, or any extension for good cause shown granted by the court, the court shall dismiss the suit.

(d) An action for dissolution of marriage or legal separation commenced by the filing a praecipe for summons without the petition shall be dismissed unless a petition for dissolution of marriage or legal separation has been filed within 6 months after the commencement of the action.

Author's Notes

Analysis

1. Commencement.
2. Praecipe for summons.
3. Temporary relief.
4. Praecipe—Form.
5. Counter pleading.
6. Dismissal: Service of the summons.
7. Dismissal: Filing of petition for dissolution or legal separation.

(1) **Commencement.** A party may commence an action for dissolution of marriage or legal separation either by filing a petition or by filing a praecipe (request) for summons.

(2) **Praecipe for summons.** The praecipe for summons is a simple temporary form that requires little input, and the praecipe is useful when it is important to file a lawsuit quickly. For example, a praecipe can be effectively used when the respondent is about to leave the jurisdiction, and it is desirable to gain jurisdiction over him before he leaves. Another situation in which a praecipe can be employed is where filing a lawsuit first is an advantage, for one reason or another, and you want to win a race to the courthouse. A divorce action commenced by the praecipe-summons procedure has precedence over any suit filed at a later time in any other county. Abbott v. Abbott, 52 Ill.App.3d 728, 10 Ill.Dec. 464, 367 N.E.2d 1073 (3d Dist.1977). Filing of a praecipe may also establish precedence in interstate or international jurisdictional disputes. A praecipe is also useful when it is desirable to initiate a lawsuit, but where the petitioner does not want to plead specific grounds or does not have the information sufficient for the preparation of a petition.

(3) **Temporary relief.** Although there is negligible authority, it should be possible to obtain temporary relief (support, custody, injunctions) when only a praecipe has been filed, in the same manner as when petitions for dissolution or legal separation are filed. But it is additionally necessary to file a petition specifically directed to the temporary relief sought. There must of course be appropriate service

FAMILIES 750 ILCS 5/411

of the praecipe and notice of the petition for temporary relief, except in cases of petitions for temporary restraining orders without notice.

(4) **Praecipe—Form.** There follows a praecipe form.

PRAECIPE FOR (DIVORCE) (SEPARATE MAINTENANCE)   (3/30/93) CCDR 0003A

IN THE CIRCUIT COURT OF COOK COUNTY, ILLINOIS
COUNTY DEPARTMENT - DIVORCE DIVISION

Praecipe for Summons in Suit for *(Divorce) (Separate Maintenance)

(*Strike out one not applicable)

Vs.   No.

To Honorable AURELIA PUCINSKI, Clerk of said Court:

Please issue summons in the above cause to the sheriff of Cook County, Illinois, directed to the above named defendant.

Name
Attorney for
Address
City
Telephone
Atty No.

AURELIA PUCINSKI, CLERK OF THE CIRCUIT COURT OF COOK COUNTY

[G17975]

750 ILCS 5/411

(5) **Counter pleading.** The respondent's counter pleading to a praecipe is a counter-petition.

(6) **Dismissal: Service of the summons.** Unless the respondent voluntarily files an appearance, the court shall dismiss the suit if the respondent is not served within 30 days after issuance of the praecipe, or within any extension granted for good cause.

(7) **Dismissal: Filing of petition for dissolution or legal separation.** The court "shall" dismiss an action initiated by a praecipe without a petition unless the petition for dissolution or legal separation is filed within six months of the filing of the praecipe. The provision for dismissal in § 411(d) is mandatory, although it is not clear whether it is reversible error for a court to allow a case to proceed after a failure to file a petition for in excess of six months, particularly in light of the permissive provisions of the second paragraph of § 411(b). The six month time period is frequently missed by lawyers and it can result in unexpected dismissals. The six months should be carefully diaried in actions begun by the filing of a praecipe.

750 ILCS 5/412

§ 412. Filing of petition—Cases requiring service by publication

In any case wherein the requisite affidavit for service by publication has been filed to obtain jurisdiction as to the party against whom a judgment of dissolution of marriage or of legal separation or of declaration of invalidity of marriage is sought, petitioner shall immediately, and without leave of court, file his or her petition.

750 ILCS 5/413

§ 413. Judgment

(a) A judgment of dissolution of marriage or of legal separation or of declaration of invalidity of marriage is final when entered, subject to the right of appeal. An appeal from the judgment of dissolution of marriage that does not challenge the finding as to grounds does not delay the finality of that provision of the judgment which dissolves the marriage, beyond the time for appealing from that provision, and either of the parties may remarry pending appeal. An order directing payment of money for support or maintenance of the spouse or the minor child or children shall not be suspended or the enforcement thereof stayed pending the appeal.

(b) The clerk of the court shall give notice of the entry of a judgment of dissolution of marriage or legal separation or a declaration of invalidity of marriage:

(1) if the marriage is registered in this State, to the county clerk of the county where the marriage is registered, who shall enter the fact of dissolution of marriage or legal separation or declaration of invalidity of marriage in the marriage registry; and within 45 days after the close of the month in which the judgment is entered, the clerk shall forward the

certificate to the Department of Public Health on a form furnished by the Department; or

(2) if the marriage is registered in another jurisdiction, to the appropriate official of that jurisdiction, with the request that he enter the fact of dissolution of marriage or legal separation or declaration of invalidity of marriage in the appropriate record.

(c) Upon request by a wife whose marriage is dissolved or declared invalid, the court shall order her maiden name or a former name restored.

(d) A judgment of dissolution of marriage or legal separation, if made, shall be awarded to both of the parties, and shall provide that it affects the status previously existing between the parties in the manner adjudged.

Author's Notes

Analysis

1. Appeal: Finality and ripeness.
2. Partial resolution of issues.
3. Appeal not challenging finding as to grounds of dissolution.
4. Appeal does not stay maintenance or support.
5. Resumption of wife's maiden name.
6. Award of judgment.
7. Cross references.
8. Judgment for Dissolution of Marriage—Form.
9. Certification and Agreement by Counsel—Form.
10. Family Support Affidavit—Form.
11. Agreement and judgment repetition.
12. Release of Errors by the Respondent; Release of Errors by the Petitioner—Forms.
13. Partial Release (Satisfaction) of Judgment—Form.

(1) **Appeal: Finality and ripeness.** Section 413(a) provides that a judgment of dissolution of marriage or of legal separation, or of declaration of invalidity of marriage is final when entered, subject to the right of appeal. Nonetheless, an appealable judgment must still meet the requirements of finality and ripeness for review. In re Marriage of Lentz, 73 Ill.App.3d 93, 29 Ill.Dec. 319, 391 N.E.2d 582 (4th Dist.1979), *aff'd*, 79 Ill.2d 400, 38 Ill.Dec. 582, 403 N.E.2d 1036 (1980).

(2) **Partial resolution of issues.** Generally, judgments that do not decide all of the issues are not final, and therefore are not appealable. A judgement is final only when the order "terminates the litigation on the merits so that, if affirmed, the trial court has only to proceed with execution." Myers v. Myers, 51 Ill.App.3d 830, 837, 9 Ill.Dec. 603, 610, 366 N.E.2d 1114, 1121 (1977).

In some instances, if all of the issues are not decided, the trial court can make a judgment final and appealable pursuant to Supreme Court Rule 304 with a specific finding that the judgment is a final order and there is no just reason to delay enforcement or appeal. However, the mere inclusion of such a special finding does not make an order final if it is not in fact final. The test of finality of a judgment order lies in the substance, not the form, of the order. In re Marriage of Nilsson, 81 Ill.App.3d 580, 37 Ill.Dec. 394, 402 N.E.2d 284 (3d Dist.1980). See Supreme Court Rules 303 and 304 and Author's Notes to Supreme Court Rule 304 for fuller discussions of finality.

(3) **Appeal not challenging finding as to grounds of dissolution.** An appeal from a judgment of dissolution of marriage that does not challenge the finding concerning the grounds for dissolution does not delay the finality of the dissolution beyond the time for appealing from that provision. For example, a dissolution is final if the finding of grounds for dissolution is not challenged on appeal, even though the appeal challenges the financial and custody issues. Either of the parties can remarry pending such an appeal.

(4) **Appeal does not stay maintenance or support.** A judgment directing the payment for the support of a spouse or a minor child is neither suspended nor its enforcement stayed pending the appeal. Acceptance of such support by the appellant does not waive her claim in the appeal that the support is insufficient. In re Marriage of Reib, 114 Ill.App.3d 993, 1003, 70 Ill.Dec. 572, 580, 449 N.E.2d 919, 927 (1st Dist.1983) (wife accepted $32,500 from the sale of the marital home and $800 per month maintenance; a litigant cannot attack a decree after enjoying its benefits, if to do so would place the opposing party at a disadvantage upon reversal; no material prejudice to husband shown).

(5) **Resumption of wife's maiden name.** The statute specifically provides in subsection 413(c) that a wife can resume her maiden name or former name after a dissolution of marriage. The name change is most easily placed in the dissolution judgment.

(6) **Award of judgment.** Pursuant to the provisions of subsection 413(d), all judgments of dissolution are now awarded to both parties. Previously, under the fault-based system, the party the court found to be free of fault was awarded a divorce from her or his spouse.

(7) **Cross references.** See 735 ILCS 5/2-1203, motions after judgment in nonjury cases; 735 ILCS 5/2-1401, relief from judgments after 30 days; Supreme Court Rule 272, time of entry of judgment; Supreme Court Rule 303, appeals from final judgments; and Supreme Court Rule 304, appeals from final judgments that do not dispose of the entire proceedings.

(8) **Judgment for Dissolution of Marriage—Form.** There follows a sample judgment that can be used to physically incorporate a settlement agreement that has been concluded by the parties. The model judgment is a basic wrap-around judgment into which the marital settlement agreement is inserted after paragraph E. Additional and alternative paragraphs that may be added or substituted follow the judgment. In contested cases, the wrap-around judgment should be modified to show a contest, to include the additional findings of the court, and, in place of the settlement agreement of the parties, should set forth the adjudication by the court of the financial and children's issues.

FAMILIES   750 ILCS 5/413

                                            FIRM #_____

IN THE CIRCUIT COURT OF COOK COUNTY, ILLINOIS
COUNTY DEPARTMENT—DOMESTIC RELATIONS DIVISION

IN RE THE MARRIAGE OF   )
)
SUSAN JELLYBY,   )
)
            Petitioner,   )
)
and   )   No. ____ D _____
)
ARTHUR JELLYBY,   )
)
            Respondent.   )

JUDGMENT FOR DISSOLUTION OF MARRIAGE

THIS CAUSE COMING ON TO BE HEARD upon the Petition for Dissolution of Marriage of the Petitioner, SUSAN JELLYBY, and the Response to the Petition for Dissolution of the Respondent, ARTHUR JELLYBY, and upon the Stipulation by the parties and their attorneys that the above entitled cause may proceed to an immediate hearing upon the Petition of the Petitioner and the Response of the Respondent as an uncontested matter; the Petitioner appearing in open Court in her own proper person, and by Samuel Kenge, of Kenge and Carboy, as her attorneys; the Respondent appearing in open court by Joseph Blowers, of Blowers & Associates, Ltd., as his attorneys; and the Court having heard testimony of the various witnesses duly sworn and examined in open Court; Petitioner offering additional proof in support of the allegations contained in her Petition (a certificate of which evidence being duly signed and sealed is filed herein), and the Court considering all of the evidence, and now being fully advised in the premises, *finds* as follows:

   A. Petitioner and Respondent *(or one of them)* are now residents of the State of Illinois, they were residents of the State of Illinois at the time this action was commenced, and the residence has been maintained for more than ninety (90) days next preceding the commencement of this action, and next preceding the making of this finding. Petitioner resides in Cook County.

   B. Petitioner and Respondent were married on _____, 19__, and the marriage is registered in _____, _____ County, _____. Petitioner and Respondent lived together as husband and wife from the time of their marriage until 19__.

   C. Two children were born to the parties as the issue of the marriage, whose names and ages are: Caddy Jellyby, 12 years of age; and Peepy Jellyby, 4 years of age. Both parties are fit and proper persons to have the custody of the minor children, Caddy and Peepy. No children were adopted by the parties, and Petitioner is not pregnant.

750 ILCS 5/413 **FAMILIES**

D. The spouses have lived separate and apart for a continuous period of in excess of two (2) years and irreconcilable differences between the parties have caused an irretrievable breakdown of the marriage. Efforts at reconciliation have failed and future attempts at reconciliation would be impracticable and not in the best interests of the family.

(If the spouses have lived apart for more than six months but less than two years, state the amount of time in the first sentence, and add the following sentence at the end of paragraph D.) The parties have waived in writing the requirement that they live separate and apart for more than two (2) years, and each has stated under oath that they have lived separate and apart for longer than six (6) months.

E. Petitioner and Respondent have entered into a written Settlement Agreement, dated _____, 19__, providing for: maintenance for the Petitioner, the custody, visitation, support, and education of the children of the parties, and a full and final settlement of all property, marital and non-marital claims, and all other rights and claims of each party against the other. *(Strike or modify topics in preceding sentence as appropriate.)* The Settlement Agreement has been presented to this Court for its consideration and approval and it is in words and figures, as follows:

(Physically insert the Settlement Agreement here.)

F. And the Court having examined the Agreement and been informed of the circumstances of the parties, FINDS that the Agreement dated _____, 199__ was entered into by the parties freely and voluntarily; the Agreement is fair, equitable under the circumstances, and is not unconscionable; and the Agreement should be approved by the Court and incorporated into this Judgment.

G. Petitioner has established by competent, material, and relevant proof the allegations in her Petition contained; and this Court has jurisdiction of the parties to this cause and of the subject matter hereof.

IT IS THEREFORE ORDERED, ADJUDGED AND DECREED, and this Court by virtue of the power and authority therein vested and the Statute in such case made and provided, DOTH HEREBY ORDER, ADJUDGE AND DECREE as follows:

1. A Judgment of Dissolution of Marriage is awarded to both of the parties. Accordingly, the bonds of matrimony existing between the Petitioner, Susan Jellyby, and the Respondent, Arthur Jellyby, be and the same are hereby dissolved, and the parties are, and each of them is, freed from the obligations thereof, and are herewith divorced from each other.

2. The Agreement of the parties dated _____, 199__ is hereby approved, and the Agreement and all of its provisions are incorporated into and made a part of this Judgment with the same full force and effect as though the Agreement and all of its provisions were written into this decretal part of this Judgment verbatim.

3. Petitioner and Respondent shall perform, execute, and carry out the provisions of the Agreement incorporated herein, and this Court reserves jurisdiction of the parties to this cause and the subject matter thereof for the following purposes: (a) to enforce the provisions of the Agreement incorporated herein; (b) to adjudicate any issue that may arise concerning the children of the parties; and (c) to adjudicate any other issues that may arise where the parties have requested that the Court reserve jurisdiction in the Settlement Agreement incorporated herein, or where jurisdiction is reserved by operation of law.

4. Petitioner and Respondent shall have the joint care, custody, control, and education of Caddy Jellyby and Peepy Jellyby, the minor children of the parties. The physical residence of Caddy and Peepy, and the visitation of them, shall be in accordance with the provisions of the Settlement Agreement, incorporated herein *(or in accordance with the Joint Parenting Agreement dated _____, 199__, or Joint Parenting Order entered on _____, 199__)*.

5. The inchoate or other right of dower, homestead, claim or title, contingent, reversionary or otherwise, and any rights of courtesy and descent, and all other rights and claims of each party in and to the marital property and the non-marital property of the other party, real, personal or mixed, shall be and the same are hereby forever relinquished, released, barred, terminated and ended, and during their respective lifetimes each of the parties hereto may deal with his or her separate estates as if the said parties hereto had never been married to each other, and upon the death of either of them, the property, real, personal or mixed, then owned by him or her shall pass by his or her Will, or under the laws of descent (as the case may be), free from any right, statutory or otherwise, inheritance, dower, title, or claim of the other party, and as if the parties hereto had never been married to each other; neither the Petitioner nor the Respondent herein shall, at any time hereafter, sue the other of them, or his or her (as the case may be) heirs, executors, administrators, or assigns for the purpose of enforcing any or all of the rights specified in and relinquished, waived, discharged, released, barred, and terminated hereunder; provided, however, that nothing herein contained shall release, limit, modify or abridge the obligations of the parties fully to perform, execute and carry out the provisions of the Agreement incorporated herein.

6. All the rights, claims and demands, of every kind, nature and description, which each party has or may hereafter have, or claim to have against the other, including all liabilities now or at any time hereinafter existing between the parties hereto, shall be and the same are forever discharged, extinguished, released and ended; and all matters and charges whatsoever, and any and all manner of actions or caused of actions, suits, debts, dues, accounts, bonds, covenants, contracts, agreements, judgments, claims, torts, and demands whatsoever in law or in equity, which each party ever had, has or which he or she, his or her heirs, executors, administrators or assigns, or any of them, hereafter can, shall or may have against the other (as the case may be) for or by reason of any cause, matter or thing whatsoever, from the beginning of the world to the date hereof, shall be and the same are forever released, dis-

750 ILCS 5/413   **FAMILIES**

charged, barred, terminated and extinguished; provided, however, nothing herein contained shall release, limit, modify, or abridge the obligation of the parties to perform, execute and carry out the provisions of the Agreement incorporated herein.

ENTER:

_____

JUDGE   Date

APPROVED:

_____   _____
SUSAN JELLYBY   ARTHUR JELLYBY

Samuel Kenge
Kenge and Carboy
Attorneys for SUSAN JELLYBY
Address
Telephone number

Judgment Additional and Alternative Provisions

7. *Deviation from children's support guidelines.* When children's support deviates from the guidelines in § 505(a)(1) of IMDMA, the following paragraph, in accordance with § 505(a)(2), should be inserted in the finding section of the judgment:

The Court hereby adopts as its finding paragraph 4(d) of the Settlement Agreement of the parties incorporated in this Judgment of Dissolution of Marriage. *(See para. 4(d) of model settlement agreement at IMDMA § 502 Author's Note (11).)*

Or:

The Court hereby finds that the application of the children's support guidelines in Section 505(a)(1) of the Illinois Marriage and Dissolution of Marriage Act are inappropriate after considering the best interests of the children in light of evidence including but not limited to one or more of the following relevant factors: *(Strike what is not relevant.)*

(a) the financial resources of the children;

(b) the financial resources and needs of the custodial parent;

(c) the standard of living the children would have enjoyed had the marriage not been dissolved;

(d) the physical and emotional condition of the children, and his and her educational needs;

(e) the financial resources and needs of the non-custodial parent.

The support that would have been required under the guidelines is $_____ *(or is not determinable)*. The reasons for deviation from the guidelines are: _____.

8. *Opting out of payments to clerk and withholding. Parties who have agreed to make maintenance and children's support payments directly, rather than through the clerk of the court pursuant to IMDMA § 507, and who have agreed to waive immediate withholding pursuant to § 706.1(B), should insert the following paragraph in the decretal section of the judgment:*

Respondent shall make the maintenance and children's support payments directly to Petitioner and not through the Clerk of the Court. The Court hereby approves: (1) the waiver by Petitioner and Respondent of the requirement in Section 706.1(B) of the Illinois Marriage and Dissolution of Marriage Act that the order for withholding take effect immediately, and (2) the parties' alternative arrangement to insure the payment of support. The parties' waiver and alternative arrangement are contained in the Settlement Agreement incorporated herein. *(See paras. 5(a) through 5(c) of the model settlement agreement at IMDMA § 502 Author's Note (11).)*

9. *Non-modifiable. Parties who have agreed to make certain provisions of their agreement non-modifiable pursuant to § 502(f) of IMDMA (usually confined to maintenance, since children's provisions are excluded by § 502(f), and property provisions are generally not modifiable pursuant to § 510(b)) should insert the following paragraph in the decretal portion of the judgment:*

The parties having so agreed in their Settlement Agreement incorporated herein, pursuant to Section 502(f) of the Illinois Marriage and Dissolution of Marriage Act, paragraphs _____ of the Settlement Agreement incorporated herein shall not be modified in any respect whatsoever, except as otherwise provided in the Settlement Agreement. *(See para. 2(g) of the model settlement agreement at IMDMA § 502 Author's Note (11).)*

10. *Incorporation by reference. For reasons of privacy, parties frequently do not want their settlement agreement to be physically incorporated into the judgment and thereby made a part of the public records. Where that is the case:*

Strike the words after "approval" in the last line of finding E of the model judgment, and do not physically insert the agreement in the judgment.

Add the following finding as finding G, and change the present G to H.

G. The parties have agreed that they will incorporate their Agreement dated _____, 199__ into this Judgment by reference. They have further agreed that the purpose of incorporating the Agreement in the Judgment by reference is only to protect the privacy of the terms of the Agreement. They further agree that it is their intention that the incorporation by reference shall have the same effect under the Illinois Marriage and Dissolution of Marriage Act as a verbatim incorporation.

In place of decretal paragraph 2, insert the following paragraph 2.

750 ILCS 5/413   **FAMILIES**

    2. The Agreement of the parties dated _____, 199__ is hereby approved and the Agreement and all of its provisions are incorporated into and made a part of this Judgment by reference. The incorporation into this Judgment by reference shall have the same force and effect and the same rights and remedies shall be available to the parties under the Illinois Marriage and Dissolution of Marriage Act as in a verbatim incorporation. *(See para. 12(b) of the model Settlement Agreement at IMDMA § 502 Author's Note (11).)*

    11. *Waiver of maintenance. If maintenance is waived by one or both of the parties, insert the following paragraph in the findings:*

    Petitioner has acknowledged that she is employed and she is capable of supporting herself from her salary and from the property and income generated therefrom allocated to her in the Agreement between the parties dated _____, 199__. Respondent has acknowledged that he is employed and he is capable of supporting himself from his salary and from the property and the income generated therefrom allocated to him in the Agreement between the parties dated _____, 199__. Both Petitioner and Respondent have acknowledged that neither requires any maintenance, alimony, or support from the other. *(See para. 2(h) of the model settlement agreement at IMDMA § 502 Author's Note (11).)*

    In addition, insert the following in the decretal paragraph section.

    The waiver by Petitioner and Respondent of her and his claims to alimony, maintenance, and support is hereby approved, and, accordingly, all rights, claims, and demands of Petitioner and Respondent, past, present, and future, to alimony, maintenance, and support, temporary and permanent, from the other, are hereby forever barred, terminated and ended.

    (9) **Certification and Agreement by Counsel—Form.** A sample Certification and Agreement by Counsel that the matter proceed to an immediate hearing as an uncontested matter is contained in this Author's Note. The documents that the court requires to enter an uncontested judgment are listed in the Certification following the first paragraph. A sample petition for dissolution is at IMDMA § 403 Author's Note (6). A sample stipulation waiving the two year requirement is at IMDMA § 401 Author's Note (7). A sample order for withholding is at IMDMA § 706.1 Author's Note (10). A sample marital settlement agreement, which contains also a joint parenting agreement is at IMDMA § 502 Author's Note (11). The same documents, except the Certification and Agreement of Counsel and the settlement agreement, are required in contested cases.

FAMILIES 750 ILCS 5/413

3231 - Stipulation to Hear Uncontested Cause   CCDCH-104

IN THE CIRCUIT COURT OF COOK COUNTY, ILLINOIS
COUNTY DEPARTMENT, DOMESTIC RELATIONS DIVISION

IN RE THE ☐ MARRIAGE ☐ CUSTODY
☐ SUPPORT OF:

PETITIONER:
AND

NO:
CALENDAR

RESPONDENT

CERTIFICATION AND AGREEMENT BY COUNSEL

We, the undersigned attorneys of record, CERTIFY that there are no contested issues in this cause, that all required court fees have been paid, that each counsel is ready to proceed in this matter by uncontested prove-up as in cases of default. We further CERTIFY that we are prepared to present to the judge on the date of trial the following documents:

1. a copy of the Petition for Dissolution and Respondent's Appearance and evidence that all court fees have been paid;
2. a copy of this Stipulation and Request to Hear Uncontested Cause signed by the parties;
3. in appropriate cases, a written stipulation executed by the parties which waives the required two year separation period;
4. a proposed Judgment including any Marital Settlement Agreement and/or Joint Parenting Agreement previously executed by the parties which may be appended thereto;
5. an immediate Order for Withholding as provided in Ch. 40 para. 706.1, ILL. REV. STAT.;
6. a completed Family Support Affidavit as required by Domestic Relations Division General Order 89-D-1; and,
7. where appropriate, a completed Application for Child Support Services with the IV-D Agency.

Attorney for Petitioner	Date	Attorney for Respondent	Date
Address		Address	
Telephone No.		Telephone No.	
Attorney's Code No.		Attorney's Code No.	

STIPULATION AND REQUEST TO HEAR UNCONTESTED CAUSE

We, the undersigned parties, STIPULATE AND AGREE that all matters pending between us have been settled, agreed and compromised, freely and voluntarily after full disclosure, and we hereby REQUEST that this cause be heard as an uncontested matter.

Petitioner	Date	Respondent	Date

8281 - Cause Assigned for Prove-up

ORDER OF ASSIGNMENT

IT IS ORDERED THAT this cause is assigned for prove-up before Judge _____
Calendar _____ on _____, 19 ____, at ____ .m.

(code no.)

ENTER: _____
Preliminary Judge   Judge Number   Date

[G17976]

750 ILCS 5/413   **FAMILIES**

(10) **Family Support Affidavit—Form.** A sample Family Support Affidavit is in this Author's Note.

IN THE CIRCUIT COURT OF COOK COUNTY
DOMESTIC RELATIONS DIVISION

In re the MARRIAGE of   )
_____   )
Petitioner   )
)
         and   ) No. ____ D _____
)
)
_____   )
Respondent   )
)

FAMILY SUPPORT AFFIDAVIT

This completed form must be attached to any judgment, decree or order of court which contains an initial order for the payment of child support and/or maintenance. Both parties may use one form or they may complete separate forms. If either party is not present, both Part I and Part II must be completed by the party who is present to the best of her/his information and belief.

PART I. To Be Completed by Custodial Parent

Full Name _____

Address _____

City _____ State _____ Zip _____

Soc. Sec. No. _____ Home phone _____ Work phone _____

Employer _____

Address _____

City _____ State _____ Zip _____

Child(ren) to be supported:

Name	Sex	Date of Birth
_____	_____	_____
_____	_____	_____
_____	_____	_____

Is child(ren) receiving Public Assistance? (Yes or No) _____

If yes, give case number _____

- -

CDSD-108(1-88)   See Reverse Side

[G17977]

FAMILIES   750 ILCS 5/413

PART II. To Be Completed by Non-Custodial Parent

Full Name _____ Date of Birth _____
Address _____
City _____ State _____ Zip Code _____
Soc. Sec. No. _____ Home phone _____ Work phone _____
Employer _____
Address _____
City _____ State _____ Zip Code _____
Height _____ Weight _____ Eyes _____ Complexion _____
Race _____ Birthplace (city, state) _____
Occupation _____ Driver's License No. _____
Father's Name (last, first) _____
Mother's Name (maiden, first) _____
Military Service? _____ If yes, which Branch? _____ Retired? _____

CERTIFICATION

Under penalties provided by law in Section 1-109 of the Code of Civil Procedure, the undersigned certifies that he/she knows the statements set forth in this document are true and correct, except as to matters therein specifically stated to be on information and belief and as to those matters the undersigned certifies that he/she believes them to be true.

_____   _____   _____   _____
Custodial Parent   Date   Non-Custodial Parent   Date

            *   *   *   *   *

_____   _____
Attorney for Custodial Parent   Attorney for Non-Custodial Parent

Atty Name:
Atty No.:
Address:
City:
Phone No. :

[G17978]

(11) **Agreement and judgment repetition.** The releases in the judgment at Author's Note (8) above, decretal paragraphs 5 and 6, may be considered redundant if similar releases are placed in the settlement agreement. See IMDMA § 502 Author's

750 ILCS 5/413 **FAMILIES**

Note (11) Article XI for settlement agreement releases. It can also be argued that it is unnecessary to repeat clauses from the settlement agreement in the judgment when the settlement agreement is adopted by the court and incorporated into the judgment, such as non-modifiability, and the like. This model judgment and its Additional and Alternative Provisions err on the side of caution.

(12) **Release of Errors by the Respondent; Release of Errors by the Petitioner—Forms.** Particularly when a contested case is settled after entry of the judgment and before an appeal, and in other situations that are vulnerable to appeal or attack by motion, it is advisable to have each side sign a release of errors in order to preclude any further proceedings. There follows sample releases of errors.

FIRM #_____

IN THE CIRCUIT COURT OF COOK COUNTY, ILLINOIS
COUNTY DEPARTMENT, DOMESTIC RELATIONS DIVISION

IN RE THE MARRIAGE OF:	)
DAVID KROOK,	)
Petitioner,	)
and	) No. ___ D _____
CHARLOTTE KROOK,	)
Respondent.	)

RELEASE OF ERRORS BY THE RESPONDENT

I, CHARLOTTE KROOK, the Respondent in the above entitled cause, for good and valuable consideration, the receipt and sufficiency whereof are hereby acknowledged and confessed, including benefits to me under the orders and judgment heretofore entered in the above entitled cause and availed of by me, do hereby release and waive any, every, and all errors that may be contained in the proceedings and record of the above entitled cause, and in the rendition of the judgment therein, and which might otherwise be taken advantage of by me by motion to set aside, reconsider, or vacate the orders or the judgment, or by petition under Section 1401 of the Code of Civil Procedure of the State of Illinois (735 ILCS 5/2–1401), or by writ of error, or by appeal, or by any other proceeding in law or in equity.

AND I, CHARLOTTE KROOK, do hereby consent and agree that this Release of Errors may be spread of record, or pleaded, or offered in evidence, to bar, defeat, and terminate any proceedings whatsoever which may hereafter be taken by me to vacate, set aside, reconsider, reverse, annul, or cancel any orders or the judgment entered in the above entitled cause.

AND I, CHARLOTTE KROOK, do hereby acknowledge and confess that this instrument is executed by me with full knowledge of the state of the record in the above entitled cause and after I have had the benefit and advice of counsel.

    IN WITNESS WHEREOF, I have hereunto set my hand and seal this _____ day of _____, 199__.

                                                _____(SEAL)
                                                CHARLOTTE KROOK

Signed, sealed and delivered in the presence of:

_____

_____

Samuel Kenge
Kenge and Carboy
Attorneys for CHARLOTTE KROOK
Address
Telephone number

                                                                     FIRM #_____

IN THE CIRCUIT COURT OF COOK COUNTY, ILLINOIS
COUNTY DEPARTMENT, DOMESTIC RELATIONS DIVISION

IN RE THE MARRIAGE OF:)
)
DAVID KROOK,   )
)
             Petitioner,   )
)
and   )   No. ____ D _____
)
CHARLOTTE KROOK,   )
)
             Respondent.   )

RELEASE OF ERRORS BY THE PETITIONER

    I, DAVID KROOK, the Petitioner in the above entitled cause, for good and valuable consideration, the receipt and sufficiency whereof are hereby acknowledged and confessed, including benefits to me under the orders and judgment heretofore entered in the above entitled cause and availed of by me, do hereby release and waive any, every, and all errors that may be contained in the proceedings and record of the above entitled cause, and in the rendition of the judgment therein, and which might otherwise be taken advantage of by me by motion to set aside, reconsider, or vacate the orders or the judgment, or by petition under Section 1401 of the Code of Civil Procedure of the State of

750 ILCS 5/413   **FAMILIES**

Illinois (735 ILCS 5/2–1401), or by writ of error, or by appeal, or by any other proceeding in law or in equity.

    AND I, DAVID KROOK, do hereby consent and agree that this Release of Errors may be spread of record, or pleaded, or offered in evidence, to bar, defeat, and terminate any proceedings whatsoever which may hereafter be taken by me to vacate, set aside, reconsider, reverse, annul, or cancel any orders or the judgment entered in the above entitled cause.

    AND I, DAVID KROOK, do hereby acknowledge and confess that this instrument is executed by me with full knowledge of the state of the record in the above entitled cause and after I have had the benefit and advice of counsel.

    IN WITNESS WHEREOF, I have hereunto set my hand and seal this _____ day of _____, 199__.

                                                _____(SEAL)
                                                DAVID KROOK

Signed, sealed and delivered in the presence of:

_____

_____

Samuel Kenge
Kenge and Carboy
Attorneys for CHARLOTTE KROOK
Address
Telephone number

    (13) **Partial Release (Satisfaction) of Judgment—Form.** A satisfaction of judgment should be used where it is necessary to have evidence independent of the performance itself that the judgment has been partially or completely performed. For example, where performance varies from the precise terms of the judgment, or where performance does not leave a paper trail of cancelled checks, deeds, or the like, a satisfaction of judgment should be obtained. There follows a sample satisfaction of judgment.

FAMILIES   750 ILCS 5/413

                                    FIRM #_____

IN THE CIRCUIT COURT OF COOK COUNTY, ILLINOIS
COUNTY DEPARTMENT—DOMESTIC RELATIONS DIVISION

IN RE THE MARRIAGE OF   )
)
SUSAN JELLYBY,   )
            Petitioner,   )
)
and   ) No. ___ D _____
)
ARTHUR JELLYBY,   )
            Respondent.   )

PARTIAL RELEASE (Satisfaction) OF JUDGMENT

SUSAN JELLYBY, the Judgment Creditor, having received full satisfaction and payment of the property paragraphs ___ through ___ of the Marital Settlement Agreement dated _____, 199__, incorporated by reference into the Judgment of Dissolution of Marriage entered on _____, 199__, hereby releases Respondent, ARTHUR JELLYBY, from any further obligation under the terms of paragraphs ___ through ___ of the Marital Settlement Agreement dated _____, 199__ incorporated in the Judgment for Dissolution of Marriage entered on _____, 199__.

DATE: _____   _____
                                    SUSAN JELLYBY

                                    APPROVED:

                                    _____
                                    SAMUEL KENGE
                                    Attorney for SUSAN JELLYBY

Joseph Blowers
Blowers & Associates, Ltd.
Attorneys for ARTHUR JELLYBY
Address
Telephone number

PART IV—A. JOINT SIMPLIFIED DISSOLUTION PROCEDURE

Analysis

Sec.
451. Applicability.
452. Petition.
453. Procedure; Judgment.
454. Affidavit.
455. Copies of judgment.
456. Forms.
457. Brochure to describe proceedings.

750 ILCS 5/451

§ 451. Applicability

In any proceeding under this Part IV-A, the provisions of this Part IV-A shall control where they conflict with other provisions of this Act.

750 ILCS 5/452

§ 452. Petition

The parties to a dissolution proceeding may file a joint petition for simplified dissolution if they certify that all of the following conditions exist when the proceeding is commenced:

(a) Neither party is dependent on the other party for support or each party is willing to waive the right to support; and the parties understand that consultation with attorneys may help them determine eligibility for spousal support.

(b) Either party has met the residency requirement of Section 401 of this Act.

(c) Irreconcilable differences have cause the irretrievable breakdown of the marriage and the parties have been separated 6 months or more and efforts at reconciliation have failed or future attempts at reconciliation would be impracticable and not in the best interests of the family.

(d) No children were born of the relationship of the parties or adopted by the parties during the marriage, and the wife, to her knowledge, is not pregnant by the husband.

(e) The duration of the marriage does not exceed 5 years.

(f) Neither party has any interest in real property.

(g) The parties waive any rights to maintenance.

(h) The total fair market value of all marital property, after deducting all encumbrances, is less than $5,000 and the combined gross annualized income from all sources is less than $25,000.

(i) The parties have disclosed to each other all assets and their tax returns for all years of the marriage.

(j) The parties have executed a written agreement dividing all assets in excess of $100 in value and allocating responsibility for debts and liabilities between the parties.

750 ILCS 5/453

§ 453. Procedure; Judgment

The parties shall use the forms provided by the circuit court clerk, and the clerk shall submit the petition to the court. The court shall expeditiously consider the cause. Both parties shall appear in person before the court and, if the court so directs, testify. The court, after examination of the petition and the parties and finding the agreement of the parties not unconscionable, shall enter a judgment granting the dissolution if the requirements of this Part IV-A have been met and the parties have submitted the affidavit required under Section 454. No transcript of proceedings shall be required.

750 ILCS 5/454

§ 454. Affidavit

At the time of the hearing, the parties shall submit to the court an affidavit executed by both parties stating that all property has been divided in accordance with the agreement of the parties and that they have executed all documents required to effectuate the agreement.

750 ILCS 5/455

§ 455. Copies of judgment

Upon entry of the judgment and upon payment of the fee, the circuit court clerk shall furnish to each party a certified copy of the final judgment of dissolution.

750 ILCS 5/456

§ 456. Forms

The contents of forms to be used in simplified dissolutions shall be provided for by court rule. The circuit court clerk shall supply forms upon request for use by parties seeking simplified dissolutions under this Part IV-A.

750 ILCS 5/457

§ 457. Brochure to describe proceedings

The circuit court clerk may make available a brochure that describes the requirements, nature, and effect of a simplified dissolution. The brochure should state, in nontechnical language, the following:

(a) It is in the best interests of each of the parties to consult attorneys regarding the dissolution of their marriage, and that the services of attorneys may be obtained.

(b) The parties should not rely exclusively on the brochure, and the brochure is intended only as a guide for self-representation.

(c) A concise summary of the provisions and procedures of the simplified dissolution procedure.

750 ILCS 5/457   **FAMILIES**

(d) The nature and availability of counseling services.

(e) If the parties waive their rights to maintenance, neither party can in the future obtain maintenance from the other.

(f) A statement in boldface type that a judgment for dissolution of marriage permanently adjudicates all financial rights arising out of the marriage, including the right to property in the name of one's spouse and the right to support from one' spouse (maintenance or alimony), that a judgment is final, and the parties waive their right to appeal, except that neither party is barred from instituting an action to set aside a final judgment for fraud, duress, accident, mistake, or other grounds at law or in equity.

(g) The parties to the marriage remain married persons and cannot remarry until a judgment dissolving the marriage is entered.

Author's Notes

Analysis

1. Effective date.
2. Joint Petition for Simplified Dissolution of Marriage—Form.
3. Agreement—Joint Petition for Simplified Dissolution of Marriage—Form.
4. Affidavit in Support of Joint Petition for Simplified Dissolution of Marriage—Form.
5. Judgment for Joint Simplified Dissolution of Marriage—Form.

(1) **Effective date.** IMDMA §§ 451–457 are effective January 1, 1994.

FAMILIES 750 ILCS 5/457

(2) Joint Petition for Simplified Dissolution of Marriage—Form.

0010   (1/1/94) CCDR-19

**IN THE CIRCUIT COURT OF COOK COUNTY, ILLINOIS
COUNTY DEPARTMENT, DOMESTIC RELATIONS DIVISION**

IN RE: THE MARRIAGE OF

_____
Co-Petitioner

and

_____
Co-Petitioner

No.

**JOINT PETITION
FOR SIMPLIFIED
DISSOLUTION OF MARRIAGE**

THE PARTIES HAVE READ THIS PETITION, AND PURSUANT TO LAW CERTIFY THAT THE INFORMATION IN THIS PETITION IS TRUE.

THE CO-PETITIONERS STATE:

1. THEIR MARRIAGE REGISTRATION AND MARITAL CIRCUMSTANCES ARE:

MARRIAGE DATE	CITY	COUNTY	STATE	SEPARATION DATE

HUSBAND			WIFE		
Name			Name		
Residence Address		County	Residence Address		County
City State		Zip Code	City State		Zip Code
Social Security Number		Birthdate	Social Security Number		Birthdate
Occupation		Age Now	Occupation		Age Now
Residence in Illinois 90 Days Immediately Before Filing		YES	Residence in Illinois 90 Days Immediately Before Filing		YES
		NO			NO
Length of Residence in Illinois		YEARS	Length of Residence in Illinois		YEARS

[G17979]

750 ILCS 5/457   **FAMILIES**

2. THE CO-PETITIONERS FURTHER STATE: (1/1/94) CCDR 19-A   Case No. [   ]

(a)   The duration of the marriage does not exceed 5 years.

(b)   Irreconcilable differences have caused the irretrievable breakdown of the marriage and the parties have been separated 6 months or more. Efforts at reconciliation have failed or future attempts at reconciliation would be impracticable and not in the best interests of the family.

(c)   No children were born of the relationship of the parties or adopted by the parties during the marriage, and the Wife, to her knowledge, is not pregnant by the Husband.

(d)   Neither party is dependent on the other party for support or each party is willing to waive the right to support. Each party understands that prior consultation with an attorney may have helped to determine eligibility for spousal support.

(e)   Each party waives any right to spousal support.

(f)   Neither party has any interest in real estate.

(g)   The total fair market value of all marital property, after deducting all debts owed, is less than $5,000.

(h)   Husband's gross annual income from all sources is [$]. Wife's gross annual income from all sources is [$]. The total annual income of both parties is less than $25,000.00.

(i)   Both parties have disclosed to each other all assets and their tax returns for all years of the marriage.

(j)   The parties have executed a written Agreement dividing all assets in excess of $100 in value and allocating responsibility for debts and liabilities between themselves. A copy of the Agreement, signed by both parties, is filed with this petition.

WHEREFORE, THE PARTIES SEEK A DISSOLUTION OF THEIR MARRIAGE, AND ASK THAT

A.   Each party's right to spousal support be forever barred and terminated.

B.   The written Agreement of the parties dividing marital assets, debts and liabilities, a copy of which is filed with this petition, be incorporated into the final order and judgment of this Court granting the petition for dissolution of marriage.

C.   (Optional) That the Wife be restored to her former maiden name: [   ]
                                                                                     (Type or print wife's maiden OR former name)

VERIFICATION BY CERTIFICATION

Under penalties of perjury as provided by Law pursuant to Sec. 1-109 of the Code of Civil Procedure, the undersigned certifies that the statements set forth in this document are true and correct except as to matters herein stated to be on information and belief.

Co-Petitioner signature   **Co-Petitioner signature**   [G17980]

FAMILIES 750 ILCS 5/457

(3) **Agreement—Joint Petition for Simplified Dissolution of Marriage—Form.**

2808 (1/1/94) CCDR 19-B

IN THE CIRCUIT COURT OF COOK COUNTY, ILLINOIS
COUNTY DEPARTMENT, DOMESTIC RELATIONS DIVISION

IN RE: THE MARRIAGE OF

_____

Co-Petitioner

and

_____

Co-Petitioner

No. _____

AGREEMENT

**JOINT PETITION FOR SIMPLIFIED
DISSOLUTION OF MARRIAGE**

WITH REGARD TO THE DIVISION OF THEIR PROPERTY AND DEBTS, THE CO-PETITIONERS AGREE THAT:

The following shall be the sole property of the Husband:	The following shall be the sole property of the Wife:
_____	_____
_____	_____
_____	_____
_____	_____
_____	_____
_____	_____
_____	_____
_____	_____

The following debts shall be the sole responsibility of the Husband:	The following debts shall be the sole responsibility of the Wife:
_____	_____
_____	_____
_____	_____
_____	_____
_____	_____
_____	_____
_____	_____

DATED THIS _____ DAY OF _____ 199___

_____   _____
Co-Petitioner signature   Co-Petitioner signature

[G17981]

750 ILCS 5/457　　　　　　　　FAMILIES

(4) **Affidavit in Support of Joint Petition for Simplified Dissolution of Marriage—Form.**

2807　　　　　　　　　　　　　　　　　　　　　　　　　　　　　(1/1/94) CCDR-20

IN THE CIRCUIT COURT OF COOK COUNTY, ILLINOIS
COUNTY DEPARTMENT, DOMESTIC RELATIONS DIVISION

IN RE: THE MARRIAGE OF

_____

Co-Petitioner

　　　　　　　　and　　　　　　　　　　　No.

_____　　　　　　　　**AFFIDAVIT IN SUPPORT OF**
　　　　　　　　　　　　　　　　　　　　　JOINT PETITION FOR SIMPLIFIED
Co-Petitioner　　　　　　　　　　　　　　**DISSOLUTION OF MARRIAGE**

THE CO-PETITIONERS STATE THAT:

1. ALL PROPERTY HAS BEEN DIVIDED IN ACCORDANCE WITH THE WRITTEN AGREEMENT OF THE PARTIES FILED WITH THE JOINT PETITION.

2. THEY HAVE EXECUTED ALL DOCUMENTS REQUIRED TO CARRY OUT THE TERMS OF THE AGREEMENT.

VERIFICATION BY CERTIFICATION

Under penalties of perjury as provided by Law pursuant to Sec. 1-109 of the Code of Civil Procedure, the undersigned certifies that the statements set forth in this instrument are true and correct except as to matters herein stated to be on information and belief.

_____　　　　　　　_____

Co-Petitioner signature　　　　　　　　**Co-Petitioner signature**　　　　　　[G17982]

FAMILIES 750 ILCS 5/457

(5) Judgment for Joint Simplified Dissolution of Marriage—Form.

8001 (1/1/94) CCDR 21

**IN THE CIRCUIT COURT OF COOK COUNTY, ILLINOIS
COUNTY DEPARTMENT, DOMESTIC RELATIONS DIVISION**

IN RE: THE MARRIAGE OF

Co-Petitioner

and No.

Co-Petitioner

**JUDGMENT FOR
JOINT SIMPLIFIED
DISSOLUTION OF MARRIAGE**

This cause was heard on the parties' Joint Petition for Simplified Dissolution of Marriage, both parties appearing in person. The Court, having jurisdiction of the parties and the subject matter and after examination of the petition and the parties, FINDS the parties' marriage registration and marital circumstances are as follows:

MARRIAGE DATE	CITY	COUNTY	STATE	SEPARATION DATE

THE COURT FINDS:

(a) One or both parties have met the residency requirement of Section 401 of the Illinois Marriage and Dissolution of Marriage Act.

(b) At filing, the duration of the marriage did not exceed 5 years.

(c) Irreconcilable differences have caused the irretrievable breakdown of the marriage and parties have been separated 6 months or more. Efforts at reconciliation have failed or future attempts at reconciliation would be impracticable and not in the best interests of the family.

(d) No children were born of the relationship of the parties or adopted by the parties during the marriage, and the Wife, to her knowledge, is not pregnant by the Husband.

(e) Neither party is dependent on the other party for support or each party is willing to waive the right to support. Each party understands that prior consultation with an attorney may have helped to determine eligibility for spousal support.

(f) Each party has waived any rights to spousal support.

(g) Neither party has any interest in real estate.

(h) The total fair market value of all marital property, after deducting all debts owed, is less than $5,000. The total annual income of both parties is less than $25,000.

[G17983]

750 ILCS 5/457　　　　　　FAMILIES

(1/1/94) CCDR-21A　　Case No.

(i)　The Parties have disclosed to each other all assets and tax returns for all years of the marriage.

(j)　The Parties have executed a written Agreement dividing all assets in excess of $100 in value and allocating responsibility for debts and liabilities between themselves. A copy of the Agreement, filed with the joint petition, has been reviewed by the Court and is not unconscionable

WHEREFORE, IT IS ORDERED:

A.　A Judgment of Dissolution of Marriage is awarded to the parties and the marriage existing between them is hereby dissolved.

B.　Spousal support is terminated and forever barred

C.　Each party shall earn income and own personal property in his/her own name, possession or control free and clear of any claims of the other

D.　Each party shall be solely liable for any debts he/she may personally incurr and neither shall be liable for any debt or liability incurred by the other

E.　The written Agreement filed with the Joint Petition is incorporated into this Judgment and shall be enforceable by this Court upon service of proper notice and petition

F　(OPTIONAL) The Wife is restored to her former maiden name of _____
　　　　　　　　　　　　　　　　　　　　　　　　　(Type or print wife's maiden OR former name)

ENTER:

_____
JUDGE:

APPROVED AND AGREED

_____　　_____
Co-Petitioner signature　　　　　　　　Co-Petitioner signature

[G17984]

PART V. PROPERTY, SUPPORT, AND ATTORNEY FEES

Analysis

Sec.
501. Temporary relief.
501.1 Dissolution action stay.
502. Agreement.
503. Disposition of property.
504. Maintenance.
505. Child support; Contempt; Penalties.
505.1 Unemployed persons owing duty of support.
505.2 Health insurance.
506. Representation of child.
507. Payment of maintenance or support to court.
508. Attorney's fees.
509. Independence of provisions of judgment or temporary order.
510. Modification and termination of provisions for maintenance, support, educational expenses, and property disposition.
511. Procedure.
512. Post-judgment venue.
513. Support for non-minor children and educational expenses.
514. Partition of real estate.
515. Partition to be filed in counties where real estate located.
516. Public Aid collection fee.

WESTLAW Electronic Research

See WESTLAW Electronic Research Guide preceding the Summary of Contents.

---

750 ILCS 5/501

§ 501. Temporary relief

In all proceedings under this Act, temporary relief shall be as follows:

(a) Either party may move for:

(1) temporary maintenance or temporary support of a child of the marriage entitled to support, accompanied by an affidavit as to the factual basis for the relief requested;

(2) a temporary restraining order or preliminary injunction, accompanied by affidavit showing a factual basis for any of the following relief:

(i) restraining any person from transferring, encumbering, concealing or otherwise disposing of any property except in the usual course of business or for the necessities of life, and, if so restrained, requiring him to notify the moving party and his attorney of any proposed extraordinary expenditures made after the order is issued;

(ii) enjoining a party from removing a child from the jurisdiction of the court;

(iii) enjoining a party from striking or interfering with the personal liberty of the other party or of any child; or

(iv) providing other injunctive relief proper in the circumstances; or

(3) other appropriate temporary relief.

(b) The court may issue a temporary restraining order without requiring notice to the other party only if it finds, on the basis of the moving affidavit or other evidence, that irreparable injury will result to the moving party if no order is issued until the time for responding has elapsed.

(c) A response hereunder may be filed within 21 days after service of notice of motion or at the time specified in the temporary restraining order.

(d) A temporary order entered under this Section:

(1) does not prejudice the rights of the parties or the child which are to be adjudicated at subsequent hearings in the proceeding;

(2) may be revoked or modified before final judgment, on a showing by affidavit and upon hearing; and

(3) terminates when the final judgment is entered or when the petition for dissolution of marriage or legal separation or declaration of invalidity of marriage is dismissed.

Author's Notes

Analysis

1. Temporary relief.
2. Temporary support.
3. Temporary support: Petitions.
4. Petition for Temporary Support—Form.
5. Income and Expense Affidavit—Form.
6. Temporary restraining orders and preliminary injunctions: Subjects.
7. Injunctions: Property.
8. Injunctions: Other injunctive relief.
9. Injunctions: Procedure.
10. Injunctions: Requirements.
11. Injunctions: Petitions.
12. Injunctions: Without notice.
13. Injunctions: Response.
14. Temporary order not a precedent.
15. Petition for an Injunction—Form.
16. Affidavit—Form.
17. Temporary Restraining Order—Form.

(1) **Temporary relief.** Temporary maintenance and children's support are obtained under IMDMA § 501. Temporary restraining orders and preliminary injunctions are obtained pursuant to IMDMA § 501 and the Illinois Code of Civil Procedure, 735 ILCS 5/11–101 et seq. Temporary attorney's fees and costs are obtained under IMDMA § 508. Temporary custody is obtained under IMDMA § 603. All of these

remedies are also available pursuant to the Illinois Domestic Violence Act when abuse is present. See 750 ILCS 60/101 et seq. and accompanying Author's Notes. IMDMA § 501(a)(3) also provides for "other appropriate temporary relief."

It has become common practice to proceed under the Illinois Domestic Violence Act in cases involving abuse where an emergency proceeding is necessary for the protection of persons or property. Such a strategy is often preferable because the petitions and orders use simple, standardized forms, and because the courts have become accustomed to granting emergency relief pursuant to the codified domestic violence law. IMDMA § 501 and the other temporary relief sections are used when abuse is not present.

(2) **Temporary support.** A party may obtain both temporary maintenance and temporary children's support under § 501(a)(1). Temporary support provides a relatively short-term remedy during the parties' pending litigation. The amount of temporary maintenance and children's support is often lower than the ultimate award of maintenance and children's support in the final judgment. The hearings also may be more abbreviated; in temporary hearings the courts are primarily concerned with providing remedies sufficient to enable the parties to complete their litigation. An award of temporary support does not stand as a precedent for the final award of support. § 501(d)(1). See Author's Note (14), this Section. Where temporary support is litigated, the issue of support can be litigated twice, on a temporary and a final basis. The same can be true for temporary and permanent custody. See IMDMA § 603.

An order providing for temporary support pending dissolution is not a final order, and therefore it is not ripe for appeal unless the court makes a special finding of finality as required by Supreme Court Rule 304(a). In re Marriage of Zymali, 94 Ill.App.3d 1145, 50 Ill.Dec. 379, 419 N.E.2d 487 (1st Dist.1981). Even with such a finding, the Appellate Court may reject the appeal because piecemeal appeals are not favored. "A judgment is final for appeal purposes if it determines the litigation on the merits or some definite part thereof so that, if affirmed, the only thing remaining is to proceed with the execution of the judgment." In re Marriage of Verdung, 126 Ill.2d 542, 553, 129 Ill.Dec. 53, 58, 535 N.E.2d 818, 823 (1989) (citations omitted). A valid finding of finality requires substance rather than form: "the trial court cannot make a nonfinal order final and appealable simply by including in its order the requisite 304(a) language." In re Marriage of Young, 244 Ill.App.3d 313, 316, 185 Ill.Dec. 289, 291, 614 N.E.2d 423, 425 (1st Dist.1993). See also In re Marriage of Ryan, 188 Ill.App.3d 679, 681, 136 Ill.Dec. 1, 2, 544 N.E.2d 454, 455 (2d Dist.1989) (dismissing appeal from temporary support judgment containing Supreme Court Rule 304(a) language).

(3) **Temporary support: Petitions.** The petition for temporary support and the supporting affidavit required by § 501(a)(1) should allege both the petitioner's financial need and the respondent's ability to furnish the necessary financial support. First, the petitioner must submit an itemized budget detailing the needs of the petitioner and of the dependent children for monetary support, as well as the petitioner's income, with a showing as to why it is insufficient to meet the demonstrated need. Second, the petitioner must present evidence of the respondent's income, with a showing as to why that income is sufficient to provide the requested support. Finally, the petition and affidavit should allege any other relevant factors, such as property interests, debts, failure to support in the past, and the like.

(4) **Petition for Temporary Support—Form.** There follows a sample of a petition for temporary maintenance and temporary children's support. See Author's

750 ILCS 5/501   **FAMILIES**

Note (5) of this Section for a supporting income and expense affidavit. Although petitions for temporary support, attorney's fees, custody, and injunctive relief are treated under separate sections in this Practice Book, where all or any number of the issues are present at one time, they can be combined in one petition.

IN THE CIRCUIT COURT OF COOK COUNTY, ILLINOIS
COUNTY DEPARTMENT, DOMESTIC RELATIONS DIVISION

IN RE THE MARRIAGE OF)
)
HAROLD SKIMPOLE,)
)
       Petitioner,)
) No. ____ D _____
and)
)
DOROTHY SKIMPOLE,)
)
       Respondent.)

PETITION FOR TEMPORARY SUPPORT

Respondent, DOROTHY SKIMPOLE ("DOROTHY"), brings the following Petition for Temporary Support and for other relief against Petitioner, HAROLD SKIMPOLE ("HAROLD"):

    1. DOROTHY and HAROLD were married on _____, 197__, after having lived together since 197__. One child was born to the parties as the issue of the marriage, Jo, who is presently twelve years of age and in the custody of DOROTHY.

    2. HAROLD withdrew from the marital home in _____, 199__. Since withdrawing from the marital home, until recently, HAROLD had paid all of the expenses of DOROTHY and the minor child of the parties, and, in addition, had paid to DOROTHY the sum of $3,000 per month.

    3. Beginning approximately eight weeks ago, HAROLD stopped paying to DOROTHY the $3,000 per month. More recently, HAROLD has either delayed in paying certain bills of DOROTHY and Jo, or has refused to pay certain bills.

    4. HAROLD is a man of substantial wealth. HAROLD is the chief operating officer of a large manufacturing business, and his annual income from salary, bonuses, and investments varies between $300,000 and $400,000. HAROLD's estate has an approximate value of $1,500,000.

    5. All of the aforedescribed income and wealth is under the control of HAROLD. DOROTHY is an unemployed mother and homemaker. DOROTHY has virtually no income nor property of her own. DOROTHY and Jo are completely dependent for their support upon HAROLD, who is well able to provide for them.

6. The parties during their marriage enjoyed an affluent lifestyle. The lifestyle included a home in Winnetka, Illinois, a condominium in Naples, Florida, membership in a country club, frequent travel, and entertaining. Over the past three years, the parties spent an average of $14,000.00 per month on their personal expenses and those of the minor child.

7. The affidavit of income and expenses attached to this Petition as an exhibit was prepared by DOROTHY from checks and bills, and the affidavit demonstrates that DOROTHY and Jo require $10,000 per month net of taxes for the temporary support of DOROTHY and the minor child. HAROLD is well able to provide this support to them.

8. Because HAROLD has made it plain that he will not continue his voluntary support of DOROTHY and Jo at the level that he established since withdrawing from the marital home ___ months ago, the Court should order temporary support for DOROTHY and Jo, taking into account the affluent lifestyle of the parties and the substantial wealth and income of HAROLD.

WHEREFORE, DOROTHY prays as follows:

1. The Court order HAROLD to pay to DOROTHY temporary support for DOROTHY and for Jo, in the amount of $10,000 per month net of taxes.

2. The Court grant such other and further relief to DOROTHY as may be appropriate under the evidence and circumstances.

DOROTHY SKIMPOLE

FREDERICK TULKINGHORN
Attorney for DOROTHY SKIMPOLE

VERIFICATION BY CERTIFICATION

Under penalties of perjury as provided by law pursuant to Section 1–109 of the Code of Civil Procedure, the undersigned certifies that the statements set forth in this instrument are true and correct, except as to matters therein stated to be on information and belief and, as to such matters, the undersigned certifies as aforesaid that I verily believe the same to be true.

DATED: _____   _____

DOROTHY SKIMPOLE

Frederick Tulkinghorn
Address
Telephone number

(5) **Income and Expense Affidavit—Form.** This Author's Note contains an income and expense affidavit form that is used to support the petition for temporary maintenance and children's support.

750 ILCS 5/501   **FAMILIES**

IN THE CIRCUIT COURT OF COOK COUNTY, ILLINOIS
COUNTY DEPARTMENT—DOMESTIC RELATIONS DIVISION

IN RE THE MARRIAGE OF   )
)
HAROLD SKIMPOLE,   )
)
          Petitioner,   )
)
and   ) No. ____ D _____
)
DOROTHY SKIMPOLE,   )
)
          Respondent.)

INCOME AND EXPENSE

AFFIDAVIT OF: DOROTHY SKIMPOLE

                                                                       Actual
                                                                       Monthly
                                                                       as of

                                                                       _____

A. STATEMENT OF INCOME AND DEDUCTIONS
   1. Gross Income Per Month $_____
      a. Salary/wages   _____
      b. Draw   _____
      c. Bonus   _____
      d. Pension   _____
      e. Annuity   _____
      f. Social Security   _____
      g. Dividends   _____
      h. Interest   _____
      i. Trusts   _____
      j. Public Aid   _____
      k. Workmen's Compensation   _____
      l. Unemployment Compensation   _____
      m. Rents   _____
      n. Disability Payments   _____
      o. Stocks   _____
      p. Bonds   _____
      q. Other (specify) _____
         _____   _____

FAMILIES 750 ILCS 5/501

TOTAL GROSS MONTHLY INCOME $_____

2. Required Deductions
   a. Taxes: Federal (based on _____ exemptions) $_____
   b. Taxes: State (based on _____ exemptions) _____
   c. Social Security (or pension equivalent) _____
   d. Mandatory retirement contributions required by law or as a condition of employment _____
   e. Union Dues _____
   f. Health/Hospitalization Insurance _____
   g. Prior obligation of support actually paid pursuant to court order _____
   h. Expenditures for repayment of debts that represent reasonable and necessary expenses for the production of income _____
   i. Medical expenditures necessary to preserve life or health _____
   j. Reasonable expenditures for the benefit of the child and the other parent exclusive of gifts (for non-custodial parent only) _____

TOTAL REQUIRED DEDUCTIONS FROM INCOME $_____

NET MONTHLY INCOME $_____

B. CASH OR CASH EQUIVALENTS ON HAND
   1. Savings and interest bearing accounts _____
   2. Checking _____
   3. Stocks and bonds _____
   4. Other (specify) _____
   _____

TOTAL CASH OR CASH EQUIVALENT ON HAND $_____

C. STATEMENT OF MONTHLY LIVING EXPENSES _____
   1. Household
      a. Mortgage or rent (specify) $_____
      b. Taxes, assessments and insurance _____
      c. Maintenance and repairs _____
      d. Heat/fuel _____
      e. Electricity _____
      f. Telephone _____
      g. Water and Sewer _____
      h. Refuse removal _____

750 ILCS 5/501 **FAMILIES**

    i. Laundry/dry cleaning _____
    j. Maid/cleaning service _____
    k. Furniture and appliance repair _____
    l. Food (groceries/milk, etc.) _____
    m. Tobacco products _____
    n. Liquor, beer, wine, etc. _____
    o. Other (specify) _____

SUBTOTAL HOUSEHOLD EXPENSES $_____

2. Transportation
    a. Gasoline $_____
    b. Repairs _____
    c. Insurance/license _____
    d. Payments/replacement _____
    e. Alternative transportation _____
    f. Other (specify) _____

SUBTOTAL TRANSPORTATION EXPENSES $_____

3. Personal:
    a. Clothing $_____
    b. Grooming _____
    c. Medical
        (1) Doctor
        (2) Dentist _____
        (3) Medication _____
    d. Insurance:
        (1) Life
        (2) Hospitalization _____
    e. Other (specify) _____

SUBTOTAL PERSONAL EXPENSES $_____

4. Miscellaneous:
    a. Clubs/social obligations/entertainment _____
    b. Newspapers, magazines, books _____
    c. Gifts/donations
    d. Vacations
    e. Other (specify) _____

SUBTOTAL MISCELLANEOUS EXPENSES $_____

FAMILIES   **750 ILCS 5/501**

5. Dependent children: Names and date of birth

      _____

      _____

      _____

      _____

      _____

      _____

    a. Clothing $_____
    b. Grooming   _____
    c. Education:
       (1) Tuition   _____
       (2) Books/fees   _____
       (3) Lunches   _____
       (4) Transportation   _____
       (5) Activities   _____
    d. Medical
       (1) Doctor   _____
       (2) Dentist   _____
       (3) Medication   _____
    e. Allowance   _____
    f. Child Care   _____
    g. Sitters   _____
    h. Lessons   _____
    i. Clubs/summer camps   _____
    j. Entertainment   _____
    k. Other (specify) _____

       _____ _____

SUBTOTAL CHILDREN'S EXPENSES: $_____

TOTAL LIVING EXPENSES: $_____

D. Debts requiring regular payments:

		MINIMUM MONTHLY
CREDITOR	BALANCE	PAYMENT
_____	_____	_____
_____	_____	_____
_____	_____	_____
_____	_____	_____
_____	_____	_____
_____	_____	_____
_____	_____	_____
_____	_____	_____

750 ILCS 5/501   **FAMILIES**

SUBTOTAL MONTHLY DEBT SERVICE: $_____
                                 Actual Monthly
                                    as of
                                 _____

NET MONTHLY INCOME $_____
TOTAL MONTHLY LIVING EXPENSES $_____
DIFFERENCE BETWEEN NET
INCOME AND EXPENSES $_____
LESS MONTHLY DEBT SERVICE $_____
INCOME AVAILABLE PER MONTH $_____

VERIFICATION BY CERTIFICATION

Under penalties of perjury as provided by law pursuant to Section 109 of the Code of Civil Procedure, the undersigned certifies that the statements set forth in the foregoing instrument are true and correct.

DATED: _____   _____
                                    DOROTHY SKIMPOLE

Frederick Tulkinghorn
Attorney for DOROTHY SKIMPOLE
Address
Telephone number

(6) **Temporary restraining orders and preliminary injunctions: Subjects.** A temporary restraining order or a preliminary injunction granted under § 501(a)(2) may restrain the transfer of property, enjoin the removal of a child from the court's jurisdiction, In re Marriage of Jaster, 222 Ill.App.3d 122, 164 Ill.Dec. 743, 583 N.E.2d 659 (2d Dist.1991), enjoin striking or interfering with the personal liberty of the other party or child, or provide other injunctive relief.

(7) **Injunctions: Property.** Injunctive property restraints cannot enjoin transfers of property for basic life necessities, or in the usual course of business. § 501(a)(2)(i). Property under a court-ordered restraint may be transferred as long as it is within the usual course of business. See, e.g., In re Marriage of De Rosa, 115 Ill.App.3d 774, 71 Ill.Dec. 525, 451 N.E.2d 13 (1st Dist.1983). Any proposed extraordinary expenditures of restrained property requires notice to the petitioner and the petitioner's attorney. The notice provision in § 501(a)(2)(i) appears to be entirely superfluous once the injunction is in place, because the extraordinary expenditure cannot be made with or without notice without violating the injunction, unless the injunction is modified. The enjoined party may apply to the court for modification of the injunctive order if he or she requires extraordinary expenditures. In re Marriage of Grauer, 133 Ill.App.3d 1019, 1023, 88 Ill.Dec. 962, 965, 479 N.E.2d 982, 985 (1st Dist.1985).

Injunctions restraining the transfer of property are frequently used to maintain the status quo, as well as to maintain the court's jurisdiction over the property so that the court can allocate property pursuant to the terms of the Illinois Marriage and Dissolution of Marriage Act. See, e.g., In re Marriage of Joerger, 221 Ill.App.3d 400,

163 Ill.Dec. 796, 581 N.E.2d 1219 (4th Dist.1991); In re Marriage of Grauer, 133 Ill.App.3d 1019, 88 Ill.Dec. 962, 479 N.E.2d 982 (1st Dist.1985).

(8) **Injunctions: Other injunctive relief.** Section 501(a)(2)(iv) provides for temporary injunctive relief beyond the statutory listed examples. For example, a party could seek to enjoin a spouse from participating in the operation of a family-owned business when the couple was unable to operate the business together due to mutual hostility. In re Marriage of Joerger, 221 Ill.App.3d 400, 163 Ill.Dec. 796, 581 N.E.2d 1219 (4th Dist.1991). A party might seek to obtain a mandatory injunction requiring a spouse to restore money to a bank account that was improperly removed by the other spouse. See, e.g., Deisenroth v. Dodge, 350 Ill.App. 20, 111 N.E.2d 575 (2d Dist.1953) (upholding a mandatory injunction requiring removal of a barrier from plaintiff's property); In re Marriage of Sherwin, 123 Ill.App.3d 748, 79 Ill.Dec. 201, 463 N.E.2d 755 (1st Dist.1984) (denying mandatory injunction requiring wife to return fixtures and furniture to marital home).

(9) **Injunctions: Procedure.** The injunction provisions of IMDMA § 501 should be read in conjunction with Article XI of the Illinois Code of Civil Procedure, which also covers injunctions. (See 735 ILCS 5/11–101 et seq. and accompanying Author's Notes.) IMDMA § 105 provides that the Code of Civil Procedure shall apply to all proceedings except as otherwise provided in IMDMA. Article XI of the Code of Civil Procedure is more detailed, and has a more developed case law than does § 501 of the Illinois Marriage and Dissolution of Marriage Act. It is therefore necessary to consult Article XI of the Code of Civil Procedure, for example, to obtain the proper procedure and time limits for temporary restraining orders without notice.

(10) **Injunctions: Requirements.** In re Marriage of Schmidt, 118 Ill.App.3d 467, 74 Ill.Dec. 93, 455 N.E.2d 123 (1st Dist.1983) sets forth the elements necessary to obtain a preliminary injunction:

> [A] party must establish: (1) that he possesses a clearly ascertainable right which needs protection; (2) that he will suffer irreparable harm without the injunction; (3) that there is no adequate remedy at law for the injury; and (4) that he is likely to be successful on the merits of his action. In addition, he generally must establish that the need for temporary relief outweighs any possible injury that the party to be enjoined might suffer by its issuance.

A party seeking only to maintain the status quo is not required to establish that he is likely to succeed on the merits of his action. The party must only establish a "fair question" of whether his right deserves protection. Status quo is defined as the "last, peaceable uncontested status which preceded the litigation." In re Marriage of Joerger, 221 Ill.App.3d 400, 404, 407, 163 Ill.Dec. 796, 801, 803, 581 N.E.2d 1219, 1223, 1225 (4th Dist.1991).

(11) **Injunctions: Petitions.** Petitions for temporary restraining orders and preliminary injunctions must be accompanied by a supporting affidavit. § 501(a)(2). The petition must be based upon facts rather than conclusions. In re Marriage of Schmidt, 118 Ill.App.3d 467, 74 Ill.Dec. 93, 455 N.E.2d 123 (1st Dist.1983). An allegation that the petitioner "fears" the respondent will cause the petitioner injury does not satisfy the requirement that the petitioner will suffer irreparable harm without the injunction. Similarly, the courts will not grant an injunction based on alleged "threats" without proof that there is a reasonable probability that a threatened act will be committed. Allott v. American Strawboard Co., 237 Ill. 55, 63, 86 N.E. 685 (1908). Finally, the petitioner must show that the perceived harm cannot be protected against with less severe measures. In re Marriage of Rayfield, 221 Ill.App.3d

763, 164 Ill.Dec. 469, 583 N.E.2d 23 (1st Dist.1991) (perceived threat that spouse may sell stock and conceal terms and proceeds from petitioner could be protected against by requiring full accounting; preliminary injunction was improper).

(12) **Injunctions: Without notice.** The provisions of §§ 501(b) and 501(c) permit the entry of a temporary restraining order without notice to the other party only upon a court finding that irreparable injury will result to the moving party if the entry of an injunction is delayed until after the time for responding has elapsed. It is insufficient to merely allege the conclusion that "irreparable injury will occur" in the petition without further pleading facts specifying what the irreparable injury will be, and why it will occur if notice of the motion for an injunction is served to the other party. In re Marriage of Schmidt, 118 Ill.App.3d 467, 473, 74 Ill.Dec. 93, 97, 455 N.E.2d 123, 127 (1st Dist.1983). See also Bashwiner v. Bashwiner, 126 Ill.App.3d 365, 81 Ill.Dec. 359, 466 N.E.2d 1161 (1st Dist.1984) (allegations that children would be irreparably harmed if removed from current environment were conclusions and insufficient grounds for issuing a temporary restraining order without notice).

Since the time periods and other provisions of the general injunction act contained in Article XI of the Code of Civil Procedure apply to procedure not expressly regulated in IMDMA, a temporary restraining order granted under IMDMA § 501 expires after 10 days as provided by the general injunction act, unless extended by the court for a like period. In re Marriage of Pick, 119 Ill.App.3d 1061, 75 Ill.Dec. 865, 458 N.E.2d 33 (2d Dist.1983). (See 735 ILCS 5/11–101 and accompanying Author's Notes.)

(13) **Injunctions: Response.** Section 501(c) provides that a response may be filed within 21 days after service of a motion seeking temporary relief, or at such time otherwise specified in the temporary restraining order. The court has the discretion to reduce the 21 days in cases of emergency motions.

(14) **Temporary order not a precedent.** Temporary support is effective only until the termination of the dissolution proceedings. In re Marriage of Bush, 209 Ill.App.3d 671, 153 Ill.Dec. 851, 567 N.E.2d 1078 (1st Dist.1991). Section 501(d)(1) provides that a temporary order is not to prejudice the rights of parties or children at subsequent hearings. For example, the sums set for temporary maintenance and children's support under § 501 are not precedent for those awards at a final hearing. In re Marriage of Schroeder, 215 Ill.App.3d 156, 158 Ill.Dec. 721, 574 N.E.2d 834 (4th Dist.1991); In re Marriage of Simmons, 221 Ill.App.3d 89, 163 Ill.Dec. 562, 581 N.E.2d 716 (5th Dist.1991).

Sections 501(d)(2) and 501(d)(3) provide that temporary orders can be modified before final judgment, and they terminate when a final judgment is entered. In contrast, orders of protection pursuant to the Illinois Domestic Violence Act can stay in full force and effect after the entry of a final judgment. See 750 ILCS 60/220(b)(1)(ii).

(15) **Petition for an Injunction—Form.** There follows a sample petition for temporary restraining order. The supporting affidavit form is in Author's Note (16) of this Section, and the temporary restraining order form is in Author's Note (17) of this Section. The sample pleadings and order pertain to assets, but IMDMA § 501 also contemplates injunctive relief where necessary against: removing a child from the jurisdiction, striking or harassing the other party or a child, or other appropriate injunctive relief. See also Illinois Code of Civil Procedure, 735 ILCS 5/11–101 to 110 and accompanying Author's Notes for injunctive procedure.

Most of the court documents in this Practice Book refer to the parties by their first names in order to clearly distinguish between the spouses. The parties can also be called Petitioner and Respondent where doing so does not cause confusion. The following pleadings and order use the latter practice.

IN THE CIRCUIT COURT FOR THE NINETEENTH
JUDICIAL CIRCUIT,
LAKE COUNTY, ILLINOIS

IN RE THE MARRIAGE OF	)
	)
LUCY DEDLOCK,	)
	)
Petitioner,	)
	)
and	) No. ___ D ___
	)
LEICESTER DEDLOCK,	)
	)
Respondent.	)

PETITION FOR AN INJUNCTION

Petitioner, LUCY DEDLOCK, brings the following Petition for a temporary restraining order, without notice, and without bond, to be followed by a preliminary injunction, against Respondent, LEICESTER DEDLOCK, pursuant to Sections 5/11–101 and 102 of the Illinois Code of Civil Procedure and pursuant to Section 501 of the Illinois Marriage and Dissolution of Marriage Act, and Petitioner alleges as follows:

1. Petitioner's name has been removed by Respondent from substantial marital assets of the parties, namely a Merrill Lynch account, formerly in the joint names of the parties, which had a value of approximately $350,000, and a Northern Trust bank account, formerly in the joint names of the parties, which contained $65,000.

2. Marital property has been put at risk and used as collateral for speculative investments by Respondent without Petitioner's consent. Respondent has placed securities that constitute marital property at risk in margin accounts to finance the purchase of additional securities.

3. A principal asset of the parties, the marital home, has been, or may about to be, used as collateral by Respondent to finance the speculative commodity trading of the Respondent.

4. Respondent has removed all of the funds from a joint checking account and a joint savings account of the parties, located at Harris Bank, in the aggregate amount of approximately $95,000.

5. Respondent, just prior to the filing of this litigation, made gifts to the children of the parties in the aggregate amount of $300,000.

6. Petitioner and the minor children of the parties are completely dependent upon Respondent for their financial support, and upon the marital assets for their future financial security.

7. Petitioner is likely to be successful in her Petition for a Dissolution of Marriage, which prays that an equitable portion of the marital estate be allocated to her and further prays that Petitioner be awarded maintenance, children's support, and the attorney's fees and costs incurred by her.

8. Petitioner will be irreparably damaged if Respondent is not enjoined from dissipating and transferring the marital assets of the parties, because Respondent has put substantial portions of the marital estate and income at risk, because Petitioner does not know the whereabouts of assets transferred out of joint tenancy, and because gifts to the children of the parties reduce the marital estate.

9. Petitioner has no adequate remedy at law to protect her interests and those of the minor children if Respondent is not restrained from reducing the marital estate, concealing assets, dissipating assets, and depriving Petitioner of her rightful share in them.

10. A temporary restraining order should issue without notice to Respondent, inasmuch as it clearly appears from Respondent's prior actions that notice will cause Respondent to accelerate the very transactions that will irreparably damage the marital estate before the time for responding has elapsed and before the injunction can issue.

11. Damage to Respondent as a result of this injunction is unlikely, and sufficient marital assets are allocable to Petitioner to pay for damages, if any, so that no bond is necessary or appropriate.

12. The entry of a temporary restraining order and thereafter a preliminary injunction will preserve the status quo during the pendency of these proceedings, and will enable the court to properly adjudicate the property rights of the parties.

13. Petitioner's affidavit in support of this Petition is attached hereto.

WHEREFORE, Petitioner, LUCY DEDLOCK, prays as follows:

A. The Court issue a temporary restraining order without notice, and without bond, and thereafter a preliminary injunction enjoining and restraining Respondent from transferring, assigning, encumbering, concealing, hypothecating, pledging, mortgaging, borrowing against, damaging, destroying, depreciating, selling, withdrawing, dissipating, making gifts of, guarantying debts with, expending, or otherwise dealing with or disposing of any real or personal property, or income in which Petitioner or Respondent have any interest whatsoever, except in the usual course of business or for the necessities of life, including, but not limited to, enjoining and restraining Respondent from removing Petitioner's name from property, using securities as collateral in a margin account, or proceeding to mortgage the marital home.

B. The Court require Respondent to notify Petitioner and her attorney at least 15 days in advance of any proposed extraordinary expenditures after the issuance of the temporary restraining order or preliminary injunction.

C. For such other and further relief as may be appropriate under the evidence and circumstances.

_____
LUCY DEDLOCK, Petitioner

_____
RICHARD VHOLES
Attorney for Petitioner

VERIFICATION BY CERTIFICATION

Under penalties of perjury as provided by law pursuant to Section 1–109 of the Code of Civil Procedure, the undersigned certifies that the statements set forth in this instrument are true and correct, except as to matters therein stated to be on information and belief and, as to such matters, the undersigned certifies as aforesaid that I verily believe the same to be true.

DATED: _____   _____
                                    LUCY DEDLOCK

Richard Vholes
Address
Telephone number

(16) **Affidavit—Form.** There follows a sample affidavit in support of the petition for a temporary restraining order.

IN THE CIRCUIT COURT FOR THE NINETEENTH
JUDICIAL CIRCUIT,
LAKE COUNTY, ILLINOIS

IN RE THE MARRIAGE OF	)
	)
	)
LUCY DEDLOCK,	)
	)
Petitioner,	)
	)
and	) No. ____ D _____
	)
LEICESTER DEDLOCK,	)
	)
Respondent.	)

AFFIDAVIT

LUCY DEDLOCK, on oath states in support of her Petition for an Injunction:

1. My name has been removed by Respondent from substantial marital assets of the parties, namely a Merrill Lynch account, formerly in the joint names of the parties, which had a value of approximately $350,000, and a Northern Trust bank account, formerly in the joint names of the parties, which contained $65,000.

2. Marital property has been put at risk and used as collateral for speculative investments by Respondent without my consent. Respondent has placed securities that constitute marital property at risk in margin accounts to finance the purchase of additional securities.

3. A principal asset, the marital home, has been, or may about to be, used as collateral by Respondent to finance the speculative commodity trading of Respondent.

4. Respondent has removed all of the funds from a joint checking account and a joint savings account of the parties, located at Harris Bank, in the aggregate amount of approximately $95,000.

5. Respondent, just prior to the filing of this litigation, made gifts to our children in the aggregate amount of $300,000.

6. I and our minor children are completely dependent upon Respondent for our financial support, and upon the marital assets for our future financial security.

7. I am likely to be successful in my Petition for a Dissolution of Marriage, which prays that an equitable portion of the marital estate be allocated to me and further prays that I be awarded maintenance, children's support, and the attorney's fees and costs incurred by me.

8. I will be irreparably damaged if Respondent is not enjoined from dissipating and transferring the marital assets, because Respondent has put substantial portions of the marital estate at risk, because I do not know the whereabouts of assets transferred out of joint tenancy, and because gifts to our children reduce the marital estate.

9. I have no adequate remedy at law to protect my interests and those of our minor children if Respondent is not restrained from reducing the marital estate, concealing assets, dissipating assets, and depriving me of my rightful share in them.

10. A temporary restraining order should issue without notice to Respondent, inasmuch as it clearly appears from Respondent's prior actions that notice will cause Respondent to accelerate the very transactions that will irreparably damage the marital estate before the time for responding has elapsed and before the injunction can issue.

11. Damage to Respondent as a result of this injunction is unlikely, and sufficient marital assets are allocable to me to pay damages, if any, so that no bond is necessary or appropriate.

12. The entry of a temporary restraining order and thereafter a preliminary injunction will preserve the status quo during the pendency of these proceedings, and will enable the court to properly adjudicate the property rights of the parties.

13. If called as a witness, I would testify as aforesaid.

_____

LUCY DEDLOCK, Petitioner

Subscribed and sworn to before me
this ___ day of _____, 199_.

_____

Notary Public

Richard Vholes
Attorney for LUCY DEDLOCK
Address
Telephone number

(17) Temporary Restraining Order—Form.

IN THE CIRCUIT COURT FOR THE NINETEENTH
JUDICIAL CIRCUIT,
LAKE COUNTY, ILLINOIS

IN RE THE MARRIAGE OF	)
	)
LUCY DEDLOCK,	)
Petitioner,	)
and	) No. ___ D _____
LEICESTER DEDLOCK,	)
Respondent.	)

TEMPORARY RESTRAINING ORDER

This matter coming on to be heard on the verified Petition of Petitioner, LUCY DEDLOCK, supported by Petitioner's affidavit, for a Temporary Restraining Order against Respondent, LEICESTER DEDLOCK, and the Court having heard the evidence, and being fully advised in the premises;

The Court finds:

1. Petitioner's name has been removed by Respondent from substantial marital assets of the parties, namely a Merrill Lynch account, formerly in the joint names of the parties, which had a value of approximately $350,000, and a Northern Trust bank account, formerly in the joint names of the parties, which contained $65,000.

2. Marital property has been put at risk and used as collateral for speculative investments by Respondent without Petitioner's consent. Respondent has placed securities that constitute marital property at risk in margin accounts to finance the purchase of additional securities.

3. A principal asset of the parties, the marital home, has been, or may about to be, used as collateral by Respondent to finance the speculative commodity trading of the Respondent.

4. Respondent has removed all of the funds from a joint checking account and a joint savings account of the parties, located at Harris Bank, in the aggregate amount of approximately $95,000.

5. Respondent, just prior to the filing of this litigation, made gifts to the children of the parties in the aggregate amount of $300,000.

6. Petitioner and the minor children of the parties are completely dependent upon Respondent for their financial support, and upon the marital assets for their future financial security.

7. Petitioner is likely to be successful in her Petition for a Dissolution of Marriage, which prays that an equitable portion of the marital estate be allocated to her and further prays that Petitioner be awarded maintenance, children's support, and the attorney's fees and costs incurred by her.

8. Petitioner will be irreparably damaged if Respondent is not enjoined from dissipating and transferring the marital assets of the parties, because Respondent has put substantial portions of the marital estate and income at risk, because Petitioner does not know the whereabouts of assets transferred out of joint tenancy, and because gifts to the children of the parties reduce the marital estate.

9. Petitioner has no adequate remedy at law to protect her interests and those of the minor children if Respondent is not restrained from reducing the marital estate, concealing assets, dissipating assets, and depriving Petitioner of her rightful share in them.

10. A temporary restraining order should issue without notice to Respondent, inasmuch as it clearly appears from Respondent's prior actions that notice will cause Respondent to accelerate the very transactions that will irreparably damage the marital estate before the time for responding has elapsed and before the injunction can issue.

11. Damage to Respondent as a result of this injunction is unlikely, and sufficient marital assets are allocable to Petitioner to pay damages, if any, so that no bond is necessary or appropriate.

12. The entry of a temporary restraining order and thereafter a preliminary injunction will preserve the status quo during the pendency of these proceedings, and will enable the court to properly adjudicate the property rights of the parties.

IT IS THEREFORE HEREBY ORDERED:

1. A Temporary Restraining Order is hereby issued against Respondent, without notice, and without bond, enjoining and restraining Respondent from transferring, assigning, encumbering, concealing, hypothecating, pledging, mortgaging, borrowing against, damaging, destroying, depreciating, selling, withdrawing, dissipating, making gifts of, guarantying debts with, expending, or otherwise dealing with or disposing of any real or personal property, or income in which Petitioner or Respondent have any interest whatsoever, except in the usual course of business or for the necessities of life, including, but not limited to, enjoining and restraining Respondent from removing Petitioner's name from property, using securities as collateral in a margin account, or proceeding to mortgage the marital home.

2. Respondent shall notify Petitioner and her attorney at least 15 days in advance of any proposed extraordinary expenditures after the date of this injunctive order.

3. The hearing on the Petition for Preliminary Injunction is set for _____, 199__ before Judge _____ at ___ a.m., in Room ___, at the courthouse located at _____.

4. This Temporary Restraining Order is entered on _____, 199__ at ___ a.m./p.m., and shall expire on _____, unless extended by the Court.

ENTER:

_____
JUDGE

Richard Vholes
Attorney for LUCY DEDLOCK
Address
Telephone number

750 ILCS 5/501.1

§ 501.1 Dissolution action stay

(a) Upon service of a summons and petition or praecipe filed under the Illinois Marriage and Dissolution of Marriage Act or upon the filing of the respondent's appearance in the proceeding, whichever first occurs, a dissolution action stay shall be in effect against both parties and their agents and employees, without bond or further notice, until a final judgement is entered, the proceeding is dismissed, or until further order of the court:

> (1) restraining both parties from transferring, encumbering, concealing, destroying, spending, damaging, or in any way disposing of any

property, without the consent of the other party or an order of the court, except in the usual course of business, for the necessities of life, or for reasonable costs, expenses, and attorney's fees arising from the proceeding, as well as requiring each party to provide written notice to the other party and his or her attorney of any proposed extraordinary expenditure or transaction;

(2) restraining both parties from physically abusing, harassing, intimidating, striking, or interfering with the personal liberty of the other party or the minor children of either party; and

(3) restraining both parties from removing any minor child of either party from the State of Illinois or from concealing any such child from the other party, without the consent of the other party or an order of the court.

A restraint of the parties' actions under this Section does not, however, affect the rights of a bona fide purchaser or mortgagee whose interest in real property or whose beneficial interest in real property under an Illinois land trust was acquired before the filing of a lis pendens notice under § 2–1901 of the Code of Civil Procedure.

(b) Notice of any proposed extraordinary expenditure or transaction, as required by subsection (a), shall be given as soon as practicable, but not less than 7 days before the proposed date for the carrying out or commencement of the carrying out of the extraordinary expenditure or transaction, except in an emergency, in which event notice shall be given as soon as practicable under the circumstances. If proper notice is given and if the party receiving the notice does not object by filing a petition for injunctive relief under the Code of Civil Procedure within 7 days of receipt of the notice, the carrying out of the proposed extraordinary expenditure or transaction is not a violation of the dissolution action stay. The dissolution action stay shall remain in full force and effect against both parties for 14 days after the date of filing of a petition for injunctive relief by the objecting party (or a shorter period if the court so orders); and no extension beyond that 14 day period shall be granted by the court. For good cause shown, a party may file a petition for a reduction in time with respect to any 7 day notice requirement under this subsection.

(c) A party making any extraordinary expenditure or carrying out any extraordinary transaction after a dissolution action stay is in effect shall account promptly to the court and to the other party for all of those expenditures and transactions. This obligation to account applies throughout the pendency of the proceeding, irrespective of (i) any notice given by any party as to any proposed extraordinary expenditure or transaction, (ii) any filing of an objection and petition under this Section or the absence of any such filing, or (iii) any court ruling as to an issue presented to it by either party.

(d) If the party making an extraordinary expenditure or transaction fails to provide proper notice or if despite proper notice the other party filed a petition and prevailed on that petition, and the extraordinary expenditure or transaction results in a loss of income or reduction in the amount or in the value of property, there is a presumption of dissipation of property, equal to the amount of the loss or reduction, charged against the party for purposes of property distribution under IMDMA § 503.

(e) In a proceeding filed under this Act, the summons shall provide notice of the entry of the automatic dissolution action stay in a form as required by applicable rules.

Author's Notes

Analysis

1. Unconstitutionality.
2. Legislative intent.
3. Advantages of an automatic stay provision.

(1) **Unconstitutionality.** The Supreme Court of Illinois held that § 501.1 is an unconstitutional denial of substantive due process insofar as § 501.1 restrained property. Messenger v. Edgar, 157 Ill.2d 162, 191 Ill.Dec. 65, 623 N.E.2d 310, (1993). Because the section restrains transfer and expenditure of non-marital property as well as marital property, the statute is excessively broad, and did not meet the rational basis standard of constitutionality. The restraints against abuse and against removing a minor child from the State or concealing a child remain valid. See Supreme Court Rule 101(d) and (e) Author's Note (1) for model summons containing restraints.

(2) **Legislative intent.** Section 501.1 was an attempt to install an automatic stay at the start of proceedings against the transfer of property, restraining abuse, and restraining the removal or concealment of a minor child. The stay would take effect without a hearing upon the service of summons and pleading or upon the filing of an appearance, whichever first occurred. The "dissolution action stay" of property is not really an injunction, except for a short time period, but a requirement for a party contemplating an extraordinary expenditure to give the other party notice. The burden is then upon the party receiving the notice to obtain the injunction.

(3) **Advantages of an automatic stay provision.** An automatic stay that conforms to the constitutional mandates would constitute a good addition to the law because one spouse often has a monopoly of knowledge about and control of the financial estate, and because non-marital property cannot be finally determined until a final adjudication of the case. Moreover, under the present law a temporary restraining order or preliminary injunction, even when warranted, can be difficult to obtain, because courts frequently insist upon the strict requirements of pleading and proof in the statutes and case law.

750 ILCS 5/502

§ 502. Agreement

(a) To promote amicable settlement of disputes between parties to a marriage attendant upon the dissolution of their marriage, the parties may enter into a written or oral agreement containing provisions for disposition of any property owned by either of them, maintenance of either of them and support, custody and visitation of their children.

(b) The terms of the agreement, except those providing for the support, custody and visitation of children, are binding upon the court unless it finds, after considering the economic circumstances of the parties and any other relevant evidence produced by the parties, on their own motion or on request of the court, that the agreement is unconscionable.

(c) If the court finds the agreement unconscionable, it may request the parties to submit a revised agreement or upon hearing, may make orders for the disposition of property, maintenance, child support and other matters.

(d) Unless the agreement provides to the contrary, its terms shall be set forth in the judgment, and the parties shall be ordered to perform under such terms, or if the agreement provides that its terms shall not be set forth in the judgment, the judgment shall identify the agreement and state that the court has approved its terms.

(e) Terms of the agreement set forth in the judgment are enforceable by all remedies available for enforcement of a judgment, including contempt, and are enforceable as contract terms.

(f) Except for terms concerning the support, custody or visitation of children, the judgment may expressly preclude or limit modification of terms set forth in the judgment if the agreement so provides. Otherwise, terms of an agreement set forth in the judgment are automatically modified by modification of the judgment.

Author's Notes

Analysis

1. Presumption of validity.
2. Terms of settlement binding upon the court.
3. Validity: Unconscionability.
4. Validity: Additional grounds for vacating settlement agreement.
5. Disclosure of assets.
6. Oral agreements.
7. Writing as a condition precedent.
8. Cross references.
9. Wrap around judgments.
10. Settlements not incorporated into judgment.
11. Settlement Agreement—Form.
12. Insurance Trust—Form.
13. Settlement Agreement Checklist.
14. Enforcement.
15. Cross reference—Form.
16. Non-modifiable.

(1) **Presumption of validity.** The law favors the amicable settlement of issues attendant to a marital dissolution by an agreement between the parties. In re Marriage of Falat, 201 Ill.App.3d 320, 326, 147 Ill.Dec. 33, 39, 559 N.E.2d 33, 37 (1st Dist.1990); In re Marriage of Cierny, 187 Ill.App.3d 334, 339, 134 Ill.Dec. 918, 924, 543 N.E.2d 201, 207 (1st Dist.1989). Therefore, there is a presumption in favor of the validity of a property settlement agreement. Flynn v. Flynn, 232 Ill.App.3d 394, 399,

173 Ill.Dec. 735, 738, 597 N.E.2d 709, 712 (1st Dist.), *appeal denied,* 146 Ill.2d 626, 176 Ill.Dec. 797, 602 N.E.2d 451 (1992). In re Marriage of Black, 133 Ill.App.3d 59, 61, 87 Ill.Dec. 831, 832, 477 N.E.2d 1359, 1360 (2d Dist.1985).

(2) **Terms of settlement binding upon the court.** The courts' bias in favor of accepting the resolution of dissolution of marriage issues by agreement of the parties is reflected in § 502(b). This Section and the case law provide that the terms of the parties' agreement, except those concerning the children of the parties, are binding upon the court, unless the court finds the agreement to be unconscionable, procured by fraud or coercion, or if contrary to any rule of law, public policy or morals. In re Marriage of Maher, 95 Ill.App.3d 1039, 1042, 51 Ill.Dec. 586, 588, 420 N.E.2d 1144, 1146 (2d Dist.1981).

Terms concerning child support, custody, and visitation are excepted from the otherwise binding terms of the parties' agreement because the court maintains continuing jurisdiction as a guardian of the children's interests. In re Marriage of Black, 133 Ill.App.3d 59, 87 Ill.Dec. 831, 477 N.E.2d 1359 (2d Dist.1985) (stipulated child custody settlements recognized unless contrary to the best interests of the child). The court retains the power to modify terms of the agreement concerning children. In re Marriage of Glickman, 211 Ill.App.3d 792, 795, 156 Ill.Dec. 162, 164, 570 N.E.2d 638, 640 (1st Dist.1991) (settlement agreement cannot preclude or limit modification of terms concerning support, custody or visitation of children). See also In re Marriage of Falat, 201 Ill.App.3d 320, 147 Ill.Dec. 33, 559 N.E.2d 33 (1st Dist.1990) (court has authority to modify a child support provision in dissolution judgment entered in accordance with settlement agreement); In re Marriage of Blisset, 144 Ill.App.3d 1088, 1092, 99 Ill.Dec. 161, 164, 495 N.E.2d 608, 611 (4th Dist.1986) ("The determination of child support is the court's responsibility and not the parties [sic]"). But see In re Marriage of Divarco, 167 Ill.App.3d 1014, 118 Ill.Dec. 949, 522 N.E.2d 619 (1st Dist.1988) (reversing order that husband pay support arrearages; husband had relied on agreement to forego visitation in exchange for being released from paying support).

(3) **Validity: Unconscionability.** A court is not obligated to accept an unconscionable agreement. Unconscionability was defined in In re Marriage of Gurin, 212 Ill.App.3d 806, 816, 156 Ill.Dec. 877, 884, 571 N.E.2d 857, 864 (1st Dist.1991), as including

> "[A]n absence of meaningful choice on the part of one of the parties together with contract terms which are unreasonably favorable to the other party." ... A contract is unconscionable when it is improvident, totally one sided or oppressive.... [T]he inquiry into unconscionability requires at least two considerations: (1) the conditions under which the agreement was made and (2) the economic circumstances of the parties that result from the agreement (citations omitted) (quoting In re Marriage of Carlson, 101 Ill.App.3d 924, 57 Ill.Dec. 325, 428 N.E.2d 1005 (1st Dist.1981); In re Marriage of Foster, 115 Ill.App.3d 969, 972, 71 Ill.Dec. 761, 764, 451 N.E.2d 915, 918 (5th Dist.1983)).

The *Gurin* court set aside a settlement agreement awarding the husband the marital home and all the vehicles because he had deliberately concealed his prospects of impending and actual employment. See also In re Marriage of Richardson, 237 Ill.App.3d 1067, 179 Ill.Dec. 224, 606 N.E.2d 56 (1st Dist.1992) (settlement agreement granting wife only 7.55% of assets was unconscionable; wife signed agreement under duress shortly after her father's death, husband replaced wife's attorney because attorney opposed the agreement, and husband substantially undervalued his assets); In re Marriage of Van Zuidam, 162 Ill.App.3d 942, 114 Ill.Dec. 176, 516 N.E.2d 331

750 ILCS 5/502 FAMILIES

(1st Dist.1987) (agreement made shortly before husband won $2.1 million was not unconscionable).

Mere unfairness or inequality does not render a marital settlement agreement unconscionable. Flynn v. Flynn, 232 Ill.App.3d 394, 400, 173 Ill.Dec. 735, 739, 597 N.E.2d 709, 713 (1st Dist.), *appeal denied*, 146 Ill.2d 626, 176 Ill.Dec. 797, 602 N.E.2d 451 (1992).

(4) **Validity: Additional grounds for vacating settlement agreement.** The statute specifically states that it will not accept an agreement that is unconscionable. Traditional grounds for setting aside contracts are not thereby eliminated, however. In re Marriage of Gurin, 212 Ill.App.3d 806, 811, 156 Ill.Dec. 877, 881, 571 N.E.2d 857, 861 (1st Dist.1991). For example, a settlement agreement may be set aside if a party agreed under coercion or duress. A finding of coercion or duress requires a showing of imposition, oppression, undue influence, or the taking of undue advantage of the stress of another whereby one is deprived of the exercise of his free will. In re Marriage of Smith, 164 Ill.App.3d 1011, 1022, 115 Ill.Dec. 925, 932, 518 N.E.2d 450, 457 (1st Dist.1987). See, e.g., In re Marriage of Moran, 136 Ill.App.3d 331, 91 Ill.Dec. 234, 483 N.E.2d 580 (1st Dist.1985) (extreme coercion and duress by court and counsel invalidated agreement); In re Marriage of Steichen, 163 Ill.App.3d 1074, 115 Ill.Dec. 234, 517 N.E.2d 645 (2d Dist.1987) (agreement was not gained through coercion or duress when husband was consulted and participated in the settlement negotiations).

Similarly, a settlement agreement procured fraudulently or by fraudulent concealment will not be upheld. One of the most common bases for a finding of fraud is inadequate financial disclosure. See e.g., In re Marriage of Burch, 205 Ill.App.3d 1082, 150 Ill.Dec. 922, 563 N.E.2d 1049 (1st Dist.1990) (wife breached affirmative duty to disclose conveyance of property allegedly purchased with marital funds); Bellow v. Bellow, 40 Ill.App.3d 442, 352 N.E.2d 427 (1st Dist.1976) (husband's fraudulent concealment of his prospective book income and wife's joint interest in an apartment rendered agreement invalid). To sustain a showing of fraud, a party must prove (1) a false statement of material fact, (2) known or believed to be false by the party making it, (3) intent to induce another party to act, (4) action by the other party in reliance on the truth of the statement, and (5) damage to the other party relying on such statement. In re Marriage of Morris, 147 Ill.App.3d 380, 393, 100 Ill.Dec. 811, 818, 497 N.E.2d 1173, 1180 (1st Dist.1986), *appeal denied*, 113 Ill.2d 574, 106 Ill.Dec. 49, 505 N.E.2d 355 (1987).

Settlement agreements, and judgments that incorporate settlement agreements, are interpreted under the same rules that govern the construction of contracts. In re Marriage of Druss, 226 Ill.App.3d 470, 475, 168 Ill.Dec. 474, 478, 589 N.E.2d 874, 878 (1st Dist.1992); In re Marriage of Agustsson, 223 Ill.App.3d 510, 518, 165 Ill.Dec. 811, 817, 585 N.E.2d 207, 213 (2d Dist.1992). An example of contract principles being applied to invalidate a settlement agreement is found in In re Marriage of Agustsson, 223 Ill.App.3d 510, 165 Ill.Dec. 811, 585 N.E.2d 207 (2d Dist.1992). There the court vacated an agreement based on mutual material mistake. See also In re Marriage of Druss, 226 Ill.App.3d 470, 168 Ill.Dec. 474, 589 N.E.2d 874 (1st Dist.1992) (discussing interpretation of ambiguous agreements to determine parties' intent). A consequence of the applicability of general contract principles to dissolution agreements is that several cases have enforced agreements made in the process of dissolution even when the dissolution action was dismissed. Such an agreement can be valid under IMDMA § 503(a)(4) rather than under § 502. See IMDMA § 503(a)(4) and accompanying Author's Notes. See also In re Marriage of Vella, 237 Ill.App.3d 194, 177 Ill.Dec. 328,

603 N.E.2d 109 (2d Dist.1992); Stern v. Stern, 105 Ill.App.3d 805, 61 Ill.Dec. 567, 434 N.E.2d 1164 (2d Dist.1982). When dissolution proceedings are abated, the parties may choose to ignore the agreement and thereby rescind it as they would any other contract. *Vella*, 237 Ill.App.3d at 200, 177 Ill.Dec. at 333, 603 N.E.2d at 113. Where the intent is to make the agreement effective only upon the entry of a judgment of dissolution, the agreement should explicitly so state. See model agreement Article XII at Author's Note (11) of this Section.

(5) **Disclosure of assets.** Spouses with significant assets tend not to want to make a complete disclosure of their assets. The better policy, however, is to make complete disclosure and then to argue a position. Inadequate financial disclosure makes settlement agreements and judgments vulnerable to being set aside. See, e.g., In re Marriage of Burch, 205 Ill.App.3d 1082, 150 Ill.Dec. 922, 563 N.E.2d 1049 (1st Dist.1990) (wife breached affirmative duty to disclose conveyance of property allegedly purchased with marital funds); Bellow v. Bellow, 40 Ill.App.3d 442, 352 N.E.2d 427 (1st Dist.1976) (husband's fraudulent concealment of his income and her joint interest in an apartment rendered agreement invalid). See Illinois Code of Civil Procedure, 735 ILCS 5/2–1401, and accompanying Author's Notes. Furthermore, post-decree litigation is untimely, because it occurs after the defending spouse believed that the case was completed, and difficult, because it involves defending what may be inadequate disclosure.

(6) **Oral agreements.** Section 502(a) provides that the settlement agreement between the parties may be either written or oral. Oral dissolution of marriage settlement agreements are not covered by the statute of frauds. The statute of frauds applies to "any agreement made upon consideration of marriage," 740 ILCS 80/1, i.e. a prenuptial agreement, but not an agreement that is part of a dissolution of the marriage.

Oral agreements are generally approved by the courts under the same considerations as written agreements. See, e.g., In re Marriage of Sherrick, 214 Ill.App.3d 92, 157 Ill.Dec. 917, 573 N.E.2d 335 (4th Dist.1991) (oral agreement referred to but not incorporated into judgment upheld as valid); In re Marriage of Lorton, 203 Ill.App.3d 823, 148 Ill.Dec. 850, 561 N.E.2d 156 (5th Dist.1990) (oral agreement found neither manifestly unfair nor unconscionable declared valid); In re Marriage of Carlson, 186 Ill.App.3d 635, 134 Ill.Dec. 414, 542 N.E.2d 760 (1st Dist.1989) (oral agreement deemed valid; parties freely entered into the agreement and terms were not unconscionable); Filko v. Filko, 127 Ill.App.2d 10, 262 N.E.2d 88 (1st Dist.1970) (oral agreement was fair and without fraud).

Because oral settlement agreements can cause complications that are not as frequently a part of written settlement agreements, an attorney should carefully consider whether submitting an oral agreement to the court for approval in a dissolution prove-up is the best course. An oral recitation of an agreement may inadvertently omit terms that should be part of the settlement, because oral agreements are seldom as well thought out as are agreements in writing. The problem is compounded when one party attempts to insert the omitted terms in the written judgment, producing inconsistencies between the record and the judgment. The potential for appeal is high.

Moreover, agreements are often oral because there is not time to reduce the agreement to writing between a last-minute settlement and the appearance before the court. Oral agreements are therefore especially susceptible to irregularities that may later affect the validity of the agreement. There is a significant line of cases rejecting oral agreements when the negotiations were too hastily contrived, suggesting that the parties did not fully grasp the terms and implications of the agreement. See In re Marriage of Moran, 136 Ill.App.3d 331, 91 Ill.Dec. 234, 483 N.E.2d 580 (1st Dist.1985) (extreme coercion, duress and misrepresentation by counsel and court made agreement unconscionable; agreement set aside); In re Marriage of Perry, 96 Ill.App.3d 370, 51 Ill.Dec. 766, 421 N.E.2d 274 (1st Dist.1981) (wife did not participate in negotiations occurring 15 minutes before hearing was scheduled, expressed her dissatisfaction with the agreement prior to and immediately after the prove up, had no knowledge of her husband's assets, no outside income and had custody of their six minor children); Crawford v. Crawford, 39 Ill.App.3d 457, 350 N.E.2d 103 (1st Dist.1976) (agreement set aside that was put together immediately before the prove-up without the wife's participation, and the wife immediately expressed aversion to it and disavowed her prior consent).

(7) **Writing as a condition precedent.** If the oral agreement submitted to the court is not meant to constitute a valid and enforceable agreement between the parties until each party signs a subsequently prepared written agreement, this contingency should be expressly told to the court as part of the oral prove-up or included in a written order. See In re Marriage of Lorton, 203 Ill.App.3d 823, 827, 148 Ill.Dec. 850, 853, 561 N.E.2d 156, 159 (5th Dist.1990) ("The [oral] agreement was clear, certain, and definite in its material provisions, and by its very nature of being presented to the court, enforceable."); In re Marriage of Carlson, 186 Ill.App.3d 635, 134 Ill.Dec. 414, 542 N.E.2d 760 (1st Dist.1989) (valid oral agreement, no intention by the parties to reduce oral agreement to writing shown). In complicated cases, it is best that the agreement not be binding until reduced to writing, particularly when the agreement is reached under the pressure of a pre-trial or other courtroom conference, and the details of the potential agreement have not been completely thought out.

(8) **Cross references.** See Illinois Code of Civil Procedure: 735 ILCS 5/2–1203 for motions to set aside agreements incorporated in judgments within 30 days after entry of the judgment, and 735 ILCS 5/2–1401 for relief from judgments after the expiration of 30 days from the entry of the judgment.

(9) **Wrap around judgments.** Pursuant to § 502(d), where there is a written settlement agreement, a simple wrap around judgment can be used that physically incorporates the written agreement into the judgment. See IMDMA § 413 Author's Note (8).

(10) **Settlements not incorporated into judgment.** Section 502(d) addresses an agreement that is not incorporated into the judgment. The usual reason for not incorporating an agreement into the judgment is to preserve the confidentiality of the agreement's terms. Where confidentiality is desired, the agreement should be incorporated in the judgment by reference, rather than physically, so that it can easily be enforced by contempt proceedings. See para. 12(b) in the model agreement at Author's Note (11) of this Section for incorporation by reference, and Author's Note (14) of this Section for enforcement.

(11) **Settlement Agreement—Form.** There follows a model settlement agreement, the support provisions of which are secured by an attached sample insurance trust in Author's Note (12). Author's Note (13) of this Section is a check list for settlement agreements. The model wrap around judgment is at IMDMA § 413 Author's Note (8).

The settlement agreement that follows contemplates a settled case. If the case is contested, all of the adjudicated terms would be placed in a judgment. The basic settlement agreement clauses can be used in the judgment, but the clauses must be made mandatory, that is, the court is ordering the property, support, custody, and other provisions; the parties are not agreeing to them.

Many settlement agreements can be simpler and will not require all of the provisions that follow. The model settlement agreement is meant to err on the side of inclusion, under the theory that it is easier to edit out than to edit in.

SETTLEMENT AGREEMENT

THIS AGREEMENT, made and entered into this _____ day of _____, 199__, by and between SUSAN JELLYBY, hereinafter referred to as "SUSAN," of _____, County of _____, and the State of Illinois, and ARTHUR JELLYBY, hereinafter referred to as "ARTHUR," of _____, County of _____, and the State of Illinois. *(The parties can be referred to as the Husband and the Wife, but settlement agreements are better personalized by giving the full names of the parties in the introductory paragraph and thereafter using the first names of the parties.)*

W I T N E S S E T H:

(a) The parties were lawfully married in _____, _____ County, Illinois on _____, 199__.

(b) Unfortunate and irreconcilable difficulties and differences have arisen between the parties, as a result of which they separated on _____, 199__.

(c) Two children were born to the parties as the issue of the marriage, whose names and ages are: Caddy Jellyby, 12 years old; and Peepy Jellyby, 4 years old. No children were adopted by the parties, and SUSAN is not pregnant.

(d) SUSAN filed a Petition for Dissolution of Marriage against ARTHUR in the Circuit Court of _____ County, Illinois, and ARTHUR filed a Response to the Petition for Dissolution of Marriage. The case is entitled "In re the Marriage of Susan Jellyby, Petitioner, and Arthur Jellyby, Respondent," Cause No. ___ D _____. The cause is pending and undetermined in the Court.

(e) Without any collusion as to the pending dissolution proceedings between the parties (but without prejudice to any right of action for dissolution which either may have), the parties hereto consider it in their best interests to settle between themselves now and forever the questions of maintenance, alimony and support of SUSAN and ARTHUR, the issues of children's custody, visitation, education, and support, and any and all rights of property and otherwise growing out of the marital or any other relationship now or previously existing between them, or which either of them now has or may hereafter have or claim to have against the other, or in or to any property of the other, of every kind, nature and description, whether real, personal or mixed, now owned or which may hereafter be acquired by either of them.

(f) SUSAN has employed and had the benefit of counsel of Samuel Kenge of Kenge and Carboy, as her attorneys. ARTHUR has employed and had the benefit of the counsel of Joseph Blowers of Blowers & Associates, Ltd., as his attorneys. SUSAN acknowledges that: she has fully informed ARTHUR of her wealth, property, estate, liabilities and income; she has been fully informed of the wealth, property, estate, liabilities and income of ARTHUR; she has been fully advised of her rights in the premises; and she is conversant with all of the wealth, property, estate, liabilities, and income possessed by ARTHUR and the value thereof. ARTHUR acknowledges that: he has fully informed SUSAN of his wealth, property, estate, liabilities and income; he has been fully informed of the wealth, property, estate, liabilities and income of SUSAN; he has been fully advised of his rights in the premises; and he is conversant with all of the wealth, property, estate, liabilities, and income possessed by SUSAN and the value thereof. The aforesaid acknowledgments are based upon the deposition of each party and upon the voluntary exchanges of information between the parties, upon which each of the parties has relied. The parties have directed their attorneys not to pursue further discovery. ARTHUR represents and warrants for himself and SUSAN represents and warrants for herself that the information supplied by him or her to the other is true, correct, and complete as of _____, 199__ (except as otherwise herein stated), and each party further represents and warrants on behalf of himself and on behalf of herself that there has been no material change in his or her financial circumstances since the information was supplied.

(g) Each party expressly states that he or she has freely and voluntarily entered into this Agreement of his or her own volition, free from any duress or coercion, and with full knowledge of each and every provision contained in this Agreement and the consequences thereof. Each party expressly states that no outside agreement has been made by either of the parties or his or her attorneys other than those agreements that are contained in this written Agreement. Each party, after carefully considering the terms and provisions of this Agreement, states that he or she believes the terms and provisions to be fair and reasonable under the present circumstances.

NOW, THEREFORE, in consideration of the foregoing, and in further consideration of the mutual and several covenants herein contained, and for other good and valuable consideration by each to the other delivered, the receipt and sufficiency whereof are hereby acknowledged, the parties do freely and voluntarily agree by and between themselves as follows:

ARTICLE I
Reservation

1. This Agreement is not one to obtain or stimulate a dissolution of marriage. SUSAN reserves the right to prosecute any action for dissolution that she has brought or may hereafter bring and defend any action that has been or may be commenced by ARTHUR. ARTHUR reserves the right to prosecute any action for dissolution that he has brought or may hereafter bring and defend any action that has been or may be commenced by SUSAN.

(In practice this paragraph is an anachronism from the days of fault divorce. But the paragraph should probably remain in agreements because of the existence of IMDMA §§ 407 and 408.)

ARTICLE II
Maintenance and Alimony
Set Years Reviewable

2(a). ARTHUR agrees, because of the marital and other family relationship, to pay to SUSAN the sum of TWO THOUSAND EIGHT HUNDRED DOLLARS ($2,800.00) per month, the first payment of $2,800.00 to be paid on the first day of the month immediately following the effective date of this Agreement, and a like monthly payment of $2,800.00 to be paid on the same day of each succeeding month thereafter until the first event to happen, in point of time, of the following five events (hereinafter referred to as "termination events"): (1) the death of SUSAN; (2) the remarriage of SUSAN; (3) the cohabitation by SUSAN with another person on a resident, continuing conjugal basis; (4) the death of ARTHUR; (5) the payment by ARTHUR to SUSAN of sixty (60) monthly payments; after which first event all of the payments pursuant to this paragraph 2(a) shall terminate (unless modified pursuant to paragraph 2(b) hereof).

2(b). The maintenance provided for in paragraph 2(a) hereof shall be reviewable and modifiable by the Circuit Court of _____ County provided that an appropriate Notice and Petition seeking review are filed with the Circuit Court of _____ County prior to the happening of the first to happen of the termination events set forth in paragraph 2(a) hereof.

Permanent Maintenance and Other Variations

(Paragraphs 2(a) and 2(b) are easily modified to provide other results. For example, for indefinite or permanent maintenance, termination event (5) in paragraph 2(a) and the provisions for review (parenthetical clause at the end of paragraph 2(a) and paragraph 2(b)) should be stricken. Maintenance that terminates upon the first of the statutory events to occur or the expiration of a set period without review can be achieved by leaving in termination event (5) and striking the review provisions. The heading should also of course be changed to conform with the paragraph. Maintenance is always modifiable pursuant to IMDMA 510(a) (including the amount and terms), unless provision is made to the contrary. Therefore, in order to protect non-reviewable maintenance against modification, model paragraph 2(g) below should be included, and the review provisions in paragraphs 2(a) and 2(b) should be deleted.)

Maintenance in Gross

2(c)(i). ARTHUR agrees to pay to SUSAN for her alimony and maintenance in gross the sum of Five Hundred Thousand Dollars ($500,000.00) payable in sixty (60) equal monthly installments as follows:

2(c)(ii). The sum of EIGHT THOUSAND THREE HUNDRED THIRTY-THREE AND 33/100 DOLLARS ($8,333.33) to be paid on _____, 199__, and the sum of $8,333.33 to be paid on the same day of each succeeding month thereafter for the following fifty-nine (59) months (60 total monthly payments).

2(c)(iii). The aforesaid monthly installments provided in paragraph 2(c)(ii) hereof shall be paid by ARTHUR to SUSAN in all events, except the death of SUSAN, regardless of the remarriage or cohabitation of either party, and regardless of the death of ARTHUR. If ARTHUR dies before he has paid to SUSAN the installments provided in paragraph 2(c)(ii) hereof, SUSAN shall have a valid and provable claim and charge against the assets of ARTHUR, assets of any living trust created by ARTHUR, and ARTHUR's estate for the unpaid monthly maintenance installments, reduced, however, by the actual payments received pursuant to the life insurance provisions of Article VII of this Agreement. ARTHUR agrees that he will at no time voluntarily reduce his estate below the gross amount of the unpaid maintenance balance due to SUSAN. If SUSAN dies, the payments accruing after the date of her death shall terminate, except that the termination shall not apply to any unpaid payments that were due and owing at the time of her death.

Tax Consequences
Taxable Maintenance

2(d). It is contemplated and understood by the parties that the alimony and maintenance payments provided to be paid by ARTHUR to SUSAN pursuant to paragraph 2__ hereof are intended to be alimony payments as defined in Sections 71(a) and 71(b) of the Internal Revenue Code of 1986, and amendments thereto, made pursuant to a "divorce instrument" as defined therein, all within the meaning and intendment of Sections 71(a) and 215 of the Internal Revenue Code of 1986, and amendments thereto, as now in effect, and of similar provisions of future laws, and that such payments will be includible in SUSAN's gross income pursuant to Section 71(a) and will be deductible by ARTHUR pursuant to Section 215 in determining their respective taxable incomes. In the event that all or any part of such payments for any year are not so includible by SUSAN or not so deductible by ARTHUR in determination of their respective taxable incomes, whether by interpretation or application of the present federal statutory provisions, or by their amendment or repeal, or as a result of the examination by the Internal Revenue Service, or by reason of recapture, the anti-Lester rules, or otherwise, at any time throughout the term of this Agreement, the parties agree that they will attempt to make an adjustment in the payments consistent with this Agreement, and, failing so to do, either party may petition the Court to adjudicate the issue upon appropriate notice. The provisions of this paragraph 2(d) shall have similar application to State income tax laws.

Non–Taxable Maintenance

(The following paragraph 2(e) should replace paragraph 2(d) in order to make the maintenance non-deductible to the payor and non-taxable to the payee.)

2(e). The cash payments from ARTHUR to SUSAN, pursuant to paragraph 2⎯ hereof, are designated under Section 71(b)(1)(B) as not includible in the gross income of SUSAN under Section 71 and not allowable as a deduction to ARTHUR under Section 215 of the Internal Revenue Code of 1986, and amendments thereto, and the parties agree to prepare their income tax returns accordingly. In the event that the payments are not so treated, whether by interpretation or application of the present statutory provisions, or as a result of the examination of the Internal Revenue Service, or otherwise, at any time throughout the term of this Agreement, the parties agree that they will attempt to make an adjustment in the payments consistent with this Agreement, and, failing so to do, either party may petition the Court to adjudicate the issue upon appropriate notice. The provisions of this paragraph 2(e) shall have similar application to State income tax laws.

(See Internal Revenue Code §§ 71 and 215, and accompanying Author's Notes for a complete discussion of the taxation of maintenance.)

(If it is desired to make the maintenance payments directly to the payee spouse instead of through the Clerk of the Court pursuant to Section 507 of IMDMA, and to waive the automatic withholding of maintenance from the payor's wages pursuant to Section 706.1(B) of IMDMA, appropriate waiver paragraphs should be included. In this Agreement the paragraphs are in Article V, which follows the children's support Article IV, because both maintenance and children's support are being paid, and it is intended that the waiver apply to both maintenance and children's support. Where only maintenance is paid, the waiver paragraphs in Article V should be inserted after the tax provisions. Even where the waiver is not desired, where only maintenance is being paid, the sentence in paragraph 5(d), which provides the payee's tax identification number, should be inserted here.)

Waiver Except as Otherwise Provided

2(f). Except as otherwise herein provided, each party agrees that he and she shall and hereby does waive and release the other from any and all claims and demands for alimony, maintenance, and support, temporary and permanent, past, present, and future.

Non–Modification

2(g). The parties hereto covenant and agree that, except as herein otherwise provided, pursuant to Section 502(f) of the Illinois Marriage and Dissolution of Marriage Act, paragraphs 2⎯ of this Agreement shall not be subject to modification in any respect whatsoever. The parties further agree that in the event there is a dissolution of the marriage between the parties in Cause No. ⎯ D ⎯⎯⎯, they will ask the Court to include in the Judgment of Dissolution of Marriage a prohibition against the modification of paragraphs 2___ of this Agreement in any respect whatsoever, except as otherwise herein provided.

(If the parties so agree, the non-modifiable clause can be used for any type of maintenance paragraphs, which are otherwise subject to modification pursuant to IMDMA § 510(a). Sometimes drafters put non-modification paragraphs at the end of an Agreement in an attempt to cover the entire Agreement, but property provisions are not subject to modification in the absence of fraud and the like with or without the non-modifiable paragraph, IMDMA § 510(b), and children's provisions cannot be made non-modifiable, IMDMA § 502(f).)

(After the court has approved the non-modifiability of maintenance, a paragraph stating the non-modifiability should be inserted in the Judgment. See IMDMA § 413 Author's Note (8), Judgment Additional and Alternative Provisions para. 9.)

Maintenance and Alimony Waiver

2(h). SUSAN acknowledges that: she is employed by Thavies Inn, her income, the property that she will receive pursuant to this Agreement, and the income generated therefrom are fully adequate to provide for her own support, and she therefore does not require any alimony, maintenance, or support from ARTHUR. SUSAN agrees that: she will not ask the court to allow her any support from ARTHUR, she will inform the court that she has property and income adequate to provide for her own support, and it is her desire to forever waive and release her rights and claims to maintenance, alimony, and support, past, present, and future, temporary and permanent, from ARTHUR. ARTHUR acknowledges that: he is employed by the Chancery Lane Bank, his income, the property that he will receive pursuant to this Agreement, and the income generated therefrom are fully adequate to provide for his own support, and he therefore does not require any alimony, maintenance, or support from SUSAN. ARTHUR agrees that: he will not ask the court to allow him any support from SUSAN, he will inform the court that he has property and income adequate to provide for his own support, and it is his desire forever to waive and release his rights and claims to maintenance, alimony and support, past, present, and future, temporary and permanent, from SUSAN. *(This waiver contemplates that appropriate paragraphs will be inserted in the Judgment after the court has approved the waiver of maintenance. See IMDMA § 413 Author's Note (8), Judgment Additional and Alternative Provisions para. 11.)*

ARTICLE III

Children's Joint Custody and Visitation

(See IMDMA § 602.1 Author's Note (2) for a sample free standing joint parenting agreement.)

3(a). Each of the parties agrees that both parties are fit and proper persons to have the joint custody of the minor children of the parties, Caddy and Peepy.

3(b). ARTHUR and SUSAN agree that they shall have the joint care, custody, control, and education of Caddy and Peepy, the minor children of the parties. The physical residence of the minor children shall be with SUSAN in her home. ARTHUR shall have the right to visit and have the company of Caddy and Peepy as follows:

(Insert a schedule of visitation, or, where appropriate: SUSAN agrees that ARTHUR shall have the right to visit and have the company of Caddy and Peepy at all reasonable times and places upon reasonable notice.)

(See IMDMA § 413 Author's Note (8), Judgment paras. C and 4 for corresponding judgment paragraphs.)

3(c). Each parent may remove either or both of the children from the State of Illinois for visitation, trips, or vacation purposes without further leave of Court or consent of the other party, provided, the party intending to remove the children shall give the other party reasonable notice of his or her intention to so do, and shall supply the other with information regarding the contemplated period of time outside of the State, the address and telephone number of where the children will be during the period of time outside the State of Illinois, and shall permit reasonable telephone communication between the children and the parent who is not with the children. Nothing contained in this provision shall be construed to permit either parent to remove the permanent residence of the minor children from the State of Illinois without first securing the written consent of the other parent or securing the approval of the Circuit Court of Cook County, Illinois.

3(d). Each party agrees to do everything within his or her power to foster the love and affection of the children of the parties for the other party, and to make every possible effort to agree on all questions involving the children, so that the children may have proper physical and emotional growth and retain their respect and affection for each of the parents. Neither party shall prevent or hinder telephone or other communication between the children and the other party. The medical and school records of the children, notices of events involving the children, and all other information concerning the children shall be made available to both parties.

3(e). The parties agree that they will jointly discuss and jointly determine, including, but not limited to: (1) the secular and religious education of the children, (2) the choice of and attendance at school and college for the children, and (3) all other significant questions relating to the health, welfare, and education of the children, including the choice of physicians in serious illnesses or injuries, except in cases of emergency. Upon the happening of an emergency, the parent with the child or first contacted in the emergency shall make all necessary decisions during the emergency. The ordinary day-to-day decisions concerning the children shall be made by the parent who at the time

750 ILCS 5/502   **FAMILIES**

is with the child or children, but care shall be taken so that ordinary decisions by one parent do not affect the time the other parent has with the children.

3(f). The parties designate the _____ County Marriage and Family Counselling Service, or such other mediator as the parties may agree upon, as their mediator. Anything herein to the contrary notwithstanding, the parties agree to first submit to the mediator before resorting to the Court issues concerning the children of the parties, including, but not limited to, changes, disputes, and alleged breaches of this Joint Parenting Agreement. The parties agree to periodically review the terms of this Joint Parenting Agreement in order to meet the changing needs of the children.

(The above provisions can be modified to provide for sole custody.)

ARTICLE IV
Children's Support

4(a). ARTHUR agrees to pay to SUSAN for the support and maintenance of Caddy, one of the children of the parties, the sum of One Thousand Dollars ($1,000.00) per month, the first monthly payment of $1,000.00 to be paid on the first day of the month immediately succeeding the month in which this Agreement become effective, and a like payment of $1,000.00 to be paid on the first day of each succeeding month thereafter during the minority of Caddy. The support for Caddy shall terminate on _____, 199__, the day on which Caddy reaches her majority, except that the termination date shall not apply to any arrearage that may remain unpaid on that date.

4(b). ARTHUR agrees to pay to SUSAN for the support and maintenance of Peepy, one of the children of the parties, the sum of One Thousand Dollars ($1,000.00) per month, the first monthly payment of $1,000.00 to be paid on the first day of the month immediately succeeding the month in which this Agreement become effective, and a like payment of $1,000.00 to be paid on the first day of each succeeding month thereafter during the minority of Peepy. The support for Peepy shall terminate on _____, 199__, the day on which Peepy reaches his majority, except that the termination date shall not apply to any arrearage that may remain unpaid on that date.

(Section 510(d) terminates child support on the "emancipation of the child," unless otherwise agreed. Some agreements elaborately define emancipation beyond just reaching majority. In most cases this is unnecessary, because emancipation of a child prior to age 18 is unusual, and, when it occurs, termination can be achieved by agreement or a petition to the court. Sometimes child support is extended to the time a child leaves for college, particularly when his 18th birthday precedes his departure from home to college by a considerable period of time.)

4(c). SUSAN agrees that ARTHUR will have the right to claim the dependency exemptions for each of the children of the parties in the computation of his Federal and State income tax returns so long as permitted by the Internal Revenue Code and the Illinois Revenue Code. SUSAN agrees to execute the appropriate Internal Revenue Service release of exemptions for Caddy and Peepy upon request by ARTHUR.

(See Author's Notes to Internal Revenue Code § 151–153 for discussion of dependency exemptions.)

(The following paragraph 4(d) should be inserted when the children's support deviates from the statutory guidelines of IMDMA § 505(a)(1). See IMDMA § 413 Author's Note (8), Judgment Additional and Alternative Provisions para. 7, for corresponding judgment finding.)

4(d). The parties acknowledge that the amounts agreed to be paid by ARTHUR hereunder as and for children's support may be below the amount that would otherwise be set as the minimum amount of support, upon application of the guidelines of IMDMA § 505(a)(1). However, the parties agree that, upon consideration of all relevant factors, the amount of children's support agreed to hereunder is reasonable and adequate, and that deviation from the guidelines set forth in IMDMA § 505(a)(1) is appropriate. The application of the guidelines would be inappropriate, considering the best interests of the children. In determining the amount of children's support to be paid by ARTHUR, the parties have considered the financial resources and needs of ARTHUR and SUSAN, including the amounts being paid to SUSAN as maintenance, the tax consequences of the maintenance and children's support awards hereunder, the property allocated to SUSAN by this Agreement and the income generated therefrom, SUSAN's income from employment, the age of the children, their physical and emotional condition, their educational needs, the standard of living the children would have enjoyed if the marriage was not dissolved, and the amounts being paid by ARTHUR to or for the benefit of the children other than in the form of periodic children's support, such as their medical insurance. SUSAN acknowledges that because of the aforesaid circumstances the children's support paid by ARTHUR together with the income from the other enumerated sources and the direct payments by ARTHUR on behalf of the children is more than sufficient to provide for the children's needs and will permit the children to continue the standard of living they enjoyed while the parties were married. The parties agree that in the event there is a dissolution of marriage between the parties, they will ask the court to include in the Judgment of Dissolution of Marriage express findings setting forth these facts as its reasons for departing from the statutory guidelines. Application of the guidelines would produce children's support of $_____, which amount would be excessive considering the above enumerated circumstances.

4(e)(i). ARTHUR agrees to maintain medical and hospital insurance covering Caddy and Peepy until each completes his or her college education or reaches his or her 23rd birthday, whichever occurs first. ARTHUR shall supply SUSAN with appropriate evidence, including medical insurance cards, that the medical and hospital insurance is in force. SUSAN shall pay for the ordinary medical expenses of Caddy and Peepy that are not paid by the medical insurance, and the parties shall attempt to agree as to the amount of each of their contributions to all extraordinary medical, psychiatric, surgical and dental bills including the cost of hospitalization of each child, when such costs are not covered by any insurance, are part of the deductible, or that portion that is in excess of the amount paid by insurance. Failing agreement, the issue shall be submitted to the Circuit Court of _____ County for determination. The term "extraordinary" includes all major dental and orthodontic work, major operations, serious illnesses or accidents requiring hospitalization, psychiatry, and the like, but shall not include routine dental care, routine medical examinations, minor ailments, and the like. SUSAN and ARTHUR agree that in the event there appears to be a need for such extraordinary care, they will obtain each other's agreement before incurring expenses for any extraordinary conditions, except in cases of emergency, when the parent with the child or first contacted in the emergency shall make any necessary decisions during the emergency. When the insurance payment is not made to the provider, or SUSAN is not reimbursed directly, SUSAN agrees to promptly transmit to ARTHUR all medical receipts for the children so that ARTHUR can apply for insurance payment. The obligations of SUSAN and ARTHUR pursuant to this paragraph 4(e) shall terminate for each child when such child completes his or her education or reaches his or her 23rd birthday, whichever first occurs.

4(e)(ii). The parties agree to cooperate to draft a Qualified Medical Child Support Order (QMCSO) acceptable to the Administrator of the _____ Medical Plan to implement the provisions of paragraph 4(e)(i) hereof. A copy of the QMCSO is attached hereto and made a part hereof as Exhibit A. The parties shall and hereby do request of the Court that it retain jurisdiction to: enter any orders that may be necessary to bring the QMCSO within the definition of a Qualified Medical Child Support Order as defined in ERISA § 609 (29 U.S.C.A. § 1169), enforce the QMCSO against successor plans, provide coverage for a child who moves out of the coverage area, amend paragraphs 4(e)(i) and 4(e)(ii) consistent with the parties' intentions, and to resolve other issues that may arise consistent with this Agreement.

(See ERISA § 609 (29 U.S.C.A. § 1169) and accompanying Author's Notes for discussion of QMCSO and a model QMCSO at Author's Note (6).)

Children's College Education

4(f). The parties shall attempt to agree on the allocation between them of the reasonable expenses incident to a college or vocational school education for each of the children of the parties, providing the child in question has the ability and desire to attend college or vocational school. Failing agreement, the issue shall be submitted to the Circuit Court of _____ County for determination in accordance with IMDMA § 513.

ARTICLE V
Withholding Waiver

5(a). The parties agree that they will request of the Court that the payments of maintenance pursuant to Article II and children's support pursuant to Article IV hereof be made directly by ARTHUR to SUSAN, rather than through the Clerk of the Court, pursuant to IMDMA § 507, and, if the Court approves, a provision so providing shall be included in the Judgment of Dissolution.

5(b). The parties further agree that the requirement in IMDMA § 706.1(B) that the Order for Withholding take effect immediately is hereby waived by ARTHUR and SUSAN.

5(c). ARTHUR and SUSAN further agree that, as an alternative arrangement, in order to insure the payment of maintenance and children's support, ARTHUR shall maintain in his checking or savings account a sum not less than the total of two months maintenance and children's support payable to SUSAN pursuant to Articles II and IV hereof for so long as ARTHUR is obligated to make payments to SUSAN pursuant to Articles II and IV hereof.

5(d). SUSAN's tax identification number is _____.

(See IMDMA § 413 Author's Note (8), Judgment Additional and Alternative Provisions para. 8, for corresponding judgment paragraph.)

ARTICLE VI
Marital and Property Settlement

6(a)(i). SUSAN and ARTHUR agree upon the following provisions set forth in paragraphs 6(b) through 6(o) below as an assignment of non-marital property to the appropriate party, as an allocation of marital property in acknowledgment of the contributions of each of the parties to the accumulated marital estate, and as a full and final settlement and satisfaction of the marital, property, and estate rights and claims of each of the parties. The allocation of the assets is set forth on Exhibit B attached hereto and made a part hereof. Exhibit B was prepared by the parties on _____, 199__. The following provisions carry out the aforedescribed asset allocation between the parties, and, where there is a conflict between the provisions of this Agreement and Exhibit B to this Agreement, the provisions of this Agreement shall control.

6(a)(ii). The parties acknowledge that any changes in values set forth on Exhibit B from the date of the preparation of Exhibit B to the effective date of this Agreement are a result of market fluctuations. Each party represents and warrants that neither he nor she has taken any action that would change any value set forth on Exhibit B.

Property in Each Name

6(b). On the effective date of this Agreement, SUSAN agrees to and does hereby assign and release to ARTHUR all of her right, title, interest, and claim in and to the following assets at their current values in ARTHUR's name (the dollar valuations below are as of the date of the preparation of Exhibit B to this Agreement):

750 ILCS 5/502   FAMILIES

(List assets and values, including:)

All benefits of employment by ———, except as otherwise herein provided.

ARTHUR shall own the aforesaid assets as his sole property, free of any right, title, or interest of SUSAN, either in assets or as a beneficiary of life insurance, and ARTHUR shall and does hereby indemnify SUSAN and hold her harmless from any liability in connection with the aforedescribed assets.

6(c). On the effective date of this Agreement, ARTHUR agrees to and does hereby assign and release to SUSAN all of his right, title, interest, and claim in and to the following assets at their current values in SUSAN's name (the dollar valuations below are as of the date of the preparation of Exhibit B to this Agreement):

(List assets and values, including:)

All benefits of employment by ———, except as otherwise herein provided.

SUSAN shall own the aforesaid assets as her sole property, free of any right, title, or interest of ARTHUR, either in assets or as a beneficiary of life insurance, and SUSAN shall and does hereby indemnify ARTHUR and hold him harmless from any liability in connection with the aforedescribed assets.

Jointly Held Assets

6(d). On the effective date of this Agreement, SUSAN agrees to and does hereby assign and release to ARTHUR all of her right, title, interest, and claim in and to the following assets at their current values presently held by the parties in their joint names (the dollar valuations below are as of the date of the preparation of Exhibit B to this Agreement):

(List assets and values.)

ARTHUR shall own the aforesaid assets as his sole property, free of any right, title, or interest of SUSAN, and ARTHUR shall and does hereby indemnify SUSAN and hold her harmless from any liability in connection with the aforedescribed assets.

6(e). On the effective date of this Agreement, ARTHUR agrees to and does hereby assign and release to SUSAN all of his right, title, interest, and claim in and to the following assets at their current values presently held by the parties in their joint names (the dollar valuations below are as of the date of the preparation of Exhibit B to this Agreement):

(List assets and values.)

SUSAN shall own the aforesaid assets as her sole property, free of any right, title, or interest in ARTHUR, and SUSAN shall and does hereby indemnify ARTHUR and hold him harmless from any liability in connection with the aforedescribed assets.

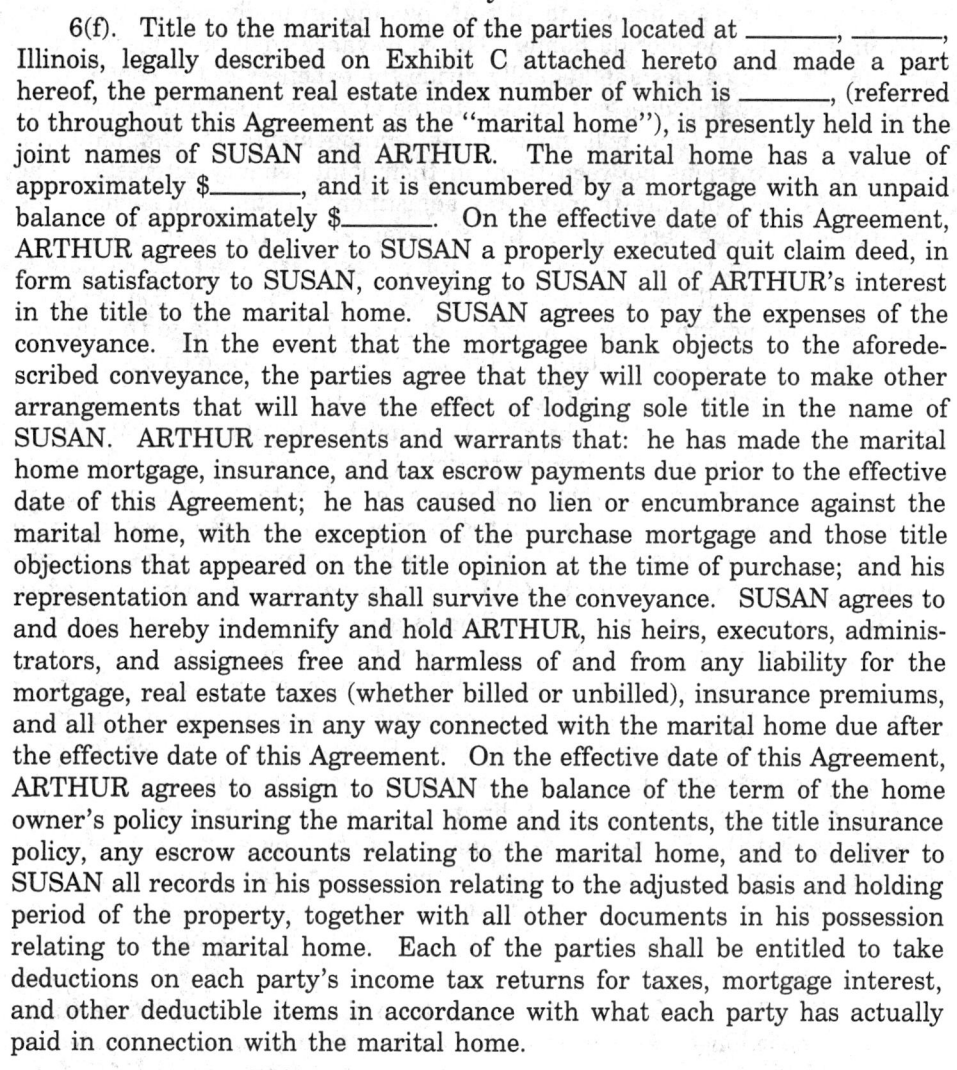

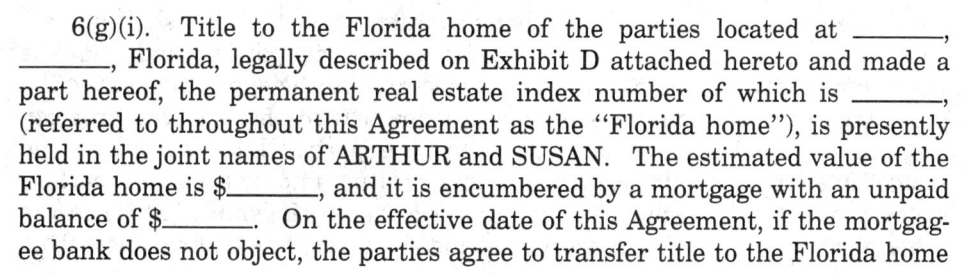

Real Estate Conveyance

6(f). Title to the marital home of the parties located at _____, _____, Illinois, legally described on Exhibit C attached hereto and made a part hereof, the permanent real estate index number of which is _____, (referred to throughout this Agreement as the "marital home"), is presently held in the joint names of SUSAN and ARTHUR. The marital home has a value of approximately $_____, and it is encumbered by a mortgage with an unpaid balance of approximately $_____. On the effective date of this Agreement, ARTHUR agrees to deliver to SUSAN a properly executed quit claim deed, in form satisfactory to SUSAN, conveying to SUSAN all of ARTHUR's interest in the title to the marital home. SUSAN agrees to pay the expenses of the conveyance. In the event that the mortgagee bank objects to the aforedescribed conveyance, the parties agree that they will cooperate to make other arrangements that will have the effect of lodging sole title in the name of SUSAN. ARTHUR represents and warrants that: he has made the marital home mortgage, insurance, and tax escrow payments due prior to the effective date of this Agreement; he has caused no lien or encumbrance against the marital home, with the exception of the purchase mortgage and those title objections that appeared on the title opinion at the time of purchase; and his representation and warranty shall survive the conveyance. SUSAN agrees to and does hereby indemnify and hold ARTHUR, his heirs, executors, administrators, and assignees free and harmless of and from any liability for the mortgage, real estate taxes (whether billed or unbilled), insurance premiums, and all other expenses in any way connected with the marital home due after the effective date of this Agreement. On the effective date of this Agreement, ARTHUR agrees to assign to SUSAN the balance of the term of the home owner's policy insuring the marital home and its contents, the title insurance policy, any escrow accounts relating to the marital home, and to deliver to SUSAN all records in his possession relating to the adjusted basis and holding period of the property, together with all other documents in his possession relating to the marital home. Each of the parties shall be entitled to take deductions on each party's income tax returns for taxes, mortgage interest, and other deductible items in accordance with what each party has actually paid in connection with the marital home.

Real Estate Sale

6(g)(i). Title to the Florida home of the parties located at _____, _____, Florida, legally described on Exhibit D attached hereto and made a part hereof, the permanent real estate index number of which is _____, (referred to throughout this Agreement as the "Florida home"), is presently held in the joint names of ARTHUR and SUSAN. The estimated value of the Florida home is $_____, and it is encumbered by a mortgage with an unpaid balance of $_____. On the effective date of this Agreement, if the mortgagee bank does not object, the parties agree to transfer title to the Florida home from ARTHUR and SUSAN as joint tenants to ARTHUR and SUSAN as tenants in common, with ARTHUR owning an undivided fifty percent (50%) interest in the Florida home and SUSAN owning an undivided fifty percent (50%) interest in the Florida home. The conveyance shall be subject to this Agreement. The parties shall equally divide the expenses of the conveyance. If the mortgagee bank does not consent to the aforedescribed conveyance, the parties agree that they will make other arrangements to eliminate the survivorship provisions between them in their joint tenancy interests. The parties agree to cooperate to make any adjustments in the homeowners and title insurance made necessary by the conveyance. ARTHUR shall have the right to occupy the Florida home on a rent free basis from the effective date of this Agreement until the closing of the sale of the Florida home. Either party shall have the right to record a Memorandum against the title to the Florida home indicating that it is subject to the terms of this Agreement.

6(g)(ii). ARTHUR and SUSAN agree that the Florida home shall be immediately placed for sale. The Florida home shall be placed for sale with a regular real estate broker, to be selected jointly by the parties, with the initial terms of the offering contract and the sale price to be determined by agreement between the parties. If the parties cannot agree upon the sale price, they shall jointly select, or select by lot if they cannot jointly select, two disinterested appraisers from the MAI list of appraisers who are qualified to appraise real estate in the _____, Florida area. The sale price shall be a sum equal to the average of the appraisals of the Florida home made by the two selected disinterested appraisers. Any reduction in the sale price, other changes in the offering contract, and acceptance or rejection of an offer shall be by agreement of the parties. When the Florida home is placed for sale, each party agrees to use his or her best efforts in accomplishing the sale of the Florida home, including, but not limited to, cooperating with the listing broker, making the Florida home available for showing at reasonable dates and times, promoting the attributes of the Florida home, maintaining the Florida home in accordance with the terms of this Agreement, and doing all other things that will help accomplish the sale of the Florida home as quickly and at as high a price as is possible.

6(g)(iii). The gross proceeds arising from the sale of the Florida home shall be apportioned, and after the payment of expenses, distributed as follows: ARTHUR, fifty percent (50%), and SUSAN, fifty percent (50%). All of the expenses of the sale, including but not limited to, appraisal fees, title expenses, broker's commissions, legal fees, unpaid balance remaining on the mortgage, real estate taxes and other prorations, and the like, shall be paid from the gross proceeds before distribution to the parties, and shall be apportioned between the parties in the same ratio as the apportionment of the gross proceeds. For purposes of capital gains tax, the basis of the property shall be allocated fifty percent (50%) to each party. Each party shall be responsible for the capital gains tax, if any, relating to only his or her portion of the proceeds, and each party shall and does hereby indemnify and hold the other party, his or her heirs, executors, and assignees, free and harmless from any liability therefor. Each party agrees to make available to the other party copies of documents in his or her possession relating to the adjusted basis and holding period of the property.

6(g)(iv). The parties agree to allow inspection of the Florida home by prospective purchasers when the Florida home is offered for sale. The parties agree to keep the Florida home fully insured against fire and accident liability, with SUSAN and ARTHUR named as beneficiaries in accordance with their respective percentage interests in the property on policies and in amounts approved in writing by both of the parties. The parties acknowledge that all payments in connection with the Florida home are current. The parties agree to each pay fifty percent (50%) of the mortgage payments, real estate taxes (billed and unbilled), insurance premiums, necessary fix up expenses, and all other expenses in connection with the Florida home from the effective date of this Agreement to the closing of any sale. The parties agree to maintain the Florida home in good condition. From the effective date of this Agreement to the closing of any sale, the parties shall consult with each other and obtain each other's approval before undertaking any major repair items, except in cases of emergency when the other party is unavailable. Each party agrees to and does hereby indemnify the other, his or her heirs, executors, administrators, and assignees from any liability for the share of expenses in connection with the marital home that each has undertaken to pay pursuant to this paragraph 6(g)(iv).

6(g)(v). SUSAN and ARTHUR each represent and warrant that neither she nor he has caused or allowed any lien or encumbrance against the Florida home, except the purchase mortgage and such title objections that were present at the time of the purchase, and each of their representations and warranties shall survive the conveyance of title into tenancy in common. Each party agrees that neither party shall cause or allow any lien or encumbrance to hereafter attach to the Florida home. Anything herein to the contrary notwithstanding, should either party cause or suffer or have caused or suffered a lien or encumbrance to be attached against the Florida home, other than as aforesaid, the amount of the lien and expenses shall be deducted from his or her share of the proceeds upon the sale of the Florida home. Either party shall have the right to contest a disputed claim prior to paying for the claim or having its amount deducted from his or her share of the proceeds from the sale of the Florida home.

6(g)(vi). Each of the parties shall be entitled to take deductions on his or her income tax returns for taxes, mortgage interest, and any other deductible items in accordance with what each party has actually paid in connection with the Florida home.

6(g)(vii). The provisions of paragraph 6(g) and its subparagraphs hereof shall be superior to the rights, if any, of the heirs, executors, administrators and assignees of either party, except as otherwise herein provided.

6(g)(viii). The parties agree that they will request of the court that it reserve jurisdiction to hear any disputes in connection with paragraph 6(g) and its subparagraphs hereof upon appropriate petition filed by either of the parties.

(The provisions of paragraph 6(g) can be modified to allow a spouse to live in a marital home with children for a specified period of time, after which the house is to be sold and the proceeds allocated between the parties.)

Furniture, Furnishings and Personalty

6(h). ARTHUR agrees to and does hereby assign to SUSAN all of his right, title, and interest in and to the furnishings, furniture, artwork, silver, womenswear, jewelry, and like personal property in the marital home, with the exception of the following "itemized exceptions": *(list or itemize on an exhibit)*, which furnishings, furniture, artwork, silver, womenswear, jewelry, and like personal property in the marital home, with the exception of the itemized exceptions, shall all be the sole and separate property of SUSAN. SUSAN agrees to and does hereby assign to ARTHUR all of her right, title and interest in and to the furniture, furnishings, artwork, silver, menswear, and like personal property located in the Florida home and the itemized exceptions listed above, which furnishings, furniture, artwork, silver, menswear, and like personal property located in the Florida home and itemized exceptions listed above shall be the sole and separate property of ARTHUR. ARTHUR agrees to remove those items assigned to him by this paragraph 6(h) from the marital home within 30 days of the effective date of this Agreement.

Automobiles

6(i). On the effective date of this Agreement, ARTHUR shall assign to SUSAN the certificate of title to and the unexpired term of insurance covering the _____ automobile in her possession. On the effective date of this Agreement, SUSAN shall assign to ARTHUR the Certificate of Title to and the unexpired term of insurance covering the _____ automobile. Both automobiles are free and clear of liens.

Cash

6(j). On the effective date of this Agreement, ARTHUR agrees to pay to SUSAN, by certified check, the sum of TEN THOUSAND DOLLARS ($10,-000.00).

Securities

6(k). The parties own the securities that are set forth on Exhibit B to this Agreement. On the effective date of this Agreement, the parties agree to and do hereby allocate the securities between them in the manner set forth on Exhibit B. Any accruals to or diminutions from the values of each of the securities set forth on Exhibit B from the date of the preparation of Exhibit B to the effective date of this Agreement shall be allocated between the parties in the same percentages as the interest of each party in each of the securities is set forth on Exhibit B. The cost bases and the unrealized gains and losses of the securities have been taken into account in the allocation of the securities between the parties, as well as the values of the securities. Each party shall own the securities allocated to him or to her as his or her sole property, free of any right, title, or interest in the other. Each party shall be entitled to the dividends and other distributions on the securities allocated to him or to her on an as paid basis and not on accrual basis, for example, if a dividend is paid the day after the allocation of a security, it shall belong in its entirety to the then owner of the shares, rather than be prorated between the parties.

Retirement Plans

QDRO

6(l)(i). ARTHUR has a vested interest in the Bleak House Retirement Plan (hereinafter referred to as the "Retirement Plan"). ARTHUR agrees that on the effective date of this Agreement he will cause to be paid by certified check the sum of TWO HUNDRED THOUSAND DOLLARS ($200,-000.00) from the Retirement Plan to an IRA in the name of SUSAN at _____ Bank, known as Account No. _____. The $200,000.00 shall be the sole property of SUSAN, free of any right, title or interest in ARTHUR. The transfer from ARTHUR's Retirement Plan to SUSAN's IRA rather than directly to SUSAN is in order to avoid the necessity of withholding. The remaining balance of the Retirement Plan after the aforedescribed payment to SUSAN shall be owned by ARTHUR as his sole property, free of any right, title or interest of SUSAN. The parties shall cooperate to draft a Qualified Domestic Relations Order (QDRO) acceptable to the Administrator of the Retirement Plan to effectuate this provision. A copy of the QDRO is attached hereto and made a part hereof as Exhibit E. The parties intend that the distribution from the Retirement Plan to SUSAN's IRA will not result in any tax consequences to SUSAN until such time as she begins to make withdrawals from her IRA, and the parties agree to prepare their income tax returns accordingly. The parties shall and hereby do ask the Court to retain jurisdiction to enter any order(s) that may be necessary to bring such order(s) within the definition of a Qualified Domestic Relations Order as defined in Section 414(p) of the Internal Revenue Code of 1986, and amendments thereto, to resolve any tax issues in a manner consistent with this Agreement, to amend this paragraph 6(l)(i), if necessary, consistent with the parties' intentions, and to adjudicate consistent with this Agreement other issues that may arise concerning this paragraph 6(l)(i). The parties shall also execute all documents, including but not limited to releases, election forms, and consent forms, that are necessary to effectuate the provisions of this paragraph 6(l)(i).

(See IMDMA § 503 Author's Notes (29)-(30) and Internal Revenue Code § 414(p) and accompanying Author's Notes for discussion of retirement plans and situations other than when cash is paid out of a retirement plan into an IRA. Internal Revenue Code § 414(p) Author's Note (6) contains a model Qualified Domestic Relations Order.)

IRA

6(*l*)(ii). ARTHUR has a vested interest in an IRA Retirement Account known as Account Number _____ at _____. ARTHUR agrees that on and as of the effective date of this Agreement, he will cause to be created a new and separate IRA Trust with _____ as Trustee ("New IRA Trust") utilizing _____ prototype trust, and he will cause to be assigned to the New IRA Trust from the existing IRA Retirement Account the sum of Two Hundred Twenty-Five Thousand Dollars ($225,000.00) in cash. ARTHUR will then transfer all of his right, title, and interest in the New IRA Trust to SUSAN as her sole property free of any right, title or interest in ARTHUR. It is intended that thereafter SUSAN will be treated as the creator of the New IRA Trust and have all rights to direct payments from it and investments in it that ARTHUR now has with respect to the existing IRA Trust. The creation of the New IRA Trust shall be pursuant to Internal Revenue Code Section 408(d)(6), and it is intended that the creation of the New IRA Trust not be treated as a distribution out of the existing IRA Retirement Account to either ARTHUR or SUSAN, and therefore not be taxable to either one of them. ARTHUR shall own the remaining assets in the existing IRA Retirement Account in his name as his sole property, free of any right, title, or interest in SUSAN.

(See Internal Revenue Code § 408(d)(6) and accompanying Author's Notes for tax provisions.)

Debts

6(m)(i). On the effective date of this Agreement, SUSAN and ARTHUR each agree to pay fifty percent (50%) of the following debts: *(list)*; and each party agrees to and does hereby hold the other harmless from any liability for what each has agreed to pay pursuant to this paragraph 6(m)(i).

6(m)(ii). Except as otherwise herein provided, each party agrees to pay the debts, obligations, tax liabilities, and bills that he or she has incurred or hereafter incurs (including also obligations regardless by whom incurred associated with assets received by each party pursuant to this Agreement), and each party agrees to and does hereby keep the other, his or her legal heirs, personal representatives and assignees, free and harmless and indemnified of and from any liability for the debts, obligations, tax liabilities, and bills that he or she has incurred or hereafter incurs (including also obligations regardless by whom incurred associated with assets received by each party pursuant to this Agreement), except as herein otherwise provided.

6(m)(iii). On the effective date of this Agreement, SUSAN agrees to deliver to ARTHUR all credit cards in SUSAN's possession that bear the name of ARTHUR.

General

6(n). Except as otherwise herein provided, each of the parties hereto covenants and agrees that each of them shall have and retain sole and exclusive right, title, and interest in and to all of the property, marital or separate, presently in his or her respective possession or name or under his or her respective control upon the date of this Agreement, including but not limited to personal bank accounts, after first giving effect to the provisions of this Agreement.

6(*o*). In connection with the aforesaid transfers and releases of property between SUSAN and ARTHUR pursuant to paragraphs 6(a) through 6(n) hereof, and the general release paragraphs of this Agreement, the parties contemplate that, except as herein otherwise provided, the property transfers and releases between the parties are not subject to Federal or State tax pursuant to Sections 1041, 408(d)(6), and 414(p) of the Internal Revenue Code of 1986, and amendments thereto, and the Illinois law, and each party, so far as is consistent with the Internal Revenue Code and the Illinois law, agrees to prepare his and her income tax returns accordingly; provided, however, that in the event of any such tax liability, the assessed party shall give timely notice to the other party, and the parties agree that they will request of the Court that it reserve jurisdiction to resolve the aforedescribed tax issues consistent with this Agreement upon appropriate petition presented by either party; provided, however, that this paragraph 6(*o*) shall not apply to transfers of assets to third parties after allocation between the parties, nor to withdrawals from retirement plans after allocation between the parties.

(For a discussion of the tax ramifications of property transfers in divorce, see Author's Notes to Internal Revenue Code §§ 1041, 408(d)(6), and 414(p).)

ARTICLE VII
Life Insurance Direct Beneficiary

7(a). ARTHUR agrees to pay the premiums on the insurance policies issued on his life by the companies listed on Exhibit F attached hereto and made a part hereof so long as he is required to keep the policies in force by this paragraph 7(a). ARTHUR represents that the aggregate proceeds of the aforesaid insurance policies payable on ARTHUR's death are in an amount not less than THREE HUNDRED THOUSAND DOLLARS ($300,000.00). If, on ARTHUR's death, the aggregate proceeds of the insurance policies are not $300,000.00, the difference between the aggregate proceeds and $300,000.00 shall be a lien and provable claim against the assets of ARTHUR, assets of any living trust created by ARTHUR, and the estate of ARTHUR on behalf of the beneficiaries as set forth in this paragraph 7(a). ARTHUR shall not borrow or create any lien on the insurance policies as long as he is obligated to keep the policies in force by the terms of this paragraph 7(a). SUSAN shall be the irrevocable beneficiary of the insurance so long as ARTHUR is obligated to pay to her or for the children: maintenance, children's support, children's medical, and children's educational expenses in accordance with Articles II and IV hereof. For purposes of this paragraph 7(a), ARTHUR's death shall not constitute a terminating event pursuant to paragraph 2(a) hereof. SUSAN, in consideration of the provisions of this paragraph 7(a), and except as otherwise provided in this paragraph 7(a), hereby releases any and

750 ILCS 5/502 **FAMILIES**

all claims that she might have against the estate of ARTHUR for children's support pursuant to IMDMA § 510(d) and (e). ARTHUR agrees to deliver the insurance policies to SUSAN and to direct the insurance companies issuing the policies to send to SUSAN copies of the beneficiary changes and the premium notices and receipts. ARTHUR's obligations pursuant to this paragraph 7(a) shall terminate when ARTHUR's obligations pursuant to Articles II and IV hereof terminate.

(Alternate)
Insurance Trust Provisions

7(b). ARTHUR agrees to pay the premiums on the life insurance policies on his life in the face amount of not less than THREE HUNDRED THOUSAND DOLLARS ($300,000.00) listed on Exhibit F, attached hereto and made a part hereof. SUSAN agrees that ARTHUR may substitute policies of insurance for the life insurance listed on Exhibit F, borrow against any policy or policies, apply the dividends accruing on the policies in reduction of premiums, or do any other thing with the policies, so long as he shall do nothing to reduce the value of the aggregate proceeds payable upon his death below $300,000.00, so long as required by paragraphs 7(b) through 7(f) hereof. ARTHUR and SUSAN agree to execute an Insurance Trust Agreement, designating _____ as Trustee, the Trust to stay in force for so long as the Trust insures obligations under this Agreement, the form of which is attached hereto as Exhibit G. ARTHUR shall designate the Trustee as the beneficiary of the insurance pursuant to the terms of the Insurance Trust. The Trust shall provide, *inter alia*, that upon ARTHUR's death, the Trustee shall collect the proceeds of the aforesaid insurance. The Trustee shall hold and administer the proceeds as a trust, upon the following terms and conditions:

7(c). If ARTHUR's death is the first termination event to occur under the terms of paragraph 2(a) hereof, the maintenance provided by paragraph 2(a) hereof shall not terminate for purposes of this paragraph 7(c), and the Trustee shall make the payments to SUSAN as if ARTHUR had not died as is provided under the terms and subject to the conditions, limitations, contingencies, and other termination events of paragraph 2(a) of this Agreement, to the extent that funds are available in the Trust. In addition, to the extent that ARTHUR has obligations to SUSAN and on behalf of the children of the parties remaining after his death pursuant to Article IV hereof, the Trustee shall make the payments to SUSAN and on behalf of the children pursuant to the terms and conditions of Article IV hereof, to the extent funds are available in the Trust. SUSAN, in consideration of the provisions of this Article VII, and except as otherwise provided in this paragraph 7(c), hereby releases any and all claims that she might otherwise have against the estate of ARTHUR for the obligations of ARTHUR under this Agreement, including, but not limited to, children's support pursuant to IMDMA § 510(d) and (e). *(This paragraph 7(c) needs to be slightly modified for use with Maintenance in Gross paragraph 2(c) and its subparagraphs where the death of the Husband is not a termination event.)*

7(d). When the payments required to be made by the Trustee, as herein provided, have been completed, the Trustee shall distribute any balance of the trust estate as provided by the terms of the Trust.

7(e). If all of the payments required to be made by ARTHUR to SUSAN and on behalf of the children, pursuant to paragraph 2(a), and Article IV hereof, have been made by ARTHUR during ARTHUR's lifetime, ARTHUR shall present to the Trustee satisfactory evidence or a statement signed by SUSAN that such payments have been made, and ARTHUR shall then be free from the obligations of paragraphs 7(b) through 7(f) hereof, and ARTHUR may terminate the Insurance Trust.

7(f). ARTHUR shall pay the expenses incident to the Trust.

ARTICLE VIII
Tax Returns

8. SUSAN and ARTHUR during their marriage have executed joint Federal and State income tax returns through the year 199__, and they agree to execute joint Federal and State income tax returns for the year 199__. Each party agrees to pay for his or her share of the taxes arising from the parties' joint returns that relates to his or her respective income and deductions. Each party also shall execute and acknowledge with the other all documents necessary and required in connection with any amendment, protest, application for refund, refund check, or suit or proceedings that hereafter may arise in connection with any joint income tax return that the parties have filed or will file. ARTHUR shall be entitled to retain any refund allowed and paid and agrees to pay any deficiency, interest, or penalties assessed, and fees and expense incurred, on or in connection with any such return that relates to his income and deductions. SUSAN shall be entitled to retain any refund allowed and paid, and agrees to pay any deficiency, interest, or penalty assessed, and fees and expense incurred, on or in connection with any such return that relates to her income and deductions. Each party agrees to and does hereby indemnify and render the other, his or her heirs, executors, and assignees free and harmless of and from any liability for that which he or she has undertaken pursuant to this Article VIII. Anything in the foregoing to the contrary notwithstanding, neither party shall be liable to the other nor shall reimburse the other for taxes heretofore withheld or paid. In the event the parties have filed a joint declaration of estimated Federal or State income tax for any year, and they do not file a joint Federal or State income tax return for such year, or in the event that either party has made an overpayment of tax, then each shall be entitled to take credit for the payment of estimated tax or overpayment of tax that he or she shall have paid.

ARTICLE IX
Medical Insurance

9. ARTHUR agrees to assist SUSAN in obtaining a continuation health insurance policy pursuant to the Federal Health Insurance Continuation

legislation contained in the Consolidated Omnibus Budget Reconciliation Act of 1985 (COBRA) (P.L. 99-272), and the Illinois Spousal Health Insurance Rights Act (SHIRA), 215 ILCS 5/367.2 (1992). ARTHUR shall fully cooperate with SUSAN to notify the _____ Insurance Company and ARTHUR's employer of the entry of the Judgment of Dissolution of Marriage. The notifications shall be made within sixty (60) days from the entry of a Judgment of Dissolution of Marriage for COBRA, and within thirty (30) days from the entry of a Judgment of Dissolution of Marriage for SHIRA. In addition, ARTHUR shall cooperate fully with SUSAN to assist her in applying for a conversion of any existing health and hospitalization insurance to a separate policy issued on her behalf pursuant to the provisions of the 215 ILCS 5/356(d) within sixty (60) days from the entry of a Judgment of Dissolution. SUSAN shall also have the conversion rights provided under COBRA and SHIRA. To the extent that the _____ medical insurance policy provides for coverage available to SUSAN that is greater than that pursuant to Illinois and Federal law, ARTHUR agrees to assist SUSAN in obtaining extended coverage. Upon obtaining continuation, conversion, or extended insurance, SUSAN shall be solely responsible for the payment of any premiums thereunder, and SUSAN agrees to and does hereby indemnify and hold ARTHUR harmless from any liability therefor. ARTHUR agrees that he will maintain SUSAN on the existing medical insurance during the election periods pursuant to COBRA, SHIRA, 215 ILCS 5/356(d), and the _____ medical policy, and ARTHUR further agrees that he will not take any action that would interfere with SUSAN's rights to continuation, conversion, or extended coverage pursuant to this Article IX.

(Delete from Article IX what is not applicable.)

ARTICLE X
Attorney's Fees

10. Each party agrees to pay his or her own attorney's fees, expert fees, and costs incurred in or related to this matrimonial litigation. Each party agrees to and does hereby indemnify and hold free and harmless the other, his or her estate, heirs, executors, administrators and personal representatives of and from any and all liability and expense in connection with the fees and costs that each party has undertaken to pay pursuant to this paragraph 10.

ARTICLE XI

(Article XI contains most of the possible releases. They can be edited for redundancy, and they should be coordinated with the releases, if any, placed in the Judgment. (See IMDMA § 413 Author's Note (8) model Judgment paras. 5 and 6.))

General Provisions

11(a). To the fullest extent by law permitted to do so, and except as herein otherwise provided, each of the parties does hereby forever relinquish, release, waive, and forever quitclaim and grant to the other, his or her heirs, personal representatives and assignees, all rights of dower, inheritance, descent, distribution, community interest, marital property, and all other right, title, claim, tort claims, interest, and estate as husband and wife, widow or widower, or otherwise, by reason of the marital relations existing between the parties hereto, under any present or future law, or which he or she otherwise has or might have or be entitled to claim in, to, or against the property and assets of the other, real, personal, or mixed, or his or her estate, whether now owned or hereafter in any manner acquired by the other party, or whether in possession or in expectancy, whether vested or contingent, and each party further covenants and agrees for himself or herself, his or her heirs, personal representatives and assignees, that neither of them will at any time hereafter sue the other or his or her heirs, personal representatives, grantees, devisees or assignees, for the purpose of enforcing any or either of the rights specified in and relinquished under this paragraph 11(a), and further agrees that in the event any suit shall be commenced, this release, when pleaded, shall be and constitute a complete defense to any claim or suit so instituted by either party hereto, and further agrees to execute, acknowledge and deliver at the request of the other party, or his or her heirs, personal representatives, grantees, devisees or assignees, any or all such deeds, releases or other instruments, and further assurances as may be required or reasonably requested to effect or evidence such release, waiver, relinquishment or extinguishment of such rights; provided, however, that nothing herein contained shall operate or be construed as a waiver or release by either party to the other party of any obligation imposed upon or undertaken by a party under this Agreement.

11(b). Each of the parties hereto hereby agrees to execute and acknowledge, concurrently with the execution hereof, good and sufficient instruments necessary or proper to vest the titles and estates in the respective parties hereto, as hereinabove provided, and hereafter, at any time and from time to time, to execute and acknowledge any and all documents that may be necessary or proper to carry out the purposes of this Agreement and establish of record the sole and separate ownership of the several properties of the parties in the manner herein agreed and provided. If either party hereto for any reason shall fail or refuse to execute any such documents, or if no document is called for, then this Agreement shall, and it is hereby expressly declared to, constitute a full and present transfer, assignment, and conveyance of all rights hereinabove designated to be relinquished and waived, and an indemnity where indemnification is hereinabove agreed. In the event after thirty (30) days from the effective date of this Agreement, there are necessary documents that either party has failed to execute or deliver, both parties hereby authorize and direct that a Judicial Officer of the Circuit Court of _____ County, Illinois shall be authorized to make, execute, and deliver any and all necessary documents on behalf of either party. This authorization includes, but shall not be limited to, any and all realty, personal property, or beneficial interests in land trusts.

11(c). Each of the parties hereby waives and relinquishes all rights to act as administrator-with-the-will-annexed of the estate of the other party, and each of the parties hereto does further relinquish all right to inherit by intestate succession any of the property of which the other party may die seized or possessed, and should either of the parties hereto die intestate, this Agreement shall operate as a relinquishment of all right of the surviving party hereafter to apply for letters of administration in any form, and the estate of such deceased party, if he or she dies intestate, shall descend to the heirs at law of such deceased party, in the same manner as though the parties hereto had never been married, each of the parties hereto respectively, by testament or otherwise, reserving the right to dispose of his or her respective property in any way that he or she may see fit, without restriction or limitation whatsoever, except as herein otherwise provided.

11(d). Save and except as herein otherwise provided, and to the fullest extent that they may lawfully do so, all the rights, claims, and demands of every kind, nature and description, which each party has, or may hereafter have, or claim to have against the other, shall be and the same hereby are forever discharged, extinguished, released, and ended, and all matters and charges whatsoever, and any and all manner of actions or causes of actions, suits, debts, dues, accounts, bonds, covenants, contracts, agreements, judgments, claims, and demands whatsoever, in law or in equity, which each party ever had, now has, or which he or she, his or her heirs, executors, administrators, or assignees, or any of them, hereafter can, shall, or may have against the other (as the case may be) for or by reason of any cause, matter or thing whatsoever, from the beginning of the world to the effective date hereof, shall be and the same are, hereby forever released, discharged, barred, terminated, and extinguished; provided, however, that nothing herein contained shall release or limit the obligation of either of the parties hereto to comply with the other provisions of this Agreement.

11(e). Except as otherwise herein provided, each party hereby waives and releases all claims that each party has or could have against the other for tort, personal, mental, physical, or emotional injury, and all damages of any nature, and each party acknowledges that any such claims that each has brought or could have brought have been considered, compromised, or waived in this Settlement Agreement, and are therefore hereafter barred.

11(f). This Agreement shall be binding upon and inure to the benefit of the respective heirs, executors, administrators, assignees, devisees, grantees, current and future trustees, and other successors of the parties hereto.

11(g). Anything herein to the contrary notwithstanding, this Agreement shall not bar any claim that SUSAN or ARTHUR has by reason of the social security laws of the United States.

11(h). This Agreement shall be construed under the laws of Illinois.

ARTICLE XII
Incorporation

12(a). In the event that any Judgment of Dissolution shall be entered in Cause No. ___ D ___, in the Circuit Court of ___ County, Illinois, this

Agreement shall be exhibited to the Court for its consideration. If the Court approves the Agreement, it shall be incorporated into the Court's Judgment. If a Judgment of Dissolution approving and incorporating this Agreement is not entered in Cause No. ___ D ___, this Agreement shall be null and void and of no force or effect.

(Use the following paragraph if the incorporation is by reference in order to protect the privacy of the terms of the Agreement.)

Incorporation by Reference

12(b). In the event the Circuit Court of _____ County, Illinois, in Cause No. ___ D ___, dissolves the marriage of the parties, this Agreement shall be submitted to such Court for its approval, and, if approved, shall be incorporated into and made a part of the Judgment of Dissolution by reference. SUSAN and ARTHUR agree that the purpose of incorporating this Agreement in the Judgment by reference is only to protect the privacy of the terms of the Agreement, and they further agree that it is their intention that the incorporation by reference have the same effect under the Illinois Marriage and Dissolution of Marriage Act as a verbatim incorporation. They further agree to do everything necessary and proper to obtain the effect of verbatim incorporation, including actually incorporating this Agreement into the Judgment, if required by the Court. If the Agreement is physically incorporated in the Judgment, the parties agree that the file shall be impounded. Each of the parties, in order to protect the privacy of the other, agrees not to publish or disclose the terms of this Agreement without the clear necessity so to do. If a Judgment of Dissolution approving and incorporating this Agreement is not entered in Cause No. ___ D ___, this Agreement shall be null and void and of no force or effect.

(See IMDMA § 413 Author's Note (8), Judgment Additional and Alternative Provisions para. 10, for corresponding incorporation by reference judgment paragraphs.)

Effective Date

12(c). This Agreement may be executed in one or more counterparts, which shall together constitute the original thereof. The effective date of this Agreement shall be the date on which a Judgment of Dissolution of Marriage is entered by the Circuit Court of _____ County approving and incorporating this Agreement, and the provisions of this Agreement shall only come into full force and effect on such date.

12(d). All transfers and payments pursuant to this Agreement shall take place on the effective date of this Agreement, except as otherwise herein provided.

Enforceability

12(e). The terms of this Agreement shall be enforceable as an independent contract and by all remedies available for the enforcement of a judgment, including but not limited to contempt proceedings.

750 ILCS 5/502 FAMILIES

IN WITNESS WHEREOF, the parties have hereunto set their hands and seals the day and year first above written.

_____   _____
SUSAN JELLYBY   ARTHUR JELLYBY

Samuel Kenge
Kenge and Carboy
Attorneys for SUSAN JELLYBY
Address
Telephone number

STATE OF ILLINOIS)
) SS
COUNTY OF COOK   )

I, the undersigned, a Notary Public in and for said County, in the State aforesaid, do hereby certify that SUSAN JELLYBY, personally known to me to be the same person whose name is subscribed to the foregoing Instrument, appeared before me this day in person and acknowledged that she signed, sealed and delivered the said Instrument as her free and voluntary act, for the uses and purposes therein set forth.

Given under my hand and notarial seal this _____ day of _____, 199__.

_____
Notary Public

STATE OF ILLINOIS)
) SS
COUNTY OF COOK   )

I, the undersigned, a Notary Public in and for said County, in the State aforesaid, do hereby certify that ARTHUR JELLYBY, personally known to me to be the same person whose name is subscribed to the foregoing Instrument, appeared before me this day in person and acknowledged that he signed, sealed and delivered the said Instrument as his free and voluntary act, for the uses and purposes therein set forth.

Given under my hand and notarial seal this _____ day of _____, 199__.

_____
Notary Public

(The notary page is not necessary to constitute a contract, but it adds to the formality of the documents and memorializes witnesses to the signing.)

EXHIBITS

Exhibit A: Qualified Medical Child Support Order (QMCSO). See ERISA § 609 (29 U.S.C.A. § 1169) Author's Note (6) for a sample form.

Exhibit B: Allocation of the parties' assets. This exhibit contemplates a summary of the allocation of all of the assets between the parties, and includes a recitation of the asset values. The exhibit is repeatedly referred to in applicable paragraphs of Article VI of the Agreement.

Exhibit C: Legal description of the marital home.

Exhibit D: Legal description of the Florida home.

Exhibit E: Qualified Domestic Relations Order (QDRO). See Internal Revenue Code § 414(p) Author's Note (6) for a sample form.

Exhibit F: Life insurance schedule.

Exhibit G: Life insurance trust sample form follows.

(12) **Insurance Trust—Form.** The following sample insurance trust is Exhibit G to the model settlement agreement in Author's Note (11) of this Section.

EXHIBIT G
ARTHUR JELLYBY INSURANCE TRUST

THIS AGREEMENT, made and executed this _____ day of _____, 199__ by and between ARTHUR JELLYBY as Settlor, and _____ as Trustee.

WITNESSETH:

I, ARTHUR JELLYBY, of _____, Illinois, have caused or shortly hereafter will cause the death benefits under the policies of insurance on my life described on Schedule I, hereto attached, to be made payable to _____, of _____, Illinois, as Trustee; the proceeds of the aforedescribed policies, and of any other policies of insurance under which I am the insured, which may become payable to the Trustee, and all investments and reinvestments thereof (referred to below as the "trust property"), to be held subject to the following trusts:

1. This Agreement and the trusts hereby evidenced, as from time to time changed and modified, shall be known as the "ARTHUR JELLYBY INSURANCE TRUST, DATED _____, 199__," and also may be designated by such number or numbers as the Trustee may determine.

2. The Trustee shall not be required to pay premiums, assessments, or other charges upon any of such policies or contracts, or to keep itself informed with respect thereto.

3. Upon my death, the Trustee shall use reasonable efforts to collect the proceeds of all of such policies and contracts that then are payable to the Trustee. The Trustee may take any action in regard to the collection of such proceeds it considers best, and may pay any expense reasonably incurred out of the trust property, but the Trustee shall not be required to incur any expense or to enter into or maintain any litigation unless indemnified in amount and manner satisfactory to it. The Trustee may compromise or otherwise adjust claims on account of any such policies or contracts. The

receipt of the Trustee to the insurance companies, and each of them, shall be a full discharge of all their liabilities under such policies and contracts.

4. At the conclusion of the litigation in the Circuit Court of _____ County between my former wife, SUSAN JELLYBY, and me, known as "In re the Marriage of Susan Jellyby, Petitioner, and Arthur Jellyby, Respondent," No. __ D ____, a Judgment for Dissolution of Marriage was entered by the Court on _____, 199__ (hereinafter referred to as the "Jellyby Judgment"), which Judgment incorporated a Settlement Agreement between the parties, dated _____, 199__ (hereinafter referred to as the "Agreement"), a copy of which Judgment and Agreement are attached hereto as Exhibit II.

5. If I should die before my obligations to make payments to SUSAN JELLYBY and on behalf of our children, Caddy Jellyby and Peepy Jellyby, terminate or have been satisfied, under the terms of paragraph 2(a) and Article IV of the Agreement incorporated in the Jellyby Judgment, the Trustee shall use the income and, if necessary, the principal of this Insurance Trust to make the payments to SUSAN JELLYBY and on behalf of our children, Caddy Jellyby and Peepy Jellyby, as provided under the terms and subject to the reductions, conditions, limitations, termination events, and contingencies of paragraph 2(a) and Article IV of the Agreement incorporated in the Jellyby Judgment. My death shall not be considered a termination event pursuant to paragraph 2(a) of the Agreement incorporated in the Jellyby Judgment for purposes of payment by this Insurance Trust.

6(a). After the Trustee's obligations to make the payments provided for in the preceding paragraph 5 hereof terminate or are satisfied, the remaining balance of the trust funds shall be distributed as I by my will appoint, and, upon my failure to appoint, to my legal heirs, *per stirpes*, as of the date that the Trustee's obligations to make the payments provided for in preceding paragraph 5 hereof terminate.

6(b). If the Trustee's obligations to make the payments provided for in the preceding paragraph 5 hereof terminate or are satisfied during my lifetime, the insurance policies and all of the other assets in the trust shall be reassigned and delivered to me and this trust shall terminate.

7. Regardless of any other provisions in this instrument, no portion of the trust property shall be retained in trust hereunder for more than twenty-one years after the death of the last to die of my former wife, SUSAN JELLYBY, my descendants who were living on _____, 199__, and myself; and any fund or share of the trust property, if any, still retained in trust at the end of the aforesaid period immediately shall be distributed to the person for whom such fund is named or in whom such share is vested, as the case may be.

8. The Trustee shall be fully protected in relying upon an instrument which has been admitted to probate in any jurisdiction as the last will of mine, or if the Trustee has no actual notice of the existence of a will of mine within three months after my death, the Trustee may presume I died without a will.

9. While a beneficiary is under a legal disability or, in the Trustee's opinion, in any way is incapacitated so as to be unable to manage his or her financial affairs, the Trustee may make the payments of income or discretionary payments of principal contemplated above to the beneficiary entitled thereto by making them directly to him or her, or to a relative or friend of the beneficiary for his or her benefit, or in such other manner as the Trustee deems best for the benefit of the beneficiary.

10. The interests of the beneficiaries in principal or income shall not be subject in any way to the claims of their creditors or others, and may not be voluntarily alienated or encumbered.

11. In reference to the trust property, including each of the separate funds and vested shares withheld from distribution as provided above, the Trustee, subject only to the limitations expressly provided in this instrument shall have the following powers and rights in addition to those vested in it elsewhere in this instrument or by law:

(a) To manage, sell, contract to sell, grant options to purchase, convey, exchange, transfer, abandon, improve, repair, insure, lease for any term even though commencing in the future or extending beyond the term of the trusts and otherwise deal with all property, real or personal, in such manner, for such considerations, and on such terms and conditions as the trustee shall decide.

(b) To retain, invest and reinvest the trust property in stocks, bonds, mortgages, notes or other property of any kind, real or personal, and irrespective of rules of law, and any investment made or retained by the trustee in good faith shall be proper although not of a kind or constituting a diversification considered by law suitable for trust investments.

(c) To borrow money for any purpose on such terms as it considers proper, and to mortgage or pledge any trust property.

(d) To compromise, contest, arbitrate or abandon claims or demands, all in its discretion.

(e) To have with respect to trust property all the rights of an individual owner, including the power to give proxies, to participate in voting trusts, mergers, consolidations, foreclosures, reorganizations or liquidations, and to exercise or sell stock subscription or conversion rights.

(f) To hold securities or other property in the name of a nominee or in such other manner as the trustee deems best with or without disclosing the trust relationship.

(g) To employ agents and counsel and to delegate to them such of its powers as it considers desirable.

(h) To divide or distribute trust property in undivided interests or in kind or partly in money and partly in kind at such valuations as the trustee considers fair; to sell property for the purpose of making division or distribution, and for administrative and investment purposes, or only to consolidate the trust property or any separate fund with any other fund, or with any other trust in which any beneficiary hereunder has any interest, and for such purposes to hold such several funds or trusts in one or more common accounts in which separate funds or trusts have undivided interests, and to make joint or several distributions of the income or principal thereof.

(i) To pay all taxes and all reasonable costs, charges and expenses incurred in the administration of the trusts hereby created, including compensation to the trustee or its agents and counsel.

(j) To purchase property from, sell property or make secured loans to, or otherwise deal without restriction with the executor, trustee or other representatives of any trust or estate in which any beneficiary has any interest, even though the trustee be such executor, trustee or representative, without liability for any loss or depreciation resulting therefrom.

(k) To receive additional property from any person by will or otherwise as part of the trust property or any fund or share thereof.

(l) To perform any and all other acts in its judgment necessary or appropriate for the proper and advantageous management, investment and distribution of the trust property.

12. All powers and directions given to the trustee shall be absolute and uncontrolled, and each exercise in good faith shall be conclusive on all persons, including persons unascertained or not born. No persons dealing with the trustee shall be obliged to see to the application of any money paid or property delivered to the Trustee. The certificate of the Trustee that it is acting according to this instrument shall fully protect all persons dealing with the Trustee.

13. Any Trustee may resign at any time by written notice to me, if I am living, otherwise to each beneficiary then entitled to receive or have the benefit of the income and/or principal from the trust. In case of the resignation, refusal, or inability to act of any Trustee, I, if living, otherwise the beneficiary or a majority in interest of the beneficiaries then entitled to receive or have the benefit of the income and/or principal from the Trust, may appoint a successor Trustee.

14. Each successor Trustee hereunder shall have the same rights, titles, powers, duties, discretions and immunities, and otherwise be in the same position, as if originally named Trustee. No successor Trustee shall be personally liable for any act or failure to act of any predecessor Trustee, and with the approval of the person or persons appointing it a successor Trustee may accept the account rendered and the property delivered to it by any predecessor trustee as a full and complete discharge to such predecessor Trustee, without incurring any liability or responsibility for so doing. Whenever the Trustee (except a substitute Trustee appointed under this paragraph)

for any reason deems it advantageous, it may substitute for itself as Trustee any person or corporation qualified to act wherever located by writing filed with the substitute Trustee so appointed. Except as limited by this paragraph and by the writing appointing him, her, or it, a substitute Trustee shall have all the rights, titles, powers, duties, discretions and immunities of the Trustee named above. A substitute Trustee shall incur no liability for any action taken or omitted to be taken pursuant to the direction of the Trustee or the writing appointing such substitute Trustee. The Trustee may remove a substitute Trustee acting hereunder, and a substitute Trustee may resign, at any time by writing filed with the other. While a substitute Trustee is acting hereunder the Trustee may reappoint itself as Trustee or may appoint another substitute Trustee.

15. I reserve the following rights, powers and authority which may be exercised by me at any time and from time to time:

(a) By written instrument delivered to the trustee to change, modify or revoke this agreement and the trusts hereby evidenced, in whole or in part, except that if changed or modified, the duties, powers and responsibilities of the trustee shall not be substantially changed without its written consent, and except that prior to the satisfaction of paragraph 5 hereof no change, modification, or revocation hereof shall be made without the prior approval of my former wife, SUSAN JELLYBY.

(b) All benefits, privileges, payments, annuities, dividends, surrender values, options and elections accorded or available to me under any and all policies of insurance which may be made payable to the trustee, including the right to change the beneficiary named in any or all of such policies or contracts, to deposit, assign, transfer or pledge them as collateral security for any loan which I may make from any lender and to withdraw any of such policies and contracts deposited with the trustee, except that none of the aforesaid powers and authorities shall be exercised contrary to the provisions of Article VII of the Agreement incorporated in the Jellyby Judgment. The Trustee shall not be obliged to see that any policy or contract so withdrawn is returned to its custody.

_____[SEAL]
ARTHUR JELLYBY

The undersigned hereby accepts the foregoing trusts as of the day and year last above-written.

_____, TRUSTEE

APPROVED:

_____
SUSAN JELLYBY

(13) **Settlement Agreement Checklist.** There follows a checklist for settlement agreements.

Settlement Agreement Checklist

(1) Preliminary provisions

    Names and places of residence of parties

    Date

    Marriage data

    Children

    Names of attorneys, and parties have had benefit of counsel

    Existence of lawsuit

    Desire of parties to settle their disputes

    Statement of discovery (voluntary exchanges, depositions, investigation, etc.)

    Representation that information provided is true and complete

    Acknowledgment by parties that they have relied on and are fully advised by discovery

    Acknowledgment that there has been no material change since completion of discovery

    Acknowledgment by parties that they are advised of rights

    Agreement freely entered into by parties

    No agreements outside of contract

    Consideration

    Agreement not to stimulate dissolution

(2) Maintenance

    (a) Types of maintenance

        Maintenance to terminate on statutory events

        Maintenance paid beyond happening of one or more statutory events

        Maintenance in gross

        Maintenance for set term of years, either to terminate or not terminate on the intervention of a statutory event before the expiration of the term of years

        Permanent or indefinite maintenance

        Reviewable maintenance

        Deductible/taxable maintenance (must terminate on death of payee)

        Unallocated maintenance and children's support

Non-deductible/non-taxable maintenance

Two streams of maintenance, e.g., one deductible/ taxable and the second neither deductible nor taxable

Percentage maintenance, with and without base and ceiling, or in addition to a stated amount (e.g., stated amount plus percent of bonus)

Maintenance to pay interest on installment property payments to gain deductions for payor

Maintenance to pay attorney's fees (beware of recapture)

Modifiable and non-modifiable maintenance

Maintenance with a specified reduction in payments (beware of recapture)

Maintenance to increase with the Consumer Price Index (or other index)

Maintenance paid by trust

Payments to third party attributable to maintenance

(b) Maintenance waiver: total or a waiver of maintenance other than the maintenance provided in the Agreement

(c) Maintenance reservation

(d) Statement of intended tax results and what happens if not realized

(e) Pay maintenance directly to recipient or through the clerk of the court

(f) Withholding of maintenance from wages provisions to take effect immediately or waived with security

(g) Tax identification number of payee

(h) Security for maintenance payments (e.g., life insurance, estate, trust, collateral trust, etc.)

(3) Children's custody

Parties or party fit and proper person to have custody

Sole custody

Joint custody

    Joint parenting agreement

    Residential custody

Shared custody

Visitation

Out of state residence

Determination of day-to-day issues

Determination of significant issues (medical, education, religion, etc.)

Issues for sole determination by a parent

Issues for joint determination by both parents

Mediation

Determination in emergencies

School and medical records

Out of state vacations

Telephone access

Each parent support the other as a parent so that the children have love and respect for both parents

(4) Children's support

Children's support neither deductible nor taxable

Unallocated maintenance and children's support, deductible/taxable, but beware of anti-Lester rules

When children's support is paid by unallocated maintenance and children's support (deductible/taxable) there should be an indemnity by the payee against seeking additional children's support while the unallocated is paid, a provision to determine children's support by agreement or through the court upon the termination of unallocated maintenance and children's support, and a statement stating reasons why there is deviation from the children's support guidelines

Stated termination date of child support

Guidelines or deviation from guidelines (if latter state reasons, amount under guidelines)

Contribution by one or both parties

Allocation of dependency exemptions

College expenses

    Determination who pays at time of agreement

    Reserve issue and determine who pays at time child goes to college

Private school

Camp, extracurricular activities, sports, lessons

Medical

    Responsibility for maintaining children on medical insurance

    Responsibility for sending medical receipts to insurance company

    Who pays medical expenses not covered by medical insurance? Deductible, not covered, or beyond limits.

    Ordinary medical expenses

    Extraordinary medical expenses

    Dental expenses

Psychiatric or psychological expenses
Joint or sole parental decisions
Emergencies
Termination of liability
Qualified Medical Children's Support Order (QMCSO)
Security (estate, life insurance, trust)
Withholding provisions to apply immediately or waived with security
Pay directly or through clerk of court

(5) Property

Introductory paragraph designating property section

(a) Assignment of non-marital property to owner
(b) Assignment of marital property that is to remain with owner
(c) Allocation of property that is to change hands
(d) Marital home and other real estate

Current title: sole, joint, land trust
Value and mortgage, home equity debt, other liens
Legal description
Real estate index number
Quit claim or other conveyance to one party or the other
Assignment of beneficial interest
Responsibility for costs, before and after effective date of Agreement
- mortgage loans
- home equity loans
- real estate taxes (In some counties billed a year late)
- insurance premiums
- utilities
- maintenance expenses (gardeners, snow removal, repairs, etc.)

Allocation of tax escrows
Assignment of title insurance
Refinancing
Delivery and assignment of real estate documents (records of cost basis, deeds, title policies, insurance policies, surveys, etc.)
Warranties of no liens and other applicable warranties
Sell and allocate proceeds
Custodial parent remains in house with children for period of time, then sell and allocate proceeds

750 ILCS 5/502   **FAMILIES**

    Mechanism to determine listing price for sales

    Mechanism to change listing price, change contract terms, accept offer

    Selection of real estate brokers

    Responsibility for sales commissions and costs

    Best efforts to accomplish sale

    Maintenance of home in good condition

    Maintenance of insurance

    Provision for repairs, fix up

    Allocation of expenses and proceeds

    Party's option to purchase

    Responsibility for capital gains tax on sale to third party

    Rollover of capital gains tax from principal residence into purchase of new principal residence

    Over 55, $125,000 credit against capital gains tax on principal residence

    Where both parties are in joint title pending a sale, transfer from joint tenants to tenancy in common to eliminate survivorship

    Operation of "due on sale" provisions of mortgages

    Reservation of court jurisdiction in joint sales

    Use of escrow of portion of sale proceeds to pay capital gains tax in joint sales

    Allocation of cost basis in joint sales

    Rights to record memorandum of judgment

(e) Allocation of personal property, furniture, furnishings, etc.

(f) Allocation of automobiles and boats

(g) Retirement plan allocations

    Defined benefit plan

    Defined contribution plan

    Allocation of plan

    Allocation paid in cash, securities, or other

    Set offs using other assets

    Rollover of IRAs

    QDROs

    Representations and warranties concerning plans

    Plan to plan or to IRA to avoid withholding

Non-qualified plans

Statement of intended tax consequences and what happens if contemplated tax consequences are not realized

Reservation of jurisdiction for court to adjudicate potential issues

(h) Allocation of:

securities

stock options

phantom stock

bonuses or other distributions after close of discovery

partnerships

bank accounts

insurance policies

art work

benefits of employment

tax bases

(i) Assignments or buyouts of closely held businesses and partnerships

Stock redemptions, caveat regarding tax consequences

(j) Allocation of joint property

(k) Installment property payments

With or without interest

Implied interest

Right of prepayment

Security by mortgage, collateral trust, life insurance, etc.

(l) Cash payments

(m) Allocation of debts

(n) Cancellation of joint credit cards

(o) Hold harmless as to assumed and future debts

(p) Indemnities against debts, taxes and other liabilities

(q) Allocation of assets held in trust or by a nominee

(r) General allocation clause covering property not specified

(s) Statement of tax intentions and what happens if contemplated tax consequences are not realized

(t) *Nota bene.* The allocation of tax bases, because of the capital gains tax upon sale to a third party, can be as important as the allocation of value, if there is to be an equitable division.

750 ILCS 5/502   **FAMILIES**

(6) Security for maintenance, children's support, installment property payments

    Life insurance

    Life insurance trust

    Collateral trust

    Mortgage lien

    Assignment of beneficial interest

    Estate

(7) Joint tax returns

    Treatment of issues, e.g., deficiencies, interest, penalties, fees, arising from previously filed joint tax returns

    Refunds

    Execution of amendments and other necessary documents

    Agreements to file or not to file joint tax returns for past year (where possible)

    Payment of tax on joint returns to be filed

    Responsibility for misstatements of income or deductions

    Allocation of estimated tax payments and overpayments

    Indemnities

(8) Medical insurance conversions and continuances

    COBRA

    SHIRA

    215 ILCS 5/356(d)

    Additional policy rights

(9) Attorney's fees, Expert's fees, costs

(10) Execution of documents pursuant to Agreement

(11) Releases

    Claims

    Estates

    Torts

(12) Effective date of Agreement

    Judgment

    Delivery of executed copies

    Specify date on which transfers to take place

(13) Agreement physically incorporated or incorporated by reference in Judgment

(14) Executed counterparts constitute originals

(15) Illinois law to control

(16) Agreement binding on successors

(17) Social Security

(18) Signatures

(19) Notary page

(14) **Enforcement.** Section 502(e) provides that the terms of the agreement set forth in the judgment are enforceable both by remedies for the enforcement of judgments, and by contract remedies. An agreement incorporated into a judgment by reference is also enforceable as part of the judgment. See, e.g., In re Marriage of Sherrick, 214 Ill.App.3d 92, 157 Ill.Dec. 917, 573 N.E.2d 335 (4th Dist.1991). The most common way of enforcing an agreement incorporated into a judgment physically or by reference is by a contempt proceeding against the party in default, who is already a party to the lawsuit. This is much simpler than initiating a new suit on the contract.

(15) **Cross reference—Form.** A sample petition for a rule to show cause, which initiates contempt proceedings, is at IMDMA § 511 Author's Note (6).

(16) **Non-modifiable.** Pursuant to § 502(f), the parties can agree to make certain terms of their settlement agreements non-modifiable. The court, however, cannot order a non-modifiable provision without an agreement of the parties. "Maintenance agreements may be modified or terminated under circumstances stated in statutory provisions, unless the parties' intent is clearly manifested in such agreement to limit or preclude such judicial modification or termination." In re Marriage of Scott, 205 Ill.App.3d 561, 564, 150 Ill.Dec. 868, 870, 563 N.E.2d 995, 997 (4th Dist.1990). See also In re Marriage of Sutton, 178 Ill.App.3d 928, 128 Ill.Dec. 37, 533 N.E.2d 1125 (3d Dist.1989) (settlement agreement did not show clear intent to preclude all judicial modification of maintenance).

Provision for non-modifiability is superfluous insofar as property terms are concerned, because, after the expiration of 30 days from the entry of the judgment, and in the absence of a ground for attacking the judgment under the Illinois Code of Civil Procedure, 735 ILCS 5/2–1401, the property terms that have been incorporated into the judgment are not modifiable pursuant to the Illinois Marriage and Dissolution of Marriage Act. See IMDMA § 510(b) and accompanying Author's Notes (9) and (10) for discussion of the non-modifiability of property terms and overriding IMDMA § 510(b).

Non-modifiability cannot apply to children's terms pursuant to IMDMA § 502(f). The provisions made for the support, custody, or visitation of the children are always modifiable, even when combined with non-modifiable maintenance. § 502(b); In re Marriage of Glickman, 211 Ill.App.3d 792, 795, 156 Ill.Dec. 162, 164, 570 N.E.2d 638, 640 (1st Dist.1991). The court reserves jurisdiction to act in the best interests of the children. In re Marriage of Falat, 201 Ill.App.3d 320, 325, 147 Ill.Dec. 33, 37, 559 N.E.2d 33, 36 (1st Dist.1990).

Non-modification agreements are therefore limited to maintenance and to other provisions that do not involve children or property, such as insurance. See e.g., In re Marriage of Tucker, 223 Ill.App.3d 671, 166 Ill.Dec. 83, 585 N.E.2d 1105 (3d Dist.

1992). See IMDMA § 510 Author's Notes (2) and (9) for caveats concerning non-modifiable maintenance and property settlements.

A sample non-modification clause is in para. 2(g) of the model settlement agreement at Author's Note (11) of this Section.

Except where agreement provisions are non-modifiable by statute or by agreement of the parties, § 502(f) provides that the terms of an agreement incorporated in a judgment are automatically modified by modification of the judgment. See IMDMA § 510 and accompanying Author's Notes for discussion of modification.

750 ILCS 5/503

§ 503. Disposition of property

(a) For purposes of this Act, "marital property" means all property acquired by either spouse subsequent to the marriage, except the following, which is known as "non-marital property":

    (1) property acquired by gift, legacy or descent;

    (2) property acquired in exchange for property acquired before the marriage or in exchange for property acquired by gift, legacy or descent;

    (3) property acquired by a spouse after a judgment of legal separation;

    (4) property excluded by valid agreement of the parties;

    (5) any judgment or property obtained by judgment awarded to a spouse from the other spouse;

    (6) property acquired before the marriage;

    (7) the increase in value of property acquired by a method listed in paragraphs (1) through (6) of this subsection, irrespective of whether the increase results from a contribution of marital property, non-marital property, the personal effort of a spouse, or otherwise, subject to the right of reimbursement provided in subsection (c) of this Section; and

    (8) income from property acquired by a method listed in paragraphs (1) through (7) of this subsection if the income is not attributable to the personal effort of a spouse.

(b) For purposes of distribution of property pursuant to this Section, all property acquired by either spouse after the marriage and before a judgment of dissolution of marriage or declaration of invalidity of marriage, including non-marital property transferred into some form of co-ownership between the spouses, is presumed to be marital property, regardless of whether title is held individually or by the spouses in some form of co-ownership such as joint tenancy, tenancy in common, tenancy by the entirety, or community property. The presumption of marital property is overcome by a showing that the property was acquired by a method listed in subsection (a) of this Section.

(c) Commingled marital and non-marital property shall be treated in the following manner, unless otherwise agreed by the spouses:

(1) When marital and non-marital property are commingled by contributing one estate of property into another resulting in a loss of identity of the contributed property, the classification of the contributed property is transmuted to the estate receiving the contribution, subject to the provisions of paragraph (2) of this subsection; provided that if marital and non-marital property are commingled into newly acquired property resulting in a loss of identity of the contributing estates, the commingled property shall be deemed transmuted to marital property, subject to the provisions of paragraph (2) of this subsection.

(2) When one estate of property makes a contribution to another estate of property, or when a spouse contributes personal effort to non-marital property, the contributing estate shall be reimbursed from the estate receiving the contribution notwithstanding any transmutation; provided, that no such reimbursement shall be made with respect to a contribution which is not retraceable by clear and convincing evidence, or was a gift, or, in the case of a contribution of personal effort of a spouse to non-marital property, unless the effort is significant and results in substantial appreciation of the non-marital property. Personal effort of a spouse shall be deemed a contribution by the marital estate. The court may provide for reimbursement out of the marital property to be divided or by imposing a lien against the non-marital property which received the contribution.

(d) In a proceeding for dissolution of marriage or declaration of invalidity of marriage, or in a proceeding for disposition of property following dissolution of marriage by a court which lacked personal jurisdiction over the absent spouse or lacked jurisdiction to dispose of the property, the court shall assign each spouse's non-marital property to that spouse. It also shall divide the marital property without regard to marital misconduct in just proportions considering all relevant factors, including:

(1) the contribution of each party to the acquisition, preservation, or increase or decrease in value of the marital or non-marital property, including the contribution of a spouse as a homemaker or to the family unit;

(2) the dissipation by each party of the marital or non-marital property;

(3) the value of the property assigned to each spouse;

(4) the duration of the marriage;

(5) the relevant economic circumstances of each spouse when the division of property is to become effective, including the desirability of awarding the family home, or the right to live therein for reasonable periods, to the spouse having custody of the children;

(6) any obligations and rights arising from a prior marriage of either party;

(7) any antenuptial agreement of the parties;

(8) the age, health, station, occupation, amount and sources of income, vocational skills, employability, estate, liabilities, and needs of each of the parties;

(9) the custodial provisions for any children;

(10) whether the apportionment is in lieu of or in addition to maintenance;

(11) the reasonable opportunity of each spouse for future acquisition of capital assets and income; and

(12) the tax consequences of the property division upon the respective economic circumstances of the parties.

(e) Each spouse has a species of common ownership in the marital property which vests at the time dissolution proceedings are commenced and continues only during the pendency of the action. Any such interest in marital property shall not encumber that property so as to restrict its transfer, assignment or conveyance by the title holder unless such title holder is specifically enjoined from making such transfer, assignment or conveyance.

(f) In a proceeding for dissolution of marriage or declaration of invalidity of marriage or in a proceeding for disposition of property following dissolution of marriage by a court that lacked personal jurisdiction over the absent spouse or lacked jurisdiction to dispose of the property, the court, in determining the value of the marital and non-marital property for purposes of dividing the property, shall value the property as of the date of trial or some other date as close to the date of trial as is practicable.

(g) The court if necessary to protect and promote the best interests of the children may set aside a portion of the jointly or separately held estates of the parties in a separate fund or trust for the support, maintenance, education, and general welfare of any minor, dependent, or incompetent child of the parties. In making a determination under this subsection, the court may consider, among other things, the conviction of a party of any of the offenses set forth in Section 12–4, 12–4.1, 12–4.2, 12–4.3, 12–13, 12–14, 12–15, or 12–16 of the Criminal Code of 1961 if the victim is a child of one or both of the parties, and there is a need for, and cost of, care, healing and counseling for the child who is the victim of the crime.

(h) Unless specifically directed by a reviewing court, or upon good cause shown, the court shall not on remand consider any increase or decrease in the value of any "marital" or "non-marital" property occurring since the assessment of such property at the original trial or hearing, but shall use only that assessment made at the original trial or hearing.

(i) The court may make such judgments affecting the marital property as may be just and may enforce such judgments by ordering a sale of marital property, with proceeds therefrom to be applied as determined by the court.

FAMILIES 750 ILCS 5/503

Author's Notes

Analysis

1. Marital property presumption. 503(a), 503(b).
2. Non-marital property: Common examples. 503(a)(1), 503(a)(6).
3. Cancelling presumptions: Property received from a parent during the marriage. 503(a), 503(b).
4. Title. 503(b).
5. Co-ownership. 503(b).
6. Homes purchased in contemplation of marriage. 503(a), 503(b).
7. Property acquired in exchange for non-marital property. 503(a)(2).
8. Property acquired after physical separation. 503(a)(3).
9. Property subject to agreements and judgments between the parties. 503(a)(4), 503(a)(5).
10. Appreciation of non-marital property. 503(a)(7).
11. Income from non-marital property. 503(a)(8).
12. Commingled non-marital property. 503(c).
13. Commingled property: Loss of identity of the contribution. 503(c)(1).
14. Loss of identity of both contributing estates. 503(c)(1).
15. Reimbursement. 503(c)(2).
16. Illustrations. 503(c)(1), 503(c)(2).
17. Allocation of reimbursement. 503(c)(2).
18. Appreciation on contribution. 503(c)(2).
19. Award of non-marital property. 503(d).
20. Award of marital property: "Just proportions." 503(d).
21. Award of marital property: Factors considered. 503(d)(1)—503(d)(12).
22. Vesting of marital property rights. 503(e).
23. Impact of valuations upon property allocation. 503(d).
24. Valuations of closely held businesses.
25. Valuation of professional good will.
26. Valuation of assets without common market value.
27. Valuation by owner.
28. Date of valuation of property. 503(f).
29. Retirement benefits: Types.
30. Retirement benefits: Allocation.
31. Cross references.
32. Debts.
33. Support trusts. 503(g).
34. Crimes by the parent against the child. 503(g).
35. Valuation of property on remand. 503(h).
36. Court-ordered sale of marital property. 503(i).

(1) **Marital property presumption. 503(a), 503(b).** The statutory presumption under IMDMA §§ 503(a) and 503(b) is that all property acquired during the marriage is marital property [see, e.g., In re Marriage of Davis, 215 Ill.App.3d 763, 768, 159 Ill.Dec. 375, 379, 576 N.E.2d 44, 48 (1st Dist.), *appeal denied*, 141 Ill.2d 538, 580 N.E.2d 110, 162 Ill.Dec. 484 (1991); In re Marriage of Eddy, 210 Ill.App.3d 450, 155 Ill.Dec. 174, 569 N.E.2d 174 (1st Dist.1991)], and therefore subject to equitable allocation by the court. See IMDMA § 503(d) and Author's Notes (20) et seq. below concerning property distribution.

750 ILCS 5/503 FAMILIES

The burden of producing evidence to show that property was acquired under an IMDMA § 503(a) non-marital exception is on the party seeking to rebut the marital property presumption. In re Marriage of Walker, 203 Ill.App.3d 632, 634, 149 Ill.Dec. 112, 113, 561 N.E.2d 390, 391 (4th Dist.1990); In re Marriage of Cook, 117 Ill.App.3d 844, 849, 73 Ill.Dec. 222, 226, 453 N.E.2d 1357, 1361 (1st Dist.1983). The presumption that property acquired during the parties' marriage is marital property may only be rebutted by clear and convincing evidence. In re Marriage of Cecil, 202 Ill.App.3d 783, 787, 148 Ill.Dec. 72, 74, 560 N.E.2d 374, 376 (3d Dist.1990).

(2) **Non-marital property: Common examples. 503(a)(1), 503(a)(6).** The most common and easily identifiable non-marital property is property acquired by a spouse by gift [see, e.g., In re Marriage of Schmidt, 242 Ill.App.3d 961, 182 Ill.Dec. 804, 610 N.E.2d 673 (4th Dist.1993)], inheritance [see, e.g., In re Marriage of Davis, 215 Ill.App.3d 763, 159 Ill.Dec. 375, 576 N.E.2d 44 (1st Dist.), *appeal denied*, 141 Ill.2d 538, 162 Ill.Dec. 484, 580 N.E.2d 110 (1991)], or prior to the marriage of the parties [In re Marriage of Werries, 247 Ill.App.3d 639, 616 N.E.2d 1379, 186 Ill.Dec. 747 (4th Dist.1993)], and kept in the owner's sole name. IMDMA §§ 503(a)(1), 503(a)(6). A gift from one spouse to the other can create non-marital property in the recipient spouse. See, e.g., In re Marriage of Weiler, 258 Ill.App.3d 454, 196 Ill.Dec. 372, 629 N.E.2d 1216 (5th Dist.1994) (wife established by clear, convincing, and unmistakable evidence that husband intended contribution to wife's IRA account to be a gift).

(3) **Cancelling presumptions: Property received from a parent during the marriage. 503(a), 503(b).** A transfer of property from parent to child is presumed to be intended as a gift. In re Marriage of Simmons, 221 Ill.App.3d 89, 91, 163 Ill.Dec. 562, 565, 581 N.E.2d 716, 719 (5th Dist.1991). When such a transfer occurs during a marriage, the presumption that the property is marital property and the conflicting presumption that it is a [non-marital] gift cancel each other out, and the trial court is "free to resolve the issue of whether the property acquired by the transaction was non-marital or marital on the facts." In re Marriage of Agazim, 147 Ill.App.3d 646, 648, 101 Ill.Dec. 418, 420, 498 N.E.2d 742, 744 (2d Dist.1986), *appeal denied*, 113 Ill.2d 574, 106 Ill.Dec. 44, 505 N.E.2d 350, (1987). See also In re Marriage of Walker, 203 Ill.App.3d 632, 634, 149 Ill.Dec. 112, 113, 561 N.E.2d 390, 391 (4th Dist.1990); In re Marriage of Rosen, 126 Ill.App. 3d 766, 772, 81 Ill.Dec. 840, 844, 467 N.E.2d 962, 966 (1st Dist.1984).

(4) **Title. 503(b).** Under the previous law, assets were in most instances distributed according to title. This often proved inequitable, especially in traditional marriages with one wage earner, who placed all the assets in his sole name. Initial modifications of the common law still required that property would pass to the title holder, unless a party alleged and established special circumstances showing that the other party had equitable ownership. Cross v. Cross, 5 Ill.2d 456, 465, 125 N.E.2d 488, 492 (1955); citing Illinois Revised Statute chapter 40, paragraph 18 (1953).

Under the IMDMA, title to the property is not determinative of whether property is marital or non-marital. Rather, the method by which the property was acquired determines its classification. All property acquired during the marriage is marital property, unless it was acquired by a method set forth in IMDMA § 503(a). Title is not critical, but the source of the property is. For example, property acquired by gift or inheritance during the marriage is non-marital property, but property accumulated from earnings during the marriage is marital property.

(5) **Co-ownership. 503(b).** IMDMA § 503(b) provides that placing non-marital property into a form of co-ownership between the spouses raises a presumption that a

gift of the non-marital property has been made to the marital estate. In re Marriage of McCoy, 225 Ill.App.3d 966, 168 Ill.Dec. 27, 589 N.E.2d 141 (3d Dist.1992). For example, when a non-marital house is conveyed into joint tenancy, there is a presumption that the house was a gift to the marital estate. In re Marriage of Cecil, 202 Ill.App.3d 783, 787, 148 Ill.Dec. 72, 74, 560 N.E.2d 374, 377 (3d Dist.1990); Atkinson v. Atkinson, 87 Ill.2d 174, 179, 57 Ill.Dec. 567, 569, 429 N.E.2d 465, 467 (1981), *cert. denied*, 456 U.S. 905, 102 S.Ct. 1751, 72 L.Ed.2d 162 (1982). This presumption of a gift to the marital estate can be rebutted by showing that no gift was intended. Factors in determining whether donative intent existed can include "the making of improvements, the payment of taxes and mortgages, the occupancy of the premises as a home or business, and the extent of control and management of the property." In re Marriage of Hunter, 223 Ill.App.3d 947, 952, 166 Ill.Dec. 242, 246, 585 N.E.2d 1264, 1268 (2d Dist.), *appeal denied*, 145 Ill.2d 634, 173 Ill.Dec. 4, 596 N.E.2d 628 (1992). A common argument against donative intent is that the conveyance was made solely for estate planning purposes. Published case law suggests that parties making this argument have not been very successful. *Cf.* In re Marriage of Davis, 215 Ill.App.3d 763, 159 Ill.Dec. 375, 576 N.E.2d 44 (1st Dist.), *appeal denied*, 141 Ill.2d 538, 162 Ill.Dec. 484, 580 N.E.2d 110 (1991); In re Marriage of Wittenauer, 103 Ill.App.3d 53, 58 Ill.Dec. 593, 430 N.E.2d 625 (5th Dist.1981). The burden of rebutting the evidentiary presumption after a conveyance into co-ownership is usually a difficult one. The "donor" spouse may rebut the presumption of a gift only by clear, convincing and unmistakable evidence. In re Marriage of McCoy, 225 Ill.App.3d 966, 969, 168 Ill.Dec. 27, 29, 589 N.E.2d 141, 143 (3d Dist.1992). See, e.g., In re Marriage of Siddens, 225 Ill.App.3d 496, 167 Ill.Dec. 680, 588 N.E.2d 321 (5th Dist.) *appeal denied*, 145 Ill.2d 644, 173 Ill.Dec. 13, 596 N.E.2d 637 (1992); In re Marriage of Orlando, 218 Ill.App.3d 312, 160 Ill.Dec. 763, 577 N.E.2d 1334 (1st Dist.1991); In re Marriage of Nicks, 177 Ill.App.3d 76, 126 Ill.Dec. 442, 531 N.E.2d 1069 (4th Dist.1988).

Conversely, if the husband, for example, placed title to the marital property home in the sole name of the wife, his conveyance would not necessarily constitute a gift from the husband to the wife that would take the home out of the marital estate and make the home the wife's non-marital property. "Mere proof that title to a tract was placed in one party's name does not rebut the presumption created by section 503 . . . (citations omitted); there must be a donative intent to pass title and relinquish all present and future dominion over the property." In re Marriage of Davis, 215 Ill.App.3d 763, 771, 159 Ill.Dec. 375, 381, 576 N.E.2d 44, 50 (1st Dist.), *appeal denied*, 141 Ill.2d 538, 162 Ill.Dec. 484, 580 N.E.2d 110 (1991) (holding that the presumption of marital property was not rebutted; conveyance of the husband's interest in the marital home to the wife was part of an estate tax scheme and without donative intent, and the house remained marital property). See also In re Marriage of Weiler, 258 Ill.App.3d 454, 196 Ill.Dec. 372, 629 N.E.2d 1216 (5th Dist.1994) (wife established by clear, convincing, and unmistakable evidence that husband intended contribution to wife's IRA account to be a gift); In re Marriage of Wittenauer, 103 Ill.App.3d 53, 58 Ill.Dec. 593, 430 N.E.2d 625 (5th Dist.1981) (mere proof that title to property was placed in wife's name as an estate planning device did not establish the requisite donative intent to remove the property from the marital estate).

There is no reimbursement when there is a gift of non-marital property to the marital estate by placing the non-marital property into co-ownership. In re Marriage of Durante, 201 Ill.App.3d 376, 382, 147 Ill.Dec. 56, 61, 559 N.E.2d 56, 61 (1st Dist.1990). See Subsection 503(c)(2) and Author's Notes (15) et seq. below. Of course, the contribution factors of IMDMA § 503(d)(1) can be considered in the distribution of the marital property. See, e.g., In re Marriage of Olson, 223 Ill.App.3d 636, 166 Ill.Dec. 60, 585 N.E.2d 1082 (2d Dist.), *appeal denied*, 145 Ill.2d 636, 173 Ill.Dec. 6, 596 N.E.2d 630 (1992).

(6) **Homes purchased in contemplation of marriage. 503(a), 503(b).** Homes acquired *before* the marriage in the sole name of the purchaser-to-be-spouse may be classified as marital property if they were bought in contemplation of the marriage. The classification of a home purchased in contemplation of marriage as marital or non-marital

> is necessarily founded upon the intention of the parties at the time the property is purchased.... The totality of the circumstances should be examined to discover the parties' intent ... [including an analysis of the] source of funds to acquire the property, who signed the offer sheet, how long prior to marriage was the property purchased and how title was held....

In re Marriage of Jacks, 200 Ill.App.3d 112, 118, 146 Ill.Dec. 143, 147, 558 N.E.2d 106, 110 (2d Dist.), *appeal denied*, 133 Ill.2d 558, 149 Ill.Dec. 322, 561 N.E.2d 692 (1990) (finding property purchased by husband one hour prior to the wedding to be marital property, where both husband and wife accompanied realtor to see the home, both names appeared on the offer sheet, all payments were made with marital funds). See, also, In re Marriage of Ohrt, 154 Ill.App.3d 738, 107 Ill.Dec. 496, 507 N.E.2d 160 (3d Dist.1987) (classifying home purchased with a loan repaid with marital funds, and with mortgage payments paid with marital funds, as marital property, although husband purchased the home two months prior to the wedding and held title solely in his name); In re Marriage of Malters, 133 Ill.App.3d 168, 88 Ill.Dec. 460, 478 N.E.2d 1068 (1st Dist.1985) (holding home to be marital property when both parties accompanied the realtor to see the property for the first time, both signed the offer to purchase the property, wife's parents provided a loan towards the down payment, and joint funds were used both towards the down payment and the mortgage); Stallings v. Stallings, 75 Ill.App.3d 96, 30 Ill.Dec. 718, 393 N.E.2d 1065 (5th Dist.1979) (finding property purchased by husband two months prior to the wedding, in contemplation of marriage, to be marital when down payment came from wife's non-marital funds, parties took title as tenants in common, and mortgage payments were made with marital funds).

Other courts, however, have declined to classify a home purchased prior to marriage as marital property. While no court has explicitly rejected the exception carved out for homes purchased in contemplation of marriage, courts have held that under an examination of the above factors, the case at bar did not qualify for the exception. In In re Marriage of Leisner, 219 Ill.App.3d 752, 162 Ill.Dec. 277, 579 N.E.2d 1091 (1st Dist.1991), the court found that the exception did not apply to the property at issue, which had been purchased 15 months prior to the parties' engagement, too long to be considered in contemplation of marriage. The court in In re Marriage of Philips, 200 Ill.App.3d 395, 146 Ill.Dec. 191, 558 N.E.2d 154 (1st Dist. 1990), declined to classify a residence purchased by the husband prior to the marriage as marital property because the property was purchased exclusively with the husband's non-marital funds.

(7) **Property acquired in exchange for non-marital property. 503(a)(2).** Property acquired in exchange for non-marital property is addressed in IMDMA

§ 503(a)(2). A common example is when non-marital investments are inherited by a spouse, sold, and the proceeds are reinvested in other investments. The new investments remain non-marital, provided the investments and proceeds are kept segregated in the inheriting spouse's name. See In re Marriage of Siddens, 225 Ill.App.3d 496, 167 Ill.Dec. 680, 588 N.E.2d 321 (5th Dist.), *appeal denied*, 145 Ill.2d 644, 173 Ill.Dec. 13, 596 N.E.2d 637 (1992) (acquisitions obtained in exchange for non-marital property kept separately maintained and titled remain non-marital, as there was no evidence of intent to transmute the property into marital property). See also In re Marriage of Jelinek, 244 Ill.App.3d 496, 506, 184 Ill.Dec. 692, 701, 613 N.E.2d 1284, 1293 (1st. Dist.), *appeal denied*, 152 Ill.2d 560, 190 Ill.Dec. 890, 622 N.E.2d 1207 (1993) (stock received in exchange for premarital equity in corporation was also non-marital); Stacke v. Bates, 200 Ill.App.3d 85, 146 Ill.Dec. 118, 557 N.E.2d 1305 (2d Dist.) *appeal denied*, 135 Ill.2d 567, 151 Ill.Dec. 393, 564 N.E.2d 848 (1990) (home purchased from proceeds of sale of non-marital asset was non-marital property); In re Marriage of Cecil, 202 Ill.App.3d 783, 148 Ill.Dec. 72, 560 N.E.2d 374 (3d Dist.1990) (without an intervening affirmative act to transmute the property into marital property, property acquired in exchange for non-marital property remains non-marital).

Inadequate segregation may compromise the non-marital character of the assets. See IMDMA § 503(c)(1) and Author's Notes (12) et seq. below.

(8) **Property acquired after physical separation. 503(a)(3).** Because the presumption of marital property in 503(b) extends until there is a judgment of dissolution or invalidity, property acquired after a physical separation of the spouses but before a judgment of dissolution is presumed to be marital. In re Marriage of Steele, 212 Ill.App.3d 425, 156 Ill.Dec. 649, 571 N.E.2d 236 (5th Dist.1991); In re Marriage of Brooks, 138 Ill.App.3d 252, 93 Ill.Dec. 166, 486 N.E.2d 267 (1st Dist.1985). The *Brooks* court argues that allowing marital property rights to be extinguished on the *de facto* termination of the spouses' relationship (as opposed to the legal status of legal separation or dissolution) would create a "common-law divorce." *Id.* at 259. See also Author's Note (28) below for an increase in value of property after separation but before divorce.

A party can stop the accrual of marital property after a physical separation pursuant to IMDMA § 503(a)(3) by obtaining a judgment of legal separation. IMDMA § 503(a)(3) provides that property acquired after a judgment of legal separation is non-marital property. In a protracted case it may be valuable to stop the accrual of marital property with a judgment of legal separation pending dissolution. See, e.g., In re Marriage of Talty, 252 Ill.App.3d 80, 191 Ill.Dec. 451, 623 N.E.2d 1041 (3d Dist.1993); *appeal allowed*, 155 Ill.2d 577, 198 Ill.Dec. 553, 633 N.E.2d 15 (1994) (substantial increase in value of marital business during the parties' nine-year separation subject to equitable distribution). See IMDMA § 402 and accompanying Author's Notes for legal separation. The reason why this practice is not widespread is that it is usually as time consuming to obtain a legal separation as it is to obtain a dissolution.

A more practical approach is to argue pursuant to IMDMA § 503(d)(1) that the non-earning spouse has not made a contribution to property acquired after a physical separation and the non-earning spouse is therefore entitled to a lesser percentage of property acquired after separation. Conversely, the non-earning spouse would argue that property acquired after separation was a result of contributions made during the time the parties lived together, or that child care, even after separation, allows the earning spouse to acquire property. Unfortunately there is little or no case authority on either side.

(9) Property subject to agreements and judgments between the parties. 503(a)(4), 503(a)(5). The parties may agree to classify property that would fall under the definition of marital property as non-marital, or vice versa. IMDMA § 503(a)(4). One example of property excluded from marital property by a valid agreement of the parties is property deemed non-marital in a prenuptial agreement between the parties. See In re Marriage of Burgess, 123 Ill.App.3d 487, 78 Ill.Dec. 345, 462 N.E.2d 203 (3d Dist.1984). Property rights can also be determined by post-nuptial agreements pursuant to IMDMA § 503(a)(4). In In re Marriage of Vella, 237 Ill.App.3d 194, 177 Ill.Dec. 328, 603 N.E.2d 109 (2d Dist.1992), the court held that the parties could determine their property rights pursuant to IMDMA § 503(a)(4), and, because the agreement was not subject to IMDMA § 502(b), the court was bound by the parties' allocation of marital and non-marital property rights, regardless of whether the provisions were conscionable.

The non-marital exception concerning property that is the subject of judgments between the spouses, under IMDMA § 503(a)(5), is self-explanatory, and rare.

(10) **Appreciation of non-marital property. 503(a)(7).** Pursuant to IMDMA § 503(a)(7), the increase in value of non-marital property, regardless of how it occurs, remains non-marital property; subject, however, to reimbursement from the non-marital to the marital estate as provided in IMDMA § 503(c). See IMDMA § 503(c) and Author's Notes (15) et seq. below. For example, the increase in value of non-marital real estate due to economic factors remains non-marital, with no reimbursement to the marital estate. In re Marriage of Eddy, 210 Ill.App.3d 450, 155 Ill.Dec. 174, 569 N.E.2d 174 (1st Dist.1991). See also In re Marriage of Leisner, 219 Ill.App.3d 752, 162 Ill.Dec. 277, 579 N.E.2d 1091 (1st Dist.1991) (holding that the trial court properly reimbursed marital estate for marital contributions made to husband's profit-sharing plan and the appreciation of those contributions; but reversing trial court's distribution to the marital estate of appreciation from contributions made to the plan prior to marriage); In re Marriage of Landfield, 209 Ill.App.3d 678, 695, 153 Ill.Dec. 834, 843, 567 N.E.2d 1061, 1070 (1st Dist.), *appeal denied*, 139 Ill.2d 597, 159 Ill.Dec. 109, 575 N.E.2d 916 (1991) (income from partnership owned by husband prior to the marriage remains non-marital). In contrast, the increase in the equity value of a non-marital house resulting from the use of marital income to pay down the mortgage debt, while non-marital, would call for a reimbursement to the marital estate. In re Marriage of Leisner, 219 Ill.App.3d 752, 763, 162 Ill.Dec. 277, 284, 579 N.E.2d 1091, 1098 (1st Dist.1991) (remanding for determination of amount of reimbursement to marital estate for contributions to reduce mortgage and improve husband's non-marital home). *Cf.* In re Marriage of Perlmutter 225 Ill.App.3d 362, 373, 167 Ill.Dec. 340, 347, 587 N.E.2d 609, 616 (2d Dist.), *appeal denied*, 146 Ill.2d 650, 176 Ill.Dec. 820, 602 N.E.2d 474 (1992), *cert. denied*, ___ U.S. ___, 113 S.Ct. 1648, 123 L.Ed.2d 269 (1993) (remanding for determination of amount of reimbursement to the marital estate for repayment of non-marital note with marital funds).

Where a non-marital business ownership increases in value due to the personal effort of one of the spouses, the right to reimbursement depends upon the reasonableness of the spouse's compensation from the business. If the spouse received reasonable compensation, the marital estate has been compensated for the marital effort, and further reimbursement is not required. In re Marriage of Perlmutter, 225 Ill.App.3d 362, 167 Ill.Dec. 340, 587 N.E.2d 609 (2d Dist.), *appeal denied*, 146 Ill.2d 650, 176 Ill.Dec. 820, 602 N.E.2d 474 (1992), *cert. denied*, ___ U.S. ___, 113 S.Ct. 1648, 123 L.Ed.2d 269 (1993); In re Marriage of Thornton, 138 Ill.App.3d 906, 93 Ill.Dec. 453, 486 N.E.2d 1288 (1st Dist.1985). If the spouse was not reasonably paid, the non-marital business owes reimbursement to the marital estate. See, e.g., In re Marriage of Pittman, 212 Ill.App.3d 99, 155 Ill.Dec. 667, 569 N.E.2d 1278 (5th Dist.1991); In re Marriage of Kamp, 199 Ill.App.3d 1080, 146 Ill.Dec. 57, 557 N.E.2d 999 (3d Dist.1990); In re Marriage of Tatham, 173 Ill.App.3d 1072, 1085, 123 Ill.Dec. 576, 583, 527 N.E.2d 1351, 1358 (5th Dist.1988) (remanding to determine if salary was unreasonable and reimbursement was therefore warranted). See IMDMA § 503(c) and Author's Note (16)(d) below.

(11) **Income from non-marital property. 503(a)(8).** The income earned from non-marital property remains non-marital, unless the income is generated by the personal effort of the spouse. For example, the salary from a non-marital business to the employed spouse results from the spouse's personal effort, and it is therefore marital property. IMDMA § 503(a)(8); In re Marriage of Perlmutter, 225 Ill.App.3d 362, 167 Ill.Dec. 340, 587 N.E.2d 609 (2d Dist.), *appeal denied*, 146 Ill.2d 650, 176 Ill.Dec. 820, 602 N.E.2d 474 (1992), *cert. denied*, ___ U.S. ___, 113 S.Ct. 1648, 123 L.Ed.2d 269 (1993). But a savings account in the wife's sole name in which she deposits only profits [and not her salary] from her non-marital business would constitute non-marital property. In re Marriage of Cook, 117 Ill.App.3d 844, 73 Ill.Dec. 222, 453 N.E.2d 1357 (1st Dist.1983). Although non-marital income is not subject to property allocation, non-marital income is available for maintenance, IMDMA § 504(a)(1), and children's support, as one factor constituting net income under IMDMA § 505(a)(3).

(12) **Commingled non-marital property. 503(c).** Non-marital property that is not segregated in the owner's name is at risk of being transmuted into marital property, In re Marriage of Nicks, 177 Ill.App.3d 76, 79, 126 Ill.Dec. 442, 444, 531 N.E.2d 1069, 1071 (4th Dist.1988), although the parties can agree to the contrary. Unfortunately, the courts have been unable to clearly define the complex criteria for transmutation and reimbursement under IMDMA § 503(c). See following Author's Notes.

(13) **Commingled property: Loss of identity of the contribution. 503(c)(1).** When one estate contributes property to another estate, resulting in the loss of identity of the contributed property (but not in the loss of identity of the receiving estate), the contributed property is transmuted into the estate receiving the contribution, subject to the right of reimbursement. Personal effort by a spouse is considered a contribution by the marital estate. § 503(c)(2).

(14) **Loss of identity of both contributing estates. 503(c)(1).** When marital and non-marital property are commingled into newly acquired property, resulting in the loss of identity of both the contributing estates (as opposed to the loss of identity of just one of the estates and the maintenance of the identity of the other; see Author's Note (13) above), the newly acquired property is transmuted into marital property, subject to the rights of reimbursement.

(15) **Reimbursement. 503(c)(2).** Reimbursement is accorded in two circumstances. First, where the contribution is personal effort from the marital estate to the non-marital receiving estate, the non-marital estate reimburses the contributing marital estate if the personal effort is significant and results in substantial appreciation of the non-marital property, provided that the marital estate has not already been reimbursed by compensation. In re Marriage of Perlmutter, 225 Ill.App.3d 362, 371, 167 Ill.Dec. 340, 346, 587 N.E.2d 609, 615 (2d Dist.), *appeal denied*, 146 Ill.2d 650, 176 Ill.Dec. 820, 602 N.E.2d 474 (1992), *cert. denied*, ___ U.S. ___, 113 S.Ct. 1648, 123 L.Ed.2d 269 (1993). Appreciation of non-marital property resulting from factors

external to the marriage, such as inflation, does not entitle the marital estate to compensation. In re Marriage of Landfield, 209 Ill.App.3d 678, 695, 153 Ill.Dec. 834, 843, 567 N.E.2d 1061, 1070 (1st Dist.1991). See also In re Marriage of Eddy, 210 Ill.App.3d 450, 155 Ill.Dec. 174, 569 N.E.2d 174 (1st Dist.1991) (no clear and convincing evidence that appreciation of the husband's non-marital property resulted from his personal effort, therefore husband was not required to reimburse the marital estate).

Second, either estate is entitled to reimbursement for other contributions, such as a contribution of the property or income from one estate into another, when the contributions are traceable by clear and convincing evidence. See, e.g., In re Marriage of Phillips, 229 Ill.App.3d 809, 171 Ill.Dec. 501, 594 N.E.2d 353 (2d Dist.1992) (reimbursement allowed); In re Marriage of Guntren, 141 Ill.App.3d 1, 95 Ill.Dec. 392, 489 N.E.2d 1120 (4th Dist.1986) (husband was unable to present documentary or other evidence of contribution of non-marital funds or property to the marital estate; therefore was not entitled to reimbursement). Tracing requires that the source of funds be identified. In re Marriage of Davis, 215 Ill.App.3d 763, 159 Ill.Dec. 375, 380, 576 N.E.2d 44, 49 (1st Dist.), *appeal denied*, 141 Ill.2d 538, 580 N.E.2d 110, 162 Ill.Dec. 484 (1991) (reimbursement not allowed).

There is no reimbursement when the contribution is a gift from one estate to another. In re Marriage of Durante, 201 Ill.App.3d 376, 382, 147 Ill.Dec. 56, 61, 559 N.E.2d 56, 61 (1st Dist.1990) (investing non-marital property in marital home does not entitle the contributing estate to reimbursement upon dissolution).

(16) **Illustrations. 503(c)(1), 503(c)(2).** The convoluted provisions of IMDMA § 503(c) are more easily understood through the use of concrete examples:

(a) **Reduction of non-marital debt with marital funds.** Non-marital property is not transmuted into marital property merely as the result of using marital funds to reduce the indebtedness on the property. In re Marriage of Leisner, 219 Ill.App.3d 752, 763, 162 Ill.Dec. 277, 284, 579 N.E.2d 1091, 1098 (1st Dist.1991) (remanding for determination of amount of reimbursement). Therefore, clearly traceable mortgage principal payments from marital salary into a non-marital home become transmuted into non-marital property. These contributions, however, are reimbursed to the marital estate upon a divorce. The reimbursements are then available for allocation between the parties as part of the marital estate.

(b) **Retention of identity of contributing estates.** In In re Marriage of Guerra, 153 Ill.App.3d 550, 106 Ill.Dec. 201, 505 N.E.2d 748 (2d Dist.), *appeal denied*, 116 Ill.2d 554, 113 Ill.Dec. 298, 515 N.E.2d 107 (1987), the husband commingled the proceeds from the sale of a non-marital business with marital funds in a joint account. The trial court found that the assets purchased from the joint account were "tainted," and had been transmuted into marital property. The Appellate Court reversed, holding that on the facts, the property had not been transmuted. The parties' practice of using and controlling separate joint bank accounts showed that the husband did not intend to make a gift to the marital estate when he placed the non-marital funds into a joint account that only he used. The joint account was only for the convenience of the parties.

(c) **Loss of identity of contributing estates.** Conversely, in In re Marriage of Davis, 215 Ill.App.3d 763, 159 Ill.Dec. 375, 576 N.E.2d 44 (1st Dist.), *appeal denied*, 141 Ill.2d 538, 162 Ill.Dec. 484, 580 N.E.2d 110 (1991), the husband deposited both non-marital securities and cash, and a smaller amount of marital funds into his cash management account. The court held that the account would have remained non-marital property if the husband had deposited nothing but the inherited securities and cash into the account. However, since he also deposited marital securities and cash, the account became marital property. The court further held that the non-marital estate was not entitled to reimbursement, because the contribution from the non-marital estate could not be traced by clear and convincing evidence. The husband actively traded his cash management account, and all but two of the inherited securities (which remained non-marital) were sold, and others were purchased. It was impossible to trace from the existing securities back to the source of the funds (marital or non-marital) in the account that were used to purchase the new securities. Each estate lost its identity through the cash management fund's acquisition of new property during the marriage. Unable to trace the contribution, the non-marital estate was not entitled to reimbursement for the original non-marital funds.

(d) **Contributions of personal effort.** In In re Marriage of Perlmutter, 225 Ill.App.3d 362, 167 Ill.Dec. 340, 587 N.E.2d 609 (2d Dist.), *appeal denied*, 146 Ill.2d 650, 176 Ill.Dec. 820, 602 N.E.2d 474 (1992), *cert. denied*, ___ U.S. ___, 113 S.Ct. 1648, 123 L.Ed.2d 269 (1993), the court held that the husband's personal effort to a non-marital real estate partnership by the husband was significant and resulted in substantial appreciation to the firm. Personal effort, under IMDMA § 503(c)(2), is considered a contribution by the marital estate. The court denied reimbursement to the marital estate, however, because the husband received an annual salary of one million dollars, which was marital property. Therefore the marital estate had already received compensation for the husband's personal effort.

The court in In re Marriage of Pittman, 212 Ill.App.3d 99, 155 Ill.Dec. 667, 569 N.E.2d 1278 (5th Dist.1991), did order that the marital estate be reimbursed for personal effort to the non-marital estate. The wife was awarded $5,000 as reimbursement for her remodeling and decorating of the husband's non-marital home.

(17) **Allocation of reimbursement.** 503(c)(2). Although the opinion in *Pittman* above skipped this step, reimbursement is made to the contributing estate and not to the contributing spouse. § 503(c)(2); In re Marriage of McCoy, 225 Ill.App.3d 966, 168 Ill.Dec. 27, 589 N.E.2d 141 (3d Dist.1992). Reimbursement can be taken into account between the parties by an adjustment in the allocation of marital property, or by lien against non-marital property, which can be foreclosed if the allocation of the reimbursement is not paid. See, e.g., In re Marriage of Sokolowski, 232 Ill.App.3d 535, 173 Ill.Dec. 701, 597 N.E.2d 675 (1st Dist.1992) (trial court awarded marital home to husband subject to a lien in favor of wife; reversed on the facts for reconsideration of amount of wife's interest).

(18) **Appreciation on contribution.** 503(c)(2). Generally, the courts in Illinois have reimbursed a contributing estate for the amount of funds contributed to an asset belonging to the other estate, while allowing the estate to which the funds were contributed to retain the benefit of the accrued appreciation. See In re Marriage of Adams, 183 Ill.App.3d 296, 131 Ill.Dec. 730, 538 N.E.2d 1286 (4th Dist.1989) (wife was reimbursed for money expended to improve husband's non-marital residence); In re Marriage of Thacker, 185 Ill.App.3d 465, 133 Ill.Dec. 573, 541 N.E.2d 784 (5th Dist.1989) (husband reimbursed for amount of down payment on marital home contributed from his non-marital estate); In re Marriage of McCoy, 225 Ill.App.3d 966, 168 Ill.Dec. 27, 589 N.E.2d 141 (3d Dist.1992) (money from wife's non-marital funds used for improvements to marital home and to increase equity was reimbursed to wife's non-marital estate). However, the Second District has held that where distinguishable marital and non-marital funds are held in the same account, the appreciation in the account should be equitably apportioned between the two estates. In re

Marriage of Hagshenas, 234 Ill.App.3d 178, 175 Ill.Dec. 506, 600 N.E.2d 437 (2d Dist.1992); *appeal denied,* 148 Ill.2d 642, 183 Ill.Dec. 19, 610 N.E.2d 1263 (1993).

(19) **Award of non-marital property. 503(d).** The court identifies the non-marital estate of each party by considering the exceptions in IMDMA § 503(a) and the reimbursements to and from the non-marital estate pursuant to IMDMA § 503(c)(2), and the court then assigns each spouse's non-marital property to that spouse in accordance with the direction in IMDMA § 503(d). Non-marital property, although available for maintenance under IMDMA § 504(a) and children's support under IMDMA § 505(a)(5), is not subject to property claims by the non-owner spouse. IMDMA § 503(d); In re Marriage of Lees, 224 Ill.App.3d 691, 694, 167 Ill.Dec. 135, 139, 587 N.E.2d 17, 21 (3d Dist.1992).

(20) **Award of marital property: "Just proportions." 503(d).** After assigning the non-marital property to its owner, the court is directed by IMDMA § 503(d) to allocate the marital property in just proportions. "Just proportions" is not necessarily 50% to each spouse. In re Marriage of Marthens, 215 Ill.App.3d 590, 598, 159 Ill.Dec. 3, 8, 575 N.E.2d 3, 8 (3d Dist.1991). The division must be equitable, but not necessarily equal. Each case rests upon its own facts. In re Marriage of Orlando, 218 Ill.App.3d 312, 319, 160 Ill.Dec. 763, 769, 577 N.E.2d 1334, 1340 (1st Dist.1991). Therefore, under an analysis of the individual facts of a case, the percentage allocation of marital property to a spouse can range from 0 to 100%. See, e.g., In re Marriage of Stallings, 75 Ill.App.3d 96, 30 Ill.Dec. 718, 393 N.E.2d 1065 (5th Dist.1979) (upholding award of 100% of marital property to wife where there was evidence of dissipation of marital assets by the husband, and wife was primary financial supporter of family); In re Marriage of Orlando, 218 Ill.App.3d 312, 160 Ill.Dec. 763, 577 N.E.2d 1334 (1st Dist.1991) (awarding two thirds of marital property to wife, where marriage had lasted 42 years, and husband had a higher education and better income potential).

Often, courts attempt to make an equal division barring exceptional circumstances. See, e.g., In re Marriage of Marthens, 215 Ill.App.3d 590, 159 Ill.Dec. 3, 575 N.E.2d 3 (3d Dist.1991) (awarding 52% of marital property to the husband, 48% to the wife); In re Marriage of Brooks, 138 Ill.App.3d 252, 93 Ill.Dec. 166, 486 N.E.2d 267 (1st Dist.1985) (award of "slightly more than 50% of the marital estate" not an abuse of discretion). This is especially true after a marriage of a short duration in which both parties work. See IMDMA § 503(d)(4) and Author's Note (21) below.

An award dividing the property into equal halves will not be overturned on that basis alone. In re Marriage of Steele, 212 Ill.App.3d 425, 432, 156 Ill.Dec. 649, 654, 571 N.E.2d 236, 241 (5th Dist.1991).

(21) **Award of marital property: Factors considered. 503(d)(1)— 503(d)(12).** The court is directed to consider all relevant factors, including the twelve factors enumerated in the statute, in arriving at an equitable result. The court need not make specific findings with reference to each of the factors. In re Marriage of Guntren, 141 Ill.App.3d 1, 5, 95 Ill.Dec. 392, 395, 489 N.E.2d 1120, 1123 (4th Dist.1986). However, it is desirable that the court do so. In re Marriage of Schmidt, 242 Ill.App.3d 961, 966, 182 Ill.Dec. 804, 808, 610 N.E.2d 673, 677 (4th Dist.1993). The court is not to consider marital misconduct. See Szesny v. Szesny, 197 Ill.App.3d 966, 145 Ill.Dec. 452, 557 N.E.2d 222 (1st Dist.1990).

The factors governing maintenance and property have become similar. See IMDMA § 504 Author's Note (3).

The enumerated IMDMA § 503 factors (which often overlap) are:

(a) **Contribution: IMDMA § 503(d)(1).** Section 503(d)(1) attempts to redress the historic disregard for the contribution of a spouse not employed outside the home. See, e.g., Debrey v. Debrey, 132 Ill.App.2d 1072, 270 N.E.2d 43 (4th Dist.1971) (wife was not entitled to home held in title in husband's name, as "there [was] no evidence suggesting that the plaintiff made any contribution to the acquisition of or the improvement of the marital home *other than the services normally rendered by a wife*") (emphasis added). The section addresses both the traditionally male contributions to the marriage: the acquisition, or preservation of marital or non-marital property, and traditionally female contributions: care of the children and the home. This balanced consideration endeavors to compensate the many women who have little, if any, experience working outside the home. They would otherwise be left without property from the marriage, because no property was purchased with their funds, and would also be unprepared to become financially self-sufficient following a dissolution. See In re Marriage of Durante, 201 Ill.App.3d 376, 383, 147 Ill.Dec. 56, 61, 559 N.E.2d 56, 61 (1st Dist.1990) ("A larger property division, as opposed to maintenance, is the preferred method of reimbursing a spouse for such things as non-monetary contributions...."); In re Marriage of Davis, 215 Ill.App.3d 763, 159 Ill.Dec. 375, 576 N.E.2d 44 (1st Dist.), *appeal denied*, 141 Ill.2d 538, 580 N.E.2d 110, 162 Ill.Dec. 484 (1991) (considering that the wife had made substantial contributions as a homemaker in allocating marital property). But see In re Marriage of Tatham, 173 Ill.App.3d 1072, 1085, 123 Ill.Dec. 576, 583, 527 N.E.2d 1351, 1358 (5th Dist.1988) (reversing trial court which "arbitrarily ascribed a monetary value to petitioner's homemaker contribution," and requiring that when "both parties worked outside the home during the marriage and one wants additional credit for his or her contributions as a homemaker, that spouse must show that she made a greater contribution as a homemaker than did the other").

Since IMDMA § 503(d) directs that marital property be divided "without regard to marital misconduct," the relative "contribution" (economic and intangible, affirmative and negative) of each spouse to the property and the marriage have become significant factors in the allocation of marital property, especially when allocating property accrued during a long marriage. Several courts have discounted homemaking contributions when the marriage is of a short duration. In re Marriage of Siddens, 225 Ill.App.3d 496, 167 Ill.Dec. 680, 588 N.E.2d 321 (5th Dist.), *appeal denied*, 145 Ill.2d 644, 173 Ill.Dec. 13, 596 N.E.2d 637 (1992) ("in some instances the court may be justified in awarding one spouse a larger share of marital property based upon that spouse having made a greater contribution to the marital assets, especially when the marriage was of short duration"); In re Marriage of Zwart, 245 Ill.App.3d 567, 575, 185 Ill.Dec. 443, 448, 614 N.E.2d 884, 889 (2d Dist.1993) ("[I]t is when the marriage is long term that the source of the assets becomes less of a factor and the spouse's role as the homemaker becomes greater." The parties' 18–month marriage "was of such short duration that this factor has little, if any, weight."). See Duration: IMDMA § 503(d)(4) below.

Although the first paragraph of IMDMA § 503(d) instructs the court to disregard marital misconduct when distributing marital property, the first enumerated factor, "contribution," immediately reintroduces the potential for the court to consider marital misconduct or negative contribution. Some courts have seized the opportunity. For instance, the court in In re Marriage of Cecil, 202 Ill.App.3d 783, 791, 148 Ill.Dec. 72, 77, 560 N.E.2d 374, 379 (3d Dist.1990), discounted the wife's contribution to the marriage as a homemaker because "the marriage lasted three years, and [the wife] moved out of the home at least six times. Thus her contribution in this regard would seem appropriately devalued." See also In re Marriage of Rai, 189 Ill.App.3d 559, 136 Ill.Dec. 922, 545 N.E.2d 446 (1st Dist.1989) (husband's contribution as a homemaker was negated by failure to contribute financially to the marital estate and blatant dissipation of assets contributed by wife).

The concept of contribution has also been introduced as a factor for the consideration of maintenance. See IMDMA § 504(a)(10) and accompanying Author's Notes.

(b) **Dissipation: IMDMA § 503(d)(2).** The dissipation of the marital or non-marital property by each party was explicitly added to the statute in 1993, although it formerly existed in the case law under the factor of contribution. See In re Marriage of Rai, 189 Ill.App.3d 559, 136 Ill.Dec. 922, 545 N.E.2d 446 (1st Dist.1989); In re Marriage of Stallings, 75 Ill.App.3d 96, 30 Ill.Dec. 718, 393 N.E.2d 1065 (5th Dist. 1979). Dissipation was originally confined to marital property. "Generally, dissipation involves one spouse's use of *marital property* for a selfish purpose unrelated to the marriage at a time when the marriage is undergoing an irretrievable breakdown." In re Marriage of Landwehr, 225 Ill.App.3d 149, 167 Ill.Dec. 260, 587 N.E.2d 529 (1st Dist.1992) (emphasis added). Dissipation was extended by the 1993 statutory amendment to include non-marital property.

Dissipation arises when property is improperly used for the sole benefit of one spouse, for a purpose unrelated to the marriage, at a time when the marriage is undergoing an irreconcilable breakdown. In re Marriage of O'Neill, 138 Ill.2d 487, 496, 150 Ill.Dec. 607, 611, 563 N.E.2d 494, 498 (1990). The party charged with dissipation has the burden of proving by clear and convincing evidence that he or she did not dissipate the assets at issue. In re Marriage of Bush, 209 Ill.App.3d 671, 676, 153 Ill.Dec. 851, 855, 567 N.E.2d 1078, 1082 (1st Dist.1991).

What specific acts constitute dissipation depend on the facts of the case, and sometimes what court is considering the issue. Generally, expenditures held to constitute dissipation are extraordinary expenses that clearly do not further common marital interests. For example, gambling losses are patently dissipation. In re Marriage of Morrical, 216 Ill.App.3d 643, 159 Ill.Dec. 796, 576 N.E.2d 465 (3d Dist.1991); In re Marriage of Sobo, 205 Ill.App.3d 357, 150 Ill.Dec. 280, 562 N.E.2d 1083 (1st Dist.1990). The payment of legal fees from marital assets has been considered dissipation. Head v. Head, 168 Ill.App.3d 697, 523 N.E.2d 17, 119 Ill.Dec. 549 (1st Dist.1988). More prosaic expenditures, such as the bona fide investment of money which proves to be a loss are generally not classified as dissipation. See, e.g., In re Marriage of Drummond, 156 Ill.App.3d 672, 109 Ill.Dec. 46, 509 N.E.2d 707 (4th Dist.), *appeal denied*, 116 Ill.2d 556, 113 Ill.Dec. 296, 515 N.E.2d 105 (1987) (finding investments made without intent to willfully dissipate assets, and prior to the time the marriage began to break down, did not constitute dissipation).

However, less than extraordinary expenses have been found to constitute dissipation. For instance, living expenses of one party after the marriage's irreconcilable breakdown were held to constitute dissipation in the First District. In re Marriage of Partyka, 158 Ill.App.3d 545, 110 Ill.Dec. 499, 511 N.E.2d 676 (1st Dist.1987) (funds spent by husband, including those to rent and maintain the residence in which he lived after leaving the marital home, were not for marital purposes and therefore constituted dissipation). See also In re Marriage of Harding, 189 Ill.App.3d 663, 676, 136 Ill.Dec. 935, 943, 545 N.E.2d 459, 467 (1st Dist.1989) (while sanctioning funds spent on "legitimate family expenses, and necessary and appropriate purposes", found that a bare assertion that funds withdrawn from living trust account were used to pay for necessary expenses was insufficient to avoid a finding of dissipation). Living expenses were held not to constitute dissipation in the Second District. In re Marriage of Hagshenas, 234 Ill.App.3d 178, 197, 175 Ill.Dec. 506, 520, 600 N.E.2d 437, 451 (2d Dist.1992), *appeal denied*, 148 Ill.2d 642, 183 Ill.Dec. 19, 610 N.E.2d 1263 (1993) ("the expenditure of marital funds by one spouse for necessary, appropriate and legitimate living expenses at a time the marriage is undergoing an irreconcilable breakdown will not be considered to be dissipation").

The timing of the alleged dissipation is an important consideration. The Illinois Supreme Court ended the debate over whether dissipation could occur before the marriage began to collapse by holding in In re Marriage of O'Neill, 138 Ill.2d 487, 150 Ill.Dec. 607, 563 N.E.2d 494 (1990) that asset dissipation must have occurred at a time when the marriage had irrevocably broken down. Allowing a spouse to charge the other with dissipation throughout the duration of the marriage would entail an accounting of all financial transactions during the marriage. Such a review would overwhelm the courts. Determining the instant when the marriage becomes irrevocably broken down can be difficult. Irreconcilable breakdown may not be viewed "as a prolonged gradual process extending from the initial signs of trouble in a marriage until actual breakdown itself." In re Marriage of Hazel, 219 Ill.App.3d 920, 921–22, 162 Ill.Dec. 451, 452–453, 579 N.E.2d 1265, 1266–67 (5th Dist.1991) (holding that marriage was not undergoing an irreconcilable breakdown five months prior to the filing of the petition for dissolution, therefore no dissipation of assets could have occurred).

The court may charge a spouse who dissipated assets the amount dissipated against his or her share of marital property in order to compensate the other party, In re Marriage of Partyka, 158 Ill.App.3d 545, 110 Ill.Dec. 499, 511 N.E.2d 676 (1st Dist.1987), but an award of cash or property equal to half of the amount dissipated is not mandated. In re Marriage of Durante, 201 Ill.App.3d 376, 386, 147 Ill.Dec. 56, 63, 559 N.E.2d 56, 63 (1st Dist.1990).

Alleged dissipation must be pleaded, or the claim may be waived at trial. Zito v. Zito, 196 Ill.App.3d 1031, 143 Ill.Dec. 606, 554 N.E.2d 541 (1st Dist.1990).

(c) **Value of property assigned: IMDMA § 503(d)(3).** The court must consider the value of non-marital property assigned to each party. In re Marriage of Landfield, 209 Ill.App.3d 678, 689, 153 Ill.Dec. 834, 839, 567 N.E.2d 1061, 1066 (1st Dist.), *appeal denied*, 139 Ill.2d 597, 159 Ill.Dec. 109, 575 N.E.2d 916 (1991). The amount of non-marital property assigned to each spouse influences the allocation of the marital property. See, e.g., In re Marriage of Forbes, 251 Ill.App.3d 133, 190 Ill.Dec. 543, 621 N.E.2d 996 (4th Dist.1993) (remanding for greater award of marital assets, partially in light of wife's substantial non-marital assets); In re Marriage of Werries, 247 Ill.App.3d 639, 186 Ill.Dec. 747, 616 N.E.2d 1379 (4th Dist.1993) (husband's large non-marital estate justified a significantly larger assignment of the marital debt). In the absence of any non-marital property assigned to either spouse, an equitable allocation of marital property might be roughly 50% to each spouse. However, if one spouse had $5,000,000 worth of non-marital property, the other spouse had no non-marital property, and the marital estate consisted of a marital home worth $200,000, the court could equitably allocate 100% of the marital home to the spouse without other property. Note that one court has held that contingent non-marital assets may be considered in making property allocations. In re Marriage of Eddy, 210 Ill.App.3d 450, 460, 155 Ill.Dec. 174, 181, 569 N.E.2d 174, 181 (1st Dist.1991) ("Potential inheritances, just as expected degrees or licenses, are not property which can be valued and awarded to a spouse, although they can be a [sic] given some consideration in determining property distribution."). But see In re Marriage of Flemming, 143 Ill.App.3d 592, 598, 97 Ill.Dec. 859, 863, 493 N.E.2d 666, 670 (3d Dist.1986) (potential inheritance cannot be considered in distribution of property; "[n]o one is an heir of a living person").

(d) **Duration of marriage: IMDMA § 503(d)(4)**. Consideration of the duration of the marriage tends to have the greatest impact on the homemaker contribution factor of IMDMA § 503(d)(1). Homemaker contribution tends to count far less in short marriages. See Contribution: IMDMA § 503(d)(1) above. In a short marriage with equal financial contributions and a modest marital estate, the court might equitably divide the marital estate between the spouses on a 50/50 basis. In an equally short marriage in which one of the spouses contributed disproportionately to accumulating a marital estate, with no children and insubstantial homemaker contributions due to the brevity of the marriage, the court might equitably apportion a larger share of the marital estate to the spouse responsible for accumulating it. In re Marriage of Philips, 200 Ill.App.3d 395, 146 Ill.Dec. 191, 558 N.E.2d 154 (1st Dist. 1990); In re Marriage of Zwart, 245 Ill.App. 567, 185 Ill.Dec. 443, 614 N.E.2d 884 (2d Dist.1993); In re Marriage of Cecil, 202 Ill.App.3d 783, 148 Ill.Dec. 72, 560 N.E.2d 374 (3d Dist.1990). A court may also just rescind a brief marriage and allow each of the parties to take what they have and go their separate ways.

On the other hand, in a lengthy marriage, where one spouse was solely responsible for the accumulation of marital property, but the other spouse raised the parties' children and contributed to the marriage as a homemaker throughout the marriage, the court might apportion the marital property on a nearly equal basis. See, e.g., In re Marriage of Davis, 215 Ill.App.3d 763, 159 Ill.Dec. 375, 576 N.E.2d 44 (1st Dist.), *appeal denied*, 141 Ill.2d 538, 580 N.E.2d 110, 162 Ill.Dec. 484 (1991).

(e) **Relative economic circumstances of the parties: IMDMA § 503(d)(5)**. The relative economic circumstances of each spouse may be considered at the time of division. For example, one spouse may be experienced and established in a job, while the other spouse is unemployed and without property. The spouse without secure employment may be entitled to a larger portion of the marital property. See, e.g., In re Marriage of Zwart, 245 Ill.App.3d 567, 185 Ill.Dec. 443, 614 N.E.2d 884 (2d Dist.1993) (awarding a larger portion of the marital assets to the unemployed spouse after he depleted most of his liquid assets in purchasing and maintaining the marital home; the wife was employed full time and owned an unencumbered non-marital home). The consideration of relative economic circumstances of the parties is similar to the consideration of the relative ownership of non-marital property between the spouses as provided in IMDMA § 503(d)(3). While a party need not liquidate his or her non-marital assets or impair capital in order to support himself or herself, In re Marriage of Pearson, 236 Ill.App.3d 337, 350, 177 Ill.Dec. 650, 660, 603 N.E.2d 720, 730 (1st Dist.1992), the asset may provide income (such as interest, dividends, rent) that can be used for support.

A custodial parent may receive favorable consideration in the property allocation, both under the preference in IMDMA § 503(d)(5) that the custodial parent be awarded the marital residence (or at least be entitled to remain there for a reasonable period of time), and under a more general recognition of the circumstances of a custodial parent under IMDMA § 503(d)(9). See Custody: IMDMA § 503(d)(9) below for a more detailed explanation of the impact of custody on the allocation of marital property.

(f) **Obligations and rights from prior marriage: IMDMA § 503(d)(6).** Courts seldom emphasize a spouse's rights and obligations from a prior marriage when dividing marital property, and there is little interpreting published case law.

(g) **Antenuptial agreements: IMDMA § 503(d)(7).** Property rights of spouses to a marriage can be altered by the parties' antenuptial agreements. In re Marriage of Burgess, 123 Ill.App.3d 487, 78 Ill.Dec. 345, 462 N.E.2d 203 (3d Dist.1984). For example, property acquired by one of the spouses during the marriage, which would statutorily be marital property, can be designated in an antenuptial agreement as the non-marital property of the acquiring spouse. See IMDMA § 503(a)(4) Author's Note (9) above; In re Marriage of Byrne, 179 Ill.App.3d 944, 128 Ill.Dec. 800, 535 N.E.2d 14 (1st Dist.1989) (parties' valid antenuptial agreement excluded all property from the marital estate).

An antenuptial agreement can also provide what specific property, whether marital or non-marital, a spouse is to receive upon a dissolution of the marriage. Such an agreement may specify that a spouse receive a tangible asset, such as a home or business, or a set monetary amount, perhaps increasing with the length of the marriage. An example of a monetary division is an agreement providing that a spouse receive the sum of $250,000 if the parties divorce during the first five years of their marriage, $500,000 if the parties' marriage is dissolved during the second five years of their marriage, and, if the parties remain married for longer than ten years, the provisions of the antenuptial agreement no longer apply. See Illinois Uniform Premarital Agreement Act, 750 ILCS 10/1 et seq. and accompanying Author's Notes.

Although IMDMA § 503(d)(7) designates only antenuptial agreements, property rights are also obviously affected by post-nuptial agreements made pursuant to IMDMA § 502 and IMDMA § 503(a)(4).

(h) **Factors bearing on economic security: IMDMA § 503(d)(8).** Factor eight sets forth various criteria by which the economic security of a party can be judged. For example, an aged, unemployable spouse in ill health might receive a greater percentage of the marital property than would a younger employable spouse. See, e.g., In re Marriage of Swigers, 176 Ill.App.3d 795, 126 Ill.Dec. 231, 531 N.E.2d 858 (1st Dist.1988). Needs and station in life are also included among the criteria.

(i) **Custody: IMDMA § 503(d)(9).** The party given custody of the children of the marriage may be entitled to adjustments in either the amount or the character of his or her share of the marital property, or both. First, the custodial parent may receive a greater proportion of the property to meet his or her increased support obligations. See, e.g., In re Marriage of Forbes, 251 Ill.App.3d 133, 190 Ill.Dec. 543, 621 N.E.2d 996 (4th Dist.1993) (remanding for larger property award to custodial father). Second, the character of the allocated property may include possession of the family home, reflecting the desirability enunciated in IMDMA § 503(d)(5) of awarding the family home, or the right to live in the family home, to the spouse having custody of the children. "[W]here possible, children should be afforded continuity in their environment in order to reduce the emotional disruption caused by the separation of their parents. One of the ways this can be accomplished is by affording the children continued residence in the family home." In re Marriage of Brenner, 95 Ill.App.3d 100, 102, 50 Ill.Dec. 292, 294, 419 N.E.2d 400, 402 (1st Dist.1981). For example, a mother with custody may receive title to the marital home as part of her allocation of the marital property, rather than awarding her some other asset, or arbitrarily allocating all of the assets between the spouses on an overall percentage basis. See In re Marriage of Wiley, 199 Ill.App.3d 169, 145 Ill.Dec. 191, 556 N.E.2d 809 (4th Dist.1990).

Section 503(d)(5) also allows the custodial spouse to remain in the marital home for some specified period of time if an unconditional award is not appropriate under the circumstances. A typical contingent award would allow the custodial spouse to remain in the marital home until the youngest child reaches 18. Such an award is often combined with other contingencies, such as remarriage. After the contingency occurs, the marital home is sold, and the proceeds are divided on a percentage basis between the spouses.

(j) **Maintenance: IMDMA § 503(d)(10).** Courts strive to seek a "high degree of finality so that parties can plan their future with certainty and need not return repeatedly to the courts." In re Marriage of Durante, 201 Ill.App.3d 376, 383, 147 Ill.Dec. 56, 61, 559 N.E.2d 56, 61 (1st Dist.1990). Accordingly, a court may award a greater portion of property in lieu of maintenance than the court would award if the property was in addition to maintenance. See, e.g., In re Marriage of Durante, 201 Ill.App. 3d 376, 383, 147 Ill.Dec. 56, 61, 559 N.E.2d 56, 61 (1st Dist.1990) ("A larger property division, as opposed to maintenance, is the preferred method of reimbursing a spouse for such things as non-monetary contributions...."). The tendency to award property without maintenance, however, has decreased since the 1993 revision of the maintenance section. See IMDMA § 504 and accompanying Author's Notes.

(k) **Economic potential: IMDMA § 503(d)(11).** The opportunity of each spouse for future income and acquisition of capital assets is an important factor in many property distributions. The share of marital assets awarded to a spouse who earns no or only nominal income at the time of the dissolution of the marriage and has no means by which to accumulate property is often increased to redress the economic imbalance. This is particularly true where the other spouse has the capability to accumulate substantial assets in the future. In Atkinson v. Atkinson, 87 Ill.2d 174, 180, 429 N.E.2d 465, 468, 57 Ill.Dec. 567, 570 (1981), the Supreme Court of Illinois affirmed the trial court's decision to award most of the marital property to the wife, noting that "[the husband's] economic circumstances, including his opportunity to acquire assets and income, were superior." See also, In re Marriage of Landfield, 209 Ill.App.3d 678, 153 Ill.Dec. 834, 567 N.E.2d 1061 (1st Dist.1991) (court awarded wife majority of marital property); In re Marriage of Thornton, 89 Ill.App.3d 1078, 45 Ill.Dec. 612, 412 N.E.2d 1336 (1st Dist.1980) (the court should consider whether one spouse has greater income and greater opportunity to acquire future income); In re Marriage of Stephenson, 121 Ill.App.3d 698, 77 Ill.Dec. 142, 460 N.E.2d 1 (5th Dist.1983) (court awarded wife 75% of marital property); In re Marriage of Jacks, 200 Ill.App.3d 112, 118, 146 Ill.Dec. 143, 147, 558 N.E.2d 106, 110 (2d Dist.), *appeal denied*, 133 Ill.2d 558, 149 Ill.Dec. 322, 561 N.E.2d 692 (1990) (allowing disproportionate award of debt to husband with much greater future earning ability than wife). Often a monetarily successful spouse can accumulate back the assets that he transfers to a spouse without his ability in a short period of time, whereas the receiving spouse will not accumulate beyond what is allocated to her upon the dissolution of marriage.

(*l*) **Tax consequences: IMDMA § 503(d)(12).** The court is explicitly directed to consider the tax consequences to the parties of the property division. See In re Marriage of Malters, 133 Ill.App.3d 168, 88 Ill.Dec. 460, 478 N.E.2d 1068 (1st Dist.1985) (trial court's failure to consider tax consequences of transferring property from husband's pension funds constituted reversible error); In re Marriage of Davis, 215 Ill.App.3d 763, 775, 159 Ill.Dec. 375, 383, 576 N.E.2d 44, 52 (1st Dist.), *appeal* *denied*, 141 Ill.2d 538, 162 Ill.Dec. 484, 580 N.E.2d 110 (1991) ("The court may consider only those tax consequences that immediately and consequentially flow from the court's division."). The tax consequences that a court will consider are generally limited to those consequences arising from the court's judgment, e.g., the capital gains taxes resulting from a court order to sell appreciated property, rather than those tax consequences that may or may not occur subsequent to the judgment. The latter are considered speculative. See In re Marriage of Benkendorf, 252 Ill.App.3d 429, 191 Ill.Dec. 863, 624 N.E.2d 1241 (1st Dist.1993) ("We find it was improper for the trial court to consider speculative tax implications from a hypothetical sale of the marital home to reduce the valuation of the home"). Generally, but not always, properly handled transfers of property between the parties pursuant to a judgment of dissolution are not taxable transactions. Subsequent sales of the property to third parties, however, are subject to applicable capital gains taxes, and withdrawals from allocated retirement plans are subject to ordinary income tax.

For a detailed discussion of the tax consequences of property divisions, see Sections 1041, 1034, 121(a), 414(p), 408(d)(6), and 3405(c) of the Internal Revenue Code, and accompanying Author's Notes.

(22) **Vesting of marital property rights. 503(e).** Section 503(e) codifies the holding of Kujawinski v. Kujawinski, 71 Ill.2d 563, 17 Ill.Dec. 801, 376 N.E.2d 1382 (1978). The *Kujawinski* court held that marital property vested only at the commencement of dissolution proceedings, continued only during the pendency of the action, and did not restrict the transfer of property by the title holder during the marriage in the absence of an injunction.

(23) **Impact of valuations upon property allocation. 503(d).** The equity of § 503(d) allocations "in just proportions" often depends on the valuations placed on the property being divided. For example, consider a couple with a marital estate consisting of (1) a marital home, (2) publicly traded securities, (3) retirement plans, and (4) the major asset, a closely held business of substantial value. An award of 50% of the marital property may or may not be equitable, depending upon the integrity of the valuation of the assets in the marital estate. Because courts seldom award a percentage of an asset, such as a business, to each spouse, the closely held business will generally be allocated entirely to one spouse. The other spouse will receive other marital assets in order to offset his or her allocable share of the business. See, e.g., In re Marriage of Thomas, 239 Ill.App.3d 992, 996, 181 Ill.Dec. 512, 515, 608 N.E.2d 585, 588 (3d Dist.1993); In re Marriage of Sales, 106 Ill.App.3d 378, 381, 62 Ill.Dec. 441, 443, 436 N.E.2d 23, 25 (1st Dist.1982) ("[C]ourts should seek to minimize further business dealings between the parties. Division of small businesses or closely held corporations is particularly disadvantageous where it would require ongoing business association between the parties...."). The fairness of the percentage allocation therefore depends on the accuracy of the valuation of the closely held business and upon the valuations of the off-setting property.

The same is true for the marital home. When the home is not sold, it is commonly awarded to one of the spouses, with the other spouse being compensated in other assets.

(24) **Valuations of closely held businesses.** Valuations of closely held businesses are usually difficult. They invariably begin with Revenue Ruling 59–60, and the principles contained in Revenue Ruling 59–60 also have application to the valuation of other business entities. Revenue Ruling 59–60 follows.

REV. RUL. 59-60

In valuing the stock of closely held corporations, or the stock of corporations where market quotations are not available, all other available financial data, as well as all relevant factors affecting the fair market value must be considered for estate tax and gift tax purposes. No general formula may be given that is applicable to the many different valuation situations arising in the valuation of such stock. However, the general approach, methods, and factors which must be considered in valuing such securities are outlined.

Revenue Ruling 54-77, C.B. 1954-1, 187, superseded.

Sec. 1. Purpose.

The purpose of this Revenue Ruling is to outline and review in general the approach, methods and factors to be considered in valuing shares of the capital stock of closely held corporations for estate tax and gift tax purposes. The methods discussed herein will apply likewise to the valuation of corporate stocks on which market quotations are either unavailable or are of such scarcity that they do not reflect the fair market value.

Sec. 2. Background and Definitions.

.01 All valuations must be made in accordance with the applicable provisions of the Internal Revenue Code of 1954 and the Federal Estate Tax and Gift Tax Regulations. Sections 2031(a), 2032 and 2512(a) of the 1954 Code (sections 811 and 1005 of the 1939 Code) require that the property to be included in the gross estate, or made the subject of a gift, shall be taxed on the basis of the value of the property at the time of death of the decedent, the alternate date if so elected, or the date of gift.

.02 Section 20.2031-1(b) of the Estate Tax Regulations (Section 81.10 of the Estate Tax Regulations 105) and Section 25.2512-1 of the Gift Tax Regulations (Section 86.19 of Gift Tax Regulations 108) define fair market value, in effect, as the price at which the property would change hands between a willing buyer and a willing seller when the former is not under any compulsion to buy and the latter is not under any compulsion to sell, both parties having reasonable knowledge of relevant facts. Court decisions frequently state in addition that the hypothetical buyer and seller are assumed to be able, as well as willing, to trade and to be well-informed about the property and concerning the market for such property.

.03 Closely held corporations are those corporations the shares of which are owned by a relatively limited number of stockholders. Often the entire stock issue is held by one family. The result of this situation is that little, if any, trading in the shares takes place. There is, therefore, no established market for the stock and such sales as occur at irregular intervals seldom reflect all of the elements of a representative transaction as defined by the term "fair market value."

Sec. 3. Approach to Valuation.

.01 A determination of fair market value, being a question of fact, will depend upon the circumstances in each case. No formula can be devised that will be generally applicable to the multitude of different valuation issues arising in estate and gift tax cases. Often, an appraiser will find wide differences of opinion as to the fair market value of a particular stock. In resolving such differences, he should maintain a reasonable attitude in recognition of the fact that valuation is not an exact science. A sound valuation will be based upon all the relevant facts, but the elements of common sense, informed judgment and reasonableness must enter into the process of weighing those facts and determining their aggregate significance.

.02 The fair market value of specific shares of stock will vary as general economic conditions change from "normal" to "boom" or "depression," that is, according to the degree of optimism or pessimism with which the investing public regards the future at the required date of appraisal. Uncertainty as to the stability or continuity of the future income from a property decreases its value by increasing the risk of loss of earnings and value in the future. The value of shares of stock of a company with very uncertain future prospects is highly speculative. The appraiser must exercise his judgment as to the degree of risk attaching to the business of the corporation which issued the stock, but that judgment must be related to all of the other factors affecting value.

.03 Valuation of securities is, in essence, a prophecy as to the future and must be based on facts available at the required date of appraisal. As a generalization, the prices of stocks which are traded in volume in a free and active market by informed persons best reflect the consensus of the investing public as to what the future holds for the corporations and industries represented. When a stock is closely held, is traded infrequently, or is traded in an erratic market, some other measure of value must be used. In many instances, the next best measure may be found in the prices at which the stocks of companies engaged in the same or a similar line of business are selling in a free and open market.

Sec. 4. Factors to Consider.

.01 It is advisable to emphasize that in the valuation of the stock of closely held corporations or the stock of corporations where market quotations are either lacking or too scarce to be recognized, all available financial data, as well as all relevant factors affecting the fair market value, should be considered. The following factors, although not all-inclusive, are fundamental and require careful analysis in each case:

(a) The nature of the business and the history of the enterprise from its inception.

(b) The economic outlook in general and the condition and outlook of the specific industry in particular.

(c) The book value of the stock and the financial condition of the business.

(d) The earning capacity of the company.

(e) The dividend-paying capacity.

(f) Whether or not the enterprise has goodwill or other intangible value.

(g) Sales of the stock and the size of the block of stock to be valued.

(h) The market price of stocks of corporations engaged in the same or a similar line of business having their stocks actively traded in a free and open market, either on an exchange or over-the-counter.

.02 The following is a brief discussion of each of the foregoing factors:

(a) The history of a corporate enterprise will show its past stability or instability, its growth or lack of growth, the diversity or lack of diversity of its operations, and other facts needed to form an opinion of the degree of risk involved in the business. For an enterprise which changed its form of organization but carried on the same or closely similar operations of its predecessor, the history of the former enterprise should be considered. The detail to be considered should increase with approach to the required date of appraisal, since recent events are of greatest help in predicting the future; but a study of gross and net income, and of dividends covering a long prior period, is highly desirable. The history to be studied should include, but need not be limited to, the nature of the business, its products or services, its operating and investment assets, capital structure, plan facilities, sales records and management, all of which should be considered as of the date of the appraisal, with due regard for recent significant changes. Events of the past that are unlikely to recur in the future should be discounted, since value has a close relation to future expectancy.

(b) A sound appraisal of a closely held stock must consider current and prospective economic conditions as of the date of appraisal, both in the national economy and in the industry or industries with which the corporation is allied. It is important to know that the company is more or less successful than its competitors in the same industry, or that it is maintaining a stable position with respect to competitors. Equal or even greater significance may attach to the ability of the industry with which the company is allied to compete with other industries. Prospective competition which has not been a factor in prior years should be given careful attention. For example, high profits due to the novelty of its product and the lack of competition often lead to increasing competition. The public's appraisal of the future prospects of competitive industries or of competitors within an industry may be indicated by price trends in the markets for commodities and for securities. The loss of the manager of a so-called "one-man" business may have a depressing effect upon the value of the stock of such business, particularly if there is a lack of trained personnel capable of succeeding to the management of the enterprise. In valuing the stock of this type of business, therefore, the effect of the loss of the manager on the future expectancy of the business, and the absence of management-succession potentialities are pertinent factors to be taken into consideration. On the other hand, there may be factors which offset, in whole or in part, the loss of the manager's services. For instance, the nature of the business and of its assets may be such that they will not be impaired by the loss of the manager. Furthermore, the loss may be adequately covered by life insurance, or competent management might be employed on the basis of the consideration paid for the former manager's services. These, or other offsetting factors, if found to exist, should be carefully weighed against the loss of the manager's services in valuing the stock of the enterprise.

(c) Balance sheets should be obtained, preferably in the form of comparative annual statements for two or more years immediately preceding the date of appraisal, together with a balance sheet at the end of the month preceding that date, if corporate accounting will permit. Any balance sheet descriptions that are not self-explanatory, and balance sheet items comprehending diverse assets or liabilities, should be clarified in essential detail by supporting supplemental schedules. These statements usually will disclose to the appraiser (1) liquid position (ratio of current assets to current liabilities); (2) gross and net book value of principal classes of fixed assets; (3) working capital; (4) long-term indebtedness; (5) capital structure; and (6) net worth. Consideration also should be given to any assets not essential to the operation of the business, such as investments in securities, real estate, etc. In general, such nonoperating asset will command a lower rate of return than do the operating assets, although in exceptional cases the reverse may be true. In computing the book value per share of stock, assets of the investment type should be revalued on the basis of their market price and the book value adjusted accordingly. Comparison of the company's balance sheets over several years may reveal, among other facts, such developments as the acquisition of additional production facilities or subsidiary companies, improvement in financial position, and details as to recapitalizations and other changes in the capital structure of the corporation. If the corporation has more than one class of stock outstanding, the charter or certificate of incorporation should be examined to ascertain the explicit rights and privileges of the various stock issues including: (1) voting powers, (2) preference as to dividends, and (3) preference as to assets in the event of liquidation.

(d) Detailed profit and loss statements should be obtained and considered for a representative period immediately prior to the required date of appraisal, preferably five or more years. Such statements should show (1) gross income by principal items; (2) principal deductions from gross income including major prior items of operating expenses, interest and other expense on each item of long-term debt, depreciation and depletion if such deductions are made, officers' salaries, in total if they appear to be reasonable or in detail if they seem to be excessive, contributions (whether or not deductible for tax purposes) that the nature of its business and its community position require the corporation to make, and taxes by principal items, including income and excess profits taxes; (3) net income available for dividends; (4) rates and amounts of dividends paid on each class of stocks; (5) remaining amount carried to surplus; and (6) adjustments to, and reconciliation with, surplus as stated on the balance sheet. With profit and loss statements of this character available, the appraiser should be able to separate recurrent from nonrecurrent items of income and expense, to distinguish between operating income and investment income, and to ascertain whether or not any line of business in which the company is engaged is operated consistently at a loss and might be abandoned with benefit to the company. The percentage of earnings retained for business expansion should be noted when dividend-paying capacity is considered. Potential future income is a major factor in many valuations of closely held stocks, and all information concerning past income which will be helpful predicting the future should be secured. Prior earnings records usually are the most reliable guide as to the future expectancy, but resort to arbitrary five-or-ten-year averages without regard to current trends or future prospects will not produce a realistic valuation. If, for instance, a record of progressively increasing or decreasing net income is found, then greater weight may be accorded the most recent years' profits in estimating earning power. It will be helpful, in judging risk and the extent to which a business is a marginal operator to consider deductions from income and net income in terms of percentage of sales. Major categories of cost and expense to be so analyzed include the consumption of raw materials and supplies in the case of manufacturers, processor and fabricators; the cost of purchased merchandise in the case of merchants; utility services; insurance; taxes; depletion or depreciation; and interest.

(e) Primary consideration should be given to the dividend-paying capacity of the company rather than to dividends actually paid in the past. Recognition must be given to the necessity of retaining a reasonable portion of profits in a company to meet competition. Dividend-paying capacity is a factor that must be considered in an appraisal, but dividends actually paid in the past may not have any relation to dividend-paying capacity. Specifically, the dividends paid by a closely held family company may be measured by the income needs of the stockholders or by their desire to avoid taxes on dividend receipts, instead of by the ability of the company to pay dividends. Where an actual or effective controlling interest in a corporation is to be valued, the dividend factor is not a material element, since the payment of such dividends is discretionary with the controlling stockholders. The individual or group in control can substitute salaries and bonuses for dividends, thus reducing net income and understating the dividend-paying capacity of the company. It follows, therefore, that dividends are less reliable criteria of fair market value than other applicable factors.

(f) In the final analysis, goodwill is based upon earning capacity. The presence of goodwill and its value, therefore, rests upon the excess of net earnings over and above a fair return on the net tangible assets. While the element of goodwill may be based primarily on earnings, such factors as the prestige and renown of the business, the ownership of a trade or brand name, and a record of successful operation over a prolonged period in a particular locality, also may furnish support for the inclusion of intangible value. In some instances it may not be possible to make a separate appraisal of the tangible and intangible assets of the business. The enterprise has a value as an entity. Whatever intangible value there is, which is supportable by the facts, may be measured by the amount by which the appraised value of the tangible assets exceeds the net book value of such assets.

(g) Sales of stock of a closely held corporation should be carefully investigated to determine whether they represent transactions at arm's length. Forced or distress sales do not ordinarily reflect fair market value nor do isolated sales in small amounts necessarily control as the measure of value. This is especially true in the valuation of a controlling interest in a corporation. Since, in the case of closely held stocks, no prevailing market prices are available, there is no basis for making an adjustment for blockage. It follows, therefore, that such stocks should be valued upon a consideration of all the evidence affecting the fair market value. The size of the block of stock itself is a relevant factor to be considered. Although it is true that a minority interest in an unlisted corporation's stock is more difficult to sell than a similar block of listed stock, it is equally true that control of a corporation, either actual or in effect, representing as it does an added element of value, may justify a higher value for a specific block of stock.

(h) Section 2031(b) of the Code states, in effect, that in valuing unlisted securities the value of stock or securities of corporations engaged in the same or a similar line of business which are listed on an exchange should be taken into consideration along with all other factors. An important consideration is that the corporations to be used for comparisons have capital stocks which are actively traded by the public. In accordance with Section 2031(b) of the Code, stocks listed on an exchange are to be considered first. However, if sufficient comparable companies whose stocks are listed on an exchange cannot be found, other comparable companies which have stocks actively traded in on the over-the-counter market also may be used. The essential factor is that whether the stocks are sold on an exchange or over-the-counter there is evidence of an active, free public market for the stock as of the valuation date. In selecting corporations for comparative purposes, care should be taken to use only comparable companies. Although the only restrictive requirement as to comparable corporations specified in the statute is that their lines of business be the same or similar, yet it is obvious that consideration must be given to other relevant factors in order that the most valid comparison possible will be obtained. For illustration, a corporation having one or more issues of preferred stock, bonds or debentures in addition to its common stock should not be considered to be directly comparable to one having only common stock outstanding. In like manner, a company with a declining business and decreasing markets is not comparable to one with a record of current progress and market expansion.

Sec. 5. Weight to Be Accorded Various Factors.

The valuation of closely held corporate stock entails the consideration of all relevant factors as stated in Section 4. Depending upon the circumstances in each case, certain factors may carry more weight than others because of the nature of the company's business. To illustrate:

(a) Earnings may be the most important criterion of value in some cases whereas asset value will receive primary consideration in others. In general, the appraiser will accord primary consideration to earnings when valuing stocks of companies which sell products or services to the public; conversely, in the investment or holding type of company, the appraiser may accord the greatest weight to the assets underlying the security to be valued.

(b) The value of the stock of a closely held investment or real estate holding company, whether or not family owned, is closely related to the value of the assets underlying the stock. For companies of this type the appraiser should determine the fair market values of the assets of the company. Operating expenses of such a company and the cost of liquidating it, if any, merit consideration when appraising the relative values of the stock and the underlying assets. The market values of the underlying assets give due weight to potential earnings and dividends of the particular items of property underlying the stock, capitalized at _____ deemed proper by the investing public at the date of appraisal. A current appraisal by the investing public should be superior to the retrospective opinion of an individual. For these reasons, adjusted net worth should be accorded greater weight in valuing the stock of a closely held investment or real estate holding company, whether or not family owned, than any of the other customary yardsticks of appraisal, such as earnings and dividend-paying capacity.

Sec. 6. Capitalization Rates.

In the application of certain fundamental valuation factors, such as earnings and dividends, it is necessary to capitalize the average or current results at some appropriate rate. A determination of the proper capitalization rate presents one of the most difficult problems in valuation. That there is no ready or simple solution will become apparent by a cursory check of the rates of return and dividend yields in terms of the selling prices of corporate shares listed on the major exchanges of the country. Wide variations will be found even for companies in the same industry. Moreover, the ratio will fluctuate from year to year depending upon economic conditions. Thus, no standard tables of capitalization rates applicable to closely held corporations can be formulated. Among the more important factors to be taken into consideration in deciding upon a capitalization rate in a particular case are: (1) the nature of the business; (2) the risk involved; and (3) the stability or irregularity of earnings.

Sec. 7. Average of Factors.

Because valuations cannot be made on the basis of a prescribed formula, there is no means whereby the various applicable factors in a particular case can be assigned mathematical weights in deriving the fair market value. For this reason, no useful purpose is served by taking an average of several factors (for example, book value, capitalized earnings and capitalized dividends) and basing the valuation on the result. Such a process excludes active consideration of other pertinent factors, and the end result cannot be supported by a realistic application of the significant facts in the case except by mere chance.

Sec. 8. Restrictive Agreements.

Frequently, in the valuation of closely held stock for estate and gift tax purposes, it will be found that the stock is subject to an agreement restricting its sale or transfer. Where shares of stock were acquired by a decedent subject to an option reserved by the issuing corporation to repurchase at a certain price, the option price is usually accepted as the fair market value for estate tax purposes. See Rev. Rul. 54–76, C.B. 1954–1, 194. However, in such a case the option price is not determinative of fair market value for gift tax purposes. Where the option, or buy and sell agreement, is the result of voluntary action by the stockholders and is binding during the life as well as the death of the stockholders, such agreement may or may not, depending upon the circumstances of each case, fix the value for estate tax purposes. However, such agreements is a factor to be considered, with other relevant factors, in determining fair market value. Where the stockholder is free to dispose of his shares during life and the option is to become effective only upon his death, the fair market value is not limited to the option price. It is always necessary to consider the relationship of the parties, the relative number of shares held by the decedent, and other material facts, to determine whether the agreement represents a bona fide business arrangement or is a device to pass the decedent's shares to the natural objects of his bounty for less than an adequate and full consideration in money or money's worth. In this connection see Rev. Rul. 157 C.B. 1953–2, 255, and Rev. Rul. 189, C.B. 1953–2, 294.

Sec. 9. Effect on Other Documents.

Revenue Ruling 54–77, C.B. 1954–1, 187, is hereby superseded.

(25) **Valuation of professional good will.** The Illinois Supreme Court held in In re Marriage of Zells, 143 Ill.2d 251, 157 Ill.Dec. 480, 572 N.E.2d 944 (1991), that professional good will is not an asset subject to equitable distribution. The court reasoned that it was not appropriate to consider good will as an asset in the valuation of the husband's law practice, because good will is responsible for the production of income. To count good will both as part of the value of an asset and in the determination of maintenance (as an indication of income potential) would be to double count.

This is a debatable proposition. An analogous situation occurs, for example, with the value of a publicly traded security. The value is influenced by the amount of dividend that the security pays, yet the dividend is legitimately counted both in value determination and in the determination of maintenance. The same is true for rental property. A fully rented building is more valuable than an empty one, and the rental proceeds are counted both in calculating value and in determining maintenance.

Nonetheless, one court has extended the *Zells* concept of impermissible double counting to the valuation of closely held corporations. Citing *Zells*, the court in In re Marriage of Brenner, 235 Ill.App.3d 840, 847, 176 Ill.Dec. 572, 577, 601 N.E.2d 1270, 1275 (1st Dist.1992), held that it was improper to count a closely held corporation's good will both as a corporate asset and as future income in calculating maintenance payments. However, the Third District disagreed with *Brenner*'s extension of *Zells* in In re Marriage of Talty, 252 Ill.App.3d 80, ___, 191 Ill.Dec. 451, 456, 623 N.E.2d 1041, 1046 (3d Dist.1993); *appeal allowed*, 155 Ill.2d 577, 198 Ill.Dec. 553, 633 N.E.2d 15 (1994), insisting that a distinction must be made between professional good will, which was in issue in *Zells*, and the good will of a business.

In a professional business situation, goodwill exists solely because professional people have skills that enable them to generate income. It is the skill, expertise and reputation of the individual that maintain the business, not the goods that they sell or the product name that may be printed on them. In a [business], the goodwill belongs to the business itself.... The concerns of duplicative valuation as addressed in *Zells* are unique to situations involving professional goodwill.

(26) **Valuation of assets without common market value.** Expert valuation of closely held businesses, professional corporations, art collections, and other assets, which either are not publicly traded or otherwise lack readily ascertainable values, is often critical in equitably distributing property and awarding appropriate maintenance. Professional valuation of stock in publicly held corporations may also be necessary. Securities may be subject to premiums when the stockholder owns large blocks of stock, or discounts reflecting restrictions or minority interests, and therefore require a valuation different from the market price.

(27) **Valuation by owner.** A party may testify as to the value of an asset of which he is the owner. Outside expert testimony is not required. In re Marriage of Vucic, 216 Ill.App.3d 692, 703, 159 Ill.Dec. 737, 744, 576 N.E.2d 406, 413 (2d Dist.1991). See also In re Marriage of Randall, 157 Ill.App.3d 892, 110 Ill.Dec. 122, 510 N.E.2d 1153 (1st Dist.1987) (wife's evaluation of her ceramics business was sufficient evidence to sustain court's valuation of the business).

In practice, parties frequently testify as to their opinion of the value of their homes. "[P]roperty ownership usually indicates knowledge of the original price paid, improvements made and the current state of the property such that the owner probably has a reasonably good idea of the property value. However, the rule is not absolute. A property owner may be shown to be incompetent to testify where it is affirmatively shown that special circumstances exist which indicate that he is unfamiliar with facts which give the property value." In re Marriage of Vucic, 216 Ill.App.3d 692, 703, 159 Ill.Dec. 737, 744, 576 N.E.2d 406, 413 (2d Dist.1991) (citations omitted). In more complex situations, it is better to call an expert to testify. Even in regard to homes, the testimony of an appraiser, or at least a realtor, is preferred evidence. See e.g., In re Marriage of Rosen, 126 Ill.App.3d 766, 81 Ill.Dec. 840, 467 N.E.2d 962 (1st Dist.1984).

(28) **Date of valuation of property. 503(f).** Subsection 503(f), effective January 1, 1993, codifies the prior case law holding that property should be valued as of the date of the entry of the judgment [see, e.g., In re Marriage of Brenner, 235 Ill.App.3d 840, 846, 176 Ill.Dec. 572, 576, 601 N.E.2d 1270, 1274 (1st Dist.1992)], with the pragmatic liberalization that the valuation should be "as of the date of trial or some other date as close to the date of trial as practicable." See, e.g., In re Marriage of Benkendorf, 252 Ill.App.3d 429, 191 Ill.Dec. 863, 624 N.E.2d 1241 (1st Dist.1993) (allowing valuation date on the last day of trial rather than the date of dissolution where property division was complex and evidence presented was lengthy).

There is frequently a disinclination on the part of the working spouse where there has been a substantial accretion to the value of the marital property after the separation of the parties to submit the increased value to the court for allocation. (The same is not true where there is a decrease in the value of the marital property after a separation.) The statute, however, is unequivocal that the valuation date shall be at or near the trial date. The answer therefore is to submit the value required by the statute, but to argue pursuant to IMDMA § 503(d)(1) that the non-working spouse did not contribute to the increase in the value of the marital property after the date of the separation of the parties, and therefore the non-working spouse is not entitled to share in the value added by the working spouse after the date of separation. Conversely, the non-working spouse would argue that the increase in value would not have occurred, but for her contributions during the time the parties lived together, continued child care, and the like. As is the situation for property acquired after physical separation but before judgment (see Author's Note (8) above), there appears to be no case authority on either side.

(29) **Retirement benefits: Types.** Retirement plans are frequently part of the divisible marital estate. There are two types of retirement plans: (1) defined benefit plans, when an employee is to receive a designated benefit after retirement; and (2) defined contribution plans, when the amount of the contribution is fixed, and the benefit to be received by the employee depends upon the value of the contributions at the time of distribution.

Retirement plans may be difficult to value. Defined benefit plans require actuarial calculations. Statements as to the current value of the assets in a spouse's account in a defined contribution plan can usually be obtained from the participant spouse or from the plan administrator.

(30) **Retirement benefits: Allocation.** Several different formulas have been developed to allocate the value of the plan between non-marital and marital property when the employed spouse accumulated retirement benefits both before and during the marriage. In In re Marriage of Davis, 215 Ill.App.3d 763, 773, 159 Ill.Dec. 375, 382, 576 N.E.2d 44, 51 (1st Dist.), *appeal denied*, 141 Ill.2d 538, 162 Ill.Dec. 484, 580 N.E.2d 110 (1991) (citations omitted), the court used the following formula to allocate a defined contribution plan that had been rolled over into an IRA between the marital and non-marital estates:

> Upon dissolution, the marital portion of such a pension or profit sharing interest, calculated by the ratio of years of accumulation during marriage to the total years of accumulation, should be divided between the spouses. An alternative method has been used in similar apportionment decisions concerning life insurance and equity in a home to determine the correct marital proportion: if the value of the pre-marital portion is known, the ratio of that figure to the value of the entire plan at the time of dissolution produces the correct marital portion.

The formulation in *Davis* may not adequately take into account variations in appreciation between the marital and non-marital portions; e.g., there may be greater appreciation in later years. Expert advice should therefore be sought for defined contribution and defined benefit plans where the reimbursement from one estate to the other is significant.

The marital property portion of a retirement plan can be distributed in several different ways. First, the most common method used to allocate qualified defined contribution plans is with a direct allocation between the parties with Qualified Domestic Relations Order (QDRO). The current value of the marital assets in the participant spouse's account is determined, and all or a portion of that value is transferred to the non-participant spouse or to her eligible retirement plan in a non-taxable transaction by means of a QDRO. See Internal Revenue Code § 414(p) Author's Note (6) for sample QDRO. The transfer can either be in kind or in cash, because the securities or other appreciated assets can be sold without incurring tax in a qualified plan, enabling the payment to be made in cash. QDROs for allocation of defined benefit plans can be complex and may require consultation with an expert.

A second alternative is the immediate offset approach. For defined benefit plans, a present value calculation is made of the future benefits to be received from the plan, and the participant spouse can then buy out his non-participant spouse's allocable share with other assets based upon the present value calculation. This approach is best used when there is sufficient actuarial evidence to determine the present value of the pension, when the employee spouse is close to retirement age, and when there is sufficient marital property to allow an offset. See In re Marriage of Wisniewski, 107 Ill.App.3d 711, 63 Ill.Dec. 378, 437 N.E.2d 1300 (4th Dist.1982). The immediate offset approach can also be used for one spouse to buy out the other's share in a defined contribution plan, which can usually be valued by obtaining a statement from the plan administrator of current value.

As a third means of allocation, in either defined benefit or defined contribution plans, the participant spouse can pay the non-participant spouse her allocable portion of retirement distributions when and if they are made. The court retains jurisdiction to enforce the decree. This latter method is particularly useful when there is doubt that the retirement program will ever be paid because of under-funding or other problems. See, e.g., Robinson v. Robinson, 146 Ill.App.3d 474, 100 Ill.Dec. 260, 497 N.E.2d 140 (3d Dist.1986).

Distributions from a retirement plan are ordinarily taxable to the participant spouse when the participant receives the distributions. If the participant spouse agrees to pay the non-participant spouse a portion of the retirement payments when he actually receives them, the participant spouse should usually make his payments to the non-participant spouse as maintenance. By doing so, the participant spouse will receive the tax alimony deduction for his payments, and the payments will constitute taxable income for the non-participant spouse. The tax is effectively shifted to the spouse who ultimately receives the retirement plan payments, without creating assignment of income problems.

In the case of Individual Retirement Accounts (IRAs), one spouse's IRA, or a portion thereof, can be transferred to the other spouse without incurring tax. See Internal Revenue Code § 408(d)(6) and accompanying Author's Notes.

(31) **Cross references.** See Sections 1041, 414(p), 408(d)(6), and 3405(c) of the Internal Revenue Code and accompanying Author's Notes for the tax ramifications of assignments of retirement plans. A sample QDRO is at IRC § 414(p) Author's Note (6). A sample settlement agreement paragraph for a QDRO is at IMDMA § 502 Author's Note (11) para. 6(*l*)(i), and a sample paragraph for an IRA transfer is at IMDMA § 502 Author's Note (11) para. 6(*l*)(ii).

(32) **Debts.** Debts must also be equitably allocated in distributing marital and non-marital property. In re Marriage of Lees, 224 Ill.App.3d 691, 693, 167 Ill.Dec. 135, 137, 587 N.E.2d 17, 19 (3d Dist.1992). Generally debts incurred to purchase property follow the property. See, e.g., In re Marriage of Guntren, 141 Ill.App.3d 1, 95 Ill.Dec. 392, 489 N.E.2d 1120 (4th Dist.1986) (ordering husband to repay debt incurred to purchase farm equipment awarded to wife was reversible error). The court has discretion to order the payment of credit card debts and the like after considering dissipation and the overall financial adjudication. In re Marriage of Moll, 232 Ill.App.3d 746, 174 Ill.Dec. 18, 597 N.E.2d 1230 (2d Dist.1992) ("the source of the marital debt, the party who signed for the debt, and the overall circumstances of the parties are appropriate considerations in apportioning debt"). See, e.g., Szesny v. Szesny, 197 Ill.App.3d 966, 145 Ill.Dec. 452, 557 N.E.2d 222 (1st Dist.1990) (upholding assignment of marital debt entirely to the husband; husband was solely responsible for credit card debts made without wife's knowledge or permission); In re Marriage of Werries, 247 Ill.App.3d 639, 186 Ill.Dec. 747, 616 N.E.2d 1379 (4th Dist.1993) (assignment of majority of marital debt to husband was proper; husband had greater ability to pay debt).

750 ILCS 5/503   FAMILIES

(33) **Support trusts. 503(g).** Subsection 503(g) provides for the creation of a support trust for children, but the clause "if necessary to protect ... the best interests of the children" has been interpreted restrictively. Special circumstances must be shown before a court is authorized to set aside a portion of the property for a children's support trust. For example, a trust may be appropriate when the father is unemployed, or incarcerated. In re Marriage of Vucic, 216 Ill.App.3d 692, 159 Ill.Dec. 737, 744, 576 N.E.2d 406 (2d Dist.1991) (remanding for finding of inability to pay, noting that evidence of father's incarceration for theft "may well support a finding that the establishment of a ... trust was reasonable because of [father's] present inability to pay"); In re Marriage of Steffen, 253 Ill.App.3d 966, 192 Ill.Dec. 709, 625 N.E.2d 864 (4th Dist.1993) (order to establish a support trust was proper after finding that husband could not or would not pay support); In re Marriage of Andrew, 258 Ill.App.3d 924, 194 Ill.Dec. 724, 628 N.E.2d 221 (1st Dist.1993) (creation of child support trust out of net proceeds of sale of marital home was proper; both wife's counsel and counsel for minor child requested trust and trust would promote best interest of minor child); In re Marriage of Hobson, 220 Ill.App.3d 1006, 163 Ill.Dec. 437, 581 N.E.2d 388 (4th Dist.1991) (child support fund was the only reasonably certain source of support).

(34) **Crimes by the parent against the child. 503(g).** Section 503(g) allows the court to consider a parent's crimes against his or her children in determining whether a children's support trust is appropriate. The court may consider convictions of aggravated battery, heinous battery, aggravated battery with a firearm, criminal sexual assault, aggravated criminal sexual assault, criminal sexual abuse and aggravated criminal sexual abuse.

(35) **Valuation of property on remand. 503(h).** Subsection 503(h) generally directs the trial court on remand not to consider any increase or decrease in the value of property occurring since the original trial. Unless otherwise specifically directed by a reviewing court, or upon good cause shown, on remand the trial court shall use only the valuation made at the original trial. The "upon good cause shown" exception was added as an amendment effective January 1, 1993.

(36) **Court-ordered sale of marital property. 503(i).** Subsection 503(i) authorizes the trial court to order the sale of marital property and allocate the proceeds. With the exception of marital homes, judge ordered sales are frequently threatened, but seldom actually ordered.

The court is empowered to order a partition sale of the marital home only if one of the parties has petitioned for partition. See IMDMA § 514 and accompanying Author's Notes. See also In re Marriage of Pieper, 79 Ill.App.3d 835, 838, 34 Ill.Dec. 877, 879, 398 N.E.2d 868, 870 (1st Dist.1979). However, this requirement may be interpreted loosely. For instance, the court in In re Marriage of Glessner, 119 Ill.App.3d 306, 312, 74 Ill.Dec. 809, 813, 456 N.E.2d 311, 315 (1st Dist.1983), upheld the trial court's order of a partition sale, holding that the wife's prayer "for use of the marital home and other equitable relief," and the husband's petition "for a division of marital property and other equitable relief" was sufficiently specific to constitute a prayer for sale.

750 ILCS 5/504

§ 504. Maintenance

(a) In a proceeding for dissolution of marriage or legal separation or declaration of invalidity of marriage, or a proceeding for maintenance following dissolution of the marriage by a court which lacked personal jurisdiction over the absent spouse, the court may grant a temporary or permanent maintenance award for either spouse in amounts and for periods of time as the court deems just, without regard to marital misconduct, in gross or for fixed or indefinite periods of time, and the maintenance may be paid from the income or property of the other spouse after consideration of all relevant factors, including:

(1) the income and property of each party, including marital property apportioned and non-marital property assigned to the party seeking maintenance;

(2) the needs of each party;

(3) the present and future earning capacity of each party;

(4) any impairment of the present and future earning capacity of the party seeking maintenance due to that party devoting time to domestic duties or having foregone or delayed education, training, employment, or career opportunities due to the marriage;

(5) the time necessary to enable the party seeking maintenance to acquire appropriate education, training, and employment, and whether that party is able to support himself or herself through appropriate employment or is the custodian of a child making it appropriate that the custodian not seek employment;

(6) the standard of living established during the marriage;

(7) the duration of the marriage;

(8) the age and the physical and emotional condition of both parties;

(9) the tax consequences of the property division upon the respective economic circumstances of the parties;

(10) contributions and services by the party seeking maintenance to the education, training, career or career potential, or license of the other spouse;

(11) any valid agreement of the parties; and

(12) any other factor that the court expressly finds to be just and equitable.

(c) The court may grant and enforce the payment of maintenance during the pendency of an appeal as the court shall deem reasonable and proper.

(d) No maintenance shall accrue during the period in which a party is imprisoned for failure to comply with the court's order for the payment of such maintenance.

(e) When maintenance is to be paid through the clerk of the court in a county of 1,000,000 inhabitants or less, the order shall direct the obligor to pay to the clerk, in addition to the maintenance payments, all fees imposed by the county board under paragraph (3) of subsection (u) of Section 27.1 of the Clerks of Courts Act. Unless paid in cash or pursuant to an order for withholding, the payment of the fee shall be by a separate instrument from the support payment and shall be made to the order of the Clerk.

Author's Notes

Analysis

1. Types of maintenance.
2. Change in legislative and judicial attitudes toward maintenance.
3. Considerations in determining maintenance.
4. Maintenance awarded irrespective of need.
5. Obligation for rehabilitation.
6. Cross references.
7. Funds for payment of maintenance.
8. Cross reference.
9. Payment of maintenance pending appeal.
10. Security for maintenance.
11. Cross reference—Forms.
12. Cross references.

(1) **Types of maintenance.** The terms in paragraph (a) of § 504 are imprecise because they overlap. "Temporary" maintenance (when not pursuant to IMDMA § 501(a)(1)) is commonly maintenance paid for a specified period of time, sometimes with a review. "Permanent" maintenance is lifetime maintenance. Maintenance "in gross" is a set amount of maintenance, paid in one or more installments. Maintenance for a "fixed" period of time comprehends temporary maintenance. Maintenance for an "indefinite" period of time can include all of the other types of maintenance when they are subject to termination by one or more of the statutory events in IMDMA § 510(c), but "indefinite" maintenance usually refers to permanent maintenance that is not subject to termination after a specified time, but only upon the happening of one of the statutory events, e.g., remarriage.

The three most common forms of maintenance awarded by Illinois courts pursuant to § 504 are permanent maintenance, rehabilitative maintenance, and reviewable maintenance. Permanent or indefinite maintenance is for the payee's life, but usually subject to termination upon the happening of one of the IMDMA § 510(c) events. A "classic case" warranting a permanent maintenance award is found in In re Marriage of Kerber, 215 Ill.App.3d 248, 158 Ill.Dec. 717, 574 N.E.2d 830 (4th Dist.1991). The *Kerber* court rejected the trial court's award of rehabilitative maintenance for one year and ordered permanent maintenance, based on the long duration of the marriage, the fact that the wife had been a homemaker during the marriage and lacked skills and experience to obtain employment by which she could support herself, the wife's bad health, and the husband's employment which made him sufficiently able to pay maintenance.

Rehabilitative maintenance is paid for a fixed period, after which it terminates, thereby presumably allowing the recipient time to become "rehabilitated" and able to support herself. See In re Marriage of Phillips, 244 Ill.App.3d 577, 186 Ill.Dec. 108, 615 N.E.2d 1165 (4th Dist.1993) (affirming rehabilitative maintenance award of $235 per month for three years; wife was homemaker during marriage, and her current job as a CPA could not support the standard of living enjoyed during the marriage); In re Marriage of Cheger, 213 Ill.App.3d 371, 157 Ill.Dec. 116, 571 N.E.2d 1135 (4th Dist.1991) (affirming rehabilitative maintenance award of $2,500 per month for first three years, $1,500 per month for next three years, and $1,000 per month for final four years of payment).

Reviewable maintenance is also paid for a specified period of time, but the court reserves jurisdiction to determine whether the maintenance should continue. The decision to then continue or terminate the maintenance is based upon a review of the parties' resources and the recipient's success in achieving financial independence. See, e.g., In re Marriage of Haas, 215 Ill.App.3d 959, 158 Ill.Dec. 983, 574 N.E.2d 1376 (3d Dist.1991) (upholding award of $600 per month maintenance reviewable at the end of 18 months; wife had been employed during marriage and had potential to become self-sufficient); In re Marriage of Marthens, 215 Ill.App.3d 590, 159 Ill.Dec. 3, 575 N.E.2d 3 (3d Dist.1991) (large disparity between husband's and wife's assets and earning capabilities warranted maintenance reviewable after five years rather than one year).

For further description of these three approaches, see In re Marriage of Pearson, 236 Ill.App.3d 337, 177 Ill.Dec. 650, 603 N.E.2d 720 (1st Dist.1992).

(2) **Change in legislative and judicial attitudes toward maintenance.** The maintenance provisions in § 504 became effective on January 1, 1993, after being substantially rewritten. Previously, the courts and the legislature focused on eliminating support dependency. The prior statute had a bias that favored property allocations over maintenance. Maintenance was authorized only when property was insufficient, and the recipient spouse was unable to support himself. The court had the power to grant a request for maintenance only if it found that the spouse seeking maintenance (1) lacks sufficient property, including marital property apportioned to him, to provide for his reasonable needs, and (2) is unable to support himself through appropriate employment or is the custodian of a child whose condition or circumstances make it appropriate that the custodian not be required to seek employment outside the home, or (3) is otherwise without sufficient income. Ill.Rev.Stat. ch. 40, para. 504(a) (1989). Even when maintenance was allowed, courts required that the spouse make a good-faith effort to become employed. In re Marriage of Jones, 187 Ill.App.3d 206, 229, 134 Ill.Dec. 836, 852, 543 N.E.2d 119, 135 (1st Dist.1989). Rehabilitative maintenance for short periods (rarely more than five years) to bridge the transition time between divorce and employment was the order of the day. See, e.g., In re Marriage of Jones, 187 Ill.App.3d 206, 229, 134 Ill.Dec. 836, 852, 543 N.E.2d 119, 135 (1st Dist.1989) ("The purpose of the act authorizing such payments ... is to provide incentive for the spouse receiving support to use diligence in procuring employment, training or other necessary skills to attain self-sufficiency."). It soon became apparent that this approach was working to the serious detriment of divorced women and children. Brief awards of maintenance were incapable of restoring the lost opportunity costs. An egregious example of rehabilitative maintenance is In re Marriage of Glessner, 119 Ill.App.3d 306, 74 Ill.Dec. 809, 456 N.E.2d 311 (1st Dist.1983) (upholding award of $400 per month for one year as rehabilitative maintenance to wife after 24 year marriage).

The 1993 amendments, following the lead of some earlier case law, created a framework that should allow judges and negotiators to use maintenance to reach more balanced results. Both "temporary [rehabilitative and reviewable] or permanent maintenance" are expressly authorized. Furthermore, courts have increasingly recognized that permanent maintenance or temporary maintenance and retaining jurisdiction for review, is appropriate when a dependent spouse's ability to become financially independent through employment is uncertain, due to the recipient's age, health, lack of education or experience, or the high standard of living established during the marriage. See, e.g., In re Marriage of Pearson, 236 Ill.App.3d 337, 177 Ill.Dec. 650, 603 N.E.2d 720 (1st Dist.1992) (rejecting trial court's 36-month limitation on rehabilitative maintenance when the wife's health and ability to obtain employment were speculative; remanding with instructions to retain jurisdiction for a future review of the need for future maintenance). The Fourth District, for instance, wrote:

> [I]t is not appropriate, regardless of age, ability, inclination, former educational experience, and with no guarantee of success, to place a duty on a dependent former spouse to seek education or training. Where the circumstances of the dependent former spouse indicate such education or training is likely to successfully enable the dependent former spouse to obtain more lucrative employment, it is reasonable to place an obligation on the spouse to obtain such training or education. However, where the dependent former spouse's circumstances indicate mandatory education or training would be little more than an exercise in futility, it is [not] appropriate to charge the dependent former spouse with the obligation to seek and accept appropriate employment.

In re Marriage of Lenkner, 241 Ill.App.3d 15, 22, 181 Ill.Dec. 646, 651, 608 N.E.2d 897, 902 (4th Dist.1993). See also Barry A. Schatz & Jacalyn Birnbaum, New Statute Promotes Homemakers' Rights, 80 Ill. B.J. 610 (1992).

(3) **Considerations in determining maintenance.** There are 12 statutory factors governing the award of maintenance. The courts and parties are directed to consider the first eleven factors, and any other factor that the court expressly finds to be just and equitable (factor 12). Although no one factor is dispositive, In re Marriage of Harlow, 251 Ill.App.3d 152, 190 Ill.Dec. 476, 621 N.E.2d 929 (4th Dist.1993), the court need not give each factor equal weight in arriving at an equitable result. In re Marriage of Miller, 231 Ill.App.3d 480, 172 Ill.Dec. 679, 595 N.E.2d 1349 (3d Dist. 1992). The same factors used to determine an initial award of maintenance are applicable in a proceeding to modify an existing award. In re Marriage of Martin, 223 Ill.App.3d 855, 166 Ill.Dec. 136, 585 N.E.2d 1158 (4th Dist.), *cert. denied*, 145 Ill.2d 635, 173 Ill.Dec. 6, 596 N.E.2d 630 (1992).

The factors governing maintenance and property have become similar. See IMDMA § 503 Author's Note (21).

The enumerated § 504 statutory factors (which often overlap) are:

(a) **Income, property, and needs: IMDMA §§ 504(a)(1), 504(a)(2).** The first two factors, the income and property of the parties and the parties' needs, are frequently the two sides of the traditional maintenance equation. The amount of maintenance is determined by considering the needs of the recipient spouse, her own ability to meet those needs, and the capacity of the payor spouse to satisfy the outstanding difference. In re Marriage of Rink, 136 Ill.App.3d 252, 91 Ill.Dec. 34, 483 N.E.2d 316 (1st Dist.1985). More often than not, both parties are required to reduce their standards of living. See, e.g., In re Marriage of Mantei, 222 Ill.App.3d 933, 164 Ill.Dec. 870, 583 N.E.2d 1192 (4th Dist.1991). Examples of cases that reverse and affirm awards of maintenance based on needs and resources are: In re Marriage of Schroeder, 215 Ill.App.3d 156, 158 Ill.Dec. 721, 574 N.E.2d 834 (4th Dist.), *cert. denied*, 141 Ill.2d 560, 162 Ill.Dec. 508, 580 N.E.2d 134 (1991) (award of maintenance in gross of $40,000, paid at $333 monthly for ten years was inadequate to meet wife's needs; together with wife's income it was insufficient to meet even her monthly mortgage and utility expenses); In re Marriage of Frederick, 218 Ill.App.3d 533, 161 Ill.Dec. 254, 578 N.E.2d 612 (2d Dist.1991) (maintenance award was sufficient; wife had received 50% of net equity in marital home and husband was ordered to pay 50% of daughter's college expenses); In re Marriage of Marcello, 247 Ill.App.3d 304, 187 Ill.Dec. 81, 617 N.E.2d 289 (1st Dist.1993) (denial of wife's petition for maintenance was error; wife's income was insufficient to maintain her household and husband had adequate resources to provide maintenance).

(b) **Earning capacity: IMDMA § 504(a)(3).** A substantial disparity in earning capacity between the two spouses may justify an award of maintenance to the spouse capable of earning relatively little. In In re Marriage of Gunn, 223 Ill.App.3d 165, 174 Ill.Dec. 381, 598 N.E.2d 1013 (5th Dist.1992), for instance, the Fifth District upheld an award of $4,000 per month maintenance when the husband had earned nearly $200,000 in the past year, far more than the $4,400 earned by his wife in the same period. See also In re Marriage of Emery, 179 Ill.App.3d 744, 128 Ill.Dec. 569, 534 N.E.2d 1014 (4th Dist.1989) (maintenance award was proper; husband earned substantial income as an electrician while wife's income was one tenth that of her husband's, coming only from child support payments and a minimum-wage job).

(c) **Lost opportunities due to marriage: IMDMA § 504(a)(4).** In many marriages, one spouse does not pursue a career outside the home in order to raise the couple's children or run the household. When the marriage is later dissolved, that spouse does not have the educational or professional experience that the other spouse obtained during the same period of time. Therefore,

> Illinois courts give consideration to a more permanent maintenance award to wives who have undertaken to have children, raise and support the family, and who have lost or been substantially impaired in maintaining their skills for continued employment during the years when [her] husband was getting his education and becoming established.

In re Marriage of Rubinstein, 145 Ill.App.3d 31, 40, 99 Ill.Dec. 212, 218, 495 N.E.2d 659, 665 (2d Dist.1986). See also In re Marriage of Gunn, 233 Ill.App.3d 165, 174 Ill.Dec. 381, 598 N.E.2d 1013 (5th Dist.1992) (upholding award of $4,000 per month maintenance until wife reaches age 60 or husband retires, whichever occurs first; wife had been a homemaker throughout the marriage and had lost her marketable skills while husband perfected his marketable skills at the same time).

(d) **Limitations to attaining employment: IMDMA § 504(a)(5).** The statute now mandates that a court consider the time and training necessary to obtain appropriate employment, whether a party is able to support herself or himself, or whether, because of the custody of a child, it is inappropriate for the party to seek employment. See, e.g., In re Marriage of Hensley, 210 Ill.App.3d 1043, 155 Ill.Dec. 486, 569 N.E.2d 1097 (4th Dist.), *appeal denied*, 141 Ill.2d 541, 162 Ill.Dec. 488, 580 N.E.2d 114 (1991) (upholding trial court's award of maintenance as a way for the custodial mother to work part-time, in order to spend more time as a homemaker to her children); In re Marriage of Kusper, 195 Ill.App.3d 494, 142 Ill.Dec. 282, 552 N.E.2d 1023 (1st Dist.1990) (three-year award of maintenance did not give wife sufficient time to pursue graduate degree and become self-sufficient); Vendredi v. Vendredi, 230 Ill.App.3d 1061, 174 Ill.Dec. 329, 598 N.E.2d 961 (1st Dist.1992) (although employed, wife's lack of formal education, sparse employment history and inadequate language skills left her incapable of supporting herself by employment). Courts frequently monitor a recipient spouse's ability to become self-sufficient through employment by awarding reviewable maintenance. See, e.g., In re Marriage of Haas, 215 Ill.App.3d 959, 158 Ill.Dec. 983, 574 N.E.2d 1376 (3d Dist.1991) (upholding award of $600 per month maintenance reviewable at the end of 18 months; wife had been employed during marriage and had potential to become self-sufficient); In re Marriage of Marthens, 215 Ill.App.3d 590, 159 Ill.Dec. 3, 575 N.E.2d 3 (3d Dist.1991) (large disparity between husband's and wife's assets and earning capabilities warranted maintenance reviewable after five years rather than one year); In re Marriage of Sisul, 234 Ill.App.3d 1038, 175 Ill.Dec. 463, 600 N.E.2d 86 (3d Dist.1992) (rejecting trial court's award of maintenance that would automatically terminate after one year; wife's injuries from automobile accident and fact that wife was a homemaker throughout marriage were evidence that wife could not become self-sufficient in one year).

(e) **Standard of living during the marriage: IMDMA § 504(a)(6).** The standard of living established during the marriage can be an important factor, particularly in long marriages, and where the spouse receiving maintenance can never realistically be expected to independently earn sufficient income to maintain the standard of living that she enjoyed during the marriage. See, e.g., In re Marriage of Martin, 223 Ill.App.3d 855, 166 Ill.Dec. 136, 585 N.E.2d 1158 (4th Dist.), *cert. denied*, 145 Ill.2d 635, 173 Ill.Dec. 6, 596 N.E.2d 630 (1992) (wife could not maintain the lavish lifestyle enjoyed during the marriage by her own employment, and was therefore entitled to rehabilitative maintenance). But see In re Marriage of O'Brien, 235 Ill.App.3d 520, 176 Ill.Dec. 529, 601 N.E.2d 1227 (1st Dist.1992) (frugal standard of living during marriage should not bar a higher award of maintenance where husband lived far more comfortably and was capable of paying additional support). Of course, it may be impossible for both parties to maintain the standard of living established during the marriage following dissolution. See, e.g., In re Marriage of Mantei, 222 Ill.App.3d 933, 164 Ill.Dec. 870, 583 N.E.2d 1192 (4th Dist.1991).

(f) **Duration of the marriage: IMDMA § 504(a)(7).** A spouse may be entitled to a lower amount of maintenance following a short marriage, or a greater amount after a long marriage. See, e.g., In re Marriage of Miller, 231 Ill.App.3d 480, 172 Ill.Dec. 679, 595 N.E.2d 1349 (3d Dist.1992) (trial court properly considered the short duration of the marriage in failing to award maintenance); In re Marriage of Kerber, 215 Ill.App.3d 248, 158 Ill.Dec. 717, 574 N.E.2d 830 (4th Dist.1991) (consideration of statutory factors, including the parties' long marriage, indicated permanent maintenance was appropriate). The duration factor has more weight the longer that the maintenance lasts. In re Marriage of Stam, 260 Ill.App.3d 754, 198 Ill.Dec. 467, 632 N.E.2d 1078 (3d Dist.1994).

(g) **Age and health: IMDMA § 504(a)(8).** Where the payor spouse has the capacity, an aged unemployed spouse may be entitled to permanent maintenance. Where one spouse is considerably older than the other, the older spouse may be entitled to additional maintenance, especially if the older spouse is beyond the age of employment and the younger spouse still works. See, e.g., In re Marriage of Toth, 224 Ill.App.3d 43, 166 Ill.Dec. 478, 586 N.E.2d 436 (1st Dist.1991) (award of maintenance paid to 61 year old wife by 49 year old husband was proper).

Similarly, if one spouse suffers from bad health and the other is relatively healthy, maintenance may be appropriate. See, e.g., In re Marriage of Shields, 167 Ill.App.3d 205, 118 Ill.Dec. 50, 521 N.E.2d 118 (4th Dist.1988) (affirming maintenance awarded to husband confined to a nursing home following a debilitating stroke).

(h) **Tax consequences: IMDMA § 504(a)(9).** Detrimental tax consequences of a property award may affect the amount of maintenance, although there does not appear to be any case law interpreting this factor.

(i) **Contribution to spouse's career: IMDMA § 504(a)(10).** The statute since 1993 requires that the trial court consider the contributions and services by the party seeking maintenance to the education, training, career or career potential, or license of the other spouse. Illustrative cases decided prior to the statutory amendment include: In re Marriage of Carpel, 232 Ill.App.3d 806, 173 Ill.Dec. 873, 597 N.E.2d 847 (4th Dist.1992); and In re Marriage of Rubinstein, 145 Ill.App.3d 31, 99 Ill.Dec. 212, 495 N.E.2d 659 (2d Dist.1986), . Factor (10) is an important addition to § 504. See Author's Note (4) below.

(j) **Agreement between the parties: IMDMA § 504(a)(11).** The parties may determine whether maintenance will be awarded, and if so, how much, in a valid prenuptial or settlement agreement, or any other valid agreement. Settlement agreements will only be accepted by a court, however, if they are conscionable. See IMDMA § 502(b) Author's Note (3). For enforceable prenuptial agreements, see 750 ILCS 10/7 and accompanying Author's Notes.

(k) **Additional factors: IMDMA § 504(a)(12).** The court may consider additional factors where applicable. For instance, in In re Marriage of Klein, 231 Ill.App.3d 901, 173 Ill.Dec. 335, 596 N.E.2d 1214 (4th Dist.1992), the court considered that the recipient wife was cohabitating with her boyfriend when it decided to deny the wife maintenance, because the cohabitation could materially affect her need for support. The court in In re Marriage of Martin, 223 Ill.App.3d 855, 166 Ill.Dec. 136, 585 N.E.2d 1158 (4th Dist.), cert. denied, 145 Ill.2d 635, 173 Ill.Dec. 6, 596 N.E.2d 630 (1992), considered, among other things, the fact that the wife had relinquished her right to receive maintenance from a former husband from whom she was receiving maintenance.

Maintenance can be reserved, for example, when the court enters a bifurcated judgment or enters a judgment without personal jurisdiction over the payor. IMDMA §§ 401(b), 504(a). Maintenance can also be waived, or denied by a court in a contested case. See, e.g., In re Marriage of Durante, 201 Ill.App.3d 376, 147 Ill.Dec. 56, 559 N.E.2d 56 (1st Dist.1990) (affirming denial of maintenance and bar from seeking maintenance in the future; wife had non-marital estate worth $420,000 and was self-sufficient); In re Marriage of Miller, 231 Ill.App.3d 480, 172 Ill.Dec. 679, 595 N.E.2d 1349 (3d Dist.1992) (denial of maintenance was proper; marriage was of a short duration, wife had beautician skills and had attended classes towards obtaining a teaching certificate, and had been awarded $13,000 in liquid assets from the marital estate).

(4) **Maintenance awarded irrespective of need.** Factor 10, contributions and services, is an important departure from prior law, because it removes maintenance from sole reliance upon the parties' needs and resources, and potentially makes maintenance serve as remuneration for contributions and services. The concept of awarding maintenance to compensate for contributions brings the maintenance section closer to the property section where "contribution" is also a factor to be considered in allocating property. See IMDMA § 503(d)(1) Author's Note (21). In other words, if a wife contributed to the career or obtaining of a professional license of her husband, she is entitled to participate in the income benefits of the career or license, in the same way that she is entitled to credit if she has contributed to the acquisition of property. See In re Marriage of Carpel, 232 Ill.App.3d 806, 173 Ill.Dec. 873, 597 N.E.2d 847 (4th Dist.1992) (denial of petition to extend maintenance was error; wife supported husband through final year of law school and did not work during the rest of the marriage, husband "may not have been able to develop his career as successfully as he did without [wife's] support"); In re Marriage of Rubinstein, 145 Ill.App.3d 31, 99 Ill.Dec. 212, 495 N.E.2d 659 (2d Dist.1986), (trial court should consider granting wife permanent maintenance on remand; wife was primary breadwinner while husband

pursued medical degree, and parties had agreed that wife would support family while husband pursued his education and then he would take care of her while she furthered her education).

The award of maintenance is supposed to be "without regard to marital misconduct," but adding "contributions" to the factors to be considered in determining maintenance will inevitably also bring in the lack of contributions (misconduct). This has already occurred in property allocation because of the "contribution" factor. *Cf.* In re Marriage of Cecil, 202 Ill.App.3d 783, 791, 148 Ill.Dec. 72, 77, 560 N.E.2d 374, 379 (3d Dist.1990); IMDMA § 503(d)(1) Author's Note (21).

The separation of maintenance from strict need factors and attaching it to considerations of contributions and services can become particularly important in cases where there cannot be property awards, either because there is no property, or because all of the property is non-marital.

Moreover, the consideration of the income and property of each party in factor 1, apart from need, can potentially allow a court to use maintenance to redress what would otherwise be inequitable property allocations. For example, a court may order maintenance to offset the award of a valuable marital business to the husband, or, where there is only non-marital property, all of which is assigned to one spouse, to provide financial benefit to the spouse without non-marital property.

Factors 4 (impairment), 9 (tax consequences of property division), and 12 (any other factor) may also be compensatory rather than tied to need.

The legislature has made maintenance a much more flexible instrument. It remains to be seen how it will be used, and how maintenance separated from need will be computed.

(5) **Obligation for rehabilitation.** The obligation of the spouse receiving maintenance to rehabilitate herself and to become independent to the extent possible undoubtedly remains in the revised maintenance provisions. See § 504(a) factors 3, 5, 8, and also compare IMDMA § 505.1 Author's Note (1). Those cases requiring a recipient spouse to actively attempt to become independent and seek employment therefore remain valid. See, e.g., In re Marriage of Martin, 223 Ill.App.3d 855, 166 Ill.Dec. 136, 585 N.E.2d 1158 (4th Dist.), *appeal denied*, 145 Ill.2d 635, 173 Ill.Dec. 6, 596 N.E.2d 630 (1992) ("The recipient of the maintenance award is under an affirmative obligation to seek appropriate training and skills to become financially independent in the future."); In re Marriage of Courtright, 229 Ill.App.3d 1089, 172 Ill.Dec. 258, 595 N.E.2d 619 (3d Dist.1992) (attempts at substitute teaching were insufficient to meet the burden of proving wife had made a good faith effort to become self-sufficient); In re Marriage of Haas, 215 Ill.App.3d 959, 158 Ill.Dec. 983, 574 N.E.2d 1376 (3d Dist.1991) (permanent maintenance was inappropriate, wife had been employed throughout the marriage and had the potential to become self-sufficient). But these cases are also tempered by the new statutory prescription that the court consider and monitor the circumstances of each case to make sure that independence is feasible. See particularly § 504(a)(5) Author's Note (3) above.

The cases that permit the payor spouse to terminate maintenance under appropriate circumstances by petitioning the court should also still apply. See IMDMA § 510(a) Author's Note (6).

(6) **Cross references.** See IMDMA § 510 and accompanying Author's Notes for maintenance modification and termination and the function of the statutory events for the termination of maintenance. See Internal Revenue Code §§ 71 and 215 and

accompanying Author's Notes for the tax treatment of maintenance. See IMDMA § 502 Author's Note (11) Article II for model maintenance agreement paragraphs, which can also be modified for use in a judgment.

(7) **Funds for payment of maintenance.** IMDMA § 504(a) provides that maintenance can be paid from the income or property of the payor spouse. The statute does not limit the source of maintenance to marital income or property, and therefore non-marital income and non-marital property are also available for the payment of maintenance. These statutory provisions can be important where marital income, the usual source of maintenance, is insufficient.

(8) **Cross reference.** See IMDMA § 703 and accompanying Author's Notes for *in rem* actions.

(9) **Payment of maintenance pending appeal.** The amendments now make provision for the payment of maintenance to an appellant or an appellee pending appeal (§ 504(c)), whereas formerly the court could grant maintenance only during an appeal that was taken against the party receiving maintenance.

(10) **Security for maintenance.** Maintenance can be secured during payor's life by the use of a collateral trust, and, after the payor's death, by life insurance, a life insurance trust or a collateral trust, or by the payor's estate. Life insurance is the most common security in settled cases. Life insurance may now also be required by courts in contested cases. In re Marriage of Vernon, 253 Ill.App.3d 783, 787–790, 192 Ill.Dec. 668, 672–673, 625 N.E.2d 823, 827–828 (4th Dist.1993) (affirming judgment requiring husband to keep wife on a life insurance policy to secure maintenance, and rejecting the reasoning of a previous case to the contrary). A life insurance trust prevents a windfall from being paid to the payee spouse. For example, if the payor dies one month before the maintenance in the amount of $3,000 per month terminates, and the payee receives $200,000 in life insurance proceeds, the payee would collect an unintended windfall. A life insurance trust is a better planning instrument, because it would pay the last month of the maintenance obligation, and the balance of the insurance proceeds would go as the payor directs in his trust.

(11) **Cross reference—Forms.** See IMDMA § 502 Author's Note (11) Article VII for model life insurance and life insurance trust provisions, and Exhibit G in IMDMA § 502 Author's Note (12) for a model life insurance trust. An estate guaranty is contained in IMDMA § 502 Author's Note (11) Article II paragraph 2(c)(iii).

(12) **Cross references.** See Internal Revenue Code §§ 71, 215, and 682 and accompanying Author's Notes for the tax effects of life insurance, trust, and estate security for the payment of maintenance.

750 ILCS 5/505

§ 505. Child support; Contempt; Penalties

(a) In a proceeding for dissolution of marriage, legal separation, declaration of invalidity of marriage, a proceeding for child support following dissolution of the marriage by a court which lacked personal jurisdiction over the absent spouse, a proceeding for modification of a previous order for child support under Section 510 of this Act, or any proceeding authorized under Section 501 or 601 of this Act, the court may order either or both parents owing a duty of support to a child of the marriage to pay an amount reasonable and necessary for his support, without regard to marital miscon-

750 ILCS 5/505 FAMILIES

duct. The duty of support owed to a minor child includes the obligation to provide for the reasonable and necessary physical, mental and emotional health needs of the child.

(1) The Court shall determine the minimum amount of support by using the following guidelines:

Number of Children	Percent of Supporting Party's Net Income
1	20%
2	25%
3	32%
4	40%
5	45%
6 or more	50%

(2) The above guidelines shall be applied in each case unless the court makes a finding that application of the guidelines would be inappropriate, after considering the best interests of the child in light of evidence including but not limited to one or more of the following relevant factors:

(a) the financial resources of the child;

(b) the financial resources and needs of the custodial parent;

(c) the standard of living the child would have enjoyed had the marriage not been dissolved;

(d) the physical and emotional condition of the child, and his educational needs; and

(e) the financial resources and needs of the non-custodial parent.

If the court deviates from the guidelines, the court's finding shall state the amount of support that would have been required under the guidelines, if determinable. The court shall include the reason or reasons for the variance from the guidelines.

(3) "Net income" is defined as the total of all income from all sources, minus the following deductions:

(a) Federal income tax (properly calculated withholding or estimated payments);

(b) State income tax (properly calculated withholding or estimated payments);

(c) Social Security (FICA payments);

(d) Mandatory retirement contributions required by law or as a condition of employment;

(e) Union dues;

(f) Dependent and individual health/hospitalization insurance premiums;

(g) Prior obligations of support or maintenance actually paid pursuant to a court order;

(h) Expenditures for repayment of debts that represent reasonable and necessary expenses for the production of income, medical expenditures necessary to preserve life or health, reasonable expenditures for the benefit of the child and the other parent, exclusive of gifts. The court shall reduce net income in determining the minimum amount of support to be ordered only for the period that such payments are due and shall enter an order containing provisions for its self-executing modification upon termination of such payment period.

(4) In cases where the court order provides for health/hospitalization insurance coverage pursuant to Section 505.2 of this Act, the premiums for that insurance, or that portion of the premiums for which the supporting party is responsible in the case of insurance provided through an employer's health insurance plan where the employer pays a portion of the premiums, shall be subtracted from net income in determining the minimum amount of support to be ordered.

(5) If the net income cannot be determined because of default or any other reason, the court shall order support in an amount considered reasonable in the particular case. The final order in all cases shall state the support level in dollar amounts.

(b) Failure of either parent to comply with an order to pay support shall be punishable as in other cases of contempt. In addition to other penalties provided by law the Court may, after finding the parent guilty of contempt, order that the parent be:

(1) placed on probation with such conditions of probation as the Court deems advisable;

(2) sentenced to periodic imprisonment for a period not to exceed 6 months; provided, however, that the Court may permit the parent to be released for periods of time during the day or night to:

(A) work; or

(B) conduct a business or other self-employed occupation.

The Court may further order any part or all of the earnings of a parent during a sentence of periodic imprisonment paid to the Clerk of the Circuit Court or to the parent having custody or to the guardian having custody of the minor children of the sentenced parent for the support of said minor children until further order of the Court.

(c) A one-time charge of 20% is imposable upon the amount of past-due child support owed on July 1, 1988 which has accrued under a support order entered by the court. The charge shall be imposed in accordance with the provisions of Section 10–21 of the Illinois Public Aid Code and shall be enforced by the court upon petition.

(d) Any new or existing support order entered by the court under this Section shall be deemed to be a series of judgments against the person obligated to pay support thereunder, each such judgment to be in the amount of each payment or installment of support and each such judgment to be deemed entered as of the date the corresponding payment or installment becomes due under the terms of the support order. Each such judgment shall have the full force, effect and attributes of any other judgment of this State, including the ability to be enforced.

(e) When child support is to be paid through the clerk of the court in a county of 1,000,000 inhabitants or less, the order shall direct the obligor to pay to the clerk, in addition to the child support payments, all fees imposed by the county board under paragraph (3) of subsection (u) of Section 27.1 of "An Act in relation to clerks of courts", approved July 1, 1874, as now or hereafter amended. Unless paid in cash or pursuant to an order for withholding, the payment of the fee shall be by a separate instrument from the support payment and shall be made to the order of the Clerk.

(f) An order for support entered or modified in a case in which a party is receiving child and spouse support services under Article X of the Illinois Public Aid Code shall include a provision requiring the obligor to notify the Illinois Department of Public Aid, within 7 days, (i) of the name and address of any new employer of the obligor, (ii) whether the obligor has access to health insurance coverage through the employer or other group coverage, and (iii) if so, the policy name and number and the names of persons covered under the policy.

(g) An order for support shall include a date on which the current support obligation terminates. The termination date shall be no earlier than the date on which the child covered by the order will attain the age of majority or is otherwise emancipated. The order for support shall state that the termination date does not apply to any arrearage that may remain unpaid on that date. Nothing in this subsection shall be construed to prevent the court from modifying this order.

Author's Notes

Analysis

1. Applicability of IMDMA § 505.
2. Contribution of support by both parents.
3. Expanded support.
4. Percentage support guidelines.
5. Deviation from statutory guidelines: Procedure.
6. Deviation from statutory guidelines: Factors considered.
7. Cross reference—Forms.
8. Net income.
9. Expenditures for debt.
10. Expenditures for child or parent.
11. Health insurance premiums.

12. Undeterminable net income.
13. Percentage support awards.
14. Enforcement by contempt.
15. Penalty on child support arrearages.
16. No judgment necessary for remedies for support arrearages.
17. Modification and termination.

(1) **Applicability of IMDMA § 505.** In addition to child support petitions in connection with actions for dissolution, invalidity, and legal separation, subsection (a) provides that IMDMA § 505 and its guidelines of minimum support apply to petitions for temporary children's support under IMDMA § 501, petitions for modification of children's support under IMDMA § 510, and petitions in connection with custody proceedings under IMDMA § 601.

(2) **Contribution of support by both parents.** IMDMA § 505(a) expressly provides that the court may order either or both parents to contribute to the support of the children of the marriage. Because child support is the joint and several obligation of the parents, In re Marriage of Schuster, 224 Ill.App.3d 958, 167 Ill.Dec. 73, 85, 586 N.E.2d 1345 (2d Dist.1992), where both parents have income, the courts commonly require both parents to contribute to the support of children. See, e.g., In re Marriage of Butler, 106 Ill.App.3d 831, 62 Ill.Dec. 535, 436 N.E.2d 561 (1st Dist.1982).

Courts may require one parent to provide all of the children's support when the other parent has no ability to contribute, or courts may impose a heavier burden of support on one parent when there is a large differential in income between the parents. Courts are reluctant to release one parent from contributing to children's support when that parent has the ability to contribute, regardless of whether the other parent has sufficient financial resources. For instance, the court in In re Marriage of Rai, 189 Ill.App.3d 559, 571, 136 Ill.Dec. 922, 929, 545 N.E.2d 446, 453 (1st Dist.1989), rejected the husband's claim that he should be excused from paying child support, although his wife earned over $200,000 per year, stating "[w]e do not believe that because children receive adequate support as a result of one parent's efforts the other parent is excused from all obligations of support." The court in In re Marriage of Reed, 100 Ill.App.3d 873, 876, 56 Ill.Dec. 202, 204, 427 N.E.2d 282, 284 (5th Dist. 1981), acknowledged that while "generally ... both parents should exercise responsibility for their children's support, this obligation is not mandatory in all situations." The wife in *Reed*, the court held, was not required to pay children's support when the children's father could adequately meet their needs, and the mother was uneducated and unemployed. See also In re Marriage of Rogliano, 198 Ill.App.3d 404, 413, 144 Ill.Dec. 595, 601, 555 N.E.2d 1114, 1120 (5th Dist.1990) ("while both divorced parents are responsible for the care and well-being of their children, it does not follow that their burden is equal and it is only equitable that the parent with the disproportionately greater income than the other bear a greater share of the costs of support, especially if it is the noncustodial parent who is earning the greater income"); In re Marriage of Schuster, 224 Ill.App.3d 958, 167 Ill.Dec. 73, 85, 586 N.E.2d 1345, 1357 (2d Dist.1992) (despite wife's high income and economic self-sufficiency, husband was neither unemployed nor unemployable, and must pay child support).

(3) **Expanded support.** The statute in IMDMA § 505(a) expands the duty of support to include the necessary physical, mental, and emotional health needs of the child. See, e.g., In re Marriage of Schroeder, 215 Ill.App.3d 156, 158 Ill.Dec. 721, 574 N.E.2d 834 (4th Dist.), *appeal denied*, 141 Ill.2d 560, 162 Ill.Dec. 508, 580 N.E.2d 134

(1991) (order that father pay health insurance premiums for children was proper; case remanded for allocation of medical expenses not covered by insurance); In re Marriage of Ingrassia, 140 Ill.App.3d 826, 95 Ill.Dec. 165, 489 N.E.2d 386 (2d Dist.1986) (trial court properly ordered husband to pay one half of daughter's psychiatric expenses if wife paid one half).

(4) **Percentage support guidelines.** IMDMA § 505(a)(1) sets forth the guidelines for the minimum amount of children's support in terms of a percentage of the supporting party's net income. Net income is calculated in accordance with IMDMA § 505(a)(3).

Where both parents have an income and are required by the court to contribute to the support of the children, the minimum percentages may not apply. See In re Marriage of Scafuri, 203 Ill.App.3d 385, 392, 149 Ill.Dec. 124, 128, 561 N.E.2d 402, 406 (2d Dist.1990) ("When dealing with above-average incomes, the specific facts of each case become more critical in determining whether the guidelines should be adhered to.").

(5) **Deviation from statutory guidelines: Procedure.** If the court deviates from the minimum guidelines (below or above), the court is required under IMDMA § 505(a)(2) to make express findings setting forth its reasons for the deviation. The 1993 amendment to the statute requires the court to find that the application of the guidelines would be inappropriate after considering the best interests of the child in light of the evidence including but not limited to one or more of the statutory factors. The enumerated factors of IMDMA § 505(a)(2) are not considered if the court follows the statutory guidelines:

> [t]he statutory factors enumerated in section 505(a)(2) are not to be considered if the circuit court is following the guidelines for child support as they are delineated in section 505(a)(1), and only if the circuit court were going to impose more or less than the minimum standard required under the statutory guidelines is a circuit court required to consider the relevant factors of section 505(a)(2).... While the court should not blindly apply the statutory guidelines in every case ... the addition of the guidelines to section 505 of the [IMDMA] shifts the burden of presenting evidence in a child support hearing to the parent who wishes to shift the non-custodial parent's contribution below or above the specified percentages.

In re Marriage of Rogliano, 198 Ill.App.3d 404, 411, 144 Ill.Dec. 595, 599, 555 N.E.2d 1114, 1118 (5th Dist.1990) (citations omitted).

(6) **Deviation from statutory guidelines: Factors considered.** The parents' resources are likely to be the primary consideration when the support level deviates from the statutory guidelines. Where one or both of the parents have an extraordinarily high income, application of the guidelines may produce children's support out of proportion to the actual needs of the children. A court may then set support payments below the statutory guidelines. In re Marriage of Bush, 191 Ill.App.3d 249, 138 Ill.Dec. 423, 547 N.E.2d 590 (4th Dist.1989), *appeal denied*, Bush v. Turner, 129 Ill.2d 561, 140 Ill.Dec. 668, 550 N.E.2d 553 (1990) (an award of 20% of husband's income, $30,000 per year, was excessive for support of one four-year-old child). An award above the conventional needs of the child may be justified when the standard of living during the marriage was high, because the children are entitled to the standard of living they would have enjoyed had the marriage not been dissolved, if it is still financially feasible. See, e.g., In re Marriage of Osborn, 206 Ill.App.3d 588, 604, 151 Ill.Dec. 663, 672, 564 N.E.2d 1325, 1334 (5th Dist.1990) (upholding award in excess of "shown needs" where it was clear that had the marriage not been dissolved the

children would have been afforded a higher standard of living); In re Marriage of Scafuri, 203 Ill.App.3d 385, 392, 149 Ill.Dec. 124, 128, 561 N.E.2d 402, 406 (2d Dist.1990) (reducing award of $10,000 per month to $6,000 when children enjoyed a "very comfortable lifestyle" but were "not accustomed to a lavish or extravagant lifestyle").

The resources of one parent's new spouse can only be considered in a limited manner in setting the level of child support.

The financial status of a current spouse may not be considered to ascertain the ability of party to fulfill a child support obligation, but it may be equitably considered to determine whether the payment of child support would endanger the ability of the support-paying party and that party's current spouse to meet their needs.

In re Marriage of Keown, 225 Ill.App.3d 808, 167 Ill.Dec. 375, 587 N.E.2d 644 (4th Dist.1992). However, courts have considered the new spouse's resources in several instances. For example, the court properly considered the new spouses's assets when the new spouse sought and received permission to intervene in the modification proceedings to protect her own financial interests, and the parent failed to object to questions pertaining to his spouse's wealth. In re Marriage of Baptist, 232 Ill.App.3d 906, 174 Ill.Dec. 81, 598 N.E.2d 278 (4th Dist.1992).

In addition to deviations based on parental resources, the court may deviate from the guidelines where children have their own resources, particularly when the parents are unable to provide for the children's needs. In re Marriage of Frazier, 205 Ill.App.3d 621, 623, 151 Ill.Dec. 130, 132, 563 N.E.2d 1236, 1238 (3d Dist.1990) (upholding reduction in father's support payments; child's estate far exceeded father's resources).

Conversely, application of the guidelines may produce less children's support than is necessary. Special circumstances concerning a child, such as an illness, may serve as reasons to deviate from the minimum guidelines when the guidelines do not yield enough child support because of the extraordinary expenses. See, e.g., IMDMA § 505(a)(2)(d).

The 1993 amendment to § 505(a)(2) requires the court's finding to state the amount of support that would have been required by the guidelines, if determinable, when there is deviation from the guidelines; and to state the reasons for the variance.

Taken as a whole, § 505 aims to balance the economic situation of the entire family. For instance, in addition to consideration of the resources of individual family members, §§ 505(b) and (e) also require that the needs of the custodial and non-custodial parent be considered. Exceptional needs will be reflected in the level of child support. For example, a non-custodial parent incurring medical payments for a serious illness may warrant a lower level of children's support than provided under the minimum guidelines. In determining whether a deviation from the guidelines is warranted, the actual needs of the children should first be determined, and then measured against the resources of the parents and the other economic factors of the family.

(7) **Cross reference—Forms.** Sample children's support paragraphs and a model paragraph when the parties agree to deviate from the statutory guidelines are provided in IMDMA § 502 Author's Note (11) Article IV. The sample judgment paragraph for deviation from the statutory guidelines is at IMDMA § 413 Author's Note (8), Judgment Additional and Alternative Provisions para. 7.

(8) **Net income.** The percentage guidelines in IMDMA § 505(a)(1) are applied to the supporting parent's net income as defined in § 505(a)(3). The starting figure is the total of income from all sources, not just earned income. See, e.g., In re Marriage of Dodds, 222 Ill.App.3d 99, 164 Ill.Dec. 692, 583 N.E.2d 608 (2d Dist.1991) (holding lump-sum worker's compensation award constitutes income under the statute); In re Marriage of Harmon, 210 Ill.App.3d 92, 154 Ill.Dec. 727, 568 N.E.2d 948 (2d Dist.1991) (money that wife received as a gift and monthly interest payments on her share of marital assets were considered income under the statute). The expenditures set forth in subparagraphs (a) through (h) of § 505(a)(3) are then subtracted from total income to get net income:

(a) Federal tax;

(b) State tax;

(c) Social Security;

(d) Mandatory retirement contributions;

(e) Union dues;

(f) Dependent and individual health insurance. See, e.g., In re Marriage of Stone, 191 Ill.App.3d 172, 138 Ill.Dec. 547, 547 N.E.2d 714 (4th Dist.1989) (reversing trial court's holding that father could not deduct the health insurance premiums covering himself and his other dependents in determining net income, in addition to the share covering his daughter).

(g) Prior obligations of support or maintenance with court order. "Prior obligation" refers to an obligation from a *previous unrelated action*, not to obligations of support and maintenance under the same dissolution order at issue. In re Marriage of Baptist, 232 Ill.App.3d 906, 914, 174 Ill.Dec. 81, 86, 598 N.E.2d 278, 283 (4th Dist.1992). Ethical, as opposed to court-ordered, support obligations are not deducted when determining net income. In re Marriage of Tatham, 173 Ill.App.3d 1072, 123 Ill.Dec. 576, 527 N.E.2d 1351 (5th Dist.1988).

(h) Expenditures for repayment of debts incurred for the production of income, certain medical expenses, and certain expenditures for the benefit of the child or the other parent, exclusive of gifts.

(9) **Expenditures for debt.** Not all expenditures for the repayment of debts are deductible pursuant to subparagraph (h). For example, in In re Marriage of Partney, 212 Ill.App.3d 586, 156 Ill.Dec. 679, 571 N.E.2d 266 (5th Dist.1991), the court rejected the husband's attempt to deduct passive real estate investment losses because he failed to show that the losses were reasonable and necessary for the production of income, and could not present a specified repayment schedule. See also In re Marriage of McBride, 166 Ill.App.3d 504, 116 Ill.Dec. 880, 519 N.E.2d 1095 (1st Dist.1988) (disallowing deductions of nonreimbursed business expenses; husband presented insufficient evidence that such expenses were debts incurred to generate income); In re Marriage of Hart, 194 Ill.App.3d 839, 141 Ill.Dec. 550, 551 N.E.2d 737 (4th Dist.1990) (upholding trial court's finding that ranch and airplane were deductible business debts).

(10) **Expenditures for child or parent.** Payments under the order of dissolution before the court do not qualify as reasonable expenditures for the benefit of the child and the other parent under IMDMA § 505(a)(3)(h): "This provision would apply when the noncustodial parent *voluntarily* contributes to necessary expenses for which

he or she is not already obligated to contribute or pay." In re Marriage of Baptist, 232 Ill.App.3d 906, 916, 174 Ill.Dec. 81, 88, 598 N.E.2d 278, 285 (4th Dist.1992).

(11) **Health insurance premiums.** IMDMA § 505(a)(4) allows premiums paid by the supporting party for health and hospitalization insurance covering a child to be subtracted from net income in cases where there is a court order providing for the insurance coverage pursuant to IMDMA § 505.2.

(12) **Undeterminable net income.** For those cases in which net income cannot be determined, IMDMA § 505(a)(5) mandates that the court provide for reasonable support. A common situation where net income cannot be determined is where the individual is self-employed, or works on a commission basis. See In re Marriage of Carpel, 232 Ill.App.3d 806, 173 Ill.Dec. 873, 597 N.E.2d 847 (4th Dist.1992) (fluctuations in husband's income as attorney working on a contingent basis made it difficult to determine net income; court held that trial court should consider previous income to determine prospective income); In re Marriage of Butler, 106 Ill.App.3d 831, 62 Ill.Dec. 535, 436 N.E.2d 561 (1st Dist.1982) (awarding child support on the basis of past income, despite an alleged decline in earnings). At least one district has rejected the attempt to approximate current net income by averaging the incomes of past years. In re Marriage of Schroeder, 215 Ill.App.3d 156, 158 Ill.Dec. 721, 574 N.E.2d 834 (4th Dist.1991).

IMDMA § 505 speaks of paying children's support only from income. IMDMA § 504(a) says that maintenance may be paid from income or property. If maintenance can be paid from property, a fortiori, support for dependent children should be payable from property when income is insufficient. The statute drafters omitted this provision, but it may be inferred from IMDMA § 505(a)(5).

(13) **Percentage support awards.** IMDMA § 505(a)(5) also prohibits percentage children's support in final orders. Relief may be possible by using non–taxable maintenance payments instead of children's support payments. See Internal Revenue Code §§ 71 and 215 Author's Note (22). At least one case has held that the prohibition does not apply to a stated base amount or a percentage, whichever is greater. In re Marriage of Liss, ___ Ill.App.4th ___, ___ Ill.Dec. ___, ___ N.E.2d ___, 1994 WL700385 (1st Dist.1994).

(14) **Enforcement by contempt.** IMDMA § 505(b) provides for contempt proceedings for failure to comply with an order for children's support. "Evidence of noncompliance with a court order of child support payments makes out a prima facie case for indirect, civil contempt. The burden then rests on the alleged contemnor to show that his noncompliance was not willful." In re Marriage of Harvey, 136 Ill.App.3d 116, 117–18, 91 Ill.Dec. 115, 116–17, 483 N.E.2d 397, 398-99 (3d Dist.1985) (citations omitted). The contempt is initiated by a petition for a rule to show cause. See model petition for a rule to show cause at IMDMA § 511 Author's Note (6).

After a finding of civil contempt and punishment, the civil contempt can be purged by compliance with the order that is the basis for the contempt. For example, the payment of the child support arrearages will purge the contempt.

In certain circumstances, the contemnor may be able to purge the contempt with partial payment of arrearages if full payment is unrealistic due to unemployment or other financial problems. See, e.g., In re Marriage of Harvey, 136 Ill.App.3d 116, 91 Ill.Dec. 115, 483 N.E.2d 397 (3d Dist.1985) (contempt order was invalid; it was

750 ILCS 5/505   FAMILIES

unrealistic to expect unemployed husband to pay support arrearages); In re Marriage of Hilkovitch, 124 Ill.App.3d 401, 79 Ill.Dec. 891, 464 N.E.2d 795 (1st Dist.1984) (husband could purge contempt by paying one-third of support arrearages).

IMDMA § 505(b) provides that a person found in contempt, in addition to other penalties provided by law, can be placed on probation or sentenced to imprisonment on a work release program. The court may order all or any part of the earnings of a parent during a sentence of periodic imprisonment paid as children's support.

(15) **Penalty on child support arrearages.** IMDMA § 505(c) imposes a penalty on past due children's support, but the paragraph applies only to public aid recipients. Baker v. Baker, 193 Ill.App.3d 294, 140 Ill.Dec. 303, 549 N.E.2d 954 (4th Dist.), *appeal denied* 131 Ill.2d 557, 142 Ill.Dec. 879, 553 N.E.2d 393 (1990).

(16) **No judgment necessary for remedies for support arrearages.** IMDMA § 505(d) makes it unnecessary for children's support arrearages to be reduced to judgment in order to have judgment remedies available to the debtor. The allowance of interest on children's support arrearages is discretionary with the Court. Baker v. Baker, 193 Ill.App.3d 294, 302, 140 Ill.Dec. 303, 308, 549 N.E.2d 954, 959 (4th Dist.), *appeal denied*, 131 Ill.2d 557, 142 Ill.Dec. 879, 553 N.E.2d 393 (1990).

(17) **Modification and termination.** Children's support is always reviewable and modifiable by the court, which retains jurisdiction over children. Children's support cannot be made non-modifiable. See Blisset v. Blisset, 123 Ill.2d 161, 121 Ill.Dec. 931, 526 N.E.2d 125 (1988). Children's support ordinarily terminates when a child reaches majority. IMDMA §§ 505(g), 510(d). In Illinois, a child reaches majority at 18 years of age. 755 ILCS 5/11–1; In re Marriage of Ferraro, 211 Ill.App.3d 797, 156 Ill.Dec. 160, 570 N.E.2d 636 (1st Dist.1991). See also IMDMA § 510 and accompanying Author's Notes in regard to modification and termination of children's support; and IMDMA § 513 and accompanying Author's Notes in regard to educational expenses and support for disabled children after they have reached their majorities.

The new 1993 language of § 505(g) requires that child support orders specify a date on which the support shall terminate, which shall not be sooner than the child's majority (18 years of age) or other emancipation, and further provide that the termination date shall not apply to arrearages that remain unpaid on the termination date. For sample language, see IMDMA § 502 Author's Note (11) paras. 4(a) and 4(b).

750 ILCS 5/505.1

§ 505.1 Unemployed persons owing duty of support

Whenever it is determined in a proceeding to establish or enforce a child support or maintenance obligation that the person owing a duty of support is unemployed, the court may order the person to seek employment and report periodically to the court with a diary, listing or other memorandum of his or her efforts in accordance with such order. Additionally, the court may order the unemployed person to report to the Department of Employment Security for job search services or to make application with the local Jobs Training Partnership Act provider for participation in job search, training or work programs and where the duty of support is owed to a child receiving support services under Article X of The Illinois Public Aid Code, as amended, the court may order the unemployed person to report to the Illinois Department of

Public Aid for participation in job search, training or work programs established under Section 9-6 of that Code.

Author's Notes

(1) **Applicability to maintenance recipients.** Although § 505.1 is directed to unemployed persons owing a duty of support, the idea of keeping a diary or other record of efforts to become employed has been extended to unemployed recipients of maintenance in an attempt to make the recipients independent of maintenance. This is particularly true for reviewable maintenance.

750 ILCS 5/505.2

§ 505.2 Health insurance

(a) Definitions. As used in this Section:

(1) "Obligee" means the individual to whom the duty of support is owed or the individual's legal representative.

(2) "Obligor" means the individual who owes a duty of support pursuant to an order for support.

(3) "Public office" means any elected official or any State or local agency which is or may become responsible by law for enforcement of, or which is or may become authorized to enforce, an order for support, including, but not limited to: the Attorney General, the Illinois Department of Public Aid, the Illinois Department of Mental Health and Developmental Disabilities, the Illinois Department of Children and Family Services, and the various State's Attorneys, Clerks of the Circuit Court and supervisors of general assistance.

(b) Order. Whenever the court establishes, modifies or enforces an order for child support or for child support and maintenance the court shall, upon request of the obligee or Public Office, order that any child covered by the order be named as a beneficiary of any health insurance plan that is available to the obligor through an employer. If the court finds that such a plan is not available to the obligor, or that the plan is not accessible to the obligee, the court may, upon request of the obligee or Public Office, order the obligor to name the child covered by the order as a beneficiary of any health insurance plan that is available to the obligor on a group basis, or as a beneficiary of an independent health insurance plan to be obtained by the obligor, after considering the following factors:

(A) the medical needs of the child;

(B) the availability of a plan to meet those needs; and

(C) the cost of such a plan to the obligor.

(2) If the employer offers more than one plan, the order shall require the obligor to name the child as a beneficiary of the plan in which the obligor is enrolled.

(3) Nothing in this Section shall be construed to limit the authority of the court to establish or modify a support order to provide for payment of expenses, including deductibles, copayments and any other health expenses, which are in addition to expenses covered by an insurance plan of which a child is ordered to be named a beneficiary pursuant to this Section.

(c) Implementation and enforcement. (1) When the court order requires that a minor child be named as a beneficiary of a health insurance plan, other than a health insurance plan available through an employer, the obligor shall provide written proof to the obligee or Public Office that the required insurance has been obtained, or that application for insurability has been made, within 30 days of receiving notice of the court order. Unless the obligor was present in court when the order was issued, notice of the order shall be given pursuant to Illinois Supreme Court Rules. If an obligor fails to provide the required proof, he may be held in contempt of court.

(2) When the court requires that a minor child be named as a beneficiary of a health insurance plan available through an employer, the court's order shall be implemented in accordance with Section 706.1, as now or hereafter amended.

(d) Failure to maintain insurance. The dollar amount of the premiums for court-ordered health insurance, or that portion of the premiums for which the obligor is responsible in the case of insurance provided under a group health insurance plan through an employer where the employer pays a portion of the premiums, shall be considered an additional child support obligation owed by the obligor. Whenever the obligor fails to provide or maintain health insurance pursuant to an order for support, the obligor shall be liable to the obligee for the dollar amount of the premiums which were not paid, and shall also be liable for all medical expenses incurred by the minor child which would have been paid or reimbursed by the health insurance which the obligor was ordered to provide or maintain. In addition, the obligee may petition the court to modify the order based solely on the obligor's failure to pay the premiums for court-ordered health insurance.

(e) Authorization for payment. The signature of the obligee is a valid authorization to the insurer to process a claim for payment under the insurance plan to the provider of the health care services or to the obligee.

(f) Disclosure of information. The obligor's employer shall disclose to the obligee or Public Office, upon request, information concerning any dependent coverage plans which would be made available to a new employee. The employer shall disclose such information whether or not a court order for medical support has been entered.

Author's Notes

Analysis

1. Applicable only to children's health insurance.

2. Withholding of salary.
3. Insurance premiums considered child support.
4. Cross references.

(1) **Applicable only to children's health insurance.** Subparagraph (b) makes § 505.2 applicable only to health insurance coverage for children. The court ordered health insurance can be established whenever a court acts on an order for children's support.

(2) **Withholding of salary.** Subparagraph (c)(2) provides that when the court requires a minor child to be named a beneficiary of a health insurance plan through an employer or union, the court's order shall be implemented in accordance with IMDMA § 706.1, which provides for enrollment of the child in the health plan and the withholding of salary for the payment of the employee's share of the premiums. See IMDMA § 706.1(G)(1) Author's Note (6).

(3) **Insurance premiums considered child support.** The premium for which the obligor is liable is considered additional children's support pursuant to IMDMA § 505.2(d), which is why it is subtracted from net income pursuant to IMDMA § 505(a)(4) in the process to establish the minimum amount of children's support in accordance with the IMDMA § 505(a)(1) guidelines. Pursuant to IMDMA § 505.2(d), an obligor who fails to obey an order to provide for health insurance is not only liable for the payment of premiums, but also for all of the medical expenses incurred by the minor child that would have been reimbursed by the insurance if the obligor had obeyed the order to maintain the health insurance.

(4) **Cross references.** See IMDMA § 510(a) Author's Note (1) for modification of child support after a parent has failed to pay the premiums for court ordered child health insurance. See 29 U.S.C.A. 1169 and accompanying Author's Notes for Qualified Medical Child Support Orders.

750 ILCS 5/506

§ 506. Representation of child

The court may appoint an attorney to represent the interests of a minor or dependent child with respect to his support, custody and visitation. The court may also appoint an attorney as the guardian-ad-litem for the child. The court shall enter an order for costs, fees and disbursements in favor of the child's attorney and guardian-ad-litem, as the case may be. The order shall be made against either or both parents, or against the child's separate estate.

Author's Notes

Analysis

1. Court's discretion to appoint attorney for child.
2. Selection.
3. Order Appointing Attorney for Minor Child(ren) and/or Guardian Ad Litem—Form.
4. Title.
5. Attorney's role.
6. Attorney's fees.

750 ILCS 5/506   FAMILIES

(1) **Court's discretion to appoint attorney for child.** It is within the discretion of the court to appoint an attorney or a guardian ad litem to represent the interests of a child in support, custody, and visitation litigation. The purpose of appointing the attorney or guardian-ad-litem for the child is to present to the court and in negotiations the perspective of the best interests of the child. See, e.g., In re Marriage of L.R., 202 Ill.App.3d 69, 85, 147 Ill.Dec. 439, 449, 559 N.E.2d 779, 789 (1st Dist.1990), *appeal denied*, 136 Ill.2d 545, 153 Ill.Dec. 375, 567 N.E.2d 333 (1991) (appointing guardian-ad-litem who is also an attorney on remand when "parties seem to have lost sight of [daughter's best interests], as evidenced by the fact that they refer to all family members by their full names in court documents, which are a matter of public record"); Hartman v. Hartman, 89 Ill.App.3d 969, 972, 45 Ill.Dec. 360, 362, 412 N.E.2d 711, 713 (4th Dist.1980) (recommending that trial court appoint attorney to represent child in any further proceedings on remand; "It is clear that the parents here are looking after only their own interests, and the interest of this child may be seriously neglected").

(2) **Selection.** Individual counties may have different methods of selecting and appointing a representative of the child. Cook County, for example, maintains an approved attorney list. Included attorneys have experience in the family law field, and have attended a training seminar. Attorneys for the parties may agree on a representative for the child, or the judge may appoint an attorney from the approved attorney list.

(3) **Order Appointing Attorney for Minor Child(ren) and/or Guardian Ad Litem—Form.** There follows a form from Cook County for the appointment of an attorney for minor children or guardian ad litem.

FAMILIES   750 ILCS 5/506

4208 - Appoint Guardian Ad Litem - Allowed   (10-90) CCDR-8

IN THE CIRCUIT COURT OF COOK COUNTY, ILLINOIS
COUNTY DEPARTMENT, DOMESTIC RELATIONS DIVISION

IN RE THE ☐ MARRIAGE ☐ CUSTODY ☐ SUPPORT OF:

NO:

CALENDAR:

_____
PETITIONER
              AND

☐ PRE JUDGMENT

☐ POST JUDGMENT - ENFORCEMENT

☐ POST JUDGMENT - MODIFICATION

_____
RESPONDENT

☐ OTHER _____

ORDER APPOINTING ATTORNEY FOR MINOR CHILD(REN) AND/OR GUARDIAN AD LITEM

On motion of _____ and pursuant to Ch. 40 Sec. 506 and the inherent power of the Court, the Court being fully advised in the premises **FINDS THAT:**

1. There are conflicts within the family adversely affecting the minor child(ren):

_____ age _____   _____ age _____
_____ age _____   _____ age _____
_____ age _____   _____ age _____

2. It is in the best interests of the child(ren) to have a legal representative appointed to protect and preserve their interests.

3. Said legal representative shall be an ATTORNEY with the same authority to act as attorneys for parties of record.

IT IS HEREBY ORDERED THAT:

1. Name: _____
    Address: _____
    Telephone: _____

is hereby appointed ☐ ATTORNEY FOR THE MINOR CHILD(REN) AND/OR ☐ GUARDIAN AD LITEM.

2. Within 7 days of the entry of this order, attorney for ☐ mother ☐ father _____ shall send the attorney for the minor child(ren) and/or the guardian ad litem copies of this order and all notices, pleadings, orders, and reports relative to this cause. The attorney for the minor child(ren) and/or the guardian ad litem shall be kept fully informed by counsel for all parties as to the status of this case and shall have the full assistance of counsel in obtaining any waivers (e.g. for school or medical records, etc.) appropriate to the representation of the minor child(ren).

3. An appearance shall be filed on behalf of the minor child(ren) within 7 days of receipt of this order and an appropriate pleading within 28 days from the date of this order.

4. The attorney for the minor child(ren) and/or the guardian ad litem shall be entitled to reasonable temporary and permanent fees and costs, as the Court sees fit, and pursuant to statute.

Mother's Attorney: _____ Telephone: _____
Father's Attorney: _____ Telephone: _____
_____ Attorney: _____ Telephone: _____

DATE: ENTER:

                                 _____
NAME: JUDGE   NO.
Attorney for:
Address:
City, State, ZIP
Telephone:
Attorney Code No. _____   [G17985]

(4) **Title.** Former practice was to appoint a guardian-ad-litem to take care of the affairs of the child, and then appoint an attorney for the guardian-ad-litem. Currently, the guardian-ad-litem and the attorney for the child are generally one and the same person.

From the attorney's perspective, it is better to have the appointment denominated "attorney" rather than "guardian ad litem". First, malpractice insurance may only cover acts as an attorney. Second, the ethical obligation of confidentiality applies to all attorney-client relationships, but not necessarily to the guardian ad litem-child relationship. Third, there is a slight difference in the perception of the two roles. The title of attorney conveys credibility both to the parties in the marital dispute, and to the represented child. It is also a more comfortable role for the attorney, and may alleviate quandaries over how much weight to give to the child's wishes, particularly frivolous wishes such as the wish to live with the parent who promises the proverbial red convertible.

(5) **Attorney's role.** Whether denominated attorney for the child, guardian ad litem, or both, the role of the child's representative often goes beyond that of the parties' representatives. The basic rights and obligations of representation are the same whether an attorney is the representative of one of the parents, or a court-appointed representative of the child. The attorney is both able and obligated to conduct necessary discovery, file appropriate pleadings, depose and present witnesses, and review experts' reports. Representation of the child, however, in addition, often requires decisions that balance the need for release of information from mental health and school records and the involvement of mental health and school personnel against the desirability of insulating the child from the stresses attendant upon every family disruption. For instance, if a parent subpoenas the child's treating therapist or teachers, this may significantly undermine the "safe harbor" that therapy or the school provides.

The unique position of representing a child in a dissolution or separation proceeding incurs other additional concerns that are not at issue when representing a parent. For example, the attorney for the child often is in a mediation role between the parents, trying to improve communication, reduce the harm to children, and initiate amicable resolutions of contested custody and visitation issues. An attorney in such a role should remain non-judgmental and objective, without compromising the ethical obligations to the represented child. The child's attorney may be the appropriate one to convene settlement conferences, and to draft proposed court orders and parenting agreements in an attempt to settle custody and visitation disputes without litigation.

Also, the attorney for the child may be asked to give his or her opinion to the court concerning the best outcome. This role is inappropriate for the attorney for the child, especially in a formal court setting, whereas a guardian ad litem may appropriately prepare a written report (and be subject to cross-examination). Nonetheless, the attorney's opinion is arguably presented de facto at trial in the opening statement, the closing argument and the plea for relief, but these positions should be based on evidence presented at the trial.

Additional concerns may arise when the attorney has a disagreement with the child, or when the parties agree to settle and the representative of the child does not.

(6) **Attorney's fees.** The court may order one or both of the parents to pay the fees and costs of the representative of the child. The factors considered to determine attorney's fees under IMDMA § 506 are the same as those under IMDMA § 508, "including the circumstances of the mother and father; the importance, novelty, and difficulty of the questions raised, especially from a family-law standpoint; the degree of responsibility involved from a management perspective; the time and labor required; the usual and customary charge in the community; and the benefits to the client." In re Marriage of Soraparu, 147 Ill.App.3d 857, 864, 101 Ill.Dec. 241, ___, 498

N.E.2d 565, 571 (1st Dist.), *appeal denied*, 113 Ill.2d 575, 106 Ill.Dec. 56, 505 N.E.2d 362 (1986). See IMDMA § 508 and accompanying Author's Notes.

In McClelland v. McClelland, 231 Ill.App.3d 214, 172 Ill.Dec. 461, 595 N.E.2d 1131 (1st Dist.1992), although the parents had equal abilities to pay the fees of the child's attorney, the court ordered the mother to pay approximately two-thirds and the father to pay approximately one-third of the fees and costs of the child's attorney because the mother caused a substantial part of the post-decree litigation, including bringing unsubstantiated charges against the husband.

As a practical consideration, the attorney should ensure that financial arrangements are made clear and explicit at the beginning of the representation. The arrangements may include an agreed to or court ordered retainer. A fee petition is an appropriate way to ask the court to monitor the payment of the attorney for the child or guardian ad litem. Because the parents' financial situations may not be adequate to include the fees of an additional attorney to represent their child, regardless of the need, pro bono representation or representation at a reduced hourly rate may be expected.

750 ILCS 5/507

§ 507. Payment of maintenance or support to court

(a) In actions instituted under this Act, the court shall order that maintenance and support payments be made to the clerk of court as trustee for remittance to the person entitled to receive the payments. However, the court in its discretion may direct otherwise where circumstances so warrant.

(b) The clerk of court shall maintain records listing the amount of payments, the date payments are required to be made and the names and addresses of the parties affected by the order. For those cases in which support is payable to the clerk of the circuit court for transmittal to the Illinois Department of Public Aid by order or court, and the Illinois Department of Public Aid collects support by assignment, offset, withholding, deduction or other process permitted by law, the Illinois Department shall notify the clerk of the date and amount of such collection. Upon notification, the clerk shall record the collection on the payment record for the case.

(c) The parties affected by the order shall inform the clerk of court of any change of address or of other condition that may affect the administration of the order.

(d) The provisions of this Section shall not apply to cases that come under the provisions of Sections 709 through 712.

Author's Notes

(1) **Cross reference—Forms.** A model Family Support Affidavit to supply the clerk with the required information is at IMDMA § 413 Author's Note (10). An agreed waiver of the payment of maintenance and support to the clerk of the court is at IMDMA § 502 Author's Note (11) para. 5(a), and the corresponding approval in the judgment is at IMDMA § 413 Author's Note (8), Judgment Additional and Alternative Provisions, para. 8.

750 ILCS 5/508

§ 508. Attorney's fees

(a) The court from time to time, after due notice and hearing, and after considering the financial resources of the parties, may order any party to pay a reasonable amount for his own costs and attorney's fees and for the costs and attorney's fees necessarily incurred or, for the purpose of enabling a party lacking sufficient financial resources to obtain or retain legal representation, expected to be incurred by any party, which award shall be made in connection with the following:

  (1) The maintenance or defense of any proceeding under this Act.

  (2) The enforcement or modification of any order or judgment under this Act.

  (3) The defense of an appeal of any order or judgment under this Act, including the defense of appeals of post-judgment orders.

  (4) The maintenance or defense of a petition brought under Section 2-1401 of the Code of Civil Procedure seeking relief from a final order or judgment under this Act.

  (5) The costs and legal services of an attorney rendered in preparation of the commencement of the proceeding brought under this Act.

(b) In every proceeding for the enforcement of an order or judgment when the court finds that the failure to comply with the order or judgment was without cause or justification, the court shall order the party against whom the proceeding is brought to pay the costs and reasonable attorney's fees of the prevailing party.

(c) The court may order that the award of attorney's fees and costs hereunder shall be paid directly to the attorney, who may enforce such order in his name, or that they be paid to the relevant party. Judgment may be entered and enforcement thereof had accordingly.

Author's Notes

Analysis

1. Attorney's fees: In general.
2. Actions by attorneys.
3. Obligation to pay legal fees.
4. Amount of fees.
5. Unreasonably litigious parties.
6. Petition.
7. Role of bankruptcy on attorney's fee awards.
8. Proceedings.
9. Penalty for failure to comply with order or judgment.
10. Petition for Temporary Attorney's Fees—Form.

(1) **Attorney's fees: In general.** Section 508(a) provides that the court can award attorney's fees and costs against a party for the services of his own attorney,

and also order a party to pay the attorney's fees and costs of the opposing party. In re Marriage of Galvin, 94 Ill.App.3d 1032, 50 Ill.Dec. 309, 419 N.E.2d 417 (1st Dist.1981). The petition can seek either fees and costs already incurred, or anticipated fees and costs. Anticipated fees and costs may include money necessary to pay a retainer so as to be able to obtain representation, to carry on future litigation, to defend an appeal (see, e.g., In re Marriage of Pittman, 213 Ill.App.3d 60, 157 Ill.Dec. 177, 571 N.E.2d 1196 (5th Dist.1991) (granting prospective award of attorney's fees to defend appeal); In re Marriage of Kennedy, 214 Ill.App.3d 849, 158 Ill.Dec. 172, 573 N.E.2d 1357 (1st Dist.1991) (affirming trial court's award of partial appellate attorney's fees to wife)), or to hire an expert needed for the litigation. See, e.g., In re Marriage of Winton, 216 Ill.App.3d 1084, 159 Ill.Dec. 933, 576 N.E.2d 856 (2d Dist.1991) (reversing award of expert fees; while a permissible award, reasonableness of fees must be established). A party often will seek temporary attorney's fees early in the litigation pursuant to § 508, in order to have money in advance with which to carry on the litigation.

The theory of § 508, grounded in Harding v. Harding, 180 Ill. 481, 54 N.E. 587 (1899), is that the parties should have equal ability to hire lawyers and bring litigation. See also In re Marriage of Mantei, 222 Ill.App.3d 933, 942, 164 Ill.Dec. 870, 876, 583 N.E.2d 1192, 1198 (4th Dist.1991) ("the purpose of the statute is to allow a spouse to contest the dissolution on an equal footing so that concerns about incurring large attorney's fees will not coerce a litigant into conceding meritorious claims"). The party without financial resources is therefore entitled to have the party with financial resources pay his attorney's fees and costs, in order to place the parties on an equal basis.

(2) **Actions by attorneys.** Section 508(a) protects lawyers in fee disputes with their own clients, but a lawyer in an adversary contest for fees and costs against his own client is not a happy proceeding. Because of the potential for abuse of the fiduciary relationship between an attorney and her client, the attorney must exercise "the utmost good faith" in all dealings with the client, and all transactions arising out of an attorney-client relationship will be subject to the closest scrutiny. In re Marriage of Pagano, 181 Ill.App.3d 547, 556, 130 Ill.Dec. 331, 336, 537 N.E.2d 398, 403 (2d Dist.1989). Therefore, the court must rigorously protect the client's interests:

> Because section 508 puts clients in a position where they are effectively before the court without representation ... precautions must be taken to ensure that any rights of the client are not relinquished unknowingly and that any resulting attorney fee is fair. At a minimum ... prior to entering an award of attorney fees on behalf of an attorney against his client, the trial court must be presented with a petition for attorney fees and an itemization of the billing including the hourly cost, the time spent on the case, and an itemization of the tasks performed. In being presented with such a petition, the trial court will have a basis for ensuring that the fees awarded are fair.

Id. 181 Ill.App.3d at 555, 537 N.E.2d at 403. It is more common for the party without sufficient funds to bring the proceeding for fees and costs against the spouse in control of the funds than it is for the attorney to bring a suit against his or her client. However,

> [T]here is a reasonable basis for permitting an attorney to proceed against his own client for fees in a dissolution proceeding, even though such claims are not permitted in other types of actions. In dissolution proceedings, a most important function of the trial court is to make divisions and allocations of property, enter

750 ILCS 5/508   **FAMILIES**

orders of support, and determine whether one spouse should pay the other spouse's attorney's fees.

In re Marriage of Galvin, 94 Ill.App.3d 1032, 1035, 50 Ill.Dec. 309, 419 N.E.2d 417, 419 (1st Dist.1981).

(3) **Obligation to pay legal fees.** The initial obligation to pay attorney's fees and costs is on the party who incurs the fees and costs. In re Marriage of Mantei, 222 Ill.App.3d 933, 941, 164 Ill.Dec. 870, 875, 583 N.E.2d 1192, 1197 (4th Dist.1991). A showing of inability to pay must therefore be made before a party can require the opposing party to pay his attorney's fees and costs. In re Marriage of Lehr, 217 Ill.App.3d 929, 940, 160 Ill.Dec. 840, 847, 578 N.E.2d 19, 26 (1st Dist.1991). See also In re Marriage of Carr, 221 Ill.App.3d 609, 612, 164 Ill.Dec. 189, 191, 582 N.E.2d 752, 754 (5th Dist.1991) (" 'inability to pay' must be determined relative to the party's standard of living, employment abilities, allocated capital assets, existing indebtedness, and income available from investments and maintenance").

A party may establish economic inability by showing that "payment of fees would strip the individual of his or her means of support and undermine his or her economic stability." In re Marriage of Smith, 128 Ill.App.3d 1017, 1027, 84 Ill.Dec. 242, 251, 471 N.E.2d 1008, 1017 (2d Dist.1984). It is insufficient to merely show that the parties' incomes differ significantly. In re Marriage of Stockton, 169 Ill.App.3d 318, 328, 119 Ill.Dec. 817, 824, 523 N.E.2d 573, 580 (4th Dist.1988).

A spouse is not required to be destitute, however, before the opposing spouse can be ordered to pay his attorney's fees and costs. In re Marriage of Orlando, 218 Ill.App.3d 312, 160 Ill.Dec. 763, 577 N.E.2d 1334 (1st Dist.1991); In re Marriage of Mantei, 222 Ill.App.3d 933, 941, 164 Ill.Dec. 870, 876, 583 N.E.2d 1192, 1198 (4th Dist.1991). A spouse need not exhaust his assets and income in order to pay attorney's fees and costs if the other spouse has the capability to pay them. Therefore, the spouse can have assets and income and still require the opposing spouse to pay all or part of his attorney's fees and costs. See, e.g., In re Marriage of Haas, 215 Ill.App.3d 959, 965, 158 Ill.Dec. 983, 987, 574 N.E.2d 1376, 1379 (3d Dist.1991) ("it is clear that petitioner will be unable to pay her attorney's fees and costs without depleting part of the marital assets awarded to her. Respondent, however, appears to be able to pay his fees as well as petitioner's fees without depleting assets, based on his income and additional bonuses. Requiring petitioner to deplete her assets is not equitable in this case where respondent is able to meet both expenses").

(4) **Amount of fees.** The fees sought must be fair and reasonable to all parties, whether already incurred or sought in advance of the work having been accomplished. In re Marriage of Powers, 252 Ill.App.3d 506, 507, 191 Ill.Dec. 541, 543, 624 N.E.2d 390, 392 (2d Dist.1993). A hearing is required to determine the financial resources of each of the spouses and the reasonableness of the fees and costs. However, "a party waives his right to a hearing on attorney's fees where he did not request a hearing before the trial court and is thereby left with the judge's ruling on the basis of the fee petition and affidavits alone." In re Marriage of Jones, 187 Ill.App.3d 206, 231, 134 Ill.Dec. 836, 853, 543 N.E.2d 119, 136 (1st Dist.1989).

Elements that make up the reasonableness of the fees include:

(1) the skill and standing of the attorneys employed; (2) the nature of the controversy, and the novelty and difficulty of the questions at issue; (3) the amount and importance of the subject matter, especially from a family law standpoint; (4) the degree of responsibility involved in the management of the

case; (5) the time and labor required; (6) the usual and customary charge in the community; and (7) the benefits resulting to the client.

In re Marriage of Landfield, 209 Ill.App.3d 678, 705, 153 Ill.Dec. 834,, 567 N.E.2d 1061, 1076 (1st Dist.1991). See, e.g., In re Marriage of Kruse, 92 Ill.App.3d 335, 48 Ill.Dec. 145, 416 N.E.2d 40 (1st Dist.1980) (reducing trial court's award of attorney's fees to reflect the relatively uncomplicated facts and issues). For a discussion of the proof required to establish the elements constituting reasonable fees, see In re Marriage of Sanda, 245 Ill.App.3d 314, 319, 184 Ill.Dec. 186, 189, 612 N.E.2d 1346, 1349 (2d Dist.1993). An additional consideration may be the allocation of time billed for different duties. For instance, attorney's fees awarded may distinguish between hours spent in the office, on the telephone, in court concerning contested matters, and in court concerning uncontested matters. See, e.g., In re Marriage of Kruse, 92 Ill.App.3d 335, 338, 48 Ill.Dec. 145, 147, 416 N.E.2d 40, 42 (1st Dist.1980). A trial judge may rely on his or her own knowledge and experience when deciding the value of the services provided. In re Marriage of Powers, 252 Ill.App.3d 506, 507, 191 Ill.Dec. 541, 544, 624 N.E.2d 390, 392 (2d Dist.1993).

A party seeking attorney's fees must present evidence of the usual and customary fees for like services in the area. In re Marriage of Girrulat, 219 Ill.App.3d 164, 161 Ill.Dec. 734, 578 N.E.2d 1380 (5th Dist.1991); In re Marriage of Morse, 143 Ill.App.3d 849, 98 Ill.Dec. 67, 493 N.E.2d 1088 (5th Dist.1986). For example, if a client hires an attorney from another, higher charging, community (such as Chicago), the court may apply the lower hourly rate charged by comparable attorneys in the community where the case is tried. Furthermore, the additional travel expenses incurred by an attorney from a distant community will not be recoverable when local counsel possesses the required expertise. See In re Marriage of Siddens, 225 Ill.App.3d 496, 167 Ill.Dec. 680, 588 N.E.2d 321 (5th Dist.1992).

An award of attorney's fees may also be reduced for double billing (charging for a partner and an associate at the same meeting where one lawyer would suffice), billing for unnecessarily applied time, and other situations when the court deems the attorney's fee request to be excessive. See, e.g., In re Marriage of Kosterka, 174 Ill.App.3d 954, 124 Ill.Dec. 295, 529 N.E.2d 12 (2d Dist.1988); Gasperini v. Gasperini, 57 Ill.App.3d 578, 15 Ill.Dec. 230, 373 N.E.2d 576 (1st Dist.1978). See also Richheimer v. Richheimer, 59 Ill.App.3d 354, 208 N.E.2d 346 (1st Dist.1965) (refusing to "subsidize the [wife's] zest for an accumulation of legal talent" with an award of attorney's fees for multiple counsel hired by the wife).

Time spent in litigation to obtain fees is normally not chargeable. In re Marriage of Powers, 252 Ill.App.3d 506, 191 Ill.Dec. 541, 624 N.E.2d 390 (2d Dist.1993), however, held that fees charged for the preparation of the wife's petition for attorney's fees were recoverable under § 508. Value billing and premiums are discussed, but seldom approved by the court. See Bellow v. Bellow, 94 Ill.App.3d 361, 50 Ill.Dec. 656, 419 N.E.2d 924 (1st Dist.1981); (rejecting request for a multiplier on attorney's fees). Contingent fee arrangements are prohibited in dissolution actions prior to a final judgment. Rule 1.5(d)(1) of the Illinois Rules of Professional Conduct provides:

(d) A lawyer shall not enter into an arrangement for, charge, or collect:

(1) any fee in a domestic relations matter, the payment or amount of which is contingent upon the securing of a dissolution of marriage or upon the amount of maintenance or support, or property settlement in lieu thereof; provided, however, that the prohibition set forth in Rule 1.5(d)(1) shall not extend to representation in matters subsequent to final judgments in such cases;

750 ILCS 5/508   **FAMILIES**

See also In re Marriage of Malec, 205 Ill.App.3d 273, 150 Ill.Dec. 207, 562 N.E.2d 1010 (1st Dist.1990), *cert. denied*, 136 Ill.2d 545, 153 Ill.Dec. 375, 567 N.E.2d 333 (1991). Rule 1.5(d)(1) of the Illinois Rules of Professional Conduct permits contingent fees in post-decree representation, e.g., the collection of support arrearages.

(5) **Unreasonably litigious parties.** In final fee awards, a factor sometimes considered is the undue litigiousness of one or both of the spouses, or the frivolity of the claims. In In re Marriage of Mantei, 222 Ill.App.3d 933, 942, 164 Ill.Dec. 870, 876, 583 N.E.2d 1192, 1198 (4th Dist.1991), for example, the court refused to order the husband to pay the wife's attorney's fees, finding that

> the attorney fees resulted from the parties' unwillingness to compromise.... [I]t is an unreasonable expectation to anticipate that the trial court will automatically require the other party to pay such attorney fees regardless of one's conduct during the litigation. There are times when the failure to compromise is frivolous.

(6) **Petition.** The petition for attorney's fees and costs must be filed within 30 days after the entry of a final judgment for the court to have jurisdiction to hear the petition. In re Marriage of Baltzer, 150 Ill.App.3d 890, 895, 104 Ill.Dec. 196, 200, 502 N.E.2d 459, 463 (2d Dist.1986) ("The court in which a dissolution proceeding is pending has jurisdiction over the matter of attorney's fees and continues to do so for a period of 30 days after entry of its final judgment").

(7) **Role of bankruptcy on attorney's fee awards.** Under the Federal Bankruptcy Act, a debtor can generally discharge a marital property obligation, but he cannot discharge a debt "for alimony to, maintenance for, or support of" a spouse, former spouse, or child of the debtor. 11 U.S.C.A. § 523(a)(5). The issue, therefore, is whether attorney's fees qualify as support or property.

> Bankruptcy law, not state law, is controlling when determining what constitutes alimony, maintenance or support.... Observance of bankruptcy law does not, however, preclude an examination of state law. State law should be considered to determine what prompted the state court to award the fees.... An award of maintenance and support is meant to provide an ex-spouse with necessary goods or services which he or she would otherwise not be able to purchase.... As such, attorney fees awarded to a spouse in an Illinois divorce action are generally considered in the nature of maintenance and support.

In re Calisoff, 92 B.R. 346, 352–53 (Bkrtcy. N.D.Ill.1988). The court concluded: "If the award tends to balance the income of the parties, then the award is in the nature of support." *Id.* at 353. See 11 U.S.C.A. § 523 and accompanying Author's Notes.

(8) **Proceedings.** Subparagraphs (a)(1) through (5) of § 508 set forth the types of proceedings for which attorney's fees may be obtained. Most conceivable proceedings are comprehended, except that § 508(a)(3) omits a prosecution of an appeal under the Act. This omission is a departure from the logic that the parties should have equal capability to hire lawyers and prosecute marital litigation. See Author's Note (1) above. The omission can work an injustice where there is error and the would be appellant is without funds to rectify the error. While subparagraph (a)(3) states that fees are recoverable for the "defense of an appeal of any order or judgment under this Act," some courts have modified the rule somewhat and awarded fees for prosecuting a successful appeal. See In re Marriage of Pick, 167 Ill.App.3d 294, 118 Ill.Dec. 53, 521 N.E.2d 121 (2d Dist.1988); *contra* In re Marriage of Wentink, 132 Ill.App.3d 71, 87 Ill.Dec. 117, 476 N.E.2d 1109 (1st Dist.1984). The court in *Pick* emphasized, however,

that the party prosecuting an appeal from a prejudgment order must be successful in the appeal in order to recover attorney's fees under § 508. Pick, 167 Ill.App.3d at 305, 118 Ill.Dec. at 60.

(9) **Penalty for failure to comply with order or judgment.** Section 508(b) provides that the court shall order the party against whom a proceeding is brought to enforce an order or judgment to pay the costs and reasonable attorney's fees of the prosecuting party when the court finds that the failure to comply with the order or judgment was without cause or justification. This award is mandatory. It does not depend upon the need of the party seeking the fees and costs. In re Marriage of Irvine, 215 Ill.App.3d 629, 635, 160 Ill.Dec. 332,336, 577 N.E.2d 462, 466 (4th Dist.1991).

(10) **Petition for Temporary Attorney's Fees—Form.** There follows a sample petition for temporary attorney's fees and costs.

IN THE CIRCUIT COURT FOR THE NINETEENTH
JUDICIAL CIRCUIT,
LAKE COUNTY, ILLINOIS

IN RE THE MARRIAGE OF	)
JOHN JARNDYCE,	)
Petitioner,	)
	) No. ___ D _____
and	)
ELLEN JARNDYCE,	)
Respondent.	)

PETITION FOR TEMPORARY ATTORNEY'S FEES

Respondent, ELLEN JARNDYCE ("ELLEN"), presents the following Petition for Temporary Attorney's Fees and Costs against Petitioner, JOHN JARNDYCE ("JOHN"):

1. JOHN filed his Petition for Dissolution of Marriage against ELLEN on _____, 199__. In _____, 199__, JOHN withdrew from the marital home.

2. Since filing his Petition for Dissolution of Marriage, JOHN has acted in a peremptory and litigious manner, making demands of ELLEN and filing Petitions against her. JOHN has filed a Petition for a Temporary Restraining Order and Preliminary Injunction, a Petition for Temporary Custody and Other Relief, a Motion to Compel Conciliation and for Other Relief, a Motion for a Protective Order and Supervision of Discovery, and a Motion for a Declaratory Judgment. It has been necessary for ELLEN to file responsive pleadings and to bring forth affirmative pleadings of her own. The matter is now set for trial on _____, 199__ on JOHN's Motion for a Declaratory

Judgment and on ELLEN's Counter-petition for a Declaratory Judgment to determine the validity of an alleged Prenuptial Agreement. In preparation for the trial, JOHN has taken the deposition of ELLEN and Harold Skimpole. It has been necessary for ELLEN to take the depositions of JOHN, Phil Squod, and Charles Krook, and she has other discovery scheduled. The trial of the issue of the validity of the alleged Prenuptial Agreement is set for three days. Regardless of the outcome of the Motion and Counter-petition for Declaratory Judgment regarding the alleged Prenuptial Agreement, it will be necessary for ELLEN to prepare for and for the Court to schedule additional trial days for litigation concerning complex financial issues which exist regardless of the validity of the Prenuptial Agreement.

3. JOHN is a man of substantial wealth. JOHN's annual income varies between $_____ AND $_____. JOHN holds in his name approximately _____ shares of _____, and approximately _____ shares of _____. JOHN has interests in homes in _____, Illinois, and in Florida. JOHN's aggregate estate is worth approximately $_____.

4. The financial issues of this case are complex and involve large sums of money. There are complicated issues of marital and non-marital property, titles, gifts, and debt transactions. In addition, JOHN has asserted issues concerning the custody of the minor child of the parties.

5. JOHN is capable of employing accountants, lawyers, psychiatrists, and other professionals in order to wage his Petition for Dissolution of Marriage, his Petition for Temporary and Permanent Custody of the minor child of the parties, his Motion for a Declaratory Judgment, and his other petitions against ELLEN. ELLEN has virtually no income or property of her own, and is completely dependent upon JOHN. In order to place ELLEN temporarily in a position equal to that of JOHN in this litigation, JOHN should pay on behalf of ELLEN temporary attorney's fees and costs of $_____. The sum would be for past services and on account for future services by ELLEN's attorneys.

6. A computer print-out of the time spent, services performed, hourly rates, and the fees and costs incurred to date on behalf of ELLEN in this litigation by ELLEN's attorneys is attached to this Petition as an exhibit. To _____, 199__, ELLEN has incurred fees of $_____ and costs of $_____ for an aggregate of $_____. ELLEN's attorneys have received no payments on her account (or have received a retainer or payments in the amount of $_____), for a net balance currently owing of $_____.

WHEREFORE, ELLEN prays as follows:

1. JOHN pay to ELLEN's attorneys on behalf of ELLEN the sum of $_____ in temporary attorney's fees and costs.

2. ELLEN have such other and further relief as may be appropriate under the evidence and circumstances.

ELLEN JARNDYCE

RICHARD VHOLES
Attorney for ELLEN JARNDYCE

VERIFICATION BY CERTIFICATION

Under penalties as provided by law pursuant to 735 ILCS 5/1-109 of the Illinois Code of Civil Procedure, the undersigned certifies that the statements set forth in the foregoing instrument are true and correct.

DATED: _____   _____

ELLEN JARNDYCE

Richard Vholes
Address
Telephone number

750 ILCS 5/509

§ 509. Independence of provisions of judgment or temporary order

If a party fails to comply with a provision of a judgment, order or injunction, the obligation of the other party to make payments for support or maintenance or to permit visitation is not suspended; but he may move the court to grant an appropriate order.

Author's Notes

(1) **Independence of support and visitation.** Section 509 is to correct the common practice of withholding support when children's visitation is denied, or, conversely, withholding visitation when support is not forthcoming. See Siegel v. Siegel, 80 Ill.App.3d 583, 35 Ill.Dec. 869, 400 N.E.3d 6 (1st Dist.1979), *aff'd in part, rev'd on other grounds*, 84 Ill.2d 212, 49 Ill.Dec. 298, 417 N.E.2d 1312 (1981); Comiskey v. Comiskey, 48 Ill.App.3d 17, 8 Ill.Dec. 925, 366 N.E.2d 87 (1st Dist.1977). The Section makes plain that neither course of action is permitted. The proper procedure is to petition the court for relief concerning the part of the judgment or order with which there has been a failure of compliance.

750 ILCS 5/510

§ 510. Modification and termination of provisions for maintenance, support, educational expenses, and property disposition

(a) Except as otherwise provided in paragraph (f) of Section 502 and, in subsection (d), clause (3) of Section 505.2, the provisions of any judgment respecting maintenance or support may be modified only as to installments accruing subsequent to due notice by the moving party of the filing of the motion for modification and, with respect to maintenance, only upon a showing of a substantial change in circumstances. An order for child support may be modified as follows:

(1) upon a showing of a substantial change in circumstances; and

(2) without the necessity of showing a substantial change in circumstances, as follows:

(A) upon a showing of an inconsistency of at least 20%, but no less than $10 per month, between the amount of the existing order and the amount of child support that results from application of the guidelines specified in Section 505 of this Act unless the inconsistency is due to the fact that the amount of the existing order resulted from a deviation from the guideline amount and there has not been a change in the circumstances that resulted in that deviation; or

(B) Upon a showing of a need to provide for the health care needs of the child under the order through health insurance or other means. In no event shall the eligibility for or receipt of medical assistance be considered to meet the need to provide for the child's health care needs.

The provisions of subparagraph (a)(2)(A) shall apply only in cases in which a party is receiving child and spouse support services from the Illinois Department of Public Aid under Article X of the Illinois Public Aid Code, and only when at least 36 months have elapsed since the order for child support was entered or last modified.

(b) The provisions as to property disposition may not be revoked or modified, unless the court finds the existence of conditions that justify the reopening of a judgment under the laws of this State.

(c) Unless otherwise agreed by the parties in a written agreement set forth in the judgment or otherwise approved by the court, the obligation to pay future maintenance is terminated upon the death of either party, or the remarriage of the party receiving maintenance, or if the party receiving maintenance cohabits with another person on a resident, continuing conjugal basis.

(d) Unless otherwise agreed in writing or expressly provided in a judgment, provisions for the support of a child are terminated by emancipation of the child, except as otherwise provided herein, but not by the death of a parent obligated to support or educate the child. An existing obligation to pay for support or educational expenses, or both, is not terminated by the death of a parent. When a parent obligated to pay support or educational expenses, or both, dies, the amount of support or educational expenses, or both, may be enforced, modified, revoked or commuted to a lump sum payment, as equity may require, and that determination may be provided for at the time of the dissolution of the marriage or thereafter.

(e) The right to petition for support or educational expenses, or both, under Sections 505 and 513 is not extinguished by the death of a parent. Upon a petition filed before or after a parent's death, the court may award sums of money out of the decedent's estate for the child's support or educational expenses, or both, as equity may require. The time within which a claim may be filed against the estate of a decedent under Sections 505 and 513 and subsection (d) and this subsection shall be governed by the provisions of the Probate Act of 1975.

Author's Notes

Analysis

1. When modification is allowed.
2. Non-modifiable maintenance: Potential problem.
3. "Substantial change in circumstances."
4. Modification of child support: Illustrations.
5. Modification of maintenance: Illustrations.
6. Termination of support or maintenance.
7. Termination of rehabilitative maintenance.
8. Amendment to Judgment—Form.
9. Revocation or modification of property allocations.
10. Reservation of jurisdiction to modify property distributions.
11. Statutory conditions for termination of maintenance.
12. Agreement for maintenance beyond statutory conditions: Tax implications.
13. Cross reference—Form.
14. Provisions for maintenance after payor's death.
15. Termination of maintenance upon remarriage.
16. Termination of maintenance upon finding of cohabitation.
17. Termination of child support upon emancipation.
18. Continuation of child support after emancipation.
19. Child support after payor's death.
20. Petition for child support and educational expenses after payor's death.

(1) **When modification is allowed.** Pursuant to § 510(a) modification is permitted only upon a showing of a substantial change in circumstances, with the following exceptions: (i) where a child or his legal representative is permitted by IMDMA § 505.2(d) to petition the court to modify a child support order after a parent or other person has been ordered to maintain health insurance for the benefit of a child, and the parent or other person has failed to pay the premiums; and (ii) under the 1993 amendments to IMDMA § 510(a) when there is a specified percentage discrepancy between a current application of the child support guidelines and the existing order for public aid recipients; or when there is a need to provide for the health needs of a child through insurance or other means.

IMDMA § 510 applies to modifications of both child support and maintenance. The analysis is the same for modifications of child support and maintenance, with one important difference. Child support is always modifiable, while the parties may agree to preclude or limit modification of maintenance pursuant to IMDMA § 502(f). Child support is always modifiable in order to protect the best interests of the child, regardless of whether the parties have agreed between themselves that it is nonmodifiable. In re Marriage of Glickman, 211 Ill.App.3d 792, 156 Ill.Dec. 162, 570 N.E.2d 638 (1st Dist.1991); Blisset v. Blisset, 123 Ill.2d 161, 121 Ill.Dec. 931, 526 N.E.2d 125 (1988). An obligation to pay children's college expenses is subject to modification under § 510 as a form of child support. In re Marriage of Loffredi, 232 Ill.App.3d 709, 173 Ill.Dec. 933, 597 N.E.2d 907 (3d Dist.1992).

Maintenance is generally modifiable, subject to a contrary agreement between the parties. Any agreement to preclude or limit modification of maintenance pursuant to IMDMA § 502(f) must be explicit. See In re Marriage of Martino, 166 Ill.App.3d 692, 117 Ill.Dec. 788, 520 N.E.2d 1139 (2d Dist.1988) (rejecting wife's argument that specific enumeration of reasons for terminating maintenance precludes modification); Schoenhard v. Schoenhard, 74 Ill.App.3d 296, 30 Ill.Dec. 109, 392 N.E.2d 764 (2d Dist.1979) (the term "permanent maintenance" does not preclude modification). However, maintenance in gross is not subject to modification under § 510. In re Marriage of Freeman, 106 Ill.2d 290, 88 Ill.Dec. 11, 478 N.E.2d 326 (1985).

Section 510 cannot be used to modify support arrearages. Only future installments accruing after due notice has been given by the moving party of the filing of his motion for modification may be modified by the court. In re Marriage of Kessler, 110 Ill.App.3d 61, 65 Ill.Dec. 707, 441 N.E.2d 1221 (1st Dist.1982). The court has the discretion to make the modification retroactive to the date on which the petition was filed; however, retroactivity is not mandatory. In re Marriage of Heil, 233 Ill.App.3d 888, 174 Ill.Dec. 622, 599 N.E.2d 168 (5th Dist.1992). But see In re Marriage of Hawking, 240 Ill.App.3d 419, 181 Ill.Dec. 254, 608 N.E.2d 327 (1st Dist.1992) (interpreting § 510(a) to allow modification retroactive only to the date the nonmoving party receives due notice of the filing of the modification petition).

(2) **Non-modifiable maintenance: Potential problem.** The exception to IMDMA § 510(a) for agreements that preclude the modification of maintenance pursuant to IMDMA § 502(f) should be subject to the caveat that non-modifiable maintenance over an extended period of time may be perilous for payors who are vulnerable to losing their jobs or suffering other financial reverses. The same caveat is applicable to non-modifiable maintenance in gross. Maintenance is not subject to discharge in bankruptcy insofar as it represents support. 11 U.S.C.A. § 523(a)(5) (a debtor cannot discharge a debt "for alimony to, maintenance for, or support of" a spouse, former spouse, or child of the debtor). See 11 U.S.C.A. § 523 and accompanying Author's Notes.

(3) **"Substantial change in circumstances."** The party seeking modification has the burden of demonstrating that there has been a substantial change of circumstances. In re Marriage of Plotz, 229 Ill.App.3d 389, 171 Ill.Dec. 514, 594 N.E.2d 366 (3d Dist.) *appeal denied*, 146 Ill.2d 651, 176 Ill.Dec. 821, 602 N.E.2d 475 (1992). The clauses allowing modification of maintenance and child support "upon a showing of a substantial change in circumstances" in subsections (a) and (a)(1) have been subject to various interpretations. The most common interpretation is that the substantial change in circumstances in order to modify maintenance or children's support payments must take place between the time of the entry of the dissolution of marriage judgment, or other prior support order, and the time of the filing of the petition for modification. For an increase, case law generally holds that the substantial change in circumstances must be bilateral: both an increase in the needs of the spouse receiving maintenance or the children who are the beneficiaries of the children's support, coupled with an increase in income on the part of the payor spouse, is required. See, e.g., In re Marriage of Plotz, 229 Ill.App.3d 389, 171 Ill.Dec. 514, 594 N.E.2d 366 (3d Dist.1992) ("Every time a paying parent's income increases it does not mean that support payments increase a like percentage."). But see Legan v. Legan, 69 Ill.App.3d 304, 307, 25 Ill.Dec. 757, 758, 387 N.E.2d 413, 414 (3d Dist.1979) (while "recogniz[ing]

that a number of cases, in prior years, have made [statements that there must be a substantial change both in the needs of the recipient and the payor's ability to pay], no such rigid and inequitable conditions are mandated by section 510(a)"); In re Marriage of Heil, 233 Ill.App.3d 888, 174 Ill.Dec. 622, 599 N.E.2d 168 (5th Dist.1992) (increased ability of the obligor parent to pay support alone can justify an increase in child support). The requirements of increased needs and abilities have been applied less stringently to children's support than to maintenance. See, e.g., Legan v. Legan, 69 Ill.App.3d 304, 309, 25 Ill.Dec. 757, 760, 387 N.E.2d 413 (3d Dist.1979) ("Only some change in circumstances of any nature which would justify equitable action by the court in the best interests of the children (with appropriate consideration of the rights and interests of the parents) is required.").

After the petitioner establishes the threshold showing of a substantial change of circumstances, the court determines whether to modify a maintenance award using the same factors as were used in the initial maintenance award. In re Marriage of Lasota, 125 Ill.App.3d 37, 80 Ill.Dec. 537, 465 N.E.2d 649 (1st Dist.1984). These factors include:

> [t]he financial resources of the party seeking maintenance, including the marital property apportioned to her; the standard of living established during the marriage; the duration of the marriage; the age and the physical and emotional condition of both parties; the ability of the spouse seeking maintenance to meet her needs independently; and the ability of the other spouse to pay.

In re Marriage of Zeman, 198 Ill.App.3d 722, 737, 145 Ill.Dec. 149, 158, 556 N.E.2d 767, 776 (2d Dist.1990).

Similarly, a petition to modify child support is determined under the same analysis as is an initial award of child support. To deviate from the minimum guidelines in IMDMA § 505(a)(1), the factors to be considered include:

> (1) the financial resources of the child; (2) the financial resources and needs of the custodial parent; (3) the standard of living the child would have enjoyed had the marriage not been dissolved; (4) the physical and emotional condition of the child and his educational needs; and (5) the financial resources and needs of the non-custodial parent or parents.

In re Marriage of Olsen, 229 Ill.App.3d 107, 115, 171 Ill.Dec. 39, 46, 593 N.E.2d 859, 866 (1st Dist.1992).

After considering the factors enumerated above, the court may deny the petition for modification, increase or extend the support or maintenance, or reduce or terminate the support or maintenance.

(4) **Modification of child support: Illustrations.**

(a) **Change in custody.** A change in custody is a substantial change in circumstances that may warrant a modification of child support. Therefore, after a change of custody occurred, the court in In re Marriage of White, 204 Ill.App.3d 579, 149 Ill.Dec. 691, 561 N.E.2d 1387 (4th Dist.1990), remanded for consideration of the statutory factors in IMDMA § 505 to determine whether a modification of child support was appropriate.

(b) **Increase in the children's need for support: Illness, increase in age, increase in living expenses.** Some increases in the needs of children who are the beneficiaries of children's support may justify a greater award of support, even in the absence of an increase in the income of the payor spouse. For example, an ill child may warrant an increase in the amount of support. See, e.g., In re Marriage of Kern, 245 Ill.App.3d 575, 185 Ill.Dec. 843, 615 N.E.2d 402 (4th Dist.1993) (affirming denial of husband's petition to reduce child support; one of the couple's children required treatment from a psychologist resulting from a learning disability and physical problems).

Both increases in the ages of the children and increases in the cost of living are appropriate considerations in determining increased need for support. See, e.g., In re Marriage of Kessler, 110 Ill.App.3d 61, 65 Ill.Dec. 707, 441 N.E.2d 1221 (1st Dist.1982) ("increased needs of children may be presumed from the fact that children have grown older and the cost of living has risen"). However, modification is not automatic. The court in In re Marriage of Glickman, 211 Ill.App.3d 792, 156 Ill.Dec. 162, 570 N.E.2d 638 (1st Dist.1991), held that while

> the fact that the children have grown older and the cost of living has risen are proper bases for establishing increased need ... an actual increase in the children's living expenses must be shown, rather than a mere increase in the cost of living generally ... and the increase in the children's needs must be balanced against the relative ability of the parents to provide for them, and where a change has occurred which creates a substantial imbalance between the children's needs and the parents' support capabilities, modification is required.

In re Marriage of Glickman, 211 Ill.App.3d at 796, 156 Ill.Dec. at 165, 570 N.E.2d at 641 (1st Dist.1991) (citations omitted). See also Harner v. Harner, 105 Ill.App.3d 430, 61 Ill.Dec. 312, 434 N.E.2d 465 (1st Dist.1982) (rejecting "rote application" of the rule that an increase is warranted if the children's ages have increased and the cost of living has increased; such a mechanical increase fails to determine whether a substantial change in circumstances has occurred). Furthermore, any increase in the cost of living is likely to affect both parties, and any increased need on the part of the recipient is likely to be offset by a decrease in the ability for the payor to pay support. In re Marriage of Geis, 159 Ill.App.3d 975, 111 Ill.Dec. 717, 512 N.E.2d 1354 (1st Dist.1987).

Children's needs may be defined above mere subsistence if the parent is able to provide them with a more luxurious lifestyle. Several courts have held that children are entitled to participate in the financial good fortune of one of their parents in the same manner as if there had not been a divorce. See, e.g., In re Marriage of Osborn, 206 Ill.App.3d 588, 604, 151 Ill.Dec. 663, 672, 564 N.E.2d 1325, 1334 (5th Dist.1990), *appeal denied*, 137 Ill.2d 666, 156 Ill.Dec. 563, 571 N.E.2d 150 (1991) (upholding initial support award in excess of "shown needs" where it was clear that had the marriage not been dissolved the children would have been afforded a higher standard of living); In re Marriage of Scafuri, 203 Ill.App.3d 385, 392, 149 Ill.Dec. 124, 128, 561 N.E.2d 402, 406 (2d Dist.1990) (reducing original support award of $10,000 per month to $6,000 when children enjoyed a "very comfortable lifestyle" but were "not accustomed to a lavish or extravagant lifestyle"); see also IMDMA § 505 Author's Note (6). Therefore an increase in children's support can be based upon an increase in income or wealth of one of the parents without a showing of a substantial change in the circumstances of the needs of the children, since, if there had not been a divorce, the children would benefit from the enlarged wealth or income of a parent. As the court noted in In re Marriage of Bussey, 108 Ill.2d 286, 91 Ill.Dec. 594, 483 N.E.2d 1229 (1985):

> A child is not expected to have to live at a minimal level of comfort while the noncustodial parent is living a life of luxury.... The child should not suffer

because the custodial parent has a limited income. We decline to accept petitioner's argument that a child is only entitled to receive support for his 'shown needs' when the noncustodial parent is obviously 'enjoying' a standard of living far above that of the child.

In re Marriage of Bussey, 108 Ill.2d at 297, 91 Ill.Dec. at 599, 483 N.E.2d at 1234 (citations omitted). See also In re Marriage of Johnson, 209 Ill.App.3d 1025, 154 Ill.Dec. 706, 568 N.E.2d 927 (3d Dist.1991) (rejecting father's argument that child support should not be increased despite increase in father's income because child's needs were met by current payments of $75 per week). Conversely, an increase in the needs of children may not require an increase in the income of an already wealthy parent.

(c) **Decrease in payor's ability to pay.** Modification may be appropriate when the payor's ability to pay support is reduced. For example, financial reverses or a fall in the payor's income may warrant a reduction of support. See, e.g., In re Marriage of Olsen, 229 Ill.App.3d 107, 171 Ill.Dec. 39, 593 N.E.2d 859 (1st Dist.1992) (father's unemployment warranted a reduction in child support obligation); People ex rel. Meyer v. Nein, 209 Ill.App.3d 1087, 154 Ill.Dec. 436, 568 N.E.2d 436 (4th Dist.1991) (affirming suspension of child support obligations for the period of father's incarceration).

However, reductions in support obligations are not allowed when the payor reduced his or her income voluntarily. See, e.g., In re Marriage of Chenowith, 134 Ill.App.3d 1015, 89 Ill.Dec. 922, 481 N.E.2d 765 (5th Dist.1985) (modification of child support was error; father's unemployment resulted from a unilateral decision to quit his job); In re Marriage of Dall, 212 Ill.App.3d 85, 155 Ill.Dec. 520, 569 N.E.2d 1131 (5th Dist.1991) (trial court properly denied petition to modify child support; father resigned from job without prospects of alternative employment or attempts to secure alternative employment). Any reduction in the ability to pay support must have been made in good faith.

> The crucial consideration in testing "good faith" is whether the change in status was prompted by a desire to evade financial responsibility for supporting the children or to otherwise jeopardize their interests.... The change in circumstances must, however, be fortuitous in nature and not the result of deliberate action or conduct of the party seeking the reduction.

Coons v. Wilder, 93 Ill.App.3d 127, 48 Ill.Dec. 512, 416 N.E.2d 785 (2d Dist.1981) (citations omitted).

Courts disfavor voluntary career changes that jeopardize the payor's financial security. For example, the court in In re Marriage of Kern, 245 Ill.App.3d 575, 579, 185 Ill.Dec. 843, 856, 615 N.E.2d 402, 405 (4th Dist.1993) rejected the father's petition to reduce his child support obligations after the father left his employment as a mechanic and attempted to make a living farming, stating

> [w]hile we respect [the father's] right to choose his field of employment, there are limitations to that right. In an intact family, a father would be reluctant to leave a job by which he supported his family for one where he could not.... Parents in intact families might wait until their children are raised before they change careers. A divorced parent should not see the fact that his child support obligation has been limited to a fixed payment based on his income as an opportunity to change careers.... If all a parent has is a crust of bread he should share it with his child.

750 ILCS 5/510 **FAMILIES**

But see In re Marriage of Webber, 191 Ill.App.3d 327, 138 Ill.Dec. 582, 547 N.E.2d 749 (4th Dist.1989) (reduction of husband's support obligation was correct; husband's voluntary decision to quit job and pursue full-time education was a good-faith attempt to increase his earning potential, and not an attempt to evade his financial responsibilities).

(d) **Increase in payor's ability to pay support.** An increase in the paying spouse's ability to pay support alone may justify an increase in his or her support obligation. See, e.g., In re Marriage of Heil, 233 Ill.App.3d 888, 174 Ill.Dec. 622, 599 N.E.2d 168 (5th Dist.1992) (upholding increase in child support after father's income increased from $10,400 to $19,400; "[t]he increased ability of the obligor parent alone can justify an increase in child support") (citing Legan v. Legan, 69 Ill.App.3d 304, 25 Ill.Dec. 757, 387 N.E.2d 413 (3d Dist.1979)). However, several courts have rejected modifications based solely on a rise in the paying parent's income. See, e.g., In re Marriage of Fazioli, 202 Ill.App.3d 245, 147 Ill.Dec. 495, 559 N.E.2d 835 (1st Dist.1990) (wife failed to show any substantial change in circumstances; although husband's income had risen, his responsibilities had also increased); In re Marriage of Plotz, 229 Ill.App.3d 389, 171 Ill.Dec. 514, 594 N.E.2d 366 (3d Dist.), *appeal denied*, 146 Ill.2d 651, 176 Ill.Dec. 821, 602 N.E.2d 475 (1992) (request to increase support payments was properly denied; "[e]very time a paying parent's income increases it does not mean that support payments increase a like percentage").

(e) **Second spouse's income.** Where a payor spouse remarries and the second spouse has income or wealth, the second spouse will undoubtedly want his or her financial circumstances protected from disclosure. The income of the second spouse is generally not relevant to the first spouse's support obligations. Robin v. Robin, 45 Ill.App.3d 365, 3 Ill.Dec. 950, 359 N.E.2d 809 (1st Dist.1977). However, the second spouse's income may be considered insofar as the income of the second spouse relieves the payor of personal expense, and therefore frees up more of the payor's income that can be used for support. See, e.g., In re Marriage of McBride, 166 Ill.App.3d 504, 116 Ill.Dec. 880, 519 N.E.2d 1095 (1st Dist.1988) (trial court's consideration of second wife's income was not improper; the court was making "an assessment of the financial circumstances and needs of [the father and his second wife] as well as the minor children, which demonstrates an effort to reach an equitable conclusion in exercising its discretion in determining the amount of child support" the father would be obliged to pay). A Fourth District case held that the court properly considered the new spouses's assets when the new spouse sought and received permission to intervene in the modification proceedings to protect her own financial interests, and the parent failed to object to questions pertaining to his spouse's wealth. In re Marriage of Baptist, 232 Ill.App.3d 906, 174 Ill.Dec. 81, 598 N.E.2d 278 (4th Dist.1992). See also IMDMA § 505 Author's Note (6).

(5) **Modification of maintenance: Illustrations.**

(a) **Increase in recipient spouse's need for support.** An increase in spousal maintenance may be justified by higher expenses and needs of the recipient. However, to warrant a modification, the increased need must be fortuitous and not deliberately assumed. For example, the court in In re Marriage of Fazioli, 202 Ill.App.3d 245, 147 Ill.Dec. 495, 559 N.E.2d 835 (1st Dist.1990), affirmed the denial of the wife's petition to increase maintenance. The court stated that the wife had "increased her financial difficulties by persisting in a failing business. The fact that her financial transactions have increased her difficulties in meeting her expenses should not cause a disadvantage to her former husband." *Fazioli*, 202 Ill.App.3d at 251, 147 Ill.Dec. at 499, 559 N.E.2d at 839. See also Faris v. Faris, 142 Ill.App.3d 987, 97 Ill.Dec. 209, 492 N.E.2d 645 (2d Dist.), *appeal denied*, 112 Ill.2d 572, 100 Ill.Dec. 603, 497 N.E.2d 781 (1986) (refusal to increase maintenance was not error; wife's only additional expenses were a mortgage taken out to improve her home and investments made in a failing business, and did not constitute a substantial change in circumstances).

(b) **Decreased need for support.** Modification of maintenance may be based upon the increased earnings or wealth of the recipient spouse which enable the recipient spouse to assume more of his or her own support. This is especially true when coupled with other factors in favor of reducing maintenance. See, e.g., In re Marriage of Martino, 166 Ill.App.3d 692, 117 Ill.Dec. 788, 520 N.E.2d 1139 (2d Dist.1988) (affirming reduction in maintenance; increase in wife's income from nothing to $19,000 per year and decrease in husband's income from $144,000 to $74,000 constituted a substantial change in circumstances warranting modification); In re Marriage of Zeman, 198 Ill.App.3d 722, 145 Ill.Dec. 149, 556 N.E.2d 767 (2d Dist.1990) (affirming reduction of maintenance although husband's income had increased substantially; recipient wife's financial condition had improved due mainly to inheritances she had received and successful investments she had made, and child in mother's custody had become emancipated).

A decrease in need may not warrant a modification if the recipient's income is still not adequate for the recipient to become financially self-sufficient. For example, in In re Marriage of Whiting, 179 Ill.App.3d 187, 128 Ill.Dec. 286, 534 N.E.2d 468 (5th Dist.), *appeal denied*, 126 Ill.2d 559, 133 Ill.Dec. 678, 541 N.E.2d 1116 (1989), the court refused to modify the $400 per month maintenance the husband was obligated to pay the wife. The court held that although the wife had an advanced college degree and had secured employment since the judgment of dissolution, she was still unable to provide for her reasonable needs. Furthermore, the court found that the husband could comfortably provide the ordered maintenance.

The parties may agree to exclude the recipient's decreased need for support from consideration in determinations to modify support. The settlement agreement incorporated into the dissolution judgment in In re Marriage of Silber, 176 Ill.App.3d 853, 126 Ill.Dec. 283, 531 N.E.2d 910 (1st Dist.1988), provided that the court was not to consider "the calculation or consideration of [the wife's] future employment or the amount derived therefrom," but only "any unfavorable change in [the husband's] economic circumstances alone." *Silber*, 176 Ill.App. at 855, 126 Ill.Dec. at 284, 531 N.E.2d at 911. The court held that this agreement precluded modification or termination of maintenance, although the wife now earned $30,000 per year and had assets worth approximately $200,000. See also In re Marriage of Lehr, 217 Ill.App.3d 929, 160 Ill.Dec. 840, 578 N.E.2d 19 (1st Dist.), *appeal denied*, 142 Ill.2d 655, 164 Ill.Dec. 918, 584 N.E.2d 130 (1991) (settlement agreement specifically precluded modification as a result of recipient wife's future earnings).

(c) **Decrease in payor's ability to pay maintenance.** Reductions in maintenance have been permitted when the payor spouse's income has declined due to unemployment or other financial reverses. See, e.g., In re Marriage of Columbo, 197 Ill.App.3d 767, 144 Ill.Dec. 159, 555 N.E.2d 56 (2d Dist.1990) (reduction in maintenance was not error; husband's financial circumstances had worsened substantially following his retirement); In re Marriage of Ingram, 185 Ill.App.3d 395, 133 Ill.Dec. 520, 541 N.E.2d 731 (5th Dist.1989) (reduction in maintenance and denial of request to terminate maintenance were proper; payor had suffered financial setbacks, but still had sufficient income to pay maintenance as reduced).

Reductions in the payor's ability to pay maintenance that are not fortuitous cannot be used to modify maintenance obligations. See, e.g., In re Marriage of Wiley, 199 Ill.App.3d 223, 145 Ill.Dec. 170, 556 N.E.2d 788 (4th Dist.), *appeal denied*, 133 Ill.2d 575, 149 Ill.Dec. 340, 561 N.E.2d 710 (1990) (upholding denial of husband's petition to decrease maintenance; evidence supported finding that job change was not in good faith, and was an attempt to evade his support responsibilities); Pierce v. Pierce, 69 Ill.App.3d 42, 25 Ill.Dec. 511, 386 N.E.2d 1175 (5th Dist.1979) (expenditures related to payor's remarriage and setting up a new household were not fortuitous but were voluntary; no substantial change in circumstances was shown and a modification was not warranted).

(6) **Termination of support or maintenance.** Modification in IMDMA § 510(a) also includes the possibility of terminating maintenance, and of terminating children's support. The statute provides that the payor can petition for the termination of maintenance upon the happening of any of the statutory events recited in IMDMA § 510(c) (unless there is a provision to the contrary), see Author's Note (11) below; and IMDMA § 510(d) provides that a payor can petition for the termination of a child's support when a child is emancipated (unless there is a provision to the contrary, or support is provided pursuant to IMDMA §§ 505.2 or 513). See Author's Note (17) below.

Termination of maintenance or support may also be justified where the change in circumstances is so extreme as to warrant a complete termination of support or maintenance, rather than a mere reduction in payments. For example, termination may be appropriate where maintenance has been paid for a sufficient amount of time to enable the recipient spouse to become self-sufficient, In re Marriage of Frus, 202 Ill.App.3d 844, 148 Ill.Dec. 240, 560 N.E.2d 638 (3d Dist.1990), *appeal denied*, 136 Ill.2d 543, 153 Ill.Dec. 373, 567 N.E.2d 331 (1991) (statutory goal of rehabilitative maintenance had been achieved; wife had obtained master's degree and was employed as a psychotherapist); or where a spouse has refused to seek employment in order to become self-sufficient, In re Marriage of McGory, 185 Ill.App.3d 517, 133 Ill.Dec. 590, 541 N.E.2d 801 (3d Dist.1989) (affirming termination of maintenance; wife had failed to complete college degree or obtain employment in five years following the dissolution), or where a recipient has become financially independent. See Author's Note (7), below; IMDMA § 504 Author's Note (5).

(7) **Termination of rehabilitative maintenance.** The recipient of maintenance has an affirmative obligation to seek the training and skills necessary to become financially independent. In re Marriage of Courtright, 229 Ill.App.3d 1089, 172 Ill.Dec. 258, 595 N.E.2d 619 (3d Dist.1992). See IMDMA § 504 Author's Note (5).

After the payor files a petition for modification pursuant to § 510, the court considers the following factors:

> [O]nce [petitioner] shows a substantial change of circumstances, the burden then shifts to [recipient] to prove she is actively acquiring skills and training, is making a good faith effort to seek appropriate employment, is appropriately employed, or,

for good reason, is unable to work toward, or obtain, financial independence. What is "appropriate" employment or whether she is able to acquire partial or full financial independence will depend, in part, on her health, age, marketable skills, education, capacity for employment, station in life, talents, financial and business ability, training, experience, physical, emotional and mental capacity, the employment market for her particular training and skills, and whether she still has minor children living with her. If the trial court, upon allowing a petition for modification under section 510(a), finds that a spouse receiving maintenance is appropriately employed, it may reduce maintenance commensurate with her ability to gain financial independence; on the other hand, if the spouse receiving maintenance is able to work but unwilling to obtain appropriate employment and is not making a good faith effort to gain financial independence, it may reduce or discontinue maintenance. Conversely, if the court finds that there is good reason for her inability to achieve full or partial financial independence, it may continue such maintenance and extend its duration.

In re Marriage of Gunn, 233 Ill.App.3d 165, 179, 174 Ill.Dec. 381, 391, 598 N.E.2d 1013, 1023 (5th Dist.1992).

For example, the court in In re Marriage of Henzler, 134 Ill.App.3d 318, 89 Ill.Dec. 261, 480 N.E.2d 147 (4th Dist.1985), terminated maintenance when the recipient wife was able to support herself. The court found that the statutory goal of rehabilitation had been realized; the wife had completed a college degree and was employed at a salary of $20,000. Conversely, the court in In re Marriage of McGory, 185 Ill.App.3d 517, 133 Ill.Dec. 590, 541 N.E.2d 801 (3d Dist.1989), terminated maintenance to the wife when she failed to become financially independent in the five years since the dissolution of marriage. The court found that the wife failed to make a reasonably diligent attempt to earn a college degree, and failed to seek employment. The application of this standard may be harsh. See, e.g., In re Marriage of Frus, 202 Ill.App.3d 844, 148 Ill.Dec. 240, 560 N.E.2d 638 (3d Dist.1990) (granting husband's petition to terminate maintenance because "the statutory goal of rehabilitative maintenance has been achieved;" despite the fact that husband earned $28,500 per month and wife earned $2,400 per month).

In certain cases, particularly following a marriage of long duration where the recipient spouse remained in the home as a full-time homemaker and parent, immediate rehabilitation may be unrealistic and inappropriate. See, e.g., In re Marriage of Carpel, 232 Ill.App.3d 806, 173 Ill.Dec. 873, 597 N.E.2d 847 (4th Dist.1992) (failure of recipient wife to secure employment enabling her to become self-sufficient did not preclude her from receiving an extension or increase in maintenance; wife had been a full-time homemaker throughout 17–year marriage and had enjoyed a comfortable lifestyle that she could not now maintain). See also the 1993 amendments to IMDMA § 504 and accompanying Author's Notes.

(8) **Amendment to Judgment—Form.** There follows a sample amendment to judgment that modifies the provisions of the original settlement agreement incorporated in the judgment pertaining to maintenance, children's support and education. See IMDMA § 502 Author's Note (11) for corresponding sample settlement agreement paragraphs that are modified by the following amendment to judgment.

IN THE CIRCUIT COURT OF COOK COUNTY, ILLINOIS
COUNTY DEPARTMENT—DOMESTIC RELATIONS DIVISION

IN RE THE MARRIAGE OF)
)
SUSAN JELLYBY,)
)
       Petitioner,)
)
and) No. ___ D _____
)
ARTHUR JELLYBY,)
)
       Respondent.)

AMENDMENT TO JUDGMENT

THIS CAUSE coming on to be heard upon the Petition of the Petitioner, SUSAN JELLYBY ("SUSAN"), filed pursuant to Section 510 of the Illinois Marriage and Dissolution of Marriage Act, to modify the provisions pertaining to maintenance, children's support, and children's education contained in the Agreement of the parties dated _____, 199_ (hereinafter the "Agreement"), incorporated in the Judgment of Dissolution of Marriage entered by this Court on _____, 199_ (hereinafter the "Judgment"), and upon the Response and Counter-petition of Respondent, ARTHUR JELLYBY ("ARTHUR"), and the Court being fully advised in the premises, FINDS:

    A. The Court has jurisdiction of the parties to and of the subject matter of this cause.

    B. The parties have come to an agreement, the provisions of which modify the Agreement incorporated into the Judgment. The provisions of the modifying agreement of the parties are incorporated in this Amendment to Judgment.

    C. The circumstances of each of the parties and the children of the parties have changed since the original Agreement, and since the entry of the Judgment.

    D. The provisions of the modifying agreement incorporated in this Amendment to Judgment settle all of the matters in dispute between the parties.

    IT IS THEREFORE HEREBY ORDERED, ADJUDGED, and DECREED that the provisions of the Agreement, incorporated into the Judgment, are modified as follows:

    1. Paragraphs 2(a) and 2(b) of the Agreement incorporated into the Judgment are stricken, and in lieu thereof is the following paragraph 2(a) (there shall no longer be a paragraph 2(b)):

2(a). ARTHUR agrees, because of the marital and other family relationship, to pay to SUSAN for the period from January 1, 1996 through December 31, 1996 the sum of ONE THOUSAND EIGHT HUNDRED DOLLARS ($1,800.00) per month, and for the period from January 1, 1997 through December 31, 1997 the sum of ONE THOUSAND DOLLARS ($1,000.00) per month, provided, however, the payments pursuant to this paragraph 2(a) shall terminate upon the first event to happen, in point of time, of the following five events (hereinafter referred to as "termination events"): (1) the death of SUSAN; (2) the remarriage of SUSAN; (3) the cohabitation by SUSAN with another person on a resident, continuing conjugal basis; (4) the death of ARTHUR; (5) the payment by ARTHUR to SUSAN of twenty-four (24) monthly payments; after which first event all of the payments pursuant to this paragraph 2(a) shall terminate, and ARTHUR shall be forever released and discharged from any and all obligation to pay to SUSAN any further maintenance.

2. Paragraphs 4(a) and 4(b) of the Agreement incorporated into the Judgment are hereby stricken, and in lieu thereof are the following:

4(a). ARTHUR agrees to pay to SUSAN for the support and maintenance of Caddy, one of the children of the parties, the sum of ONE THOUSAND TWO HUNDRED DOLLARS ($1,200.00) per month, the first monthly payment of $1,200.00 to be paid on January 1, 1996, and a like payment of $1,200.00 to be paid on the first day of each succeeding month thereafter during the minority of Caddy. The support for Caddy shall terminate on _____, 199__, the day on which Caddy reaches her majority, except that the termination date shall not apply to any arrearage that may remain unpaid on that date.

4(b). ARTHUR agrees to pay to SUSAN for the support and maintenance of Peepy, one of the children of the parties, the sum of ONE THOUSAND TWO HUNDRED DOLLARS ($1,200.00) per month, the first monthly payment of $1,200.00 to be paid on January 1, 1996, and a like payment of $1,200.00 to be paid on the first day of each succeeding month thereafter during the minority of Peepy. The support for Peepy shall terminate on _____, 199__, the day on which Peepy reaches his majority, except that the termination date shall not apply to any arrearage that may remain unpaid on that date.

3. Paragraph 4(f) of the Agreement incorporated into the Judgment is hereby stricken, and in lieu thereof is the following:

4(f). ARTHUR agrees, to the extent of his financial ability, to pay all reasonable costs of room, board and tuition for four consecutive years of college immediately following graduation from high school for Caddy and Peepy, providing the child in question has the ability and desire to attend college, and providing the choice of college is jointly approved by ARTHUR and SUSAN, after considering the wishes of the child in question.

750 ILCS 5/510 FAMILIES

IT IS THEREFORE HEREBY FURTHER ORDERED, ADJUDGED, and DECREED:

4. Each party shall pay his or her own attorney's fees and costs incurred in connection with the post-decree litigation and this Amendment to Judgment.

5. To the extent that this Amendment to Judgment changes or modifies the Agreement incorporated into the Judgment, or is in conflict with them, the terms and provisions of this Amendment to Judgment shall and are hereby deemed to be controlling. In all other respects, the Agreement incorporated into the Judgment remains in full force and effect.

6. The Court retains jurisdiction of the parties hereto and of this matter to enforce the terms of the Agreement incorporated into the Judgment, and this Amendment to Judgment.

ENTER:

_____
JUDGE

APPROVED:

_____
SUSAN JELLYBY

_____
ARTHUR JELLYBY

Samuel Kenge
Kenge and Carboy
Attorneys for SUSAN JELLYBY
Address
Telephone number

(9) **Revocation or modification of property allocations.** Under IMDMA § 510(b), dispositions of property cannot be revoked or modified, unless the court finds the existence of conditions that justify reopening the judgment. The conditions that may justify reopening a property distribution can include fraud, misrepresentation, concealment, coercion, mutual mistake of fact, and the like. See 735 ILCS 5/2–1401 and accompanying Author's Notes. Property dispositions can also be modified by motions brought within 30 days of the entry of a judgment to modify or to vacate the judgment, or for a re-hearing. See 735 ILCS 5/2–1203 and accompanying Author's Notes.

IMDMA § 510(b) is important, because it means that under most situations, property provisions of an agreement or a judgment are not modifiable. The non-modifiability of property dispositions pursuant to IMDMA § 510(b) would seem to make IMDMA § 502(f) (agreement to limit modification) redundant insofar as property is concerned. The non-modifiability of property provisions should be kept in mind when installment property payments are contemplated over a substantial period of time by a payor who may be vulnerable to financial reverses. While property obligations are not subject to modification, in most cases they are dischargeable in bankruptcy. 11 U.S.C.A. § 523(a)(5). See 11 U.S.C.A. § 523 and accompanying Author's Notes.

(10) **Reservation of jurisdiction to modify property distributions.** Because of the prohibition in § 510(b) against revoking or modifying property allocations under most circumstances, in those situations where adjustments in property allocations may be necessary, it is wise for the parties to override the statute and specify in the agreement or judgment that the court shall reserve jurisdiction to make the required property adjustments. For example (the following citations are to model forms), the parties may desire modification to cause QDROs to satisfy the demands of retirement plans, see IMDMA § 502 Author's Note (11) para. 6(l)(i); to adjust for potential tax assessments, see IMDMA § 502 Author's Note (11) para. 6(o); or in situations where real estate is to be sold after the entry of the judgment of dissolution of marriage and it may be necessary to have court ordered reductions in the listing price or for other details, see IMDMA § 502 Author's Note (11) para. 6(g)(viii).

(11) **Statutory conditions for termination of maintenance.** The statutory events for the termination of maintenance are set forth in IMDMA § 510(c): (1) the death of either party, (2) the remarriage of the party receiving maintenance, or (3) the cohabitation of the party receiving maintenance with another person on a resident, continuing conjugal basis. Pursuant to § 510(c) one or more of the statutory termination events can be overridden by written agreement of the parties, or "otherwise approved by the court." See, e.g., In re Marriage of Arvin, 184 Ill.App.3d 644, 133 Ill.Dec. 53, 540 N.E.2d 919 (2d Dist.1989) (provisions for termination of maintenance in parties' settlement agreement did not include cohabitation, and the parties' agreement superseded the statutory termination provisions). "Otherwise approved by the court" has been interpreted by the Illinois Supreme Court to mean "that another arrangement is 'approved by the court,' ... ", e.g., alimony in gross. In re Marriage of Freeman, 106 Ill.2d 290, 298, 88 Ill.Dec. 11, 14, 478 N.E.2d 326, 329 (1985).

(12) **Agreement for maintenance beyond statutory conditions: Tax implications.** In a situation where the parties have agreed to the payment of alimony in gross of a fixed amount for a set period of time regardless of the happening of the statutory events, but where they want to maintain the deductibility/taxation characteristics of alimony, the parties will want to override the statutory termination events in IMDMA § 510(c), by agreement, except for the statutory termination event of the death of the payee. *Cf.* In re Marriage of Freeman, 106 Ill.2d 290, 88 Ill.Dec. 11, 478 N.E.2d 326 (1985). It is necessary to maintain the statutory termination event of the death of the payee in order to gain deductibility/taxation under the Internal Revenue Code. See Internal Revenue Code §§ 71, 215 and accompanying Author's Notes.

(13) **Cross reference—Form.** See IMDMA § 502 Author's Note (11) para. 2(c) for a model clause in which the maintenance in gross is to be paid in all events except the death of the payee.

(14) **Provisions for maintenance after payor's death.** The parties may want to provide for the continuation of maintenance after the death of the payor. This is usually accomplished by means of an estate guaranty, life insurance, or an insurance trust. Care should be taken to use appropriate language to avoid the potential inconsistency of terminating the payments on the death of the payor in the maintenance part of the agreement and continuing them in the security part of the agreement. See IMDMA § 502 Author's Note (11) para. 2(c)(iii) (estate guaranty), and Article VII (life insurance and life insurance trust).

(15) **Termination of maintenance upon remarriage.** Maintenance terminates upon the remarriage of the party receiving the maintenance. IMDMA § 510(c). See, e.g., In re Marriage of Erickson, 136 Ill.App.3d 907, 91 Ill.Dec. 346, 483 N.E.2d 692 (2d Dist.1985). This is true even if the remarriage is subsequently declared invalid. In re Marriage of Harris, 203 Ill.App.3d 241, 148 Ill.Dec. 541, 560 N.E.2d 1138 (1st Dist.1990) (affirming denial of maintenance to wife after her subsequent marriage was invalidated; the statutory use of "remarriage" referred to the marriage ceremony, not a marital status) (relying upon Kolb v. Kolb, 99 Ill.App.3d 895, 55 Ill.Dec. 128, 425 N.E.2d 1301 (1st Dist.1981)). Unallocated maintenance and child support cannot be unilaterally reduced by the payor spouse when the recipient spouse remarries; the payor spouse must petition the court for modification pursuant to IMDMA § 510. In re Marriage of Erickson, 136 Ill.App.3d 907, 91 Ill.Dec. 346, 483 N.E.2d 692 (2d Dist.1985).

(16) **Termination of maintenance upon finding of cohabitation.** IMDMA § 510(c) provides that maintenance terminates if the recipient cohabits with another person on a resident, continuing conjugal basis. Cohabitation as defined by the statute has all the characteristics of a marriage except for the license. In the absence of common law marriage in Illinois, the question is whether a de facto marriage exists. In re Marriage of Caradonna, 197 Ill.App.3d 155, 143 Ill.Dec. 175, 553 N.E.2d 1161 (2d Dist.1990) ("the most likely reason the legislature added the provision allowing termination of maintenance when there is conjugal cohabitation is that it intended to end the inequities caused when a former spouse had in fact entered into a husband-wife relationship, although not formalized legally, and was still entitled to maintenance merely because Illinois does not recognize common-law marriages"). The burden of proof to show that there is cohabitation sufficient to terminate the maintenance is on the party seeking to terminate the maintenance. In re Marriage of Lambdin, 245 Ill.App.3d 797, 184 Ill.Dec. 789, 613 N.E.2d 1381 (4th Dist.1993).

The courts consider both the nature of the relationship and the financial circumstances. Although a casual relationship is insufficient to constitute the type of cohabitation that will terminate maintenance, it is not necessary that there be a sexual relationship. In re Marriage of Sappington, 106 Ill.2d 456, 88 Ill.Dec. 61, 478 N.E.2d 376 (1985); In re Marriage of Johnson, 215 Ill.App.3d 174, 158 Ill.Dec. 742, 574 N.E.2d 855 (4th Dist.1991). There is not yet a case in Illinois determining whether a homosexual relationship constitutes cohabitation under subsection 510(c).

The courts also consider the financial arrangements of the relationship. Several courts have insisted that maintenance does not terminate when the recipient cohabits with another person because the cohabitation is immoral; rather, the maintenance terminates because the cohabitation may "materially affec[t] the recipient spouse's need for support because [the recipient] either receive[s] support from her co-resident or use[s] maintenance monies to support" the co-resident. In re Marriage of Bramson, 83 Ill.App.3d 657, 39 Ill.Dec. 85, 404 N.E.2d 469 (1st Dist.1980). A short term relationship, even if intense, where there was no mixing of finances, has been held not to constitute cohabitation nor to reduce the wife's need for support so as to terminate maintenance under the statute. See, e.g., In re Marriage of Caradonna, 197 Ill.App.3d 155, 143 Ill.Dec. 175, 553 N.E.2d 1161 (2d Dist.1990) (although recipient wife resided in other man's home for six months, the payor spouse did not establish continual conjugal cohabitation; there was no evidence of commingled funds and the cohabitation did not affect the wife's need for support); In re Marriage of Bramson, 83 Ill.App.3d 657, 39 Ill.Dec. 85, 404 N.E.2d 469 (1st Dist.1980) (cohabitation for four and one half months did not constitute continual cohabitation, especially when there was no commingling of funds "as might be expected in a husband-wife relationship"). But see In re Marriage of Herrin, 262 Ill.App.3d 573, 199 Ill.Dec. 814, 634 N.E.2d 1168 (4th Dist.1994) ("if the court finds the required relationship exists based on its assessment of the totality of the circumstances ... it need not make any specific finding as to the maintenance recipient's financial need;" termination of maintenance due to wife's cohabitation was proper although wife's companion slept elsewhere most nights in another residence, wife and companion saw each other every day, engaged in sexual relations and took vacations together).

Cohabitation between the parties, rather than with another person, does not operate to terminate maintenance. The court in In re Marriage of Antonich, 148 Ill.App.3d 575, 102 Ill.Dec. 97, 499 N.E.2d 654 (2d Dist.1986) *appeal dismissed*, 113 Ill.2d 574, 106 Ill.Dec. 44, 505 N.E.2d 350 (1987), reasoned that the former spouse did not qualify as "another person" under the statutory language. Furthermore, the recipient spouse's need for support was not diminished during the cohabitation, there was no issue of the payor indirectly supporting a cohabitant, and the public policy of encouraging reconciliation was furthered.

The parties may agree that cohabitation will not be grounds for termination. See, e.g., In re Marriage of Arvin, 184 Ill.App.3d 644, 133 Ill.Dec. 53, 540 N.E.2d 919 (2d Dist.1989) (valid separation agreement expressly provided that maintenance would terminate upon recipient's death or remarriage; conjugal cohabitation was not a basis for termination under the agreement). However, even if an agreement specifically enumerates reasons for termination, a party may still petition the court for modification because of a change in economic circumstances under IMDMA § 510(a). *Id.*

The court in In re Marriage of Klein, 231 Ill.App.3d 901, 173 Ill.Dec. 335, 596 N.E.2d 1214 (4th Dist.1992), interpreted IMDMA § 510 as prohibiting an initial award of maintenance if the would be recipient is cohabiting at the time the initial award is to be made. The wife in *Klein* conceded that any maintenance award would be terminated if she continued to cohabit after the initial judgment was entered, but argued that IMDMA § 510 did not apply to initial awards of maintenance. The court rejected her argument, stating that "[t]here should be no distinction between whether the petitioner's obligation is terminated before it ripens or after maintenance is ordered," and that an award of maintenance despite her admission that she was cohabitating "would be inconsistent with the policy of section 510(c)." In re Marriage of Klein, 231 Ill.App.3d at 906, 173 Ill.Dec. at 337–38, 596 N.E.2d at 1216–17. The court remanded the action for a determination of whether the wife was cohabiting within the definition of the statute.

(17) **Termination of child support upon emancipation.** IMDMA § 510(d) terminates support for a child upon the emancipation of the child, unless otherwise agreed in writing or expressly provided in the judgment, or as otherwise provided in the statute. Emancipation is most commonly the child's attainment of majority, which in Illinois is 18 years of age. In re Marriage of Ferraro, 211 Ill.App.3d 797, 156 Ill.Dec. 160, 570 N.E.2d 636 (1st Dist.1991). See also 755 ILCS 5/11–1. Emancipation, however, can also occur before the age of 18, but only upon a showing of extraordinary circumstances. Meyer v. Meyer, 222 Ill.App.3d 357, 164 Ill.Dec. 800, 583 N.E.2d 716 (5th Dist.1991) (minor child was emancipated under the meaning of the statute; child had enrolled in Job Corps, lived in a state other than where the custodial mother lived, and was financially self-sufficient). The marriage of the child may also a basis for a finding of emancipation.

While child support for one child in most instances terminates by the terms of § 510(d) when the child is emancipated, the modification of unallocated child support and maintenance payments must be pursuant to a IMDMA § 510 petition for modification. Unallocated support payments comprehending support for a single child and spousal maintenance may be modified only with court approval. See, e.g., Potocki v. Potocki, 98 Ill.App.3d 501, 53 Ill.Dec. 923, 424 N.E.2d 714 (1st Dist.1981) (unallocated maintenance and support award for parties' only child modifiable after child's emancipation only upon petition to the court for modification).

Moreover, unless the parties agree to the contrary, a payor parent is not permitted to reduce support payments for more than one child that are paid by lump sum payments on a pro rata basis when one child is emancipated:

> the unilateral reduction of child-support payments constitutes a modification of the support order.... It is the function of the court to determine whether there should be a *pro rata* reduction in lump-sum periodic support payments when one of several children is emancipated, or whether other equitable considerations require that the reduction be a lower amount, or in fact whether there should be any reduction in the payments.... The responsible parent should petition the court for a judicial determination of the amount the support payments should be reduced due to changed circumstances.

Finley v. Finley, 81 Ill.2d 317, 329, 43 Ill.Dec. 12, 17–18, 410 N.E.2d 12, 17–18 (1980) (citations omitted). See also Meyer v. Meyer, 222 Ill.App.3d 357, 164 Ill.Dec. 800, 583 N.E.2d 716 (5th Dist.1991) (child support payments automatically ended by operation of law when sole child was emancipated, however, court "would reach a different conclusion had the case involved unallocated support payments for multiple children, for in such cases the parent responsible for tendering the payments cannot make a unilateral pro rata reduction in the amount he or she pays when one of the children becomes emancipated, absent agreement to the contrary"); In re Marriage of Henry, 156 Ill.2d 541, 190 Ill.Dec. 773, 622 N.E.2d 803 (1993) ("the amount required to support a second child is incrementally less than that necessary to support one child"). For example, the court in In re Marriage of Wettstein, 160 Ill.App.3d 554, 113 Ill.Dec. 1, 514 N.E.2d 783 (4th Dist.1987), *appeal denied*, 118 Ill.2d 544, 117 Ill.Dec. 233, 520 N.E.2d 394 (1988), only reduced the father's child support payments from $335 to $275 after three of the four children covered by the payments had attained the age of majority. Although the modified payments were to support only one child, rather than four, the court found that the remaining child was older and the expenses of her maintenance had increased.

The problem of the courts not permitting pro rata reduction of lump sum payments for multiple children can be avoided by stating the support for each child separately in settlement agreements. See IMDMA § 502 Author's Note (11) paras. 4(a) and 4(b). The provisions for children support are, however, still susceptible to increase by modification.

(18) **Continuation of child support after emancipation.** Judgments and agreements seldom provide for support for children after majority, except pursuant to IMDMA § 513 for disabled children or for educational expenses. See IMDMA § 513 and accompanying Author's Notes. In some instances, however, the parties may want to provide for support after the majority of a child, for example, in order to provide the custodial parent of a child with money for the child when he or she returns home for a college summer vacation. This can be accomplished through an agreement between the parties. Medical insurance is also commonly provided for children until they

complete college or they can no longer be covered on the policy of one of their parents, pursuant to IMDMA § 513. See also IMDMA § 502 Author's Note (11) para. 4(e) for medical insurance sample paragraph.

(19) **Child support after payor's death.** IMDMA § 510 (d) expressly provides that an existing obligation to pay child support or educational expenses is not terminated by the death of the payor spouse. The obligation may be enforced, modified, revoked, or commuted to a lump sum at any time.

(20) **Petition for child support and educational expenses after payor's death.** IMDMA § 510(e) provides that a petition seeking to have a court order child support and educational expenses is not extinguished by the death of a parent, and it may be filed either before or after the parent's death. Prior to the 1992 amendment, case law did not allow children to obtain educational support from their divorced parents' estates unless there was an obligation for the parent to provide such support prior to his death. See Treacy v. Treacy, 204 Ill.App.3d 282, 149 Ill.Dec. 802, 562 N.E.2d 266 (1st Dist.1990).

When, pursuant to § 510(d), provision is made at the time of the dissolution of the marriage for payment of child support and educational expenses in case of the death of the payor parent, for example, by an insurance trust, and the parties intend that the provision be in lieu of a claim against the payor's estate pursuant to § 510(e), the agreement should expressly set forth that the insurance trust is in lieu of the claim against the estate. See § 502 Author's Note (11) para. 7(c). If the provision in lieu of the claim against the estate is insufficient to pay the children's support or the educational expenses, however, the court probably retains the jurisdiction to order additional money from the deceased payor parent's estate pursuant to § 510(e).

The time for filing a claim for child support or educational expenses against the estate of a deceased payor parent is governed by § 18-3 of the Probate Act, 755 ILCS 5/18-3, and is six months from the date of the first publication of notice of the death of the decedent, or three months from the date of mailing or delivery of notice, whichever is later.

750 ILCS 5/511

§ 511. Procedure

A judgment of dissolution or of legal separation or of declaration of invalidity of marriage may be enforced or modified by order of court pursuant to petition.

(a) Any judgment entered within this State may be enforced or modified in the judicial circuit wherein such judgment was entered or last modified by the filing of a petition with notice mailed to the respondent at his last known address, or by the issuance of summons to the respondent. If neither party continues to reside in the county wherein such judgment was entered or last modified, the court on the motion of either party or on its own motion may transfer a post-judgment proceeding, including a proceeding under Section 706.1 of this Act, to another county or judicial circuit, as appropriate, where either party resides. If the post-judgment proceeding is with respect to maintenance or support, any such transfer shall be to the county or judicial circuit wherein the recipient or proposed recipient of such maintenance or support resides.

(b) In any post-judgment proceeding to enforce or modify in one judicial circuit the judgment of another judicial circuit of this State, the moving party shall commence the proceeding by filing a petition establishing the judgment and attaching a copy of the judgment as a part of the petition. The parties shall continue to be designated as in the original proceeding. Notice of the filing of the petition shall be mailed to the clerk of the court wherein the judgment was entered and last modified in the same manner as notice is mailed when registering a foreign judgment. Summons shall be served as provided by law.

(c) In any post-judgment proceeding to enforce or modify the judgment of another state, the moving party shall commence the proceeding by filing a petition to enroll that judgment, attaching a copy thereof as a part of the petition and proceed as provided for in paragraph (b) hereof.

(d) In any post-judgment proceeding to enforce a judgment or order for payment of maintenance or support, including a proceeding under Section 706.1 of this Act, where the terms of such judgment or order provide that payments of such maintenance or support are to be made to the clerk of the court and where neither party continues to reside in the county wherein such judgment or order was entered or last modified, the court on the motion of either party or on its own motion may transfer the collection of the maintenance or support to the clerk of the court in another county or judicial circuit, as appropriate, wherein the recipient of the maintenance or support payments resides.

Author's Notes

Analysis

1. Enforcement and modifications outside county of judgment.
2. Notice.
3. Petition for rule to show cause.
4. Procedure.
5. Civil and criminal contempt: Sanctions.
6. Petition for Rule to Show Cause—Form.
7. Rule to Show Cause Order—Form.
8. Attachment Order—Form.
9. Interplay with IMDMA § 512.
10. Petition for rule to show cause: Defenses.
11. Appeal.

(1) **Enforcement and modifications outside county of judgment.** Most enforcement or modification proceedings take place pursuant to § 511 in the county where the original judgment or order was entered. Section 511 also sets forth the procedure for enforcement or modification proceedings where it is inappropriate for the action to take place in the county in which the original pleadings were held. In addition, subparagraph (c) sets forth the procedure for enforcing or modifying a judgment of another state.

(2) **Notice.** Where the judgment sought to be modified or enforced is in the same county where it was entered or last modified, notice is sufficient either when it is mailed to the respondent at his last known address, or by issuance of summons to the respondent. *Nota bene* that notice to the respondent's attorney is not sufficient. See In re Marriage of Mullins, 135 Ill.App.3d 279, 89 Ill.Dec. 771, 481 N.E.2d 322 (4th Dist.1985). "The attorney-client relationship terminates after the judgment of divorce is entered." In re Marriage of Ponsart, 118 Ill.App.3d 664, 667–668, 74 Ill.Dec. 241, 242–243, 455 N.E.2d 271, 272–273 (1st Dist.1983) (citations omitted). Where the action takes place in a judicial circuit other than where the judgment was entered or last modified, summons to the respondent is necessary. Notice to the clerk of the court where the judgment was entered or last modified or, to the foreign jurisdiction where the judgment was entered, is required. See 735 ILCS 5/12–650 et seq. and accompanying Author's Notes for the enrollment of a foreign judgment.

(3) **Petition for rule to show cause.** The most effective way to enforce a judgment for dissolution of marriage, legal separation, or declaration of invalidity of marriage is by a petition for a rule to show cause why the respondent should not be held in contempt of court for failure to obey the judgment. See, e.g., In re Marriage of Lavelle, 206 Ill.App.3d 607, 152 Ill.Dec. 49, 565 N.E.2d 291 (5th Dist.1990) (regarding wife's petition for rule to show cause in response to husband's failure to pay child support, maintain health insurance for the parties' children, and make a good effort to find employment); In re Marriage of Havens, 213 Ill.App.3d 151, 156 Ill.Dec. 737, 571 N.E.2d 521 (3d Dist.1991) (both parties filed petitions for rules to show cause to enforce the terms of a divorce judgment); In re Marriage of Herkert, 245 Ill.App.3d 1068, 186 Ill.Dec. 29, 615 N.E.2d 833 (4th Dist.1993) (affirming trial court's denial of husband's petition for rule to show cause for wife's failure to allow husband visitation with parties' children). The availability of this remedy is an obvious advantage that attaches to incorporating marital settlement agreements in judgments for dissolutions, since the petition for a rule is far more efficient than initiating a new suit on the contract. Petitions for a rule to show cause can also be used to enforce temporary orders of the court.

(4) **Procedure.** Evidence of noncompliance with a court order to pay maintenance (or support) establishes a prima facie case of civil contempt. In re Marriage of Scordo, 176 Ill.App.3d 269, 125 Ill.Dec. 761, 530 N.E.2d 1170 (3d Dist.1988). If the petitioner for a rule to show cause makes a prima facie showing to the court, the burden shifts to the respondent, and the court orders a rule to issue against the respondent, directing the respondent to show cause why he should not be held in contempt of court for failure to obey the court's order. In the absence of the appearance of the respondent or his attorney in court at the time of the issuance of the rule to show cause, the rule and a copy of the petition for a rule should be served in accordance with Supreme Court Rule 105(b). See, e.g., Circuit Court of Cook County Rule 6.1(a). An affidavit of appropriate service should be attached to the rule and filed with the court. If the respondent fails to appear in response to proper service of the rule, he can be brought before the court by an order of attachment. A hearing is then held at the time and date specified in the rule, or when the respondent is produced pursuant to the attachment.

(5) **Civil and criminal contempt: Sanctions.** The court can impose various sanctions, including fines and imprisonment, against a party found to be in contempt of court for failure to obey a court order. Contempt may be either civil or criminal contempt. The primary distinction between civil and criminal contempt is the purpose for which the sanctions are imposed: sanctions intended to coerce the contemnor to

perform a particular act are civil in nature, and sanctions imposed as a punishment for past misconduct are criminal in nature. Contempt may also be either direct or indirect: direct contempt occurs in the presence of the court, and indirect contempt does not. For a lengthy review of the different types of contempt, the requisite procedure for each, and the rights of the respondent, see In re Marriage of Betts, 200 Ill.App.3d 26, 146 Ill.Dec. 441, 558 N.E.2d 404 (4th Dist.1990), cert. denied, 136 Ill.2d 541, 153 Ill.Dec. 370, 567 N.E.2d 328 (1991).

The contempt imposed in family law actions is usually indirect civil contempt for failure to obey a court order, e.g, the payment of children's support. The respondent can purge himself or herself of the contempt and terminate the punishment by complying with the court's order. In effect, the respondent holds the keys to the jailhouse. See, e.g., In re Marriage of Havens, 213 Ill.App.3d 151, 156 Ill.Dec. 737, 571 N.E.2d 521 (3d Dist.1991) (contemnor could purge contempt by returning items of value to husband as ordered by the court, or by paying the replacement value of items she could not return); In re Marriage of Hilkovitch, 124 Ill.App.3d 401, 79 Ill.Dec. 891, 464 N.E.2d 795 (1st Dist.1984) (husband could regain freedom if he paid one-third of unallocated maintenance and child support arrearages). In Sanders v. Shephard, 258 Ill.App.3d 626, 196 Ill.Dec. 845, 630 N.E.2d 1010 (1st Dist.), *appeal allowed*, 156 Ill.2d 566, 202 Ill.Dec. 931, 638 N.E.2d 1125 (1994), the court upheld the father's fourth consecutive contempt order incarcerating him for failing to comply with a protective order issued under the Domestic Violence Act requiring him to return his daughter to her mother. The father had been incarcerated for six years for his contempt. The court wrote

> Incarceration for civil contempt can continue only so long as it serves a coercive purpose. Once it is clear that a contemnor will not be compelled to comply, the rationale for the incarceration ceases—its character changes from remedial to punitive—and due process requires the contemnor's release.... The test to determine whether confinement no longer is coercive is whether the contemnor has shown there is no "realistic possibility" or "substantial likelihood" that continued confinement will accomplish its coercive purpose.

Sanders v. Shephard, 258 Ill.App.3d at 630, 196 Ill.Dec. at 849, 630 N.E.2d at 1014 (citations omitted). The court held that "the passage of time, standing alone, is insufficient to show an unwillingness forever to reveal the whereabouts of the child." Id.

An example of criminal contempt is where a court punishes a person for something that is an affront to the court, e.g., a violation of an order of protection, or a lawyer continuing to argue when instructed by the judge to stop, and the punishment is not abated upon compliance. See, e.g., In re Marriage of Betts, 200 Ill.App.3d 26, 146 Ill.Dec. 441, 558 N.E.2d 404 (4th Dist.1990) (husband's practice of refusing to make child support payments until after contempt proceedings were commenced constituted sufficient basis for punishing him for indirect criminal contempt).

A respondent is entitled to greater due process protection if charged with criminal contempt than if charged with civil contempt. The contemnor must be given notice that criminal sanctions may be imposed against him, must have the opportunity to answer, has the privilege against self-incrimination, and must be proven guilty beyond a reasonable doubt. In re Marriage of Betts, 200 Ill.App.3d 26, 146 Ill.Dec. 441, 558 N.E.2d 404 (4th Dist.1990); In re Marriage of Morse, 240 Ill.App.3d 296, 180 Ill.Dec. 563, 607 N.E.2d 632 (2d Dist.1993).

The alleged contemnor is entitled to a jury trial if the aggregate punishments for a particular course of criminally contemptuous conduct exceeds the punishment normally imposed for misdemeanors and the punishments are not imposed immediately after the contemptuous conduct occurs. In re Marriage of Betts, 200 Ill.App.3d at 50, 146 Ill.Dec. at 457, 558 N.E.2d at 420.

(6) **Petition for Rule to Show Cause—Form.**

IN THE CIRCUIT COURT OF COOK COUNTY, ILLINOIS
COUNTY DEPARTMENT—DOMESTIC RELATIONS DIVISION

IN RE THE MARRIAGE OF)
)
LUCY DEDLOCK,)
)
        Petitioner,)
)
and) No. ___ D _____
)
LEICESTER DEDLOCK,)
)
        Respondent.)

PETITION FOR RULE TO SHOW CAUSE

Petitioner, LUCY DEDLOCK ("LUCY"), brings the following Petition for a Rule to Show Cause against Respondent, LEICESTER DEDLOCK ("LEICESTER"):

1. On _____, 19__, a Judgment of Dissolution of Marriage was entered between the parties which incorporated a Settlement Agreement of the same date, and which Settlement Agreement provided as follows in regard to the payment of unallocated maintenance and children's support by LEICESTER to LUCY:

    2(a). LEICESTER agrees, because of the marital and other family relationship, and in complete discharge of his obligation to pay alimony, maintenance, and support to LUCY, to pay to LUCY the sum of SIX THOUSAND DOLLARS ($6,000) per month, the first payment of $6,000 to be paid on the 1st day of _____, 19__, and a like payment of $6,000 to be paid on the same day of each succeeding month thereafter for the following 59 months (60 total monthly payments).

2. Contrary to the provisions of the Settlement Agreement dated _____, 19__, incorporated in the Judgment of Dissolution of Marriage entered on _____, 19__, LEICESTER has failed and refused to make the payments to LUCY required to be made by paragraph 2(a) of the Settlement Agreement for the months of September, October, November, and December, 199__. LEICESTER therefore owes to LUCY the sum of $24,000.

3. LEICESTER has the financial capacity to make the aforedescribed payments, and his failure and refusal to make the payments to LUCY is willful and contemptuous of the Judgment of this Court.

750 ILCS 5/511 **FAMILIES**

4. LEICESTER's failure to comply with paragraph 2(a) of the Settlement Agreement incorporated in the Judgment of Dissolution of Marriage entered on _____, 19__, is without cause or justification, and LUCY is entitled to attorney's fees and costs pursuant to Section 508(b) of the Illinois Marriage and Dissolution of Marriage Act.

WHEREFORE, Petitioner, LUCY DEDLOCK, prays as follows against Respondent, LEICESTER DEDLOCK.

1. The Court issue a rule requiring Respondent, LEICESTER DEDLOCK, to show cause, if any he can, why he should not be held in contempt of this court and punished for failure to comply with the Judgment of Dissolution entered by this Court.

2. The Court enter a Judgment in favor of Petitioner, LUCY DEDLOCK, and against Respondent, LEICESTER DEDLOCK, for the arrearages in unallocated maintenance and children's support in the amount of $24,000.

3. The Court require Respondent, LEICESTER DEDLOCK, to pay the attorney's fees and costs incurred by Petitioner, LUCY DEDLOCK, in bringing this Petition.

4. Petitioner, LUCY DEDLOCK, have such other and further relief as may be appropriate under the evidence and circumstances.

_____
LUCY DEDLOCK, Petitioner

_____
Samuel Kenge
Attorney for Petitioner

VERIFICATION BY CERTIFICATION

Under penalties of perjury as provided by law pursuant to Section 1–109 of the Illinois Code of Civil Procedure, the undersigned certifies that the statements set forth in the foregoing instrument are true and correct.

DATED: _____   _____
                                                              LUCY DEDLOCK

Samuel Kenge
Kenge and Carboy
Address
Telephone number

(7) **Rule to Show Cause Order—Form.**

IN THE CIRCUIT COURT OF COOK COUNTY, ILLINOIS
COUNTY DEPARTMENT—DOMESTIC RELATIONS DIVISION

IN RE THE MARRIAGE OF)
)
LUCY DEDLOCK,)
)
       Petitioner,)
)
and) No. ____ D _____
)
LEICESTER DEDLOCK,)
)
       Respondent.)

ORDER

The matter having come on to be heard upon the verified Petition of Petitioner, LUCY DEDLOCK, to show cause why Respondent, LEICESTER DEDLOCK, should not be held in contempt of Court, notice having been properly served, and it appearing to the Court that Respondent has willfully failed to comply with the provisions of paragraph 2(a) the Settlement Agreement incorporated in the Judgment for Dissolution of Marriage entered on _____, 19__, concerning the payment of unallocated maintenance and children's support, and the Court being fully advised in the premises.

IT IS THEREFORE HEREBY ORDERED that Respondent, LEICESTER DEDLOCK, appear before this Court on _____, 19__, at ____ a.m., and show cause, if any he can, why he should not be punished for contempt of Court for willfully refusing to comply with the provisions of paragraph 2(a) of the Settlement Agreement incorporated in the Judgment of Dissolution of Marriage entered by the Court on _____, 19__.

                      ENTER:

                        _____

                      JUDGE

                      Date: _____

Samuel Kenge
Attorney for LUCY DEDLOCK
Kenge and Carboy
Address
Telephone number

CERTIFICATE OF DELIVERY

The undersigned hereby certifies under penalties of perjury as provided by law pursuant to Section 1-109 of the Code of Civil Procedure, that the

750 ILCS 5/511   FAMILIES

above Petition for Rule to Show Cause and Order for a rule to show cause were mailed via Certified Mail (Return Receipt Requested) to LEICESTER DEDLOCK at _____, and were placed in the U.S. Mail properly addressed and mailed with first class postage prepaid to LEICESTER DEDLOCK's Attorneys at Blowers & Associates, Ltd. at _____ on the _____ day of _____, 19 __, before the hour of 5:00 p.m.

_____   _____
(Signature)   (Print Name)

(8) **Attachment Order—Form.** See also IMDMA § 713 and accompanying Author's Notes for attachments in cases of support delinquencies.

IN THE CIRCUIT COURT OF COOK COUNTY, ILLINOIS
COUNTY DEPARTMENT—DOMESTIC RELATIONS DIVISION

IN RE THE MARRIAGE OF)
)
LUCY DEDLOCK,)
)
      Petitioner,)
)
and) No. ___ D _____
)
LEICESTER DEDLOCK,)
)
      Respondent.)

ATTACHMENT ORDER

This matter coming for hearing on this date pursuant to the Order of this Court heretofore entered on _____ (date) and a rule being entered and made returnable forthwith directed to the Respondent, LEICESTER DEDLOCK, to show cause why the said Respondent should not have sanctions imposed in accordance with relief prayed for in the petition heretofore filed on _____ (date); and this matter coming on for hearing on the request for certain other relief as is set forth in the petition; and it appearing that the Respondent has been duly and properly served with the petition as aforesaid in accordance with the law as made and provided; and that the Respondent has had due notice of the hearing set for this date, and the Respondent having failed to appear; and the Court being in all respects fully informed;

IT IS ORDERED as follows:

1. That the Sheriff of _____ County, State of Illinois, is directed to take and bring the person of the Respondent, LEICESTER DEDLOCK, before this Court in Room _____, Richard J. Daley Center, Chicago, Illinois forthwith to answer to the Rule to show cause heretofore entered and to respond to the matter of relief set forth in the petition filed herein and heretofore continued for hearing to this date.

2. That the costs of processing this attachment as provided under law shall be charged to and paid by the Respondent unless otherwise ordered by the Court hereafter.

Date: _____

ENTER: _____

Judge   Judge's No.

Samuel Kenge
Kenge and Carboy
Attorneys for LUCY DEDLOCK
Address
Telephone number

(9) Interplay with IMDMA § 512. Section 511 should be read together with IMDMA § 512 "Post-judgment Venue."

(10) Petition for rule to show cause: Defenses. There are several defenses to petitions for a rule to show cause, beside the obvious one that the provision of the judgment or order has not in fact been violated. See, e.g., In re Marriage of Lavelle, 206 Ill.App.3d 607, 152 Ill.Dec. 49, 565 N.E.2d 291 (5th Dist.1990) (husband was not in contempt of court order to make child support payments through circuit court's office; husband and wife had a mutual agreement that husband would make payments directly to wife).

A party is in contempt of court when he or she willfully violates an order of the court. In re Marriage of Hartian, 222 Ill.App.3d 566, 165 Ill.Dec. 66, 584 N.E.2d 245 (1st Dist.1991). A valid defense therefore is that the violation of the court order was not a willful violation. For example, a party who has failed to pay support cannot be held in contempt for his failure so to do if he did not have the capacity to make the payment:

> A clear defense to contempt exists where the failure of a person to obey an order to pay is due to poverty, insolvency, or other misfortune, unless that inability to pay is the result of a wrongful or illegal act.... However, the defense of poverty and misfortune as a valid excuse for nonpayment has been found applicable only in the most extreme cases.... [the burden of proof to show financial inability to comply] is not met by testimony of a general nature with regard to financial status.

In re Marriage of Dall, 212 Ill.App.3d 85, 155 Ill.Dec. 520, 569 N.E.2d 1131 (5th Dist.1991) (husband failed to show that failure to pay child support was due to financial inability to comply with court order) (citations omitted). See, also, In re Marriage of Lavelle, 206 Ill.App.3d 607, 152 Ill.Dec. 49, 565 N.E.2d 291 (5th Dist.1990) (nonpayment of child support was due to lack of sufficient income).

Another possible defense is that of equitable estoppel. A claim of equitable estoppel exists where a person induces a second person to rely to his detriment on the first person's statements or conduct. Baker v. Baker, 193 Ill.App.3d 294, 140 Ill.Dec. 303, 549 N.E.2d 954 (4th Dist.), *cert. denied*, 131 Ill.2d 557, 142 Ill.Dec. 879, 553 N.E.2d 393 (1990). See, e.g., Blisset v. Blisset, 123 Ill.2d 161, 121 Ill.Dec. 931, 526 N.E.2d 125 (1988) (wife was not barred from collecting child support arrearages under theory of equitable estoppel; husband was on notice that agreement between husband

and wife that wife would not pursue support arrearages in exchange for husband not exercising his visitation rights was not enforceable, therefore any reliance on the part of the husband was not reasonable). The respondent may also claim the defense of laches, if the petitioner did not pursue her claim for an unreasonably long time, and the respondent relied upon this inaction to his detriment. See, e.g., In re Marriage of Azotea, 200 Ill.App.3d 182, 146 Ill.Dec. 587, 558 N.E.2d 550 (4th Dist.1990); In re Marriage of Yakubec, 154 Ill.App.3d 540, 107 Ill.Dec. 453, 507 N.E.2d 117 (1st Dist.1987).

(11) **Appeal.** Orders finding a person in contempt of court which impose a fine or other penalty are immediately appealable. No finding that there is no just reason for delaying appeal is required. See Supreme Court Rule 304(b)(5) Author's Note (4).

750 ILCS 5/512

§ 512. Post-judgment venue

After 30 days from the entry of a judgment of dissolution of marriage or the last modification thereof, any further proceedings to enforce or modify the judgment shall be as follows:

(a) If the respondent does not then reside within this State, further proceedings shall be had either in the judicial circuit wherein the moving party resides or where the judgment was entered or last modified.

(b) If one or both of the parties then resides in the judicial circuit wherein the judgment was entered or last modified, further proceedings shall be had in the judicial circuit that last exercised jurisdiction in the matter; provided, however, that the court may in its discretion, transfer matters involving a change in child custody to the judicial circuit where the minor or dependent child resides.

(c) If neither party then resides in the judicial circuit wherein the judgment was entered or last modified, further proceedings shall be had in that circuit or in the judicial circuit wherein either party resides or where the respondent is actively employed; provided, however, that the court may, in its discretion, transfer matters involving a change in child custody to the judicial circuit where the minor or dependent child resides.

(d) Objection to venue is waived if not made within such time as the respondent's answer is due. Counter relief shall be heard and determined by the court hearing any matter already pending.

Author's Notes

(1) **Interplay with IMDMA § 511.** The provisions of § 512, "Post-judgment Venue," should be read in connection with the provisions of IMDMA § 511, "Procedure," in order to obtain the proper venue and the appropriate way of bringing the respondent into the post-decree action. Note that objection to improper venue is waived in post-judgment proceedings if it is not raised "within such time as respondent's answer is due." § 512(d). See also IMDMA § 104 and 735 ILCS 5/2–104 for objections to improper venue.

750 ILCS 5/513

§ 513. Support for non-minor children and educational expenses

(a) The court may award sums of money out of the property and income of either or both parties or the estate of a deceased parent, as equity may require, for the support of the child or children of the parties who have attained majority in the following instances:

(1) When the child is mentally or physically disabled and not otherwise emancipated, an application for support may be made before or after the child has attained majority.

(2) The court may also make provision for the educational expenses of the child or children of the parties, whether of minor or majority age, and an application for educational expenses may be made before or after the child has attained majority, or after the death of either parent. The authority under this Section to make provision for educational expenses extends not only to periods of college education or professional or other training after graduation from high school, but also to any period during which the child of the parties is still attending high school, even though he or she attained the age 18. The educational expenses may include, but shall not be limited to, room, board, dues, tuition, transportation, books, fees, registration and application costs, medical expenses including medical insurance, dental expenses, and living expenses during the school year and periods of recess, which sums may be ordered payable to the child, to either parent, or to the educational institution, directly or through a special account or trust created for that purpose, as the court sees fit.

(b) In making awards under paragraph (1) or (2) of subsection (a), the court shall consider all relevant factors that appear reasonable and necessary, including:

(1) The financial resources of both parents.

(2) The standard of living the child would have enjoyed had the marriage not been dissolved.

(3) The financial resources of the child.

Author's Notes

Analysis

1. § 513: In general.
2. Parents' financial resources and contribution.
3. Child's financial resources and contribution.
4. Agreements on higher education made for young children.
5. Child's standing under § 513.
6. Petition for support of disabled child or educational expenses: Timing.

(1) **§ 513: In general.** Parents are usually not held financially responsible for children over the age of majority. Section 513 concerns two exceptions to this rule.

750 ILCS 5/513   **FAMILIES**

Under this Section, a divorced parent may be held responsible for a disabled non-minor child's support (see, e.g., In re Marriage of Kennedy, 170 Ill.App.3d 726, 121 Ill.Dec. 362, 525 N.E.2d 168 (5th Dist.1988)) (holding that wife was entitled to receive child support for mentally handicapped child even after child reached majority); Rosche v. Rosche, 163 Ill.App.3d 308, 114 Ill.Dec. 846, 516 N.E.2d 1001 (5th Dist.1987), *appeal denied*, 119 Ill.2d 575, 119 Ill.Dec. 397, 522 N.E.2d 1256 (1988) (denying husband's petition to require wife to continue child support payments for disabled adult child; child was not unemployable nor incapable of supporting himself), and for a non-minor child's educational expenses. The statute does not mandate that the divorced parents finance a non-minor child's education. The statute merely allows the trial court, in its discretion, to require a divorced parent to provide educational expenses after the child reaches majority. In re Support of Pearson, 111 Ill.2d 545, 551, 96 Ill.Dec. 69, 72, 490 N.E.2d 1274, 1277 (1986).

The most common controversies in litigation involving § 513 concern the extent of the need of the children, and the financial resources of the parents. For example, even if the parents have agreed upon the portion each parent will contribute to the child's education, a common dispute is whether the child should attend a state university or a private university. The choice is within the discretion of the court, after considering the financial resources of the parents, the academic record of the child, the lifestyle of the parties, and other relevant factors. The court does not actually mandate which university the child attends. The court merely determines the amount of financial assistance that the parent is obligated to provide. If the court requires that the parents only contribute enough to finance a public education and the child has no other source of income, the effect is the same as if the court had decided that the child attend a public university rather than a more expensive private university. See, e.g., In re Marriage of Calisoff, 176 Ill.App.3d 721, 126 Ill.Dec. 183, 531 N.E.2d 810 (1st Dist.1988) (remanding decision requiring husband to bear entire burden for children's educational costs because he had "limited financial resources" and "the children themselves have an obligation to lessen their parents' financial burden" by attending a less costly state university); Greiman v. Friedman, 90 Ill.App.3d 941, 46 Ill.Dec. 355, 414 N.E.2d 77 (1st Dist.1980) (remanding with directions that trial court consider husband's financial obligations to new family in addition to children's academic performance, and the lower cost of public education in determining obligation to continue payment of educational expenses for adult children).

(2) **Parents' financial resources and contribution.** The statute directs that the financial resources of both of the parents be considered. This often results in disputes over the extent of each parent's contribution to the college educations of their children. Courts frequently require each parent to make a contribution. See, e.g., In re Marriage of Kuhn, 221 Ill.App.3d 1, 163 Ill.Dec. 429, 581 N.E.2d 380 (2d Dist.1991), *appeal denied*, 143 Ill.2d 639, 167 Ill.Dec. 401, 587 N.E.2d 1016, *cert. denied*, ___ U.S. ___, 113 S.Ct. 62, 121 L.Ed.2d 30 (1992); In re Marriage of Albiani, 159 Ill.App.3d 519, 111 Ill.Dec. 126, 512 N.E.2d 30 (1st Dist.1987) (both affirming decisions requiring each parent to pay 50% of child's educational expenses). See also In re Marriage of Korte, 193 Ill.App.3d 243, 140 Ill.Dec. 255, 549 N.E.2d 906 (4th Dist.1990) (upholding order requiring husband to carry entire financial burden of child's educational expenses; wife provided indirect contributions such as laundry, hosting the child's friends, buying child's clothes, and providing housing for the summer months). However, courts usually require the parent with the superior financial resources to make the largest contribution. See, e.g., In re Marriage of Olson, 223 Ill.App.3d 636, 166 Ill.Dec. 60, 585 N.E.2d 1082 (2d Dist.), *appeal denied*, 145 Ill.2d 636, 173 Ill.Dec. 6, 596 N.E.2d

630 (1992) (upholding order that father pay 75% of children's college education; father had superior abilities to generate financial resources). But see In re Marriage of Stockton, 169 Ill.App.3d 318, 119 Ill.Dec. 817, 523 N.E.2d 573 (4th Dist.1988) (apportioning educational expenses based on a ratio of the parents' gross incomes was reversible error).

(3) **Child's financial resources and contribution.** Section 513(b) expressly directs the court to consider not only the financial resources of both parents and the standard of living the child would have enjoyed had the marriage not been dissolved, but also the financial resources of the child. A child therefore may be required to contribute to his own college education. This can include contribution from the child's assets as well as earnings that the child may have from work. See, e.g., In re Marriage of McGory, 185 Ill.App.3d 517, 133 Ill.Dec. 590, 541 N.E.2d 801 (3d Dist.1989) (denying wife's petition to continue husband's payment of daughter's educational expenses; daughter was employed, had established credit and lived with maternal grandmother); Larsen v. Larsen, 126 Ill.App.3d 1072, 82 Ill.Dec. 103, 468 N.E.2d 165 (3d Dist.1984) (requiring child to contribute proceeds of part-time employment but not other assets to her educational expenses when settlement agreement provided that father would be responsible for the expenses).

(4) **Agreements on higher education made for young children.** Provision for the payment of college educations can be made in settlement agreements or judgments. But because dissolutions frequently take place while the children are young, when many divorcing spouses do not know what their financial circumstances will be when their children reach college age, the determination of each spouse's contribution to the cost of their children's college educations is often delayed in the agreement or by the court until the children are ready for college. (See IMDMA § 502 Author's Note (11) para. 4(f).)

(5) **Child's standing under § 513.** Actions under § 513 are usually brought by one parent against the other. However, several children have attempted to use the statute to obtain educational assistance from a parent. The reaction of the courts has been varied. Two 1987 cases, both entitled Miller v. Miller, disagreed whether a child has standing to sue a parent under § 513. The Third District held that a child has no standing under § 513 to bring an action for support payments covering his educational expenses. Miller v. Miller, 160 Ill.App.3d 354, 112 Ill.Dec. 191, 513 N.E.2d 605 (3d Dist.1987). The First District, on the other hand, held that the child did possess standing as a third-party beneficiary to enforce his father's obligation to pay for the child's education. Miller v. Miller, 163 Ill.App.3d 602, 114 Ill.Dec. 682, 516 N.E.2d 837 (1st Dist.1987). A later case, Orr v. Orr, 228 Ill.App.3d 234, 170 Ill.Dec. 117, 592 N.E.2d 553 (1st Dist.1992) reconciled the two cases, holding that a child had standing to sue as a third-party beneficiary if, as in the First District's *Miller*, the child was attempting to enforce her parents' divorce decree that specifically provided for the child's educational expenses. The child would not have standing if, as in the *Miller* case in the Third District, there was no provision in the divorce decree requiring that the parents fund the child's education.

(6) **Petition for support of disabled child or educational expenses: Timing.** Application for both the support of a disabled child and for educational expenses can be made to the court either before or after the child has attained his majority. A petition may also be made pursuant to § 513 after the death of a parent for payment out of the decedent's estate, as provided for in IMDMA § 510(e).

750 ILCS 5/514

§ 514. Partition of real estate

A court having jurisdiction in an action for dissolution of marriage may, upon petition of one of the parties, hear and decide an action for partition subject to the provisions of Article XVII of the Code of Civil Procedure, as now or hereafter amended, except as otherwise provided in this Act.

Author's Notes

Analysis

1. Procedure.
2. Not an absolute right.
3. Pleading.
4. Petition for the Partition of Real Estate—Form.
5. Cross reference—Lis pendens.

(1) **Procedure.** See 735 ILCS 5/17-101 et seq. for procedural rules governing partition.

(2) **Not an absolute right.** Partition of real estate held in joint tenancy or tenancy in common was formerly an absolute right in divorce proceedings. In re Marriage of Kush, 106 Ill.App.3d 233, 236, 62 Ill.Dec. 123, 125, 435 N.E.2d 921, 923 (3d Dist.1982), however, held "Under the new act, partition of property owned jointly by a husband and wife is no longer an absolute right. Section 514 of the new act permits a court to entertain a petition for partition, but any rights to partition must yield to the court's disposition of marital property."

(3) **Pleading.** The cases have held that where the sale of real estate is sought in a dissolution action, the sale must be pleaded, In re Marriage of Pieper, 79 Ill.App.3d 835, 838, 34 Ill.Dec. 877, 879, 398 N.E.2d 868, 870 (1st Dist.1979), although pleading "for use of the marital home and other equitable relief" has also been held to be adequate. In re Marriage of Glessner, 119 Ill.App.3d 306, 312, 74 Ill.Dec. 809, 813, 456 N.E.2d 311, 315 (1st Dist.1983).

(4) **Petition for the Partition of Real Estate—Form.** There follows a sample partition form.

IN THE CIRCUIT COURT OF COOK COUNTY, ILLINOIS
COUNTY DEPARTMENT—DOMESTIC RELATIONS DIVISION

IN RE THE MARRIAGE OF)
)
ROSA ROUNCEWELL,)
)
      Petitioner and)
      Counter-Respondent,)
)
and) No. ____ D _____
)
WATT ROUNCEWELL,)
)
      Respondent and)
      Counter-Petitioner.)

PETITION FOR THE PARTITION OF REAL ESTATE

Respondent and Counter–Petitioner, WATT ROUNCEWELL ("WATT"), brings the following Petition for the Partition of Real Estate against Petitioner and Counter–Respondent, ROSA ROUNCEWELL ("ROSA"), pursuant to Section 514 of the Illinois Marriage and Dissolution of Marriage Act and Sections 5/17–101 et. seq. of the Illinois Code of Civil Procedure, and WATT alleges as follows:

1. The marital home of the parties, located at _____, Northfield, Cook County, Illinois (hereinafter the "Northfield home"), is held by the parties in joint tenancy. The legal description of the Northfield home is attached to this petition as an Exhibit.

2. WATT has withdrawn from the Northfield home. ROSA is currently living in the Northfield home with the two minor children of the parties.

3. The Northfield home is elaborate. It contains 12 rooms, including five bedrooms, that occupy 6,512 square feet. There is an exercise room, a swimming pool, and extensive grounds. The Northfield home is a larger house than is required by ROSA and the two minor children of the parties. ROSA and the two minor children could live comfortably in a more modest home in the Northfield area.

4. The Northfield home is excessively expensive to maintain, particularly because WATT is currently required to support the Northfield home and maintain independent housing for himself. ROSA has insisted that she requires household help, gardeners, snow removers, painters, and various repairmen in order to maintain the Northfield home. ROSA is currently unemployed and unable to contribute to the maintenance of the Northfield home. The continued maintenance of the Northfield home constitutes a drain on the financial resources of WATT and is an unnecessary waste of income and assets.

5. The Northfield home has an approximate value of $925,000. It is encumbered by a loan owed to the Lincoln's Inn Bank with an unpaid balance of $315,000. The Lincoln's Inn Bank should be made a party defendant to this action.

6. Inasmuch as the premises constitute a home held in joint tenancy by WATT and ROSA, who are in the midst of dissolution of marriage proceedings, a division and partition of the premises cannot be made without manifest prejudice to the owners. The court should therefore order an immediate sale of the premises.

7. After the closing of the sale, the costs of the sale should be paid out of the proceeds. Inasmuch as a sale will trigger a potential capital gains tax, an escrow should be created from the proceeds for the payment of the tax. After

the deduction of the costs and the amount required to fund the tax escrow, the balance of the proceeds should be divided equally between WATT and ROSA.

WHEREFORE Respondent and Counter-Petitioner, WATT ROUNCEWELL, prays as follows:

   A. The Lincoln's Inn Bank be named as an additional party defendant, and the Court order that summons issue to the Lincoln's Inn Bank, instanter.

   B. The Court order the immediate sale of the Northfield home.

   C. The Court appoint the three commissioners required by Section 5/17-106 of the Illinois Code of Civil Procedure to conduct the evaluation and sale of the Northfield home.

   D. The Court order that the costs of partition and sale of the Northfield home be paid out of the proceeds from the sale of the Northfield home, and the Court further order that a tax escrow be created for the payment of the potential capital gains tax due upon the sale of the Northfield home.

   E. The Court order that the net proceeds from the sale of the Northfield home after the payment of costs and the creation of the tax escrow be divided equally between the joint tenants, WATT and ROSA.

   F. WATT have such other and further relief as may be appropriate under the evidence and circumstances.

WATT ROUNCEWELL
Respondent and Counter-Petitioner

CONRAD SNAGSBY
Attorney for
Respondent and Counter-Petitioner

VERIFICATION BY CERTIFICATION

Under penalties of perjury as provided by law pursuant to Section 1-109 of the Illinois Code of Civil Procedure, the undersigned certifies that the statements set forth in the foregoing instrument are true and correct.

DATED: _____   _____
                                                  WATT ROUNCEWELL

Conrad Snagsby
Address
Telephone number

   (5) **Cross reference—Lis pendens.** See 735 ILCS 5/2-1901 et seq. and accompanying Author's Notes for recording notice of litigation affecting property.

750 ILCS 5/515

§ 515. Partition to be filed in counties where real estate located

A court hearing an action for partition pursuant to Section 514 of this Act may determine and declare the rights, titles and interests of all parties to that action without regard to the location within this State of the land in question. However, if the land in question is located in a county other than that in which the dissolution of marriage action is commenced, notice of the action for partition and a certified copy of the judgment of dissolution of marriage must be filed, by the party filing the petition for partition, in the office of the recorder or registrar of titles in each county, other than that where the action is brought, where any part of the land in question is located.

750 ILCS 5/516

§ 516. Public Aid collection fee

In all cases instituted by the Illinois Department of Public Aid on behalf of a child or spouse, other than one receiving a grant of financial aid under Article IV of The Illinois Public Aid Code, on whose behalf an application has been made and approved for support services as provided by Section 10-1 of that Code, the court shall impose a collection fee on the individual who owes a child or spouse support obligation in an amount equal to 10% of the amount so owed as long as such collection is required by federal law, which fee shall be in addition to the support obligation. The imposition of such fee shall be in accordance with provisions of Title IV, Part D, of the Social Security Act and regulations duly promulgated thereunder. The fee shall be payable to the clerk of the circuit court for transmittal to the Illinois Department of Public Aid and shall continue until support services are terminated by that Department.

PART VI. CUSTODY

Analysis

Sec.
601. Jurisdiction—Commencement of proceeding.
602. Best interest of child.
602.1 Parental powers—Joint custody—Criteria.
603. Temporary orders.
604. Interviews.
605. Investigations and reports.
606. Hearings.
607. Visitation.
607.1 Enforcement of visitation orders; Visitation abuse.
608. Judicial supervision.
609. Leave to remove children.
610. Modification.

611. Enforcement of custody order or order prohibiting removal of child from the jurisdiction of the court.

750 ILCS 5/601   **FAMILIES**

WESTLAW Electronic Research

See WESTLAW Electronic Research Guide preceding the Summary of Contents.

---

750 ILCS 5/601

§ 601. Jurisdiction—Commencement of proceeding

(a) A court of this State competent to decide child custody matters has jurisdiction to make a child custody determination in original or modification proceedings as provided in Section 4 of the Uniform Child Custody Jurisdiction Act as adopted by this State.

(b) A child custody proceeding is commenced in the court:

    (1) by a parent, by filing a petition:

        (i) for dissolution of marriage or legal separation or declaration of invalidity of marriage; or

        (ii) for custody of the child, in the county in which he is permanently resident or found; or

    (2) by a person other than a parent, by filing a petition for custody of the child in the county in which he is permanently resident or found, but only if he is not in the physical custody of one of his parents.

(c) Notice of a child custody proceeding, including an action for modification of a previous custody order, shall be given to the child's parents, guardian and custodian, who may appear, be heard, and file a responsive pleading. The court, upon showing of good cause, may permit intervention of other interested parties.

(d) Proceedings for modification of a previous custody order commenced more than 30 days following the entry of a previous custody order must be initiated by serving a written notice and a copy of the petition for modification upon the child's parent, guardian and custodian at least 30 days prior to hearing on the petition. Nothing in this Section shall preclude a party in custody modification proceedings from moving for a temporary order under Section 603 of this Act.

(e) In a custody proceeding involving an out-of-state party, the court, prior to granting or modifying a custody judgment, shall consult the registry of out-of-state judgments to determine whether there exists any communications or documents alleging that the child who is the subject of custody proceedings may have been improperly removed from the physical custody of the person entitled to custody or may have been improperly retained after a visit or other temporary relinquishment of physical custody. Where, on the basis of such documents or communications contained in the registry of out-of-state judgments, the court determines that the child who is the subject of custody may have been improperly removed or retained, the court shall notify the person or agency who submitted such communications as to the location of the child, as soon as is practicable.

Author's Notes

Analysis

1. Standing and standards.
2. Rights of the natural parent.
3. Rights of an unmarried parent.
4. Venue and notice.
5. Modification of custody orders.

(1) **Standing and standards.** Before a nonparent has standing under the Dissolution Act to file a petition for custody of a child, the nonparent must show that the child is not in the physical custody of one of her parents. In re Custody of Peterson, 112 Ill.2d 48, 96 Ill.Dec. 690, 491 N.E.2d 1150 (1986). However, standing "should not turn on who is in physical possession ... of the child at the moment of filing the petition for custody." In re Custody of Peterson, 112 Ill.2d at 53, 96 Ill.Dec. at 692, 491 N.E.2d at 1152 (holding that grandmother did not have standing although granddaughter lived with her). See also In re Marriage of Dile, 248 Ill.App.3d 683, 188 Ill.Dec. 595, 618 N.E.2d 1165 (5th Dist.1993) (holding that grandparents lacked standing under Marriage and Dissolution Act; father had allowed daughter to live with grandparents only to spare daughter further trauma after mother's suicide). The rationale for this distinction is to deter abductions of children in order to satisfy the literal terms of the statute. *Peterson*, 112 Ill.2d at 54, 96 Ill.Dec. at 693, 491 N.E.2d at 1153.

If the nonparent can make an adequate showing, the standard as to whether the nonparent can obtain custody is the best interests of the child. Montgomery v. Roudez, 156 Ill.App.3d 262, 267, 108 Ill.Dec. 803, 806, 509 N.E.2d 499, 502 (1st Dist.1987). Courts may apply the best interests of the child standard even though nonparent lacked standing under the Marriage and Dissolution of Marriage Act when the court finds that the parent waived issue of standing. See In re Marriage of Sechrest, 202 Ill.App.3d 865, 148 Ill.Dec. 615, 560 N.E.2d 1212 (4th Dist.1990), *appeal denied*, 136 Ill.2d 554, 153 Ill.Dec.384, 567 N.E.2d 342 (1991) (standing waived in previous custody proceedings); In re Custody of Gonzalez, 204 Ill.App.3d 28, 149 Ill.Dec. 580, 561 N.E.2d 1276 (3d Dist.1990) (standing waived when father agreed to continue temporary custody with nonparents during the pendency of their petition for permanent custody). There is no requirement to establish parental unfitness or parental fault. *Montgomery*, 156 Ill.App.3d at 266, 108 Ill.Dec. at 806, 509 N.E.2d at 502. If the nonparent fails to establish standing under the Illinois Marriage and Dissolution of Marriage Act, the nonparent must seek custody under the higher standard of the Juvenile Court Act or the Adoption Act. These statutes require that the nonparent show that the natural parents are unfit to have custody of the child. See Juvenile Court Act, 705 ILCS 405/1 et seq.; Adoption Act, 750 ILCS 50/0.01 et seq. and accompanying Author's Notes.

(2) **Rights of the natural parent.** A natural parent is presumed to have the right to custody of his of her child over all other persons.

> In child-custody disputes it is an accepted presumption that the right or interest of a natural parent in the care, custody and control of a child is superior to the claim of a third person. The presumption is not absolute and serves only as one of

several factors used by courts in resolving the ultimately controlling question of where the best interests of the child lie.

In re Custody of Townsend, 86 Ill.2d 502, 508, 56 Ill.Dec. 685, 688, 427 N.E.2d 1231, 1234 (1981). This presumption is often referred to as the superior right doctrine.

However, this right is not absolute. A parent may lose custody to a nonparent with standing under IMDMA § 601 if it is not in the best interests of the child to remain with the parent. See, e.g., Montgomery v. Roudez, 156 Ill.App.3d 262, 108 Ill.Dec. 803, 509 N.E.2d 499 (1st Dist.1987) (affirming award of custody to great-aunt when mother was a ward of the state and had failed to demonstrate any maturity, responsibility or stability). A parent may also lose custody to a nonparent if the parent is found unfit under the Juvenile Court Act, 705 ILCS 405/1 et seq., or the Adoption Act, 750 ILCS 50/0.01 et seq.

(3) **Rights of an unmarried parent.** An unmarried parent may commence child custody proceedings pursuant to IMDMA § 601(b)(ii). Such an action may be independent of any dissolution litigation. Myer v. Alvarado, 100 Ill.App.3d 27, 32, 55 Ill.Dec. 358, 360, 426 N.E.2d 333, 335 (4th Dist.1981). However, the Third Circuit held in Kapp v. Alexander, 218 Ill.App.3d 412, 161 Ill.Dec. 158, 578 N.E.2d 285 (3d Dist.1991), that the father of a child born out of wedlock who had never legally established parentage of the child could not pursue an action for visitation or custody through the Marriage and Dissolution of Marriage Act. Instead, because "parentage was at issue", the father must seek custody or visitation rights through the Parentage Act. Id., 218 Ill.App. at 416, 161 Ill.Dec. at 160, 578 N.E.2d at 287.

(4) **Venue and notice.** Section 601(b) sets forth the venue in which independent custody actions can be brought. See IMDMA § 104 and 735 ILCS 5/2–104 for objections to improper venue. Notice of the custody proceedings and of custody modification petitions within 30 days of the custody order must be made on the child's parent, guardian, and custodian, not just their attorneys, pursuant to § 601(c).

(5) **Modification of custody orders.** Section 601(d) became effective January 7, 1993. It provides that proceedings for a modification of a previous custody order commenced more than 30 days following the entry of the previous custody order must be initiated by serving written notice and a copy of the Petition for Modification upon the child's parent, guardian, and custodian (notice to the attorneys alone is insufficient), at least 30 days prior to hearing on the petition. Temporary custody, however, can be obtained pursuant to IMDMA § 603 of the Act in fewer than 30 days prior to the hearing in appropriate circumstances. See IMDMA § 603 and accompanying Author's Notes.

750 ILCS 5/602

§ 602. Best interest of child

(a) The court shall determine custody in accordance with the best interest of the child. The court shall consider all relevant factors including:

(1) the wishes of the child's parent or parents as to his custody;

(2) the wishes of the child as to his custodian;

(3) the interaction and interrelationship of the child with his parent or parents, his siblings and any other person who may significantly affect the child's best interest;

(4) the child's adjustment to his home, school and community;

(5) the mental and physical health of all individuals involved;

(6) the physical violence or threat of physical violence by the child's potential custodian, whether directed against the child or directed against another person;

(7) the occurrence of ongoing abuse as defined in Section 103 of the Illinois Domestic Violence Act of 1986, whether directed against the child or directed against another person; and

(8) the willingness and ability of each parent to facilitate and encourage a close and continuing relationship between the other parent and the child.

(b) The court shall not consider conduct of a present or proposed custodian that does not affect his relationship to the child.

(c) Unless the court finds the occurrence of ongoing abuse as defined in Section 103 of the Illinois Domestic Violence Act of 1986, the court shall presume that the maximum involvement and cooperation of both parents regarding the physical, mental, moral, and emotional well-being of their child is in the best interest of the child. There shall be no presumption in favor of or against joint custody.

Author's Notes

Analysis

1. Best interest of the child.
2. Preference of the child.
3. In court or in camera testimony.
4. Separation of siblings.
5. Relocation of children.
6. Cross reference—Form.
7. Impact of parental conduct.
8. Desirability of involvement of both parents.
9. Tender years doctrine.
10. Expert testimony of mental health professionals.
11. Representation of children.
12. Admissibility of hearsay evidence.
13. Effect of custody agreements between parties.
14. Mediation of custody issues.
15. Illegitimate custody claims.

(1) **Best interest of the child.** Section 602 codifies the long-standing policy that custody be awarded in accordance with the best interests of the child, rather than in accordance with any need or interest of a parent. In re Marriage of Radae, 208 Ill.App.3d 1027, 1029, 153 Ill.Dec. 802, 803, 567 N.E.2d 760, 761 (5th Dist.1991). The focus of the court is therefore on the child, not on the parent: "Charged with guaranteeing the best interest of the children in a custody dispute, it is proper that [the court] look at the situation from their perspective." De Franco v. De Franco, 67 Ill.App.3d 760, 769, 24 Ill.Dec. 130, 137, 384 N.E.2d 997, 1004 (1978).

Section 602(a) sets forth salient factors comprising the best interests of a child. The statutory list, however, is not exhaustive, and the court can consider other relevant factors. See, e.g., In re Marriage of Fahy, 208 Ill.App.3d 677, 695, 153 Ill.Dec. 594, 605, 567 N.E.2d 552, 563 (1st Dist.1991) ("The factors that are relevant to a custody determination include, in addition to those enumerated in section 602, the sufficiency and stability of the respective parties' homes and surroundings, the interaction and relationship of the child to his parent and the child's adjustment to his home"); Montgomery v. Roudez, 156 Ill.App.3d 262, 108 Ill.Dec. 803, 509 N.E.2d 499 (1st Dist.1987) (trial court's consideration of relative economic positions was not error); In re Marriage of Soraparu, 147 Ill.App.3d 857, 101 Ill.Dec. 241, 498 N.E.2d 565 (1st Dist.1986), *appeal denied*, 113 Ill.2d 575, 106 Ill.Dec. 56, 505 N.E.2d 362 (1987) (trial court properly considered husband's child support arrearage in custody determination); In re Marriage of McKeever, 117 Ill.App.3d 905, 73 Ill.Dec. 164, 453 N.E.2d 1153 (3d Dist.1983) (trial court adequately considered mother's regular church attendance with children).

(2) **Preference of the child.** The court may inquire as to the preference of a child concerning who shall be his custodian. However, the preference of a child is not binding upon a court. In re Marriage of Balzell, 207 Ill.App.3d 310, 152 Ill.Dec. 492, 566 N.E.2d 20 (3d Dist.1991) ("Even if [a child] unequivocally indicated a preference for living with [one parent], this preference, while entitled to consideration, would not be binding on the trial court.") The court is not compelled to ask a child for his or her preference. In re Marriage of Balzell, 207 Ill.App.3d 310, 314, 152 Ill.Dec. 492, 494, 566 N.E.2d 20, 22 (3d Dist.1991).

The court can hear the preference of a child of any age. While the age 14 is sometimes given as a time when a child can make an intelligent preference, courts have questioned children considerably younger as well. See, e.g., In re Marriage of Andersen, 236 Ill.App.3d 679, 177 Ill.Dec. 289, 603 N.E.2d 70 (2d Dist.1992) (preference of fourteen year old was determinative); In re Marriage of Seymour, 206 Ill.App.3d 506, 152 Ill.Dec. 27, 565 N.E.2d 269 (2d Dist.1990) (considering preference of a "relatively mature" eight year old girl). But see In re Marriage of Shoff, 179 Ill.App.3d 178, 128 Ill.Dec. 280, 534 N.E.2d 462 (5th Dist.1989) (disregarding preference of eight year old that was not based on sound reasoning). Some children, particularly teenagers, may manipulate their parents by expressing the preference for the one who is less of a disciplinarian. As the court noted in In re Marriage of Allen, 81 Ill.App.3d 517, 520, 36 Ill.Dec. 767, 770, 401 N.E.2d 608, 611 (3d Dist.1980), a child's stated preference "may not always accord with the child's best interest. Frequently, a child will favor a non-custodial parent, whom he sees only on weekends, to his custodial parent, who is responsible for his day-to-day schooling and discipline, irrespective of the quality of care he receives at home."

(3) **In court or in camera testimony.** The testimony of a child can be heard either in open court or in camera. See IMDMA § 604 and accompanying Author's Notes.

(4) **Separation of siblings.** A court will generally prefer to keep siblings together in one household. See e.g., In re Marriage of Lovejoy, 84 Ill.App.3d 53, 39 Ill.Dec. 501, 404 N.E.2d 1092 (3d Dist.1980) ("Generally, it is thought that children ought not to be separated if some semblance of a family unit is to be maintained."); In re Marriage of Ford, 91 Ill.App.3d 1066, 47 Ill.Dec. 541, 415 N.E.2d 546 (1st Dist. 1980), ("there is much to commend the keeping together of the siblings of a family in order to preserve what remains of the family"). Separation of the children may,

however, occasionally be in the children's best interest. In re Marriage of Slavenas, 139 Ill.App.3d 581, 587, 93 Ill.Dec. 914, 917, 487 N.E.2d 739, 742 (2d Dist.1985) (citations omitted). In appropriate circumstances, the courts may order divided custody, giving one parent custody of one or more of the children and the other parent custody of one or more of the children. See, e.g., In re Marriage of Seymour, 206 Ill.App.3d 506, 152 Ill.Dec. 27, 565 N.E.2d 269 (2d Dist.1990) (granting custody of nine year old daughter to mother and eighteen year old son to father; daughter preferred to live with mother and son would soon depart to attend college); In re Marriage of Lovejoy, 84 Ill.App.3d 53, 39 Ill.Dec. 501, 404 N.E.2d 1092 (3d Dist.1980) (awarding custody of all three children to their mother although one child expressed preference to live with father).

(5) **Relocation of children.** A court will frequently attempt to keep children in their homes so that they may remain in their neighborhoods and in their schools. A common means of accomplishing this is by allowing the custodial parent to remain in the marital home while the children are minors, or until the happening of some other event, such as the completion of a school year or their entire education. For example, the marital home can be placed in tenancy in common in accordance with the relative property interests of the parents, as determined in the Judgment of Dissolution of Marriage. Upon the happening of the termination event, the marital home can then be sold, and the proceeds can be divided in accordance with the percentage tenancies. See IMDMA §§ 503(d)(5) and 503(d)(9) Author's Note (21).

(6) **Cross reference—Form.** See IMDMA § 502 Author's Note (11) para. 6(g) for model paragraph that can be modified to delay the sale of a marital home.

(7) **Impact of parental conduct.** Pursuant to § 602(b), the court cannot consider the conduct of a potential custodian that does not affect his or her relationship to the child. In re Marriage of Radae, 208 Ill.App.3d 1027, 1030, 153 Ill.Dec. 802, 804, 567 N.E.2d 760, 762 (5th Dist.1991). For example, a parent who has intercourse with another person is not necessarily disqualified as a custodian, so long as the conduct does not take place in the presence of the children, and does not otherwise affect the parent's ability to be an appropriate custodian. *Cf.* Nolte v. Nolte, 241 Ill.App.3d 320, 182 Ill.Dec. 78, 609 N.E.2d 381 (3d Dist.1993) (mother's cohabitation with lover did not justify change in custody). See also In re Custody of Gonzalez, 204 Ill.App.3d 28, 34, 149 Ill.Dec. 580, 583, 561 N.E.2d 1276, 1279 (3d Dist.1990) (parent's use of drugs is relevant to custody dispute only if the conduct "can be shown to affect his mental or physical health and his relationship with the child").

Violence or abuse, on the other hand, may disqualify a parent from being a custodian whether or not it takes place in the presence of the child. §§ 602(a)(6) and 602(a)(7). For instance, the court in In re Custody of Williams, 104 Ill.App.3d 16, 59 Ill.Dec. 791, 432 N.E 2d 375 (3d Dist.1982), refused to ignore the violent beating that the husband inflicted upon the wife, even though the child did not witness the beating. The court insisted that the beatings were significant in determining the child's best interest. *Id.*, 104 Ill.App.3d at 18, 59 Ill.Dec. at 792, 432 N.E.2d at 376.

Homosexuality may disqualify a parent from becoming a custodian in Illinois, even if it is not in the presence of the child. The court in In re Marriage of Diehl, 221 Ill.App.3d 410, 164 Ill.Dec. 73, 582 N.E.2d 281 (2d Dist.1991) *cert. denied*, 144 Ill.2d 632, 169 Ill.Dec. 140, 591 N.E.2d 20 (1992), rejected applying a "clear nexus test," under which homosexuality would be considered only insofar as there is a proven adverse impact on the child. The court stated that an "intimate cohabitation relationship of a parent, be it heterosexual, homosexual or lesbian in nature is a proper factor to be considered by the trial court in making a custody determination." *Diehl* is unique, however, in addressing the subject directly. Homosexuality or homosexual conduct outside the presence of the child has been held not to disqualify visitation. Pleasant v. Pleasant, 256 Ill.App.3d 742, 195 Ill.Dec. 169, 628 N.E.2d 633 (1st Dist.1993) ("sexual orientation is not relevant to a parent's visitation rights.... It is ... irrelevant that respondent lives with her lesbian lover. What is relevant is whether [the child] is adversely affected by that cohabitation").

(8) **Desirability of involvement of both parents.** The potential jeopardy to children of divorce is almost never that they will suffer from too much involvement by each parent. More frequently children are emotionally malnourished because of minimal or no involvement on the part of one of the parents. The statute in § 602(c) seems to recognize this threat by establishing a presumption that the maximum involvement of both parents with the children is in the best interests of the children. The last sentence of § 602(c), however, backs away from creating a presumption in favor of joint custody. See IMDMA § 602.1 and accompanying Author's Notes.

Unfortunately, a parent will often conclude that because the other parent has been a bad husband or wife, he or she is therefore also a bad father or mother. This faulty logic often leads to an attempt to "protect" the children from the other parent, while the best interests of the children dictate just the opposite, namely the maximum involvement of both parents in their lives. In almost all circumstances, it is appropriate for an attorney to support and encourage the full participation by both parents in the lives of their children.

(9) **Tender years doctrine.** In custody litigation, mothers and fathers have an equal opportunity to obtain the custody of their children. The tender years doctrine, under which mothers were preferred as the custodians of very young children, no longer exists as a legal presumption.

> [C]hanging social and legal trends have cast the tender years doctrine aside. The doctrine rested on a sociological presumption that maternal affection is more active and better adapted to the care of the child than that of the father. With the advent of new lifestyles for both men and women, however, the factual basis for the doctrine, if there ever was one, has vanished.... The sex of the candidate for custody is but one of the many factors that may be considered in determining which parent receives the child.

In re Marriage of Kennedy, 94 Ill.App.3d 537, 545, 49 Ill.Dec. 927, 933, 418 N.E.2d 947, 953 (1st Dist.1981) (citations omitted).

Although mothers are no longer favored custodians under the tender years presumption, courts may give added weight to the parent who served as the child's primary care giver. In practice, because more mothers than fathers are primary care givers, this often means that there is again a slight preference for the mother. See, e.g., In re Marriage of Dall, 191 Ill.App.3d 652, 138 Ill.Dec. 879, 548 N.E.2d 109 (5th Dist.1989); In re Marriage of Bush, 191 Ill.App.3d 249, 138 Ill.Dec. 423, 547 N.E.2d 590 (4th Dist.1989).

(10) **Expert testimony of mental health professionals.** Psychiatrists, psychologists, and other mental health professionals are regularly called upon to evaluate the parents and children in custody litigation, and to testify at trial as experts. Mental health professionals may testify as to how the best interests of the children will be served. However, their testimony is not determinative. In re Marriage of Siegel, 123 Ill.App.3d 710, 79 Ill.Dec. 219, 463 N.E.2d 773 (1st Dist.1984).

(11) **Representation of children.** In custody litigation, the court may appoint a guardian or lawyer to represent the interests of the children upon its own motion, or on the motion of either party. See IMDMA §§ 506, 604(b), and Supreme Court Rule 215 and accompanying Author's Notes.

(12) **Admissibility of hearsay evidence.** Courts have admitted hearsay evidence of statements of children outside the courtroom in custody proceedings in appropriate circumstances. The most common hearsay exception is when the testimony concerns a child's preference for custody, which may fit into the state of mind exception for hearsay. See, e.g., Rizzo v. Rizzo, 95 Ill.App.3d 636, 51 Ill.Dec. 141, 420 N.E.2d 555 (1st Dist.1981) (hearsay statements made by children to third parties stating the children's state of mind should have been admitted if made under conditions ensuring trustworthiness); In re Marriage of Sieck, 78 Ill.App.3d 204, 33 Ill.Dec. 490, 396 N.E.2d 1214 (1st Dist.1979) (hearsay testimony by psychiatrist admissible; statements were offered as evidence of the children's state of mind, not to prove the truth of the statements). *Cf.* In re Marriage of Gustafson, 187 Ill.App.3d 551, 135 Ill.Dec. 192, 543 N.E.2d 575 (4th Dist.1989) (disallowing grandmother's testimony concerning what children allegedly told her about father's conduct and living conditions because it did not fit into an exception to the rule against hearsay).

(13) **Effect of custody agreements between parties.** An agreement between the parties concerning the custody of their children does not bind the court if the agreement is contrary to the best interests of the children. In re Marriage of Solomon, 84 Ill.App.3d 901, 907, 40 Ill.Dec. 197, 202, 405 N.E.2d 1289, 1294 (1st Dist.1980). See IMDMA § 502 Author's Note (2).

(14) **Mediation of custody issues.** Custody litigation can often be harmful to children regardless of its result. Sometimes the custody litigation itself is more damaging to the children than would be custody with either parent. Custody litigation represents confrontation, a public broadcasting of family failure, children who are witnesses to and unavoidably a part of a struggle over their lives, judgment, large expense, and lasting enmity that often poisons the possibility of future cooperation between parents in regard to their children. A potential way to obviate the necessity for custody litigation is through mediation of custody issues by mental health professionals or other trained mediators. This process, which avoids most of the perils of open court custody litigation, should almost always be first attempted before placing children in the middle of a court contest. Many courts have established mediation programs to which reference is generally made before litigation of custody or visitation issues.

(15) **Illegitimate custody claims.** At the earliest stage, genuine as opposed to manipulative claims to custody should be shaken out. As an officer of the court, every lawyer must be mindful that the standard is the best interests of the child. Custody claims that do not address the best interests of the child, for example to threaten the other spouse with a loss of custody in order to reduce her financial demands, are therefore not acceptable.

750 ILCS 5/602.1

§ 602.1 Parental powers—Joint custody—Criteria.

(a) The dissolution of marriage, the declaration of invalidity of marriage, the legal separation of the parents, or the parents living separate and apart shall not diminish parental powers, rights, and responsibilities except as the court for good reason may determine under the standards of Section 602.

(b) Upon the application of either or both parents, or upon its own motion, the court shall consider an award of joint custody. Joint custody means custody determined pursuant to a Joint Parenting Agreement or a Joint Parenting Order. In such cases, the court shall initially request the parents to produce a Joint Parenting Agreement. Such Agreement shall specify each parent's powers, rights and responsibilities for the personal care of the child and for major decisions such as education, health care, and religious training. The Agreement shall further specify a procedure by which proposed changes, disputes and alleged breaches may be mediated or otherwise resolved and shall provide for a periodic review of its terms by the parents. In producing a Joint Parenting Agreement, the parents shall be flexible in arriving at resolutions which further the policy of this State as expressed in Sections 102 and 602. For the purpose of assisting the court in making a determination whether an award of joint custody is appropriate, the court may order mediation and may direct that an investigation be conducted pursuant to the provisions of Section 605. In the event the parents fail to produce a Joint Parenting Agreement, the court may enter an appropriate Joint Parenting Order under the standards of Section 602 which shall specify and contain the same elements as a Joint Parenting Agreement, or it may award sole custody under the standards of Sections 602, 607, and 608.

(c) The court may enter an order of joint custody if it determines that joint custody would be in the best interests of the child, taking into account the following:

> (1) the ability of the parents to cooperate effectively and consistently in matters that directly affect the joint parenting of the child. "Ability of the parents to cooperate" means the parents' capacity to substantially comply with a Joint Parenting Order. The court shall not consider the inability of the parents to cooperate effectively and consistently in matters that do not directly affect the joint parenting of the child;
>
> (2) The residential circumstances of each parent; and
>
> (3) all other factors which may be relevant to the best interest of the child.

(d) Nothing within this section shall imply or presume that joint custody shall necessarily mean equal parenting time. The physical residence of the child in joint custodial situations shall be determined by:

> (1) express agreement of the parties; or
>
> (2) order of the court under the standards of this Section.

(e) Notwithstanding any other provision of law, access to records and information pertaining to a child, including but not limited to medical, dental, child care and school records, shall not be denied to a parent for the reason that such parent is not the child's custodial parent; however, no parent shall have access to the school records of a child if the parent is prohibited by an order of protection from inspecting or obtaining such records pursuant to the Illinois Domestic Violence Act of 1986, as now or hereafter amended.

Author's Notes

Analysis

1. Joint parenting agreements: Contents.
2. Joint Parenting Agreement—Form.
3. Joint parenting agreements: Suitable situations.
4. Terminology.

(1) **Joint parenting agreements: Contents.** Joint parenting agreements should first state that the parents have agreed to have joint custody of the child or children. Additionally, the agreement should specify the physical residence of the child, a visitation schedule for the other parent (or other arrangements such as shared physical custody or divided custody), how major and day-to-day decisions will be made (for instance, major decisions will be made jointly, and day-to-day decisions will be made by the parent with the children at that time), and a method for resolving disputes and for periodic review (usually by an appointed mediator). All other details pertinent to the case should be included in the joint parenting agreement.

(2) **Joint Parenting Agreement—Form.** There follows a sample joint parenting agreement. Joint agreements will vary considerably with the circumstances and schedules of the parties and their children in each case. See IMDMA § 502 Author's Note (11) Article III for a joint parenting agreement that is incorporated into the settlement agreement itself. Where the joint parenting agreement is a separate document, it should be identified in the settlement agreement or judgment and attached as an exhibit.

Firm #_____

IN THE CIRCUIT COURT OF COOK COUNTY, ILLINOIS
COUNTY DEPARTMENT—DOMESTIC RELATIONS DIVISION

IN RE THE MARRIAGE OF	)
	)
SUSAN JELLYBY,	)
	)
Petitioner,	)
	)
and	) No. ____ D _____
	)
ARTHUR JELLYBY,	)
	)
Respondent.	)

JOINT PARENTING AGREEMENT

1. SUSAN JELLYBY ("SUSAN") and ARTHUR JELLYBY ("ARTHUR") agree that both parties are fit and proper persons to have the joint legal custody of the minor children of the parties, Caddy and Peepy. SUSAN

and ARTHUR both recognize the continuing need of the children for close and frequent contact with both parents and the importance of both parents remaining actively involved in the lives of the minor children, and therefore SUSAN and ARTHUR agree that they shall have the joint care, custody, control, and education of Caddy and Peepy. The physical residence of Caddy and Peepy shall be with ARTHUR, and SUSAN shall have frequent and liberal visitation. Each party shall make the day-to-day routine decisions concerning Caddy or Peepy when one or both are with ARTHUR or SUSAN, except as otherwise herein provided. SUSAN will have the right to visit and have the company of Caddy and Peepy at such reasonable times and places as the parties may from time to time decide, but not less than the schedule set out herein.

2. Either parent may remove the children from the State of Illinois for visitation, trips, or vacation purposes without further leave of Court or consent of the other party, provided that the party intending to remove the children shall give the other parent reasonable notice of his or her intention to do so, and shall supply the other with information regarding the contemplated period of time outside the state, the address and telephone number where they will be located, and shall permit reasonable telephone communication between the children and the parent who is not with the children. Nothing contained in this provision shall be construed to permit either parent to remove the permanent residence of the minor children from the State of Illinois without first securing the written consent of the other parent, or securing the approval of the Circuit Court of Cook County, Illinois.

3. Each party agrees to do everything within his or her power to foster the respect, love, and affection of the children of the parties for the other party, and to make every possible effort to agree on all questions involving the children so that they may have proper physical and emotional growth and retain their respect and affection for both of their parents. Neither party shall prevent or hinder telephone or other communication between the children and the other parent. Neither party shall make disparaging remarks about the other parent to, or in the presence of, the children, and shall request that friends and relatives refrain from doing so as well.

4. The parties agree that they will jointly discuss and determine major decisions concerning Caddy and Peepy, including, but not limited to: (a) education; (b) choice of and attendance at after-school care and religious services; (c) medical care and choice of physicians, dentists, and the like; and (d) all other significant questions relating to the health, welfare, and education of the children, except in the case of an emergency. Upon the happening of a medical emergency, the parent with the child, or first making contact with the child, shall make all necessary decisions during the emergency and shall promptly notify the other parent. Medical and school records, as well as all other information concerning or related to Caddy and Peepy, shall be made available to both parties. SUSAN shall be notified of any and all communications between the school and ARTHUR concerning Caddy and Peepy, and both parents shall be welcome at parent activities, such as teacher

conferences, and attendance at Caddy's and Peepy's extracurricular activities. Both parties shall have the right to communicate with teachers, school personnel, counsellors, and physicians to discuss Caddy's and Peepy's standing and progress. In the event there are school or extracurricular programs open to parents, ARTHUR shall immediately inform SUSAN of the same and cooperate to facilitate her attendance.

5. SUSAN shall have liberal and reasonable visitation with Caddy and Peepy. The visitation shall include the following:

(a) SUSAN shall have visitation with Caddy and Peepy one weekend day each week, alternating Friday after school to Saturday at 7:00 p.m. with Saturday from 7:00 p.m. to Sunday at 7:00 p.m., and once every two months the whole weekend (from 6:00 p.m. Friday night to 6:00 p.m. Sunday night). In addition, Caddy and Peepy shall spend at least two week night evenings (after school until one-half hour before bedtime) with SUSAN, presently to coincide with ARTHUR's teaching commitment.

(i) ARTHUR and SUSAN shall equally share driving related to visitation.

(ii) ARTHUR and SUSAN agree that neither shall move farther than 20 miles from _____ so that the intention of this Agreement, that Caddy and Peepy spend substantial amounts of time with both parents, is facilitated.

(iii) Each parent will be responsible for driving the children to routine activities scheduled during the time they are with that parent. Neither parent will schedule activities that occur during the other parent's time with the children without the prior consent of that parent, and, whenever possible, such activities shall be scheduled so that they do not disproportionately interfere with visitation.

(b) The summer break between spring and fall school terms shall be equally shared by the parties. Each may choose to allow Caddy and Peepy to spend time visiting relatives or friends during the summer so long as it does not interfere with the time allocated to the other parent. Each parent shall have the right to two consecutive weeks of vacation with the children. Since SUSAN is not employed, and therefore able to be more flexible, ARTHUR shall notify SUSAN of his preference as soon as he knows his vacation dates or by March 1 of each year, whichever is earlier. SUSAN shall notify ARTHUR of her preference not later than one month after receiving ARTHUR's notification. On or about May 1 of each year the parties shall meet to schedule the summer allocation of time for Caddy and Peepy. If no agreement is reached by May 15, they shall confer with a mediator as provided for herein to arrange a summer schedule.

(c) SUSAN shall have visitation with Caddy and Peepy on each child's birthday in alternating years.

(d) SUSAN shall be entitled to have Caddy and Peepy with her on her birthday and on Mother's Day. In the event that either such day falls on a weekend when SUSAN does not normally have visitation, she shall nonetheless have visitation on her birthday and Mother's Day. ARTHUR shall have the right to have Caddy and Peepy with him on his birthday and on Father's Day. In the event that either day falls on a weekend that is normally SUSAN's visitation, Caddy and Peepy shall be returned to ARTHUR on that particular day.

(e) SUSAN shall have visitation with Caddy and Peepy on alternating holidays in alternating years. For purposes of this, Christmas Eve and Christmas Day and New Year's Eve and New Year's Day shall be treated as separate holidays. The other holidays shall include Easter, Memorial Day, Independence Day, Labor Day, Thanksgiving and legal school holidays. In addition, the parties shall equally divide school vacations at Christmas and in the Spring.

(f) The parties shall encourage ongoing telephone contact between Caddy and Peepy and the absent parent.

6. It is the intention of the parties that the children continue to attend schools in their present school district and ARTHUR and SUSAN agree to make good faith efforts to live close enough so that the children can have easy access to their schools and to both parents' homes after they separate.

7. The parties agree to confer with a mediator before instituting any litigation to settle conflicts in implementing this Joint Parenting Agreement. They have previously consulted with Dr. Prince Turveydrop and agree to schedule appointments with him to resolve future disputes and prevent misunderstandings. ARTHUR and SUSAN agree to abide by the summer schedule already worked out by them with the mediator for this summer.

8. The parents agree to review the Joint Parenting Agreement with Dr. Prince Turveydrop at the end of one year and periodically every three years thereafter, but acknowledge that changes in the schedules of the children or parents' employment may require earlier review.

_____   _____
ARTHUR JELLYBY   SUSAN JELLYBY

Samuel Kenge
Kenge and Carboy
Attorneys for SUSAN JELLYBY
Address
Telephone number

(3) **Joint parenting agreements: Suitable situations.** Where the husband and wife cannot agree, courts have tended to not order joint custody. The parties, they reason, would never be able to implement an agreement that requires their cooperation to reach joint decisions. See, e.g. Kocal v. Holt, 229 Ill.App.3d 1023, 172 Ill.Dec. 106, 595 N.E.2d 169 (3d Dist.1992) (reversing joint custody order when the

parties had not demonstrated a capacity to cooperate effectively regarding their child's upbringing); In re Marriage of Bush, 191 Ill.App.3d 249, 138 Ill.Dec. 423, 547 N.E.2d 590 (4th Dist.1989) (joint parenting agreement between hostile parties was manifest abuse of discretion).

Even more rarely have courts authorized a shared form of joint custody in which each parent spends equal time with the children. For example, the court in In re Marriage of Oros, 256 Ill.App.3d 167, 194 Ill.Dec. 604, 627 N.E.2d 1246 (4th Dist. 1994), rejected a joint parenting agreement that transferred the child's custody between the two parents' homes in different cities every three months. The child had been "subjected to a merry-go-round of changing preschools, doctors, playmates, households and environments" and suffered emotional problems as a result of "this rotational existence." *Oros*, 256 Ill.App.3d at 170, 194 Ill.Dec. at 607, 627 N.E.2d at 1249. The court remanded to the trial court, directing it to grant one parent sole custody. See also In re Marriage of Hacker, 239 Ill.App.3d 658, 179 Ill.Dec. 816, 606 N.E.2d 648 (4th Dist.1992) (rejecting joint custody arrangement transferring physical custody of the parties' three children weekly, and remanding to issue a custody order giving "some permanency to the physical custody of the children").

It is unwise for courts to reason, as they frequently do, that § 602.1(c)(1) mandates that if parties cannot agree during their divorce, there can be no joint custody. Contending spouses usually find their divorce to be the most difficult time to cooperate. This may not continue to be true after their divorce is concluded, at least concerning their mutual children. Once the court eliminates the possibility of joint custody, the "best interests of the children" takes over and produces a divisive contest in which one parent is effectively adjudged a winner and the other a loser. The chances for cooperation after that contest ends are small. A far better policy is to work toward joint custody in the beginning, by agreeing upon or moving the court to appoint a mediator (pursuant to IMDMA §§ 602.1(b), 604(b), and Supreme Court Rule 215) to assist in negotiating the terms of joint custody. The mediator should be kept in place after the joint parenting agreement is formulated, pursuant to § 602.1(b), in order to resolve future disputes. The parties are drawn together in such a joint project concerning their children, rather than driven apart by custody litigation or negotiations over who is to have sole custody. Neither party is adjudged unfit or demeaned by losing custody. A mediator is appointed to exercise continuing supervision over the joint parenting of the children. This process can be successful in the most difficult situations, and should replace the facile "if the parties cannot agree, there cannot be joint custody." Litigation over sole custody should take place in only the most egregious circumstances.

(4) **Terminology.** Although frequently the subject of litigation, the terms joint custody, sole custody, shared custody, and divided custody are not as important as the manner in which each of those labels is defined by agreement of the parties or by order of the court. The issues which are actually before the court are how much time the children will spend with each parent and how decisions will be made concerning the children. Concentrating on these concrete issues, rather than what the arrangement will be called, is usually the most productive course for lawyers and courts.

750 ILCS 5/603

§ 603. Temporary orders

(a) A party to a custody proceeding may move for a temporary custody order. The court may award temporary custody under the standards of

Section 602 and the standards and procedures of Section 602.1, after a hearing, or, if there is no objection, solely on the basis of the affidavits.

(b) If a proceeding for dissolution of marriage or legal separation or declaration of invalidity of marriage is dismissed, any temporary custody order is vacated unless a parent or the child's custodian moves that the proceeding continue as a custody proceeding and the court finds, after a hearing, that the circumstances of the parents and the best interest of the child requires that a custody judgment be issued.

(c) If a custody proceeding commenced in the absence of a petition for dissolution of marriage or legal separation, under either subparagraph (ii) of paragraph (1), or paragraph (2), of subsection (d) of Section 601, is dismissed, any temporary custody order is vacated.

Author's Notes

Analysis

1. Temporary custody proceedings: Scope.
2. Temporary custody proceedings: Statutory provisions.

(1) **Temporary custody proceedings: Scope.** Because temporary custody is determined after a hearing on the same best interests of the child standard that govern permanent custody, and because the parties inevitably believe that critical issues are at stake, temporary custody proceedings have the potential for mushrooming into major hearings. In re Marriage of Lombaer, 200 Ill.App.3d 712, 722–23, 146 Ill.Dec. 425, 431, 558 N.E.2d 388, 394 (1st Dist.1990). Nonetheless, temporary custody awards lack precedential value in the court's final determination of custody. Custody has a propensity for being litigated twice: once for temporary custody and once for permanent custody.

Note that the standard for modification is different for temporary and permanent custody awards. Temporary custody proceedings are modified under IMDMA § 603 pursuant to the best interest of the child standard. Final awards are modified under the stricter standards of IMDMA § 610. See, e.g., In re Marriage of Goldman, 196 Ill.App.3d 785, 796–97, 143 Ill.Dec. 944, 952, 554 N.E.2d 1016, 1024 (1st Dist.), *appeal denied*, 132 Ill.2d 544, 144 Ill.Dec. 257, 555 N.E.2d 376 (1990). See IMDMA § 610 Author's Notes (1) and (2).

(2) **Temporary custody proceedings: Statutory provisions.** Temporary custody can be obtained both under IMDMA § 603, and, in cases of abuse, under the Domestic Violence Act. 750 ILCS 60/214(b)(6).

750 ILCS 5/604

§ 604. Interviews

(a) The court may interview the child in chambers to ascertain the child's wishes as to his custodian and as to visitation. Counsel shall be present at the interview unless otherwise agreed upon by the parties. The court shall cause a court reporter to be present who shall make a complete record of the interview instantaneously to be part of the record in the case.

(b) The court may seek the advice of professional personnel, whether or not employed by the court on a regular basis. The advice given shall be in writing and made available by the court to counsel. Counsel may examine, as a witness, any professional personnel consulted by the court, designated as a court's witness.

Author's Notes

Analysis

1. Interplay with § 602(a)(2).
2. Court-appointed guardians ad litem and mental health professionals.

(1) **Interplay with § 602(a)(2).** The court may seek to learn the preference of the child in a custody proceeding, although it is not compelled to so do. In re Marriage of Balzell, 207 Ill.App.3d 310, 314, 152 Ill.Dec. 492,, 566 N.E.2d 20, 22 (3d Dist.1991). See IMDMA § 602(a)(2) Author's Note (2). If the trial court chooses to interview the child, the court has the discretion to decide whether the testimony is heard in court or in camera. In re Marriage of Willis, 234 Ill.App.3d 156, 159, 174 Ill.Dec. 633, 636, 599 N.E.2d 179, 182 (3d Dist.1992). In camera testimony may protect the child from a contentious battle between his or her parents in court:

> [t]he acrimonious atmosphere in which a child is required to state in open court his preference as to custody is well known. Often the primary concern, the welfare of the child, is lost in the violent charges and counter-charges of the contesting parties. This atmosphere is heightened when the contesting parties or relatives are present in the courtroom. To have a child face such an array of belligerence and state on which side his preference lies is inhuman....

Oakes v. Oakes, 45 Ill.App.2d 387, 393, 195 N.E.2d 840, 843 (1st Dist.1964). If the testimony is heard in camera, the lawyers for each of the parents have the right to be present, which can be waived. See, e.g., In re Marriage of Hindenburg, 227 Ill.App.3d 228, 169 Ill.Dec. 187, 591 N.E.2d 67 (2d Dist.1992) (parties' attorneys waived their right to be present at in camera interview). A court reporter must be present to produce a contemporaneous record. A record of the in camera interview is mandatory and cannot be waived by the parties. DeYoung v. DeYoung, 62 Ill.App.3d 837, 19 Ill.Dec. 732, 379 N.E.2d 396 (3d Dist.1978). But see In re Marriage of Slavenas, 139 Ill.App.3d 581, 93 Ill.Dec. 914, 487 N.E.2d 739 (2d Dist.1985) (error in conducting interview without making a record was not reversible error).

(2) **Court-appointed guardians ad litem and mental health professionals.** Pursuant to § 604(b) a court may appoint a guardian ad litem for the children to investigate the circumstances of the custody case and to report back to the court. See also IMDMA § 506 and accompanying Author's Notes. The court may also appoint a psychiatrist or other mental health professional to negotiate a joint parenting agreement, to conduct evaluations of the parties and the children, and to report back to the court. See, e.g., In re Marriage of Ford, 91 Ill.App.3d 1066, 47 Ill.Dec. 541, 415 N.E.2d 546 (1st Dist.1980). The professional who reports to the court pursuant to this Section is designated a court's witness. Therefore, counsel for both parties may cross examine him or her. IMDMA § 604(b). Michael H. Graham, *Cleary & Graham's Handbook of Illinois Evidence* §§ 614.1, 706.1 (6th ed. 1994).

750 ILCS 5/604   **FAMILIES**

Mental and physical examinations can also be ordered on the motion of the parties or on the court's own motion pursuant to Supreme Court Rule 215. See Supreme Court Rule 215 and accompanying Author's Notes.

750 ILCS 5/605

§ 605. Investigations and reports

(a) In contested custody proceedings, and in other custody proceedings if a parent or the child's custodian so requests, the court may order an investigation and report concerning custodial arrangements for the child. The investigation and report may be made by a child welfare agency approved by the Department of Children and Family Services, but shall not be made by that Department unless the court determines either that there is no child welfare agency available or that the parent or the child's custodian is financially unable to pay for the investigation or report.

(b) In preparing his report concerning a child, the investigator may consult any person who may have information about the child and his potential custodial arrangements. Under order of the court, the investigator may refer the child to professional personnel for diagnosis. The investigator may consult with and obtain information from medical, psychiatric or other expert persons who have served the child in the past, without obtaining the consent of the parent or the child's custodian. The child's consent must be obtained if he has reached the age of 16, unless the court finds that he lacks mental capacity to consent.

(c) The investigator shall mail the report to counsel, and to any party not represented by counsel, at least 10 days prior to the hearing. The court may examine and consider the investigator's report in determining custody. The investigator shall make available to counsel, the investigator's file of underlying data, reports, and the complete texts of diagnostic reports made to the investigator pursuant to the provisions of subsection (b) of this Section, and the names and addresses of all persons whom the investigator has consulted. Any party to the proceeding may call the investigator, or any person whom he has consulted, as a court's witness, for cross-examination. A party may not waive his right of cross-examination prior to the hearing.

Author's Notes

Analysis

1. Admissibility of investigative reports containing hearsay.
2. Examination of court-appointed investigator.

(1) **Admissibility of investigative reports containing hearsay.** Courts have taken both sides in determining the admissibility of investigative reports that contain hearsay. For instance, the court in In re Marriage of Noble, 192 Ill.App.3d 501, 139 Ill.Dec. 133, 548 N.E.2d 518 (2d Dist.1989), stated that § 605 "provides an exception to the hearsay rule," and therefore held that the trial court's refusal to admit the court-appointed investigator's report was error. Courts in the First and Third Circuits, however, have upheld trial courts' rulings that the investigator's reports or

testimony were inadmissible hearsay. In re Marriage of Hazard, 167 Ill.App.3d 61, 117 Ill.Dec. 770, 520 N.E.2d 1121 (1st Dist.1988) (conclusions in investigator's report based on hearsay correctly ruled inadmissible); In re Marriage of Theis, 121 Ill.App.3d 1092, 77 Ill.Dec. 608, 460 N.E.2d 912 (3d Dist.1984) (investigator's testimony concerning what child told investigator correctly ruled inadmissible; "any underlying facts contained in the report which are outside the personal knowledge of the investigator are hearsay").

(2) **Examination of court-appointed investigator.** Any party to the proceedings may call the investigator, or any person that the investigator has consulted, for cross-examination pursuant to § 605(c).

750 ILCS 5/606
§ 606. Hearings

(a) Custody proceedings shall receive priority in being set for hearing.

(b) The court may tax as costs the payment of necessary travel and other expenses incurred by any person whose presence at the hearing the court deems necessary to determine the best interest of the child.

(c) The court, without a jury, shall determine questions of law and fact. If it finds that a public hearing may be detrimental to the child's best interest, the court may exclude the public from a custody hearing, but may admit any person who has a direct and legitimate interest in the particular case or a legitimate educational or research interest in the work of the court.

(d) If the court finds it necessary, in order to protect the child's welfare, that the record of any interview, report, investigation, or testimony in a custody proceeding be kept secret, the court may make an appropriate order sealing the record.

(e) Previous statements made by the child relating to any allegations that the child is an abused or neglected child within the meaning of the Abused and Neglected Child Reporting Act, or an abused or neglected minor within the meaning of the Juvenile Court Act of 1987, shall be admissible in evidence in a hearing concerning custody of or visitation with the child. No such statement, however, if uncorroborated and not subject to cross examination, shall be sufficient in itself to support a finding of abuse or neglect.

Author's Notes

(1) **Admissibility of hearsay statements by child.** Paragraph (e), added in 1993, apparently makes hearsay statements of a child concerning abuse or neglect admissible in custody or visitation hearings, even though the statements are not sufficient in themselves to support a finding of abuse or neglect.

750 ILCS 5/607
§ 607. Visitation

(a) A parent not granted custody of the child is entitled to reasonable visitation rights unless the court finds, after a hearing, that visitation would endanger seriously the child's physical, mental, moral or emotional health. If the custodian's street address is not identified, pursuant to Section 708, the court shall require the parties to identify reasonable alternative arrangements for visitation by a non-custodial parent, including but not limited to visitation of the minor child at the residence of another person or at a local public or private facility.

(b) (1) The court may grant reasonable visitation privileges to a grandparent, great-grandparent, or sibling of any minor child upon petition to the court by the grandparents or great-grandparents or on behalf of the sibling, with notice to the parties required to be notified under Section 601 of this Act, if the court determines that it is in the best interests and welfare of the child, and may issue any necessary orders to enforce such visitation privileges. Except as provided in paragraph (2) of this subsection (b), a petition for visitation privileges may be filed under this subsection (b) whether or not a petition pursuant to this Act has been previously filed or is currently pending if one or more of the following circumstances exist:

(A) the parents are not currently cohabiting on a permanent or an indefinite basis;

(B) one of the parents has been absent from the marital abode for more than one month without the spouse knowing his or her whereabouts;

(C) one of the parents is deceased;

(D) one of the parents joins in the petition with the grandparents, great-grandparents, or sibling; or

(E) a sibling is in State custody.

(2)(A) A petition for visitation privileges shall not be filed pursuant to this subsection (b) by the parents or grandparents of a putative father if the paternity of the putative father has not been legally established.

(B) A petition for visitation privileges may not be filed under this subsection (b) if the child who is the subject of the grandparents' or great-grandparents' petition has been voluntarily surrendered by the parent or parents, except for a surrender to the Illinois Department of Children and Family Services or a foster care facility, or has been previously adopted by an individual or individuals who are not related to the biological parents of the child or is the subject of a pending adoption petition by an individual or individuals who are not related to the biological parents of the child.

(3) When one parent is deceased, the surviving parent shall not interfere with the visitation rights of the grandparents.

(c) The court may modify an order granting or denying visitation rights whenever modification would serve the best interest of the child; but the court shall not restrict a parent's visitation rights unless it finds that the visitation would endanger seriously the child's physical, mental, moral or emotional health.

(d) If any court has entered an order prohibiting a non-custodial parent of a child from any contact with a child or restricting the non-custodial parent's contact with the child, the following provisions shall apply:

(1) If an order has been entered granting visitation privileges with the child to a grandparent or great-grandparent who is related to the child through the non-custodial parent, the visitation privileges of the grandparent or great-grandparent may be revoked if:

(i) a court has entered an order prohibiting the non-custodial parent from any contact with the child, and the grandparent or great-grandparent is found to have used his or her visitation privileges to facilitate contact between the child and the non-custodial parent; or

(ii) a court has entered an order restricting the non-custodial parent's contact with the child, and the grandparent or great-grandparent is found to have used his or her visitation privileges to facilitate contact between the child and the non-custodial parent's contact with the child.

Nothing in this subdivision (1) limits the authority of the court to enforce its orders in any manner permitted by law.

(2) Any order granting visitation privileges with the child to a grandparent or great-grandparent who is related to the child through the non-custodial parent shall contain the following provisions:

"If the (grandparent or great-grandparent, whichever is applicable) who has been granted visitation privileges under this order uses the visitation privileges to facilitate contact between the child and the child's non-custodial parent, the visitation privileges granted under this order shall be permanently revoked."

(e) No parent, not granted custody of the child, or grandparent, or great-grandparent, or sibling of any minor child, convicted of any offense involving an illegal sex act perpetrated upon a victim less than 18 years of age including but not limited to offenses for violations of Article 12 of the Criminal Code of 1961, is entitled to visitation rights while on parole or mandatory supervised release for that offense, and upon discharge from parole or mandatory supervised release, visitation shall be denied until said person successfully completes a treatment program approved by the court.

Author's Notes

Analysis

1. Visitation rights of non-custodial parent.
2. Restriction of visitation rights.
3. Visitation rights of grandparents.
4. Independence of support and visitation rights.

(1) **Visitation rights of non-custodial parent.** Because "parents have a natural or inherent right of access to their children," and because "sound public policy encourages the maintenance of strong family relationships" (In re Marriage of L.R., 202 Ill.App.3d 69, 85, 147 Ill.Dec. 439, 449, 559 N.E.2d 779, 789 (1st Dist.1990)), courts rarely completely deny visitation rights to a parent who is not granted custody of a child. Section 607 "creates something of an 'entitlement' to reasonable visitation." Lyons v. Lyons, 228 Ill.App.3d 407, 410, 169 Ill.Dec. 502, 591 N.E.2d 1006, 1007 (5th Dist.1992).

However, in appropriate circumstances, visitation may be denied or temporarily denied. See, e.g., In re Marriage of Ashby, 193 Ill.App.3d 366, 140 Ill.Dec. 272, 549 N.E.2d 923 (5th Dist.1990) (visitation rights of father found to have sexually abused two-year old daughter during visitation properly terminated).

In circumstances where there has been abuse, or other dangerous behavior by a parent, a court can order that visitation of the children by the parent only take place under supervision. See, e.g., In re Marriage of Gocal, 216 Ill.App.3d 221, 159 Ill.Dec. 1023, 576 N.E.2d 946 (1st Dist.1991) (upholding supervised visitation for father suffering from manic depression); In re Marriage of Oertel, 216 Ill.App.3d 806, 159 Ill.Dec. 766, 576 N.E.2d 435 (2d Dist.1991) (affirming supervised visitation for alcoholic father).

(2) **Restriction of visitation rights.** Section 607(c) provides two different standards for modifying visitation rights. While the court may modify visitation orders when such a modification would further the best interests of the child, any modification that would restrict a parent's visitation rights must meet the higher serious endangerment standard. A parent's visitation rights may be restricted only if the trial court first finds that the visitation as it exists seriously endangers the child's physical, mental, moral, or emotional health. See, e.g., In re Marriage of Solomon, 84 Ill.App.3d 901, 40 Ill.Dec. 197, 405 N.E.2d 1289 (1st Dist.1980) (trial court incorrectly applied best interest standard to restrict visitation from "almost concurrent custody to the trial court's conception of more reasonable visitation"); In re Marriage of Lombaer, 200 Ill.App.3d 712, 723, 146 Ill.Dec. 425, 432, 558 N.E.2d 388, 395 (1st Dist.1990) (mother's hospitalization and failure to take medication was insufficient to meet standard of serious endangerment). The endangerment standard applies only if the modification of the court order in question is deemed a "restriction" of the noncustodial parent's visitation rights. "Restrict" is given "its ordinary and everyday meaning, indicat[ing] action to limit, restrain, or confine within bounds." In re Marriage of Tisckos, 161 Ill.App.3d 302, 310, 112 Ill.Dec. 860, ___, 514 N.E.2d 523, 528 (4th Dist.1987).

(3) **Visitation rights of grandparents.** At common law, grandparents generally had no rights of visitation. Grandparents seeking visitation privileges at common law had to prove that special circumstances existed that entitled them to legally enforceable rights. See, e.g., Hawkins v. Hawkins, 102 Ill.App.3d 1037, 1039, 58 Ill.Dec. 620, 621–22, 430 N.E.2d 652, 653–54 (3d Dist.1981). The courts were reluctant to intrude upon the parent's right to determine who would participate in their children's lives. See, e.g., Chodzko v. Chodzko, 66 Ill.2d 28, 4 Ill.Dec. 313, 360 N.E.2d 60 (1976). Section 607(b) reflects the current trend toward recognition of at least limited rights of visitation for grandparents. A trial court may now award grandparents visitation either (1) when there are special circumstances, or (2) under a best interests and welfare standard when a grandparent petitions the court under § 607(b). In re Marriage of Balzell, 207 Ill.App.3d 310, 314, 152 Ill.Dec. 492, 495, 566

N.E.2d 20, 23 (3d Dist.1991). Examples of circumstances where courts have granted grandparents visitation rights include following the parents' divorce, In re Marriage of Spomer, 123 Ill.App.3d 31, 78 Ill.Dec. 605, 462 N.E.2d 724 (5th Dist.1984); after the grandparents' child's post-dissolution death, McVey v. Fredrickson, 226 Ill.App.3d 1082, 169 Ill.Dec. 77, 590 N.E.2d 996 (3d Dist.1992); and when the grandparent's child lost visitation rights after a divorce and the grandchild was subsequently adopted by the ex-spouse's new spouse, Lingwall v. Hoener, 108 Ill.2d 206, 91 Ill.Dec. 166, 483 N.E.2d 512 (1985). Section 607 does not guarantee that the grandparents will receive visitation, however, and rights granted may be limited. See, e.g., Weybright v. Puckett, 262 Ill.App.3d 605, 200 Ill.Dec. 18, 635 N.E.2d 119 (4th Dist.1994) (denying visitation to parents of child's deceased father who had not seen child for four years; child was unlikely to recognize grandparents and visitation was not in the child's best interests); In re Marriage of Lindsey, 158 Ill.App.3d 769, 110 Ill.Dec. 363, 511 N.E.2d 198 (4th Dist.1987) (limiting visitation to six hours per month at home of children's custodial parent).

The 1993 amendments added § 607(d) which seeks to curtail a grandparent from using his visitation to facilitate visitation by a non-custodial parent, where the visitation by the non-custodial parent has been restricted or denied.

(4) **Independence of support and visitation rights.** The courts have not accepted the withholding of support by a parent whose visitation has been interfered with by the other parent. See, e.g., Hess v. Hess, 87 Ill.App.3d 947, 952, 42 Ill.Dec. 882, 886, 409 N.E.2d 497, 501 (3d Dist.1980) (admonishing custodial mother that "lack of payment [of child support] has no bearing, per se, on visitation rights.") See also IMDMA § 509 and accompanying Author's Notes. The appropriate remedy for the parent whose visitation has been interfered with is to bring a petition setting forth the violation of the visitation order before the court, but not to withhold support. See IMDMA § 607.1 for enforcement of visitation orders.

750 ILCS 5/607.1

§ 607.1 Enforcement of visitation orders; Visitation abuse

(a) The circuit court shall provide an expedited procedure for enforcement of court ordered visitation in cases of visitation abuse. Visitation abuse occurs when a party has willfully and without justification: (1) denied another party visitation as set forth by the court; or (2) exercised his or her visitation rights in a manner that is harmful to the child or child's custodian.

(b) An Action may be commenced by filing a petition setting forth: (i) the petitioner's name, residence address or mailing address, and telephone number; (ii) respondent's name and place of residence, place of employment, or mailing address; (iii) the nature of the visitation abuse, giving dates and other relevant information; (iv) that a reasonable attempt was made to resolve the dispute; and (v) the relief sought.

Notice of the filing of the petitions shall be given as provided in Section 511.

(c) After hearing all of the evidence, the court may order one or more of the following:

(1) Modification of the visitation order to specifically outline periods of visitation or restrict visitation as provided by law.

(2) Supervised visitation with a third party or public agency.

(3) Make up visitation of the same time period, such as weekend for weekend, holiday for holiday.

(4) Counseling or mediation, except in cases where there is evidence of domestic violence, as defined in Section 1 of the Domestic Violence Shelters Act, occurring between the parties.

(5) Other appropriate relief deemed equitable.

(d) Nothing contained in this Section shall be construed to limit the court's contempt power, except as provided in subsection (g) of this Section.

(e) When the court issues an order holding a party in contempt of court for violation of a visitation order, the clerk shall transmit a copy of the contempt order to the sheriff of the county. The sheriff shall furnish a copy of each contempt order to the Department of State Police on a daily basis in the form and manner required by the Department. The Department shall maintain a complete record and index of the contempt orders and make this data available to all local law enforcement agencies.

(f) Attorney fees and costs shall be assessed against a party if the court finds that the enforcement action is vexatious and constitutes harassment.

(g) A person convicted of unlawful visitation interference under Section 10–5.5 of the Criminal Code of 1961 shall not be subject to the provisions of this Section and the court may not enter a contempt order for visitation abuse against any person for the same conduct for which the person was convicted of unlawful visitation interference or subject that person to the sanctions provided for in this Section.

Author's Notes

Analysis

1. Visitation under the Illinois Domestic Violence Act.
2. Cross reference—Form.
3. Cross reference.

(1) **Visitation under the Illinois Domestic Violence Act.** See also 750 ILCS 60/214(b)(7) for visitation under the Illinois Domestic Violence Act.

(2) **Cross reference—Form.** For a model Petition for a Rule to Show Cause in order to initiate contempt proceedings, see IMDMA § 511 Author's Note (6).

(3) **Cross reference.** IMDMA § 607.1(g) provides that a person shall not be subject to sanctions under § 607.1 for the same conduct for which that person was convicted under 720 ILCS 5/10–5.5, Unlawful visitation interference. Both IMDMA § 607.1(g) and § 5/10–5.5 of the Criminal Code were effective January 1, 1994.

750 ILCS 5/608

§ 608. Judicial supervision

(a) Except as otherwise agreed by the parties in writing at the time of the custody judgment or as otherwise ordered by the court, the custodian may determine the child's upbringing, including but not limited to, his education, health care and religious training, unless the court, after hearing, finds, upon motion by the noncustodial parent, that the absence of a specific limitation of the custodian's authority would clearly be contrary to the best interests of the child.

(b) If both parents or all contestants agree to the order, or if the court finds that in the absence of agreement the child's physical health would be endangered or his emotional development significantly impaired, the court may order the Department of Children and Family Services to exercise continuing supervision over the case to assure that the custodial or visitation terms of the judgment are carried out. Supervision shall be carried out under the provisions of Section 5 of the Children and Family Services Act.

Author's Notes

(1) **Right of custodial parent to make major decisions concerning child.** It should be carefully noted that pursuant to § 608(a), in the absence of an agreement by the parties in writing at the time of the custody judgment, or as otherwise ordered by the court, a custodian determines major questions relating to a child, unless the court, upon motion by the non-custodial parent, limits the custodian's authority. In sole custody agreements or orders, a non-custodial parent should therefore be vigilant to protect his voice in the child's life.

750 ILCS 5/609

§ 609. Leave to remove children

(a) The court may grant leave, before or after judgment, to any party having custody of any minor child or children to remove such child or children from Illinois whenever such approval is in the best interests of such child or children. The burden of proving that such removal is in the best interests of such child or children is on the party seeking the removal. When such removal is permitted, the court may require the party removing such child or children from Illinois to give reasonable security guaranteeing the return of such children.

(b) Before a minor child is temporarily removed from Illinois, the parent responsible for the removal shall inform the other parent, or the other parent's attorney, of the address and telephone number where the child may be reached during the period of temporary removal, and the date on which the child shall return to Illinois.

The State of Illinois retains jurisdiction when the minor child is absent from the State pursuant to this subsection.

Author's Notes

Analysis

1. Standard for removal from Illinois.
2. Conditions warranting removal from Illinois.
3. Visitation of non-custodial parent after child is removed from Illinois.
4. Security requirements.

(1) **Standard for removal from Illinois.** Removal of a child from Illinois is not favored because it disrupts the remaining parent's visitation and involvement with the child, and makes it more difficult for the court to exercise its jurisdiction over the absent child and parent outside of the state. Therefore, the best interests of the child standard is again the criterion applied to determine whether a child can be removed from the State of Illinois. In re Marriage of Davis, 229 Ill.App.3d 653, 660, 171 Ill.Dec. 590, 595, 594 N.E.2d 734, 739 (4th Dist.), *appeal denied*, 146 Ill.2d 625, 176 Ill.Dec. 795, 602 N.E.2d 449 (1992). The parent seeking removal bears the burden of showing that the move is in the child's best interests. In re Marriage of Gratz, 193 Ill.App.3d 142, 148, 139 Ill.Dec. 611, 614, 548 N.E.2d 1325, 1328 (2d Dist.1989).

(2) **Conditions warranting removal from Illinois.** The Illinois Supreme Court set forth the following factors to be considered in determining the best interests of the child regarding the proposed removal:

> The court should consider the proposed move in terms of likelihood for enhancing the general quality of life for both the custodial parent and the children. The court should also consider the motives of the custodial parent in seeking the move to determine whether the removal is merely a ruse intended to defeat or frustrate visitation. Similarly, the court should consider the motives of the noncustodial parent in resisting the removal. It is also in the best interests of a child to have a healthy and close relationship with both parents, as well as other family members. Therefore, the visitation rights of the noncustodial parent should be carefully considered. Another factor is whether, in a given case, a realistic and reasonable visitation schedule can be reached if the move is allowed.

In re Marriage of Eckert, 119 Ill.2d 316, 327–28, 116 Ill.Dec. 220, 224, 518 N.E.2d 1041, 1045 (1988) (citations omitted).

The court may consider the enhancement of the custodial parent's life resulting from the proposed removal insofar as it also enhances the life of the child. Several courts have reasoned that a move that enhances the life of the custodial parent may also indirectly enhance the life of the child, and therefore may be considered in the child's best interests. See, e.g., In re Marriage of Taylor, 202 Ill.App.3d 740, 147 Ill.Dec. 810, 559 N.E.2d 1150 (3d Dist.1990) (custodial mother would see more of her new husband, would have to maintain only one household and would receive camaraderie from military community if allowed to relocate with the child; this would enhance the general quality of her life and indirectly benefit the child's quality of life); In re Marriage of Roppo, 225 Ill.App.3d 721, 167 Ill.Dec. 416, 587 N.E.2d 1031 (1st Dist.1991) (custodial mother would be "happier and more fulfilled" living near her family and family surroundings; this would indirectly increase the child's quality of life). Several courts have strongly rejected this reasoning. *Cf.* In re Marriage of Berk, 215 Ill.App.3d 459, 158 Ill.Dec. 971, 574 N.E.2d 1364 (2d Dist.1991); In re Marriage of Davis, 229 Ill.App.3d 653, 171 Ill.Dec. 590, 594 N.E.2d 734 (4th Dist.), *appeal denied*, 146 Ill.2d 625, 176 Ill.Dec. 795, 602 N.E.2d 449 (1992).

Courts may allow removal when the custodial parent remarries a person from another state. Courts allowing removal in order to be closer to a new spouse often reason that the child will be indirectly benefited if his or her custodial parent is directly benefitted by increased time with the new spouse. See, e.g., In re Marriage of Taylor, 202 Ill.App.3d 740, 147 Ill.Dec. 810, 559 N.E.2d 1150 (3d Dist.1990); In re Marriage of Miroballi, 225 Ill.App.3d 1094, 168 Ill.Dec. 165, 589 N.E.2d 565 (1st Dist.1991). But see In re Marriage of Berk, 215 Ill.App.3d 459, 466–67, 158 Ill.Dec. 971, 976, 574 N.E.2d 1364, 1369 (2d Dist.1991):

> It is virtually impossible to envision a situation wherein the custodial parent does not wish to live with a new spouse. If the obvious happiness the spouse would receive from being able to live with a new spouse were sufficient to prove removal in the child's best interests, court supervision of the proceedings would be unnecessary, and at best, ceremonial. A custodial parent must prove more than his or her own desire to live with a new spouse to prove that a child's best interests will be served by removal.

Accord, In re Marriage of Davis, 229 Ill.App.3d 653, 171 Ill.Dec. 590, 594 N.E.2d 734 (4th Dist.), *appeal denied*, 146 Ill.2d 625, 176 Ill.Dec. 795, 602 N.E.2d 449 (1992).

Removal has also been allowed when the parent seeking removal has better job opportunities in another state, and the increased earnings will provide a better lifestyle for the child. See, e.g., In re Marriage of Taylor, 202 Ill.App.3d 740, 147 Ill.Dec. 810, 559 N.E.2d 1150 (3d Dist.1990). Similarly, removal has been allowed when the move would increase the family's income, and as a result the custodial parent would be able to cease working outside the home and spend more time with the child. See, e.g., In re Marriage of Pribble and Wagenblast, 239 Ill.App.3d 761, 180 Ill.Dec. 455, 607 N.E.2d 349 (5th Dist.1993); In re Marriage of Miroballi, 225 Ill.App.3d 1094, 168 Ill.Dec. 165, 589 N.E.2d 565 (1st Dist.1991); In re Marriage of Gratz, 193 Ill.App.3d 142, 139 Ill.Dec. 611, 548 N.E.2d 1325 (2d Dist.1989).

Earlier cases generally permitted removal more readily than do later cases, which concentrate more on the benefits to the children than on the opportunities for the parent seeking removal. See, e.g, In re Marriage of Siklossy, 87 Ill.App.3d 124, 128, 42 Ill.Dec. 534, 409 N.E.2d 29, 32 (1st Dist.1980) ("a court should not oppose the removal of the children from Illinois unless there is a specific showing that the move would be against the children's best interest").

(3) **Visitation of non-custodial parent after child is removed from Illinois.** Where removal is allowed, the visitation of the parent who remains in the State of Illinois is adjusted, usually to allow him less frequent visitation, but for extended periods of time. See, e.g., In re Marriage of Gratz, 193 Ill.App.3d 142, 149, 139 Ill.Dec. 611, 615, 548 N.E.2d 1325, 1329 (2d Dist.1989) (rejecting noncustodial parent's preference for regular contact, rather than exclusive contact with the child over longer periods of time). Transportation costs are frequently assessed to the party who removes the children from the State of Illinois. See, e.g., In re Marriage of Gratz, 193 Ill.App.3d 142, 139 Ill.Dec. 611, 548 N.E.2d 1325 (2d Dist.1989) (custodial parent would pay for child's flights to see noncustodial parent during summer vacation); In re Marriage of Zamarripa–Gesundheit, 175 Ill.App.3d 184, 124 Ill.Dec. 799, 529 N.E.2d 780 (1st Dist.1988), *appeal denied*, 124 Ill.2d 563, 129 Ill.Dec. 157, 535 N.E.2d 922 (1989) (child support payments placed in escrow account to fund transportation for visitation).

(4) **Security requirements.** A bond, the posting of a bank account, or other security may be required to guarantee the return of children to the State of Illinois for

750 ILCS 5/609   **FAMILIES**

visitation or when their removal is temporary. See, e.g., Gray v. Gray, 57 Ill.App.3d 1, 14 Ill.Dec. 630, 372 N.E.2d 909 (1st Dist.1978); Reddig v. Reddig, 12 Ill.App.3d 1009, 299 N.E.2d 353 (3d Dist.1973).

750 ILCS 5/610
§ 610. Modification

(a) Unless by stipulation of the parties, no motion to modify a custody judgment may be made earlier than 2 years after its date, unless the court permits it to be made on the basis of affidavits that there is reason to believe the child's present environment may endanger seriously his physical, mental, moral or emotional health.

(b) The court shall not modify a prior custody judgment unless it finds by clear and convincing evidence, upon the basis of facts that have arisen since the prior judgment or that were unknown to the court at the time of entry of the prior judgment, that a change has occurred in the circumstances of the child or his custodian, or in the case of a joint custody arrangement that a change has occurred in the circumstances of the child or either or both parties having custody, and that the modification is necessary to serve the best interest of the child. In the case of joint custody, if the parties agree to a termination of a joint custody arrangement, the court shall so terminate the joint custody and make any modification which is in the child's best interest. The court shall state in its decision specific findings of fact in support of its modification or termination of joint custody if either parent opposes the modification or termination.

(c) Attorney fees and costs shall be assessed against a party seeking modification if the court finds that the modification action is vexatious and constitutes harassment.

(d) Notice under this section shall be given as provided in subsection (c) and (d) of Section 601.

Author's Notes

Analysis

1. Two year stay on custody modifications.
2. Precedence of initial custody arrangements.
3. Attorney's fees.
4. Notice of modification.
5. Modification: Findings of fact.

(1) **Two year stay on custody modifications.** Because the courts desire stability and finality in child custody arrangements, a custody order may not be modified within two years after the judgment is entered, unless the parties stipulate to the modification, or unless a serious endangerment criterion is satisfied.

> Section 610 of the Marriage Act was enacted to provide a degree of finality to child custody cases. The rationale for this provision was to provide stability and permanency in children's custodial and environmental relationships. The law favors the preservation of the existing custody judgment. Additionally, reviewing

courts are reluctant to interfere with the disposition of the trial court in child custody matters.

In re Marriage of Pease, 106 Ill.App.3d 617, 621, 62 Ill.App.3d 617, 622, 435 N.E.2d 1361, 1366 (2d Dist.1982) (citations omitted).

To warrant a modification within the first two years, the petitioner must submit affidavits showing a serious endangerment to the physical, mental, moral, or emotional health of a child. If the affidavits are sufficient, the court must then proceed to a hearing that presents sufficient evidence to show serious endangerment before a change will be granted. In re Custody of Carter, 137 Ill.App.3d 439, 92 Ill.Dec. 320, 484 N.E.2d 1175 (2d Dist.1985). See, e.g., In re Marriage of Eleopoulos, 186 Ill.App.3d 374, 134 Ill.Dec. 326, 542 N.E.2d 505 (4th Dist.1989) (affidavit reporting incident when custodial father struck daughter, causing bruises, was sufficient to warrant modification hearing within two years of enactment of custody order); In re Marriage of Olson, 98 Ill.App.3d 316, 53 Ill.Dec. 751, 424 N.E.2d 386 (3d Dist.1981) (custodial mother's sexual relationship with unmarried man did not threaten the moral, emotional or mental health of the child; modification within two years was properly denied).

After two years, the standard applied to a petition to modify custody is lower. The petitioner must first show that there is a change in circumstances in regard to either the child or the custodian, or material facts have come to light that were unknown at the time of the original judgment. The petitioner must then show that modification is necessary to serve the best interests of the child. A showing of changed circumstances alone is insufficient to warrant modification of custody. In re Marriage of Fuesting, 228 Ill.App.3d 339, 169 Ill.Dec. 456, 591 N.E.2d 960 (5th Dist.1992) (custodial mother's cohabitation with fiance was insufficient grounds for modification without showing that child's welfare was affected). See also, In re Marriage of Valter, 191 Ill.App.3d 584, 138 Ill.Dec. 799, 548 N.E.2d 29 (5th Dist.1989) (substantial changes warranted modification; custodial father acknowledged alcohol dependency, remarried and brought four new children into the house); In re Marriage of Eldert, 158 Ill.App.3d 798, 110 Ill.Dec. 768, 511 N.E.2d 945 (3d Dist.1987), *appeal denied*, 118 Ill.2d 542, 117 Ill.Dec. 224, 520 N.E.2d 385 (1988) (child's behavioral and emotional problems constituted sufficient showing of changed circumstances, evidence supported finding that modification was in the child's best interest); Vollmer v. Mattox, 137 Ill.App.3d 1, 91 Ill.Dec. 752, 484 N.E.2d 311 (5th Dist.1985) (remanding modification of custody; although trial court found that modification would be in the child's best interests, it did not first find any change of circumstances as required under § 610); Ehr v. Ehr, 77 Ill.App.3d 540, 33 Ill.Dec. 11, 396 N.E.2d 87 (2d Dist.1979) (custodial parent's past promiscuity and marijuana use did not seriously endanger child).

Even though the standard for custody modification after two years is lower, it is also true that a court may be less inclined to disturb a custody arrangement that has endured for that period of time in the absence of egregious circumstances.

(2) **Precedence of initial custody arrangements.** It is critical that custody arrangements be well thought out or adjudicated prior to the entry of a final custody judgment. Custody questions should never be glossed over in an effort to get to an agreement. Because the courts favor stability in custody arrangements, alterations in custody after a final judgment can be difficult. The serious endangerment standard

applied within two years of the original custody judgment is not easy to establish, and, even after the two years, the court will likely be predisposed to favor stability and continuity, and deny a request to alter custody. Furthermore, the burden of proof is on the parent seeking a change of custody, Nolte v. Nolte, 241 Ill.App.3d 320, 182 Ill.Dec. 78, 609 N.E.2d 381 (3d Dist.1993), and the standard of "clear and convincing evidence" that a change in custody is in the best interests of the children after two years is a higher standard than the usual preponderance of the evidence. *Id.*

(3) **Attorney's fees.** Section 610(c) allows the court to assess attorney's fees against a party who has brought a modification action found to be vexatious and harassing. Repeated unsuccessful modification actions may be vexatious, and may warrant an award of attorney's fees. See, e.g., In re Marriage of Lewis, 188 Ill.App.3d 142, 135 Ill.Dec. 667, 544 N.E.2d 24 (5th Dist.1989).

(4) **Notice of modification.** Effective January, 1993, notice for a modification of custody is to be given as provided in subsections (c) and (d) of IMDMA § 601. See IMDMA §§ 601(c), 601(d) Author's Notes (4) and (5).

(5) **Modification: Findings of fact.** IMDMA § 610(b) requires that specific findings of fact be set forth in support of orders modifying custody judgments or terminating joint custody in contested proceedings. In re Marriage of Oliver, 155 Ill.App.3d 181, 107 Ill.Dec. 929, 507 N.E.2d 1298 (5th Dist.1987).

750 ILCS 5/611

§ 611. Enforcement of custody order or order prohibiting removal of child from the jurisdiction of the court

(a) The court may enter a judgment to enforce a custody order or a court order prohibiting removal of the child from the jurisdiction of the court if it finds that the respondent has violated the terms of the court order by having improperly removed the child from the physical custody of the petitioner or another person entitled to custody or by having improperly retained the child after a visit or other temporary relinquishment of physical custody.

If the general whereabouts of the child are known, the judgment shall direct any sheriff or law enforcement officer to provide assistance to the petitioner in apprehending the child and shall further authorize any child care personnel, babysitter, teacher or any person having physical custody of the child to surrender the child to such sheriff or law enforcement officer.

(b) The court may enter a judgment pursuant to subsection (a) of this Section without prior notice to the respondent if the court finds that prior notice would be likely to cause the respondent's flight from the jurisdiction or cause further removal or concealment of the child. If an ex parte order is entered pursuant to this subsection, the respondent may, upon 2 days notice to the petitioner or upon such shorter notice as the court may prescribe, appear and move for the dissolution or modification of the judgment and in that event the court shall proceed to hear and determine such motion as expeditiously as possible.

(c) Nothing contained in this Section shall be construed to limit the court's contempt power.

PART VII. MISCELLANEOUS

Analysis

Sec.
701. Marital residence—Order granting possession to spouse.
702. Maintenance in case of bigamy.
703. Lien of judgment—Sales.
704. Public Aid provisions.
705. Support payments—Receiving and disbursing agents.
706.1 Withholding of income to secure payment of support.
706.2 Posting security, bond or guarantee to secure payment.
707. Certificate of dissolution or invalidity of marriage—Filing with Department of Public Health.
708. Disclosure of address.
709. Mandatory child support payments to clerk.
710. Enforcement; Penalties.
711. Fees.
712. Child support enforcement program—Certification—Child and Spouse Support Unit in Department of Public Aid—Powers and duties—Financial assistance in counties.
713. Attachment of the body.

WESTLAW Electronic Research

See WESTLAW Electronic Research Guide preceding the Summary of Contents.

---

750 ILCS 5/701

§ 701. Marital residence—Order granting possession to spouse

Where there is on file a verified complaint or verified petition seeking temporary eviction from the marital residence, the court may, during the pendency of the proceeding, only in cases where the physical or mental well being of either spouse or their children is jeopardized by occupancy of the marital residence by both spouses, and only upon due notice and full hearing, unless waived by the court on good cause shown, enter orders of injunction, mandatory or restraining, granting the exclusive possession of the marital residence to either spouse, by eviction from, or restoration of, the marital residence, until the final determination of the cause. No such order shall in any manner affect any estate in homestead property of either party.

Author's Notes

Analysis

1. Stringent requirements.
2. Domestic Violence Act.
3. Balancing of hardships.

(1) **Stringent requirements.** The standard for granting exclusive possession of a marital residence to a spouse in IMDMA § 701 is of a high order, requiring the petitioner to show that his or his children's physical or mental well-being is jeopar-

750 ILCS 5/701

dized by the occupancy of the marital residence by both spouses. There is also a requirement of due notice and full hearing unless waived by the court for good cause shown. Both the standard of showing jeopardy and the requirement of full hearing unless there is good cause have been protected by the courts with the result that only serious cases of jeopardy have resulted in evictions from the marital residence pursuant to § 701. See, e.g., In re Marriage of Lombaer, 200 Ill.App.3d 712, 146 Ill.Dec. 425, 558 N.E.2d 388 (1st Dist.1990) (wife's hospitalization for mental problems and failure to take medication prescribed there were "insufficient to meet the onerous standard of serious endangerment"); In re Marriage of Hoffsetter, 102 Ill.App.3d 392, 58 Ill.Dec. 137, 430 N.E.2d 79 (1st Dist.1981) (wife's testimony that husband struck her with his fist, an iron and a gun, and husband's admission that he beat wife were sufficient evidence to justify award of exclusive possession of the marital home to the wife).

(2) **Domestic Violence Act.** As a result of the requirement for a showing of serious jeopardy pursuant to IMDMA § 701, where there is "abuse," most petitions for exclusive possession of the marital home are brought under the Illinois Domestic Violence Act. See 750 ILCS 60/101 et seq. and accompanying Author's Notes. "Abuse" includes "harassment." 750 ILCS 60/103(1).

(3) **Balancing of hardships.** Section 214(b)(2) of the Illinois Domestic Violence Act, 750 ILCS 60/214(b)(2), expressly states that, in determining exclusive possession, the court shall not be limited by the standard set forth in IMDMA § 701. In determining whether to grant exclusive possession of the marital home, § 214(b)(2) of the Illinois Domestic Violence Act provides for a balancing of hardships between the petitioner and the respondent and those dependent upon them, rather than applying the IMDMA § 701 standard of jeopardy to the physical or mental well-being of the petitioner. Rather than the requirement of good cause shown in IMDMA § 701, in order to waive due notice and a full hearing, § 217(a)(3)(ii) of the Illinois Domestic Violence Act, 750 ILCS 60/217(a)(3)(ii), allows a balancing of immediate danger to petitioner against hardships to respondent of granting an emergency order of exclusive possession without prior notice to the respondent and without a full hearing.

750 ILCS 5/702

§ 702. Maintenance in case of bigamy

When a dissolution of marriage is granted to a person who shall, in good faith, have intermarried with a person having at the time of such marriage, another spouse or spouses living, the court may, nevertheless, allow the petitioner maintenance in the same manner as in other cases of dissolution of marriage; but no such allowance shall be made as will be inconsistent with the rights of such other spouse or spouses, which shall first be ascertained by the court before the granting of such maintenance.

750 ILCS 5/703

§ 703. Lien of judgment—Sales

Whenever, in any case of dissolution of marriage, a judgment orders that maintenance be made a lien on any real estate to arise to secure the payment of any money to become due by installments, and a sale of such real estate to be made if necessary to satisfy any of such installments, the property shall be sold subject to the lien of the installments not then due, unless the court shall at the same time direct otherwise, and subsequent sales may, from time to time, be made to enforce such lien as the installments may become due, until all installments are paid.

Author's Notes

Analysis

1. Maintenance from real property.
2. Cross reference—Form.
3. *In rem* actions.
4. Cross reference.

(1) **Maintenance from real property.** Where a respondent does not have income, but does own real property, maintenance can be obtained from the real property pursuant to IMDMA § 703 and IMDMA § 504(a), which provide that maintenance can be paid from property. See, e.g., Varap v. Varap, 76 Ill.App.2d 402, 222 N.E.2d 77 (1st Dist.1966) (affirming wife's lien for maintenance against husband's real property); Wilson v. Smart, 324 Ill. 276, 281–282, 155 N.E. 288, 291(1927). The real property sought to be sold in order to provide support must be described in the petition. Interstate Bank of Oak Forest v. Cardona, 167 Ill.App.3d 214, 218, 118 Ill.Dec. 72, 75, 521 N.E.2d 140, 143 (3d Dist.1988). A *lis pendens* notice should be filed at the start of the litigation in order for the petitioner seeking support to gain priority to the proceeds of the property over other creditors.

(2) **Cross reference—Form.** For *lis pendens* sample form and explanation see 735 ILCS 5/2–1901 Author's Notes (1) through (3).

(3) ***In rem* actions.** In situations where the party seeking support cannot obtain actual service of process on the respondent because his whereabouts are unknown or he is not reachable under the long arm statute, support can be obtained from any real estate owned by the respondent and located in the jurisdiction by means of an *in rem* action against the real estate. See Schneider v. Schneider, 312 Ill.App. 59, 69, 37 N.E.2d 911, 916 (1st Dist.1941):

> While a purely personal decree awarding alimony against a nonresident defendant who is notified of the proceeding by publication and who does not appear is not binding upon him, the proceeding will partake of the nature of a proceeding in rem where the complainant describes property of the defendant within the court's jurisdiction and prays that alimony and solicitor's fees be made a lien on said property, and the decree may provide that in the event of the defendant's failure to pay the sum fixed for alimony and solicitor's fees within a stated time the property shall be sold to satisfy the decree.

(4) **Cross reference.** See 750 ILCS 65/11 for *in rem* actions in cases of abandonment which requires absence for one year. Query, whether the one year absence is necessary if the proceeding is brought under IMDMA §§ 504(a) and 703 rather than 750 ILCS 65/11?

750 ILCS 5/704

§ 704. Public Aid provisions

Except as provided in Sections 709 through 712, if maintenance, child support or both, is awarded to persons who are recipients of aid under "The

Illinois Public Aid Code", the court shall direct the husband or wife, as the case may be, to make the payments to (1) the Illinois Department of Public Aid if the persons are recipients under Articles III, IV or V of the Code, or (2) the local governmental unit responsible for their support if they are recipients under Article VI or VII of the Code. The order shall permit the Illinois Department of Public Aid or the local governmental unit, as the case may be, to direct that subsequent payments be made directly to the former spouse, the children, or both, or to some person or agency in their behalf, upon removal of the former spouse or children from the public aid rolls; and upon such direction and removal of the recipients from the public aid rolls, the Illinois Department or local governmental unit, as the case requires, shall give written notice of such action to the court.

750 ILCS 5/705

§ 705. Support payments—Receiving and disbursing agents

(1) The provisions of this Section shall apply, except as provided in Sections 709 through 712.

(2) In a dissolution of marriage action filed in a county of less than 3 million population in which an order or judgment for child support is entered, and in supplementary proceedings in any such county to enforce or vary the terms of such order or judgment arising out of an action for dissolution of marriage filed in such county, the court, except as it otherwise orders, under subsection (4) of this Section, may direct that child support payments be made to the clerk of the court.

(3) In a dissolution of marriage action filed in any county of 3 million or more population in which an order or judgment for child support is entered, and in supplementary proceedings in any such county to enforce or vary the terms of such order or judgment arising out of an action for dissolution of marriage filed in such county, the court, except as it otherwise orders under subsection (4) of this Section, may direct that child support payments be made either to the clerk of the court or to the Court Service Division of the County Department of Public Aid. After the effective date of this Act, the court, except as it otherwise orders under subsection (4) of this Section, may direct that child support payments be made either to the clerk of the court or to the Illinois Department of Public Aid.

(4) In a dissolution of marriage action or supplementary proceedings involving maintenance or child support payments, or both, to persons who are recipients of aid under The Illinois Public Aid Code, the court shall direct that such payments be made to (a) the Illinois Department of Public Aid if the persons are recipients under Articles III, IV, or V of the Code, or (b) the local governmental unit responsible for their support if they are recipients under Articles VI or VII of the Code. The Illinois Department of Public Aid may continue to collect current maintenance or child support payments, or both, for a period not to exceed three months from the month following the month in which such persons cease to receive public assistance, and pay all amounts

so collected to such persons. At the end of such three month period, the Illinois Department of Public Aid may continue to collect such payments if authorized by such persons to do so, and pay the net amount so collected to such persons after deducting any costs incurred in making the collection or any collection fee from the amount of any recovery made. The order shall permit the Illinois Department of Public Aid or the local governmental unit, as the case may be, to direct that subsequent payments be made directly to the former spouse, the children, or both, or to some person or agency in their behalf, upon removal of the former spouse or children from the public aid rolls or upon termination of any extended collection period; and upon such direction, the Illinois Department or local governmental unit, as the case requires, shall give written notice of such action to the court.

(5) All clerks of the court and the Court Service Division of a County Department of Public Aid and, after the effective date of this Act, all clerks of the court and the Illinois Department of Public Aid, receiving child support payments under subsections (2) and (3) of this Section shall disburse the payments to the person or persons entitled thereto under the terms of the order or judgment. They shall establish and maintain current records of all moneys received and disbursed and of defaults and delinquencies in required payments. The court, by order or rule, shall make provision for the carrying out of these duties.

Payments under this Section to the Illinois Department of Public Aid pursuant to the Child Support Enforcement Program established by Title IV-D of the Social Security Act shall be paid into the Child Support Enforcement Trust Fund. All other payments under this Section to the Illinois Department of Public Aid shall be deposited in the Public Assistance Recoveries Trust Fund. Disbursements from these funds shall be as provided in The Illinois Public Aid Code. Payments received by a local governmental unit shall be deposited in that unit's General Assistance Fund. Any order of court directing payment of child support to a clerk of court or the Court Service Division of a County Department of Public Aid, which order has been entered on or after August 14, 1961, and prior to the effective date of this Act, may be amended by the court in line with this Act; and orders involving payments of maintenance or child support to recipients of public aid may in like manner be amended to conform to this Act.

(6) No filing fee or costs will be required in any action brought at the request of the Illinois Department of Public Aid in any proceeding under this Act. However, any such fees or costs may be assessed by the court against the respondent in the court's order of support or any modification thereof in a proceeding under this Act.

(7) For those cases in which child support is payable to the clerk of the circuit court for transmittal to the Illinois Department of Public Aid by order of court, the clerk shall transmit all such payments, within 4 working days of receipt, to insure that funds are available for immediate distribution by the Department to the person or entity entitled thereto in accordance with

750 ILCS 5/705 FAMILIES

standards of the Child Support Enforcement Program established under Title IV–D of the Social Security Act. The clerk shall notify the Department of the date of receipt and amount thereof at the time of transmittal. Where the clerk has entered into an agreement of cooperation with the Department to record the terms of child support orders and payments made thereunder directly into the Department's automated data processing system, the clerk shall account for, transmit and otherwise distribute child support payments in accordance with such agreement in lieu of the requirements contained herein.

In any action filed in a county with a population of 1,000,000 or less, the court shall assess against the respondent in any order of maintenance or child support any sum up to $36 annually authorized by ordinance of the county board to be collected by the clerk of the court as costs for administering the collection and disbursement of maintenance and child support payments. Such sum shall be in addition to and separate from amounts ordered to be paid as maintenance or child support.

Author's Notes

Analysis

1. Payments to court or Public Aid.
2. Cross reference—Forms.

(1) **Payments to court or Public Aid.** IMDMA § 705 governs payments of child support and payments of maintenance to recipients of public aid through the clerk of the court or to the Department of Public Aid. Section 705, except as is provided in §§ 709 through 712 of the Illinois Marriage and Dissolution of Marriage Act, is discretionary as to children's support payments for persons not on public aid, but mandatory for those persons receiving public aid. Sections 709 through 712, in regard to those persons receiving public aid, are mandatory in those counties covered by these Sections. They are discretionary whether the court may direct that payments be made to the clerk of the court in cases not covered by public aid. Section 705 can apply to any county, although there are some differences depending upon whether the county has more or less than 3,000,000 in population.

(2) **Cross reference—Forms.** See IMDMA § 502 Author's Note (11) para. 5(a) for model agreement paragraph waiving payment of maintenance and children's support to the clerk of court, and see IMDMA § 413 Author's Note (8), Judgment and Alternative Provisions para. 8, for corresponding judgment paragraph. IMDMA §§ 705 and 709 through 712 govern the payments to the Clerk of the Court or to the Public Aid. See IMDMA § 507 for corresponding provision for those not on public aid.

750 ILCS 5/706.1

§ 706.1 Withholding of income to secure payment of support

(A) Definitions.

(1) "Order for support" means any order of the court which provides for periodic payment of funds for the support of a child or maintenance of a spouse, whether temporary or final, and includes any such order which provides for:

(a) Modification or resumption of, or payment of arrearage accrued under, a previously existing order;

(b) Reimbursement of support; or

(c) Enrollment in a health insurance plan that is available to the obligor through an employer.

(2) "Arrearage" means the total amount of unpaid support obligations.

(3) "Delinquency" means any payment under an order for support which becomes due and remains unpaid after an order for withholding has been entered under subsection (B) or, for purposes of subsection (K), after the last order for support was entered for which no order for withholding was entered.

(4) "Income" means any form of periodic payment to an individual, regardless of source, including, but not limited to: wages, salary, commission, compensation as an independent contractor, workers' compensation, disability, annuity and retirement benefits, lottery prize awards, insurance proceeds, vacation pay, bonuses, profit-sharing payments and any other payments, made by any person, private entity, federal or state government, any unit of local government, school district or any entity created by Public Act; however, "income" excludes:

(a) Any amounts required by law to be withheld, other than creditor claims, including, but not limited to, federal, State and local taxes, Social Security and other retirement and disability contributions;

(b) Union dues;

(c) Any amounts exempted by the federal Consumer Credit Protection Act;

(d) Public assistance payments; and

(e) Unemployment insurance benefits except as provided by law.

Any other State or local laws which limit or exempt income or the amount or percentage of income that can be withheld shall not apply.

(5) "Obligor" means the individual who owes a duty to make payments under an order for support.

(6) "Obligee" means the individual to whom a duty of support is owed or the individual's legal representative.

(7) "Payor" means any payor of income to an obligor.

(8) "Public office" means any elected official or any State or local agency which is or may become responsible by law for enforcement of, or which is or may become authorized to enforce, an order for support, including, but not limited to: the Attorney General, the Illinois Department of Public Aid, the Illinois Department of Mental Health and Developmental Disabilities, the Illinois Department of Children and Family Services, and the various State's Attorneys, Clerks of the Circuit Court and supervisors of general assistance.

750 ILCS 5/706.1   FAMILIES

(9) "Premium" means the dollar amount for which the obligor is liable to his employer and which must be paid to enroll or maintain a child in a health insurance plan that is available to the obligor through an employer.

(B) Entry of an order for withholding.

(1) Upon entry of any order for support on or after January 1, 1984, the court shall enter a separate order for withholding which shall not take effect unless the obligor becomes delinquent in paying the order for support or the obligor requests an earlier effective date; except that the court may require the order for withholding to take effect immediately.

On or after January 1, 1989, the court shall require the order for withholding to take effect immediately, unless a written agreement is reached between both parties providing for an alternative arrangement, approved by the court, which insures payment of support. In that case, the court shall enter the order for withholding which will not take effect unless the obligor becomes delinquent in paying the order for support.

Upon entry of any order of support on or after September 11, 1989, if the obligor is not a United States citizen, the obligor shall provide to the court the obligor's alien registration number, passport number, and home country's social security or national health number, if applicable; the court shall make the information part of the record in the case.

(2) An order for withholding shall be entered upon petition by the obligee or public office where an order for withholding has not been previously entered.

(3) The order for withholding shall:

(a) Direct any payor to withhold a dollar amount equal to the order for support; and

(b) Direct any payor to withhold an additional dollar amount, not less than 20% of the order for support, until payment in full of any delinquency stated in the notice of delinquency provided for in subsection (C) or (F) of this Section; and

(c) Direct any payor to enroll a child as a beneficiary of a health insurance plan and withhold any required premiums; and

(d) State the rights, remedies and duties of the obligor under this Section; and

(e) Include the obligor's Social Security Number, which the obligor shall disclose to the court.

(f) Include the date that withholding for current support terminates, which shall be the date of termination of the current support obligation set forth in the order for support.

(4) At the time the order for withholding is entered, the Clerk of the Circuit Court shall provide a copy of the order for withholding and the order for support to the obligor and shall make copies available to the obligee and

public office. Any copy of the order for withholding furnished to the parties under this subsection shall be stamped "Not Valid".

(5) The order for withholding shall remain in effect for as long as the order for support upon which it is based.

(6) The failure of an order for withholding to state an arrearage is not conclusive of the issue of whether an arrearage is owing.

(7) Notwithstanding the provisions of this subsection, if the court finds at the time of any hearing that an arrearage has accrued in an amount equal to at least one month's support obligation or that the obligor is 30 days late in paying all or part of the order for support, the court shall order immediate service of the order for withholding upon the payor.

(C) Notice of delinquency.

(1) Whenever an obligor becomes delinquent in payment of an amount equal to at least one month's support obligation pursuant to the order for support or is at least 30 days late in complying with all or part of the order for support, whichever occurs first, the obligee or public office may prepare and serve a verified notice of delinquency, together with a form petition to stay service, pursuant to paragraph (3) of this subsection.

(2) The notice of delinquency shall recite the terms of the order for support and contain a computation of the period and total amount of the delinquency, as of the date of the notice. The notice shall clearly state that it will be sent to the payor, together with a specially certified copy of the order for withholding, except as provided in subsection (F), unless the obligor files a petition to stay service in accordance with paragraph (1) of subsection (D).

(3) The notice of delinquency shall be served by ordinary mail addressed to the obligor at his or her last known address.

(4) The obligor may execute a written waiver of the provisions of paragraphs (1) through (3) of this subsection and request immediate service upon the payor.

(D) Procedures to avoid income withholding.

(1) Except as provided in subsection (F), the obligor may prevent an order for withholding from being served by filing a petition to stay service with the Clerk of the Circuit Court, within 20 days after service of the notice of delinquency; however, the grounds for the petition to stay service shall be limited to:

(a) A dispute concerning the amount of current support or the existence or amount of the delinquency;

(b) The identity of the obligor.

The Clerk of the Circuit Court shall notify the obligor and the obligee or public office, as appropriate, of the time and place of the hearing on the petition to stay service. The court shall hold such hearing pursuant to the provisions of subsection (H).

(2) Except as provided in subsection (F), filing of a petition to stay service, within the 20-day period required under this subsection, shall prohibit the obligee or public office from serving the order for withholding on any payor of the obligor.

(E) Initial service of order for withholding.

(1) Except as provided in subsection (F), in order to serve an order for withholding upon a payor, an obligee or public office shall follow the procedures set forth in this subsection. After 20 days following service of the notice of delinquency, the obligee or public office shall file with the Clerk of the Circuit Court an affidavit, with the copy of the notice of delinquency attached thereto, stating:

(a) that the notice of delinquency has been duly served and the date on which service was effected; and

(b) that the obligor has not filed a petition to stay service, or in the alternative

(c) that the obligor has waived the provisions of subparagraphs (a) and (b) of this paragraph (1) in accordance with subsection (C)(4).

(2) Upon request of the obligee or public office, the Clerk of the Circuit Court shall: (a) make available any record of payment; and (b) determine that the file contains a copy of the affidavit described in paragraph (1). The Clerk shall then provide to the obligee or public office a specially certified copy of the order for withholding and the notice of delinquency indicating that the preconditions for service have been met.

(3) The obligee or public office may then serve the notice of delinquency and order for withholding on the payor, its superintendent, manager or other agent, by certified mail or personal delivery. A proof of service shall be filed with the Clerk of the Circuit Court.

(F) Subsequent service of order for withholding.

(1) Notwithstanding the provisions of this Section, at any time after the court has ordered immediate service of an order for withholding or after initial service of an order for withholding pursuant to subsection (E), the obligee or public office may serve the order for withholding upon any payor of the obligor without further notice to the obligor. The obligee or public office shall provide notice to the payor, pursuant to paragraph (6) of subsection (I), of any payments that have been made through previous withholding or any other method.

(2) The Clerk of the Circuit Court shall, upon request, provide the obligee or public office with specially certified copies of the order for withholding or the notice of delinquency or both whenever the Court has ordered immediate service of an order for withholding or an affidavit has been placed in the court file indicating that the preconditions for service have been previously met. The obligee or public office may then serve the order for withholding on the payor, its superintendent, manager or other agent by certified mail or person-

al delivery. A proof of service shall be filed with the Clerk of the Circuit Court.

(3) If a delinquency has accrued for any reason, the obligee or public office may serve a notice of delinquency upon the obligor pursuant to subsection (C). The obligor may prevent the notice of delinquency from being served upon the payor by utilizing the procedures set forth in subsection (D). If no petition to stay service has been filed within the required 20 day time period, the obligee or public office may serve the notice of delinquency on the payor by utilizing the procedures for service set forth in subsection (E).

(G) Duties of payor.

(1) It shall be the duty of any payor who has been served with a copy of the specially certified order for withholding and any notice of delinquency to deduct and pay over income as provided in this subsection. The payor shall deduct the amount designated in the order for withholding, as supplemented by the notice of delinquency and any notice provided pursuant to paragraph (6) of subsection (I), beginning no later than the next payment of income which is payable to the obligor that occurs 14 days following the date the order and any notice were mailed by certified mail or placed for personal delivery. The payor may combine all amounts withheld for the benefit of an obligee or public office into a single payment and transmit the payment with a listing of obligors from whom withholding has been effected. The payor shall pay the amount withheld to the obligee or public office within 3 business days of the date income is paid to the obligor in accordance with the order for withholding and any subsequent notification received from the public office redirecting payments. If the payor knowingly fails to pay any amount withheld to the obligee or public office within 3 business days of the date income is paid to the obligor, the payor shall pay a penalty of $100 for each day that the withheld amount is paid to the obligee or public office after the period of 3 business days has expired. The failure of a payor, on more than one occasion, to pay amounts withheld to the obligee or public office within 3 business days of the date income is paid to the obligor creates a presumption that the payor knowingly failed to pay the amounts. This penalty may be collected in a civil action which may be brought against the payor in favor of the obligee. For purposes of this Section, a withheld amount shall be considered paid by a payor on the date it is mailed by the payor, or on the date an electronic funds transfer of the amount has been initiated by the payor, or on the date delivery of the amount has been initiated by the payor. For each deduction, the payor shall provide the obligee or public office, at the time of transmittal, with the date income was paid from which support was withheld.

Upon receipt of an order requiring that a minor child be named as a beneficiary of a health insurance plan available through an employer, the employer shall immediately enroll the minor child as a beneficiary in the health insurance plan designated by the court order. The employer shall withhold any required premiums and pay over any amounts so withheld and any additional amounts the employer pays to the insurance carrier in a timely manner. The employer shall mail to the obligee, within 15 days of enrollment or upon request, notice of the date of coverage, information on the dependent coverage plan, and all forms necessary to obtain reimbursement for covered health expenses, such as would be made available to a new employee. When an order for dependent coverage is in effect and the insurance coverage is terminated or changed for any reason, the employer shall notify the obligee within 10 days of the termination or change date along with notice of conversion privileges.

For withholding of income, the payor shall be entitled to receive a fee not to exceed $5 per month to be taken from the income to be paid to the obligor.

(2) Whenever the obligor is no longer receiving income from the payor, the payor shall return a copy of the order for withholding to the obligee or public office and shall provide information for the purpose of enforcing this Section.

(3) Withholding of income under this Section shall be made without regard to any prior or subsequent garnishments, attachments, wage assignments, or any other claims of creditors. Withholding of income under this Section shall not be in excess of the maximum amounts permitted under the federal Consumer Credit Protection Act. If the payor has been served with more than one order for withholding pertaining to the same obligor, the payor shall allocate income available for withholding on a proportionate share basis, giving priority to current support payments. If there is any income available for withholding after withholding for all current support obligations, the payor shall allocate the income to past due support payments ordered in non-AFDC matters and then to past due support payments ordered in AFDC matters, both on a proportionate share basis. Payment as required by the order for withholding shall be a complete defense by the payor against any claims of the obligor or his creditors as to the sum so paid.

(4) No payor shall discharge, discipline, refuse to hire or otherwise penalize any obligor because of the duty to withhold income.

(H) Petitions to stay service or to modify, suspend or terminate orders for withholding.

(1) When an obligor files a petition to stay service, the court, after due notice to all parties, shall hear the matter as soon as practicable and shall enter an order granting or denying relief, amending the notice of delinquency, amending the order for withholding, where applicable, or otherwise resolving the matter. If the court finds that a delinquency existed when the notice of delinquency was served upon the obligor, in an amount of at least one month's support obligation, or that the obligor was at least 30 days late in paying all or part of the order for support, the court shall order immediate service of the order for withholding. Where the court cannot promptly resolve any dispute over the amount of the delinquency, the court may order immediate service of the order for withholding as to any undisputed amounts

specified in an amended notice of delinquency, and may continue the hearing on the disputed amounts.

(2) At any time, an obligor, obligee, public office or Clerk of the Circuit Court may petition the court to:

(a) Modify, suspend or terminate the order for withholding because of a modification, suspension or termination of the underlying order for support; or

(b) Modify the amount of income to be withheld to reflect payment in full or in part of the delinquency or arrearage by income withholding or otherwise; or

(c) Suspend the order for withholding because of inability to deliver income withheld to the obligee due to the obligee's failure to provide a mailing address or other means of delivery.

(3) The obligor, obligee or public office shall serve on the payor, by certified mail or personal delivery, a copy of any order entered pursuant to this subsection that affects the duties of the payor.

(4) The order for withholding shall continue to be binding upon the payor until service of any order of the court entered under this subsection.

(I) Additional duties.

(1) An obligee who is receiving income withholding payments under this Section shall notify the payor, if the obligee receives the payments directly from the payor, or the public office or the Clerk of the Circuit Court, as appropriate, of any change of address within 7 days of such change.

(2) An obligee who is a recipient of public aid shall send a copy of any notice of delinquency filed pursuant to subsection (C) to the Bureau of Child Support of the Illinois Department of Public Aid.

(3) Each obligor shall notify the obligee and the Clerk of the Circuit Court of any change of address within 7 days.

(4) An obligor whose income is being withheld or who has been served with a notice of delinquency pursuant to this Section shall notify the obligee and the Clerk of the Circuit Court of any new payor, within 7 days.

(5) When the Illinois Department of Public Aid is no longer authorized to receive payments for the obligee, it shall, within 7 days, notify the payor or, where appropriate, the Clerk of the Circuit Court, to redirect income withholding payments to the obligee.

(6) The obligee or public office shall provide notice to the payor and Clerk of the Circuit Court of any other support payment made, including but not limited to, a set-off under federal and State law or partial payment of the delinquency or arrearage, or both.

(7) Any public office and Clerk of the Circuit Court which collects, disburses or receives payments pursuant to orders for withholding shall maintain complete, accurate, and clear records of all payments and their

750 ILCS 5/706.1 FAMILIES

disbursements. Certified copies of payment records maintained by a public office or Clerk of the Circuit Court shall, without further proof, be admitted into evidence in any legal proceedings under this Section.

(8) The Illinois Department of Public Aid shall design suggested legal forms for proceeding under this Section and shall make available to the courts such forms and informational materials which describe the procedures and remedies set forth herein for distribution to all parties in support actions.

(9) At the time of transmitting each support payment, the clerk of the circuit court shall provide the obligee or public office, as appropriate, with any information furnished by the payor as to the date income was paid from which such support was withheld.

(J) Penalties.

(1) Where a payor wilfully fails to withhold or pay over income pursuant to a properly served, specially certified order for withholding and any notice of delinquency, or wilfully discharges, disciplines, refuses to hire or otherwise penalizes an obligor as prohibited by subsection (G), or otherwise fails to comply with any duties imposed by this Section, the obligee, public office or obligor, as appropriate, may file a complaint with the court against the payor. The clerk of the circuit court shall notify the obligee or public office, as appropriate, and the obligor and payor of the time and place of the hearing on the complaint. The court shall resolve any factual dispute including, but not limited to, a denial that the payor is paying or has paid income to the obligor. Upon a finding in favor of the complaining party, the court:

(a) Shall enter judgment and direct the enforcement thereof for the total amount that the payor wilfully failed to withhold or pay over; and

(b) May order employment or reinstatement of or restitution to the obligor, or both, where the obligor has been discharged, disciplined, denied employment or otherwise penalized by the payor and may impose a fine upon the payor not to exceed $200.

(2) Any obligee, public office or obligor who wilfully initiates a false proceeding under this Section or who wilfully fails to comply with the requirements of this Section shall be punished as in cases of contempt of court.

(K) Alternative procedures for entry and service of an order for withholding.

(1) Effective January 1, 1987, in any matter in which an order for withholding has not been entered for any reason, based upon the last order for support that has been entered, and in which the obligor has become delinquent in payment of an amount equal to at least one month's support obligation pursuant to the last order for support or is at least 30 days late in complying with all or part of the order for support, the obligee or public office may prepare and serve an order for withholding pursuant to the procedures set forth in this subsection.

(2) The obligee or public office shall:

(a) Prepare a proposed order for withholding for immediate service as provided by paragraphs (1) and (3) of subsection (B), except that the minimum 20% delinquency payment shall be used;

(b) Prepare a notice of delinquency as provided by paragraphs (1) and (2) of subsection (C), except the notice shall state further that the order for withholding has not been entered by the court and the conditions under which the order will be entered; and

(c) Serve the notice of delinquency and form petition to stay service as provided by paragraph (3) of subsection (C), together with the proposed order for withholding, which shall be marked "COPY ONLY".

(3) After 20 days following service of the notice of delinquency and proposed order for withholding, in lieu of the provisions of subsection (E), the obligee or public office shall file with the Clerk of the Circuit Court an affidavit, with a copy of the notice of delinquency and proposed order for withholding attached thereto, stating that:

(a) The notice of delinquency and proposed order for withholding have been served upon the obligor and the date on which service was effected;

(b) The obligor has not filed a petition to stay service within 20 days of service of such notice and order; and

(c) The proposed order for withholding accurately states the terms and amounts contained in the last order for support.

(4) Upon the court's satisfaction that the procedures set forth in this subsection have been met, it shall enter the order for withholding.

(5) The Clerk shall then provide to the obligee or public office a specially certified copy of the order for withholding and the notice of delinquency indicating that the preconditions for service have been met.

(6) The obligee or public office shall serve the specially certified copies of the order for withholding and the notice of delinquency on the payor, its superintendent, manager or other agent by certified mail or personal delivery. A proof of service shall be filed with the Clerk of the Circuit Court.

(7) If the obligor requests in writing that income withholding become effective prior to becoming delinquent in payment of an amount equal to one month's support obligation pursuant to the last order for support, or prior to becoming 30 days late in paying all or part of the order for support, the obligee or public office shall file an affidavit with the Clerk of the Circuit Court, with a proposed order for withholding attached, stating that the proposed order accurately states the terms and amounts contained in the last order for support and the obligor's request for immediate service. The provisions of paragraphs (4) through (6) of this subsection shall apply, except that a notice of delinquency shall not be required.

(8) All other provisions of this Section shall be applicable with respect to the provisions of this subsection (K), except that under paragraph (1) of

subsection (H), the court may also amend the proposed order for withholding to conform to the last order for support.

(9) Nothing in this subsection shall be construed as limiting the requirements of paragraph (1) of subsection (B) with respect to the entry of a separate order for withholding upon entry of any order for support.

(L) Remedies in addition to other laws.

(1) The rights, remedies, duties and penalties created by this Section are in addition to and not in substitution for any other rights, remedies, duties and penalties created by any other law.

(2) Nothing in this Section shall be construed as invalidating any assignment of wages or benefits executed prior to January 1, 1984.

Author's Notes

Analysis

1. Applicable to all support orders.
2. Two steps.
3. Step one: Immediate effect.
4. Option out.
5. Step two: Service.
6. Employer duties.
7. Modification.
8. Penalties.
9. Alternative procedures.
10. Order for Withholding—Form.
11. Petition to Stay Service of Order for Withholding and Notice of Delinquency—Form.

(1) **Applicable to all support orders.** The withholding provisions of § 706.1 apply to all child support and maintenance orders, whether temporary or final. § 706.1(A)(1).

(2) **Two steps.** There are two steps under § 706.1 for requiring the withholding of children's support and maintenance by the employer from the party obligated to pay the maintenance and children's support. The Section refers to an employer as a "payor," which it defines as "any payor of income to an obligor." § 706.1(A)(7). The first step is that the court require the order for withholding to take effect immediately, and the second step is for the order of withholding to be served upon the employer.

(3) **Step one: Immediate effect.** The court is required to make orders of withholding effective immediately, "unless a written agreement is reached between and signed by both parties providing for an alternative arrangement, approved and entered into the record by the court, which ensures payment of support." § 706.1(B)(1). The order for withholding remains valid as long as order for support upon which it is based remains valid. § 706.1(B)(5).

(4) **Option out.** If the parties seek to avoid the immediate effect of the order of withholding, the written agreement of the parties should follow the words of the statute and should provide some form of insuring the payment of the maintenance and children's support. The security must then be approved by the court in an order.

Often this can be accomplished in the settlement agreement with approval in the judgment. Insuring payment of the support can take any form that the court will approve. For example, an obligor may be required to maintain at all times in his bank account a sum equal to at least two months of maintenance and children's support. See IMDMA § 502 Author's Note (11) paras. 5(b) and 5(c) and IMDMA § 413 Author's Note (8) Judgment Additional and Alternative Provisions para. 8 for sample agreement and judgment language. Where the court has not required that the order of withholding take effect immediately, the court can order that it subsequently take effect pursuant to the provisions of IMDMA § 706.1(B)(8).

(5) **Step two: Service.** Once the withholding order is in effect, the second step required in order to cause the employer to withhold the children's support and maintenance is service of the withholding order upon the employer. The court can order immediate service upon the employer when the court finds at the time of any hearing that there is an arrearage pursuant to the provisions of § 706.1(B)(7). Otherwise, the following series of events must take place before the order of withholding can be served upon the employer: (1) there must be a payment delinquency of one month's support obligation or a delinquency of all or part of a support order for 30 days, whichever occurs first; (2) a notice of delinquency must be served upon the obligor pursuant to the provisions of § 706.1(C); and (3) the obligor either does not seek, or is unsuccessful in seeking, a court stay of the service of the order of withholding, pursuant to the procedures set forth in § 706.1(D), within 20 days of service upon the obligor of the notice of delinquency. The hearing pursuant to a petition filed by the obligor to stay the service of the withholding order is pursuant to the procedures set forth in § 706.1(H)(1). Initial service of the order of withholding pursuant to the delinquency notice (other than where immediate service has been ordered pursuant to § 706.1(B)(7)), and where the obligor has not filed a petition to stay service, are pursuant to the procedures set forth in § 706.1(E). Subsequent service of orders of withholding, after the immediate service or initial service of an order of withholding, can be made by the obligee or by the public office without further notice to the obligor. § 706.1(F). There are also provisions for the service of a further delinquency notice in § 706.1(F)(3).

(6) **Employer duties.** The duties of the payor employer who has been served with an order for withholding and a notice of delinquency are set forth in § 706.1(G). Penalties for failure of the payor employer to comply are also set forth in subsection (G). Willful non-compliance may result in fines of $100 for each day overdue, and may subject the employer to liability in a civil action. See IMDMA § 706.1(J) and Author's Note (8) below. Provisions are also set forth in subparagraph (G)(1) for enrolling a minor child as a beneficiary on a health insurance plan when the employer receives an order requiring that the minor child be so named. IMDMA § 505.2 and accompanying Author's Notes.

(7) **Modification.** Provisions for the modification suspension or termination of the order for withholding are contained in § 706.1(H)(2).

(8) **Penalties.** Procedures for acting against an employer who willfully fails to comply are contained in § 706.1(J). Non-compliance includes both failing to pay the obligee, and firing, not hiring, or otherwise discriminating against the obligor.

(9) **Alternative procedures.** Section 706.1(K) provides for alternative procedures to subsection (B)(8) for the immediate entry of an order of withholding and for service of a proposed order for withholding upon the payor where the court has not

750 ILCS 5/706.1   **FAMILIES**

previously required that the order of withholding take effect. Subsection (K) utilizes the notice of delinquency type of proceeding set forth in subsection (C).

(10) **Order for Withholding—Form.** There follows a sample of the Order for Withholding from Cook County.

IN THE CIRCUIT COURT OF COOK COUNTY, ILLINOIS   (1-89) CCG-512

IN RE THE

    and

)
)
)
) No.
)
) IV-D No.

ORDER FOR WITHHOLDING

THIS CAUSE is before the Court on the matter of withholding income to secure payment of support and/or maintenance (hereinafter support), the Court having jurisdiction of the parties and subject matter and being fully advised:

THE COURT FINDS:
1. A support order was entered in this cause on _____.
2. The Court is required to enter an Order for Withholding pursuant to law.

THEREFORE, IT IS ORDERED:
1. That this order may be served:
   ( ) Immediately
   ( ) Only when the conditions set forth on the reverse side of this Order have been met. Subsequent service may be effected pursuant to statute.
2. Any Payor who is served with a specially certified copy of this Order for Withholding shall withhold from the income of the Obligor, _____ Social Security Number _____:
   ( ) $ _____ per _____ current support;
   ( ) and $ _____ per _____ on a(n) (arrearage) (reimbursement) of $ _____ owed to (Obligee designated below) (Illinois Department of Public Aid) until paid in full; and then on a(n) (arrearage) (reimbursement) of _____ owed to the (Obligee designated below) (Department of Public Aid) until paid in full;
   ( ) and _____
   ( ) $ _____ per _____ until payment in full of the delinquency stated in any separate Notice of Delinquency served with or after this Order. [If this subsection is checked but the dollar amount is left blank, Payor shall withhold an additional dollar amount equal to 20% of the total amount being withheld herein (current support plus any arrearage and reimbursement).]

THE PAYOR IS NOT TO WITHHOLD FOR PAYMENT OF DELINQUENCY UNLESS THE PAYOR IS SERVED WITH A SEPARATE NOTICE OF DELINQUENCY EITHER AT THE TIME OF SERVICE OF THIS ORDER FOR WITHHOLDING OR AFTER SERVICE OF THIS ORDER.

3. The Payor shall pay over any amounts withheld pursuant to paragraph 2 above to the:
   ( ) OBLIGEE, _____
       NAME   ADDRESS   STATE   ZIP
   ( ) CLERK OF THE CIRCUIT COURT FOR _____ County, _____, Illinois
4. IMPORTANT NOTICE: THE CONDITIONS FOR SERVICE AND RIGHTS, REMEDIES AND DUTIES OF THE PAYOR, OBLIGOR AND OBLIGEE APPEARING ON THE REVERSE SIDE OF THIS ORDER ARE INCORPORATED HEREIN AND SHOULD BE READ.

DATE: _____

ENTER: _____
                 Judge   Judge's No.

Name:
Attorney for:
Address:
City/State/Zip:
Telephone:

BELOW.

PAYOR: EXECUTE AGAINST INCOME ONLY WHEN CERTIFIED

CLERK: CERTIFY BELOW PURSUANT TO LAW

I HEREBY CERTIFY THE FOREGOING TO BE A TRUE AND CORRECT COPY OF AN ORDER FOR WITHHOLDING FILED WITH THIS OFFICE.

By: _____
    Clerk of the Circuit Court of Cook County, Illinois
Date: _____

THIS ORDER IS THE COMMAND OF THE CIRCUIT COURT AND VIOLATION THEREOF IS SUBJECT TO DUE PENALTY OF LAW.

[G17986]

FAMILIES   **750 ILCS 5/706.1**

IMPORTANT NOTICE: CONDITIONS FOR SERVICE AND RIGHTS, REMEDIES AND DUTIES OF OBLIGOR, PAYOR AND OBLIGEE

CONDITIONS FOR SERVICE:
Where immediate service of the Order for Withholding has not been ordered, the following conditions must be met before this Order can be served on a Payor for the first time: (a) the Obligor becomes delinquent in payment of an amount equal to at least one month's support obligation pursuant to the Order for Support or is at least 30 days late in paying all or part of the Order for Support, whichever occurs first; **and** (b) the Obligor is served with a Notice of Delinquency containing a computation of delinquency accrued; **and** (c) either (1) the Obligor fails to file a Petition to Stay Service with the court within 20 days after he or she is served with the Notice of Delinquency, **or** (2) the Obligor's Petition to Stay Service is denied, **or** (3) the Obligor waives the conditions stated in (a) (b) and (c) (1) above and requests immediate service upon the Payor.

TO THE OBLIGOR:
Under the law, an Obligor is the individual who owes a duty to make payments under an order of support.

1. The Obligor may file a Petition to Stay Service within 20 days after service of a Notice of Delinquency for the following reasons: (1) a dispute concerning the amount of current support or the existence of amount of delinquency, (2) misidentification of the Obligor. The Obligor may file a Petition at any time to modify, suspend or terminate the Order for Withholding pursuant to statute.

2. An Obligor may not be discharged, disciplined, denied employment or otherwise penalized because of Payor's duty to withhold income. An Obligor shall notify the Obligee and the Clerk of the Circuit Court within 7 days of any change of address and/or new Payor when he or she is having income withheld or has been served a Notice of Delinquency.

TO THE PAYOR:
Under the law, a Payor is any Payor of monies to an Obligor.

1. The Payor must begin withholding no later than the next payment of income to the Obligor that occurs 14 days after the Order for Withholding is mailed to the Payor and continue to withhold until further notified by the Obligee or Public Office or until ordered by the Circuit Court.

2. The Order for withholding shall be given priority over any prior or subsequent garnishments, attachments, wage assignments or claims of any creditors.

3. No Payor shall withhold income in excess of the maximum amount permitted by Section 303(b) of the Federal Consumer Credit Protection Act (FCCPA) 15 USC 1673(b): 50% of net income if the Obligor is supporting other dependents; or, 55% of net income if the Obligor is supporting other dependents and the arrearage is owed for 12 weeks or more; or, 60% of net income if the Obligor is not supporting other dependents, or 65% of net income if the Obligor is not supporting other dependents and arrearage is owed for 12 weeks or more. The Payor may deduct and keep as a service fee from the Obligor's income an additional five dollars, or the actual check processing cost, whichever is less, after deducting the total to be withheld. The total withheld from the Obligor's income, including any processing fee, may not exceed the limits of the FCCP.

4. If the Order for Withholding contains payments periods that do not conform with the regular pay period of the Payor, the Payor must convert the support terms to the applicable pay period by using the following conversions: Weekly payment amount x 4.33 = monthly amount; bi-weekly payment amount x 2.17 = monthly amount; semi-monthly payment amount x 2 = monthly amount.

5. The amount withheld by the Payor must be paid to the Obligee or Public Office within 10 days of the date income is paid to the Obligor. The Payor may combine into a single payment all amounts to be transmitted to the Clerk of the Circuit Court, along with a list of Obligors from whom withholding has been effected.

6. If the Payor has been served with more than one Order for Withholding pertaining to a single Obligor and if there is insufficient income available to satisfy all obligations, the Payor shall allocate income on a proportionate share basis giving priority to (a) current support, then to (b) arrearage and delinquency payments owed to the Obligee, then to (c) arrearage and delinquency payments owed to the Public Office.

7. The Payor must take into account any other support payment made, such as set-offs under Federal and State law, partial payment of delinquency, arrearage or both, when notified by the Obligee or Public Office.

8. Whenever the Obligor is no longer receiving income from the Payor, the Payor shall (a) return a copy of the Order for Withholding to the Obligee or Public Office, and (b) cooperate in furnishing information about the Obligor's whereabouts and subsequent employment.

9. No Payor shall discharge, discipline, refuse to hire or otherwise penalize any Obligor because of the duty to withhold. Any Payor who does so may be ordered to employ or reinstate or pay restitution to the Obligor, or both and may be fined up to $200.

10. If the Payor willfully fails to withhold or pay over income pursuant to a valid Order for Withholding, he or she may be liable for the total amount that was not withheld or paid over.

TO THE OBLIGEE:
Under the law, an Obligee is the individual to whom a duty or support is owed or the individual's legal representative.

1. An Obligee who is receiving income withholding payments shall notify the Payor, if receiving payments directly from Payor, or the Public Office or Clerk of the Circuit Court, as appropriate, of any change of address within 7 days of such change. An Obligee shall provide notice to the Payor, the Clerk of the Circuit Court, or the Public Office, as appropriate of any support payment made other than under this order for withholding.

2. An Obligee who receives Public Aid shall send a copy of any Notice of Delinquency filed to the Bureau of Child Support of the Illinois Department of Public Aid.

[G17987]

(11) **Petition to Stay Service of Order for Withholding and Notice of Delinquency—Form.** There follows a sample Petition to Stay Service from Cook County.

750 ILCS 5/706.1   **FAMILIES**

IN THE CIRCUIT COURT OF COOK COUNTY
_____ DEPARTMENT, _____ DIVISION/DISTRICT

```
                              )
_____     )
                              )
           vs.                )   NO. _____
                              )
_____     )   IV–D NO. _____
                              )
```

PETITION TO STAY SERVICE OF ORDER FOR
WITHHOLDING AND NOTICE OF DELINQUENCY

Now comes Petitioner, _____, the _____ in the above entitled case and states:

That service of the Order for Withholding dated _____, 19__ and the attached Notice of Delinquency dated _____, 19__ should be stayed for the following reason(s) (complete at least one, as appropriate):

( ) There is no delinquency in this case in that _____.

( ) The amount of delinquency stated in the notice is incorrect in that _____.

( ) There has been a substantial change in circumstances beyond the control of the Petitioner as follows: _____.

WHEREFORE PETITIONER PRAYS:

1. That service of the Order for Withholding dated _____, 19__ and the Notice of Delinquency dated _____, 19__ be stayed.

2. For such other and further relief as the court deems just.

Attorney for petitioner: _____

                                                 PETITIONER

Address: Subscribed and sworn to before me this ___ day of _____, 19__

Telephone: _____
                                                NOTARY PUBLIC

DPA 2581A (N-11-83)

750 ILCS 5/706.2

§ 706.2 Posting security, bond or guarantee to secure payment

The court may require a parent to post security, bond or give some other guarantee of a character and amount sufficient to assure payment of any amount of support due.

750 ILCS 5/707

§ 707. Certificate of dissolution or invalidity of marriage—Filing with Department of Public Health

A certificate of each dissolution of marriage or declaration of invalidity of marriage ordered in this State shall be filed with the Illinois Department of Public Health on a form furnished by such Department. This form shall be prepared by the person filing the petition for dissolution of marriage or declaration of invalidity of marriage and shall be presented to the judge of the court for his inspection prior to the entry of the final order. Failure to comply with this Act shall not invalidate any judgment of dissolution of marriage or declaration of invalidity of marriage. Immediately after the judgment is granted, the clerk of the court shall complete the remaining entries on the certificate. Within 45 days after the close of the month in which the judgment is rendered, the clerk shall forward the certificate to the Illinois Department of Public Health.

Author's Notes

(1) **Certificate of Dissolution, Invalidity of Marriage or Legal Separation—Form.** There follows a sample copy of the certificate that is required pursuant to § 707.

750 ILCS 5/707   FAMILIES

[Certificate of Dissolution, Invalidity of Marriage or Legal Separation form — State of Illinois, Illinois Department of Public Health, Division of Vital Records, VR700 (1989)]

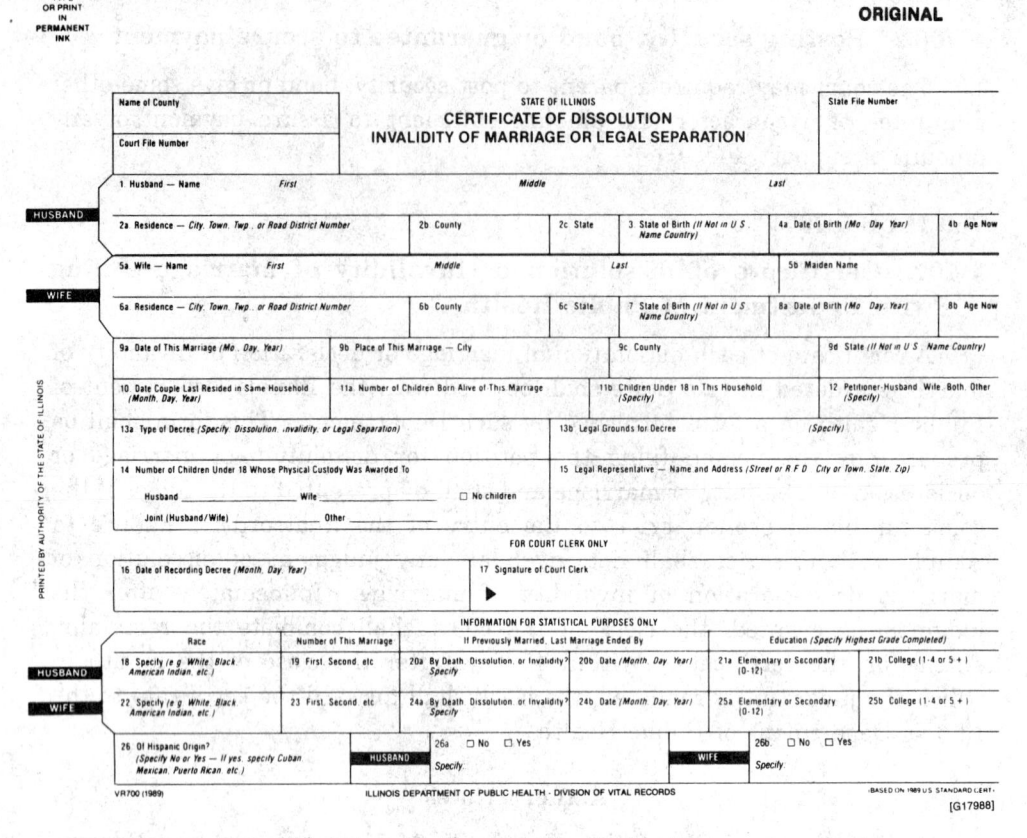

750 ILCS 5/708

§ 708. Disclosure of address

In any proceeding brought under this Act, the identification of a party's street address shall not be required for any purpose if the court finds that the physical, mental or emotional health of a party or that of a minor child, or both, would be seriously endangered by disclosure of the party's address.

750 ILCS 5/709

§ 709. Mandatory child support payments to clerk

(a) As of January 1, 1982, child support orders entered in any county covered by this subsection shall be made pursuant to the provisions of Sections 709 through 712 of this Act. For purposes of these Sections, the term "child support payment" or "payment" shall include any payment ordered to be made solely for the purpose of the support of a child or children or any payment ordered for general support which includes any amount for support of any child or children.

The provisions of Sections 709 through 712 shall be applicable to any county with a population of 2 million or more and to any other county which notifies the Supreme Court of its desire to be included within the coverage of these Sections and is certified pursuant to Supreme Court Rules.

The effective date of inclusion, however, shall be subject to approval of the application for reimbursement of the costs of the support program by the Department of Public Aid as provided in Section 712.

(b) In any proceeding for a dissolution of marriage, legal separation, or declaration of invalidity of marriage, or in any supplementary proceedings in which a judgment or modification thereof for the payment of child support is entered on or after January 1, 1982, in any county covered by Sections 709 through 712, and the person entitled to payment is receiving a grant of financial aid under Article IV of "The Illinois Public Aid Code" or has applied and qualified for support services under Section 10-1 of that Code, the court shall direct: (1) that such payments be made to the clerk of the court and (2) that the parties affected shall each thereafter notify the clerk of any change of address or change in other conditions that may affect the administration of the order, including the fact that a party who was previously not on public aid has become a recipient of public aid, within 10 days of such change. All notices sent to the obligor's last known address on file with the clerk shall be deemed sufficient to proceed with enforcement pursuant to the provisions of Sections 709 through 712.

(c) Except as provided in subsection (d) of this Section, the clerk shall disburse the payments to the person or persons entitled thereto under the terms of the order or judgment.

(d) The court shall determine, prior to the entry of the support order, if the party who is to receive the support is presently receiving public aid or has a current application for public aid pending and shall enter the finding on the record.

If the person entitled to payment is a recipient of aid under The Illinois Public Aid Code, the clerk, upon being informed of this fact by finding of the court, by notification by the party entitled to payment, by the Illinois Department of Public Aid or by the local governmental unit, shall make all payments to: (1) the Illinois Department of Public Aid if the person is a recipient under Article III, IV, or V of the Code or (2) the local governmental unit responsible for his or her support if the person is a recipient under Article VI or VII of the Code. The Illinois Department of Public Aid may continue to collect current maintenance or child support payments, or both, for a period not to exceed 3 months from the month following the month in which such persons cease to receive public assistance, and pay all amounts so collected to such persons. At the end of such 3 month period, the Illinois Department of Public Aid may continue to collect such payments if authorized by such persons to do so, and pay the net amount so collected to such persons after deducting any costs incurred in making the collection or any collection fee from the amount of any recovery made. Upon termination of public aid payments to such a recipient, the Illinois Department of Public Aid or the appropriate local governmental unit shall notify the clerk that all subsequent payments are to be sent directly to the person entitled thereto.

Payments under this Section to the Illinois Department of Public Aid pursuant to the Child Support Enforcement Program established by Title IV-D of the Social Security Act shall be paid into the Child Support Enforcement Trust Fund. All other payments under this Section to the Illinois Department of Public Aid shall be deposited in the Public Assistance Recoveries Trust Fund. Disbursements from these funds shall be as provided in The Illinois Public Aid Code. Payments received by a local governmental unit shall be deposited in that unit's General Assistance Fund.

(e) Any order or judgment may be amended by the court, upon its own motion or upon the motion of either party, to conform with the provisions of Sections 709 through 712, either as to the requirement of making payments to the clerk or, where payments are already being made to the clerk, as to the statutory fees provided for under Section 711.

(f) The clerk may invest in any interest bearing account or in any securities, monies collected for the benefit of a payee, where such payee cannot be found; however, the investment may be only for the period until the clerk is able to locate and present the payee with such monies. Any interest or capital gains accrued shall be for the benefit of the county and shall be paid into the special fund established in subsection (b) of Section 711.

(g) The clerk shall establish and maintain a payment record of all monies received and disbursed and such record shall constitute prima facie evidence of such payment and non-payment, as the case may be.

(h) For those cases in which child support is payable to the clerk of the circuit court for transmittal to the Illinois Department of Public Aid by order of court, the clerk shall transmit all such payments, within 4 working days of receipt, to insure that funds are available for immediate distribution by the Department to the person or entity entitled thereto in accordance with standards of the Child Support Enforcement Program established under Title IV-D of the Social Security Act. The clerk shall notify the Department of the date of receipt and amount thereof at the time of transmittal. Where the clerk has entered into an agreement of cooperation with the Department to record the terms of child support orders and payments made thereunder directly into the Department's automated data processing system, the clerk shall account for, transmit and otherwise distribute child support payments in accordance with such agreement in lieu of the requirements contained herein.

Author's Notes

Analysis

1. Mandatory for Public Aid.
2. Child Support Enforcement Program.
3. Cross reference.

(1) **Mandatory for Public Aid.** IMDMA §§ 709 through 712 are parallel provisions to § 705 in many respects and provide for the payments of children's support or maintenance when it is part of children's support to the Clerk of the Court and to Public Aid. They are mandatory for public aid recipients, but discretionary in all other cases. Sections 709 through 712 apply to counties of 2 million or more people and counties who receive certification from the Illinois Supreme Court that they want to be included in the enforcement and disbursing provisions.

(2) **Child Support Enforcement Program.** Pursuant to Title IV–D of the Social Security Act, 42 U.S.C.A. § 651 et seq., the states are to enact enabling legislation for the enforcement of children's support obligations. IMDMA §§ 709 through 712, 750 ILCS 25/1 et seq., Expedited Child Support Act of 1990, and Supreme Court Rules 100.1 through 100.13, Expedited Child Support Rules, are part of the enabling legislation.

(3) **Cross reference.** See Expedited Child Support Rules, Supreme Court Rules 100.1 through 100.13 and accompanying Author's Notes for an explanation of the system.

750 ILCS 5/710

§ 710. Enforcement; Penalties

(a) In counties certified as included under the provisions of Sections 709 through 712 and whose application for reimbursement is approved, there shall be instituted a child support enforcement program to be conducted by the clerk of the circuit court and the state's attorney of the county. The program is to be limited to enforcement of child support orders entered pursuant to this Act.

The child support enforcement program is to be conducted only on behalf of dependent children included in a grant of financial aid under Article IV of The Illinois Public Aid Code and parties who apply and qualify for support services pursuant to Section 10–1 of such Code.

(b) In the event of a delinquency in payment, as determined from the record maintained by the clerk in a county covered by the child support enforcement program, such clerk shall notify both the party obligated to make the payment, hereinafter called the payor, and the recipient of such payment, hereinafter called the payee, of such delinquency and that if the amount then due and owing is not remitted in the time period required by circuit court rules, the matter will be referred to the state's attorney for enforcement proceedings. Upon failure of the payor to remit as required, the clerk shall refer the matter to the state's attorney, except as provided by rule of the circuit court.

(c) Upon referral from the clerk, the state's attorney shall promptly initiate enforcement proceedings against the payor. Legal representation by the state's attorney shall be limited to child support and shall not extend to visitation, custody, property or other matters; however, if the payor properly files pleadings raising such matters during the course of the child support hearing and the court finds that it has jurisdiction of such matters, the payee shall be granted the opportunity to obtain a continuance in order to secure

750 ILCS 5/710   **FAMILIES**

representation for those other matters, and the court shall not delay entry of an appropriate support order pending the disposition of such other matters.

If the state's attorney does not commence enforcement proceedings within 30 days, the clerk shall inform the court which, upon its own motion, shall appoint counsel for purposes of enforcement. The fees and expenses of such counsel shall be paid by the payor and shall not be paid by the State.

Nothing in this Section shall be construed to prevent a payee from instituting independent enforcement proceedings or limit the remedies available to payee in such proceedings. However, absent the exercise under this provision of a private right of enforcement, enforcement shall be as otherwise provided in this Section.

(d) At the time any support order is entered, the payee shall be informed of the procedure used for enforcement and shall be given the address and telephone number both of the clerk and of the Child and Spouse Support Unit as provided in Section 712.

The payee shall be informed that, if no action is taken within 2 months of any complaint to the clerk, payee may contact the Unit to seek assistance in obtaining enforcement.

(e) Upon a finding that payor is in default and that such non-payment is for a period of two months and that such non-payment is without good cause, the court shall order the payor to pay a sum equal to 2% of the arrearage as a penalty along with his payment.

The court may further assess against the payor any fees and expenses incurred in the enforcement of any order or the reasonable value thereof and may impose any penalty otherwise available to it in a case of contempt.

All penalties, fees and expenses assessed against the payor pursuant to this subsection are to cover the expenses of enforcement, are to be paid to the clerk and are to be placed by him in the special fund provided for in Section 711.

(f) Any person not covered by the child support enforcement program may institute private and independent proceedings to enforce payment of support.

750 ILCS 5/711

§ 711. Fees

(a) To reimburse any covered county for the cost of maintaining the child support enforcement program pursuant to Section 710, the court shall order any payor making payments directly to the clerk to pay the clerk a fee at the rate of $3.00 per month for every month the order is in effect. However, any fee collected for any case not included in such program as provided in subsection (a) of Section 710 may be used by the county for any purpose.

The fee shall be payable semi-annually, being due with the support payment due on or next immediately following January 1 and July 1. The fee shall be payable in advance as herein provided, except for the initial payment which shall be paid at the time of the initial child support payment to the clerk. The amount of the fee due for the initial period shall be computed from the date the support order first takes effect to the next January 1 or July 1, whichever occurs first.

Unless paid in cash, the payment of the fee shall be by a separate instrument from the support payment and shall be made to the order of the clerk.

(b) All monies collected in fees by the clerk and all monies received by him upon assessment under Section 710 for reimbursement for the costs of enforcement shall be held in a special fund, the contents of which the clerk shall pay over to the county treasury every month or at such other period as the treasurer shall determine.

750 ILCS 5/712

§ 712. Child support enforcement program—Certification—Child and Spouse Support Unit in Department of Public Aid—Powers and duties—Financial assistance in counties

(a) The Supreme Court may make Rules concerning the certification of counties for inclusion in the child support enforcement program and the application of the procedures created by Sections 709 through 712 in the various counties.

The Supreme Court shall inform each circuit court and clerk of the court of the availability of the program to reimburse counties desiring to participate in the program of enforcement of child support payments.

The Supreme Court shall also distribute to each circuit court and clerk of the court any materials prepared by the Child and Spouse Support Unit comparing child support enforcement in counties included and not included in this program.

(b) The Illinois Department of Public Aid, through the Child and Spouse Support Unit provided for by Section 10–3.1 of The Illinois General supervision of the child support programs created by Sections 709 through 712 and shall have the powers and duties provided in this Section, including the following:

   (1) to make advance payments to any county included in the program for expenses in preparing programs to enforce payment of child support to the clerk from appropriations made for such purposes by the General Assembly;

   (2) to make payments to each covered county to pay for its reasonable expenses actually necessary to maintain a continuing program not paid for by fees, penalties, or other monies; provided that, with respect to that portion of the program on behalf of dependent children included in a grant of financial aid under Article IV of The Illinois Public Aid Code the Unit shall pay only such expenses as is its current practice or as it may

750 ILCS 5/712   **FAMILIES**

deem appropriate; provided further that the Unit shall only pay expenses of the entire program subject to the availability of federal monies to pay the majority of expenses of the entire child support enforcement program; provided further that the Unit or Department may set standards relating to enforcement which have to be met by any county seeking to enter a contract with the Department for reimbursement of expenses of the entire enforcement program prior to an application for reimbursement being approved and the contract granted; and provided further that such standards may relate to, but are not limited to the following factors: maintenance of the payment record, the definition of delinquency; the period of time in which a delinquency must be determined, the payor notified, the remittance received, the referral to the state's attorney made, and the payment remitted by the clerk to the payee or other party entitled to the payment; the conditions under which referral will not be made to the state's attorney; and the definitions and procedures for other matters necessary for the conduct and operation of the program;

(3) to monitor the various local programs for enforcement of child support payments to the clerk;

(4) to act to encourage enforcement whenever local enforcement procedures are inadequate;

(5) to receive monies from any source for assistance in enforcement of child support; and

(6) to assist any county desirous of assistance in establishing and maintaining a child support enforcement program.

(c) Any county may apply for financial assistance to the Unit to initiate or maintain a program of child support enforcement. Every county which desires such assistance shall apply according to procedures established by the Unit. In its application, it shall state the following: financial needs, personnel requirements, anticipated caseloads, any amounts collected or anticipated in fees or penalties, and any other information required by the Unit.

(d) In the case that any advance money is given to any county under this Section to initiate an enforcement system, the county shall reimburse the state within 2 years from the date such monies are given to it. The Unit may establish an appropriate schedule of reimbursement for any county.

(e) In the event of the unavailability of federal monies to pay for the greater part of the costs to a county of the child support enforcement program under Sections 709 through 712 and the resulting cessation of state participation, the operation of the child support enforcement program under Sections 709 through 712 shall terminate. The date and the method of termination shall be determined by Supreme Court Rule.

750 ILCS 5/713

§ 713. Attachment of the body

As used in this Section, "obligor" has the same meaning ascribed to such term in Section 706.1 of this Act.

(1) In any proceeding to enforce an order for support, where the obligor has failed to appear in court pursuant to Order of court and after due notice thereof, the court may enter an order for the attachment of the body of the obligor. Notices under this Section shall be served upon the obligor either (1) by prepaid certified mail with delivery restricted to the obligor, or (2) by personal service on the obligor. The attachment order shall fix an amount of escrow which is equal to a minimum of 20% of the total child support arrearage alleged by the obligee in sworn testimony to be due and owing. The attachment order shall direct the Sheriff of any county in Illinois to take the obligor into custody and shall set the number of days following release from custody for a hearing to be held at which the obligor must appear, if he is released under subsection (c) of this Section.

(b) If the obligor is taken into custody, the Sheriff shall take the obligor before the court which entered the attachment order. However, the Sheriff may release the person after he or she has deposited the amount of escrow ordered by the court pursuant to local procedures for the posting of bond. The Sheriff shall advise the obligor of the hearing date at which the obligor is required to appear.

(c) Any escrow deposited pursuant to this Section shall be transmitted to the Clerk of the Circuit Court for the county in which the order for attachment of the body of the obligor was entered. Any Clerk who receives money deposited into escrow pursuant to this Section shall notify the obligee, public office or legal counsel whose name appears on the attachment order of the court date at which the obligor is required to appear and the amount deposited into escrow. The Clerk shall disburse such money to the obligee only under an order from the court that entered the attachment order pursuant to this Section.

(d) Whenever an obligor is taken before the court by the Sheriff, or appears in court after the court has ordered the attachment of his body, the court shall:

(1) hold a hearing on the complaint or petition that gave rise to the attachment order. For purposes of determining arrearages that are due and owing by the obligor, the court shall accept the previous sworn testimony of the obligee as true and the appearance of the obligee shall not be required. The court shall require sworn testimony of the obligor as to his or her Social Security number, income, employment, bank accounts, property and any other assets. If there is a dispute as to the total amount of arrearages, the court shall proceed as in any other case as to the undisputed amounts; and

(2) order the Clerk of the Circuit Court to disburse to the obligee or public office money held in escrow pursuant to this Section if the court finds that the amount of arrearages exceeds the amount of the escrow. Amounts received by the obligee or public office shall be deducted from the amount of the arrearages.

(e) If the obligor fails to appear in court after being notified of the court date by the Sheriff upon release from custody, the court shall order any monies deposited into escrow to be immediately released to the obligee or public office and shall proceed under subsection (a) of this Section by entering another order for the attachment of the body of the obligor.

(f) This Section shall apply to any order for support issued under the "Illinois Marriage and Dissolution of Marriage Act", approved September 22, 1977, as amended; the "Illinois Parentage Act of 1984", effective July 1, 1985, as amended; the "Revised Uniform Reciprocal Enforcement of Support Act", approved August 28, 1969, as amended; "The Illinois Public Aid Code", approved April 11, 1967, as amended; and the "Non-support of Spouse and Children Act", approved June 8, 1953, as amended.

(g) Any escrow established pursuant to this Section for the purpose of providing support shall not be subject to fees collected by the Clerk of the Circuit Court for any other escrow.

Author's Notes

(1) **Cross reference—Form.** See IMDMA § 511 Author's Note (8) for sample attachment order. Note that for an order of attachment pursuant to IMDMA § 713, there must be added provisions for an escrow, release, and hearing pursuant to §§ 713(a) and (b).

PART VIII. APPLICATION AND SEVERABILITY

Analysis

Sec.
801. Application.
802. Court rules.

WESTLAW Electronic Research

See WESTLAW Electronic Research Guide preceding the Summary of Contents.

---

750 ILCS 5/801

§ 801. Application

(a) This Act applies to all proceedings commenced on or after its effective date.

(b) This Act applies to all pending actions and proceedings commenced prior to its effective date with respect to issues on which a judgment has not been entered. Evidence adduced after the effective date of this Act shall be in compliance with this Act.

(c) This Act applies to all proceedings commenced after its effective date for the modification of a judgment or order entered prior to the effective date of this Act. Alimony in gross or settlements in lieu of alimony provided for in judgments entered prior to October 1, 1977 shall not be modifiable or terminable as maintenance thereafter.

(d) In any action or proceeding in which an appeal was pending or a new trial was ordered prior to the effective date of this Act, the law in effect at the time of the order sustaining the appeal or the new trial governs the appeal, the new trial, and any subsequent trial or appeal.

750 ILCS 5/802

§ 802. Court rules

The Supreme Court and, subject to the Rules of the Supreme Court, the respective circuit courts, may adopt such rules as they deem necessary and expedient to carry out the provisions of this Act.

ACT 10. ILLINOIS UNIFORM PREMARITAL AGREEMENT ACT

Analysis

Sec.
1. Short title.
2. Definitions.
3. Formalities.
4. Content.
5. Effect of marriage.
6. Amendment, revocation.
7. Enforcement.
8. Enforcement: Void marriage.
9. Limitation of actions.
10. Application and construction.
11. Time of taking effect.

WESTLAW Electronic Research

See WESTLAW Electronic Research Guide preceding the Summary of Contents.

---

750 ILCS 10/1

§ 1. Short title

This Article shall be known and may be cited as the Illinois Uniform Premarital Agreement Act.

Author's Notes

Analysis

1. Difficulty of premarital agreements.
2. Segregation of non-marital property.
3. Disposition of non-marital property upon death.
4. *Inter vivos* trusts.

5. *Johnson* case: Content of the probate estate.
6. *Inter vivos* trust protection not complete.
7. Trust together with premarital agreement.

(1) **Difficulty of premarital agreements.** Premarital agreements are presented as the rational way to handle financial and property affairs that arise upon marriage. In appropriate circumstances premarital agreements are useful.

> Today, divorce is a "common-place fact of life." ... As a result there is a concurrent increase in second and third marriages—often of mature people with substantial means and separate families from earlier marriages. The conflicts that naturally inhere in such relationships make the litigation that follows even more uncertain, unpleasant and costly. Consequently, people with previous "bad luck" with domestic life may not be willing to risk marriage again without the ability to safeguard their financial interests. In other words, without the ability to order their own affairs as they wish, many people may simply forgo marriage for more "informal" relationships. Prenuptial agreements, on the other hand, provide such people with the opportunity to ensure predictability, plan their future with more security, and, most importantly, decide their own destiny. Moreover, allowing couples to think through the financial aspects of their marriage beforehand can only foster strength and permanency in that relationship.

Brooks v. Brooks, 733 P.2d 1044, 1050 (Alaska 1987) (citations omitted) (footnotes omitted). The focus of the engagement period prior to marriage, however, is generally on emotional rather than material concerns, and the suggestion of negotiations over money and property during an engagement is not always well-received. As a result, many premarital agreements are discussed, and even drawn, but never actually executed.

There are viable alternatives to prenuptial agreements that parties can use to protect their property in marriage, even though the alternatives do not possess the same security and comprehensive coverage that can be achieved by a prenuptial agreement. See Author's Notes (2) through (7) below.

Furthermore, there are at least two important caveats in prenuptial agreements. First: particularly because there are alternative measures for protection, it may not be wise to press a prenuptial agreement so hard upon an unwilling party that it spoils the marriage that it is supposed to improve. Second: a lawyer drawing a prenuptial agreement may well be disqualified from representing his client if there is a subsequent divorce, because the lawyer is a potential witness. See Supreme Court Rule of Professional Conduct 3.6 ("A lawyer shall not accept or continue employment in contemplated or pending litigation if the lawyer knows or reasonably should know that the lawyer may be called as a witness on behalf of the client.... ").

(2) **Segregation of non-marital property.** Even in the absence of a premarital agreement, in a dissolution proceeding, a spouse can shelter non-marital property and its income (but not marital property) from property claims (but not from maintenance or child support claims; see Author's Note (6) below). Section 503(a) of the Illinois Marriage and Dissolution of Marriage Act sets forth the criteria which establish non-marital property, including, property acquired before the marriage, property acquired by gift, and property acquired by inheritance. Income from non-marital property, if it is not attributable to the personal effort of a spouse, is also non-marital (IMDMA § 503(a)(8)). In order to remain non-marital property, the non-marital property and its income must be kept in the owner's name, carefully segregated and clearly identified, separate and apart from marital property and marital income. The segrega-

tion of the non-marital property must include a separate bank account in the sole name of the owner of the non-marital property to receive and disburse the non-marital income and the proceeds from the sale of any non-marital property. If non-marital income or proceeds are placed in a joint account, or mixed with marital money, the non-marital is compromised. See IMDMA § 503 Author's Notes (12) through (16). A party who brings a large estate to a marriage (as opposed to earning it during the marriage) can therefore at least be partially protected by careful segregation in the event of a divorce without a premarital agreement.

(3) **Disposition of non-marital property upon death.** Although the careful segregation of non-marital property protects it from property allocation to the other spouse in dissolution proceedings, non-marital property is not similarly protected upon the death of the owner spouse. The surviving spouse may take an intestate share if the decedent dies without a will, or, if the decedent leaves a will, the surviving spouse can waive the will of the deceased spouse and take his or her statutory share. An intestate share is ½ of the estate if the decedent is survived by one or more descendants, and all of the estate if the decedent leaves no descendants. 755 ILCS 5/2-1. Renunciation of the decedent's will by the surviving spouse entitles the surviving spouse to ⅓ of the testator's estate if the testator leaves a descendant, or ½ of the estate if the testator does not leave a descendant. 755 ILCS 5/2-8. The intestate share or the share resulting from a waiver of the decedent's will includes the decedent's non-marital property that is in his probate estate.

(4) *Inter vivos* **trusts.** Additional security without a premarital agreement in the event of divorce or a hostile spouse at death can be obtained through the use of a revocable *inter vivos* trust, for which the settlor can be both the lifetime beneficiary and the trustee. Non-marital property can be placed into an *inter vivos* trust, which can also collect the income generated by the non-marital property. Purchases and sales of non-marital property take place in the trust and in its accounts, separate from marital property. Provided that the *inter vivos* trust is not vitiated by a contribution of marital property or marital income, the *inter vivos* trust will clearly segregate and identify the non-marital property and the income generated by it from marital property and income. The non-marital property and income is therefore safe from property claims in a dissolution proceeding. Additionally, because the *inter vivos* trust takes the non-marital property and its income out of the probate estate of the decedent, the non-marital property and its income in the trust are not subject to an intestate share or to the statutory share upon the renunciation of the decedent's will by the surviving spouse. See Author's Note (5) below.

(5) *Johnson* **case: Content of the probate estate.** In Johnson v. LaGrange State Bank, 73 Ill.2d 342, 22 Ill.Dec. 709, 383 N.E.2d 185 (1978), the Illinois Supreme Court held:

> In Illinois ... and by the weight of authority in other jurisdictions, the owner of property has an absolute right to dispose of his property during his lifetime in any manner he sees fit, and he may do so even though the transfer is for the precise purpose of minimizing or defeating the statutory marital interests of the spouse in the property conveyed.

Johnson v. LaGrange State Bank, 73 Ill.2d at 357, 22 Ill.Dec. at 716, 383 N.E.2d at 185 (citations omitted). The court in *Johnson* sustained a transfer of property by a wife into an *inter vivos* revocable trust of which she was the trustee and lifetime beneficiary against an attempt by her surviving husband to obtain his statutory share of the trust property by waiving the decedent wife's will. Therefore the trust property was not a

750 ILCS 10/1

part of the wife's probate estate, and the husband could not obtain any part of it. The attempts in the Illinois legislature to change the result of *Johnson* have so far been unsuccessful, and *Johnson* is still good law.

(6) **Inter vivos trust protection not complete.** In the absence of a premarital agreement, a large measure of protection against both death and dissolution of marriage can be obtained by segregating non-marital property and income in an *inter vivos* revocable trust. See Author's Notes (2) through (5), above. The protection is not complete, because the income, and even the property, may be subject to claims for maintenance and children's support pursuant to §§ 504 and 505 of the Illinois Marriage and Dissolution of Marriage Act. See IMDMA § 504 Author's Note (7), IMDMA § 505 Author's Note (12). The court could merely order the [spouse] trustee to so apply the income and property.

(7) **Trust together with premarital agreement.** The maximum security for non-marital property and income is to both place the non-marital property and income in an *inter vivos* revocable trust, and, in addition, where it is possible, conclude a premarital agreement, which spells out the intentions of the parties.

750 ILCS 10/2

§ 2. Definitions

As used in this Article:

(1) "Premarital agreement" means an agreement between prospective spouses made in contemplation of marriage and to be effective upon marriage.

(2) "Property" means an interest, present or future, legal or equitable, vested or contingent, in real or personal property, including income and earnings.

750 ILCS 10/3

§ 3. Formalities

A premarital agreement must be in writing and signed by both parties. It is enforceable without consideration.

750 ILCS 10/4

§ 4. Content

(a) Parties to a premarital agreement may contract with respect to:

(1) the rights and obligations of each of the parties in any of the property of either or both of them whenever and wherever acquired or located;

(2) the right to buy, sell, use, transfer, exchange, abandon, lease, consume, expend, assign, create a security interest in, mortgage, encumber, dispose of, or otherwise manage and control property;

(3) the disposition of property upon separation, marital dissolution, death, or the occurrence or nonoccurrence of any other event;

(4) the modification or elimination of spousal support;

(5) the making of a will, trust, or other arrangement to carry out the provisions of the agreement;

(6) the ownership rights in and disposition of the death benefit from a life insurance policy;

(7) the choice of law governing the construction of the agreement; and

(8) any other matter, including their personal rights and obligations, not in violation of public policy or a statute imposing a criminal penalty.

(b) The right of a child to support may not be adversely affected by a premarital agreement.

750 ILCS 10/5
§ 5. Effect of marriage

A premarital agreement becomes effective upon marriage.

750 ILCS 10/6
§ 6. Amendment, revocation

After marriage, a premarital agreement may be amended or revoked only by a written agreement signed by the parties. The amended agreement or the revocation is enforceable without consideration.

750 ILCS 10/7
§ 7. Enforcement

(a) A premarital agreement is not enforceable if the party against whom enforcement is sought proves that:

(1) that party did not execute the agreement voluntarily; or

(2) the agreement was unconscionable when it was executed and, before execution of the agreement, that party:

(i) was not provided a fair and reasonable disclosure of the property or financial obligations of the other party;

(ii) did not voluntarily and expressly waive, in writing, any right to disclosure of the property or financial obligations of the other party beyond the disclosure provided; and

(iii) did not have, or reasonably could not have had, an adequate knowledge of the property or financial obligations of the other party.

(b) If a provision of a premarital agreement modifies or eliminates spousal support and that modification or elimination causes one party to the agreement undue hardship in light of circumstances not reasonably foreseeable at the time of the execution of the agreement, a court, notwithstanding the terms of the agreement, may require the other party to provide support to the extent necessary to avoid such hardship.

(c) An issue of unconscionability of a premarital agreement shall be decided by the court as a matter of law.

Author's Notes

Analysis

1. Premarital agreements easier to enforce.
2. Requirements for setting aside.
3. Premarital superior to post-marital agreements.
4. Sources of case law.
5. Duress.
6. Unconscionability.
7. Disclosure.
8. Waiver of disclosure.
9. Support and foreseeable circumstances.
10. Unconscionability a matter of law.

(1) **Premarital agreements easier to enforce.** Section 7 of the Uniform Premarital Agreement Act makes the enforcement of premarital agreements easier than was the case under the previous law. Because the emotions of an engagement make it undesirable to take adversarial positions or create conflict, the party without wealth will frequently acquiesce in the requests for financial protection from the party with wealth when premarital agreements are negotiated. Women, more often than men, are in this disadvantageous bargaining position, which might be colloquially described as "let's get married and I will worry about the finances afterwards." Section 7 can therefore be expected to work hardships against women. The situation is not different from the quixotic but unrealistic expectations of spousal independence under the maintenance section, IMDMA § 504, that led to the impoverishment of so many women before the amendment of IMDMA § 504 in 1993. See IMDMA § 504 Author's Note (2).

(2) **Requirements for setting aside.** Largely because § 7 is stated in negatives, the language is unnecessarily complex. Stated affirmatively, a prenuptial agreement may be set aside if:

(1) The agreement was executed under duress or coercion; or

(2) The agreement was unconscionable at the time when it was executed (not when enforcement is sought), and, before execution of the agreement, the party against whom enforcement is sought:

(i) was not provided with fair financial disclosure; or

(ii) did not voluntarily waive in writing the right to financial disclosure; or

(iii) did not have adequate knowledge of the other party's financial circumstances.

In other words, if the agreement was conscionable at the time it was executed, paragraphs (i), (ii), and (iii) are irrelevant and the contract is enforceable. Moreover, even if the premarital agreement was unconscionable at the time it was executed, if any one of the following occurred, the agreement is enforceable:

(i) The party was given fair disclosure; or

(ii) the party voluntarily waived the disclosure; or

(iii) the party had knowledge of the financial circumstances.

(3) **Premarital superior to post-marital agreements.** Premarital agreements, for no logical reason, are therefore given a superior position to post-nuptial agreements that are drawn while the spouses are undergoing dissolution proceedings. A court can find a post-nuptial divorce settlement agreement unconscionable at the time of the dissolution without any limits of disclosure, waiver, or knowledge on its authority to so do. See IMDMA § 502(b) Author's Note (3). The same court cannot set aside a premarital agreement that is unconscionable at the time of the dissolution if it was not unconscionable at the time of its execution (maybe 10 years or more previous), or, even if it was unconscionable at the time of its execution, the court cannot set it aside if there was disclosure, waiver, or knowledge. The statute takes no account of the unequal bargaining positions of many engaged couples that may not amount to coercion.

(4) **Sources of case law.** Because very few cases have been decided in Illinois under the new Uniform Premarital Agreement Act, the best sources for case law are cases construing premarital agreements prior to the Act, cases construing post-nuptial settlement agreements, and cases from other states that have enacted the Uniform Act.

(5) **Duress.** The Illinois Supreme Court defined duress as "a condition where one is induced by a wrongful act or threat of another to make a contract under circumstances which deprive him of the exercise of his free will ... " Kaplan v. Kaplan, 25 Ill.2d 181, 185, 182 N.E.2d 706, 708 (1962). The *Kaplan* court found that the wife's threat to publicize the husband's affair was not sufficient to prove duress. The threat, while potentially embarrassing, did not control the will of the husband in executing the settlement agreement because the threat was merely annoying and vexatious. *Id.* at 188, 182 N.E.2d at ___. The Second District found an Antenuptial Agreement to be invalid because of concealment and coercion in In re Estate of Gigele, 64 Ill.App.3d 136, 20 Ill.Dec. 935, 380 N.E.2d 1144 (1st Dist.1978) ("The provisions made for the [wife] were disproportionate to the extent and value of the decedent's estate, giving rise to the presumption that there was concealment." Furthermore, wife was not informed of her right to consult an attorney, she had not read the instrument, it was not explained to her, her husband told her it was for her protection, and she had no knowledge of her husband's finances.).

(6) **Unconscionability.** The Illinois Appellate Court has defined unconscionability as

> includ[ing] "an absence of meaningful choice on the part of one of the parties together with contract terms which are unreasonably favorable to the other party." ... A contract is unconscionable when it is improvident, totally one sided or oppressive.... [t]he inquiry into unconscionability requires at least two considerations: (1) the conditions under which the agreement was made and (2) the economic circumstances of the parties that result from the agreement.

In re Marriage of Gurin, 212 Ill.App.3d 806, 815, 156 Ill.Dec. 877, 884, 571 N.E.2d 857, 864 (1st Dist.1991).

Compare In re Marriage of Richardson, 237 Ill.App.3d 1067, 179 Ill.Dec. 224, 606 N.E.2d 56 (1st Dist.1992), in which the court found a post-nuptial agreement invalid because of coercion, concealment, and unconscionability.

(7) **Disclosure.** In Watson v. Watson, 5 Ill.2d 526, 126 N.E.2d 220 (1955), the Illinois Supreme Court noted that "specific knowledge is required before a prospective wife can intelligently choose to take a small sum in payment for a release of her rights and interests in her prospective husband's property." *Watson*, 5 Ill.2d at 532, 126 N.E.2d at 223 (1955). But the Uniform Act has also codified the prior case law that in the absence of specific disclosure, a party is held to have constructive knowledge where she in fact knew or was in a position to know the other party's financial circumstances. (§ 7(a)(2)(iii)) See, e.g., Warren v. Warren, 169 Ill.App.3d 226, 119 Ill.Dec. 924, 523 N.E.2d 680 (5th Dist.1988) (wife held to have made prenuptial agreement with full knowledge although husband did not give full financial disclosure due to her experience in the business world and familiarity with his property gained from working and living with him).

(8) **Waiver of disclosure.** The statutory authority in § 7(a)(2)(ii) for making an unconscionable agreement enforceable against a party who waives financial disclosure creates the potential for an even further imbalance in the negotiating positions, because the weaker negotiator can accept an unconscionable contract without even knowing the financial context.

(9) **Support and foreseeable circumstances.** Section 7(b) also has the potential for problems. For example, query, whether placing in a prenuptial agreement a clause to the effect that illness is a reasonably foreseeable possibility at the time of the execution of the agreement is sufficient to support a waiver of maintenance in the prenuptial agreement by a wife who becomes ill and unemployable after 20 years of marriage? Moreover, even in specifically foreseeable circumstances, why should the state be preferred as a source of support for a spouse who is ill and unemployable at dissolution when she waived support years previously in a premarital agreement?

(10) **Unconscionability a matter of law.** Section 7(c), which mandates that the unconscionability of a premarital agreement be decided by the court as a matter of law, is misleading. In the situation where no financial disclosure is attached to the premarital agreement against which the court could measure the conscionability of the premarital agreement provisions, the court, despite the provisions of § 7(c), would obviously have to take evidence concerning the financial circumstances that existed at the time of the execution of the prenuptial agreement and determine what they were as a question of fact, before deciding as a question of law whether the agreement was unconscionable.

750 ILCS 10/8

§ 8. Enforcement: Void marriage

If a marriage is determined to be void, an agreement that would otherwise have been a premarital agreement is enforceable only to the extent necessary to avoid an inequitable result.

750 ILCS 10/9

§ 9. Limitation of actions

Any statute of limitations applicable to an action asserting a claim for relief under a premarital agreement is tolled during the marriage of the parties to the agreement. However, equitable defenses limiting the time for enforcement, including laches and estoppel, are available to either party.

750 ILCS 10/10
§ 10. Application and construction

This Act shall be applied and construed to effectuate its general purpose to make uniform the law with respect to the subject of this Act among states enacting it.

750 ILCS 10/11
§ 11. Time of taking effect

This Article applies to any premarital agreement executed on or after January 1, 1990.

Author's Notes

Analysis

1. Premarital agreement powers of attorney.
2. Internal Revenue Code § 417.
3. Premarital Agreement—Form.

(1) **Premarital agreement powers of attorney.** Powers of attorney in premarital agreements are used to authorize one spouse to take actions on behalf of the other spouse, e.g., the signing of documents. Premarital agreements are drawn with powers of attorney included within the agreement, with separate powers of attorney attached to the premarital agreement, or with powers of attorney omitted altogether. The best practice is to use separate powers of attorney, which are signed after the wedding, because the powers are then independent documents which contain the married names (not the pre-marriage names) of the parties, and because of the requirements of § 417 of the Internal Revenue Code. The practice of eliminating the separate powers of attorney signed after the marriage ceremony is a hazardous one if the premarital agreement includes a waiver of an interest in a qualified retirement plan, because Internal Revenue Code § 417(a)(2)(A)(i) requires that a "spouse" consent to a waiver of a survivor annuity under the plan, and premarital agreements are executed before marriage. Marjorie A. O'Connell, *Divorce Taxation*, Report Bulletin ¶11.2 (Nov. 16, 1993). IRC § 417(a)(2)(A)(i) also requires that the spousal consent be witnessed before a plan representative or a notary public, so that the notary page for the power of attorney should not be eliminated.

(2) **Internal Revenue Code § 417.** Section 417 of the Internal Revenue Code follows.

SEC. 417. DEFINITIONS AND SPECIAL RULES FOR PURPOSES OF MINIMUM SURVIVOR ANNUITY REQUIREMENTS.

(a) ELECTION TO WAIVE QUALIFIED JOINT AND SURVIVOR ANNUITY OR QUALIFIED PRERETIREMENT SURVIVOR ANNUITY.

(1) IN GENERAL. A plan meets the requirements of section 401(a)(11) only if—

(A) under the plan, each participant—

(i) may elect at any time during the applicable election period to waive the qualified joint and survivor annuity form of benefit or the qualified preretirement survivor annuity form of benefit (or both), and

(ii) may revoke any such election at any time during the applicable election period, and

(B) the plan meets the requirements of paragraphs (2), (3) and (4) of this subsection.

(2) SPOUSE MUST CONSENT TO ELECTION. Each plan shall provide that an election under paragraph (1)(A)(i) shall not take effect unless—

(A)(i) the spouse of the participant consents in writing to such election, (ii) such election designates a beneficiary (or a form of benefits) which may not be changed without spousal consent (or the consent of the spouse expressly permits designations by the participant without any requirement of further consent by the spouse), and (iii) the spouse's consent acknowledges the effect of such election and is witnessed by a plan representative or a notary public, or

(B) it is established to the satisfaction of a plan representative that the consent required under subparagraph (A) may not be obtained because there is no spouse, because the spouse cannot be located, or because of such other circumstances as the Secretary may by regulations prescribe.

Any consent by a spouse (or establishment that the consent of a spouse may not be obtained) under the preceding sentence shall be effective only with respect to such spouse.

(3) **Premarital Agreement—Form.** There follows a sample premarital agreement with separate powers of attorney attached as exhibits. If separate powers are used, the premarital agreement itself should be signed before the marriage ceremony, and the powers signed afterwards.

PREMARITAL AGREEMENT

THIS AGREEMENT, made and entered into this _____ day of _____, 199__, by and between ESTHER SUMMERSON, of Chicago, Cook County, Illinois (hereinafter referred to as "ESTHER") and JOHN JARNDYCE, of Chicago, Cook County, Illinois (hereinafter referred to as "JOHN").

WHEREAS:

(a) ESTHER is 29 years of age;

(b) ESTHER states that her present aggregate gross income is approximately $36,000.00 annually, although she does not plan to continue working after her marriage to JOHN;

(c) ESTHER is possessed of an estate consisting of the assets listed and described in the schedule attached hereto and made a part hereof, as Exhibit A;

(d) JOHN is 54 years of age, has been divorced, and is the father of four children;

(e) JOHN states that his present aggregate gross income is approximately $500,000.00 annually;

(f) JOHN is possessed of an estate consisting of the assets listed and described in the schedule attached hereto and made a part hereof as Exhibit B;

(g) ESTHER and JOHN have agreed to be married in the near future;

(h) ESTHER has employed and had the benefit of the counsel of Conrad Snagsby as her attorney. JOHN has employed and had the benefit of the counsel of Frederick Tulkinghorn as his attorney.

(i) ESTHER acknowledges that she has reviewed the financial statement of JOHN attached hereto as Exhibit B, and that she has been advised that as a result of her marriage to JOHN she will, in case of a dissolution of the marriage, or if she survives JOHN as his wife, acquire certain rights and interests in and claims against the income, property, and estate of JOHN under the statutes and laws of the State of Illinois and other states of the United States of America;

(j) JOHN acknowledges that he has reviewed the financial statement of ESTHER attached hereto as Exhibit A and that he has been advised that as a result of his marriage he will, in case of a dissolution of the marriage, or if he survives ESTHER as her husband, acquire certain rights and interests in and claims against the income, property and estate of ESTHER under the statutes and laws of the State of Illinois and other states of the United States of America;

(k) So as to avoid any possible differences between them and to make for peace and harmony in their contemplated marriage, ESTHER and JOHN are desirous of forever settling and determining the rights and claims of each party in and to the property and estate of the other, and the rights and claims of each party to alimony, maintenance and support from the other in the event of a separation or divorce;

NOW, THEREFORE, and in consideration of their Agreement to marry and of such marriage, and of the mutual promises, agreements, and waivers herein contained, the parties do hereby agree as follows:

Article I

Waivers

1(a). ESTHER hereby waives, releases and quitclaims to JOHN all right, title, and interest that she may acquire as wife, widow or otherwise upon and by reason of her marriage to JOHN, and that she may acquire after such marriage under any present or future law of the State of Illinois or of any state of the United States of America or of the United States Federal Government or of any foreign country in and to all property and estate, legal and equitable, real, personal and mixed of JOHN, whether now owned or hereafter acquired by him, and wheresoever situated, including, but in no way limited to: (a) dower, (b) statutory allowance in lieu of dower, (c) statutory intestate or other distributive share, (d) right of election against the will, (e) statutory Widow's or Spouse's Award, (f) Homestead rights, (g) interest in marital, non-marital, separate or community property, (h) right to act as administrator or executor, and (i) any interest under Federal or State law to the pension, profit sharing, retirement plan, or other employee benefits of JOHN. Immediately after their marriage, ESTHER shall make, execute and deliver to JOHN a deed, waiving, releasing and quitclaiming all such interest as she may then have by virtue of such marriage in and to all property then owned or thereafter acquired by JOHN, together with a power of attorney authorizing and empowering JOHN to make and execute for and on her behalf, as her attorney-in-fact, any deeds or other instruments waiving, releasing or otherwise transferring all of her right, title and interest in and to all such property and real estate of JOHN then owned or thereafter acquired, a copy of which deed and power of attorney is attached hereto as Exhibit C and made a part hereof; and ESTHER hereby acknowledges that the aforedescribed instrument is given for a valuable consideration, coupled with an interest, and that the power of attorney contained therein is and shall be in all respects absolutely irrevocable; and ESTHER shall from time to time make, execute and deliver such other and further deeds and instruments as may be necessary or appropriate or which JOHN may request in order to waive, release and quitclaim to JOHN or his grantee or assigns any and all such rights, title and interest in his property, and join JOHN in making, executing and delivering such deeds and other instruments as may be necessary or appropriate or which he may request for the purpose of waiving, releasing and quitclaiming any and all such rights, title and interest in his property.

1(b). ESTHER hereby, pursuant to Section 417(a) of the Internal Revenue Code of 1986, and amendments thereto, consents in writing and waives any interest that she may have in any qualified retirement plan of JOHN, including, but not limited to, a waiver of any interest in the qualified joint and survivor annuity form of benefit and the qualified preretirement survivor annuity form of benefit. ESTHER hereby further grants permission to JOHN to designate, without further consent by ESTHER, the beneficiary or a form of benefits of any qualified plan in place of ESTHER. ESTHER acknowledges that the effect of this consent and waiver is that ESTHER will receive no benefits under any qualified retirement plan of JOHN, and JOHN may designate the beneficiary of or form of benefits of any qualified plan in place of ESTHER without the further consent by ESTHER.

1(c). JOHN and ESTHER hereby agree that the property hereinabove released by ESTHER to JOHN in paragraphs 1(a) and 1(b) hereof, any appreciation of the property, any proceeds of the property, any acquisitions of or exchanges for new property, and any income generated by the property, including but not limited to salary from _____, Inc., shall not be considered marital property or marital income for any purpose whatsoever, but shall instead be designated the non-marital property and non-marital income of JOHN for all purposes, pursuant to the Illinois Marriage and Dissolution of Marriage Act.

1(d). JOHN hereby waives, releases and quitclaims to ESTHER all right, title and interest that he may acquire as husband, widower, or otherwise upon or by reason of his marriage to ESTHER or that he may acquire after such marriage under any present or future law of the State of Illinois or of any other state of the United States of America or of the United States Federal Government, or of any foreign country in and to any and all property and estate, legal or equitable, real, personal and mixed of ESTHER, whether now owned or hereafter any time acquired by her, and wheresoever situated, including, but in no way limited to: (a) dower and curtesy, (b) statutory allowance in lieu of dower and curtesy, (c) statutory intestate or other distributive share, (d) right of election against the will, (e) statutory widower's or surviving spouse's award, (f) Homestead rights, (g) interest in marital, non-marital, separate or community property, (h) right to act as administrator or executor, and (i) any interest under Federal or State law to the pension, profit sharing, retirement plan, or other employee benefits of ESTHER. Immediately after their marriage, JOHN shall make, execute and deliver to ESTHER a deed, waiving, releasing and quitclaiming all such interest as he may then have by virtue of such marriage in and to all property then owned or thereafter acquired by ESTHER, together with a power of attorney authorizing and empowering ESTHER to make and execute for and on his behalf, as his attorney-in-fact, any deeds or other instruments waiving, releasing, or otherwise transferring all of his right, title and interest in and to all such property and real estate of ESTHER then owned or thereafter acquired, a copy of which deed and power of attorney is attached hereto as Exhibit D and made a part hereof; and JOHN hereby acknowledges that the instrument is given for a valuable consideration coupled with an interest, and that the power of attorney contained therein is and shall be in all respects absolutely irrevocable; and JOHN shall from time to time make, execute and deliver such other and further deeds and instruments as may be necessary or appropriate or which ESTHER may request in order to waive, release and quitclaim to ESTHER or her grantee or assigns any and all such rights, title and interest in her property, and join ESTHER in making, executing and delivering such deeds and other instruments as may be necessary or appropriate or which she may request for the purpose of waiving, releasing, and quitclaiming any and all such right, title and interest in her property.

1(e). JOHN hereby, pursuant to Section 417(a) of the Internal Revenue Code of 1986, and amendments thereto, consents in writing and waives any interest that he may have in any qualified retirement plan of ESTHER, including, but not limited to, a waiver of any interest in the qualified joint and survivor annuity form of benefit and the qualified preretirement survivor annuity form of benefit. JOHN hereby further grants permission to ESTHER to designate, without further consent by JOHN, the beneficiary or a form of benefits of any qualified plan in place of JOHN. JOHN acknowledges that the effect of this consent and waiver is that JOHN will receive no benefits under any qualified retirement plan of ESTHER, and ESTHER may designate the beneficiary of or form of benefits of any qualified plan in place of JOHN without the further consent by JOHN.

1(f). ESTHER and JOHN hereby agree that the property hereinabove released by JOHN to ESTHER in paragraphs 1(d) and 1(e) hereof, any appreciation of the property, any proceeds of the property, any acquisitions of or exchanges for new property, and any income generated by the property, shall not be considered marital property or marital income for any purpose whatsoever, but shall instead be designated the non-marital property and non-marital income of ESTHER for all purposes, pursuant to the Illinois Marriage and Dissolution of Marriage Act.

1(g). Except as otherwise herein expressly provided, during the continuance of their marriage and thereafter, each of the parties is to have the full right to own, control, bequeath, and dispose of his or her separate property in the same manner as if the marriage did not exist, and each of the parties is to have the full right to dispose of and sell any and all real or personal property now or hereafter owned by either of them without the other party joining, and the transfer by either of the parties to this Agreement will convey the same title that the transfer would convey if the marriage had not existed.

1(h). ESTHER acknowledges that her income from her separate property and her prior training and experience as a realtor is sufficient and adequate to provide for and to enable her to provide for the support and maintenance of herself, and, as a result, she does not require any alimony, maintenance or support from JOHN. ESTHER agrees that in the event the parties hereto are hereafter divorced, or their marriage is dissolved, or declared invalid, or the parties are legally separated, in any proceeding now or hereafter instituted by either party in any court, she will not ask the court to allow her any alimony or maintenance from JOHN, and she will inform the court that she has sufficient income and wealth and employment experience to adequately provide for her support and maintenance, temporarily and permanently; and that it is her desire forever to waive and release her rights and claims to alimony, maintenance and support, temporary and permanent, past, present, and future, including also attorney's fees, from JOHN.

1(i). JOHN acknowledges that his separate income and wealth, and his salary from _____, Inc., is sufficient and adequate to provide for the support and maintenance of himself, and that he does not require any alimony, maintenance or support from ESTHER. JOHN agrees that in the event the parties hereto are hereafter divorced or their marriage is dissolved or declared invalid, or the parties are legally separated in any proceedings now or hereafter instituted by either party in any court, he will not ask the court to allow him any alimony or maintenance from ESTHER and he will inform the court that he has sufficient income and wealth to provide for his own support and maintenance temporarily and permanently; and that it is his desire forever to waive and release his rights and claims to alimony, maintenance and support, temporary and permanent, past, present and future, including also attorney's fees, from ESTHER.

Article II
Death

2(a). Anything in the foregoing to the contrary notwithstanding, in the event of JOHN's death prior to ESTHER's death (and if they die simultaneously, JOHN shall not be presumed to have died prior to ESTHER), JOHN agrees by valid will or other testamentary instrument to bequeath to ESTHER at least the following:

2(b). *(Insert bequests.)*

2(c). ESTHER's right to receive the amounts set forth in paragraph 2(b) hereof shall be extinguished and barred in the event that: ESTHER makes any attempt at any time to challenge the validity of this Agreement; ESTHER makes any attempt at any time to challenge the validity of any part of a will drawn in accordance with this Agreement; ESTHER makes any attempt at any time to waive the will and take a statutory share; the parties at the time of JOHN's death are divorced, their marriage has been dissolved or declared invalid, they are not living together, or they have litigation pending between them.

2(d). Anything in the foregoing to the contrary notwithstanding, in the event of ESTHER's death prior to JOHN's death (and if they die simultaneously, ESTHER shall not be presumed to have died prior to JOHN), ESTHER agrees by valid will or other testamentary instrument to bequeath to JOHN at least the following:

2(e). *(Insert bequests.)*

2(f). JOHN's right to receive the amounts set forth in paragraph 2(e) hereof shall be extinguished and barred in the event that: JOHN makes any attempt at any time to challenge the validity of this Agreement; JOHN makes any attempt at any time to challenge the validity of any part of a will drawn in accordance with this Agreement; JOHN makes any attempt at any time to waive the will and take a statutory share; the parties at the time of ESTHER's death are divorced, their marriage has been dissolved or declared invalid, they are not living together, or they have litigation pending between them.

Article III
Dissolution

3(a). Anything in the foregoing to the contrary notwithstanding, in the event of dissolution of marriage or divorce (but not in the event of a declaration of invalidity or legal separation), JOHN agrees to pay the following to ESTHER as a property settlement and in lieu of maintenance, in complete discharge of his obligation to pay temporary and permanent alimony, maintenance, and support to ESTHER:

3(b). *(A frequently used formula is to increase the amounts of property transferred to the spouse in accordance with the number of years that the parties remain married, in some cases causing the premarital agreement to terminate if the parties stay married a specified number of years. A similar technique can also be used for maintenance payments and bequests.)*

3(c). The principal payment to be paid by JOHN to ESTHER pursuant to the terms of this Article III shall be a property settlement and shall be neither deductible to JOHN nor taxable to ESTHER for purposes of Federal or State income tax. *(If maintenance is provided instead of or in addition to property, an appropriate tax paragraph designating the maintenance as taxable and deductible or neither taxable nor deductible should be included. See IMDMA § 502 Author's Note (11), paragraphs 2(d) and 2(e) of the model Marital Settlement Agreement from which the paragraphs for the premarital agreement can be fashioned.)*

3(d). ESTHER's right to receive the amounts set forth in this Article III shall be extinguished and barred in the event ESTHER makes any attempt at any time to challenge the validity of any part of this Agreement.

3(e). Amounts, if any, awarded by a court as temporary maintenance, attorney's fees, or other awards to ESTHER outside the scope of this Agreement, shall be a credit against and a reduction of the amounts to be paid pursuant to Article III hereof.

3(f). Pursuant to Sections 502(f), 503(a)(4), and 510(b) of the Illinois Marriage and Dissolution of Marriage Act, the parties agree that Article III hereof shall not be subject to modification in any respect whatsoever. The parties further agree that in the event there is a dissolution of marriage or divorce between the parties, they will ask the court to include in the Judgment a prohibition against the modification of Article III hereof in any respect whatsoever.

Article IV

Care, Gifts

4(a). Nothing herein contained shall be construed as a release or waiver of the liability of either party to care for the other party, so long as they are husband and wife, not involved in litigation against one another, and are living together.

4(b). Nothing herein contained shall be construed as a waiver or renunciation by ESTHER or JOHN of any gift, bequest, or devise which may be made to him or her by the other, provided, however, that this paragraph shall not be construed as a promise or representation that any such gift, bequest, or devise shall be made by the one to the other.

4(c). The effect of placing property in any form of joint ownership shall be to make each party the owner of the percentage interest in his or her name, either in recognition of the contribution of each party to the jointly owned property, or as a gift by one to the other, anything herein to the contrary notwithstanding.

Article V

Tax

5. Each party agrees that he and she shall indemnify and hold the other, his or her heirs, executors, administrators and personal representatives, free and harmless from any liability for capital gains, income, gift taxes or other Federal and State taxes, if any, assessed in the first instance on the releasing or transferring party in connection with the aforesaid releases and transfers of property pursuant to this Agreement, and for costs, interest, penalties, professional fees, and other expenses in connection therewith, but the releasing or transferring party, his or her heirs, executors, administrators and personal representatives, shall have no further liability for taxes resulting from subsequent transfers of the property.

Article VI

Acknowledgments

6(a). ESTHER hereby acknowledges that the disclosure of JOHN's property, income, and financial obligations set forth herein and on Exhibit B attached hereto and made a part hereof was reviewed by ESTHER prior to execution of this Agreement and determined by ESTHER to be fair, reasonable, and complete, and ESTHER hereby voluntarily and expressly waives any right to disclosure of the property, income, and financial obligations of JOHN beyond the disclosure herein provided.

6(b). JOHN hereby acknowledges that the disclosure of ESTHER's property, income, and financial obligations set forth herein and on Exhibit A attached hereto and made a part hereof was reviewed by JOHN prior to execution of this Agreement and determined by JOHN to be fair, reasonable, and complete, and JOHN hereby voluntarily and expressly waives any right to disclosure of the property, income, and financial obligations of ESTHER beyond the disclosure herein provided.

6(c). Each party hereby acknowledges that: each party has entered into this Agreement freely and voluntarily; each party has reviewed all of its terms with an attorney of his or her choice; and each party has determined that the Agreement was conscionable at the time it was executed.

6(d). Each party acknowledges that the circumstances reasonably foreseeable at the time of the execution of this Agreement include, but are not limited to, the illness, incapacity, or unemployability of either of the parties.

Article VII
General

7(a). The parties agree that if any of the provisions of this Agreement are held to be invalid for any reason whatsoever, such invalidity shall relate only to the provision or provisions so declared to be invalid and shall not affect in any way the remaining provisions of this Agreement, which shall remain in full force and effect.

7(b). It is further mutually agreed that each party will make, execute and deliver from time to time such papers or other instruments as may be necessary or appropriate or as may be requested by either party to carry into effect any of the terms, provisions or conditions of this Agreement.

7(c). This Agreement is made and executed in contemplation of an agreement to marry and of the marriage pursuant thereto. The provisions hereof shall be effective upon the marriage of the parties hereto.

7(d). The provisions of this Agreement shall be governed by the laws of the State of Illinois.

IN WITNESS WHEREOF, the parties hereto have hereunto set their hands and seals on the day and year first above written.

ESTHER SUMMERSON

JOHN JARNDYCE

Frederick Tulkinghorn
Attorney for ESTHER
SUMMERSON
Address
Telephone number

FAMILIES   750 ILCS 10/11

EXHIBIT A

ESTHER SUMMERSON'S ASSETS AND LIABILITIES AS OF 199__

                              Net worth $17,000

750 ILCS 10/11   **FAMILIES**

EXHIBIT B

JOHN JARNDYCE'S ASSETS AND LIABILITIES AS OF 199__

                                        Net worth $7,000,000

STATE OF ILLINOIS)
) SS
COUNTY OF COOK   )

    I, the undersigned, a Notary Public in and for said County, in the State aforesaid, do hereby certify that ESTHER SUMMERSON, personally known to me to be the same person whose name is subscribed to the foregoing Instrument, appeared before me this day in person and acknowledged that she signed, sealed and delivered the said Instrument as her free and voluntary act, for the uses and purposes therein set forth.

    Given under my hand and notarial seal this _____ day of _____, 199__.

                                        Notary Public

STATE OF ILLINOIS)
) SS
COUNTY OF COOK   )

I, the undersigned, a Notary Public in and for said County, in the State aforesaid, do hereby certify that JOHN JARNDYCE, personally known to me to be the same person whose name is subscribed to the foregoing Instrument, appeared before me this day in person and acknowledged that he signed, sealed and delivered the said Instrument as his free and voluntary act, for the uses and purposes therein set forth.

Given under my hand and notarial seal this _____ day of _____, 199__.

_____
Notary Public

EXHIBIT C

KNOW ALL MEN BY THESE PRESENTS that ESTHER JARNDYCE of Chicago, Illinois (wife of JOHN JARNDYCE of Chicago, Illinois), for and in consideration of TEN DOLLARS ($10.00) and other good and valuable consideration and of the mutual promises, agreements, covenants, waivers and releases contained in a certain agreement dated the _____ day of _____, 199__, by and between ESTHER SUMMERSON and JOHN JARNDYCE, hereby conveys, releases, waives and quitclaims to JOHN JARNDYCE all of her rights, title and interest that she, as the wife of JOHN JARNDYCE, now has or may hereafter acquire under any present or future law of the State of Illinois or of any state of the United States of America or of the United States Federal Government or of any foreign country, including but not limited to: (a) dower, (b) statutory allowance in lieu of dower, (c) statutory intestate or other distributive share, (d) right of election against the will, (e) statutory Widow's or Spouse's Award, (f) Homestead rights, (g) interest in marital, nonmarital, separate, or community property, (h) right to act as administrator or executor, and (i) any interest under Federal or State law to the pension, profit sharing, retirement plan, or other employee benefits of JOHN JARNDYCE, and in and to any and all property and estate, legal or equitable, real, personal and mixed of JOHN JARNDYCE, now owned or hereafter at any time acquired by him and wheresoever situated, except as otherwise provided in the Agreement dated the _____ day of _____, 199__, between ESTHER SUMMERSON and JOHN JARNDYCE.

ESTHER JARNDYCE hereby, pursuant to Section 417(a) of the Internal Revenue Code of 1986, and amendments thereto, consents in writing and waives any interest that she may have in any qualified retirement plan of JOHN JARNDYCE, including, but not limited to, a waiver of any interest in the qualified joint and survivor annuity form of benefit and the qualified preretirement survivor annuity form of benefit. ESTHER JARNDYCE hereby further grants permission to JOHN JARNDYCE to designate, without

750 ILCS 10/11   **FAMILIES**

further consent by ESTHER JARNDYCE, the beneficiary or a form of benefits of any qualified plan in place of ESTHER JARNDYCE. ESTHER JARNDYCE acknowledges that the effect of this consent and waiver is that ESTHER JARNDYCE will receive no benefits under any qualified retirement plan of JOHN JARNDYCE, and JOHN JARNDYCE may designate the beneficiary of or form of benefits of any qualified plan in place of ESTHER JARNDYCE without the further consent by ESTHER JARNDYCE.

And ESTHER JARNDYCE does hereby irrevocably constitute and appoint JOHN JARNDYCE as her true and lawful attorney for and in her place and stead, in her name and on her behalf to make, execute and deliver deeds and other instruments conveying, assigning, waiving, releasing, or otherwise transferring any and all right, title and interest which she now has or may hereafter acquire as the wife of JOHN JARNDYCE under any present or future law of the State of Illinois or of any other state of the United States of America or of the United States Federal Government, or of any foreign country in and to any and all property and estate, legal or equitable, real, personal or mixed, of JOHN JARNDYCE, now owned or hereafter at any time acquired by him, and wheresoever situated, except as otherwise provided in the Agreement dated the _____ day of _____, 199__, between ESTHER SUMMERSON and JOHN JARNDYCE; and ESTHER JARNDYCE does hereby acknowledge that the power of attorney herein granted is given for a valuable consideration and is coupled with an interest and is absolutely irrevocable.

IN WITNESS WHEREOF, ESTHER JARNDYCE has hereunto set her hand and seal this _____ day of _____, 199__.

                                              ESTHER JARNDYCE

STATE OF ILLINOIS)
) SS
COUNTY OF COOK)

I, the undersigned, a Notary Public in and for said County, in the State aforesaid, do hereby certify that ESTHER JARNDYCE, personally known to me to be the same person whose name is subscribed to the foregoing Instrument, appeared before me this day in person and acknowledged that she signed, sealed and delivered the said Instrument as her free and voluntary act, for the uses and purposes therein set forth.

Given under my hand and notarial seal this _____ day of _____, 199__.

                                              Notary Public

EXHIBIT D

KNOW ALL MEN BY THESE PRESENTS that JOHN JARNDYCE of Chicago, Illinois (husband of ESTHER JARNDYCE of Chicago, Illinois), for and in consideration of TEN DOLLARS ($10.00) and other good and valuable consideration and of the mutual promises, agreements, covenants, waivers and releases contained in a certain agreement dated the _____ day of _____, 199__, by and between ESTHER SUMMERSON and JOHN JARNDYCE, hereby conveys, releases, waives and quitclaims to ESTHER JARNDYCE all of his rights, title and interest that he, as the husband of ESTHER JARNDYCE, now has or may hereafter acquire under any present or future law of the State of Illinois or of any state of the United States of America or of the United States Federal Government or of any foreign country, including but not limited to: (a) dower, (b) statutory allowance in lieu of dower, (c) statutory intestate or other distributive share, (d) right of election against the will, (e) statutory Widow's or Spouse's Award, (f) Homestead rights, (g) interest in marital, non-marital, separate, or community property, (h) right to act as administrator or executor, and (i) any interest under Federal or State law to the pension, profit sharing, retirement plan, or other employee benefits of ESTHER JARNDYCE, and in and to any and all property and estate, legal or equitable, real, personal and mixed of ESTHER JARNDYCE, now owned or hereafter at any time acquired by her and wheresoever situated, except as otherwise provided in the Agreement dated the _____ day of _____, 199__, between ESTHER SUMMERSON and JOHN JARNDYCE.

JOHN JARNDYCE hereby, pursuant to Section 417(a) of the Internal Revenue Code of 1986, and amendments thereto, consents in writing and waives any interest that he may have in any qualified retirement plan of ESTHER JARNDYCE, including, but not limited to, a waiver of any interest in the qualified joint and survivor annuity form of benefit and the qualified preretirement survivor annuity form of benefit. JOHN JARNDYCE hereby further grants permission to ESTHER JARNDYCE to designate, without further consent by JOHN JARNDYCE, the beneficiary or a form of benefits of any qualified plan in place of JOHN JARNDYCE. JOHN JARNDYCE acknowledges that the effect of this consent and waiver is that JOHN will receive no benefits under any qualified retirement plan of ESTHER JARNDYCE, and ESTHER JARNDYCE may designate the beneficiary of or form of benefits of any qualified plan in place of JOHN JARNDYCE without the further consent by JOHN JARNDYCE.

And JOHN JARNDYCE does hereby irrevocably constitute and appoint ESTHER JARNDYCE as his true and lawful attorney for and in his place and stead, in his name and on his behalf to make, execute and deliver deeds and other instruments conveying, assigning, waiving, releasing, or otherwise transferring any and all right, title and interest which he now has or may hereafter acquire as the husband of ESTHER JARNDYCE under any present or future law of the State of Illinois or of any other state of the United States of America or of the United States Federal Government, or of any foreign country in and to any and all property and estate, legal or equitable, real, personal or mixed, of ESTHER JARNDYCE, now owned or hereafter at any time acquired by her, and wheresoever situated, except as otherwise provided in the Agreement dated the _____ day of _____, 199__, between ESTHER

750 ILCS 10/11   **FAMILIES**

SUMMERSON and JOHN JARNDYCE; and JOHN JARNDYCE does hereby acknowledge that the power of attorney herein granted is given for a valuable consideration and is coupled with an interest and is absolutely irrevocable.

    IN WITNESS WHEREOF, JOHN JARNDYCE has hereunto set his hand and seal this _____ day of _____, 199__.

                                       JOHN JARNDYCE

STATE OF ILLINOIS)
) SS
COUNTY OF COOK)

    I, the undersigned, a Notary Public in and for said County, in the State aforesaid, do hereby certify that JOHN JARNDYCE, personally known to me to be the same person whose name is subscribed to the foregoing Instrument, appeared before me this day in person and acknowledged that he signed, sealed and delivered the said Instrument as his free and voluntary act, for the uses and purposes therein set forth.

    Given under my hand and notarial seal this _____ day of _____, 199__.

                                       Notary Public

ACT 15. NON–SUPPORT OF SPOUSE AND CHILDREN ACT

Analysis

Sec.
1. Neglect to support wife or child; Punishment; Civil action.
1a. Citation of Act.
1b. Prosecutions by Attorney General.
2. Proceedings.
2.1 Support money; Receiving and disbursement agents.
3. Temporary order for support.
4. Fine; Release of defendant on probation; Orders to be series of judgments.
4.1 Withholding of income to secure payment of support.
5. Violation of order; Forfeiture or recognizance.
6. Evidence.
7. Husband or wife as competent witness.
8. Actions may be prosecuted during existence of marriage relations.
9. Prosecutions; Age of children.
10. Offenses, how construed.
11. Public Aid collection fee.
12. Unemployed persons owing duty of support.
12.1 Order of protection; Status.

750 ILCS 15/1
§ 1. Neglect to support wife or child; Punishment; Civil action

Every person who shall, without any lawful excuse, neglect or refuse to provide for the support or maintenance of his spouse, said spouse being in need of such support or maintenance, or any person who shall, without lawful excuse, desert or neglect or refuse to provide for the support or maintenance of his or her child or children under the age of 18 years, in need of such support or maintenance, shall be deemed guilty of a Class A misdemeanor and shall be liable under the provisions of the "Public Aid Code of Illinois", approved April 11, 1967, to the Supervisor of General Assistance or to the Illinois Department of Public Aid, as the case may be, in a civil action, for the amount of general assistance or assistance provided to his spouse or children, or both his spouse and children.

Author's Notes

(1) **Support.** Although the Non–Support of Spouse and Children Act is a criminal statute providing misdemeanor penalties for non-support, limited maintenance and children's support orders can be obtained under §§ 3 and 4 of the Act.

750 ILCS 15/1a
§ 1a. Citation of Act

This Act shall be known and may be cited as the "Non–Support of Spouse and Children Act".

750 ILCS 15/1b
§ 1b. Prosecutions by Attorney General

In addition to enforcement proceedings by the several State's Attorneys, a proceeding for the enforcement of this Act may be instituted and prosecuted by the Attorney General in cases referred to his office by the Department of Public Aid as provided in Section 12–16 of "The Illinois Public Aid Code", wherever, as a consequence of the defendant's failure to provide support, the Department of Public Aid has expended assistance as defined in "The Illinois Public Aid Code" to or in behalf of the spouse or child or children of the defendant.

750 ILCS 15/2
§ 2. Proceedings

Proceedings under this act may be by indictment or information.

750 ILCS 15/2.1

§ 2.1 Support money; Receiving and disbursement agents

(1) In actions instituted under this Act on and after August 14, 1961, involving a minor child or children, the Court, except in actions instituted on or after August 26, 1969, in which the support payments are in behalf of a recipient of aid under "The Illinois Public Aid Code", approved April 11, 1967, as amended, shall direct that moneys ordered to be paid for support under Sections 3 and 4 of this Act shall be paid to the clerk of the court in counties of less than 3 million population, and in counties of 3 million or more population, to the clerk or probation officer of the court or to the Court Service Division of the County Department of Public Aid. After the effective date of this amendatory Act of 1975, the court shall direct that such support moneys be paid to the clerk or probation officer or the Illinois Department of Public Aid. However, the court in its discretion may direct otherwise where exceptional circumstances so warrant. If payment is to be made to persons other than the clerk or probation officer, the Court Service Division of the County Department of Public Aid, or the Illinois Department of Public Aid, the judgment or order of support shall set forth the facts of the exceptional circumstances.

(2) In actions instituted after August 26, 1969, where the support payments are in behalf of spouses, children, or both, who are recipients of aid under The Illinois Public Aid Code, the court shall order the payments to be made directly to (1) the Illinois Department of Public Aid if the person is a recipient under Articles III, IV or V of the Code, or (2) to the local governmental unit responsible for the support of the person if he or she is a recipient under Articles VI or VII of the Code. The Illinois Department of Public Aid may continue to collect current maintenance or child support payments, or both, for a period not to exceed 3 months from the month following the month in which such persons cease to receive public assistance, and pay all amounts so collected to such persons. At the end of such 3 month period, the Illinois Department of Public Aid may continue to collect such payments if authorized by such persons to do so, and pay the net amount so collected to such persons after deducting any costs incurred in making the collection or any collection fee from the amount of any recovery made. The order shall permit the Illinois Department of Public Aid or the local governmental unit, as the case may be, to direct that subsequent support payments be made directly to the spouse, children, or both, or to some person or agency in their behalf, upon removal of the spouse or children from the public aid rolls or upon termination of any extended collection period; and upon such direction, the Illinois Department or the local governmental unit, as the case requires, shall give written notice of such action to the court.

(3) The clerks, probation officers, and the Court Service Division of the County Department of Public Aid in counties of 3 million or more population, and, after the effective date of this amendatory Act of 1975, the clerks, probation officers, and the Illinois Department of Public Aid, shall disburse moneys paid to them to the person or persons entitled thereto under the order

of the Court. They shall establish and maintain current records of all moneys received and disbursed and of delinquencies and defaults in required payments. The Court, by order or rule, shall make provision for the carrying out of these duties. Upon certification by the Illinois Department of Public Aid that a person who is receiving support payments under this Section is a public aid recipient, any support payments subsequently received by the clerk of the court shall be transmitted to the Illinois Department of Public Aid until the Department gives notice to cease such transmittal.

(4) Payments under this Section to the Illinois Department of Public Aid pursuant to the Child Support Enforcement Program established by Title IV–D of the Social Security Act shall be paid into the Child Support Enforcement Trust Fund. All other payments under this Section to the Illinois Department of Public Aid shall be deposited in the Public Assistance Recoveries Trust Fund. Disbursements from these funds shall be as provided in The Illinois Public Aid Code. Payments received by a local governmental unit shall be deposited in that unit's General Assistance Fund.

(5) Orders and assignments entered or executed prior to the Act approved August 14, 1961 shall not be affected thereby. Employers served with wage assignments executed prior to that date shall comply with the terms thereof. However, the Court, on petition of the state's attorney, or of the Illinois Department of Public Aid or local governmental unit in respect to recipients of public aid, may order the execution of new assignments and enter new orders designating the clerk, probation officer, or the Illinois Department of Public Aid or appropriate local governmental unit in respect to payments in behalf of recipients of public aid, as the person or agency authorized to receive and disburse the salary or wages assigned. On like petition the Court may enter new orders designating such officers, agencies or governmental units to receive and disburse the payments ordered under Section 4.

(6) For those cases in which child support is payable to the clerk of the circuit court for transmittal to the Illinois Department of Public Aid by order of court, the clerk shall transmit all such payments, within 4 working days of receipt, to insure that funds are available for immediate distribution by the Department to the person or entity entitled thereto in accordance with standards of the Child Support Enforcement Program established under Title IV–D of the Social Security Act. The clerk shall notify the Department of the date of receipt and amount thereof at the time of transmittal. Where the clerk has entered into an agreement of cooperation with the Department to record the terms of child support orders and payments made thereunder directly into the Department's automated data processing system, the clerk shall account for, transmit and otherwise distribute child support payments in accordance with such agreement in lieu of the requirements contained herein.

750 ILCS 15/3
§ 3. Temporary order for support

At any time before the trial, upon motion of the State's Attorney, or of the Attorney General if the action has been instituted by his office, and upon

750 ILCS 15/3   FAMILIES

notice to the defendant, or at the time of arraignment or as a condition of the postponement of arraignment, the court at any time may enter such temporary order as may seem just, providing for the support or maintenance of the spouse or child or children of the defendant, or both, pendente lite.

The Court shall determine the amount of child support by using the guidelines and standards set forth in subsection (a) of Section 505 and in Section 505.2 of the Illinois Marriage and Dissolution of Marriage Act.

The Court shall determine the amount of maintenance using the standards set forth in Section 504 of the Illinois Marriage and Dissolution of Marriage Act.

The court may for violation of any order under this Section punish the offender as for a contempt of court, but no pendente lite order shall remain in force for a longer term than 4 months, or after the discharge of any panel of jurors summoned for service thereafter in such court, whichever is the sooner.

Any new or existing support order entered by the court under this Section shall be deemed to be a series of judgments against the person obligated to pay support thereunder, each such judgment to be in the amount of each payment or installment of support and each such judgment to be deemed entered as of the date the corresponding payment or installment becomes due under the terms of the support order. Each such judgment shall have the full force, effect and attributes of any other judgment of this State, including the ability to be enforced. Any such judgment is subject to modification or termination only in accordance with Section 510 of the Illinois Marriage and Dissolution of Marriage Act.

A one-time interest charge of 20% is imposable upon the amount of past-due child support owed on July 1, 1988 which has accrued under a support order entered by the court. The charge shall be imposed in accordance with the provisions of Section 10–21 of the Illinois Public Aid Code and shall be enforced by the court upon petition.

750 ILCS 15/4

§ 4. Fine; Release of defendant on probation; Orders to be series of judgments

Whenever a fine is imposed it may be directed by the court to be paid, in whole or in part, to the spouse, or if the support of a minor child or children is involved, to the clerk, probation officer, the Court Service Division of the County Department of Public Aid in counties of 3 million or more population or to the Illinois Department of Public Aid or a local governmental unit if a recipient of public aid is involved, in accordance with Section 2.1, as the case requires, to be disbursed by such officers, agency or governmental unit under the terms of the order. However, before the trial with the consent of the defendant, or at the trial on entry of a plea of guilty, or after conviction, instead of imposing the penalty provided in this Act, or in addition thereto, the court in its discretion, having regard to the circumstances and the financial ability or earning capacity of the defendant, may make an order, subject to change by the court from time to time as circumstances may require, directing the defendant to pay a certain sum periodically for a term not exceeding 3 years to the spouse or, if the support of a minor child or children is involved, to the clerk, probation officer, the Court Service Division of the County Department of Public Aid in counties of 3 million or more population or to the Illinois Department of Public Aid or a local governmental unit if a recipient of public aid is involved in accordance with Section 2.1, as the case requires, to be disbursed by such officers, agency or governmental unit under the terms of the order.

The Court shall determine the amount of child support by using the standards set forth in subsection (a) of Section 505 and in Section 505.2 of the Illinois Marriage and Dissolution of Marriage Act.

The Court shall determine the amount of maintenance using the standards set forth in Section 504 of the Illinois Marriage and Dissolution of Marriage Act.

The court may also relieve the defendant from custody on probation for the period fixed in the order or judgment upon his or her entering into a recognizance, with or without surety, in such sum as the court orders and approves. The condition of the recognizance shall be such that if the defendant makes his or her personal appearance in court whenever ordered to do so by the court, during such period as may be so fixed, and further complies with the terms of the order of support, or of any subsequent modification thereof, then the recognizance shall be void; otherwise in full force and effect.

Any new or existing support order entered by the court under this Section shall be deemed to be a series of judgments against the person obligated to pay support thereunder, each such judgment to be in the amount of each payment or installment of support and each such judgment to be deemed entered as of the date the corresponding payment or installment becomes due under the terms of the support order. Each such judgment shall have the full force, effect and attributes of any other judgment of this State, including the ability to be enforced. Any such judgment is subject to modification or termination only in accordance with Section 510 of the Illinois Marriage and Dissolution of Marriage Act.

A one-time charge of 20% is imposable upon the amount of past-due child support owed on July 1, 1988 which has accrued under a support order entered by the court. The charge shall be imposed in accordance with the provisions of Section 10–21 of the Illinois Public Aid Code and shall be enforced by the court upon petition.

750 ILCS 15/4.1

§ 4.1 Withholding of income to secure payment of support

(A) Definitions.

(1) "Order for support" means any order of the court which provides for periodic payment of funds for the support of a child or maintenance of a spouse, whether temporary or final, and includes any such order which provides for:

    (a) Modification or resumption of, or payment of arrearage accrued under, a previously existing order;

    (b) Reimbursement of support; or

    (c) Enrollment in a health insurance plan that is available to the obligor through an employer.

(2) "Arrearage" means the total amount of unpaid support obligations.

(3) "Delinquency" means any payment under an order for support which becomes due and remains unpaid after an order for withholding has been entered under subsection (B) or, for purposes of subsection (K), after the last order for support was entered for which no order for withholding was entered.

(4) "Income" means any form of periodic payment to an individual, regardless of source, including, but not limited to: wages, salary, commission, compensation as an independent contractor, workers' compensation, disability, annuity and retirement benefits, lottery prize awards, insurance proceeds, vacation pay, bonuses, profit-sharing payments and any other payments, made by any person, private entity, federal or state government, any unit of local government, school district or any entity created by Public Act; however, "income" excludes:

    (a) Any amounts required by law to be withheld, other than creditor claims, including, but not limited to, federal, State and local taxes, Social Security and other retirement and disability contributions;

    (b) Union dues;

    (c) Any amounts exempted by the federal Consumer Credit Protection Act;

    (d) Public assistance payments; and

    (e) Unemployment insurance benefits except as provided by law.

Any other State or local laws which limit or exempt income or the amount or percentage of income that can be withheld shall not apply.

(5) "Obligor" means the individual who owes a duty to make payments under an order for support.

(6) "Obligee" means the individual to whom a duty of support is owed or the individual's legal representative.

(7) "Payor" means any payor of income to an obligor.

(8) "Public office" means any elected official or any State or local agency which is or may become responsible by law for enforcement of, or which is or may become authorized to enforce, an order for support, including, but not limited to: the Attorney General, the Illinois Department of Public Aid, the

Illinois Department of Mental Health and Developmental Disabilities, the Illinois Department of Children and Family Services, and the various State's Attorneys, Clerks of the Circuit Court and supervisors of general assistance.

(9) "Premium" means the dollar amount for which the obligor is liable to his employer and which must be paid to enroll or maintain a child in a health insurance plan that is available to the obligor through an employer or union.

(B) Entry of an order for withholding.

(1) Upon entry of any order for support on or after January 1, 1984, the court shall enter a separate order for withholding which shall not take effect unless the obligor becomes delinquent in paying the order for support or the obligor requests an earlier effective date; except that the court may require the order for withholding to take effect immediately.

On or after January 1, 1989, the court shall require the order for withholding to take effect immediately, unless a written agreement is reached between both parties providing for an alternative arrangement, approved by the court, which insures payment of support. In that case, the court shall enter the order for withholding which will not take effect unless the obligor becomes delinquent in paying the order for support.

Upon entry of any order of support on or after September 11, 1989, if the obligor is not a United States citizen, the obligor shall provide to the court the obligor's alien registration number, passport number, and home country's social security or national health number, if applicable; the court shall make the information part of the record in the case.

(2) An order for withholding shall be entered upon petition by the obligee or public office where an order for withholding has not been previously entered.

(3) The order for withholding shall:

(a) Direct any payor to withhold a dollar amount equal to the order for support; and

(b) Direct any payor to withhold an additional dollar amount, not less than 20% of the order for support, until payment in full of any delinquency stated in the notice of delinquency provided for in subsection (C) or (F) of this Section; and

(c) Direct any payor to enroll a child as a beneficiary of a health insurance plan and withhold any required premiums; and

(d) State the rights, remedies and duties of the obligor under this Section; and

(e) Include the obligor's Social Security Number, which the obligor shall disclose to the court.

(4) At the time the order for withholding is entered, the Clerk of the Circuit Court shall provide a copy of the order for withholding and the order for support to the obligor and shall make copies available to the obligee and

public office. Any copy of the order for withholding furnished to the parties under this subsection shall be stamped "Not Valid".

(5) The order for withholding shall remain in effect for as long as the order for support upon which it is based.

(6) The failure of an order for withholding to state an arrearage is not conclusive of the issue of whether an arrearage is owing.

(7) Notwithstanding the provisions of this subsection, if the court finds at the time of any hearing that an arrearage has accrued in an amount equal to at least one month's support obligation or that the obligor is 30 days late in paying all or part of the order for support, the court shall order immediate service of the order for withholding upon the payor.

(C) Notice of delinquency.

(1) Whenever an obligor becomes delinquent in payment of an amount equal to at least one month's support obligation pursuant to the order for support or is at least 30 days late in complying with all or part of the order for support, whichever occurs first, the obligee or public office may prepare and serve a verified notice of delinquency, together with a form petition to stay service, pursuant to paragraph (3) of this subsection.

(2) The notice of delinquency shall recite the terms of the order for support and contain a computation of the period and total amount of the delinquency, as of the date of the notice. The notice shall clearly state that it will be sent to the payor, together with a specially certified copy of the order for withholding, except as provided in subsection (F), unless the obligor files a petition to stay service in accordance with paragraph (1) of subsection (D).

(3) The notice of delinquency shall be served by ordinary mail addressed to the obligor at his or her last known address.

(4) The obligor may execute a written waiver of the provisions of paragraphs (1) through (3) of this subsection and request immediate service upon the payor.

(D) Procedures to avoid income withholding.

(1) Except as provided in subsection (F), the obligor may prevent an order for withholding from being served by filing a petition to stay service with the Clerk of the Circuit Court, within 20 days after service of the notice of delinquency; however, the grounds for the petition to stay service shall be limited to:

    (a) A dispute concerning the amount of current support or the existence or amount of the delinquency;

    (b) The identity of the obligor.

The Clerk of the Circuit Court shall notify the obligor and the obligee or public office, as appropriate, of the time and place of the hearing on the petition to stay service. The court shall hold such hearing pursuant to the provisions of subsection (H).

(2) Except as provided in subsection (F), filing of a petition to stay service, within the 20-day period required under this subsection, shall prohibit the obligee or public office from serving the order for withholding on any payor of the obligor.

(E) Initial service of order for withholding.

(1) Except as provided in subsection (F), in order to serve an order for withholding upon a payor, an obligee or public office shall follow the procedures set forth in this subsection. After 20 days following service of the notice of delinquency, the obligee or public office shall file with the Clerk of the Circuit Court an affidavit, with the copy of the notice of delinquency attached thereto, stating:

(a) that the notice of delinquency has been duly served and the date on which service was effected; and

(b) that the obligor has not filed a petition to stay service, or in the alternative

(c) that the obligor has waived the provisions of subparagraphs (a) and (b) of this paragraph (1) in accordance with subsection (C)(4).

(2) Upon request of the obligee or public office, the Clerk of the Circuit Court shall: (a) make available any record of payment; and (b) determine that the file contains a copy of the affidavit described in paragraph (1). The Clerk shall then provide to the obligee or public office a specially certified copy of the order for withholding and the notice of delinquency indicating that the preconditions for service have been met.

(3) The obligee or public office may then serve the notice of delinquency and order for withholding on the payor, its superintendent, manager or other agent, by certified mail or personal delivery. A proof of service shall be filed with the Clerk of the Circuit Court.

(F) Subsequent service of order for withholding.

(1) Notwithstanding the provisions of this Section, at any time after the court has ordered immediate service of an order for withholding or after initial service of an order for withholding pursuant to subsection (E), the obligee or public office may serve the order for withholding upon any payor of the obligor without further notice to the obligor. The obligee or public office shall provide notice to the payor, pursuant to paragraph (6) of subsection (I), of any payments that have been made through previous withholding or any other method.

(2) The Clerk of the Circuit Court shall, upon request, provide the obligee or public office with specially certified copies of the order for withholding or the notice of delinquency or both whenever the Court has ordered immediate service of an order for withholding or an affidavit has been placed in the court file indicating that the preconditions for service have been previously met. The obligee or public office may then serve the order for withholding on the payor, its superintendent, manager or other agent by certified mail or person-

750 ILCS 15/4.1   **FAMILIES**

al delivery. A proof of service shall be filed with the Clerk of the Circuit Court.

(3) If a delinquency has accrued for any reason, the obligee or public office may serve a notice of delinquency upon the obligor pursuant to subsection (C). The obligor may prevent the notice of delinquency from being served upon the payor by utilizing the procedures set forth in subsection (D).

If no petition to stay service has been filed within the required 20 day time period, the obligee or public office may serve the notice of delinquency on the payor by utilizing the procedures for service set forth in subsection (E).

(G) Duties of payor.

(1) It shall be the duty of any payor who has been served with a copy of the specially certified order for withholding and any notice of delinquency to deduct and pay over income as provided in this subsection. The payor shall deduct the amount designated in the order for withholding, as supplemented by the notice of delinquency and any notice provided pursuant to paragraph (6) of subsection (I), beginning no later than the next payment of income which is payable to the obligor that occurs 14 days following the date the order and any notice were mailed by certified mail or placed for personal delivery. The payor may combine all amounts withheld for the benefit of an obligee or public office into a single payment and transmit the payment with a listing of obligors from whom withholding has been effected. The payor shall pay the amount withheld to the obligee or public office within 3 business days of the date income is paid to the obligor in accordance with the order for withholding and any subsequent notification received from the public office redirecting payments. If the payor knowingly fails to pay any amount withheld to the obligee or public office within 3 business days of the date income is paid to the obligor, the payor shall pay a penalty of $100 for each day that the withheld amount is paid to the obligee or public office after the period of 3 business days has expired. The failure of a payor, on more than one occasion, to pay amounts withheld to the obligee or public office within 3 business days of the date income is paid to the obligor creates a presumption that the payor knowingly failed to pay the amounts. This penalty may be collected in a civil action which may be brought against the payor in favor of the obligee. For purposes of this Section, a withheld amount shall be considered paid by a payor on the date it is mailed by the payor, or on the date an electronic funds transfer of the amount has been initiated by the payor, or on the date delivery of the amount has been initiated by the payor. For each deduction, the payor shall provide the obligee or public office, at the time of transmittal, with the date income was paid from which support was withheld.

Upon receipt of an order requiring that a minor child be named as a beneficiary of a health insurance plan available through an employer, the employer shall immediately enroll the minor child as a beneficiary in the health insurance plan designated by the court order. The employer shall withhold any required premiums and pay over any amounts so withheld and any additional amounts the employer pays to the insurance carrier in a timely manner. The employer shall mail to the obligee, within 15 days of enrollment or upon request, notice of the date of coverage, information on the dependent coverage plan, and all forms necessary to obtain reimbursement for covered health expenses, such as would be made available to a new employee. When an order for dependent coverage is in effect and the insurance coverage is terminated or changed for any reason, the employer shall notify the obligee within 10 days of the termination or change date along with notice of conversion privileges.

For withholding of income, the payor shall be entitled to receive a fee not to exceed $5 per month or the actual check processing cost to be taken from the income to be paid to the obligor.

(2) Whenever the obligor is no longer receiving income from the payor, the payor shall return a copy of the order for withholding to the obligee or public office and shall provide information for the purpose of enforcing this Section.

(3) Withholding of income under this Section shall be made without regard to any prior or subsequent garnishments, attachments, wage assignments, or any other claims of creditors. Withholding of income under this Section shall not be in excess of the maximum amounts permitted under the federal Consumer Credit Protection Act. If the payor has been served with more than one order for withholding pertaining to the same obligor, the payor shall allocate income available for withholding on a proportionate share basis, giving priority to current support payments. If there is any income available for withholding after withholding for all current support obligations, the payor shall allocate the income to past due support payments ordered in non-AFDC matters and then to past due support payments ordered in AFDC matters, both on a proportionate share basis. Payment as required by the order for withholding shall be a complete defense by the payor against any claims of the obligor or his creditors as to the sum so paid.

(4) No payor shall discharge, discipline, refuse to hire or otherwise penalize any obligor because of the duty to withhold income.

(H) Petitions to stay service or to modify, suspend or terminate orders for withholding.

(1) When an obligor files a petition to stay service, the court, after due notice to all parties, shall hear the matter as soon as practicable and shall enter an order granting or denying relief, amending the notice of delinquency, amending the order for withholding, where applicable, or otherwise resolving the matter. If the court finds that a delinquency existed when the notice of delinquency was served upon the obligor, in an amount of at least one month's support obligation, or that the obligor was at least 30 days late in paying all or part of the order for support, the court shall order immediate service of the order for withholding. Where the court cannot promptly resolve any dispute over the amount of the delinquency, the court may order immediate service of the order for withholding as to any undisputed amounts

specified in an amended notice of delinquency, and may continue the hearing on the disputed amounts.

(2) At any time, an obligor, obligee, public office or Clerk of the Circuit Court may petition the court to:

(a) Modify, suspend or terminate the order for withholding because of a modification, suspension or termination of the underlying order for support; or

(b) Modify the amount of income to be withheld to reflect payment in full or in part of the delinquency or arrearage by income withholding or otherwise; or

(c) Suspend the order for withholding because of inability to deliver income withheld to the obligee due to the obligee's failure to provide a mailing address or other means of delivery.

(3) The obligor, obligee or public office shall serve on the payor, by certified mail or personal delivery, a copy of any order entered pursuant to this subsection that affects the duties of the payor.

(4) The order for withholding shall continue to be binding upon the payor until service of any order of the court entered under this subsection.

(I) Additional duties.

(1) An obligee who is receiving income withholding payments under this Section shall notify the payor, if the obligee receives the payments directly from the payor, or the public office or the Clerk of the Circuit Court, as appropriate, of any change of address within 7 days of such change.

(2) An obligee who is a recipient of public aid shall send a copy of any notice of delinquency filed pursuant to subsection (C) to the Bureau of Child Support of the Illinois Department of Public Aid.

(3) Each obligor shall notify the obligee and the Clerk of the Circuit Court of any change of address within 7 days.

(4) An obligor whose income is being withheld or who has been served with a notice of delinquency pursuant to this Section shall notify the obligee and the Clerk of the Circuit Court of any new payor, within 7 days.

(5) When the Illinois Department of Public Aid is no longer authorized to receive payments for the obligee, it shall, within 7 days, notify the payor or, where appropriate, the Clerk of the Circuit Court, to redirect income withholding payments to the obligee.

(6) The obligee or public office shall provide notice to the payor and Clerk of the Circuit Court of any other support payment made, including but not limited to, a set-off under federal and State law or partial payment of the delinquency or arrearage, or both.

(7) Any public office and Clerk of the Circuit Court which collects, disburses or receives payments pursuant to orders for withholding shall maintain complete, accurate, and clear records of all payments and their

disbursements. Certified copies of payment records maintained by a public office or Clerk of the Circuit Court shall, without further proof, be admitted into evidence in any legal proceedings under this Section.

(8) The Illinois Department of Public Aid shall design suggested legal forms for proceeding under this Section and shall make available to the courts such forms and informational materials which describe the procedures and remedies set forth herein for distribution to all parties in support actions.

(9) At the time of transmitting each support payment, the clerk of the circuit court shall provide the obligee or public office, as appropriate, with any information furnished by the payor as to the date income was paid from which such support was withheld.

(J) Penalties.

(1) Where a payor wilfully fails to withhold or pay over income pursuant to a properly served, specially certified order for withholding and any notice of delinquency, or wilfully discharges, disciplines, refuses to hire or otherwise penalizes an obligor as prohibited by subsection (G), or otherwise fails to comply with any duties imposed by this Section, the obligee, public office or obligor, as appropriate, may file a complaint with the court against the payor. The clerk of the circuit court shall notify the obligee or public office, as appropriate, and the obligor and payor of the time and place of the hearing on the complaint. The court shall resolve any factual dispute including, but not limited to, a denial that the payor is paying or has paid income to the obligor. Upon a finding in favor of the complaining party, the court:

> (a) Shall enter judgment and direct the enforcement thereof for the total amount that the payor wilfully failed to withhold or pay over; and

> (b) May order employment or reinstatement of or restitution to the obligor, or both, where the obligor has been discharged, disciplined, denied employment or otherwise penalized by the payor and may impose a fine upon the payor not to exceed $200.

(2) Any obligee, public office or obligor who wilfully initiates a false proceeding under this Section or who wilfully fails to comply with the requirements of this Section shall be punished as in cases of contempt of court.

(K) Alternative procedures for entry and service of an order for withholding.

(1) Effective January 1, 1987, in any matter in which an order for withholding has not been entered for any reason, based upon the last order for support that has been entered, and in which the obligor has become delinquent in payment of an amount equal to at least one month's support obligation pursuant to the last order for support or is at least 30 days late in complying with all or part of the order for support, the obligee or public office may prepare and serve an order for withholding pursuant to the procedures set forth in this subsection.

(2) The obligee or public office shall:

(a) Prepare a proposed order for withholding for immediate service as provided by paragraphs (1) and (3) of subsection (B), except that the minimum 20% delinquency payment shall be used;

(b) Prepare a notice of delinquency as provided by paragraphs (1) and (2) of subsection (C), except the notice shall state further that the order for withholding has not been entered by the court and the conditions under which the order will be entered; and

(c) Serve the notice of delinquency and form petition to stay service as provided by paragraph (3) of subsection (C), together with the proposed order for withholding, which shall be marked "COPY ONLY".

(3) After 20 days following service of the notice of delinquency and proposed order for withholding, in lieu of the provisions of subsection (E), the obligee or public office shall file with the Clerk of the Circuit Court an affidavit, with a copy of the notice of delinquency and proposed order for withholding attached thereto, stating that:

(a) The notice of delinquency and proposed order for withholding have been served upon the obligor and the date on which service was effected;

(b) The obligor has not filed a petition to stay service within 20 days of service of such notice and order; and

(c) The proposed order for withholding accurately states the terms and amounts contained in the last order for support.

(4) Upon the court's satisfaction that the procedures set forth in this subsection have been met, it shall enter the order for withholding.

(5) The Clerk shall then provide to the obligee or public office a specially certified copy of the order for withholding and the notice of delinquency indicating that the preconditions for service have been met.

(6) The obligee or public office shall serve the specially certified copies of the order for withholding and the notice of delinquency on the payor, its superintendent, manager or other agent by certified mail or personal delivery. A proof of service shall be filed with the Clerk of the Circuit Court.

(7) If the obligor requests in writing that income withholding become effective prior to becoming delinquent in payment of an amount equal to one month's support obligation pursuant to the last order for support, or prior to becoming 30 days late in paying all or part of the order for support, the obligee or public office shall file an affidavit with the Clerk of the circuit Court, with a proposed order for withholding attached, stating that the proposed order accurately states the terms and amounts contained in the last order for support and the obligor's request for immediate service. The provisions of paragraphs (4) through (6) of this subsection shall apply, except that a notice of delinquency shall not be required.

(8) All other provisions of this Section shall be applicable with respect to the provisions of this subsection (K), except that under paragraph (1) of

subsection (H), the court may also amend the proposed order for withholding to conform to the last order for support.

(9) Nothing in this subsection shall be construed as limiting the requirements of paragraph (1) of subsection (B) with respect to the entry of a separate order for withholding upon entry of any order for support.

(L) Remedies in addition to other laws.

(1) The rights, remedies, duties and penalties created by this Section are in addition to and not in substitution for any other rights, remedies, duties and penalties created by any other law.

(2) Nothing in this Section shall be construed as invalidating any assignment of wages or benefits executed prior to January 1, 1984.

Author's Notes

(1) **Cross references.** The provisions of § 4.1 are substantially the same as IMDMA § 706.1. See therefore 750 ILCS 5/706.1 and accompanying Author's Notes. See also 750 ILCS 20/1 Author's Note (4) for other remedies.

750 ILCS 15/5

§ 5. Violation of order; Forfeiture or recognizance

If the court be satisfied by testimony in open court, that at any time during said period of one year the defendant has violated the terms of such order, it may forthwith proceed with the trial of the defendant under the original charge, or sentence him or her under the original conviction, or enforce the suspended sentence, as the case may be. In case of forfeiture or recognizance, and enforcement thereof by execution, the sum so recovered may, in the discretion of the court, be paid, in whole or in part, to the spouse, or to the guardian or custodian or trustee of the said minor child or children.

750 ILCS 15/6

§ 6. Evidence

No other or greater evidence shall be required to prove the marriage of such husband and wife, or that the defendant is the father or mother of such child or children, than is or shall be required to prove such fact in a civil action.

750 ILCS 15/7

§ 7. Husband or wife as competent witness

In no prosecution under this act shall any existing statute or rule of law prohibiting the disclosure of confidential communications between husband and wife apply. And both husband and wife shall be competent witnesses to testify to any and all relevant matters, including the fact of such marriage and of the parentage of such child or children: Provided, that neither shall be compelled to give evidence incriminating himself or herself.

750 ILCS 15/8

§ 8. Actions may be prosecuted during existence of marriage relations

Actions against persons under this act who shall without any reasonable cause, neglect or refuse to provide for the support or maintenance of his wife may be prosecuted at any time during the existence of the marriage relations.

750 ILCS 15/9

§ 9. Prosecutions; Age of children

Actions against persons under this act who shall without lawful excuse, neglect or refuse to provide for the support or maintenance of his or her child or children, may be prosecuted at any time until said child or children reaches the age of eighteen years.

750 ILCS 15/10

§ 10. Offenses, how construed

It is hereby expressly declared that the offenses as hereinbefore set forth in this act, are and shall be so taken and construed to be continuing offenses.

750 ILCS 15/11

§ 11. Public Aid collection fee

In all cases instituted by the Illinois Department of Public Aid on behalf of a child or spouse, other than one receiving a grant of financial aid under Article IV of The Illinois Public Aid Code, on whose behalf an application has been made and approved for support services as provided by Section 10-1 of that Code, the court shall impose a collection fee on the individual who owes a child or spouse support obligation in an amount equal to 10% of the amount so owed as long as such collection is required by federal law, which fee shall be in addition to the support obligation. The imposition of such fee shall be in accordance with provisions of Title IV, Part D, of the Social Security Act and regulations duly promulgated thereunder. The fee shall be payable to the clerk of the circuit court for transmittal to the Illinois Department of Public Aid and shall continue until support services are terminated by that Department.

750 ILCS 15/12

§ 12. Unemployed persons owing duty of support

Whenever it is determined in a proceeding to establish or enforce a child support or maintenance obligation that the person owing a duty of support is unemployed, the court may order the person to seek employment and report periodically to the court with a diary, listing or other memorandum of his or her efforts in accordance with such order. Additionally, the court may order the unemployed person to report to the Department of Employment Security for job search services or to make application with the local Jobs Training

Partnership Act provider for participation in job search, training or work programs and where the duty of support is owed to a child receiving support services under Article X of The Illinois Public Aid Code, as amended, the court may order the unemployed person to report to the Illinois Department of Public Aid for participation in job search, training or work programs established under Section 9–6 of that Code.

750 ILCS 15/12.1

§ 12.1 Order of protection; Status

Whenever relief sought under this Act is based on allegations of domestic violence, as defined in the Illinois Domestic Violence Act of 1986, the court, before granting relief, shall determine whether any order of protection has previously been entered in the instant proceeding or any other proceeding in which any party, or a child of any party, or both, if relevant, has been designated as either a respondent or a protected person.

ACT 20. REVISED UNIFORM RECIPROCAL ENFORCEMENT OF SUPPORT ACT

PART I. GENERAL PROVISIONS

Analysis

Sec.
1. Short title; Purposes.
2. Definitions.
3. Remedies additional to those now existing.
4. Extent of duties of support.
4.1 Convention Country.

WESTLAW Electronic Research

See WESTLAW Electronic Research Guide preceding the Summary of Contents.

---

750 ILCS 20/1

§ 1. Short title; Purposes

This Act may be cited as the Revised Uniform Reciprocal Enforcement of Support Act.

The purposes of this Act are to improve and extend by reciprocal legislation the enforcement of duties of support.

Author's Notes

Analysis

1. Citation.
2. Purpose.

750 ILCS 20/1   **FAMILIES**

3. Cross reference.
4. Other remedies.
5. Prospective modification.
6. Cross reference.

(1) **Citation.** The Revised Uniform Reciprocal Enforcement of Support Act is sometimes cited herein by its acronym "RURESA."

(2) **Purpose.** The Revised Uniform Reciprocal Enforcement of Support Act is one of many acts that seeks to enforce obligations of support. RURESA provides a mechanism to enforce obligations of support in the common circumstance when one party resides in one state and the other party resides in a different state. Under RURESA the enforcement can take place without the parties meeting in a common courtroom, through the cooperation of state's attorneys and the judicial systems in each state.

(3) **Cross reference.** On January 1, 1995, the Uniform Interstate Family Support Act, 750 ILCS 22/100 et seq., is scheduled to become effective. As of the time of this writing, however, an effort is being made to postpone the effective date. The new Act does not supersede RURESA, but it does amend § 24 of RURESA. See 750 ILCS 22/100 et seq.

(4) **Other remedies.** There are a proliferation of remedies to enforce support, which include: Non-support of Spouse and Children Act, 750 ILCS 15/1 et seq.; RURESA, 750 ILCS 20/1 et seq.; Registration of Foreign Support Orders, 750 ILCS 20/35 et seq.; Uniform Interstate Family Support Act, 750 ILCS 22/100 et seq.; Expedited Child Support Act of 1990, 750 ILCS 25/1 et seq.; Expedited Child Support Rules, Supreme Court Rules 100.1 et seq.; Supreme Court Rule 296; Uniform Enforcement of Foreign Judgments Act, 735 ILCS 5/12–650 et seq.; and the enforcement provisions of the Illinois Marriage and Dissolution of Marriage Act, 750 ILCS 5 Parts V and VII. The provisions are overlapping, and have not begun to solve the problem of collecting delinquent support.

Part IV of RURESA, which is the Registration of Foreign Support Orders, 750 ILCS 20/35 et seq., permits a foreign support order to be made an order in the responding state without the necessity required by Part III of RURESA of starting an action in the initiating state. The Uniform Enforcement of Foreign Judgments Act, 735 ILCS 5/12–650 et seq. has similar procedures for establishing a foreign order, with the differences that Part IV of RURESA allows representation by the State's Attorney, and there is more of an automatic confirmation process of the foreign order if the obligor does not petition the court within 30 days after the mailing of notice.

(5) **Prospective modification.** Foreign support orders that are enrolled in Illinois are subject to prospective modification, in the same manner that Illinois support orders are subject to prospective modification pursuant to IMDMA § 510, 750 ILCS 5/510. See Part III of RURESA § 24(3); Part IV of RURESA § 40(a); Uniform Enforcement of Foreign Judgments Act § 12–652, 735 ILCS 5/12–652; but see the Uniform Interstate Family Support Act §§ 611 and 950, 750 ILCS 22/611, 950, which limit the modification of support orders of another state. See 750 ILCS 22/999 Author's Note (1) for effective date.

(6) **Cross reference.** RURESA cases can be brought under the Expedited Child Support Rules. See Supreme Court Rule 100.1 Author's Note (2).

750 ILCS 20/2

§ 2. Definitions

(a) "Court" means the circuit court of this State and when the context requires means the court of any other state as defined in a substantially similar reciprocal law.

(b) "Duty of support" means a duty of support whether imposed or imposable by law or by order or judgment of any court, whether interlocutory or final or whether incidental to an action for dissolution of marriage, legal separation, or otherwise and includes the duty to pay arrearages of support past due and unpaid.

(c) "Governor" includes any person performing the functions of Governor or the executive authority of any state covered by this Act.

(d) "Initiating state" means a state in which a proceeding pursuant to this or a substantially similar reciprocal law is commenced. "Initiating court" means the court in which a proceeding is commenced.

(e) "Law" includes both common and statutory law.

(f) "Obligee" means a person including a state or political subdivision to whom a duty of support is owed or a person including a state or political subdivision that has commenced a proceeding for enforcement of an alleged duty of support or for registration of a support order. It is immaterial if the person to whom a duty of support is owed is a recipient of public assistance.

(g) "Obligor" means any person owing a duty of support or against whom a proceeding for the enforcement of a duty of support or registration of a support order is commenced.

(h) "Prosecuting attorney" means the public official in the appropriate place who has the duty to enforce criminal laws relating to the failure to provide for the support of any person.

(i) "Register" means to record in the Registry of Foreign Support Orders.

(j) "Registering court" means any court of this State in which a support order of a rendering state is registered.

(k) "Rendering state" means a state in which the court has entered a support order for which registration is sought or granted in the court of another state.

(*l*) "Responding state" means a state in which any responsive proceeding pursuant to the proceeding in the initiating state is commenced. "Responding court" means the court in which the responsive proceeding is commenced.

(m) "State" includes a state, territory, or possession of the United States, the District of Columbia, the Commonwealth of Puerto Rico, and any foreign jurisdiction in which this or a substantially similar reciprocal law is in effect.

(n) "Support order" means any judgment or order of support in favor of an obligee whether temporary or final, or subject to modification, revocation, or remission, regardless of the kind of action or proceeding in which it is entered.

750 ILCS 20/3
§ 3. Remedies additional to those now existing

The remedies herein provided are in addition to and not in substitution for any other remedies.

750 ILCS 20/4
§ 4. Extent of duties of support

Duties of support arising under the law of this State, when applicable under Section 7, bind the obligor present in this State regardless of the presence or residence of the obligee.

750 ILCS 20/4.1
§ 4.1 Convention Country

Illinois shall become a "Convention Country" as provided in the international Revised Uniform Reciprocal Enforcement of Support Act as enacted by the United Kingdom, and shall execute whatever agreements are necessary to foster cooperation between this State and the United Kingdom in the matter of the collection of support.

PART II. CRIMINAL ENFORCEMENT

Analysis

Sec.
5. Interstate rendition.
6. Conditions of interstate rendition.

WESTLAW Electronic Research
See WESTLAW Electronic Research Guide preceding the Summary of Contents.

---

750 ILCS 20/5
§ 5. Interstate rendition

The Governor of this State may

(1) demand of the Governor of another state the surrender of a person found in that state who is charged criminally in this State with failing to provide for the support of any person; or

(2) surrender on demand by the Governor of another state a person found in this State who is charged criminally in that state with failing to provide for the support of any person. Provisions for extradition of criminals not inconsistent with this Act apply to the demand even if the person whose surrender is demanded was not in the demanding state at the time of the

commission of the crime and has not fled therefrom. The demand, the oath, and any proceedings for extradition pursuant to this section need not state or show that the person whose surrender is demanded has fled from justice or at the time of the commission of the crime was in the demanding state.

750 ILCS 20/6
§ 6. Conditions of interstate rendition

(a) Before making the demand upon the Governor of another state for the surrender of a person charged criminally in this State with failing to provide for the support of a person, the Governor of this State may require any prosecuting attorney of this State to satisfy him that at least 60 days prior thereto the obligee initiated proceedings for support under this Act or that any proceeding would be of no avail.

(b) If, under a substantially similar Act, the Governor of another state makes a demand upon the Governor of this State for the surrender of a person charged criminally in that state with failure to provide for the support of a person, the Governor may require any prosecuting attorney to investigate the demand and to report to him whether proceedings for support have been initiated or would be effective. If it appears to the Governor that a proceeding would be effective but has not been initiated he may delay honoring the demand for a reasonable time to permit the initiation of a proceeding.

(c) If proceedings have been initiated and the person demanded has prevailed therein the Governor may decline to honor the demand. If the obligee prevailed and the person demanded is subject to a support order, the Governor may decline to honor the demand if the person demanded is complying with the support order.

PART III. CIVIL ENFORCEMENT

Analysis

Sec.
7. Choice of law.
8. Remedies of state or political subdivision furnishing support.
9. How duties of support enforced.
10. Jurisdiction.
11. Contents and filing of petition for support; Venue.
12. Officials to represent obligee.
13. Petition for a minor.
14. Duty of initiating court.
15. Costs and fees.
15a. Public Aid collection fee.
16. Jurisdiction by arrest.
17. State information agency.
18. Duty of the court and officials of this state as responding state.
19. Further duties of court and officials in the responding state.
20. Hearing and continuance.
21. Immunity from criminal prosecution.
22. Evidence of husband and wife.
23. Rules of evidence.

Sec.
24. Order of support.
24.1 Unemployed persons owing duty of support.
25. Responding court to transmit copies to initiating court.
26. Additional powers of responding court.
26.1 Withholding of income to secure payment of support.
27. Paternity.
28. Additional duties of responding court.
29. Additional duty of initiating court.
29A. Notice to clerk of initiating or responding circuit court of payment received by Illinois Department of Public Aid for recording.
29B. Time of payment transmittal by circuit court to Department of Public Aid.
30. Proceedings not to be stayed.
31. Application of payments.
32. Effect of participation in proceeding.
33. Intrastate application.
34. Appeals.

WESTLAW Electronic Research

See WESTLAW Electronic Research Guide preceding the Summary of Contents.

---

750 ILCS 20/7

§ 7. Choice of law

Duties of support applicable under this Act are those imposed under the laws of any state where the obligor was present for the period during which support is sought. The obligor is presumed to have been present in the responding state during the period for which support is sought until otherwise shown.

Author's Notes

(1) **Duties of support.** The duty of support that is enforceable under the Act is not only where a support order exists, but also where there is a duty of support under the law of the state in which the obligor is present. See also RURESA § 2(b).

750 ILCS 20/8

§ 8. Remedies of state or political subdivision furnishing support

If a state or a political subdivision furnishes support to an individual obligee it has the same right to initiate a proceeding under this Act as the individual obligee for the purpose of securing reimbursement for support furnished and of obtaining continuing support.

750 ILCS 20/9

§ 9. How duties of support enforced

All duties of support, including the duty to pay arrearages, are enforceable by a proceeding under this Act including a proceeding for civil contempt. The defense that the parties are immune to suit because of their relationship as husband and wife or parent and child is not available to the obligor.

750 ILCS 20/10
§ 10. Jurisdiction

Jurisdiction of any proceeding under this Act is vested in the circuit court.

750 ILCS 20/11
§ 11. Contents and filing of petition for support; Venue

(a) The petition shall be verified and shall state the name and, so far as known to the obligee, the address and circumstances of the obligor and the persons for whom support is sought, and all other pertinent information. The obligee may include in or attach to the petition any information which may help in locating or identifying the obligor including a photograph of the obligor, a description of any distinguishing marks on his person, other names and aliases by which he has been or is known, the name of his employer, his fingerprints, and his Social Security number.

(b) The petition may be filed in the appropriate court of any state in which the obligee resides. The court shall not decline or refuse to accept and forward the petition on the ground that it should be filed with some other court of this or any other state where there is pending another action for dissolution of marriage, declaration of invalidity of marriage, legal separation, habeas corpus, adoption, or custody between the same parties or where another court has already issued a support order in some other proceeding and has retained jurisdiction for its enforcement.

750 ILCS 20/12
§ 12. Officials to represent obligee

If this State is acting as an initiating state the prosecuting attorney upon the request of the court, the County Department of Public Aid or the Supervisor of General Assistance shall represent the obligee in any proceeding under this Act, except where a claim is referred to the Attorney General under Section 10-15 of "The Illinois Public Aid Code", approved April 11, 1967, as amended. If the prosecuting attorney neglects or refuses to represent the obligee, the Attorney General may undertake the representation.

Author's Notes

Analysis

1. Representation by state's attorneys.
2. Representation by private attorneys.

(1) **Representation by state's attorneys.** The utility of the Revised Uniform Reciprocal Enforcement of Support Act is that an obligee who is owed support can obtain representation by the state's attorney in her home state, and thereby prosecute her case against the obligor in another state, the obligee being also represented by the state's attorney in the home state of the obligor. See RURESA § 18 for duties of responding state.

750 ILCS 20/12   **FAMILIES**

(2) **Representation by private attorneys.** Actions under the Revised Uniform Reciprocal Enforce of Support Act can also be brought by private attorneys as well as public prosecuting attorneys.

750 ILCS 20/13

§ 13. Petition for a minor

A petition on behalf of a minor obligee may be executed and filed by a person having legal custody of the minor without appointment as guardian ad litem.

750 ILCS 20/14

§ 14. Duty of initiating court

If the initiating court finds that the petition sets forth facts from which it may be determined that the obligor owes a duty of support and that a court of the responding state may obtain jurisdiction of the obligor or his property it shall so certify and cause 3 copies of the petition and its certificate and one copy of this Act to be sent to the responding court. Certification shall be in accordance with the requirements of the initiating state. If the name and address of the responding court is unknown and the responding state has an information agency comparable to that established in the initiating state it shall cause the copies to be sent to the state information agency or other proper official of the responding state, with a request that the agency or official forward them to the proper court and that the court of the responding state acknowledge their receipt to the initiating court.

750 ILCS 20/15

§ 15. Costs and fees

An initiating court shall not require payment of either a filing fee or other costs from the obligee but may request the responding court to collect fees and costs from the obligor. A responding court shall not require payment of a filing fee or other costs from the obligee but it may direct that all fees and costs requested by the initiating court and incurred in this State when acting as a responding state, including fees for filing of pleadings, service of process, seizure of property, stenographic or duplication service, or other service supplied to the obligor, be paid in whole or in part by the obligor or by the county. These costs or fees do not have priority over amounts due to the obligee.

750 ILCS 20/15a

§ 15a. Public Aid collection fee

In all cases instituted by the Illinois Department of Public Aid on behalf of a child or spouse, other than one receiving a grant of financial aid under Article IV of The Illinois Public Aid Code, on whose behalf an application has been made and approved for support services as provided by Section 10–1 of that Code, the court shall impose a collection fee on the individual who owes a child or spouse support obligation in an amount equal to 10% of the amount so owed as long as such collection is required by federal law, which fee shall be in addition to the support obligation. The imposition of such fee shall be in accordance with provisions of Title IV, Part D, of the Social Security Act and regulations duly promulgated thereunder. The fee shall be payable to the clerk of the circuit court for transmittal to the Illinois Department of Public Aid and shall continue until support services are terminated by that Department.

750 ILCS 20/16
§ 16. Jurisdiction by arrest

If the court of this State believes that the obligor may flee it may

(1) as an initiating court, request in its certificate that the responding court obtain the body of the obligor by appropriate process; or

(2) as a responding court, obtain the body of the obligor by appropriate process. Thereupon it may release him upon his own recognizance or upon his giving a bond in an amount set by the court to assure his appearance at the hearing.

750 ILCS 20/17
§ 17. State information agency

(a) The State Department of Public Aid is designated as the state information agency under this Act, it shall

(1) compile a list of the courts and their addresses in this State having jurisdiction under this Act and transmit it to the state information agency of every other state which has adopted this or a substantially similar Act. Upon the adjournment of each session of the General Assembly the agency shall distribute copies of any amendments to the Act and a statement of their effective date to all other state information agencies;

(2) maintain a register of lists of courts received from other states and transmit copies thereof promptly to every court in this state having jurisdiction under this Act; and

(3) forward to the court in this State which has jurisdiction over the obligor or his property petitions, certificates and copies of the Act it receives from courts or information agencies of other states.

(b) If the state information agency does not know the location of the obligor or his property in the state and no state location service is available it shall use all means at its disposal to obtain this information, including the examination of official records in the state and other sources such as telephone directories, real property records, vital statistics records, police records, requests for the name and address from employers who are able or willing to cooperate, records of motor vehicle license offices, requests made to the tax offices both state and federal where such offices are able to cooperate, and requests made to the Social Security Administration as permitted by the Social Security Act as amended.

(c) After the deposit of 3 copies of the petition and certificate and one copy of the Act of the initiating state with the clerk of the appropriate court, if the state information agency knows or believes that the prosecuting attorney is not prosecuting the case diligently it shall inform the Attorney General who may undertake the representation.

750 ILCS 20/18

§ 18. Duty of the court and officials of this state as responding state

(a) After the responding court receives copies of the petition, certificate and Act from the initiating court the clerk of the court shall docket the case and notify the prosecuting attorney of his action.

(b) The prosecuting attorney shall prosecute the case diligently. He shall take all action necessary in accordance with the laws of this State to enable the court to obtain jurisdiction over the obligor or his property and shall request the clerk of the court to set a time and place for a hearing and give notice thereof to the obligor in accordance with law.

(c) If the prosecuting attorney neglects or refuses to represent the obligee, the Attorney General may undertake the representation.

750 ILCS 20/19

§ 19. Further duties of court and officials in the responding state

(a) The prosecuting attorney on his own initiative shall use all means at his disposal to locate the obligor or his property, and if because of inaccuracies in the petition or otherwise the court cannot obtain jurisdiction the prosecuting attorney shall inform the court of what he has done and request the court to continue the case pending receipt of more accurate information or an amended petition from the initiating court.

(b) If the obligor or his property is not found in the county, and the prosecuting attorney discovers that the obligor or his property may be found in another county of this State or in another state he shall so inform the court. Thereupon the clerk of the court shall forward the documents received from the court in the initiating state to a court in the other county or to a court in the other state or to the information agency or other proper official of the other state with a request that the documents be forwarded to the proper court. All powers and duties provided by this Act apply to the recipient of the documents so forwarded. If the clerk of a court of this State forwards documents to another court he shall forthwith notify the initiating court.

(c) If the prosecuting attorney has no information as to the location of the obligor or his property he shall so inform the initiating court.

750 ILCS 20/20

§ 20. Hearing and continuance

If the obligee is not present at the hearing and the obligor denies owing the duty of support alleged in the petition or offers evidence constituting a defense the court, upon request of either party, shall continue the hearing to permit evidence relative to the duty to be adduced by either party by deposition or by appearing in person before the court. The court may designate the judge of the initiating court as a person before whom a deposition may be taken.

Author's Notes

(1) **Depositions.** Since evidence by evidence deposition is expressly authorized, it is unnecessary for the obligee who is located in another state to actually appear in the responding state to testify.

750 ILCS 20/21

§ 21. Immunity from criminal prosecution

If at the hearing the obligor is called for examination as an adverse party and he declines to answer upon the ground that his testimony may tend to incriminate him, the court may require him to answer, in which event he is immune from criminal prosecution with respect to matters revealed by his testimony, except for perjury committed in this testimony.

750 ILCS 20/22

§ 22. Evidence of husband and wife

Laws attaching a privilege against the disclosure of communications between husband and wife are inapplicable to proceedings under this Act. Husband and wife are competent witnesses and may be compelled to testify to any relevant matter, including marriage and parentage.

750 ILCS 20/23

§ 23. Rules of evidence

In any hearing for the civil enforcement of this Act the court is governed by the rules of evidence applicable in a civil court action in the Circuit Court. If the action is based on a support order issued by a court or administrative body of this or any other State, a certified copy of the order shall be received as evidence of the duty of support, subject only to any defenses available to an obligor with respect to paternity (Section 27) or to a defendant in an action or a proceeding to enforce a foreign money judgment. The determination or enforcement of a duty of support owed to one obligee is unaffected by any interference by another obligee with rights of custody or visitation granted by a court.

750 ILCS 20/24

§ 24. Order of support

If the responding court finds a duty of support it may order the obligor to furnish support or reimbursement therefor and subject the property of the obligor to the order.

Any new or existing support order entered by a court or administrative body of this or any other State shall be deemed to be a series of judgments against the person obligated to pay support thereunder, each such judgment to be in the amount of each payment or installment of support and each such judgment to be deemed entered as of the date the corresponding payment or installment becomes due under the terms of the support order. Each such judgment shall:

(1) have the full force, effect, and attributes of any other judgment of such State, including the ability to be enforced;

(2) be entitled as a judgment to full faith and credit in this and any other State; and

(3) not be subject to retroactive modification by this or any other State; except that modification is permitted with respect to any period during which there is pending a petition for modification, but only from the date that notice of such petition has been given in accordance with law.

Where the terms of a support order entered by a court or administrative body of this or any other State are subject to modification, or where action is not based upon such order, the Illinois court shall determine the amount of maintenance or child support by using the guidelines and standards set forth in Section 504, or in subsection (a) of Section 505 and in Section 505.2 of the Illinois Marriage and Dissolution of Marriage Act, respectively.

Support orders made pursuant to this Act shall require that payments be made to the clerk of the court of the responding state. The court and prosecuting attorney of any county in which the obligor is present or has property have the same powers and duties to enforce the order as have those of the county in which it was first issued. If enforcement is impossible or cannot be completed in the county in which the order was issued, the prosecuting attorney shall send a certified copy of the order to the prosecuting attorney of any county in which it appears that proceedings to enforce the order would be effective. The prosecuting attorney to whom the certified copy of the order is forwarded shall proceed with enforcement and report the results of the proceedings to the court first issuing the order.

A one-time charge of 20% is imposable upon the amount of past-due child support owed on July 1, 1988 which has accrued under a support order entered by the court. The charge shall be imposed in accordance with the provisions of Section 10–21 of The Illinois Public Aid Code and shall be enforced by the court upon petition.

A court or administrative body of this State may modify a support order of another state only if that other state no longer has continuing, exclusive jurisdiction of the proceeding in which the support order was entered. The order must be registered under Section 609 of the Uniform Interstate Family Support Act and may be modified only if permitted under Section 611 of the Uniform Interstate Family Support Act.

An order for support entered or modified in a case in which a party is receiving child and spouse support services under Article X of the Illinois Public Aid Code shall include a provision requiring the non-custodial parent to notify the Illinois Department of Public Aid, within 7 days, of the name and address of any new employer of the non-custodial parent, whether the non-custodial parent has access to health insurance coverage through the employer or other group coverage, and, if so, the policy name and number and the names of persons covered under the policy.

An order for support shall include a date on which the current support obligation terminates. The termination date shall be no earlier than the date on which the child covered by the order will attain the age of majority or is otherwise emancipated. The order for support shall state that the termination date does not apply to any arrearage that may remain unpaid on that date. Nothing in this paragraph shall be construed to prevent the court from modifying the order.

Author's Notes

(1) **Powers of the responding state.** The responding state can, *inter alia*, require the payment of arrearages, enter a new order of support, or prospectively modify an existing order of support. See also RURESA § 26. See also § 611 of the Uniform Interstate Family Support Act, 750 ILCS 22/611, which limits modification of support orders of another state. See 750 ILCS 22/999 Author's Note (1) for effective date of Uniform Interstate Family Support Act.

750 ILCS 20/24.1

§ 24.1 Unemployed persons owing duty of support

Whenever it is determined in a proceeding to establish or enforce a child support or maintenance obligation that the person owing a duty of support is unemployed, the court may order the person to seek employment and report periodically to the court with a diary, listing or other memorandum of his or her efforts in accordance with such order. Additionally, the court may order the unemployed person to report to the Department of Employment Security for job search services or to make application with the local Jobs Training Partnership Act provider for participation in job search, training or work programs and where the duty of support is owed to a child receiving support services under Article X of The Illinois Public Aid Code, as amended, the court may order the unemployed person to report to the Illinois Department of Public Aid for participation in job search, training or work programs established under Section 9–6 of that Code.

750 ILCS 20/25

§ 25. Responding court to transmit copies to initiating court

The responding court shall cause a copy of all support orders to be sent to the initiating court.

750 ILCS 20/26

§ 26. Additional powers of responding court

In addition to the foregoing powers a responding court may subject the obligor to any terms and conditions proper to assure compliance with its orders and in particular to:

(1) require the obligor to furnish a cash deposit or a bond of a character and amount to assure payment of any amount due;

(2) require the obligor to report personally and to make payments at specified intervals to the clerk of the court; and

(3) punish under the power of contempt the obligor who violates any order of the court.

750 ILCS 20/26.1

§ 26.1 Withholding of income to secure payment of support

(A) Definitions.

(1) "Order for support" means any order of the court which provides for periodic payment of funds for the support of a child or maintenance of a spouse, whether temporary or final, and includes any such order which provides for:

(a) modification or resumption of, or payment of arrearage accrued under, a previously existing order;

(b) reimbursement of support; or

(c) enrollment in a health insurance plan that is available to the obligor through an employer.

(2) "Arrearage" means the total amount of unpaid support obligations.

(3) "Delinquency" means any payment under an order for support which becomes due and remains unpaid after an order for withholding has been entered under subsection (B) or, for purposes of subsection (K), after the last order for support was entered for which no order for withholding was entered.

(4) "Income" means any form of periodic payment to an individual, regardless of source, including, but not limited to: wages, salary, commission, compensation as an independent contractor, workers' compensation, disability, annuity and retirement benefits, lottery prize awards, insurance proceeds, vacation pay, bonuses, profit-sharing payments and any other payments, made by any person, private entity, federal or state government, any unit of local government, school district or any entity created by Public Act; however, "income" excludes:

(a) any amounts required by law to be withheld, other than creditor claims, including, but not limited to, federal, State and local taxes, Social Security and other retirement and disability contributions;

(b) union dues;

(c) any amounts exempted by the federal Consumer Credit Protection Act;

(d) public assistance payments; and

(e) unemployment insurance benefits except as provided by law.

Any other State or local laws which limit or exempt income or the amount or percentage of income that can be withheld shall not apply.

(5) "Obligor" means the individual who owes a duty to make payments under an order for support.

(6) "Obligee" means the individual to whom a duty of support is owed or the individual's legal representative.

(7) "Payor" means any payor of income to an obligor.

(8) "Public office" means any elected official or any State or local agency which is or may become responsible by law for enforcement of, or which is or may become authorized to enforce, an order for support, including, but not limited to: the Attorney General, the Illinois Department of Public Aid, the Illinois Department of Mental Health and Developmental Disabilities, the Illinois Department of Children and Family Services, and the various State's Attorneys, Clerks of the Circuit Court and supervisors of general assistance.

(9) "Premium" means the dollar amount for which the obligor is liable to his employer and which must be paid to enroll or maintain a child in a health insurance plan that is available to the obligor through an employer.

(B) Entry of an order for withholding.

(1) Upon entry of any order for support on or after January 1, 1984, the court shall enter a separate order for withholding which shall not take effect unless the obligor becomes delinquent in paying the order for support or the obligor requests an earlier effective date; except that the court may require the order for withholding to take effect immediately.

On or after January 1, 1989, the court shall require the order for withholding to take effect immediately, unless a written agreement is reached between both parties providing for an alternative arrangement, approved by the court, which insures payment of support. In that case, the court shall enter the order for withholding which will not take effect unless the obligor becomes delinquent in paying the order for support.

Upon entry of any order of support on or after September 11, 1989, if the obligor is not a United States citizen, the obligor shall provide to the court the obligor's alien registration number, passport number, and home country's social security or national health number, if applicable; the court shall make the information part of the record in the case.

(2) An order for withholding shall be entered upon petition by the obligee or public office where an order for withholding has not been previously entered.

(3) The order for withholding shall:

(a) direct any payor to withhold a dollar amount equal to the order for support; and

(b) direct any payor to withhold an additional dollar amount, not less than 20% of the order for support, until payment in full of any delinquency stated in the notice of delinquency provided for in subsection (C) or (F) of this Section; and

(c) direct any payor to enroll a child as a beneficiary of a health insurance plan and withhold any required premiums; and

(d) state the rights, remedies and duties of the obligor under this Section; and

(e) include the obligor's Social Security Number, which the obligor shall disclose to the court.

(4) At the time the order for withholding is entered, the Clerk of the Circuit Court shall provide a copy of the order for withholding and the order for support to the obligor and shall make copies available to the obligee and public office. Any copy of the order for withholding furnished to the parties under this subsection shall be stamped "Not Valid".

(5) The order for withholding shall remain in effect for as long as the order for support upon which it is based.

(6) The failure of an order for withholding to state an arrearage is not conclusive of the issue of whether an arrearage is owing.

(7) Notwithstanding the provisions of this subsection, if the court finds at the time of any hearing that an arrearage has accrued in an amount equal to at least one month's support obligation or that the obligor is 30 days late in paying all or part of the order for support, the court shall order immediate service of the order for withholding upon the payor.

(C) Notice of delinquency.

(1) Whenever an obligor becomes delinquent in payment of an amount equal to at least one month's support obligation pursuant to the order for support or is at least 30 days late in complying with all or part of the order for support, whichever occurs first, the obligee or public office may prepare and serve a verified notice of delinquency, together with a form petition to stay service, pursuant to paragraph (3) of this subsection.

(2) The notice of delinquency shall recite the terms of the order for support and contain a computation of the period and total amount of the delinquency, as of the date of the notice. The notice shall clearly state that it will be sent to the payor, together with a specially certified copy of the order

for withholding, except as provided in subsection (F), unless the obligor files a petition to stay service in accordance with paragraph (1) of subsection (D).

(3) The notice of delinquency shall be served by ordinary mail addressed to the obligor at his or her last known address.

(4) The obligor may execute a written waiver of the provisions of paragraphs (1) through (3) of this subsection and request immediate service upon the payor.

(D) Procedures to avoid income withholding.

(1) Except as provided in subsection (F), the obligor may prevent an order for withholding from being served by filing a petition to stay service with the Clerk of the Circuit Court, within 20 days after service of the notice of delinquency; however, the grounds for the petition to stay service shall be limited to a dispute concerning: (a) the amount of current support or the existence or amount of the delinquency; or (b) the identity of the obligor.

The Clerk of the Circuit Court shall notify the obligor and the obligee or public office, as appropriate, of the time and place of the hearing on the petition to stay service. The court shall hold such hearing pursuant to the provisions of subsection (H).

(2) Except as provided in subsection (F), filing of a petition to stay service, within the 20–day period required under this subsection, shall prohibit the obligee or public office from serving the order for withholding on any payor of the obligor.

(E) Initial service of order for withholding.

(1) Except as provided in subsection (F), in order to serve an order for withholding upon a payor, an obligee or public office shall follow the procedures set forth in this subsection. After 20 days following service of the notice of delinquency, the obligee or public office shall file with the Clerk of the Circuit Court an affidavit, with the copy of the notice of delinquency attached thereto, stating:

(a) that the notice of delinquency has been duly served and the date on which service was effected; and

(b) that the obligor has not filed a petition to stay service, or in the alternative

(c) that the obligor has waived the provisions of subparagraphs (a) and (b) of this paragraph (1) in accordance with subsection (C)(4).

(2) Upon request of the obligee or public office, the Clerk of the Circuit shall: (a) make available any record of payment; and (b) determine that the file contains a copy of the affidavit described in paragraph (1). The Clerk shall then provide to the obligee or public office a specially certified copy of the order for withholding and the notice of delinquency indicating that the preconditions for service have been met.

(3) The obligee or public office may then serve the notice of delinquency and order for withholding on the payor, its superintendent, manager or other agent, by certified mail or personal delivery. A proof of service shall be filed with the Clerk of the Circuit Court.

(F) Subsequent service of order for withholding.

(1) Notwithstanding the provisions of this Section, at any time after the court has ordered immediate service of an order for withholding or after initial service of an order for withholding pursuant to subsection (E), the obligee or public office may serve the order for withholding upon any payor of the obligor without further notice to the obligor. The obligee or public office shall provide notice to the payor, pursuant to paragraph (6) of subsection (I), of any payments that have been made through previous withholding or any other method.

(2) The Clerk of the Circuit Court shall, upon request, provide the obligee or public office with specially certified copies of the order for withholding or the notice of delinquency or both whenever the Court has ordered immediate service of an order for withholding or an affidavit has been placed in the court file indicating that the preconditions for service have been previously met. The obligee or public office may then serve the order for withholding on the payor, its superintendent, manager or other agent by certified mail or personal delivery. A proof of service shall be filed with the Clerk of the Circuit Court.

(3) If a delinquency has accrued for any reason, the obligee or public office may serve a notice of delinquency upon the obligor pursuant to subsection (C). The obligor may prevent the notice of delinquency from being served upon the payor by utilizing the procedures set forth in subsection (D). If no petition to stay service has been filed within the required 20 day time period, the obligee or public office may serve the notice of delinquency on the payor by utilizing the procedures for service set forth in subsection (E).

(G) Duties of payor.

(1) It shall be the duty of any payor who has been served with a copy of the specially certified order for withholding and any notice of delinquency to deduct and pay over income as provided in this subsection. The payor shall deduct the amount designated in the order for withholding, as supplemented by the notice of delinquency and any notice provided pursuant to paragraph (6) of subsection (I), beginning no later than the next payment of income which is payable to the obligor that occurs 14 days following the date the order and any notice were mailed by certified mail or placed for personal delivery. The payor may combine all amounts withheld for the benefit of an obligee or public office into a single payment and transmit the payment with a listing of obligors from whom withholding has been effected. The payor shall pay the amount withheld to the obligee or public office within 3 business days of the date income is paid to the obligor in accordance with the order for withholding and any subsequent notification received from the public office redirecting payments. If the payor knowingly fails to pay any amount

withheld to the obligee or public office within 3 business days of the date income is paid to the obligor, the payor shall pay a penalty of $100 for each day that the withheld amount is paid to the obligee or public office after the period of 3 business days has expired. The failure of a payor, on more than one occasion, to pay amounts withheld to the obligee or public office within 3 business days of the date income is paid to the obligor creates a presumption that the payor knowingly failed to pay the amounts. This penalty may be collected in a civil action which may be brought against the payor in favor of the obligee. For purposes of this Section, a withheld amount shall be considered paid by a payor on the date it is mailed by the payor, or on the date an electronic funds transfer of the amount has been initiated by the payor, or on the date delivery of the amount has been initiated by the payor. For each deduction, the payor shall provide the obligee or public office, at the time of transmittal, with the date income was paid from which support was withheld.

Upon receipt of an order requiring that a minor child be named as a beneficiary of a health insurance plan available through an employer, the employer shall immediately enroll the minor child as a beneficiary in the health insurance plan designated by the court order. The employer shall withhold any required premiums and pay over any amounts so withheld and any additional amounts the employer pays to the insurance carrier in a timely manner. The employer shall mail to the obligee, within 15 days of enrollment or upon request, notice of the date of coverage, information on the dependent coverage plan, and all forms necessary to obtain reimbursement for covered health expenses, such as would be made available to a new employee. When an order for dependent coverage is in effect and the insurance coverage is terminated or changed for any reason, the employer shall notify the obligee within 10 days of the termination or change date along with notice of conversion privileges.

For withholding of income, the payor shall be entitled to receive a fee not to exceed $5 per month to be taken from the income to be paid to the obligor.

(2) Whenever the obligor is no longer receiving income from the payor, the payor shall return a copy of the order for withholding to the obligee or public office and shall provide information for the purpose of enforcing this Section.

(3) Withholding of income under this Section shall be made without regard to any prior or subsequent garnishments, attachments, wage assignments, or any other claims of creditors. Withholding of income under this Section shall not be in excess of the maximum amounts permitted under the federal Consumer Credit Protection Act. If the payor has been served with more than one order for withholding pertaining to the same obligor, the payor shall allocate income available for withholding on a proportionate share basis, giving priority to current support payments. If there is any income available for withholding after withholding for all current support obligations, the payor shall allocate the income to past due support payments ordered in non-

AFDC matters and then to past due support payments ordered in AFDC matters, both on a proportionate share basis. Payment as required by the order for withholding shall be a complete defense by the payor against any claims of the obligor or his creditors as to the sum so paid.

(4) No payor shall discharge, discipline, refuse to hire or otherwise penalize any obligor because of the duty to withhold income.

(H) Petitions to stay service or to modify, suspend or terminate orders for withholding.

(1) When an obligor files a petition to stay service, the court, after due notice to all parties, shall hear the matter as soon as practicable and shall enter an order granting or denying relief, amending the notice of delinquency, amending the order for withholding where applicable, or otherwise resolving the matter. If the court finds that a delinquency existed when the notice of delinquency was served upon the obligor, in an amount of at least one month's support obligation, or that the obligor was at least 30 days late in paying all or part of the order for support, the court shall order immediate service of the order for withholding. Where the court cannot promptly resolve any dispute over the amount of the delinquency, the court may order immediate service of the order for withholding as to any undisputed amounts specified in an amended notice of delinquency, and may continue the hearing on the disputed amounts.

(2) At any time, an obligor, obligee, public office or Clerk of the Circuit Court may petition the court to:

(a) modify, suspend or terminate the order for withholding because of a modification, suspension or termination of the underlying order for support; or

(b) modify the amount of income to be withheld to reflect payment in full or in part of the delinquency or arrearage by income withholding or otherwise; or

(c) suspend the order for withholding because of inability to deliver income withheld to the obligee due to the obligee's failure to provide a mailing address or other means of delivery.

(3) The obligor, obligee or public office shall serve on the payor, by certified mail or personal delivery, a copy of any order entered pursuant to this subsection that affects the duties of the payor.

(4) The order for withholding shall continue to be binding upon the payor until service of any order of the court entered under this subsection.

(I) Additional duties.

(1) An obligee who is receiving income withholding payments under this Section shall notify the payor, if the obligee receives the payments directly from the payor, or the public office or the Clerk of the Circuit Court, as appropriate, of any change of address within 7 days of such change.

(2) An obligee who is a recipient of public aid shall send a copy of any notice of delinquency filed pursuant to subsection (C) to the Bureau of Child Support of the Illinois Department of Public Aid.

(3) Each obligor shall notify the obligee and the Clerk of the Circuit Court of any change of address within 7 days.

(4) An obligor whose income is being withheld or who has been served with a notice of delinquency pursuant to this Section shall notify the obligee and the Clerk of the Circuit Court of any new payor, within 7 days.

(5) When the Illinois Department of Public Aid is no longer authorized to receive payments for the obligee, it shall, within 7 days, notify the payor or, where appropriate, the Clerk of the Circuit Court, to redirect income withholding payments to the obligee.

(6) The obligee or public office shall provide notice to the payor and Clerk of the Circuit Court of any other support payment made, including but not limited to, a set-off under federal and State law or partial payment of the delinquency or arrearage, or both.

(7) Any public office and Clerk of the Circuit Court which collects, disburses or receives payments pursuant to orders for withholding shall maintain complete, accurate, and clear records of all payments and their disbursements. Certified copies of payment records maintained by a public office or Clerk of the Circuit Court shall, without further proof, be admitted into evidence in any legal proceedings under this Section.

(8) The Illinois Department of Public Aid shall design suggested legal forms for proceeding under this Section and shall make available to the courts such forms and informational materials which describe the procedures and remedies set forth herein for distribution to all parties in support actions.

(9) At the time of transmitting each support payment, the clerk of the circuit court shall provide the obligee or public office, as appropriate, with any information furnished by the payor as to the date income was paid from which such support was withheld.

(J) Penalties.

(1) Where a payor wilfully fails to withhold or pay over income pursuant to a properly served, specially certified order for withholding and any notice of delinquency, or wilfully discharges, disciplines, refuses to hire or otherwise penalizes an obligor as prohibited by subsection (G), or otherwise fails to comply with any duties imposed by this Section, the obligee, public office or obligor, as appropriate, may file a complaint with the court against the payor. The clerk of the circuit court shall notify the obligee or public office, as appropriate, and the obligor and payor of the time and place of the hearing on the complaint. The court shall resolve any factual dispute including, but not limited to, a denial that the payor is paying or has paid income to the obligor. Upon a finding in favor of the complaining party, the court:

(a) shall enter judgment and direct the enforcement thereof for the total amount that the payor wilfully failed to withhold or pay over; and

(b) may order employment or reinstatement of or restitution to the obligor, or both, where the obligor has been discharged, disciplined, denied employment or otherwise penalized by the payor and may impose a fine upon the payor not to exceed $200.

(2) Any obligee, public office or obligor who wilfully initiates a false proceeding under this Section or who wilfully fails to comply with the requirements of this Section shall be punished as in cases of contempt of court.

(K) Alternative procedures for entry and service of an order for withholding.

(1) Effective January 1, 1987, in any matter in which an order for withholding has not been entered for any reason, based upon the last order for support that has been entered, and in which the obligor has become delinquent in payment of an amount equal to at least one month's support obligation pursuant to the last order for support or is at least 30 days late in complying with all or part of the order for support, the obligee or public office may prepare and serve an order for withholding pursuant to the procedures set forth in this subsection.

(2) The obligee or public office shall:

(a) prepare a proposed order for withholding for immediate service as provided by paragraphs (1) and (3) of subsection (B), except that the minimum 20% delinquency payment shall be used;

(b) prepare a notice of delinquency as provided by paragraphs (1) and (2) of subsection (C), except the notice shall state further that the order for withholding has not been entered by the court and the conditions under which the order will be entered; and

(c) serve the notice of delinquency and form petition to stay service as provided by paragraph (3) of subsection (C), together with the proposed order for withholding, which shall be marked "COPY ONLY".

(3) After 20 days following service of the notice of delinquency and proposed order for withholding, in lieu of the provisions of subsection (E), the obligee or public office shall file with the Clerk of the Circuit Court an affidavit, with a copy of the notice of delinquency and proposed order for withholding attached thereto, stating that:

(a) the notice of delinquency and proposed order for withholding have been served upon the obligor and the date on which service was effected;

(b) the obligor has not filed a petition to stay service within 20 days of service of such notice and order; and

(c) the proposed order for withholding accurately states the terms and amounts contained in the last order for support.

(4) Upon the court's satisfaction that the procedures set forth in this subsection have been met, it shall enter the order for withholding.

(5) The Clerk shall then provide to the obligee or public office a specially certified copy of the order for withholding and the notice of delinquency indicating that the preconditions for service have been met.

(6) The obligee or public office shall serve the specially certified copies of the order for withholding and the notice of delinquency on the payor, its superintendent, manager or other agent by certified mail or personal delivery. A proof of service shall be filed with the Clerk of the Circuit Court.

(7) If the obligor requests in writing that income withholding become effective prior to becoming delinquent in payment of an amount equal to one month's support obligation pursuant to the last order for support, or prior to becoming 30 days late in paying all or part of the order for support, the obligee or public office shall file an affidavit with the Clerk of the circuit Court, with a proposed order for withholding attached, stating that the proposed order accurately states the terms and amounts contained in the last order for support and the obligor's request for immediate service. The provisions of paragraphs (4) through (6) of this subsection shall apply, except that a notice of delinquency shall not be required.

(8) All other provisions of this Section shall be applicable with respect to the provisions of this subsection (K), except that under paragraph (1) of subsection (H), the court may also amend the proposed order for withholding to conform to the last order for support.

(9) Nothing in this subsection shall be construed as limiting the requirements of paragraph (1) of subsection (B) with respect to the entry of a separate order for withholding upon entry of any order for support.

(L) Remedies in addition to other laws.

(1) The rights, remedies, duties and penalties created by this Section are in addition to and not in substitution for any other rights, remedies, duties and penalties created by any other law.

(2) Nothing in this Section shall be construed as invalidating any assignment of wages or benefits executed prior to January 1, 1984.

Author's Notes

(1) **Cross reference.** The provisions of RURESA § 26.1 are substantially the same as IMDMA § 706.1. See 750 ILCS 5/706.1 and accompanying Author's Notes.

750 ILCS 20/27

§ 27. Paternity

If the obligor asserts as a defense that he is not the father of the child for whom support is sought and it appears to the court that the defense is not frivolous, and if both of the parties are present at the hearing or the proof required in the case indicates that the presence of either or both of the parties

750 ILCS 20/27   **FAMILIES**

is not necessary, the court may adjudicate the paternity issue. Otherwise the court may adjourn the hearing until the paternity issue has been adjudicated.

750 ILCS 20/28

§ 28. Additional duties of responding court

A responding court has the following duties which may be carried out through the clerk of the court:

(1) to transmit to the initiating court any payment made by the obligor pursuant to any order of the court or otherwise; and

(2) to furnish to the initiating court upon request a certified statement of all payments made by the obligor.

750 ILCS 20/29

§ 29. Additional duty of initiating court

An initiating court shall receive and disburse forthwith all payments made by the obligor or sent by the responding court. This duty may be carried out through the clerk of the court. If the obligee and other dependents for whom support or reimbursement therefor has been ordered pursuant to Section 24 of this Act are recipients of public aid under "The Illinois Public Aid Code", approved April 11, 1967, as amended, each court of this State, in respect to payments received by it as initiating court, shall order such payments to be transmitted to (1) the Illinois Department of Public Aid if the obligee, other dependents, or both, are recipients of aid under Articles III, IV or V of the Code, or (2) the local governmental unit responsible for the support of the obligee, other dependents, or both, if they are recipients under Articles VI or VII of the Code. The Illinois Department of Public Aid may continue to collect current maintenance or child support payments, or both, for a period not to exceed three months from the month following the month in which such obligee, other dependents, or both, cease to receive public assistance, and pay all amounts so collected to such persons. At the end of such three month period, the Illinois Department of Public Aid may continue to collect such payments if authorized by such persons to do so, and pay the net amount so collected to such persons after deducting any costs incurred in making the collection or any collection fee from the amount of any recovery made. Upon removal of the obligee, other dependents, or both, from the public aid rolls or upon termination of any extended collection period, the Illinois Department or the local governmental unit, as the case requires, shall give written notice of such action to the court, together with request that subsequent payments be made directly to the obligee, the other dependents, or both, or to some other person or agency in their behalf. Payments under this Section to the Illinois Department of Public Aid pursuant to the Child Support Enforcement Program established by Title IV–D of the Social Security Act shall be paid into the Child Support Enforcement Trust Fund. All other payments under this Section to the Illinois Department of Public Aid shall be deposited in the Public Assistance Recoveries Trust Fund. Disbursements from these funds shall be as provided in The Illinois Public Aid Code. Payments received by a local governmental unit shall be deposited in that unit's General Assistance Fund.

750 ILCS 20/29A

§ 29A. Notice to clerk of initiating or responding circuit court of payment received by Illinois Department of Public Aid for recording

For those cases in which support is payable to the clerk of the initiating or responding circuit court for transmittal to the Illinois Department of Public Aid by order of court, and the Illinois Department of Public Aid collects support by assignment, offset, withholding, deduction or other process permitted by law, the Illinois Department of Public Aid shall notify the clerk of the date and amount of such collection. Upon notification, the clerk shall record the collection on the payment record for the case.

750 ILCS 20/29B

§ 29B. Time of payment transmittal by circuit court to Department of Public Aid

For those cases in which child support is payable to the clerk of the circuit court for transmittal to the Illinois Department of Public Aid by order of court, the clerk shall transmit all such payments, within 4 working days of receipt, to insure that funds are available for immediate distribution by the Department to the person or entity entitled thereto in accordance with standards of the Child Support Enforcement Program established under Title IV–D of the Social Security Act. The clerk shall notify the Department of the date of receipt and amount thereof at the time of transmittal. Where the clerk has entered into an agreement of cooperation with the Department to record the terms of child support orders and payments made thereunder directly into the Department's automated data processing system, the clerk shall account for, transmit and otherwise distribute child support payments in accordance with such agreements in lieu of the requirements contained herein.

750 ILCS 20/30

§ 30. Proceedings not to be stayed

A responding court shall not stay the proceeding or refuse a hearing under this Act because of any pending or prior action or proceeding for dissolution of marriage, declaration of invalidity of marriage, legal separation, habeas corpus, adoption, or custody in this or any other state. The court shall hold a hearing and may issue a support order pendente lite. In aid thereof it may require the obligor to give a bond for the prompt prosecution of the pending proceeding. If the other action or proceeding is concluded before the hearing in the instant proceeding and the judgment therein provides for the support demanded in the petition being heard the court must conform its

750 ILCS 20/30

support order to the amount allowed in the other action or proceeding. Thereafter the court shall not stay enforcement of its support order because of the retention of jurisdiction for enforcement purposes by the court in the other action or proceeding.

750 ILCS 20/31

§ 31. Application of payments

A support order made by a court of this State pursuant to this Act does not nullify and is not nullified by a support order made by a court of this State pursuant to any other law or by a support order made by a court of any other state pursuant to a substantially similar act or any other law, regardless of priority of issuance, unless otherwise specifically provided by the court. Amounts paid for a particular period pursuant to any support order made by the court of another state shall be credited against the amounts accruing or accrued for the same period under any support order made by the court of this State.

750 ILCS 20/32

§ 32. Effect of participation in proceeding

Participation in any proceeding under this Act does not confer jurisdiction upon any court over any of the parties thereto in any other proceeding.

750 ILCS 20/33

§ 33. Intrastate application

This Act applies if both the obligee and the obligor are in this State but in different counties. If the court of the county in which the petition is filed finds that the petition sets forth facts from which it may be determined that the obligor owes a duty of support and finds that a court of another county in this State may obtain jurisdiction over the obligor or his property, the clerk of the court shall send the petition and a certification of the findings to the court of the county in which the obligor or his property is found. The clerk of the court of the county receiving these documents shall notify the prosecuting attorney of their receipt. The prosecuting attorney and the court in the county to which the copies are forwarded then shall have duties corresponding to those imposed upon them when acting for this State as a responding state.

750 ILCS 20/34

§ 34. Appeals

If the Attorney General is of the opinion that a support order is erroneous and presents a question of law warranting an appeal in the public interest, he may

(a) perfect an appeal to the proper appellate court if the support order was issued by a court of this State, or

(b) if the support order was issued in another state, cause the appeal to be taken in the other state. In either case expenses of appeal may be paid on his order from funds appropriated for his office.

PART IV. REGISTRATION OF FOREIGN SUPPORT ORDERS

Analysis

Sec.
35. Additional remedies.
36. Registration.
37. Registry of Foreign Support Orders.
38. Official to represent obligee.
39. Registration procedure; Notice.
40. Effect of registration; Enforcement procedure.
41. Uniformity of interpretation.
42. Severability.

WESTLAW Electronic Research

See WESTLAW Electronic Research Guide preceding the Summary of Contents.

---

750 ILCS 20/35

§ 35. Additional remedies

If the duty of support is based on a foreign support order, the obligee has the additional remedies provided in the following sections.

750 ILCS 20/36

§ 36. Registration

The obligee may register the foreign support order in a court of this State in the manner, with the effect, and for the purposes herein provided.

750 ILCS 20/37

§ 37. Registry of Foreign Support Orders

The clerk of the court shall maintain a Registry of Foreign Support Orders in which he shall file foreign support orders.

750 ILCS 20/38

§ 38. Official to represent obligee

If this State is acting either as a rendering or a registering state the prosecuting attorney upon the request of the court, the County Department of Public Aid or the Supervisor of General Assistance shall represent the obligee in proceedings under this Part.

If the prosecuting attorney neglects or refuses to represent the obligee, the Attorney General may undertake the representation.

750 ILCS 20/38   FAMILIES

Author's Notes

(1) **Private attorney.** A private attorney, as well as public prosecuting attorneys, can register foreign support orders under this Act.

750 ILCS 20/39

§ 39. Registration procedure; Notice

(a) An obligee seeking to register a foreign support order in a court of this State shall transmit to the clerk of the court (1) three certified copies of the order with all modifications thereof, (2) one copy of the reciprocal enforcement of support act of the state in which the order was made, and (3) a statement verified and signed by the obligee, showing the post office address of the obligee, the last known place of residence and post office address of the obligor, the amount of support remaining unpaid, a description and the location of any property of the obligor available upon execution, and a list of the states in which the order is registered. Upon receipt of these documents the clerk of the court, without payment of a filing fee or other cost to the obligee, shall file them in the Registry of Foreign Support Orders. The filing constitutes registration under this Act.

(b) Promptly upon registration the clerk of the court shall send by certified or registered mail to the obligor at the address given a notice of the registration with a copy of the registered support order and the post office address of the obligee. He shall also docket the case and notify the prosecuting attorney of his action. The prosecuting attorney shall proceed diligently to enforce the order.

Author's Notes

(1) **Cross reference.** For a comparison of available remedies for the civil enforcement of foreign orders among Part III of RURESA, Part IV of RURESA, and other statutes, see RURESA § 1 Author's Notes (4) and (5).

750 ILCS 20/40

§ 40. Effect of registration; Enforcement procedure

(a) Upon registration the registered foreign support order shall be treated in the same manner as a support order entered by a court of this State. It has the same effect and is subject to the same procedures, defenses, and proceedings for reopening, vacating, or staying as a support order of this State and may be enforced and satisfied in like manner.

(b) The obligor has 30 days after the mailing of notice of the registration in which to petition the court to vacate the registration or for other relief. If he does not so petition the registered support order is confirmed.

(c) At the hearing to enforce the registered support order the obligor may present only matters that would be available to him as defenses in an action to enforce a foreign money judgment. If he shows to the court that an appeal from the order is pending or will be taken or that a stay of enforcement has been granted the court shall stay enforcement of the order until the appeal is concluded, the time for appeal has expired, or the order is vacated, upon satisfactory proof that the obligor has furnished security for payment of the support ordered as required by the rendering state. If he shows to the court any ground upon which enforcement of a support order of this State may be stayed the court shall stay enforcement of the order for an appropriate period if the obligor furnishes the same security for payment of the support ordered that is required for a support order of this State.

750 ILCS 20/41

§ 41. Uniformity of interpretation

This Act shall be so construed as to effectuate its general purpose to make uniform the law of those states which enact it.

750 ILCS 20/42

§ 42. Severability

If any provision of this Act or the application thereof to any person or circumstance is held invalid, the invalidity does not affect other provisions or applications of the Act which can be given effect without the invalid provision or application, and to this end the provisions of this Act are severable.

ACT 22. UNIFORM INTERSTATE FAMILY SUPPORT ACT

ARTICLE I. GENERAL PROVISIONS

Analysis

Sec.
100. Short title.
101. Definitions.
102. Tribunal of this State.
103. Remedies cumulative.

WESTLAW Electronic Research

See WESTLAW Electronic Research Guide preceding the Summary of Contents.

---

750 ILCS 22/100

§ 100. Short title

This Act may be cited as the Uniform Interstate Family Support Act.

750 ILCS 22/101

§ 101. Definitions

In this Act:

"Child" means an individual, whether over or under the age of 18, who is or is alleged to be owed a duty of support by the individual's parent or who is or is alleged to be the beneficiary of a support order directed to the parent.

"Child support order" means a support order for a child, including a child who has attained the age of 18.

"Duty of support" means an obligation imposed or imposable by law to provide support for a child, spouse, or former spouse including an unsatisfied obligation to provide support.

"Home state" means the state in which a child lived with a parent or a person acting as parent for at least 6 consecutive months immediately preceding the time of filing of a petition or comparable pleading for support, and if a child is less than 6 months old, the state in which the child lived from birth with any of them. A period of temporary absence of any of them is counted as part of the 6–month or other period.

"Income" includes earnings or other periodic entitlements to money from any source and any other property subject to withholding for support under the law of this State.

"Income-withholding order" means an order or other legal process directed to an obligor's employer or other debtor, as defined by the Illinois Marriage and Dissolution of Marriage Act, the Non–Support of Spouse and Children Act, the Illinois Public Aid Code, and the Illinois Parentage Act of 1984, to withhold support from the income of the obligor.

"Initiating state" means a state in which a proceeding under this Act or a law substantially similar to this Act, is filed for forwarding to a responding state.

"Initiating tribunal" means the authorized tribunal in an initiating state.

"Issuing state" means the state in which a tribunal issues a support order or renders a judgment determining parentage.

"Issuing tribunal" means the tribunal that issues a support order or renders a judgment determining parentage.

"Obligee" means: (i) an individual to whom a duty of support is or is alleged to be owed or in whose favor a support order has been issued or a judgment determining parentage has been rendered; (ii) a state or political subdivision to which the rights under a duty of support or support order have been assigned or which has independent claims based on financial assistance provided to an individual obligee; or (iii) an individual seeking a judgment determining parentage of the individual's child.

"Obligor" means an individual, or the estate of a decedent: (i) who owes or is alleged to owe a duty of support; (ii) who is alleged but has not been adjudicated to be a parent of a child; or (iii) who is liable under a support order.

"Register" means to record a support order or judgment determining parentage in the appropriate Registry of Foreign Support Orders.

"Registering tribunal" means a tribunal in which a support order is registered.

"Responding state" means a state to which a proceeding is forwarded under this Act or a law substantially similar to this Act.

"Responding tribunal" means the authorized tribunal in a responding state.

"Spousal-support order" means a support order for a spouse or former spouse of the obligor.

"State" means a state of the United States, the District of Columbia, the Commonwealth of Puerto Rico, or any territory or insular possession subject to the jurisdiction of the United States. The term "state" includes an Indian tribe and includes a foreign jurisdiction that has established procedures for issuance and enforcement of support orders which are substantially similar to the procedures under this Act.

"Support enforcement agency" means a public official or agency authorized to seek:

(1) enforcement of support orders or laws relating to the duty of support;

(2) establishment or modification of child support;

(3) determination of parentage; or

(4) to locate obligors or their assets.

"Support order" means a judgment, decree, or order, whether temporary, final, or subject to modification, for the benefit of a child, a spouse, or a former spouse, which provides for monetary support, health care, arrearages, or reimbursement, and may include related costs and fees, interest, income withholding, attorney's fees, and other relief.

"Tribunal" means a court, administrative agency, or quasi-judicial entity authorized to establish, enforce, or modify support orders or to determine parentage.

750 ILCS 22/102

§ 102. Tribunal of this State

The circuit court is the tribunal of this State.

750 ILCS 22/103

§ 103. Remedies cumulative

Remedies provided by this Act are cumulative and do not affect the availability of remedies under other law.

750 ILCS 22/201   FAMILIES

ARTICLE II. JURISDICTION

Analysis

PART A. EXTENDED PERSONAL JURISDICTION

Sec.
201. Bases for jurisdiction over nonresident.
202. Procedure when exercising jurisdiction over nonresident.

PART B. PROCEEDINGS INVOLVING TWO OR MORE STATES

203. Initiating and responding tribunal of this State.
204. Simultaneous proceedings in another state.
205. Continuing, exclusive jurisdiction.
206. Enforcement and modification of support order by tribunal having continuing jurisdiction.

PART C. RECONCILIATION WITH ORDERS OF OTHER STATES

207. Recognition of child support orders.
208. Multiple child support orders for two or more obligees.
209. Credit for payments.

WESTLAW Electronic Research

See WESTLAW Electronic Research Guide preceding the Summary of Contents.

PART A. EXTENDED PERSONAL JURISDICTION

750 ILCS 22/201

§ 201. Bases for jurisdiction over nonresident

In a proceeding to establish, enforce, or modify a support order or to determine parentage, a tribunal of this State may exercise personal jurisdiction over a nonresident individual or the individual's guardian or conservator if:

(1) the individual is personally served with notice within this State;

(2) the individual submits to the jurisdiction of this State by consent, by entering a general appearance, or by filing a responsive document having the effect of waiving any contest to personal jurisdiction;

(3) the individual resided with the child in this State;

(4) the individual resided in this State and provided prenatal expenses or support for the child;

(5) the child resides in this State as a result of the acts or directives of the individual;

(6) the individual engaged in sexual intercourse in this State and the child may have been conceived by that act of intercourse;

(7) (Blank); or

(8) there is any other basis consistent with the constitutions of this State and the United States for the exercise of personal jurisdiction.

750 ILCS 22/202

§ 202. Procedure when exercising jurisdiction over nonresident

A tribunal of this State exercising personal jurisdiction over a nonresident under Section 201 may apply Section 316 to receive evidence from another state, and Section 318 to obtain discovery through a tribunal of another state. In all other respects, Articles 3 through 7 do not apply and the tribunal shall apply the procedural and substantive law of this State, including the rules on choice of law other than those established by this Act.

PART B. PROCEEDINGS INVOLVING TWO OR MORE STATES

750 ILCS 22/203

§ 203. Initiating and responding tribunal of this State

Under this Act, a tribunal of this State may serve as an initiating tribunal to forward proceedings to another state and as a responding tribunal for proceedings initiated in another state.

750 ILCS 22/204

§ 204. Simultaneous proceedings in another state

(a) A tribunal of this State may exercise jurisdiction to establish a support order if the petition is filed after a petition or comparable pleading is filed in another state only if:

(1) the petition in this State is filed before the expiration of the time allowed in the other state for filing a responsive pleading challenging the exercise of jurisdiction by the other state;

(2) the contesting party timely challenges the exercise of jurisdiction in the other state; and

(3) if relevant, this State is the home state of the child.

(b) A tribunal of this State may not exercise jurisdiction to establish a support order if the petition is filed before a petition or comparable pleading is filed in another state if:

(1) the petition or comparable pleading in the other state is filed before the expiration of the time allowed in this State for filing a responsive pleading challenging the exercise of jurisdiction by this State;

(2) the contesting party timely challenges the exercise of jurisdiction in this State; and

(3) if relevant, the other state is the home state of the child.

750 ILCS 22/205

§ 205. Continuing, exclusive jurisdiction

(a) A tribunal of this State issuing a support order consistent with the law of this State has continuing, exclusive jurisdiction over a child support order:

>(1) as long as this State remains the residence of the obligor, the individual obligee, or the child for whose benefit the support order is issued; or

>(2) until each individual party has filed written consent with the tribunal of this State for a tribunal of another state to modify the order and assume continuing, exclusive jurisdiction.

(b) A tribunal of this State issuing a child support order consistent with the law of this State may not exercise its continuing jurisdiction to modify the order if the order has been modified by a tribunal of another state pursuant to a law substantially similar to this Act.

(c) If a child support order of this State is modified by a tribunal of another state pursuant to a law substantially similar to this Act, a tribunal of this State loses its continuing, exclusive jurisdiction with regard to prospective enforcement of the order issued in this State, and may only:

>(1) enforce the order that was modified as to amounts accruing before the modification;

>(2) enforce nonmodifiable aspects of that order; and

>(3) provide other appropriate relief for violations of that order which occurred before the effective date of the modification.

(d) A tribunal of this State shall recognize the continuing, exclusive jurisdiction of a tribunal of another state which has issued a child support order pursuant to a law substantially similar to this Act.

(e) A temporary support order issued ex parte or pending resolution of a jurisdictional conflict does not create continuing, exclusive jurisdiction in the issuing tribunal.

(f) A tribunal of this State issuing a support order consistent with the law of this State has continuing, exclusive jurisdiction over a spousal support order throughout the existence of the support obligation. A tribunal of this State may not modify a spousal support order issued by a tribunal of another state having continuing, exclusive jurisdiction over that order under the law of that state.

750 ILCS 22/206

§ 206. Enforcement and modification of support order by tribunal having continuing jurisdiction

(a) A tribunal of this State may serve as an initiating tribunal to request a tribunal of another state to enforce or modify a support order issued in that state.

(b) A tribunal of this State having continuing, exclusive jurisdiction over a support order may act as a responding tribunal to enforce or modify the order. If a party subject to the continuing, exclusive jurisdiction of the tribunal no longer resides in the issuing state, in subsequent proceedings the tribunal may apply Section 316 (Special Rules of Evidence and Procedure) to receive evidence from another state and Section 318 (Assistance with Discovery) to obtain discovery through a tribunal of another state.

(c) A tribunal of this State which lacks continuing, exclusive jurisdiction over a spousal support order may not serve as a responding tribunal to modify a spousal support order of another state.

PART C. RECONCILIATION WITH ORDERS OF OTHER STATES

750 ILCS 22/207

§ 207. Recognition of child support orders

(a) If a proceeding is brought under this Act, and one or more child support orders have been issued in this or another state with regard to an obligor and a child, a tribunal of this State shall apply the following rules in determining which order to recognize for purposes of continuing, exclusive jurisdiction:

(1) If only one tribunal has issued a child support order, the order of that tribunal must be recognized.

(2) If two or more tribunals have issued child support orders for the same obligor and child, and only one of the tribunals would have continuing, exclusive jurisdiction under this Act, the order of that tribunal must be recognized.

(3) If two or more tribunals have issued child support orders for the same obligor and child, and more than one of the tribunals would have continuing, exclusive jurisdiction under this Act, an order issued by a tribunal in the current home state of the child must be recognized, but if an order has not been issued in the current home state of the child, the order most recently issued must be recognized.

(4) If two or more tribunals have issued child support orders for the same obligor and child, and none of the tribunals would have continuing, exclusive jurisdiction under this Act, the tribunal of this State may issue a child support order, which must be recognized.

(b) The tribunal that has issued an order recognized under subsection (a) is the tribunal having continuing, exclusive jurisdiction.

750 ILCS 22/208

§ 208. Multiple child support orders for two or more obligees

In responding to multiple registrations or petitions for enforcement of two or more child support orders in effect at the same time with regard to the same obligor and different individual obligees, at least one of which was

750 ILCS 22/208   **FAMILIES**

issued by a tribunal of another state, a tribunal of this State shall enforce those orders in the same manner as if the multiple orders had been issued by a tribunal of this State.

750 ILCS 22/209

§ 209. Credit for payments

Amounts collected and credited for a particular period pursuant to a support order issued by a tribunal of another state must be credited against the amounts accruing or accrued for the same period under a support order issued by the tribunal of this State.

ARTICLE III. CIVIL PROVISIONS OF GENERAL APPLICATION

Analysis

Sec.
301. Proceedings under this Act.
302. Action of minor parent.
303. Application of law of this State.
304. Duties of initiating tribunal.
305. Duties and powers of responding tribunal.
306. Inappropriate tribunal.
307. Duties of support enforcement agency.
308. Duty of Attorney General.
309. Private Counsel.
310. Duties of the Illinois Department of Public Aid.
311. Pleadings and accompanying documents.
312. Nondisclosure of information in exceptional circumstances.
313. Costs and fees.
314. Limited immunity of obligee.
315. Nonparentage as defense.
316. Special rules of evidence and procedure.
317. Communications between tribunals.
318. Assistance with discovery.
319. Receipt and disbursement of payments.

WESTLAW Electronic Research

See WESTLAW Electronic Research Guide preceding the Summary of Contents.

---

750 ILCS 22/301

§ 301. Proceedings under this Act

(a) Except as otherwise provided in this Act, this Article applies to all proceedings under this Act.

(b) This Act provides for the following proceedings:

    (1) establishment of an order for spousal support or child support pursuant to Article 4;

(2) enforcement of a support order and income-withholding order of another state without registration pursuant to Article 5;

(3) registration of an order for spousal support or child support of another state for enforcement pursuant to Article 6;

(4) modification of an order for child support or spousal support issued by a tribunal of this State pursuant to Article 2, Part B;

(5) registration of an order for child support of another state for modification pursuant to Article 6;

(6) determination of parentage pursuant to Article 7; and

(7) assertion of jurisdiction over nonresidents pursuant to Article 2, Part A.

(c) An individual obligee or a support enforcement agency may commence a proceeding authorized under this Act by filing a petition in an initiating tribunal for forwarding to a responding tribunal or by filing a petition or a comparable pleading directly in a tribunal of another state which has or can obtain personal jurisdiction over the obligor.

750 ILCS 22/302

§ 302. Action by minor parent

A minor parent or a guardian or other legal representative of a minor parent may maintain a proceeding on behalf of or for the benefit of the minor's child.

750 ILCS 22/303

§ 303. Application of law of this State

Except as otherwise provided by this Act, a responding tribunal of this State:

(1) shall apply the procedural and substantive law, including the rules on choice of law, generally applicable to similar proceedings originating in this State and may exercise all powers and provide all remedies available in those proceedings; and

(2) shall determine the duty of support and the amount payable in accordance with the law and support guidelines of this State.

750 ILCS 22/304

§ 304. Duties of initiating tribunal

Upon the filing of a petition authorized by this Act, an initiating tribunal of this State shall forward three copies of the petition and its accompanying documents:

(1) to the responding tribunal or appropriate support enforcement agency in the responding state; or

750 ILCS 22/304

(2) if the identity of the responding tribunal is unknown, to the state information agency of the responding state with a request that they be forwarded to the appropriate tribunal and that receipt be acknowledged.

750 ILCS 22/305

§ 305. Duties and powers of responding tribunal

(a) When a responding tribunal of this State receives a petition or comparable pleading from an initiating tribunal or directly pursuant to Section 301(c), it shall cause the petition or pleading to be filed and notify the obligee by first class mail where and when it was filed.

(b) A responding tribunal of this State, to the extent otherwise authorized by law, may do one or more of the following:

(1) issue or enforce a support order, modify a child support order, or render a judgment to determine parentage;

(2) order an obligor to comply with a support order, specifying the amount and the manner of compliance;

(3) order income withholding;

(4) determine the amount of any arrearages, and specify a method of payment;

(5) enforce orders by civil or criminal contempt, or both;

(6) set aside property for satisfaction of the support order;

(7) place liens and order execution on the obligor's property;

(8) order an obligor to keep the tribunal informed of the obligor's current residential address, telephone number, employer, address of employment, and telephone number at the place of employment;

(9) issue a bench warrant for an obligor who has failed after proper notice to appear at a hearing ordered by the tribunal and enter the bench warrant in any local and state computer systems for criminal warrants;

(10) order the obligor to seek appropriate employment by specified methods;

(11) award reasonable attorney's fees and other fees and costs; and

(12) grant any other available remedy.

(c) A responding tribunal of this State shall include in a support order issued under this Act, or in the documents accompanying the order, the calculations on which the support order is based.

(d) A responding tribunal of this State may not condition the payment of a support order issued under this Act upon compliance by a party with provisions for visitation.

(e) If a responding tribunal of this State issues an order under this Act, the tribunal shall send a copy of the order by first class mail to the obligee and the obligor and to the initiating tribunal, if any.

750 ILCS 22/306

§ 306. Inappropriate tribunal

If a petition or comparable pleading is received by an inappropriate tribunal of this State, it shall forward the pleading and accompanying documents to an appropriate tribunal in this State or another state and notify the obligee by first class mail where and when the pleading was sent.

750 ILCS 22/307

§ 307. Duties of support enforcement agency

(a) A support enforcement agency of this State, upon request, shall provide services to an obligee in a proceeding under this Act. This subsection does not affect any ability the support enforcement agency may have to require an application for services, charge fees, or recover costs in accordance with federal or State law and regulations.

(b) A support enforcement agency that is providing services to the obligee as appropriate shall:

(1) take all steps necessary to enable an appropriate tribunal in this State or another state to obtain jurisdiction over the obligor;

(2) request an appropriate tribunal to set a date, time, and place for a hearing;

(3) make a reasonable effort to obtain all relevant information, including information as to income and property of the parties;

(4) within 2 days, exclusive of Saturdays, Sundays, and legal holidays, after receipt of a written notice from an initiating, responding, or registering tribunal, send a copy of the notice by first class mail to the obligee;

(5) within 2 days, exclusive of Saturdays, Sundays, and legal holidays, after receipt of a written communication from the obligor or the obligor's attorney, send a copy of the communication by first class mail to the obligee; and

(6) notify the obligee if jurisdiction over the obligor cannot be obtained.

(c) This Act does not create or negate a relationship of attorney and client or other fiduciary relationship between a support enforcement agency or the attorney for the agency and the individual being assisted by the agency.

750 ILCS 22/308

§ 308. Duty of Attorney General

If the support enforcement agency is a prosecuting attorney of this State and if the Attorney General determines that the support enforcement agency is neglecting or refusing to provide services to an individual, the Attorney

750 ILCS 22/308 FAMILIES

General may order the agency to perform its duties under this Act or may provide those services directly to the individual.

750 ILCS 22/309

§ 309. Private counsel

An individual may employ private counsel to represent the individual in proceedings authorized by this Act.

750 ILCS 22/310

§ 310. Duties of the Illinois Department of Public Aid

(a) The Illinois Department of Public Aid is the state information agency under this Act.

(b) The state information agency shall:

(1) compile and maintain a current list, including addresses, of the tribunals in this State which have jurisdiction under this Act and any support enforcement agencies in this State and transmit a copy to the state information agency of every other state;

(2) maintain a register of tribunals and support enforcement agencies received from other states;

(3) forward to the appropriate tribunal in the place in this State in which the individual obligee or the obligor resides, or in which the obligor's property is believed to be located, all documents concerning a proceeding under this Act received from an initiating tribunal or the state information agency of the initiating state; and

(4) obtain information concerning the location of the obligor and the obligor's property within this State not exempt from execution, by such means as postal verification and federal or state locator services, examination of telephone directories, requests for the obligor's address from employers, and examination of governmental records, including, to the extent not prohibited by other law, those relating to real property, vital statistics, law enforcement, taxation, motor vehicles, driver's licenses, and social security.

750 ILCS 22/311

§ 311. Pleadings and accompanying documents

(a) An obligee seeking to establish or modify a support order or to determine parentage in a proceeding under this Act must verify the petition. Unless otherwise ordered under Section 312, the petition or accompanying documents must provide, so far as known, the name, residential address, and social security numbers of the obligor and the obligee, and the name, sex, residential address, social security number, and date of birth of each child for whom support is sought. The petition must be accompanied by a certified copy of any support order in effect. The petition may include any other information that may assist in locating or identifying the obligor.

(b) The petition must specify the relief sought. The petition and accompanying documents must conform substantially with the requirements imposed by the forms mandated by federal law for use in cases filed by a support enforcement agency.

750 ILCS 22/312

§ 312. Nondisclosure of information in exceptional circumstances

Upon a finding, which may be made ex parte, that the health, safety, or liberty of a party or child would be unreasonably put at risk by the disclosure of identifying information, or if an existing order so provides, a tribunal shall order that the address of the child or party or other identifying information not be disclosed in a pleading or other document filed in a proceeding under this Act.

750 ILCS 22/313

§ 313. Costs and fees

(a) The obligee may not be required to pay a filing fee or other costs.

(b) If an obligee prevails, a responding tribunal may assess against an obligor filing fees, reasonable attorney's fees, other costs, and necessary travel and other reasonable expenses incurred by the obligee and the obligee's witnesses. The tribunal may not assess fees, costs, or expenses against the obligee or the support enforcement agency of either the initiating or the responding state, except as provided by other law. Attorney's fees may be taxed as costs, and may be ordered paid directly to the attorney, who may enforce the order in the attorney's own name. Payment of support owed to the obligee has priority over fees, costs and expenses.

(c) The tribunal shall order the payment of costs and reasonable attorney's fees if it determines that a hearing was requested primarily for delay. In a proceeding under Article 6, a hearing is presumed to have been requested primarily for delay if a registered support order is confirmed or enforced without change.

750 ILCS 22/314

§ 314. Limited immunity of obligee

(a) Participation by an obligee in a proceeding before a responding tribunal, whether in person, by private attorney, or through services provided by the support enforcement agency, does not confer personal jurisdiction over the obligee in another proceeding.

(b) An obligee is not amenable to service of civil process while physically present in this State to participate in a proceeding under this Act.

750 ILCS 22/314 FAMILIES

(c) The immunity granted by this Section does not extend to civil litigation based on acts unrelated to a proceeding under this Act committed by a party while present in this State to participate in the proceeding.

750 ILCS 22/315

§ 315. Nonparentage as defense

A party whose parentage of a child has been previously determined by or pursuant to law may not plead nonparentage as a defense to a proceeding under this Act.

750 ILCS 22/316

§ 316. Special rules of evidence and procedure

(a) The physical presence of the obligee in a responding tribunal of this State is not required for the establishment, enforcement, or modification of a support order or the rendition of a judgment determining parentage.

(b) A verified petition, affidavit, document substantially complying with federally mandated forms, and a document incorporated by reference in any of them, not excluded under the hearsay rule if given in person, is admissible in evidence if given under oath by a party or witness residing in another state.

(c) A copy of the record of child support payments certified as a true copy of the original by the custodian of the record may be forwarded to a responding tribunal. The copy is evidence of facts asserted in it, and is admissible to show whether payments were made.

(d) Copies of bills for testing for parentage, and for prenatal and postnatal health care of the mother and child, furnished to the adverse party at least 10 days before trial, are admissible in evidence to prove the amount of the charges billed and that the charges were reasonable, necessary, and customary.

(e) Documentary evidence transmitted from another state to a tribunal of this State by telephone, telecopier, or other means that do not provide an original writing may not be excluded from evidence on an objection based on the means of transmission.

(f) In a proceeding under this Act, a tribunal of this State may permit a party or witness residing in another state to be deposed or to testify by telephone, audiovisual means, or other electronic means at a designated tribunal or other location in that state. A tribunal of this State shall cooperate with tribunals of other states in designating an appropriate location for the deposition or testimony.

(g) If a party called to testify at a civil hearing refuses to answer on the ground that the testimony may be self-incriminating, the trier of fact may draw an adverse inference from the refusal.

(h) A privilege against disclosure of communications between spouses does not apply in a proceeding under this Act.

(i) The defense of immunity based on the relationship of husband and wife or parent and child does not apply in a proceeding under this Act.

750 ILCS 22/317
§ 317. Communications between tribunals

A tribunal of this State may communicate with a tribunal of another state in writing, or by telephone or other means, to obtain information concerning the laws of that state, the legal effect of a judgment, decree, or order of that tribunal, and the status of a proceeding in the other state. A tribunal of this State may furnish similar information by similar means to a tribunal of another state.

750 ILCS 22/318
§ 318. Assistance with discovery

A tribunal of this State may:

(1) request a tribunal of another state to assist in obtaining discovery; and

(2) upon request, compel a person over whom it has jurisdiction to respond to a discovery order issued by a tribunal of another state.

750 ILCS 22/319
§ 319. Receipt and disbursement of payments

A support enforcement agency or tribunal of this State shall disburse promptly any amounts received pursuant to a support order, as directed by the order. The agency or tribunal shall furnish to a requesting party or tribunal of another state a certified statement by the custodian of the record of the amounts and dates of all payments received.

ARTICLE IV. ESTABLISHMENT OF SUPPORT ORDER

Analysis

Sec.
401. Petition to establish support order.

WESTLAW Electronic Research

See WESTLAW Electronic Research Guide preceding the Summary of Contents.

---

750 ILCS 22/401
§ 401. Petition to establish support order

(a) If a support order entitled to recognition under this Act has not been issued, a responding tribunal of this State may issue a support order if:

(1) the individual seeking the order resides in another state; or

(2) the support enforcement agency seeking the order is located in another state.

(b) The tribunal may issue a temporary child support order if:

(1) the obligor has signed a verified statement acknowledging parentage;

(2) the obligor has been determined by or pursuant to law to be the parent; or

(3) there is other clear and convincing evidence that the obligor is the child's parent.

(c) Upon finding, after notice and opportunity to be heard, that an obligor owes a duty of support, the tribunal shall issue a support order directed to the obligor and may issue other orders pursuant to Section 305.

ARTICLE V. DIRECT ENFORCEMENT OF ORDER OF ANOTHER STATE WITHOUT REGISTRATION

Analysis

Sec.
501. Recognition of income-withholding order of another state.
502. Administrative enforcement of orders.

WESTLAW Electronic Research

See WESTLAW Electronic Research Guide preceding the Summary of Contents.

---

750 ILCS 22/501

§ 501. Recognition of income-withholding order of another state

(a) An income-withholding order issued in another state may be sent by first class mail to the person or entity defined as the obligor's employer without first filing a petition or comparable pleading or registering the order with a tribunal of this State. Upon receipt of the order, the employer shall:

(1) treat an income-withholding order issued in another state which appears regular on its face as if it had been issued by a tribunal of this State;

(2) immediately provide a copy of the order to the obligor; and

(3) distribute the funds as directed in the withholding order.

(b) An obligor may contest the validity or enforcement of an income-withholding order issued in another state in the same manner as if the order had been issued by a tribunal of this State. Section 604 applies to the contest. The obligor shall give notice of the contest to any support enforcement agency providing services to the obligee and to:

> (1) the person or agency designated to receive payments in the income-withholding order; or

> (2) if no person or agency is designated, the obligee.

750 ILCS 22/502
§ 502. Administrative enforcement of orders

(a) A party seeking to enforce a support order or an income-withholding order, or both, issued by a tribunal of another state may send the documents required for registering the order to a support enforcement agency of this State.

(b) Upon receipt of the documents, the support enforcement agency, without initially seeking to register the order, shall consider and, if appropriate, use any administrative procedure authorized by the law of this State to enforce a support order or an income-withholding order, or both. If the obligor does not contest administrative enforcement, the order need not be registered. If the obligor contests the validity or administrative enforcement of the order, the support enforcement agency shall register the order pursuant to this Act.

ARTICLE VI. ENFORCEMENT AND MODIFICATION OF SUPPORT ORDER AFTER REGISTRATION

Analysis

PART A. REGISTRATION AND ENFORCEMENT OF SUPPORT ORDER

Sec.
601. Registration of order for enforcement.
602. Procedure to register order for enforcement.
603. Effect of registration for enforcement.
604. Choice of law.

PART B. CONTEST OF VALIDITY OR ENFORCEMENT

605. Notice of registration of order.
606. Procedure of contest validity or enforcement of registered order.
607. Contest of registration or enforcement.
608. Confirmed order.

PART C. REGISTRATION AND MODIFICATION OF CHILD SUPPORT ORDER

609. Procedure to register child support order of another state for modification.
610. Effect of registration for modification.
611. Modification of child support order of another state.
612. Recognition of order modified in another state.

WESTLAW Electronic Research
See WESTLAW Electronic Research Guide preceding the Summary of Contents.

750 ILCS 22/601 FAMILIES

PART A. REGISTRATION AND ENFORCEMENT OF SUPPORT ORDER

750 ILCS 22/601

§ 601. Registration of order for enforcement

A support order or an income-withholding order issued by a tribunal of another state may be registered in this State for enforcement.

750 ILCS 22/602

§ 602. Procedure to register order for enforcement

(a) A support order or income-withholding order of another state may be registered in this State by sending the following documents and information to the appropriate circuit court in this State:

(1) a letter of transmittal to the tribunal requesting registration and enforcement;

(2) 2 copies, including one certified copy, of all orders to be registered, including any modification of an order;

(3) a sworn statement by the party seeking registration or a certified statement by the custodian of the records showing the amount of any arrearage;

(4) the name of the obligor and, if known:

(i) the obligor's address and social security number;

(ii) the name and address of the obligor's employer and any other source of income of the obligor; and

(iii) a description and the location of property of the obligor in this State not exempt from execution; and

(5) the name and address of the obligee and, if applicable, the agency or person to whom support payments are to be remitted.

(b) On receipt of a request for registration, the registering tribunal shall cause the order to be filed as a foreign judgment, together with one copy of the documents and information, regardless of their form.

(c) A petition or comparable pleading seeking a remedy that must be affirmatively sought under other law of this State may be filed at the same time as the request for registration or later. The pleading must specify the grounds for the remedy sought.

750 ILCS 22/603

§ 603. Effect of registration for enforcement

(a) A support order or income-withholding order issued in another state is registered when the order is filed in the registering tribunal of this State.

(b) A registered order issued in another state is enforceable in the same manner and is subject to the same procedures as an order issued by a tribunal of this State.

(c) Except as otherwise provided in this article, a tribunal of this State shall recognize and enforce, but may not modify, a registered order if the issuing tribunal had jurisdiction.

750 ILCS 22/604

§ 604. Choice of law

(a) The law of the issuing state governs the nature, extent, amount, and duration of current payments and other obligations of support and the payment of arrearages under the order.

(b) In a proceeding for arrearages, the statute of limitation under the laws of this State or of the issuing state, whichever is longer, applies.

PART B. CONTEST OF VALIDITY OR ENFORCEMENT

750 ILCS 22/605

§ 605. Notice of registration of order

(a) When a support order or income-withholding order issued in another state is registered, the registering tribunal shall notify the nonregistering party. Notice must be given by first class, certified, or registered mail or by any means of personal service authorized by the law of this State. The notice must be accompanied by a copy of the registered order and the documents and relevant information accompanying the order.

(b) The notice must inform the nonregistering party:

(1) that a registered order is enforceable as of the date of registration in the same manner as an order issued by a tribunal of this State;

(2) that a hearing to contest the validity or enforcement of the registered order must be requested within 20 days after the date of mailing or personal service of the notice;

(3) that failure to contest the validity or enforcement of the registered order in a timely manner will result in confirmation of the order and enforcement of the order and the alleged arrearages and precludes further contest of that order with respect to any matter that could have been asserted; and

(4) of the amount of any alleged arrearages.

(c) Upon registration of an income-withholding order for enforcement, the registering tribunal shall notify the obligor's employer pursuant to Section 10–16.2 of the Illinois Public Aid Code, Section 706.1 of the Illinois Marriage and Dissolution of Marriage Act, Section 4.1 of the Non–Support of Spouse and Children Act, and Section 20 of the Illinois Parentage Act of 1989.

750 ILCS 22/606

§ 606. Procedure to contest validity or enforcement of registered order

(a) A nonregistering party seeking to contest the validity or enforcement of a registered order in this State shall request a hearing within 20 days after the date of mailing or personal service of notice of the registration. The nonregistering party may seek to vacate the registration, to assert any defense to an allegation of noncompliance with the registered order, or to contest the remedies being sought or the amount of any alleged arrearages pursuant to Section 607.

(b) If the nonregistering party fails to contest the validity or enforcement of the registered order in a timely manner, the order is confirmed by operation of law.

(c) If a nonregistering party requests a hearing to contest the validity or enforcement of the registered order, the registering tribunal shall schedule the matter for hearing and give notice to the parties by first class mail of the date, time, and place of the hearing.

750 ILCS 22/607

§ 607. Contest of registration or enforcement

(a) A party contesting the validity or enforcement of a registered order or seeking to vacate the registration has the burden of proving one or more of the following defenses:

(1) the issuing tribunal lacked personal jurisdiction over the contesting party;

(2) the order was obtained by fraud;

(3) the order has been vacated, suspended, or modified by a later order;

(4) the issuing tribunal has stayed the order pending appeal;

(5) there is a defense under the law of this State to the remedy sought;

(6) full or partial payment has been made; or

(7) the statute of limitation under Section 604 precludes enforcement of some or all of the arrearages.

(b) If a party presents evidence establishing a full or partial defense under subsection (a), a tribunal may stay enforcement of the registered order, continue the proceeding to permit production of additional relevant evidence, and issue other appropriate orders. An uncontested portion of the registered order may be enforced by all remedies available under the law of this State.

(c) If the contesting party does not establish a defense under subsection (a) to the validity or enforcement of the order, the registering tribunal shall issue an order confirming the order.

750 ILCS 22/608

§ 608. Confirmed order

Confirmation of a registered order, whether by operation of law or after notice and hearing, precludes further contest of the order with respect to any matter that could have been asserted at the time of registration.

PART C. REGISTRATION AND MODIFICATION OF CHILD SUPPORT ORDER

750 ILCS 22/609

§ 609. Procedure to register child support order of another state for modification

A party or support enforcement agency seeking to modify, or to modify and enforce, a child support order issued in another state shall register that order in this State in the same manner provided in Part A of this Article if the order has not been registered. A petition for modification may be filed at the same time as a request for registration, or later. The pleading must specify the grounds for modification.

750 ILCS 22/610

§ 610. Effect of registration for modification

A tribunal of this State may enforce a child support order of another state registered for purposes of modification, in the same manner as if the order had been issued by a tribunal of this State, but the registered order may be modified only if the requirements of Section 611 have been met.

750 ILCS 22/611

§ 611. Modification of child support order of another state

(a) After a child support order issued in another state has been registered in this State, the responding tribunal of this State may modify that order only if, after notice and hearing, it finds that:

(1) the following requirements are met:

(i) the child, the individual obligee, and the obligor do not reside in the issuing state;

(ii) an obligee who is a nonresident of this State seeks modification; and

(iii) the obligor is subject to the personal jurisdiction of the tribunal of this State; or

(2) an individual party or the child is subject to the personal jurisdiction of the tribunal and all of the individual parties have filed a written consent in the issuing tribunal providing that a tribunal of this State may modify the support order and assume continuing, exclusive jurisdiction over the order.

750 ILCS 22/611   **FAMILIES**

(b) Modification of a registered child support order is subject to the same requirements, procedures, and defenses that apply to the modification of an order issued by a tribunal of this State and the order may be enforced and satisfied in the same manner.

(c) A tribunal of this State may not modify any aspect of a child support order that may not be modified under the law of the issuing state.

(d) On issuance of an order modifying a child support order issued in another state, a tribunal of this State becomes the tribunal of continuing, exclusive jurisdiction.

(e) Within 30 days after issuance of a modified child support order, the party obtaining the modification shall file a certified copy of the order with the issuing tribunal which had continuing, exclusive jurisdiction over the earlier order, and in each tribunal in which the party knows that earlier order has been registered.

750 ILCS 22/612

§ 612. Recognition of order modified in another state

A tribunal of this State shall recognize a modification of its earlier child support order by a tribunal of another state which assumed jurisdiction pursuant to a law substantially similar to this Act and, upon request, except as otherwise provided in this Act, shall:

(1) enforce the order that was modified only as to amounts accruing before the modification;

(2) enforce only nonmodifiable aspects of that order;

(3) provide other appropriate relief only for violations of that order which occurred before the effective date of the modification; and

(4) recognize the modifying order of the other state, upon registration, for the purpose of enforcement.

ARTICLE VII. DETERMINATION OF PARENTAGE

Analysis

Sec.
701. Proceeding to determine parentage.

WESTLAW Electronic Research
See WESTLAW Electronic Research Guide preceding the Summary of Contents.

---

750 ILCS 22/701

§ 701. Proceeding to determine parentage

(a) A tribunal of this State may serve as an initiating or responding tribunal in a proceeding brought under this Act or a law substantially similar to this Act, to determine that the obligee is a parent of a particular child or to determine that an obligor is a parent of that child.

(b) In a proceeding to determine parentage, a responding tribunal of this State shall apply the Illinois Parentage Act of 1984, and the rules of this State on choice of law.

ARTICLE VIII. INTERSTATE RENDITION

Analysis

Sec.
801. Grounds for rendition.
802. Conditions of rendition.

WESTLAW Electronic Research

See WESTLAW Electronic Research Guide preceding the Summary of Contents.

750 ILCS 22/801

§ 801. Grounds for rendition

(a) For purposes of this article, "governor" includes an individual performing the functions of governor or the executive authority of a state covered by this Act.

(b) The governor of this State may:

(1) demand that the governor of another state surrender an individual found in the other state who is charged criminally in this State with having failed to provide for the support of an obligee; or

(2) on the demand by the governor of another state, surrender an individual found in this State who is charged criminally in the other state with having failed to provide for the support of an obligee.

(c) A provision for extradition of individuals not inconsistent with this Act applies to the demand even if the individual whose surrender is demanded was not in the demanding state when the crime was allegedly committed and has not fled therefrom.

750 ILCS 22/802

§ 802. Conditions of rendition

(a) Before making demand that the governor of another state surrender an individual charged criminally in this State with having failed to provide for the support of an obligee, the Governor of this State may require a prosecutor of this State to demonstrate that at least 60 days previously the obligee had initiated proceedings for support pursuant to this Act or that the proceeding would be of no avail.

750 ILCS 22/802   **FAMILIES**

(b) If, under this Act or a law substantially similar to this Act, the Uniform Reciprocal Enforcement of Support Act, or the Revised Uniform Reciprocal Enforcement of Support Act, the Governor of another state makes a demand that the governor of this State surrender an individual charged criminally in that state with having failed to provide for the support of a child or other individual to whom a duty of support is owed, the governor may require a prosecutor to investigate the demand and report whether a proceeding for support has been initiated or would be effective. If it appears that a proceeding would be effective but has not been initiated, the governor may delay honoring the demand for a reasonable time to permit the initiation of a proceeding.

(c) If a proceeding for support has been initiated and the individual whose rendition is demanded prevails, the governor may decline to honor the demand. If the obligee prevails and the individual whose rendition is demanded is subject to a support order, the governor may decline to honor the demand if the individual is complying with the support order.

ARTICLE IX. MISCELLANEOUS PROVISIONS

Analysis

Sec.
901. Uniformity of application and construction.
902. Short title.
903. Severability clause.
904. Effective date.
905. Repeal.
910. Conflict.
999. Effective date.

WESTLAW Electronic Research
See WESTLAW Electronic Research Guide preceding the Summary of Contents.

---

750 ILCS 22/901
§ 901. Uniformity of application and construction

This Act shall be applied and construed to effectuate its general purpose to make uniform the law with respect to the subject of this Act among states enacting it.

750 ILCS 22/902
§ 902. Short title

(See Section 100 for short title.)

750 ILCS 22/903
§ 903. Severability clause

If any provision of this Act or its application to any person or circumstance is held invalid, the invalidity does not affect other provisions or applications of this Act which can be given effect without the invalid provision or application, and to this end the provisions of this Act are severable.

750 ILCS 22/904
§ 904. Effective date

(See Section 999 for effective date.)

750 ILCS 22/905
§ 905. Repeal. (Blank)

750 ILCS 22/910
§ 910. Conflict

If there is an apparent conflict between a provision of this Act and a provision of any other law of this State, those provisions must be construed so as to give effect to both of them if possible. If the conflict is irreconcilable, the later of the provisions as passed by the General Assembly governs.

750 ILCS 22/999
§ 999. Effective date

This Act takes effect upon becoming law, except that Sections 100 through 910, Section 965, and the provisions amending Section 24 of the Revised Uniform Reciprocal Enforcement of Support Act take effect January 1, 1995.

Author's Notes

(1) **Postponement of effective date.** As of the time of this writing, an effort is being made to postpone from January 1, 1995 the effective date of the Uniform Interstate Family Support Act.

ACT 25. EXPEDITED CHILD SUPPORT ACT OF 1990

Analysis

Sec.
1. Short title.
2. Purpose.
3. Definitions.
4. Establishment of the Expedited Child Support System.
5. Actions subject to expedited child support hearings.
6. Authority of hearing officers.
7. Expedited child support hearings.
8. Authority retained by the court.
9. Judicial hearings.
10. Failure to appear.

WESTLAW Electronic Research

See WESTLAW Electronic Research Guide preceding the Summary of Contents.

750 ILCS 25/1

§ 1. **Short title**

This Act may be cited as the Expedited Child Support Act of 1990.

750 ILCS 25/2

§ 2. **Purpose**

It is the express public policy of this State to ensure the expeditious establishment, enforcement and modification of child support orders and to ensure the expeditious establishment of parentage.

Author's Notes

Analysis

1. Provisions.
2. Cross reference.

(1) **Provisions.** The Expedited Child Support Act establishes an administrative system to hasten determination of child support and parentage questions. The program provides for an Administrative Hearing Officer who occupies a managerial and advisory role, and reserves final determination for the court. Under the act, the Administrative Hearing Officer is authorized, *inter alia*, to accept voluntary agreements between the parties and recommend that the court enter such agreements, to accept voluntary admissions of parentage and recommend that the court enter an order establishing parentage, manage discovery, take testimony, and make written recommendations and proposed findings to the court based on the evidence gathered. 750 ILCS 25/6. The court retains the power to enter final orders and resolve disputed issues. 750 ILCS 25/7(e), 8. The court may enter orders consistent with the recommendations of the Administrative Hearing Officer, refer the matter back to the Administrative Hearing Officer, or hold judicial hearings as the court deems necessary. 750 ILCS 25/9.

Participating counties must offer the program to all participants of the IV-D public aid program, and may offer the program to non-participants as well. 750 ILCS 25/4(a)(1), 4(d).

(2) **Cross reference.** The expedited child support system is in use in Cook County. See Supreme Court Rules 100.1 et seq. and accompanying Author's Notes for an explanation of the system. See also IMDMA §§ 709 through 712, 750 ILCS 709-712 and accompanying Author's Notes.

750 ILCS 25/3

§ 3. **Definitions**

For the purposes of this Act, the following terms shall have the following meaning:

(a) "Administrative Hearing Officer" shall mean the person employed by the Chief Judge of the Circuit Court of each county establishing an Expedited Child Support System for the purpose of hearing child support and parentage matters and making recommendations.

(b) "Administrative expenses" shall mean, but not be limited to, the costs of personnel, travel, equipment, telecommunications, postage, space, contractual services, and other related costs necessary to implement the provisions of this Act.

(c) "Arrearage" shall mean the total amount of unpaid child support obligations.

(d) "Department" shall mean the Illinois Department of Public Aid.

(e) "Expedited child support hearing" shall mean a hearing before an Administrative Hearing Officer pursuant to this Act.

(f) "Federal time frames" shall mean the time frames established for the IV–D program in regulations promulgated by the United States Department of Health and Human Services, Office of Child Support Enforcement, (codified at 45 C.F.R. 303), for the disposition of parentage and child support cases and shall, for purposes of this Act, apply to all parentage and child support matters, whether IV–D or non-IV–D.

(g) "System" shall mean the procedures and personnel created by this Act for the expedited establishment, modification, and enforcement of child support orders, and for the expedited establishment of parentage.

(h) "IV–D program" shall mean the Child Support Enforcement Program established pursuant to Title IV, Part D of the Social Security Act, (42 U.S.C. 651 et seq.) as administered by the Illinois Department of Public Aid.

(i) "Medical support" shall mean support provided pursuant to Section 505.2 of the Illinois Marriage and Dissolution of Marriage Act.

(j) "Obligee" shall mean the individual to whom a duty of support is owed or that individual's legal representative.

(k) "Obligor" shall mean the individual who owes a duty to make payments under an order of support.

(*l*) "Plan" shall mean the plan submitted by the Chief Judge of a Judicial Circuit to the Supreme Court for the creation of an Expedited Child Support System in such circuit pursuant to this Act.

(m) "Pre-hearing motions" shall mean all motions, the disposition of which requires a court order, except motions for the ultimate relief requested in the petition to commence the action.

(n) "Recommendations" shall mean the Administrative Hearing Officer's proposed findings of fact, recommended orders and any other recommendations made by the Administrative Hearing Officer.

750 ILCS 25/4

§ 4. Establishment of the Expedited Child Support System

(a) Creation of Expedited Child Support System.

(1) Beginning July 1, 1991, an Expedited Child Support System may be established in accordance with this Act in one or more counties for

actions to establish parentage and to establish, modify, and enforce child support obligations. The System shall be available to all participants in the IV–D program, and may be made available to all persons, regardless of participation in the IV–D program, in accordance with subsection (d) of this Section.

(2) Implementation. To implement this System, the Chief Judge of any Circuit shall develop and submit to the Supreme Court a Plan for the creation of a System.

(3) The Plan. The Plan shall indicate whether the System is to be available to non-participants in the IV–D program; designate the number of Administrative Hearing Officers to be employed; describe the facilities to be made available for Expedited Child Support Hearings, including days and hours of availability; describe the procedure for presentation to a judge of contested pre-hearing motions that require a court order; describe the procedure for transmittal of recommendations to a judge; describe the procedure for action on recommendations by a judge; describe the procedure for transfer of matters from a judge to an Administrative Hearing Officer; and describe the procedure for referral of matters from an Administrative Hearing Officer to a judge. The Plan shall otherwise be in accordance with the provisions of this Act, with Supreme Court rules promulgated pursuant to this Act, and with the standards, policies and rules of the IV–D program to the extent federal reimbursement is sought. At the option of the Chief Judge, the Plan may create a circuit-wide System or may create a separate System for each county within the circuit. The Chief Judges of 2 or more contiguous judicial circuits may jointly submit a Plan that creates a single System for those judicial circuits.

(4) Supreme Court review and approval. The Supreme Court shall review and approve or modify any submitted Plan to assure that it is consistent with the standards, policies and rules of the Supreme Court, the provisions and policies of this Act, and with the standards, policies and rules of the IV–D program to the extent federal reimbursement is sought, but shall not require Department or county approval.

(5) Implementation. The System shall be administered by the Supreme Court. The Supreme Court may delegate, to the Chief Judge of each Judicial Circuit, the day-to-day administration of the System in the county or counties in such circuit in a manner consistent with the standards, policies, and rules established by the Supreme Court. Day-to-day administration includes, but is not limited to, engagement and termination of services, and periodic evaluation and assessment of work performed by all Administrative Hearing Officers.

(6) Hearing officers. At a minimum, Administrative Hearing Officers must be licensed to practice law in Illinois and shall otherwise meet the qualifications established by the Supreme Court in rules promulgated pursuant to this Act.

(7) Reporting.

(A) The Supreme Court may promulgate rules for the collection and reporting of data with respect to compliance with the Federal time frames for all counties within the State. The reports shall be submitted at such intervals as the Supreme Court may prescribe and shall otherwise be in accordance with rules promulgated by the Supreme Court pursuant to this Act.

(B) Beginning in 1992, the Supreme Court shall file with the General Assembly a report no later than April 1, of each year, describing the implementation status of this Act, which shall include, but not be limited to, an assessment of the System's effectiveness in all implementing counties, data reported pursuant to subparagraph (A) of this paragraph, and recommendations regarding continuation of the System in the implementing counties and expansion of the System into other counties.

(b) Demonstration program. The Department may establish a demonstration program in one or more counties selected by the Department for the use of the Expedited Child Support System in IV–D cases beginning July 1, 1991, or as soon thereafter as practicable. The program shall remain operative until June 30, 1994; provided, that if funds become unavailable the program shall terminate. The portion of the administrative expenses for such program attributable to use by the IV–D program which is not funded by the federal government shall be paid out of funds in the Child Support Enforcement Trust Fund as established in Section 12–10.2 of the Illinois Public Aid Code.

The Supreme Court shall notify the Chief Judge of each judicial circuit of the Department's intent to establish a demonstration program in one or more counties. Any Chief Judge may submit a demonstration Plan to the Supreme Court for its review; approval or modification pursuant to subsection (a) of this Section; and for potential submission to the Department. The demonstration Plan, in addition to the elements described in subsection (a) of this Section, shall include a projected budget for the operation of the System and may provide for participation in the System by parties who are not participants in the IV–D program provided that the portion of administrative expenses attributable to use by non-participants in the IV–D program has been appropriated by the respective county and the conditions of subsection (d) of this Section shall apply. The Department may select, after reviewing the submitted Plans, one or more counties to participate in a demonstration program and shall notify the Supreme Court of its decision.

The Department shall file, no later than April 1, 1993, an interim report assessing the effectiveness of the program in the demonstration county or counties, including specific data on the disposition of child support cases covered by this Act. The Department shall file no later than April 1, 1994, a final report updating the assessment and data provided in the interim report, making recommendations regarding continuation of the program in the participating county or counties and making recommendations regarding implementation in non-participating counties.

(c) Non-demonstration counties. Upon Supreme Court approval of a submitted Plan, any non-demonstration county, circuit or multi-circuit area may implement an Expedited Child Support System, provided that funding has been appropriated by the respective County Board or Boards for administrative expenses incurred in the establishment and maintenance of the non-IV–D portion of the System and the IV–D portion that is not subject to federal reimbursement and that a plan for cost sharing has been filed with and approved by the Department. The Chief Judge of each implementing circuit shall maintain records of the number of IV–D and non-IV–D cases pending and disposed of in the System. The administrative expenses that are subject to federal reimbursement shall be documented and recorded in such a fashion as to insure eligibility for federal reimbursement under the IV–D program. The Supreme Court shall co-operate with the Department in providing information necessary to obtain reimbursement from the federal government pursuant to the IV–D program.

(d) Use of the Expedited Child Support System when neither party is a IV–D participant. Any Plan submitted by the Chief Judge of a Judicial Circuit may provide, but may not require, that the Expedited Child Support System be available, on a case by case basis, when neither party is a participant in the IV–D program, provided that funding for administrative expenses relating to non-IV-D participants has been appropriated by the respective County Board or Boards and that a plan for cost sharing has been filed with and approved by the Department. Provided that, the petitioner may elect to file an action under this Act before the Administrative Hearing Officer; in such a case, the other party, notwithstanding any other provision of this Act, on or before the hearing date, may elect to have the case transferred for judicial hearing.

750 ILCS 25/5

§ 5. Actions subject to expedited child support hearings

(a) The Chief Judge of each Judicial Circuit that establishes a System shall delegate to the Administrative Hearing Officer the authority to hear the following actions:

(1) Petitions for child support and for medical support, pursuant to Section 505.2 of the Illinois Marriage and Dissolution of Marriage Act, for post-judgment dissolution of marriage and post-judgment parentage actions where child support or medical support was reserved or could not be ordered at the time of entry of the judgment because the court lacked personal jurisdiction over the obligor.

(2) Petitions for modification of child support and medical support in post-judgment dissolution of marriage and post-judgment parentage actions.

(3) Parentage actions, including the establishment of child support orders after parentage has been acknowledged.

(4) Actions for the enforcement of any existing order for child support or medical support in post-judgment dissolution of marriage and post-judgment parentage actions.

(5) Actions for the establishment of child support and medical support orders involving parties who are married and living separately, pursuant to Section 402 of the Marriage and Dissolution of Marriage Act.

(6) Temporary orders for support in any action in which the custodial parent is a participant in the IV-D program.

(7) Any other child support matter provided for in the Plan for the creation of the System approved by the Illinois Supreme Court.

(8) Actions brought pursuant to Article X of the Illinois Public Aid Code.

(b) Notwithstanding the provisions of subsection (a) of this Section, if the custodial parent is not a participant in the IV-D program and maintenance is in issue, the case shall be presented directly to the court.

(c) Except as provided in subsection (b), the Plan may provide that the System be available in pre-judgment proceedings for dissolution of marriage, declaration of invalidity of marriage and legal separation.

750 ILCS 25/6

§ 6. Authority of hearing officers

(a) With the exception of judicial functions exclusively retained by the court in Section 8 of this Act and in accordance with Supreme Court rules promulgated pursuant to this Act, Administrative Hearing Officers shall be authorized to:

(1) Accept voluntary agreements reached by the parties setting the amount of child support to be paid and medical support liability and recommend the entry of orders incorporating such agreements.

(2) Accept voluntary acknowledgments of parentage and recommend entry of an order establishing parentage based on such acknowledgement. Prior to accepting such acknowledgment, the Administrative Hearing Officer shall advise the putative father of his rights and obligations in accordance with Supreme Court rules promulgated pursuant to this Act.

(3) Manage all stages of discovery, including setting deadlines by which discovery must be completed; and directing the parties to submit to appropriate tests pursuant to Section 11 of the Illinois Parentage Act of 1984.

(4) Cause notices to be issued requiring the Obligor to appear either before the Administrative Hearing Officer or in court.

(5) Administer the oath or affirmation and take testimony under oath or affirmation.

(6) Analyze the evidence and prepare written recommendations based on such evidence, including but not limited to: (i) proposed findings as to the amount of the Obligor's income; (ii) proposed findings as to the amount and nature of appropriate deductions from the Obligor's income to determine the Obligor's net income; (iii) proposed findings as to the existence of relevant factors as set forth in subsection (a)(2) of Section 505 of the Illinois Marriage and Dissolution of Marriage Act, which justify setting child support payment levels above or below the guidelines; (iv) recommended orders for temporary child support; (v) recommended orders setting the amount of current child support to be paid; (vi) proposed findings as to the existence and amount of any arrearages; (vii) recommended orders reducing any arrearages to judgement and for the payment of amounts towards such arrearages; (viii) proposed findings as to whether there has been a substantial change of circumstances since the entry of the last child support order, or other circumstances justifying a modification of the child support order; and (ix) proposed findings as to whether the Obligor is employed.

(7) With respect to any unemployed Obligor who is not making child support payments or is otherwise unable to provide support, recommend that the Obligor be ordered to seek employment and report periodically of his or her efforts in accordance with such order. Additionally, the Administrative Hearing Officer may recommend that the Obligor be ordered to report to the Department of Employment Security for job search services or to make application with the local Jobs Training Partnership Act provider for participation in job search, training or work programs and, where the duty of support is owed to a child receiving support services under Article X of The Illinois Public Aid Code, the Administrative Hearing Officer may recommend that the Obligor be ordered to report to the Illinois Department of Public Aid for participation in the job search, training or work programs established under Section 9-6 of the Public Aid Code; and

(8) Recommend the registration of any foreign support judgments or orders as the judgments or orders of Illinois.

(b) In any case in which the Obligee is not participating in the IV-D program or has not applied to participate in the IV-D program, the Administrative Hearing Officer shall:

(1) inform the Obligee of the existence of the IV-D program and provide applications on request; and

(2) inform the Obligee and the Obligor of the option of requesting payment to be made through the Clerk of the Circuit Court.

If a request for payment through the Clerk is made, the Administrative Hearing Officer shall note this fact in the recommendations to the court.

(c) The Administrative Hearing Officer may make recommendations in addition to the proposed findings of fact and recommended order to which the parties have agreed.

750 ILCS 25/7
§ 7. Expedited child support hearings

(a) Service. Except as otherwise provided in this subsection and in Section 11 of this Act, the service of notice to commence an action under this Act may be made by regular mail. The notice shall be sent to the last known address of the Obligor. Parentage actions, actions for the establishment of child support orders involving parties who are married and living separately, and any other proceedings in which no court has yet acquired jurisdiction over the subject matter shall be commenced as provided in the Code of Civil Procedure and Supreme Court Rules. The notice or summons shall indicate the date set for hearing.

(b) Rules of evidence. Except as provided in this Section, the established rules of evidence shall be followed in all Expedited Child Support Hearings. A party may offer in evidence, without foundation or other proof:

(1) the Obligor's pay stubs or other employer-provided statement of gross income, deductions, and net income prepared by the employer in the usual course of business;

(2) documents provided by the Obligor's insurance company that describe the dependent care coverage available to the Obligor; and

(3) records kept by the Clerk of the Circuit Court as to payment of child support.

(c) Other domestic relations matters. Petitions for visitation, custody, distribution of property, petitions pursuant to Section 513 of the Illinois Marriage and Dissolution of Marriage Act, spousal maintenance as otherwise provided, and any domestic relations matters other than parentage and child support shall be transferred by the Administrative Hearing Officer for a judicial hearing as provided in the Plan. Transfer of such matters shall not delay the proceeding before the Administrative Hearing Officer relative to parentage or child support.

(d) Transfers for judicial hearings. All actions and matters requiring a judicial hearing, as provided for in this Act and in Supreme Court rules promulgated pursuant to this Act, shall be transferred to the court as provided in the Plan.

(e) All pre-hearing motions and other matters that require a court order, as defined in this Act and in the Supreme Court rules promulgated pursuant to this Act, shall be presented to the court for resolution and the court shall make every effort to dispose of the motion in an expeditious manner. However, if the parties are in agreement with respect to the pre-hearing motion or other matters, the Administrative Hearing Officer shall transmit a recommended order, signed by both parties, to the court.

750 ILCS 25/7   **FAMILIES**

(f) Notice to parties and transmittal of recommendations. The Administrative Hearing Officer shall provide each party with a copy of the recommendations, together with a notice informing the parties of their right to request a judicial hearing. The recommendations and notice shall be given to the parties at the time of the hearing. If either party is not present at the time of the hearing, either in person or through his or her attorney, the provisions of Section 10 of this Act shall apply. If both parties are present at the hearing and agree to the recommended order of the Administrative Hearing Officer, they shall sign the recommended order and the Administrative Hearing Officer shall transmit the recommendations to the Court as provided in the Plan.

(1) If either party does not agree to the recommended order or any part thereof, a judicial hearing shall immediately be scheduled as to those matters on which the parties disagree. The Administrative Hearing Officer shall record the date, time, and place of the judicial hearing on a notice and provide a copy of the notice to each party either in person at the time of the expedited hearing or by regular mail. The Administrative Hearing Officer shall transmit to the court a written statement indicating that the parties do not agree to all or part of the recommendations. No part of the recommendations on which the parties disagree shall be made a part of the record in court unless both parties stipulate to its admission and the court so orders. However, those matters on which the parties agree may be made a part of the record in court.

(2) If either party does not agree to the Administrative Hearing Officer's recommendations and the case is transferred for a judicial hearing, neither the parties nor the court may compel the Administrative Hearing Officer to testify at the judicial hearing.

(g) Forms. The Supreme Court may develop and provide a standard form for proposed findings and recommended orders, and any other necessary standard forms, for use by Administrative Hearing Officers in Expedited Child Support Hearings.

750 ILCS 25/8

§ 8. Authority retained by the court

The following shall be deemed judicial functions and shall only be performed by a judge or associate judge:

(a) review the recommendations of the Administrative Hearing Officer and enter such order as it deems appropriate;

(b) conduct judicial hearings on all pre-hearing motions and other matters that require a court order and enter such orders as it deems appropriate;

(c) conduct judicial hearings on all child support matters in which the parties disagree with the Administrative Hearing Officer's recommendations;

(d) conduct trials in contested parentage cases;

(e) issue body attachment orders and rules to show cause, conduct contempt proceedings, and impose such sanctions or relief as may be appropriate;

(f) conduct judicial hearings on visitation, custody, distribution of property, petitions pursuant to Section 513 of the Illinois Marriage and Dissolution of Marriage Act, spousal maintenance as otherwise provided, and any domestic relations matters other than parentage and child support;

(g) conduct judicial hearings on objections to the entry of orders pursuant to Section 10 of this Act, where the hearing has been requested by the absent party in a timely manner;

(h) conduct judicial hearings on such other matters as are provided in Supreme Court Rules promulgated pursuant to this Act; and

(i) impose sanctions pursuant to Supreme Court Rule 137.

750 ILCS 25/9

§ 9. Judicial hearings

(a) Upon receipt of any recommended order to which both parties agree, the court shall review the Administrative Hearing Officer's recommendations. The court may enter an order consistent with these recommendations, may refer the matter to the Administrative Hearing Officer for further proceedings, or may hold such additional hearing as it deems necessary.

(b) Upon receipt of a statement from the Administrative Hearing Officer indicating that the parties do not agree to the Administrative Hearing Officer's recommended order, or any part thereof, the court shall conduct a judicial hearing on those matters to which the parties do not agree and enter such orders following the hearing as it deems appropriate.

(c) A copy of all court orders shall be mailed to the parties within 5 days of entry, unless the parties were present in court at the time the order was entered, in which case the parties shall be given a copy of the order in open court. The specially certified copy of the order for withholding, if any, shall be mailed only to the Obligee or his or her attorney, and not the Obligor.

750 ILCS 25/10

§ 10. Failure to appear

(a) In any case in which the responding party fails to appear at the hearing, the Administrative Hearing Officer shall proceed to hear the case based upon the testimony of the petitioning party and other evidence presented, and shall recommend that the court enter an appropriate order. If the petitioning party agrees to the Administrative Hearing Officer's recommended order, a copy of such order signed by the petitioning party and a notice advising the absent party of his or her right to object shall be served upon the absent party in the following manner:

(1) If service to commence the proceeding before the Administrative Hearing Officer was by regular mail, the notice and recommended order shall be served in the same manner as summonses are served in other civil proceedings, or, in lieu of personal service, by certified mail, return receipt requested, mailed to the absent party's last known address. If service is made by certified mail, the return receipt shall constitute proof of service.

(2) If service to commence the proceeding before the Administrative Hearing Officer was as provided in the Code of Civil Procedure and Supreme Court Rules, the notice and recommended order shall be served by regular mail to the absent party's last known address.

(b) At any time within 14 days after the recommended order has been mailed, the absent party may file a written objection with the court to the entry of the recommended order. The court shall hold a hearing on the objection and enter the appropriate orders. If the court determines that the recommended order not be entered, the court may refer the case back to the Administrative Hearing Officer for further proceedings or may conduct a judicial hearing.

(c) If the petitioning party does not agree to the recommended order or any part thereof, a judicial hearing shall immediately be scheduled. The Administrative Hearing Officer shall record the date, time and place of the judicial hearing on a notice and provide a copy of the notice to the petitioning party at the time of the expedited hearing and to the responding party by regular mail.

ACT 30. EMANCIPATION OF MATURE MINORS ACT

Analysis

Sec.
1. Short title.
2. Purpose and policy.
3. Definitions.
3–1. Minor.
3–2. Mature minor.
3–3. Parents.
3–4. Guardian.
3–5. Petition.
4. Jurisdiction.
5. Rights and responsibilities of an emancipated minor.
6. Duration of emancipation and discharge of proceedings.
7. Petition.
8. Notice.
9. Hearing.
10. Joinder, juvenile court proceedings.
11. Appeal.

750 ILCS 30/1
§ 1. Short title.

This Act shall be known and may be cited as the Emancipation of Mature Minors Act.

750 ILCS 30/2
§ 2. Purpose and policy

The purpose of this Act is to provide a means by which a mature minor who has demonstrated the ability and capacity to manage his own affairs and to live wholly or partially independent of his parents or guardian, may obtain the legal status of an emancipated person with power to enter into valid legal contracts. This Act is not intended to interfere with the integrity of the family or the rights of parents and their children. No order of complete or partial emancipation may be entered under this Act if there is any objection by the minor, his parents or guardian. This Act does not limit or exclude any other means either in statute or case law by which a minor may become emancipated.

750 ILCS 30/3
§ 3. Definitions

Terms used in this Act, unless the context otherwise requires, have the meanings ascribed to them in Sections 3–1 through 3–5.

750 ILCS 30/3–1
§ 3–1. Minor

"Minor" means a person 16 years of age or over, and under the age of 18 years, subject to this Act.

750 ILCS 30/3–2
§ 3–2. Mature minor

"Mature minor" means a person 16 years of age or over and under the age of 18 years who has demonstrated the ability and capacity to manage his own affairs and to live wholly or partially independent of his parents or guardian.

750 ILCS 30/3–3
§ 3–3. Parents

"Parent" means the father or mother of a legitimate or illegitimate child, and includes any adoptive parent. It does not include a parent whose rights in respect to the minor have been terminated in any manner provided by law.

750 ILCS 30/3-4
§ 3-4. Guardian

"Guardian" means any person, association or agency appointed guardian of the person of the minor under the Juvenile Court Act, the Juvenile Court Act of 1987, the "Probate Act of 1975", or any other statute or court order.

750 ILCS 30/3-5
§ 3-5. Petition

"Petition" means the petition provided for in Sec. 7 of this Act, or any other petition filed under the Juvenile Court Act or the Juvenile Court Act of 1987, seeking the emancipation of a minor in accordance with the provisions of this Act.

750 ILCS 30/4
§ 4. Jurisdiction

The circuit court in the county where the minor resides, is found, owns property, or in which a court action affecting the interests of the minor is pending, may, upon the filing of a petition on behalf of the minor by his next friend, parent or guardian and after a hearing on notice to all persons as set forth in Sections 7 and 8 of this Act, enter a finding that the minor is a mature minor as defined in this Act and order complete or partial emancipation of the minor. The court in its order for partial emancipation may specifically limit the rights and responsibilities of the minor seeking emancipation.

750 ILCS 30/5
§ 5. Rights and responsibilities of an emancipated minor

(a) A mature minor ordered emancipated under this Act shall have the right to enter into valid legal contracts, and shall have such other rights and responsibilities as the court may order that are not inconsistent with the specific age requirements of the State or federal constitution or any State or federal law.

(b) A mature minor who is partially emancipated under this Act shall have only those rights and responsibilities specified in the order of the court.

750 ILCS 30/6
§ 6. Duration of emancipation and discharge of proceedings

The court shall retain continuing jurisdiction over the proceedings until the emancipated minor reaches age 18, and may modify or terminate its previous emancipation orders. However, any subsequent modification or termination of a previous order shall be effective only prospectively and shall not affect any rights, duties, obligations or causes of action existing prior to the modification or termination of any order under this Act.

750 ILCS 30/7
§ 7. Petition

The petition for emancipation shall be verified and shall set forth: (1) the age of the minor; (2) that the minor is a resident of Illinois at the time of the filing of the petition, or owns real estate in Illinois, or has an interest or is a party in any case pending in Illinois; (3) the cause for which the minor seeks to obtain partial or complete emancipation; (4) the names of the minor's parents, and the address, if living; (5) the names and addresses of any guardians or custodians appointed for the minor; (6) that the minor is a mature minor who has demonstrated the ability and capacity to manage his own affairs; and (7) that the minor has lived wholly or partially independent of his parents or guardian.

750 ILCS 30/8
§ 8. Notice

All persons named in the petition shall be given written notice 21 days prior to the hearing and shall have a right to be present and be represented by counsel.

All notices shall be served on persons named in the petition by personal service or by "certified mail, return receipt requested, addressee only". If personal service cannot be made in accordance with the provisions of this Act, substitute service or service by publication shall be made in accordance with the Civil Practice Law.

750 ILCS 30/9
§ 9. Hearing

Before proceeding to a hearing on the petition the court shall advise all persons present of the nature of the proceedings, and their rights and responsibilities if an order of emancipation should be entered.

If, after the hearing, the court determines that the minor is a mature minor who is of sound mind and has the capacity and maturity to manage his own affairs including his finances, and that the best interests of the minor and his family will be promoted by declaring the minor an emancipated minor, the court shall enter a finding that the minor is an emancipated minor within the meaning of this Act, or that the mature minor is partially emancipated with such limitations as the court by order deems appropriate. No order of complete or partial emancipation may be entered under this Act if there is any objection by the minor, his parents or guardian.

750 ILCS 30/10
§ 10. Joinder, juvenile court proceedings

The petition for declaration of emancipation may, with leave of the court, be joined with any pending litigation affecting the interests of the minor including a petition filed under the Juvenile Court Act or the Juvenile Court Act of 1987.

If any minor seeking emancipation is a ward of the court under the Juvenile Court Act or the Juvenile Court Act of 1987 at the time of the filing of the petition for emancipation, the petition shall be set for hearing in the juvenile court.

750 ILCS 30/11

§ 11. Appeal

Any judgment or order allowing or denying a complete or partial emancipation is a final order for purposes of appeal.

ACT 35. UNIFORM CHILD CUSTODY JURISDICTION ACT

Analysis

Sec.
1. Short title.
2. Purposes of Act; Construction of provisions.
3. Definitions.
4. Jurisdiction.
5. Notice and opportunity to be heard.
6. Process and notice to persons outside this State.
7. Simultaneous proceedings in other states.
8. Inconvenient forum.
9. Jurisdiction declined by reason of conduct.
10. Information under oath to be submitted to the court.
11. Additional parties.
12. Appearance of parties and the child.
13. Binding force and res judicata effect of custody judgment.
14. Recognition of out-of-state custody judgments.
15. Modification of custody judgment of another state.
16. Filing and enforcement of custody judgment of another state.
17. Registry of out-of-state custody judgments and proceedings.
18. Certified copies of custody judgment.
19. Testimony by deposition in another state.
20. Hearings and studies in another state.
21. Assistance to courts of other states.
22. Preservation of documents for use in other states.
23. Request for court records of another state.
24. International application.
25. Priority.
26. Severability.

WESTLAW Electronic Research

See WESTLAW Electronic Research Guide preceding the Summary of Contents.

750 ILCS 35/1

§ 1. Short title

This Act shall be known and may be cited as the "Uniform Child Custody Jurisdiction Act".

Author's Notes

(1) **Citation.** The Uniform Child Custody Jurisdiction Act is sometimes cited herein by its acronym "UCCJA."

750 ILCS 35/2

§ 2. Purposes of Act; Construction of provisions

(a) The general purposes of this Act are to:

1. avoid jurisdictional competition and conflict with courts of other states in matters of child custody which have in the past resulted in the shifting of children from state to state with harmful effects on their well-being;

2. promote co-operation with the courts of other states to the end that a custody judgment is rendered in that state which can best decide the case in the interest of the child;

3. assure that litigation concerning the custody of a child take place ordinarily in the state with which the child and his family have the closest connection and where significant evidence concerning his care, protection, training, and personal relationships is most readily available, and that courts of this State decline the exercise of jurisdiction when the child and his family have a closer connection with another state;

4. discourage continuing controversies over child custody in the interest of greater stability of home environment and of secure family relationships for the child;

5. deter abductions and other unilateral removals of children undertaken to obtain custody awards;

6. avoid relitigation of custody decisions of other states in this State to the extent to which the avoidance of such relitigation is feasible;

7. facilitate the enforcement of custody judgments of other states;

8. promote and expand the exchange of information and other forms of mutual assistance between the courts of this State and those of other states concerned with the same child; and

9. make uniform the law of those states which enact it.

(b) This Act shall be construed to promote the general purposes stated in this Section.

Author's Notes

Analysis

1. Purpose.
2. Cross references: Additional bases for child custody actions.

(1) **Purpose.** The UCCJA controls actions taken in interstate custody litigation. Child custody controversies present special problems when the courts of more than one state become involved. As the Supreme court explained in Thompson v. Thompson, 484 U.S. 174, 108 S.Ct. 513, 98 L.Ed.2d 512 (1988), custody orders traditionally held a unique position under the full faith and credit doctrine, which generally requires that each state give effect to other States' judicial proceedings:

> [C]ustody orders characteristically are subject to modification as required by the best interests of the child. As a consequence, some courts doubted whether custody orders were sufficiently "final" to trigger full faith and credit requirements ... and [the U.S. Supreme] Court had declined expressly to settle the question.... Even if custody orders were subject to full faith and credit requirements, the Full Faith and Credit Clause obliges States only to accord the same force to judgments as would be accorded by the courts of the State in which the judgment was entered. Because courts entering custody orders generally retain the power to modify them, courts in other States were no less entitled to change the terms of custody according to their own views of the child's best interest....
>
> [A] parent who lost a custody battle in one State had an incentive to kidnap the child and move to another State to relitigate the issue. This circumstance contributed to widespread jurisdictional deadlocks ... and more importantly, to a national epidemic of parental kidnapping.

Thompson, 484 U.S. at 180, 108 S.Ct. at 516–17, 98 L.Ed.2d at 520.

The UCCJA was enacted to "prescrib[e] uniform standards for deciding which State could make a custody determination and obligat[e] enacting States to enforce the determination made by the State with proper jurisdiction." *Thompson*, 484 U.S. at 181, 108 S.Ct. at 517, 98 L.Ed.2d at 521. The principal purposes of the UCCJA are "to avoid conflict with courts of other States, to protect the best interests of the child, and to discourage forum shopping." Levy v. Levy, 105 Ill.App.3d 355, 358, 61 Ill.Dec. 247, 250, 434 N.E.2d 400, 403 (1st Dist.1982). In addition, the Act attempts to deter unilateral removal of children to obtain custody awards. Dagher v. Dagher, 145 Ill.App.3d 379, 382, 99 Ill.Dec. 269, 271, 495 N.E.2d 1004, 1006 (1st Dist.1986).

Judges often implement the Uniform Child Custody Jurisdiction Act simply by phoning the judge in another jurisdiction to determine which court better meets the jurisdictional requirements of UCCJA § 4(a). See UCCJA § 4(a) and accompanying Author's Notes. Alexander Graham Bell himself could not want for a better use of the telephone.

(2) **Cross references: Additional bases for child custody actions.** Besides the UCCJA, there are other laws that may be involved in international or interstate custody jurisdiction disputes. These include the Hague Convention, 42 U.S.C.A. 11601 et seq.; the federal Parental Kidnapping Prevention Act, 28 U.S.C.A. 1738A et seq. (The PKPA provides that states must give full faith and credit to valid child custody determinations of sister states, however, no independent cause of action exists under the PKPA. Thompson v. Thompson, 484 U.S. 174, 108 S.Ct. 513, 98 L.Ed.2d 512 (1988)); the Indian Child Welfare Act, 25 U.S.C.A. 1901–23; state criminal statutes

such as the Illinois child abduction law, 720 ILCS 5/10–5; and tort actions for intentional interference with parent-child relationships such as custody and visitation.

750 ILCS 35/3
§ 3. Definitions

As used in this Act unless the context otherwise requires, the terms specified in Sections 3.01 through 3.10 have the meanings ascribed to them in those Sections.

3.01. "Contestant" means a person, including a parent, who claims a right to custody or visitation rights with respect to a child.

3.02. "Custody determination" means a court decision and court orders and instructions providing for the custody of a child, including visitation rights but such term does not include a decision relating to child support or any other monetary obligation of any person.

3.03. "Custody proceeding" means proceedings in which a custody determination is one of several issues, and includes child neglect and dependency proceedings.

3.04. "Home state" means the state in which the child immediately preceding the time involved lived with his parents, a parent, or a person acting as parent, for at least 6 consecutive months, and in the case of a child less than 6 months old the state in which the child lived from birth with any of the persons mentioned, however, periods of temporary absence of any of the named persons are counted as part of the 6–month or other period.

3.05. "Initial judgment" means the first custody judgment concerning a particular child.

3.06. "Judgment" or "custody judgment" means a custody determination made in a custody proceeding, and includes an initial judgment and a modification judgment.

3.07. "Modification judgment" means a custody judgment which modifies or replaces a prior judgment, whether made by the court which rendered the prior judgment or by another court.

3.08. "Physical custody" means actual possession and control of a child.

3.09. "Person acting as parent" means a person, other than a parent, who has physical custody of a child and who has either been awarded custody by a court or claims a right to custody.

3.10. "State" means any state, territory, or possession of the United States, the Commonwealth of Puerto Rico, and the District of Columbia.

750 ILCS 35/4
§ 4. Jurisdiction

(a) The circuit courts have jurisdiction to make a child custody determination by initial or modification judgment if:

1. this State

(i) is the home state of the child at the time of commencement of the proceeding, or

(ii) had been the child's home state within 6 months before commencement of the proceeding and the child is absent from this State because of his removal or retention by a person claiming his custody or for other reasons, and a parent or person acting as parent continues to live in this State; or

2. it is in the best interest of the child that a court of this State assume jurisdiction because

(i) the child and his parents, or the child and at least one contestant, have a significant connection with this State, and

(ii) there is available in this State substantial evidence concerning the child's present or future care, protection, training, and personal relationships; or

3. the child is physically present in this State and

(i) the child has been abandoned or

(ii) it is necessary in an emergency to protect the child because he has been subjected to or threatened with mistreatment or abuse or is otherwise neglected or dependent; or

4. (i) it appears that no other state would have jurisdiction under prerequisites substantially in accordance with paragraphs 1., 2., or 3., or another state has declined to exercise jurisdiction on the ground that this State is the more appropriate forum to determine the custody of the child, and

(ii) it is in the best interest of the child that this court assume jurisdiction.

(b) A court, once having obtained jurisdiction over a child, shall retain such jurisdiction unless it concedes jurisdiction to a foreign state or none of the parties to the action, including the child, remain in Illinois.

(c) Except under paragraphs 3 and 4 of subsection (a), physical presence in this State of the child, or of the child and one of the contestants, is not alone sufficient to confer jurisdiction on a court of this State to make a child custody determination.

(d) Physical presence of the child, while desirable, is not a prerequisite for jurisdiction to determine his custody.

Author's Notes

Analysis

1. Definition of jurisdiction.
2. Analysis.

3. Jurisdiction: Home state.
4. Jurisdiction: Significant connection and substantial evidence.
5. Jurisdiction: Presence in the state, abandonment and emergency situations.
6. Jurisdiction: No alternate forum.
7. Retained jurisdiction.

(1) **Definition of jurisdiction.** Jurisdiction under the UCCJA is subject matter jurisdiction in the sense of "a limitation on the existing jurisdiction conferred on the courts by the Illinois Constitution." Levy v. Levy, 105 Ill.App.3d 355, 360, 61 Ill.Dec. 247, 250, 434 N.E.2d 400, 403 (1st Dist.1982). Personal jurisdiction over either parent is not necessary under the UCCJA. In re Marriage of Schuham, 120 Ill.App.3d 339, 345–46, 76 Ill.Dec. 159, 163, 458 N.E.2d 559, 563 (1st Dist.1983). Accord, In re Marriage of Los, 229 Ill.App.3d 357, 361, 170 Ill.Dec. 584, 587, 593 N.E.2d 126, 129 (2d Dist.1992) ("personal jurisdiction is an irrelevant issue under the Custody Act") (citing In re Marriage of Bueche, 193 Ill.App.3d 594, 140 Ill.Dec. 566, 550 N.E.2d 48 (2d Dist.1990)); In re Marriage of Mobley, 210 Ill.App.3d 936, 155 Ill.Dec. 323, 569 N.E.2d 323 (5th Dist.1991) ("while it is true that personal jurisdiction is necessary to impose child support obligations ... the same is not true with regard to orders establishing or modifying custody arrangements under the Uniform Child Custody Jurisdiction Act.") (citations omitted).

(2) **Analysis.** The circuit courts of Illinois have jurisdiction under UCCJA § 4(a) if (1) Illinois is the child's home state as defined by UCCJA § 3.04; (2) it is in the child's best interest that the Illinois courts exercise jurisdiction, either because there is a significant connection with this state or because there is substantial evidence concerning the child in this state; (3) the child is physically present in this state, and has either been abandoned or needs emergency protection; or (4) no other state has jurisdiction, or another state has declined to exercise jurisdiction because it believed that Illinois is the more appropriate forum. In addition, once a state has jurisdiction over a custody matter, it retains jurisdiction, unless and until that state concedes jurisdiction to another state, or none of the parties remain in the state. UCCJA § 4(b). See Author's Note (7), below. Subject matter jurisdiction under the UCCJA cannot be established by consent of the parties. In re Marriage of Rogers, 141 Ill.App.3d 561, 95 Ill.Dec. 908, 490 N.E.2d 1000 (5th Dist.1986).

Even if jurisdiction is properly established under § 4, a court may decline jurisdiction because it is an inconvenient forum for the dispute. See UCCJA § 8 and accompanying Author's Notes.

Once a court has proper jurisdiction over the subject matter and parties in a case, the court does not lose jurisdiction before the case is resolved. For instance, in Kelly v. Warner, 119 Ill.App.3d 217, 77 Ill.Dec. 273, 460 N.E.2d 329 (3d Dist.1983), the wife argued that the Illinois court had lost jurisdiction over the custody proceeding when, following a remand from the Court of Appeals, both parties and the child had relocated to Indiana. The court held that the Illinois court was not deprived of jurisdiction although all parties lived in another state:

> [W]e do not believe that section 4(b) was intended to divest a court of jurisdiction in the midst of a custody modification proceeding based on a change in circumstances occurring after the proceeding had commenced but prior to final determination. The jurisdiction of a court over the subject matter and parties in a case, once fully attached, continues until all issues of fact and law have been decided. Once jurisdiction has been vested, it cannot be divested by subsequent events.

Generally, a court's jurisdiction ceases upon rendition of a final judgment *except for such purposes as the enforcement or correction of the judgment.* Kelly v. Warner, 119 Ill.App.3d 217, 219, 77 Ill.Dec. 273, 274, 460 N.E.2d 329, 330 (3d Dist.1983) (citing Fiore v. City of Highland Park, 93 Ill.App.2d 24, 31, 235 N.E.2d 23, 27 (2d Dist.1968), *cert. denied*, 393 U.S. 1084, 89 S.Ct. 867, 21 L.Ed.2d 776 (1969) (emphasis in original)).

(3) **Jurisdiction: Home state.** The concept of home state jurisdiction is defined in UCCJA § 3.04 as the state in which the child lived for the six months preceding "the time involved." UCCJA § 4(a)(1)(ii) refers to "6 months before *commencement of the proceeding*." (Emphasis added.) See In re Marriage of Miche, 131 Ill.App.3d 1029, 87 Ill.Dec. 72, 476 N.E.2d 774 (2d Dist.1985) (petitioner did not establish jurisdiction under § 4(a)(1)(ii); the custody proceeding commenced at the date the petition for dissolution was filed, and only three months had elapsed).

For example, the court in In re Marriage of Doehner, 215 Ill.App.3d 570, 158 Ill.Dec. 987, 574 N.E.2d 1380 (3d Dist.1991), found that North Carolina, not Illinois, was the child's home state, because the child had moved from Illinois with her father to North Carolina a full year before her mother filed a petition to modify custody. In contrast, the court in In re Custody of Bozarth, 182 Ill.App.3d 345, 131 Ill.Dec. 410, 538 N.E.2d 785 (2d Dist.1989), found that Illinois was the home state of the child at issue because she had lived in Illinois with her grandmother who was a "person acting as a parent" for at least six months prior to the filing of her father's petition to modify custody.

It is possible that no home state exists. For example, in Hollo v. Hollo, 131 Ill.App.3d 119, 85 Ill.Dec. 867, 474 N.E.2d 827 (5th Dist.1985), the child and his custodial mother moved among several states and could not establish any one state as the child's home state at the time the proceedings were commenced. The court ruled that Illinois was the appropriate forum because the child and his parents had a significant connection to Illinois, because Illinois was the only state in which all three had resided prior to the commencement of the proceedings.

(4) **Jurisdiction: Significant connection and substantial evidence.** UCCJA § 4(a)(2) grants a state jurisdiction if it is in the child's best interest that this state's courts exercise jurisdiction; either because this state has a significant connection with the child and at least one parent or other contestant, or because the state possesses substantial evidence concerning the child in this state. See Levy v. Levy, 105 Ill.App.3d 355, 362, 61 Ill.Dec. 247, 252, 434 N.E.2d 400, 405 (1st Dist.1982) (because the purpose of the UCCJA "is to limit jurisdiction rather than to proliferate it," there "must be maximum rather than minimum contact with the state," and "substantial evidence" rather than merely "some evidence" available in the state).

A significant connection may consist, *inter alia*, of present or recent residence in the state, or a prior custody proceeding in the state. See, e.g., In re Marriage of Bass, 176 Ill.App.3d 249, 125 Ill.Dec. 559, 530 N.E.2d 717 (3d Dist.1988) (Illinois had a significant connection with the children; although the children lived in Wisconsin, they had spent their entire lives in Illinois up to one year before proceedings were commenced); In re Marriage of Miche, 131 Ill.App.3d 1029, 87 Ill.Dec. 72, 476 N.E.2d 774 (2d Dist.1985) (California, not Illinois, had the more significant connection with the children; children spent majority of their lives in California, although two of the three children lived in Illinois with the petitioner father).

The determination of which state possesses more evidence concerning the child's care, education, and personal relationships is based on similar factors. See, e.g., Levy v. Levy, 105 Ill.App.3d 355, 61 Ill.Dec. 247, 434 N.E.2d 400 (1st Dist.1982) (Illinois had substantial evidence concerning the child's education, personal relationships and well-being; child had spent entire life in Illinois prior to the divorce proceeding, father and other family members remained in Illinois); Hollo v. Hollo, 131 Ill.App.3d 119, 85 Ill.Dec. 867, 474 N.E.2d 827 (5th Dist.1985) (father's "continued residence in Illinois and the fact that he represents a potential custodian indicate that there is available within this State substantial evidence concerning the child's future care").

(5) **Jurisdiction: Presence in the state, abandonment and emergency situations.** Under UCCJA § 4(c), it is not necessary for the child to be present in the state for the court to assert jurisdiction. See Hollo v. Hollo, 131 Ill.App.3d 119, 85 Ill.Dec. 867, 474 N.E.2d 827 (5th Dist.1985); In re Custody of Bozarth, 182 Ill.App.3d 345, 131 Ill.Dec. 410, 538 N.E.2d 785 (2d Dist.1989). Removal of the child from the state after the state has established proper jurisdiction does not divest the state of jurisdiction. Lewis v. Canty, 115 Ill.App.3d 306, 71 Ill.Dec. 176, 450 N.E.2d 864 (1st Dist.1983). Conversely, the child's presence alone is not enough to confer jurisdiction, except under emergency circumstances and where no other state has jurisdiction. See, e.g., Gainey v. Gainey, 237 Ill.App.3d 868, 871, 178 Ill.Dec. 427, 429, 604 N.E.2d 950, 952 (3d Dist.1992) (the "emergency jurisdiction provision is meant solely to prevent irreparable and immediate harm to children, and absent other jurisdictional prerequisites, does not confer on the State exercising emergency jurisdiction the authority to make a permanent custody determination").

(6) **Jurisdiction: No alternate forum.** Finally, Illinois may properly exercise jurisdiction if no other state has jurisdiction under the statute, or another state with proper jurisdiction deferred to the jurisdiction of Illinois. See, e.g., In re Marriage of Kehres, 164 Ill.App.3d 148, 115 Ill.Dec. 206, 517 N.E.2d 617 (5th Dist.1987) (Illinois court had jurisdiction when Virginia court determined that it would not exercise jurisdiction over dispute).

(7) **Retained jurisdiction.** Once an Illinois court has jurisdiction over a custody matter, it retains jurisdiction, unless it concedes jurisdiction to a foreign state or none of the parties remain in Illinois. UCCJA § 4(b). See, e.g., In re Marriage of Bass, 176 Ill.App.3d 249, 125 Ill.Dec. 559, 530 N.E.2d 717 (3d Dist.1988) (Illinois retained jurisdiction over custody proceedings; Illinois did not concede jurisdiction to Wisconsin, Illinois possessed substantial evidence concerning the children's future care and a significant connection to the parties). Note, however, that § 4(b) (also called the Marovitz Amendment) is strictly an Illinois amendment, and not a part of the Uniform Act. In re Marriage of Bueche, 193 Ill.App.3d 594, 140 Ill.Dec. 566, 550 N.E.2d 48 (2d Dist.1990) (Marovitz Amendment does not apply to a Michigan court modifying a Michigan decree where the Michigan court would otherwise lose jurisdiction). See also UCCJA § 15 and accompanying Author's Notes.

750 ILCS 35/5

§ 5. Notice and opportunity to be heard

Before making a judgment under this Act, reasonable notice and opportunity to be heard shall be given to the contestants, any parent whose parental rights have not been previously terminated, and any person who has physical custody of the child. If any of these persons is outside this State, notice and opportunity to be heard shall be given pursuant to Section 6.

750 ILCS 35/6

750 ILCS 35/6

§ 6. Process and notice to persons outside this State

(a) Process in initial custody proceedings shall be governed by the Civil Practice Law.

(b) Notice in all custody proceedings required for the exercise of jurisdiction over a person outside this State shall be given in a manner best calculated to give actual notice, and shall be either:

    1. by personal delivery outside this State in the manner prescribed for service of process within this State; or

    2. in the manner prescribed by the law of the place in which the service is made for service of process in that place in an action in any of its courts of general jurisdiction; or

    3. by any form of mail addressed to the person to be served and requesting a receipt; or

    4. as directed by the court if other means of notification are ineffective.

(c) Notice under this Section shall be served, mailed or delivered at least 10 days before any hearing in this State.

(d) Proof of service outside this State may be made by affidavit of the individual who made the service, or in the manner prescribed by the law of this State, the order pursuant to which the service is made, or the law of the place in which the service is made. If service is made by mail, proof may be a receipt signed by the addressee or other evidence of delivery to the addressee.

750 ILCS 35/7

§ 7. Simultaneous proceedings in other states

(a) A court of this State shall not exercise its jurisdiction under this Act if at the time of filing the petition a proceeding concerning the custody of the child was pending in a court of another state exercising jurisdiction substantially in conformity with this Act, unless the proceeding is stayed by the court of the other state because this State is a more appropriate forum or for other reasons.

(b) Before hearing the petition in a custody proceeding the court shall examine the pleadings and other information supplied by the parties under Section 10 and shall consult the child custody registry established under Section 17 concerning the pendency of proceedings with respect to the child in other states. If the court has reason to believe that proceedings may be pending in another state it shall direct an inquiry to the state court administrator or other appropriate official of the other state.

(c) If the court is informed during the course of the proceeding that a proceeding concerning the custody of the child was pending in another state before the court assumed jurisdiction it shall stay the proceeding and communicate with the court in which the other proceeding is pending to the end that the issue may be litigated in the more appropriate forum and that information be exchanged in accordance with Sections 20 through 23 of this Act. If a court of this State has made a custody judgment before being informed of a pending proceeding in a court of another state it shall immediately inform that court of the fact. If the court is informed that a proceeding was commenced in another state after it assumed jurisdiction it shall likewise inform the other court to the end that the issues may be litigated in the most appropriate forum.

750 ILCS 35/8

§ 8. Inconvenient forum

(a) A court which has jurisdiction under this Act to make an initial or modification judgment may decline to exercise its jurisdiction any time before making a judgment if it finds that it is an inconvenient forum to make a custody determination under the circumstances of the case and that a court of another state is a more appropriate forum.

(b) A finding of inconvenient forum may be made upon the court's own motion or upon motion of a party or a guardian ad litem or other representative of the child.

(c) In determining if it is an inconvenient forum, the court shall consider if it is in the interest of the child that another state assume jurisdiction. For this purpose it may take into account the following factors, among others:

    1. if another state is or recently was the child's home state;

    2. if another state has a closer connection with the child and his family or with the child and one or more of the contestants;

    3. if substantial evidence concerning the child's present or future care, protection, training, and personal relationships is more readily available in another state;

    4. if the parties have agreed on another forum which is no less appropriate; and

    5. if the exercise of jurisdiction by a court of this State would contravene any of the purposes stated in Section 2 of this Act.

(d) Before determining whether to decline or retain jurisdiction the court may communicate with a court of another state and exchange information pertinent to the assumption of jurisdiction by either court with a view to assuring that jurisdiction will be exercised by the most appropriate court and that a forum will be available to the parties.

(e) If the court finds that it is an inconvenient forum and that a court of another state is a more appropriate forum, it may dismiss the proceedings upon condition that a custody proceeding be promptly commenced in another named state or upon any other conditions which may be just and proper, including the condition that a moving party stipulate his consent and submission to the jurisdiction of the other forum.

(f) The court may decline to exercise its jurisdiction under this Act if a custody determination is incidental to an action for dissolution of marriage or another proceeding while retaining jurisdiction over the action for dissolution of marriage or other proceeding.

(g) If it appears to the court that it is clearly an inappropriate forum it may require the party who commenced the proceedings to pay, in addition to the costs of the proceedings in this State, necessary travel and other expenses, including attorneys' fees, incurred by other parties or their witnesses. Payment is to be made to the clerk of the court for remittance to the proper party.

(h) Upon dismissal or stay of proceedings under this Section the court shall inform the court found to be the more appropriate forum of this fact, or if the court which would have jurisdiction in the other state is not certainly known, shall transmit the information to the court administrator or other appropriate official for forwarding to the appropriate court.

(i) Any communication received from another state informing this State of a finding of inconvenient forum because a court of this State is the more appropriate forum shall be filed in the custody registry of the appropriate court. Upon assuming jurisdiction the court of this State shall inform the original court of this fact.

Author's Notes

Analysis

1. Forum non-convenience.
2. Bifurcated proceedings.
3. Sanctions for bringing actions in an inappropriate forum.

(1) **Forum non-convenience.** Even where a court could exercise jurisdiction pursuant to UCCJA § 4(a), it may decline to do so on a forum non-convenience basis. In order to decline jurisdiction, the court must determine that the interests of the child would be best served by having the matter heard elsewhere. The court should consider, *inter alia*, (1) if another state is or recently was the child's home state; (2) if another state has a closer connection with the child and his or her family or with the child and one or more of the contestants; (3) if substantial evidence concerning the child's present or future care, protection, training, and personal relationships is more readily available in another state; (4) if the parties have agreed on another forum which is no less appropriate; and (5) if the exercise of jurisdiction by a court of this State would contravene any of the purposes of the UCCJA.

For example, the court in In re Marriage of Breyley, 247 Ill.App.3d 486, 187 Ill.Dec. 215, 617 N.E.2d 423 (3d Dist.1993), held that Illinois was not an inconvenient forum, although the wife and child now lived in Texas. The *Breyley* court held that the child retained a significant connection with Illinois, and that conceding jurisdiction to Texas would condone the wife's removal of the child from Illinois without the court's knowledge or consent. See UCCJA § 9 and accompanying Author's Notes.

The court in In re Marriage of Doehner, 215 Ill.App.3d 570, 158 Ill.Dec. 987, 574 N.E.2d 1380 (3d Dist.1991), reversed the trial court's denial of the husband's motion to dismiss the wife's petition to modify custody which she filed in Illinois. Illinois was an inconvenient forum, the court held, because North Carolina was the child's home state, the child had developed closer connections to North Carolina, and North Carolina had greater access to relevant evidence. See also In re Marriage of Hilliard, 178 Ill.App.3d 620, 127 Ill.Dec. 671, 533 N.E.2d 543 (3d Dist.1989) (Illinois was not an inconvenient forum; motion to transfer jurisdiction was properly denied); In re Marriage of Rizza, 237 Ill.App.3d 83, 177 Ill.Dec. 353, 603 N.E.2d 134 (2d Dist.1992) (Illinois was an inconvenient forum; both parties had participated in a determination on the merits of jurisdictional claims in the courts of Louisiana).

The touchstone consideration must be a determination of what court is most able to act in the best interests of the child. In In re Marriage of Pavelcik, 138 Ill.App.3d 1060, 93 Ill.Dec. 589, 487 N.E.2d 33 (1st Dist.1985), the court stated:

> [T]he trial court is required to engage in an often difficult balancing act: while the court is obligated to act in the best interests of the child, it is called upon to exercise its discretion based upon motions filed not by the children, but by the parents. The parents' interests often do not parallel, or even approximate, the child's interests. In such circumstances, the child often becomes the pawn in a contest between the parents, to his or her detriment.... This places an even more significant responsibility on the trial court to ensure that the hearing is held in the *locus* best able to gather information requisite to the interests of the child.

In re Marriage of Pavelcik, 138 Ill.App.3d at 1065, 93 Ill.Dec. at 592, 487 N.E.2d at 36. A jurisdiction may be inconvenient to a parent who lives far away, and yet in the best interests of the child. As the Illinois Supreme Court wrote in Siegel v. Siegel, 84 Ill.2d 212, 228, 49 Ill.Dec. 298, 305, 417, N.E.2d 1312, 1319 (1981):

> [C]ontesting visitation, support and custody questions in California, rather than in Illinois [where the father resided], will be more inconvenient and costly for the father if such contests become necessary. It is, however, an unpleasant fact that, in a highly mobile society with a high incidence of marital instability, problems such as this are not infrequent.

The court is supposed to communicate its finding of forum non-convenience to the court of the state more appropriately exercising jurisdiction. The state receiving such notification is to file it in its custody registry. UCCJA § 8(h).

(2) **Bifurcated proceedings.** A court can retain jurisdiction over a dissolution of marriage proceeding but decline to hear the custody portion when another jurisdiction is the more appropriate forum to hear the custody proceeding. UCCJA § 8(f).

(3) **Sanctions for bringing actions in an inappropriate forum.** When a party has commenced proceedings in a clearly inappropriate forum, the court may require that party to pay the costs incurred by the other parties and witnesses, including travel expenses and attorney's fees. UCCJA § 8(g).

750 ILCS 35/9

§ 9. Jurisdiction declined by reason of conduct

(a) If the petitioner for an initial judgment has wrongfully taken the child from another state or has engaged in similar reprehensible conduct the court may decline to exercise jurisdiction if this is just and proper under the circumstances.

(b) Unless required in the interest of the child and subject to Section 15, paragraph (a), the court shall not exercise its jurisdiction to modify a custody judgment of another state if the petitioner, without consent of the person entitled to custody, has improperly removed the child from the physical custody of the person entitled to custody or has improperly retained the child after a visit or other temporary relinquishment of physical custody. If the petitioner has violated any other provision of a custody judgment of another state the court subject to Section 15, paragraph (a), may decline to exercise jurisdiction if this is just and proper under the circumstances.

(c) In appropriate cases a court dismissing a petition under this Section may charge the petitioner with necessary travel and other expenses, including attorneys' fees, incurred by other parties or their witnesses. Where the court finds that the petitioner has improperly removed the child from the physical custody of the person entitled to custody or has improperly retained the child after a visit or other temporary relinquishment of physical custody, the court shall notify the person entitled to custody as to the location of the child, as soon as is practicable.

Author's Notes

(1) **Denial of jurisdiction due to wrongful conduct.** A court may decline to exercise jurisdiction, even if it is a proper forum under UCCJA § 4, if the child's initial removal was wrongful. If a child is wrongfully removed from a state, the state from which he or she was removed retains jurisdiction. One of the purposes of the UCCJA is to discourage unilateral removals, see UCCJA § 2(a)(5), and the denial of jurisdiction after a parent wrongfully removes the child from the state serves to condemn such actions. It is similar to the "clean hands" concept applied to equity matters. See, e.g., In re Marriage of Breyley, 247 Ill.App.3d 486, 187 Ill.Dec. 215, 617 N.E.2d 423 (3d Dist.1993) (Illinois was not an inconvenient forum, although the wife and child now lived in Texas; conceding jurisdiction to Texas would condone the wife's removal of the child from Illinois without the court's knowledge or consent); In re Marriage of Rizza, 237 Ill.App.3d 83, 89, 177 Ill.Dec. 353, 358, 603 N.E.2d 134, 139 (2d Dist.1992) (although court "condemn[ed] in no uncertain terms" the mother's conduct of removing children from the State in violation of an Illinois court order, she was the custodial parent and therefore did not "unilaterally remove the children from Illinois for the purpose of obtaining custody").

750 ILCS 35/10

§ 10. Information under oath to be submitted to the court

(a) Every party in a custody proceeding in his first pleading or in an affidavit attached to that pleading shall give information under oath as to the child's present address, the places where the child has lived within the last 5 years, and the names and present addresses of the persons with whom the child has lived during that period. In this pleading or affidavit every party shall further declare under oath if:

1. he has participated (as a party, witness, or in any other capacity) in any other litigation concerning the custody of the same child in this or any other state;

2. he has information of any custody proceeding concerning the child pending in a court of this or any other state; and

3. he knows of any person not a party to the proceedings who has physical custody of the child or claims to have custody or visitation rights with respect to the child.

(b) If the declaration as to any of the above items is in the affirmative the declarant shall give additional information under oath as required by the court. The court may examine the parties under oath as to details of the information furnished and as to other matters pertinent to the court's jurisdiction and the disposition of the case.

(c) Each party has a continuing duty to inform the court of any custody proceeding concerning the child in this or any other state of which he obtained information during this proceeding.

Author's Notes

(1) **Content of initial pleadings.** Initial pleadings in custody and modification matters must set forth, under oath, the chronology of the child's residency for the previous five years, the petitioning party's participation in any capacity in other litigation anywhere concerning custody of the child, whether there are other persons with custody or visitation claims, and whether other proceedings involving the child are pending anywhere else.

750 ILCS 35/11

§ 11. Additional parties

If the court learns from information furnished by the parties pursuant to Section 10 or from other sources that a person not a party to the custody proceeding has physical custody of the child or claims to have custody or visitation rights with respect to the child, pursuant to an existing court order, it shall order that person to be joined as a party and to be duly notified of the pendency of the proceeding and of his joinder as a party. If the person joined as a party is outside this State he shall be served with process or otherwise notified in accordance with Section 6.

750 ILCS 35/12

§ 12. Appearance of parties and the child

(a) The court may order any party to the proceeding who is in this State or over whom the court has personal jurisdiction to appear personally before the court. If that party has physical custody of the child the court may order that he appear personally with the child. For the protection of the child's best interests, the court may appoint counsel for the child. Reasonable attorney's fees shall be assessed in an equitable manner.

(b) If a party to the proceeding whose presence is desired by the court is outside this State with or without the child the court may order that the notice given under Section 5 include a statement directing that party to appear personally with or without the child and declaring that failure to appear may result in a decision adverse to that party.

(c) If a party to the proceeding who is outside this State is directed to appear under subsection (b) or desires to appear personally before the court with or without the child, the court may require another party to pay travel and other necessary expenses of the party so appearing and of the child if that is just and proper under the circumstances.

750 ILCS 35/13
§ 13. Binding force and res judicata effect of custody judgment

A custody judgment rendered by a court of this State which had jurisdiction under Section 4 binds all parties who have been served in this State or notified in accordance with Section 6 or who have submitted to the jurisdiction of the court, and who have been given an opportunity to be heard. As to these parties the custody judgment is conclusive as to all issues of law and fact decided and as to the custody determination made unless and until that determination is modified pursuant to law, including the provisions of this Act.

750 ILCS 35/14
§ 14. Recognition of out-of-state custody judgments

The courts of this State shall recognize and enforce an initial or modification judgment of a court of another state which had assumed jurisdiction under statutory provisions substantially in accordance with this Act or which was made under factual circumstances meeting the jurisdictional standards of the Act, so long as this judgment has not been modified in accordance with jurisdictional standards substantially similar to those of this Act.

Author's Notes

(1) **Signatory states.** As of January, 1994, the UCCJA has been adopted by all states as well as the District of Columbia and the U.S. Virgin Islands. Forty-one countries have become signatories to the Hague Convention. See 42 U.S.C.A. § 11601 et seq. and accompanying Author's Notes.

750 ILCS 35/15
§ 15. Modification of custody judgment of another state

(a) If a court of another state has made a custody judgment, a court of this State shall not modify that judgment unless:

    1. it appears that the court which rendered the judgment does not have jurisdiction under jurisdictional prerequisites substantially in accordance with this Act or has declined to assume jurisdiction to modify the judgment or

    2. the court of this State has jurisdiction.

(b) In a custody proceeding involving an out-of-state party, the court, prior to modifying a custody judgment, shall consult the registry of out-of-state judgments to determine whether there exists any communications or documents alleging that the child who is the subject of custody proceedings may have been improperly removed from the physical custody of the person entitled to custody or may have been improperly retained after a visit or other temporary relinquishment of physical custody. Where the court determines the existence of any such documents or communications, the court shall direct that notice of the pending custody proceedings be provided to the out-of-state party.

(c) If a court of this State is authorized under subsection (a) and Section 9 to modify a custody judgment of another state it shall give due consideration to the transcript of the record and other documents of all previous proceedings submitted to it in accordance with Section 23.

Author's Notes

(1) **Modification.** UCCJA § 15 describes the modification process. Illinois has amended the Uniform Act, in that UCCJA § 4(b) requires that in most circumstances if Illinois initially entered the custody judgment, Illinois must decline jurisdiction before another state may exercise jurisdiction to modify the initial judgment. Moreover, UCCJA § 15 undermines the Uniform Act's goal of avoiding jurisdictional competition by accepting jurisdiction to modify another state's custody judgment if that state no longer has jurisdiction, *or*, rather than *and*, the Illinois court has jurisdiction. At the same time UCCJA § 15 limits Illinois' deference to the judgments of other states, the provisions of UCCJA § 4(b), which require Illinois to concede jurisdiction before an Illinois judgment can be modified by another state, elevate the deference that Illinois expects other states to give to Illinois judgments. These deviations from the Uniform Act encourage, rather than avoid, jurisdictional competition between the courts of Illinois and the courts of other states.

750 ILCS 35/16

§ 16. Filing and enforcement of custody judgment of another state

(a) A certified copy of a custody judgment of another state may be filed in the office of the clerk of any circuit court of this State. The clerk shall treat the judgment in the same manner as a custody judgment of a circuit court of this State. A custody judgment so filed has the same effect and shall be enforced in like manner as a custody judgment rendered by a court of this State.

(b) A person violating a custody judgment of another state which makes it necessary to enforce the judgment in this State may be required to pay necessary travel and other expenses, including attorneys' fees, incurred by the party entitled to the custody or his witnesses.

750 ILCS 35/17

§ 17. Registry of out-of-state custody judgments and proceedings

The clerk of each circuit court shall maintain a registry in which he shall enter the following:

(a) certified copies of custody judgments of other states received for filing;

(b) communications as to the pendency of custody proceedings in other states;

(c) communications concerning a finding of inconvenient forum by a court of another state;

(d) communications or documents concerning a child who may have been improperly removed from the physical custody of the person entitled to custody or may have been improperly retained after a visit or other temporary relinquishment of physical custody; and

(e) other communications or documents concerning custody proceedings in another state which may affect the jurisdiction of a court of this State or the disposition to be made by it in a custody proceeding.

The clerk of the court may provide for a schedule of fees for the registration of such judgments, communications or documents.

Author's Notes

(1) **Registry of out-of-state judgments.** Each state is to maintain a registry of out-of-state custody judgments. The registry also should contain other documents and communications relevant to the jurisdiction of custody matters. Only when the out-of-state judgment is registered may it be enforced by the courts of Illinois. See, e.g., In re Marriage of Alush, 172 Ill.App.3d 646, 122 Ill.Dec. 694, 527 N.E.2d 66 (2d Dist.1988) (wife was improperly held in contempt for violation of foreign custody decree when conduct occurred prior to the recognition of the decree by the Illinois courts); UCCJA § 14. Under the language of UCCJA § 16, the terms recognition and registration are interchangeable.

750 ILCS 35/18

§ 18. Certified copies of custody judgment

The clerk of a circuit court of this State, at the request of the court of another state or at the request of any person who is affected by or has a legitimate interest in a custody judgment, shall certify and forward a copy of the judgment to that court or person.

The clerk of the court may charge a customary fee for such certification.

750 ILCS 35/19

§ 19. Testimony by deposition in another state

In addition to other procedural devices available to a party any party to the proceeding or a guardian ad litem or other representative of the child may adduce testimony of witnesses, including parties and the child, by evidence or discovery deposition or otherwise, in another state. The court on its own motion may direct that the testimony of a person be taken in another state and may prescribe the manner in which and the terms upon which the testimony shall be taken.

750 ILCS 35/20

§ 20. Hearings and studies in another state

(a) A court of this State may request the appropriate court of another state to hold a hearing to adduce evidence, to order a party to produce or give evidence under other procedures of that state, or to have social studies made with respect to the custody of a child involved in proceedings pending in the court of this State; and to forward to the court of this State certified copies of the transcript of the record of the hearing, the evidence otherwise adduced, or any social studies prepared in compliance with the request. The cost of the services may be assessed against the parties or, if necessary, ordered paid by the county.

(b) A court of this State may request the appropriate court of another state to order a party to custody proceedings pending in the court of this State to appear in the proceedings, and if that party has physical custody of the child, to appear with the child. The request may state that travel and other necessary expenses of the party and of the child whose appearance is desired will be assessed against another party or will otherwise be paid.

Author's Notes

(1) **Assistance among courts.** Courts may ask for assistance from, and shall give assistance to, courts of other states in the process of gathering the information and eliciting the evidence needed to make custody determinations. This includes ordering depositions in other states, holding hearings, processing home studies, and forwarding records and reports to the state having jurisdiction to hear the custody matter. See also UCCJA §§ 19 and 21.

750 ILCS 35/21

§ 21. Assistance to courts of other states

(a) Upon request of the court of another state the circuit courts of this State may order a person in this State to appear at a hearing to adduce evidence or to produce or give evidence under other procedures available in this State or may order social studies to be made for use in a custody proceeding in another state. A certified copy of the transcript of the record of the hearing or the evidence otherwise adduced and any social studies prepared shall be forwarded by the clerk of the court to the requesting court.

(b) A person within this State may voluntarily give his testimony or statement in this State for use in a custody proceeding outside this State.

(c) Upon request of the court of another state a circuit court of this State may order a person in this State to appear alone or with the child in a custody proceeding in another state. The court may condition compliance with the request upon assurance by the other state that travel and other necessary expenses will be advanced or reimbursed.

750 ILCS 35/22

§ 22. Preservation of documents for use in other states

In any custody proceeding in this State the court shall preserve the pleadings, orders and judgments, any record that has been made of its hearings, social studies, and other pertinent documents until the child reaches 21 years of age. Upon appropriate request of the court of another state the court shall forward to the other court certified copies of any or all of such documents.

750 ILCS 35/23

§ 23. Request for court records of another state

If a custody judgment has been rendered in another state concerning a child involved in a custody proceeding pending in a court of this State, the court of this State upon taking jurisdiction of the case shall request of the court of the other state a certified copy of the transcript of any court record and other documents mentioned in Section 22.

750 ILCS 35/24

§ 24. International application

The general policies of this Act extend to the international area. The provisions of this Act relating to the recognition and enforcement of custody judgments of other states apply to custody judgments and judgments involving legal institutions similar in nature to custody institutions rendered by appropriate authorities of other nations if reasonable notice and opportunity to be heard were given to all affected persons.

Author's Notes

(1) **International custody disputes.** The Hague Convention, 42 U.S.C.A. § 11601, et seq., applies to international custody jurisdictional disputes (provided the countries involved are signatories to the agreement); and so does the Uniform Child Custody Jurisdiction Act, so long as the legal institutions of the other country are similar, and the procedures followed in the other country in reaching a custody adjudication resemble ours as to reasonable notice and an opportunity to be heard. See, e.g., In re Marriage of Silvestri–Gagliardoni, 186 Ill.App.3d 46, 134 Ill.Dec. 106, 542 N.E.2d 106 (1st Dist.1989) ("the UCCJA compels Illinois courts not only to recognize proper custody decrees from foreign nations, but also that they must decline to accept jurisdiction to modify custody decrees in the absence of the showing of conditions in the custodial household that are physically or emotionally harmful to the child").

750 ILCS 35/25

§ 25. Priority

Upon the request of a party to a custody proceeding which raises a question of existence or exercise of jurisdiction under this Act the case shall be given calendar priority and handled expeditiously.

Author's Notes

(1) **Priority of custody hearings.** When getting a court date from a clerk, it is important to mention that it is a custody matter involving a jurisdictional question, because the courts are supposed to hear such cases on an expedited basis.

750 ILCS 35/26

§ 26. Severability

If any provision of this Act or the application thereof to any person or circumstance is held invalid, its invalidity does not affect other provisions or applications of the Act which can be given effect without the invalid provision or application, and to this end the provisions of this Act are severable.

ACT 40. ILLINOIS PARENTAGE ACT

Analysis

Sec.
1. Short title.
2. Child born as result of artificial insemination; Treatment as naturally conceived legitimate child.
3. Husband of wife artificially inseminated; Treatment as natural father.

WESTLAW Electronic Research

See WESTLAW Electronic Research Guide preceding the Summary of Contents.

---

750 ILCS 40/1

§ 1. Short title

This Act may be cited as the Illinois Parentage Act.

750 ILCS 40/2

§ 2. Child born as result of artificial insemination; Treatment as naturally conceived legitimate child

Any child or children born as the result of heterologous artificial insemination shall be considered at law in all respects the same as a naturally conceived legitimate child of the husband and wife so requesting and consenting to the use of such technique.

750 ILCS 40/3

§ 3. Husband of wife artificially inseminated; Treatment as natural father

(a) If, under the supervision of a licensed physician and with the consent of her husband, a wife is inseminated artificially with semen donated by a man not her husband, the husband shall be treated in law as if he were the natural father of a child thereby conceived. The husband's consent must be in writing executed and acknowledged by both the husband and wife. The physician who is to perform the technique shall certify their signatures and the date of the insemination, and file the husband's consent in the medical record where it shall be kept confidential and held by the patient's physician. However, the physician's failure to do so shall not affect the legal relationship between father and child. All papers and records pertaining to the insemination, whether part of the permanent medical record held by the physician or not, are subject to inspection only upon an order of the court for good cause shown.

(b) The donor of semen provided to a licensed physician for use in artificial insemination of a woman other than the donor's wife shall be treated in law as if he were not the natural father of a child thereby conceived.

ACT 45. ILLINOIS PARENTAGE ACT OF 1984

Analysis

Sec.
1. Short title.
1.1 Public policy.
2. Parent and child relationship defined.
3. Relationship and support not dependent on marriage.
3.1 Minor parent obligation.
4. How parent and child relationship established.
5. Presumption of paternity.
6. Establishment of parent and child relationship by consent of the parties.
7. Determination of father and child relationship; Who may bring action; Parties.
8. Statute of limitations.
9. Jurisdiction; Venue.
9.1 Notice to presumed father.
10. Pre-trial proceedings.
11. Blood tests.
12. Pre-trial recommendations.
12.1 Settlement orders.
13. Civil action; Jury.
14. Judgment.
15. Enforcement of judgment or order.
15.1 Unemployed persons owing duty of support.
15.2 Order of protection; Status.
16. Modification of judgment.
17. Costs.
18. Right to counsel; Free transcript on appeal.
19. Action to declare mother and child relationship.
20. Withholding of income to secure payment of support.
21. Support payments—Duties of person or agencies receiving or disbursing support monies.
22. Public Aid collection fee.
23. Notice to clerk of circuit court of payment received by Illinois Department of Public Aid for recording.
25. Savings clause.
26. Severability.

750 ILCS 45/1
§ 1. Short title
This Act shall be known and may be cited as the "Illinois Parentage Act of 1984".

750 ILCS 45/1.1
§ 1.1 Public policy
Illinois recognizes the right of every child to the physical, mental, emotional and monetary support of his or her parents under this Act.

750 ILCS 45/2
§ 2. Parent and child relationship defined
As used in this Act, "parent and child relationship" means the legal relationship existing between a child and his natural or adoptive parents incident to which the law confers or imposes rights, privileges, duties, and obligations. It includes the mother and child relationship and the father and child relationship.

750 ILCS 45/3
§ 3. Relationship and support not dependent on marriage
The parent and child relationship, including support obligations, extends equally to every child and to every parent, regardless of the marital status of the parents.

750 ILCS 45/3.1
§ 3.1 Minor parent obligation
A child's mother or a person found to be the father of a child under this Act, is not relieved of support and maintenance obligations to the child because he or she is a minor.

750 ILCS 45/4
§ 4. How parent and child relationship established
The parent and child relationship between a child and

(1) the natural mother may be established by proof of her having given birth to the child, or under this Act;

(2) the natural father may be established under this Act;

750 ILCS 45/4

(3) an adoptive parent may be established by proof of adoption, or by records established pursuant to Section 16 of the "Vital Records Act", approved August 8, 1961, as amended.

750 ILCS 45/5

§ 5. Presumption of paternity

(a) A man is presumed to be the natural father of a child if:

(1) he and the child's natural mother are or have been married to each other, even though the marriage is or could be declared invalid, and the child is born or conceived during such marriage; or

(2) after the child's birth, he and the child's natural mother have married each other, even though the marriage is or could be declared invalid, and he is named, with his consent, as the child's father on the child's birth certificate pursuant to Section 12 of the "Vital Records Act", approved August 8, 1961, as amended.

(b) A presumption under this Section may be rebutted only by clear and convincing evidence.

750 ILCS 45/6

§ 6. Establishment of parent and child relationship by consent of the parties

(a) A parent and child relationship may be established pursuant to a verified petition filed with the clerk of the appropriate circuit court. The petition shall state the names and dates and places of birth of the parents and the name and date and place of birth of the child. The petition shall be signed by:

(1) the father; and

(2) the mother; and

(3) the guardian of the child, if different from the mother or father; and

(4) any man presumed under Section 5 of this Act to be the child's father, if different from the father signing the petition; except that in lieu of the presumed father's signature, the mother may attach an affidavit stating that she has complied with the notice provision of Section 9.1 of this Act; and

(5) a parent or guardian of a father, presumed father or mother who is not of legal age; unless the father, presumed father, or mother is emancipated pursuant to the Emancipation of Mature Minors Act, as amended. The signature shall be made only in such person's capacity as parent or guardian.

(b) The petition shall ask that the circuit court enter an order establishing the existence of the parent and child relationship. The petition may ask that an order for support or that an order for visitation, custody or guardianship be entered. In any case where a public agency is providing assistance to the child, the parties requesting an order for support shall serve a copy of the petition and proposed order upon the agency. The filing and appearance fees provided under "An Act to Revise the Law in Relation to Clerks of Court", as now or hereafter amended, shall be waived for all cases in which the parent and child relationship is established by consent of the parties.

(c) A proposed order signed by the parties shall be filed with the petition.

(d) The signature of any party on a petition and proposed order filed pursuant to this Section shall constitute a waiver of service, entry of a general appearance and consent to the entry of the proposed order, for purposes of the petition.

(e) The clerk of the circuit court shall make available suggested legal forms for proceeding under this Section.

(f) Evidence derived from proceeding under this Section shall be inadmissible against a defendant in a criminal proceeding involving the crimes of fornication under Section 11–8, adultery under Section 11–7, or criminal sexual abuse under subsection (b) of Section 12–15 of the "Criminal Code of 1961," approved July 28, 1961, as amended, wherein the defendant was a petitioner in the proceeding from which the evidence was derived.

750 ILCS 45/7

§ 7. Determination of father and child relationship; Who may bring action; Parties

(a) An action to determine the existence of the father and child relationship, whether or not such a relationship is already presumed under Section 5 of this Act, may be brought by the child; the mother; a pregnant woman; any person or public agency who has custody of, or is providing or has provided financial support to, the child; or a man presumed or alleging himself to be the father of the child or expected child. The complaint shall be verified and shall name the person or persons alleged to be the father of the child.

(b) An action to declare the non-existence of the parent and child relationship may be brought by the child, the natural mother or a man presumed to be the father under Section 5 of this Act. The complaint shall be verified. After the presumption has been rebutted, paternity of the child by another man may be determined in the same action, if he has been made a party.

(c) If any party is a minor, he or she may be represented by his or her general guardian or a guardian ad litem appointed by the court, which may include an appropriate agency. The court may align the parties.

(d) Regardless of its terms, an agreement, other than a settlement approved by the court, between an alleged or presumed father and the mother or child, does not bar an action under this Section.

(e) If an action under this Section is brought before the birth of the child, all proceedings shall be stayed until after the birth, except for service or process, the taking of depositions to perpetuate testimony, and the ordering of blood tests under appropriate circumstances.

750 ILCS 45/8
§ 8. Statute of limitations

(a) (1) An action brought by or on behalf of a child shall be barred if brought later than 2 years after the child reaches the age of majority; however, if the action on behalf of the child is brought by a public agency, it shall be barred 2 years after the agency has ceased to provide assistance to the child.

(2) An action brought on behalf of any person other than the child shall be barred if brought later than 2 years after the birth of the child. Failure to bring an action within 2 years shall not bar any party from asserting a defense in any action to declare the non-existence of the parent and child relationship.

(3) An action to declare the non-existence of the parent and child relationship shall be barred if brought later than 2 years after the petitioner obtains knowledge of relevant facts. Failure to bring an action within 2 years shall not bar any party from asserting a defense in any action to declare the existence of the parent and child relationship.

(b) The time during which any party is not subject to service of process or is otherwise not subject to the jurisdiction of the courts of this State shall toll the aforementioned periods.

(c) This Act does not affect the time within which any rights under the Probate Act of 1975, as amended, may be asserted beyond the time provided by law relating to distribution and closing of decedent's estates or to the determination of heirship, or otherwise.

750 ILCS 45/9
§ 9. Jurisdiction; Venue

(a) The circuit courts shall have jurisdiction of an action brought under this Act. In any civil action not brought under this Act, the provisions of this Act shall apply if parentage is at issue. The Court may join any action under this Act with any other civil action where applicable.

(b) The action may be brought in the county in which any party resides or is found or, if the father is deceased, in which proceedings for probate of his estate have been or could be commenced.

(c) The summons that is served on a defendant shall include the return date on or by which the defendant must appear and shall contain the following information, in a prominent place and in conspicuous language, in addition to the information required to be provided by the laws of this State: "If you do not appear as instructed in this summons, you may be required to support the child named in this petition until the child is at least 18 years old. You may also have to pay the pregnancy and delivery costs of the mother."

750 ILCS 45/9.1

§ 9.1 Notice to presumed father

(a) In any action brought under Section 6 or 7 of this Act where the man signing the petition for an order establishing the existence of the parent and child relationship by consent or the man alleged to be the father in a complaint is different from a man who is presumed to be father of the child under Section 5, a notice shall be served on the presumed father in the same manner as summonses are served in other civil proceedings or, in lieu of personal service, service may be made as follows:

(1) The person requesting notice shall pay to the Clerk of the Court a mailing fee of $1.50 and furnish to the Clerk an original and one copy of a notice together with an affidavit setting forth the presumed father's last known address. The original notice shall be retained by the Clerk.

(2) The Clerk shall promptly mail to the presumed father, at the address appearing in the affidavit, the copy of the notice, certified mail, return receipt requested. The envelope and return receipt shall bear the return address of the Clerk. The receipt for certified mail shall state the name and address of the addressee, and the date of mailing, and shall be attached to the original notice.

(3) The return receipt, when returned to the Clerk, shall be attached to the original notice, and shall constitute proof of service.

(4) The Clerk shall note the fact of service in a permanent record.

(b) The notice shall read as follows:

IN THE MATTER OF NOTICE TO _____ PRESUMED FATHER.

You have been identified as the presumed father of _____ born on _____.

The mother of the child is _____.

An action is being brought to establish the parent and child relationship between the named child and a man named by the mother, _____.

Under the law, you are presumed to be the father if (1) you and the child's mother are or have been married to each other, and the child was born or conceived during the marriage; or if (2) upon the child's birth, you and the child's mother married each other and you were named, with your consent, as the child's father on the child's birth certificate.

As the presumed father, you have certain legal rights with respect to the named child, including the right to notice of the filing of proceedings instituted for the establishment of parentage of said child. If you wish to retain your rights with respect to said child, you must file with the Clerk of this Circuit Court of _____ County, Illinois whose address is _____, Illinois, within 30

750 ILCS 45/9.1   FAMILIES

days after the date of receipt of this notice, a declaration of parentage stating that you are, in fact, the father of said child and that you intend to retain your legal rights with respect to said child, or request to be notified of any further proceedings with respect to the parentage of said child.

If you do not file such declaration of parentage, or a request for notice, then whatever legal rights you have with respect to the named child, including the right to notice of any future proceedings for the establishment of parentage of the child, may be terminated without any further notice to you. When your legal rights with respect to the named child are so terminated, you will not be entitled to notice of any future proceedings.

(c) The notice to presumed fathers provided for in this Section in any action brought by a public agency shall be prepared and mailed by such public agency and the mailing fee to the Clerk shall be waived.

750 ILCS 45/10

§ 10. Pre-trial proceedings

(a) As soon as practicable after an action to declare the existence or non-existence of the father and child relationship has been brought, and the parties are at issue, the court may conduct a pre-trial conference.

750 ILCS 45/11

§ 11. Blood tests

(a) As soon as practicable, the court or Administrative Hearing Officer in an Expedited Child Support System may, and upon request of a party shall, order or direct the mother, child and alleged father to submit to appropriate tests to determine inherited characteristics, including, but not limited to, blood types and genetic markers such as those found by Human Leucocyte Antigen (HLA) tests. If any party refuses to submit to these tests, the court may resolve the question of paternity against that party or enforce its order if the rights of others and the interests of justice so require.

(b) The tests shall be conducted by an expert or experts appointed by the court. The court shall determine the types of tests to be conducted. The expert or experts shall determine the testing procedures. However, any interested party, for good cause shown, in advance of the scheduled tests, may request a hearing to object to the types of tests, the number and qualifications of the expert or experts or the testing procedures. The expert or experts appointed by the court shall testify at the pre-test hearing at the expense of the party requesting the hearing, except as provided in subsection (h) of this Section for an indigent party. An expert not appointed by the court shall testify at the pre-test hearing at the expense of the party retaining the expert. Inquiry into an expert's qualifications at the pre-test hearing shall not affect either parties' right to have the expert qualified at trial.

(c) The expert or experts shall prepare a written report of the test results. The expert may be called by the court as a witness to testify to his or her findings and, if called, shall be subject to cross-examination by the parties. Any party may demand that other experts, qualified as examiners of blood or tissue types, perform independent tests under order of court, the results of which may be offered in evidence. The number and qualifications of the experts shall be determined by the court.

(d) Documentation of the chain of custody of the blood and tissue samples, accompanied by an affidavit or certification in accordance with Section 1–109 of the Code of Civil Procedure, is competent evidence to establish the chain of custody.

(e) The report of the blood and tissue tests prepared by the appointed expert shall be made by affidavit or by certification as provided in Section 1–109 of the Code of Civil Procedure and shall be mailed to all parties. A proof of service shall be filed with the court. The verified report shall be admitted into evidence at trial, unless a written motion challenging the admissibility of the report is filed by either party within 28 days of receipt of the report, in which case expert testimony shall be required. Before trial, the court shall determine whether the motion is sufficient to deny admission of the report by verification. Failure to make that timely motion constitutes a waiver of the right to object to admission by verification and shall not be grounds for a continuance of the hearing to determine paternity.

(f) Tests taken pursuant to this Section shall have the following effect:

(1) If the court finds that the conclusion of all the experts, as disclosed by the evidence based upon the tests, is that the alleged father is not the parent of the child, the question of paternity shall be resolved accordingly.

(2) If the experts disagree in their findings or conclusions, the question shall be weighed with other competent evidence of paternity.

(3) If the blood or tissue tests show that the alleged father is not excluded and that the combined paternity index is less than 500 to 1, this evidence shall be admitted by the court and shall be weighed with other competent evidence of paternity.

(4) If the blood or tissue tests show that the alleged father is not excluded and combined paternity index is at least 500 to 1, the alleged father is presumed to be the father, and this evidence shall be admitted. This presumption may be rebutted by clear and convincing evidence.

(g) Any presumption of parentage as set forth in Section 5 of this Act is rebutted if the court finds that the conclusion of the experts excludes paternity of the presumed father.

(h) The expense of the tests shall be paid by the party who requests the tests. Where the tests are requested by the party seeking to establish paternity and that party is found to be indigent by the court, the expense shall be paid by the public agency providing representation; except that where a public agency is not providing representation, the expense shall be paid by the county in which the action is brought. Where the tests are ordered by the court on its own motion or are requested by the alleged or presumed father and that father is found to be indigent by the court, the expense shall be paid by the county in which the action is brought. Any part of the expense may be taxed as costs in the action, except that no costs may be taxed against a public agency that has not requested the blood test.

(i) The compensation of each expert witness appointed by the court shall be paid as provided in subsection (h) of this Section. Any part of the payment may be taxed as costs in the action, except that no costs may be taxed against a public agency that has not requested the services of the expert witness.

(j) Nothing in this Section shall prevent any party from obtaining tests of his or her own blood independent of those ordered by the court or from presenting expert testimony interpreting those tests or any other blood tests ordered pursuant to this Section. Reports of all the independent tests, accompanied by affidavit or certification pursuant to Section 1–109 of the Code of Civil Procedure, and notice of any expert witnesses to be called to testify to the results of those tests shall be submitted to all parties at least 30 days before any hearing set to determine the issue of parentage.

750 ILCS 45/12

§ 12. Pre-trial recommendations

(a) On the basis of the information produced at a pretrial conference, the court shall evaluate the probability of determining the existence or non-existence of the father and child relationship in a trial and whether a judicial declaration of the relationship would be in the best interest of the child. On the basis of the evaluation, an appropriate recommendation for settlement shall be made to the parties, which may include that the alleged father consent to a finding of his paternity of the child, or that the action be dismissed with or without prejudice.

(b) If the parties accept a recommendation made in accordance with subsection (a) of this Section, judgment shall be entered accordingly.

750 ILCS 45/12.1

§ 12.1 Settlement orders

In cases where the alleged father has not consented to a finding of paternity and where the parties have requested a settlement, the court shall review the proposed settlement in light of the allegations made, the probable evidence and the circumstances of the parties. If the court is satisfied that the best interests of the child and of the parties will be served by entry of an order incorporating the settlement, and if the court is satisfied that the financial security of the child is adequately provided for and that the child and its mother are not likely to become public charges, it may enter an order so incorporating the settlement. The order may be directed to the defendant, or the mother, or both. Notwithstanding subsection (d) of Section 7 of this Act, neither the entry of a settlement order, nor the terms of a settlement order shall bar an action brought under this Act by a child to ascertain paternity.

750 ILCS 45/13

§ 13. Civil action; Jury

(a) An action under this Act is a civil action governed by the provisions of the "Code of Civil Procedure", approved August 19, 1981, as amended, and the Supreme Court rules applicable thereto, except where otherwise specified in this Act.

(b) Any party who desires a trial by jury on the issue of parentage must file a demand therefor pursuant to and within the time limits set forth in the "Code of Civil Procedure", approved August 19, 1981, as amended.

750 ILCS 45/14

§ 14. Judgment

(a) (1) The judgment shall contain or explicitly reserve provisions concerning any duty and amount of child support and may contain provisions concerning the custody and guardianship of the child, visitation privileges with the child, the furnishing of bond or other security for the payment of the judgment, which the court shall determine in accordance with the relevant factors set forth in the "Illinois Marriage and Dissolution of Marriage Act", approved September 22, 1977, as amended, and any other applicable law of Illinois, to guide the court in a finding in the best interests of the child. Specifically, in determining the amount of any child support award, the court shall use the guidelines and standards set forth in subsection (a) of Section 505 and in Section 505.2 of the Illinois Marriage and Dissolution of Marriage Act, approved September 22, 1977, as amended. For purposes of Section 505 of the Illinois Marriage and Dissolution of Marriage Act, "net income" of the non-custodial parent shall include any benefits available to that person under The Illinois Public Aid Code or from other federal, State or local government-funded programs. The court shall, in any event and regardless of the amount of the non-custodial parent's net income, in its judgment order the non-custodial parent to pay child support to the custodial parent in a minimum amount of not less than $10 per month. Subject to the limitations on actions brought on behalf of persons other than the child as provided in Section 8 of this Act, the judgment or order may direct the father to pay the reasonable expenses of the mother's pregnancy and delivery.

(2) If a judgment of parentage contains no explicit award of custody, the establishment of a support obligation or of visitation rights in one parent shall be considered a judgment granting custody to the other parent. If the parentage judgment contains no such provisions, custody shall be presumed to be with the mother; however, the presumption shall not apply if the father has had physical custody for at least 6 months prior to the date that the mother seeks to enforce custodial rights.

(b) The court shall order all child support payments, determined in accordance with such guidelines, to commence with the date summons is served. The level of current periodic support payments shall not be reduced because of payments set for the period prior to the date of entry of the support order. The Court may order any child support payments to be made for a period prior to the commencement of the action, including payments to reimburse any public agency for assistance granted on behalf of the child. In determining whether and the extent to which such payments shall be made for any prior period, the court shall consider all relevant facts, including the factors for determining the amount of support specified in the "Illinois Marriage and Dissolution of Marriage Act", approved September 22, 1977, as amended, and other equitable factors including but not limited to:

(1) the father's prior knowledge of the fact and circumstances of the child's birth;

(2) the father's prior willingness or refusal to help raise or support the child;

(3) the extent to which the mother or the public agency bringing the action previously informed the father of the child's needs or attempted to seek or require his help in raising or supporting the child;

(4) the reasons the mother or the public agency did not file the action earlier; and

(5) the extent to which the father would be prejudiced by the delay in bringing the action.

(c) Any new or existing support order entered by the court under this Section shall be deemed to be a series of judgments against the person obligated to pay support thereunder, each such judgment to be in the amount of each payment or installment of support and each such judgment to be deemed entered as of the date the corresponding payment or installment becomes due under the terms of the support order. Each such judgment shall have the full force, effect and attributes of any other judgment of this State, including the ability to be enforced.

(d) If the judgment or order of the court is at variance with the child's birth certificate, the court shall order that a new birth certificate be issued under the "Vital Records Act", approved August 8, 1961, as amended.

(e) On request of the mother and the father, the court shall order a change in the child's name. After hearing evidence the court may stay payment of support during the period of the father's minority or period of disability.

(f) If, upon proper service, the father fails to appear in court, or otherwise appear as provided by law, the court may proceed to hear the cause upon testimony of the mother or other parties taken in open court and shall enter a judgment by default. The court may reserve any order as to the amount of child support until the father has received notice, by regular mail, of a hearing on the matter.

(g) A one-time charge of 20% is imposable upon the amount of past-due child support owed on July 1, 1988 which has accrued under a support order entered by the court. The charge shall be imposed in accordance with the provisions of Section 10–21 of the Illinois Public Aid Code and shall be enforced by the court upon petition.

750 ILCS 45/15

§ 15. Enforcement of judgment or order

(a) If existence of the parent and child relationship is declared, or paternity or duty of support has been established under this Act or under prior law or under the law of any other jurisdiction, the judgment rendered thereunder may be enforced in the same or other proceedings by any party or any person or agency that has furnished or may furnish financial assistance or services to the child. Sections 14, 16 and 20 of this Act shall also be applicable with respect to entry, modification and enforcement of any support judgment entered under provisions of the "Paternity Act", approved July 5, 1957, as amended, repealed July 1, 1985.

(b) Failure to comply with any order of the court shall be punishable as contempt as in other cases of failure to comply under the "Illinois Marriage and Dissolution of Marriage Act", as now or hereafter amended. In addition to other penalties provided by law, the court may, after finding the party guilty of contempt, order that the party be:

(1) Placed on probation with such conditions of probation as the court deems advisable;

(2) Sentenced to periodic imprisonment for a period not to exceed 6 months. However, the court may permit the party to be released for periods of time during the day or night to work or conduct business or other self-employed occupation. The court may further order any part of all the earnings of a party during a sentence of periodic imprisonment to be paid to the Clerk of the Circuit Court or to the person or parent having custody of the minor child for the support of said child until further order of the court.

(c) In any post-judgment proceeding to enforce or modify the judgment the parties shall continue to be designated as in the original proceeding.

750 ILCS 45/15.1

§ 15.1 Unemployed persons owing duty of support

Whenever it is determined in a proceeding to establish or enforce a child support obligation that the person owing a duty of support is unemployed, the court may order the person to seek employment and report periodically to the court with a diary, listing or other memorandum of his or her efforts in accordance with such order. Additionally, the court may order the unemployed person to report to the Department of Employment Security for job search services or to make application with the local Jobs Training Partnership Act provider for participation in job search, training or work programs and where the duty of support is owed to a child receiving support services under Article X of The Illinois Public Aid Code, as amended, the court may order the unemployed person to report to the Illinois Department of Public Aid for participation in job search, training or work programs established under Section 9–6 of that Code.

750 ILCS 45/15.2

§ 15.2 Order of protection; Status

Whenever relief is sought under this Act, the court, before granting relief, shall determine whether any order of protection has previously been entered in the instant proceeding or any other proceeding in which any party, or a child of any party, or both, if relevant, has been designated as either a respondent or a protected person.

750 ILCS 45/16

§ 16. Modification of judgment

The court has continuing jurisdiction to modify an order for support, custody or visitation included in a judgment entered under this Act. Any custody or visitation judgment modification shall be in accordance with the relevant factors specified in the "Illinois Marriage and Dissolution of Marriage Act", approved September 22, 1977, as now or hereafter amended. Any support judgment is subject to modification or termination only in accordance with Section 510 of the Illinois Marriage and Dissolution of Marriage Act.

750 ILCS 45/17

§ 17. Costs

Except as otherwise provided in this Act, the court may order reasonable fees of counsel, experts, and other costs of the action, pre-trial proceedings, post-judgment proceedings to enforce or modify the judgment, and the appeal or the defense of an appeal of the judgment, to be paid by the parties in accordance with the relevant factors specified in Section 508 of the Illinois Marriage and Dissolution of Marriage Act, as amended.

750 ILCS 45/18

§ 18. Right to counsel; Free transcript on appeal

(a) Any party may be represented by counsel at all proceedings under this Act. In the best interests of the child, the court may appoint counsel to represent a child whose parentage is at issue.

(b) Upon the request of a mother or child seeking to establish the existence of a father and child relationship, the State's Attorney shall represent the mother or child in the trial court. If the child is an applicant for or a recipient of assistance as defined in Section 2–6 of "The Illinois Public Aid Code", approved April 11, 1967, as amended, or has applied to the Illinois Department of Public Aid for services under Article X of such Code, the Department may file a complaint in the child's behalf under this Act. The

Department shall refer the complaint to the Public Aid Claims Enforcement Division of the Office of the Attorney General as provided in Section 12–16 of "The Illinois Public Aid Code" for enforcement by the Attorney General. Legal representation by the State's Attorney or the Attorney General shall be limited to the establishment and enforcement of an order for support, and shall not extend to visitation, custody, property or other matters. If visitation, custody, property or other matters are raised by a party and considered by the court in any proceeding under this Act, the court shall provide a continuance sufficient to enable the mother or child to obtain representation for such matters.

(c) The Court shall appoint the Public Defender, or if there is no Public Defender other counsel, to represent any indigent defendant in the trial court, except that this representation shall be limited to the establishment of a parent and child relationship and an order for support, and shall not extend to visitation, custody, property, enforcement of an order for support, or other matters. If visitation, custody, property or other matters are raised by a party and considered by the court in any proceeding under this Act, the court shall provide a continuance sufficient to enable the defendant to obtain representation for such matters.

(d) The court shall furnish on request of any indigent party a transcript for purposes of appeal.

750 ILCS 45/19

§ 19. Action to declare mother and child relationship

Any interested party may bring an action to determine the existence or non-existence of a mother and child relationship. Insofar as practicable, the provisions of this Act applicable to the father and child relationship shall apply to the mother and child relationship, including, but not limited to the obligation to support.

750 ILCS 45/20

§ 20. Withholding of income to secure payment of support

(A) Definitions.

(1) "Order for support" means any order of the court which provides for periodic payment of funds for the support of a child, whether temporary or final, and includes any such order which provides for:

    (a) modification or resumption of, or payment of arrearage accrued under, a previously existing order;

    (b) reimbursement of support;

    (c) payment or reimbursement of the expense of pregnancy and delivery; or

    (d) enrollment in a health insurance plan that is available to the obligor through an employer.

(2) "Arrearage" means the total amount of unpaid support obligations.

(3) "Delinquency" means any payment under an order for support which becomes due and remains unpaid after an order for withholding has been entered under subsection (B) or, for purposes of subsection (K), after the last order for support was entered for which no order for withholding was entered.

(4) "Income" means any form of periodic payment to an individual, regardless of source, including, but not limited to: wages, salary, commission, compensation as an independent contractor, workers' compensation, disability, annuity and retirement benefits, lottery prize awards, insurance proceeds, vacation pay, bonuses, profit-sharing payments and any other payments, made by any person, private entity, federal or state government, any unit of local government, school district or any entity created by Public Act; however, "income" excludes:

(a) any amounts required by law to be withheld, other than creditor claims, including, but not limited to, federal, State and local taxes, Social Security and other retirement and disability contributions;

(b) union dues;

(c) any amounts exempted by the federal Consumer Credit Protection Act;

(d) public assistance payments; and

(e) unemployment insurance benefits except as provided by law. Any other State or local laws which limit or exempt income or the amount or percentage of income that can be withheld shall not apply.

(5) "Obligor" means the individual who owes a duty to make payments under an order for support.

(6) "Obligee" means the individual to whom a duty of support is owed or the individual's legal representative.

(7) "Payor" means any payor of income to an obligor.

(8) "Public office" means any elected official or any State or local agency which is or may become responsible by law for enforcement of, or which is or may become authorized to enforce, an order for support, including, but not limited to: the Attorney General, the Illinois Department of Public Aid, the Illinois Department of Mental Health and Developmental Disabilities, the Illinois Department of Children and Family Services, and the various State's Attorneys, Clerks of the Circuit Court and supervisors of general assistance.

(9) "Premium" means the dollar amount for which the obligor is liable to his employer and which must be paid to enroll or maintain a child in a health insurance plan that is available to the obligor through an employer.

(B) Entry of an order for withholding.

(1) Upon entry of any order for support on or after July 1, 1985, the court shall enter a separate order for withholding which shall not take effect unless the obligor becomes delinquent in paying the order for support or the

obligor requests an earlier effective date; except that the court may require the order for withholding to take effect immediately.

On or after January 1, 1989, the court shall require the order for withholding to take effect immediately, unless a written agreement is reached between both parties providing for an alternative arrangement, approved by the court, which insures payment of support. In that case, the court shall enter the order for withholding which will not take effect unless the obligor becomes delinquent in paying the order for support.

Upon entry of any order of support on or after September 11, 1989, if the obligor is not a United States citizen, the obligor shall provide to the court the obligor's alien registration number, passport number, and home country's social security or national health number, if applicable; the court shall make the information part of the record in the case.

(2) An order for withholding shall be entered upon petition by the obligee or public office where an order for withholding has not been previously entered.

(3) The order for withholding shall:

(a) direct any payor to withhold a dollar amount equal to the order for support; and

(b) direct any payor to withhold an additional dollar amount, not less than 20% of the order for support, until payment in full of any delinquency stated in the notice of delinquency provided for in subsection (C) or (F) of this Section; and

(c) direct any payor to enroll a child as a beneficiary of a health insurance plan and withhold any required premiums; and

(d) state the rights, remedies and duties of the obligor under this Section; and

(e) include the obligor's Social Security Number, which the obligor shall disclose to the court.

(4) At the time the order for withholding is entered, the Clerk of the Circuit Court shall provide a copy of the order for withholding and the order for support to the obligor and shall make copies available to the obligee and public office. Any copy of the order for withholding furnished to the parties under this subsection shall be stamped "Not Valid".

(5) The order for withholding shall remain in effect for as long as the order for support upon which it is based.

(6) The failure of an order for withholding to state an arrearage is not conclusive of the issue of whether an arrearage is owing.

(7) Notwithstanding the provisions of this subsection, if the court finds at the time of any hearing that arrearage has accrued in an amount equal to at least one month's support obligation or that the obligor is 30 days late in

paying all or part of the order for support, the court shall order immediate service of the order for withholding upon the payor.

(C) Notice of delinquency.

(1) Whenever an obligor becomes delinquent in payment of an amount equal to at least one month's support obligation pursuant to the order for support or is at least 30 days late in complying with all or part of the order for support, whichever occurs first, the obligee or public office may prepare and serve a verified notice of delinquency, together with a form petition to stay service, pursuant to paragraph (3) of this subsection.

(2) The notice of delinquency shall recite the terms of the order for support and contain a computation of the period and total amount of the delinquency, as of the date of the notice. The notice shall clearly state that it will be sent to the payor, together with a specially certified copy of the order for withholding, except as provided in subsection (F), unless the obligor files a petition to stay service in accordance with paragraph (1) of subsection (D).

(3) The notice of delinquency shall be served by ordinary mail addressed to the obligor at his or her last known address.

(4) The obligor may execute a written waiver of the provisions of paragraphs (1) through (3) of this subsection and request immediate service upon the payor.

(D) Procedures to avoid income withholding.

(1) Except as provided in subsection (F), the obligor may prevent an order for withholding from being served by filing a petition to stay service with the Clerk of the Circuit Court, within 20 days after service of the notice of delinquency; however, the grounds for the petition to stay service shall be limited to a dispute concerning: (a) the amount of current support or the existence or amount of the delinquency; or (b) the identity of the obligor.

The Clerk of the Circuit Court shall notify the obligor and the obligee or public office, as appropriate, of the time and place of the hearing on the petition to stay service. The court shall hold such hearing pursuant to the provisions of subsection (H).

(2) Except as provided in subsection (F), filing of a petition to stay service, within the 20-day period required under this subsection, shall prohibit the obligee or public office from serving the order for withholding on any payor of the obligor.

(E) Initial service of order for withholding.

(1) Except as provided in subsection (F), in order to serve an order for withholding upon a payor, an obligee or public office shall follow the procedures set forth in this subsection. After 20 days following service of the notice of delinquency, the obligee or public office shall file with the Clerk of the Circuit Court an affidavit, with the copy of the notice of delinquency attached thereto, stating:

(a) that the notice of delinquency has been duly served and the date on which service was effected; and

(b) that the obligor has not filed a petition to stay service, or in the alternative

(c) that the obligor has waived the provisions of subparagraphs (a) and (b) of this paragraph (1) in accordance with subsection (C)(4).

(2) Upon request of the obligee or public office, the Clerk of the Circuit Court shall: (a) make available any record of payment; and (b) determine that the file contains a copy of the affidavit described in paragraph (1). The Clerk shall then provide to the obligee or public office a specially certified copy of the order for withholding and the notice of delinquency indicating that the preconditions for service have been met.

(3) The obligee or public office may then serve the notice of delinquency and order for withholding on the payor, its superintendent, manager or other agent, by certified mail or personal delivery. A proof of service shall be filed with the Clerk of the Circuit Court.

(F) Subsequent service of order for withholding.

(1) Notwithstanding the provisions of this Section, at any time after the court has ordered immediate service of an order for withholding or after initial service of an order for withholding pursuant to subsection (E), the obligee or public office may serve the order for withholding upon any payor of the obligor without further notice to the obligor. The obligee or public office shall provide notice to the payor, pursuant to paragraph (6) of subsection (I), of any payments that have been made through previous withholding or any other method.

(2) The Clerk of the Circuit Court shall, upon request, provide the obligee or public office with specially certified copies of the order for withholding or the notice of delinquency or both whenever the Court has ordered immediate service of an order for withholding or an affidavit has been placed in the court file indicating that the preconditions for service have been previously met. The obligee or public office may then serve the order for withholding on the payor, its superintendent, manager or other agent by certified mail or personal delivery. A proof of service shall be filed with the Clerk of the Circuit Court.

(3) If a delinquency has accrued for any reason, the obligee or public office may serve a notice of delinquency upon the obligor pursuant to subsection (C). The obligor may prevent the notice of delinquency from being served upon the payor by utilizing the procedures set forth in subsection (D). If no petition to stay service has been filed within the required 20 day time period, the obligee or public office may serve the notice of delinquency on the payor by utilizing the procedures for service set forth in subsection (E).

(G) Duties of payor.

(1) It shall be the duty of any payor who has been served with a copy of the specially certified order for withholding and any notice of delinquency to deduct and pay over income as provided in this subsection. The payor shall deduct the amount designated in the order for withholding, as supplemented by the notice of delinquency and any notice provided pursuant to paragraph (6) of subsection (I), beginning no later than the next payment of income which is payable to the obligor that occurs 14 days following the date the order and any notice were mailed by certified mail or placed for personal delivery. The payor may combine all amounts withheld for the benefit of an obligee or public office into a single payment and transmit the payment with a listing of obligors from whom withholding has been effected. The payor shall pay the amount withheld to the obligee or public office within 3 business days of the date income is paid to the obligor in accordance with the order for withholding and any subsequent notification received from the public office redirecting payments. If the payor knowingly fails to pay any amount withheld to the obligee or public office within 3 business days of the date income is paid to the obligor, the payor shall pay a penalty of $100 for each day that the withheld amount is paid to the obligee or public office after the period of 3 business days has expired. The failure of a payor, on more than one occasion, to pay amounts withheld to the obligee or public office within 3 business days of the date income is paid to the obligor creates a presumption that the payor knowingly failed to pay the amounts. This penalty may be collected in a civil action which may be brought against the payor in favor of the obligee. For purposes of this Section, a withheld amount shall be considered paid by a payor on the date it is mailed by the payor, or on the date an electronic funds transfer of the amount has been initiated by the payor, or on the date delivery of the amount has been initiated by the payor. For each deduction, the payor shall provide the obligee or public office, at the time of transmittal, with the date income was paid from which support was withheld.

Upon receipt of an order requiring that a minor child be named as a beneficiary of a health insurance plan available through an employer, the employer shall immediately enroll the minor child as a beneficiary in the health insurance plan designated by the court order. The employer shall withhold any required premiums and pay over any amounts so withheld and any additional amounts the employer pays to the insurance carrier in a timely manner. The employer shall mail to the obligee, within 15 days of enrollment or upon request, notice of the date of coverage, information on the dependent coverage plan, and all forms necessary to obtain reimbursement for covered health expenses, such as would be made available to a new employee. When an order for dependent coverage is in effect and the insurance coverage is terminated or changed for any reason, the employer shall notify the obligee within 10 days of the termination or change date along with notice of conversion privileges.

For withholding of income, the payor shall be entitled to receive a fee not to exceed $5 per month to be taken from the income to be paid to the obligor.

(2) Whenever the obligor is no longer receiving income from the payor, the payor shall return a copy of the order for withholding to the obligee or public office and shall provide information for the purpose of enforcing this Section.

(3) Withholding of income under this Section shall be made without regard to any prior or subsequent garnishments, attachments, wage assignments, or any other claims of creditors. Withholding of income under this Section shall not be in excess of the maximum amounts permitted under the federal Consumer Credit Protection Act. If the payor has been served with more than one order for withholding pertaining to the same obligor, the payor shall allocate income available for withholding on a proportionate share basis, giving priority to current support payments. If there is any income available for withholding after withholding for all current support obligations, the payor shall allocate the income to past due support payments ordered in non-AFDC matters and then to past due support payments ordered in AFDC matters, both on a proportionate share basis. Payment as required by the order for withholding shall be a complete defense by the payor against any claims of the obligor or his creditors as to the sum so paid.

(4) No payor shall discharge, discipline, refuse to hire or otherwise penalize any obligor because of the duty to withhold income.

(H) Petitions to stay service or to modify, suspend or terminate orders for withholding.

(1) When an obligor files a petition to stay service, the court, after due notice to all parties, shall hear the matter as soon as practicable and shall enter an order granting or denying relief, amending the notice of delinquency, amending the order for withholding, where applicable, or otherwise resolving the matter. If the court finds that a delinquency existed when the notice of delinquency was served upon the obligor, in an amount of at least one month's support obligation, or that the obligor was at least 30 days late in paying all or part of the order for support, the court shall order immediate service of the order for withholding. Where the court cannot promptly resolve any dispute over the amount of the delinquency, the court may order immediate service of the order for withholding as to any undisputed amounts specified in an amended notice of delinquency, and may continue the hearing on the disputed amounts.

(2) At any time, an obligor, obligee, public office or Clerk of the Circuit Court may petition the court to:

(a) modify, suspend or terminate the order for withholding because of a modification, suspension or termination of the underlying order for support; or

(b) modify the amount of income to be withheld to reflect payment in full or in part of the delinquency or arrearage by income withholding or otherwise; or

(c) suspend the order for withholding because of inability to deliver income withheld to the obligee due to the obligee's failure to provide a mailing address or other means of delivery.

(3) The obligor, obligee or public office shall serve on the payor, by certified mail or personal delivery, a copy of any order entered pursuant to this subsection that affects the duties of the payor.

(4) The order for withholding shall continue to be binding upon the payor until service of any order of the court entered under this subsection.

(I) Additional duties.

(1) An obligee who is receiving income withholding payments under this Section shall notify the payor, if the obligee receives the payments directly from the payor, or the public office or the Clerk of the Circuit Court, as appropriate, of any change of address within 7 days of such change.

(2) An obligee who is a recipient of public aid shall send a copy of any notice of delinquency filed pursuant to subsection (C) to the Bureau of Child Support of the Illinois Department of Public Aid.

(3) Each obligor shall notify the obligee and the Clerk of the Circuit Court of any change of address within 7 days.

(4) An obligor whose income is being withheld or who has been served with a notice of delinquency pursuant to this Section shall notify the obligee and the Clerk of the Circuit Court of any new payor, within 7 days.

(5) When the Illinois Department of Public Aid is no longer authorized to receive payments for the obligee, it shall, within 7 days, notify the payor or, where appropriate, the Clerk of the Circuit Court, to redirect income withholding payments to the obligee.

(6) The obligee or public office shall provide notice to the payor and Clerk of the Circuit Court of any other support payment made, including but not limited to, a set-off under federal and State law or partial payment of the delinquency or arrearage, or both.

(7) Any public office and Clerk of the Circuit Court which collects, disburses or receives payments pursuant to orders for withholding shall maintain complete, accurate, and clear records of all payments and their disbursements. Certified copies of payment records maintained by a public office or Clerk of the Circuit Court shall, without further proof, be admitted into evidence in any legal proceedings under this Section.

(8) The Illinois Department of Public Aid shall design suggested legal forms for proceeding under this Section and shall make available to the courts such forms and informational materials which describe the procedures and remedies set forth herein for distribution to all parties in support actions.

(9) At the time of transmitting each support payment, the clerk of the circuit court shall provide the obligee or public office, as appropriate, with any information furnished by the payor as to the date income was paid from which such support was withheld.

(J) Penalties.

(1) Where a payor wilfully fails to withhold or pay over income pursuant to a properly served, specially certified order for withholding and any notice of delinquency, or wilfully discharges, disciplines, refuses to hire or otherwise penalizes an obligor as prohibited by subsection (G), or otherwise fails to comply with any duties imposed by this Section, the obligee, public office or obligor, as appropriate, may file a complaint with the court against the payor. The clerk of the circuit court shall notify the obligee or public office, as appropriate, and the obligor and payor of the time and place of the hearing on the complaint. The court shall resolve any factual dispute including, but not limited to, a denial that the payor is paying or has paid income to the obligor. Upon a finding in favor of the complaining party, the court:

(a) shall enter judgment and order the enforcement thereof for the total amount that the payor wilfully failed to withhold or pay over; and

(b) may order employment or reinstatement of or restitution to the obligor, or both, where the obligor has been discharged, disciplined, denied employment or otherwise penalized by the payor and may impose a fine upon the payor not to exceed $200.

(2) Any obligee, public office or obligor who wilfully initiates a false proceeding under this Section or who wilfully fails to comply with the requirements of this Section shall be punished as in cases of contempt of court.

(K) Alternative procedures for entry and service of an order for withholding.

(1) Effective January 1, 1987, in any matter in which an order for withholding has not been entered for any reason, based upon the last order for support that has been entered, and in which the obligor has become delinquent in payment of an amount equal to at least one month's support obligation pursuant to the last order for support or is at least 30 days late in complying with all or part of the order for support, the obligee or public office may prepare and serve an order for withholding pursuant to the procedures set forth in this subsection.

(2) The obligee or public office shall:

(a) prepare a proposed order for withholding for immediate service as provided by paragraphs (1) and (3) of subsection (B), except that the minimum 20% delinquency payment shall be used;

(b) prepare a notice of delinquency as provided by paragraphs (1) and (2) of subsection (C), except the notice shall state further that the order for withholding has not been entered by the court and the conditions under which the order will be entered; and

(c) serve the notice of delinquency and form petition to stay service as provided by paragraph (3) of subsection (C), together with the proposed order for withholding, which shall be marked "COPY ONLY".

(3) After 20 days following service of the notice of delinquency and proposed order for withholding, in lieu of the provisions of subsection (E), the obligee or public office shall file with the Clerk of the Circuit Court an affidavit, with a copy of the notice of delinquency and proposed order for withholding attached thereto, stating that:

    (a) the notice of delinquency and proposed order for withholding have been served upon the obligor and the date on which service was effected;

    (b) the obligor has not filed a petition to stay service within 20 days of service of such notice and order; and

    (c) the proposed order for withholding accurately states the terms and amounts contained in the last order for support.

(4) Upon the court's satisfaction that the procedures set forth in this subsection have been met, it shall enter the order for withholding.

(5) The Clerk shall then provide to the obligee or public office a specially certified copy of the order for withholding and the notice of delinquency indicating that the preconditions for service have been met.

(6) The obligee or public office shall serve the specially certified copies of the order for withholding and the notice of delinquency on the payor, its superintendent, manager or other agent by certified mail or personal delivery. A proof of service shall be filed with the Clerk of the Circuit Court.

(7) If the obligor requests in writing that income withholding become effective prior to becoming delinquent in payment of an amount equal to one month's support obligation pursuant to the last order for support, or prior to becoming 30 days late in paying all or part of the order for support, the obligee or public office shall file an affidavit with the Clerk of the Circuit Court, with a proposed order for withholding attached, stating that the proposed order accurately states the terms and amounts contained in the last order for support and the obligor's request for immediate service. The provisions of paragraphs (4) through (6) of this subsection shall apply, except that a notice of delinquency shall not be required.

(8) All other provisions of this Section shall be applicable with respect to the provisions of this subsection (K), except that under paragraph (1) of subsection (H), the court may also amend the proposed order for withholding to conform to the last order for support.

(9) Nothing in this subsection shall be construed as limiting the requirements of paragraph (1) of subsection (B) with respect to the entry of a separate order for withholding upon entry of any order for support.

(L) Remedies in addition to other laws.

(1) The rights, remedies, duties and penalties created by this Section are in addition to and not in substitution for any other rights, remedies, duties and penalties created by any other law.

(2) Nothing in this Section shall be construed as invalidating any assignment of wages or benefits executed prior to July 1, 1985.

750 ILCS 45/21

§ 21. Support payments—Duties of person or agencies receiving or disbursing support monies

(1) In an action filed in counties of less than 3 million population in which an order for child support is entered, and in supplementary proceedings in such counties to enforce or vary the terms of such order arising out of an action filed in such counties, the court, except in actions or supplementary proceedings in which the pregnancy and delivery expenses of the mother or the child support payments are for a recipient of aid under "The Illinois Public Aid Code", approved April 11, 1967, as amended, shall direct that child support payments be made to the clerk of the court unless in the discretion of the court exceptional circumstances warrant otherwise. In cases where payment is to be made to persons other than the clerk of the court the judgment or order of support shall set forth the facts of the exceptional circumstances.

(2) In an action filed in counties of 3 million or more population in which an order for child support is entered, and in supplementary proceedings in such counties to enforce or vary the terms of such order arising out of an action filed date in such counties, the court, except in actions or supplementary proceedings in which the pregnancy and delivery expenses of the mother or the child support payments are for a recipient of aid under The Illinois Public Aid Code, shall direct that child support payments be made either to the clerk of the court or to the Court Service Division of the County Department of Public Aid, or to the clerk of the court or to the Illinois Department of Public Aid, unless in the discretion of the court exceptional circumstances warrant otherwise. In cases where payment is to be made to persons other than the clerk of the court, the Court Service Division of the County Department of Public Aid, or the Illinois Department of Public Aid, the judgment or order of support shall set forth the facts of the exceptional circumstances.

(3) Where the action or supplementary proceeding is in behalf of a mother for pregnancy and delivery expenses or for child support, or both, and the mother, child, or both, are recipients of aid under the Illinois Public Aid Code, the court shall order that the payments be made directly to (a) the Illinois Department of Public Aid if the mother or child, or both, are recipients under Articles IV or V of the Code, or (b) the local governmental unit responsible for the support of the mother or child, or both, if they are recipients under Articles VI or VII of the Code. The Illinois Department of Public Aid may continue to collect current child support payments for a period not to exceed 3 months from the month following the month in which such mother or child, or both, cease to receive public assistance, and pay all amounts so collected to such persons. At the end of such 3 month period, the Illinois Department of Public Aid may continue to collect such payments if

authorized by such persons to do so, and pay the net amount so collected to such persons after deducting any costs incurred in making the collection or any collection fee from the amount of any recovery made. The Illinois Department of Public Aid or the local governmental unit, as the case may be, may direct that subsequent payments be made directly to the mother of the child, or to some other person or agency in the child's behalf, upon the removal of the mother and child from the public aid rolls or upon termination of any extended collection period; and upon such direction, the Illinois Department or the local governmental unit, as the case requires, shall give written notice of such action to the court.

(4) All clerks of the court and the Court Service Division of a County Department of Public Aid and the Illinois Department of Public Aid, receiving child support payments under paragraphs (1) or (2) shall disburse the same to the person or persons entitled thereto under the terms of the order. They shall establish and maintain clear and current records of all moneys received and disbursed and of defaults and delinquencies in required payments. The court, by order or rule, shall make provision for the carrying out of these duties. Upon notification in writing by the Illinois Department of Public Aid that a person who is receiving support payments under this Section is a public aid recipient, any support payments subsequently received by the clerk of the court shall be transmitted to the Illinois Department of Public Aid until the Department gives notice to cease such transmittal. Payments under this Section to the Illinois Department of Public Aid pursuant to the Child Support Enforcement Program established by Title IV–D of the Social Security Act shall be paid into the Child Support Enforcement Trust Fund. All other payments under this Section to the Illinois Department of Public Aid shall be deposited in the Public Assistance Recoveries Trust Fund. Disbursement from these funds shall be as provided in The Illinois Public Aid Code. Payments received by a local governmental unit shall be deposited in that unit's General Assistance Fund.

(5) The moneys received by persons or agencies designated by the court shall be disbursed by them in accordance with the order. However, the court, on petition of the state's attorney, may enter new orders designating the clerk of the court or the Illinois Department of Public Aid, as the person or agency authorized to receive and disburse child support payments and, in the case of recipients of public aid, the court, on petition of the Attorney General or State's Attorney, shall direct subsequent payments to be paid to the Illinois Department of Public Aid or to the appropriate local governmental unit, as provided in paragraph (3). Payments of child support by principals or sureties on bonds, or proceeds of any sale for the enforcement of a judgment shall be made to the clerk of the court, the Illinois Department of Public Aid or the appropriate local governmental unit, as the respective provisions of this Section require.

(6) For those cases in which child support is payable to the clerk of the circuit court for transmittal to the Illinois Department of Public Aid by order of court, the clerk shall transmit all such payments, within 4 working days of

receipt, to insure that funds are available for immediate distribution by the Department to the person or entity entitled thereto in accordance with standards of the Child Support Enforcement Program established under Title IV–D of the Social Security Act. The clerk shall notify the Department of the date of receipt and amount thereof at the time of transmittal. Where the clerk has entered into an agreement of cooperation with the Department to record the terms of child support orders and payments made thereunder directly into the Department's automated data processing system, the clerk shall account for, transmit and otherwise distribute child support payments in accordance with such agreement in lieu of the requirements contained herein.

750 ILCS 45/22
§ 22. Public Aid collection fee

In all cases instituted by the Illinois Department of Public Aid on behalf of a child or spouse, other than one receiving a grant of financial aid under Article IV of The Illinois Public Aid Code, on whose behalf an application has been made and approved for support services as provided by Section 10–1 of that Code, the court shall impose a collection fee on the individual who owes a child or spouse support obligation in an amount equal to 10% of the amount so owed as long as such collection is required by federal law, which fee shall be in addition to the support obligation. The imposition of such fee shall be in accordance with provisions of Title IV, Part D, of the Social Security Act and regulations duly promulgated thereunder. The fee shall be payable to the clerk of the circuit court for transmittal to the Illinois Department of Public Aid and shall continue until support services are terminated by that Department.

750 ILCS 45/23
§ 23. Notice to clerk of circuit court of payment received by Illinois Department of Public Aid for recording

For those cases in which support is payable to the clerk of the circuit court for transmittal to the Illinois Department of Public Aid by order of court, and the Illinois Department of Public Aid collects support by assignment offset, withhold, deduction or other process permitted by law, the Illinois Department of Public Aid shall notify the clerk of the date and amount of such collection. Upon notification, the clerk shall record the collection on the payment record for the case.

750 ILCS 45/25
§ 25. Savings clause

Except as provided in Section 8 of this Act, the repeal of the "Paternity Act", approved July 5, 1957, as amended, shall not affect rights or liabilities which have accrued thereunder and which have been determined, settled or adjudicated prior to the effective date of this Act or which are the subject of proceedings pending thereunder on such effective date. Provided further,

750 ILCS 45/25

this Act shall not be construed to bar an action which would have been barred because the action had not been filed within the then applicable time limitation, or which could not have been maintained under the "Paternity Act," approved July 5, 1957 and repealed hereunder, as long as the limitations periods set forth in Section 8 of this Act are complied with.

750 ILCS 45/26

§ 26. Severability

If any provision of this Act or the application thereof to any person or circumstance is held invalid, the invalidity does not affect other provisions or applications of the Act which can be given effect without the invalid provision or application, and to this end the provisions of this Act are severable.

ACT 50. THE ADOPTION ACT

Analysis

Sec.	
0.01	Short title.
1.	Definitions.
2.	Who may adopt a child.
2.1	Construction of Act.
3.	Who may be adopted.
4.	Jurisdiction and venue.
4.1	Placements—Compliance with law—Rules.
5.	Petition, contents, verification, filing.
6.	Investigation.
7.	Process.
8.	Consents to adoption and surrenders for purposes of adoption.
9.	Time for taking a consent or surrender.
10.	Forms of consent and surrender; Execution and acknowledgment thereof.
11.	Consents, surrenders, irrevocability.
12.	Consent of child or adult.
12.1	Putative Father Registry.
12a.	Notice to putative father.
13.	Interim order.
14.	Judgment.
14a.	Death of child prior to final judgment.
15.	Welfare of child—Same religious belief.
15.1	Licensed foster parent.
16.	Entry of judgment.
17.	Effect of order terminating parental rights or judgment of adoption.
18.	Records confidential.
18.1	Procedure for the disclosure of identifying information—Confidentiality.
18.2	Forms.
18.3	Biological parents—Written statement—Identifying information—Disclosure of information.
18.3a	Confidential intermediary.
18.4	Information given to adoptive parents.
18.4a	Medical and mental health histories—Contents—Release.
18.5	Exemption from liability.
18.6	Fees and charges.
19.	Registration new birth certificate.

FAMILIES 750 ILCS 50/0.01

Sec.
20. Practice.
20a. Construction of Act.
20b. Time limit for relief from final judgment or order.
21. Compensation for placing of children prohibited.
22. Partial invalidity.
23. Repeal—Saving.
24. Effective date.

WESTLAW Electronic Research

See WESTLAW Electronic Research Guide preceding the Summary of Contents.

---

750 ILCS 50/0.01

§ 0.01. Short title

This Act may be cited as the Adoption Act.

Author's Notes

Analysis

1. Statutory basis of adoption.
2. Persons available for adoption; Persons able to adopt.
3. Termination of parental rights.
4. Cross references: Additional statutory bases for termination of parental rights.
5. Administrative requirements.
6. Petition requirements.
7. Obtaining personal jurisdiction.
8. Consent.
9. Seventy-two hour waiting period following birth of child.
10. Irrevocable consents and surrenders.
11. Forms.
12. Consents or surrenders executed outside Illinois.
13. Interim hearings.
14. Disclosure of financial expenditures.
15. Religion of the child and adopting parents.
16. Foster parent adoptions.
17. Rights of inheritance and support after adoption.
18. Confidentiality.
19. Disclosure of medical histories.
20. Non-identifying information.
21. Revised birth certificate.
22. Payment for placement of children.
23. Expedited court proceedings.

(1) **Statutory basis of adoption.** Adoption is a statutorily created process, and did not exist at common law. Houston v. Brackett, 38 Ill.App.2d 463, 187 N.E.2d 545 (2d Dist.1963). The provisions of the adoption act should be followed as precisely as possible. However, unlike other statutes in derogation of common law mandating "strict construction," the adoption act is to be "liberally construed." § 20.

(2) **Persons available for adoption, Persons able to adopt.** The two major components of adoption are (1) a child (or adult) available for adoption; and (2) a person eligible to be an adoptive parent. These are further defined in §§ 1(F), 2, respectively. The adoption act applies to the adoption of children and adults, and to the adoption of related and unrelated persons. Note that the death of a person otherwise available for adoption does not necessarily prevent the adoption. § 14a.

The act states that "the best interests and welfare of the person to be adopted shall be of paramount consideration in the construction and interpretation of this act." § 20a.

(3) **Termination of parental rights.** Section 1, the definitional section, describes how a child becomes available for adoption: either by voluntary action of the biological parent[s] (consent or surrender), or by involuntary termination of parental rights (unfitness). Note that a "consent" is to an adoption, whereas a "surrender" is to an agency having the right later to place a child for adoption. Either one effectively relinquishes parental rights. If the child who is the subject of the adoption is over 14, the consent of the child is needed also.

Section 1(D) allows parental rights to be terminated even when there are no specific adoptive plans in place. The various subsections of this paragraph try to balance the two sometimes opposing positions of preserving families of origin but allowing them to be permanently divided where the best interests of the child require it. These paragraphs give guidance to people involved in the adoption process, so that parental rights are protected from improper termination but children are not left in limbo indefinitely, without the ability to create new families when biological ones are seriously dysfunctional. See, e.g., In Interest of Austin, 61 Ill.App.3d 344, 351, 19 Ill.Dec. 37, 42, 378 N.E.2d 538, 543 (1st Dist.1978) (requirement that parents make "reasonable efforts" to improve their performance as a parent "clearly manifests the intention of the legislature that determinations of unfitness under this subsection be made as soon as possible so that children will not be left for an unnecessarily long time in an impermanent home").

(4) **Cross references: Additional statutory bases for termination of parental rights.** Section 2.1 requires that the Adoption Act be construed together with other statutes relating to adoption procedures, including the Juvenile Court Act, which provides another venue for the termination of parental rights. Another statute that occasionally but importantly relates to adoptions is the Indian Child Welfare Act. 25 U.S.C.A. § 1901 et seq. If a child is even part Native–American, jurisdiction over matters relating to the child may not be with the Illinois courts at all and different procedures will apply, e.g., a consent taken before 10 days after the child's birth is not valid. See 43 U.S.C.A. § 1606 defining who is an "Indian child" under the ICWA. To avoid possible future problems, it should be established at the initial stages of any adoption that a child has no Native–American ancestry. Cf. In Interest of Armell, 194 Ill.App.3d 31, 141 Ill.Dec. 14, 550 N.E.2d 1060 (1st Dist.), *appeal denied* sub nom. Armell v. Prairie Band of Potawatomi Indians, 132 Ill.2d 545, 144 Ill.Dec. 255, 555 N.E.2d 374, *cert. denied* sub nom. Armell Through Murphy v. Prairie Band of Potawatomi Indians, 498 U.S. 940, 111 S.Ct. 345, 112 L.Ed.2d 310 (1990) (ICWA applied to neglect and dependency proceeding where both parents and the child were members of Indian tribe); In re Stiarwalt, 190 Ill.App.3d 547, 137 Ill.Dec. 420, 546 N.E.2d 44 (2d Dist.1989), *appeal denied* sub nom. People v. Stiarwalt, 129 Ill.2d 571, 140 Ill.Dec. 679, 550 N.E.2d 564 (1990) (ICWA did not apply to proceeding to terminate parental rights when child was a member of a Canadian Indian tribe).

(5) **Administrative requirements.** Adoptions across state and national boundaries are subject to the "importing" regulations of § 4.1, and the implementing administrative rules of the Department of Children and Family Services. These procedures exist to protect the children, the biological parents, the adoptive parents, and the states' resources (in the case of failed adoptions). Adequate exchange of information and adherence to procedural legalities serve to lessen the likelihood of improper adoptions which may be vulnerable to later legal attack.

(6) **Petition requirements.** The petition requirements of § 5 are very specific. The requirements for related adoptions, § 5(C), are slightly different. There must be an acceptable investigation of the petition's allegations pursuant to § 6, including an investigation of the prospective adoptive parents. Such an investigation is not routinely required for a related child, but may be requested by the court in its discretion. § 6(D). The contents of the report are confidential, except the court shall inform the petitioners of adverse findings, without necessarily making the entire report available.

(7) **Obtaining personal jurisdiction.** Section 7 discusses obtaining jurisdiction over everyone involved. The child who is the subject of the adoption must be served with summons. Anyone over the age of 14 may waive service by voluntarily filing an appearance.

(8) **Consent.** Unless a parent has been found unfit pursuant to § 1 of the act, consent to the adoption of a child is required, except that the putative father of a child born out of wedlock is excused from this requirement under certain circumstances, §§ 8, 12a and 12.1, unless he has registered and commenced paternity proceedings in a timely manner.

The recent amendments establishing a Putative Father Registry have tightened the requirements placed on the putative father in order to be able to contest an adoption.

(9) **Seventy-two hour waiting period following birth of child.** The 72 hour period after the birth of a child is crucial to the validity of the consent or the surrender. Under § 9, consent taken from the father even prior to the birth of the child may be revoked within that time frame; a consent taken from the mother is revocable unless taken after the 72 hours has passed. See also § 11 and Author's Note (10) below. The persons before whom a consent or surrender may be acknowledged are specifically enumerated in § 10(H), (I).

(10) **Irrevocable consents and surrenders.** Under § 11, consents and surrenders properly obtained are irrevocable, even those from parents who are minors. Consents and surrenders are revocable on the basis of fraud or duress only if an action to void the consent or surrender is instituted within 12 months of the date of the consent or surrender *and* the fraud or duress was on the part of the adopting parties or their agents, or the person before whom the consent or surrender was acknowledged. The biological mother must now supply an affidavit identifying the putative father of the child. That identification creates a rebuttable presumption of the father's true identity.

(11) **Forms.** The adoption act contains within it the actual forms to be used for consents, surrenders, notices, and affidavits of identification. §§ 10, 11, 12a. These should be followed carefully, and the form used should be the proper one for the circumstances. If the biological mother is married but her spouse is not the father of the child, consents should be obtained from him as well as from the biological father.

750 ILCS 50/0.01   FAMILIES

If a man is named as putative father, his role in later adoption proceedings concerning the child can be determined even before any adoption is pending. Section 12a provides for notice to the putative father that he has the right to file a declaration or disclaimer of paternity, if he meets the standards in § 12a(1.5). If he is not the father of the child and files such a disclaimer, he need not participate in later adoption proceedings. If he claims paternity and wishes to oppose the adoption, he must take steps to do so within thirty days of receipt of the notice, and also establish paternity pursuant to the Parentage Act, within thirty days of the notice, or if the child is not yet born, within thirty days after the birth of the child. The putative father must now follow the procedures of the Putative Father Registry established under § 12.1.

(12) **Consents or surrenders executed outside Illinois.** Consents or surrenders signed outside of Illinois will be valid if they are executed and acknowledged in conformance with Illinois law or that of the state where signed, or valid if they are executed and acknowledged in conformance with the law of the foreign country where signed. § 10(L), (M). Note that the wording of § 10(M) makes consents and surrenders signed in another country valid only if the procedure conforms to that country's law; there is no provision parallel with § 10(L) recognizing consents and surrenders of another state if valid under Illinois law.

(13) **Interim hearings.** Section 13 deals with the interim hearing, at which time the court may determine the validity of any consents, appoint an attorney to serve as guardian ad litem for the child, appoint an attorney for others as described, terminate parental rights, enter an order telling a hospital to release a newborn to the adoption petitioners, and determine suitable temporary custodial care for the child sought to be adopted. In Cook County, this is sometimes the only court appearance that may be necessary for adopting parents, since once reports approving the adoption are received, assuming all papers are in order, and the required amount of time elapses (six months, unless waived under § 16, for non-related, non-agency adoptions; any time after the return date on the summons served in related adoptions, adult adoptions, or adoptions consented to by an agency or other legally authorized persons), the final order of adoption may be obtained from the court by the attorney, without any of the parties needing to be present.

(14) **Disclosure of financial expenditures.** A financial affidavit must be filed in all adoptions except related or adult adoptions. When total expenses exceed $3,500, the listing needs to be itemized. All past, present, or promised expenditures, relating to any aspect of the adoption or parties thereto, must be included; such as payments or things of value given to the biological parents, expenses paid on their behalf, contributions, fees, attorney and medical costs, and the like. Improper payments might jeopardize the adoption itself. See In re Adoption of Kindgren, 184 Ill.App.3d 661, 132 Ill.Dec. 745, 540 N.E.2d 485 (2d Dist.) *appeal denied*, 127 Ill.2d 617, 136 Ill.Dec. 588, 545 N.E.2d 112 (1989) (consent given by biological mother to allow adoption was invalid; payment by adopting parents in excess of actual medical expenses was contrary to public policy and vitiated consent); In re Adoption of Baby Girls Mandell, 213 Ill.App.3d 670, 157 Ill.Dec. 290, 572 N.E.2d 359 (2d Dist.), appeal denied 141 Ill.2d 541, 162 Ill.Dec. 489, 580 N.E.2d 115 (1991) (judgment of adoption based on mother's consent could not be attacked because consent was given in return for monetary compensation; purported illegality of consent must be raised within the prescribed 12–month period); In re Nadler, 91 Ill.2d 326, 63 Ill.Dec. 460, 438 N.E.2d 198 (1982) (suspending attorney for three years after, *inter alia*, committing fraud on court by instructing adopting couples to sign false affidavits and remaining silent when

couples testify that affidavits are complete and accurate). See also 720 ILCS 525/4, 4.1 and Cook County Circuit Court Rule 10.7.

(15) **Religion of the child and adopting parents.** Section 15 of the Adoption Act suggests that the religion of the adopting parents be the same as that of the child "whenever possible." Biological parents may be asked whether they prefer or wish to waive religious matchings as part of the consent or surrender process, or during the interview and investigation.

(16) **Foster parent adoptions.** Foster parents who have cared for a child for more than a year are given some preference in adopting the child placed with them. There are several factors relevant to approval of such an adoption, enumerated in § 15.1, and the final decision is based on the welfare and best interests of the child, and is discretionary with the court. The foster parent must apply to the "guardian with the power to consent" to the proposed adoption, and the court has the right to overrule either the guardian's consent or refusal to consent if the court finds that the guardian has abused its discretion.

(17) **Rights of inheritance and support after adoption.** The adoption act specifically states in § 17 that the entry of an order terminating parental rights or granting a judgment of adoption ends all responsibilities and rights between the child and biological parents. However, the biological parents retain a residual duty to support their child, and adopted children may inherit from both biological and adoptive parents. In re M.M., 156 Ill.2d 53, 189 Ill. Dec 1, 619 N.E.2d 702 (1993).

(18) **Confidentiality.** The statute ensures the confidentiality of all aspects of the adoption proceeding. Court records are impounded, and even the adopting parties need a court order to get certified copies of the adoption decree if more than 30 days has passed since its entry. Access to the court file is by court order, except that the guardian ad litem of the child sought to be adopted may access the file without leave of court while the proceeding is pending. § 18(c).

Attorneys and others connected to an adoption are sometimes asked for information from their office files by parties to an adoption. The confidentiality provisions of the adoption act require that attorneys and others be bound by the same restrictions as are imposed on the court: no identifying information should be given, even if their information is obtained from out-of-court sources.

There is now in place a Registry process whereby the biological parents, biological siblings, and adoptees who have reached the age of 18 may gain access to identifying information if they all have authorized it. The forms for the registry are found at § 18.2. Consent to the release of identifying information may be revoked at any time by any party pursuant to § 18.1. The Registry process applies to past adoptions as well. Now, at the time consents or surrenders are given, the biological parents must sign a statement indicating that they know they can allow or deny access to identifying information, or that they have not yet decided but may do so in the future.

(19) **Disclosure of medical histories.** When a physician attests to the need by the adoptee for background information related to a "psychological or genetically-based medical problem," and no information exchange authorization or denial exists, the Adoption Act allows the court to appoint a confidential intermediary. This person has the right to examine otherwise confidential records, including the court file, and to actually contact the biological parent. The biological parent controls the amount of disclosure that occurs, which can range from none, to cooperating in the treatment process openly. It is also possible to preserve the privacy of the biological parent who

wishes to assist but does not wish identifying information revealed. Section 18.3 allows for sanctions, including fines, for violations of confidentiality contrary to the wishes of the biological parent.

(20) **Non-identifying information.** Non-identifying information, including medical and mental health histories, must be shared to the extent known upon the request of prospective adoptive parents and adoptees over the age of 18. This provision applies to adoptions completed at any time. See §§ 18.4, 18.4a. Informational records are to be maintained by agencies and governmental bodies until such time as the adoptee would have reached the age of 99 years. The provisions related to access to information, and the Biological Parent Registration are relatively recent, becoming effective in the 1980's and 1990's.

(21) **Revised birth certificate.** Following the finalization of an adoption, the clerk of the court that entered the judgment of adoption must send a certificate of adoption to the Department of Public Health, which then issues the adopted child a new birth certificate. § 19. This usually requires a certified copy of the adoption decree. The name in the adoption decree should be exactly as the parties wish it to be on the birth certificate, including any middle names. It is best to accomplish this as soon as possible after the adoption decree is entered.

(22) **Payment for placement of children.** Section 21 states that it is illegal for any person or entity, other than a licensed child welfare agency, to be paid or given, directly or indirectly, anything of value for the placement of children. See also the Adoption Compensation Prohibition Act, 720 ILCS 525/1 et seq.

(23) **Expedited court proceedings.** Section 20 of the Adoption Act describes the preferential timetable to be given contest of adoption proceedings at the trial and appellate levels.

750 ILCS 50/1

§ 1. Definitions

When used in this Act, unless the context otherwise requires:

A. "Child" means a person under legal age subject to adoption under this Act.

B. "Related child" means a child subject to adoption where either or both of the adopting parents stands in any of the following relationships to the child by blood or marriage: parent, grand-parent, brother, sister, step-parent, step-grandparent, step-brother, step-sister, uncle, aunt, great-uncle, great-aunt, or cousin of first degree. A child whose parent has executed a final irrevocable consent to adoption or a final irrevocable surrender for purposes of adoption, or whose parent has had his or her parental rights terminated, is not a related child to that person.

C. "Agency" for the purpose of this Act means a public child welfare agency or a licensed child welfare agency.

D. "Unfit person" means any person whom the court shall find to be unfit to have a child, without regard to the likelihood that the child will be placed for adoption. The grounds of unfitness are any one or more of the following:

(a) Abandonment of the child.

(b) Failure to maintain a reasonable degree of interest, concern or responsibility as to the child's welfare.

(c) Desertion of the child for more than 3 months next preceding the commencement of the Adoption proceeding.

(d) Substantial neglect of the child if continuous or repeated.

(e) Extreme or repeated cruelty to the child.

(f) Two or more findings of physical abuse to any children under Section 4–8 of the Juvenile Court Act or Section 2–21 of the Juvenile Court Act of 1987, the most recent of which was determined by the juvenile court hearing the matter to be supported by clear and convincing evidence; a criminal conviction resulting from the death of any child by physical child abuse; or a finding of physical child abuse resulting from the death of any child under Section 4–8 of the Juvenile Court Act or Section 2–21 of the Juvenile Court Act of 1987.

(g) Failure to protect the child from conditions within his environment injurious to the child's welfare.

(h) Other neglect of, or misconduct toward the child; provided that in making a finding of unfitness the court hearing the adoption proceeding shall not be bound by any previous finding, order or judgment affecting or determining the rights of the parents toward the child sought to be adopted in any other proceeding except such proceedings terminating parental rights as shall be had under either this Act, the Juvenile Court Act or the Juvenile Court Act of 1987.

(i) Depravity.

(j) Open and notorious adultery or fornication.

(k) Habitual drunkenness or addiction to drugs, other than those prescribed by a physician, for at least one year immediately prior to the commencement of the unfitness proceeding.

(*l*) Failure to demonstrate a reasonable degree of interest, concern or responsibility as to the welfare of a new born child during the first 30 days after its birth.

(m) Failure by a parent to make reasonable efforts to correct the conditions that were the basis for the removal of the child from the parent, or to make reasonable progress toward the return of the child to the parent within 12 months after an adjudication of neglected or abused minor under Section 2–3 or dependent minor under Section 2–4 of the Juvenile Court Act of 1987. For purposes of this Act, failure to make reasonable progress toward the return of the child to the parents may be defined as failure to complete the service plan established to correct the conditions that were the basis for the removal of the child from his or her parents as required under Section 8.2 of the Abused and Neglected Child

Reporting Act within 12 months after the adjudication under Section 2-3 or 2-4 of the Juvenile Court Act of 1987.

(n) Evidence of intent to forego his or her parental rights, whether or not the child is a ward of the court, (1) as manifested by his or her failure for a period of 12 months: (i) to visit the child, (ii) to communicate with the child or agency, although able to do so and not prevented from doing so by an agency or by court order, or (iii) to maintain contact with or plan for the future of the child, although physically able to do so, or (2) as manifested by the father's failure, where he and the mother of the child were unmarried to each other at the time of the child's birth, (i) to commence legal proceedings to establish his paternity under the Illinois Parentage Act of 1984 or the law of the jurisdiction of the child's birth within 30 days of being informed, pursuant to Section 12a of this Act, that he is the father or the likely father of the child or, after being so informed where the child is not yet born, within 30 days of the child's birth, or (ii) to make a good faith effort to pay a reasonable amount of the expenses related to the birth of the child and to provide a reasonable amount for the financial support of the child, the court to consider in its determination all relevant circumstances, including the financial condition of both parents; provided that the ground for termination provided in this subparagraph (n)(2)(ii) shall only be available where the petition is brought by the mother or the husband of the mother.

Contact or communication by a parent with his or her child that does not demonstrate affection and concern does not constitute reasonable contact and planning under subdivision (n). In the absence of evidence to the contrary, the ability to visit, communicate, maintain contact, pay expenses and plan for the future shall be presumed. The subjective intent of the parent, whether expressed or otherwise, unsupported by evidence of the foregoing parental acts manifesting that intent, shall not preclude a determination that the parent has intended to forego his or her parental rights. In making this determination, the court may consider but shall not require a showing of diligent efforts by an authorized agency to encourage the parent to perform the acts specified in subdivision (n).

It shall be an affirmative defense to any allegation under paragraph (2) of this subsection that the father's failure was due to circumstances beyond his control or to impediments created by the mother or any other person having legal custody. Proof of that fact need only be by a preponderance of the evidence.

(o) repeated or continuous failure by the parents, although physically and financially able, to provide the child with adequate food, clothing, or shelter.

(p) inability to discharge parental responsibilities supported by competent evidence from a psychiatrist, licensed clinical social worker, or clinical psychologist of mental impairment, mental illness or mental retardation as defined in Section 1–116 of the Mental Health and Developmental Disabilities Code, or developmental disability as defined in Section 1–106 of that Code, and there is sufficient justification to believe that the inability to discharge parental responsibilities shall extend beyond a reasonable time period. However, this subdivision (p) shall not be construed so as to permit a licensed clinical social worker to conduct any medical diagnosis to determine mental illness or mental impairment.

(q) a finding of physical abuse of the child under Section 4–8 of the Juvenile Court Act or Section 2–21 of the Juvenile Court Act of 1987 and a criminal conviction of aggravated battery of the child.

E. "Parent" means the father or mother of a legitimate or illegitimate child. For the purpose of this Act, a person who has executed a final and irrevocable consent to adoption or a final and irrevocable surrender for purposes of adoption, or whose parental rights have been terminated by a court, is not a parent of the child who was the subject of the consent or surrender.

F. A person is available for adoption when the person is:

(a) a child who has been surrendered for adoption to an agency and to whose adoption the agency has thereafter consented;

(b) a child to whose adoption a person authorized by law, other than his parents, has consented, or to whose adoption no consent is required pursuant to Section 8 of this Act;

(c) a child who is in the custody of persons who intend to adopt him through placement made by his parents; or

(d) an adult who meets the conditions set forth in Section 3 of this Act.

A person who would otherwise be available for adoption shall not be deemed unavailable for adoption solely by reason of his or her death.

G. The singular includes the plural and the plural includes the singular and the "male" includes the "female", as the context of this Act may require.

H. "Adoption disruption" occurs when an adoptive placement does not prove successful and it becomes necessary for the child to be removed from placement before the adoption is finalized.

I. "Foreign placing agency" is an agency or individual operating in a country or territory outside the United States that is authorized by its country to place children for adoption either directly with families in the United States or through United States based international agencies.

J. "Immediate relatives" means the biological parents, the parents of the biological parents and siblings of the biological parents;

K. "Intercountry adoption" is a process by which a child from a country other than the United States is adopted.

L. "Intercountry Adoption Coordinator" is a staff person of the Department of Children and Family Services appointed by the Director to coordinate the provision of services by the public and private sector to prospective parents of foreign-born children.

M. "Interstate Compact on the Placement of Children" is a law enacted by most states for the purpose of establishing uniform procedures for handling the interstate placement of children in foster homes, adoptive homes, or other child care facilities.

N. "Non–Compact state" means a state that has not enacted the Interstate Compact on the Placement of Children.

O. "Preadoption requirements" are any conditions established by the laws or regulations of the Federal Government or of each state that must be met prior to the placement of a child in an adoptive home.

P. "Abused child" means a child whose parent or immediate family member, or any person responsible for the child's welfare, or any individual residing in the same home as the child, or a paramour of the child's parent:

(a) inflicts, causes to be inflicted, or allows to be inflicted upon the child physical injury, by other than accidental means, that causes death, disfigurement, impairment of physical or emotional health, or loss or impairment of any bodily function;

(b) creates a substantial risk of physical injury to the child by other than accidental means which would be likely to cause death, disfigurement, impairment of physical or emotional health, or loss or impairment of any bodily function;

(c) commits or allows to be committed any sex offense against the child, as sex offenses are defined in the Criminal Code of 1961 and extending those definitions of sex offenses to include children under 18 years of age; (d) commits or allows to be committed an act or acts of torture upon the child; or

(e) inflicts excessive corporal punishment.

Q. "Neglected child" means any child whose parent or other person responsible for the child's welfare withholds or denies nourishment or medically indicated treatment including food or care denied solely on the basis of the present or anticipated mental or physical impairment as determined by a physician acting alone or in consultation with other physicians or otherwise does not provide the proper or necessary support, education as required by law, or medical or other remedial care recognized under State law as necessary for a child's well-being, or other care necessary for his or her well-being, including adequate food, clothing and shelter; or who is abandoned by his or her parents or other person responsible for the child's welfare.

A child shall not be considered neglected or abused for the sole reason that the child's parent or other person responsible for his or her welfare depends upon spiritual means through prayer alone for the treatment or cure of disease or remedial care as provided under Section 4 of the Abused and Neglected Child Reporting Act.

R. "Putative father" means a man who may be a child's father, but who (1) is not married to the child's mother on or before the date that the child was or is to be born and (2) has not established paternity of the child in a court proceeding before the filing of a petition for the adoption of the child. The term includes a male who is less than 18 years of age.

750 ILCS 50/2

§ 2. Who may adopt a child

A. Any of the following persons, who is under no legal disability (except the minority specified in sub-paragraph (b)) and who has resided in the State of Illinois continuously for a period of at least 6 months immediately preceding the commencement of an adoption proceeding, or any member of the armed forces of the United States who has been domiciled in the State of Illinois for 90 days, may institute such proceeding:

(a) A reputable person of legal age and of either sex, provided that if such person is married, his or her spouse shall be a party to the adoption proceeding, including a husband or wife desiring to adopt a child of the other spouse, in all of which cases the adoption shall be by both spouses jointly;

(b) A minor, by leave of court upon good cause shown.

B. The residence requirement specified in paragraph A of this Section shall not apply to an adoption of a related child or to an adoption of a child placed by an agency.

750 ILCS 50/2.1

§ 2.1 Construction of Act

This Act shall be construed in concert with the Juvenile Court Act of 1987, the Child Care Act of 1969, and the Interstate Compact on the Placement of Children.

750 ILCS 50/3

§ 3. Who may be adopted

A male or female child, or an adult, may be adopted, provided the other conditions set forth in this Act are met, and further provided, with respect to an adult, that such adult has resided in the home of the persons intending to adopt him at any time for more than 2 years continuously preceding the commencement of an adoption proceeding, or in the alternative that such persons are related to him within a degree set forth in the definition of a related child in Section 1 of this Act.

750 ILCS 50/4

§ 4. Jurisdiction and venue

An adoption proceeding may be commenced in the circuit court of the county in which petitioners reside, or the county in which the person to be adopted resides, or was born, or the county in which the parents of such person reside, provided, however, if an agency has acquired the custody and control of a child and such agency is authorized to consent to the adoption of such child, the proceeding may be commenced in any county, and provided further that if a guardian of the person of such child has been appointed by a court of competent jurisdiction, the proceeding may be commenced in any county.

750 ILCS 50/4.1

§ 4.1 Placements—Compliance with law—Rules

Placements under this Act shall comply with the Child Care Act of 1969 and the Interstate Compact on the Placement of Children. Placements of children born outside the United States or a territory thereof shall comply with rules promulgated by the United States Department of Immigration and Naturalization.

Rules promulgated by the Department of Children and Family Services shall include but not be limited to the following:

(a) Any agency which places such children for adoption in this State:

(i) Shall be licensed in this State as a child welfare agency as defined in Section 2.08 of the Child Care Act of 1969; or

(ii) Shall be licensed as a child placement agency in a state which is a party to the Interstate Compact on the Placement of Children; or

(iii) Shall be licensed as a child placement agency in a country other than the United States or, if located in such a country but not so licensed, shall provide information such as a license or court document which authorizes that agency to place children for adoption and to establish that such agency has legal authority to place children for adoption; or

(iv) Shall be a child placement agency which is so licensed in a non-compact state, if such agency first files with the Department of Children and Family Services a bond with surety in the amount of $5,000 for each such child to ensure that such child shall not become a public charge upon this State. Such bond shall remain in effect until a judgment for adoption is entered with respect to such child pursuant to this Act. The Department of Children and Family Services may accept, in lieu of such bond, a written agreement with such agency which provides that such agency shall be liable for all costs associated with the placement of such child in the event a judgement of adoption is not entered, upon such terms and conditions as the Department deems appropriate.

(b) As an alternative to requiring the bond provided for in paragraph (a)(iv) of this Section, the Department of Children and Family Services may require the filing of such a bond by the individual or individuals seeking to adopt such a child through placement of such child by a child placement agency located in a state which is not a party to the Interstate Compact on the Placement of Children.

(c) In the case of any foreign-born child brought to the United States for adoption in this State, the following preadoption requirements shall be met:

(1) Documentation that the child is legally free for adoption prior to entry into the United States shall be submitted.

(2) A medical report on the child, by authorized medical personnel in the country of the child's origin, shall be provided when such personnel are available.

(3) Verification that the adoptive family has been licensed as a foster family home pursuant to the Child Care Act of 1969, as now or hereafter amended, shall be provided.

(4) A valid home study conducted by a licensed child welfare agency that complies with guidelines established by the United States Immigration and Naturalization Service at 8 CFR 204.4(d)(2)(i), as now or hereafter amended, shall be submitted. A home study is considered valid if it contains:

(i) A factual evaluation of the financial, physical, mental and moral capabilities of the prospective parent or parents to rear and educate the child properly.

(ii) A detailed description of the living accommodations where the prospective parent or parents currently reside.

(iii) A detailed description of the living accommodations in the United States where the child will reside, if known.

(iv) A statement or attachment recommending the proposed adoption signed by an official of the child welfare agency which has conducted the home study.

(5) The placing agency located in a non-compact state or a family desiring to adopt through an authorized placement party in a non-compact state or a foreign country shall file with the Department of Children and Family Services a bond with surety in the amount of $5,000 as protection that a foreign-born child accepted for care or supervision not become a public charge upon the State of Illinois.

(6) In lieu of the $5,000 bond, the placement agency may sign a binding agreement with the Department of Children and Family Services to assume full liability for all placements should, for any reason, the adoption be disrupted or not be completed, including financial and planning responsibility until the child is either returned to the country of

750 ILCS 50/4.1   **FAMILIES**

its origin or placed with a new adoptive family in the United States and that adoption is finalized.

(7) Compliance with the requirements of the Interstate Compact on the Placement of Children, when applicable, shall be demonstrated.

(8) When a child is adopted in a foreign country and a final, complete and valid Order of Adoption is issued in that country, as determined by both the United States Department of State and the United States Department of Justice, this State shall not impose any additional preadoption requirements. The adoptive family, however, must comply with applicable requirements of the United States Department of Immigration and Naturalization as provided in 8 CFR 204.4 (d)(2)(ii), as now or hereafter amended.

(d) The Department of Children and Family Services shall maintain the office of Intercountry Adoption Coordinator, shall maintain and protect the rights of families and children participating in adoption of foreign born children, and shall develop ongoing programs of support and services to such families and children. The Intercountry Adoption Coordinator shall determine that all preadoption requirements have been met and report such information to the Department of Immigration and Naturalization.

750 ILCS 50/5

§ 5. Petition, contents, verification, filing

A. A proceeding to adopt a child, other than a related child, shall be commenced by the filing of a petition within 30 days after such child has become available for adoption, provided that such petition may be filed at a later date by leave of court upon a showing that the failure to file such petition within such 30 day period was not due to the petitioners' culpable negligence or their wilful disregard of the provisions of this Section. In the case of a child born outside the United States or a territory thereof, if the prospective adoptive parents of such child have been appointed guardians of such child by a court of competent jurisdiction in a country other than the United States or a territory thereof, such parents shall file a petition as provided in this Section within 30 days after entry of the child into the United States. A petition to adopt an adult or a related child may be filed at any time. A petition for adoption may include more than one person sought to be adopted.

B. A petition to adopt a child other than a related child shall state:

(a) The full names of the petitioners and, if minors, their respective ages;

(b) The place of residence of the petitioners and the length of residence of each in the State of Illinois immediately preceding the filing of the petition;

(c) When the petitioners acquired, or intend to acquire, custody of the child, and the name and address of the persons or agency from whom the child was or will be received;

(d) The name, the place and date of birth if known, and the sex of the child sought to be adopted;

(e) The relationship, if any, of the child to each petitioner;

(f) The names, if known, and the place of residence, if known, of the parents; and whether such parents are minors, or otherwise under any legal disability. The names and addresses of the parents shall be omitted and they shall not be made parties defendant to the petition if (1) the rights of the parents have been terminated by a court of competent jurisdiction, or (2) if the child has been surrendered to an agency, or (3) if the parent or parents have been served with the notice provided in Section 12a of this Act and said parent or parents have filed a disclaimer of paternity as therein provided or have failed to file such declaration of paternity or a request for notice as provided in said Section.

(g) If it is alleged that the child has no living parent, then the name of the guardian, if any, of such child and the court which appointed such guardian;

(h) If it is alleged that the child has no living parent and that no guardian of such child is known to petitioners, then the name of a near relative, if known, shall be set forth, or an allegation that no near relative is known and on due inquiry cannot be ascertained by petitioners:

(i) The name to be given the child or adult;

(j) That the person or agency, having authority to consent under Section 8 of this Act, has consented, or has indicated willingness to consent, to the adoption of the child by the petitioners, or that the person having authority to consent is an unfit person and the ground therefor, or that no consent is required under paragraph (f) of Section 8 of this Act;

(k) Whatever orders, judgments or decrees have heretofore been entered by any court affecting (1) adoption or custody of the child, or (2) the adoptive, custodial or parental rights of either petitioner, including the prior denial of any petition for adoption pertaining to such child, or to the petitioners, or either of them.

C. A petition to adopt a related child shall include the information specified in sub-paragraphs (a), (b), (d), (e), (f), (i) and (k) of paragraph B and a petition to adopt an adult shall contain the information required by sub-paragraphs (a), (b) and (i) of paragraph B in addition to the name, place, date of birth and sex of such adult.

D. The petition shall be verified by the petitioners.

E. Upon the filing of the petition the petitioners shall furnish the Clerk of the Court in which the petition is pending such information not contained

750 ILCS 50/5 FAMILIES

in such petition as shall be necessary to enable the Clerk of such Court to complete a certificate of adoption as hereinafter provided.

750 ILCS 50/6

§ 6. Investigation

A. Investigation; all cases. Within 10 days after the filing of a petition for the adoption of a child other than a related child, the court shall appoint a child welfare agency approved by the Department of Children and Family Services or a probation officer of the court, or in Cook County the Court Services Division of the Cook County Department of Public Aid, or the Department of Children and Family Services if the court determines that no child welfare agency is available or that the petitioner is financially unable to pay for the investigation, to investigate accurately, fully and promptly, the allegations contained in the petition; the character; reputation, health and general standing in the community of the petitioners; the religious faith of the petitioners and, if ascertainable, of the child sought to be adopted; and whether the petitioners are proper persons to adopt the child and whether the child is a proper subject of adoption.

B. Investigation; foreign-born child. In the case of a child born outside the United States or a territory thereof, in addition to the investigation required under subsection (A) of this Section, a post-placement investigation shall be conducted in accordance with the requirements of the Child Care Act of 1969, the Interstate Compact on the Placement of Children, and regulations of the foreign placing agency and the supervising agency.

The requirements of a post-placement investigation shall be deemed to have been satisfied if a valid final order or judgment of adoption has been entered by a court of competent jurisdiction in a country other than the United States or a territory thereof with respect to such child and the petitioners.

C. Report of investigation. The court shall determine whether the costs of the investigation shall be charged to the petitioners. The information obtained as a result of such investigation shall be presented to the court in a written report. The Court, in its discretion, may accept the report of the investigation previously made by a licensed child welfare agency, if made within one year prior to the entry of the judgment. Such report shall be treated as confidential and withheld from inspection unless findings adverse to the petitioners or to the child sought to be adopted are contained therein, and in that event the court shall inform the petitioners of the relevant portions pertaining to the adverse findings. In no event shall any facts set forth in the report be considered at the hearing of the proceeding, unless established by competent evidence. The report shall be filed with the record of the proceeding. If the file relating to the proceeding is not impounded, the report shall be impounded by the clerk of the court and shall be made available for inspection only upon order of the court.

D. Related adoption. Such investigation shall not be made when the petition seeks to adopt a related child or an adult unless the court, in its discretion, shall so order. In such an event the court may appoint a person deemed competent by the court.

750 ILCS 50/7
§ 7. Process

A. All persons named in the petition for adoption, other than the petitioners and any party who has previously either denied being a parent pursuant to Section 12a of this Act or whose rights have been terminated pursuant to Section 12a of this Act, but including the person sought to be adopted, shall be made parties defendant by name, and if the name or names of any such persons are alleged in the petition to be unknown such persons shall be made parties defendant under the name and style of "All whom it may concern". In all such actions petitioner or his attorney shall file, at the office of the clerk of the court in which the action is pending, an affidavit showing that the defendant resides or has gone out of this State, or on due inquiry cannot be found, or is concealed within this State, so that process cannot be served upon him, and stating the place of residence of the defendant, if known, or that upon diligent inquiry his place of residence cannot be ascertained, the clerk shall cause publication to be made in some newspaper published in the county in which the action is pending. If there is no newspaper published in that county, then the publication shall be in a newspaper published in an adjoining county in this State, having a circulation in the county in which such action is pending. In the event there is service on any of the parties by publication, the publication shall contain notice of pendency of the action, the name of the person to be adopted and the name of the parties to be served by publication, and the date on or after which default may be entered against such parties. Neither the name of petitioners nor the name of any party who has either surrendered said child, has given their consent to the adoption of the child, or whose parental rights have been terminated by a court of competent jurisdiction shall be included in the notice of publication. The Clerk shall also, within ten (10) days of the first publication of the notice, send a copy thereof by mail, addressed to each defendant whose place of residence is stated in such affidavit. The certificate of the Clerk that he sent the copies pursuant to this section is evidence that he has done so. Except as provided in this section pertaining to service by publication, all parties defendant shall be notified of the proceedings in the same manner as is now or may hereafter be required in other civil cases or proceedings. Any party defendant who is of age of 14 years or upward may waive service of process by entering an appearance in writing. The form to be used for publication shall be substantially as follows: "ADOPTION NOTICE—STATE OF ILLINOIS, County of _____, ss.—Circuit Court of _____ County. In the matter of the Petition for the Adoption of _____, a _____ male child. Adoption No. _____. To— _____ (whom it may concern or the named parent) Take notice that a petition was filed in the Circuit

Court of _____ County, Illinois, for the adoption of a child named _____. Now, therefore, unless you _____, and all whom it may concern, file your answer to the Petition in the action or otherwise file your appearance therein, in the said Circuit Court of _____ County, Room ___, ___, in the City of _____, Illinois, on or before the _____ day of _____, a default may be entered against you at any time after that day and a judgment entered in accordance with the prayer of said Petition. Dated, _____, Illinois, _____, Clerk. (Name and address of attorney for petitioners.)"

B. A minor defendant who has been served in accordance with this Section may be defaulted in the same manner as any other defendant.

750 ILCS 50/8

§ 8. Consents to adoption and surrenders for purposes of adoption

(a) Except as hereinafter provided in this Section consents or surrenders shall be required in all cases, unless the person whose consent or surrender would otherwise be required shall be found by the court:

(1) to be an unfit person as defined in Section 1 of this Act, by clear and convincing evidence; or

(2) not to be the biological or adoptive father of the child; or

(3) to have waived his parental rights to the child under Section 12a or 12.1 of this Act; or

(4) to be the parent of an adult sought to be adopted.

(b) Where consents are required in the case of an adoption of a minor child, the consents of the following persons shall be sufficient:

(1)(A) The mother of the minor child; and

(B) The father of the minor child, if the father:

(i) was married to the mother on the date of birth of the child or within 300 days before the birth of the child, except for a husband or former husband who has been found by a court of competent jurisdiction not to be the biological father of the child; or

(ii) is the father of the child under a judgment for adoption or an order of parentage; or

(iii) in the case of a child placed with the adopting parents less than 6 months after birth, openly lived with the child, the child's biological mother, or both, and held himself out to be the child's biological father during the first 30 days following the birth of the child; or

(iv) in the case of a child placed with the adopting parents less than 6 months after birth, made a good faith effort to pay a reasonable amount of the expenses related to the birth of the child and to provide a reasonable amount for the financial support of the child before the expiration of 30 days following the birth of the child, provided that the court may consider in its determination all relevant circumstances, including the financial condition of both biological parents; or

(v) in the case of a child placed with the adopting parents more than 6 months after birth, has maintained substantial and continuous or repeated contact with the child as manifested by: (I) the payment by the father toward the support of the child of a fair and reasonable sum, according to the father's means, and either (II) the father's visiting the child at least monthly when physically and financially able to do so and not prevented from doing so by the person or authorized agency having lawful custody of the child, or (III) the father's regular communication with the child or with the person or agency having the care or custody of the child, when physically and financially unable to visit the child or prevented from doing so by the person or authorized agency having lawful custody of the child. The subjective intent of the father, whether expressed or otherwise unsupported by evidence of acts specified in this subparagraph as manifesting such intent, shall not preclude a determination that the father failed to maintain substantial and continuous or repeated contact with the child; or

(vi) in the case of a child placed with the adopting parents more than six months after birth, openly lived with the child for a period of six months within the one year period immediately preceding the placement of the child for adoption and openly held himself out to be the father of the child; or

(vii) has timely registered with Putative Father Registry, as provided in Section 12.1 of this Act, and within 30 days of the date of such registration, commenced legal proceedings to establish paternity under the Illinois Parentage Act of 1984 or under the law of the jurisdiction of the child's birth; or

(2) The legal guardian of the person of the child, if there is no surviving parent; or

(3) An agency, if the child has been surrendered for adoption to such agency; or

(4) Any person or agency having legal custody of a child by court order if the parental rights of the parents have been judicially terminated, and the court having jurisdiction of the guardianship of the child has authorized the consent to the adoption; or

(5) The execution and verification of the petition by any petitioner who is also a parent of the child sought to be adopted shall be sufficient evidence of such parent's consent to the adoption.

(c) Where surrenders to an agency are required in the case of a placement for adoption of a minor child by an agency, the surrenders of the following persons shall be sufficient:

750 ILCS 50/8 FAMILIES

(1)(A) The mother of the minor child; and

(B) The father of the minor child, if the father;

(i) was married to the mother on the date of birth of the child or within 300 days before the birth of the child, except for a husband or former husband who has been found by a court of competent jurisdiction not to be the biological father of the child; or

(ii) is the father of the child under a judgment for adoption or an order of parentage; or

(iii) in the case of a child placed with the adopting parents less than 6 months after birth, openly lived with the child, the child's biological mother, or both, and held himself out to be the child's biological father during the first 30 days following the birth of a child; or

(iv) in the case of a child placed with the adopting parents less than 6 months after birth, made a good faith effort to pay a reasonable amount of the expenses related to the birth of the child and to provide a reasonable amount for the financial support of the child before the expiration of 30 days following the birth of the child, provided that the court may consider in its determination all relevant circumstances, including the financial condition of both biological parents; or

(v) in the case of a child placed with the adopting parents more than six months after birth, has maintained substantial and continuous or repeated contact with the child as manifested by: (I) the payment by the father toward the support of the child of a fair and reasonable sum, according to the father's means, and either (II) the father's visiting the child at least monthly when physically and financially able to do so and not prevented from doing so by the person or authorized agency having lawful custody of the child or (III) the father's regular communication with the child or with the person or agency having the care or custody of the child, when physically and financially unable to visit the child or prevented from doing so by the person or authorized agency having lawful custody of the child. The subjective intent of the father, whether expressed or otherwise, unsupported by evidence of acts specified in this subparagraph as manifesting such intent, shall not preclude a determination that the father failed to maintain substantial and continuous or repeated contact with the child; or

(vi) in the case of a child placed with the adopting parents more than six months after birth, openly lived with the child for a period of six months within the one year period immediately preceding the placement of the child for adoption and openly held himself out to be the father of the child; or

(vii) has timely registered with the Putative Father Registry, as provided in Section 12.1 of this Act, and within 30 days of the date of such registration, commenced legal proceedings to establish paternity under the Illinois Parentage Act of 1984, or under the law of the jurisdiction of the child's birth.

(d) In making a determination under subparagraphs (b)(1) and (c)(1), no showing shall be required of diligent efforts by a person or agency to encourage the father to perform the acts specified therein.

(e) In the case of the adoption of an adult, only the consent of such adult shall be required.

750 ILCS 50/9

§ 9. Time for taking a consent or surrender

A. A consent or a surrender taken not less than 72 hours after the birth of the child is irrevocable except as provided in Section 11 of this Act.

B. No consent or surrender shall be taken within the 72 hour period immediately following the birth of the child.

C. A consent or a surrender may be taken from the father prior to the birth of the child. Such consent or surrender shall be revoked if, within 72 hours after the birth of the child, the father who gave such consent or surrender, notifies in writing the person, agency or court representative who took the surrender or consent or any individual representing or connected with such person, agency or court representative of the revocation of the consent or surrender.

D. Any consent or surrender taken in accordance with paragraph C above which is not revoked within 72 hours after the birth of the child is irrevocable except as provided in Section 11 of this Act.

750 ILCS 50/10

§ 10. Forms of consent and surrender; Execution and acknowledgment thereof

A. The form of consent required for the adoption of a born child shall be substantially as follows:

FINAL AND IRREVOCABLE CONSENT TO ADOPTION

I, _____, (relationship, e.g., mother, father, relative, guardian) of _____, a ____male child, state:

That such child was born on _____ at _____.

That I reside at _____, County of _____ and State of _____.

That I am of the age of _____ years.

That I hereby enter my appearance in this proceeding and waive service of summons on me.

That I do hereby consent and agree to the adoption of such child.

That I wish to and understand that by signing this consent I do irrevocably and permanently give up all custody and other parental rights I have to such child.

That I understand such child will be placed for adoption and that I cannot under any circumstances, after signing this document, change my mind and revoke or cancel this consent or obtain or recover custody or any other rights over such child. That I have read and understand the above and I am signing it as my free and voluntary act.

Dated this _____ day of _____, 19__.

_____

If under Section 8 the consent of more than one person is required, then each such person shall execute a separate consent.

B. The form of consent required for the adoption of an unborn child shall be substantially as follows:

CONSENT TO ADOPTION OF UNBORN CHILD

I, _____, state:

That I am the father of a child expected to be born on or about _____ to _____ (name of mother).

That I reside at _____ County of _____, and State of _____.

That I am of the age of _____ years.

That I hereby enter my appearance in such adoption proceeding and waive service of summons on me.

That I do hereby consent and agree to the adoption of such child, and that I have not previously executed a consent or surrender with respect to such child.

That I wish to and do understand that by signing this consent I do irrevocably and permanently give up all custody and other parental rights I have to such child, except that I have the right to revoke this consent by giving written notice of my revocation not later than 72 hours after the birth of the child.

That I understand such child will be placed for adoption and that, except as hereinabove provided, I cannot under any circumstances, after signing this document, change my mind and revoke or cancel this consent or obtain or recover custody or any other rights over such child.

That I have read and understand the above and I am signing it as my free and voluntary act.

Dated this _____ day of _____, 19__.

_____

FAMILIES   750 ILCS 50/10

C. The form of surrender to any agency given by a parent of a born child who is to be subsequently placed for adoption shall be substantially as follows and shall contain such other facts and statements as the particular agency shall require.

FINAL AND IRREVOCABLE SURRENDER
FOR PURPOSES OF ADOPTION

I, _____ (relationship, e.g., mother, father, relative, guardian) of _____, a ____male child, state:

That such child was born on _____, at _____.

That I reside at _____, County of _____, and State of _____.

That I am of the age of _____ years.

That I do hereby surrender and entrust the entire custody and control of such child to the _____ (the "Agency"), a (public) (licensed) child welfare agency with its principal office in the City of _____, County of _____ and State of _____, for the purpose of enabling it to care for and supervise the care of such child, to place such child for adoption and to consent to the legal adoption of such child.

That I hereby grant to the Agency full power and authority to place such child with any person or persons it may in its sole discretion select to become the adopting parent or parents and to consent to the legal adoption of such child by such person or persons; and to take any and all measures which, in the judgment of the Agency, may be for the best interests of such child, including authorizing medical, surgical and dental care and treatment including inoculation and anaesthesia for such child.

That I wish to and understand that by signing this surrender I do irrevocably and permanently give up all custody and other parental rights I have to such child.

That I understand I cannot under any circumstances, after signing this surrender, change my mind and revoke or cancel this surrender or obtain or recover custody or any other rights over such child.

That I have read and understand the above and I am signing it as my free and voluntary act.

Dated this _____ day of _____, 19__.

D. The form of surrender to an agency given by a parent of an unborn child who is to be subsequently placed for adoption shall be substantially as follows and shall contain such other facts and statements as the particular agency shall require.

SURRENDER OF UNBORN CHILD FOR PURPOSES OF ADOPTION

I, _____ (father), state:

That I am the father of a child expected to be born on or about _____ to _____ (name of mother).

That I reside at _____, County of _____, and State of _____.

That I am of the age of _____ years.

That I do hereby surrender and entrust the entire custody and control of such child to the _____ (the "Agency"), a (public) (licensed) child welfare agency with its principal office in the City of _____, County of _____ and State of _____, for the purpose of enabling it to care for and supervise the care of such child, to place such child for adoption and to consent to the legal adoption of such child, and that I have not previously executed a consent or surrender with respect to such child.

That I hereby grant to the Agency full power and authority to place such child with any person or persons it may in its sole discretion select to become the adopting parent or parents and to consent to the legal adoption of such child by such person or persons; and to take any and all measures which, in the judgment of the Agency, may be for the best interests of such child, including authorizing medical, surgical and dental care and treatment, including inoculation and anaesthesia for such child.

That I wish to and understand that by signing this surrender I do irrevocably and permanently give up all custody and other parental rights I have to such child.

That I understand I cannot under any circumstances, after signing this surrender, change my mind and revoke or cancel this surrender or obtain or recover custody or any other rights over such child, except that I have the right to revoke this surrender by giving written notice of my revocation not later than 72 hours after the birth of such child.

That I have read and understand the above and I am signing it as my free and voluntary act.

Dated this _____ day of _____, 19__.

_____

E. The form of consent required from the parents for the adoption of an adult, when such adult elects to obtain such consent, shall be substantially as follows:

CONSENT

I, _____, (father) (mother) of _____, an adult, state:

That I reside at _____, County of _____ and State of _____.

That I do hereby consent and agree to the adoption of such adult by _____ and _____.

Dated this _____ day of _____, 19__.

_____

F. The form of consent required for the adoption of a child of the age of 14 years or upwards, or of an adult, to be given by such person, shall be substantially as follows:

CONSENT

I, _____, state:

That I reside at _____, County of _____ and State of _____. That I am of the age of _____ years. That I consent and agree to my adoption by _____ and _____.

Dated this _____ day of _____, 19__.

_____

G. The form of consent given by an agency to the adoption by specified persons of a child previously surrendered to it shall set forth that the agency has the authority to execute such consent. The form of consent given by a guardian of the person of a child sought to be adopted, appointed by a court of competent jurisdiction, shall set forth the facts of such appointment and the authority of the guardian to execute such consent.

H. A consent (other than that given by an agency, or guardian of the person of the child sought to be adopted appointed by a court of competent jurisdiction) shall be acknowledged by a parent before the presiding judge of the court in which the petition for adoption has been, or is to be filed or before any other judge designated or subsequently approved by the court, or the circuit clerk if so authorized by the presiding judge or, except as otherwise provided in this Act, before a representative of the Department of Children and Family Services or a licensed child welfare agency, or before social service personnel under the jurisdiction of a court of competent jurisdiction, or before social service personnel of the Cook County Department of Supportive Services designated by the presiding judge.

I. A surrender, or any other document equivalent to a surrender, by which a child is surrendered to an agency shall be acknowledged by the person signing such surrender, or other document, before a judge or the clerk of any court of record, either in this State or any other state of the United States, or before a representative of an agency or before any other person designated or approved by the presiding judge of the court in which the petition for adoption has been, or is to be, filed.

J. The form of the certificate of acknowledgment for a consent, a surrender, or any other document equivalent to a surrender, shall be substantially as follows:

750 ILCS 50/10   FAMILIES

STATE OF _____)
) SS.
COUNTY OF _____)

    I, _____ (Name of judge or other person), _____ (official title, name and location of court or status or position of other person), certify that _____, personally known to me to be the same person whose name is subscribed to the foregoing (consent) (surrender), appeared before me this day in person and acknowledged that (she) (he) signed and delivered such (consent) (surrender) as (her) (his) free and voluntary act, for the specified purpose.

    I have fully explained that by signing such (consent) (surrender) (she) (he) is irrevocably relinquishing all parental rights to such child or adult and (she) (he) has stated that such is (her) (his) intention and desire.

    Dated _____ 19__.

    Signature _____

    K. When the execution of a consent or a surrender is acknowledged before someone other than a judge or the clerk of a court of record, such other person shall have his signature on the certificate acknowledged before a notary public, in form substantially as follows:

STATE OF _____)
) SS.
COUNTY OF _____)

    I, a Notary Public, in and for the _____ County, in the State _____, certify that _____, personally known to me to be the same person whose name is subscribed to the foregoing certificate of acknowledgment, appeared before me in person and acknowledged that (she) (he) signed such certificate as (her) (his) free and voluntary act and that the statements made in the certificate are true.

    Dated _____ 19__.

                                     Signature _____
                                           Notary Public
                                           (official seal)

    There shall be attached a certificate of magistracy, or other comparable proof of office of the notary public satisfactory to the court, to a consent signed and acknowledged in another state.

    L. A surrender or consent executed and acknowledged outside of this State, either in accordance with the law of this State or in accordance with the law of the place where executed, is valid.

    M. Where a consent or a surrender is signed in a foreign country, the execution of such consent shall be acknowledged or affirmed in a manner conformable to the law and procedure of such country.

N. If the person signing a consent or surrender is in the military service of the United States, the execution of such consent or surrender may be acknowledged before a commissioned officer and the signature of such officer on such certificate shall be verified or acknowledged before a notary public or by such other procedure as is then in effect for such division or branch of the armed forces.

750 ILCS 50/11

§ 11. Consents, surrenders, irrevocability

(a) A consent to adoption by a parent, including a minor, executed and acknowledged in accordance with the provisions of Section 8 of this Act, or a surrender of a child by a parent, including a minor, to an agency for the purpose of adoption shall be irrevocable unless it shall have been obtained by fraud or duress on the part of the person before whom such consent, surrender, or other document equivalent to a surrender is acknowledged pursuant to the provisions of Section 10 of this Act or on the part of the adopting parents or their agents and a court of competent jurisdiction shall so find. No action to void or revoke a consent to or surrender for adoption, including an action based on fraud or duress, may be commenced after 12 months from the date the consent or surrender was executed. The consent or surrender of a parent who is a minor shall not be voidable because of such minority.

(b) The petitioners in an adoption proceeding are entitled to rely upon a sworn statement of the biological mother of the child to be adopted identifying the father of her child. The affidavit shall be conclusive evidence as to the biological mother regarding the facts stated therein, and shall create a rebuttable presumption of truth as to the biological father only. Except as provided in Section 11 of this Act, the biological mother of the child shall be permanently barred from attacking the proceeding thereafter. The biological mother shall execute such affidavit in writing and under oath. The affidavit shall be executed by the biological mother before or at the time of execution of the consent or surrender, and shall be retained by the court and be a part of the Court's files. The form of affidavit shall be substantially as follows:

AFFIDAVIT OF IDENTIFICATION

I, _____, the mother of a (male or female) child, state under oath or affirm as follows:

(1) That the child was born, or is expected to be born, on the _____ day of _____, 199__, at _____, in the State of _____.

(2) That I reside at _____, in the City or Village of _____, State of _____.

(3) That I am of the age of _____ years.

(4) That I acknowledge that I have been asked to identify the father of my child.

750 ILCS 50/11   **FAMILIES**

(5) (CHECK ONE)

___ I know and am identifying the biological father.

___ I do not know the identity of the biological father.

___ I am unwilling to identify the biological father.

(6A) If I know and am identifying the father:

That the name of the biological father is _____; his last known home address is _____; his last known work address is _____; and he is _____ years of age; or he is deceased, having died on the _____ day of _____, 19__, at _____, in the State of _____.

(6B) If I do now know the identity of the biological father:

I do not know who the biological father is; the following is an explanation of why I am unable to identify him:

_____
_____
_____

(6C) If I am unwilling to identify the biological father:

I do not wish to name the biological father of the child for the following reasons:

_____
_____
_____

(7) The physical description of the biological father is:

_____
_____
_____

(8) I reaffirm that the information contained in paragraphs 5, 6, and 7, inclusive, is true and correct.

(9) I have been informed and understand that if I am unwilling, refuse to identify, or misidentify the biological father of the child, absent fraud or duress, I am permanently barred from attacking the proceedings for the adoption of the child at any time after I sign this document.

(10) I have read this Affidavit and have had the opportunity to review and question it; it was explained to me by _____; and I am signing it as my free and voluntary act and understand the contents and the results of signing it.

Dated this _____ day of _____, 199__.

_____
Signature

Under penalties as provided by law under Section 1–109 of the Code of Civil Procedure, the undersigned certifies that the statements set forth in this Affidavit are true and correct.

_____
Signature

750 ILCS 50/12
§ 12. Consent of child or adult

If, upon the date of the entry of the judgment the person sought to be adopted is of the age of 14 years or upwards, the adoption shall not be made without the consent of such person. Such consent shall be in writing and shall be acknowledged by such person as provided in Section 10 of this Act, provided, that if such person is in need of mental treatment or mentally retarded, the court may waive the provisions of this Section. No consent shall be required under this Section if the person sought to be adopted has died before giving such consent.

750 ILCS 50/12.1
§ 12.1 Putative Father Registry

The Department of Children and Family Services shall establish a Putative Father Registry for the purpose of determining the identity and location of a putative father of a minor child who is, or is expected to be, the subject of an adoption proceeding, in order to provide notice of such proceeding to the putative father. The Department of Children and Family Services shall establish rules and informational material necessary to implement the provisions of this Section. The Department shall have the authority to set reasonable fees for the use of the Registry.

(a) The Department shall maintain the following information in the Registry:

(1) With respect to the putative father:

(i) Name, including any other names by which the putative father may be known and that he may provide to the Registry;

(ii) Address at which he may be served with notice of a petition under this Act, including any change of address;

(iii) Social Security Number;

(iv) Date of birth; and

(v) If applicable, a certified copy of an order by a court of another state or territory of the United States adjudicating the putative father to be the father of the child.

(2) With respect to the mother of the child:

(i) Name, including all other names known to the putative father by which the mother may be known;

(ii) If known to the putative father, her last address;

(iii) Social Security Number; and

(iv) Date of birth.

(3) If known to the putative father, the name, gender, place of birth, and date of birth or anticipated date of birth of the child.

(4) The date that the Department received the putative father's registration.

(5) Other information as the Department may by rule determine necessary for the orderly administration of the Registry.

(b) A putative father may register with the Department before the birth of the child but shall register no later than 30 days after the birth of the child. All registrations shall be in writing and signed by the putative father. No fee shall be charged for the initial registration. The Department shall have no independent obligation to gather the information to be maintained.

(c) An interested party, including persons intending to adopt a child, a child welfare agency with whom the mother has placed or has given written notice of her intention to place a child for adoption, the mother of the child, or an attorney representing an interested party may request that the Department search the Registry to determine whether a putative father is registered in relation to a child who is or may be the subject to an adoption petition.

(d) A search of the Registry may be proven by the production of a certified copy of the registration form, or by the certified statement of the administrator of the Registry form, or by the certified statement of the administrator of the Registry that after a search, no registration of a putative father in relation to a child who is or may be the subject of an adoption petition could be located.

(e) Except as otherwise provided, information contained within the Registry is confidential and shall not be published or open to public inspection.

(f) A person who knowingly or intentionally registers false information under this Section commits a Class B misdemeanor. A person who knowingly or intentionally releases confidential information in violation of this Section commits a Class B misdemeanor.

(g) Except as provided in Section 8(b) of this Act, a putative father who fails to register with the Putative Father Registry as provided in this Section is barred from thereafter bringing or maintaining any action to assert any interest in the child, unless he proves by clear and convincing evidence that:

(1) it was not possible for him to register within the period of time specified in subsection (b) of this Section; and

(2) his failure to register was through no fault of his own; and

(3) he registered within 10 days after it became possible for him to file.

A lack of knowledge of the pregnancy or birth is not an acceptable reason for failure to register.

(h) Except as provided in Section 8(b) of this Act, failure to timely register with the Putative Father Registry (i) shall be deemed to be a waiver and surrender of any right to notice of any hearing in any judicial proceeding for adoption of the child, and the consent of that person to the adoption of the child is not required, and (ii) shall constitute an abandonment of the child and shall be prima facie evidence of sufficient grounds to support termination of such father's parental rights under this Act.

(i) In any adoption proceeding pertaining to a child born out of wedlock, if there is no showing that a putative father has consented to or waived his rights regarding the proposed adoption, certification as specified in subsection (d) shall be filed with the court prior to entry of a final judgment order of adoption.

750 ILCS 50/12a

§ 12a. Notice to putative father

1. Upon the written request to any Clerk of any Circuit Court, and upon the payment of a filing fee of $10.00, by any interested party, including persons intending to adopt a child, a child welfare agency with whom the mother has placed or has given written notice of her intention to place a child for adoption, the mother of a child, or any attorney representing an interested party, a notice, the declaration of paternity and the disclaimer of paternity may be served on a putative father in the same manner as Summons is served in other civil proceedings, or, in lieu of personal service, service may be made as follows:

(a) The person requesting notice shall pay to the Clerk of the Court a mailing fee of $2 plus the cost of U.S. postage for certified or registered mail and furnish to the Clerk an original and one copy of a notice, the declaration of paternity and the disclaimer of paternity together with an Affidavit setting forth the putative father's last known address. The original notice, the declaration of paternity and the disclaimer of paternity shall be retained by the Clerk.

(b) The Clerk shall forthwith mail to the putative father, at the address appearing in the Affidavit, the copy of the notice, the declaration of paternity and the disclaimer of paternity, by certified mail, return receipt requested; the envelope and return receipt shall bear the return address of the Clerk. The receipt for certified mail shall state the name and address of the addressee, and the date of mailing, and shall be attached to the original notice.

(c) The return receipt, when returned to the Clerk, shall be attached to the original notice, the declaration of paternity and the disclaimer of paternity, and shall constitute proof of service.

(d) The Clerk shall note the fact of service in a permanent record.

750 ILCS 50/12a   **FAMILIES**

    1.5 Notwithstanding any inconsistent provision of this or any other law, and in addition to the notice requirements of any law pertaining to persons other than those specified in this subsection, the persons entitled to notice that a petition has been filed under Section 5 of the Act shall include:

        (a) any person adjudicated by a court in this State to be the father of the child;

        (b) any person adjudicated by a court of another state or territory of the United States to be the father of the child, when a certified copy of the court order has been filed with the Putative Father Registry under Section 12.1 of the Act;

        (c) any person who at the time of the filing of the petition is registered in the Putative Father Registry under Section 12.1 of the Act as the putative father of the child;

        (d) any person who is recorded on the child's birth certificate as the child's father;

        (e) any person who is openly living with the child or the child's mother at the time the proceeding is initiated and who is holding himself out to be the child's father;

        (f) any person who has been identified as the child's father by the mother in a written, sworn statement, including an Affidavit of Identification as specified under Section 11 of the Act;

        (g) any person who was married to the child's mother on the date of the child's birth or within 300 days prior to the child's birth.

The sole purpose of notice under this Section shall be to enable the person receiving notice to appear in the adoption proceedings to present evidence to the court relevant to the best interests of the child.

    2. The notice shall be signed by the Clerk, and may be served on the putative father at any time after conception, and shall read as follows:

    "IN THE MATTER OF NOTICE TO _____, PUTATIVE FATHER.

    You have been identified as the father of a child born on the _____ day of _____, 19__, (or expected to be born on or about the _____ day of _____, 19__).

    The mother of the child is _____.

    The mother has indicated that she intends to place the child for adoption.

    As the alleged father of the child, you have certain legal rights with respect to the child, including the right to notice of the filing of proceedings instituted for the adoption of the child. If you wish to retain your rights with respect to the child, you must file with the Clerk of this Circuit Court of _____ County, Illinois, whose address is _____, Illinois, within 30 days after the date of receipt of this notice, the declaration of paternity enclosed herewith stating that you are, in fact, the father of the child and that you intend to retain your legal rights with respect to the child, or request to be notified of any further proceedings with respect to custody or adoption of the child.

If you do not file such a declaration of paternity, or a request for notice, then whatever legal rights you have with respect to the child, including the right to notice of any future proceedings for the adoption of the child, may be terminated without any further notice to you. When your legal rights with respect to the child are so terminated, you will not be entitled to notice of any proceeding instituted for the adoption of the child.

If you are not the father of the child, you may file with the Clerk of this Court the disclaimer of paternity enclosed herewith which will be noted in the Clerk's file and you will receive no further notice with respect to the child."

The declaration of paternity shall be substantially as follows:

"IN THE CIRCUIT COURT OF THE _____
JUDICIAL CIRCUIT, ILLINOIS
_____ County

)
)
) No.
)

DECLARATION OF PATERNITY WITH ENTRY OF APPEARANCE

I, _____ state as follows:

(1) That I am _____ years of age; and I reside at _____ in the County of _____, State of _____.

(2) That I have been advised that _____ is the mother of a _____ male child named _____ born or expected to be born on or about _____ and that such mother has stated that I am the father of this child.

(3) I declare that I am the father of this child.

(4) I understand that the mother of this child wishes to consent to the adoption of this child. I do not consent to the adoption of this child, and I understand that I must return this initial declaration of parentage form to the Clerk of the Circuit Court of _____ County, located at _____, within 30 days of receipt of this notice.

(5) I further understand that I am also obligated to establish my paternity pursuant to the Parentage Act of 1984 within 30 days of my receiving this notice or, if the child is not yet born, within 30 days after the birth of the child. This proceeding is separate and distinct from the above mailing of initial declaration of paternity; in this second notice, I must state that I am, in fact, the father of said child, and that I intend to retain my legal rights with respect to said child, and request to be notified of any further proceedings with respect to custody or adoption of the child.

(6) I hereby enter my appearance in the above entitled cause.

750 ILCS 50/12a   **FAMILIES**

OATH

I have been duly sworn and I say under oath that I have read and understand this Declaration of Paternity With Entry of Appearance. The facts that it contains are true and correct to the best of my knowledge, and I understand that by signing this document I admit my paternity. I have signed this document as my free and voluntary act.

_____
Signature

Dated this _____ day of _____, 19__.

Signed and Sworn Before Me This _____ day of _____, 19__.

_____
(notary public)".

The disclaimer of paternity shall be substantially as follows:

"IN THE CIRCUIT COURT OF THE _____
JUDICIAL CIRCUIT, ILLINOIS
_____ County

)
)
) No.
)

DENIAL OF PATERNITY WITH ENTRY OF APPEARANCE AND CONSENT TO ADOPTION

I, _____, state as follows:

(1) That I am _____ years of age; and I reside at _____ in the County of _____, State of _____.

(2) That I have been advised that _____ is the mother of a _____ male child named _____ born or expected to be born on or about _____ and that such mother has stated that I am the father of this child.

(3) I deny that I am the father of this child.

(4) I further understand that the mother of this child wishes to consent to the adoption of the child. I hereby consent to the adoption of this child, and waive any rights, remedies and defenses that I may now or in the future have as a result of the mother's allegation of the paternity of this child. This consent is being given in order to facilitate the adoption of the child and so that the court may terminate what rights I may have to the child as a result of being named the father by the mother. This consent is not in any manner an admission of paternity.

(5) I hereby enter my appearance in the above entitled cause and waive service of summons and other pleading.

OATH

I have been duly sworn and I say under oath that I have read and understood this Denial of Paternity With Entry of Appearance and Consent to Adoption. The facts it contains are true and correct to the best of my knowledge, and I understand that by signing this document I have not admitted paternity. I have signed this document as my free and voluntary act in order to facilitate the adoption of the child.

_____
Signature

Dated this _____ day of _____, 19__.

Signed and Sworn Before Me This _____ day of _____, 19__.

_____
(notary public)".

The names of adoptive parents shall not be included in the notice.

3. If the putative father files a disclaimer of paternity, he shall be deemed not to be the father of the child with respect to any adoption or other proceeding held to terminate the rights of parents as respects such child.

4. In the event the putative father does not file a declaration of paternity of the child or request for notice within 30 days of service of the above notice, he need not be made a party to or given notice of any proceeding brought for the adoption of the child. An Order or judgment may be entered in such proceeding terminating all of his rights with respect to the child without further notice to him.

5. If the putative father files a declaration of paternity or a request for notice in accordance with subsection 2, with respect to the child, he shall be given notice in event any proceeding is brought for the adoption of the child.

6. The Clerk shall maintain separate numbered files and records of requests and proofs of service and all other documents filed pursuant to this article. All such records shall be impounded.

750 ILCS 50/13

§ 13. Interim order

As soon as practicable after the filing of a petition for adoption the court shall hold a hearing for the following purposes:

A. In other than an adoption of a related child or an adoption through an agency, or of an adult:

750 ILCS 50/13   **FAMILIES**

(a) To determine the validity of the consent, provided that the execution of a consent pursuant to this Act shall be prima facie evidence of its validity, and provided that the validity of a consent shall not be affected by the omission therefrom of the names of the petitioners or adopting parents at the time the consent is executed or acknowledged, and further provided that the execution of a consent prior to the filing of a petition for adoption shall not affect its validity;

(b) To determine whether there is available suitable temporary custodial care for a child sought to be adopted.

B. In all cases:

(a) The court shall appoint the State's Attorney of the county in which the proceeding is pending, or some other licensed attorney as guardian ad litem to represent a child sought to be adopted. Such guardian ad litem shall have power to consent to the adoption of the child, if such consent is required;

(b) The court shall appoint a guardian ad litem for all named minors or defendants who are persons under legal disability, if any.

(c) If the petition alleges a person to be unfit pursuant to the provisions of subparagraph (p) of paragraph D of Section 1 of this Act, such person shall be represented by counsel. If such person is indigent or an appearance has not been entered on his behalf at the time the matter is set for hearing, the court shall appoint as counsel for him either the Guardianship and Advocacy Commission, the public defender, or, only if no attorney from the Guardianship and Advocacy Commission or the public defender is available, an attorney licensed to practice law in this State.

(d) If it is proved to the satisfaction of the court, after such investigation as the court deems necessary, that termination of parental rights and temporary commitment of the child to an agency or to a person deemed competent by the court, including petitioners, will be for the welfare of the child, the court may order the child to be so committed and may terminate the parental rights of the parents and declare the child a ward of the court or, if it is not so proved, the court may enter such other order as it shall deem necessary and advisable.

C. In the case of a child born outside the United States or a territory thereof, if the petitioners have previously been appointed guardians of such child by a court of competent jurisdiction in a country other than the United States or a territory thereof, the court may order that the petitioners continue as guardians of such child.

750 ILCS 50/14

§ 14. Judgment

Prior to the entry of the order of adoption in any case other than an adoption of a related child or of an adult, each petitioner and each person, agency, association, corporation, institution, society or organization consenting to said adoption shall execute an affidavit setting forth the costs, expenses, contributions, fees, compensation or other thing of value which has been given, promised or received unless the total of contributions, fees, compensation or other things of value which have been given, promised or received is less than $3,500, in which case the execution of an affidavit to such effect shall be sufficient. The Court, in its discretion, may require any person or agency to file a full affidavit of costs. No affidavit need be filed by a nonconsenting parent, or by any judge, or clerk, involved in the adoption proceedings. Such affidavit shall be under penalty of perjury and shall include, but is not limited to, hospital and medical costs, legal fees, social services, living expenses or any other expenses related to the adoption. Upon the expiration of 6 months after the date of any interim order vesting temporary care, custody and control of a child, other than a related child, in the petitioners, entered pursuant to this Act, the petitioners may apply to the court for a judgment of adoption. Notice of such application shall be served by the petitioners upon the investigating agency or the person making such investigation, and the guardian ad litem. After the hearing on such application, at which the petitioners and the child shall appear in person, unless their presence is waived by the court for good cause shown, the court may enter an order of adoption, provided the court is satisfied from the report of the investigating agency or the person making the investigation, and from the evidence, if any, introduced, that the adoption is for the welfare of the child and that there is a valid consent, or that no consent is required as provided in Section 8 of this Act.

A judgment for adoption of a related child, an adult, or a child as to whose adoption an agency or person authorized by law has the right of authority to consent may be entered at any time after service of process and after the return day designated therein.

No special findings of fact or certificate of evidence shall be necessary in any case to support the judgment.

750 ILCS 50/14a
§ 14a. Death of child prior to final judgment

After any court has acquired jurisdiction over the person of any child in an adoption proceeding, if such child dies before entry of final judgment, upon petition by the intended adoptive parent or parents suggesting the death of the child and asking that the court proceed in absence of the child to enter a final judgment, in the presence of the adoptive parent or parents and the State's attorney who are parties to the record, the court shall proceed to hearing and final judgment to enable the child to have the intended name by adoption. Otherwise the court may dismiss the proceeding.

In the case of an adoption proceeding commenced after the death of the person sought to be adopted, the intended adoptive parent or parents shall not, by reason of such adoption, acquire any interest in the estate of such deceased person, nor shall the intended adoptive parent or parents acquire any other right or incur any duty or obligation with respect to such deceased person.

750 ILCS 50/15

§ 15. Welfare of child—Same religious belief

The welfare of the child shall be the prime consideration in all adoption proceedings. The court in entering a judgment of adoption shall, whenever possible, give custody through adoption to a petitioner or petitioners of the same religious belief as that of the child.

750 ILCS 50/15.1

§ 15.1 Licensed foster parent

(a) Any person over the age of 18, who has cared for a child for a continuous period of one year or more as a foster parent licensed under the Child Care Act of 1969 to operate a foster family home, may apply to the child's guardian with the power to consent to adoption, for such guardian's consent.

(b) Such guardian shall give preference and first consideration to that application over all other applications for adoption of the child but the guardian's final decision shall be based on the welfare and best interest of the child. In arriving at this decision, the guardian shall consider all relevant factors including but not limited to:

(1) the wishes of the child;

(2) the interaction and interrelationship of the child with the applicant to adopt the child;

(3) the child's need for stability and continuity of relationship with parent figures;

(4) the wishes of the child's parent as expressed in writing prior to that parent's execution of a consent or surrender for adoption;

(5) the child's adjustment to his present home, school and community;

(6) the mental and physical health of all individuals involved;

(7) the family ties between the child and the applicant to adopt the child and the value of preserving family ties between the child and the child's relatives, including siblings;

(8) the background, race, ethnic heritage, behavior, age and living arrangements of the applicant to adopt the child.

(c) The final determination of the propriety of the adoption shall be within the sole discretion of the court, which shall base its decision on the welfare and best interest of the child. In arriving at this decision, the court shall consider all relevant factors including but not limited to the factors in subsection (b).

(d) If the court specifically finds that the guardian has abused his discretion by withholding consent to an adoption in violation of the child's welfare and best interests, then the court may grant an adoption, after all of the other provisions of this Act have been complied with, with or without the consent of the guardian with power to consent to adoption. If the court specifically finds that the guardian has abused his discretion by granting consent to an adoption in violation of the child's welfare and best interests, then the court may deny an adoption even though the guardian with power to consent to adoption has consented to it.

750 ILCS 50/16

§ 16. Entry of judgment

If, after examination of the report required by Section 6, the court finds a waiver to be for the welfare of the child, the court may, in its discretion, waive the waiting period of 6 months provided in Section 14 and enter a judgment of adoption.

750 ILCS 50/17

§ 17. Effect of order terminating parental rights or judgment of adoption

After the entry either of an order terminating parental rights or the entry of a judgment of adoption, the natural parents of a child sought to be adopted shall be relieved of all parental responsibility for such child and shall be deprived of all legal rights as respects the child, and the child shall be free from all obligations of maintenance and obedience as respects such natural parents.

750 ILCS 50/18

§ 18. Records confidential

(a) The word "illegitimate", the words "born out of wedlock", and words of similar import shall not be used in any adoption proceeding in any respect.

(b) The court call of adoption proceedings shall not identify any of the parties by name. The parties may be identified by initials or pseudonyms. The case shall be identified by its general number. The names of the lawyers representing the parties may appear on the court call, and the type of application that is being made to the court may also be identified.

(c) All adoption records maintained by each circuit clerk shall be impounded in accordance with the procedures provided by the Illinois Supreme Court's General Administrative Order on Recordkeeping and shall be opened for examination only upon specific order of the court, which order shall name the person or persons who are to be permitted to examine the file. Certified copies of all papers and documents contained in any file so impounded shall be

750 ILCS 50/18   FAMILIES

made only on like order. The guardian ad litem for a minor sought to be adopted shall have the right to inspect the court file without leave of court during the pendency of the proceeding. The attorney of record for the petitioners and other parties may inspect the file only with leave of court. The petitioners to the adoption, the attorney of record for the petitioners, and the guardian ad litem of the person who is the subject of the proceeding shall be entitled to receive certified copies of the order of adoption in the proceeding at any time within 30 days after the entry of the judgment of adoption without order of court. After 30 days from the entry of the judgment of adoption, no copies may be obtained without prior order of court, but good cause is not necessary to be shown by one of the petitioners to the adoption.

(d) If an appeal is taken from an adoption proceeding, the papers filed in the court of review and the opinion of the reviewing court shall not identify the true names of the parties; instead, initials or pseudonyms shall be used to identify the parties.

750 ILCS 50/18.1
§ 18.1 Procedure for the disclosure of identifying information—Confidentiality

(a) The Department of Public Health shall establish a Registry for the purpose of providing identifying information to mutually consenting children surrendered for adoption or adoptees and biological parents and to mutually consenting biological siblings. Identifying information for the purpose of this Act shall mean only the name and last known address of the consenting person or persons.

(b) At any time after a child is surrendered for adoption, or at any time during the adoption proceedings or at any time thereafter, either biological parent or both of them may file with the Registry a Biological Parent Registration Identification Form and an Information Exchange Authorization.

(c) Any adoptee, or any child who has been surrendered for adoption but not adopted ("surrendered child"), may file with the Registry an Adoptee Registration Identification Form or a Surrendered Child Registration Identification Form and an Information Exchange Authorization if such adoptee or surrendered child is 21 years of age or over; or, if over 18 years of age and under 21 years of age, if there is attached to the Information Exchange Authorization (1) written consent of both adoptive parents, or (2) written consent of a single adoptive parent with a certified copy of the Judgment of Adoption, or (3) proof of the death of one adoptive parent and written consent of the surviving adoptive parent, or (4) written consent of the guardian of the adoptee or surrendered child with a certified copy of the Order of Guardianship.

(d) The Department of Public Health shall supply to the adoptee or surrendered child and to the biological parents identifying information only if both the adoptee or surrendered child and the biological parents have filed with the Registry an Information Exchange Authorization and the information at the Registry indicates that the consenting adoptee or surrendered child is the child of the consenting biological parents.

The Department of Public Health shall supply to adoptees or surrendered children who are biological siblings identifying information only if both siblings have filed with the Registry an Information Exchange Authorization and the information at the Registry indicates that the consenting siblings have one or both biological parents in common. Identifying information shall be supplied to consenting biological siblings if any such sibling is 21 years of age or over; or, if over 18 years of age and under 21 years of age, if there is attached to the Information Exchange Authorization (1) written consent of both adoptive parents, or (2) written consent of a single adoptive parent with a certified copy of the Judgment of Adoption, or (3) proof of the death of one adoptive parent and written consent of the surviving adoptive parent, or (4) written consent of the guardian of the adoptee or surrendered child with a certified copy of the Order of Guardianship.

(e) A biological parent, adoptee or surrendered child may notify the Registry of his desire not to have his identity revealed or may revoke any previously filed Information Exchange Authorization by completing and filing with the Registry a Registry Identification Form along with a Denial of Information Exchange. Any adoptee, surrendered child or biological parent may revoke a Denial of Information Exchange by filing an Information Exchange Authorization. The Department of Public Health shall act in accordance with the most recently filed Authorization.

(f) Identifying information ascertained from the Registry shall be confidential and may be disclosed only (1) upon a Court Order, which order shall name the person or persons entitled to the information, or (2) to the adoptee, surrendered child, adopted or surrendered sibling, or biological parent if both the adoptee, or surrendered child, and his or her biological parent, or both adopted or surrendered siblings, have filed with the Registry an Information Exchange Authorization, or (3) as authorized under subsection (h) of Section 18.3 of this Act. Any person who willfully provides unauthorized disclosure of any information filed with the Registry shall be guilty of a Class A misdemeanor and shall be liable for damages.

750 ILCS 50/18.2

§ 18.2 Forms

(a) The form of the Biological Parent Registration Identification Form shall be substantially as follows:

BIOLOGICAL PARENT IDENTIFICATION
(Insert all known information)

I, _____, state that I am the _____ (mother or father) of the following child:

750 ILCS 50/18.2   **FAMILIES**

      Child's original name: _____ (first) _____ (middle) _____ (last), _____ (hour of birth), _____ (date of birth), _____ (city and state of birth), _____ (name of hospital).

      Father's full name: _____ (first) _____ (middle) _____ (last), _____ (date of birth), _____ (city and state of birth).

      Name of mother inserted on birth certificate: _____ (first) _____ (middle) _____ (last), _____ (race), _____ (date of birth), _____ (city and state of birth).

      That I surrendered my child to: _____ (name of agency), _____ (city and state of agency), _____ (approximate date child surrendered).

      That I gave up my child by private adoption: _____ (date), _____ (city and state).

Name of adoptive parents, if known: _____.
Other identifying information: _____.

                                                              (Signature of parent)

                                                           (printed name of parent)

(date)

      (b) The form of Adoptee Registration Identification shall be substantially as follows:

ADOPTEE REGISTRATION IDENTIFICATION
                (Insert all known information)

I, _____, state the following:

      Adoptee's present name: _____ (first) _____ (middle) _____ (last).

      Adoptee's name at birth (if known): _____ (first) _____ (middle) _____ (last), _____ (birth date), _____ (city and state of birth), _____ (sex), _____ (race).

      Name of adoptive father: _____ (first) _____ (middle) _____ (last), _____ (race).

      Maiden name of adoptive mother: _____ (first) _____ (middle) _____ (last), _____ (race).

      Name of biological mother (if known): _____ (first) _____ (middle) _____ (last), _____ (race).

      Name of biological father (if known): _____ (first) _____ (middle) _____ (last), _____ (race).

I was adopted through: _____ (name of agency).

I was adopted privately: _____ (state "yes" if known).
I was adopted in _____ (city and state), _____ (approximate date).
Other identifying information: _____.

_____
(Signature of adoptee)

_____
(printed name of adoptee)

_____
(date)

(c) The form of Surrendered Child Registration Identification shall be substantially as follows:

SURRENDERED CHILD REGISTRATION IDENTIFICATION
(Insert all known information)

I, _____, state the following:

Surrendered Child's present name: _____ (first) _____ (middle) _____ (last).

Surrendered Child's name at birth (if known): _____ (first) _____ (middle) _____ (last), _____ (birth date), _____ (city and state of birth), _____ (sex), _____ (race).

Name of guardian father: _____ (first) _____ (middle) _____ (last), _____ (race).

Maiden name of guardian mother: _____ (first) _____ (middle) _____ (last), _____ (race).

Name of biological mother (if known): _____ (first) _____ (middle) _____ (last) _____ (race).

Name of biological father (if known): _____ (first) _____ (middle) _____ (last), _____ (race).

I was surrendered for adoption to: _____ (name of agency).

I was surrendered for adoption in _____ (city and state), _____ (approximate date).

Other identifying information: _____.

_____
(Signature of surrendered child)

_____
(printed name of child surrendered for adoption)

_____
(date)

750 ILCS 50/18.2   **FAMILIES**

(d) The form of Information Exchange Authorization shall be substantially as follows:

INFORMATION EXCHANGE AUTHORIZATION

I, _____, state that I am the person who completed the Registration Identification; that I am of the age of _____ years; that I hereby authorize the Department of Public Health to give to my (biological parent) (child) the necessary information so I can be contacted; that I am fully aware that I can only be supplied with the name and last known address of my (biological parent) (child) if such person has duly executed an Information Exchange Authorization which has not been revoked; that I can be contacted by writing to: _____ (own name or name of person to contact) (address) (phone number). Dated this _____ day of _____, 19__.

_____   _____
(witness)   (signature)

(e) The form of Denial of Information Exchange shall be substantially as follows:

DENIAL OF INFORMATION EXCHANGE

I, _____, state that I am the person who completed the Registration Identification; that I am of the age of _____ years; that I hereby instruct the Department of Public Health not to give any identifying information about me to my (biological parent) (child); that I do not wish to be contacted.

Dated this _____ day of _____, 19__.

_____   _____
(witness)   (signature)

(f) The Information Exchange Authorization and the Denial of Information Exchange shall be acknowledged by the biological parent, adoptee or surrendered child before a notary public, in form substantially as follows:

State of _____

County of _____

I, a Notary Public, in and for the said County, in the State aforesaid, do hereby certify that _____ personally known to me to be the same person whose name is subscribed to the foregoing certificate of acknowledgement, appeared before me in person and acknowledged that (he or she) signed such certificate as (his or her) free and voluntary act and that the statements in such certificate are true.

Given under my hand and notarial seal this _____ day of _____, 19__.

_____
(signature)

(g) When the execution of an Information Exchange Authorization or a Denial of Information Exchange is acknowledged before a representative of an agency, such representative shall have his signature on said Certificate acknowledged before a notary public, in form substantially as follows:

State of _____

County of _____

I, a Notary Public, in and for the said County, in the State aforesaid, do hereby certify that _____ personally known to me to be the same person whose name is subscribed to the foregoing certificate of acknowledgement, appeared before me in person and acknowledged that (he or she) signed such certificate as (his or her) free and voluntary act and that the statements in such certificate are true.

Given under my hand and notarial seal this _____ day of _____, 19__.

_____
(signature)

(h) Where an Information Exchange Authorization or a Denial of Information Exchange is signed in a foreign country, the execution of such document shall be acknowledged or affirmed in a manner conformable to the law and procedure of such country.

(i) If the person signing an Information Exchange Authorization or a Denial of Information is in the military service of the United States, the execution of such document may be acknowledged before a commissioned officer and the signature of such officer on such certificate shall be verified or acknowledged before a notary public or by such other procedure as is then in effect for such division or branch of the armed forces.

750 ILCS 50/18.3

§ 18.3 Biological parents—Written statement—Identifying information—Disclosure of information

(a) The agency, Department of Children and Family Services, Court Supportive Services, Juvenile Division of the Circuit Court, Probation Officers of the Circuit Court and any other party to the surrender of a child for adoption or in an adoption proceeding shall obtain from any biological parent or parents giving up a child for purposes of adoption after the effective date of this Act a written statement which indicates:

(1) a desire to have identifying information shared with the adopted or surrendered child at a later date;

(2) a desire not to have identifying information revealed; or

(3) that no decision is made at that time.

(b) When the written statement is signed, the biological parent or parents shall be informed in writing that their decision regarding the sharing of identifying information can be made or changed by such biological parent or parents at any future date.

(c) The biological parent shall be informed in writing that if sharing of identifying information with the adopted or surrendered child is to occur, that the child must be 21 years of age or over; or if under the age of 21 with written consent of both adoptive parents, with written consent of a single adoptive parent, with proof of death of one adoptive parent and written consent of the surviving adoptive parent, or with written consent of the guardian of the child.

(d) If the biological parent or parents indicate a desire to share identifying information with the child, the statement shall contain information regarding means to communicate with the biological parent.

(e) Any biological parent or parents requesting that no identifying information be revealed to the adoptee or surrendered child shall be informed that such request will be conveyed to the adoptee or surrendered child if the adoptee or surrendered child requests such information; and such identifying information shall not be revealed.

(f) Any adoptee or surrendered child 21 years of age or over, and any adoptee under 21 years of age with written consent of the adoptive parents, the surviving adoptive parent, a single adoptive parent or the guardian of the child may also indicate in writing his desire or lack of desire to share identifying information with the biological parent or parents or biological sibling or siblings. Any adoptee or surrendered child requesting that no identifying information be revealed to the biological parent or biological sibling shall be informed that such request shall be conveyed to the parent if such biological parent or biological sibling requests such information; and such identifying information shall not be revealed.

(g) Any biological parents and adoptees or surrendered children indicating their desire to have identifying information shall be informed of the existence of the Registry and assistance shall be given to such biological parent, adoptee or surrendered child to also legally record his name with the Registry.

(h) The agency, Department of Children and Family Services, Court Supportive Services, Juvenile Division of the Circuit Court, Probation Officers of the Circuit Court and any other organization involved in the surrender of a child for adoption in an adoption proceeding which has written statements from an adoptee or surrendered child and the biological parent or a biological sibling indicating a desire to receive identifying information shall supply such information to the mutually consenting parties, except that no identifying information shall be supplied to consenting biological siblings if any such sibling is under 21 years of age. However, both the Registry having an Information Exchange Authorization and the organization having a written statement requesting identifying information shall communicate with each other to determine if the adoptee or surrendered child or the biological parent or biological sibling has signed a form at a later date indicating a change in his desires regarding the sharing of information. The agreement of the biological parent shall be binding.

750 ILCS 50/18.3a
§ 18.3a Confidential intermediary

(a) General purposes. Notwithstanding any other provision of this Act, any adoptee over the age of 18 or any adoptive parent or legal guardian of an adoptee under the age of 18 may petition the court for appointment of a confidential intermediary as provided in this Section for the purpose of obtaining from one or both biological parents or a sibling or siblings of the adoptee information concerning the background of a psychological or genetically-based medical problem experienced or which may be expected to be experienced in the future by the adoptee or obtaining assistance in treating such a problem.

(b) Petition. The court shall appoint a confidential intermediary for the purposes described in subsection (f) if the petitioner shows the following:

(1) the adoptee is suffering or may be expected to suffer in the future from a life-threatening or substantially incapacitating physical illness of any nature, or a psychological disturbance which is substantially incapacitating but not life-threatening, or a mental illness which, in the opinion of a physician licensed to practice medicine in all its branches, is or could be genetically based to a significant degree;

(2) the treatment of the adoptee, in the opinion of a physician licensed to practice medicine in all of its branches, would be materially assisted by information obtainable from the biological parents or might benefit from the provision of organs or other bodily tissues, materials, or fluids by the biological parents or other close biological relatives; and

(3) there is neither an Information Exchange Authorization nor a Denial of Information Exchange filed in the Registry as provided in Section 18.1.

The affidavit or testimony of the treating physician shall be conclusive on the issue of the utility of contact with the biological parents unless the court finds that the relationship between the illness to be treated and the alleged need for contact is totally without foundation.

(c) Fees and expenses. The court shall condition the appointment of the confidential intermediary on the payment of the intermediary's fees and expenses in advance, unless the intermediary waives the right to full advance payment or to any reimbursement at all.

(d) Eligibility of intermediary. The court may appoint as confidential intermediary either an employee of the Illinois Department of Children and Family Services designated by the Department to serve as such, any other person certified by the Department as qualified to serve as a confidential intermediary, or any employee of a licensed child welfare agency certified by the agency as qualified to serve as a confidential intermediary.

(e) Access. Notwithstanding any other provision of law, the confidential intermediary shall have access to all records of the court or any agency, public or private, which relate to the adoption or the identity and location of any biological parent.

(f) Purposes of contact. The confidential intermediary has only the following powers and duties:

(1) To contact one or both biological parents, inform the parent or parents of the basic medical problem of the adoptee and the nature of the information or assistance sought from the biological parent, and inform the parent or parents of the following options:

(A) The biological parent may totally reject the request for assistance or information, or both, and no disclosure of identity or location shall be made to the petitioner.

(B) The biological parent may file an Information Exchange Authorization as provided in Section 18.1. The confidential intermediary shall explain to the biological parent the consequences of such a filing, including that the biological parent's identity will be available for discovery by the adoptee. If the biological parent agrees to this option, the confidential intermediary shall supply the parent with the appropriate forms, shall be responsible for their immediate filing with the Registry, and shall inform the petitioner of their filing.

(C) If the biological parent wishes to provide the information or assistance sought but does not wish his or her identity disclosed, the confidential intermediary shall arrange for the disclosure of the information or the provision of assistance in as confidential a manner as possible so as to protect the privacy of the biological parent and minimize the likelihood of disclosure of the biological parent's identity.

(2) If a biological parent so desires, to arrange for a confidential communication with the treating physician to discuss the need for the requested information or assistance.

(3) If a biological parent agrees to provide the information or assistance sought but wishes to maintain his or her privacy, to arrange for the provision of the information or assistance to the physician in as confidential a manner as possible so as to protect the privacy of the biological parent and minimize the likelihood of disclosure of the biological parent's identity.

(g) Oath. The confidential intermediary shall sign an oath of confidentiality substantially as follows:

"I, _____, being duly sworn, on oath depose and say: As a condition of appointment as a confidential intermediary, I affirm that:

(1) I will not disclose to the petitioner, directly or indirectly, any information about the identity or location of the biological parent whose

assistance is being sought for medical reasons except in a manner consistent with the law.

(2) I recognize that violation of this oath subjects me to civil liability and to being found in contempt of court.

_____

SUBSCRIBED AND SWORN to before me, a Notary Public, this _____ day of _____, 19__.

_____

(h) Sanctions.

(1) Any confidential intermediary who improperly discloses information identifying a biological parent shall be liable to the biological parent for damages and may also be found in contempt of court.

(2) Any physician or other person who learns a biological parent's identity, directly or indirectly, through the use of procedures provided in this Section and who improperly discloses information identifying the biological parent shall be liable to the biological parent for actual damages plus minimum punitive damages of $10,000.

(i) Death of biological parent. Notwithstanding any other provision of this Act, if the confidential intermediary discovers that the person whose assistance is sought has died, he or she shall report this fact to the court, along with a copy of the death certificate if possible.

750 ILCS 50/18.4

§ 18.4 Information given to adoptive parents

(a) The agency, Department of Children and Family Services, Court Supportive Services, Juvenile Division of the Circuit Court, or the Probation Officers of the Circuit Court involved in the adoption proceedings shall give in writing the following information, if known, to the adoptive parents not later than the date of placement with the petitioning adoptive parents: (i) age of biological parents; (ii) their race, religion and ethnic background; (iii) general physical appearance of biological parents; (iv) their education, occupation, hobbies, interests and talents; (v) existence of any other children born to the biological parents; (vi) information about biological grandparents; reason for emigrating into the United States, if applicable, and country of origin; (vii) relationship between biological parents; and (viii) detailed medical and mental health histories of the child, the biological parents, and their immediate relatives. However, no information provided under this subsection shall disclose the name or last known address of the biological parents, grandparents, the siblings of the biological parents, or any other relative of the adopted.

750 ILCS 50/18.4   **FAMILIES**

(b) Any adoptee 18 years of age or over shall be given the information in subsection (a) upon request.

(c) Any of the above available information for any adoption proceedings completed before the effective date of this Act shall be supplied to the adoptive parents or an adoptee 18 years of age or over upon request.

(d) The agency, Department of Children and Family Services, Court Supportive Services, Juvenile Division of the Circuit Court, the Probation Officers of the Circuit Court and any other governmental bodies having any of the above information shall retain the file until the adoptee would have reached the age of 99 years.

750 ILCS 50/18.4a

§ 18.4a. Medical and mental health histories—Contents—Release

(a) Notwithstanding any other provision of law to the contrary, to the extent currently in possession of the agency, the medical and mental health histories of a child legally freed for adoption and of the biological parents, with information identifying the biological parents eliminated, shall be provided by an agency to the child's prospective adoptive parent and shall be provided upon request to an adoptive parent when a child has been adopted. The medical and mental health histories shall include all the following available information:

(1) Conditions or diseases believed to be hereditary.

(2) Drugs or medications taken by the child's biological mother during pregnancy.

(3) Psychological and psychiatric information.

(4) Any other information that may be a factor influencing the child's present or future health.

(b) The Department of Children and Family Services may promulgate rules and regulations governing the release of medical histories under this Section.

750 ILCS 50/18.5

§ 18.5 Exemption from liability

No liability shall attach to the State, any agency thereof, any licensed agency, any judge, any officer or employee of the court, or any party or employee thereof involved in the surrender of a child for adoption or in an adoption proceeding for acts or efforts made within the scope of Sections 18.1 thru 18.5, inclusive, of this Act and pursuant to its provisions, except for subsection (f) of Section 18.1.

750 ILCS 50/18.6

§ 18.6 Fees and charges

The Department of Public Health shall levy a fee for each registrant under Sections 18.1 through 18.5. No charge of any kind shall be made for the withdrawal of a registration or consent form.

750 ILCS 50/19

§ 19. Registration new birth certificate

Upon the entry of a judgment of adoption, the clerk of the court that entered the judgment shall prepare a certificate of adoption and send the certificate to the Department of Public Health, pursuant to Sections 16 and 17 of the Vital Records Act. The statutory fee of the clerk of the court for that certificate shall be paid by the petitioners.

750 ILCS 50/20

§ 20. Practice

The provisions of the Civil Practice Law and all existing and future amendments of that Law and the Supreme Court Rules now or hereafter adopted in relation to that Law shall apply to all adoption proceedings except as otherwise specifically provided in this Act.

Proceedings under this Act shall receive priority over other civil cases in being set for hearing.

No matters not germane to the distinctive purpose of a proceeding under this Act shall be introduced by joinder, counterclaim or otherwise.

An appeal from a judgment order for adoption or other appealable orders under this Act shall be prosecuted and heard on an expedited basis, unless good cause for doing otherwise is shown.

In the event a judgment order for adoption is vacated or a petition for adoption is denied, the court shall promptly conduct a hearing as to the temporary and permanent custody of the minor child who is the subject of the proceedings pursuant to Part VI of the Illinois Marriage and Dissolution of Marriage Act. The parties to said proceedings shall be the petitioners to the adoption proceedings, the minor child, any biological parents whose parental rights have not been terminated, and other parties who have been granted leave to intervene in the proceedings.

This Act shall be liberally construed, and the rule that statutes in derogation of the common law must be strictly construed shall not apply to this Act.

All defects in pleadings, either in form or substance, not objected 45 prior to the entry of final judgment, shall be deemed to be waived.

As to persons over whom the court had jurisdiction or persons claiming under them, it shall be no basis for attack as to the validity of an adoption judgment that the court lacked jurisdiction over some other person or persons over whom it should have had jurisdiction. If, upon attack by a person or persons over whom the court lacked jurisdiction, or persons claiming under them, an adoption judgment is set aside, it shall be set aside only insofar as it affects such person or persons.

This amendatory Act of 1994 applies to cases pending on and after its effective date.

750 ILCS 50/20a

§ 20a. Construction of Act

The best interests and welfare of the person to be adopted shall be of paramount consideration in the construction and interpretation of this Act. It is in the best interests of persons to be adopted that this Act be construed and interpreted so as not to result in extending time limits beyond those set forth herein.

750 ILCS 50/20b

§ 20b. Time limit for relief from final judgment or order

A petition for relief from a final order or judgment entered in a proceeding under this Act, after 30 days from the entry thereof under the provisions of Section 2-1401 of the Code of Civil Procedure or otherwise, must be filed not later than one year after the entry of the order or judgment.

An appeal from a judgment order for adoption or other appealable order under this Act shall be heard on an expedited basis. In the event that an order for adoption is vacated, the court shall promptly conduct a hearing as to the temporary and permanent custody of the minor child who is the subject of the proceeding pursuant to Part VI of the Illinois Marriage and Dissolution of Marriage Act. The parties to the proceeding shall be the petitioners to the adoption proceeding, the minor child, the biological parents whose rights have been terminated, and other parties who have been granted leave to intervene in the proceeding. The provisions of this Section shall apply to all cases pending on and after the effective date of this amendatory Act of 1994.

750 ILCS 50/21

§ 21. Compensation for placing of children prohibited

No person, agency, association, corporation, institution, society or other organization, except a child welfare agency as defined by the "Child Care Act", approved July 10, 1957, as now or hereafter amended, shall receive or accept, or pay or give any compensation or thing of value, directly or indirectly, for placing out of a child as is more specifically provided in "An Act to prevent the payment or receipt of compensation for placing out children for adoption or for the purpose of providing care", approved July 14, 1955, as now or hereafter amended.

750 ILCS 50/22

§ 22. Partial invalidity

If any part of this Act is held by any court to be unconstitutional or invalid, such decision or judgment shall not affect the validity of the remaining portions of this Act.

750 ILCS 50/23

§ 23. Repeal—Saving

"An Act in relation to the adoption of children and to repeal an Act therein named", approved June 30, 1945, as amended is repealed.

Such repeal shall not in any way affect an act done or a right, power or remedy given or accrued under any statute in force prior to the effective date of this Act.

The execution of a consent or surrender, prior to the effective date of this Act, shall not affect its validity for use in a proceeding under this Act, if such consent or surrender was executed in accordance with law then in effect.

750 ILCS 50/24

§ 24. Effective date

This Act shall take effect January 1, 1960.

ACT 55. CONTEST OF ADOPTIONS ACT

Analysis

Sec.
0.01. Short title.
1. Notice—Attack on proceedings for failure to give.

WESTLAW Electronic Research

See WESTLAW Electronic Research Guide preceding the Summary of Contents.

---

750 ILCS 55/0.01

§ 0.01 Short title

This Act may be cited as the Contest of Adoptions Act.

750 ILCS 55/1

§ 1. Notice—Attack on proceedings for failure to give

No attack upon or proceedings contesting the validity of an adoption decree heretofore entered shall be made either directly or collaterally because of the failure to serve notice on or give notice to the reputed father, unless such attack or proceedings shall be instituted within one year after the effective date of this Act.

Author's Notes

(1) **Effective date.** The effective date of the Act was August 3, 1949. The Act appears to apply to only adoption decrees entered prior to the effective date of the Act. See Adoption Act, 750 ILCS 50/8 and 50/12.1.

ACT 60. ILLINOIS DOMESTIC VIOLENCE ACT OF 1986
ARTICLE I. GENERAL PROVISIONS

Analysis

Sec.
101. Short title.
102. Purposes; Rules of construction.
103. Definitions.

WESTLAW Electronic Research

See WESTLAW Electronic Research Guide preceding the Summary of Contents.

---

750 ILCS 60/101

§ 101. Short title

This Act shall be known and may be cited as the "Illinois Domestic Violence Act of 1986".

750 ILCS 60/102

§ 102. Purposes; Rules of construction

This Act shall be liberally construed and applied to promote its underlying purposes, which are to:

(1) Recognize domestic violence as a serious crime against the individual and society which produces family disharmony in thousands of Illinois families, promotes a pattern of escalating violence which frequently culminates in intra-family homicide, and creates an emotional atmosphere that is not conducive to healthy childhood development;

(2) Recognize domestic violence against high risk adults with disabilities, who are particularly vulnerable due to impairments in ability to seek or obtain protection, as a serious problem which takes on many forms, including physical abuse, sexual abuse, neglect, and exploitation, and facilitate accessibility of remedies under the Act in order to provide immediate and effective assistance and protection.

(3) Recognize that the legal system has ineffectively dealt with family violence in the past, allowing abusers to escape effective prosecution or financial liability, and has not adequately acknowledged the criminal nature of domestic violence; that, although many laws have changed, in practice there is still widespread failure to appropriately protect and assist victims;

(4) Support the efforts of victims of domestic violence to avoid further abuse by promptly entering and diligently enforcing court orders which prohibit abuse and, when necessary, reduce the abuser's access to the victim

and address any related issues of child custody and economic support, so that victims are not trapped in abusive situations by fear of retaliation, loss of a child, financial dependence, or loss of accessible housing or services;

(5) Clarify the responsibilities and support the efforts of law enforcement officers to provide immediate, effective assistance and protection for victims of domestic violence, recognizing that law enforcement officers often become the secondary victims of domestic violence, as evidenced by the high rates of police injuries and deaths that occur in response to domestic violence calls; and

(6) Expand the civil and criminal remedies for victims of domestic violence; including, when necessary, the remedies which effect physical separation of the parties to prevent further abuse.

750 ILCS 60/103

§ 103. Definitions

For the purposes of this Act, the following terms shall have the following meanings:

(1) "Abuse" means physical abuse, harassment, intimidation of a dependent, interference with personal liberty or willful deprivation but does not include reasonable direction of a minor child by a parent or person in loco parentis.

(2) "Adult with disabilities" means an elder adult with disabilities or a high-risk adult with disabilities. A person may be an adult with disabilities for purposes of this Act even though he or she has never been adjudicated an incompetent adult. However, no court proceeding may be initiated or continued on behalf of an adult with disabilities over that adult's objection, unless such proceeding is approved by his or her legal guardian, if any.

(3) "Domestic violence" means abuse as defined in paragraph (1).

(4) "Elder adult with disabilities" means an adult prevented by advanced age from taking appropriate action to protect himself or herself from abuse by a family or household member.

(5) "Exploitation" means the illegal, including tortious, use of a high-risk adult with disabilities or of the assets or resources of a high-risk adult with disabilities. Exploitation includes, but is not limited to, the misappropriation of assets or resources of a high-risk adult with disabilities by undue influence, by breach of a fiduciary relationship, by fraud, deception, or extortion, or the use of such assets or resources in a manner contrary to law.

(6) "Family or household members" include spouses, former spouses, parents, children, stepchildren and other persons related by blood or by present or prior marriage, persons who share or formerly shared a common dwelling, persons who have or allegedly have a child in common, persons who share or allegedly share a blood relationship through a child, persons who have or have had a dating or engagement relationship, and persons with

disabilities and their personal assistants. For purposes of this paragraph, neither a casual acquaintanceship nor ordinary fraternization between 2 individuals in business or social contexts shall be deemed to constitute a dating relationship. In the case of a high-risk adult with disabilities, "family or household members" includes any person who has the responsibility for a high-risk adult as a result of a family relationship or who has assumed responsibility for all or a portion of the care of a high-risk adult with disabilities voluntarily, or by express or implied contract, or by court order.

(7) "Harassment" means knowing conduct which is not necessary to accomplish a purpose that is reasonable under the circumstances; would cause a reasonable person emotional distress; and does cause emotional distress to the petitioner. Unless the presumption is rebutted by a preponderance of the evidence, the following types of conduct shall be presumed to cause emotional distress:

(i) creating a disturbance at petitioner's place of employment or school;

(ii) repeatedly telephoning petitioner's place of employment, home or residence;

(iii) repeatedly following petitioner about in a public place or places;

(iv) repeatedly keeping petitioner under surveillance by remaining present outside his or her home, school, place of employment, vehicle or other place occupied by petitioner or by peering in petitioner's windows;

(v) improperly concealing a minor child from petitioner, repeatedly threatening to improperly remove a minor child of petitioner's from the jurisdiction or from the physical care of petitioner, repeatedly threatening to conceal a minor child from petitioner, or making a single such threat following an actual or attempted improper removal or concealment, unless respondent was fleeing an incident or pattern of domestic violence; or

(vi) threatening physical force, confinement or restraint on one or more occasions.

(8) "High-risk adult with disabilities" means a person aged 18 or over whose physical or mental disability impairs his or her ability to seek or obtain protection from abuse, neglect, or exploitation.

(9) "Interference with personal liberty" means committing or threatening physical abuse, harassment, intimidation or willful deprivation so as to compel another to engage in conduct from which she or he has a right to abstain or to refrain from conduct in which she or he has a right to engage.

(10) "Intimidation of a dependent" means subjecting a person who is dependent because of age, health or disability to participation in or the witnessing of: physical force against another or physical confinement or restraint of another which constitutes physical abuse as defined in this Act, regardless of whether the abused person is a family or household member.

(11) (A) "Neglect" means the failure to exercise that degree of care toward a high-risk adult with disabilities which a reasonable person would exercise under the circumstances and includes but is not limited to:

(i) the failure to take reasonable steps to protect a high-risk adult with disabilities from acts of abuse;

(ii) the repeated, careless imposition of unreasonable confinement;

(iii) the failure to provide food, shelter, clothing, and personal hygiene to a high-risk adult with disabilities who requires such assistance;

(iv) the failure to provide medical and rehabilitative care for the physical and mental health needs of a high-risk adult with disabilities; or

(v) the failure to protect a high-risk adult with disabilities from health and safety hazards.

(B) Nothing in this subsection (10) shall be construed to impose a requirement that assistance be provided to a high-risk adult with disabilities over his or her objection in the absence of a court order, nor to create any new affirmative duty to provide support to a high-risk adult with disabilities.

(12) "Order of protection" means an emergency order, interim order or plenary order, granted pursuant to this Act, which includes any or all of the remedies authorized by Section 214 of this Act.

(13) "Petitioner" may mean not only any named petitioner for the order of protection and any named victim of abuse on whose behalf the petition is brought, but also any other person protected by this Act.

(14) "Physical abuse" includes sexual abuse and means any of the following:

(i) knowing or reckless use of physical force, confinement or restraint;

(ii) knowing, repeated and unnecessary sleep deprivation; or

(iii) knowing or reckless conduct which creates an immediate risk of physical harm.

(15) "Willful deprivation" means wilfully denying a person who because of age, health or disability requires medication, medical care, shelter, accessible shelter or services, food, therapeutic device, or other physical assistance, and thereby exposing that person to the risk of physical, mental or emotional harm, except with regard to medical care or treatment when the dependent person has expressed an intent to forgo such medical care or treatment. This paragraph does not create any new affirmative duty to provide support to dependent persons.

Author's Notes

Analysis

1. Citation.
2. Broad definitions.
3. Coverage.
4. High risk adults and exploitation.
5. Family or household members.
6. Neglect.

(1) **Citation.** The Illinois Domestic Violence Act is sometimes cited herein as the DVA.

(2) **Broad definitions.** The broad definition section forms the basis of the Illinois Domestic Violence Act. Abuse is defined in DVA § 103(1) to not only include physical abuse but also harassment, intimidation of a dependent, and interference with personal liberty or willful deprivation. Domestic violence is defined by DVA § 103(3) to mean abuse as defined by paragraph DVA § 103(1). These terms are further defined in subsequent paragraphs. For example, physical abuse is defined in DVA § 103(14) to include sexual abuse, physical force, sleep deprivation, and reckless conduct which creates an immediate risk of physical harm. Harassment is presumed by DVA § 103(7) because of actual conduct, but also as a result of threats concerning a child or physical force.

(3) **Coverage.** The Domestic Violence Act covers, *inter alia*, persons abused by family or household members and high risk adults with disabilities who are abused, neglected, or exploited by a family or household member. See DVA § 201 and accompanying Author's Notes.

(4) **High risk adults and exploitation.** Exploitation is defined in DVA § 103(5) to include the misappropriation of assets of a high risk adult with disabilities. A high risk adult with disabilities is an adult whose physical or mental disability impairs his ability to seek protection from abuse, neglect, or exploitation. DVA § 103(8).

(5) **Family or household members.** The terms "family" and "household members" are also very broadly defined. Section 103(6) extends "family or household members" to include former spouses, persons who share or formerly shared a common dwelling, persons who have a child in common, or even allegedly have a child in common, and persons who have or had a dating or engagement relationship. Personal assistants for persons with disabilities are also included.

(6) **Neglect.** Neglect is defined in DVA § 103(11) to be a failure to exercise reasonable care toward a high risk adult with disabilities.

ARTICLE II. ORDERS OF PROTECTION

Analysis

Sec.
201. Persons protected by this Act.
201.1 Access of high-risk adults.
202. Commencement of action; Filing fees; Dismissal.
203. Pleading; Non-disclosure of address.
204. Petitions of indigent persons.
205. Application of rules of civil procedure; Domestic abuse advocates.
206. Trial by jury.
207. Subject matter jurisdiction.
208. Jurisdiction over persons.
209. Venue.

Sec.
210. Process.
210.1 Service of notice in conjunction with a pending civil case.
211. Service of notice of hearings.
212. Hearings.
213. Continuances.
213.1 Hearsay exception.
213.2 Waiver of privilege.
213.3 Independent counsel; Temporary substitute guardian.
214. Order of protection; Remedies.
215. Mutual orders of protection; Correlative separate orders.
216. Accountability for actions of others.
217. Emergency order of protection.
218. 30–Day interim order of protection.
219. Plenary order of protection.
220. Duration and extension of orders.
221. Contents of orders.
222. Notice of orders.
223. Enforcement of orders of protection.
223.1 Order of protection; status.
224. Modification and re-opening of orders.
225. Immunity from prosecution.
226. Untrue statements.
227. Privileged communications between domestic violence counselors and victims.
227.1 Other privileged information.

WESTLAW Electronic Research

See WESTLAW Electronic Research Guide preceding the Summary of Contents.

750 ILCS 60/201

§ 201. Persons protected by this Act

(a) The following persons are protected by this Act:

(i) any person abused by a family or household member;

(ii) any high-risk adult with disabilities who is abused, neglected, or exploited by a family or household member;

(iii) any minor child or dependent adult in the care of such person; and

(iv) any person residing or employed at a private home or public shelter which is housing an abused family or household member.

(b) A petition for an order of protection may be filed only: (i) by a person who has been abused by a family or household member or by any person on behalf of a minor child or an adult who has been abused by a family or household member and who, because of age, health, disability, or inaccessibility, cannot file the petition, or (ii) by any person on behalf of a high-risk adult with disabilities who has been abused, neglected, or exploited by a family or household member. However, any petition properly filed under this Act may seek protection for any additional persons protected by this Act.

750 ILCS 60/201   **FAMILIES**

Author's Notes

Analysis

1. Protected persons.
2. Limited to abused persons.
3. Act not available to other than abused persons.

(1) **Protected persons.** Persons protected by the Act include any person abused by a family or household member; any high risk adult with disability who is abused, neglected or exploited by a family or household member; any minor child or dependent adult in the care of such abused persons; and any person residing in or employed at a private home or public shelter which is housing an abused family or household member. In construing this Section it is important to refer back to the broad definitions of "abuse," "family or household members," and other terms. See DVA § 103 and accompanying Author's Notes.

(2) **Limited to abused persons.** DVA § 201(b) provides that a petition for an order of protection may be filed only by a person who has been abused by a family or household member, or by a person on behalf of a minor child or an adult under disability who has been abused by a family or household member, or by a person on behalf of a high risk adult with disabilities who has been abused, neglected or exploited by a family or household member.

(3) **Act not available to other than abused persons.** The limitation of persons who can file a petition under the Domestic Violence Act prevents the use of the Act by persons other than abused persons and neglected or exploited high risk adults for the broad relief that is provided under DVA § 214. For example, if a person is not an abused person or a neglected or exploited high risk adult, he or she cannot use the Domestic Violence Act to restrain the transfer of property or to obtain court orders for child support or visitation. If the person does not qualify under the Domestic Violence Act, relief must be obtained pursuant to the Illinois Marriage and Dissolution of Marriage Act and the Injunction Act. See 750 ILCS 5/501 (temporary relief and temporary injunctions), 750 ILCS 5/505 (child support), 750 ILCS 5/601 et seq. (custody and visitation), and 735 ILCS 5/11-101 et seq. (injunctions).

750 ILCS 60/201.1
§ 201.1 Access of high-risk adults

No person shall obstruct or impede the access of a high-risk adult with disabilities to any agency or organization authorized to file a petition for an order of protection under Section 201 of this Act for the purpose of a private visit relating to legal rights, entitlements, claims and services under this Act and Section 1 of "An Act in relation to domestic relations and domestic violence shelters and service programs", approved September 24, 1981, as now or hereafter amended. If a person does so obstruct or impede such access of a high-risk adult with disabilities, local law enforcement agencies shall take all appropriate action to assist the party seeking access in petitioning for a search warrant or an ex parte injunctive order. Such warrant or order may issue upon a showing of probable cause to believe that the high-risk adult with disabilities is the subject of abuse, neglect, or exploitation which constitutes a criminal offense or that any other criminal offense is occurring which affects the interests or welfare of the high-risk adult with disabilities. When, from the personal observations of a law enforcement officer, it appears probable that delay of entry in order to obtain a warrant or order would cause the high-risk adult with disabilities to be in imminent danger of death or great bodily harm, entry may be made by the law enforcement officer after an announcement of the officer's authority and purpose.

750 ILCS 60/202

§ 202. Commencement of action; Filing fees; Dismissal

(a) How to commence action. Actions for orders of protection are commenced:

(1) Independently: By filing a petition for an order of protection in any civil court, unless specific courts are designated by local rule or order.

(2) In conjunction with another civil proceeding: By filing a petition for an order of protection under the same case number as another civil proceeding involving the parties, including but not limited to: (i) any proceeding under the Illinois Marriage and Dissolution of Marriage Act, Illinois Parentage Act of 1984, Nonsupport of Spouse and Children Act, Revised Uniform Reciprocal Enforcement of Support Act or an action for nonsupport brought under Article 10 of the Illinois Public Aid Code, provided that a petitioner and the respondent are a party to or the subject of that proceeding or (ii) a guardianship proceeding under the Probate Act of 1975, or a proceeding for involuntary commitment under the Mental Health and Developmental Disabilities Code, or any proceeding, other than a delinquency petition, under the Juvenile Court Act of 1987, provided that a petitioner or the respondent is a party to or the subject of such proceeding.

(3) In conjunction with a delinquency petition or a criminal prosecution: By filing a petition for an order of protection, under the same case number as the delinquency petition or criminal prosecution, to be granted during pre-trial release of a defendant, with any dispositional order issued under Section 5–23 of the Juvenile Court Act of 1987 or as a condition of release, supervision, conditional discharge, probation, periodic imprisonment, parole or mandatory supervised release, or in conjunction with imprisonment or a bond forfeiture warrant; provided that:

(i) the violation is alleged in an information, complaint, indictment or delinquency petition on file, and the alleged offender and victim are family or household members or persons protected by this Act; and

(ii) the petition, which is filed by the State's Attorney, names a victim of the alleged crime as a petitioner.

(b) Filing and service fees. No fee shall be charged for filing or service by the sheriff of a petition in an action commenced under this Section.

(c) Dismissal and consolidation. Withdrawal or dismissal of any petition for an order of protection prior to adjudication where the petitioner is represented by the State shall operate as a dismissal without prejudice. No action for an order of protection shall be dismissed because the respondent is being prosecuted for a crime against the petitioner. An independent action may be consolidated with another civil proceeding, as provided by paragraph (2) of subsection (a) of this Section. For any action commenced under paragraph (2) or (3) of subsection (a) of this Section, dismissal of the conjoined case (or a finding of not guilty) shall not require dismissal of the action for the order of protection; instead, it may be treated as an independent action and, if necessary and appropriate, transferred to a different court or division. Dismissal of any conjoined case shall not affect the validity of any previously issued order of protection, and thereafter subsections (b)(1) and (b)(2) of Section 220 shall be inapplicable to such order.

(d) Pro se petitions. The court shall provide, through the office of the clerk of the court, simplified forms and clerical assistance to help with the writing and filing of a petition under this Section by any person not represented by counsel. In addition, that assistance may be provided by the state's attorney.

Author's Notes

Analysis

1. Bringing of action.
2. Petition for Order of Protection—Form.

(1) **Bringing of action.** DVA § 202(a) provides that the petition for an order of protection can be brought as an independent action or in conjunction with other actions, including proceedings under the Illinois Marriage and Dissolution of Marriage Act. The petition for an order of protection can also be brought, within the limitations of DVA § 202(a)(3), in conjunction with a criminal prosecution or a delinquency petition. DVA § 202(c) provides that the dismissal of a case including a petition for an order of protection does not require dismissal of the action for the order of protection, which may continue as an independent action.

(2) **Petition for Order of Protection—Form.** The clerks of the court are required to provide form petitions. A sample copy follows.

FAMILIES   750 ILCS 60/202

PETITION: 1 of 5 Pages   0007
                            3501   CCG84-1-20M-9/1/92(21464)

IN THE CIRCUIT COURT OF COOK COUNTY, ILLINOIS

People ex rel. _____
_____ on behalf of
_____ self and/or behalf of

_____
         Petitioner

         -vs-

_____
         Respondent

Case No. _____

☐ Independent Proceeding
☐ Other Civil Proceeding
    (*Specify*) _____
☐ Criminal Proceeding
☐ Juvenile Proceeding

PETITION FOR ORDER OF PROTECTION

[Fill in lines and check boxes as applicable]

Now comes the Petitioner _____ on his/her own behalf or on behalf of _____, a minor child, or on behalf of _____, an adult who cannot file a petition because of age, health, disability or inaccessibility on his/her own behalf, pursuant to the **Illinois Domestic Violence Act (IDVA)**, and moves this Honorable Court to issue an Order of Protection in this cause and in support thereof states as follows:

ALLEGATIONS

THIS COURT HAS JURISDICTION OF THE SUBJECT MATTER AND OVER ALL NECESSARY PERSONS, WITH APPROPRIATE VENUE, BECAUSE:

A. ☐ **Petitioner resides at** _____,
       (Street Address, City)   **OR**
     in the County of _____ State of _____;

  ☐ **Petitioner resides at** _____,
       (Street Address, City)
     in the County of _____ State of _____, and _____,
     the person on whose behalf this Petition is brought, resides at _____
                                                                      (Street Address, City)
     in the County of _____ State of _____; **OR**

  ☐ Petitioner's address is omitted pursuant to statute. [Alternative address for notice of any motion is _____
     _____.]

B. ☐ **Respondent resides** _____,
                             (Street Address, City)
     in the County of _____ State of _____.

C.   Respondent stands in relationship to the Petitioner or alleged abused person/s as:

      ☐ Spouse;   ☐ Former spouse;   ☐ Parent;
      ☐ Child;   ☐ Having or allegedly   ☐ Stepchild;
                                      having a child in common;
      ☐ Sharing or formerly sharing a   ☐ Having or having had a dating   ☐ Other person related by
         common dwelling;   or engagement relationship;   blood or marriage.
      ☐ Sharing a blood relationship   ☐ Personal assistant to person with
         through a child;   disabilities or a person who has
                                          responsibility for a high-risk adult
                                          with disabilities;

[G17989]

1.) CLERK OF THE CIRCUIT COURT

750 ILCS 60/202   **FAMILIES**

- D. ☐ There is no other pending court action involving the parties. **OR**
  ☐ There is another pending court action involving the parties in _____ Court, County of _____ State of _____ known as Case No. _____.
- E. ☐ As referred to herein, "the minor child/ren" are _____
  ☐ The Court has jurisdiction over the minor child/ren because:
    ☐ 1. This state
      ☐ a. is the home state (as defined in the Illinois Uniform Child Custody Jurisdiction Act) of the child/ren at the time of the commencement of this proceeding, or
      ☐ b. had been the child/ren's home state within 6 months before commencement of the proceeding and the child is absent from this State because of his removal or retention by a person claiming his custody or for other reasons, and a parent or person acting as parent continues to live in this state;
      OR
    ☐ 2. It is in the best interest of the child that a court of this State assume jurisdiction because the child and his parents, or the child and at least one contestant, have a significant connection with this State, and there is available in this State substantial evidence concerning the child's present or future care, protection, training and personal relationships;
      OR
    ☐ 3. The child is physically present in this State and
      ☐ a. the child has been abandoned, or
      ☐ b. it is necessary in an emergency to protect the child because he has been subjected to or threatened with mistreatment or abuse or is otherwise neglected or dependent;
      OR
    ☐ 4. It appears that no other state would have jurisdiction under prerequisites substantially in accordance with paragraphs 1, 2, or 3, or another state has declined to exercise jurisdiction on the grounds that this State is the more appropriate forum to determine the custody of the child, and it is in the best interest of the child that this Court assume jurisdiction.
- F. ☐ No "father and child relationship" (pursuant to the Illinois Parentage Act of 1984) has been established with the following child/ren: _____
- G. ☐ The primary caretaker of the minor child/ren is or has been _____.
- H. ☐ Venue in civil proceedings is appropriate because:
    ☐ Petitioner resides in the County of Cook, State of Illinois; **OR**
    ☐ Respondent resides in the County of Cook, State of Illinois; **OR**
    ☐ The alleged abuse occurred in the County of Cook, State of Illinois; **OR**
    ☐ The Petitioner is temporarily located in the County of Cook, State of Illinois, to avoid further abuse, and could not obtain safe, accessible, and adequate temporary housing in the county of his/her residence.

PETITIONER ALLEGES AS TO RESPONDENT THAT:
- I. ☐ The following individuals are alleged to be persons who need to be protected from abuse by Respondent: _____
- J. ☐ Respondent has acted in the following manner towards the Petitioner:
  [State details of incident(s) of abuse (including time and place), as well as effects of incident(s) on Petitioner.]
  Incident(s): _____
  _____
  _____
  _____
  _____
  _____

  Effect(s): _____
  _____
  _____

1.) CLERK OF THE CERCUIT COURT   CASE NO. _____

FAMILIES   750 ILCS 60/202

- K. ☐ Petitioner should be granted exclusive possession of the residence, the special venue rules of sec. 209(b) of IDVA (applicable only in civil proceedings) having been met, because:
  - ☐ Petitioner has a right to occupancy and Respondent has no right to occupancy. **OR**
  - ☐ Both parties have a right to occupancy; and, considering the risk of further abuse by Respondent interfering with the Petitioner's safe and peaceful occupancy, the balance of hardships favors the Petitioner because of the following relevant factors:
    - ☐ Availability, accessibility, cost, safety, adequacy, location, and other characteristics of alternative housing for each party and any minors or other dependents; and/or
    - ☐ Effect on each party's employment; and/or
    - ☐ Other factors, as follows: _____

- L. ☐ Respondent should be ordered to stay away from Petitioner and the protected persons.
  - ☐ Respondent should be prohibited from entering or remaining present at Petitioner's school, place of employment, or (specify) _____ because:
    - ☐ Respondent has no right to enter/remain present at such place(s); **OR**
    - ☐ The balance of hardships favors the Petitioner in prohibiting the Respondent from entering or remaining at such place(s).

- M. ☐ The likelihood of future abuse would be minimized by appropriate counseling.

- N. ☐ Petitioner should be granted physical care of the minor child/ren or granted other appropriate relief because there exists a danger that the minor child/ren will be:
  - ☐ Abused or neglected; and/or
  - ☐ Separated in an unwarranted manner from the child/ren's primary caretaker; and/or
  - ☐ Unprotected as to his/her/their well-being.

- O. ☐ Petitioner should be granted temporary legal custody of the minor child/ren.

- P. ☐ The Respondent's visitation with the minor child/ren should be restricted or denied because the Respondent has or is likely to:
  - ☐ abuse or endanger the minor child/ren during visitation; and/or
  - ☐ use visitation as an opportunity to abuse or harass Petitioner or Petitioner's family or household members; and/or
  - ☐ improperly conceal or detain the minor child/ren; and/or
  - ☐ otherwise act in a manner that is not in the best interest of the minor child/ren.

- Q. ☐ There exists a danger that the minor child/ren will be removed from this jurisdiction or concealed within the State.

- R. ☐ Respondent has knowledge of the whereabouts of or access to the minor child/ren.

- S. ☐ Petitioner should be granted exclusive possession of the following items of personal property: _____ ,
  because:
  - ☐ Petitioner, but not Respondent, owns such property;
    OR
  - ☐ Sharing the property creates a further risk of abuse or is impractical; the balance of hardships favors temporary possession by Petitioner; and
    - ☐ Petitioner and Respondent own the property jointly, or
    - ☐ The property is alleged to be marital property and a proceeding has been filed under the IMDMA.

- T. ☐ An order should be granted protecting the following items of personal property : _____ ,
  because:
  - ☐ Petitioner, but not Respondent, owns such property;
    OR
  - ☐ The balance of hardships favors Petitioner, and
    - ☐ Petitioner and Respondent own the property jointly, or
    - ☐ The property is alleged to be marital property and a proceeding has been filed under the IMDMA.

- U. ☐ Respondent has a legal obligation to support Petitioner and/or the minor child/ren, and Respondent is able to provide such support.

- V. ☐ As a direct result of the above described abuse, Petitioner has suffered certain losses, incurred certain expenses, and/or has been provided temporary shelter/counseling services, as follows:
  _____
  _____
  _____

CASE NO. _____

1. CLERK OF THE CIRCUIT COURT

750 ILCS 60/202   **FAMILIES**

- W. ☐ There is a threat to the safety and well-being of Petitioner's family or household when Respondent enters or remains on the premises while under the influence of alcohol or drugs.
- X. ☐ Respondent should be denied access to school or other records of the minor child/ren because:
  - ☐ Respondent is or will be prohibited from having contact with the minor child/ren; or
  - ☐ Petitioner's address is omitted pursuant to statute; or
  - ☐ It is necessary to prevent abuse or wrongful removal or concealment of the minor child/ren.
- Y. ☐ Allegations for other injunctive relief:
  _____
  _____
- Z. ☐ Disclosure of Petitioner's address would risk further abuse to her/him or to another protected person, or such disclosure would reveal the confidential location of a shelter for domestic violence victims.

Additional Allegations for Emergency Orders Only

- ☐ (i) For requested remedies 1, 3, 5, 7, 8, 9, 11, 14, 15, and 17, the harm which that remedy is intended to prevent would be likely to occur if Respondent were given any prior notice, or greater notice than was actually given, of Petitioner's efforts to obtain judicial relief.
- ☐ (ii) For requested remedy 2, the immediate danger of further abuse of Petitioner by Respondent if Petitioner chose or had chosen to remain in the household while Respondent was given any prior notice or greater notice than was actually given, outweighs the hardship to Respondent of an emergency order granting Petitioner exclusive possession of the residence or household.
- ☐ (iii) For requested remedy 10, improper disposition of the personal property would be likely to occur if Respondent were given any prior notice or greater notice than was actually given of Petitioner's effort to obtain judicial relief, or that Petitioner has an immediate and pressing need for possession of that property.

REMEDIES REQUESTED

PETITIONER REQUESTS THAT THE COURT FIND THAT THE FOLLOWING ARE PROTECTED PERSONS:
_____
_____

WHEREFORE, PETITIONER REQUESTS THE ENTRY OF AN ORDER OF PROTECTION SETTING FORTH THE FOLLOWING REMEDIES:

- ☐ 1. With respect to Petitioner and other Protected Persons, Respondent be prohibited from committing the following:
  - ☐ Physical abuse; ☐ Harassment; ☐ Interference with personal liberty; ☐ Intimidation of a dependent;
  - ☐ Willful deprivation; ☐ Neglect; ☐ Exploitation; ☐ Stalking.
- ☐ 2. Petitioner be granted exclusive possession of the residence and Respondent be prohibited from entering or remaining at such premises: (Address) _____.
- ☐ 3. ☐ a. Respondent be ordered to stay away from Petitioner and other protected persons; and/or
     ☐ b. Respondent be prohibited from entering or remaining at _____
         _____ while any Protected Person is present; and/or
     ☐ c. Respondent be allowed access to the residence on (date) _____ at (time) _____ in the presence of (name) _____ to remove items of clothing, personal adornments, medications used exclusively by the Respondent and other items, as follows: _____.
- ☐ 4. Respondent be ordered to undergo counseling for a period of time to be determined by this court. *[Not available in Emergency Order]*
- ☐ 5. ☐ a. Petitioner be granted physical care and possession of the minor child/ren; and/or
     ☐ b. Respondent be ordered to:
       ☐ Return the minor child/ren _____ to the physical care of _____ ; and/or
       ☐ Not remove the minor child/ren _____ from the physical care of Petitioner or _____ .
- ☐ 6. Petitioner be granted temporary legal custody of the minor child/ren _____.
     [Not available in Emergency Order]

CASE NO. _____

1. CLERK OF THE CIRCUIT COURT

FAMILIES   750 ILCS 60/202

☐ 7. ☐ a. **Respondent be awarded visitation rights on the following dates and times or under the following conditions or parameters:**
             [No order shall merely refer to the term " reasonable visitation"]
             _____
             _____

      ☐ b. **Respondent's visitation be restricted as follows:**
             _____
             _____

      ☐ c. **Respondent's visitation be denied.**

☐ 8.   Respondent be prohibited from removing the minor chiId/ren from Illinois or concealing them within Illinois.
☐ 9.   Respondent be ordered to appear in this Court with/without the child/ren on a date certain.
☐ 10. Petitioner be granted exclusive temporary possession of the following personal property and the Respondent be ordered to deliver to Petitioner said property that is in Respondent's possession or control, to wit: _____
       _____

☐ 11. Respondent be ordered not to take, encumber, conceal, damage or otherwise dispose of any of the following real or personal property, to wit: _____
       _____

☐ 12. Respondent be ordered to pay temporary support for Petitioner and/or the minor child/ren of the parties as follows: $ _____
       per _____ , starting _____ payable ☐ through the Clerk of the Circuit Court, or
       ☐ directly to Petitioner . *[Not available in Emergency Order]*

☐ 13. Respondent be ordered to pay $ _____ respecting losses and expenses within the scope of sec. 214(b)(13) of the
       IDVA to _____ on or before _____ . *[Not available in Emergency Order]*

☐ 14. Respondent be prohibited from entering or remaining at the household or residence located at _____
       _____ while under
       the influence of alcohol or drugs and so constituting a threat to the safety and well-being of any Protected Person.

☐ 15. Respondent be denied access to school or any other records of the minor child/ren and prohibited from inspecting, obtaining, or attempting to inspect or obtain such records.

☐ 16. Respondent be ordered to pay $ _____ to the following shelter _____
       on or before _____ . *[Not available in Emergency Order]*

☐ 17. Respondent be further enjoined as follows: _____
       _____
       _____

                                                   _____
                                                   Signature of Petitioner

_____
Signature of Attorney or State's Attorney

UNDER THE PENALTIES OF PERJURY AND AS PROVIDED BY LAW PURSUANT TO SECTION 1-109 OF THE CODE OF CIVIL PROCEDURE, THE UNDERSIGNED CERTIFIES THAT THE STATEMENTS SET FORTH IN THIS INSTRUMENT ARE TRUE AND CORRECT, EXCEPT AS TO MATTERS THEREIN STATED TO BE ON INFORMATION AND BELIEF AND AS TO SUCH MATTERS THE UNDERSIGNED CERTIFIES AS AFORESAID THAT THE UNDERSIGNED VERILY BELIEVES THE SAME TO BE TRUE.

                                                   _____
                                                   Signature of Petitioner

Attorney (or Pro Se Petitioner) Name: _____
Address _____
City _____
Phone _____
Attorney # _____
Service by Facsimile ☐ will be accepted ☐ will not be accepted.
Facsimile Number _____
                 (Must be included if service by facsimile is accepted)

                                          CASE NO. _____

1. CLERK OF THE CIRCUIT COURT

750 ILCS 60/203

§ 203. Pleading; Non-disclosure of address

(a) A petition for an order of protection shall be in writing and verified or accompanied by affidavit and shall allege that petitioner has been abused by respondent, who is a family or household member. The petition shall further set forth whether there is any other pending action between the parties. During the pendency of this proceeding, each party has a continuing duty to inform the court of any subsequent proceeding for an order of protection in this or any other state.

(b) If the petition states that disclosure of petitioner's address would risk abuse of petitioner or any member of petitioner's family or household or reveal the confidential address of a shelter for domestic violence victims, that address may be omitted from all documents filed with the court. If disclosure is necessary to determine jurisdiction or consider any venue issue, it shall be made orally and in camera. If petitioner has not disclosed an address under this subsection, petitioner shall designate an alternative address at which respondent may serve notice of any motions.

Author's Notes

(1) **Verification.** Note that petitions for orders of protection must be verified or accompanied by an affidavit.

750 ILCS 60/204

§ 204. Petitions of indigent persons

(a) Emergency petitions. A petition for an emergency order of protection shall be filed without payment of the filing fee, if any, or without a prior court order waiving or deferring that fee, if accompanied by an affidavit, in compliance with Illinois Supreme Court Rule 298, stating that petitioner lacks the funds to pay filing fees. At the hearing for that emergency order, the court shall determine petitioner's eligibility for waiver or deferral of court costs.

(b) Other petitions. A petition for a 30-day interim order or a plenary order of protection may be filed without payment of the filing fee, if any, only if accompanied by a court order waiving or deferring that fee. Application for such an order shall be in accordance with Illinois Supreme Court Rule 298.

(c) Denial of petitions. A decision to deny indigent status shall not be based, in whole or in part, on any of the following factors:

   (i) Petitioner is the sole or joint owner of his or her residence;

   (ii) Petitioner is the sole or joint owner of a single automobile worth less than $5,000; or

   (iii) Petitioner receives income, if that income is less than 125% of the official poverty threshold set by the U.S. Office of Management and Budget.

(d) Deferral of costs. If petitioner is not eligible for waiver of court costs, the court may nevertheless defer payment of filing and service fees upon evidence that:

(i) Petitioner seeks an order of protection to deter future abuse and lacks immediate resources to pay filing and service fees; and

(ii) either petitioner or respondent will have the means to pay deferred court costs prior to entry of a final order.

(e) Income of alleged abuser. The income of the family or household member alleged to be abusing the petitioner shall not be considered in determining petitioner's eligibility for waiver of court costs. However, such waiver shall not diminish the court's authority to order payment of court costs by the abusive party.

750 ILCS 60/205

§ 205. Application of rules of civil procedure; Domestic abuse advocates

(a) Any proceeding to obtain, modify, reopen or appeal an order of protection, whether commenced alone or in conjunction with a civil or criminal proceeding, shall be governed by the rules of civil procedure of this State. The standard of proof in such a proceeding is proof by a preponderance of the evidence, whether the proceeding is heard in criminal or civil court. The Code of Civil Procedure and Supreme Court and local court rules applicable to civil proceedings, as now or hereafter amended, shall apply, except as otherwise provided by law.

(b)(1) In all circuit court proceedings under this Act, domestic abuse advocates shall be allowed to attend and sit at counsel table and confer with the victim, unless otherwise directed by the court.

(2) In criminal proceedings in circuit courts, domestic abuse advocates shall be allowed to accompany the victim and confer with the victim, unless otherwise directed by the court.

(3) Court administrators shall allow domestic abuse advocates to assist victims of domestic violence in the preparation of petitions for orders of protection.

(4) Domestic abuse advocates are not engaged in the unauthorized practice of law when providing assistance of the types specified in this subsection (b).

750 ILCS 60/206

§ 206. Trial by jury

There shall be no right to trial by jury in any proceeding to obtain, modify, vacate or extend any order of protection under this Act. However, nothing in this Section shall deny any existing right to trial by jury in a criminal proceeding.

750 ILCS 60/207

§ 207. Subject matter jurisdiction

Each of the circuit courts shall have the power to issue orders of protection.

750 ILCS 60/208

§ 208. Jurisdiction over persons

In child custody proceedings, the court's personal jurisdiction is determined by this State's Uniform Child Custody Jurisdiction Act, as now or hereafter amended. Otherwise, the courts of this State have jurisdiction to bind (i) State residents and (ii) non-residents having minimum contacts with this State, to the extent permitted by the long-arm statute, Section 2–209 of the Code of Civil Procedure, as now or hereafter amended.

750 ILCS 60/209

§ 209. Venue

(a) Filing. A petition for an order of protection may be filed in any county where (i) petitioner resides, (ii) respondent resides, (iii) the alleged abuse occurred or (iv) the petitioner is temporarily located if petitioner left petitioner's residence to avoid further abuse and could not obtain safe, accessible, and adequate temporary housing in the county of that residence.

(b) Exclusive possession. With respect to requests for exclusive possession of the residence under this Act, venue is proper only in the county where the residence is located, except in the following circumstances:

(1) If a request for exclusive possession of the residence is made under this Act in conjunction with a proceeding under the Illinois Marriage and Dissolution of Marriage Act, venue is proper in the county or judicial circuit where the residence is located or in a contiguous county or judicial circuit.

(2) If a request for exclusive possession of the residence is made under this Act in any other proceeding, provided the petitioner meets the requirements of item (iv) of subsection (a), venue is proper in the county or judicial circuit where the residence is located or in a contiguous county or judicial circuit. In such case, however, if the court is not located in the county where the residence is located, it may grant exclusive possession of the residence under subdivision (b)(2) of Section 214 only in an emergency order under Section 217, and such grant may be extended thereafter beyond the maximum initial period only by a court located in the county where the residence is located.

(c) Inconvenient forum. If an order of protection is issued by a court in a county in which neither of the parties resides, the court may balance hardships to the parties and accordingly transfer any proceeding to extend, modify, re-open, vacate or enforce any such order to a county wherein a party resides.

(d) Objection. Objection to venue is waived if not made within such time as respondent's response is due, except as otherwise provided in subsection (b). In no event shall venue be deemed jurisdictional.

750 ILCS 60/210

§ 210. Process

(a) Summons. Any action for an order of protection, whether commenced alone or in conjunction with another proceeding, is a distinct cause of action and requires that a separate summons be issued and served, except that in pending cases the following methods may be used:

(1) By delivery of the summons to respondent personally in open court in pending civil or criminal cases.

(2) By notice in accordance with Section 210.1 in civil cases in which the defendant has filed a general appearance.

The summons shall be in the form prescribed by Supreme Court Rule 101(d), except that it shall require respondent to answer or appear within 7 days. Attachments to the summons or notice shall include the petition for order of protection and supporting affidavits, if any, and any emergency order of protection that has been issued. The enforcement of an order of protection under Section 223 shall not be affected by the lack of service, delivery, or notice, provided the requirements of subsection (d) of that Section are otherwise met.

(b) Fees. No fee shall be charged for service of summons in any action commenced in conjunction with (i) another civil proceeding, if the summons for both proceedings are filed together or (ii) any criminal proceeding.

(c) Expedited service. The summons shall be served by the sheriff or other law enforcement officer at the earliest time and shall take precedence over other summonses except those of a similar emergency nature. Special process servers may be appointed at any time, and their designation shall not affect the responsibilities and authority of the sheriff or other official process servers.

(d) Remedies requiring actual notice. The counseling, payment of support, payment of shelter services, and payment of losses remedies provided by paragraphs 4, 12, 13, and 16 of subsection (b) of Section 214 may be granted only if respondent has been personally served with process, has answered or has made a general appearance.

(e) Remedies upon constructive notice. Service of process on a member of respondent's household or by publication shall be adequate for the remedies provided by paragraphs 1, 2, 3, 5, 6, 7, 8, 9, 10, 11, 14, 15, and 17 of subsection (b) of Section 214, but only if: (i) petitioner has made all reasonable efforts to accomplish actual service of process personally upon respondent, but respondent cannot be found to effect such service and (ii) petitioner files an affidavit or presents sworn testimony as to those efforts.

750 ILCS 60/210

(f) *Default.* A plenary order of protection may be entered by default as follows:

(1) For any of the remedies sought in the petition, if respondent has been served or given notice in accordance with subsection (a) and if respondent then fails to appear as directed or fails to appear on any subsequent appearance or hearing date agreed to by the parties or set by the court; or

(2) For any of the remedies provided in accordance with subsection (e), if respondent fails to answer or appear in accordance with the date set in the publication notice or the return date indicated on the service of a household member.

750 ILCS 60/210.1

§ 210.1 Service of notice in conjunction with a pending civil case

(a) *Notice.* When an action for an order of protection is sought in conjunction with a pending civil case in which the court has obtained jurisdiction over respondent, and respondent has filed a general appearance, then a separate summons need not issue. Original notice of a hearing on a petition for an order of protection may be given, and the documents served, in accordance with Illinois Supreme Court Rules 11 and 12. When, however, an emergency order of protection is sought in such a case on an ex parte application, then the procedure set forth in subsection (a) of Section 210 (other than in subsection (a)(2)) shall be followed. If an order of protection is issued using the notice provisions of this Section, then the order of protection or extensions of that order may survive the disposition of the main civil case. The enforcement of any order of protection under Section 223 shall not be affected by the lack of notice under this Section, provided the requirements of subsection (d) of that Section are otherwise met.

(b) *Default.* The form of notice described in subsection (a) shall include the following language directed to the respondent:

A 2-year plenary order of protection may be entered by default for any of the remedies sought in the petition if you fail to appear on the specified hearing date or on any subsequent hearing date agreed to by the parties or set by the court.

(c) *Party to give notice.* Notice in the pending civil case shall be given (i) by either party under this Section, with respect to extensions, modifications, hearings, or other relief pertinent to an order of protection, in accordance with Illinois Supreme Court Rules 11 and 12 or (ii) by the respondent as provided in subsection (c) of Section 224.

Author's Notes

Analysis

1. DVA §§ 210 and 210.1 together.
2. Service (DVA §§ 210(a), 210.1).
3. Summons (DVA § 210(a)).
4. Remedies and types of service (DVA §§ 210(d), (e), and (f)).
5. Notice statement.
6. Notice.

(1) **DVA §§ 210 and 210.1 together.** Section 210 should be read in conjunction with § 210.1.

(2) **Service (DVA §§ 210(a), 210.1).** An action for an order of protection, whether commenced independently or in conjunction with another proceeding, is started by a separate summons that shall be issued and personally served (see 735 ILCS 5/2–203 and accompanying Author's Notes), with the following exceptions: (1) in pending cases, the separate summons can be delivered to the respondent personally in open court; and (2) in cases in which the respondent has filed a general appearance, a separate summons need not issue, and the petition for an order of protection may be initiated by notice served in accordance with Illinois Supreme Court Rules 11 and 12. However, where an emergency order of protection is sought on an *ex parte* application, even though the respondent has filed a general appearance in a pending action, notice of the entry of the *ex parte* order is not sufficient. A separate summons must be issued and, with a copy of the *ex parte* order, personally served, or delivered to the respondent in open court. See DVA §§ 210.1(a), 217, and 222(c).

(3) **Summons (DVA § 210(a)).** The summons in an action for an order of protection shall be in the form prescribed by Supreme Court Rule 101(d), except that it must require the respondent to answer or appear within seven days. See Supreme Court Rule 101(d) and (e) Author's Note (1) for a model summons used in Cook County. The model summons has a box to check if an order of protection is part of the relief sought, and a box to check when the respondent must answer or appear within seven, rather than 30 days after service. The summons must have attached to it the petition for the order of protection, any supporting affidavits, and any previously issued emergency order of protection.

(4) **Remedies and types of service (DVA §§ 210(d), (e), and (f)).** Remedies of restraint generally do not require actual personal service on the affected party or a general appearance. Constructive service of process on a member of the respondent's household or publication, accompanied by an affidavit that all reasonable efforts have been made to effectuate actual service, is adequate. However, counselling and payment remedies generally require actual personal service on the affected party or a general appearance.

A plenary order of protection may be entered by default for any remedies sought in the petition if the respondent has been personally served, the summons has been delivered to him personally in open court, or he has entered a general appearance and has been given notice in accordance with DVA §§ 210(a)(2) and 210.1. The court may enter a plenary order of protection for the restraining remedies if the respondent fails to answer or appear after publication notice or service upon a household member.

(5) **Notice statement.** Pursuant to DVA § 210.1, notice to a respondent who has filed a general appearance must include the statement in § 210.1(b) to the effect that a two year plenary order of protection may be entered by default upon failure to appear.

(6) **Notice.** DVA § 210.1(c) requires notice concerning hearings and other actions in regard to orders of protection to be in accordance with Supreme Court Rules

750 ILCS 60/210.1

11 and 12. The reference in § 210.1(c) to notice by respondent in accordance with § 224(c) should undoubtedly refer to § 224(d).

750 ILCS 60/211

§ 211. Service of notice of hearings

Except as provided in Sections 210 and 210.1, notice of hearings on petitions or motions shall be served in accordance with Supreme Court Rules 11 and 12, unless notice is excused by Section 217 of this Act, or by the Code of Civil Procedure, Supreme Court Rules, or local rules, as now or hereafter amended.

750 ILCS 60/212

§ 212. Hearings

(a) A petition for an order of protection shall be treated as an expedited proceeding, and no court shall transfer or otherwise decline to decide all or part of such petition except as otherwise provided herein. Nothing in this Section shall prevent the court from reserving issues when jurisdiction or notice requirements are not met.

(b) Any court or a division thereof which ordinarily does not decide matters of child custody and family support may decline to decide contested issues of physical care, custody, visitation, or family support unless a decision on one or more of those contested issues is necessary to avoid the risk of abuse, neglect, removal from the state or concealment within the state of the child or of separation of the child from the primary caretaker. If the court or division thereof has declined to decide any or all of these issues, then it shall transfer all undecided issues to the appropriate court or division. In the event of such a transfer, a government attorney involved in the criminal prosecution may, but need not, continue to offer counsel to petitioner on transferred matters.

(c) If the court transfers or otherwise declines to decide any issue, judgment on that issue shall be expressly reserved and ruling on other issues shall not be delayed or declined.

750 ILCS 60/213

§ 213. Continuances

(a) Petitions for emergency orders. Petitions for emergency remedies shall be granted or denied in accordance with the standards of Section 217, regardless of respondent's appearance or presence in court.

(b) Petitions for interim and plenary orders. Any action for an order of protection is an expedited proceeding. Continuances should be granted only for good cause shown and kept to the minimum reasonable duration, taking into account the reasons for the continuance. If the continuance is necessary for some, but not all, of the remedies requested, hearing on those other remedies shall not be delayed.

Author's Notes

(1) **Limitation of continuances.** The limitation on continuances in DVA § 213, and the authority of the court to grant emergency relief regardless of respondent's appearance or presence in court, give the court a great deal of flexibility to intervene in abusive situations. The court can also grant relief in regard to some of the remedies requested, and grant a continuance in regard to others.

750 ILCS 60/213.1

§ 213.1 Hearsay exception

In an action for an order of protection on behalf of a high-risk adult with disabilities, a finding of lack of capacity to testify shall not render inadmissible any statement as long as the reliability of the statement is ensured by circumstances bringing it within the scope of a hearsay exception. The following evidence shall be admitted as an exception to the hearsay rule whether or not the declarant is available as a witness:

(1) A statement relating to a startling event or condition made spontaneously while the declarant was under the contemporaneous or continuing stress of excitement caused by the event or condition.

(2) A statement made for the purpose of obtaining, receiving, or promoting medical diagnosis or treatment, including psychotherapy, and describing medical history, or past or present symptoms, pain, or sensations, or the inception or general character of the cause or external source thereof insofar as reasonably pertinent to diagnosis or treatment. For purposes of obtaining a protective order, the identity of any person inflicting abuse or neglect as defined in this Act shall be deemed reasonably pertinent to diagnosis or treatment.

(3) A statement not specifically covered by any of the foregoing exceptions but having equivalent circumstantial guarantees of trustworthiness, if the court determines that (A) the statement is offered as evidence of a material fact, and (B) the statement is more probative on the point for which it is offered than any other evidence which the proponent can procure through reasonable efforts.

Circumstantial guarantees of trustworthiness include:

(1) the credibility of the witness who testifies the statement was made;

(2) assurance of the declarant's personal knowledge of the event;

(3) the declarant's interest or bias and the presence or absence of capacity or motive to fabricate;

(4) the presence or absence of suggestiveness or prompting at the time the statement was made;

(5) whether the declarant has ever reaffirmed or recanted the statement; and

(6) corroboration by physical evidence or behavioral changes in the declarant.

The record shall reflect the court's findings of fact and conclusions of law as to the trustworthiness requirement.

A statement shall not be admitted under the exception set forth in this Section unless its proponent gives written notice stating his or her intention to offer the statement and the particulars of it to the adverse party sufficiently in advance of offering the statement to provide the adverse party with a fair opportunity to prepare to meet the statement.

Author's Notes

(1) **Hearsay exception: Notification requirement.** The Domestic Violence Act provides a broad hearsay exception in actions brought on behalf of a high risk adult with disabilities. The exception is tempered by the requirement that when a party proposes to introduce a statement under the exceptions in DVA § 213.1, she must give the adverse party notice of her intention to do so a sufficient time in advance to allow the adverse party to prepare to meet the statement.

750 ILCS 60/213.2

§ 213.2 Waiver of privilege

When the subject of any proceeding under this Act is a high-risk adult with disabilities for whom no guardian has been appointed, no party other than the high-risk adult or the attorney for the high-risk adult shall be entitled to invoke or waive a common law or statutory privilege on behalf of the high-risk adult which results in the exclusion of evidence.

750 ILCS 60/213.3

§ 213.3 Independent counsel; Temporary substitute guardian

If the petitioner is a high-risk adult with disabilities for whom a guardian has been appointed, the court shall appoint independent counsel other than a guardian ad litem and, may appoint a temporary substitute guardian under the provisions of Article XIa of the Probate Act of 1975. The court shall appoint a temporary substitute guardian if the guardian is named as a respondent in a petition under this Act.

750 ILCS 60/214

§ 214. Order of protection; Remedies

(a) Issuance of order. If the court finds that petitioner has been abused by a family or household member or that petitioner is a high-risk adult who has been abused, neglected, or exploited, as defined in this Act, an order of protection prohibiting the abuse, neglect, or exploitation shall issue; provided that petitioner must also satisfy the requirements of one of the following Sections, as appropriate: Section 217 on emergency orders, Section 218 on interim orders, or Section 219 on plenary orders. Petitioner shall not be denied an order of protection because petitioner or respondent is a minor. The court, when determining whether or not to issue an order of protection, shall not require physical manifestations of abuse on the person of the victim.

Modification and extension of prior orders of protection shall be in accordance with this Act.

(b) Remedies and standards. The remedies to be included in an order of protection shall be determined in accordance with this Section and one of the following Sections, as appropriate: Section 217 on emergency orders, Section 218 on interim orders, and Section 219 on plenary orders. The remedies listed in this subsection shall be in addition to other civil or criminal remedies available to petitioner.

(1) Prohibition of abuse, neglect, or exploitation. Prohibit respondent's harassment, interference with personal liberty, intimidation of a dependent, physical abuse, or willful deprivation, neglect or exploitation, as defined in this Act, or stalking of the petitioner, as defined in Section 12–7.3 of the Criminal Code of 1961, if such abuse, neglect, exploitation, or stalking has occurred or otherwise appears likely to occur if not prohibited.

(2) Grant of exclusive possession of residence. Prohibit respondent from entering or remaining in any residence or household of the petitioner, including one owned or leased by respondent, if petitioner has a right to occupancy thereof. The grant of exclusive possession of the residence shall not affect title to real property, nor shall the court be limited by the standard set forth in Section 701 of the Illinois Marriage and Dissolution of Marriage Act.

(A) Right to occupancy. A party has a right to occupancy of a residence or household if it is solely or jointly owned or leased by that party, that party's spouse, a person with a legal duty to support that party or a minor child in that party's care, or by any person or entity other than the opposing party that authorizes that party's occupancy (e.g., a domestic violence shelter). Standards set forth in subparagraph (B) shall not preclude equitable relief.

(B) Presumption of hardships. If petitioner and respondent each has the right to occupancy of a residence or household, the court shall balance (i) the hardships to respondent and any minor child or dependent adult in respondent's care resulting from entry of this remedy with (ii) the hardships to petitioner and any minor child or dependent adult in petitioner's care resulting from continued exposure to the risk of abuse (should petitioner remain at the residence or household) or from loss of possession of the residence or household (should petitioner leave to avoid the risk of abuse). When determining the balance of hardships, the court shall also take into account the accessibility of the residence or household. Hardships need not be balanced if respondent does not have a right to occupancy.

The balance of hardships is presumed to favor possession by petitioner unless the presumption is rebutted by a preponderance of the evidence, showing that the hardships to respondent substantially outweigh the hardships to petitioner and any minor child or dependent adult in petitioner's care. The court, on the request of petitioner or on its own motion, may order respondent to provide suitable, accessible, alternate housing for petitioner instead of excluding respondent from a mutual residence or household.

(3) Stay away order and additional prohibitions. Order respondent to stay away from petitioner or any other person protected by the order of protection, or prohibit respondent from entering or remaining present at petitioner's school, place of employment, or other specified places at times when petitioner is present, or both, if reasonable, given the balance of hardships. Hardships need not be balanced for the court to enter a stay away order or prohibit entry if respondent has no right to enter the premises.

If an order of protection grants petitioner exclusive possession of the residence, or prohibits respondent from entering the residence, or orders respondent to stay away from petitioner or other protected persons, then the court may allow respondent access to the residence to remove items of clothing and personal adornment used exclusively by respondent, medications, and other items as the court directs. The right to access shall be exercised on only one occasion as the court directs and in the presence of an agreed-upon adult third party or law enforcement officer.

(4) Counseling. Require or recommend the respondent to undergo counseling for a specified duration with a social worker, psychologist, clinical psychologist, psychiatrist, family service agency, alcohol or substance abuse program, mental health center guidance counselor, agency providing services to elders, program designed for domestic violence abusers or any other guidance service the court deems appropriate.

(5) Physical care and possession of the minor child. In order to protect the minor child from abuse, neglect, or unwarranted separation from the person who has been the minor child's primary caretaker, or to otherwise protect the well-being of the minor child, the court may do either or both of the following: (i) grant petitioner physical care or possession of the minor child, or both, or (ii) order respondent to return a minor child to, or not remove a minor child from, the physical care of a parent or person in loco parentis.

If a court finds, after a hearing, that respondent has committed abuse (as defined in Section 103) of a minor child, there shall be a rebuttable presumption that awarding physical care to respondent would not be in the minor child's best interest.

(6) Temporary legal custody. Award temporary legal custody to petitioner in accordance with this Section, the Illinois Marriage and Dissolution of Marriage Act, the Illinois Parentage Act of 1984, and this State's Uniform Child Custody Jurisdiction Act.

If a court finds, after a hearing, that respondent has committed abuse (as defined in Section 103) of a minor child, there shall be a rebuttable presumption that awarding temporary legal custody to respondent would not be in the child's best interest.

(7) Visitation. Determine the visitation rights, if any, of respondent in any case in which the court awards physical care or temporary legal custody of a minor child to petitioner. The court shall restrict or deny respondent's visitation with a minor child if the court finds that respondent has done or is likely to do any of the following: (i) abuse or endanger the minor child during visitation; (ii) use the visitation as an opportunity to abuse or harass petitioner or petitioner's family or household members; (iii) improperly conceal or detain the minor child; or (iv) otherwise act in a manner that is not in the best interests of the minor child. The court shall not be limited by the standards set forth in Section 607.1 of the Illinois Marriage and Dissolution of Marriage Act. If the court grants visitation, the order shall specify dates and times for the visitation to take place or other specific parameters or conditions that are appropriate. No order for visitation shall refer merely to the term "reasonable visitation".

Petitioner may deny respondent access to the minor child if, when respondent arrives for visitation, respondent is under the influence of drugs or alcohol and constitutes a threat to the safety and well-being of petitioner or petitioner's minor children or is behaving in a violent or abusive manner.

If necessary to protect any member of petitioner's family or household from future abuse, respondent shall be prohibited from coming to petitioner's residence to meet the minor child for visitation, and the parties shall submit to the court their recommendations for reasonable alternative arrangements for visitation. A person may be approved to supervise visitation only after filing an affidavit accepting that responsibility and acknowledging accountability to the court.

(8) Removal or concealment of minor child. Prohibit respondent from removing a minor child from the State or concealing the child within the State.

(9) Order to appear. Order the respondent to appear in court, alone or with a minor child, to prevent abuse, neglect, removal or concealment of the child, to return the child to the custody or care of the petitioner or to permit any court-ordered interview or examination of the child or the respondent.

(10) Possession of personal property. Grant petitioner exclusive possession of personal property and, if respondent has possession or control, direct respondent to promptly make it available to petitioner, if:

(i) petitioner, but not respondent, owns the property; or

(ii) the parties own the property jointly; sharing it would risk abuse of petitioner by respondent or is impracticable; and the balance of hardships favors temporary possession by petitioner.

If petitioner's sole claim to ownership of the property is that it is marital property, the court may award petitioner temporary possession thereof under the standards of subparagraph (ii) of this paragraph only if a proper proceeding has been filed under the Illinois Marriage and Dissolution of Marriage Act, as now or hereafter amended.

No order under this provision shall affect title to property.

(11) Protection of property. Forbid the respondent from taking, transferring, encumbering, concealing, damaging or otherwise disposing of any real or personal property, except as explicitly authorized by the court, if:

(i) petitioner, but not respondent, owns the property; or

(ii) the parties own the property jointly, and the balance of hardships favors granting this remedy.

If petitioner's sole claim to ownership of the property is that it is marital property, the court may grant petitioner relief under subparagraph (ii) of this paragraph only if a proper proceeding has been filed under the Illinois Marriage and Dissolution of Marriage Act, as now or hereafter amended.

The court may further prohibit respondent from improperly using the financial or other resources of an aged member of the family or household for the profit or advantage of respondent or of any other person.

(12) Order for payment of support. Order respondent to pay temporary support for the petitioner or any child in the petitioner's care or custody, when the respondent has a legal obligation to support that person, in accordance with the Illinois Marriage and Dissolution of Marriage Act, which shall govern, among other matters, the amount of support, payment through the clerk and withholding of income to secure payment. An order for child support may be granted to a petitioner with lawful physical care or custody of a child, or an order or agreement for physical care or custody, prior to entry of an order for legal custody. Such a support order shall expire upon entry of a valid order granting legal custody to another, unless otherwise provided in the custody order.

(13) Order for payment of losses. Order respondent to pay petitioner for losses suffered as a direct result of the abuse, neglect, or exploitation. Such losses shall include, but not be limited to, medical expenses, lost earnings or other support, repair or replacement of property damaged or taken, reasonable attorney's fees, court costs and moving or other travel expenses, including additional reasonable expenses for temporary shelter and restaurant meals.

(i) Losses affecting family needs. If a party is entitled to seek maintenance, child support or property distribution from the other party under the Illinois Marriage and Dissolution of Marriage Act, as now or hereafter amended, the court may order respondent to reimburse petitioner's actual losses, to the extent that such reimbursement would be "appropriate temporary relief", as authorized by subsection (a)(3) of Section 501 of that Act.

(ii) Recovery of expenses. In the case of an improper concealment or removal of a minor child, the court may order respondent to pay the reasonable expenses incurred or to be incurred in the search for and recovery of the minor child, including but not limited to legal fees, court costs, private investigator fees, and travel costs.

(14) Prohibition of entry. Prohibit the respondent from entering or remaining in the residence or household while the respondent is under the influence of alcohol or drugs and constitutes a threat to the safety and well-being of the petitioner or the petitioner's children.

(15) Prohibition of access to records. If an order of protection prohibits respondent from having contact with the minor child, or if petitioner's address is omitted under subsection (b) of Section 203, or if necessary to prevent abuse or wrongful removal or concealment of a minor child, the order shall deny respondent access to, and prohibit respondent from inspecting, obtaining, or attempting to inspect or obtain, school or any other records of the minor child who is in the care of petitioner.

(16) Order for payment of shelter services. Order respondent to reimburse a shelter providing temporary housing and counseling services to the petitioner for the cost of the services, as certified by the shelter and deemed reasonable by the court.

(17) Order for injunctive relief. Enter injunctive relief necessary or appropriate to prevent further abuse of a family or household member or further abuse, neglect, or exploitation of a high-risk adult with disabilities or to effectuate one of the granted remedies, if supported by the balance of hardships. If the harm to be prevented by the injunction is abuse or any other harm that one of the remedies listed in paragraphs (1) through (16) of this subsection is designed to prevent, no further evidence is necessary that the harm is an irreparable injury.

(c) Relevant factors; findings.

(1) In determining whether to grant a specific remedy, other than payment of support, the court shall consider relevant factors, including but not limited to the following:

(i) the nature, frequency, severity, pattern and consequences of the respondent's past abuse, neglect or exploitation of the petitioner or any family or household member, including the concealment of his or her location in order to evade service of process or notice, and the likelihood of danger of future abuse, neglect, or exploitation to petitioner or any member of petitioner's or respondent's family or household; and

(ii) the danger that any minor child will be abused or neglected or improperly removed from the jurisdiction, improperly concealed within the State or improperly separated from the child's primary caretaker.

(2) In comparing relative hardships resulting to the parties from loss of possession of the family home, the court shall consider relevant factors, including but not limited to the following:

(i) availability, accessibility, cost, safety, adequacy, location and other characteristics of alternate housing for each party and any minor child or dependent adult in the party's care;

(ii) the effect on the party's employment; and

(iii) the effect on the relationship of the party, and any minor child or dependent adult in the party's care, to family, school, church and community.

(3) Subject to the exceptions set forth in paragraph (4) of this subsection, the court shall make its findings in an official record or in writing, and shall at a minimum set forth the following:

(i) That the court has considered the applicable relevant factors described in paragraphs (1) and (2) of this subsection.

(ii) Whether the conduct or actions of respondent, unless prohibited, will likely cause irreparable harm or continued abuse.

(iii) Whether it is necessary to grant the requested relief in order to protect petitioner or other alleged abused persons.

(4) For purposes of issuing an ex parte emergency order of protection, the court, as an alternative to or as a supplement to making the findings described in paragraphs (c)(3)(i) through (c)(3)(iii) of this subsection, may use the following procedure:

When a verified petition for an emergency order of protection in accordance with the requirements of Sections 203 and 217 is presented to the court, the court shall examine petitioner on oath or affirmation. An emergency order of protection shall be issued by the court if it appears from the contents of the petition and the examination of petitioner that the averments are sufficient to indicate abuse by respondent and to support the granting of relief under the issuance of the emergency order of protection.

(5) Never married parties. No rights or responsibilities for a minor child born outside of marriage attach to a putative father until a father and child relationship has been established under the Illinois Parentage Act of 1984. Absent such an adjudication, no putative father shall be granted temporary custody of the minor child, visitation with the minor child, or physical care and possession of the minor child, or physical care and possession of the minor child, nor shall an order of payment for support of the minor child be entered.

(d) Balance of hardships; findings. If the court finds that the balance of hardships does not support the granting of a remedy governed by paragraph (2), (3), (10), (11), or (16) of subsection (b) of this Section, which may require such balancing, the court's findings shall so indicate and shall include a finding as to whether granting the remedy will result in hardship to respondent that would substantially outweigh the hardship to petitioner from denial of the remedy. The findings shall be an official record or in writing.

(e) Denial of remedies. Denial of any remedy shall not be based, in whole or in part, on evidence that:

(1) Respondent has cause for any use of force, unless that cause satisfies the standards for justifiable use of force provided by Article VII of the Criminal Code of 1961;

(2) Respondent was voluntarily intoxicated;

(3) Petitioner acted in self-defense or defense of another, provided that, if petitioner utilized force, such force was justifiable under Article VII of the Criminal Code of 1961;

(4) Petitioner did not act in self-defense or defense of another;

(5) Petitioner left the residence or household to avoid further abuse, neglect, or exploitation by respondent;

(6) Petitioner did not leave the residence or household to avoid further abuse, neglect, or exploitation by respondent;

(7) Conduct by any family or household member excused the abuse, neglect, or exploitation by respondent, unless that same conduct would have excused such abuse, neglect, or exploitation if the parties had not been family or household members.

Author's Notes

Analysis

1. Lower standards of proof.
2. Remedies.
3. Evidence and findings.
4. Cross reference—Form.

(1) **Lower standards of proof.** DVA § 214 provides for a myriad of remedies, usually with lower standards of proof than are required by comparable Sections in other statutes. For example, exclusive possession of a marital residence and injunctive restraints against abuse and transfers of property can be obtained more easily under the Domestic Violence Act than they can be obtained under comparable Sections of the Illinois Marriage and Dissolution of Marriage Act and the Injunction Act. See 750 ILCS 5/501 (temporary relief), 5/701 (exclusive possession), and 735 ILCS 5/11–101 et seq. (injunctions) and accompanying Author's Notes. The limitation of course is that an action can be brought under the Domestic Violence Act pursuant to DVA § 201(b) only by, or on behalf of, a person who has been the victim of some form of abuse by a family or a household member.

(2) **Remedies.** Before a domestic violence remedy can be obtained, the petitioner must satisfy the requirements for the entry of an emergency order (§ 217), an interim order (§ 218), or a plenary order (§ 219).

The remedies pursuant to DVA § 214 are spelled out in detail. A summary of the available remedies follows: (1) injunction-like restraints on abuse, stalking, harassment, interference with personal liberty, intimidation, willful deprivation, neglect, or exploitation; (2) exclusive possession of the marital home under a balancing of hardship standard; (3) injunction-like stay away order; (4) order of counselling; (5) grant of physical care of a minor child; (6) order of temporary custody; (7) order of visitation, including restricted visitation; (8) prohibition against the removal of a minor child; (9) order directed to respondent and a child to appear in court; (10) grant of exclusive possession or return of personal property; (11) restraint against the transfer, encumbrance, concealment, and the like of property; including a restraint against the use of an aged family member's resources; (12) order of support or children's support to the petitioner; (13) order of payment of losses suffered by the petitioner as a result of abuse, such as medical expenses, attorneys' fees, moving or travel expenses, loss of maintenance, child support, or property, if the petitioner is entitled to any of those awards as temporary relief under § 501(a)(3) of the Illinois Marriage and Dissolution of Marriage Act, and payment of expenses incurred in the search and recovery of a minor child; (14) order restraining respondent from entering the residence or household while intoxicated or under the influence of drugs; (15) restraint against access to the minor child's school and similar records; (16) order of payment of shelter expenses; and (17) other such injunctive relief as is necessary to prevent further abuse, neglect, or exploitation.

(3) **Evidence and findings.** In actions to prevent the types of future abuse or harm described in paragraphs (1) through (16) of DVA § 214(b), DVA § 214(b)(17) provides that it is unnecessary to prove irreparable injury beyond the proof of the likelihood of, e.g., future abuse. *Cf.* 750 ILCS 5/501 Author's Notes (10), (11), and (12) (requirement of irreparable harm under IMDMA and the Injunction Act).

In determining whether to grant a remedy other than the payment of support, the court by DVA § 214(c) is directed to consider the severity and frequency of past abuse and the likelihood that it will be repeated, as well as the danger that a minor child will be abused, neglected, or removed. When the petitioner is seeking exclusive possession of the family home where the respondent has a legal right of entry, the court is instructed to balance the relative hardships. The court is directed to make specific minimal findings either in writing or on an official record; except, in the case of an *ex parte* emergency order, the court may determine whether there is a sufficient basis to support the granting of an emergency order of protection on the basis of the contents of the petition together with an examination of the petitioner. Subsection 214(d) requires that the court make findings for certain remedies which are denied. Subsection 214(e) precludes certain defenses to abuse.

(4) **Cross reference—Form.** For model orders of protection see DVA § 221 Author's Notes (5) and (6).

750 ILCS 60/215

§ 215. Mutual orders of protection; Correlative separate orders

Mutual orders of protection are prohibited. Correlative separate orders of protection undermine the purposes of this Act and are prohibited unless

(2) Certification and transfer. Any order issued under this Section and any documentation in support thereof shall be certified on the next court day to the appropriate court. The clerk of that court shall immediately assign a case number, file the petition, order and other documents with the court, and enter the order of record and file it with the sheriff for service, in accordance with Section 222. Filing the petition shall commence proceedings for further relief under Section 202. Failure to comply with the requirements of this subsection shall not affect the validity of the order.

Author's Notes

Analysis

1. Summary.
2. Emergency order without notice.
3. Unavailable remedies.
4. Holidays and evenings.

(1) **Summary.** Before the court can enter either an emergency order of protection (§ 217), a 30-day interim order of protection (§ 218), or a plenary order of protection (§ 219), the court must have jurisdiction under DVA § 208, and the requirements of DVA § 214 (remedies) must be satisfied. Thereafter, the requirements differ for each type of order. For an emergency order of protection, neither prior notice to nor service upon the respondent is required, but there must be a likelihood that prior notice would cause the harm that the order of protection seeks to prevent. A 30-day interim order of protection requires, at a minimum, notice to the respondent pursuant to DVA § 211 coupled with a diligent attempt to complete service of process on the respondent. A plenary order of protection requires, at a minimum, notice to the respondent pursuant to DVA § 211 coupled with service on the respondent pursuant to DVA § 210, and either an answer or a default by the respondent. A general appearance by the respondent obviates the necessity for service of process, except after the entry of an *ex parte* emergency order. See DVA § 210.1 Author's Note (2).

(2) **Emergency order without notice.** An emergency order of protection can be entered regardless of prior notice to the respondent or prior service of process, if the petitioner can establish for each remedy requested that the harm that the petition is seeking to prevent is more likely to occur if notice is given. Specific standards are set forth for different types of relief under DVA § 217(a)(3). For example, in the case of petitions seeking exclusive possession of a residence, the test is whether the likelihood of harm caused to the petitioner by prior notice to the respondent outweighs the hardship to the respondent of an emergency order granting exclusive possession of a household to the petitioner.

(3) **Unavailable remedies.** Emergency orders cannot include remedies of counselling, legal custody (but can include physical care and possession of a minor child), payment of support, or monetary compensation.

(4) **Holidays and evenings.** During court holidays and evenings, a petition for an emergency order of protection can be filed before any available circuit court or associate judge who is capable of granting relief under the Act.

750 ILCS 60/218

759 ILCS 60/218

§ 218. 30–Day interim order of protection

(a) Prerequisites. An interim order of protection shall issue if petitioner has served notice of the hearing for that order on respondent, in accordance with Section 211, and satisfies the requirements of this subsection for one or more of the requested remedies. For each remedy requested, petitioner shall establish that:

    (1) The court has jurisdiction under Section 208;

    (2) The requirements of Section 214 are satisfied; and

    (3) A general appearance was made or filed by or for respondent; or process was served on respondent in the manner required by Section 210; or the petitioner is diligently attempting to complete the required service of process.

An interim order may not include the counseling, payment of support or monetary compensation remedies, unless the respondent has filed a general appearance or has been personally served.

(b) Appearance by respondent. If respondent appears in court for this hearing for an interim order, he or she may elect to file a general appearance and testify. Any resulting order may be an interim order, governed by this Section. Notwithstanding the requirements of this Section, if all requirements of Section 219 have been met, the court may issue a plenary order of protection.

Author's Notes

Analysis

1. Requirements.
2. Remedies not available.

    (1) **Requirements.** After satisfying the prerequisites of DVA §§ 208 and 214 (see DVA § 217 Author's Note (1)), an interim 30–day order of protection can be entered: (i) if the petitioner has served notice of the hearing for an interim order on respondent in accordance with the requirements of DVA § 211, and (ii) a general appearance was filed by the respondent, or process was served on respondent in the manner required by DVA § 210, or the petitioner is diligently attempting to complete the required service of process.

    (2) **Remedies not available.** An interim order cannot include an order for counselling, the payment of support, or monetary compensation, unless the respondent has filed a general appearance or has been personally served.

750 ILCS 60/219

§ 219. Plenary order of protection

A plenary order of protection shall issue if petitioner has served notice of the hearing for that order on respondent, in accordance with Section 211, and satisfies the requirements of this Section for one or more of the requested remedies. For each remedy requested, petitioner must establish that:

(1) The court has jurisdiction under Section 208;

(2) The requirements of Section 214 are satisfied; and

(3) A general appearance was made or filed by or for respondent or process was served on respondent in the manner required by Section 210; and

(4) Respondent has answered or is in default.

Author's Notes

Analysis

1. Requirements.
2. Upgrading orders.

(1) **Requirements.** After satisfying the prerequisites of DVA §§ 208 and 214 (see DVA § 217 Author's Note (1)), a plenary order of protection can be entered: (i) if the petitioner has served notice of the hearing for that order on respondent in accordance with DVA § 211, and (ii) a general appearance was made or filed by the respondent, or process was served on the respondent in the manner required by DVA § 210, and respondent has answered or is in default.

(2) **Upgrading orders.** DVA § 217(b) allows an emergency order to be upgraded to an interim order if the respondent appears in court, testifies, enters a general appearance, and the requirements of DVA § 218 have been met. DVA § 218(b) has the same criteria for upgrading interim orders to plenary orders of protection, provided that the requirements of DVA § 219 are met.

750 ILCS 60/220

§ 220. Duration and extension of orders

(a) Duration of emergency and interim orders. Unless re-opened or extended or voided by entry of an order of greater duration:

(1) Emergency orders issued under Section 217 shall be effective for not less than 14 nor more than 21 days;

(2) Interim orders shall be effective for up to 30 days.

(b) Duration of plenary orders. Except as otherwise provided in this Section, a plenary order of protection shall be valid for a fixed period of time, not to exceed two years.

(1) A plenary order of protection entered in conjunction with another civil proceeding shall remain in effect as follows:

(i) if entered as preliminary relief in that other proceeding, until entry of final judgment in that other proceeding;

(ii) if incorporated into the final judgment in that other proceeding, until the order of protection is vacated or modified; or

(iii) if incorporated in an order for involuntary commitment, until termination of both the involuntary commitment and any voluntary commitment, or for a fixed period of time not exceeding 2 years.

(2) A plenary order of protection entered in conjunction with a criminal prosecution shall remain in effect as follows:

(i) if entered during pre-trial release, until disposition, withdrawal, or dismissal of the underlying charge; if, however, the case is continued as an independent cause of action, the order's duration may be for a fixed period of time not to exceed 2 years;

(ii) if in effect in conjunction with a bond forfeiture warrant, until final disposition or an additional period of time not exceeding 2 years; no order of protection, however, shall be terminated by a dismissal that is accompanied by the issuance of a bond forfeiture warrant;

(iii) until expiration of any supervision, conditional discharge, probation, periodic imprisonment, parole or mandatory supervised release and for an additional period of time thereafter not exceeding 2 years; or

(iv) until the date set by the court for expiration of any sentence of imprisonment and subsequent parole or mandatory supervised release and for an additional period of time thereafter not exceeding 2 years.

(c) Computation of time. The duration of an order of protection shall not be reduced by the duration of any prior order of protection.

(d) Law enforcement records. When a plenary order of protection expires upon the occurrence of a specified event, rather than upon a specified date as provided in subsection (b), no expiration date shall be entered in Department of State Police records. To remove the plenary order from those records, either party shall request the clerk of the court to file a certified copy of an order stating that the specified event has occurred or that the plenary order has been vacated or modified with the Sheriff, and the Sheriff shall direct that law enforcement records shall be promptly corrected in accordance with the filed order.

(e) Extension of orders. Any emergency, interim or plenary order may be extended one or more times, as required, provided that the requirements of Section 217, 218 or 219, as appropriate, are satisfied. If the motion for extension is uncontested and petitioner seeks no modification of the order, the order may be extended on the basis of petitioner's motion or affidavit stating that there has been no material change in relevant circumstances since entry of the order and stating the reason for the requested extension. Extensions may be granted only in open court and not under the provisions of subsection (c) of Section 217, which applies only when the court is unavailable at the close of business or on a court holiday.

(f) Termination date. Any order of protection which would expire on a court holiday shall instead expire at the close of the next court business day.

(g) **Statement of purpose.** The practice of dismissing or suspending a criminal prosecution in exchange for the issuance of an order of protection undermines the purposes of this Act. This Section shall not be construed as encouraging that practice.

Author's Notes

Analysis

1. Emergency and interim orders: Duration.
2. Plenary orders.
3. Post-judgment restraint.
4. Court Holidays.
5. Extensions.
6. Order of Extension—Form.

(1) **Emergency and interim orders: Duration.** Emergency orders entered under DVA § 216 are effective for not less than 14 days nor for more than 21 days. Interim orders entered pursuant to DVA § 218 are effective for up to 30 days.

(2) **Plenary orders.** Plenary orders entered pursuant to DVA § 219 are valid for fixed periods of time, not to exceed two years, with the following exceptions: (1) if a plenary order is part of a final judgment entered in conjunction with another civil proceeding, the order remains in effect until vacated or modified; and (2) if a plenary order is entered as preliminary relief in another proceeding, then the order expires upon the entry of a final judgment in that proceeding, unless the final judgment incorporates the order of protection. Special rules are provided for plenary orders of protection entered in conjunction with orders for involuntary commitment or criminal proceedings.

(3) **Post-judgment restraint.** The Domestic Violence Act expressly provides for a plenary order of protection incorporated into a final judgment that remains in force after the entry of the judgment (§ 220(b)(1)(ii)). There is no similar authority in the Illinois Marriage and Dissolution of Marriage Act, nor in the Injunction Act. Both provide for relief only *pendente lite*. See 750 ILCS 5/501; 735 ILCS 5/11–101, 102. The Domestic Violence Act has therefore provided a valuable post-decree restraint for use in cases where abuse can be expected to continue after the entry of judgment.

(4) **Court holidays.** Orders of protection that are set to expire on a court holiday instead expire at the close of the next court business day.

(5) **Extensions.** Orders of protection can be extended one or more times, provided the requirements of the Section pursuant to which they were entered remain satisfied. All extensions must be made in open court, and, when they are uncontested, they can be granted on the basis of a motion or affidavit setting forth the reason for the requested extension and stating that there has been no material change in the relevant circumstances.

(6) **Order of Extension—Form.** A sample order of extension from Cook County follows.

750 ILCS 60/220 FAMILIES

PROTECTION ORDER EXTENSION (5-82) CCG-81

IN THE CIRCUIT COURT OF COOK COUNTY, ILLINOIS

v.

Case No. ....

LEEDS NO. ....

[ ] Independent Petition
[ ] Criminal Proceeding
[ ] Domestic Relations

ORDER

The Court Finds that

[ ] A Ex Parte Order of Protection was issued on ....

[ ] An Order of Protection was issued on ....

THE COURT HAVING JURISDICTION OF THE SUBJECT MATTER, IT IS HEREBY ORDERED THAT:

[ ] 1. An extension of the Ex Parte Order of Protection is granted and is hereby extended to ....

.............................., 19...., at ....m.

[ ] 2. A hearing on the Ex Parte Order of Protection is set for ....m., on ....

.... 19...., in Courtroom No. ....

[ ] 3. The Ex Parte Order of Protection is vacated.

[ ] 4. The Order of Protection previously issued is extended to ...., 19....

[ ] 5. A hearing on the Order of Protection is set for ....m., on......................., 19....,

in Courtroom No. ....

[ ] 6. The Order of Protection is vacated.

[ ] 7. [ ] The Ex Parte Order of Protection is modified as follows

[ ] The Order of Protection is modified as follows

_____

_____

Name
Attorney for   Enter: ....
Address   Judge   Judge's No.
City
Telephone   Date: ....

AURELIA PUCINSKI, CLERK OF THE CIRCUIT COURT OF COOK COUNTY, ILLINOIS

[G17994]

---

750 ILCS 60/221

§ 221. Contents of orders

(a) Any order of protection shall describe the following:

(1) Each remedy granted by the court, in reasonable detail and not by reference to any other document, so that respondent may clearly understand what he or she must do or refrain from doing. Pre-printed form orders of protection shall include the definitions of the types of abuse, neglect, and exploitation, as provided in Section 103. Remedies set forth in pre-printed form orders shall be numbered consistently with and corresponding to the numerical sequence of remedies listed in Section 214 (at least as of the date the form orders are printed).

(2) The reason for denial of petitioner's request for any remedy listed in Section 214.

(b) An order of protection shall further state the following:

(1) The name of each petitioner that the court finds was abused, neglected, or exploited by respondent, and that respondent is a member of the family or household of each such petitioner, and the name of each other person protected by the order and that such person is protected by this Act.

(2) For any remedy requested by petitioner on which the court has declined to rule, that that remedy is reserved.

(3) The date and time the order of protection was issued, whether it is an emergency, interim or plenary order and the duration of the order.

(4) The date, time and place for any scheduled hearing for extension of that order of protection or for another order of greater duration or scope.

(5) For each remedy in an emergency order of protection, the reason for entering that remedy without prior notice to respondent or greater notice than was actually given.

(6) For emergency and interim orders of protection, that respondent may petition the court, in accordance with Section 224, to re-open that order if he or she did not receive actual prior notice of the hearing, in accordance with Section 211, and alleges that he or she had a meritorious defense to the order or that the order or any of its remedies was not authorized by this Act.

(c) Any order of protection shall include the following notice, printed in conspicuous type: "Any knowing violation of an order of protection forbidding physical abuse, neglect, exploitation, harassment, intimidation, interference with personal liberty, willful deprivation, or entering or remaining present at specified places when the protected person is present, or granting exclusive possession of the residence or household, or granting a stay away order is a Class A misdemeanor. Grant of exclusive possession of the residence or household shall constitute notice forbidding trespass to land. Any knowing violation of an order awarding legal custody of physical care of a child or prohibiting removal or concealment of a child may be a Class 4 felony. Any willful violation of any order is contempt of court. Any violation may result in fine or imprisonment."

750 ILCS 60/221   FAMILIES

Author's Notes

Analysis

1. Simple forms.
2. Findings.
3. Emergency order findings.
4. Appeals.
5. Emergency Order of Protection—Form.
6. Order of Protection (interim or plenary)—Form.

(1) **Simple forms.** The requirements for orders of protection are set forth in DVA § 221, and clerks of the court are directed to include these requirements in their preprinted forms. The Domestic Violence Act is a comprehensive and complicated codification of substantive and procedural law. A less comprehensive statute might have been expected to grow into a coherent body of law only on a case by case basis over an extended period of time. The Act was saved from inoperativeness because of its own complexity when it was implemented with easily understood form petitions and orders. The two form orders in use in Cook County are an Emergency Order of Protection and an Order of Protection; the latter for use as either an interim or a plenary order, depending upon which box is checked. See Author's Note (6) below.

(2) **Findings.** Both the emergency order of protection and the order of protection provided at Author's Notes (5) and (6) below contemplate (in the first printed paragraph at the top of their second pages) that the findings required by DVA §§ 214(c) and 214(d) be made either orally on the official transcript or by a separate instrument filed by the court. Paragraph 18 in both orders contains space for stating the reasons why the relief requested was denied (DVA § 221(a)(2)), or reserved (DVA § 221(b)(2)).

(3) **Emergency order findings.** DVA § 221(b)(5) requires that, for each remedy in an emergency order of protection, the reason for entering that remedy without prior notice to the respondent, or greater notice than was actually given, must be stated in the order of protection. An express direction to that effect is not contained in the Cook County reprinted form located at Author's Note (5) below. Because of the mandatory nature of the DVA § 221(b)(5), such a finding for each remedy should be made part of the emergency order of protection, either at the top of the second page in the "Finding" section, in the space at the end, or by a separate instrument.

(4) **Appeals.** An interlocutory appeal should exist of right from those remedies in orders of protection that are injunctive in nature. See Supreme Court Rule 307. See, e.g., In re Marriage of Healy, 263 Ill.App.3d 596, 200 Ill.Dec. 327, 635 N.E.2d 666 (1st Dist.1994); In re Marriage of McCoy, 253 Ill.App.3d 958, 192 Ill.Dec. 728, 625 N.E.2d 883 (4th Dist.1993); Glater v. Fabianich, 252 Ill.App.3d 372, 192 Ill.Dec. 136, 625 N.E.2d 96 (1st Dist.1993).

(5) **Emergency Order of Protection—Form.** There follows the Emergency Order of Protection form in use in Cook County.

FAMILIES   **750 ILCS 60/221**

EMERGENCY ORDER OF PROTECTION: 1 of 4 Pages   [4553]   CCG-96-1-REV. 12/02/92

IN THE CIRCUIT COURT OF COOK COUNTY

People ex rel. _____

_____ on behalf of

_____ self and/or behalf of

_____
Petitioner

-vs-

_____
Respondent

Case No. _____

☐ Independent Proceeding
☐ Other Civil Proceeding
(*Specify*) _____
☐ Criminal Proceeding
☐ Juvenile Proceeding

LEADS NO. _____

PETITIONER	ADDRESS	CITY
	☐ (Check if omitted pursuant to Statute)	
RESPONDENT	ADDRESS	CITY

Birthdate	Sex	Race	Height	Weight	Hair	Eyes	Social Security Number (*if known*)
(Required for LEADS)							

EMERGENCY ORDER OF PROTECTION

ANY KNOWING VIOLATION OF ANY ORDER OF PROTECTION FORBIDDING PHYSICAL ABUSE, NEGLECT, EXPLOITATION, HARASSMENT, INTIMIDATION, INTERFERENCE WITH PERSONAL LIBERTY, WILLFUL DEPRIVATION, OR ENTERING OR REMAINING PRESENT AT SPECIFIED PLACES WHEN THE PROTECTED PERSON IS PRESENT OR GRANTING EXCLUSIVE POSSESSION OF THE RESIDENCE OR HOUSEHOLD, PROHIBITING ENTERING OR REMAINING AT THE HOUSEHOLD WHILE UNDER THE INFLUENCE OF ALCOHOL OR DRUGS AND SO CONSTITUTING A THREAT TO THE SAFETY AND WELL-BEING OF ANY PROTECTED PERSON, OR GRANTING A STAY AWAY ORDER, IS A CLASS A MISDEMEANOR. GRANT OF EXCLUSIVE POSSESSION OF THE RESIDENCE OR HOUSEHOLD SHALL CONSTITUTE NOTICE FORBIDDING TRESPASS TO LAND. ANY KNOWING VIOLATION OF ANY ORDER AWARDING LEGAL CUSTODY OR PHYSICAL CARE OF A CHILD, OR PROHIBITING REMOVAL OR CONCEALMENT OF A CHILD MAY BE A CLASS 4 FELONY. ANY WILLFUL VIOLATION OF ANY ORDER IS CONTEMPT OF COURT. ANY VIOLATION MAY RESULT IN FINE OR IMPRISONMENT. STALKING IS A FELONY.

[Definitions of prohibited conduct on reverse.]

The following persons are protected by this Order: _____
_____
"The minor child/ren" referred to herein are: _____
_____

Date, time and place for further hearing:

Date _____ Time _____ Courtroom/Calendar No. _____

Location _____

This Order was issued on:	This Order will be in effect until:
Date _____ Time _____	☐ Date _____ Time _____

1. CLERK OF CIRCUIT COURT

[G17995]

750 ILCS 60/221 **FAMILIES**

EMERGENCY ORDER OF PROTECTION: 2 of 4 Pages   CCG-96-2-REV. 12/02/92

BASED ON THE FINDINGS OF THIS COURT, ☐ WHICH WERE MADE ORALLY FOR TRANSCRIPTION, OR ☐ WHICH ARE SET OUT IN A SEPARATE INSTRUMENT FILED WITH THE COURT, AND WITH THE COURT HAVING JURISDICTION OF THE SUBJECT MATTER AND OVER ALL NECESSARY PARTIES, IT IS HEREBY ORDERED THAT:

☐ 1. With respect to all Protected Persons, Respondent is prohibited from committing the following:
  ☐ Physical abuse; ☐ Harassment; ☐ Interference with personal liberty; ☐ Intimidation of a dependent;
  ☐ Willful deprivation; ☐ Neglect; ☐ Exploitation; ☐ Stalking.

☐ 2. Petitioner is granted exclusive possession of the residence and Respondent shall not enter or remain in the household or premises located at: _____
  [This remedy does not affect title to property]

☐ 3. ☐ a. Respondent is ordered to stay away from Petitioner and other protected persons; and/or
  ☐ b. Respondent is prohibited from entering or remaining at _____
  _____ while any Protected Person is present; and/or

  ☐ c. Respondent is allowed access to the residence on (date)_____ at (time)_____ in the presence of (name)_____ to remove items of clothing, personal adornments, medications used exclusively by the Respondent and other items, as follows: _____

☐ 5. ☐ a. Petitioner is granted physical care and possession of the minor child/ren; and/or
  ☐ b. Respondent is ordered to:
    ☐ Return the minor child/ren _____ to the physical care of _____ ; and/or
    ☐ Not remove the minor child/ren _____ from the physical care of Petitioner or _____

☐ 7. ☐ a. Respondent is awarded visitation rights on the following dates and times or under the following conditions or parameters: *[No order shall merely refer to the term " reasonable visitation"]*
  _____

  ☐ b. Respondent's visitation is restricted as follows: _____

  ☐ c. Respondent's visitation is reserved/ denied.
  (Petitioner may deny Respondent access to the minor child/ren if, when Respondent arrives for visitation, Respondent is under the influence of drugs or alcohol and constitutes a threat to the safety and well-being of Petitioner or Petitioner's minor child/ren or is behaving in a violent or abusive manner.)

☐ 8. Respondent is prohibited from removing the minor child/ren from Illinois or concealing them within Illinois.

☐ 9. Respondent is ordered to appear in Courtroom/Calendar _____ at _____ on _____ at _____ AM/PM, with/without the minor child/ren

☐ 10. Petitioner is granted exclusive possession of the following personal property and the Respondent is ordered to promptly make available to Petitioner said property that is in Respondent's possession or control, to wit: _____
  [This remedy does not affect title to property]

☐ 11. Respondent is prohibited from taking, encumbering, concealing, damaging or otherwise disposing of the following personal property:
  _____ , except as explicitly authorized by the Court
  ☐ Further, Respondent is prohibited from improperly using the financial or other resources of an aged member of the family or household for the profit or advantage of Respondent or any other person.

1. CLERK OF CIRCUIT COURT   CASE NO. _____

[G17996]

EMERGENCY ORDER OF PROTECTION: 3 of 4 Pages   CCG-96-3-REV. 12/02/92

☐ 14. Respondent is prohibited from entering or remaining at the household or residence located at _____
_____ while under
the influence of alcohol or drugs and so constituting a threat to the safety and well-being of any Protected Person.
☐ 15. Respondent is denied access to school and/or any other records of the minor child/ren and is prohibited from inspecting, obtaining, or attempting to inspect or obtain such records.
☐ 17. Respondent is further ordered and/or enjoined as follows: _____
_____

☐ 18. The relief requested in paragraph(s) _____ of the petition is (*DENIED*) (*RESERVED*), because:
_____

NOTICE: Upon 2 days notice to Petitioner, or such shorter notice as the Court may prescribe, a Respondent subject to an Emergency Order of Protection issued under the IDVA may appear and petition the Court to re-hear the original or amended Petition. Respondent's petition shall be verified and shall allege lack of notice and a meritorious defense.

Date: _____
Judge: _____
                        Judge's No.

Attorney (or Pro Se Petitioner) Name: _____
Address _____
City _____
Phone _____
Attorney # _____
Service by Facsimile ☐ will be accepted ☐ will not be accepted.
Facsimile Number _____
(Must be included if service by facsimile is accepted)

1. CLERK OF CIRCUIT COURT   CASE NO. _____
                                                    [G17997]

750 ILCS 60/221　　　　　　FAMILIES

EMERGENCY ORDER OF PROTECTION: 4 of 4 Pages

DEFINITIONS
PURSUANT TO THE ILLINOIS DOMESTIC VIOLENCE ACT

1. "Petitioner" may mean not only any named petitioner for the order of protection and any named victim of abuse on whose behalf the petition is brought, but also any other person protected by this Act.
2. "Abuse" means physical abuse, harassment, intimidation of a dependent, interference with personal liberty or willful deprivation, but does not include reasonable direction of a minor child by a parent or person in loco parentis.
3. "Physical abuse" includes sexual abuse and means any of the following:
    (a) knowing or reckless use of physical force, confinement or restraint;
    (b) knowing, repeated and unnecessary sleep deprivation; or
    (c) knowing or reckless conduct which creates an immediate risk of physical harm.
4. "Harassment" means knowing conduct which is not necessary to accomplish a purpose that is reasonable under the circumstances; would cause a reasonable person emotional distress; and does cause emotional distress to the petitioner. Unless the presumption is rebutted by a preponderance of the evidence, the following types of conduct shall be presumed to cause emotional distress:
    (a) creating a disturbance at petitioner's place of employment or school;
    (b) repeatedly telephoning petitioner's place of employment, home, or residence;
    (c) repeatedly following petitioner about in a public place or places;
    (d) repeatedly keeping petitioner under surveillance by remaining present outside his or her home, school, place of employment, vehicle or other place occupied by petitioner or by peering in petitioner's windows;
    (e) improperly concealing a minor child from petitioner, repeatedly threatening to improperly remove a minor child of petitioner's from the jurisdiction or from the physical care of petitioner, repeatedly threatening to conceal a minor child from petitioner, or making a single such threat following an actual or attempted improper removal or concealment, unless respondent was fleeing an incident or pattern of domestic violence;
    (f) threatening physical force, confinement or restraint on one or more occasions.
5. "Interference with personal liberty" means committing or threatening physical abuse, harassment, intimidation or willful deprivation so as to compel another to engage in conduct from which she or he has a right to abstain or to refrain from conduct in which she or he has a right to engage.
6. "Willful deprivation" means willfully denying a person who because of age, health or disability requires medication, medical care, shelter, accessible shelter or services, food, therapeutic device, or other physical assistance, and thereby exposing that person to the risk of physical, mental or emotional harm, except with regard to medical care or treatment when the dependent person has expressed an intent to forgo such medical care or treatment. This paragraph does not create any new affirmative duty to provide support to dependent persons.
7. "Intimidation of dependent" means subjecting a person who is dependent because of age, health or disability to participation in or the witnessing of: physical force against another or physical confinement or restraint of another which constitutes physical abuse as defined in this Act, regardless of whether the abused person is a family or household member.
8. "Exploitation" means the illegal, including tortious, use of a high-risk adult with disabilities or of the assets or resources of a high-risk adult with disabilities. Exploitation includes, but is not limited to, the misappropriation of assets or resources of a high-risk adult with disabilities by undue influence, by breach of a fiduciary relationship, by fraud, deception, or extortion, or the use of such assets or resources in a manner contrary to law.
9. "Neglect" means the failure to exercise that degree of care toward a high-risk adult with disabilities which a reasonable person would exercise under the circumstances and includes but is not limited to:
    (a) the failure to take reasonable steps to protect a high-risk adult with disabilities from acts of abuse;
    (b) the repeated, careless imposition of unreasonable confinement;
    (c) the failure to provide food, shelter, clothing, and personal hygiene to a high-risk adult with disabilities who requires such assistance;
    (d) the failure to provide medical and rehabilitative care for the physical and mental health needs of a high-risk adult with disabilities; or
    (e) the failure to protect a high-risk adult with disabilities from health and safety hazards.

CASE NO. _____

[G17998]

(6) **Order of Protection (interim or plenary)—Form.** There follows the Order of Protection (interim or plenary) form in use in Cook County.

FAMILIES 750 ILCS 60/221

INTERIM/PLENARY ORDER OF PROTECTION: 1 of 3 Pages   CCG-83-1-25M-9-1-92(20417)

IN THE CIRCUIT COURT OF COOK COUNTY

People ex rel. _____
_____ on behalf of
_____ self and/or behalf of

_____
Petitioner

-vs-

_____
Respondent

Case No. _____
☐ Independent Proceeding
☐ Other Civil Proceeding
   (Specify) _____
☐ Criminal Proceeding
☐ Juvenile Proceeding
LEADS NO. _____

PETITIONER	ADDRESS	CITY
	☐ (Check if omitted pursuant to Statute)	
RESPONDENT	ADDRESS	CITY

Birthdate	Sex	Race	Height	Weight	Hair	Eyes	Social Security Number *(if known)*
(Required for LEADS)							

ORDER OF PROTECTION

4552 ☐ INTERIM   4652 ☐ PLENARY

ANY KNOWING VIOLATION OF ANY ORDER OF PROTECTION FORBIDDING PHYSICAL ABUSE, NEGLECT, EXPLOITATION, HARASSMENT, INTIMIDATION, INTERFERENCE WITH PERSONAL LIBERTY, WILLFUL DEPRIVATION, OR ENTERING OR REMAINING PRESENT AT SPECIFIED PLACES WHEN THE PROTECTED PERSON IS PRESENT OR GRANTING EXCLUSIVE POSSESSION OF THE RESIDENCE OR HOUSEHOLD, PROHIBITING ENTERING OR REMAINING AT THE HOUSEHOLD WHILE UNDER THE INFLUENCE OF ALCOHOL OR DRUGS AND SO CONSTITUTING A THREAT TO THE SAFETY AND WELL-BEING OF ANY PROTECTED PERSON, OR GRANTING A STAY AWAY ORDER, IS A CLASS A MISDEMEANOR. GRANT OF EXCLUSIVE POSSESSION OF THE RESIDENCE OR HOUSEHOLD SHALL CONSTITUTE NOTICE FORBIDDING TRESPASS TO LAND. ANY KNOWING VIOLATION OF ANY ORDER AWARDING LEGAL CUSTODY OR PHYSICAL CARE OF A CHILD, OR PROHIBITING REMOVAL OR CONCEALMENT OF A CHILD MAY BE A CLASS 4 FELONY. ANY WILLFUL VIOLATION OF ANY ORDER IS CONTEMPT OF COURT. ANY VIOLATION MAY RESULT IN FINE OR IMPRISONMENT. STALKING IS A FELONY.

(Definitions of prohibited conduct on reverse)

The following persons are protected by this Order: _____
_____
"The minor child/ren" referred to herein are: _____
_____

Date, time and place for further hearing *(if Interim Order)*:

Date _____ Time _____ Courtroom/Calendar No. _____
                                  Location _____

This Order was issued on:	This Order will be in effect until:
Date _____ Time _____	☐ Date _____ Time _____
	☐ Vacated by court order.
	☐ Specified event: _____

[G17999]

1.) CLERK OF THE CIRCUIT COURT

750 ILCS 60/221   FAMILIES

INTERIM/PLENARY ORDER OF PROTECTION: 2 of 3 Pages   CCG-83-2-25M-9-1-92(20417)

BASED ON THE FINDINGS OF THIS COURT, ☐ WHICH WERE MADE ORALLY FOR TRANSCRIPTION, OR ☐ WHICH ARE SET OUT IN A SEPARATE INSTRUMENT FILED WITH THE COURT, AND WITH THE COURT HAVING JURISDICTION OF THE SUBJECT MATTER AND OVER ALL NECESSARY PARTIES, IT IS HEREBY ORDERED THAT:

☐ 1. With respect to all Protected Persons, Respondent is prohibited from committing the following:
    ☐ Physical abuse;   ☐ Harassment;   ☐ Interference with personal liberty;   ☐ Intimidation of a dependent;
    ☐ Willful deprivation;   ☐ Neglect;   ☐ Exploitation;   ☐ Stalking.

☐ 2. Petitioner is granted exclusive possession of the residence and Respondent shall not enter or remain in the household or premises located at: _____
(This remedy does not affect title to property)

☐ 3. ☐ a. Respondent is ordered to stay away from Petitioner and other protected persons; and/or
    ☐ b. Respondent is prohibited from entering or remaining at _____ while any Protected Person is present; and/or

    ☐ c. Respondent is allowed access to the residence on (date) _____ at (time) _____ in the presence of (name) _____ to remove items of clothing, personal adornments, medications used exclusively by the Respondent and other items, as follows: _____

☐ 4. Respondent is ordered to undergo counseling at _____ for a duration of _____

☐ 5. ☐ a. Petitioner is granted physical care and possession of the minor child/ren; and/or
    ☐ b. Respondent is ordered to:
        ☐ Return the minor child/ren _____ to the physical care of _____ ; and/or
        ☐ Not remove the minor child/ren _____ from the physical care of Petitioner or _____

☐ 6. Petitioner is granted temporary legal custody of the minor child/ren _____

☐ 7. ☐ a. Respondent is awarded visitation rights on the following dates and times or under the following conditions or parameters:
(No order shall merely refer to the term "reasonable visitation")
_____

    ☐ b. Respondent's visitation is restricted as follows: _____

    ☐ c. Respondent's visitation is denied.
(Petitioner may deny Respondent access to the minor child/ren if, when Respondent arrives for visitation, Respondent is under the influence of drugs or alcohol and constitutes a threat to the safety and well-being of Petitioner or Petitioner's minor child/ren or is behaving in a violent or abusive manner.)

☐ 8. Respondent is prohibited from removing the minor child/ren from Illinois or concealing them within Illinois.

☐ 9. Respondent is ordered to appear in Courtroom/Calendar _____ at _____ on _____ at _____ AM/PM, with/without the minor child/ren.

☐ 10. Petitioner is granted exclusive possession of the following personal property and the Respondent is ordered to promptly make available to Petitioner said property that is in Respondent's possession or control, to wit: _____
(This remedy does not affect title to property)

☐ 11. Respondent is prohibited from taking, encumbering, concealing, damaging or otherwise disposing of the following personal property: _____ , except as explicitly authorized by the Court.
    ☐ Further, Respondent is prohibited from improperly using the financial or other resources of an aged member of the family or household for the profit or advantage of Respondent or any other person.

☐ 12. Respondent is ordered to pay temporary support for ☐ Petitioner and/or ☐ the minor child/ren of the parties as follows: $ _____ per _____ , starting _____ , payable ☐ through the Clerk of the Circuit Court, or ☐ directly to Petitioner.

☐ 13. Respondent is ordered to pay $ _____ as actual monetary compensation for loss(es) to _____ on or before _____ .
    ☐ Further, Respondent is ordered to pay court costs in the amount of $ _____ and attorney fees in the amount of $ _____ to _____ in connection with any action to obtain, modify, enforce, appeal or reopen any order of protection, on or before _____ .

1.) CLERK OF THE CIRCUIT COURT   CASE NO. _____

[G19001]

INTERIM/PLENARY ORDER OF PROTECTION: 3 of 3 Pages   CCG-83-3-25M-9-1-92(20417)

☐ 14. Respondent is prohibited from entering or remaining at the household or residence located at _____
_____ while under
the influence of alcohol or drugs and so constituting a threat to the safety and well-being of any Protected Person.

☐ 15. Respondent is denied access to school and/or any other records of the minor child/ren and is prohibited from inspecting, obtaining, or attempting to inspect or obtain such records.

☐ 16. Respondent is ordered to pay $ _____ to the following shelter _____
on or before _____ .

☐ 17. Respondent is further ordered and/or enjoined as follows: _____
_____
_____

☐ 18. The relief requested in paragraph(s) _____ of the petition is *(DENIED) (RESERVED)*, because:
_____
_____

PLENARY ORDERS ONLY

This order shall remain in effect until:

☐ 1. Two years following the date of entry of such Order, such expiration date being _____ , or such earlier date, as ordered by the Court, such expiration date being _____ .

☐ 2. Final judgment in conjoined proceeding is rendered.

☐ 3. This Order is modified or vacated (provided such Order is incorporated into the final judgment of another civil proceeding).

☐ 4. Termination of any voluntary or involuntary commitment, or until _____ .
(not to exceed 2 years)

☐ 5. Final disposition when a Bond Forfeiture Warrant has issued, or until _____ .
(not to exceed 2 years)

☐ 6. Expiration of any supervision, conditional discharge, probation, periodic imprisonment, parole, or supervised mandatory release, plus 2 years.

☐ 7. Expiration of a term of imprisonment set by this Court, plus 2 years.

NOTICE: Upon 2 days notice to Petitioner, or such shorter notice as the Court may prescribe, a Respondent subject to an Interim Order of Protection issued under the IDVA may appear and petition the Court to re-hear the original or amended Petition. Respondent's petition shall be verified and shall allege lack of notice and a meritorious defense.

Date _____

Judge _____
Judge's No.

Attorney (or Pro Se Petitioner) Name _____

Address _____

City _____

Phone _____

Attorney # _____

Service by Facsimile ☐ will be accepted ☐ will not be accepted.

Facsimile Number _____
(Must be included if service by facsimile is accepted)

1.) CLERK OF THE CIRCUIT COURT   CASE NO. _____

750 ILCS 60/222
§ 222. Notice of orders

(a) Entry and issuance. Upon issuance of any order of protection, the clerk shall immediately (i) enter the order on the record and file it in accordance with the circuit court procedures and (ii) provide a file stamped copy of the order to respondent, if present, and to petitioner.

(b) Filing with sheriff. The clerk of the issuing judge shall, or the petitioner may, on the same day that an order of protection is issued, file a certified copy of that order with the sheriff or other law enforcement officials charged with maintaining Department of State Police records or charged with serving the order upon respondent.

(c) Service by sheriff. Unless respondent was present in court when the order was issued, the sheriff, other law enforcement official or special process server shall promptly serve that order upon respondent and file proof of such service, in the manner provided for service of process in civil proceedings. If process has not yet been served upon the respondent, it shall be served with the order. A single fee may be charged for service of an order obtained in civil court, or for service of such an order together with process, unless waived or deferred under Section 210.

(d) Extensions, modifications and revocations. Any order extending, modifying or revoking any order of protection shall be promptly recorded, issued and served as provided in this Section.

(e) Notice to schools. Upon request and at the expense of the petitioner, the clerk of the issuing judge shall file a certified copy of an order of protection with the private school or schools or the principal office of the school district or districts in which any children of the petitioner are enrolled.

(f) Disclosure by schools. A private school may prohibit the disclosure by any school employee to any person against whom the school has received a certified copy of an order of protection the location or address of the petitioner for the order of protection. The school shall maintain the copy of the order of protection in the records of the child or children enrolled in the school whose parent is the petitioner of an order of protection. A public school district may prohibit disclosure in accordance with Section 10–22.3c or 34–18.6a of the School Code.

Author's Notes

(1) **Filing and notice.** DVA § 222 provides for the filing and service of orders of protection. The sheriff or a special process server is required to serve a respondent who was not present in court. In cases where there is a potential for physical abuse or the like, it is also advisable to notify the local police that the court has entered the order of protection.

750 ILCS 60/223

§ 223. Enforcement of orders of protection

(a) When violation is crime. A violation of any order of protection, whether issued in a civil or criminal proceeding, may be enforced by a criminal court when:

(1) The respondent commits the crime of violation of order of protection pursuant to Section 12-30 of the Criminal Code of 1961, by having knowingly violated remedies described in paragraphs (1), (2), (3), or (14) of subsection (b) of Section 214 of this Act or any other remedy when the act constitutes a crime against the protected parties as defined by the Criminal Code of 1961. Prosecution for a violation of an order of protection shall not bar concurrent prosecution for any other crime, including any crime that may have been committed at the time of the violation of the order of protection; or

(2) The respondent commits the crime of child abduction pursuant to Section 10-5 of the Criminal Code of 1961, by having knowingly violated remedies described in paragraphs (5), (6) or (8) of subsection (b) of Section 214 of this Act.

(b) When violation is contempt of court. A violation of any valid Illinois order of protection, whether issued in a civil or criminal proceeding, may be enforced through civil or criminal contempt procedures, as appropriate, by any court with jurisdiction, regardless where the act or acts which violated the order of protection were committed, to the extent consistent with the venue provisions of this Act. Nothing in this Act shall preclude any Illinois court from enforcing any valid order of protection issued in another state. Illinois courts may enforce orders of protection through both criminal prosecution and contempt proceedings, unless the action which is second in time is barred by collateral estoppel or the constitutional prohibition against double jeopardy.

(1) In a contempt proceeding where the petition for a rule to show cause sets forth facts evidencing an immediate danger that the respondent will flee the jurisdiction, conceal a child, or inflict physical abuse on the petitioner or minor children or on dependent adults in petitioner's care, the court may order the attachment of the respondent without prior service of the rule to show cause or the petition for a rule to show cause. Bond shall be set unless specifically denied in writing.

(2) A petition for a rule to show cause for violation of an order of protection shall be treated as an expedited proceeding.

(c) Violation of custody or support orders. A violation of remedies described in paragraphs (5), (6), (8), or (9) of subsection (b) of Section 214 of this Act may be enforced by any remedy provided by Section 611 of the Illinois Marriage and Dissolution of Marriage Act. The court may enforce any order for support issued under paragraph (12) of subsection (b) of Section 214 in the manner provided for under Articles V and VII of the Illinois Marriage and Dissolution of Marriage Act.

(d) Actual knowledge. An order of protection may be enforced pursuant to this Section if the respondent violates the order after the respondent has actual knowledge of its contents as shown through one of the following means:

(1) By service, delivery, or notice under Section 210.

(2) By notice under Section 210.1 or 211.

(3) By service of an order of protection under Section 222.

(4) By other means demonstrating actual knowledge of the contents of the order.

(e) The enforcement of an order of protection in civil or criminal court shall not be affected by either of the following:

(1) The existence of a separate, correlative order, entered under Section 215.

(2) Any finding or order entered in a conjoined criminal proceeding.

(f) Circumstances. The court, when determining whether or not a violation of an order of protection has occurred, shall not require physical manifestations of abuse on the person of the victim.

(g) Penalties.

(1) Except as provided in paragraph (3) of this subsection, where the court finds the commission of a crime or contempt of court under subsections (a) or (b) of this Section, the penalty shall be the penalty that generally applies in such criminal or contempt proceedings, and may include one or more of the following: incarceration, payment of restitution, a fine, payment of attorneys' fees and costs, or community service.

(2) The court shall hear and take into account evidence of any factors in aggravation or mitigation before deciding an appropriate penalty under paragraph (1) of this subsection.

(3) To the extent permitted by law, the court is encouraged to:

(i) increase the penalty for the knowing violation of any order of protection over any penalty previously imposed by any court for respondent's violation of any order of protection or penal statute involving petitioner as victim and respondent as defendant;

(ii) impose a minimum penalty of 24 hours imprisonment for respondent's first violation of any order of protection; and

(iii) impose a minimum penalty of 48 hours imprisonment for respondent's second or subsequent violation of an order of protection unless the court explicitly finds that an increased penalty or that period of imprisonment would be manifestly unjust.

(4) In addition to any other penalties imposed for a violation of an order of protection, a criminal court may consider evidence of any violations of an order of protection:

(i) to increase, revoke or modify the bail bond on an underlying criminal charge pursuant to Section 110–6 of the Code of Criminal Procedure of 1963;

(ii) to revoke or modify an order of probation, conditional discharge or supervision, pursuant to Section 5-6-4 of the Unified Code of Corrections;

(iii) to revoke or modify a sentence of periodic imprisonment, pursuant to Section 5-7-2 of the Unified Code of Corrections.

Author's Notes

Analysis

1. Criminal prosecution.
2. Contempt.
3. Custody and support.
4. Knowledge.
5. Imprisonment.

(1) **Criminal prosecution.** DVA § 223(a) provides that a knowing violation of the remedies in an order of protection under DVA §§ 214(b)(1), (2), (3) or (14) (prohibitions of abuse, grants of exclusive possession, stay away orders, prohibitions of entry); DVA § 214(b)(5), (6) or (8) (physical care of a child, temporary custody, prohibitions against removal); or any other remedy when the act constitutes a crime against the protected party, can be prosecuted under the Criminal Code. The first violation of an order of protection is a Class A misdemeanor. A second or subsequent violation is a Class 4 felony and is accompanied by a minimum of 24 hours imprisonment. Fines and restitution to the victim are also permitted. See 720 ILCS 5/12-30 (set forth at DVA § 301 Author's Note (2)), 720 ILCS 5/10-5.

(2) **Contempt.** DVA § 223(b) provides that any violation of an order of protection can be enforced by criminal or civil contempt proceedings. Pursuant to DVA § 223(b)(1), where it is shown in the petition for a rule to show cause that there is immediate danger, a court may order an attachment against the respondent without prior service of the petition or the rule to show cause. See 750 ILCS 5/511 Author's Note (5) for explication of civil and criminal contempt proceedings. 750 ILCS 5/511 Author's Notes (6) through (8) contain a sample petition for a rule to show cause, an order for a rule to show cause, and an attachment order.

(3) **Custody and support.** DVA § 223(c) provides that violations of custody and support provisions of orders of protection may, in addition, be enforced under § 611 and Articles V and VII of the Illinois Marriage and Dissolution of Marriage Act.

(4) **Knowledge.** Enforcement of an order of protection against a respondent requires that, in accordance with DVA § 223(d), the respondent have actual knowledge of the contents of the order, either through service or notice pursuant to the Act, or otherwise demonstrate actual knowledge.

(5) **Imprisonment.** Courts are encouraged by DVA § 223(g)(3)(ii) to impose a minimum of 24 hours imprisonment for the first violation of any order of protection.

750 ILCS 60/223.1

§ 223.1. Order of protection; Status

Whenever relief is sought under this Act, the court, before granting relief, shall determine whether any order of protection has previously been entered in the instant proceeding or any other proceeding in which any party, or a child of any party, or both, if relevant, has been designated as either a respondent or a protected person.

750 ILCS 60/224

§ 224. Modification and re-opening of orders

(a) Except as otherwise provided in this Section, upon motion by petitioner, the court may modify an emergency, interim, or plenary order of protection:

> (1) If respondent has abused petitioner since the hearing for that order, by adding or altering one or more remedies, as authorized by Section 214; and

> (2) Otherwise, by adding any remedy authorized by Section 214 which was:

>> (i) reserved in that order of protection;

>> (ii) not requested for inclusion in that order of protection; or

>> (iii) denied on procedural grounds, but not on the merits.

(b) Upon motion by petitioner or respondent, the court may modify any prior order of protection's remedy for custody, visitation or payment of support in accordance with the relevant provisions of the Illinois Marriage and Dissolution of Marriage Act. Each order of protection shall be entered in the Law Enforcement Automated Data System on the same day it is issued by the court.

(c) After 30 days following entry of a plenary order of protection, a court may modify that order only when changes in the applicable law or facts since that plenary order was entered warrant a modification of its terms.

(d) Upon 2 days' notice to petitioner, in accordance with Section 211 of this Act, or such shorter notice as the court may prescribe, a respondent subject to an emergency or interim order of protection issued under this Act may appear and petition the court to re-hear the original or amended petition. Any petition to re-hear shall be verified and shall allege the following:

> (1) that respondent did not receive prior notice of the initial hearing in which the emergency, interim, or plenary order was entered under Sections 211 and 217; and

> (2) that respondent had a meritorious defense to the order or any of its remedies or that the order or any of its remedies was not authorized by this Act.

(e) In the event that the emergency or interim order granted petitioner exclusive possession and the petition of respondent seeks to re-open or vacate that grant, the court shall set a date for hearing within 14 days on all issues relating to exclusive possession. Under no circumstances shall a court continue a hearing concerning exclusive possession beyond the 14th day, except by agreement of the parties. Other issues raised by the pleadings may be consolidated for the hearing if neither party nor the court objects.

(f) This Section does not limit the means, otherwise available by law, for vacating or modifying orders of protection.

Author's Notes

Analysis

1. Modification.
2. Modification of appealed order.

(1) **Modification.** Section 224 sets out the procedures for modifying of orders of protection. Most importantly, DVA § 224(d) permits the respondent to an emergency or interim order of protection to petition the court to rehear the petition on two days notice, which is shorter than the notice usually required. The petition for rehearing must be verified, allege that respondent did not receive prior notice of the initial hearing, and set forth a meritorious defense. In the case of an emergency or interim order granting exclusive possession, the court is required to conduct the hearing within 14 days, unless the parties agree to the contrary.

(2) **Modification of appealed order.** Orders of protection that are entered *pendente lite* remain with the court and can be modified by the trial court. This is not affected by whether the original entry of the order has been appealed. See In re Marriage of Fischer, 228 Ill.App.3d 482, 170 Ill.Dec. 168, 592 N.E.2d 604 (4th Dist.1992).

750 ILCS 60/225
§ 225. Immunity from prosecution

Any individual or organization acting in good faith to report the abuse of any person 60 years of age or older or to do any of the following in complying with the provisions of this Act shall not be subject to criminal prosecution or civil liability as a result of such action: providing any information to the appropriate law enforcement agency, providing that the giving of any information does not violate any privilege of confidentiality under law; assisting in any investigation; assisting in the preparation of any materials for distribution under this Act; or by providing services ordered under an order of protection.

Any individual, agency, or organization acting in good faith to report or investigate alleged abuse, neglect, or exploitation of a high-risk adult with disabilities, to testify in any proceeding on behalf of a high-risk adult with disabilities, to take photographs or perform an examination, or to perform any other act in compliance with the provisions of this Act shall not be the subject of criminal prosecution, civil liability, or other penalty, sanction, restriction, or retaliation as a result of such action.

750 ILCS 60/226
§ 226. Untrue statements

Allegations and denials, made without reasonable cause and found to be untrue, shall subject the party pleading them to the payment of reasonable expenses actually incurred by the other party by reason of the untrue pleading, together with a reasonable attorney's fee, to be summarily taxed by the court upon motion made within 30 days of the judgment or dismissal, as provided in Supreme Court Rule 137. The court may direct that a copy of an order entered under this Section be provided to the State's Attorney so that he or she may determine whether to prosecute for perjury. This Section shall not apply to proceedings heard in Criminal Court or to criminal contempt of court proceedings, whether heard in Civil or Criminal Court.

Author's Notes

(1) The sanctions for untrue statements in DVA § 226 should deter abuse of Domestic Violence Act petitions in order to gain advantage in custody litigation and similar proceedings. *Cf.* Supreme Court Rule 137 and accompanying Author's Notes.

750 ILCS 60/227

§ 227. Privileged communications between domestic violence counselors and victims

(a) As used in this Section:

(1) "Domestic violence program" means any unit of local government, organization, or association whose major purpose is to provide one or more of the following: information, crisis intervention, emergency shelter, referral, counseling, advocacy, or emotional support to victims of domestic violence.

(2) "Domestic violence advocate or counselor" means any person (A) who has undergone a minimum of forty hours of training in domestic violence advocacy, crisis intervention, and related areas, and (B) who provides services to victims through a domestic violence program either on an employed or volunteer basis.

(3) "Confidential communication" means any communication between an alleged victim of domestic violence and a domestic violence advocate or counselor in the course of providing information, counseling, or advocacy. The term includes all records kept by the advocate or counselor or by the domestic violence program in the course of providing services to an alleged victim concerning the alleged victim and the services provided. The confidential nature of the communication is not waived by the presence at the time of the communication of any additional persons, including but not limited to an interpreter, to further express the interests of the domestic violence victim or by the advocate's or counselor's disclosure to such an additional person with the consent of the victim when reasonably necessary to accomplish the purpose for which the advocate or counselor is consulted.

(4) "Domestic violence victim" means any person who consults a domestic violence counselor for the purpose of securing advice, counseling or assistance related to one or more alleged incidents of domestic violence.

(5) "Domestic violence" means abuse as defined in the Illinois Domestic Violence Act.

(b) No domestic violence advocate or counselor shall disclose any confidential communication or be examined as a witness in any civil or criminal case or proceeding or in any legislative or administrative proceeding without the written consent of the domestic violence victim except (1) in accordance with the provisions of the Abused and Neglected Child Reporting Act or (2) in cases where failure to disclose is likely to result in an imminent risk of serious bodily harm or death of the victim or another person.

(c) A domestic violence advocate or counselor who knowingly discloses any confidential communication in violation of this Act commits a Class A misdemeanor.

(d) When a domestic violence victim is deceased or has been adjudged incompetent by a court of competent jurisdiction, the guardian of the domestic violence victim or the executor or administrator of the estate of the domestic violence victim may waive the privilege established by this Section, except where the guardian, executor or administrator of the estate has been charged with a violent crime against the domestic violence victim or has had an Order of Protection entered against him or her at the request of or on behalf of the domestic violence victim or otherwise has an interest adverse to that of the domestic violence victim with respect to the waiver of the privilege. In that case, the court shall appoint an attorney for the estate of the domestic violence victim.

(e) A minor may knowingly waive the privilege established by this Section. Where a minor is, in the opinion of the court, incapable of knowingly waiving the privilege, the parent or guardian of the minor may waive the privilege on behalf of the minor, except where such parent or guardian has been charged with a violent crime against the minor or has had an Order of Protection entered against him or her on request of or on behalf of the minor or otherwise has any interest adverse to that of the minor with respect to the waiver of the privilege. In that case, the court shall appoint an attorney for the minor child who shall be compensated in accordance with Section 506 of the Illinois Marriage and Dissolution of Marriage Act.

(f) Nothing in this Section shall be construed to limit in any way any privilege that might otherwise exist under statute or common law.

(g) The assertion of any privilege under this Section shall not result in an inference unfavorable to the State's cause or to the cause of the domestic violence victim.

Author's Notes

Analysis

1. Extension of privilege.
2. Waiver.

(1) **Extension of privilege.** DVA § 227 extends the concept of privileged communications to include domestic violence counsellors. The privilege is not compromised by the presence of a third person to further express the interests of the victim, or even, within limitations, by disclosure to such third person. DVA § 227(a)(3).

(2) **Waiver.** In order to waive the privilege, DVA § 227(b) requires written consent of the domestic violence victim, not just oral consent. The privilege does not apply if contrary to the Abused and Neglected Child Reporting Act, see 325 ILCS 5/10, or if failure to disclose the communication is likely to result in imminent risk of serious bodily harm or death.

750 ILCS 60/227.1
§ 227.1 Other privileged information

Except as otherwise provided in this Section, no court or administrative or legislative body shall compel any person or domestic violence program to disclose the location of any domestic violence program or the identity of any domestic violence advocate or counselor in any civil or criminal case or proceeding or in any administrative or legislative proceeding. A court may compel disclosure of the location of a domestic violence program or the identity of a domestic violence advocate or counselor if the court finds, following a hearing, that there is clear and convincing evidence that failure to disclose would be likely to result in an imminent risk of serious bodily harm or death to a domestic violence victim or another person. If the court makes such a finding, then disclosure shall take place in camera, under a restrictive protective order that does not frustrate the purposes of compelling the disclosure, and the information disclosed shall not be made a part of the written record of the case.

ARTICLE III. LAW ENFORCEMENT RESPONSIBILITIES

Analysis

Sec.
301.   Arrest without warrant.
301.1 Law enforcement policies.
302.   Data maintenance by law enforcement agencies.
303.   Reports by law enforcement officers.
304.   Assistance by law enforcement officers.
305.   Limited law enforcement liability.
306.   Domestic Violence Training and Curriculum Task Force.

WESTLAW Electronic Research Guide
See WESTLAW Electronic Research Guide preceding the Summary of Contents.

---

750 ILCS 60/301
§ 301. Arrest without warrant

(a) Any law enforcement officer may make an arrest without warrant if the officer has probable cause to believe that the person has committed or is committing any crime, including but not limited to violation of an order of protection, under Section 12–30 of the Criminal Code of 1961, even if the crime was not committed in the presence of the officer.

(b) The law enforcement officer may verify the existence of an order of protection by telephone or radio communication with his or her law enforcement agency or by referring to the copy of the order provided by the petitioner or respondent.

Author's Notes

Analysis

1. Police enforcement.
2. Violation of order of protection.

(1) **Police enforcement.** The police are very aware of orders of protection. They are more likely to act to enforce an order of protection than they are to enforce similar injunctions. Because the police will often ask to see a copy of an order of protection, it is advisable that the petitioner retains a stamped or certified copy.

(2) **Violation of order of protection.** 720 ILCS 5/12–30, referred to in § 60/301(a), pertains to violations of prohibitions against abuse and exclusive possession. Section 5/12–30 of the Criminal Code is as follows:

720 ILCS 5/12–30. Violation of order of protection.

(a) A person commits violation of an order of protection if he or she:

(1) Commits an act which was prohibited by a court or fails to commit an act which was ordered by a court in violation of a remedy in a valid order of protection authorized under paragraphs (1) or (2) of subsection (b) of Section 214 of the Illinois Domestic Violence Act of 1986, enacted by the 84th General Assembly.

(2) Such violation occurs after the offender has been served notice of the contents of the order, pursuant to the Illinois Domestic Violence Act, or otherwise has acquired actual knowledge of the contents of the order.

(b) For purposes of this Section, an "order of protection" may have been issued by any circuit or associate judge in the State of Illinois in a criminal or civil proceeding.

(c) Nothing in this Section shall be construed to diminish the inherent authority of the courts to enforce their lawful orders through civil or criminal contempt proceedings.

(d) Violation of an order of protection under subsection (a) of this Section is a Class A misdemeanor. The court should:

(1) increase the penalty, within a range of penalties available for a Class A misdemeanor, for the knowing violation of any order of protection over any penalty previously imposed by any court for the defendant's prior violation of an order of protection; and

(2) impose a minimum penalty of 24 hours imprisonment for defendant's second or subsequent violation of any order of protection; unless the court explicitly finds that an increased penalty of such period of imprisonment would be manifestly unjust. In addition to any other penalties, the court may order the defendant to pay a fine as authorized under Section 5-9-1 of the Unified Code of

750 ILCS 60/301   FAMILIES

Corrections or to make restitution to the victim under Section 5-5-6 of the Unified Code of Corrections.

750 ILCS 60/301.1

§ 301.1 Law enforcement policies

Every law enforcement agency shall develop, adopt, and implement written policies regarding arrest procedures for domestic violence incidents consistent with the provisions of this Act. In developing these policies, each law enforcement agency is encouraged to consult with community organizations and other law enforcement agencies with expertise in recognizing and handling domestic violence incidents.

750 ILCS 60/302

§ 302. Data maintenance by law enforcement agencies

(a) All sheriffs shall furnish to the Department of State Police, on the same day as received, in the form and detail the Department requires, copies of any recorded emergency, interim, or plenary orders of protection issued by the court and transmitted to the sheriff by the clerk of the court pursuant to subsection (b) of Section 222 of this Act. Each order of protection shall be entered in the Law Enforcement Automated Data System on the same day it is issued by the court.

(b) The Department of State Police shall maintain a complete and systematic record and index of all valid and recorded orders of protection issued pursuant to this Act. The data shall be used to inform all dispatchers and law enforcement officers at the scene of an alleged incident of abuse, neglect, or exploitation or violation of an order of protection of any recorded prior incident of abuse, neglect, or exploitation involving the abused, neglected, or exploited party and the effective dates and terms of any recorded order of protection.

(c) The data, records and transmittals required under this Section shall pertain to any valid emergency, interim or plenary order of protection, whether issued in a civil or criminal proceeding.

750 ILCS 60/303

§ 303. Reports by law enforcement officers

(a) Every law enforcement officer investigating an alleged incident of abuse, neglect, or exploitation between family or household members shall make a written police report of any bona fide allegation and the disposition of such investigation. The police report shall include the victim's statements as to the frequency and severity of prior incidents of abuse, neglect, or exploitation by the same family or household member and the number of prior calls for police assistance to prevent such further abuse, neglect, or exploitation.

(b) Every police report completed pursuant to this Section shall be recorded and compiled as a domestic crime within the meaning of Section 5.1 of the Criminal Identification Act.

750 ILCS 60/304

§ 304. Assistance by law enforcement officers

(a) Whenever a law enforcement officer has reason to believe that a person has been abused, neglected, or exploited by a family or household member, the officer shall immediately use all reasonable means to prevent further abuse, neglect, or exploitation, including:

(1) Arresting the abusing, neglecting and exploiting party, where appropriate;

(3) Accompanying the victim of abuse, neglect, or exploitation to his or her place of residence for a reasonable period of time to remove necessary personal belongings and possessions;

(4) Offering the victim of abuse, neglect, or exploitation immediate and adequate information (written in a language appropriate for the victim or in Braille or communicated in appropriate sign language), which shall include a summary of the procedures and relief available to victims of abuse under subsection (c) of Section 217 and the officer's name and badge number;

(5) Providing the victim with one referral to an accessible service agency;

(6) Advising the victim of abuse about seeking medical attention and preserving evidence (specifically including photographs of injury or damage and damaged clothing or other property); and

(7) Providing or arranging accessible transportation for the victim of abuse (and, at the victim's request, any minors or dependents in the victim's care) to a medical facility for treatment of injuries or to a nearby place of shelter or safety; or, after the close of court business hours, providing or arranging for transportation for the victim (and, at the victim's request, any minors or dependents in the victim's care) to the nearest available circuit judge or associate judge so the victim may file a petition for an emergency order of protection under subsection (c) of Section 217. When a victim of abuse chooses to leave the scene of the offense, it shall be presumed that it is in the best interests of any minors or dependents in the victim's care to remain with the victim or a person designated by the victim, rather than to remain with the abusing party.

(b) Whenever a law enforcement officer does not exercise arrest powers or otherwise initiate criminal proceedings, the officer shall:

(1) Make a police report of the investigation of any bona fide allegation of an incident of abuse, neglect, or exploitation and the disposition of the investigation, in accordance with subsection (a) of Section 303;

750 ILCS 60/304   **FAMILIES**

(2) Inform the victim of abuse neglect, or exploitation of the victim's right to request that a criminal proceeding be initiated where appropriate, including specific times and places for meeting with the State's Attorney's office, a warrant officer, or other official in accordance with local procedure; and

(3) Advise the victim of the importance of seeking medical attention and preserving evidence (specifically including photographs of injury or damage and damaged clothing or other property).

750 ILCS 60/305

§ 305. Limited law enforcement liability

Any act of omission or commission by any law enforcement officer acting in good faith in rendering emergency assistance or otherwise enforcing this Act shall not impose civil liability upon the law enforcement officer or his or her supervisor or employer, unless the act is a result of willful or wanton misconduct.

750 ILCS 60/306

§ 306. Domestic Violence Training and Curriculum Task Force

(a) Creation of the Task Force. There is hereby created within the Illinois Local Governmental Law Enforcement Officers Training Board a Domestic Violence Training and Curriculum Task Force. The Task Force shall be composed of the Directors, or their designees, of the Department on Aging, Department of Children and Family Services, Department of State Police, Office of the State's Attorneys' Appellate Prosecutor, the Executive Directors, or their designees, of the Illinois Criminal Justice Information Authority and the Local Governmental Law Enforcement Officers Training Board, the Attorney General, or his or her designee, the Chief Justice of the Illinois Supreme Court, or his or her designee, and 6 persons appointed by the Governor, 2 of whom shall be representative of domestic violence victims and 2 of whom shall be representative of sexual assault victims, and one each who shall be representative of police chiefs and county sheriffs in Illinois. The first meeting of the Task Force shall be held within 60 days of the effective date of this amendatory Act of 1992. At its first meeting, the Task Force shall select a chairperson from among its members.

(b) Scope and functions. The Domestic Violence Training and Curriculum Task Force shall:

(1) gather and review current curricula and training programs utilized by law enforcement officers, prosecutors, and the judiciary on domestic violence;

(2) develop a model coordinated response protocol to incidents of domestic violence;

(3) recommend a regionally based system for providing training to, and coordinating the activities of, law enforcement officers, prosecutors, and the judiciary; and

(4) provide a plan for implementation.

(c) Meetings. The Task Force shall meet at least quarterly, and at such other times at the call of the chairperson of the Task Force.

(d) Reporting requirements. On or before September 1, 1993, the Task Force shall make a written report to the Governor and the General Assembly concerning its findings and recommendations for administrative or legislative changes.

(e) This Section is repealed on September 1, 1994.

ARTICLE IV. HEALTH CARE SERVICES

Analysis

Sec.
401. Health care services—Liability.

WESTLAW Electronic Research

See WESTLAW Electronic Research Guide preceding the Summary of Contents.

---

750 ILCS 60/401

§ 401. Health care services—Liability

Any person who is licensed, certified or otherwise authorized by the law of this State to administer health care in the ordinary course of business or practice of a profession shall offer to a person suspected to be a victim of abuse immediate and adequate information regarding services available to victims of abuse.

Any person who is licensed, certified or otherwise authorized by the law of this State to administer health care in the ordinary course of business, or practice of a profession and who in good faith offers to a person suspected to be a victim of abuse information regarding services available to victims of abuse shall not be civilly liable for any act or omission of the agency providing those services to the victims of abuse or for the inadequacy of those services provided by the agency.

ACT 65. RIGHTS OF MARRIED PERSONS ACT

Analysis

Sec.
0.01 Short title.
1. Rights to sue and be sued.
2. Defending in own right or for other.

750 ILCS 65/0.01 — FAMILIES

Sec.
3. Desertion by one spouse; Other may use deserter's name.
4. Recovery of damages.
5. Not liable for each other's debts.
6. Contracts.
7. Earnings.
8. Repealed.
9. Property.
10. Suit for property unlawfully obtained.
11. Abandonment by one spouse; Proceedings to sell property by other.
12. Acts binding on both spouses.
13. When order may be set aside.
14. Attorney in fact.
15. Expenses of family.
16. Removal from homestead; Custody of children.
17. Legal disability; Conveyances; Petitioner.
18. Oath; Notice; Proceedings.
19. Judgment.
20. Mentally ill person's rights secured.
21. Effect of conveyances.
22. Devise, conveyance, assignment or other transfer of homestead; Tenancy by the entirety.

WESTLAW Electronic Research

See WESTLAW Electronic Research Guide preceding the Summary of Contents.

---

750 ILCS 65/0.01

§ 0.01 Short title

This Act may be cited as the Rights of Married Persons Act.

750 ILCS 65/1

§ 1. Rights to sue and be sued

A married person may, in all cases, sue and be sued without joining his or her spouse as if unmarried. A husband or wife may sue the other for a tort committed during the marriage. No finding by any court under Section 401 of the Illinois Marriage and Dissolution of Marriage Act shall be admissible or be used as prima facie evidence of a tort in any civil action brought under this Act. An attachment or judgment in an action may be enforced by or against a married person as if unmarried.

Author's Notes

Analysis

1. Interspousal torts.
2. Cross references.

(1) **Interspousal torts.** A husband or wife may sue the other for a tort committed during marriage. 750 ILCS 65/1. Therefore, a husband or wife may successfully bring an intentional tort action if, for example, one spouse infects the other with a venereal disease, or abuses the other sexually or physically. See, e.g.,

Heyman v. Heyman, 548 F.Supp. 1041 (N.D.Ill.1982) (wife stated a cause of action in claim to recover damages for husband's illegal wiretapping; although Illinois law then prohibited interspousal tort actions, the husband's conduct was actionable under the federal Omnibus Crime Control and Safe Streets Act of 1968). There is little illustrative case law, because previous law did not allow interspousal tort actions. See, e.g., Wartell v. Formusa, 34 Ill.2d 57, 213 N.E.2d 544 (1966) (interspousal tort immunity statute then in effect prohibited interspousal torts: "neither husband nor wife may sue the other for a tort to the person committed during coverture").

(2) **Cross references.** See 740 ILCS 5/7 Author's Notes (1) and (2) for alienation of affections, and 740 ILCS 15/10 Author's Note (1) for breach of promise. See 735 ILCS 5/8–801 for ability of husbands and wives to testify against each other in tort actions. See 750 ILCS 5/502 Author's Note (11) para. 11(e) for mutual waiver of tort actions in a settlement agreement.

750 ILCS 65/2

§ 2. Defending in own right or for other

If husband and wife are sued together, either may defend for his or her own right and, if either neglects to defend, the other may defend for both.

750 ILCS 65/3

§ 3. Desertion by one spouse; Other may use deserter's name

When the husband has deserted his family, the wife may prosecute or defend, in his name, any action which he might have prosecuted or defended, and, under like circumstances, the same right shall apply to the husband upon the desertion of the wife.

750 ILCS 65/4

§ 4. Recovery of damages

For all civil injuries committed by a married person, damages may be recovered from that person alone, and his or her spouse shall not be responsible for those damages, except in cases where he or she would be jointly responsible with that person if the marriage did not exist.

750 ILCS 65/5

§ 5. Not liable for each other's debts

Neither husband or wife shall be liable for the debts or liabilities of the other incurred before marriage, and (except as herein otherwise provided) they shall not be liable for the separate debts of each other, nor shall the wages, earnings or property of either, nor the rent or income of such property, be liable for the separate debts of the other.

Author's Notes

(1) **Cross reference.** See Rights of Married Persons Act § 15, 750 ILCS 65/15, Author's Note (1) for the limited liability of one spouse for debts incurred by the other.

750 ILCS 65/6

§ 6. Contracts

Contracts may be made and liabilities incurred by any married person and may be enforced against that person to the same extent and in the same manner as if unmarried.

750 ILCS 65/7

§ 7. Earnings

A married person may receive, use, and possess his or her own earnings and sue for those earnings in his or her own name, free from the interference of his or her spouse or the creditors of his or her spouse.

750 ILCS 65/8

§ 8. Repealed by P.A.80-923, § 901, eff. Oct. 1, 1977

750 ILCS 65/9

§ 9. Property

A married person may own in his or her own right real and personal property obtained by descent, gift, or purchase and may manage, sell, and convey that property to the same extent and in the same manner as an unmarried person. When husband and wife live together, however, no transfer or conveyance of goods and chattels between the husband and wife shall be valid as against the rights and interests of any third person unless the transfer or conveyance is in writing and filed in the same manner as security interests are required to be filed by the laws of this State in cases where the possession of the property is to remain with the person giving the security.

Author's Notes

(1) **Homestead.** The apparent meaning of the statute to the contrary notwithstanding, homestead property cannot be conveyed without both spouses joining in the conveyance. 735 ILCS 5/12-901 et seq. See also 750 ILCS 65/17-21 for conveyance of homestead by a spouse under disability.

750 ILCS 65/10

§ 10. Suit for property unlawfully obtained

Should either the husband or wife unlawfully obtain or retain possession or control of property belonging to the other, either before or after marriage, the owner of the property may maintain an action therefor, or for any right growing out of the same, in the same manner and to the same extent as if they were unmarried.

750 ILCS 65/11

§ 11. Abandonment by one spouse; Proceedings to sell property by other

In case the husband or wife abandons the other and leaves the state, and is absent therefrom for one year, without providing for the maintenance and support of his or her family, or is imprisoned in the penitentiary, the circuit court in the county where the husband or wife so abandoned or, not confined, resides, may, on application by petition, setting forth fully the facts, if the court is satisfied of the necessity by the evidence, authorize him or her to manage, control, sell or incumber the property of the other, as shall be necessary, in the judgment of the court, for the support and maintenance of the family, and for the purpose of paying debts of the other, or debts contracted for the support of the family. Notice of such proceedings shall be given as in other civil actions, and anything done under or by virtue of the order or judgment of the court, shall be valid to the same extent as if the same were done by the party owning the property.

Author's Notes

(1) *In rem* actions. See 750 ILCS 5/703 and accompanying Author's Notes for *in rem* actions.

750 ILCS 65/12
§ 12. Acts binding on both spouses

All contracts, sales or incumbrances made by either the husband or wife, by virtue of the power contemplated in the preceding section, shall be binding on both, and during such absence or confinement, the person acting under such power may sue and be sued thereon; and for all acts done the property of both shall be liable, and execution may be levied or attachment issued accordingly. No suit or proceeding shall abate, or be in anywise affected, by the return or release of the person absent or confined, but he or she shall be permitted to prosecute or defend jointly with the other.

750 ILCS 65/13
§ 13. When order may be set aside

The husband or wife affected by the proceedings contemplated in the 2 preceding sections may have the order or judgment of the court set aside or annulled, by filing a petition therefor and serving a notice on the person in whose favor the same was granted, as in other civil actions. But the setting aside of such judgment or order shall in nowise affect any act done thereunder.

750 ILCS 65/14
§ 14. Attorney in fact

A husband or wife may constitute the other his or her attorney in fact, to control and dispose of his or her property for their mutual benefit or otherwise, and may revoke the same to the same extent and in the same manner as other persons.

750 ILCS 65/15
§ 15. Expenses of family

(a) (1) The expenses of the family and of the education of the children shall be chargeable upon the property of both husband and wife, or of either of them, in favor of creditors therefor, and in relation thereto they may be sued jointly or separately.

(2) No creditor, who has a claim against a spouse or former spouse for an expense incurred by that spouse or former spouse which is not a family expense, shall maintain an action against the other spouse or former spouse for that expense except:

    (A) an expense for which the other spouse or former spouse agreed, in writing, to be liable; or

    (B) an expense for goods or merchandise purchased by or in the possession of the other spouse or former spouse, or for services ordered by the other spouse or former spouse.

(3) Any creditor who maintains an action in violation of this subsection (a) for an expense other than a family expense against a spouse or former spouse other than the spouse or former spouse who incurred the expense, shall be liable to the other spouse or former spouse for his or her costs, expenses and attorney's fees incurred in defending the action.

(4) No creditor shall, with respect to any claim against a spouse or former spouse for which the creditor is prohibited under this subsection (a) from maintaining an action against the other spouse or former spouse, engage in any collection efforts against the other spouse or former spouse, including, but not limited to, informal or formal collection attempts, referral of the claim to a collector or collection agency for collection from the other spouse or former spouse, or making any representation to a credit reporting agency that the other spouse or former spouse is any way liable for payment of the claim.

(b) No spouse shall be liable for any expense incurred by the other spouse when an abortion is performed on such spouse, without the consent of such other spouse, unless the physician who performed the abortion certifies that such abortion is necessary to preserve the life of the spouse who obtained such abortion.

(c) No parent shall be liable for any expense incurred by his or her minor child when an abortion is performed on such minor child without the consent of both parents of such child, if they both have custody, or the parent having custody, or legal guardian of such child, unless the physician who performed the abortion certifies that such abortion is necessary to preserve the life of the minor child who obtained such abortion.

Author's Notes

(1) **Liability of one spouse for debts of the other.** The effect of §§ 5 and 15 is that a debtor's spouse is only liable for the debts incurred by the debtor when: the debts are for family expenses or for the education of their children, when the debtor's spouse has agreed in writing to be liable, or when the goods or merchandise were purchased by or are in the possession of the debtor's spouse, or for services ordered by the debtor's spouse. Family expenses for which the debtor's spouse is liable, even though the debts were incurred by the debtor, include food, clothing, and shelter.

Under [§ 15], a debtor's spouse can be held liable for a debtor's bills if a family "in fact" existed at the time of the expenditures ... and the expenditures were incurred for a family expense. A family expense is defined as one which contributes to the welfare of the family or maintains its integrity.

Peoples Gas Light and Coke Co. v. Commerce Comm'n, 222 Ill.App.3d 738, 740, 165 Ill.Dec. 162, 164, 584 N.E.2d 341, 343 (1st Dist.1991) (citations omitted).

750 ILCS 65/16
§ 16. Removal from homestead; Custody of children

Neither the husband nor wife can remove the other or their children from their homestead without the consent of the other, unless the owner of the property shall, in good faith, provide another homestead suitable to the condition in life of the family; and if he abandons her, she is entitled to the custody of their minor children, unless a court of competent jurisdiction, upon application for that purpose, shall otherwise direct.

750 ILCS 65/17
§ 17. Legal disability; Conveyances; Petitioner

When the husband or wife is under legal disability and therefore incapable of executing a deed or mortgage, and relinquishing or conveying his or her right to homestead in the real property of the other, such other person may present his or her petition to the circuit court in the county where the petitioner resides, or where the real estate to be affected is situated, setting forth the facts, and particularly describing the real estate sought to be conveyed or mortgaged, and asking for an order authorizing the petitioner, or some other person, to execute a deed or mortgage for the person who is under legal disability, and thereby relinquish his or her right of homestead in the real estate.

750 ILCS 65/18
§ 18. Oath; Notice; Proceedings

The petition shall be verified by the oath of the petitioner, and shall be filed in the office of the clerk of the circuit court. Notice of the filing of such petition shall be given to such person who is under disability, by service of summons or by publication, as provided in other civil cases. The court shall appoint some discreet person or attorney as guardian for the person alleged to be under disability, and the appointed person shall ascertain as to the propriety, good faith and necessity of the petition, and shall have power to resist such application and subpoena witnesses and take depositions to disprove any of the matters in the petition, or show the impropriety of granting the same.

750 ILCS 65/19
§ 19. Judgment

If the court is satisfied upon the hearing that the petition was made in good faith, and the prayer thereof ought to be granted, then the court shall

750 ILCS 65/19   **FAMILIES**

enter a judgment granting such prayer, and authorizing some discreet and proper person to make, execute, acknowledge and deliver jointly with said petitioner all such conveyances or mortgages, and of such parcels of land as shall in said judgment be specified.

750 ILCS 65/20
§ 20. Mentally ill person's rights secured

The court shall require of the petitioner, at the time and as one of the conditions of entering the judgment, such security for the protection of the interests, and for the proper support of such person under legal disability, as the court deems satisfactory, and may from time to time renew or change the same, or require additional security. Such security shall be deposited with the clerk of the court, and actions may be maintained thereon for the benefit of such person under legal disability in any court of competent jurisdiction; or the court may order such portion of the money received from the sale of such property as the court deems just, to be set apart in such manner as the court shall direct, for the use and benefit of such person under legal disability; and such sum so set apart shall be and remain subject to the control and order of the court.

750 ILCS 65/21
§ 21. Effect of conveyances

All deeds or mortgages authorized by and executed under the order of any court, made as hereinbefore provided, shall be valid and shall convey all the homestead interest of such person under legal disability in and to the real estate so conveyed or mortgaged, as fully as if such person had been under no legal disability, and executed and acknowledged the same in due form of law.

750 ILCS 65/22
§ 22. Devise, conveyance, assignment or other transfer of homestead; Tenancy by the entirety

Nothing in this Act abolishes or prevents the creation and enjoyment of the estate of tenancy by the entirety with respect to any devise, conveyance, assignment, or other transfer of homestead property maintained as a homestead by both husband and wife during coverture made or executed on or after October 1, 1990.

Author's Notes

(1) **Protection from creditors.** Tenancy by the entirety is a joint tenancy with the right of survivorship that a husband and wife can hold during their marriage. Tenancy by the entirety differs from joint tenancy with the right of survivorship in that it protects real estate conveyed into tenancy by the entirety from the creditors of either the husband or the wife. Only real estate that is maintained as the homestead by both the husband and wife during their marriage can be conveyed into tenancy by the entirety. The entire value of the homestead property is protected from claims by creditors of the husband or the wife, and not just the homestead value of the property. See Celeste M. Hammond and Ronald L. Otto, The Illusion of Reform: Illinois Statutory Tenancy by the Entirety, 78 Ill.B.J. 198 (1990).

CHAPTER 325

CHILDREN

ACT 5. ABUSED AND NEGLECTED CHILD REPORTING ACT

Analysis

Sec.
1. Short title.
2. Protective services; Application of Act.
2.1 Persons eligible to use services and facilities; Referral.
3. Definitions.
4. Persons required to report; Medical personnel; Privileged communications; Transmitting false report.
4.02 Failure to report suspected abuse or neglect.
4.1 Death caused by abuse or neglect; Reports.
5. Temporary protective custody.
6. Photographs and x-rays of child; Photographs of environment.
7. Time and manner of making report; Confirmation of report.
7.1 Cooperation of agencies; Multi-disciplinary teams.
7.2 Child protective service unit; Establishment.
7.3 Investigations; Responsibilities of department.
7.3a Perinatal coordinator; Appointment; Duties.
7.3b Referral of addicted pregnant persons; Services.
7.4 Time and manner of making investigations; Emergency services.
7.5 Access to child for examination or interview; Intervention of law enforcement agencies; Court orders.
7.6 Toll-free telephone number; Posted notice of criminal offense.
7.7 Register of reported cases.
7.8 Notification of previous reports to child protective service units.
7.9 Form and contents of reports.
7.10 Copies of reports; Transmission to central register; Contents of preliminary reports.
7.12 Determination of classification of report.
7.13 Additional information; Reports.
7.14 Categories of classification; Reports.
7.15 Contents of central register; Additional information; Expungement of records.
7.16 Application of expungement; Hearing; Review under Administrative Review Law.
7.17 Notice of amendment on expungement; Local records.
7.18 Amendment of reports.
7.19 Copies of report to subject.
8.1 Disposition by Child Protective Service Unit.
8.2 Service plan.
8.3 Court proceedings; Assistance of Child Protective Services Unit.
8.4 Rehabilitative services; Monitoring.
8.5 Local child abuse and neglect index.
9. Immunity from liability; Presumption.
9.1 Employer discrimination.

FAMILIES

Sec.
10. Testimony by person making report.
11. Confidentiality of records; Violations.
11.1 Access to records.
11.2 Disclosure to mandated reporting sources.
11.3 Publicizing disclosed information; Court actions; Violations.
11.4 Court and criminal records; Effect of Act.
11.5 Continuing education program.
11.6 Review under Administrative Review Law.
11.7 State-wide citizens committee on child abuse and neglect.

WESTLAW Electronic Research

See WESTLAW Electronic Research Guide preceding the Summary of Contents.

325 ILCS 5/1

§ 1. Short title

This Act shall be known and may be cited as the Abused and Neglected Child Reporting Act.

325 ILCS 5/2

§ 2. Protective services; Application of Act

The Illinois Department of Children and Family Services shall, upon receiving reports made under this Act, protect the best interests of the child, offer protective services in order to prevent any further harm to the child and to other children in the same environment or family, stabilize the home environment, preserve family life whenever possible and protect the health and safety of children in all situations in which they are vulnerable to child abuse or neglect. Recognizing that children also can be abused and neglected while living in public or private residential agencies or institutions meant to serve them, while attending day care centers or schools, or when in contact with adults who are responsible for the welfare of the child at that time, this Act also provides for the reporting and investigation of child abuse and neglect in such instances. In performing any of these duties, the Department may utilize such protective services of voluntary agencies as are available.

325 ILCS 5/2.1

§ 2.1 Persons eligible to use services and facilities; Referral

Any person or family seeking assistance in meeting child care responsibilities may use the services and facilities established by this Act which may assist in meeting such responsibilities. Whether or not the problem presented constitutes child abuse or neglect, such persons or families shall be referred to appropriate resources or agencies. No person seeking assistance under this Section shall be required to give his name or any other identifying information.

325 ILCS 5/3
§ 3. Definitions

As used in this Act unless the context otherwise requires:

"Child" means any person under the age of 18 years, unless legally emancipated by reason of marriage or entry into a branch of the United States armed services.

"Department" means Department of Children and Family Services.

"Local law enforcement agency" means the police of a city, town, village or other incorporated area or the sheriff of an unincorporated area or any sworn officer of the Illinois Department of State Police.

"Abused child" means a child whose parent or immediate family member, or any person responsible for the child's welfare, or any individual residing in the same home as the child, or a paramour of the child's parent:

    a. inflicts, causes to be inflicted, or allows to be inflicted upon such child physical injury, by other than accidental means, which causes death, disfigurement, impairment of physical or emotional health, or loss or impairment of any bodily function;

    b. creates a substantial risk of physical injury to such child by other than accidental means which would be likely to cause death, disfigurement, impairment of physical or emotional health, or loss or impairment of any bodily function;

    c. commits or allows to be committed any sex offense against such child, as such sex offenses are defined in the Criminal Code of 1961, as amended, and extending those definitions of sex offenses to include children under 18 years of age;

    d. commits or allows to be committed an act or acts of torture upon such child; or

    e. inflicts excessive corporal punishment.

"Neglected child" means any child who is not receiving the proper or necessary nourishment or medically indicated treatment including food or care not provided solely on the basis of the present or anticipated mental or physical impairment as determined by a physician acting alone or in consultation with other physicians or otherwise is not receiving the proper or necessary support or medical or other remedial care recognized under State law as necessary for a child's well-being, or other care necessary for his or her well-being, including adequate food, clothing and shelter; or who is abandoned by his or her parents or other person responsible for the child's welfare without a proper plan of care; or who is a newborn infant whose blood or urine contains any amount of a controlled substance as defined in subsection (f) of Section 102 of the Illinois Controlled Substances Act or a metabolite thereof, with the exception of a controlled substance or metabolite thereof whose presence in the newborn infant is the result of medical treatment administered to the mother or the newborn infant. A child shall not be considered neglected for the sole reason that the child's parent or other person responsible for his or her welfare has left the child in the care of an adult relative for any period of

325 ILCS 5/3   **FAMILIES**

time as a plan of care. A child shall not be considered neglected or abused for the sole reason that such child's parent or other person responsible for his or her welfare depends upon spiritual means through prayer alone for the treatment or cure of disease or remedial care as provided under Section 4 of this Act. A child shall not be considered neglected or abused solely because the child is not attending school in accordance with the requirements of Article 26 of The School Code, as amended.

"Child Protective Service Unit" means certain specialized State employees of the Department assigned by the Director to perform the duties and responsibilities as provided under Section 7.2 of this Act.

"Person responsible for the child's welfare" means the child's parent; guardian; foster parent; any person responsible for the child's welfare in a public or private residential agency or institution; any person responsible for the child's welfare within a public or private profit or not for profit child care facility; or any other person responsible for the child's welfare at the time of the alleged abuse or neglect, or any person who came to know the child through an official capacity or position of trust, including but not limited to health care professionals, educational personnel, recreational supervisors, and volunteers or support personnel in any setting where children may be subject to abuse or neglect.

"Temporary protective custody" means custody within a hospital or other medical facility or a place previously designated for such custody by the Department, subject to review by the Court, including a licensed foster home, group home, or other institution; but such place shall not be a jail or other place for the detention of criminal or juvenile offenders.

"An unfounded report" means any report made under this Act for which it is determined after an investigation that no credible evidence of abuse or neglect exists.

"An indicated report" means a report made under this Act if an investigation determines that credible evidence of the alleged abuse or neglect exists.

"An undetermined report" means any report made under this Act in which it was not possible to initiate or complete an investigation on the basis of information provided to the Department.

"Subject of report" means any child reported to the central register of child abuse and neglect established under Section 7.7 of this Act and his or her parent, guardian or other person responsible who is also named in the report.

"Perpetrator" means a person who, as a result of investigation, has been determined by the Department to have caused child abuse or neglect.

325 ILCS 5/4

§ 4. Persons required to report; Medical personnel; Privileged communications; Transmitting false report

Any physician, resident, intern, hospital, hospital administrator and personnel engaged in examination, care and treatment of persons, surgeon, dentist, dentist hygienist, osteopath, chiropractor, podiatrist, substance abuse treatment personnel, Christian Science practitioner, coroner, medical examiner, emergency medical technician, crisis line or hotline personnel, school personnel, educational advocate assigned to a child pursuant to The School Code, truant officers, social worker, social services administrator, domestic violence program personnel, registered nurse, licensed practical nurse, director or staff assistant of a nursery school or a child day care center, recreational program or facility personnel, law enforcement officer, registered psychologist and assistants working under the direct supervision of a psychologist, psychiatrist, or field personnel of the Illinois Department of Public Aid, Public Health, Mental Health and Developmental Disabilities, Corrections, Human Rights, Rehabilitation Services, or Children and Family Services, supervisor and administrator of general assistance under The Illinois Public Aid Code, probation officer, or any other foster parent, homemaker or child care worker having reasonable cause to believe a child known to them in their professional or official capacity may be an abused child or a neglected child shall immediately report or cause a report to be made to the Department. Whenever such person is required to report under this Act in his capacity as a member of the staff of a medical or other public or private institution, school, facility or agency, he shall make report immediately to the Department in accordance with the provisions of this Act and may also notify the person in charge of such institution, school, facility or agency or his designated agent that such report has been made. Under no circumstances shall any person in charge of such institution, school, facility or agency, or his designated agent to whom such notification has been made, exercise any control, restraint, modification or other change in the report or the forwarding of such report to the Department. The privileged quality of communication between any professional person required to report and his patient or client shall not apply to situations involving abused or neglected children and shall not constitute grounds for failure to report as required by this Act. In addition to the above persons required to report suspected cases of abused or neglected children, any other person may make a report if such person has reasonable cause to believe a child may be an abused child or a neglected child. Any person who enters into employment on and after July 1, 1986 and is mandated by virtue of that employment to report under this Act, shall sign a statement on a form prescribed by the Department, to the effect that the employee has knowledge and understanding of the reporting requirements of this Act. The statement shall be signed prior to commencement of the employment. The signed statement shall be retained by the employer. The cost of printing, distribution, and filing of the statement shall be borne by the employer. The Department shall provide copies of this Act, upon request, to all employers employing persons who shall be required under the provisions of this Section to report under this Act.

Any person who knowingly transmits a false report to the Department commits the offense of disorderly conduct under subsection (a)(7) of Section

26-1 of the "Criminal Code of 1961". Any person who violates this provision a second or subsequent time shall be guilty of a Class 4 felony.

Any person who knowingly and willfully violates any provision of this Section other than a second or subsequent violation of transmitting a false report as described in the preceding paragraph, shall be guilty of a Class A misdemeanor.

A child whose parent, guardian or custodian in good faith selects and depends upon spiritual means through prayer alone for the treatment or cure of disease or remedial care may be considered neglected or abused, but not for the sole reason that his parent, guardian or custodian accepts and practices such beliefs.

A child shall not be considered neglected or abused solely because the child is not attending school in accordance with the requirements of Article 26 of The School Code, as amended.

Author's Notes

Analysis

1. Required reporting.
2. Misuse of the Abused and Neglected Child Reporting Act.

(1) **Required reporting.** Medical and mental health professionals, and others covered by the Act (the Act does not include lawyers), "having reasonable cause to believe a child known in their professional or official capacity may be an abused child or a neglected child," are required to immediately make a report to the Illinois Department of Children and Family Services. Failure to so do can result in disciplinary action against physicians or conviction of a misdemeanor for others. See 325 ILCS 5/4.02. The physician-patient privilege does not excuse a professional required to report under the Act from reporting knowledge of incidents of child abuse or neglect.

(2) **Misuse of the Abused and Neglected Child Reporting Act.** A false allegation of child abuse may be made in dissolution and custody actions as a dangerous and misguided attempt to gain a strategic advantage over the opposing party. Because it is difficult to disprove reports of child abuse, care must be taken in the initial interview of the alleged child victim to avoid confusing or leading the child. It is also difficult to prove that an unsubstantiated allegation was made in bad faith. However, the courts may impose severe penalties for false reports of child abuse or neglect. See 325 ILCS 5/7 concerning criminal sanctions for false reports. See also Brown v. Farkas, 158 Ill.App.3d 772, 110 Ill.Dec. 823, 511 N.E.2d 1143 (1st Dist.1986), *appeal denied*, 117 Ill.2d 542, 115 Ill.Dec. 398, 517 N.E.2d 1084 (1987) (upholding award of $50,000 compensatory damages in defamation action regarding false report of child abuse; reversing $1,000,000 punitive damages award).

325 ILCS 5/4.02

§ 4.02 Failure to report suspected abuse or neglect

Any physician who willfully fails to report suspected child abuse or neglect as required by this Act shall be referred to the Illinois State Medical Disciplinary Board for action in accordance with paragraph 22 of Section 22 of the Medical Practice Act of 1987. Any other person required by this Act to report suspected child abuse and neglect who willfully fails to report such shall be guilty of a Class A misdemeanor.

325 ILCS 5/4.1
§ 4.1 Death caused by abuse or neglect; Reports

Any person required to report under this Act who has reasonable cause to suspect that a child has died as a result of abuse or neglect shall also immediately report his suspicion to the appropriate medical examiner or coroner. Any other person who has reasonable cause to believe that a child has died as a result of abuse or neglect may report his suspicion to the appropriate medical examiner or coroner. The medical examiner or coroner shall investigate the report and communicate his apparent gross findings, orally, immediately upon completion of the gross autopsy, but in all cases within 72 hours and within 21 days in writing, to the local law enforcement agency, the appropriate State's attorney, the Department and, if the institution making the report is a hospital, the hospital. The child protective investigator assigned to the death investigation shall have the right to require a copy of the completed autopsy report from the coroner or medical examiner.

325 ILCS 5/5
§ 5. Temporary protective custody

An officer of a local law enforcement agency, designated employee of the Department, or a physician treating a child may take or retain temporary protective custody of the child without the consent of the person responsible for the child's welfare, if (1) he has reason to believe that the circumstances or conditions of the child are such that continuing in his place of residence or in the care and custody of the person responsible for the child's welfare, presents an imminent danger to that child's life or health; and (2) there is not time to apply for a court order under the Juvenile Court Act of 1987 for temporary custody of the child. The person taking or retaining a child in temporary protective custody shall immediately make every reasonable effort to notify the person responsible for the child's welfare and shall immediately notify the Department. The Department shall provide to the temporary caretaker of a child any information in the Department's possession concerning the positive results of a test performed on the child to determine the presence of the antibody or antigen to Human Immunodeficiency Virus (HIV), or of HIV infection, as well as any communicable diseases or communicable infections that the child has. The temporary caretaker of a child shall not disclose to another person any information received by the temporary caretaker from the Department concerning the results of a test performed on the child to determine the presence of the antibody or antigen to HIV, or of HIV infection, except pursuant to Section 9 of the AIDS Confidentiality Act, as now or hereafter amended. The Department shall promptly initiate proceedings under the Juvenile Court Act of 1987 for the continued temporary custody of the child.

325 ILCS 5/5

Where the physician keeping a child in his custody does so in his capacity as a member of the staff of a hospital or similar institution, he shall notify the person in charge of the institution or his designated agent, who shall then become responsible for the further care of such child in the hospital or similar institution under the direction of the Department.

Said care includes, but is not limited to the granting of permission to perform emergency medical treatment to a minor where the treatment itself does not involve a substantial risk of harm to the minor and the failure to render such treatment will likely result in death or permanent harm to the minor, and there is not time to apply for a court order under the Juvenile Court Act of 1987.

Any person authorized and acting in good faith in the removal of a child under this Section shall have immunity from any liability, civil or criminal that might otherwise be incurred or imposed as a result of such removal. Any physician authorized and acting in good faith and in accordance with acceptable medical practice in the treatment of a child under this Section shall have immunity from any liability, civil or criminal, that might otherwise be incurred or imposed as a result of granting permission for emergency treatment.

With respect to any child taken into temporary protective custody pursuant to this Section, the Department of Children and Family Services Guardianship Administrator or his designee shall be deemed the child's legally authorized representative for purposes of consenting to an HIV test if deemed necessary and appropriate by the Department's Guardianship Administrator or designee and obtaining and disclosing information concerning such test pursuant to the AIDS Confidentiality Act if deemed necessary and appropriate by the Department's Guardianship Administrator or designee and for purposes of consenting to the release of information pursuant to the Illinois Sexually Transmissible Disease Control Act if deemed necessary and appropriate by the Department's Guardianship Administrator or designee.

Any person who administers an HIV test upon the consent of the Department of Children and Family Services Guardianship Administrator or his designee, or who discloses the results of such tests to the Department's Guardianship Administrator or his designee, shall have immunity from any liability, civil, criminal or otherwise, that might result by reason of such actions. For the purpose of any proceedings, civil or criminal, the good faith of any persons required to administer or disclose the results of tests, or permitted to take such actions, shall be presumed.

325 ILCS 5/6

§ 6. Photographs and x-rays of child; Photographs of environment

Any person required to investigate cases of suspected child abuse or neglect may take or cause to be taken, at Department expense, color photographs and x-rays of the child who is the subject of a report, and color photographs of the physical environment in which the alleged abuse or neglect has taken place. The person seeking to take such photographs or x-rays shall make every reasonable effort to notify the person responsible for the child's welfare.

325 ILCS 5/7
§ 7. Time and manner of making report; Confirmation of report

All reports of suspected child abuse or neglect made under this Act shall be made immediately by telephone to the central register established under Section 7.7 on the single, State-wide, toll-free telephone number established in Section 7.6, or in person or by telephone through the nearest Department office. The Department shall, in cooperation with school officials, distribute appropriate materials in school buildings listing the toll-free telephone number established in Section 7.6, including methods of making a report under this Act.

Wherever the Statewide number is posted, there shall also be posted the following notice:

"Any person who knowingly transmits a false report to the Department commits the offense of disorderly conduct under subsection (a)(7) of Section 26–1 of the Criminal Code of 1961. A first violation of this subsection is a Class A misdemeanor, punishable by a term of imprisonment for up to one year, or by a fine not to exceed $1,000, or by both such term and fine. A second or subsequent violation is a Class 4 felony."

The report required by this Act shall include, if known, the name and address of the child and his parents or other persons having his custody; the child's age; the nature of the child's condition including any evidence of previous injuries or disabilities; and any other information that the person filing the report believes might be helpful in establishing the cause of such abuse or neglect and the identity of the person believed to have caused such abuse or neglect. Reports made to the central register through the Statewide, toll-free telephone number shall be immediately transmitted to the appropriate Child Protective Service Unit. The Department shall within 24 hours orally notify local law enforcement personnel and the office of the State's Attorney of the involved county of the receipt of any report alleging the death of a child, serious injury to a child including, but not limited to, brain damage, skull fractures, subdural hematomas, and, internal injuries, torture of a child, malnutrition of a child, and sexual abuse to a child, including, but not limited to, sexual intercourse, sexual exploitation, sexual molestation, and venereal disease in a child age twelve and under. All oral reports made by the Department to local law enforcement personnel and the office of the State's Attorney of the involved county shall be confirmed in writing within 48 hours of the oral report. All reports by persons mandated to report under this Act shall be confirmed in writing to the appropriate Child Protective Service Unit, which may be on forms supplied by the Department, within 48 hours of any initial report.

325 ILCS 5/7   **FAMILIES**

Written confirmation reports from persons not required to report by this Act may be made to the appropriate Child Protective Service Unit. Written reports from persons required by this Act to report shall be admissible in evidence in any judicial proceeding relating to child abuse or neglect. Reports involving known or suspected child abuse or neglect in public or private residential agencies or institutions shall be made and received in the same manner as all other reports made under this Act.

325 ILCS 5/7.1

§ 7.1 Cooperation of agencies; Multi-disciplinary teams

(a) To the fullest extent feasible, the Department shall cooperate with and shall seek the cooperation and involvement of all appropriate public and private agencies, including health, education, social service and law enforcement agencies, courts of competent jurisdiction, and agencies, organizations, or programs providing or concerned with human services related to the prevention, identification or treatment of child abuse or neglect.

Such cooperation and involvement shall include joint consultation and services, joint planning, joint case management, joint public education and information services, joint utilization of facilities, joint staff development and other training, and the creation of multidisciplinary case diagnostic, case handling, case management, and policy planning teams. Such cooperation and involvement shall also include consultation and planning with the Illinois Department of Public Health regarding referrals to designated perinatal centers of newborn children requiring protective custody under this Act, whose life or development may be threatened by a developmental disability or handicapping condition.

For implementing such intergovernmental cooperation and involvement, units of local government and public and private agencies may apply for and receive federal or State funds from the Department under this Act or seek and receive gifts from local philanthropic or other private local sources in order to augment any State funds appropriated for the purposes of this Act.

(b) The Department may establish up to 5 demonstrations of multidisciplinary teams to advise, review and monitor cases of child abuse and neglect brought by the Department or any member of the team. The Director shall determine the criteria by which certain cases of child abuse or neglect are brought to the multidisciplinary teams. The criteria shall include but not be limited to geographic area and classification of certain cases where allegations are of a severe nature. Each multidisciplinary team shall consist of 7 to 10 members appointed by the Director, including, but not limited to representatives from the medical, mental health, educational, juvenile justice, law enforcement and social service fields.

325 ILCS 5/7.2

§ 7.2 Child protective service unit; Establishment

The Department shall establish a Child Protective Service Unit within each geographic region as designated by the Director of the Department. The

Child Protective Service Unit shall perform those functions assigned by this Act to it and only such others that would further the purposes of this Act. It shall have a sufficient staff of qualified personnel to fulfill the purpose of this Act and be organized in such a way as to maximize the continuity of responsibility, care and service of the individual workers toward the individual children and families.

The Child Protective Service Unit shall designate members of each unit to receive specialty training to serve as special consultants to unit staff and the public in the areas of child sexual abuse, child deaths and injuries, and out-of-home investigations.

325 ILCS 5/7.3

§ 7.3 Investigations; Responsibilities of department

The Department shall be the sole agency responsible for receiving and investigating reports of child abuse or neglect made under this Act, except where investigations by other agencies may be required with respect to reports alleging the death of a child, serious injury to a child or sexual abuse to a child made pursuant to Sections 4.1 or 7 of this Act, and except that the Department may delegate the performance of the investigation to the Department of State Police, a law enforcement agency and to those private social service agencies which have been designated for this purpose by the Department prior to July 1, 1980.

325 ILCS 5/7.3a

§ 7.3a Perinatal coordinator; Appointment; Duties

The Director of the Department shall appoint a Perinatal Coordinator who shall be a physician licensed to practice medicine in all its branches with a specialty certification in pediatric care. Such coordinator, or other designated medical specialists, shall review all reports of suspected medical neglect involving newborns or infants, coordinate the evaluation of the subject of such report, and assist in necessary referrals to appropriate perinatal medical care and treatment. When the Perinatal Coordinator or other designated medical specialists, alone or in consultation with an infant care review committee established by a medical facility, determine that a newborn or infant child is being neglected as defined in Section 3 of this Act, a designated employee of the Department shall take the steps necessary to protect such newborn or infant child's life or health, including but not limited to taking temporary protective custody.

325 ILCS 5/7.3b

§ 7.3b Referral of addicted pregnant persons; Services

All persons required to report under Section 4 may refer to the Department of Public Health any pregnant person in this State who is addicted as defined in the Illinois Alcoholism and Other Drug Dependency Act. The Department of Public Health shall notify the local Infant Mortality Reduction

Network service provider or Department funded prenatal care provider in the area in which the person resides. The service provider shall prepare a case management plan and assist the pregnant woman in obtaining counseling and treatment from a local substance abuse service provider licensed by the Department of Alcoholism and Substance Abuse or a licensed hospital which provides substance abuse treatment services. The local Infant Mortality Reduction Network service provider and Department funded prenatal care provider shall monitor the pregnant woman through the service program. The Department of Public Health shall have the authority to promulgate rules and regulations to implement this Section.

325 ILCS 5/7.4

§ 7.4 Time and manner of making investigations; Emergency services

(a) The Department shall be capable of receiving reports of suspected child abuse or neglect 24 hours a day, 7 days a week. Whenever the Department receives a report alleging that a child is a truant as defined in Section 26-2a of The School Code, as now or hereafter amended, the Department shall notify the superintendent of the school district in which the child resides and the appropriate superintendent of the educational service region. The notification to the appropriate officials by the Department shall not be considered an allegation of abuse or neglect under this Act.

(b) (1) The following procedures shall be followed in the investigation of all reports of suspected abuse or neglect of a child, except as provided in subsection (c) of this Section.

(2) If it appears that the immediate safety or well-being of a child is endangered, that the family may flee or the child disappear, or that the facts otherwise so warrant, the Child Protective Service Unit shall commence an investigation immediately, regardless of the time of day or night. In all other cases, investigation shall be commenced within 24 hours of receipt of the report. Upon receipt of a report, the Child Protective Service Unit shall make an initial investigation and an initial determination whether the report is a good faith indication of alleged child abuse or neglect.

(3) If the Unit determines the report is a good faith indication of alleged child abuse or neglect, then a formal investigation shall commence and, pursuant to Section 7.12 of this Act, may or may not result in an indicated report. The formal investigation shall include: direct contact with the subject or subjects of the report as soon as possible after the report is received; an evaluation of the environment of the child named in the report and any other children in the same environment; a determination of the risk to such children if they continue to remain in the existing environments, as well as a determination of the nature, extent and cause of any condition enumerated in such report; the name, age and condition of other children in the environment; and an evaluation as to whether there would be an immediate and urgent necessity to remove the child from the environment if

appropriate family preservation services were provided. After seeing to the safety of the child or children, the Department shall forthwith notify the subjects of the report in writing, of the existence of the report and their rights existing under this Act in regard to amendment or expungement. To fulfill the requirements of this Section, the Child Protective Service Unit shall have the capability of providing or arranging for comprehensive emergency services to children and families at all times of the day or night.

(4) If (i) at the conclusion of the Unit's initial investigation of a report, the Unit determines the report to be a good faith indication of alleged child abuse or neglect that warrants a formal investigation by the Unit, the Department, any law enforcement agency or any other responsible agency and (ii) the person who is alleged to have caused the abuse or neglect is employed or otherwise engaged in an activity resulting in frequent contact with children and the alleged abuse or neglect are in the course of such employment or activity, then the Department shall, except in investigations where the Director determines that such notification would be detrimental to the Department's investigation, inform the appropriate supervisor or administrator of that employment or activity that the Unit has commenced a formal investigation pursuant to this Act, which may or may not result in an indicated report. The Department shall also notify the person being investigated, unless the Director determines that such notification would be detrimental to the Department's investigation.

(c) In an investigation of a report of suspected abuse or neglect of a child by a school employee at a school or on school grounds, the Department shall make reasonable efforts to follow the following procedures:

(1) Investigations involving teachers shall not, to the extent possible, be conducted when the teacher is scheduled to conduct classes. Investigations involving other school employees shall be conducted so as to minimize disruption of the school day. The school employee accused of child abuse or neglect may have his superior, his association or union representative and his attorney present at any interview or meeting at which the teacher or administrator is present. The accused school employee shall be informed by a representative of the Department, at any interview or meeting, of the accused school employee's due process rights and of the steps in the investigation process. The information shall include, but need not necessarily be limited to the right, subject to the approval of the Department, of the school employee to confront the accuser, if the accuser is 14 years of age or older, or the right to review the specific allegations which gave rise to the investigation, and the right to review all materials and evidence that have been submitted to the Department in support of the allegation. These due process rights shall also include the right of the school employee to present countervailing evidence regarding the accusations.

(2) If a report of neglect or abuse of a child by a teacher or administrator does not involve allegations of sexual abuse or extreme physical abuse, the Child Protective Service Unit shall make reasonable efforts to conduct the

initial investigation in coordination with the employee's supervisor. If the Unit determines that the report is a good faith indication of potential child abuse or neglect, it shall then commence a formal investigation under paragraph (3) of subsection (b) of this Section.

(3) If a report of neglect or abuse of a child by a teacher or administrator involves an allegation of sexual abuse or extreme physical abuse, the Child Protective Unit shall commence an investigation under paragraph (2) of subsection (b) of this Section.

(d) If the Department has contact with an employer in the course of its investigation, the Department shall notify the employer, in writing, when a report is unfounded so that any record of the investigation can be expunged from the employee's personnel records. The Department shall also notify the employee, in writing, that notification has been sent to the employer informing the employer that the Department's investigation has resulted in an unfounded report.

325 ILCS 5/7.5

§ 7.5 Access to child for examination or interview; Intervention of law enforcement agencies; Court orders

If the Child Protective Service Unit is denied reasonable access to a child by the parents or other persons and it deems that the best interests of the child so require, it shall request the intervention of a local law enforcement agency or seek an appropriate court order to examine and interview the child.

325 ILCS 5/7.6

§ 7.6 Toll-free telephone number; Posted notice of criminal offense

There shall be a single State-wide, toll-free telephone number established and maintained by the Department which all persons, whether or not mandated by law, may use to report suspected child abuse or neglect at any hour of the day or night, on any day of the week. Immediately upon receipt of such reports, the Department shall transmit the contents of the report, either orally or electronically, to the appropriate Child Protective Service Unit. Any other person may use the State-wide number to obtain assistance or information concerning the handling of child abuse and neglect cases.

Wherever the Statewide number is posted, there shall also be posted the following notice:

"Any person who knowingly transmits a false report to the Department commits the offense of disorderly conduct under subsection (a)(7) of Section 26–1 of the Criminal Code of 1961. A violation of this subsection is a Class B misdemeanor, punishable by a term of imprisonment for not more than 6 months, or by a fine not to exceed $500, or by both such term and fine."

325 ILCS 5/7.7

§ 7.7 Register of reported cases

There shall be a central register of all cases of suspected child abuse or neglect reported and maintained by the Department under this Act. Through the recording of initial, preliminary, and final reports, the central register shall be operated in such a manner as to enable the Department to: (1) immediately identify and locate prior reports of child abuse or neglect; (2) continuously monitor the current status of all reports of child abuse or neglect being provided services under this Act; and (3) regularly evaluate the effectiveness of existing laws and programs through the development and analysis of statistical and other information.

The Department shall maintain in the central register a listing of unfounded reports where the subject of the unfounded report requests that the record not be expunged because the subject alleges an intentional false report was made. Such a request must be made by the subject in writing to the Department, within 10 days of the investigation.

325 ILCS 5/7.8

§ 7.8 Notification of previous reports to child protective service units

Upon receiving an oral or written report of suspected child abuse or neglect, the Department shall immediately notify, either orally or electronically, the Child Protective Service Unit of a previous report concerning a subject of the present report or other pertinent information. In addition, upon satisfactory identification procedures, to be established by Department regulation, any person authorized to have access to records under Section 11.1 relating to child abuse and neglect may request and shall be immediately provided the information requested in accordance with this Act. However, no information shall be released unless it prominently states the report is "indicated", and only information from "indicated" reports shall be released, except that information concerning pending reports may be released to any person authorized under paragraphs (1), (2), (3) and (11) of Section 11.1. In addition, State's Attorneys are authorized to receive unfounded reports for prosecution purposes related to the transmission of false reports of child abuse or neglect in violation of subsection (a), paragraph (7) of Section 26–1 of the Criminal Code of 1961 and guardians ad litem appointed under Article II of the Juvenile Court Act of 1987 shall receive the classified reports set forth in Section 7.14 of this Act in conformance with paragraph (19) of Section 11.1 and Section 7.14 of this Act. The names and other identifying data and the dates and the circumstances of any persons requesting or receiving information from the central register shall be entered in the register record.

325 ILCS 5/7.9

§ 7.9 Form and contents of reports

The Department shall prepare, print, and distribute initial, preliminary, and final reporting forms to each Child Protective Service Unit. Initial written reports from the reporting source shall contain the following information to the extent known at the time the report is made: (1) the names and addresses of the child and his parents or other persons responsible for his welfare; (2) the child's age, sex, and race; (3) the nature and extent of the child's abuse or neglect, including any evidence of prior injuries, abuse, or neglect of the child or his siblings; (4) the names of the persons apparently responsible for the abuse or neglect; (5) family composition, including names, ages, sexes, and races of other children in the home; (6) the name of the person making the report, his occupation, and where he can be reached; (7) the actions taken by the reporting source, including the taking of photographs and x-rays, placing the child in temporary protective custody, or notifying the medical examiner or coroner; (8) and any other information the person making the report believes might be helpful in the furtherance of the purposes of this Act.

325 ILCS 5/7.10

§ 7.10 Copies of reports; Transmission to central register; Contents of preliminary reports

Upon the receipt of each oral report made under this Act, the Child Protective Service Unit shall immediately transmit a copy thereof to the state central register of child abuse and neglect. A preliminary report from a Child Protective Service Unit shall be made at the time of the first of any 30–day extensions made pursuant to Section 7.12 and shall describe the status of the related investigation up to that time, including an evaluation of the present family situation and danger to the child or children, corrections or up-dating of the initial report, and actions taken or contemplated.

325 ILCS 5/7.12

§ 7.12 Determination of classification of report

The Child Protective Service Unit shall determine, within 60 days, whether the report is "indicated" or "unfounded" and report it forthwith to the central register; where it is not possible to initiate or complete an investigation within 60 days the report may be deemed "undetermined" provided every effort has been made to undertake a complete investigation. The Department may extend the period in which such determinations must be made in individual cases for additional periods of up to 30 days each for good cause shown. The Department shall by rule establish what shall constitute good cause.

325 ILCS 5/7.13

§ 7.13 Additional information; Reports

The reports made under this Act may contain such additional information in the furtherance of the purposes of this Act as the Department, by rule, may require.

325 ILCS 5/7.14

§ 7.14 Categories of classification; Reports

All reports in the central register shall be classified in one of three categories: "indicated", "unfounded" or "undetermined", as the case may be.

After the report is classified, the person making the classification shall determine whether the child named in the report is the subject of an action under Article II of the Juvenile Court Act of 1987. If the child is the subject of an action under Article II of the Juvenile Court Act, the Department shall transmit a copy of the report to the guardian ad litem appointed for the child under Section 2-17 of the Juvenile Court Act. All information identifying the subjects of an unfounded report shall be expunged from the register forthwith, except as provided in Section 7.7. Identifying information on all other records shall be removed from the register no later than 5 years after the report is indicated. However, if another report is received involving the same child, his sibling or offspring, or a child in the care of the persons responsible for the child's welfare, the identifying information may be maintained in the register until 5 years after the subsequent case or report is closed.

Notwithstanding any other provision of this Section, identifying information in indicated reports involving the sexual abuse of a child, the death of a child, or serious physical injury to a child as defined by the Department in rules, may be retained longer than 5 years after the report is indicated or after the subsequent case or report is closed, and may not be removed from the register except as provided by the Department in rules.

325 ILCS 5/7.15

§ 7.15 Contents of central register; Additional information; Expungement of records

The central register may contain such other information which the Department determines to be in furtherance of the purposes of this Act. Pursuant to the provisions of Sections 7.14 and 7.16, the Department may amend, expunge, or remove from the central register appropriate records upon good cause shown and upon notice to the subjects of the report and the Child Protective Service Unit.

325 ILCS 5/7.16

§ 7.16 Application for expungement; Hearing; Review under Administrative Review Law

Within 60 days after the notification of the completion of the Child Protective Service Unit investigation, determined by the date of the notification sent by the Department, a subject of a report may request the Department to amend, expunge identifying information from, or remove the record of the report from the register. Such request shall be in writing and directed to such person as the Department designates in the notification. The Department shall disregard any request not made in such manner. If the Department refuses to do so or does not act within 30 days, the subject shall have the right to a hearing within the Department to determine whether the record of the report should be amended, expunged, or removed on the grounds that it is inaccurate or it is being maintained in a manner inconsistent with this Act, except that there shall be no such right to a hearing on the ground of the report's inaccuracy if there has been a court finding of child abuse or neglect, the report's accuracy being conclusively presumed on such finding. Such hearing shall be held within a reasonable time after the subject's request and at a reasonable place and hour. The appropriate Child Protective Service Unit shall be given notice of the hearing. In such hearings, the burden of proving the accuracy and consistency of the record shall be on the Department and the appropriate Child Protective Service Unit. The hearing shall be conducted by the Director or his designee, who is hereby authorized and empowered to order the amendment, expunction, or removal of the record to make it accurate and consistent with this Act. The decision shall be made, in writing, at the close of the hearing, or within 30 days thereof, and shall state the reasons upon which it is based. Decisions of the Department under this Section are administrative decisions subject to judicial review under the Administrative Review Law.

325 ILCS 5/7.17

§ 7.17 Notice of amendment on expungement; Local records

To the fullest extent possible, written notice of any amendment, expunction, or removal of any record made under this Act shall be served upon each subject of such report and the appropriate Child Protective Service Unit. Upon receipt of such notice, the Child Protective Service Unit shall take similar action in regard to the local child abuse and neglect index and shall inform, for the same purpose, any other individuals or agencies which received such record under this Act or in any other manner. Nothing in this Section is intended to require the destruction of case records.

325 ILCS 5/7.18

§ 7.18 Amendment of reports

Pursuant to Sections 7.15 and 7.16 and for good cause shown, the Child Protective Service Unit may amend any report previously sent to the Statewide center. Unless otherwise prescribed by this Act, the content, form, manner and timing of making the reports shall be established by rules of the Department.

325 ILCS 5/7.19

§ 7.19 Copies of report to subject

Upon request, a subject of a report shall be entitled to receive a copy of all information contained in the central register pertaining to his case. However, the Department may prohibit the release of data that would identify or locate a person who, in good faith, made a report or cooperated in a subsequent investigation. In addition, the Department may seek a court order from the circuit court prohibiting the release of any information which the court finds is likely to be harmful to the subject of the report.

325 ILCS 5/8.1
§ 8.1 Disposition by Child Protective Service Unit

If the Child Protective Service Unit determines after investigating a report that there is no credible evidence that a child is abused or neglected, it shall deem the report to be an unfounded report. However, if it appears that the child or family could benefit from other social services, including services under Section 8.2, the local service may suggest such services for the family's voluntary acceptance or refusal. If the family declines such services, the Department shall take no further action.

325 ILCS 5/8.2
§ 8.2 Service plan

If the Child Protective Service Unit determines, following an investigation made pursuant to Section 7.4 of this Act, that there is credible evidence that the child is abused or neglected, the Department shall assess the family's need for services, and, as necessary, develop, with the family, an appropriate service plan for the family's voluntary acceptance or refusal. In any case where there is evidence that the perpetrator of the abuse or neglect is an addict or alcoholic as defined in the Illinois Alcoholism and Other Drug Dependency Act, as now or hereafter amended, the Department, when making referrals for drug or alcohol abuse services, shall make such referrals to facilities licensed by the Department of Alcoholism and Substance Abuse or the Department of Public Health. The Department shall comply with Section 8.1 by explaining its lack of legal authority to compel the acceptance of services and may explain its noncomitant authority to petition the Circuit court under the Juvenile Court Act of 1987 or refer the case to the local law enforcement authority or State's attorney for criminal prosecution.

For purposes of this Act, the term "family preservation services" refers to all services to prevent the placement of children in substitute care, to reunite them with their families if so placed and if reunification is an appropriate goal, or to maintain an adoptive placement. The term "homemaker" includes emergency caretakers, homemakers, caretakers, housekeepers and chore services. The term "counseling" includes individual therapy, infant stimulation therapy, family therapy, group therapy, self-help groups, drug and alcohol abuse counseling, vocational counseling and post-adoptive services. The term "day care" includes protective day care and day care to meet educational, prevocational or vocational needs. The term "emergency assistance and advocacy" includes coordinated services to secure emergency cash, food, housing and medical assistance or advocacy for other subsistence and family protective needs.

The Department shall promptly notify children and families of the Department's responsibility to offer and provide family preservation services as identified in the service plan. Such plans may include but are not limited to: case management services; homemakers; counseling; parent education; day care; emergency assistance and advocacy assessments; respite care; in-home health care; transportation to obtain any of the above services; and medical assistance.

The availability of family preservation services shall be phased in, so that orderly development may occur, during the first 5 fiscal years after the effective date (December 22, 1987) of this amendatory Act of 1987. The Department shall develop a phase-in plan and rules in consultation with the Child Welfare Advisory Committee.

During the phase-in period, any type of service enumerated in this Act and made available pursuant to the phase-in plan to any client population in one geographic area shall be made equally available to the same client population throughout the State within 3 full years. By July 1, 1995, the family preservation services shall be uniformly available throughout the State.

The Department shall provide a preliminary report to the General Assembly no later than January 1, 1991, in regard to the provision of services authorized pursuant to this Section. The report shall include:

(a) the number of families and children served, by type of services;

(b) the outcome from the provision of such services, including the number of families which remained intact at least 6 months following the termination of services;

(c) the number of families which have been subjects of founded reports of abuse following the termination of services;

(d) an analysis of general family circumstances in which family preservation services have been determined to be an effective intervention;

(e) information regarding the number of families in need of services but unserved due to budget or program criteria guidelines;

(f) an estimate of the time necessary for and the annual cost of statewide implementation of such services;

(g) an estimate of the length of time before expansion of these services will be made to include families with children over the age of 6; and

(h) recommendations regarding any proposed legislative changes to this program.

Each Department field office shall maintain on a local basis directories of services available to children and families in the local area where the Department office is located.

The Department shall refer children and families served pursuant to this Section to private agencies and governmental agencies, where available.

Where there are 2 equal proposals from both a not-for-profit and a for-profit agency to provide services, the Department shall give preference to the proposal from the not-for-profit agency.

No service plan shall compel any child or parent to engage in any activity or refrain from any activity which is not reasonably related to remedying a condition or conditions that gave rise or which could give rise to any finding of child abuse or neglect.

325 ILCS 5/8.3

§ 8.3 Court proceedings; Assistance of Child Protective Services Unit

The Department shall assist a Circuit Court during all stages of the court proceeding in accordance with the purposes of this Act and the Juvenile Court Act of 1987 by providing full, complete, and accurate information to the court and by appearing in court if requested by the court. Failure to provide assistance requested by a court shall be enforceable through proceedings for contempt of court.

325 ILCS 5/8.4

§ 8.4 Rehabilitative services; Monitoring

The Department shall provide or arrange for and monitor, as authorized by this Act, rehabilitative services for children and their families on a voluntary basis or under a final or intermediate order of the Court.

325 ILCS 5/8.5

§ 8.5 Local child abuse and neglect index

The Child Protective Service Unit shall maintain a local child abuse and neglect index of all cases reported under this Act which will enable it to determine the location of case records and to monitor the timely and proper investigation and disposition of cases. The index shall include the information contained in the initial, progress, and final reports required under this Act, and any other appropriate information.

325 ILCS 5/9

§ 9. Immunity from liability; Presumption

Any person, institution or agency, under this Act, participating in good faith in the making of a report or referral, or in the investigation of such a report or referral or in the taking of photographs and x-rays or in the retaining a child in temporary protective custody shall have immunity from any liability, civil, criminal or that otherwise might result by reason of such actions. For the purpose of any proceedings, civil or criminal, the good faith of any persons required to report or refer, or permitted to report, cases of suspected child abuse or neglect or permitted to refer individuals under this Act, shall be presumed.

325 ILCS 5/9.1

§ 9.1 Employer discrimination

Employer discrimination. No employer shall discharge, demote or suspend, or threaten to discharge, demote or suspend, or in any manner discrimi-

325 ILCS 5/9.1   **FAMILIES**

nate against any employee who makes any good faith oral or written report of suspected child abuse or neglect, or who is or will be a witness or testify in any investigation or proceeding concerning a report of suspected child abuse or neglect.

325 ILCS 5/10

§ 10. Testimony by person making report

Any person who makes a report or who investigates a report under this Act shall testify fully in any judicial proceeding resulting from such report, as to any evidence of abuse or neglect, or the cause thereof. Any person who is required to report a suspected case of abuse or neglect under Section 4 of this Act shall testify fully in any administrative hearing resulting from such report, as to any evidence of abuse or neglect or the cause thereof. No evidence shall be excluded by reason of any common law or statutory privilege relating to communications between the alleged perpetrator of abuse or neglect, or the child subject of the report under this Act and the person making or investigating the report.

§ 11. Confidentiality of records; Violations

All records concerning reports of child abuse and neglect or records concerning referrals under this Act and all records generated as a result of such reports or referrals, shall be confidential and shall not be disclosed except as specifically authorized by this Act or other applicable law. It is a Class A misdemeanor to permit, assist, or encourage the unauthorized release of any information contained in such reports, referrals or records.

325 ILCS 5/11.1

§ 11.1 Access to records

A person shall have access to the records described in Section 11 only in furtherance of purposes directly connected with the administration of this Act or the Intergovernmental Missing Child Recovery Act of 1984. Such persons and purposes for access include:

(1) Department staff in the furtherance of their responsibilities under this Act, or for the purpose of completing background investigations on persons or agencies licensed by the Department or with whom the Department contracts for the provision of child welfare services.

(2) A law enforcement agency investigating known or suspected child abuse or neglect, known or suspected involvement with child pornography, known or suspected criminal sexual assault, known or suspected criminal sexual abuse, or any other sexual offense when a child is alleged to be involved.

(3) The Department of State Police when administering the provisions of the Intergovernmental Missing Child Recovery Act of 1984.

(4) A physician who has before him a child whom he reasonably suspects may be abused or neglected.

(5) A person authorized under Section 5 of this Act to place a child in temporary protective custody when such person requires the information in the report or record to determine whether to place the child in temporary protective custody.

(6) A person having the legal responsibility or authorization to care for, treat, or supervise a child or a parent, guardian, or other person responsible for the child's welfare who is the subject of a report.

(7) Except in regard to harmful or detrimental information as provided in Section 7.19, any subject of the report, and if the subject of the report is a minor, his guardian or guardian ad litem.

(8) A court, upon its finding that access to such records may be necessary for the determination of an issue before such court; however, such access shall be limited to in camera inspection, unless the court determines that public disclosure of the information contained therein is necessary for the resolution of an issue then pending before it.

(9) A grand jury, upon its determination that access to such records is necessary in the conduct of its official business.

(10) Any person authorized by the Director, in writing, for audit or bona fide research purposes.

(11) Law enforcement agencies, coroners or medical examiners, physicians, courts, school superintendents and child welfare agencies in other states who are responsible for child abuse or neglect investigations or background investigations.

(12) The Department of Professional Regulation, the State Board of Education and school superintendents in Illinois, who may use or disclose information from the records as they deem necessary to conduct investigations or take disciplinary action, as provided by law.

(13) A coroner or medical examiner who has reason to believe that a child has died as the result of abuse or neglect.

(14) The Director of a State-operated facility when an employee of that facility is the perpetrator in an indicated report.

(15) The operator of a licensed child care facility or a facility licensed by the Department of Alcoholism and Substance Abuse in which children reside when a current or prospective employee of that facility is the perpetrator in an indicated child abuse or neglect report, pursuant to Section 4.3 of the Child Care Act of 1969.

(16) Members of a multidisciplinary team in the furtherance of its responsibilities under subsection (b) of Section 7.1. All reports concerning child abuse and neglect made available to members of such multidisciplinary teams and all records generated as a result of such reports shall be confidential and shall not be disclosed, except as specifically authorized by this Act or other applicable law. It is a Class A misdemeanor to

permit, assist or encourage the unauthorized release of any information contained in such reports or records.

(17) The Department of Rehabilitation Services, as provided in Section 17 of the Disabled Persons Rehabilitation Act.

(18) Any other agency or investigative body, including the Department of Public Health and a local board of health, authorized by State law to conduct an investigation into the quality of care provided to children in hospitals and other State regulated care facilities. The access to and release of information from such records shall be subject to the approval of the Director of the Department or his designee.

(19) The person appointed, under Section 2-17 of the Juvenile Court Act, as the guardian ad litem of a minor who is the subject of a report or records under this Act.

325 ILCS 5/11.2

§ 11.2 Disclosure to mandated reporting sources

Upon request, a mandated reporting source as provided in Section 4 of this Act may receive appropriate information about the findings and actions taken by the Child Protective Service Unit in response to its report.

325 ILCS 5/11.3

§ 11.3 Publicizing disclosed information; Court actions; Violations

A person given access to the names or other information identifying the subjects of the report, except the subject of the report, shall not make public such identifying information unless he is a State's attorney or other law enforcement official and the purpose is to initiate court action. Violation of this Section is a Class A misdemeanor.

325 ILCS 5/11.4

§ 11.4 Court and criminal records; Effect of Act

Nothing in this Act affects existing policies or procedures concerning the status of court and criminal justice system records.

325 ILCS 5/11.5

§ 11.5 Continuing education program

Within the appropriation available, the Department shall conduct a continuing education and training program for State and local staff, persons and officials required to report, the general public, and other persons engaged in or intending to engage in the prevention, identification, and treatment of child abuse and neglect. The program shall be designed to encourage the fullest degree of reporting of known and suspected child abuse and neglect, and to improve communication, cooperation, and coordination among all agencies in the identification, prevention, and treatment of child abuse and neglect. The program shall inform the general public and professionals of the nature and extent of child abuse and neglect and their responsibilities, obligations, powers and immunity from liability under this Act. It may include information on the diagnosis of child abuse and neglect and the roles and procedures of the Child Protective Service Unit, the Department and central register, the courts and of the protective, treatment, and ameliorative services available to children and their families. Such information may also include special needs of mothers at risk of delivering a child whose life or development may be threatened by a handicapping condition, to ensure informed consent to treatment of the condition and understanding of the unique child care responsibilities required for such a child. The program may also encourage parents and other persons having responsibility for the welfare of children to seek assistance on their own in meeting their child care responsibilities and encourage the voluntary acceptance of available services when they are needed. It may also include publicity and dissemination of information on the existence and number of the 24 hour, State-wide, toll-free telephone service to assist persons seeking assistance and to receive reports of known and suspected abuse and neglect.

Within the appropriation available, the Department also shall conduct a continuing education and training program for State and local staff involved in investigating reports of child abuse or neglect made under this Act. The program shall be designed to train such staff in the necessary and appropriate procedures to be followed in investigating cases which it appears may result in civil or criminal charges being filed against a person. Program subjects shall include but not be limited to the gathering of evidence with a view toward presenting such evidence in court and the involvement of State or local law enforcement agencies in the investigation. The program shall be conducted in cooperation with State or local law enforcement agencies, State's Attorneys and other components of the criminal justice system as the Department deems appropriate.

325 ILCS 5/11.6

§ 11.6 Review under Administrative Review Law

All final administrative decisions of the Department under this Act are subject to judicial review under the Administrative Review Law, as now or hereafter amended, and the rules adopted pursuant thereto. The term "administrative decision" is defined as in Section 3–101 of the Code of Civil Procedure.

325 ILCS 5/11.7

§ 11.7 State-wide citizens committee on child abuse and neglect

(a) The Director shall appoint the chairperson and members of a "State-wide Citizen's Committee on Child Abuse and Neglect" to consult with and advise the Director. The Committee shall be composed of individuals of distinction in human services, neonatal medical care, needs and rights of the disabled, law and community life, broadly representative of social and economic communities across the State, who shall be appointed to 3 year staggered terms. The chairperson and members of the Committee shall serve without compensation, although their travel and per diem expenses shall be reimbursed in accordance with standard State procedures. Under procedures adopted by the Committee, it may meet at any time, confer with any individuals, groups, and agencies; and may issue reports or recommendations on any aspect of child abuse or neglect it deems appropriate.

(b) The Committee shall advise the Director on setting priorities for the administration of child abuse prevention, shelters and service programs, as specified in Section 4a of "An Act creating the Department of Children and Family Services, codifying its powers and duties, and repealing certain Acts and Sections herein named", approved June 4, 1963, as amended.

(c) The Committee shall advise the Director on policies and procedures with respect to the medical neglect of newborns and infants.

CHAPTER 720
CRIMINAL OFFENSES

ACT 5. CRIMINAL CODE OF 1961
ARTICLE X. KIDNAPING AND RELATED OFFENSES

Analysis

Sec.
10–5. Child abduction.
10–5.5 Unlawful visitation interference.
10–6. Harboring a runaway.
10–7. Aiding and abetting child abduction.

WESTLAW Electronic Research

See WESTLAW Electronic Research Guide preceding the Summary of Contents.

720 ILCS 5/10–5

§ 10–5. Child abduction

(a) For purposes of this Section, the following terms shall have the following meanings:

(1) "Child" means a person under the age of 18 or an institutionalized severely or profoundly mentally retarded person at the time the alleged violation occurred; and

(2) "Detains" means taking or retaining physical custody of a child, whether or not the child resists or objects; and

(3) "Lawful custodian" means a person or persons granted legal custody of a child or entitled to physical possession of a child pursuant to a court order. It is presumed that, when the parties have never been married to each other, the mother has legal custody of the child unless a valid court order states otherwise. If an adjudication of paternity has been completed and the father has been assigned support obligations or visitation rights, such a paternity order should, for the purposes of this Section, be considered a valid court order granting custody to the mother.

(b) A person commits child abduction when he or she:

(1) Intentionally violates any terms of a valid court order granting sole or joint custody, care or possession to another, by concealing or

detaining the child or removing the child from the jurisdiction of the court; or

(2) Intentionally violates a court order prohibiting the person from concealing or detaining the child or removing the child from the jurisdiction of the court; or

(3) Intentionally conceals, detains or removes the child without the consent of the mother or lawful custodian of the child if the person is a putative father and either: (A) the paternity of the child has not been legally established or (B) the paternity of the child has been legally established but no orders relating to custody have been entered. However, notwithstanding the presumption created by paragraph (3) of subsection (a), a mother commits child abduction when she intentionally conceals or removes a child, whom she has abandoned or relinquished custody of, from an unadjudicated father who has provided sole ongoing care and custody of the child in her absence; or

(4) Intentionally conceals or removes the child from a parent after filing a petition or being served with process in an action affecting marriage or paternity but prior to the issuance of a temporary or final order determining custody; or

(5) At the expiration of visitation rights outside the State, intentionally fails or refuses to return or impedes the return of the child to the lawful custodian in Illinois; or

(6) Being a parent of the child, and where the parents of such child are or have been married and there has been no court order of custody, conceals the child for 15 days, and fails to make reasonable attempts within the 15 day period to notify the other parent as to the specific whereabouts of the child, including a means by which to contact such child, or to arrange reasonable visitation or contact with the child. It is not a violation of this Section for a person fleeing domestic violence to take the child with him or her to housing provided by a domestic violence program; or

(7) Being a parent of the child, and where the parents of the child are or have been married and there has been no court order of custody, conceals, detains, or removes the child with physical force or threat of physical force; or

(8) Conceals, detains, or removes the child for payment or promise of payment at the instruction of a person who has no legal right to custody; or

(9) Retains in this State for 30 days a child removed from another state without the consent of the lawful custodian or in violation of a valid court order of custody; or

(10) Intentionally lures or attempts to lure a child under the age of 16 into a motor vehicle, building, housetrailer, or dwelling place without

the consent of the parent or lawful custodian of the child for other than a lawful purpose.

For the purposes of this subsection (b), paragraph (10), the luring or attempted luring of a child under the age of 16 into a motor vehicle, building, housetrailer, or dwelling place without the consent of the parent or lawful custodian of the child shall be prima facie evidence of other than a lawful purpose.

(c) It shall be an affirmative defense that:

(1) The person had custody of the child pursuant to a court order granting legal custody or visitation rights which existed at the time of the alleged violation; or

(2) The person had physical custody of the child pursuant to a court order granting legal custody or visitation rights and failed to return the child as a result of circumstances beyond his or her control, and the person notified and disclosed to the other parent or legal custodian the specific whereabouts of the child and a means by which such child can be contacted or made a reasonable attempt to notify the other parent or lawful custodian of the child of such circumstances and make such disclosure within 24 hours after the visitation period had expired and returned the child as soon as possible; or

(3) The person was fleeing an incidence or pattern of domestic violence; or

(4) The person lured or attempted to lure a child under the age of 16 into a motor vehicle, building, housetrailer, or dwelling place for a lawful purpose in prosecutions under subsection (b), paragraph (10).

(d) A person convicted of child abduction under this Section is guilty of a Class 4 felony. It shall be a factor in aggravation for which a court may impose a more severe sentence under Section 5-8-1 of the Unified Code of Corrections, if upon sentencing the court finds evidence of any of the following aggravating factors:

(1) that the defendant abused or neglected the child following the concealment, detention or removal of the child; or

(2) that the defendant inflicted or threatened to inflict physical harm on a parent or lawful custodian of the child or on the child with intent to cause such parent or lawful custodian to discontinue criminal prosecution of the defendant under this Section; or

(3) that the defendant demanded payment in exchange for return of the child or demanded that he or she be relieved of the financial or legal obligation to support the child in exchange for return of the child; or

(4) that the defendant has previously been convicted of child abduction; or

(5) that the defendant committed the abduction while armed with a deadly weapon or the taking of the child resulted in serious bodily injury to another.

(e) The court may order the child to be returned to the parent or lawful custodian from whom the child was concealed, detained or removed. In addition to any sentence imposed, the court may assess any reasonable expense incurred in searching for or returning the child against any person convicted of violating this Section.

(f) Nothing contained in this Section shall be construed to limit the court's contempt power.

(g) Every law enforcement officer investigating an alleged incident of child abduction shall make a written police report of any bona fide allegation and the disposition of such investigation. Every police report completed pursuant to this Section shall be compiled and recorded within the meaning of Section 5.1 of "An Act in relation to criminal identification and investigation", approved July 2, 1931, as now or hereafter amended.

(h) Whenever a law enforcement officer has reasons to believe a child abduction has occurred, he shall provide the lawful custodian a summary of her or his rights under this Act, including the procedures and relief available to her or him.

(i) If during the course of an investigation under this Section the child is found in the physical custody of the defendant or another, the law enforcement officer shall return the child to the parent or lawful custodian from whom the child was concealed, detained or removed, unless there is good cause for the law enforcement officer or the Department of Children and Family Services to retain temporary protective custody of the child pursuant to the Abused and Neglected Child Reporting Act, as now or hereafter amended.

720 ILCS 5/10–5.5

§ 10–5.5 Unlawful visitation interference

(a) As used in this Section, the terms "child", "detain", and "lawful custodian" shall have the meanings ascribed to them in Section 10–5 of this Code.

(b) Every person who, in violation of the visitation provisions of a court order relating to child custody, detains or conceals a child with the intent to deprive another person of his or her rights to visitation shall be guilty of unlawful visitation interference.

(c) A person committing unlawful visitation interference is guilty of a petty offense. However, any person violating this Section after 2 prior convictions of unlawful visitation interference is guilty of a Class A misdemeanor.

(d) Any law enforcement officer who has probable cause to believe that a person has committed or is committing an act in violation of this Section shall issue to that person a notice to appear.

(e) The notice shall:

(1) be in writing;

(2) state the name of the person and his address, if known;

(3) set forth the nature of the offense;

(4) be signed by the officer issuing the notice; and

(5) request the person to appear before a court at a certain time and place.

(f) Upon failure of the person to appear, a summons or warrant of arrest may be issued.

(g) It is an affirmative defense that:

(1) a person or lawful custodian committed the act to protect the child from imminent physical harm, provided that the defendant's belief that there was physical harm imminent was reasonable and that the defendant's conduct in withholding visitation rights was a reasonable response to the harm believed imminent;

(2) the act was committed with the mutual consent of all parties having a right to custody and visitation of the child; or

(3) the act was otherwise authorized by law.

(h) A person convicted of unlawful visitation interference shall not be subject to a civil contempt citation for the same conduct for violating visitation provisions of a court order issued under the Illinois Marriage and Dissolution of Marriage Act.

720 ILCS 5/10-6

§ 10-6. Harboring a runaway

(a) Any person, other than an agency or association providing crisis intervention services as defined in Section 3-5 of the Juvenile Court Act of 1987, or an operator of a youth emergency shelter as defined in Section 2.21 of the Child Care Act of 1969, who, without the knowledge and consent of the minor's parent or guardian, knowingly gives shelter to a minor, other than a mature minor who has been emancipated under the Emancipation of Mature Minors Act, for more than 48 hours without the consent of the minor's parent or guardian, and without notifying the local law enforcement authorities of the minor's name and the fact that the minor is being provided shelter commits the offense of harboring a runaway.

(b) Any person who commits the offense of harboring a runaway is guilty of a Class A misdemeanor.

720 ILCS 5/10-7

§ 10-7. Aiding and abetting child abduction

(a) A person violates this Section when:

(i) Before or during the commission of a child abduction as defined in Section 10-5 and with the intent to promote or facilitate such offense, he or she intentionally aids or abets another in the planning or commission of child abduction, unless before the commission of the offense he or she makes proper effort to prevent the commission of the offense; or

(ii) With the intent to prevent the apprehension of a person known to have committed the offense of child abduction, or with the intent to obstruct or prevent efforts to locate the child victim of a child abduction, he or she knowingly destroys, alters, conceals or disguises physical evidence or furnishes false information.

(b) Sentence. A person who violates this Section commits a Class 4 felony.

ACT 525. ADOPTION COMPENSATION PROHIBITION ACT

Analysis

Sec.
0.01 Short title.
1. Receipt of compensation for placing out prohibited; Exception.
2. Payment of compensation for placing out prohibited; Exception.
3. "Placing out" defined.
4. Certain payments of salaries and medical expenses not prevented.
5. Violations.

WESTLAW Electronic Research

See WESTLAW Electronic Research Guide preceding the Summary of Contents.

---

720 ILCS 525/0.01

§ 0.01. Short title

This Act may be cited as the Adoption Compensation Prohibition Act.

720 ILCS 525/1

§ 1. Receipt of compensation for placing out prohibited; Exception

No person and no agency, association, corporation, institution, society, or other organization, except a child welfare agency as defined by the Child Care Act of 1969, as now or hereafter amended, shall request, receive or accept any compensation or thing of value, directly or indirectly, for placing out of a child.

720 ILCS 525/2

§ 2. Payment of compensation for placing out prohibited; Exception

No person shall pay or give any compensation or thing of value, directly or indirectly, for placing out of a child to any person or to any agency, association, corporation, institution, society, or other organization except a child welfare agency as defined by the Child Care Act of 1969, as now or hereafter amended.

720 ILCS 525/3

§ 3. "Placing out" defined

As used in this Act the term "placing out" means to arrange for the free care of a child in a family other than that of the child's parent, stepparent, grandparent, brother, sister, uncle or aunt or legal guardian, for the purpose of adoption or for the purpose of providing care.

720 ILCS 525/4

§ 4. Certain payments of salaries and medical expenses not prevented

The provisions of this Act shall not be construed to prevent the payment of salaries or other compensation by a licensed child welfare agency, as that term is defined by the Child Care Act of 1969, as now or hereafter amended, to the officers or employees thereof; nor shall it be construed to prevent the payment by a person with whom a child has been placed out of reasonable and actual medical fees or hospital charges for services rendered in connection with the birth of such child, if such payment is made to the physician or hospital who or which rendered the services or to the natural mother of the child or to prevent the receipt of such payment by such physician, hospital, or mother.

720 ILCS 525/5

§ 5. Violations

Any person, agency, association, corporation, institution, society, or other organization violating the provisions of this Section shall be guilty of illegal placement of children and upon first conviction for an offense under this Act shall be guilty of a Class 4 felony; and upon conviction for any subsequent offense under this Act shall be guilty of a Class 3 felony.

DIVISION B. CIVIL LIABILITIES

CHAPTER 740
CIVIL LIABILITIES

ACT 5. ALIENATION OF AFFECTIONS ACT

Analysis

Sec.
0.01 Short title.
1. Declaration of public policy.
2. Actual damages, only, recoverable.
3. Punitive, exemplary, vindictive or aggravated damages not recoverable.
4. Elements not to be considered in determining damages.
5. Application of Act.
6. Criminal laws not affected.
7. Liberal construction; Partial invalidity.

WESTLAW Electronic Research

See WESTLAW Electronic Research Guide preceding the Summary of Contents.

---

740 ILCS 5/0.01

§ 0.01 Short title

This Act may be cited as the Alienation of Affections Act.

740 ILCS 5/1

§ 1. Declaration of public policy

It is hereby declared, as a matter of legislative determination, that the remedy heretofore provided by law for the enforcement of the action for alienation of affections has been subjected to grave abuses and has been used as an instrument for blackmail by unscrupulous persons for their unjust enrichment, due to the indefiniteness of the damages recoverable in such actions and the consequent fear of persons threatened with such actions that exorbitant damages might be assessed against them. It is also hereby declared that the award of monetary damages in such actions is ineffective as a recompense for genuine mental or emotional distress. Accordingly, it is hereby declared as the public policy of the state that the best interests of the people of the state will be served by limiting the damages recoverable in such actions and by leaving any punishment of wrongdoers guilty of alienation of affections to proceedings under the criminal laws of the state, rather than to the imposition of punitive, exemplary, vindictive, or aggravated damages in actions for alienation of affections. Consequently, in the public interest, the necessity for the enactment of this chapter is hereby declared as a matter of legislative determination.

740 ILCS 5/2

§ 2. Actual damages, only, recoverable

The damages to be recovered in any action for alienation of affections shall be limited to the actual damages sustained as a result of the injury complained of.

740 ILCS 5/3

§ 3. Punitive, exemplary, vindictive or aggravated damages not recoverable

No punitive, exemplary, vindictive or aggravated damages shall be allowed in any action for alienation of affections.

740 ILCS 5/4

§ 4. Elements not to be considered in determining damages

In determining the damages to be allowed in any action for alienation of affections, none of the following elements shall be considered: the wealth or position of defendant or the defendant's prospects of wealth or position; mental anguish suffered by plaintiff; any injury to plaintiff's feelings; shame, humiliation, sorrow or mortification suffered by plaintiff; defamation or injury to the good name or character of plaintiff or his or her spouse resulting from the alienation of affections complained of; or dishonor to plaintiff's family resulting from the alienation of affections.

740 ILCS 5/5

§ 5. Application of Act

This Act shall apply to all actions for alienation of affections begun after the effective date of this Act, even though the alleged alienations of affections on which the action is based occurred prior to such effective date.

740 ILCS 5/6

§ 6. Criminal laws not affected

Nothing herein contained shall be deemed to repeal or amend any provisions of the criminal laws of this state.

740 ILCS 5/7

§ 7. Liberal construction; Partial invalidity

This Act shall be liberally construed to effectuate the objects and purposes thereof and the public policy as herein declared. If any section, clause, sentence, paragraph or part of this Act shall for any reason be adjudged by any court of competent jurisdiction to be invalid, such judgment shall not affect, impair or invalidate the remainder thereof, but shall be confined in its operation to the section, clause, sentence, paragraph or part thereof directly involved in the controversy in which such judgment shall have been rendered. If the application of this act, or any part thereof, to any person or circumstance shall be adjudged by such court to be invalid or ineffectual for any reason, such judgment shall not affect the application of this act, or part thereof, to any other person or circumstance.

Author's Notes

Analysis

1. Action not favored.
2. Cross reference.

(1) **Action not favored.** Because of the legislative declaration that alienation of affection actions are not favored, and because of the severe limitation on damages that can be recovered, successful alienation of affections actions are currently rare to almost non-existent. See, e.g., Wheeler v. Fox, 16 Ill.App.3d 1089, 307 N.E.2d 633 (4th Dist.1974) (reversing jury verdict awarding husband damages for alienation of wife's affections; husband did not prove that the wife and husband loved each other, that he suffered actual damages, or that the defendant was the blamable party).

(2) **Cross reference.** See 740 ILCS 15/10 Author's Note (1) for breach of promise, 750 ILCS 65/1 Author's Notes (1) and (2) for interspousal torts, and 750 ILCS 5/502 Author's Note (11) para. 11(e) for mutual waiver of tort actions in a settlement agreement.

ACT 15. BREACH OF PROMISE ACT

Analysis

Sec.
0.01 Short title.
1. Legislative declaration of necessity.
2. Actual damages only recoverable.
3. Punitive, exemplary, vindictive or aggravated damages not recoverable.
4. Notice required before bringing action for breach of promise.
5. Action barred unless notice is given.
6. Limitations.
7. Retroactive effect.
8. Criminal laws not affected.
9. Liberal construction; Partial invalidity.
10. Effective date.

WESTLAW Electronic Research

See WESTLAW Electronic Research Guide preceding the Summary of Contents.

740 ILCS 15/0.01

§ 0.01. Short title

This Act may be cited as the Breach of Promise Act.

740 ILCS 15/1

§ 1. Legislative declaration of necessity

It is hereby declared, as a matter of legislative determination, that the remedy heretofore provided by law for the enforcement of actions based upon breaches of promises or agreements to marry has been subject to grave abuses and has been used as an instrument for blackmail by unscrupulous persons for their unjust enrichment, due to the indefiniteness of the damages recoverable in such actions and the consequent fear of persons threatened with such actions that exorbitant damages might be assessed against them. It is also hereby declared that the award of monetary damages in such actions is ineffective as a recompense for genuine mental or emotional distress. Accordingly, it is hereby declared as the public policy of the state that the best interests of the people of the state will be served by limiting the damages recoverable in such actions, and by leaving any punishments of wrongdoers guilty of seduction to proceedings under the criminal laws of the state, rather than to the imposition of punitive, exemplary, vindictive or aggravated damages in actions for breach of promise or agreement to marry. Consequently, in the public interest, the necessity for the enactment of this chapter is hereby declared as a matter of legislative determination.

740 ILCS 15/2

§ 2. Actual damages only recoverable

The damages to be recovered in any action for breach of promise or agreement to marry shall be limited to the actual damages sustained as a result of the injury complained of.

740 ILCS 15/3

§ 3. Punitive, exemplary, vindictive or aggravated damages not recoverable

No punitive, exemplary, vindictive or aggravated damages shall be allowed in any action for breach of promise or agreement to marry.

740 ILCS 15/4

§ 4. Notice required before bringing action for breach of promise

Within three months from the date that the breach of promise or agreement to marry occurred, unless such breach occurred prior to the effective date of the act, any person who is about to commence any civil action in any court for breach of promise or agreement to marry shall give to the person against whom said action is to be brought, or send in a sealed envelope with first class postage prepaid and deposited in the United States mail to such person at his or her last known address, notice in writing, signed by the person who is about to commence said action, giving the date upon which the promise or agreement to marry was made, and the date upon which the marriage ceremony was to have been performed, stating the damages suffered by the person signing said notice and stating whether the person signing said notice is or is not still willing to marry the person to whom the statement is given. If the breach occurred prior to the effective date of this Act the notice herein required shall be served within three months after such effective date.

740 ILCS 15/5
§ 5. Action barred unless notice is given

If the notice provided for by Section 4 is not given as provided in that section, any such civil action for breach of promise or agreement to marry shall be dismissed and the person to whom any such cause of action accrued shall be forever barred from further suing.

740 ILCS 15/6
§ 6. Limitations

Actions on promises or agreements to marry shall be commenced within one year next after the cause of action accrued.

740 ILCS 15/7
§ 7. Retroactive effect

This Act shall apply to all actions for breach of promise or agreement to marry begun after the effective date of this act, even though the alleged breach of promise or agreement to marry on which the action is based occurred prior to such effective date.

740 ILCS 15/8
§ 8. Criminal laws not affected

Nothing herein contained shall be deemed to repeal or amend any provisions of the criminal laws of this state.

740 ILCS 15/9
§ 9. Liberal construction; Partial invalidity

This Act shall be liberally construed to effectuate the objects and purposes thereof and the public policy as herein declared. If any section, clause, sentence, paragraph or part of this Act shall for any reason be adjudged by any court of competent jurisdiction to be invalid, such judgment shall not affect, impair or invalidate the remainder thereof, but shall be confined in its operation to the section, clause, sentence, paragraph or part thereof directly involved in the controversy in which such judgment shall have been rendered. If the application of this act, or any part thereof, to any person or circumstance shall be adjudged by such court to be invalid or ineffectual for any

740 ILCS 15/9   CIVIL LIABILITIES

reason, such judgment shall not affect the application of this act, or part thereof, to any other person or circumstance.

740 ILCS 15/10

§ 10. Effective date

This Act shall become effective on January 1, 1948.

Author's Notes

(1) **Action not favored.** The legislative policy against breach of promise actions is the same as that against alienation of affection actions, and breach of promise actions are likewise rare to almost non-existent. See 740 ILCS 5/7 Author's Notes (1) and (2).

ACT 110. MENTAL HEALTH AND DEVELOPMENTAL DISABILITIES CONFIDENTIALITY ACT

Analysis

Sec.
1. Short title.
2. Definitions.
3. Records and communications—Personal notes of therapist—Psychological test material.
4. Persons entitled to inspect and copy recipient's record.
5. Written consent for disclosure of records and communications.
6. Information used in application for benefits—Disclosure without consent.
7. Review of therapist or agency; Use of recipient's record.
7.1 Interagency disclosures.
8. Regional human rights authority—Consent to inspect or copy recipient's records during investigations.
8.1 Access to records of developmentally disabled residing in facilities.
9. Disclosure by therapist without consent.
9.1 Disclosure without consent.
9.2. Interagency disclosure of recipient information.
10. Civil, criminal, administrative, or legislative proceedings.
11. Disclosure of records and communications.
12. Information to be furnished to United States Secret Service and Department of State Police.
12.1. Report of violation or incident—Investigation.
12.2 Recipients on unauthorized absence—Disclosure of identifying information.
12.3 Notice of discharge.
13. Disclosure without consent.
14. Agreement to waive Act—Void.
15. Actions by aggrieved parties for violation of Act—Fees and costs.
16. Violations—Penalty.
17. Rules and regulations.

WESTLAW Electronic Research

See WESTLAW Electronic Research Guide preceding the Summary of Contents.

740 ILCS 110/1

§ 1. Short title

This Act shall be known and may be cited as the "Mental Health and Developmental Disabilities Confidentiality Act".

Author's Notes

Analysis

1. Citation.
2. Purpose.

(1) **Citation.** The Mental Health and Developmental Disabilities Confidentiality Act is sometimes cited herein by its acronym "MHDDCA" or as the "Confidentiality Act."

(2) **Purpose.** The Confidentiality Act, enacted in 1979, addresses the conflict between encouraging individuals to seek treatment and obtaining necessary information in judicial proceedings.

> The statutory privilege is a legislative balancing between relationships which society thinks should be fostered through the shield of confidentiality and the interests served by disclosure of the information in court. The legislature has determined that except for limited purposes, there is more value to encouraging and sustaining this kind of relationship.... The beneficent purposes of psychiatry can only be fully realized when the patient knows that what is revealed in the evaluation conferences or communications are free from judicial scrutiny unless the patient affirmatively places her mental condition in issue.

In re Marriage of Lombaer, 200 Ill.App.3d 712, 722, 146 Ill.Dec. 425, 430–31, 558 N.E.2d 388, 393–94 (1st Dist.1990) (citations omitted). The circumstances where the need for information prevails over the interest of confidentiality are very limited. The Confidentiality Act should be interpreted in light of the judgment that people must feel protected and encouraged in their efforts to get help for mental conditions, and that in the long run everyone benefits from this assurance of confidentiality.

740 ILCS 110/2

§ 2. Definitions

The terms used in this Act, unless the context requires otherwise, have the meanings ascribed to them in this Section.

"Agent" means a person who has been legally appointed as an individual's agent under a power of attorney for health care or for property.

"Confidential communication" or "communication" means any communication made by a recipient or other person to a therapist or to or in the presence of other persons during or in connection with providing mental health or developmental disability services to a recipient. Communication includes information which indicates that a person is a recipient.

"Guardian" means a legally appointed guardian or conservator of the person.

"Mental health or developmental disabilities services" or "services" includes but is not limited to examination, diagnosis, evaluation, treatment, training, pharmaceuticals, aftercare, habilitation or rehabilitation.

"Personal notes" means:

(i) information disclosed to the therapist in confidence by other persons on condition that such information would never be disclosed to the recipient or other persons;

(ii) information disclosed to the therapist by the recipient which would be injurious to the recipient's relationships to other persons, and

(iii) the therapist's speculations, impressions, hunches, and reminders.

"Parent" means a parent or, in the absence of a parent or guardian, a person in loco parentis.

"Recipient" means a person who is receiving or has received mental health or developmental disabilities services.

"Record" means any record kept by a therapist or by an agency in the course of providing mental health or developmental disabilities service to a recipient concerning the recipient and the services provided. Record does not include the therapist's personal notes, if such notes are kept in the therapist's sole possession for his own personal use and are not disclosed to any other person, except the therapist's supervisor, consulting therapist or attorney. If at any time such notes are disclosed, they shall be considered part of the recipient's record for purposes of this Act.

"Record custodian" means a person responsible for maintaining a recipient's record.

"Therapist" means a psychiatrist, physician, psychologist, social worker, or nurse providing mental health or developmental disabilities services or any other person not prohibited by law from providing such services or from holding himself out as a therapist if the recipient reasonably believes that such person is permitted to do so. Therapist includes any successor of the therapist.

740 ILCS 110/3

§ 3. Records and communications—Personal notes of therapist—Psychological test material

(a) All records and communications shall be confidential and shall not be disclosed except as provided in this Act.

(b) A therapist is not required to but may, to the extent he determines it necessary and appropriate, keep personal notes regarding a recipient. Such personal notes are the work product and personal property of the therapist and shall not be subject to discovery in any judicial, administrative or legislative proceeding or any proceeding preliminary thereto.

(c) Psychological test material whose disclosure would compromise the objectivity or fairness of the testing process may not be disclosed to anyone including the subject of the test and is not subject to disclosure in any administrative, judicial or legislative proceeding. However, any recipient who has been the subject of the psychological test shall have the right to have all records relating to that test disclosed to any psychologist designated by the recipient. Requests for such disclosure shall be in writing and shall comply with the requirements of subsection (b) of Section 5 of this Act.

Author's Notes

(1) **Personal notes.** A therapist's records and communications are distinguished in § 2 of the Confidentiality Act from his or her personal notes. Under § 3(b), personal notes need never be disclosed if the therapist keeps the notes separate and uses them only to consult with the therapist's professional supervisor or attorney.

740 ILCS 110/4

§ 4. Persons entitled to inspect and copy recipient's record

(a) The following persons shall be entitled, upon request, to inspect and copy a recipient's record or any part thereof:

(1) the parent or guardian of a recipient who is under 12 years of age;

(2) the recipient if he is 12 years of age or older;

(3) the parent or guardian of a recipient who is at least 12 but under 18 years, if the recipient is informed and does not object or if the therapist does not find that there are compelling reasons for denying the access. The parent or guardian who is denied access by either the recipient or the therapist may petition a court for access to the record;

(4) the guardian of a recipient who is 18 years or older;

(5) an attorney or guardian ad litem who represents a minor 12 years of age or older in any judicial or administrative proceeding, provided that the court or administrative hearing officer has entered an order granting the attorney this right; or

(6) an agent appointed under a recipient's power of attorney for health care or for property, when the power of attorney authorizes the access.

(b) Assistance in interpreting the record may be provided without charge and shall be provided if the person inspecting the record is under 18 years of age. However, access may in no way be denied or limited if the person inspecting the record refuses the assistance. A reasonable fee may be charged for duplication of a record. However, when requested to do so in writing by any indigent recipient, the custodian of the records shall provide at no charge to the recipient, or to the Guardianship and Advocacy Commission, the agency designated by the Governor under Section 1 of the protection and advocacy for Developmentally Disabled Persons Act or to any other not-for-profit agency whose primary purpose is to provide free legal services or advocacy for the indigent and who has received written authorization from the recipient under Section 5 of this Act to receive his records, one copy of any records in its possession whose disclosure is authorized under this Act.

(c) Any person entitled to access to a record under this Section may submit a written statement concerning any disputed or new information, which statement shall be entered into the record. Whenever any disputed part of a record is disclosed, any submitted statement relating thereto shall accompany the disclosed part. Additionally, any person entitled to access may request modification of any part of the record which he believes is incorrect or misleading. If the request is refused, the person may seek a court order to compel modification.

(d) Whenever access or modification is requested, the request and any action taken thereon shall be noted in the recipient's record.

Author's Notes

(1) **Access to child's records.** Under the Illinois Marriage and Dissolution of Marriage Act, the consent of a child over the age of 16 is necessary to release records from the child's therapist to the custody investigator. See 750 ILCS 5/605(b). However, § 4(a)(2) of the Confidentiality Act allows a 12 year old to see and copy such records, and presumably consent to their release.

Either parent's consent to access to a child's mental health records is sufficient. Furthermore, the fact that the parent requesting access is not the custodial parent "is not relevant to the issue" of access. See In re Marriage of Markey, 223 Ill.App.3d 1055, 166 Ill.Dec. 392, 586 N.E.2d 350 (1st Dist.1991) (the use of the word "parent" rather than "parents" in MHDDCA § 4(a)(1) allows either parent to consent to disclosure, without regard to which one of the parents may have legal custody of the child).

740 ILCS 110/5

§ 5. Written consent for disclosure of records and communications

(a) Except as provided in Sections 6 through 12.2 of this Act, records and communications may be disclosed to someone other than those persons listed in Section 4 of this Act only with the written consent of those persons who are entitled to inspect and copy a recipient's record pursuant to Section 4 of this Act.

(b) Every consent form shall be in writing and shall specify the following:

    (1) the person or agency to whom disclosure is to be made;

    (2) the purpose for which disclosure is to be made;

    (3) the nature of the information to be disclosed;

    (4) the right to inspect and copy the information to be disclosed;

    (5) the consequences of a refusal to consent, if any; and

(6) the calendar date on which the consent expires, provided that if no calendar date is stated, information may be released only on the day the consent form is received by the therapist; and

(7) the right to revoke the consent at any time.

The consent form shall be signed by the person entitled to give consent and the signature shall be witnessed by a person who can attest to the identity of the person so entitled. A copy of the consent and a notation as to any action taken thereon shall be entered in the recipient's record. Any revocation of consent shall be in writing, signed by the person who gave the consent and the signature shall be witnessed by a person who can attest to the identity of the person so entitled. No written revocation of consent shall be effective to prevent disclosure of records and communications until it is received by the person otherwise authorized to disclose records and communications.

(c) Only information relevant to the purpose for which disclosure is sought may be disclosed. Blanket consent to the disclosure of unspecified information shall not be valid. Advance consent may be valid only if the nature of the information to be disclosed is specified in detail and the duration of the consent is indicated. Consent may be revoked in writing at any time; any such revocation shall have no effect on disclosures made prior thereto.

(d) No person or agency to whom any information is disclosed under this Section may redisclose such information unless the person who consented to the disclosure specifically consents to such redisclosure.

(e) Except as otherwise provided in this Act, records and communications shall remain confidential after the death of a recipient and shall not be disclosed unless the recipient's representative, as defined in the Probate Act of 1975 and the therapist consent to such disclosure or unless disclosure is authorized by court order after in camera examination and upon good cause shown.

(f) Paragraphs (a) through (e) of this Section shall not apply to and shall not be construed to limit insurance companies writing Life, Accident or Health insurance as defined in Section 4 of the Illinois Insurance Code, and Non-Profit Health Care Service Plan Corporations, writing Health Care Service contracts, under The Non-profit Health Care Service Plan Act, in obtaining general consents for the release to them or their designated representatives of any and all confidential communications and records kept by agencies, hospitals, therapists or record custodians, and utilizing such information in connection with the underwriting of applications for coverage for such policies or contracts, or in connection with evaluating claims or liability under such policies or contracts, or coordinating benefits pursuant to policy or contract provisions.

Author's Notes

(1) **Consent to disclosure of confidential records and communications.** A party may consent to release information that would otherwise be confidential. Under

740 ILCS 110/5   CIVIL LIABILITIES

Confidentiality Act § 5, consent must be in writing and explicitly state what is to be released, to whom, and why. Consent is revocable at any time. A party may also waive his or her privilege of confidentiality. For example, a party may waive the privilege by placing his or her mental health at issue. See MHDDCA § 10(a).

740 ILCS 110/6

§ 6. Information used in application for benefits—Disclosure without consent

Such information from a recipient's record as is necessary to enable him to apply for or receive benefits may be disclosed with consent obtained pursuant to Section 5 of this Act. Disclosure may be made without consent when despite every reasonable effort it is not possible to obtain consent because the person entitled to give consent is not capable of consenting or is not available to do so. The recipient shall be informed of any disclosure made without consent. The information disclosed without consent under this Section may include only the identity of the recipient and therapist and a description of the nature, purpose, quantity, and date of the services provided. Any request for additional information shall state with particularity what further information is needed and the reasons therefor. Refusal to consent to the disclosure of more information than is necessary to apply for or receive direct benefits shall not be grounds for in any way denying, limiting, or cancelling such benefits or refusing to accept an application or renew such benefits. Such information shall not be redisclosed except with the consent of the person entitled to give consent.

740 ILCS 110/7

§ 7. Review of therapist or agency; Use of recipient's record

(a) When a therapist or agency which provides services is being reviewed for purposes of licensure, statistical compilation, research, evaluation, or other similar purpose, a recipient's record may be used by the person conducting the review to the extent that this is necessary to accomplish the purpose of the review, provided that personally identifiable data is removed from the record before use. Personally identifiable data may be disclosed only with the consent obtained under Section 5 of this Act. Licensure and the like may not be withheld or withdrawn for failure to disclose personally identifiable data if consent is not obtained.

(b) When an agency which provides services is being reviewed for purposes of funding, accreditation, reimbursement or audit by a State or federal agency or accrediting body, a recipient's record may be used by the person conducting the review and personally identifiable information may be disclosed without consent, provided that the personally identifiable information is necessary to accomplish the purpose of the review.

For the purpose of this subsection, an inspection investigation or site visit by the United States Department of Justice regarding compliance with a pending consent decree is considered an audit by a federal agency.

(c) The Mental Health and Developmental Disabilities Medical Review Board shall be entitled to inspect and copy the records of any recipient. Information disclosed under this subsection may not be redisclosed without the written consent of one of the persons identified in Section 4 of this Act.

740 ILCS 110/7.1
§ 7.1 Interagency disclosures

(a) Nothing in this Act shall be construed to prevent the interagency disclosure of the name, social security number, and information concerning services rendered, currently being rendered, or proposed to be rendered regarding a recipient of services. This disclosure may be made only between agencies or departments of the State including, but not limited to: (i) the Department of Mental Health and Developmental Disabilities, (ii) the Department of Public Aid, (iii) the Department of Public Health, (iv) the Department of Rehabilitation Services, (v) the Department of Alcoholism and Substance Abuse, and (vi) the State Board of Education, when one or more agencies or departments of the State have entered into a prior interagency agreement, memorandum of understanding, or similar agreement to jointly provide or cooperate in the provision of or funding of mental health or developmental disabilities services.

(b) This Section applies to, but is not limited to, interagency disclosures under interagency agreements entered into in compliance with the Early Intervention Services System Act.

(c) Information disclosed under this Section shall be for the limited purpose of coordinating State efforts in providing efficient interagency service systems and avoiding duplication of interagency services.

(d) Information disclosed under this Section shall be limited to the recipient's name, address, social security number or other individually assigned identifying number, or information generally descriptive of services rendered or to be rendered. The disclosure of individual clinical or treatment records or other confidential information is not authorized by this Section.

740 ILCS 110/8
§ 8. Regional human rights authority—Consent to inspect or copy recipient's records during investigations

In the course of an investigation, or in the course of monitoring issues concerning the rights of recipients or the services provided to recipients as authorized by subsection (l) of Section 5 of the Guardianship and Advocacy Act, a regional human rights authority of the Guardianship and Advocacy Commission created by the Guardianship and Advocacy Act may inspect and copy any recipient's records in the possession of a therapist, agency, Department or facility which provides services to a recipient, including reports of suspected abuse or neglect of a recipient and information regarding the disposition of such reports. However, a regional authority may not inspect or copy records containing personally identifiable data which cannot be removed without imposing an unreasonable burden on the therapist, agency, Department or facility which provides services, except as provided herein. The regional authority shall give written notice to the person entitled to give consent for the identifiable recipient of services under Section 4 that it is conducting an investigation or monitoring and indicating the nature and purpose of the investigation or monitoring and the need to inspect and copy the recipient's record. If the person notified objects in writing to such inspection and copying, the regional authority may not inspect or copy the record. The therapist, agency, Department or facility which provides services may not object on behalf of a recipient.

740 ILCS 110/8.1

§ 8.1 Access to records of developmentally disabled residing in facilities

The agency designated by the Governor under Section 1 of "An Act in relation to the protection and advocacy of the rights of persons with developmental disabilities, and amending Acts therein named", approved September 20, 1985, as now or hereafter amended, shall have access, for the purpose of inspection and copying, to the records of a person with developmental disabilities who resides in a developmental disability facility or mental health facility, as defined in Sections 1-107 and 1-114, respectively, of the Mental Health and Developmental Disabilities Code, as now or hereafter amended, if (a) a complaint is received by such agency from or on behalf of the person with a developmental disability, and (b) such person does not have a guardian of the person or the State or the designee of the State is his or her guardian of the person. The designated agency shall provide written notice of the receipt of a complaint to the custodian of the records of the person from whom or on whose behalf a complaint is received. The designated agency shall provide to the person with developmental disabilities and to his or her State guardian, if appointed, written notice of the nature of the complaint based upon which the designated agency has gained access to the records. No record or the contents of any record shall be redisclosed by the designated agency unless the person with developmental disabilities and the State guardian are provided 7 days advance written notice, except in emergency situations, of the designated agency's intent to redisclose such record, during which time the person with developmental disabilities or the State guardian may seek to judicially enjoin the designated agency's redisclosure of such record on the grounds that such redisclosure is contrary to the interests of the person with developmental disabilities. If a person with developmental disabilities resides in a developmental disability or mental health facility and has a guardian other than the State or the designee of the State, the facility director shall disclose the guardian's name, address and telephone number to the designated agency at the agency's request.

Upon written request and after the provision of written notice to the agency, facility or other body from which records and other materials are sought of the designated agency's investigation of problems affecting numbers of persons with developmental disabilities, the designated agency shall be entitled to inspect and copy any records or other materials which may further the agency's investigation of problems affecting numbers of persons with developmental disabilities. When required by law any personally identifiable information of persons with developmental disabilities shall be removed from the records. However, the designated agency may not inspect or copy records or other materials when the removal of personally identifiable information imposes an unreasonable burden on mental health and developmental disabilities facilities.

For the purposes of this Section, "developmental disability" means a severe, chronic disability of a person which—

(A) is attributable to a mental or physical impairment or combination of mental and physical impairments;

(B) is manifested before the person attains age 22;

(C) is likely to continue indefinitely;

(D) results in substantial functional limitations in 3 or more of the following areas of major life activity: (i) self-care, (ii) receptive and expressive language, (iii) learning, (iv) mobility, (v) self-direction, (vi) capacity for independent living, and (vii) economic self-sufficiency; and

(E) reflects the person's need for a combination and sequence of special, interdisciplinary or generic care, treatment or other services which are of lifelong or extended duration and are individually planned and coordinated.

740 ILCS 110/9

§ 9. Disclosure by therapist without consent

In the course of providing services and after the conclusion of the provision of services, a therapist may disclose a record or communications without consent to:

(1) the therapist's supervisor, a consulting therapist, members of a staff team participating in the provision of services, a record custodian, or a person acting under the supervision and control of the therapist;

(2) persons conducting a peer review of the services being provided;

(3) the Institute for Juvenile Research and the Institute for the Study of Developmental Disabilities; and

(4) an attorney or advocate consulted by a therapist or agency which provides services concerning the therapist's or agency's legal rights or duties in relation to the recipient and the services being provided.

In the course of providing services, a therapist may disclose a record or communications without consent to any department, agency, institution or facility which has custody of the recipient pursuant to State statute or any court order of commitment.

740 ILCS 110/9   CIVIL LIABILITIES

Information may be disclosed under this Section only to the extent that knowledge of the record or communications is essential to the purpose for which disclosure is made and only after the recipient is informed that such disclosure may be made. A person to whom disclosure is made under this Section shall not redisclose any information except as provided in this Act.

740 ILCS 110/9.1

§ 9.1 Disclosure without consent

The Department of Mental Health and Developmental Disabilities, and other agencies and institutions which provide services, may disclose a recipient's record or communications, without consent, to the Institute for Juvenile Research and the Institute for the Study of Developmental Disabilities for purposes of research, education and treatment. The Institutes shall not redisclose any personally identifiable information, unless necessary for treatment of the identified recipient.

740 ILCS 110/9.2

§ 9.2 Interagency disclosure of recipient information

For the purposes of continuity of care, the Department of Mental Health and Developmental Disabilities and community agencies funded by the Department of Mental Health and Developmental Disabilities may disclose a recipient's record or communications, without consent, to each other, but only for the purpose of admission, treatment, planning, or discharge. Entities shall not redisclose any personally identifiable information, unless necessary for admission, treatment, planning, or discharge of the identified recipient to another setting.

740 ILCS 110/10

§ 10. Civil, criminal, administrative, or legislative proceedings

(a) Except as provided herein, in any civil, criminal, administrative, or legislative proceeding, or in any proceeding preliminary thereto, a recipient, and a therapist on behalf and in the interest of a recipient, has the privilege to refuse to disclose and to prevent the disclosure of the recipient's record or communications.

    (1) Records and communications may be disclosed in a civil, criminal or administrative proceeding in which the recipient introduces his mental condition or any aspect of his services received for such condition as an element of his claim or defense, if and only to the extent the court in which the proceedings have been brought, or, in the case of an administrative proceeding, the court to which an appeal or other action for review of an administrative determination may be taken, finds, after in camera examination of testimony or other evidence, that it is relevant, probative, not unduly prejudicial or inflammatory, and otherwise clearly admissible; that other satisfactory evidence is demonstrably unsatisfactory as evidence of the facts sought to be established by such evidence; and that

disclosure is more important to the interests of substantial justice than protection from injury to the therapist-recipient relationship or to the recipient or other whom disclosure is likely to harm. Except in a criminal proceeding in which the recipient, who is accused in that proceeding, raises the defense of insanity, no record or communication between a therapist and a recipient shall be deemed relevant for purposes of this subsection, except the fact of treatment, the cost of services and the ultimate diagnosis unless the party seeking disclosure of the communication clearly establishes in the trial court a compelling need for its production. However, for purposes of this Act, in any action brought or defended under the Illinois Marriage and Dissolution of Marriage Act, or in any action in which pain and suffering is an element of the claim, mental condition shall not be deemed to be introduced merely by making such claim and shall be deemed to be introduced only if the recipient or a witness on his behalf first testifies concerning the record or communication.

(2) Records or communications may be disclosed in a civil proceeding after the recipient's death when the recipient's physical or mental condition has been introduced as an element of a claim or defense by any party claiming or defending through or as a beneficiary of the recipient, provided the court finds, after in camera examination of the evidence, that it is relevant, probative, and otherwise clearly admissible; that other satisfactory evidence is not available regarding the facts sought to be established by such evidence; and that disclosure is more important to the interests of substantial justice than protection from any injury which disclosure is likely to cause.

(3) In the event of a claim made or an action filed by a recipient, or, following the recipient's death, by any party claiming as a beneficiary of the recipient for injury caused in the course of providing services to such recipient, the therapist and other persons whose actions are alleged to have been the cause of injury may disclose pertinent records and communications to an attorney or attorneys engaged to render advice about and to provide representation in connection with such matter and to persons working under the supervision of such attorney or attorneys, and may testify as to such records or communication in any administrative, judicial or discovery proceeding for the purpose of preparing and presenting a defense against such claim or action.

(4) Records and communications made to or by a therapist in the course of examination ordered by a court for good cause shown may, if otherwise relevant and admissible, be disclosed in a civil, criminal, or administrative proceeding in which the recipient is a party or in appropriate pretrial proceedings, provided such court has found that the recipient has been as adequately and as effectively as possible informed before submitting to such examination that such records and communications would not be considered confidential or privileged. Such records and communications shall be admissible only as to issues involving the

recipient's physical or mental condition and only to the extent that these are germane to such proceedings.

(5) Records and communications may be disclosed in a proceeding under the Probate Act of 1975, to determine a recipient's competency or need for guardianship, provided that the disclosure is made only with respect to that issue.

(6) Records and communications may be disclosed when such are made during treatment which the recipient is ordered to undergo to render him fit to stand trial on a criminal charge, provided that the disclosure is made only with respect to the issue of fitness to stand trial.

(7) Records and communications of the recipient may be disclosed in any civil or administrative proceeding involving the validity of or benefits under a life, accident, health or disability insurance policy or certificate, or Health Care Service Plan Contract, insuring the recipient, but only if and to the extent that the recipient's mental condition, or treatment or services in connection therewith, is a material element of any claim or defense of any party, provided that information sought or disclosed shall not be redisclosed except in connection with the proceeding in which disclosure is made.

(8) Records or communications may be disclosed when such are relevant to a matter in issue in any action brought under this Act and proceedings preliminary thereto, provided that any information so disclosed shall not be utilized for any other purpose nor be redisclosed except in connection with such action or preliminary proceedings.

(9) Records and communications of the recipient may be disclosed in investigations of and trials for homicide when the disclosure relates directly to the fact or immediate circumstances of the homicide.

(10) Records and communications of a deceased recipient may be disclosed to a coroner conducting a preliminary investigation into the recipient's death under Section 3–3013 of the Counties Code. However, records and communications of the deceased recipient disclosed in an investigation shall be limited solely to the deceased recipient's records and communications relating to the factual circumstances of the incident being investigated in a mental health facility.

(b) Before a disclosure is made under subsection (a), any party to the proceeding or any other interested person may request an in camera review of the record or communications to be disclosed. The court or agency conducting the proceeding may hold an in camera review on its own motion. When, contrary to the express wish of the recipient, the therapist asserts a privilege on behalf and in the interest of a recipient, the court may require that the therapist, in an in camera hearing, establish that disclosure is not in the best interest of the recipient. The court or agency may prevent disclosure or limit disclosure to the extent that other admissible evidence is sufficient to establish the facts in issue. The court or agency may enter such orders as may be necessary in order to protect the confidentiality, privacy, and safety of the recipient or of other persons. Any order to disclose or to not disclose shall be considered a final order for purposes of appeal and shall be subject to interlocutory appeal.

(c) A recipient's records and communications may be disclosed to a duly authorized committee, commission or subcommittee of the General Assembly which possesses subpoena and hearing powers, upon a written request approved by a majority vote of the committee, commission or subcommittee members. The committee, commission or subcommittee may request records only for the purposes of investigating or studying possible violations of recipient rights. The request shall state the purpose for which disclosure is sought.

The facility shall notify the recipient, or his guardian, and therapist in writing of any disclosure request under this subsection within 5 business days after such request. Such notification shall also inform the recipient, or guardian, and therapist of their right to object to the disclosure within 10 business days after receipt of the notification and shall include the name, address and telephone number of the committee, commission or subcommittee member or staff person with whom an objection shall be filed. If no objection has been filed within 15 business days after the request for disclosure, the facility shall disclose the records and communications to the committee, commission or subcommittee. If an objection has been filed within 15 business days after the request for disclosure, the facility shall disclose the records and communications only after the committee, commission or subcommittee has permitted the recipient, guardian or therapist to present his objection in person before it and has renewed its request for disclosure by a majority vote of its members.

Disclosure under this subsection shall not occur until all personally identifiable data of the recipient and provider are removed from the records and communications. Disclosure under this subsection shall not occur in any public proceeding.

(d) No party to any proceeding described under paragraphs (1), (2), (3), (4), (7), or (8) of subsection (a) of this Section, nor his or her attorney, shall serve a subpoena seeking to obtain access to records or communications under this Act unless the subpoena is accompanied by a written order issued by a judge, authorizing the disclosure of the records or the issuance of the subpoena. No person shall comply with a subpoena for records or communications under this Act, unless the subpoena is accompanied by a written order authorizing the issuance of the subpoena or the disclosure of the records.

Author's Notes

Analysis

1. Confidentiality: In general.
2. Confidentiality Act applied to family law actions.

3. *In camera* review.
4. Comparison: Physician-patient privilege.
5. Cross reference: Other applicable laws concerning privileged communications.

(1) **Confidentiality: In general.** Section 10 of the Confidentiality Act protects communications between a person and his or her therapist from disclosure to others. However, that protection is not absolute, and the rest of the Act must be reviewed to see if any exceptions apply, such as voluntary disclosure with consent pursuant to § 4 of the Act. See, e.g., Gottemoller v. Gottemoller, 37 Ill.App.3d 689, 346 N.E.2d 393 (3d Dist.1976) (wife waived privilege of confidentiality by authorizing her physician to release records of her treatment to her husband's attorney and therefore could not invoke it later at trial). Thus therapists' records and even the fact that a person may be undergoing therapy (see MHDDCA § 2), are not subject to subpoena, unless the judge orders the disclosure of records or the issuance of the subpoena. The mental health professional receiving a subpoena demanding disclosure of confidential communications or records must not comply unless it is accompanied by such an order. § 10(d). Furthermore, there may be grounds to quash or limit the subpoena even if the summons is correctly served with the necessary court order.

The court can and should limit disclosure and enter protective orders to preserve the privacy and safety of the recipient and others. The court may prevent disclosure if the information is available elsewhere, such as through a court ordered examination under Supreme Court Rule 215, or a custody evaluation under IMDMA § 605. See, e.g., In re Marriage of Lombaer, 200 Ill.App.3d 712, 146 Ill.Dec. 425, 558 N.E.2d 388 (1st Dist.1990) (order directing wife's psychiatrist to testify in custody action was error; wife did not put her mental condition at issue and psychiatric testimony necessary to determine the children's best interests could be obtained via the court-ordered psychiatric examination).

(2) **Confidentiality Act applied to family law actions.** Marriage counsellors qualify as therapists under § 3, and therefore are within the purview of the confidentiality provisions of the MHDDCA. See Martino v. Family Serv. Agency of Adams County, 112 Ill.App.3d 593, 67 Ill.Dec. 714, 445 N.E.2d 6 (4th Dist.1982).

Records and communications of the recipient are subject to disclosure only if the party puts his mental condition in issue. Section 10(a)(1) specifically states that in a dissolution of marriage proceeding, "mental condition shall not be deemed to be introduced merely by making [a claim under the IMDMA] and shall be deemed to be introduced only if the recipient or witness on his behalf first testifies concerning the record of communication." See, e.g., In re Marriage of Lombaer, 200 Ill.App.3d 712, 146 Ill.Dec. 425, 558 N.E.2d 388 (1st Dist.1990) (order directing wife's psychiatrist to testify in custody action was error; wife did not introduce her mental condition into the proceedings by first testifying about the privileged communications or records). *Cf.* Bland v. Department of Children and Family Serv., 141 Ill.App.3d 818, 96 Ill.Dec. 122, 490 N.E.2d 1327 (3d Dist.1986) (mental condition not placed in issue by filing petition for adoption).

(3) ***In camera* review.** Section 10(b) provides for an *in camera* review before disclosure under subsection 10(a), either on the court's own motion, or on the motion of the party or another interested person. Because a therapist has the right to block disclosure even where the recipient consents if the therapist shows that disclosure is not in the best interest of the recipient, the *in camera* review also provides an opportunity to hear from the therapist as to why disclosure should not be made. Ideally, the *in camera* review should be before a judge other than the one hearing the

CIVIL LIABILITIES 740 ILCS 110/11

case. If the judge hearing the main case conducts the *in camera* review, he or she will hear the information whether it is admissible or inadmissible, defeating the purpose of confidentiality and potentially coloring the outcome of the case.

(4) **Comparison: Physician-patient privilege.** The protection of the Confidentiality Act is broader than the physician-patient privilege. All communications and records generated in connection with providing mental health services to a recipient are protected unless excepted by law. People v. Kaiser, 239 Ill.App.3d 295, 179 Ill.Dec. 863, 606 N.E.2d 695 (2d Dist.1992). When there is a conflict between the Mental Health and Developmental Disabilities Confidentiality Act and the Physician–Patient Privilege, the Mental Health and Developmental Disabilities Confidentiality Act controls. In re Marriage of Lombaer, 200 Ill.App.3d 712, 146 Ill.Dec. 425, 558 N.E.2d 388 (1st Dist.1990).

(5) **Cross reference: Other applicable laws concerning privileged communications.** Other statutes may also be relevant to issues that arise in dissolution cases. The Abused and Neglected Child Reporting Act (ANCRA), mandates that certain persons, including mental health professionals, report suspected incidents of child abuse and neglect. See 325 ILCS 5/1 et seq. and accompanying Author's Notes. Communications between victims of domestic violence and domestic violence counselors, who often do not qualify as mental health professionals under the Confidentiality Act, are privileged from disclosure; as are records of any domestic violence program. See 750 ILCS 60/227.

740 ILCS 110/11

§ 11. Disclosure of records and communications

Records and communications may be disclosed, (i) in accordance with the provisions of the Abused and Neglected Child Reporting Act; (ii) when, and to the extent, a therapist, in his or her sole discretion, determines that disclosure is necessary to initiate or continue civil commitment proceedings under the laws of this State or to otherwise protect the recipient or other person against a clear, imminent risk of serious physical or mental injury or disease or death being inflicted upon the recipient or by the recipient on himself or another; (iii) when, and to the extent disclosure is, in the sole discretion of the therapist, necessary to the provision of emergency medical care to a recipient who is unable to assert or waive his or her rights hereunder; (iv) when disclosure is necessary to collect sums or receive third party payment representing charges for mental health or developmental disabilities services provided by a therapist or agency to a recipient under Chapter V of the Mental Health and Developmental Disabilities Code or to transfer debts under the Uncollected States Claims Act; however, disclosure shall be limited to information needed to pursue collection, and the information so disclosed shall not be used for any other purposes nor shall it be redisclosed except in connection with collection activities; (v) when requested by a family member, the Department of Mental Health and Developmental Disabilities may assist in the location of the interment site of a deceased recipient who is interred in a cemetery established under Section 100–26 of the Department of Mental Health and Developmental Disabilities Act; (vi) in commitment proceedings under the Mental Health and Developmental Disabilities Code and proceedings and investigations preliminary thereto, to the State's Attorney for the county or residence of a person for whom involuntary or judicial admission is sought, or in which the person is found, or in which the facility is located, and to the attorney representing the recipient in the commitment proceedings, provided that the information so disclosed shall not be utilized for any other purpose nor be redisclosed except in connection with the proceedings or investigations; (vii) when, and to the extent disclosure is necessary to comply with the requirements of the Census Bureau in taking the federal Decennial Census; and (viii) when, and to the extent, in the therapist's sole discretion, disclosure is necessary to warn or protect a specific individual against whom a recipient has made a specific threat of violence where there exists a therapist-recipient relationship or a special recipient-individual relationship. Any person, institution, or agency, under this Act, participating in good faith in the making of a report under the Abused and Neglected Child Reporting Act or in the disclosure of records and communications under this Section, shall have immunity from any liability, civil, criminal or otherwise, that might result by reason of such action. For the purpose of any proceeding, civil or criminal, arising out of a report or disclosure under this Section, the good faith of any person, institution, or agency so reporting or disclosing shall be presumed.

740 ILCS 110/12

§ 12. Information to be furnished to United States Secret Service and Department of State Police

(a) If the United States Secret Service or the Department of State Police requests information from a mental health or developmental disability facility, as defined in Section 1–107 and 1–114 of the Mental Health and Developmental Disabilities Code, relating to a specific recipient and the facility director determines that disclosure of such information may be necessary to protect the life of, or to prevent the infliction of great bodily harm to, a public official, or a person under the protection of the United States Secret Service, only the following information may be disclosed: the recipient's name, address, and age and the date of any admission to or discharge from a facility; and any information which would indicate whether or not the recipient has a history of violence or presents a danger of violence to the person under protection. Any information so disclosed shall be used for investigative purposes only and shall not be publicly disseminated. Any person participating in good faith in the disclosure of such information in accordance with this provision shall have immunity from any liability, civil, criminal or otherwise, if such information is disclosed relying upon the representation of an officer of the United States Secret Service or the Department of State Police that a person is under the protection of the United States Secret Service or is a public official.

For the purpose of this subsection (a), the term "public official" means the Governor, Lieutenant Governor, Attorney General, Secretary of State, State Comptroller, State Treasurer or member of the General Assembly. The term shall also include the spouse, child or children of a public official.

(b) The Department of Mental Health and Developmental Disabilities and all private hospitals are required, as hereafter described in this subsection, to furnish the Department of State Police only such information as may be required for the sole purpose of determining whether an individual who may be or may have been a patient is disqualified because of that status from receiving or retaining a Firearm Owner's Identification Card under subsection (e) of Section 8 of the Firearm Owners Identification Card Act. All private hospitals shall, in the form and manner required by the Department, provide such information as shall be necessary for the Department to comply with the reporting requirements to the Department of State Police. Such information shall be furnished within 30 days after admission to a private hospital. Any such information disclosed under this subsection shall remain privileged and confidential, and shall not be redisclosed nor utilized for any other purpose. The method of requiring the providing of such information shall guarantee that no information is released beyond what is necessary for this purpose. In addition, the information disclosed shall be provided by the Department within the time period established by Section 24-3 of the Criminal Code of 1961 regarding the delivery of firearms. The method used shall be sufficient to provide the necessary information within the prescribed time period, which may include periodically providing lists to the Department of Mental Health and Developmental Disabilities or any private hospital of Firearm Owner's Identification Card applicants on which the Department or hospital shall indicate the identities of those individuals who are to its knowledge disqualified from having a Firearm Owner's Identification Card for reasons described herein. The Department may provide for a centralized source of information for the State on this subject under its jurisdiction.

Any person, institution, or agency, under this Act, participating in good faith in the reporting or disclosure of records and communications otherwise in accordance with this provision or with rules, regulations or guidelines issued by the Department shall have immunity from any liability, civil, criminal or otherwise, that might result by reason of the action. For the purpose of any proceeding, civil or criminal, arising out of a report or disclosure in accordance with this provision, the good faith of any person, institution, or agency so reporting or disclosing shall be presumed. The full extent of the immunity provided in this subsection (b) shall apply to any person, institution or agency that fails to make a report or disclosure in the good faith belief that the report or disclosure would violate federal regulations governing the confidentiality of alcohol and drug abuse patient records implementing 42 U.S.C. 290dd-3 and 290ee-3.

For purposes of this subsection (b) only, the following terms shall have the meaning prescribed:

(1) "Hospital" means only that type of institution which is providing full-time residential facilities and treatment for in-patients and excludes institutions, such as community clinics, which only provide treatment to out-patients.

740 ILCS 110/12 CIVIL LIABILITIES

(2) "Patient" shall mean only a person who is an in-patient or resident of any hospital, not an out-patient or client seen solely for periodic consultation.

(c) Upon the request of a peace officer who takes a person into custody and transports such person to a mental health or developmental disability facility pursuant to Section 3–606 or 4–404 of the Mental Health and Developmental Disabilities Code or who transports a person from such facility, a facility director shall furnish said peace officer the name, address, age and name of the nearest relative of the person transported to or from the mental health or developmental disability facility. In no case shall the facility director disclose to the peace officer any information relating to the diagnosis, treatment or evaluation of the person's mental or physical health.

For the purposes of this subsection (c), the terms "mental health or developmental disability facility", "peace officer" and "facility director" shall have the meanings ascribed to them in the Mental Health and Developmental Disabilities Code.

740 ILCS 110/12.1

§ 12.1 Report of violation or incident—Investigation

A facility director who has reason to believe that a violation of criminal law or other serious incident has occurred within a mental health or developmental disability facility shall report that violation or incident and the identity of individuals with personal knowledge of the facts related to the violation or incident to the appropriate law enforcement and investigating agencies.

In the course of any investigation conducted pursuant to a report made under this Section, any person with personal knowledge of the incident or the circumstances surrounding the incident shall disclose that information to the individuals conducting the investigation, except that information regarding a recipient of services shall be limited solely to information relating to the factual circumstances of the incident.

740 ILCS 110/12.2

§ 12.2 Recipients on unauthorized absence—Disclosure of identifying information

(a) When a recipient who has been judicially or involuntarily admitted, or is a forensic recipient admitted to a developmental disability or mental health facility, as defined in Section 1–107 or 1–114 of the Mental Health and Developmental Disabilities Code, is on an unauthorized absence or otherwise has left the facility without being discharged or being free to do so, the facility director shall immediately furnish and disclose to the appropriate local law enforcement agency identifying information, as defined in this Section, and all further information unrelated to the diagnosis, treatment or evaluation of the recipient's mental or physical health that would aid the law enforcement agency in locating and apprehending the recipient and returning him to the facility.

(b) If a law enforcement agency requests information from a developmental disability or mental health facility, as defined in Section 1–107 or 1–114 of the Mental Health and Developmental Disabilities Code, relating to a recipient who has been admitted to the facility and for whom a missing person report has been filed with a law enforcement agency, the facility director shall, except in the case of a voluntary recipient wherein the recipient's permission in writing must first be obtained, furnish and disclose to the law enforcement agency identifying information as is necessary to confirm or deny whether that person is, or has been since the missing person report was filed, a resident of that facility. The facility director shall notify the law enforcement agency if the missing person is admitted after the request. Any person participating in good faith in the disclosure of information in accordance with this provision shall have immunity from any liability, civil, criminal, or otherwise, if the information is disclosed relying upon the representation of an officer of a law enforcement agency that a missing person report has been filed.

(c) Upon the request of a law enforcement agency in connection with the investigation of a particular felony or sex offense, when the investigation case file number is furnished by the law enforcement agency, a facility director shall immediately disclose to that law enforcement agency identifying information on any forensic recipient who is admitted to a developmental disability or mental health facility, as defined in Section 1–107 or 1–114 of the Mental Health and Developmental Disabilities Code, who was or may have been away from the facility at or about the time of the commission of a particular felony or sex offense, and: (1) whose description, clothing, or both reasonably match the physical description of any person allegedly involved in that particular felony or sex offense; or (2) whose past modus operandi matches the modus operandi of that particular felony or sex offense.

(d) For the purposes of this Section and Section 12.1, "law enforcement agency" means an agency of the State or unit of local government that is vested by law or ordinance with the duty to maintain public order and to enforce criminal laws or ordinances, the Federal Bureau of Investigation, the Central Intelligence Agency, and the United States Secret Service.

(e) For the purpose of this Section, "identifying information" means the name, address, age, and a physical description, including clothing, of the recipient of services, the names and addresses of the recipient's nearest known relatives, where the recipient was known to have been during any past unauthorized absences from a facility, whether the recipient may be suicidal, and the condition of the recipient's physical health as it relates to exposure to the weather. Except as provided in Section 11, in no case shall the facility director disclose to the law enforcement agency any information relating to the diagnosis, treatment, or evaluation of the recipient's mental or physical

740 ILCS 110/12.2   CIVIL LIABILITIES

health, unless the disclosure is deemed necessary by the facility director to insure the safety of the investigating officers or general public.

(f) For the purpose of this Section, "forensic recipient" means a recipient who is placed in a developmental disability facility or mental health facility, as defined in Section 1–107 or 1–114 of the Mental Health and Developmental Disabilities Code, pursuant to Article 104 of the Code of Criminal Procedure or Sections 3–8–5, 3–10–5 or 5–2–4 of the Unified Code of Corrections.

740 ILCS 110/12.3

§ 12.3 Notice of discharge

Nothing in this Act shall be construed to prevent compliance with the notice requirement of Section 4–704 of the Mental Health and Developmental Disabilities Code.

740 ILCS 110/13

§ 13. Disclosure without consent

Whenever disclosure of a record or communication is made without consent pursuant to this Act or whenever a record is used pursuant to Sections 7 and 8 of this Act, a notation of the information disclosed and the purpose of such disclosure or use shall be noted in the recipient's record together with the date and the name of the person to whom disclosure was made or by whom the record was used.

740 ILCS 110/14

§ 14. Agreement to waive Act—Void

Any agreement purporting to waive any of the provisions of this Act is void.

740 ILCS 110/15

§ 15. Actions by aggrieved parties for violation of Act—Fees and costs

Any person aggrieved by a violation of this Act may sue for damages, an injunction, or other appropriate relief. Reasonable attorney's fees and costs may be awarded to the successful plaintiff in any action under this Act.

Author's Notes

(1) **Damages for wrongful disclosure.** A recipient may sue for damages, an injunction, or other appropriate relief if a therapist wrongfully discloses communications protected under the MHDDCA. See, e.g., Renzi v. Morrison, 249 Ill.App.3d 5, 188 Ill.Dec. 224, 618 N.E.2d 794 (1st Dist.), *appeal denied*, 152 Ill.2d 579, 190 Ill.Dec. 909, 622 N.E.2d 1226 (1993) (therapist who voluntarily disclosed patient's confidential communications while a witness for patient's husband in dissolution proceeding could be held liable for damages). Damages may include attorney's fees and costs.

740 ILCS 110/16
§ 16. Violations—Penalty

Any person who knowingly and wilfully violates any provision of this Act is guilty of a Class A misdemeanor.

740 ILCS 110/17
§ 17. Rules and regulations

The Director of the Department of Mental Health and Developmental Disabilities shall adopt rules and regulations to implement this Act.

ACT 115. PARENTAL RESPONSIBILITY LAW

Analysis

Sec.
1. Short title and citation.
2. Definitions.
3. Parent or legal guardian; Liability; Willful or malicious acts of minor.
4. Persons or entities entitled to enforce Act.
5. Limitation on damages; Damages allowable.
6. Common law damages.
7. Judgments; Applicability of other Act.

WESTLAW Electronic Research

See WESTLAW Electronic Research Guide preceding the Summary of Contents.

---

740 ILCS 115/1
§ 1. Short title and citation

This Act shall be known and may be cited as the Parental Responsibility Law.

740 ILCS 115/2
§ 2. Definitions

As used in this Act, unless the context otherwise requires, the terms specified have the meanings ascribed to them:

(1) "Legal guardian" means a person appointed guardian, or given custody, of a minor by a circuit court of the State, but does not include a person appointed guardian, or given custody, of a minor under the Juvenile Court Act or the Juvenile Court Act of 1987.

(2) "Minor" means a person who is above the age of 11 years, but not yet 19 years of age.

740 ILCS 115/3

§ 3. Parent or legal guardian; Liability; Willful or malicious acts of minor

The parent or legal guardian of an unemancipated minor who resides with such parent or legal guardian is liable for actual damages for the wilful or malicious acts of such minor which cause injury to a person or property.

740 ILCS 115/4

§ 4. Persons or entities entitled to enforce Act

Any municipal corporation, county, township, village or any other political subdivision or department of the State of Illinois, or any person, partnership, corporation, association or any incorporated or unincorporated religious, educational or charitable organization is entitled to enforce the liability imposed by this Act.

740 ILCS 115/5

§ 5. Limitation on damages; Damages allowable

No recovery under this Act may exceed $1,000 actual damages for each person, or legal entity as provided in Section 4 of this Act, for each occurrence of such wilful or malicious acts by the minor causing injury, in addition to taxable court costs. In determining the damages to be allowed in an action under this Act for personal injury, only medical, dental and hospital expenses and expenses for treatment by Christian Science practitioners and nursing care appropriate thereto may be considered.

740 ILCS 115/6

§ 6. Common law damages

This Act shall not affect the recovery of damages in any other cause of action where the liability of the parent or legal guardian is predicated on a common law basis.

740 ILCS 115/7

§ 7. Judgments; Applicability of other Act

Section 12–107 of the Code of Civil Procedure, as now or hereafter amended, is not applicable to judgments obtained under this Act.

Author's Notes

(1) **Cross reference.** 735 ILCS 5/12–107 allows imprisonment of tort judgment debtors where there is malice.

DIVISION C. PROBATE

CHAPTER 755
ESTATES

ACT 5. PROBATE ACT OF 1975
ARTICLE IV. WILLS

Analysis

Sec.
4–7. Revocation—Revival.

WESTLAW Electronic Research

See WESTLAW Electronic Research Guide preceding the Summary of Contents.

---

755 ILCS 5/4–7

§ 4–7. Revocation—Revival

(a) A will may be revoked only (1) by burning, cancelling, tearing or obliterating it by the testator himself or by some person in his presence and by his direction and consent, (2) by the execution of a later will declaring the revocation, (3) by a later will to the extent that it is inconsistent with the prior will or (4) by the execution of an instrument declaring the revocation and signed and attested in the manner prescribed by this Article for the signing and attestation of a will.

(b) No will or any part thereof is revoked by any change in the circumstances, condition or marital status of the testator, except that dissolution of marriage or declaration of invalidity of the marriage of the testator revokes every legacy or interest or power of appointment given to or nomination to fiduciary office of the testator's former spouse in a will executed before the entry of the judgment of dissolution of marriage or declaration of invalidity of marriage and the will takes effect in the same manner as if the former spouse had died before the testator.

(c) A will which is totally revoked in any manner is not revived other than by its re-execution or by an instrument declaring the revival and signed and attested in the manner prescribed by this Article for the signing and attestation of a will. If a will is partially revoked by an instrument which is

755 ILCS 5/4-7 PROBATE

itself revoked, the revoked part of the will is revived and takes effect as if there had been no revocation.

Author's Notes

(1) **Wills in divorce.** Caution requires that consideration be given to revising an estate plan when a spouse enters into dissolution proceedings. For those wills that are executed prior to the entry of a judgment of dissolution of marriage or declaration of invalidity of marriage, and not revised, in which a divorced spouse therefore retains an interest, 755 ILCS 5/4-7(b) provides that the will shall take effect in the same manner as if the former spouse had predeceased the testator. Section 4-7(b) is an important savings provision for those spouses who divorce and neglect to change their wills. Section 4-7(b) does not, however, help the testator who fails to revise his will during dissolution litigation, and who dies before the entry of judgment.

ARTICLE XI. MINORS

Analysis

Sec.
11-1.   Minor defined.
11-3.   Who may act as guardian.
11-5.   Appointment of guardian.
11-6.   Venue.
11-7.   Parental right to custody.
11-7.1   Visitation rights.
11-8.   Petition for guardian of minor.
11-9.   Domestic violence: Order of protection.
11-10.1 Procedure for appointment of a guardian of a minor.
11-11.   Costs in certain cases.
11-13.   Duties of guardian of a minor.
11-14.1 Revocation of letters.
11-18.   Successor guardian.

WESTLAW Electronic Research

See WESTLAW Electronic Research Guide preceding the Summary of Contents.

---

755 ILCS 5/11-1

§ 11-1. Minor defined

A minor is a person who has not attained the age of 18 years. A person who has attained the age of 18 years is of legal age for all purposes except as otherwise provided in the Illinois Uniform Transfers to Minors Act.

755 ILCS 5/11-3

§ 11-3. Who may act as guardian

(a) A person who has attained the age of 18 years and is a resident of the United States, is not of unsound mind, is not an adjudged disabled person as defined in this Act and has not been convicted of a felony, is qualified to act as guardian of the person and, if he is a resident of this State, as guardian of the estate. One person may be appointed guardian of the person and another person appointed guardian of the estate.

(b) The Department of Mental Health and Developmental Disabilities or the Department of Children and Family Services may with the approval of the court designate one of its employees to serve without fees as guardian of the estate of a minor patient in a State mental hospital or a resident in a State institution when the value of the personal estate does not exceed $1,000.

755 ILCS 5/11-5
§ 11-5. Appointment of guardian

(a) Upon the filing of a petition by a reputable citizen of this State or on its own motion, the court may appoint a guardian of the person or estate, or both, of a minor whenever it appears necessary or convenient.

(b) A parent of an unmarried minor or of a child likely to be born may by will nominate a guardian of the person and of the estate of such child to continue during his minority or for a less time, but if the surviving parent is a fit and competent person, no such nomination deprives him of the custody, nurture, tuition and education of the child or the right to nominate by his will the guardian of the person of the child. Before a testamentary guardian of the estate of the minor can act, he must be appointed by the court of the proper county and give the bond prescribed in Section 12-2.

(c) If the minor is 14 years of age or more, he may nominate the guardian of his person and of his estate, subject to approval of the court. If the minor's nominee is not approved by the court, or if the minor resides out of the State, or if, after notice to the minor, he fails to nominate a guardian of his person or estate, the court may appoint the guardian without nomination.

(d) The court shall not appoint as guardian of the person of the minor, any person whom the court has determined had caused or substantially contributed to the minor becoming a neglected or abused minor as defined in the Juvenile Court Act of 1987, as amended, unless two years has elapsed since the last proven incident of abuse or neglect and the court determines that appointment of such person as guardian is in the best interests of the minor.

755 ILCS 5/11-6
§ 11-6. Venue

If the minor is a resident of this State, the proceeding shall be instituted in the court of the county in which he resides. If the minor is not a resident of this State, the proceeding shall be instituted in the court of a county in which his real or personal estate is located.

755 ILCS 5/11-7
§ 11-7. Parental right to custody

If both parents of a minor are living and are competent to transact their own business and are fit persons, they are entitled to the custody of the

755 ILCS 5/11-7

person of the minor and the direction of his education. If one parent is dead and the surviving parent is competent to transact his own business and is a fit person, he is similarly entitled. The parents have equal powers, rights and duties concerning the minor. If the parents live apart, the court for good reason may award the custody and education of the minor to either parent or to some other person.

755 ILCS 5/11-7.1

§ 11-7.1 Visitation rights

Whenever both natural or adoptive parents of a minor are deceased, visitation rights shall be granted to the grandparents of the minor who are the parents of the minor's legal parents unless it is shown that such visitation would be detrimental to the best interests and welfare of the minor. In the discretion of the court, reasonable visitation rights may be granted to any other relative of the minor or other person having an interest in the welfare of the child. However, the court shall not grant visitation privileges to any person who otherwise might have visitation privileges under this Section where the minor has been adopted subsequent to the death of both his legal parents except where such adoption is by a close relative. For the purpose of this Section, "close relative" shall include, but not be limited to, a grandparent, aunt, uncle, first cousin, or adult brother or sister.

Where such adoption is by a close relative, the court shall not grant visitation privileges under this Section unless the petitioner alleges and proves that he or she has been unreasonably denied visitation with the child. The court may grant reasonable visitation privileges upon finding that such visitation would be in the best interest of the child.

An order denying visitation rights to grandparents of the minor shall be in writing and shall state the reasons for denial. An order denying visitation rights is a final order for purposes of appeal.

755 ILCS 5/11-8

§ 11-8. Petition for guardian of minor

The petition for appointment of a guardian of the person or of the estate of a minor must state, if known:

(a) The name, date of birth and residence of the minor; (b) the names and post office addresses of the nearest relatives of the minor in the following order: (1) the spouse, if any; if none, (2) the parents and adult brothers and sisters, if any; if none, (3) the nearest adult kindred; (c) the name and post office address of the person having the custody of the minor; (d) the approximate value of the personal estate; (e) the amount of the anticipated gross annual income and other receipts; (f) the name, post office address and, in case of an individual, the age and occupation of the proposed guardian; and (g) if a testamentary guardian is designated, the facts concerning admission of the will to probate, a copy of which shall be attached to or filed with the petition.

755 ILCS 5/11-9

§ 11-9. Domestic violence: Order of protection

An order of protection, as defined in the Illinois Domestic Violence Act of 1986, enacted by the 84th General Assembly, may be issued in conjunction with a proceeding for appointment of a guardian for a minor if the petition for an order of protection alleges that a person who is party to or the subject of the proceeding has been abused by or has abused a family or household member. The Illinois Domestic Violence Act of 1986 shall govern the issuance, enforcement and recording of orders of protection issued under this Section.

755 ILCS 5/11-10.1

§ 11-10.1 Procedure for appointment of a guardian of a minor

(a) Unless excused by the court for good cause shown, it is the duty of the petitioner to give notice of the time and place of the hearing on the petition, in person or by mail, to the minor, if he is 14 years, or older, and to the relatives of the minor whose names and addresses are stated in the petition, not less than 3 days before the hearing, but failure to give notice to any relative is not jurisdictional.

(b) In any proceeding for the appointment of a guardian the court may appoint a guardian ad litem to represent the minor in the proceeding.

755 ILCS 5/11-11

§ 11-11. Costs in certain cases

No costs may be taxed or charged by any public officer in any proceeding for the appointment of a guardian or for any subsequent proceeding or report made in pursuance of the appointment when the primary purpose of the appointment is any of the following:

(a) The proper expenditure of public assistance awarded to the ward under the provisions of any act of the General Assembly;

(b) The collection, disbursement or administering of money or assets derived from money awarded to the ward by the Veterans Administration or by any state or territory of the United States or the District of Columbia as a veteran's benefit, but costs may be allowed, in the discretion of the court, whenever there are assets from sources other than the Veterans Administration;

(c) The management of the estate of a minor patient in a State mental health or developmental disabilities facility when the value of the personal estate does not exceed $1,000.

755 ILCS 5/11-13

§ 11-13. Duties of guardian of a minor

The court shall have control over the person and estate of the ward. Under the direction of the court:

(a) The guardian of the person shall have the custody, nurture and tuition and shall provide education of the ward and of his children, but the ward's spouse may not be deprived of the custody and education of the spouse's children, without consent of the spouse, unless the court finds that the spouse is not a fit and competent person to have such custody and education. If the ward's estate is insufficient to provide for the ward's education and the guardian of his person fails to provide education, the court may award the custody of the ward to some other person for the purpose of providing education. If a person makes a settlement upon or provision for the support or education of a ward and if either parent of the ward is dead, the court may make such order for the visitation of the ward by the person making the settlement or provision as the court deems proper.

(b) The guardian or other representative of the ward's estate shall have the care, management and investment of the estate, shall manage the estate frugally and shall apply the income and principal of the estate so far as necessary for the comfort and suitable support and education of the ward, his children, and persons related by blood or marriage who are dependent upon or entitled to support from him, or for any other purpose which the court deems to be for the best interests of the ward, and the court may approve the making on behalf of the ward of such agreements as the court determines to be for the ward's best interests. The representative may make disbursement of his ward's funds and estate directly to the ward or other distributee or in such other manner and in such amounts as the court directs. If the estate of a ward is derived in whole or in part from payments of compensation, adjusted compensation, pension, insurance or other similar benefits made directly to the estate by the Veterans Administration, notice of the application for leave to invest or expend the ward's funds or estate, together with a copy of the petition and proposed order, shall be given to the Veterans' Administration Regional Office in this State at least 7 days before the hearing on the application.

(c) Upon the direction of the court which issued his letters a representative may perform the contracts of his ward which were legally subsisting at the time of the commencement of the guardianship. The court may authorize the guardian to execute and deliver any bill of sale, deed or other instrument.

(d) The representative of the estate of a ward shall appear for and represent the ward in all legal proceedings unless another person is appointed for that purpose as representative or next friend. This does not impair the power of any court to appoint a representative or next friend to defend the interests of the ward in that court, or to appoint or allow any person as the next friend of a ward to commence, prosecute or defend any proceeding in his behalf. Any proceeding on behalf of a minor may be commenced and prosecuted by his next friend, without any previous authority or appointment by the court if the next friend enters bond for costs and files it in the court where the proceeding is pending.

755 ILCS 5/11–14.1

§ 11–14.1 Revocation of letters

Upon the minor reaching the age of majority, the letters of office shall be revoked and the guardianship shall be terminated.

755 ILCS 5/11–18

§ 11–18. Successor guardian

Upon the death, incapacity, resignation or removal of a guardian, the court may appoint a successor guardian.

*

DIVISION D. PROCEDURE

CHAPTER 735
CIVIL PROCEDURE

ACT 5. CODE OF CIVIL PROCEDURE
ARTICLE I. GENERAL PROVISIONS

Analysis

Sec.
1-109. Verification by certification.

WESTLAW Electronic Research

See WESTLAW Electronic Research Guide preceding the Summary of Contents.

---

735 ILCS 5/1-109

§ 1-109. Verification by certification

Unless otherwise expressly provided by rule of the Supreme Court, whenever in this Code any complaint, petition, answer, reply, bill of particulars, answer to interrogatories, affidavit, return or proof of service, or other document or pleading filed in any court of this State is required or permitted to be verified, or made, sworn to or verified under oath, such requirement or permission is hereby defined to include a certification of such pleading, affidavit or other document under penalty of perjury as provided in this Section.

Whenever any such pleading, affidavit or other document is so certified, the several matters stated shall be stated positively or upon information and belief only, according to the fact. The person or persons having knowledge of the matters stated in a pleading, affidavit or other document certified in accordance with this Section shall subscribe to a certification in substantially the following form: Under penalties as provided by law pursuant to Section 1-109 of the Code of Civil Procedure, the undersigned certifies that the statements set forth in this instrument are true and correct, except as to matters therein stated to be on information and belief and as to such matters the undersigned certifies as aforesaid that he verily believes the same to be true.

Any pleading, affidavit or other document certified in accordance with this Section may be used in the same manner and with the same force and effect as though subscribed and sworn to under oath.

Any person who makes a false statement, material to the issue or point in question, which he does not believe to be true, in any pleading, affidavit or other document certified by such person in accordance with this Section shall be guilty of a Class 3 felony.

ARTICLE II. CIVIL PRACTICE

Analysis

Sec.
2–104.	Wrong venue—Waiver—Motion to transfer.
2–106.	Transfer.
2–107.	Costs and expenses of transfer.
2–202.	Persons authorized to serve process; Place of service; Failure to make return.
2–203.	Service on individuals.
2–203.1	Service by special order of court.
2–206.	Service by publication—Affidavit—Mailing—Certificate.
2–207.	Period of publication—Default.
2–208.	Personal service outside State.
2–209.	Act submitting to jurisdiction—Process.
2–620.	Practice on motions.
2–701.	Declaratory judgments.
2–1001.	Substitution of judge.
2–1001.5	Change of Venue.
2–1102.	Examination of adverse party or agent.
2–1203.	Motions after judgment in non-jury cases.
2–1301.	Judgments—Default—Confession.
2–1302.	Notice of entry of default order.
2–1303.	Interest on judgment.
2–1401.	Relief from judgments.
2–1501.	Writs abolished.
2–1901.	Lis pendens—Operative date of notice.
84.	Torrens Act Notice.

WESTLAW Electronic Research

See WESTLAW Electronic Research Guide preceding the Summary of Contents.

---

735 ILCS 5/2–104

§ 2–104. Wrong venue—Waiver—Motion to transfer

(a) No order or judgment is void because rendered in the wrong venue, except in case of judgment by confession as provided in subsection (c) of Section 2–1301 of this Act. No action shall abate or be dismissed because commenced in the wrong venue if there is a proper venue to which the cause may be transferred.

(b) All objections of improper venue are waived by a defendant unless a motion to transfer to a proper venue is made by the defendant on or before the date upon which he or she is required to appear or within any further time that may be granted him or her to answer or move with respect to the complaint, except that if a defendant upon whose residence venue depends is dismissed upon motion of plaintiff, a remaining defendant may promptly move for transfer as though the dismissed defendant had not been a party.

(c) Motions for transfer to a proper venue may be supported and opposed by affidavit. In determining issues of fact raised by affidavits, any competent evidence adduced by the parties shall also be considered. The determination of any issue of fact in connection with a motion to transfer does not constitute a determination of the merits of the case or any aspect thereof.

Author's Notes

(1) **IMDMA.** Venue under the Illinois Marriage and Dissolution of Marriage Act is determined by IMDMA § 104 and other sections. See IMDMA § 104, 750 ILCS 5/104, and accompanying Author's Notes.

735 ILCS 5/2-106

§ 2-106. Transfer

(a) Transfer for wrong venue. If a motion to transfer is allowed on the ground that the action was commenced in a wrong venue, the cause shall be transferred to the court in a proper venue, subject to any equitable terms and conditions that may be prescribed.

(b) Method of transfer. The clerk of the court from which a transfer is granted shall immediately certify and transmit to the clerk of the court to which the transfer is ordered the originals of all papers filed in the case together with copies of all orders entered therein. In the event of a severance, certified copies of papers filed and orders entered shall be transmitted. The clerk of the court to which the transfer is ordered shall file the papers and transcript transmitted to him or her and docket the case, and the action shall proceed and be determined as if it had originated in that court.

735 ILCS 5/2-107

§ 2-107. Costs and expenses of transfer

The costs attending a transfer shall be taxed by the clerk of the court from which the transfer is granted, and, together with the filing fee in the transferee court, shall be paid by plaintiff. If the court granting the transfer finds that venue was fixed by plaintiff in bad faith and without probable cause, then it may order the reasonable expenses of defendant in attending and obtaining a transfer to a proper venue, including a reasonable attorney's fee, to be paid by plaintiff. If the costs and expenses are not paid within a reasonable time, the transferring court shall on motion dismiss the action.

735 ILCS 5/2-202

§ 2-202. Persons authorized to serve process; Place of service; Failure to make return

(a) Process shall be served by a sheriff, or if the sheriff is disqualified, by a coroner of some county of the State. A sheriff of a county with a population of less than 1,000,000 may employ civilian personnel to serve process. In counties with a population of less than 1,000,000, process may be served, without special appointment, by a person who is licensed or registered as a private detective under the Private Detective, Private Alarm and Private Security Act of 1983 or by a registered employee of a private detective agency certified under that Act. A private detective or licensed employee must supply the sheriff of any county in which he serves process with a copy of his license or certificate; however, the failure of a person to supply the copy shall not in any way impair the validity of process served by the person. The court may, in its discretion upon motion, order service to be made by a private person over 18 years of age and not a party to the action. It is not necessary that service be made by a sheriff or coroner of the county in which service is made. If served or sought to be served by a sheriff or coroner, he or she shall endorse his or her return thereon, and if by a private person the return shall be by affidavit.

(b) Summons may be served upon the defendants wherever they may be found in the State, by any person authorized to serve process. An officer may serve summons in his or her official capacity outside his or her county, but fees for mileage outside the county of the officer cannot be taxed as costs. The person serving the process in a foreign county may make return by mail.

(c) If any sheriff, coroner, or other person to whom any process is delivered, neglects or refuses to make return of the same, the plaintiff may petition the court to enter a rule requiring the sheriff, coroner, or other person, to make return of the process on a day to be fixed by the court, or to show cause on that day why that person should not be attached for contempt of the court. The plaintiff shall then cause a written notice of the rule to be served on the sheriff, coroner, or other person. If good and sufficient cause be not shown to excuse the officer or other person, the court shall adjudge him or her guilty of a contempt, and shall impose punishment as in other cases of contempt.

(d) If process is served by a sheriff or coroner, the court may tax the fee of the sheriff or coroner as costs in the proceeding. If process is served by a private person or entity, the court may establish a fee therefor and tax such fee as costs in the proceedings.

Author's Notes

(1) **Motion for Appointment of Special Process Server—Form.** There follows a sample motion and order for a special process server that is used in Cook County.

CIVIL PROCEDURE   735 ILCS 5/2–202

3149-Motion   (10-90) CCDR-3
4209-Order

IN THE CIRCUIT COURT OF COOK COUNTY, ILLINOIS
COUNTY DEPARTMENT, DOMESTIC RELATIONS DIVISION

IN RE THE MARRIAGE OF:)
)
ESTHER SUMMERSON,   )
            Petitioner,   )
)
and   ) No. ____ D _____
) Calendar:
WILLIAM GUPPY,   )
            Respondent.)

MOTION FOR APPOINTMENT OF SPECIAL PROCESS SERVER

I. Petitioner moves this Court to order service of process in this cause to be made by the following individual, who is over the age of eighteen and not a party to this cause:

NAME: Inspector Bucket
ADDRESS: _____

II. The appointment of a special process server will better facilitate the administration of justice.

     1. It is necessary to serve Respondent immediately in order to obtain the effect of an injunction.

     2. Inspector Bucket is best suited to serve all necessary court documents upon Respondent.

                                                      _____
                                                      Petitioner/Attorney

Attorney Signature: _____

NAME: Conrad Snagsby
Attorney for: Petitioner
Address:
City, State, ZIP:
Telephone:
Attorney Code No. _____

ORDER APPOINTING SPECIAL PROCESS SERVER

     IT IS HEREBY ORDERED that _____ Inspector Bucket _____, an individual over 18 years of age and not a party to this cause, is appointed to make service of process in this cause and to file an affidavit of proof of service with the Clerk of the Circuit Court immediately thereafter.

DATE: ENTER:

                                    JUDGE   NO.

735 ILCS 5/2-203

§ 2-203. Service on individuals

(a) Except as otherwise expressly provided, service of summons upon an individual defendant shall be made (1) by leaving a copy of the summons with the defendant personally, (2) by leaving a copy at the defendant's usual place of abode, with some person of the family or a person residing there, of the age of 13 years or upwards, and informing that person of the contents of the summons, provided the officer or other person making service shall also send a copy of the summons in a sealed envelope with postage fully prepaid, addressed to the defendant at his or her usual place of abode, or (3) as provided in Section 1-2-9.2 of the Illinois Municipal Code with respect to violation of an ordinance governing parking or standing of vehicles in cities with a population over 500,000. The certificate of the officer or affidavit of the person that he or she has sent the copy in pursuance of this Section is evidence that he or she has done so.

(b) The officer, in his or her certificate or in a record filed and maintained in the Sheriff's office, or other person making service, in his or her affidavit or in a record filed and maintained in his or her employer's office, shall (1) identify as to sex, race and approximate age the defendant or other person with whom the summons was left and (2) state the place where (whenever possible in terms of an exact street address) and the date and time of the day when the summons was left with the defendant or other person.

(c) Any person who knowingly sets forth in such certificate or affidavit any false statement, shall be liable in civil contempt. When the court holds a person in civil contempt under this Section, it shall award such damages as it determines to be just and, when the contempt is prosecuted by a private attorney, may award reasonable attorney's fees.

Author's Notes

Analysis

1. Copy of petition.
2. Some person of the family.

(1) **Copy of petition.** See Supreme Court Rule 104(a), which requires that a copy of the Petition for Dissolution of Marriage or other petition be attached to the summons for service.

(2) **Some person of the family.** Abode service is made by leaving a copy of the summons at the respondent's usual place of abode, with some person of the family or a person residing there aged 13 or older, informing him of the contents of the summons, and thereafter mailing copies of the summons and petition to the respondent. 735 ILCS 5/2-203(a). Prior to January 1, 1994, abode service was proper only if the summons was left with some person of the family of sufficient age. "Some person of the family" cannot include a temporary guest. See Cumbo v. Cumbo, 9 Ill.App.3d 1056, 293 N.E.2d 694 (1st Dist.1973) ("a temporary guest in the defendant's usual place of abode is not a member of the family within the meaning of the statute ... [and w]e do not think that ... the fact that this temporary guest was related by blood to the defendant is enough to make him a member of the family for purposes of the statute"); Conley v. McNamara, 334 Ill.App. 396, 79 N.E.2d 645 (1st Dist.1948) (stepdaughter residing in separate apartment in defendant's home did not qualify as "some person of the family" under the statute). There is, however, case law extending the term "some person of the family" to maids, Lewis v. West Side Trust & Savings Bank, 286 Ill.App. 130, 2 N.E.2d 976 (1st Dist.1936), and to tenants in a single apartment, Sanchez v. Randall, 31 Ill.App.2d 41, 175 N.E.2d 645 (1st Dist.1961). Both maids and tenants in a single apartment would be proper recipients of the summons under the amended statute which also allows the summons to be left with "a person residing there" at the respondent's usual place of abode.

735 ILCS 5/2-203.1

§ 2-203.1 Service by special order of court

If service upon an individual defendant is impractical under items (1) and (2) of subsection (a) of Section 2-203, the plaintiff may move, without notice, that the court enter an order directing a comparable method of service. The motion shall be accompanied with an affidavit stating the nature and extent of the investigation made to determine the whereabouts of the defendant and the reasons why service is impractical under items (1) and (2) of subsection (a) of Section 2-203, including a specific statement showing that a diligent inquiry as to the location of the individual defendant was made and reasonable efforts to make service have been unsuccessful. The court may order service to be made in any manner consistent with due process.

735 ILCS 5/2-206

§ 2-206. Service by publication—Affidavit—Mailing—Certificate

(a) Whenever, in any action affecting property or status within the jurisdiction of the court, including an action to obtain the specific performance, reformation, or rescission of a contract for the conveyance of land, plaintiff or his or her attorney shall file, at the office of the clerk of the court in which the action is pending, an affidavit showing that the defendant resides or has gone out of this State, or on due inquiry cannot be found, or is concealed within this State, so that process cannot be served upon him or her, and stating the place of residence of the defendant, if known, or that upon diligent inquiry his or her place of residence cannot be ascertained, the clerk shall cause publication to be made in some newspaper published in the county in which the action is pending. If there is no newspaper published in that

735 ILCS 5/2-206   PROCEDURE

county, then the publication shall be in a newspaper published in an adjoining county in this State, having a circulation in the county in which action is pending. The publication shall contain notice of the pendency of the action, the title of the court, the title of the case, showing the names of the first named plaintiff and the first named defendant, the number of the case, the names of the parties to be served by publication, and the date on or after which default may be entered against such party. The clerk shall also, within 10 days of the first publication of the notice, send a copy thereof by mail, addressed to each defendant whose place of residence is stated in such affidavit. The certificate of the clerk that he or she has sent the copy in pursuance of this Section is evidence that he or she has done so.

* * *

735 ILCS 5/2-207

§ 2-207. Period of publication—Default

The notice required in the preceding section may be given at any time after the commencement of the action, and shall be published at least once in each week for 3 successive weeks. No default or proceeding shall be taken against any defendant not served with summons, or a copy of the complaint, and not appearing, unless the first publication be at least 30 days prior to the time when the default or other proceeding is sought to be taken.

735 ILCS 5/2-208

§ 2-208. Personal service outside State

(a) Personal service of summons may be made upon any party outside the State. If upon a citizen or resident of this State or upon a person who has submitted to the jurisdiction of the courts of this State, it shall have the force and effect of personal service of summons within this State; otherwise it shall have the force and effect of service by publication.

(b) The service of summons shall be made in like manner as service within this State, by any person over 18 years of age not a party to the action. No order of court is required. An affidavit of the server shall be filed stating the time, manner and place of service. The court may consider the affidavit, or any other competent proofs, in determining whether service has been properly made.

(c) No default shall be entered until the expiration of at least 30 days after service. A default judgment entered on such service may be set aside only on a showing which would be timely and sufficient to set aside a default judgment entered on personal service within this State.

Author's Notes

(1) **Letter and Affidavit—Forms.** There follows a sample letter and affidavit for service outside of the State.

CIVIL PROCEDURE   735 ILCS 5/2-208

_____, 199__

Sheriff of New York County
New York, NY

Dear Sir:

　　Enclosed please find an original and two copies of the summons and two copies of the Petition for Dissolution of Marriage in the case of In re Marriage of Ellen Jarndyce and John Jarndyce now pending in the Circuit Court of Cook County, Illinois, No. ___ D _____. Under the provisions of the Illinois Code of Civil Procedure, summons may be served outside of Illinois in cases such as this by any person over 18 years of age, not a party to the litigation. Service can be made either (1) by leaving a copy of the summons and Petition for Dissolution of Marriage with the Respondent John Jarndyce personally, or (2) by leaving a copy of the summons and Petition for Dissolution of Marriage at his usual place of abode, with some person of the family or a person residing there, of the age of 13 years or upwards, and informing that person of the contents of the summons, and thereafter mailing a copy of the summons and Petition for Dissolution of Marriage in a sealed envelope with postage fully prepaid addressed to the Respondent John Jarndyce at his usual place of abode.

　　Kindly serve a copy of the enclosed summons and Petition for Dissolution of Marriage on Respondent John Jarndyce in one of the two alternative methods indicated above.

　　After service has been made, the following should be accomplished:

(1) The one who serves the summons should make a return of summons on the back of the original copy of the summons stating the place, time, and manner of service;

(2) The enclosed affidavit should be completed;

(3) The original of the summons and the completed affidavit should be returned to me.

　　If you will inform me of your fees, I will make prompt remittance.

　　　　　　　　　　　　　　　　　Sincerely yours,

　　　　　　　　　　　　　　　　　Richard Vholes

XX/xx
Enclosures

735 ILCS 5/2-208 PROCEDURE

IN THE CIRCUIT COURT OF COOK COUNTY, ILLINOIS
COUNTY DEPARTMENT—DOMESTIC RELATIONS DIVISION

IN RE THE MARRIAGE OF)
)
ELLEN JARNDYCE,)
)
      Petitioner,)
)
and) No. ____ D _____
)
JOHN JARNDYCE,)
)
      Respondent.)

AFFIDAVIT

  1. _____ on oath states:

  2. I am a person over 18 years of age, not a party to the above entitled action.

  3. I served John Jarndyce at _____ a.m./p.m. on _____, 199__, at the following address: _____, New York, New York, by: (1) leaving a copy of the Summons and Petition for Dissolution of Marriage with the Respondent personally, or (2) leaving a copy of the Summons and Petition for Dissolution of Marriage at his usual place of abode with some person of the family or a person residing there, of the age of 13 years or upwards, and informing that person of the contents of the summons, and thereafter mailing a copy of the Summons and Petition for Dissolution of Marriage in a sealed envelope with postage fully prepaid addressed to the Respondent at his usual place of abode *(cross out the inapplicable form of service)*.

  4. The Respondent or other person served had the following identity: Name, _____ sex, _____ race, _____ approximate age of _____.

  5. Where a person of the family is served, his or her relationship to the family was _____.

  6. If called as a witness, I would testify as aforesaid.

_____

Subscribed and sworn to
before me this _____ day
of _____, 199__.

_____
Notary Public

735 ILCS 5/2-209

§ 2-209. Act submitting to jurisdiction—Process

(a) Any person, whether or not a citizen or resident of this State, who in person or through an agent does any of the acts hereinafter enumerated, thereby submits such person, and, if an individual, his or her personal representative, to the jurisdiction of the courts of this State as to any cause of action arising from the doing of any of such acts:

* * *

(2) The commission of a tortious act within this State;

(3) The ownership, use, or possession of any real estate situated in this State;

* * *

(5) With respect to actions of dissolution of marriage, declaration of invalidity of marriage and legal separation, the maintenance in this State of a matrimonial domicile at the time this cause of action arose or the commission in this State of any act giving rise to the cause of action;

(6) With respect to actions brought under the Illinois Parentage Act of 1984, as now or hereafter amended, the performance of an act of sexual intercourse within this State during the possible period of conception;

(7) The making or performance of any contract or promise substantially connected with this State;

(8) The performance of sexual intercourse within this State which is claimed to have resulted in the conception of a child who resides in this State;

(9) The failure to support a child, spouse or former spouse who has continued to reside in this State since the person either formerly resided with them in this State or directed them to reside in this State;

(10) The acquisition of ownership, possession or control of any asset or thing of value present within this State when ownership, possession or control was acquired;

(11) The breach of any fiduciary duty within this State;

* * *

(13) The ownership of an interest in any trust administered within this State; or

* * *

(b) A court may exercise jurisdiction in any action arising within or without this State against any person who:

(1) Is a natural person present within this State when served;

(2) Is a natural person domiciled or resident within this State when the cause of action arose, the action was commenced, or process was served;

* * *

(4) Is a natural person . . . doing business within this State.

(c) A court may also exercise jurisdiction on any other basis now or hereafter permitted by the Illinois Constitution and the Constitution of the United States.

(d) Service of process upon any person who is subject to the jurisdiction of the courts of this State, as provided in this Section, may be made by personally serving the summons upon the defendant outside this State, as provided in this Act, with the same force and effect as though summons had been personally served within this State.

* * *

(f) Only causes of action arising from acts enumerated herein may be asserted against a defendant in an action in which jurisdiction over him or her is based upon subsection (a).

(g) Nothing herein contained limits or affects the right to serve any process in any other manner now or hereafter provided by law.

Author's Notes

Analysis

1. Personal jurisdiction.
2. Service.

(1) **Personal jurisdiction.** A party moving into Illinois without her spouse may be able to obtain a dissolution of marriage after 90 days of residence, even without personal jurisdiction over him, IMDMA § 401, 750 ILCS 5/401; In re Marriage of Passiales, 144 Ill.App.3d 629, 637, 98 Ill.Dec. 419, 426, 494 N.E.2d 541, 548 (1st Dist.1986). She may not be able to obtain personal jurisdiction over her husband if he remains out of state, unless the matrimonial domicile at the time the action arose was in Illinois; an act giving rise to the cause of action occurred in Illinois, 735 ILCS 5/2-209(5); or another section of § 2-209(5) is satisfied. Failure to obtain personal jurisdiction over her husband means that no financial issue can be conclusively adjudicated. See Wilson v. Smart 324 Ill. 276, 281, 155 N.E. 288, 291 (1927) ("A purely personal decree in a divorce suit awarding alimony against a non-resident defendant who is notified of the proceeding constructively by publication and who does not appear is not binding upon him."); Duncan v. Duncan, 94 Ill.App.3d 868, 50 Ill.Dec. 592, 419 N.E.2d 700 (3d Dist.1981) (Illinois courts could not exercise in personam jurisdiction over nonresident, nondomiciliary father of minor children in Illinois for purposes of children's support). But see the Uniform Child Custody Jurisdiction Act, 750 ILCS 35/4, Author's Note (1), for issues of child custody where personal jurisdiction over either parent is unnecessary. See IMDMA § 703, 750 ILCS

CIVIL PROCEDURE 735 ILCS 5/2-620

5/703, and accompanying Author's Notes regarding in rem actions for support and property where there is no personal jurisdiction.

(2) **Service.** See 735 ILCS 5/2-208 and accompanying Author's Notes for personal service of summons outside of the State.

735 ILCS 5/2-620

§ 2-620. Practice on motions

The form and contents of motions, notices regarding the same, hearings on motions, and all other matters of procedure relative thereto, shall be according to rules.

Author's Notes

Analysis

1. Notice of Motion—Form.
2. Cross reference.
3. Notice of Filing—Form.

(1) **Notice of Motion—Form.** There follows a sample notice of motion, which is used to give notice of the presentation of a motion to the court.

FIRM #_____

IN THE CIRCUIT COURT OF COOK COUNTY, ILLINOIS
COUNTY DEPARTMENT—DOMESTIC RELATIONS DIVISION

IN RE THE MARRIAGE OF	)
	)
DOROTHY SKIMPOLE,	)
	)
Petitioner,	)
	)
and	) No. ____ D _____
	)
HAROLD SKIMPOLE,	)
	)
Respondent.	)

NOTICE OF MOTION

To:

PLEASE TAKE NOTICE that on _____, 199__ at __.m., or as soon thereafter as counsel may be heard, I shall appear before the Honorable Judge _____ or any judge sitting in his stead, in the courtroom usually occupied by him in Room _____ of The Richard J. Daley Center, Chicago, Illinois, and

735 ILCS 5/2-620   **PROCEDURE**

then and there present a Motion to _____, a copy of which is attached hereto.

_____
RICHARD VHOLES

Richard Vholes
Attorney for HAROLD SKIMPOLE
Address
Telephone number

CERTIFICATE OF DELIVERY

The undersigned hereby certifies under penalties of perjury as provided by law pursuant to Section 1-109 of the Code of Civil Procedure, that the above notice and any attached pleadings were [ ]placed in the U.S. Mail properly addressed and mailed with first class postage prepaid, [ ]sent via messenger, [ ]sent via facsimile (___ pages, from the office of _____, sender's facsimile number ___, to recipient's facsimile number _____), to the party at the address set forth above on the ___ day of _____, 199__, before the hour of 5:00 p.m.

_____   _____
(Signature)   (Print Name)

(2) **Cross reference.** See Supreme Court Rule 11 for manner of service; Supreme Court Rule 12 for proof of service; and § 1-109 of the Code of Civil Procedure, 735 ILCS 5/1-109, for certification.

(3) **Notice of Filing—Form.** There follows a sample notice of filing, which is used when a paper is filed with the clerk of the court. Alternatively, the document can be filed with just the certificate of service placed at the end of the document.

FIRM #_____

IN THE CIRCUIT COURT OF COOK COUNTY, ILLINOIS
COUNTY DEPARTMENT—DOMESTIC RELATIONS DIVISION

IN RE THE MARRIAGE OF	)
	)
DOROTHY SKIMPOLE,	)
	)
Petitioner,	)
	)
and	) No. ___ D _____
	)
HAROLD SKIMPOLE,	)
	)
Respondent.	)

640

CIVIL PROCEDURE 735 ILCS 5/2-701

NOTICE OF FILING

To:

PLEASE TAKE NOTICE that on the ___ day of _____, 199__, there was filed with the Clerk of the Circuit Court of Cook County, Illinois: _____, a copy of which is attached.

RICHARD VHOLES

Richard Vholes
Attorney for HAROLD SKIMPOLE
Address
Telephone number

CERTIFICATE OF DELIVERY

The undersigned hereby certifies under penalties of perjury as provided by law pursuant to Section 1-109 of the Code of Civil Procedure, that the above notice and any attached pleadings were [ ]placed in the U.S. Mail properly addressed and mailed with first class postage prepaid, [ ]sent via messenger, [ ]sent via facsimile (___ pages, from the office of _____, sender's facsimile number _____, to recipient's facsimile number _____), to the party at the address set forth above on the ___ day of _____, 199__, before the hour of 5:00 p.m.

(Signature) (Print Name)

735 ILCS 5/2-701

§ 2-701. Declaratory judgments

(a) No action or proceeding is open to objection on the ground that a merely declaratory judgment or order is sought thereby. The court may, in cases of actual controversy, make binding declarations of rights, having the force of final judgments, whether or not any consequential relief is or could be claimed, including the determination, at the instance of anyone interested in the controversy, of the construction of any statute, municipal ordinance, or other governmental regulation, or of any deed, will, contract or other written instrument, and a declaration of the rights of the parties interested. The foregoing enumeration does not exclude other cases of actual controversy. The court shall refuse to enter a declaratory judgment or order, if it appears that the judgment or order, would not terminate the controversy or some part thereof, giving rise to the proceeding. In no event shall the court entertain any action or proceeding for a declaratory judgment or order involving any political question where the defendant is a State officer whose election is provided for by the Constitution; however, nothing herein shall prevent the court from entertaining any such action or proceeding for a declaratory

735 ILCS 5/2-701   **PROCEDURE**

judgment or order if such question also involves a constitutional convention or the construction of a statute involving a constitutional convention.

(b) Declarations of rights, as herein provided for, may be obtained by means of a pleading seeking that relief alone, or as incident to or part of a complaint, counterclaim or other pleading seeking other relief as well, and if a declaration of rights is the only relief asked, the case may be set for early hearing as in the case of a motion.

(c) If further relief based upon a declaration of right becomes necessary or proper after the declaration has been made, application may be made by petition to any court having jurisdiction for an order directed to any party or parties whose rights have been determined by the declaration to show cause why the further relief should not be granted forthwith, upon reasonable notice prescribed by the court in its order.

(d) If a proceeding under this Section involves the determination of issues of fact triable by a jury, they shall be tried and determined in the same manner as issues of fact are tried and determined in other civil actions in the court in which the proceeding is pending.

(e) Unless the parties agree by stipulation as to the allowance thereof, costs in proceedings authorized by this Section shall be allowed in accordance with rules. In the absence of rules the practice in other civil actions shall be followed if applicable, and if not applicable, the costs may be taxed as to the court seems just.

Author's Notes

(1) **Dissolution actions.** Petitions for declaratory judgments are commonly used as part of dissolution actions in order to determine the validity of prenuptial agreements prior to adjudication of the issues allegedly governed by the prenuptial agreement. See, e.g., In re Marriage of Byrne, 179 Ill. App.3d 944, 128 Ill.Dec. 800, 535 N.E.2d 14 (1st Dist.1989). It may be possible to obtain an interlocutory appeal of the adjudication of the prenuptial agreement pursuant to Supreme Court Rule 304(a). See Supreme Court Rule 304(a) and accompanying Author's Notes.

735 ILCS 5/2-1001

§ 2-1001. Substitution of judge

(a) A substitution of judge in any civil action may be had in the following situations:

    (1) Involvement of judge. When the judge is a party or interested in the action, or his or her testimony is material to either of the parties to the action, or he or she is related to or has been counsel for any party in regard to the matter in controversy. In any such situation a substitution of judge may be awarded by the court with or without the application of either party.

(2) Substitution as a right. When a party timely exercises his or her right to a substitution without cause as provided in this paragraph (2).

(i) Each party shall be entitled to one substitution of judge without cause as a matter of right.

(ii) An application for substitution of judge as of right shall be made by motion and shall be granted if it is presented before trial or hearing begins and before the judge to whom it is presented has ruled on any substantial issue in the case, or if it is presented by consent of the parties.

(iii) If any party has not entered an appearance in the case and has not been found in default, rulings in the case by the judge on any substantial issue before the party's appearance shall not be grounds for denying an otherwise timely application for substitution of judge as of right by the party.

(3) Substitution for cause. When cause exists.

(i) Each party shall be entitled to a substitution or substitutions for judge for cause.

(ii) Every application for substitution of judge for cause shall be made by petition, setting forth the specific cause for substitution and praying a substitution of judge. The petition shall be verified by the affidavit of the applicant.

(iii) Upon the filing of a petition for substitution of judge for cause, a hearing to determine whether the cause exists shall be conducted as soon as possible by a judge other than the judge named in the petition.

(4) Substitution in contempt proceedings. When any defendant in a proceeding for contempt arising from an attack upon the character or conduct of a judge occurring otherwise than in open court, and the proceeding is pending before the judge whose character or conduct was impugned, fears that he or she will not receive a fair and impartial trial before that judge. In any such situation the application shall be by petition, verified by the applicant, and shall be filed before the trial of the contempt proceeding.

(b) An application for substitution of judge may be made to the court in which the case is pending, reasonable notice of the application having been given to the adverse party or his or her attorney.

(c) When a substitution of judge is granted, the case may be assigned to some other judge in the same county, or in some other convenient county, to which there is no valid objection. If the case is assigned to a judge in some other county, the provisions of subsections (f) through (m) of Section 2.1001.5 shall apply.

735 ILCS 5/2-1001   PROCEDURE

Author's Notes

Analysis

1. Amendment.
2. Substitution of judge.

(1) **Amendment.** The legislature amended 735 ILCS 5/2-1001 and added § 2-1001.5 to distinguish between changes of judge and changes of the place of trial in cases of perceived prejudice. Both were formerly comprehended under the single term change of venue. See In re Marriage of Roach, 245 Ill.App.3d 742, 185 Ill.Dec. 735, 615 N.E.2d 30 (4th Dist.1993); Gerald L. Angst and Dennis M. Coghlan, Substitution of Judges: Recent Statute Codifies and Modifies Existing Law, 82 Ill. B.J. 240 (1994).

(2) **Substitution of judge.** Section 2-1001 provides for four categories of substitution of judges:

> (a) **Relationship.** A substitution of judge may be had where the judge is involved in the action, is related, or has been counsel for one of the parties in the matter in controversy. The change may be initiated by the court or upon application of either party at any time.
>
> (b) **Without cause.** Either party is entitled as a matter of right to one substitution of judge without cause, if the application is presented before there is a trial or a hearing and before the judge has ruled on any substantial issue in the case, or if the application is presented by consent of the parties.
>
>> Pre-trial conferences, where no decisions were made affecting the merits of the case, and rulings on motions for continuance, unopposed motions for leave to amend, discovery motions, and motions for severance have all been held not to be rulings on substantial issues which would prevent a change of judge as of right.... Even when the trial court has not ruled on a substantial issue ... the motion may be denied if the movant has had an opportunity to test the waters and form an opinion as to the court's reaction to his claim ... or if the movant is simply attempting to delay or avoid trial.
>
> In re Marriage of Roach, 245 Ill.App.3d 742, 746, 185 Ill.Dec. 735, 737–738, 615 N.E.2d 30, 33 (4th Dist.), *appeal denied*, 152 Ill.2d 579, 190 Ill.Dec. 910, 622 N.E.2d 1227 (1993). See also In re Marriage of Birt, 157 Ill.App.3d 363, 109 Ill.Dec. 691, 510 N.E.2d 559 (2d Dist.), *appeal denied*, 116 Ill.2d 556, 113 Ill.Dec. 292, 515 N.E.2d 101 (1987), and cases cited therein; Paschen Contractors, Inc. v. Illinois State Toll Highway Authority, 225 Ill.App.3d 930, 168 Ill.Dec. 902, 590 N.E.2d 539 (2d Dist.1992) (motion for substitution of judge was properly denied; judge had stated his position regarding the law as applied to certain issues of the case, and the petitioner had an opportunity to determine the trial judge's thinking). Post-decree actions do not constitute new actions, but are merely continuations of the dissolution proceedings, and therefore a change of venue as of right is not available in a post-decree proceeding. In re Marriage of Roach, 245 Ill.App.3d at 746, 185 Ill.Dec. at 737, 615 N.E.2d at 32.
>
> (c) **Cause.** After a ruling on any substantial issue has been made, a party is entitled to a change of judge only if he or she can demonstrate substantial prejudice. In re Marriage of Hartian, 222 Ill.App.3d 566, 165 Ill.Dec. 66, 584 N.E.2d 245 (1st Dist.1991). The application is made by petition verified by the affidavit of the applicant. The petition must be brought at the earliest practical

moment after the prejudice is discovered, and the change of judge is a matter of judicial discretion. In re Marriage of Roach, 245 Ill.App.3d 742, 185 Ill.Dec. 735, 615 N.E.2d 30 (4th Dist.), *appeal denied*, 152 Ill.2d 579, 190 Ill.Dec. 910, 622 N.E.2d 1227 (1993). The hearing as to whether cause exists is conducted by a judge other than the judge from whom the change is sought.

General allegations of prejudice are insufficient to support a charge of prejudice on the part of the trial court. See Wier v. Isenberg, 95 Ill.App.3d 839, 51 Ill.Dec. 376, 420 N.E.2d 790 (2d Dist.1981). Furthermore,

[a] trial judge is presumed to be impartial and the burden of overcoming this presumption rests on the party making the charge of prejudice, who must present evidence of prejudicial trial conduct.

In re Marriage of Hartian, 222 Ill.App.3d 566, 569, 165 Ill.Dec. 66, 68, 584 N.E.2d 245, 247 (1st Dist.1991) (adverse rulings were insufficient to predicate a motion for substitution of judge) (citation omitted). See also Schlenz v. Castle, 132 Ill.App.3d 993, 87 Ill.Dec. 571, 477 N.E.2d 697 (2d Dist.1985) *aff'd, remanded*, 115 Ill.2d 135, 104 Ill.Dec. 684, 503 N.E.2d 241 (1986) (general allegations of prejudice against all judges in Lake County due to duration of the litigation at bar were insufficient to establish prejudice warranting a substitution of judge; however, specific allegation against individual judge because judge had opposed plaintiff's attorney in a bitterly contested case was sufficient to require removal for cause); Palmisano v. Connell, 179 Ill.App.3d 1089, 1096, 128 Ill.Dec. 638, 643, 534 N.E.2d 1243, 1248 (2d Dist.) *appeal denied*, 127 Ill.2d 621, 136 Ill.Dec. 591, 545 N.E.2d 115 (1989) ("the fact that a judge's mind is closed on a point of law is not considered personal prejudice for purposes of a petition for change of venue.") (citations omitted).

(d) **Contempt.** The statute also allows a change of judge in contempt proceedings where the character of the judge has been attacked out of court and the defendant fears that he will not receive an impartial trial before that judge.

735 ILCS 5/2-1001.5

§ 2-1001.5 Change of venue

(a) A change of venue in any civil action may be had when the court determines that any party may not receive a fair trial in the court in which the action is pending because the inhabitants of the county are prejudiced against the party, or his or her attorney, or the adverse party has an undue influence over the minds of the inhabitants.

(b) Every application for a change of venue by a party or his or her attorney shall be by petition, verified by the affidavit of the application. The petition shall set forth the facts upon which the petitioner bases his or her belief of prejudice of the inhabitants of the county or the undue influence of the adverse party over their minds, and must be supported by the affidavits of at least 2 other reputable persons residing in the county. The adverse party may controvert the petition by counter affidavits, and the court may grant or deny the petition as shall appear to be according to the right of the case.

(c) A petition for change of venue shall not be granted unless it is presented before trial or hearing begins and before the judge to whom it is

735 ILCS 5/2-1001.5   PROCEDURE

presented has ruled on any substantial issue in the case, but if any ground for such change of venue occurs thereafter, a petition for change of venue may be presented based upon such ground.

(d) The application may be made to the court in which the case is pending, reasonable notice thereof having been given to the adverse party or his or her attorney.

(e) When a change of venue is granted, it shall be to some other convenient county to which there is no valid objection.

(f) The order for a change of venue may be made subject to such equitable terms and conditions as safety to the rights of the parties may seem to require, and the court in its discretion may prescribe.

(g) The expenses attending a change of venue shall be taxed by the clerk of the court from which the case is certified according to the rates established by law for like services, and shall be paid by the petitioner and not allowed as part of the costs in the action.

(h) The order shall be void unless the party obtaining a change of venue shall, within 15 days, or such shorter time as the court may prescribe, pay to the clerk the expenses attending the change.

(i) Where the venue is changed without the application of either party, the costs of such change shall abide the event of the action.

(j) In all cases of change of venue, the clerk of the court from which the change is granted shall immediately prepare a full transcript of the record and proceedings in the case, and of the petition, affidavits and order for the change of venue, and transmit the same, together with all the papers filed in the case, to the proper court, but when the venue is changed, on behalf of a part of the defendants in a condemnation proceeding, it shall not be necessary to transmit the original papers in the case, and it shall be sufficient to transmit certified copies of so much thereof as pertains to the case so changed. Such transcript and papers or copies may be transmitted by mail, or in such other ways as the court may direct.

(k) The clerk of the court to which the change of venue is granted shall file the transcript and papers transmitted and docket the cause, and such cause shall be proceeded in and determined before and after judgment, as if it had originated in such court.

(*l*) All questions concerning the regularity of the proceedings in a change of venue, and the right of the court to which the change is made to try the cause and enforce the judgment, shall be considered as waived after trial and verdict.

(m) Upon the entry of judgment of any civil cause in which the venue has been changed, it shall be lawful for the party in whose favor judgment is entered, to file in the office of the clerk of the court where the action was instituted a transcript of such judgment, and the clerk shall file the same of record, and enforcement may be had thereon, and the same shall, from the time of filing such transcript, have the same operation and effect as if originally recovered in such court.

735 ILCS 5/2-1102
§ 2-1102. Examination of adverse party or agent

Upon the trial of any case any party thereto or any person for whose immediate benefit the action is prosecuted or defended, or the officers, directors, managing agents or foreman of any party to the action, may be called and examined as if under cross-examination at the instance of any adverse party. The party calling for the examination is not concluded thereby but may rebut the testimony thus given by countertestimony and may impeach the witness by proof of prior inconsistent statements.

Author's Notes

(1) **Examination of person other than adverse party or agent.** Section 2-1102 applies only to an adverse party or agent. For other witnesses the calling party may want to attack, see Supreme Court Rule 238 and accompanying Author's Notes.

735 ILCS 5/2-1203
§ 2-1203. Motions after judgment in non-jury cases

(a) In all cases tried without a jury, any party may, within 30 days after the entry of the judgment or within any further time the court may allow within the 30 days or any extensions thereof, file a motion for a rehearing, or a retrial, or modification of the judgment or to vacate the judgment or for other relief.

(b) A motion filed in apt time stays enforcement of the judgment.

Author's Notes

(1) **Cross references.** See Supreme Court Rule 303(a) for the timing of a notice of appeal when a motion has been filed after judgment. See Supreme Court Rule 366(b)(3)(i) and 366(b)(3)(ii) for the necessity of a post-trial motion to preserve issues for review.

735 ILCS 5/2-1301
§ 2-1301. Judgments—Default—Confession

(a) The court shall determine the rights of the parties and grant to any party any affirmative relief to which the party may be entitled on the pleadings and proofs. Judgments shall be in the form required by the nature of the case and by the recovery or relief awarded. More than one judgment may be rendered in the same cause. If relief is granted against a party who upon satisfying the same in whole or in part will be entitled by operation of law to be reimbursed by another party to the action, the court may determine the rights of the parties as between themselves, and may thereafter upon motion and notice in the cause, and upon a showing that satisfaction has been made render a final judgment against the other party accordingly.

735 ILCS 5/2-1301 PROCEDURE

(b) A determination in favor of the plaintiff on an issue as to the truth or validity of any defense in abatement shall be that the defendant answer or otherwise plead.

* * *

(d) Judgment by default may be entered for want of an appearance, or for failure to plead, but the court may in either case, require proof of the allegations of the pleadings upon which relief is sought.

(e) The court may in its discretion, before final order or judgment, set aside any default, and may on motion filed within 30 days after entry thereof set aside any final order or judgment upon any terms and conditions that shall be reasonable.

(f) The fact that any order or judgment is joint does not deprive the court of power to set it aside as to fewer than all the parties, and if so set aside it remains in full force and effect as to the other parties.

(g) If any final judgment is entered against any defendant who has been served by publication with notice of the commencement of the action and who has not been served with a copy of the complaint, or received the notice required to be sent him or her by mail, or otherwise brought into court, and such defendant or his or her heirs, legatees, or personal representatives, as the case may require, shall, within 90 days after notice in writing given him or her of the judgment, or within 1 year after the judgment, if no notice has been given, appear in open court and petition to be heard touching the matter of the judgment, the court shall upon notice being given to the parties to such action who appeared therein and the purchaser at a sale made pursuant to the judgment, or their attorneys, set the petition for hearing and may allow the parties and the purchaser to answer the petition. If upon the hearing it appears that the judgment ought not to have been made against the defendant, it may be set aside, altered or amended as appears just; otherwise the petition shall be dismissed at petitioner's costs. If, however, a sale has been had under and pursuant to the final judgment, the court, in altering or amending the judgment may, upon terms just and equitable to the defendant, permit the sale to stand. If upon the hearing of the petition it appears that the defendant was entitled under the law to redeem from the sale, the court shall permit redemption to be made at any time within 90 days thereafter, upon terms that are equitable and just.

735 ILCS 5/2-1302

§ 2-1302. Notice of entry of default order

(a) Upon the entry of an order of default, the attorney for the moving party shall immediately give notice thereof to each party who has appeared, against whom the order was entered, or such party's attorney of record. However, the failure of the attorney to give the notice does not impair the force, validity or effect of the order.

CIVIL PROCEDURE 735 ILCS 5/2-1401

(b) The notice shall contain the title, number, court, date of entry, name of the judge, and state that the order was one of default. The notice may be given by postal card or in any manner provided by rules.

* * *

(d) No notice of the entry of an order of dismissal for want of prosecution shall be necessary provided plaintiff has been notified in advance that the court is considering the entry of such an order, unless required by local rule.

735 ILCS 5/2-1303

§ 2-1303. Interest on judgment

Judgments recovered in any court shall draw interest at the rate of 9% per annum from the date of the judgment until satisfied or 6% per annum when the judgment debtor is a unit of local government, as defined in Section 1 of Article VII of the Constitution, a school district, a community college district, or any other governmental entity. When judgment is entered upon any award, report or verdict, interest shall be computed at the above rate, from the time when made or rendered to the time of entering judgment upon the same, and included in the judgment. Interest shall be computed and charged only on the unsatisfied portion of the judgment as it exists from time to time. The judgment debtor may by tender of payment of judgment, costs and interest accrued to the date of tender, stop the further accrual of interest on such judgment notwithstanding the prosecution of an appeal, or other steps to reverse, vacate or modify the judgment.

735 ILCS 5/2-1401

§ 2-1401. Relief from judgments

(a) Relief from final orders and judgments, after 30 days from the entry thereof, may be had upon petition as provided in this Section. Writs of error coram nobis and coram vobis, bills of review and bills in the nature of bills of review are abolished. All relief heretofore obtainable and the grounds for such relief heretofore available, whether by any of the foregoing remedies or otherwise, shall be available in every case, by proceedings hereunder, regardless of the nature of the order or judgment from which relief is sought or of the proceedings in which it was entered. There shall be no distinction between actions and other proceedings, statutory or otherwise, as to availability of relief, grounds for relief or the relief obtainable.

(b) The petition must be filed in the same proceeding in which the order or judgment was entered but is not a continuation thereof. The petition must be supported by affidavit or other appropriate showing as to matters not of record. All parties to the petition shall be notified as provided by rule.

(c) Except as provided in Section 20b of the Adoption Act, the petition must be filed not later than 2 years after the entry of the order or judgment. Time during which the person seeking relief is under legal disability or duress or the ground for relief is fraudulently concealed shall be excluded in computing the period of 2 years.

(d) The filing of a petition under this Section does not affect the order or judgment, or suspend its operation.

(e) Unless lack of jurisdiction affirmatively appears from the record proper, the vacation or modification of an order or judgment pursuant to the provisions of this Section does not affect the right, title or interest in or to any real or personal property of any person, not a party to the original action, acquired for value after the entry of the order or judgment but before the filing of the petition, nor affect any right of any person not a party to the original action under any certificate of sale issued before the filing of the petition, pursuant to a sale based on the order or judgment.

(f) Nothing contained in this Section affects any existing right to relief from a void order or judgment, or to employ any existing method to procure that relief.

Author's Notes

Analysis

1. Notice.
2. Grounds.
3. Time limit.

(1) **Notice.** See Supreme Court Rules 105 and 106 for service of notice.

(2) **Grounds.** Section 2–1401 applies to petitions for relief of judgments more than 30 days after the date the judgment was entered.

> The elements required to establish a section 2–1401 claim for relief are: (1) the existence of a meritorious claim or defense; (2) due diligence in presenting the claim or defense to the circuit court in the original action; and (3) due diligence in filing the section 2–1401 petition.

In re Marriage of Halas, 173 Ill.App.3d 218, 223, 123 Ill.Dec. 11, 15, 527 N.E.2d 474, 478 (1st Dist.), *appeal denied*, 123 Ill.2d 558, 128 Ill.Dec. 890, 535 N.E.2d 401 (1988) (citations omitted). For example, dissolution judgments may be set aside after 30 days pursuant to § 2–1401 because of fraud that was not discoverable within 30 days of judgment. See, e.g, Spengler v. Spengler, 53 Ill.App.3d 620, 11 Ill.Dec. 432, 368 N.E.2d 1040 (2d Dist.1977) (wife presented sufficient evidence to establish that husband fraudulently concealed increase in his salary); Zieske v. Zieske, 41 Ill.App.3d 746, 354 N.E.2d 513 (1st Dist.1976) (court erred in refusing to allow husband to present evidence supporting his petition to vacate dissolution decree after wife concealed fact that she planned to remarry and remove children from Illinois); Deahl v. Deahl, 13 Ill.App.3d 150, 300 N.E.2d 497 (1st Dist.1973) (husband's motion to vacate dissolution decree satisfied requirements of the statute; wife intentionally concealed fact that she planned to remarry, inducing court to order maintenance in gross instead of maintenance which would terminate upon the wife's remarriage). Judgments may also be vacated if based on mutual mistake of fact which violates the understanding of both parties. See In re Marriage of Breyley, 247 Ill.App.3d 486, 187 Ill.Dec. 215, 617 N.E.2d 423 (3d Dist.1993).

(3) **Time limit.** The time limit for § 2-1401 petitions is two years from the date of judgment, but time is excluded for any periods that the petitioner is under legal disability or duress, or, more commonly, the subject matter of the petition for relief has been fraudulently concealed from the petitioner. See In re Marriage of Halas, 173 Ill.App.3d 218, 223-24, 123 Ill.Dec. 11, 15, 527 N.E.2d 474, 478 (1st Dist.), *appeal denied*, 123 Ill.2d 558, 128 Ill.Dec. 890, 535 N.E.2d 401 (1988) ("if the petition is filed more than two years after the initial judgment was entered, petitioner must also present evidence of fraudulent concealment ... and the issue of fraudulent concealment is necessarily analyzed in the context of the due diligence requirement"). See also In re Marriage of Frazier, 203 Ill.App.3d 847, 148 Ill.Dec. 854, 561 N.E.2d 160 (5th Dist.1990) (dismissal of husband's petition to vacate order dividing marital and non-marital property was error; allegations that wife concealed the fact that the property awarded to husband had been stolen in a robbery more than two years previously were sufficient to toll the running of the two year statutory period); Spengler v. Spengler, 53 Ill.App.3d 620, 11 Ill.Dec. 432, 368 N.E.2d 1040 (2d Dist.1977) (wife presented sufficient evidence to establish fraudulent concealment by husband of increase in his salary to toll two year statutory period).

735 ILCS 5/2-1501

§ 2-1501. Writs abolished

The function which was prior to January 1, 1979, performed by a writ of execution to enforce a judgment or order for the payment of money, or by the writs of mandamus, injunction, prohibition, sequestration, habeas corpus, replevin, ne exeat or attachment, or by the writ of possession in an action of ejectment, or by the writ of restitution in an action of forcible entry and detainer, or by the writ of assistance for the possession of real estate, or by a temporary restraining order, shall hereafter be performed by a copy of the order of judgment to be enforced, certified by the clerk of the court which entered the judgment or order.

The clerk's certification shall bear a legend substantially as follows:

I hereby certify the above to be correct.

Dated _____

(Seal of Clerk of Circuit Court)

_____

Clerk of the Circuit Court of _____ Illinois.

This order is the command of the Circuit Court and violation thereof is subject to the penalty of the law.

Author's Notes

(1) **Sequestration.** The action of sequestration is used in dissolution cases when assets are being mismanaged or dissipated. The action seeks to have the court appoint a sequestrator, who takes control of the assets and manages them subject to court supervision during the pendency of the dissolution litigation. See, e.g, Hellwig v. Hellwig, 100 Ill.App.3d 452, 55 Ill.Dec. 762, 426 N.E.2d 1087 (1st Dist.1981) (upholding

735 ILCS 5/2-1501   PROCEDURE

appointment of sequestrator to protect assets from dissipation by the husband and ensure husband's payment of maintenance to the wife).

735 ILCS 5/2-1901

§ 2-1901. Lis pendens—Operative date of notice

Except as otherwise provided in Section 15-1503, every condemnation proceeding, proceeding to sell real estate of decedent to pay debts, or other action seeking equitable relief, affecting or involving real property shall, from the time of the filing in the office of the recorder in the county where the real estate is located, of a notice signed by any party to the action or his attorney of record or attorney in fact, on his or her behalf, setting forth the title of the action, the parties to it, the court where it was brought and a description of the real estate, be constructive notice to every person subsequently acquiring an interest in or a lien on the property affected thereby, and every such person and every person acquiring an interest or lien as above stated, not in possession of the property and whose interest or lien is not shown of record at the time of filing such notice, shall, for the purposes of this Section, be deemed a subsequent purchaser and shall be bound by the proceedings to the same extent and in the same manner as if he or she were a party thereto. If in any such action plaintiff or petitioner neglects or fails for the period of 6 months after the filing of the complaint or petition to cause notice to be given the defendant or defendants, either by service of summons or publication as required by law, then such notice shall cease to be such constructive notice until service of summons or publication as required by law is had.

This Section authorizes a notice of any of these actions concerning real property pending in any United States district court to be recorded and indexed in the same manner and in the same place as herein provided with respect to notices of such actions pending in courts of this State.

However, no such action or proceeding shall be constructive notice, either before or after service of summons or publication, as to property subject to the provisions of "An Act concerning land titles", approved May 1, 1897, as amended, until the provisions of Section 84 of that Act are complied with.

At any time during the pendency of an action or proceeding initiated after July 1, 1959, which is constructive notice, the court, upon motion, may for good cause shown, provided a finding of specific performance is not necessary for final judgment in the action or proceeding, and upon such terms and conditions, including the posting of suitable bond, if any, as it may deem equitable, authorize the making of a deed, mortgage, lease or other conveyance of any or all of the real estate affected or involved, in which event the party to whom the deed, mortgage, lease or other conveyance of the real estate is made and those claiming under him or her shall not be bound by such action or proceeding.

CIVIL PROCEDURE 735 ILCS 5/2-1901

Author's Notes

Analysis

1. References.
2. Effect.
3. Lis Pendens Notice—Form.
4. 765 ILCS 35/84.

(1) **References.** The reference in the first paragraph to § 15-1503 is to special requirements for notices of foreclosure. The reference in the third paragraph to "an Act concerning land titles," is to the Torrens Act. For property registered under the Torrens Act, there is no constructive notice of the pendency of litigation concerning the property until 765 ILCS 35/84 is complied with. See Author's Note 4 below.

(2) **Effect.** The recording of the lis pendens notice in the county where the real estate is located prevents a purchaser of the real estate from taking the property out from under the proceedings. See, e.g., Security Savings and Loan Ass'n v. Hofmann, 181 Ill.App.3d 419, 130 Ill.Dec. 197, 537 N.E.2d 18 (3d Dist.1989) (lis pendens notice recorded by wife in divorce action gave mortgagee constructive notice of pending litigation). An injunction restraining the parties from transferring assets affects the parties to the lawsuit, but will not affect a bona fide purchaser of real estate in the absence of a recorded lis pendens notice.

(3) **Lis Pendens Notice—Form.** A sample lis pendens notice follows.

IN THE CIRCUIT COURT OF COOK COUNTY, ILLINOIS
COUNTY DEPARTMENT—DOMESTIC RELATIONS DIVISION

IN RE THE MARRIAGE OF	)
	)
CHARLOTTE KROOK,	)
	)
Petitioner,	)
	)
and	) No. ___ D _____
	)
DAVID KROOK,	)
	)
Respondent.	)

LIS PENDENS NOTICE

I, the undersigned, do hereby certify that the above entitled cause was filed in the above court on _____, 199__, as a Petition for Dissolution of Marriage, is now pending in the court, and that the property affected by the cause is described as follows:

735 ILCS 5/2-1901 PROCEDURE

(INSERT LEGAL DESCRIPTION)

                                    Conrad Snagsby
                                    Attorney of Record for Petitioner

Conrad Snagsby
Address
Telephone number

CERTIFICATE OF DELIVERY

    The undersigned hereby certifies under penalties of perjury as provided by law pursuant to Section 1–109 of the Code of Civil Procedure, that the above Lis Pendens Notice was [ ]placed in the U.S. Mail properly addressed and mailed with first class postage prepaid, [ ] sent via messenger, [ ] sent via facsimile (___ pages, from the office of _____, sender's facsimile number _____, to recipient's facsimile number _____), to _____(attorney for Respondent) at _____, on the ____ day of _____, 199__, before the hour of 5:00 p.m.

_____   _____
(Signature)   (Print Name)

    (4) **765 ILCS 35/84.** 765 ILCS 35/84 follows:

§ 84. Torrens Act Notice. (This Section is scheduled to be repealed on July 1, 1997.)

    Notice pursuant to "An Act concerning constructive notice of condemnation proceedings, proceedings to sell real property of decedents to pay debts, or other suits seeking equitable relief involving real property, and proceedings in bankruptcy", approved June 11, 1917, as amended, concerning registered land shall be registered and memorialized in the same manner and in the same place as herein provided.

    No civil action affecting registered land or any estate or interest therein, or any charge upon the same, is lis pendens or notice to any person dealing with the same, until a certificate of the pendency of such civil action under the signature and official seal of the clerk of the court, shall be filed with the registrar and a memorial thereof entered by him upon the register of the last certificate to be affected.

    The termination of lis pendens proceedings shall be recorded by the registrar for a fee of $5.

    This Section authorizes a notice of an action affecting registered land pending in any United States District Court to be registered and memorialized in the same manner and in the same place as herein provided with respect to notice of actions pending in courts of this State.

    The provisions of this Section are not applicable to proceedings under Part 1 of Article IV of the Code of Civil Procedure, as amended.

CIVIL PROCEDURE   735 ILCS 5/8-2601

ARTICLE VIII. EVIDENCE

Analysis

Sec.
8-801.   Privileged communications, husband and wife.
8-2601. Admissibility of evidence; Out of court statements; Child abuse.

WESTLAW Electronic Research

See WESTLAW Electronic Research Guide preceding the Summary of Contents.

---

735 ILCS 5/8-801

§ 8-801. Privileged communications, husband and wife

In all actions, husband and wife may testify for or against each other, provided that neither may testify as to any communication or admission made by either of them to the other or as to any conversation between them during marriage, except in actions between such husband and wife, and in actions where the custody, support, health or welfare of their children or children in either spouse's care, custody or control is directly in issue, and as to matters in which either has acted as agent for the other.

735 ILCS 5/8-2601

§ 8-2601. Admissibility of evidence; Out of court statements; Child abuse

(a) An out-of-court statement made by a child under the age of 13 describing any act of child abuse or any conduct involving an unlawful sexual act performed in the presence of, with, by, or on the declarant child, or testimony by such of an out-of-court statement made by such child that he or she complained of such acts to another, is admissible in any civil proceeding, if: (1) the court conducts a hearing outside the presence of the jury and finds that the time, content, and circumstances of the statement provide sufficient safeguards of reliability; and (2) the child either: (i) testifies at the proceeding; or (ii) is unavailable as a witness and there is corroborative evidence of the act which is the subject of the statement.

(b) If a statement is admitted pursuant to this Section, the court shall instruct the jury that it is for the jury to determine the weight and credibility to be given to the statement and that, in making its determination, it shall consider the age and maturity of the child, the nature of the statement, the circumstances under which the statement was made, and any other relevant factors.

(c) The proponent of the statement shall give the adverse party reasonable notice of an intention to offer the statement and the particulars of the statement.

ARTICLE XI. INJUNCTION

Analysis

Sec.
11–101. Temporary restraining order.
11–102. Preliminary injunction.
11–103. Bond.
11–104. Bond before court or clerk.
11–105. Filing of bond.
11–106. Injunctive relief on Saturday, Sunday or legal holiday.
11–107. Seeking wrong remedy not fatal.
11–107.1 Injunctive relief for the father of an unborn child in an abortion related decision by the mother.
11–108. Motion to dissolve.
11–109. Affidavits in support of motion to dissolve.
11–110. Assessing damages.

WESTLAW Electronic Research

See WESTLAW Electronic Research Guide preceding the Summary of Contents.

---

735 ILCS 5/11–101

§ 11–101. Temporary restraining order

No temporary restraining order shall be granted without notice to the adverse party unless it clearly appears from specific facts shown by affidavit or by the verified complaint that immediate and irreparable injury, loss, or damage will result to the applicant before notice can be served and a hearing had thereon. Every temporary restraining order granted without notice shall be indorsed with the date and hour of signing; shall be filed forthwith in the clerk's office; shall define the injury and state why it is irreparable and why the order was granted without notice; and shall expire by its terms within such time after the signing of the order, not to exceed 10 days, as the court fixes, unless within the time so fixed the order, for good cause shown, is extended for a like period or unless the party against whom the order is directed consents that it may be extended for a longer period. The reasons for the granting of the extension shall be stated in the written order of the court. In case a temporary restraining order is granted without notice, the motion for a preliminary injunction shall be set for hearing at the earliest possible time and takes precedence over all matters except older matters of the same character; and when the motion comes on for hearing the party who obtained the temporary restraining order shall proceed with the application for a preliminary injunction and, if he or she does not do so, the court shall dissolve the temporary restraining order.

On 2 days' notice to the party who obtained the temporary restraining order without notice or on such shorter notice to that party as the court may prescribe, the adverse party may appear and move its dissolution or modification and in that event the court shall proceed to hear and determine such motion as expeditiously as the ends of justice require.

Every order granting an injunction and every restraining order shall set forth the reasons for its entry; shall be specific in terms; shall describe in reasonable detail, and not by reference to the complaint or other document, the act or acts sought to be restrained; and is binding only upon the parties to the action, their officers, agents, employees, and attorneys, and upon those persons in active concert or participation with them who receive actual notice of the order by personal service or otherwise.

735 ILCS 5/11-102

§ 11-102. Preliminary injunction

No court or judge shall grant a preliminary injunction without previous notice of the time and place of the application having been given the adverse party.

Author's Notes

Analysis

1. IMDMA and Code of Civil Procedure.
2. Domestic Violence Act.
3. Cross reference—Form.
4. TRO procedure.
5. Status quo.
6. Mutual injunctions.
7. Appeals.

(1) **IMDMA and Code of Civil Procedure.** In seeking temporary injunctive relief pursuant to § 501 of the Illinois Marriage and Dissolution of Marriage Act, 750 ILCS 5/501, IMDMA § 501 must be read in conjunction with Article XI of the Code of Civil Procedure, 735 ILCS 5/11-101 et seq. Section 501(a)(2) of IMDMA specifically requires that the petition for a temporary restraining order or a preliminary injunction be accompanied by an affidavit showing the factual basis for the relief sought. Section 11-101 of the Code of Civil Procedure requires an affidavit or a verified complaint. Courts acting under the dissolution act frequently require both the petition and the affidavit. Section 501(a)(2) of the Illinois Marriage and Dissolution of Marriage Act enumerates the injunctive relief that can be obtained.

(2) **Domestic Violence Act.** The high standards of pleading and proof that are required for an injunction pursuant to IMDMA § 501 (see 750 ILCS 5/501 Author's Notes (10) and (11)), and Article XI of the Code of Civil Procedure, have been relaxed under the provisions of the Illinois Domestic Violence Act, 750 ILCS 60/101 et seq. Injunctive-like relief can be obtained pursuant to § 214 of the Domestic Violence Act for abuse, exclusive possession of a residence, removal or concealment of a child, and property. The petition for relief under the Domestic Violence Act, however, can be filed only by or on behalf of an abused person pursuant to § 201(b) of the Domestic Violence Act. Injunctive relief is therefore not available except in the cases of abuse, neglect, or exploitation. See 750 ILCS 60/201 Author's Note (3). The practitioner

with a client who does not qualify under the Domestic Violence Act is therefore left with IMDMA § 501 and §§ 11-101 and 11-102 of the Code of Civil Procedure.

(3) **Cross reference—Form.** See 750 ILCS 5/501 Author's Notes (15) through (17) for a sample petition for a temporary restraining order without notice and without bond, a supporting affidavit, and a temporary restraining order.

(4) **TRO procedure.** Frequently a temporary restraining order, without notice, is obtained from the court immediately after the petition for dissolution of marriage is filed; and the summons, petition for dissolution of marriage, and temporary restraining order are served on the respondent simultaneously. Pursuant to § 11-101 of the Code of Civil Procedure, the temporary restraining order expires not later than 10 days after entry, unless it is extended for a like period by the court for good cause, or unless the party against whom it is entered agrees to a longer extension. After receiving the summons, petition, and TRO, the respondent has notice of the time and place of the hearing on the application to extend the temporary restraining order to a preliminary injunction, because the notice is placed in the temporary restraining order itself. See 750 ILCS 5/501 Author's Note (17) for sample temporary restraining order. A preliminary injunction continues during the pendency of the litigation, unless dissolved sooner by the court. See, e.g., Bullard v. Bullard, 66 Ill.App.3d 132, 22 Ill.Dec. 876, 383 N.E.2d 684 (5th Dist.1978) (primary purpose of preliminary injunction was to provide relief to petitioner and "maintain the status quo until the trial on the merits").

(5) **Status quo.** The general purpose of temporary restraining orders and preliminary injunctions is to maintain the status quo during the litigation so that the court will have the opportunity to adjudicate the property and support rights of the parties. The status quo that is to be maintained is the last peaceful status quo that preceded the controversy.

> The primary purpose of a preliminary injunction is to preserve the status quo until there can be a final hearing on the merits. The status quo which will be preserved by a preliminary injunction is "the last actual, peaceful, uncontested status which preceded the pending controversy."

Deisenroth v. Dodge, 350 Ill.App. 20, 23, 111 N.E.2d 575, 577 (2d Dist.1953) (citations omitted). *Cf.* Seagram Distillers Company v. Foremost Sales Promotions, Inc., 13 Ill.App.3d 166, 300 N.E.2d 490 (1st Dist.1973). It may therefore be necessary to seek a mandatory injunction in order to reestablish the last peaceful status quo. For example, a mandatory injunction may require that the respondent restore funds that he has removed from the joint accounts of the parties.

(6) **Mutual injunctions.** A practical compromise to a protracted hearing on a petition for a preliminary injunction is to enter into a mutual agreed injunction restraining both parties from transferring property or abusing one another, and the like. See 750 ILCS 60/215 Author's Note (1) regarding the prohibition against mutual orders of protection under the Domestic Violence Act.

(7) **Appeals.** For interlocutory appeals involving injunctions, see Supreme Court Rule 307.

735 ILCS 5/11-103
§ 11-103. Bond

The court in its discretion, may before entering a restraining order or a preliminary injunction, require the applicant to give bond in such sum, upon such condition and with such security as may be deemed proper by the court, for the payment of such costs and damages as may be incurred or suffered by any party who is found to have been wrongfully enjoined or restrained.

No such bond shall be required of any governmental office or agency.

A surety upon a bond or undertaking under Article XI of this Act submits to the jurisdiction of the court and irrevocably appoints the clerk of the court as the surety's agent upon whom any papers affecting the surety's liability on the bond or undertaking may be served. Such liability may be enforced on motion without the necessity of an independent action. The motion and such notice of motion as the court prescribes may be served on the clerk of the court who shall forthwith mail copies to the persons giving the security if their addresses are known.

Author's Notes

(1) **Purpose.** The court may require the applicant for an injunction post a bond.

> The purpose of requiring a bond ... where a preliminary injunction is issued, is to allow the plaintiff his temporary relief while at the same time assuring the defendant that in the event the preliminary injunction is later dissolved and damages for the unlawful suing out of the injunction are assessed against the plaintiff, such damages will be paid.

Hoffman v. City of Evanston, 101 Ill.App.2d 440, 444, 243 N.E.2d 478, 480 (1st Dist.1968).

Bonds are almost never required in marital litigation. See, e.g., In re Marriage of Meyer, 146 Ill.App.3d 83, 100 Ill.Dec. 128, 496 N.E.2d 1193 (1st Dist.1986) (requirement that wife post bond in order to prevent husband from evicting wife's mother from parties' condominium was error; there was no showing of any financial hardship on the husband).

735 ILCS 5/11-104

§ 11-104. Bond before court or clerk

The bond may be entered into before the court granting or ordering the injunction, or before the clerk of the court, if the court has approved the security.

735 ILCS 5/11-105

§ 11-105. Filing of bond

All bonds required by Article XI of this Act shall be filed with the clerk of the court who is to certify the injunctive order or judgment.

735 ILCS 5/11-106

§ 11-106. Injunctive relief on Saturday, Sunday or legal holiday

When an application is made on a Saturday, Sunday, legal holiday or on a day when courts are not in session for injunctive relief and there is filed with the complaint an affidavit of the plaintiff, or his, her or their agent or attorney, stating that the benefits of injunctive relief will be lost or endangered, or irremediable damage occasioned unless such injunctive relief is immediately granted, and stating the bases for such alleged consequence, and if it appears to the court from such affidavit that the benefits of injunctive relief will be lost or endangered, or irremediable damage occasioned unless such injunctive relief is immediately granted, and if the plaintiff otherwise is entitled to such relief under the law, the court may grant injunctive relief on a Saturday, Sunday, legal holiday, or on a day when courts are not in session; and it shall be lawful for the clerk to certify, and for the sheriff or coroner to serve such order for injunctive relief on a Saturday, Sunday, legal holiday or on a day when courts are not in session as on any other day, and all affidavits and bonds made and proceedings had in such case shall have the same force and effect as if made or had on any other day.

735 ILCS 5/11-107
§ 11-107. Seeking wrong remedy not fatal

Where relief is sought under Article XI of this Act and the court determines, on motion directed to the pleadings, or on motion for summary judgment or upon trial, that the plaintiff has pleaded or established facts which entitle the plaintiff to relief but that the plaintiff has sought the wrong remedy, the court shall permit the pleadings to be amended, on just and reasonable terms, and the court shall grant the relief to which plaintiff is entitled on the amended pleadings or upon the evidence. In considering whether a proposed amendment is just and reasonable, the court shall consider the right of the defendant to assert additional defenses, to demand a trial by jury, to plead a counterclaim or third party complaint, and to order the plaintiff to take additional steps which were not required under the pleadings as previously filed.

735 ILCS 5/11-107.1
§ 11-107.1 Injunctive relief for the father of an unborn child in an abortion related decision by the mother

In any case when a married woman wishes to have an abortion performed upon her, and her spouse, who is the father of the unborn child, is opposed to the performance of that abortion, a court may hear testimony from both parties and balance the rights and interests of those parties.

When the interests of the husband in preventing the abortion outweigh those of the wife in having an abortion performed after the unborn child is viable, the court may issue an injunction against the performance of the abortion but only where the court makes a finding that the mother's life or physical health are not in danger.

735 ILCS 5/11-108
§ 11-108. Motion to dissolve

A motion to dissolve an injunction may be made at any time before or after answer is filed. Upon a motion to dissolve an injunction after answer is filed the court shall decide the motion upon the weight of the evidence.

735 ILCS 5/11-109

§ 11-109. Affidavits in support of motion to dissolve

The plaintiff may support the complaint and the defendant may support the answer by affidavits filed with the same, which may be read in evidence on the hearing of the motion to dissolve the injunction.

735 ILCS 5/11-110

§ 11-110. Assessing damages

In all cases where a temporary restraining order or a preliminary injunction is dissolved by the circuit court or by the reviewing court, the circuit court, after the dissolution of the temporary restraining order or preliminary injunction, and before finally disposing of the action shall, upon the party claiming damages by reason of such temporary restraining order or preliminary injunction, filing a petition under oath setting forth the nature and amount of damages suffered, determine and enter judgment in favor of the party who was injured by such temporary restraining order or preliminary injunction for the damages which the party suffered as a result thereof, which judgment may be enforced as other judgments for the payment of money. However, a failure so to assess damages as hereinabove set out shall not operate as a bar to an action upon the injunction bond.

ARTICLE XII. JUDGMENTS—ENFORCEMENT

Analysis

Sec.
12–650. Short title.
12–651. Definition.
12–652. Filing and status of foreign judgments.
12–653. Notice of filing.
12–654. Stay.
12–655. Fees.
12–656. Optional procedure.
12–657. Uniformity of interpretation.

WESTLAW Electronic Research

See WESTLAW Electronic Research Guide preceding the Summary of Contents.

735 ILCS 5/12-650

§ 12-650. Short title

Sections 12–650 through 12–657 of this Act may be cited as the Uniform Enforcement of Foreign Judgments Act.

735 ILCS 5/12-651

§ 12-651. Definition

As used in Sections 12-650 through 12-657, "foreign judgment" means any judgment, decree, or order of a court of the United States or of any other court which is entitled to full faith and credit in this State.

735 ILCS 5/12-652

§ 12-652. Filing and status of foreign judgments

A copy of any foreign judgment authenticated in accordance with the acts of Congress or the statutes of this State may be filed in the office of the circuit clerk for any county of this State. The clerk shall treat the foreign judgment in the same manner as a judgment of the circuit court for any county of this State. A judgment so filed has the same effect and is subject to the same procedures, defenses and proceedings for reopening, vacating, or staying as a judgment of a circuit court for any county of this State and may be enforced or satisfied in like manner.

Author's Notes

Analysis

1. Modification.
2. Cross references.

(1) **Modification.** A foreign judgment that is enrolled in Illinois is capable of being prospectively modified pursuant to § 12-652.

(2) **Cross references.** For a comparison of available remedies and rights to prospective modification among the various statutes for the enforcement of out-of-state support orders, see 750 ILCS 20/1 Author's Notes (4) and (5). For modification of foreign custody orders in Illinois, see 750 ILCS 35/15 Author's Note (1).

735 ILCS 5/12-653

§ 12-653. Notice of filing

(a) At the time of the filing of the foreign judgment, the judgment creditor or his lawyer shall make and file with the circuit clerk an affidavit setting forth the name and last known post office address of the judgment debtor, and the judgment creditor.

(b) Promptly upon the filing of the foreign judgment and the affidavit, the clerk shall mail notice of the filing of the foreign judgment to the judgment debtor at the address given and shall make a note of the mailing in the docket. The notice shall include the name and post office address of the judgment creditor and the judgment creditor's lawyer, if any, in this State. In addition, the judgment creditor may mail a notice of the filing of the judgment to the judgment debtor and may file proof of mailing with the clerk. Lack of mailing notice of filing by the clerk shall not affect the enforcement proceedings if proof of mailing by the judgment creditor has been filed.

(c) No order or other process for enforcement of a foreign judgment filed hereunder shall issue until 30 days after the date the judgment is filed.

735 ILCS 5/12-654
§ 12-654. Stay

(a) If the judgment debtor shows the circuit court that an appeal from the foreign judgment is pending or will be taken, or that a stay of execution has been granted, the court shall stay enforcement of the foreign judgment until the appeal is concluded, the time for appeal expires, or the stay of execution expires or is vacated, upon proof that the judgment debtor has furnished the security for the satisfaction of the judgment required by the state in which is was rendered.

(b) If the judgment debtor shows the circuit court any ground upon which enforcement of a judgment of any circuit court for any county of this State would be stayed, the court shall stay enforcement of the foreign judgment for an appropriate period, upon requiring the same security for satisfaction of the judgment which is required in this State.

735 ILCS 5/12-655
§ 12-655. Fees

Any person filing a foreign judgment shall pay a fee to the circuit clerk equivalent to the fee which would be required were the person filing a complaint seeking the amount awarded in the foreign judgment. Fees for docketing, transcription or other enforcement proceedings shall be as provided for judgments of the circuit court.

735 ILCS 5/12-656
§ 12-656. Optional procedure

The right of a judgment creditor to bring an action to enforce his judgment instead of proceeding under this Act remains unimpaired.

735 ILCS 5/12-657
§ 12-657. Uniformity of interpretation

This Act shall be so interpreted and construed as to effectuate its general purpose to make uniform the law of those states which enact it.

ARTICLE XXI. CHANGE OF NAME

Analysis

Sec.
21–101. Change of name; Proceedings; Parties.
21–102. Petition.
21–103. Notice by publication.
21–104. Process and notice to persons outside this State.

735 ILCS 5/21-101

§ 21-101. Change of name; Proceedings; Parties

If any person who is a resident of this State and has resided in this State for 6 months desires to change his or her name and to assume another name by which to be afterwards called and known, the person may file a petition in the circuit court of the county wherein he or she resides praying for that relief. If it appears to the court that the conditions hereinafter mentioned have been complied with and that there is no reason why the prayer should not be granted, the court, by an order to be entered of record, may direct and provide that the name of that person be changed in accordance with the prayer in the petition. The filing of a petition in accordance with this Section shall be the sole and exclusive means by which any person committed under the laws of this State to a penal institution may change his or her name and assume another name. However, any person convicted of a felony in this State or any other state who has not been pardoned may not file a petition for a name change until 2 years have passed since completion and discharge from his or her sentence. A petitioner may include his or her spouse and adult unmarried children, with their consent, and his or her minor children where it appears to the court that it is for their best interest, in the petition and prayer, and the court's order shall then include the spouse and children. Whenever any minor has resided in the family of any person for the space of 3 years and has been recognized and known as an adopted child in the family of that person, the application herein provided for may be made by the person having that minor in his or her family.

An order shall be entered as to a minor only if the court finds by clear and convincing evidence that the change is necessary to serve the best interest of the child. In determining the best interest of a minor child under this Section, the court shall consider all relevant factors, including:

(1) The wishes of the child's parents and any person acting as a parent who has physical custody of the child.

(2) The wishes of the child and the reasons for those wishes. The court may interview the child in chambers to ascertain the child's wishes with respect to the change of name. Counsel shall be present at the interview unless otherwise agreed upon by the parties. The court shall cause a court reporter to be present who shall make a complete record of the interview instantaneously to be part of the record in the case.

(3) The interaction and interrelationship of the child with his or her parents or persons acting as parents who have physical custody of the

child, step-parents, siblings, step-siblings, or any other person who may significantly affect the child's best interest.

(4) The child's adjustment to his or her home, school, and community.

Author's Notes

Analysis

1. Not exclusive.
2. Change of child's name.

(1) **Not exclusive.** Chapter 735 ILCS 5/21–101 et seq. is not the exclusive means by which an adult not in a penal institute may change his or her name. By agreement between the husband and wife, a maiden or previous name of a wife may be authorized in a dissolution of marriage decree, or the wife may petition to change her name as part of the dissolution proceedings. See IMDMA § 413(c), 750 ILCS 5/413(c). Under the common law, "every person is free not only to assume any surname he or she pleases, but also to change it at any time." Thomas v. Thomas, 100 Ill.App.3d 1080, 1081, 56 Ill.Dec. 604, 605, 427 N.E.2d 1009, 1010 (1st Dist.1981). However, the common law right is valid only if such action does not interfere with the rights of others. See Chaney v. Civil Service Commission, 82 Ill.2d 289, 45 Ill.Dec. 146, 412 N.E.2d 497 (1980). Therefore, a person may also change his or her name without any judicial proceeding simply by using another name, provided that the purpose is not to defraud creditors or otherwise interfere with the rights of others.

(2) **Change of child's name.** If a parent or guardian petitions the court to change the name of a child, the court must determine if such a change is in the best interests of the child. In re Marriage of Presson, 102 Ill.2d 303, 80 Ill.Dec. 294, 465 N.E.2d 85 (1984) (the fact that child had a different surname from his remarried mother and stepsiblings was not enough to warrant a change of the child's last name). The court should consider

> the expressed wishes of the child and of both parents, the stated reasons for the proposed change, the child's age and maturity, the nature of the family situation, the strength of the ties between the child and each parent, any misconduct toward or neglect of the child by the parent opposing the change, and the name by which the child has customarily been called.

Id., 102 Ill.2d at 309, 80 Ill.Dec. at 297, 465 N.E.2d at 88. See also In re Mattson, 240 Ill.App.3d 993, 181 Ill.Dec. 810, 608 N.E.2d 1284 (2d Dist.1993) (testimony that the child had been teased by classmates because her surname differed from the surname of her custodial mother was insufficient to establish that a name change was in the child's best interest).

735 ILCS 5/21–102

§ 21–102. Petition

The petition shall set forth the name then held, the name sought to be assumed, the residence of the petitioner, the length of time the petitioner has resided in this State, and the state or country of the petitioner's nativity or supposed nativity. The petition shall be signed by the person petitioning or,

735 ILCS 5/21-102   **PROCEDURE**

in case of minors, by the parent or guardian having the legal custody of the minor. The petition shall be verified by the affidavit of some credible person.

735 ILCS 5/21-103

§ 21-103. Notice by publication

(a) Previous notice shall be given of the intended application by publishing a notice thereof in some newspaper published in the municipality in which the person resides if the municipality is in a county with a population under 2,000,000, or if the person does not reside in a municipality in a county with a population under 2,000,000, or if no newspaper is published in the municipality or if the person resides in a county with a population of 2,000,000 or more, then in some newspaper published in the county where the person resides, or if no newspaper is published in that county, then in some convenient newspaper published in this State. The notice shall be inserted for 3 consecutive weeks, the first insertion to be at least 6 weeks before the return day upon which the petition is to be filed, and shall be signed by the petitioner or, in case of a minor, the minor's parent or guardian, and shall set forth the return day of court on which the petition is to be filed and the name sought to be assumed.

(b) The publication requirement of subsection (a) shall not be required in any application for a change of name involving a minor if, before making judgment under this Article, reasonable notice and opportunity to be heard is given to any parent whose parental rights have not been previously terminated and to any person who has physical custody of the child. If any of these persons are outside this State, notice and opportunity to be heard shall be given under Section 21-104.

735 ILCS 5/21-104

§ 21-104. Process and notice to persons outside this State

(a) Process in change of name proceedings shall be governed by this Code.

(b) Notice in all change of name proceedings required for the exercise of jurisdiction over a person outside this State shall be given in a manner best calculated to give actual notice and shall be given in one of the following manners:

 (1) By personal delivery outside this State in the manner prescribed for service of process within this State.

 (2) In the manner prescribed by the law of the place in which the service is made for service of process in that place in an action in any of its courts of general jurisdiction.

 (3) By any form of mail addressed to the person to be served and requesting a receipt.

 (4) As directed by the court if other means of notification are ineffective.

(c) Notice under this Section shall be served, mailed, or delivered at least 10 days before any hearing in this State.

(d) Proof of service outside this State may be made by affidavit of the individual who made the service or in the manner prescribed by the law of this State, the order pursuant to which the service is made, or the law of the place in which the service is made. If service is made by mail, proof may be a receipt signed by the addressee or other evidence of delivery to the addressee.

ILLINOIS SUPREME COURT RULES

Analysis

Rule
11.	Manner of serving papers other than process and complaint on parties not in default in the trial and reviewing courts.
12.	Proof of service in the trial and reviewing courts; Effective date of service.
13.	Appearances—Time to plead—Withdrawal.
100.1	Expedited child support rules. Implementation of Expedited Child Support System.
100.2	Appointment, qualification and compensation of administrative hearing officers.
100.3	Actions subject to expedited child support hearings.
100.4	Authority of administrative hearing officers.
100.5	Blood tests.
100.6	Scheduling of the hearings.
100.7	Conduct of the hearing.
100.8	Absence of party at hearing.
100.9	Transfers for judicial hearings.
100.10	Submission of recommendations to the court.
100.11	Authority retained by the court.
100.12	Judicial hearings.
100.13	Definitions.
101.	Summons and original process—Form and issuance.
102.	Service of summons and complaint—Return.
104.	Service of pleadings and other papers—Filing.
105.	Additional relief against parties in default—Notice.
106.	Notice of petitions filed for relief from, or revival of, judgments.
137.	Signing of pleadings, motions and other papers—Sanctions.
201.	General discovery provisions.
202.	Purposes for which depositions may be taken in pending action.
203.	Where depositions may be taken.
204.	Compelling appearance of deponent.
206.	Method of taking depositions on oral examination.
207.	Signing and filing depositions.
208.	Fees and charges—Copies.
209.	Failure to attend or serve subpoena—Expenses.
210.	Depositions on written questions.
211.	Effect of errors and irregularities in depositions—Objections.
212.	Use of depositions.
213.	Written interrogatories to parties.
214.	Discovery of documents, objects, and tangible things—Inspection of real estate.
215.	Physical and mental examination of parties and other persons.
216.	Admission of fact or of genuineness of documents.
218.	Pretrial procedure.
219.	Consequences of refusal to comply with rules or order relating to discovery or pretrial conferences.
220.	Expert witnesses.
231.	Motions for continuance.
236.	Admission of business records in evidence.
237.	Compelling appearance of witnesses at trial.
238.	Impeachment of witnesses—Hostile witnesses.

Rule
272. When judgment is entered.
296. Enforcement of order for support.
301. Method of review.
303. Appeals from final judgments of the circuit courts in civil cases.
304. Appeals from final judgments that do not dispose of an entire proceeding.
305. Stay of judgments pending appeal.
306. Appeals from orders of the circuit court granting new trials and granting or denying certain motions.
307. Interlocutory appeals as of right.
308. Interlocutory appeals by permission.
311. Accelerated docket.
312. Docketing statement.
366. Powers of reviewing court—Scope of review and procedure—Lien of judgment.

WESTLAW Electronic Research

See WESTLAW Electronic Research Guide preceding the Summary of Contents.

Rule 11. Manner of serving papers other than process and complaint on parties not in default in the trial and reviewing courts

(a) On whom made. If a party is represented by an attorney of record, service shall be made upon the attorney. Otherwise service shall be made upon the party.

(b) Method. Papers shall be served as follows:

(1) by delivering them to the attorney or party personally;

(2) by leaving them in the office of the attorney with his clerk, or with a person in charge of the office; or if a party is not represented by counsel, by leaving them at his residence with a family member of the age of 13 years or upwards;

(3) by depositing them in a United States post office or postoffice box, enclosed in an envelope, plainly addressed to the attorney at his business address, or to the party at his business address or residence, with postage fully prepaid; or

(4) by transmitting them via facsimile machine to the office of the attorney or party, who has consented to receiving service by facsimile transmission. Briefs filed in reviewing courts shall not be served by facsimile transmission.

(i) A party or attorney electing to serve pleadings by facsimile must include on the certificate of service transmitted the telephone number of the sender's facsimile transmitting device. Use of service by facsimile shall be deemed consent by that party or attorney to receive service by facsimile transmission. Any party may rescind consent of service by facsimile transmission in a case by filing with the court and serving a notice on all parties or their attorneys who have filed appearances that facsimile service will not be accepted. A party or attorney who has rescinded consent to service by facsimile transmission in a case may not serve another party or attorney by facsimile transmission in that case.

(ii) Each page of notices and documents transmitted by facsimile pursuant to this rule should bear the circuit court number, the title of the document, and the page number.

(c) *Multiple parties or attorneys.* In cases in which there are two or more plaintiffs or defendants who appear by different attorneys, service of all papers shall be made on the attorney for each of the parties. If one attorney appears for several parties, he is entitled to only one copy of any paper served upon him by the opposite side. When more than one attorney appears for a party, service of a copy upon one of them is sufficient.

Rule 12. Proof of service in the trial and reviewing courts; Effective date of service

(a) *Filing.* When service of a paper is required, proof of service shall be filed with the clerk.

(b) *Manner of proof.* Service is proved:

(1) by written acknowledgment signed by the person served;

(2) in case of service by personal delivery, by certificate of the attorney, or affidavit of a person, other than an attorney, who made delivery;

(3) in case of service by mail, by certificate of the attorney, or affidavit of a person other than the attorney, who deposited the paper in the mail, stating the time and place of mailing, the complete address which appeared on the envelope, and the fact that proper postage was prepaid; or

(4) in case of service by facsimile transmission, by certificate of the attorney or affidavit of a person other than the attorney, who transmitted the paper via facsimile machine, stating the time and place of transmission, the telephone number to which the transmission was sent, and the number of pages transmitted.

(c) *Effective date of service by mail.* Service by mail is complete four days after mailing.

(d) *Effective date of service by facsimile transmission.* Service by facsimile machine is complete on the first court day following transmission.

Author's Notes

Analysis

1. Facsimile service.
2. Cross reference—Form.

mended orders, and any other matters that require transfer or should be referred to a judge;

(12) describe the procedure for transfer of matters from a judge to an administrative hearing officer; and

(13) describe the procedure for action by a judge on an administrative hearing officer's recommendations.

(d) Availability of system to non-IV–D participants. A Plan may provide that the System is available in cases where both parties are non-IV–D participants and request access to the System.

(e) Establishment of demonstration programs. The Illinois Department of Public Aid may notify the Supreme Court of its desire to establish a demonstration program in one or more circuits or counties. Any such program shall be available to IV–D participants. Upon receipt of such notification, the Supreme Court will notify the chief judge of each judicial circuit of the department's desire to establish a demonstration program. Each chief judge may submit a demonstration Plan to the Supreme Court which, upon approval, will submit the Plan to the Department. The Department may select one or more circuits or counties to participate in the demonstration program after reviewing the submitted Plans. The Department shall notify the Supreme Court of its decision. The submitted demonstration Plan shall include each element listed in subsection (c) above. In addition, each demonstration Plan shall include a projected budget for operation of the System. The demonstration Plan shall specify whether it is available to non-IV–D participants, and if so, shall provide that the portion of the administrative costs attributable to use by non-IV–D participants has been appropriated by the demonstration county and meets the requirements of subsection (g) below.

(f) Supreme Court review and approval. The Supreme Court shall review and approve or request that the chief judge modify any submitted Plan or demonstration Plan for compliance with the Act, these rules and, to the extent Federal reimbursement is sought, the rules of the IV–D program. Upon Supreme Court approval of a Plan, any nondemonstration county, circuit, multicircuit area or multicounty area may establish a System. Approved demonstration Plans will be submitted to the Department of Public Aid for review based on Department standards.

(g) Funding. Before establishment of a System according to a Supreme Court approved Plan, each participating nondemonstration county board or boards must appropriate the administrative expenses incurred to establish and maintain the non-IV–D portion of the System and the IV–D portion that is not subject to Federal reimbursement. A Plan for cost-sharing must be submitted to the Department of Public Aid for approval. Each chief judge shall be responsible for documenting and recording the number of IV–D and non-IV–D cases pending and disposed of in the System each month, and the portion of administrative expenses eligible for Federal reimbursement under the IV–D program, in such a manner as to insure Federal reimbursement.

S. Ct. Rule 100.1   **PROCEDURE**

Information necessary for Federal reimbursement shall be submitted to the Department of Public Aid 14 days after the end of each month. The chief judge shall also submit copies of such information to the Supreme Court. Reimbursement shall be made to the Supreme Court, which shall pay for the expenses incurred by the System. Employees of the System are employees of the State of Illinois.

(h) Administration. Pursuant to rule, the chief judge of each judicial circuit shall be responsible for administering the System on a day-to-day basis, shall employ and terminate administrative hearing officers and other necessary staff, and shall review and evaluate the performance of each administrative hearing officer. Reviews shall be conducted quarterly in the first year of employment, and annually thereafter.

(i) Reporting of data. The chief judge shall file a report with the Supreme Court within 35 days of the end of each State fiscal year detailing the number of:

    (1) matters initially assigned to an administrative hearing officer;

    (2) matters transferred to an administrative hearing officer;

    (3) matters returned to an administrative hearing officer from a judge;

    (4) matters submitted to a judge from an administrative hearing officer with recommendation for a court order;

    (5) recommended court orders entered by a judge;

    (6) recommended court orders rejected by a judge;

    (7) matters submitted by an administrative hearing officer to a judge for hearings;

    (8) IV–D and non-IV–D matters pending and disposed of in the System; and

    (9) matters which complied or failed to comply with Federal time frames. The above data shall be reported for each fiscal year with respect to each administrative hearing office and for the System as a whole.

(j) Local rules. Each judicial circuit may adopt rules for the conduct of expedited child support hearings which are consistent with these rules and may determine which matters within the general classification of eligible actions shall be heard by administrative hearing officers.

(k) Applicability of other Acts, the Code of Civil Procedure and Rules of the Supreme Court. The provisions of the Illinois Marriage and Dissolution of Marriage Act, the Illinois Parentage Act of 1984, the Illinois Public Aid Code, the Revised Uniform Reciprocal Enforcement of Support Act, the Nonsupport of Spouse and Children Act, the State Mandates Act, the Code of Civil Procedure and the rule of the Supreme Court shall be applicable to expedited child support hearings except insofar as these rules otherwise provide.

Author's Notes

Analysis

1. Cook County.
2. Cases heard.
3. Who qualifies?
4. Hearing officers and judges.
5. Advantages and disadvantages.
6. Cross references.

(1) **Cook County.** The Expedited Child Support System is operating in Cook County where there are currently ten hearing officers. The System started in Cook County on June 28, 1993. No other Illinois counties are presently operating the Expedited Child Support System, although it is in operation in several other states. The System is part of the Domestic Relations Division, and it is located at 32 W. Randolph Street in Chicago.

(2) **Cases heard.** The Cook County System is hearing parentage cases, establishment of child support cases, and enforcement of child support cases, including the enforcement of orders where one party is out of state under the Revised Uniform Reciprocal Enforcement of Support Act. See 750 ILCS 20/1 et seq. It does not hear maintenance cases.

(3) **Who qualifies?** The System will hear any Title IV–D cases, which can be anyone who is a custodial parent, whether or not the custodial parent is on Public Aid. Public Aid initially fills out the forms for the petitioner, and the State's Attorney prosecutes the case, although a custodial parent can also hire a private attorney.

(4) **Hearing officers and judges.** Hearing officers take evidence and agreements by the parties; and, from the evidence and agreements, submit recommendations to the judges. Judges can accept, reject, modify, or send back the recommendations of the hearing officers. Hearing officers cannot sign orders nor hold parties in contempt. Although the functions of the hearing officers appear to be new, they are not remarkably different from the masters in chancery system that formerly existed in Illinois.

(5) **Advantages and disadvantages.** The advantages of the Expedited Child Support System for those on Public Aid are apparent. For others, there is the advantage of the capability of intercepting income tax refunds and unemployment compensation for application to children's support arrearages. Also the System allows access to W–2 records in order to locate an employed obligor and garnish his wages. The major disadvantage is the necessity of dealing with a huge bureaucracy, which is slow and inefficient.

(6) **Cross references.** See also Expedited Child Support Act of 1990, 750 ILCS 25/1 et seq., and IMDMA §§ 705, 709 through 712, 750 ILCS 5/705, 709 through 712, and accompanying Author's Notes. See also Supreme Court Rule 296 and accompanying Author's Notes.

Rule 100.2 Appointment, qualification and compensation of administrative hearing officers

(a) Appointment. Administrative hearing officers shall be hired by the chief judge of each judicial circuit, after satisfying the qualifications set by the Supreme Court. Candidates for the position of administrative hearing officer must apply for appointment with the chief judge of each judicial circuit.

(b) Qualifications. Administrative hearing officers must be licensed to practice law in Illinois and must have been engaged in the active practice of law for a minimum of three years.

(c) Disqualification. A full-time administrative hearing officer shall not practice law before any court. A part-time administrative hearing officer shall not practice law in any domestic relations matter or other matter which would qualify for an expedited hearing before an administrative hearing officer without the written consent of both parties. Upon appointment to a case, an administrative hearing officer shall notify the judge and withdraw from the case if any grounds appear to exist for disqualification under Supreme Court Rules 61 through 67.

(d) Oath of office. Each administrative hearing officer shall take an oath of office similar to a judicial oath.

(e) Compensation. Each administrative hearing officer shall be compensated as provided in the Plan.

(f) Communications with attorneys. Disciplinary rules governing the conduct of attorneys before a court remain applicable in expedited child support hearings. Disciplinary rules governing communications between an attorney and a judge govern communications between attorneys and administrative hearing officers.

Rule 100.3 Actions subject to expedited child support hearings

(a) Eligible actions. The following actions, if so provided for in the Plan, are eligible to be heard by an administrative hearing officer:

(1) actions pursuant to the Illinois Public Aid Code, as amended, to establish temporary and final child support and medical support, and to enforce or modify existing orders of child support and medical support;

(2) actions pursuant to the Illinois Parentage Act of 1984, as amended, to establish a parent and child relationship; to establish child support and medical support after parentage has been acknowledged or established, whether or not these issues were reserved at the time judgment was entered; and to enforce or modify existing child support and medical support orders;

(3) actions pursuant to the Illinois Marriage and Dissolution of Marriage Act, as amended, to establish temporary and final child support and medical support, whether or not these issues were reserved or could not be ordered at the time judgment was entered because the court lacked

personal jurisdiction over the obligor; and to enforce or modify existing orders of child support and medical support;

(4) actions pursuant to the Nonsupport of Spouse and Children Act to establish temporary child support and to enforce and modify such orders;

(5) actions pursuant to the Revised Uniform Reciprocal Enforcement of Support Act to establish temporary and final child support and medical support, whether or not these issues were reserved or could not be ordered at the time judgment was entered because the court lacked personal jurisdiction over the obligor; and to enforce and modify existing child support and medical support orders; and

(6) any other child support or medical support matter.

(b) Other eligible prejudgment proceedings. If provided for in the Plan, the System may be available in prejudgment proceedings for dissolution of marriage, declaration of invalidity of marriage and legal separation.

Rule 100.4 Authority of administrative hearing officers

(a) Powers of administrative hearing officers. Administrative hearing officers shall have the authority to conduct child support hearings, to administer oaths and affirmations, to take testimony under oath or affirmation, to determine the admissibility of evidence, to propose findings of fact, and to recommend orders to the judge based on such evidence as prescribed by the Act.

(b) Accept voluntary agreements of parties. Administrative hearing officers may accept stipulations of fact and voluntary agreements of the parties setting the amount of child support to be paid or medical support liability and to recommend to the judge the entry of orders incorporating such agreements.

(c) Accept voluntary acknowledgments of parentage. Administrative hearing officers may accept voluntary orders of parentage and recommend to the judge the entry of orders based on such acknowledgments. Prior to accepting an acknowledgment of parentage, administrative hearing officers shall advise the putative father of his rights and obligations.

(d) Discovery. Administrative hearing officers shall manage all stages of discovery, including hearings on citations to discover assets and setting deadlines for the completion of discovery, and to direct the submission to tests pursuant to section 11 of the Illinois Parentage Act of 1984 and Rule 100.5 below. Administrative hearing officers may not enter orders with respect to disputed discovery matters though they may recommend the entry of such orders to a judge. Discovery shall be conducted in accordance with these rules and shall be completed prior to the expedited child support hearing. No discovery shall be permitted after the hearing, except upon leave of court and good cause shown.

S. Ct. Rule 100.4   PROCEDURE

(e) *Compelling appearance of the obligor.* The person designated in the Plan may recommend that the judge issue a notice requiring the obligor to appear before the administrative hearing officer or in court.

(f) *Recommend default orders.* Administrative hearing officers may recommend that the judge issue a default order to absent parties who fail to respond to a notice to appear before the administrative hearing officer or such other orders as are specified in Rule 100.11(d).

(g) *Authority over unemployed obligor.* Administrative hearing officers may recommend that an unemployed obligor who is not making child support payments or who is unable to provide support be ordered to seek employment and may recommend that the obligor be required to submit periodic reports as to such efforts. Administrative hearing officers may recommend that the obligor be ordered to report to the appropriate agency to participate in job search, training or work programs.

(h) *Foreign support matters.* Administrative hearing officers may recommend that foreign support judgments or orders be registered as Illinois judgments or orders.

(i) *Non–IV–D obligees.* Administrative hearing officers shall inform non-IV–D obligees of the existence and services of the IV–D program and provide applications if requested. Administrative hearing officers shall also inform such obligees that payment may be requested through the clerk of the circuit court. Any such request that payment be made through the clerk shall be noted in the recommended order to the judge.

Rule 100.5 Blood tests

(a) *Order to submit to tests.* Administrative hearing officers may recommend, upon the request of a party, that the judge order the mother, child and alleged father to submit to appropriate tests to determine inherited characteristics including, but not limited to, blood types and genetic markers such as those found by Human Leucocyte Antigen (HLA) tests. The judge shall determine the appropriate tests to be conducted and appoint an expert to determine the testing procedures and conduct the tests.

Rule 100.6 Scheduling of the hearings

(a) *Assignment of hearing date.* If an action or a motion filed by a IV–D participant qualifies as an action over which an administrative hearing officer has authority, the person designated in the Plan shall assign a hearing date before an administrative hearing officer. The procedure for fixing the date, time and place of a hearing before an administrative hearing officer shall be prescribed by circuit rule provided that not less than seven days' notice in writing shall be given to the parties or their attorneys of record. In cases in which the court has previously acquired jurisdiction over the responding party, the hearing shall be held on the scheduled date and not less than 21 days or more than 35 days of the date of filing of the action, unless continued by the administrative hearing officer or court upon good cause shown. In cases in which the court has not previously acquired jurisdiction over the responding party, the hearing shall be held on the scheduled date and not less than 21 days or more than 45 days of the date of filing of the action, unless continued by the administrative hearing officer or court upon good cause shown. The hearing shall be held at a location provided or authorized by the chief judge of the circuit.

(b) Providing notice of hearing date. The person designated in the Plan shall serve notice of the action and the hearing date on respondent by regular mail to his or her last known address, unless the action is one over which no court has previously acquired personal jurisdiction, in which case service will be in the same manner as summonses are served in other civil proceedings. If service is made by mail, the person serving notice shall prepare a certificate of mailing to be included in the file.

(c) Subpoenas. The clerk of the circuit court may issue subpoenas upon, or prior to, the filing of a petition if the court has previously acquired jurisdiction over the subject matter of the underlying action.

(d) Affidavit of income and expenses. A form affidavit of income and expenses, in such form as the Supreme Court shall prescribe, may be served on the respondent with the petition initiating the proceedings before the administrative hearing officer. Each party should be requested to complete the form prior to the first appearance before the administrative hearing officer.

Rule 100.7 Conduct of the hearing

(a) Established rules of evidence apply. Except as provided by this rule, the rules of evidence shall be liberally construed in all expedited child support hearings.

(b) Documents presumptively admissible. A party may offer in evidence, without foundation or other proof:

> (1) the obligor's pay stubs or other employer-provided statement of gross income, deductions and net income or other records prepared by the employer in the usual course of business.

> (2) documents provided by the obligor's insurance company which describe the dependent care coverage available to the obligor; and

> (3) records kept by the clerk of the circuit court as to payment of child support.

If at least seven days written notice of the intention to offer the following documents in evidence is given to every other party, accompanied by a copy of the document, or if at the expedited child support hearing the other party does not object, a party may offer in evidence without foundation or other proof:

> (1) the deposition of a witness, the statement of a witness which the witness would be allowed to express if testifying in person, if the state-

S. Ct. Rule 100.7 **PROCEDURE**

ment is made by affidavit or by certification as provided in section 1–109 of the Code of Civil Procedure;

(2) computer-generated documents and records, unless objected to by a party; and

(3) any other document not specifically covered by any of the foregoing provisions, and which is otherwise admissible under the rules of evidence.

(c) Opinions of expert witnesses. Notwithstanding the provisions of Rule 220, a party who proposes to use a written opinion of an expert witness or the testimony of an expert witness at the hearing may do so provided a written notice of such intention is given to every other party not less than seven days prior to the date of hearing, accompanied by a statement containing the identity of the expert, his qualifications, the subject matter, the basis of his conclusions, and his opinion.

(d) Right to subpoena maker of a document. Any other party may subpoena the author or maker of a document admissible under this rule, at that party's expense, and examine the author or maker as if under cross-examination. The provisions of the Code of Civil Procedure relative to subpoenas, section 2–1101, shall be applicable to expedited child support hearings and it shall be the duty of the party requesting the subpoena to modify the form to show that the appearance is set before an administrative hearing officer and to give the time and place set for the hearing.

(e) Adverse examination of parties or agents. The provisions of the Code of Civil Procedure relative to the adverse examination of parties or agents, section 2–1102, shall be applicable to expedited child support hearings as upon the trial of a case.

(f) Compelling appearance of witness at hearing. The provisions of Supreme Court Rule 237 shall be equally applicable to expedited child support hearings as they are to trials.

Rule 100.8 Absence of party at hearing

(a) Failure to be present at hearing. The expedited child support hearing may proceed in the absence of the responding party if service has been made and the petitioning party and/or his or her attorney is present. Based upon the testimony of the petitioning party and any other evidence that may have been presented, the administrative hearing officer shall recommend that the judge enter an appropriate order. If the petitioning party does not agree to the recommended order, the administrative hearing officer shall immediately schedule a judicial hearing, record the date, time and place of the hearing upon a notice and provide such notice to the petitioning party at the expedited hearing. Such notice shall be sent to the nonappearing party by regular mail. If the petitioning party agrees to and signs the order, a copy of the signed order and a notification of the right to object to the order shall be served upon the nonappearing party as directed in subsection (b) below. If the petitioning party is not present, either in person or through an attorney, the administrative hearing officer may continue the matter or may strike the matter with leave to reinstate. Notification of such action shall be served upon the petitioning party by regular mail.

(b) Service of recommended order and notice. If service to commence the hearing before the administrative hearing officer was made by regular mail, the notice and recommended order shall be served in the same manner as summonses are served in other civil proceedings or by certified mail, return receipt requested, mailed to the nonappearing party's last known address. If service to commence the hearing was as provided in the Code of Civil Procedure, the notice and recommended order shall be served by regular mail to the nonappearing party's last known address.

(c) Objections. The nonappearing party may file with the judge a written objection to the entry of the recommended order within 14 days after the order was mailed. If no objection is filed within 14 days, the nonappearing party is deemed to have accepted the recommended order. The judge may then enter the order, refer the case back to the administrative hearing officer for further proceedings, or conduct a judicial hearing. If a timely objection is filed, the judge must hold a judicial hearing and shall enter an appropriate order.

Rule 100.9 Transfers for judicial hearings

(a) Domestic relations matters other than child support and parentage. Any domestic relations matter other than child support and parentage, including but not limited to petitions for visitation, custody, distribution of property, petitions pursuant to section 513 of the Illinois Marriage and Dissolution of Marriage Act, and spousal maintenance shall be transferred according to the judicial circuit's Plan to a judge for a judicial hearing. The administrative hearing officer shall proceed as scheduled with matters relative to child support or parentage. In actions to establish parentage where the putative father voluntarily acknowledges paternity, the recommended order shall include provisions for custody of the child in the mother and reasonable visitation for the father if both parties agree. If either party wishes to contest custody or visitation, the recommended order will be silent on those issues, but the contest will not delay the entry of the order establishing parentage and child support.

(b) Prehearing motions and other matters that require a court order. All prehearing motions and other matters that require a court order or judicial hearing, as defined in the Act and in these rules, shall be transferred to a judge for resolution in an expeditious manner. However, if the parties are in agreement as to the prehearing motion or other such matter, the administrative hearing officer shall transmit a recommended order, signed by both parties to a judge.

(c) Matters requiring judicial hearing. All other matters requiring a judicial hearing, as provided for in the Act and in these rules, shall be

S. Ct. Rule 100.9   PROCEDURE

immediately transferred according to the judicial circuit's Plan to a judge for a judicial hearing.

(d) *Service of orders of withholding pending judicial hearing.* Whenever the parties disagree with part of the administrative hearing officer's recommendations, but do agree as to the existing obligation and no order for withholding was previously served upon the obligor's employer, the order for withholding shall be served upon the obligor's employer as to the existing support obligation pending judicial hearing on the contested matter.

Rule 100.10   Submission of recommendations to the court

(a) *Notice to parties.* The administrative hearing officer shall present each party with a copy of the recommended order to be submitted to a judge. The administrative hearing officer shall also present each party with a written notice informing the parties of their right to request a judicial hearing and the procedures for so doing. The recommended order and notice shall be presented to each party at the conclusion of the hearing, either in person or through an attorney, the recommendation and order shall be mailed by regular mail to the party's last known address.

(b) *Acceptance of recommended order.* If both parties are present at the hearing and agree to the recommended order, they shall sign the recommended order. The administrative hearing officer shall transmit the signed recommended order to a judge as provided for in the Plan of Implementation.

(c) *Rejection of recommended order.* If either party does not agree to the recommended order or any part thereof, the administrative hearing officer shall immediately request a judicial hearing to resolve the contested matter. The administrative hearing officer shall record the date, time and place of such judicial hearing on a notice which shall be presented to the parties at the conclusion of the hearing. Notice shall be sent to nonappearing parties by regular mail. The administrative hearing officer shall transmit to a judge a written statement indicating those issues to which the parties agree and disagree, all documentary evidence and all schedules presented at the expedited child support hearing.

(d) *Administrative hearing officer may not testify.* An administrative hearing officer may not be called or compelled to testify as to what transpired before the administrative hearing officer with respect to contested matters.

Rule 100.11   Authority retained by the court

(a) *Review recommendations of administrative hearing officers.* The judge shall review all recommended orders of an administrative hearing officer upon which parties agree and enter such orders as are appropriate as to all or part of the matters indicated on the recommended order.

(b) *Conduct judicial hearings.* The judge shall conduct judicial hearings on all prehearing motions the parties disagree with, the recommended order of the administrative hearing officer on any domestic relations matters other than uncontested child support and parentage matters, on objections to the entry of orders as provided for in Rule 100.6 and section 10 of the Act, and on any other matters properly before the court.

(c) Hear contested parentage matters. Only the judge may conduct trials in contested parentage cases.

(d) Issue special orders. Only the judge may issue body attachment orders, rules to show cause, or conduct contempt proceedings. The judge shall impose sanctions or relief in such cases as are appropriate.

(e) Impose sanctions. Only the judge may impose sanctions pursuant to Supreme Court Rule 137.

Rule 100.12 Judicial hearings

(a) Recommended orders agreed upon by the parties. The judge shall review the recommended orders of administrative hearing officers in a timely fashion. The judge (1) may enter an order consistent with the recommended order, (2) may reject all or part of the recommended order and refer the matter to the administrative hearing officer for further proceedings, or (3) may conduct judicial hearings as are necessary. The judge shall provide the administrative hearing officer with a copy of the entered order and may inform the administrative hearing officer if a recommended order was not accepted by the judge and the reasons for the changes or rejection. If the judge enters an order consistent with a recommended order, the effective date of the order shall be (1) the date on which the recommended order was signed by both parties, or (2) if the respondent party failed to appear and failed to file a timely objection to the recommended order pursuant to Rule 100.8(c), the date the recommended order was signed by the petitioning party. The order may specify the date payments of support are to begin, which may be different from the effective date of the order.

(b) Recommended orders rejected by the parties. Upon receipt of a statement from the administrative hearing officer that the parties do not agree to all or part of a recommended order, the judge shall promptly conduct a judicial hearing to resolve any contested matters and shall enter an appropriate order.

(c) Presentation of order to the parties. The clerk of the circuit court shall mail a copy of all orders to the parties within five days of entry. If the parties are present in court at the time the order is entered, a copy shall be given to both parties in open court. If an order sets forth an amount for support, an immediate withholding order shall be specially certified and mailed to the obligee or his or her attorney for service.

Rule 100.13 Definitions

For purposes of these rules, the following terms shall have the following meanings:

(a) "Act" shall mean the Expedited Child Support Act of 1990.

(b) "Administrative hearing officer" shall mean the person employed by the chief judge of the circuit court of each circuit, county, multicounty area or multicircuit area establishing an expedited child support system for the purpose of hearing child support and parentage matters and recommending orders.

(c) "Expedited child support hearing" shall mean a hearing before an administrative hearing officer pursuant to the Act and these rules.

(d) "Plan" shall mean the plan submitted by the chief judge of a judicial circuit to the Supreme Court for the creation of an expedited child support system in such circuit pursuant to the Act and these rules.

(e) "System" shall mean the procedures and personnel created by the Act and these rules for the expedited establishment, modification, and enforcement of child support orders, and for the expedited establishment of parentage.

(f) "IV-D program" shall mean the Child Support Enforcement Program established pursuant to Title IV, Part D, of the Social Security Act (42 U.S.C. § 651 et seq.) as administered by the Illinois Department of Public Aid.

Author's Notes

(1) **Federal statutes.** The Federal Child Support Act is at 42 U.S.C.A. § 651 et seq. Excerpted from the Act there follows §§ 659, 666. Federal criminal sanctions for failure to pay legal child support obligations are found at 18 U.S.C.A. § 228, which follows. Overdue child support obligations are included in consumer reports by consumer reporting agencies pursuant to 15 U.S.C.A. § 1681s-1, which also follows.

42 U.S.C.A. 659

§ 659. Enforcement of individual's legal obligations to provide child support or make alimony payments.

(a) United States and District of Columbia to be subject to legal process. Notwithstanding any other provision of law (including section 407 of this title) effective January 1, 1975, moneys (the entitlement to which is based upon remuneration for employment) due from, or payable by, the United States or the District of Columbia (including any agency, subdivision, or instrumentality thereof) to any individual, including members of the armed services, shall be subject, in like manner and to the same extent as if the United States or the District of Columbia were a private person, to legal process brought for the enforcement, against such individual of his legal obligations to provide child support or make alimony payments.

(b) Methods of service of legal process. Service of legal process brought for the enforcement of an individual's obligation to provide child support or make alimony payments shall be accomplished by certified or registered mail, return receipt requested, or by personal service, upon the appropriate agent designated for receipt of such service of process pursuant to regulations promulgated pursuant to section 661 of this title (or, if no agent has been designated for the governmental entity having payment responsibility for the moneys involved, then upon the head of such governmental entity). Such process shall be accompanied by sufficient data to permit prompt identification of the individual and the moneys involved.

(c) Disclosure of information in answering interrogatories; disciplinary action or civil or criminal liability or penalty prohibited. No Federal employee whose duties include responding to interrogatories pursuant to requirements imposed by section 661(b)(3) of this title shall be subject under any law to any disciplinary action or civil or criminal liability or penalty for, or on account of, any disclosure of information made by him in connection with the carrying out of any of his duties which pertain (directly or indirectly) to the answering of any such interrogatory.

(d) Notice. Whenever any person, who is designated by law or regulation to accept service of process to which the United States is subject under this section, is effectively served with any such process or with interrogatories relating to an individual's child support or alimony payment obligations, such person shall respond thereto within thirty days (or within such longer period as may be prescribed by applicable State law) after the date effective service thereof is made, and shall, as soon as possible but not later than fifteen days after the date effective service is so made of any such process, send written notice that such process has been so served (together with a copy thereof) to the individual whose moneys are affected thereby at his duty station or last-known home address.

(e) Variance in normal pay and disbursement cycles not required. Governmental entities affected by legal processes served for the enforcement of an individual's child support or alimony payment obligations shall not be required to vary their normal pay and disbursement cycles in order to comply with any such legal process.

(f) Non-liability of United States, disbursing officers, and governmental entities with respect to payments. Neither the United States, any disbursing officer, nor governmental entity shall be liable with respect to any payment made from moneys due or payable from the United States to any individual pursuant to legal process regular on its face, if such payment is made in accordance with this section and the regulations issued to carry out this section.

42 U.S.C.A. 666

§ 666. Requirement of statutorily prescribed procedures to improve effectiveness of child support enforcement.

(a) Types of procedures required. In order to satisfy section 654(20)(A) of this title [requiring states to enact laws to improve the effectiveness of child support enforcement in accordance with the Federal statutes], each State must have in effect laws requiring the use of the following procedures, consistent with this section and with regulations of the Secretary, to increase the effectiveness of the program which the State administers under this part:

S. Ct. Rule 100.13   **PROCEDURE**

(1) Procedures described in subsection (b) of this section for the withholding from income of amounts payable as support.

(2) Procedures under which expedited processes (determined in accordance with regulations of the Secretary) are in effect under the State judicial system or under State administrative processes (A) for obtaining and enforcing support orders, and (B) for establishing paternity. The Secretary may waive the provisions of this paragraph with respect to one or more political subdivisions within the State on the basis of the effectiveness and timeliness of support order issuance and enforcement or paternity establishment within the political subdivision (in accordance with the general rule for exemptions under subsection (d) of this section).

(3) Procedures under which the State child support enforcement agency shall request, and the State shall provide, that for the purpose of enforcing a support order under any State plan approved under this part—

    (A) any refund of State income tax which would otherwise be payable to an absent parent will be reduced, after notice has been sent to that absent parent of the proposed reduction and the procedures to be followed to contest it (and after full compliance with all procedural due process requirements of the State), by the amount of any overdue support owed by such absent parent;

    (B) the amount by which such refund is reduced shall be distributed in accordance with section 657(b)(4) or (d)(3) of this title in the case of overdue support assigned to a State pursuant to section 602(a)(26) or 671(a)(17) of this title, or, in the case of overdue support which a State has agreed to collect under section 654(6) of this title, shall be distributed, after deduction of any fees imposed by the State to cover the costs of collection, to the child or parent to whom such support is owed; and

    (C) notice of the absent parent's social security account number (or numbers, if he has more than one such number) and home address shall be furnished to the State agency requesting the refund offset, and to the State agency enforcing the order.

(4) Procedures under which liens are imposed against real and personal property for amounts of overdue support owed by an absent parent who resides or owns property in the State.

(5)(A)(i) Procedures which permit the establishment of the paternity of any child at any time prior to such child's eighteenth birthday.

    (ii) As of August 16, 1984, the requirement of clause (i) shall also apply to any child for whom paternity has not yet been established and any child for whom a paternity action was brought but dismissed because a statute of limitations of less than 18 years was then in effect in the State.

(B) Procedures under which the State is required (except in cases where the individual involved has been found under section 602(a)(26)(B) of this title to have good cause for refusing to cooperate) to require the child and all other parties, in a contested paternity case, to submit to genetic tests upon the request of any such party.

(C) Procedures for a simple civil process for voluntarily acknowledging paternity under which the State must provide that the rights and responsibilities of acknowledging paternity are explained and ensure that due process safeguards are afforded. Such procedures must include a hospital-based program for the voluntary acknowledgment of paternity during the period immediately before or after the birth of a child.

(D) Procedures under which the voluntary acknowledgment of paternity creates a rebuttable, or at the option of the State, conclusive presumption of paternity, and under which such voluntary acknowledgment is admissible as evidence of paternity.

(E) Procedures under which the voluntary acknowledgement of paternity must be recognized as a basis for seeking a support order without requiring any further proceedings to establish paternity.

(F) Procedures which provide that (i) any objection to genetic testing results must be made in writing within a specified number of days before any hearing at which such results may be introduced into evidence, and (ii) if no objection is made, the test results are admissible as evidence of paternity without the need for foundation testimony or other proof of authenticity or accuracy.

(G) Procedures which create a rebuttable or, at the option of the State, conclusive presumption of paternity upon genetic testing results indicating a threshold probability that the alleged father is the father of the child.

(H) Procedures requiring a default order to be entered in a paternity case upon a showing of service of process on the defendant and any additional showing required by law.

(6) Procedures which require that an absent parent give security, post a bond, or give some other guarantee to secure payment of overdue support, after notice has been sent to such absent parent of the proposed action and of the procedures to be followed to contest it (and after full compliance with all procedural due process requirements of the State).

(7) Procedures by which information regarding the amount of overdue support owed by an absent parent residing in the State will be made available to any consumer reporting agency (as defined in section 1681a(f) of Title 15) upon the request of such agency; except that (A) if the amount of the overdue support involved in any case is less than $1,000, information regarding such amount shall be made available only at the option of the State, (B) any information with respect to an absent parent shall be made available under such procedures only after notice has been

sent to such absent parent of the proposed action, and such absent parent has been given a reasonable opportunity to contest the accuracy of such information (and after full compliance with all procedural due process requirements of the State), and (C) a fee for furnishing such information, in an amount not exceeding the actual cost thereof, may be imposed on the requesting agency by the State.

(8)(A) Procedures under which all child support orders not described in subparagraph (B) will include provision for withholding from wages, in order to assure that withholding as a means of collecting child support is available if arrearages occur without the necessity of filing application for services under this part.

(B) Procedures under which all child support orders which are initially issued in the State on or after January 1, 1994, and are not being enforced under this part will include the following requirements:

    (i) The wages of an absent parent shall be subject to withholding, regardless of whether support payments by such parent are in arrears, on the effective date of the order; except that such wages shall not be subject to withholding under this clause in any case where (I) one of the parties demonstrates, and the court (or administrative process) finds, that there is good cause not to require immediate income withholding, or (II) a written agreement is reached between both parties which provides for an alternative arrangement.

    (ii) The requirements of subsection (b)(1) of this section (which shall apply in the case of each absent parent against whom a support order is or has been issued or modified in the State, without regard to whether the order is being enforced under the State plan).

    (iii) The requirements of paragraphs (2), (5), (6), (7), (8), (9), and (10) of subsection (b) of this section, where applicable.

    (iv) Withholding from income of amounts payable as support must be carried out in full compliance with all procedural due process requirements of the State.

(9) Procedures which require that any payment or installment of support under any child support order, whether ordered through the State judicial system or through the expedited processes required by paragraph (2), is (on and after the date it is due)—

    (A) a judgment by operation of law, with the full force, effect, and attributes of a judgment of the State, including the ability to be enforced,

    (B) entitled as a judgment to full faith and credit in such State and in any other State, and

    (C) not subject to retroactive modification by such State or by any other State; except that such procedures may permit modification with respect to any period during which there is pending a petition for modification, but only from the date that notice of such petition has been given, either directly or through the appropriate agent, to the obligee or (where the obligee is the petitioner) to the obligor.

(10)(A) Procedures to ensure that, beginning 2 years after October 13, 1988, if the State determines (pursuant to a plan indicating how and when child support orders in effect in the State are to be periodically reviewed and adjusted) that a child support order being enforced under this part should be reviewed, the State must, at the request of either parent subject to the order, or of a State child support enforcement agency, initiate a review of such order, and adjust such order, as appropriate, in accordance with the guidelines established pursuant to section 667(a) of this title.

(B) Procedures to ensure that, beginning 5 years after October 13, 1988, or such earlier date as the State may select, the State must implement a process for the periodic review and adjustment of child support orders being enforced under this part under which the order is to be reviewed not later than 36 months after the establishment of the order or the most recent review, and adjusted, as appropriate, in accordance with the guidelines established pursuant to section 667(a) of this title, unless—

(i) in the case of an order with respect to an individual with respect to whom an assignment under section 602(a)(26) of this title is in effect, the State has determined, in accordance with regulations of the Secretary, that such a review would not be in the best interests of the child and neither parent has requested review; and

(ii) in the case of any other order being enforced under this part, neither parent has requested review.

(C) Procedures to ensure that the State notifies each parent subject to a child support order in effect in the State that is being enforced under this part—

(i) of any review of such order, at least 30 days before the commencement of such review; and

(ii) of the right of such parent under subparagraph (B) to request the State to review such order; and

(iii) of a proposed adjustment (or determination that there should be no change) in the child support award amount, and such parent is afforded not less than 30 days after such notification to initiate proceedings to challenge such adjustment (or determination).

(11) Procedures under which a State must give full faith and credit to a determination of paternity made by any other State, whether established through voluntary acknowledgment or through administrative or judicial processes.

S. Ct. Rule 100.13 PROCEDURE

Notwithstanding section 654(20)(B) of this title, the procedures which are required under paragraphs (3), (4), (6), and (7) need not be used or applied in cases where the State determines (using guidelines which are generally available within the State and which take into account the payment record of the absent parent, the availability of other remedies, and other relevant considerations) that such use or application would not carry out the purposes of this part or would be otherwise inappropriate in the circumstances.

(b) Withholding from income of amounts payable as support.

The procedures referred to in subsection (a)(1) of this section (relating to the withholding from income of amounts payable as support) must provide for the following:

(1) In the case of each absent parent against whom a support order is or has been issued or modified in the State, and is being enforced under the State plan, so much of such parent's wages (as defined by the State for purposes of this section) must be withheld, in accordance with the succeeding provisions of this subsection, as is necessary to comply with the order and provide for the payment of any fee to the employer which may be required under paragraph (6)(A), up to the maximum amount permitted under section 1673(b) of Title 15. If there are arrearages to be collected, amounts withheld to satisfy such arrearages, when added to the amounts withheld to pay current support and provide for the fee, may not exceed the limit permitted under such section 1673(b), but the State need not withhold up to the maximum amount permitted under such section in order to satisfy arrearages.

(2) Such withholding must be provided without the necessity of any application therefor in the case of a child (whether or not eligible for aid under part A of this subchapter) with respect to whom services are already being provided under the State plan under this part, and must be provided in accordance with this subsection on the basis of an application for services under the State plan in the case of any other child in whose behalf a support order has been issued or modified in the State. In either case such withholding must occur without the need for any amendment to the support order involved or for any further action (other than those actions required under this part) by the court or other entity which issued such order.

(3)(A) The wages of an absent parent shall be subject to such withholding, regardless of whether support payments by such parent are in arrears, in the case of a support order being enforced under this part that is issued or modified on or after the first day of the 25th month beginning after October 13, 1988, on the effective date of the order; except that such wages shall not be subject to such withholding under this subparagraph in any case where (i) one of the parties demonstrates, and the court (or administrative process) finds, that there is good cause not to require immediate income withholding, or (ii) a written agreement is reached between both parties which provides for an alternative arrangement.

(B) The wages of an absent parent shall become subject to such withholding, in the case of wages not subject to withholding under subparagraph (A), on the date on which the payments which the absent parent has failed to make under a support order are at least equal to the support payable for one month or, if earlier, and without regard to whether there is an arrearage, the earliest of—

(i) the date as of which the absent parent requests that such withholding begin,

(ii) the date as of which the custodial parent requests that such withholding begin, if the State determines, in accordance with such procedures and standards as it may establish, that the request should be approved, or

(iii) such earlier date as the State may select.

(4)(A) Such withholding must be carried out in full compliance with all procedural due process requirements of the State, and (subject to subparagraph (B)) the State must send advance notice to each absent parent to whom paragraph (1) applies regarding the proposed withholding and the procedures such absent parent should follow if he or she desires to contest such withholding on the grounds that withholding (including the amount to be withheld) is not proper in the case involved because of mistakes of fact. If the absent parent contests such withholding on those grounds, the State shall determine whether such withholding will actually occur, shall (within no more than 45 days after the provision of such advance notice) inform such parent of whether or not withholding will occur and (if so) of the date on which it is to begin, and shall furnish such parent with the information contained in any notice given to the employer under paragraph (6)(A) with respect to such withholding.

(B) The requirement of advance notice set forth in the first sentence of subparagraph (A) shall not apply in the case of any State which has a system of income withholding for child support purposes in effect on August 16, 1984, if such system provides on that date, and continues to provide, such procedures as may be necessary to meet the procedural due process requirements of State law.

(5) Such withholding must be administered by a public agency designated by the State, and the amounts withheld must be expeditiously distributed by the State or such agency in accordance with section 657 of this title under procedures (specified by the State) adequate to document payments of support and to track and monitor such payments, except that the State may establish or permit the establishment of alternative procedures for the collection and distribution of such amounts (under the supervision of such public agency) otherwise than through such public agency so long as the entity making such collection and distribution is

publicly accountable for its actions taken in carrying out such procedures, and so long as such procedures will assure prompt distribution, provide for the keeping of adequate records to document payments of support, and permit the tracking and monitoring of such payments.

(6)(A)(i) The employer of any absent parent to whom paragraph (1) applies, upon being given notice as described in clause (ii), must be required to withhold from such absent parent's wages the amount specified by such notice (which may include a fee, established by the State, to be paid to the employer unless waived by such employer) and pay such amount (after deducting and retaining any portion thereof which represents the fee so established) to the appropriate agency (or other entity authorized to collect the amounts withheld under the alternative procedures described in paragraph (5)) for distribution in accordance with section 657 of this title.

(ii) The notice given to the employer shall contain only such information as may be necessary for the employer to comply with the withholding order.

(B) Methods must be established by the State to simplify the withholding process for employers to the greatest extent possible, including permitting any employer to combine all withheld amounts into a single payment to each appropriate agency or entity (with the portion thereof which is attributable to each individual employee being separately designated).

(C) The employer must be held liable to the State for any amount which such employer fails to withhold from wages due an employee following receipt by such employer of proper notice under subparagraph (A), but such employer shall not be required to vary the normal pay and disbursement cycles in order to comply with this paragraph.

(D) Provision must be made for the imposition of a fine against any employer who discharges from employment, refuses to employ, or takes disciplinary action against any absent parent subject to wage withholding required by this subsection because of the existence of such withholding and the obligations or additional obligations which it imposes upon the employer.

(7) Support collection under this subsection must be given priority over any other legal process under State law against the same wages.

(8) The State may take such actions as may be necessary to extend its system of withholding under this subsection so that such system will include withholding from forms of income other than wages, in order to assure that child support owed by absent parents in the State will be collected without regard to the types of such absent parents' income or the nature of their income-producing activities.

(9) The State must extend its withholding system under this subsection so that such system will include withholding from income derived

within such State in cases where the applicable support orders were issued in other States, in order to assure that child support owed by absent parents in such State or any other State will be collected without regard to the residence of the child for whom the support is payable or of such child's custodial parent.

(10) Provision must be made for terminating withholding.

(c) Administration of support payments through State agency or other entity. Any State may at its option, under its plan approved under section 654 of this title, establish procedures under which support payments under this part will be made through the State agency or other entity which administers the State's income withholding system in any case where either the absent parent or the custodial parent requests it, even though no arrearages in child support payments are involved and no income withholding procedures have been instituted; but in any such case an annual fee for handling and processing such payments, in an amount not exceeding the actual costs incurred by the State in connection therewith or $25, whichever is less, shall be imposed on the requesting parent by the State.

(d) Exemption of States. If a State demonstrates to the satisfaction of the Secretary, through the presentation to the Secretary of such data pertaining to caseloads, processing times, administrative costs, and average support collections, and such other data or estimates as the Secretary may specify, that the enactment of any law or the use of any procedure or procedures required by or pursuant to this section will not increase the effectiveness and efficiency of the State child support enforcement program, the Secretary may exempt the State, subject to the Secretary's continuing review and to termination of the exemption should circumstances change, from the requirement to enact the law or use the procedure or procedures involved.

(e) "Overdue support" defined. For purposes of this section, the term "overdue support" means the amount of a delinquency pursuant to an obligation determined under a court order, or an order of an administrative process established under State law, for support and maintenance of a minor child which is owed to or on behalf of such child, or for support and maintenance of the absent parent's spouse (or former spouse) with whom the child is living if and to the extent that spousal support (with respect to such spouse or former spouse) would be included for purposes of paragraph (4) or (6) of section 654 of this title. At the option of the State, overdue support may include amounts which otherwise meet the definition in the first sentence of this subsection but which are owed to or on behalf of a child who is not a minor child. The option to include support owed to children who are not minors shall apply independently to each procedure specified under this section.

18 U.S.C.A. 228

§ 228. Failure to pay legal child support obligations.

(a) Offense. Whoever willfully fails to pay a past due support obligation with respect to a child who resides in another State shall be punished as provided in subsection (b).

(b) Punishment. The punishment for an offense under this section is—

   (1) in the case of a first offense under this section, a fine under this title, imprisonment for not more than 6 months, or both; and

   (2) in any other case, a fine under this title, imprisonment for not more than 2 years, or both.

(c) Restitution. Upon a conviction under this section, the court shall order restitution under section 3663 in an amount equal to the past due support obligation as it exists at the time of sentencing.

(d) Definitions. As used in this section—

   (1) the term "past due support obligation" means any amount—

      (A) determined under a court order or an order of an administrative process pursuant to the law of a State to be due from a person for the support and maintenance of a child or of a child and the parent with whom the child is living; and

      (B) that has remained unpaid for a period longer than one year, or is greater than $5,000; and

   (2) the term "State" includes the District of Columbia, and any other possession or territory of the United States.

15 U.S.C.A. 1681s–1

§ 1681s–1. Information on overdue child support obligations.

Notwithstanding any other provision of this subchapter, a consumer reporting agency shall include in any consumer report furnished by the agency in accordance with section 1681b of this title, any information on the failure of the consumer to pay overdue support which—

(1) is provided—

   (A) to the consumer reporting agency by a State or local child support enforcement agency; or

   (B) to the consumer reporting agency and verified by any local, State, or Federal Government agency; and

(2) antedates the report by 7 years or less.

Rule 101. Summons and original process—Form and issuance

(a) General. The summons shall be issued under the seal of the court, tested in the name of the clerk, and signed with his name. It shall be dated on the date it is issued, shall be directed to each defendant, and shall bear the address and telephone number of the plaintiff or his attorney, and if service or notices of motions or filings by facsimile transmission will be accepted, the telephone number of the facsimile machine of the plaintiff or his attorney.

* * *

(d) Summons requiring appearance within 30 days after service. In all other cases the summons shall require each defendant to file his answer or otherwise file his appearance within 30 days after service, exclusive of the date of service (see Rule 181(a)), and shall be in substantially the following form:

In the Circuit Court of the _____ Judicial Circuit, _____ County, Illinois.

(Or, In the Circuit Court of Cook County, Illinois.)

A.B., C.D. etc. (naming all plaintiffs),
    Plaintiffs
              No. _____
v.

H.J., K.L. etc. (naming all defendants),
    Defendants.

SUMMONS

To each defendant:

You are summoned and required to file an answer to the complaint in this case, a copy of which is hereto attached, or otherwise file your appearance, in the office of the clerk of this court within 30 days after service of this summons, not counting the day of service. If you fail to do so, a judgment by default may be entered against you for the relief asked in the complaint.

To the officer:

This summons must be returned by the officer or other person to whom it was given for service, with indorsement of service and fees, if any, immediately after service. If service cannot be made, this summons shall be returned so indorsed.

This summons may not be served later than 30 days after its date.

                      Witness _____, 19__

(Seal of Court)
                                    Clerk of Court

Plaintiff's Attorney (or plaintiff, if he is not represented by attorney) _____

Address _____

Telephone No. _____

Facsimile Telephone No. _____

(If service by facsimile transmission will be accepted, the telephone number of the plaintiff or plaintiff's attorney's facsimile machine is additionally required.)

Date of service _____, 19__ (to be inserted by officer on copy left with defendant or other person).

(e) Summons in cases under the Illinois Marriage and Dissolution of Marriage Act. In all proceedings under the Illinois Marriage and Dissolution of Marriage Act, the summons shall include a notice on its reverse side referring to a dissolution action stay being in effect on service of summons, and shall state that any person who fails to obey a dissolution action stay may be subject to punishment for contempt, and shall include language:

(1) restraining both parties from physically abusing, harassing, intimidating, striking, or interfering with the personal liberty of the other party or the minor children of either party; and

(2) restraining both parties from removing any minor child of either party from the State of Illinois or from concealing any such child from the other party, without the consent of the other party or an order of the court.

(f) Use of wrong form of summons. The use of the wrong form of summons shall not affect the jurisdiction of the court.

Author's Notes

Analysis

1. Summons—Form.
2. Constitutionality of stay.

(1) **Summons—Form.** The summons that follows is the form used by the Circuit Court of Cook County, Domestic Relations Division.

ILLINOIS S. CT. RULES   S. Ct. Rule 101

(Rev. 9/28/93) CCDR 0001

IN THE CIRCUIT COURT OF COOK COUNTY, ILLINOIS
COUNTY DEPARTMENT, DOMESTIC RELATIONS DIVISION

IN RE THE ☐ MARRIAGE ☐ CUSTODY   NO:
☐ SUPPORT OF:
                                             CALENDAR
_____
PETITIONER   Please serve the Respondent at:
            AND
_____   _____
RESPONDENT
(SS # If known) _____   _____

2120 - Summons - Retd. P.S.   2220 - Summons - Retd. N.S.
2121 - Alias Summons - Retd. P.S.   2221 - Alias Summons - Retd. N.S.
2700 - Return of Service P.S. - Ord. of Protect   2702 - Return of Service N.S. - Ord. of Protect

SUMMONS

TO THE RESPONDENT
    The Petitioner is suing you for one or more of the following

☐ Dissolution of Marriage ☐ Legal Separation ☐ Declaration of Invalidity ☐ Custody ☐ Child Support
☐ Order of Protection under the Domestic Violence Act ☐ Other: _____

YOU ARE SUMMONED and required to file your WRITTEN APPEARANCE AND RESPONSE in this case in the Office of the Clerk of Court ☐ Located in Room 802, Richard J. Daley Center, Chicago, IL 60602 ☐ Other: _____

not later than ☐ 30 days ☐ 7 days after service of this summons, not counting the day of service.

IF YOU FAIL TO FILE YOUR WRITTEN APPEARANCE WITHIN THE TIME STATED ABOVE, DEFAULT MAY BE ENTERED AGAINST YOU AND THE COURT MAY GRANT THE PETITIONER ALL OR PART OF THE RELIEF THAT SHE OR HE IS REQUESTING IN HER OR HIS PETITION.

TO THE OFFICER: This summons must be returned by the officer or other person to whom it was given for service, with endorsement thereon of service and fees, if any, immediately after service. If service cannot be made, this summons shall be returned so endorsed.

                        WITNESS, _____, 19____

                        Clerk of Court

                        Date of Service: _____, 19____
                        [To be inserted by officer on copy left with respondent or other person]

Name:
Attorney for: SEE REVERSE SIDE
Address:
City, State, Zip
Telephone:
Atty Code No.
**Service by Facsimile Transmission will be accepted at:_____
                                         (Area Code) (Facsimile Telephone Number)

AURELIA PUCINSKI, CLERK OF THE CIRCUIT COURT OF COOK COUNTY, ILLINOIS   [G19002]

S. Ct. Rule 101   PROCEDURE

(Rev. 9/28/93) CCDR 0001

NOTICE:

ON SERVICE OF THIS SUMMONS, A DISSOLUTION ACTION STAY SHALL BE IN EFFECT, RESTRAINING BOTH PARTIES, AS PROVIDED BY STATUTE

750 ILCS 5/501.1(a) of the Illinois Marriage and Dissolution of Marriage Act includes the following:

Dissolution action stay.

a) Upon service of a summons and petition or praecipe filed under the Illinois Marriage and Dissolution of Marriage Act or upon the filing of the respondent's appearance in the proceedings, whichever first occurs, a dissolution action stay shall be in effect against both parties and their agents and employees, without bond or further notice, until a final judgment is entered, the proceeding is dismissed, or until further order of the court:

   (1) **This provision declared unconstitutional by the Illinois Supreme Court (# 75132 Carrie Messenger v. Jim Edgar, Et Al.)**

   (2) restraining both parties from physically abusing, harassing, intimidating, striking or interfering with the personal liberty of the other party or the minor children of either party; and

   (3) restraining both parties from removing any minor child of either party from the State of Illinois or from concealing any such child from the other party without the consent of the other party or an order of the court.

* * * * * * * *

ANY PERSON WHO FAILS TO OBEY A DISSOLUTION ACTION STAY MAY BE SUBJECT TO PUNISHMENT FOR CONTEMPT.

(2) **Constitutionality of stay.** The dissolution action stay was held unconstitutional insofar as it restrained property in Messenger v. Edgar, 157 Ill.2d 162, 191 Ill.Dec. 65, 623 N.E.2d 310 (1993). See 750 ILCS 5/501.1 and accompanying Author's

Notes. Therefore, the immediate mutual restraint carried on the summons remains only against abuse, harassment and against removing or concealing a minor child.

Rule 102. Service of summons and complaint—Return

(a) Placement for service. Promptly upon issuance, summons (together with copies of the complaint as required by Rule 104), shall be placed for service with the sheriff or other officer or person authorized to serve process.

Author's Notes

(1) **Cross reference—Form.** See 735 ILCS 5/2-202 Author's Note (1) for a sample motion and order to authorize a private person to serve the summons and complaint. Such authorization is useful when it is anticipated that service will be difficult for the sheriff to accomplish, or where immediate service is necessary.

Rule 104. Service of pleadings and other papers—Filing

(a) Delivery of copy of complaint. Every copy of a summons used in making service shall have attached thereto a copy of the complaint, which shall be furnished by plaintiff.

(b) Filing of papers and proof of service. Pleadings subsequent to the complaint, written motions, and other papers required to be filed shall be filed with the clerk with a certificate of counsel or other proof that copies have been served on all parties who have appeared and have not theretofore been found by the court to be in default for failure to plead.

(c) Excusing service. For good cause shown on ex parte application, the court or any judge thereof may excuse the delivery or service of any complaint, pleading, or written motion or part thereof on any party, but the attorney filing it shall furnish a copy promptly and without charge to any party requesting it.

(d) Failure to serve copies. Failure to deliver or serve copies as required by this rule does not in any way impair the jurisdiction of the court over the person of any party, but the aggrieved party may obtain a copy from the clerk and the court shall order the offending party to reimburse the aggrieved party for the expense thereof.

Rule 105. Additional relief against parties in default—Notice

(a) Notice—Form and contents. If new or additional relief, whether by amendment, counterclaim, or otherwise, is sought against a party not entitled to notice under Rule 104, notice shall be given him as herein provided. The notice shall be captioned and numbered in the case and directed to the party. It shall state that a pleading seeking new or additional relief against him has been filed and that a judgment by default may be taken against him for the new or additional relief unless he files an answer or otherwise files an appearance in the office of the clerk of the court within 30 days after service, receipt by certified or registered mail, or the first publication of the notice, as the case may be, exclusive of the day of service, receipt or first publication. Except in case of publication, a copy of the new or amended pleading shall be attached to the notice, unless excused by the court for good cause shown on ex parte application.

(b) Service. The notice may be served by any of the following methods:

(1) By any method provided by law for service of summons, either within or without this State. Service may be made by an officer or by any person over 18 years of age not a party to the action. Proof of service by an officer may be made by return as in the case of a summons. Otherwise proof of service shall be made by affidavit of the server, stating the time, manner, and place of service. The court may consider the affidavit and any other competent proofs in determining whether service has been properly made.

(2) By prepaid certified or registered mail addressed to the party, restricted delivery, return receipt requested showing to whom, date and address of delivery. Service is not complete until the notice is received by the defendant, and the registry receipt is prima facie evidence thereof.

(3) By publication, upon the filing of an affidavit as required for publication of notice of pendency of the action in the manner of but limited to the cases provided for, and with like effect as, publication of notice of pendency of the action.

Rule 106. Notice of petitions filed for relief from, or revival of, judgments

Notice of the filing of a petition under section 2–1401, section 2–1601 or section 12–183 of the Code of Civil Procedure shall be given by the same methods provided in Rule 105 for the giving of notice of additional relief to parties in default.

Rule 137. Signing of pleadings, motions and other papers—Sanctions

Every pleading, motion and other paper of a party represented by an attorney shall be signed by at least one attorney of record in his individual name, whose address shall be stated. A party who is not represented by an attorney shall sign his pleading, motion, or other paper and state his address. Except when otherwise specifically provided by rule or statute, pleadings need not be verified or accompanied by affidavit. The signature of an attorney or party constitutes a certificate by him that he has read the pleading, motion or other paper; that to the best of his knowledge, information, and belief formed after reasonable inquiry it is well grounded in fact and is warranted by existing law or a good-faith argument for the extension, modification, or reversal of existing law, and that it is not interposed for any improper purpose, such as to harass or to cause unnecessary delay or needless increase in the cost of litigation. If a pleading, motion, or other paper is not signed, it shall be stricken unless it is signed promptly after the omission is called to the attention of the pleader or movant. If a pleading, motion, or other paper is signed in violation of this rule, the court, upon motion or upon its own initiative, may impose upon the person who signed it, a represented party, or both, an appropriate sanction, which may include an order to pay to the other party or parties the amount of reasonable expenses incurred because of the filing of the pleading, motion or other paper, including a reasonable attorney fee.

All proceedings under this rule shall be brought within the civil action in which the pleading, motion or other paper referred to has been filed, and no violation or alleged violation of this rule shall give rise to a separate civil suit, but shall be considered a claim within the same civil action. Motions brought pursuant to this rule must be filed within 30 days of the entry of final judgment, or if a timely post-judgment motion is filed, within 30 days of the ruling on the post-judgment motion.

This rule shall apply to the State of Illinois or any agency of the State in the same manner as any other party. Furthermore, where the litigation involves review of a determination of an administrative agency, the court may include in its award for expenses an amount to compensate a party for costs actually incurred by that party in contesting on the administrative level an allegation or denial made by the State without reasonable cause and found to be untrue.

Where a sanction is imposed under this rule, the judge shall set forth with specificity the reasons and basis of any sanction so imposed either in the judgment order itself or in a separate written order.

Author's Notes

Analysis

1. Responsibility.
2. Sanctions.
3. Verification.

(1) **Responsibility.** Supreme Court Rule 137 requires that an attorney take responsibility for the pleadings that he or she files. The attorney certifies by his signature that, *inter alia*, after "reasonable inquiry," he or she believes that the pleading is well grounded in fact, warranted either by existing law, or a good-faith argument for the extension, modification or reversal of existing law, and is not filed for any improper purpose, such as delay or to increase cost. The inquiry must be reasonable under the circumstances that exist at the time the pleading is signed, not with the benefit of hindsight. See Couri v. Korn, 202 Ill.App.3d 848, 148 Ill.Dec. 77, 560 N.E.2d 379 (3d Dist.1990), and Lewy v. Koeckritz Intern, Inc., 211 Ill.App.3d 330, 155 Ill.Dec. 848, 570 N.E.2d 361 (1st Dist.1991).

(2) **Sanctions.** Sanctions for violation of Supreme Court Rule 137 may be imposed upon the attorney, party, or both.

(3) **Verification.** Petitions for dissolution of marriage or legal separation are required to be verified by IMDMA § 403(a), 750 ILCS 5/403(a).

Rule 201. General discovery provisions

(a) Discovery methods. Information is obtainable as provided in these rules through any of the following discovery methods: depositions upon oral or written questions, written interrogatories to parties, discovery or inspection of documents or property, and physical and mental examination of persons. Duplication of discovery methods to obtain the same information should be avoided.

(b) Scope of discovery.

(1) Full disclosure required. Except as provided in these rules, a party may obtain by discovery full disclosure regarding any matter relevant to the subject matter involved in the pending action, whether it relates to the claim or defense of the party seeking disclosure or of any other party, including the existence, description, nature, custody, condition, and location of any documents or tangible things, and the identity and location of persons having knowledge of relevant facts. The word "documents," as used in these rules, includes, but is not limited to, papers, photographs, films, recordings, memoranda, books, records, accounts, and communications.

(2) Privilege and work product. All matters that are privileged against disclosure on the trial, including privileged communications between a party or his agent and the attorney for the party, are privileged against disclosure through any discovery procedure. Material prepared by or for a party in preparation for trial is subject to discovery only if it does not contain or disclose the theories, mental impressions, or litigation plans of the party's attorney. The court may apportion the cost involved in originally securing the discoverable material, including when appropriate a reasonable attorney's fee, in such manner as is just.

(c) Prevention of abuse.

(1) Protective orders. The court may at any time on its own initiative, or on motion of any party or witness, make a protective order as justice requires, denying, limiting, conditioning, or regulating discovery to prevent unreasonable annoyance, expense, embarrassment, disadvantage, or oppression.

(2) Supervision of discovery. Upon the motion of any party or witness, on notice to all parties, or on its own initiative without notice, the court may supervise all or any part of any discovery procedure.

(d) Time discovery may be initiated. Prior to the time all defendants have appeared or are required to appear, no deposition or other discovery procedure shall be noticed or otherwise initiated without leave of court granted upon good cause shown.

(e) Sequence of discovery. Unless the court upon motion, for the convenience of parties and witnesses and in the interests of justice, orders otherwise, methods of discovery may be used in any sequence, and the fact that a party is conducting discovery, whether by deposition or otherwise, shall not operate to delay any other party's discovery.

(f) Diligence in discovery. The trial of a case shall not be delayed to permit discovery unless due diligence is shown.

* * *

(i) Stipulations. If the parties so stipulate, depositions and discovery may take place before any person, for any purpose, at any time or place, and in any manner.

(j) Effect of discovery disclosure. Disclosure of any matter obtained by discovery is not conclusive, but may be contradicted by other evidence.

(k) Reasonable attempt to resolve differences required. Every motion with respect to discovery shall incorporate a statement that after personal consultation and reasonable attempts to resolve differences the parties have been unable to reach an accord. The court may order that reasonable costs, including attorneys' fees, be assessed against a party or his attorney who unreasonably fails to facilitate discovery under this provision.

(l) Discovery pursuant to special appearance. Discovery shall be permitted on the issues raised in a special appearance filed pursuant to section 2-301 of the Code of Civil Procedure, provided such discovery is limited to the court's jurisdiction over the person of the defendant.

(m) Filing materials with the clerk of the circuit court. Nothing in these rules concerning discovery shall be construed to prohibit a circuit court from adopting local rules to regulate or prohibit the filing of designated discovery materials with the clerk of the circuit court without leave of court.

Author's Notes

Analysis

1. Liberal scope of discovery.
2. Full disclosure.
3. Abuse of discovery.
4. Duration of discovery.
5. Discovery by agreement.
6. Cross reference.
7. Protective Order—Form.

(1) **Liberal scope of discovery.** Supreme Court Rule 201 establishes a liberal standard of discovery. See Evers v. Edward Hosp. Ass'n, 247 Ill.App.3d 717, 735, 187 Ill.Dec. 490, 504, 617 N.E.2d 1211, 1225 (2d Dist.1993) ("the purpose of discovery is to determine the truth.... To achieve this end, the scope of discovery may be very broad.") (citations omitted); Monier v. Chamberlain, 35 Ill.2d 351, 357, 221 N.E.2d 410, 415 (1966) ("discovery before trial 'presupposes a range of relevance and materiality which includes not only what is admissible at the trial, but also that which leads to what is admissible at the trial'") (citation omitted). A litigant is able to obtain all facts concerning a claim or a defense, including information that may lead to other information concerning a claim or defense.

Discovery is not unlimited, however. Subparagraph (b)(2) denies access to privileged communications, and to work product prepared by or for a party in preparation of trial. Work product is subject to discovery only if it does not contain the party's or the attorney's theories, mental impressions, or litigation plans. On the other hand, a party cannot prevent discovery by placing a relevant document in his attorney's file. See, e.g., Johnson v. Frontier Ford, Inc., 68 Ill.App.3d 315, 24 Ill.Dec. 908, 386 N.E.2d 112 (2d Dist.1979).

(2) **Full disclosure.** An attorney should resist a client's inclination to suppress legitimately sought information, not only because of the important ethical considerations, but also because of the practical considerations of potential sanctions and post-decree litigation. See 750 ILCS 5/502 Author's Note (5), and 735 ILCS 5/2–1401 and accompanying Author's Notes.

(3) **Abuse of discovery.** Subparagraph (c) empowers the court to prevent abuse of discovery procedures, either by issuing protective orders, or by supervising discovery.

(4) **Duration of discovery.** Subparagraph (f) provides that a trial shall not be delayed to permit discovery, in the absence of a showing of due diligence. See, e.g., Carlisle v. Harp, 200 Ill.App.3d 908, 146 Ill.Dec. 355, 558 N.E.2d 318 (5th Dist.1990) (denial of requested trial continuance to permit discovery was not error; defendant did not establish due diligence when requesting independent physical examination of plaintiff only nine days before trial).

Individual courts may place additional time constraints upon the discovery process in domestic relations litigation. In the Circuit Court of Cook County, for instance, Rule 13.4(h) provides that, except for the disclosure of the identity and location of persons having knowledge of relevant facts (provision for which is in Supreme Court Rule 213(e)), discovery in domestic relations cases shall be concluded within 15 months after the case is filed, or as is otherwise provided by the preliminary judge.

(5) **Discovery by agreement.** Court supervision of discovery is time-consuming for the court, and expensive for the parties. To encourage discovery by agreement, subparagraph (k) requires a statement accompanying every motion concerning discovery that the parties have been unable, despite reasonable attempts, to reach an accord. See Brandt v. John S. Tilley Ladders Co., 145 Ill.App.3d 304, 99 Ill.Dec. 534, 495 N.E.2d 1269 (1st Dist.1986) (failure to include a statement in compliance with Rule 201(k) should result in dismissal of the motion.) Economic sanctions are available against a party who fails to reasonably facilitate discovery. See, e.g., Lavaja v. Carter, 153 Ill.App.3d 317, 106 Ill.Dec. 147, 505 N.E.2d 694 (2d Dist.), appeal denied 116 Ill.2d 560, 113 Ill.Dec. 301, 515 N.E.2d 110 (1987) (upholding sanctions imposed for noncompliance with discovery requests).

(6) **Cross reference.** See Supreme Court Rule 213 Author's Note (4) for a sample interrogatory seeking the identity of persons having knowledge of the relevant facts, pursuant to Supreme Court Rules 201(b)(1) and 213(e).

(7) **Protective Order—Form.** Frequently, in discovery, there is a desire for confidentiality, particularly when closely held corporations or partnerships are involved. There follows a sample agreed confidentiality order. The terms of confidentiality orders are usually negotiated, so the sample will undoubtedly be subject to modification.

ILLINOIS S. CT. RULES **S. Ct. Rule 201**

IN THE CIRCUIT COURT OF COOK COUNTY, ILLINOIS
COUNTY DEPARTMENT, DOMESTIC RELATIONS DIVISION

IN RE THE MARRIAGE OF)
)
ELLEN JARNDYCE,)
)
          Petitioner,)
)
and) No. ____ D _____
)
JOHN JARNDYCE,)
)
          Respondent.)

PROTECTIVE ORDER

BY AGREEMENT of the parties;

IT IS HEREBY ORDERED that the following conditions shall govern the use of any document or information relating to ELLEN JARNDYCE, JOHN JARNDYCE, and JARNDYCE ENTERPRISES, LTD., either of their interests in assets, income, expenses, and needs, and any documents or information supplied by Petitioner, Respondent, Jarndyce Enterprises, Ltd., or any agent on his, her, or its behalf, that is obtained or learned through discovery or other proceedings in this case, whether by way of depositions, interrogatories, subpoenas, testimony, stipulations or voluntary or involuntary disclosure, the representation of counsel, or in any other way:

    1. Petitioner and Respondent and their attorneys of record shall refrain from disclosing, either directly or indirectly, to any person or entity any such document or information without the prior written consent of Petitioner and Respondent except as otherwise provided in this Order.

    2. If Petitioner and Respondent consent to disclosure to others of the documents or information otherwise protected herein, such individuals shall not make any further disclosure, either directly or indirectly, of such documents or information without the prior written consent of Petitioner and Respondent. Such individuals, prior to being given any document or information, shall sign a copy of this Order whereby they agree to be bound by the terms hereof, and a copy of such agreement shall be delivered to Petitioner's and Respondent's attorneys of record.

    3. Petitioner and Respondent hereby consent to disclosure to those of the following, provided they have first signed and delivered a copy of this Order pursuant to the terms and conditions of paragraph 2 hereof: professionals used for consultation and as experts during these proceedings.

    4. This Order shall not prevent the disclosure of the documents or information protected herein to employees of the parties' law firms, experts' firms (both of whom shall be deemed to have signed and be bound by the

terms of this Order), or to this Court for purposes of trial or other proceedings in any Court concerning this action; provided, however, any disclosure to any Court shall be subject to this Order or further Orders as the Court may at the time deem reasonable and necessary to preserve the confidentiality of the material involved.

    5. All such documents and information produced in this case shall be used for purposes of this litigation only.

    6. The attorneys of record may modify any terms of this Order by written agreement, without leave of Court.

    7. This Order is without prejudice to the right of either party to seek relief from the Court, good cause shown, from any of the restrictions provided herein.

AGREED:

_____   _____
Attorney for Petitioner   ELLEN JARNDYCE

_____   _____
Attorney for Respondent   JOHN JARNDYCE

                                       ENTER:

                                         _____
                                         JUDGE

Richard Vholes
Attorney for ELLEN JARNDYCE
Address
Telephone number

Rule 202. Purposes for which depositions may be taken in pending action

    Any party may take the testimony of any party or person by deposition upon oral examination or written questions for the purpose of discovery or for use as evidence in the action. The notice, order, or stipulation to take a deposition shall specify whether the deposition is to be a discovery deposition or an evidence deposition. In the absence of specification a deposition is a discovery deposition only. If both discovery and evidence depositions are desired of the same witness they shall be taken separately, unless the parties stipulate otherwise or the court orders otherwise upon notice and motion.

Rule 203. Where depositions may be taken

    Unless otherwise agreed, depositions shall be taken in the county in which the deponent resides or is employed or transacts his business in person, or, in the case of a plaintiff-deponent, in the county in which the action is pending. However, the court, in its discretion, may order a party or a person who is currently an officer, director, or employee of a party to appear at a designated place in this State or elsewhere for the purpose of having his deposition taken. The order designating the place of a deposition may impose any terms and conditions that are just, including payment of reasonable expenses.

Rule 204. Compelling appearance of deponent

(a) Action pending in this state.

(1) Subpoenas. Except as provided in paragraph (c) hereof, the clerk of the court shall issue subpoenas on request. The subpoena may command the person to whom it is directed to produce documents or tangible things which constitute or contain evidence relating to any of the matters within the scope of the examination permitted under these rules.

(2) Service of subpoenas. A deponent shall respond to any lawful subpoena of which he has actual knowledge, if payment of the fee and mileage has been tendered. Service of a subpoena by mail may be proved *prima facie* by a return receipt showing delivery to the deponent or his authorized agent by certified or registered mail at least 7 days before the date on which appearance is required and an affidavit showing that the mailing was prepaid and was addressed to the deponent, restricted delivery, return receipt requested, showing to whom, date and address of delivery, with a check or money order for the fee and mileage enclosed.

(3) Notice to parties, et al. Service of notice of the taking of the deposition of a party or person who is currently an officer, director, or employee of a party is sufficient to require the appearance of the deponent and the production of any documents or tangible things listed in the notice.

(b) Action pending in another state, territory, or country. Any officer or person authorized by the laws of another State, territory, or country to take any deposition in this State, with or without a commission, in any action pending in a court of that State, territory, or country may petition the circuit court in the country [sic] in which the deponent resides or is employed or transacts his business in person or is found for a subpoena to compel the appearance of the deponent or for an order to compel the giving of testimony by him. The court may hear and act upon the petition with or without notice as the court directs.

(c) Depositions of physicians and surgeons. The discovery depositions of physicians and surgeons being deposed in their professional capacity may be taken only with the agreement of the parties and the subsequent consent of the deponent or under a subpoena issued upon order of court. A party shall pay a reasonable fee to a physician or surgeon for the time he or she will spend testifying at any such deposition. Unless the physician or surgeon was retained by a party for the purpose of rendering an expert opinion at trial (see

S. Ct. Rule 204   **PROCEDURE**

Rule 220(c)(6)), or unless otherwise ordered by the court, the fee shall be paid by the party at whose instance the deposition is taken.

Author's Notes

Analysis

1. Witness fees: Amount.
2. Notice of Subpoena for Deposition—Form.
3. Subpoena for Deposition—Form.
4. Subpoena for Deposition (Records Only)—Form.
5. Notice of Deposition—Form.
6. Document production limited to documents already in existence.
7. Depositions outside Illinois.
8. Motion—Form.
9. Order—Form.
10. Notice of Deposition—Form.

(1) **Witness fees: Amount.** The witness fee is $20.00 for each day's attendance, and $.20 per mile each way for necessary travel. 55 ILCS 45/47. The fees should accompany service of the subpoena.

(2) **Notice of Subpoena for Deposition—Form.** There follows a sample notice of subpoena for deposition. The attorney for the opposing party should be notified by the notice of subpoena for deposition of the service of the subpoenas for deposition upon the deponents.

IN THE CIRCUIT COURT OF COOK COUNTY, ILLINOIS
COUNTY DEPARTMENT—DOMESTIC RELATIONS DIVISION

IN RE THE MARRIAGE OF)	
)	
LEICESTER DEDLOCK,)	
Petitioner,)	
)	
and)	No. ____ D _____
)	
LUCY DEDLOCK,)	
Respondent.)	

NOTICE OF SUBPOENA FOR DEPOSITION

TO: Frederick Tulkinghorn

    Address

PLEASE TAKE NOTICE that on _____, 199__, we served the attached Subpoenas for Deposition on Joshua Smallweed and on the Chancery Lane Bank.

                                            BLOWERS & ASSOCIATES, LTD.

ILLINOIS S. CT. RULES   S. Ct. Rule 204

CERTIFICATE OF DELIVERY

The undersigned hereby certifies under penalties of perjury as provided by law pursuant to Section 1–109 of the Code of Civil Procedure, that the above Notice of Subpoena for Deposition was [ ]placed in the U.S. Mail properly addressed and mailed with first class postage prepaid, [ ]sent via messenger, [ ]sent via facsimile (___ pages, from the office of _____, sender's facsimile number _____, to recipient's facsimile number _____), to the party at the address set forth above on the ___ day of _____, 199__, before the hour of 5:00 p.m.

_____   _____
(Signature)   (Print Name)

Joseph Blowers
Blowers & Associates, Ltd.
Attorneys for LUCY DEDLOCK
Address
Telephone number

(3) **Subpoena for Deposition—Form.** There follows a sample subpoena for deposition.

IN THE CIRCUIT COURT OF COOK COUNTY, ILLINOIS
COUNTY DEPARTMENT—DOMESTIC RELATIONS DIVISION

IN RE THE MARRIAGE OF)	
)	
LEICESTER DEDLOCK,)	
Petitioner,)	
)	
and)	No. ___ D _____
)	
LUCY DEDLOCK,)	
Respondent.)	

SUBPOENA FOR DEPOSITION

TO: Joshua Smallweed
    Address

YOU ARE COMMANDED to appear to give your deposition before a notary public at _____, Room ___, _____, Illinois, _____, on Tuesday, _____, 199__ at 2:00 p.m.

YOU ARE COMMANDED ALSO to bring the following in your possession or control:

S. Ct. Rule 204 PROCEDURE

YOUR FAILURE TO APPEAR IN RESPONSE TO THIS SUBPOENA WILL SUBJECT YOU TO PUNISHMENT FOR CONTEMPT OF THIS COURT.

WITNESS _____, 199__

_____
Clerk of Court

I served this subpoena by mailing a copy via prepaid certified mail, return receipt requested, restricted delivery, to the above-named person at the above address on _____, 199__. I paid the witness $_____ for witness and mileage fees.

_____

Subscribed and sworn before me this __ day of _____, 199__.

_____
Notary Public

Joseph Blowers
Blowers & Associates, Ltd.
Attorneys for LUCY DEDLOCK
Address
Telephone number

(4) **Subpoena for Deposition (Records Only)—Form.** There follows a sample subpoena for deposition limited to records only.

IN THE CIRCUIT COURT OF COOK COUNTY, ILLINOIS
COUNTY DEPARTMENT—DOMESTIC RELATIONS DIVISION

IN RE THE MARRIAGE OF   )
)
LEICESTER DEDLOCK,   )
            Petitioner,   )
)
and   ) No. ___ D _____
)
LUCY DEDLOCK,   )
            Respondent.   )

SUBPOENA FOR DEPOSITION (RECORDS ONLY)

TO: Keeper of the Records
    Chancery Lane Bank
    Address

YOU ARE COMMANDED TO APPEAR to give your deposition before a notary public at _____, Room ___, _____, Illinois, _____, on _____, 19__ at ___.m.

ILLINOIS S. CT. RULES   S. Ct. Rule 204

YOU ARE COMMANDED ALSO to bring the following in your possession or control:

All financial statements, appraisals, accounting records, loan files, and other documents pertaining to loans made by the Chancery Lane Bank to Leicester Dedlock from 199__ to 199__.

YOUR FAILURE TO APPEAR IN RESPONSE TO THIS SUBPOENA WILL SUBJECT YOU TO PUNISHMENT FOR CONTEMPT OF THIS COURT.

This Subpoena will not necessitate your personal appearance if you submit all your original records by the due date indicated on the Subpoena.

WITNESS _____, 199__

_____
Clerk of Court

Joseph Blowers
Blowers & Associates, Ltd.
Attorneys for LUCY DEDLOCK
Address
Telephone number

I served this subpoena by handing a copy to _____ on _____, 199__. I paid the witness $__ for witness and mileage fees.

_____

SUBSCRIBED AND SWORN
BEFORE ME THIS __ DAY OF
_____, 199__.

_____

NOTARY PUBLIC

(5) **Notice of Deposition—Form.** There follows a model notice of deposition to a party, together with a rider illustrating documents that might be requested from the deponent pursuant to Supreme Court Rule 204(a)(3). See also Supreme Court Rules 206(a) and 214 for more detailed provisions pertaining to the notice of deposition and the production of documents. The requested documents are broken down into categories. A number of the document requests may apply to more than one category, but they are not repeated. The last paragraph on the second page of the deposition notice specifies a date for the production of the requested documents. The purpose of this paragraph is to obtain the documents before the deposition date in order to review

S. Ct. Rule 204   **PROCEDURE**

them before taking the deposition. Although the sample notice of deposition is for taking of the husband's deposition, the document request seeks documents that a wife as well as a husband might hold. The sample document request is obviously not definitive, and it should therefore be edited for the particular case.

IN THE CIRCUIT COURT OF COOK COUNTY, ILLINOIS
COUNTY DEPARTMENT—DOMESTIC RELATIONS DIVISION

IN RE THE MARRIAGE OF   )
)
LEICESTER DEDLOCK,   )
)
        Petitioner,   )
)
and   )   No. ____ D _____
)
LUCY DEDLOCK,   )
)
        Respondent.)

NOTICE OF DEPOSITION

TO: Frederick Tulkinghorn, Esq.

    Address

PLEASE TAKE NOTICE that pursuant to Section 2–1003 of the Code of Civil Procedure and Illinois Supreme Court Rule 201 et seq., the discovery deposition of LEICESTER DEDLOCK, _____, Chicago, Illinois, will be taken before a Notary Public in and for the County of Cook and State of Illinois on _____, 199__, at the hour of 2:00 p.m., at the offices of Blowers & Associates, Ltd., _____, Chicago, Illinois, upon oral interrogatories to be propounded to the deponent, at which time and place you may appear if you so desire. As counsel of record for the deponent, this is a demand upon you to produce the deponent at the stated time and place. If the deponent is required to produce any documents or other matter pursuant to Supreme Court Rules 204(a)(3) and 214, the items, if any, are specified on a Rider attached hereto and made a part hereof.

This request for documents is addressed to the deponent, his or her agents, employees and attorneys. If the requested documents are known to deponent to exist but are not in the possession or control of the deponent, his or her agents, employees or attorneys, deponent shall produce documents that show the names of the persons or entities having possession or control of the documents.

As used herein, the term "document" means any written, printed, typed or graphic matter of every kind, nature or description, including also computer disks, computer printouts, "E" mail, computer storage, and microfilms in the possession or control of the deponent, as well as all notes, previous drafts and copies of documents made by whatever means if the copy bears any additional marking, notation, interlineation, amendment or deletion.

The documents requested should be produced at the offices of Blowers & Associates, Ltd. not later than _____, 199__.

Joseph Blowers, Attorney for
LUCY DEDLOCK

Joseph Blowers
Blowers & Associates, Ltd.
Address
Telephone number

In re the Marriage of Dedlock

RIDER TO NOTICE OF DEPOSITION

Income and Gift Tax Returns

1. Complete copies, including all schedules, of individual Federal and State income tax returns and amended Income Tax Returns for Petitioner and Respondent for the years 199__ through 199__.

2. Federal and State estimated tax returns, cancelled checks in payment of estimated tax, and estimated tax work sheets for 199__ and 199__ for Petitioner and Respondent. All documents reflecting income received, or to be received, during 199__ and 199__ by Petitioner.

3. Federal and State applications to extend time for the filing of 199__ income tax returns of Petitioner and Respondent. Cancelled checks submitted to the Federal and State Revenue Services with applications for extension. All work papers, documents, and preliminary drafts of returns prepared for 199__ even if incomplete.

4. Pay stubs and W-2 statements from all employers of Petitioner from 199__ to the present time.

5. 1099 statements issued to Petitioner from 199__ to the present.

6. K-1 statements issued to Petitioner from 199__ to the present date.

7. Copies of all gift tax returns in the possession of or filed by Petitioner or Respondent in the last three years, for gifts given or received.

8. Complete copies of audit reports issued by the Internal Revenue Service or State Revenue Service for any tax returns referred to herein.

9. Federal and State partnership income tax returns as well as federal and state corporation income tax returns for entities in which Petitioner or Respondent have or had any partnership interest or stock ownership or participation at any time during the past three calendar years and the current year to date.

S. Ct. Rule 204   **PROCEDURE**

10. Computer printouts, disks, or other documents containing income, expenses, checks, or tax information of Petitioner from 199__ to the current date.

11. Form 4789, Currency Transaction Report, filed with the Internal Revenue Service during the past three years.

Financial Statements and Personal Records

12. All personal financial statements and financial documents prepared by Petitioner or on his behalf during the past three years.

13. Personal ledgers, computer discs or printouts, and other documents reflecting securities or other assets owned or income received by Petitioner or Respondent.

14. Documents reflecting current beneficial ownership of any assets.

15. Documents reflecting nominee ownership of any assets or income either by or on behalf of Petitioner.

16. All budgets or affidavits or schedules of income and expenses compiled by Petitioner, including all documents, notes, previous drafts, and computer disks and printouts related thereto.

17. Memoranda, notes, compilations, accountings, computer runs, and other documents reflecting expenses of the family.

18. Statements of account for the most current 12 months from all clubs of which Petitioner is a member.

19. Records of ownership by, access to, and inventories of any safety deposit box in the name of Petitioner alone, with another, or in the name of a nominee.

20. All documents reflecting transfers of property or assignments of income by Petitioner or Respondent within in the last three years.

21. Divorce Decrees and Settlement Agreements from the previous marriages of Petitioner.

22. All calendars and other documents reflecting appointments of Petitioner during 199__.

23. All diaries of Petitioner.

24. All contracts of employment, documents reflecting benefits, expense account records, documents reflecting current salary and bonus, deferred compensation, and other compensation and benefits resulting from Petitioner's employment during the past three years.

Children

25. All documents reflecting assets and their current value and income owned, received, or held for the benefit of any or all of the children of Petitioner and Respondent.

26. Plan documents for the benefit of children of Petitioner and Respondent, including, but not limited to, trusts, Uniform Gifts to Minors Act accounts, and the like.

27. Federal and State tax returns of children of Petitioner and Respondent for the past three years.

28. All documents reflecting expenditures from the children's accounts for tuitions and for other expenses for the past three years.

Medical Insurance

29. Copies of all medical insurance policies or plans covering Petitioner or Respondent or their children.

Retirement Plans

30. All plan documents, amendments, plan descriptions, summaries, and statements showing current balances or current vested interests in any retirement plans of which Petitioner is a beneficiary.

Real Estate

31. Title policies, home owners policies, deeds, surveys, trust agreements, and other documents reflecting ownership of any real estate by Petitioner or Respondent, directly or beneficially, solely or with others, including, but not limited to, investment real estate, inherited real estate, real estate received by gift, conservation real estate, and the homes located in _____, Illinois and _____, Florida.

32. All appraisals, closing statements, records of improvements, and other documents indicating value and tax bases of all real estate owned by Petitioner or Respondent.

33. All documents reflecting the change in title of the _____, Florida house from joint ownership by Petitioner and Respondent to sole ownership by Petitioner, and all documents reflecting a change in title in other real estate during the time either Petitioner or Respondent had an interest in the real estate.

34. All documents reflecting Petitioner's interests in a farm in _____, a shopping center and store in _____, Florida, and other real estate, including appraisals, contracts of sale, correspondence relating to sales, offers, tax assessments, deeds, title opinions, loan documents, plats of subdivisions, and other documents relating to those properties.

35. All contracts, leases, and other documents reflecting agreements for the payment to Petitioner or Respondent of rental income, farm income, or royalty income.

Securities

36. Brokerage statements, reports, inventories, and other documents reflecting activities in the accounts of Petitioner for the past three years from

investment counsellors employed by Petitioner, any company through which Petitioner has bought or sold securities, bonds, or mutual funds, or which holds securities on behalf of Petitioner.

37. All documents reflecting the tax bases of securities owned by Petitioner.

38. Current statements relating to mutual funds, stock funds, bond funds, money market funds, certificates of deposit and the like, in the name of Petitioner or his nominee.

39. Copies of stock certificates, bonds, CDs, options, and all other securities owned by Petitioner.

40. All reports, financial statements, accountings, prospectuses and other documents for investments of and interests of Petitioner, received by Petitioner during the past three years.

41. All documents and accounts reflecting dividends, interest, stock splits, stock dividends or other distributions received by Petitioner as a result of the ownership of securities during the year 199__.

42. All reports filed by Petitioner with the Securities and Exchange Commission or with other Governmental regulatory agencies relating to securities or trading in securities.

43. Documents reflecting that any securities owned by Petitioner should be sold at a premium or a discount above or below their recognized price.

Trading Accounts

44. Statements of monthly activity for each month for each account utilized by Petitioner to trade commodities or other assets from January 1, 199__ to current date.

45. Any year-end tax summary issued for the above accounts for years 199__ to current date.

46. Federal and State tax returns for _____ Clearing House or other clearing firms in which Petitioner has any interest for years 199__ to current date.

47. Audited and unaudited financial statements or reports prepared for the clearing firms described in paragraph 46 hereof for years 199__ to current date.

48. Interim financial statements and reports for the clearing firms described in paragraph 46 hereof issued since December 31, 199__.

49. Lists of all stockholders or owners of the clearing firms described in paragraph 46 hereof.

50. Copies of stock certificates in the name of Petitioner, and corporate minutes which describe the capital structure for the clearing firms described in paragraph 46 hereof, or if a clearing firm is not a corporation, the partnership agreement or the like.

51. All documents, including corporate minutes, that describe financial arrangements between Petitioner and the clearing firms which clear Petitioner's trades.

52. All documents, including corporate minutes, that describe financial arrangements for the clearing firms described in paragraph 46 hereof to clear owners other than Petitioner or customers other than owners' trades.

53. Statement of monthly activity for each month for each account of the clearing firms that is in the name of Petitioner, or in the name of any entity in which Petitioner has an interest, from January 1, 199__ to current date.

54. Schedule of life insurance policies, if any, on the life of Petitioner payable to the clearing firm.

55. Pension, profit sharing, and documents concerning deferred compensation arrangements, if any, of the clearing firms described in paragraph 46 hereof.

56. Filings with government or any regulatory agencies from January 1, 199__ to present date for Petitioner or the clearing firms described in paragraph 46 hereof.

57. The same documents as requested in paragraphs 44 through 56 of this Rider for _____ Trading Company or any other trading company in which Petitioner has any interest.

58. Documents of organizations and tax returns and financial statements for the past five years for any company or partnership or joint venture in which Petitioner has any interest, which is not publicly traded, and which is not covered by paragraphs 44 through 57 of this Rider.

Closely Held Businesses

59. Federal and State corporate tax returns for _____ Company from 199__ through the most current available tax return and any other closely held business in which Petitioner has an interest.

60. Financial statements for the past three years, including the most current annual and interim financial statement, for _____ Company and any other closely held business in which Petitioner has an interest.

61. All documents reflecting any options of Petitioner to purchase stock in _____ Company or any other company.

62. The corporate minutes and stock record book for _____ Company.

63. All appraisals, stock valuations, asset valuations, or other studies of value relating to _____ Company.

64. Documents and reports indicating that Petitioner's stock in _____ Company would be sold at a premium or a discount above or below the recognized price for the shares.

65. All offers to purchase _____ Company.

66. All documents reflecting stock sales or offers to purchase or sell stock of _____ Company.

67. Stock redemption agreements or buy-sell agreements to which Petitioner was or is a party that were in effect at any time during the past three calendar years and the current year to date.

68. All documents reflecting restrictions on stock owned by Petitioner.

Partnerships

69. Copy of the partnership agreement of Petitioner's law firm, _____.

70. Documents reflecting accounts receivable, work in progress, unbilled time, unbilled costs, insofar as those records are attributable to Petitioner's percentage interest in his law firm partnership.

71. Documents reflecting assets and investments of Petitioner's law firm, _____.

72. Documents reflecting Petitioner's current capital account in his law firm, _____.

73. Federal and State tax returns of any partnership in which Petitioner has had an interest for the past three most current years.

74. K–1 statements, reports, statements reflecting Petitioner's share of partnership income, financial statements, prospectuses, appraisals, and other documents received by Petitioner during the past two years relating to partnerships, drilling programs, real estate partnerships, and the like, in which Petitioner has an interest.

Sole Proprietorships

75. Ledgers, income and expense reports, balance sheets, and all other documents reflecting income, expenses, assets and liabilities of Petitioner's therapy practice or any other sole proprietorship of Petitioner.

Income and Benefits

76. All correspondence, memoranda, agreements, notes, and all other documents relating to deferred compensation, bonuses, stock options, retirement plans, and the like, to which Petitioner is entitled currently or in the future.

77. All contracts of employment, documents reflecting benefits, expense account records, documents reflecting current salary and bonus, deferred compensation, share ownership and beneficial share ownership, executive incentive plans, stock plans, phantom stock, retirement plans, ESOPs, stock options, and other compensation and benefits resulting from Petitioner's employment or otherwise at _____ and other places of Petitioner's employment.

78. Most current proxy statements of _____ and other places of Petitioner's employment.

79. Documents and proxy statements setting forth Petitioner's compensation and other benefits resulting from Petitioner's service as a director, officer, or trustee of any company, trust, or entity.

80. All documents reflecting any options to purchase stock in _____, Inc., owned by Petitioner.

Death, Estates, Gifts

81. The current will of Petitioner.

82. Copies of all life insurance policies on Petitioner's life and copies of current statements reflecting cash surrender values, loans, and interest paid.

83. All correspondence, receipts, inventories, appraisals, court documents, notices, income and gift tax returns, accounts, receipts, estate or inheritance tax returns, and any other documents of estates of deceased persons in which Petitioner has any interest. This paragraph refers to the estate of, including but not limited to, Petitioner's mother.

84. The same documents are requested as in the previous paragraph for any assets received by way of gift from any persons.

Trusts and Foundations

85. For the _____ Revocable Trust and any other trusts of which Petitioner or Respondent are beneficiaries, settlors, or in which they have any other interest, contingent or otherwise: statements or other documents describing the corpus of the trusts and reflecting the current value and yield of the corpus of the trusts; all trust agreements and documents; and all trust tax returns for the past three years.

86. The same documents as were requested in the previous paragraph of this Rider for any trusts of which the children of Petitioner and Respondent are beneficiaries.

87. Documents of organization, statements describing assets and stating current values and yields, and tax returns for the past three years, for all foundations, corporations, and trusts through which Petitioner invests for himself and others, including but not limited to _____.

88. Documents of organization, statements describing assets and stating current values and yields, and tax returns for the past three years, for all foundations, corporations, and trusts through which Petitioner makes charitable contributions for himself and others, including, but not limited to _____.

Personal Property

89. Copies of all current homeowners, personal property, and automobile insurance policies insuring jewelry, personal property, and other assets of Petitioner or Respondent.

90. All appraisals and inventories of jewelry, furniture, antiques, collections, and other personal property owned by Petitioner or Respondent.

S. Ct. Rule 204   PROCEDURE

91. Certificates of title and all other documents relating to automobiles, boats, airplanes, and the like owned by Petitioner.

Checking and Savings Accounts and Credit Cards

92. All credit card statements and receipts reflecting charges by Petitioner for the past two years.

93. All cancelled checks, bank statements, and deposit slips for all checking accounts at banks, and for all other money market or cash management accounts, trust accounts, and the like on which checks are drawn bearing the name of Petitioner or his nominee, for the past three years.

94. Savings account statements and passbooks for all savings accounts bearing the name of Petitioner or his nominee, for the past three years.

Debts

95. All documents reflecting current indebtednesses, mortgages, home equity loans, and loan guarantees by Petitioner.

Transfers

96. All documents reflecting transfers of property or assignments of income by Petitioner or Respondent within the last three years.

Marital and Non-marital Property

97. All documents reflecting the source of any assets owned by Petitioner or Respondent to have been premarital, or to have been the result of gifts or inheritance, or reflecting the non-marital nature of any property. This request includes, but is not limited to, all documents used in the tracing of a current asset to a non-marital source.

98. All documents reflecting the marital nature of any property.

99. All documents reflecting reimbursement owed by: the non-marital estate to the marital estate or the marital estate to the non-marital estate.

100. All documents reflecting a change in the character of property from non-marital to marital property or from marital to non-marital property, whether through contribution, commingling, placing in co-ownership, or otherwise.

Affidavit

101. An affidavit pursuant to Supreme Court Rule 214 signed under oath by Petitioner stating that his production of documents is complete in accordance with this Request for Production of Documents.

Joseph Blowers
Blowers & Associates, Ltd.
Attorneys for LUCY DEDLOCK
Address
Telephone number

ILLINOIS S. CT. RULES   **S. Ct. Rule 204**

CERTIFICATE OF DELIVERY

The undersigned hereby certifies under penalties of perjury as provided by law pursuant to Section 1–109 of the Code of Civil Procedure, that the above Notice of Deposition was [ ]placed in the U.S. Mail properly addressed and mailed with first class postage prepaid, [ ]sent via messenger, [ ]sent via facsimile (__ pages, from the office of _____, sender's facsimile number _____, to recipient's facsimile number ___), to the party at the address set forth above on the __ day of _____, 199__, before the hour of 5:00 p.m.

_____   _____
(Signature)   (Print Name)

(6) **Document production limited to documents already in existence.** A deponent is not required to respond to a request for production of documents by making lists, preparing budgets, or otherwise creating documents that are not already in existence. Mendelson v. Feingold, 69 Ill.App.3d 227, 25 Ill.Dec. 707, 387 N.E.2d 363 (2d Dist.1979). Such requests are more properly made by written interrogatories. See Supreme Court Rule 213.

(7) **Depositions outside Illinois.** Deposing a witness in a state other than Illinois when the action is pending in Illinois generally requires a motion in Illinois to obtain an order authorizing the deposition, which is then enrolled in the foreign jurisdiction. The foreign state issues subpoenas for the deposition pursuant to the enrolled order from Illinois. A notice of subpoena for deposition must be served upon the opposing attorneys as in the case of local depositions. See Author's Note (2) above. Usually a discovery deposition is first taken, followed by an evidence deposition for use at the trial. It is a good practice to initially contact a lawyer in the foreign jurisdiction in order to determine the precise requirements of the foreign state (corresponding to Supreme Court Rule 204(b) in Illinois) concerning the process of enrollment, the necessity for certified copies, and the like.

(8) **Motion—Form.** A model motion to use for the taking of a deposition in a foreign state for an action pending in Illinois follows. The corresponding order and notice of deposition are at Author's Notes (9) and (10) below.

IN THE CIRCUIT COURT OF COOK COUNTY, ILLINOIS
COUNTY DEPARTMENT—DOMESTIC RELATIONS DIVISION

IN RE THE MARRIAGE OF   )
)
WILLIAM GUPPY,   )
)
             Petitioner,   )
)
and   )   No. __ D _____
)
ESTHER SUMMERSON,   )
)
            Respondent.   )

S. Ct. Rule 204   PROCEDURE

MOTION

RESPONDENT, ESTHER SUMMERSON, by her attorneys, Blowers & Associates, Ltd., moves:

1. The Court enter the attached Order authorizing the issuance of a subpoena duces tecum and the taking of a discovery and an evidence deposition of DAVID KROOK in Santa Barbara, California.

2. ESTHER SUMMERSON have such other and further relief as may be appropriate under the evidence and circumstances.

In support of the foregoing Motion, ESTHER SUMMERSON, by her attorneys, alleges:

1. In order to take a deposition in the State of California, counsel has been advised that it is necessary to have the Illinois Court enter an Order authorizing the taking of the deposition and the issuance of a subpoena to the deponent. The Illinois Order is then enrolled in the California Court and the deposition and subpoena are thereby authorized.

2. The deposition of and the production of documents by DAVID KROOK is relevant to the pending litigation, inasmuch as DAVID KROOK may have been connected with the dissipation of assets from the marital estate, and may, in fact, hold some assets belonging to the marital estate. DAVID KROOK resides in Santa Barbara, California.

                                                                 Joseph Blowers, Attorney for
                                                                 ESTHER SUMMERSON

Joseph Blowers
Blowers & Associates, Ltd.
Address
Telephone number

(9) **Order—Form.** A sample Illinois order to be enrolled in the appropriate foreign state court for the taking of the out-of-state deposition follows.

ILLINOIS S. CT. RULES   S. Ct. Rule 204

IN THE CIRCUIT COURT OF COOK COUNTY, ILLINOIS
COUNTY DEPARTMENT—DOMESTIC RELATIONS DIVISION

IN RE THE MARRIAGE OF)
)
WILLIAM GUPPY,)
)
        Petitioner,)
)
and) No. ___ D _____
)
ESTHER SUMMERSON,)
)
        Respondent.)

ORDER

ON THE MOTION OF RESPONDENT, ESTHER SUMMERSON, and the Court being fully advised,

IT IS THEREFORE HEREBY ORDERED:

1. The discovery and the evidence depositions of DAVID KROOK are hereby authorized for the purposes of discovery and providing evidence in this pending litigation. DAVID KROOK resides in Santa Barbara, California. The depositions shall be taken as soon as practical after notification of the time, date, and place of the depositions is served upon Samuel Kenge, Kenge and Carboy, _____, Chicago, Illinois 60606, attorney for WILLIAM GUPPY, and upon Joseph Blowers, Blowers & Associates, Ltd., Chicago, Illinois 60603, attorney for ESTHER SUMMERSON.

2. The Clerk of the Court in the State of California in which this Order is enrolled is requested to issue appropriate subpoena duces tecum to DAVID KROOK, _____, Santa Barbara, California 93105, specifying the time, date, and place of the deposition and directing the production of documents.

3. This Order is entered in the State of Illinois for purposes of being enrolled in the appropriate court in the State of California in order to provide authority for the production of documents by and the taking of the discovery

S. Ct. Rule 204   PROCEDURE

and evidence depositions of DAVID KROOK, and for the purpose of causing the issuance of an appropriate subpoena duces tecum to DAVID KROOK.

                      ENTER:

                      _____

                      JUDGE

DATE: _____

Joseph Blowers
Blowers & Associates, Ltd.
Attorneys for ESTHER SUMMERSON
Address
Telephone number

(10) **Notice of Deposition—Form.** There follows a sample notice of deposition to which the foreign deposition subpoena should be attached.

IN THE CIRCUIT COURT OF COOK COUNTY, ILLINOIS
COUNTY DEPARTMENT—DOMESTIC RELATIONS DIVISION

IN RE THE MARRIAGE OF	)
WILLIAM GUPPY,	)
Petitioner,	)
and	) No. ____ D _____
ESTHER SUMMERSON,	)
Respondent.	)

NOTICE OF DEPOSITION

TO: Samuel Kenge   Joseph Blowers
    Kenge and Carboy   Blowers & Associates, Ltd.
    Address   Address

PLEASE TAKE NOTICE that pursuant to the provisions of Section 2-1003 of the Illinois Code of Civil Procedure and the Illinois Supreme Court Rule 201, et seq., and the Cook County Court Order of _____, 199__, the undersigned counsel shall take the discovery and evidence depositions of DAVID KROOK, _____, Santa Barbara, California, on _____, 199__ through _____, 199__ beginning at 2:00 p.m. on each day, at the law offices of Morgan Snagsby, _____, Santa Barbara, California. A copy of the subpoena served in this matter is attached hereto.

                                              Morgan Snagsby, Attorney for
                                              ESTHER SUMMERSON

Morgan Snagsby
Address
Santa Barbara, California
Telephone number

CERTIFICATE OF DELIVERY

The undersigned hereby certifies under penalties of perjury as provided by law pursuant to Section 1–109 of the Code of Civil Procedure, that the above Notice of Deposition was [ ]placed in the U.S. Mail properly addressed and mailed with first class postage prepaid, [ ]sent via messenger, [ ]sent via facsimile (____ pages, from the office of _____, sender's facsimile number _____, to recipient's facsimile number _____), to the party at the address set forth above on the ___ day of _____, 199__, before the hour of 5:00 p.m.

(Signature)   (Print Name)

Rule 206. Method of taking depositions on oral examination

(a) Notice of examination; Time and place. A party desiring to take the deposition of any person upon oral examination shall serve notice in writing a reasonable time in advance on the other parties. The notice shall state the time and place for taking the deposition; the name and address of each person to be examined, if known, or, if unknown, information sufficient to identify him; and whether the deposition is for purposes of discovery or for use in evidence.

    (1) Representative deponent. A party may in the notice and in a subpoena, if required, name as the deponent a public or private corporation or a partnership or association or governmental agency and describe with reasonable particularity the matters on which examination is requested. In that event, the organization so named shall designate one or more officers, directors, or managing agents, or other persons to testify on its behalf, and may set forth, for each person designated, the matters on which he will testify. The subpoena shall advise a nonparty organization of its duty to make such a designation. The persons so designated shall testify as to matters known or reasonably available to the organization.

    (2) Audio-visual recording to be used. If a party serving notice of deposition intends to record the deponent's testimony by use of an audio-visual recording device, the notice of deposition must so advise all parties to the deposition. If any other party intends to record the testimony of

S. Ct. Rule 206 PROCEDURE

the witness by use of an audio-visual recording device, notice of that intent must likewise be served upon all other parties a reasonable time in advance. Such notices shall contain the name of the recording-device operator. After notice is given that a deposition will be recorded by an audio-visual recording device, any party may make a motion for relief in the form of a protection order under Rule 201. If a hearing is not held prior to the taking of the deposition, the recording shall be made subject to the court's ruling at a later time.

If the deposition is to be taken pursuant to a subpoena, a copy of the subpoena shall be attached to the notice. On motion of any party upon whom the notice is served, the court, for cause shown, may extend or shorten the time. Unless otherwise agreed by the parties or ordered by the court, depositions shall not be taken on Saturdays, Sundays, or court holidays.

(b) Any party entitled to take deposition pursuant to a notice. When a notice of the taking of a deposition has been served, any party may take a deposition under the notice, in which case he shall pay the fees and charges payable by a party at whose instance a deposition is taken.

(c) Scope and manner of examination and cross-examination.

(1) The deponent in a discovery deposition may be examined regarding any matter subject to discovery under these rules. He may be questioned by any party as if under cross-examination.

(2) In an evidence deposition the examination and cross-examination shall be the same as though the deponent were testifying at the trial.

(d) Motion to terminate or limit examination. At any time during the taking of the deposition, on motion of any party or of the deponent and upon a showing that the examination is being conducted in bad faith or in any manner that unreasonably annoys, embarrasses, or oppresses the deponent or party, the court may order that the examination cease forthwith or may limit the scope and manner of taking the examination as provided by these rules. An examination terminated by the order shall be resumed only upon further order of the court. Upon the demand of the objecting party or deponent, the taking of the deposition shall be suspended for the time necessary to present a motion for an order. The court may require either party or the deponent to pay costs or expenses, including reasonable attorney's fees, or both, as the court may deem reasonable.

(e) Record of examination; Oath; Objections. The officer before whom the deposition is to be taken shall put the witness on oath and shall personally, or by someone acting under his direction and in his presence, record the testimony of the witness. The testimony shall be taken stenographically, by sound-recording device, by audio-visual recording device, or by any combination of all three. The testimony shall be transcribed at the request of any party. Objections made at the time of the examination to the qualifications of the officer taking the deposition, to the manner of taking it, to the evidence presented, or to the conduct of any person, and any other objection to the proceedings, shall be included in the deposition. Evidence objected to shall be taken subject to the objection. In lieu of participating in the oral examination, parties served with notice of taking a deposition may transmit written questions to the officer, who shall propound them to the witness and record the answers verbatim.

(f) *Videotaped depositions.* Except as otherwise provided in this rule, the rules governing the practice, procedures and use of depositions shall apply to videotaped depositions.

(1) Depositions which are to be recorded on an audio-visual recording device shall begin by the operator of the device stating, on camera, (1) his name and address, (2) the date, time and place of the deposition, (3) the caption of the case, (4) the name of the witness, (5) the party on whose behalf the deposition is being taken, and (6) the party at whose instance the deposition is being recorded on an audio-visual recording device. The officer before whom the deposition is being taken shall identify himself and swear the witness on camera. At the conclusion of the deposition the operator shall state on camera that the deposition is concluded. If the deposition requires the use of more than one videotape, the end of each videotape and the beginning of each succeeding tape shall be announced on camera by the operator.

(2) The operator shall initially take custody of the videotape of the deposition and shall run through the videotape to determine the exact length of time of the deposition. The operator shall sign an affidavit stating the length of time of the deposition and shall certify that the videotape is a true record of the deposition and shall certify that the operator has not edited or otherwise altered the videotape. A deposition so certified requires no further proof of authenticity. If requested by any party at the conclusion of the taking of the deposition, the operator shall make a copy of the videotape and deliver it to the party requesting it at the cost of that party.

(3) A videotape of a deposition for purposes of discovery only shall be returned to the attorney for the party at whose instance the deposition was videotaped. Said attorney is responsible for the safeguarding of the videotape and shall permit the viewing of and shall provide a copy of the videotape upon the request and at the cost of any party. A videotape of a discovery deposition shall not be filed with the court except by leave of court for good cause shown.

(4) A videotape of a deposition for use in evidence shall be securely sealed by the operator, in an envelope bearing the title and number of the action, and marked "Deposition(s) of (here insert name(s) of deponent(s))," and promptly filed or sent by certified mail to the clerk of the court for filing. Upon payment of reasonable charges therefor, the operator shall furnish a copy of the videotape to any party or the deponent.

S. Ct. Rule 206   PROCEDURE

(5) The party at whose instance the videotaped deposition is taken shall pay the charges of the videotape operator for attending and shall pay any charges for filing the videotape of an evidence deposition.

(6) The videotape of a deposition may be presented at trial in lieu of reading from the stenographic transcription of the deposition.

Author's Notes

Analysis

1. Objections during deposition.
2. Objection: Procedure.

(1) **Objections during deposition.** Supreme Court Rule 206(e) provides that "evidence objected to shall be taken subject to the objection." Generally this is true for both discovery and evidence depositions. See Supreme Court Rule 211 for the circumstances when objections not made before or during the deposition are waived, and for the making of objections at trial when the deposition evidence is offered at the trial. There may be occasions when a deponent's lawyer instructs his witness not to answer an objectionable question, rather than merely making the objection and allowing the witness to testify subject to the objection; for example, where the question put to the deponent seeks privileged information or work product information. The remedy of the party taking the deposition is to submit to the court a motion to compel the deponent to answer the questions pursuant to Supreme Court Rule 219. See, e.g., Lynch v. Mullenix, 48 Ill.App.3d 963, 6 Ill.Dec. 831, 363 N.E.2d 645 (3d Dist.1977) (court correctly ordered deponent to answer questions, and correctly awarded the opposing party costs as restitution). The technique of a deponent's lawyer instructing his witness not to answer and the remedy of the questioner presenting a motion to compel the answer to the court is not confined to privilege and work product, but can also be used for other allegedly improper questions, such as those that are irrelevant or harassing. See, e.g., Carlson v. Healey, 69 Ill.App.2d 236, 215 N.E.2d 831 (2d Dist.1966) (court properly sustained deponent's refusal to answer irrelevant and argumentative questions).

(2) **Objection: Procedure.** The proper objection exchange is as follows:

Questioner: (Question.)

Deponent's lawyer: Objection; attorney-client privilege. I instruct the witness not to answer.

Questioner: Mr. Krook, do you refuse to answer the question?

Deponent: Yes, I refuse to answer the question upon the advice of my counsel.

Questioner: Reporter, please certify the question for presentation to the court.

Rule 207. Signing and filing depositions

(a) Submission to deponent; Changes; Signing. Unless signature is waived by the deponent, the officer shall instruct the deponent that if the testimony is transcribed he will be afforded an opportunity to examine the deposition at the office of the officer or reporter, or elsewhere by reasonable arrangement at the deponent's expense, and that any changes in form or substance which the deponent desires to make will be entered upon the deposition with a statement of the reasons he gives for making them. The deponent shall provide the officer with an address to which notice is to be sent when the transcript is available for examination and signing. When the deposition is fully transcribed, the officer shall mail to the deponent, at the address last supplied, notice that it is available and may be examined at a stated place at stated times, or pursuant to arrangement. After the deponent has examined the deposition, the officer shall enter upon it any changes the deponent desires to make, with the reasons the deponent gives for making them. If the deponent does not appear at the place specified in the notice within 28 days after the mailing of the notice, or within the same 28 days make other arrangements for examination of the deposition, or after examining the deposition refuses to sign it, or after it has been made available to him by arrangement it remains unsigned for 28 days, the officer's certificate shall state the reason for the omission of the signature, including any reason given by the deponent for a refusal to sign. The deposition may then be used as fully as though signed, unless on a motion to suppress under Rule 211(d) the court holds that the reasons given by the deponent for a refusal to sign require rejection of the deposition in whole or in part.

(b) Certification, filing, and notice of filing.

(1) If the testimony is transcribed, the officer shall certify on the deposition that the deponent was duly sworn by him and that the deposition is a true record of the testimony given by the deponent. A deposition so certified requires no further proof of authenticity. At the request of any party, the officer shall then securely seal the deposition, together with all exhibits, or copies thereof, in an envelope bearing the title and number of the action and marked "Deposition(s) of (here insert name(s) of deponent(s))" and promptly file it or send it by registered or certified mail to the clerk of the court for filing.

(2) The party causing a deposition to be filed shall promptly serve notice thereof on the other parties.

Author's Notes

(1) **Reading and signing deposition.** When representing a deponent, it is prudent to have the deponent read the deposition and sign it. Reading and signing the deposition not only allows the deponent an opportunity to correct any errors, but also fixes in the deponent's mind that to which he or she has testified. Waiving the signature is not a worthwhile expediency.

Rule 208. Fees and charges—Copies

(a) Who shall pay. The party at whose instance the deposition is taken shall pay the fees of the witness and of the officer and the charges of the recorder or stenographer for attending. The party at whose request a deposition is transcribed and filed shall pay the charges for transcription and filing. The party at whose request a tape recorded deposition is filed without having been transcribed shall pay the charges for filing, and if such deposition is subsequently transcribed the party requesting it shall pay the charges for such transcription. If, however, the scope of the examination by any other party exceeds the scope of examination by the party at whose instance the deposition is taken, the fees and charges due to the excess shall be summarily taxed by the court and paid by the other party.

(b) Amount. The officer taking and certifying a deposition is entitled to any fees provided by statute, together with the reasonable and necessary charges for a recorder or stenographer for attending and transcribing the deposition. Every witness attending before the officer is entitled to the fees and mileage allowance provided by statute for witnesses attending courts in this state.

(c) Copies. Upon payment of reasonable charges therefor, the officer shall furnish a copy of the deposition to any party or to the deponent.

(d) Taxing as costs. The aforesaid fees and charges may in the discretion of the trial court be taxed as costs.

Rule 209. Failure to attend or serve subpoena—Expenses

(a) Failure to attend or to proceed; Expenses. If the party serving notice of the taking of a deposition fails to attend or to proceed therewith and another party attends in person or by attorney pursuant to the notice, the court may order the party serving the notice to pay to the other party the amount of the reasonable expenses incurred by him and his attorney in so attending, including reasonable attorney's fees.

(b) Failure to serve subpoena or notice; Expenses. If the party serving notice of the taking of a deposition fails to serve a subpoena or notice, as may be appropriate, requiring the attendance of the deponent and because of that failure the deponent does not attend, and if another party attends in person or by attorney because he expects the deposition of that deponent to be taken, the court may order the party serving the notice to pay to the other party the amount of the reasonable expenses incurred by him and his attorney in attending, including reasonable attorney's fees.

Rule 210. Depositions on written questions

(a) Serving questions; Notice. A party desiring to take the deposition of any person upon written questions shall serve them upon the other parties with a notice stating the name and address of the person who is to answer them if known, or, if the name is not known, a general description sufficient to identify him, and the name or descriptive title and address of the officer before whom the deposition is to be taken. Within 14 days thereafter a party so served may likewise serve cross questions. Within 7 days after being served with cross questions a party may likewise serve redirect questions. Within 7 days after being served with redirect questions, a party may likewise serve recross questions.

(b) Officer to take responses and prepare record. The party at whose instance the deposition is taken shall transmit a copy of the notice and copies of the initial and subsequent questions served to the officer designated in the notice who shall proceed promptly, in the manner provided by Rules 206(e) and 207, to take the testimony of the deponent in response to the questions and to prepare, certify, and file or mail the deposition, attaching thereto the copy of the notice and the questions received by him. No party, attorney, or person interested in the event of the action (unless he is the deponent) shall be present during the taking of the deposition or dictate, write, or draw up any answer to the questions.

(c) Notice of filing. The party causing a deposition to be filed shall promptly serve notice thereof on the other parties.

Author's Notes

(1) **Disuse of depositions on written questions.** Depositions on written questions are seldom used. It is not a recommended procedure, because, like written interrogatories, it does not provide the questioner with the valuable tool of the follow-up question.

Rule 211. Effect of errors and irregularities in depositions—Objections

(a) As to notice. All errors and irregularities in the notice for taking a deposition are waived unless written objection is promptly served upon the party giving the notice.

(b) As to disqualification of officer or person. Objection to taking a deposition because of disqualification of the officer or person before whom it is to be taken is waived unless made before the taking of the deposition begins or as soon thereafter as the disqualification becomes known or could have been discovered with reasonable diligence.

(c) As to competency of deponent; Admissibility of testimony; Questions and answers; Misconduct; Irregularities.

(1) Grounds of objection to the competency of the deponent or admissibility of testimony which might have been corrected if presented during the taking of the deposition are waived by failure to make them at that time; otherwise objections to the competency of the deponent or admissibility of testimony may be made when the testimony is offered in evidence.

(2) Objections to the form of a question or answer, errors and irregularities occurring at the oral examination in the manner of taking the deposition, in the oath or affirmation, or in the conduct of any person, and errors and irregularities of any kind which might be corrected if promptly presented, are waived unless seasonable objection thereto is made at the taking of the deposition.

(3) Objections to the form of written questions are waived unless served in writing upon the party propounding them within the time allowed for serving succeeding questions and, in the case of the last questions authorized, within 7 days after service thereof.

(4) A motion to suppress is unnecessary to preserve an objection seasonably made. Any party may, but need not, on notice and motion obtain a ruling by the court on the objections in advance of the trial.

(d) As to completion and return of deposition. Errors and irregularities in the manner in which the testimony is transcribed or the deposition is prepared, signed, certified, sealed, indorsed, transmitted, filed, or otherwise dealt with by the officer are waived unless a motion to suppress the deposition or some part thereof is made with reasonable promptness after the defect is, or with due diligence might have been, ascertained.

Author's Notes

Analysis

1. Waiver of objections.
2. Timing of ruling.
3. Cross reference.

(1) **Waiver of objection.** Supreme Court Rule 211(c) provides, *inter alia*, that objections to the admissibility of testimony that might have been corrected if the objection was presented during the taking of the deposition are waived by a failure to make them at the deposition; otherwise most objections may be made when the testimony is offered in evidence. For example, if the questioner asks a leading question or poses an improper hypothetical question, the objections are waived if not made at the deposition, because the questions could have been corrected by the questioner. Similarly, an objection to the admission of secondary evidence concerning the contents of unavailable letters may be waived if not made at the time of the deposition testimony, because the deponent may be able to account for the whereabouts of the original documents if asked. Hutchinson v. Bambas, 249 Ill. 624, 94 N.E. 987 (1911).

Because it is often difficult during the pressure of a deposition to comprehend both whether a question is objectionable and whether it is subject to correction when the testimony is offered in evidence, it is a good idea to present all important objections during the deposition. This is true whether the purpose of the deposition is discovery or evidence, because both discovery and evidence depositions may find their way into evidence. See Supreme Court Rule 212. Discovery depositions are commonly introduced into evidence for purposes of impeachment, as an admission of a party opponent, or as support for motions for summary judgment.

(2) **Timing of ruling.** Supreme Court Rule 211(c)(4) provides that a party may, but need not, obtain a ruling upon the propriety of objections asserted at a deposition prior to the trial. It is just as appropriate to obtain the ruling when the deposition is offered as evidence at the trial, provided that the objection has not been waived. Obviously, the questioner may seek to compel a deponent to testify prior to trial where the deponent's lawyer has not only made an objection but instructed his client not to answer the question. See Supreme Court Rule 219 for procedures to obtain relief. A prompt motion to suppress is required pursuant to Supreme Court Rule 211(d) in regard to irregularities by the officer transcribing the deposition.

(3) **Cross reference.** See Supreme Court Rule 206 Author's Note (2) for the proper objection procedure for the deponent, his lawyer, and the questioner.

Rule 212. Use of depositions

(a) Purposes for which discovery depositions may be used. Discovery depositions taken under the provisions of this rule may be used only:

(1) for the purpose of impeaching the testimony of the deponent as a witness in the same manner and to the same extent as any inconsistent statement made by a witness;

(2) as an admission made by a party or by an officer or agent of a party in the same manner and to the same extent as any other admission made by that person;

(3) if otherwise admissible as an exception to the hearsay rule; or

(4) for any purpose for which an affidavit may be used.

(b) Use of evidence depositions. The evidence deposition of a physician or surgeon may be introduced in evidence at trial on the motion of either party regardless of the availability of the deponent, without prejudice to the right of either party to subpoena or otherwise call the physician or surgeon for attendance at trial. All or any part of other evidence depositions may be used for any purpose for which a discovery deposition may be used, and may be used by any party for any purpose if the court finds that at the time of the trial:

(1) the deponent is dead or unable to attend or testify because of age, sickness, infirmity, or imprisonment;

(2) the deponent is out of the county, unless it appears that the absence was procured by the party offering the deposition, provided, that a party who is not a resident of this State may introduce his own deposition if he is absent from the county; or

(3) the party offering the deposition has exercised reasonable diligence but has been unable to procure the attendance of the deponent by subpoena; or finds, upon notice and motion in advance of trial, that exceptional circumstances exist which make it desirable, in the interest of justice and with due regard for the importance of presenting the testimony of witnesses orally in open court, to allow the deposition to be used.

(c) Partial use. If only a part of a deposition is read or used at the trial by a party, any other party may at that time read or use or require him to read any other part of the deposition which ought in fairness to be considered in connection with the part read or used.

(d) Use after substitution, dismissal, or remandment. Substitution of parties does not affect the right to use depositions previously taken. If any action in any court of this or any other jurisdiction of the United States is dismissed and another action involving the same subject matter is afterward brought between the same parties or their representatives or successors in interest, or if any action is remanded by a court of the United States to a court of this State, all depositions lawfully taken and duly filed in the former action, or before remandment, may be used as if taken in the later action, or after remandment.

Author's Notes

Analysis

1. Admission of evidence deposition at trial.
2. Use of deposition to impeach witness.

(1) **Admission of evidence deposition at trial.** Where the party who has taken an evidence deposition fails or refuses to offer it into evidence, the other party may offer the evidence deposition into evidence at the trial. See Dobkowski v. Lowe's Inc., 20 Ill.App.3d 275, 279, 314 N.E.2d 623, 627 (1974) ("a party who takes an evidence deposition should not have the power to suppress the evidence contained therein merely be [sic] refusing to offer it into evidence").

(2) **Use of deposition to impeach witness.** To use a deposition to impeach the testimony of a witness after the witness has given testimony at trial which is contrary to a noncollateral prior statement, the examining attorney must first lay a proper foundation for admission of the prior inconsistent statement. The proper procedure is to inquire of the witness: (1) whether he recalls having his deposition taken on such and such a date; (2) whether he recalls the impeaching questions and answers at such and such pages of the deposition, which should be read to him. If he admits that he was asked the questions and gave the testimony that is read to him from the deposition, sufficient proof has been made and extrinsic evidence is not necessary. If he denies being asked the questions or giving the answers, the impeaching portion of the deposition should be offered into evidence. See Michael H. Graham, *Cleary & Graham's Handbook of Illinois Evidence* §§ 613.3, 607.2 (6th ed. 1994).

In either event, unless the deposition testimony is admissible as substantive evidence under an exception to the hearsay rule, the prior inconsistent statement is admitted for impeachment purposes only, and not for its truth. People v. Morgan, 28 Ill.2d 55, 190 N.E.2d 755 (1963).

Rule 213. Written interrogatories to parties

(a) Directing interrogatories. A party may direct written interrogatories to any other party. One copy of the interrogatories shall be filed with proof of service on all other parties entitled to notice. Written interrogatories shall be reasonably spaced so as to permit the answering party to make his answer on the interrogatories served upon him. The answering party may attach an addendum to the copies if the space provided is insufficient.

(b) Duty of attorney. It is the duty of an attorney directing interrogatories to restrict them to the subject matter of the particular case, to avoid undue detail, and to avoid the imposition of any unnecessary burden or expense on the answering party.

(c) Answers and objections. Within 28 days after service of the interrogatories upon the party to whom they are directed, he shall file a sworn answer or an objection to each interrogatory, with proof of service upon all other parties entitled to notice. Any objection to an answer or to the refusal to answer an interrogatory shall be heard by the court upon prompt notice and motion of the party propounding the interrogatory. The answering party shall set forth in full each interrogatory being answered immediately preceding the answer. Sworn answers to interrogatories directed to a public or private corporation, or a partnership or association, shall be made by an officer, partner, or agent, who shall furnish such information as is available to the party.

(d) Option to produce documents. When the answer to an interrogatory may be obtained from documents in the possession or control of the party on whom the interrogatory was served, it shall be a sufficient answer to the interrogatory to specify those documents and to afford the party serving the interrogatory a reasonable opportunity to inspect the documents and to make copies thereof or compilations, abstracts, or summaries therefrom.

(e) Supplemental interrogatories. If a party makes an answer that is complete when made, he has no duty to supplement the answer to include information thereafter received, unless requested to do so by a timely supplemental interrogatory. However, upon request made at any time before the trial, a party must furnish the identity and location of persons, in addition to those previously disclosed, having knowledge of relevant facts.

(f) Use of answers to interrogatories. Answers to interrogatories may be used in evidence to the same extent as a discovery deposition.

Author's Notes

Analysis

1. Value of general interrogatories.
2. Best use of interrogatories.
3. Avoiding work product objection.
4. Interrogatories seeking identity of persons having knowledge of relevant facts—Form.
5. Interrogatories regarding non-marital property—Form.
6. Supplemental answers to interrogatories.
7. Expert witnesses.
8. Interrogatories to non-parties.

(1) **Value of general interrogatories.** General interrogatories that are sometimes served at the beginning of litigation are often of little use because of the frequency of incomplete or evasive answers, and the inability of the questioner to ask his follow-up questions. Oral depositions are therefore a better tool for broad based discovery.

(2) **Best use of interrogatories.** Interrogatories are of greatest use in narrow areas to obtain specific information that is not subject to evasive or incomplete answers. For example, interrogatories may be highly effective in seeking the identity and location of persons having knowledge of relevant facts, pursuant to Supreme Court Rules 201(b)(1) and 213(e). Names and addresses of such persons are not subject to

S. Ct. Rule 213   PROCEDURE

evasion, and, if a name is omitted, and that person is subsequently called as a witness, a sustainable objection can be made to his appearance. Among the factors the court should consider in determining whether to exclude a witness not listed in the interrogatories from testifying at trial are the surprise to the adverse party, the prejudicial effect of the testimony, the nature of the testimony, the diligence of the adverse party, the timely objection to the testimony and the good faith of the party calling the witness. Kirkwood v. Checker Taxi Co., 12 Ill.App.3d 129, 298 N.E.2d 233 (1st Dist.1973) (five minute interview prior to examination was inadequate remedy when opposing party called undisclosed witness at trial). Also, at any time prior to the trial (even after discovery is otherwise closed) a party can demand that the opposite party furnish the identity and location of persons, having knowledge of relevant facts, in addition to those previously disclosed, pursuant to Supreme Court Rule 213(e).

(3) **Avoiding work product objection.** An interrogatory seeking the identity and location of the persons an attorney plans to call as witnesses at the trial would be improper, since it would constitute an invasion of his work product. Requesting the names and locations of persons having knowledge of the relevant facts is a legitimate question since it avoids the thinking of the attorney.

(4) **Interrogatories seeking identity of persons having knowledge of relevant facts—Form.** There follows a sample interrogatory seeking the identity of persons having knowledge of the relevant facts.

IN THE CIRCUIT COURT OF COOK COUNTY, ILLINOIS

COUNTY DEPARTMENT—DOMESTIC RELATIONS DIVISION

IN RE THE MARRIAGE OF   )
)
LEICESTER DEDLOCK,   )
)
               Petitioner,   )
)
and   ) No. ____ D _____
)
LUCY DEDLOCK,   )
)
               Respondent.)

INTERROGATORIES

TO: Frederick Tulkinghorn

    Address

Respondent, LUCY DEDLOCK, by Joseph Blowers, her attorney, requests that the Petitioner, LEICESTER DEDLOCK, answer under oath, in accordance with Supreme Court Rules 201(b)(1) and 213(e) the following Interrogatories:

> State the names and addresses of all persons who have knowledge of the relevant facts involving the allegations contained in Petitioner's Petition for Dissolution of Marriage.

ILLINOIS S. CT. RULES **S. Ct. Rule 213**

Please take notice that a copy of the answers to these Interrogatories should be served upon the undersigned within 28 days after the service of these Interrogatories.

Joseph Blowers
Attorney for LUCY DEDLOCK

CERTIFICATE OF DELIVERY

The undersigned hereby certifies under penalties of perjury as provided by law pursuant to Section 1–109 of the Code of Civil Procedure, that the above Interrogatories were [ ]placed in the U.S. Mail properly addressed and mailed with first class postage prepaid, [ ]sent via messenger, [ ]sent via facsimile (__ pages, from the office of _____, sender's facsimile number _____, to recipient's facsimile number _____), to the party at the address set forth above on the __ day of _____, 199_, before the hour of 5:00 p.m.

(Signature)   (Print Name)

Joseph Blowers
Blowers & Associates, Ltd.
Address
Telephone Number

(5) **Interrogatories regarding non-marital property—Form.** As noted in Author's Note (2) above, interrogatories are best used to obtain specific information on a narrow subject. One such use is when a party claims property to be non-marital. There follows a sample set of interrogatories directed at a claim of non-marital property.

IN THE CIRCUIT COURT OF COOK COUNTY, ILLINOIS
COUNTY DEPARTMENT—DOMESTIC RELATIONS DIVISION

IN RE THE MARRIAGE OF	)
	)
DOROTHY SKIMPOLE,	)
	)
Petitioner,	)
	)
and	) No. __ D _____
	)
HAROLD SKIMPOLE,	)
	)
Respondent.	)

S. Ct. Rule 213   PROCEDURE

INTERROGATORIES

TO: Richard Vholes
    Address

The Petitioner requests that the Respondent answer under oath in accordance with Supreme Court Rule 213 the following Interrogatories:

1. List and describe all assets presently owned by you that you claim: were acquired by gift, inheritance, owned by you prior to the marriage, or otherwise are your non-marital property.

ANSWER NO. 1:

2. For each asset identified in paragraph 1:
   (a) Give the date of its acquisition.
   (b) Give the manner of its acquisition, whether by gift, bequest, devise, descent, purchase, or otherwise.
   (c) Identify the name and address of the donor, testator, seller, or other source for each asset.
   (d)(i) Describe how title to each asset is presently held.
   (d)(ii) Has title to the asset ever been changed during your ownership? If so, describe and explain reasons for change.
   (e) Give the market value or other tax basis at the time of acquisition of each asset.
   (f) Explain how the tax basis is calculated.
   (g) Identify by description and location documents supporting the tax basis.
   (h) Give the present market value of each asset.
   (i) Identify the authority for the present market value for each asset, and whether or not the authority is in writing. If in writing, produce, or describe and give the location of the documents.

ANSWER NO. 2:

3. If any of the property identified in paragraph 1 is claimed to constitute non-marital property because it is traceable to a non-marital source, for each such asset:

(a) Identify the non-marital source.

(b) Identify and describe the nature of all intervening transactions from the current asset to the claimed non-marital source, with dates of each transaction.

(c)(i) Describe how title was held in the non-marital source and in each intervening transaction.

(c)(ii) Was title to any of the traced assets ever in co-ownership with Petitioner? If so, describe ownership, with dates, and reason for co-ownership.

(d) Where the mesne transactions constituted purchases or sales or both:

    (i) Give the institution, account number, account title, and persons authorized on the account, for each deposit and withdrawal of funds for each transaction.

    (ii) Give the amount of the sale proceeds and the purchase price for each transaction.

ANSWER NO. 3:

4. For each asset claimed to be non-marital, and for each asset in a claim of tracing to a non-marital source, after the date of the marriage:

(a) State any increase in value.

(b) Describe the cause of the increase.

(c) Identify all monetary contributions, dates of contributions, and source of monetary contributions to the asset. For the source, identify the institution, account number, account title, and persons authorized on the account.

(d) Identify all personal contributions of effort by Petitioner or Respondent to each asset. Describe the personal effort, with dates. State the amount of compensation received, if any, for the personal effort.

(e) Identify and describe with dates any other type of contributions by Petitioner or Respondent to each asset.

(f) If the contribution described in paragraphs 4(c) through 4(e) is claimed to be non-marital, explain the basis of the claim.

(g) Identify the amount and use of all income produced by each asset. If held in an account or reinvested, describe and identify how title is held.

S. Ct. Rule 213　　　　　　　PROCEDURE

ANSWER NO. 4:

5(i). Has claimed non-marital property ever been contributed to marital property?

5(ii). Has marital property ever been contributed to claimed non-marital property?

5(iii). Has claimed non-marital property ever been used with marital property to purchase or otherwise obtain a new asset?

5(iv). If the answer to any of the aforesaid questions in this paragraph 5 is yes, describe the transaction in detail, identify the assets and accounts, and give dates. For accounts, give the institution, account number, account title, and persons authorized on the account.

5(v). Is reimbursement claimed? If the answer is yes, give reasons and amount.

ANSWER NO. 5:

6. Identify by description and location all writings reflecting the source of any assets owned by you to have been premarital, or to have been the result of gifts or inheritance, or reflecting the non-marital nature of any property. This request includes, but is not limited to, all writings used in the tracing of a current asset to a non-marital source.

ANSWER NO. 6:

7. When the answer to one of these Interrogatories may be obtained from documents, it shall be a sufficient answer to the Interrogatories to specify the documents and to produce the documents for inspection and copying.

8. As used herein, the term "document" or "writing" means any written, printed, typed or graphic matter of every kind, nature or description, including also computer disks, computer printouts, "E" mail, computer stor-

age, and microfilms in the possession or control of the party, as well as all notes, previous drafts and copies of documents made by whatever means if the copy bears any additional marking, notation, interlineation, amendment or deletion.

PLEASE TAKE NOTICE that a copy of the answers to these Interrogatories should be served upon the undersigned within 28 days after the service of these Interrogatories.

Samuel Kenge
Attorney for DOROTHY SKIMPOLE

Samuel Kenge
Kenge and Carboy
Address
Telephone number

CERTIFICATE OF DELIVERY

The undersigned hereby certifies under penalties of perjury as provided by law pursuant to Section 1-109 of the Code of Civil Procedure, that the above Interrogatories were [ ]placed in the U.S. Mail properly addressed and mailed with first class postage prepaid, [ ]sent via messenger, [ ]sent via facsimile (___ pages, from the office of _____, sender's facsimile number _____, to recipient's facsimile number _____), to the party at the address set forth above on the ___ day of _____, 199__, before the hour of 5:00 p.m.

(Signature)   (Print Name)

(6) **Supplemental answers to interrogatories.** Pursuant to Supreme Court Rule 213(e), the initiative in supplementing complete answers to interrogatories that have been previously given with information received thereafter lies with the party asking the questions.

(7) **Expert witnesses.** Interrogatories are also useful in discovery concerning expert witnesses. Unlike interrogatories pursuant to Supreme Court Rule 213, Supreme Court Rule 220 interrogatories are required to be supplemented by the party to whom they are directed as additional information becomes known to the party or his counsel. See Supreme Court Rule 220(c)(3) Author's Note (7).

(8) **Interrogatories to non-parties.** Written interrogatories pursuant to Supreme Court Rule 213 can be directed only to a party. If a questioner desires to submit written questions to a non-party witness, he must do so following the procedure of Supreme Court Rule 210.

Rule 214. Discovery of documents, objects, and tangible things—Inspection of real estate

Any party may by written request direct any other party to produce for inspection, copying, reproduction, photographing, testing or sampling specified documents, objects or tangible things, or to permit access to real estate for the purpose of making surface or sub-surface inspections or surveys or photographs, or tests or taking samples, or to disclose information calculated to lead to the discovery of the whereabouts of any of these items, whenever the nature, contents, or condition of such documents, objects, tangible things, or real estate is relevant to the subject matter of the action. The request shall specify a reasonable time, which shall not be less than 28 days except by agreement or by order of court, and the place and manner of making the inspection and performing the related acts. One copy of the request shall be filed with the proof of service on all other parties entitled to notice. A party served with the written request shall (1) comply with the request within the time specified, or (2) serve upon the party so requesting written objections on the ground that the request is improper in whole or in part. If written objections to a part of the request are made, the remainder of the request shall be complied with. Any objection to the request or the refusal to respond shall be heard by the court upon prompt notice and motion of the party submitting the request. If the party claims that the item is not in his possession or control or that he does not have information calculated to lead to the discovery of its whereabouts, he may be ordered to submit to examination in open court or by deposition regarding such claim. If requested, the party producing documents shall furnish an affidavit stating whether the production is complete in accordance with the request.

This rule does not preclude an independent action against a person not a party for production of documents and things and permission to enter upon real estate.

Author's Notes

Analysis

1. Applicable only to parties.
2. Notice to Produce—Form.

(1) **Applicable only to parties.** Supreme Court Rule 214 is available only when the request is directed to a party. Discovery of documents and other tangible objects in the possession of a person who is not a party to the litigation may be obtained by serving the non-party witness with a subpoena duces tecum for the taking of his deposition. This subpoena may be limited to the production of documents only when oral testimony is not sought. See Supreme Court Rule 204 Author's Notes (2) through (4) for model subpoenas and notice. The last paragraph of Supreme Court Rule 214 was inserted in order not to preclude an independent discovery action in the occasional case in which a party seeks to inspect real estate that is in the control of a person not a party to the litigation. Supreme Court Rule 214 committee cmt.

(2) **Notice to Produce—Form.** There follows a sample request for the discovery of documents pursuant to Supreme Court Rule 214. Documents are usually requested from a party by a rider to a notice of deposition. See sample in Supreme Court Rule 204 Author's Note (5). Requests pursuant to Supreme Court Rule 214 are usually used to supplement the documents requested in the notice of deposition. For example, when documents not produced pursuant to the notice of deposition are discovered during the oral deposition, if the documents are not voluntarily produced by

ILLINOIS S. CT. RULES   **S. Ct. Rule 214**

the party deponent, the deponent should be served with a notice pursuant to Supreme Court Rule 214.

IN THE CIRCUIT COURT OF COOK COUNTY, ILLINOIS
COUNTY DEPARTMENT—DOMESTIC RELATIONS DIVISION

IN RE THE MARRIAGE OF   )
)
LEICESTER DEDLOCK,   )
)
        Petitioner,)
)
and   ) No. ___ D _____
)
LUCY DEDLOCK,   )
)
        Respondent.)

NOTICE TO PRODUCE

TO: Frederick Tulkinghorn
    Address

YOU ARE HEREBY NOTIFIED pursuant to Supreme Court Rule 214 that within 28 days, in the offices of LUCY DEDLOCK's attorneys, _____, _____, Illinois, you are to produce the documents of Leicester Dedlock on the attached Rider for inspection and copying.

                                                          Joseph Blowers
                                                          Attorney for LUCY DEDLOCK

Joseph Blowers
Blowers & Associates, Ltd.
Address
Telephone number

In re the Marriage of Dedlock

RIDER TO NOTICE TO PRODUCE

1. Deed to Bleak House.
2.
3.
4.
5.
6.
7.

745

S. Ct. Rule 214   PROCEDURE

8.
9.
10.
11. An affidavit pursuant to Supreme Court Rule 214 signed under oath by Petitioner stating that his production of documents is complete in accordance with this Request for Production of Documents.

Joseph Blowers
Blowers & Associates, Ltd.
Address
Telephone number

CERTIFICATE OF DELIVERY

The undersigned hereby certifies under penalties of perjury as provided by law pursuant to Section 1–109 of the Code of Civil Procedure, that the above Notice to Produce was [ ]placed in the U.S. Mail properly addressed and mailed with first class postage prepaid, [ ]sent via messenger, [ ]sent via facsimile (___ pages, from the office of _____, sender's facsimile number _____, to recipient's facsimile number _____), to the party at the address set forth above on the ___ day of _____, 199__, before the hour of 5:00 p.m.

_____   _____
(Signature)   (Print Name)

Rule 215. Physical and mental examination of parties and other persons

(a) *Notice; Motion; Order.* In any action in which the physical or mental condition of a party or of a person in his custody or legal control in controversy, the court upon notice and for good cause shown on motion made within a reasonable time before the trial, may order the party to submit to a physical or mental examination by a physician suggested by the party requesting the examination, or to produce for such examination the person in custody or under legal control who is to be examined. The court may refuse to order examination by the physician suggested but in that event shall permit the party seeking the examination to suggest others. A party or person shall not be required to travel an unreasonable distance for the examination. The order shall fix the time, place, conditions, and scope of the examination and designate the examining physician.

(b) *Physician's fee and compensation for loss of earnings.* The party requesting the examination shall pay the fee of the examining physician and compensation for any loss of earnings incurred or to be incurred by the party or person to be examined in complying with the order for examination, and shall advance all reasonable expenses incurred or to be incurred by the party or person in complying with the order.

(c) *Physician's report.* Within 21 days after the completion of the examination, and in no event later than 14 days before trial, the examining physician shall prepare duplicate originals of a written report of the examination, setting out his findings, results of all tests made, his diagnosis and conclusions, and deliver or mail an original of his report and of all corrections, supplements, or additions thereto, to the attorney for the party requesting the examination and a duplicate original thereof to the attorney for the party examined or for the party who produced the person who was examined. The court may enforce compliance with this requirement. If the report is not delivered or mailed to the attorney for the party examined, or for the party who produced the person who was examined, within the time herein specified or within any extensions or modifications thereof granted by the court, neither the physician's report nor his testimony or his findings or X-ray films or the results of any tests he has made may be received in evidence except at the instance of the party examined or who produced the person examined.

(d) Impartial medical experts.

(1) Examination before trial. A reasonable time in advance of the trial, the court may on its own motion or that of any party, order an impartial physical or mental examination of a party whose mental or physical condition is in issue, when in the court's discretion it appears that such an examination will materially aid in the just determination of the case. The examination shall be made by a member or members of a panel of physicians chosen for their special qualifications by the Illinois State Medical Society.

(2) Examination during trial. Should the court at any time during the trial find that compelling considerations make it advisable to have an examination and report at that time, the court may in its discretion so order.

(3) Copies of report. A copy of the report of examination shall be given to the court and to the attorneys for the parties.

(4) Testimony of examining physician. Either party or the court may call the examining physician or physicians to testify. Any physician so called shall be subject to cross-examination.

(5) Costs and compensation of physician. The examination shall be made, and the physician or physicians, if called, shall testify without cost to the parties. The court shall determine the compensation of the physician or physicians.

(6) Administration of rule. The Administrative Director and the Deputy Administrative Director are charged with the administration of the rule.

Author's Notes

Analysis

1. Appointment of physicians.
2. Good cause required.

3. Reports.
4. Impartial examination.
5. Cross reference.
6. 215 Motion—Form.

(1) **Appointment of physicians.** Rule 215 provides for the appointment of a physician to conduct a physical or mental examination. The physician may either be suggested by the party requesting the examination, Rule 215(a); or may be independent, appointed by the court on its own motion or that of any party pursuant to Rule 215(d)(1). Supreme Court Rule 215 may be of great utility in dissolution cases, for example, when a party's capacity to work is in question because of alleged illness or mental disability, or in evaluating parents and children in custody cases.

(2) **Good cause required.** Where a party seeks to have the opposite party or the children examined by a physician of his own choice pursuant to Supreme Court Rule 215(a), the examination can only be "for good cause shown." Courts have discretion in determining good cause, but the burden is on the moving party to show that the examination is necessary to present evidence concerning a bona fide issue. See, e.g, In re Stevenson's Estate, 44 Ill.2d 525, 256 N.E.2d 766, *cert. denied*, 400 U.S. 850, 91 S.Ct. 50, 27 L.Ed.2d 87 (1970).

(3) **Reports.** Supreme Court Rule 215(c) precludes the results of the examination from being put into evidence if written reports of the examination are not served on the attorneys within 21 days of completion of the examination, and in no event later than 14 days before trial. See, e.g., Wehmeier v. UNR Indus., Inc., 213 Ill.App.3d 6, 157 Ill.Dec. 251, 572 N.E.2d 320 (4th Dist.1991) (trial court erred in allowing examining physician to testify when report was furnished less than 14 days before trial); Harris v. Minardi, 74 Ill.App.2d 262, 220 N.E.2d 39 (2d Dist.1966) (permitting doctor's testimony when report was submitted to opposing counsel five days before trial was reversible error; Rule prohibiting use of untimely medical report is mandatory, except at the instance of the party examined or at the instance of the party who produced the person examined).

(4) **Impartial examination.** Pursuant to Supreme Court Rule 215(d)(1), the court on its own motion can order an impartial physical or mental examination, and can also do so on the motion of any party. The burden of proof necessary to obtain the impartial physical or mental examination on the motion of a party appears to be less than that for the physician suggested by a party pursuant to Supreme Court Rule 215(a), which requires that the mental or physical condition be at issue, and good cause is shown. Subparagraph (d)(1) requires only that the "mental or physical condition is in issue, when in the court's discretion it appears that such an examination will materially aid in the just determination of the case." Also, there are no time periods specified in Supreme Court Rule 215(d)(3) for the service of the medical reports of an impartial examination. The less stringent standards of an impartial examination presumably exist because the Supreme Court Rule 215(d)(1) examination is conducted by an impartial physician, as opposed to an expert expected to advocate a position. The Rule 215(d)(1) physician is to be selected from a list prepared by the Illinois State Medical Society.

(5) **Cross reference.** See also 750 ILCS 5/604(b) and accompanying Author's Notes for appointment by the court of professional personnel in cases involving children.

(6) **215 Motion—Form.** There follows a sample motion for a physical and mental examination of a party pursuant to Supreme Court Rule 215(a).

IN THE CIRCUIT COURT OF COOK COUNTY, ILLINOIS
COUNTY DEPARTMENT—DOMESTIC RELATIONS DIVISION

IN RE THE MARRIAGE OF)
)
ROSA ROUNCEWELL,)
       Petitioner and)
       Counter-Respondent,)
)
and) No. ____ D _____
)
WATT ROUNCEWELL,)
       Respondent and)
       Counter-Petitioner.)

215(a) MOTION

Counter-Petitioner, WATT ROUNCEWELL ("WATT"), moves pursuant to Supreme Court Rule 215(a) as follows:

1. The Court order Counter-Respondent, ROSA ROUNCEWELL ("ROSA"), to undergo a psychological examination by Dr. Prince Turveydrop, a psychiatrist at _____ Hospital, Chicago, Illinois.

2. The Court order ROSA to undergo a physical examination by Dr. Lawrence Boythorn, a medical doctor at _____ Hospital, Chicago, Illinois.

3. WATT have such other and further relief as may be appropriate under the evidence and circumstances.

In support of his 215(a) Motion for a psychological and medical examination of ROSA, WATT alleges as follows:

1. Each party has prayed for the temporary and permanent sole care, custody, and control of the minor children of the parties, Clarissa and Conrad. Custody is therefore at issue. On information and belief, WATT alleges that because of ROSA's psychological instability it would not be in the best interests of the children for ROSA to be the sole custodian of the children. In order to assist the Court in making a proper determination of custody, there should be a psychological evaluation of ROSA.

2. ROSA has called upon WATT to pay an extraordinary number of medical bills and medication bills. ROSA has also taken the position that she requires household help because of her medical condition in order to take care of the house and in order to take care of the minor children of the parties, Clarissa, who is 10 years of age, and Conrad, who is 7 years of age. The necessity of the medical, medication, and household help expenses is therefore at issue.

3. ROSA is presently not employed. ROSA has told WATT that she is not capable of employment because of her medical condition. ROSA's capacity for employment is therefore at issue.

S. Ct. Rule 215   PROCEDURE

4. ROSA complains of depression, stomach disorders, back disorders, and headaches.

5. Because of ROSA's alleged medical and psychological problems, ROSA has frequently been too sick to take care of the children.

6. ROSA has frequently complained how hard it is to take care of two children. She has said that she cannot lift the children and other objects because of her back pain.

7. ROSA has insisted upon bringing nurses, household help, and relatives into the home in order to assist her in taking care of the children.

8. Because of her alleged depression, ROSA isolates herself, refuses to engage in normal human interaction, and does not go out of the house for unusual lengths of time.

9. ROSA has seen the following doctors in regard to her alleged medical problems: *(list doctors and approximate dates).*

10. This Motion is brought under the authority of Supreme Court Rule 215(a), which is as follows:

(a) Notice; Motion; Order. In any action in which the physical or mental condition of a party or of a person in his custody or legal control is in controversy, the court upon notice and for good cause shown on motion made within a reasonable time before the trial, may order the party to submit to a physical or mental examination by a physician suggested by the party requesting the examination, or to produce for such examination the person in custody or under legal control who is to be examined. The court may refuse to order examination by the physician suggested but in that event shall permit the party seeking the examination to suggest others. A party or person shall not be required to travel an unreasonable distance for the examination. The order shall fix the time, place, conditions, and scope of the examination and designate the examining physician.

11. It will aid the Court to have available expert testimony from the medical and psychological evaluation of ROSA in determining the issues of custody, the possibility of joint custody, visitation, the necessity of the medical and psychological and household help expenses that ROSA is seeking to have WATT pay, and the capacity of ROSA for employment.

_____
WATT ROUNCEWELL

_____
Samuel Kenge
Attorney for WATT ROUNCEWELL

ILLINOIS S. CT. RULES   S. Ct. Rule 216

VERIFICATION BY CERTIFICATION

Under penalties as provided by law pursuant to 735 ILCS 5/1–109 of the Illinois Code of Civil Procedure, the undersigned certifies that the statements set forth in the foregoing instrument are true and correct, except as to matters therein stated to be on information and belief and as to such matters the undersigned certifies as aforesaid that he verily believes the same to be true.

DATED: _____   _____
                                     WATT ROUNCEWELL

Samuel Kenge
Kenge and Carboy
Address
Telephone number

Rule 216. Admission of fact or of genuineness of documents

(a) Request for admission of fact. A party may serve on any other party a written request for the admission by the latter of the truth of any specified relevant fact set forth in the request.

(b) Request for admission of genuineness of document. A party may serve on any other party a written request for admission of the genuineness of any relevant documents described in the request. Copies of the documents shall be served with the request unless copies have already been furnished.

(c) Admission in the absence of denial. Each of the matters of fact and the genuineness of each document of which admission is requested is admitted unless, within 28 days after service thereof, the party to whom the request is directed serves upon the party requesting the admission either (1) a sworn statement denying specifically the matters of which admission is requested or setting forth in detail the reasons why he cannot truthfully admit or deny those matters or (2) written objections on the ground that some or all of the requested admissions are privileged or irrelevant or that the request is otherwise improper in whole or in part. If written objections to a part of the request are made, the remainder of the request shall be answered within the period designated in the request. A denial shall fairly meet the substance of the requested admission. If good faith requires that a party deny only a part, or requires qualification, of a matter of which an admission is requested, he shall specify so much of it as is true and deny only the remainder. Any objection to a request or to an answer shall be heard by the court upon prompt notice and motion of the party making the request.

(d) Public records. If any public records are to be used as evidence, the party intending to use them may prepare a copy of them insofar as they are to be used, and may seasonably present the copy to the adverse party by notice in writing, and the copy shall thereupon be admissible in evidence as admitted facts in the case if otherwise admissible, except insofar as its inaccuracy is pointed out under oath by the adverse party in an affidavit filed and served within 14 days after service of the notice.

S. Ct. Rule 216　　　　　　PROCEDURE

(e) **Effect of admission.** Any admission made by a party pursuant to request under this rule is for the purpose of the pending action and any action commenced pursuant to the authority of section 13–217 of the Code of Civil Procedure (Ill.Rev.Stat. 1983, ch. 110, par. 13–217) only. It does not constitute an admission by him for any other purpose and may not be used against him in any other proceeding.

Author's Notes

Analysis

1. Most useful concerning narrowly defined subject matter.
2. Requests for the Admission of Facts and the Genuineness of Documents—Form.

(1) **Most useful concerning narrowly defined subject matter.** As noted in the Committee Comments, requests for admissions of fact or of the genuineness of documents are seldom used in actual Illinois practice. Supreme Court Rule 216 committee cmt. More frequently, admissions are obtained through depositions. For narrowly defined subject matter, however, requests for admissions can be useful. Admissions can save trial time, for example, by eliminating the necessity to call some witnesses if admissions are obtained in advance of trial as to the authenticity of documents.

A procedure is also established by Supreme Court Rule 216(d) for admitting public records into evidence, which, in any event, are an exception to the hearsay rule. See Michael H. Graham, *Cleary and Graham's Illinois Handbook of Evidence* § 803.12 (6th ed. 1994).

(2) **Requests for the Admission of Facts and the Genuineness of Documents—Form.** There follows a sample request for admissions.

IN THE CIRCUIT COURT OF COOK COUNTY, ILLINOIS
COUNTY DEPARTMENT—DOMESTIC RELATIONS DIVISION

IN RE THE MARRIAGE OF　　　)
　　　　　　　　　　　　　　)
LUCY DEDLOCK,　　　　　　　)
　　　　　　　　　　　　　　)
　　　　　　Petitioner,　　　)
　　　　　　　　　　　　　　)
and　　　　　　　　　　　　) No. ____ D _____
　　　　　　　　　　　　　　)
LEICESTER DEDLOCK,　　　　)
　　　　　　　　　　　　　　)
　　　　　　Respondent. 　　)

REQUESTS FOR THE ADMISSION OF
FACTS AND THE GENUINENESS OF DOCUMENTS

To: Frederick Tulkinghorn
　　Address

Petitioner, LUCY DEDLOCK, presents the following Requests for the Admission of Facts and the Genuineness of Documents pursuant to Supreme Court Rule 216. Within 28 days after service of this Request for Admissions, Respondent, LEICESTER DEDLOCK, is requested to admit in writing the truth of the following specified facts and the genuineness of the following specified documents, copies of which are attached to this Request to Admit.

1. The attached financial statements are true and correct copies of financial statements dated April 23, 1992 and April 23, 1993 that were prepared by LEICESTER DEDLOCK or prepared on his behalf and submitted to the Chancery Lane Bank in connection with LEICESTER DEDLOCK's line of credit at that bank.

2. The current outstanding unpaid balance on LEICESTER DEDLOCK's line of credit at the Chancery Lane Bank is $943,000.

3. The attached bank statements for LEICESTER DEDLOCK's checking account and savings account at the Chancery Lane Bank for the years 1991, 1992, and 1993 are true and correct copies of statements kept in the ordinary course of business by the Chancery Lane Bank and issued to LEICESTER DEDLOCK, and the attached checking and savings account statements require no further authentication to be admissible as business records under Supreme Court Rule 236.

PLEASE TAKE NOTICE that a copy of the admissions, denials, or objections to the foregoing Requests for Admissions should be served upon the undersigned within 28 days after the service of these Requests for Admissions.

Richard Vholes
Attorney for LUCY DEDLOCK

CERTIFICATE OF DELIVERY

The undersigned hereby certifies under penalties of perjury as provided by law pursuant to Section 1-109 of the Code of Civil Procedure, that the above Requests for the Admission of Facts and the Genuineness of Documents was [ ]placed in the U.S. Mail properly addressed and mailed with first class postage prepaid, [ ]sent via messenger, [ ]sent via facsimile (___ pages, from the office of _____, sender's facsimile number _____, to recipient's facsimile number _____), to the party at the address set forth above on the ___ day of _____, 199__, before the hour of 5:00 p.m.

(Signature)   (Print Name)

Richard Vholes
Address
Telephone Number

S. Ct. Rule 218 — PROCEDURE

Rule 218. Pretrial procedure

(a) Conference. In any civil case, the court may hold a pretrial conference. At the conference counsel familiar with the case and authorized to act shall appear, with or without the parties as the court directs, to consider:

(1) the simplification of the issues;

(2) amendments to the pleadings;

(3) the possibility of obtaining admissions of fact and of documents which will avoid unnecessary proof;

(4) the limitation of the number of expert witnesses; and

(5) any other matters which may aid in the disposition of the action.

(b) Order. The court shall make an order which recites any action taken by the court and the agreements made by the parties as to any of the matters considered, and which specifies as the issues for trial those not disposed of at the conference. The order controls the subsequent course of the action unless modified.

(c) Calendar. The court shall establish a pretrial calendar on which actions shall be placed for consideration, as above provided, either by the court on its own motion or on motion of any party.

(d) Enforcement. The court shall make and enforce all rules and orders necessary to compel compliance with this rule, and may apply the remedies provided in paragraph (c) of Rule 219.

Author's Notes

Analysis

1. Pre-trial Memorandum—Form.
2. Motions in limine.
3. Pre-marked exhibits.

(1) **Pre-trial Memorandum—Form.** The pre-trial memorandum form used by the Domestic Relations Courts in Cook County at pre-trial conferences follows. The form is cumbersome and often not well adapted to tell your client's story. It is therefore good practice to attach your own memorandum as an exhibit.

ILLINOIS S. CT. RULES   S. Ct. Rule 218

3400 Pre-Trial Memorandum, Revised 1991   (10-90) CCDR - 10

IN THE CIRCUIT COURT OF COOK COUNTY, ILLINOIS
COUNTY DEPARTMENT, DOMESTIC RELATIONS DIVISION

IN RE THE ☐ MARRIAGE ☐ CUSTODY
☐ SUPPORT OF:

NO:

CALENDAR:

_____
PETITIONER

AND

_____
RESPONDENT

PRE-TRIAL MEMORANDUM

A pre-trial memorandum is to be prepared by each attorney of record. Failure to prepare a pre-trial memorandum shall be considered a violation of rules and result in appropriate sanctions.

Schedules A and C shall be filed with the pre-trial judge seven (7) days prior to the initial pre-trial conference.

Schedule B shall be filed with the judge to whom the case is assigned before the date set for the mediation intake session.

The ☐ Petitioner ☐ Respondent ☐ Attorney for Child ☐ Other   presents the following information:

All items are to be filled in.

NAME: _____
ADDRESS: _____
DATE OF BIRTH: _____
SS#: _____

CONDITION OF HEALTH (SPECIFY CONDITION):
_____
_____

EDUCATIONAL BACKGROUND:
_____
_____

DATE OF MARRIAGE: _____

DATE OF SEPARATION: _____

[G19004]

S. Ct. Rule 218 PROCEDURE

(10-90) CCDR - 10.1

CHILDREN:

      NAME   AGE   DATE OF BIRTH

_____

_____

_____

_____

GROUNDS: (Specify party alleging grounds:)

_____

SUMMARY OF DISPUTED ISSUES: (CHECK DISPUTED ISSUES. ISSUES NOT CHECKED WILL BE DEEMED UNDISPUTED.)

☐ Dissolution	☐ Dissipation
☐ Legal Separation	☐ Value of property
☐ Declaration of Invalidity	☐ Amount of Income H ☐ W ☐
☐ Custody/Custody Modification	☐ Whether property is marital or non-marital
☐ Visitation	☐ Division of marital property
☐ Removal	☐ Reimbursement
☐ Child Support/Support Modification	☐ Disposition of debts
☐ Maintenance	☐ Attorney's Fees
☐ Educational Expenses	☐ Division of personal property

Briefly describe other issues to be resolved:

_____

_____

_____

Prepared By:
NAME:

_____

Attorney for:

Address:

City:

Telephone:

Attorney Code No:

[G19005]

ILLINOIS S. CT. RULES   S. Ct. Rule 218

SCHEDULE A - ASSETS

The date of valuation(s) is _____ unless otherwise specified. Please designate value and whether the property is marital (M) non-marital husband (NMH) or non-marital wife (NMW).

Titled In Name Of		Value	
		H	W
	1. Cash, Bank Accounts and Equivalents, i.e., checking, savings, IRA, CD, etc; Location; Account Number.		
	2. Stock, Bonds and other Securities:		
	3. Real Property: Address; Physical Description; How title is held; Amounts of any Mortgages or Liens.		
	4. Motor Vehicle (s): Model/Year; Lien; Debtor; Amount; How Title is held.		

S. Ct. Rule 218   PROCEDURE

Present Value & Whether the Property is Marital (M) Non-Marital Husband (NMH) or Non-Marital Wife (NMW)

Titled In Name Of		Value	
	5. Business Interests; Name of Business, Type of Business (e.g., corporation, partnership, sole proprietorship); Percentage Interest.	H	W
	6. Insurance Policies: Type of Insurance (life, medical, etc.); Policy Number; Face Amount; Beneficiary. Show surrender value and loans on policies.		
	7. Retirement Plans: Name and Type of Plan; Trustee of Plan; Nature of Interest; Beneficiary; Vested or non-vested.		
	8. Income Tax Refunds: Amount Federal; Amount State.		
	9. Choses in Action: Date of Occurrence; Nature and Amount of Claim; Date Lawsuit Filed; Case Number.		
	10. All other property not previously listed (except for tangible personal property):		

ILLINOIS S. CT. RULES   S. Ct. Rule 218

A-3   (10-90) CCDR - A-3

TANGIBLE PERSONAL PROPERTY

Set forth any disputed items of tangible personal property (including household goods and personal effects) on a separate inventory attached to Schedule A. Provide the following information: description and location of the goods; category claimed (M, NMW, or NMH); value; and recommendation as to award.

DEBTS

Debtor (H,W,JT)	Nature/ Purpose	Date Incurred	Original Amount	Current Balance	Who Incurred (H, W, JT)

CONTINGENT LIABILITIES

Potential Obligor(s) (H, W, JT)	Claimant	Basis of Claim	Date Incurred	Amount Claimed	Who Incurred (H, W, JT)

[G19008]

S. Ct. Rule 218 PROCEDURE

A-4 (10-90) CCDR-10 A.4

SETTLEMENT POSITION WITH REFERENCE TO SPECIFIC ASSETS

IN THE EVENT SETTLEMENT DOES NOT OCCUR, THIS PAGE SHALL BE DELETED FROM THE PRE-TRIAL MEMORANDUM AND RETURNED TO THE RESPECTIVE PARTIES' ATTORNEYS.

(State items to be received by each party; whether any items are to be liquidated and if so, the division of proceeds from said liquidation; the tax consequences of said division; and the percentage of the estate each receives, together with the reasons for said division.)

[G19009]

ILLINOIS S. CT. RULES   S. Ct. Rule 218

A-5   (Rev. 7/21/93) CCDR 10 A5 J

IN THE CIRCUIT COURT OF COOK COUNTY, ILLINOIS
COUNTY DEPARTMENT, DOMESTIC RELATIONS DIVISION

IN RE THE MARRIAGE OF:

_____   NO:
PETITIONER
                    AND   CALENDAR:

_____
RESPONDENT

INCOME AND EXPENSE
AFFIDAVIT: OF:_____
                        (NAME)

Actual Monthly as of
_____

A. STATEMENT OF INCOME AND DEDUCTIONS
   1. Gross Income Per Month $ _____
      a. Salary/wages   _____
      b. Draw   _____
      c. Bonus   _____
      d. Pension   _____
      e. Annuity   _____
      f. Social Security   _____
      g. Dividends   _____
      h. Interest   _____
      i. Trusts   _____
      j. Public Aid   _____
      k. Workmen's Compensation   _____
      l. Unemployment Compensation   _____
      m. Rents   _____
      n. Disability Payments   _____
      o. Stocks   _____
      p. Bonds   _____
      q. Other (specify) _____   _____

      TOTAL GROSS MONTHLY INCOME $ _____

   2. Required Deductions
      a. Taxes: Federal (based on_____exemptions) $ _____
      b. Taxes: State (based on_____exemptions)   _____
      c. Social Security (or pension equivalent)   _____
      d. Mandatory retirement contributions required
         by law or as a condition of employment   _____
      e. Union Dues   _____
      f. Health/Hospitalization Insurance   _____
      g. Prior obligation of support actually paid
         pursuant to Court order   _____
      h. Expenditure for repayment of debts that represent reasonable
         and necessary expenses for the production of income _____
      i. Medical expenditures necessary to preserve life or health _____

AURELIA PUCINSKI, CLERK OF THE CIRCUIT COURT OF COOK COUNTY   [G19010]

S. Ct. Rule 218 **PROCEDURE**

A-6   (Rev. 7/21/93) CCDR 10 A6 J

    j. Reasonable expenditures for the benefit of the child
        and the other parent exclusive of gifts
        (for non-custodial parent only)   _____

            TOTAL REQUIRED DEDUCTIONS FROM INCOME $ _____

            NET MONTHLY INCOME $ _____

B. CASH OR CASH EQUIVALENTS ON HAND
   1. Savings and interest bearing accounts $ _____
   2. Checking   _____
   3. Stocks and bonds   _____
   4. Other (specify) _____   _____

        TOTAL CASH OR CASH EQUIVALENT ON HAND $ _____

                                                         Actual Monthly as of:
                                                          _____

C. STATEMENT OF MONTHLY LIVING EXPENSES
   1. Household
      a. Mortgage or rent (specify) $ _____
      b. Taxes, assessments and insurance   _____
      c. Maintenance and repairs   _____
      d. Heat/fuel   _____
      e. Electricity   _____
      f. Telephone   _____
      g. Water and Sewer   _____
      h. Refuse removal   _____
      i. Laundry/dry cleaning   _____
      j. Maid/cleaning service   _____
      k. Furniture and appliance replacement   _____
      l. Food (groceries/milk, etc.)   _____
      m. Tobacco products   _____
      n. Liquor, beer, wine, etc.   _____
      o. Other (specify)_____   _____

            SUBTOTAL HOUSEHOLD EXPENSES $ _____

   2. Transportation
      a. Gasoline $ _____
      b. Repairs
      c. Insurance/license   _____
      d. Payments/replacement   _____
      e. Alternative/replacement   _____
      f. Other (specify) _____   _____

            SUBTOTAL TRANSPORTATION EXPENSES: $ _____

[G19011]

ILLINOIS S. CT. RULES S. Ct. Rule 218

(Rev. 7/21/93) CCDR 10 A7 J

3. Personal: $ _____
   a. Clothing _____
   b. Grooming _____
   c. Medical: _____
      (1) Doctor _____
      (2) Dentist _____
      (3) Medication _____
   d. Insurance: _____
      (1) Life _____
      (2) Hospitalization _____
   e. Other (specify) _____ _____

   SUBTOTAL PERSONAL EXPENSES: $ _____

4. Miscellaneous
   a. Clubs/social obligations/entertainment $ _____
   b. Newspaper, magazines and books _____
   c. Gifts/donations _____
   d. Vacations _____
   e. Other (specify) _____ _____

   SUBTOTAL MISCELLANEOUS EXPENSES: $ _____

5. Dependent children: Names and date of birth:
   _____
   _____
   _____
   _____
   _____

   a. Clothing $ _____
   b. Grooming _____
   c. Education: _____
      (1) Tuition _____
      (2) Books/fees _____
      (3) Lunches _____
      (4) Transportation _____
      (5) Activities _____
   d. Medical: _____
      (1) Doctor _____
      (2) Dentist _____
      (3) Medication _____
   e. Allowance _____
   f. Child care _____
   g. Sitters _____
   h. Lessons _____
   i. Clubs/summer camps _____
   j. Entertainment _____
   k. Other (specify) _____ _____

   SUBTOTAL CHILDREN'S EXPENSES: $ _____

   TOTAL LIVING EXPENSES: $ _____

S. Ct. Rule 218   PROCEDURE

A-8   (7/21/93) CCDR 10 A8 J

D. Debts requiring regular payments:

CREDITOR	BALANCE	MINIMUM MONTHLY PAYMENT

SUB TOTAL MONTHLY DEBT SERVICE: $_____

Actual Monthly as of
_____

NET MONTHLY INCOME $_____

TOTAL MONTHLY LIVING EXPENSES $_____

DIFFERENCE BETWEEN NET
INCOME AND EXPENSES $_____

LESS MONTHLY DEBT SERVICE $_____

INCOME AVAILABLE PER MONTH $_____

STATE OF ILLINOIS | SS
COUNTY OF COOK

VERIFICATION BY CERTIFICATION

    Under penalties of perjury as provided by law pursuant to Section 1-109 of the Code of Civil Procedure (735 ILCS 5/1-109), the undersigned certifies that the statements set forth in this instrument are true and correct, except as to matters therein stated to be on information and belief and as to such matters the undersigned certifies as aforesaid, that I verily believe the same to be true.

DATE:_____   _____

Schedule A prepared by:
_____

Attorney:
Address:
City, State, ZIP:
Telephone: [G19013]

ILLINOIS S. CT. RULES **S. Ct. Rule 218**

B-1   (10-90) CCDR - 11 - B-1

──────── **SCHEDULE B: CUSTODY, VISITATION & CHILD SUPPORT** ────────

This Schedule was prepared by ☐ Petitioner ☐ Respondent ☐ Attorney for Child ☐ Other

1. Name of Child	Sex	Date of Birth	School and Grade	Special Problems

2. Current order in effect relating to custody, visitation and child support.

3. Present medical policies covering children. (Specify company and how obtained.)

[G19014]

S. Ct. Rule 218   PROCEDURE

B-2   (10-90) CCDR - 11.1 - B-2

4. Professional Examinations and Reports: Unless objected to by specific motion, include the following information: name and type of profession or agency, date, purpose of examination and findings. Reports, if not protected by confidentiality shall be presented to the pre-trial judge for pre-trial purposes only and shall not be a part of the court file unless otherwise ordered.

5. Other court proceedings having a bearing on custody, visitation and support. (Name of case, type of action and last order)

[G19015]

6. Recommendations of ☐ Petitioner ☐ Respondent

Indicate: (A) type of custody; (B) location and time spent at child(ren)'s residence; (C) visitation schedule, including, holidays and vacation time.

S. Ct. Rule 218   PROCEDURE

B-4   (Revised 5-91) CCDR 10-B-4

6. Recommendations continued:

   Indicate: (D) child support, specifying to whom support will be paid and the reasons supporting the amount recommended; (E) medical, dental and hospital expenses, specifying type of treatment, provider, and method of payment (including insurance); (F) each child's school expenses, specifying the name and type of school, (e.g., pre-school, religious school, elementary/high school, college, public/private, etc.) and amount of expense; and (G) any special problems of each child.

Submitted By:
NAME:

_____

Attorney for:

Address:

City, State, Zip:

Telephone:

Attorney Code No.:

[G19017]

ILLINOIS S. CT. RULES   S. Ct. Rule 218

C-1   (10-90) CCDR - 11.2 - C-1

─────────────── **SCHEDULE C: EXPERTS** ───────────────

This Schedule is prepared by the attorney for ☐ Petitioner ☐ Respondent ☐ Attorney for the Child(ren) ☐ Other

Name experts of whom you are aware who will testify at trial, and indicate the date of disclosure pursuant to Supreme Court Rule 220.

Submitted By:
NAME:

_____

Attorney for:

Address:

City, State, Zip:

Telephone:

Attorney Code No.:   [G19018]

S. Ct. Rule 218 PROCEDURE

D1 (10-90) CCDR - 12 - D-1

IN THE CIRCUIT COURT OF COOK COUNTY, ILLINOIS
COUNTY DEPARTMENT, DOMESTIC RELATIONS DIVISION

IN RE THE ☐ MARRIAGE ☐ CUSTODY
☐ SUPPORT OF:

NO:

CALENDAR:

_____
PETITIONER

AND

_____
RESPONDENT

SCHEDULE D - TRIAL INFORMATION

This Schedule need not be completed before the pre-trial conference. If the matter is not settled at the pre-trial conference, the Court will enter an order designating the date by which Schedule D must be filed.

Any stipulations entered into by the parties including exhibits, are attached hereto. If none, so indicate.

All discovery is completed.

1. ☐ The parties' stipulations are attached hereto.

   ☐ There are no stipulations.

2. The expected length of the trial is _____ full days. Petitioner represents that Petitioner's case in chief will take _____ ; Respondent represents that Respondent's case in chief will take _____ ; Attorney for the Child(ren) represents that their case in chief will take _____ .

3. Describe all issues still in dispute, on following page (D-2).

4. The parties reaffirm the items contained in Schedules A, B, and C, except for the following:

[G19019]

770

ILLINOIS S. CT. RULES			S. Ct. Rule 218

(10-90) CCDR - 12.1 - D-2

DESCRIPTION OF DISPUTED ISSUES

The following issues are in dispute

Issue	Petitioner's Position	Respondent's Position

Any other party shall submit their position separately.

[G19020]

S. Ct. Rule 218   PROCEDURE

D-3   (10-90) CCDR - 12.2 - D-3

Submitted By:

PARTY
☐ Petitioner ☐ Respondent ☐ Other

Name: _____

Address: _____

Telephone: _____

Signature: _____

ATTORNEY FOR
☐ Petitioner ☐ Respondent ☐ Children ☐ Other

Client Name(s): _____

Attorney Name: _____

Address: _____

Telephone: _____

Signature: _____

Attorney No: _____

THE COURT, having received the pre-trial memoranda presented by counsel, CERTIFIES this case ready for trial.

ENTER:

_____   _____
JUDGE   NO.   [G19021]

(2) **Motions in limine.** Motions in limine are useful prior to trial to gain early rulings on, for example, anticipated important evidentiary problems. See, e.g., In re Marriage of Madoch, 212 Ill.App.3d 1007, 157 Ill.Dec. 10, 571 N.E.2d 1029 (1st Dist.1991) (motion in limine to block evidence contrary to alleged admission made by opposing party); In re Marriage of Marcello, 247 Ill.App.3d 304, 187 Ill.Dec. 81, 617 N.E.2d 289 (1st Dist.1993) (motion in limine to bar witness who never responded to deposition subpoena from testifying at trial). For instance, where discovery has revealed that an opponent will seek to introduce extensive testimony on the value of the goodwill of a professional practice, a motion in limine can be made to seek a pre-

trial ruling on whether the evidence is admissible under In re Marriage of Zells, 143 Ill.2d 251, 157 Ill.Dec. 480, 572 N.E.2d 944 (1991), and, if so, for what purposes.

(3) **Pre-marked exhibits.** Trials are expedited when exhibits are marked before the trials commence.

Rule 219. Consequences of refusal to comply with rules or order relating to discovery or pretrial conferences

(a) Refusal to answer or comply with request for production. If a party or other deponent refuses to answer any question propounded upon oral examination, the examination shall be completed on other matters or adjourned, as the proponent of the question may prefer. Thereafter, on notice to all persons affected thereby, he may move the court for an order compelling an answer. If a party or other deponent refuses to answer any written question upon the taking of his deposition or if a party fails to answer any interrogatory served upon him, or to comply with a request for the production of documents or tangible things or inspection of real property, the proponent of the question or interrogatory or the party serving the request may on like notice move for an order compelling an answer or compliance with the request. If the court finds that the refusal or failure was without substantial justification, the court shall require the offending party or deponent, or the party whose attorney advised the conduct complained of, or either of them, to pay to the aggrieved party the amount of the reasonable expenses incurred in obtaining the order, including reasonable attorney's fees. If the motion is denied and the court finds that the motion was made without substantial justification, the court shall require the moving party to pay to the refusing party the amount of the reasonable expenses incurred in opposing the motion, including reasonable attorney's fees.

(b) Expenses on refusal to admit. If a party, after being served with a request to admit the genuineness of any documents or the truth of any matters of fact, serves a sworn denial thereof, and if the party requesting the admissions thereafter proves the genuineness of the document or the truth of the matter of fact, he may apply to the court for an order requiring the other party to pay him the reasonable expenses incurred in making the proof, including reasonable attorney's fees. Unless the court finds that there were good reasons for the denial or that the admissions sought were of no substantial importance, the order shall be made.

(c) Failure to comply with order or rules. If a party, or any person at the instance of or in collusion with a party, unreasonably refuses to comply with any provision of part E of article II of the rules of this court (Discovery, Requests for Admission, and Pretrial Procedure) or fails to comply with any order entered under these rules, the court, on motion, may enter, in addition to remedies elsewhere specifically provided, such orders as are just, including, among others, the following:

    (i) that further proceedings be stayed until the order or rule is complied with;

S. Ct. Rule 219   PROCEDURE

(ii) that the offending party be debarred from filing any other pleading relating to any issue to which the refusal or failure relates;

(iii) that he be debarred from maintaining any particular claim, counterclaim, third-party complaint, or defense relating to that issue;

(iv) that a witness be barred from testifying concerning that issue;

(v) that, as to claims or defenses asserted in any pleading to which that issue is material, a judgment by default be entered against the offending party or that his action be dismissed with or without prejudice; or

(vi) that any portion of his pleadings relating to that issue be stricken and, if thereby made appropriate, judgment be entered as to that issue.

In lieu of or in addition to the foregoing, the court may order that the offending party or his attorney pay the reasonable expenses, including attorney's fees incurred by any party as a result of the misconduct, and by contempt proceedings compel obedience by any party or person to any subpoena issued or order entered under the rules. Notwithstanding the entry of a judgment or an order of dismissal, whether voluntary or involuntary, the trial court shall retain jurisdiction to enforce, on its own motion or on the motion of any party, any order imposing monetary sanctions, including such orders as may be entered on motions which were pending hereunder prior to the filing of a notice or motion seeking a judgment or order of dismissal.

(d) Abuse of discovery procedures. The court may order that information obtained through abuse of discovery procedures be suppressed. If a party wilfully obtains or attempts to obtain information by an improper discovery method, wilfully obtains or attempts to obtain information to which he is not entitled, or otherwise abuses these discovery rules, the court may enter any order provided for in paragraph (c) of this rule.

Author's Notes

Analysis

1. Sanctions for failure to comply with discovery.
2. Required statement of attempted resolution of discovery disputes.
3. Motion for Sanctions for Failure to Comply with Discovery—Form.

(1) **Sanctions for failure to comply with discovery.** Supreme Court Rule 219 provides for discovery sanctions against parties and non-party witnesses. Rule 219(c) authorizes, *inter alia*, contempt proceedings against a witness who does not respond to a discovery proceeding, attorney's fees, debarring claims, debarring the filing of pleadings, debarring testimony, or a default judgment.

(2) **Required statement of attempted resolution of discovery disputes.** All discovery motions must contain the statement from Supreme Court Rule 201(k) that "after personal consultation and reasonable attempts to resolve differences the parties have been unable to reach an accord." See para. 8 in sample motion in Author's Note (3) below.

ILLINOIS S. CT. RULES   S. Ct. Rule 219

(3) **Motion for Sanctions for Failure to Comply with Discovery—Form.** There follows a sample Motion for Sanctions for Failure to Comply with Discovery.

IN THE CIRCUIT COURT OF COOK COUNTY, ILLINOIS
COUNTY DEPARTMENT—DOMESTIC RELATIONS DIVISION

IN RE THE MARRIAGE OF   )
)
WILLIAM GUPPY,   )
)
            Petitioner,   )
)
and   )   No. ___ D _____
)
ESTHER SUMMERSON,   )
)
            Respondent.   )

MOTION FOR SANCTIONS FOR FAILURE TO COMPLY WITH DISCOVERY

Respondent, ESTHER SUMMERSON ("ESTHER"), brings the following Motion pursuant to Supreme Court Rule 219 against Petitioner, WILLIAM GUPPY ("WILLIAM"), for the failure by WILLIAM to comply with discovery:

1. On June ___, 199_, ESTHER properly served upon WILLIAM's attorneys a Notice to Produce certain documents pursuant to Supreme Court Rule 214. A copy of the Notice to Produce is attached to this Petition as an exhibit.

2. WILLIAM at his deposition taken on June ___, 199_ agreed to produce the documents requested in the Notice to Produce served upon his attorneys on June ___, 199_.

3. WILLIAM has not produced the requested documents and WILLIAM has failed to comply with the Notice to Produce pursuant to Supreme Court Rule 214.

4. The documents requested in the Notice to Produce served upon WILLIAM's attorneys on June ___, 199_ are relevant to this litigation because they concern the value of the marital estate.

5. At the deposition taken of WILLIAM on June ___, 199_, WILLIAM refused to answer the following question:

"What is the present value of the accounts receivable to your medical practice?"

6. A copy of pages ___ to ___ of the deposition containing the question and WILLIAM's refusal to answer are attached to this Motion as an Exhibit.

7. The question is relevant to this litigation because accounts receivable are part of the value of WILLIAM's medical practice. *In re Marriage of*

S. Ct. Rule 219   PROCEDURE

Weiss, 129 Ill.App.3d 166, 172, 84 Ill.Dec. 378, 382, 472 N.E.2d 128, 132 (1st Dist.1984).

    8. After personal consultation and reasonable attempts to resolve their differences, the parties have been unable to reach an accord concerning their discovery differences. The requirements of Supreme Court Rule 201(k) have been satisfied prior to bringing this Motion.

    9. WILLIAM's failure to produce the documents requested and refusal to answer the deposition question are without substantial justification, and WILLIAM should therefore pay the fees and costs incurred by ESTHER in bringing this Motion.

    10. ESTHER is entitled to sanctions against WILLIAM for WILLIAM's failure to comply with discovery.

    11. By order of Court, discovery closes on September ___, 199__.

WHEREFORE, Respondent, ESTHER SUMMERSON, prays for relief against Petitioner, WILLIAM GUPPY, as follows:

    1. WILLIAM be ordered to produce the documents requested from him in the Notice to Produce served upon his attorneys on June ___, 199__.

    2. WILLIAM be ordered to answer the question set forth in paragraph 5 of this Motion.

    3. The Court allow to ESTHER reasonable attorney's fees and costs incurred by her in bringing this Motion for Sanctions for failure to comply with discovery pursuant to Supreme Court Rule 219.

    4. Further proceedings be stayed and the discovery deadline be extended for 30 days beyond the time that WILLIAM produces the documents requested in the Notice to Produce served upon his attorneys on June ___, 199__.

    5. WILLIAM be barred from testifying concerning the value of the marital estate.

    6. WILLIAM be barred from testifying concerning the value of his medical practice.

    7. The Court enter such other sanctions against WILLIAM as may be appropriate pursuant to Supreme Court Rule 219.

    8. ESTHER have such other relief as may be appropriate under the evidence and circumstances.

_____
ESTHER SUMMERSON

_____
Conrad Snagby
Attorney for ESTHER SUMMERSON

ILLINOIS S. CT. RULES **S. Ct. Rule 220**

VERIFICATION BY CERTIFICATION

Under penalties as provided by law pursuant to 735 ILCS 5/1–109 of the Illinois Code of Civil Procedure, the undersigned certifies that the statements set forth in the foregoing instrument are true and correct.

DATED: _____   _____
                                    ESTHER SUMMERSON

Conrad Snagsby
Address
Telephone number

Rule 220. Expert witnesses

(a) Definitions.

(1) Definition of expert witness. An expert is a person who, because of education, training or experience, possesses knowledge of a specialized nature beyond that of the average person on a factual matter material to a claim or defense in pending litigation and who may be expected to render an opinion within his expertise at trial. He may be an employee of a party, a party or an independent contractor.

(2) Consulting expert. A consulting expert is a person who possesses the same qualifications as an expert witness and who has been retained or specially employed in anticipation of litigation or preparation for trial but who is not to be called at trial to render opinions within his area of expertise.

(b) Disclosure.

(1) Expert witness. Where the testimony of experts is reasonably contemplated, the parties will act in good faith to seasonably:

(i) ascertain the identity of such witnesses, and

(ii) obtain from them the opinions upon which they may be requested to testify.

In order to insure fair and equitable preparation for trial by all parties the identity of an expert who is retained to render an opinion at trial on behalf of a party must be disclosed by that party either within 90 days after the substance of the expert's opinion first becomes known to that party or his counsel or, if the substance of the expert's opinion is then known, at the first pretrial conference in the case, whichever is later. In any event, as to all expert witnesses not previously disclosed, the trial court, on its own motion, or on the motion of any party after the first pretrial conference, shall enter an order scheduling the dates upon which all expert witnesses, including rebuttal experts, shall be disclosed. The schedule established by the trial court will sequence the disclosure of expert witnesses in accordance with the complexities of the issues involved and the burdens of proof of the respective parties as to those issues. All dates set by the trial court shall be chosen to insure that discovery regarding such expert witnesses will be completed not later than 60 days before the date on which the trial court reasonably anticipates the trial will commence. Upon disclosure, the expert's opinion may be the subject of discovery as provided in paragraph (c) hereof. Failure to make the disclosure required by this rule or to comply with the discovery contemplated herein will result in disqualification of the expert as a witness.

(2) Consulting expert. Except as provided in paragraph (c)(5) hereof, a party need not disclose the identity of a consulting expert.

(c) Discovery.

(1) Upon interrogatory propounded for that purpose, the party retaining or employing an expert witness shall be required to state:

(i) the subject matter on which the expert is expected to testify;

(ii) his conclusions and opinions and the bases therefor; and

(iii) his qualifications.

(2) The party answering such interrogatories may respond by submitting the signed report of the expert containing the required information.

(3) A party shall be required to seasonably supplement his answers to interrogatories propounded under this rule as additional information becomes known to the party or his counsel.

(4) The provisions of paragraphs (c) and (d) hereof also apply to a party or an employee of a party who will render an opinion within his expertise at the time of trial. However, the provisions of paragraphs (c) and (d) do not apply to parties or employees of entities whose professional acts or omissions are the subject of the litigation. The opinions of these latter persons may be the subject of disclosure by deposition only.

(5) The identity, opinions and work product of consulting experts are discoverable only upon a showing of exceptional circumstances under which it is impracticable for the party seeking discovery to obtain facts or opinions on the same subject matter by other means. However, documents, objects and tangible things as defined in Rule 214 which are in the possession of a consulting expert and which do not contain his opinions may be obtained by a request for that purpose served upon the party retaining him.

(6) Unless manifest injustice would result, each party shall bear the expense of all fees charged by his expert witness or witnesses.

(d) Scope of testimony. To the extent that the facts known or opinions held by an expert have been developed in discovery proceedings through interrogatories, deposition, or requests to produce, his direct testimony at trial may not be inconsistent with nor go beyond the fair scope of the facts known or opinions disclosed in such discovery proceedings. However, he shall not be prevented from testifying as to facts or opinions on matters regarding which inquiry was not made in the discovery proceedings.

Author's Notes

Analysis

1. Disqualification.
2. Two steps.
3. Disclosure timetable: Outline.
4. Sixty day rule.
5. Burden of disclosure.
6. Diary.
7. Discovery.
8. Interrogatories Pursuant to Supreme Court Rule 220—Form.
9. Rule 220 Disclosure Statement—Form.
10. Experts, consulting experts, and occurrence witnesses.
11. Other remedies.
12. Motion to Allow Testimony of Experts, or, in Alternative, to Set Discovery Schedule, or to Continue Trial—Form.
13. Scope of testimony.

(1) **Disqualification.** Supreme Court Rule 220 is a complex and potentially hazardous rule because failure to comply with it can result in the disqualification of a critical expert witness pursuant to 220(b). Keating v. Dominick's Finer Foods, Inc., 224 Ill.App.3d 981, 984, 167 Ill.Dec. 175, 177, 587 N.E.2d 57, 59 (2d Dist.1992) ("failure to respond, or to properly or sufficiently respond, to Rule 220 interrogatories seeking discovery of an expert's qualifications will result in debarring of such expert from testifying"). For example, an important accounting or valuation expert upon whom a wife is relying to prove the value of a closely held corporation predominantly owned by the husband can be barred from testifying if the disclosure provisions of Supreme Court Rule 220 have not been satisfied.

(2) **Two steps.** There are two steps to Supreme Court Rule 220: disclosure of the identity of expert witnesses, (220(b)); and discovery of their opinions, (220(c)).

(3) **Disclosure timetable: Outline.** There follows in outline form the disclosure provisions of Supreme Court Rule 220(b).

(A) Expert witness shall be disclosed by the party employing the expert witness

(i) 90 days after the substance of the expert's opinion becomes known to the party or counsel; or

(ii) at the first pre-trial conference, if the substance of the expert's opinion is then known;

(iii) whichever is later.

(B) In any event, as to all expert witnesses not previously disclosed

(i) the trial court on its own or a party's motion shall schedule the disclosure of all expert witnesses, including rebuttal experts,

S. Ct. Rule 220 PROCEDURE

(ii) so that discovery regarding expert witnesses is completed not later than 60 days before trial.

(4) **Sixty day rule.** The 60 day rule is not well adapted to divorce litigation. In practice, experts are seldom disclosed prior to the first pre-trial conference, and often not even at the pre-trial conference. The primary reason for this is that preliminary pre-trial conferences are generally focused on settlement rather than litigation. Expert witnesses also may not be employed until after the failure of the pre-trial conference to settle the case, thereby making the 90 day portion of the Rule moot. Compounding the problem is that the parties and the court rarely take the initiative contemplated by the rule to enter an order scheduling the disclosure of expert witnesses. In this common situation, the appellate court has held,

> if a trial court does not set deadlines for disclosure of expert witnesses, such disclosure must occur in time to enable discovery concerning the witnesses to be completed at least 60 days prior to trial.

In re Marriage of Gorsich, 208 Ill.App.3d 852, 153 Ill.Dec. 643, 567 N.E.2d 601 (2d Dist.1991).

(5) **Burden of disclosure.** Disclosure of expert witnesses does not require receipt of interrogatories from the opposing party. The burden of disclosure is on the party intending to use the expert witness at trial, regardless of the receipt of an interrogatory. See Author's Note (9) below for a model Rule 220 disclosure statement.

(6) **Diary.** Because the pre-trial conference rarely addresses experts, because expert witnesses are often employed late in the case, because Supreme Court Rule 220 orders are not frequently entered by the court, and because often no Rule 220 interrogatory is served, it is easy to allow the required disclosure of and discovery from expert witnesses 60 days before trial to slip, with potentially disastrous results. The solution is two-fold:

> (a) Diary all cases at least 90 days prior to when you reasonably anticipate that the trial will commence, in order to assure that: (i) your expert witnesses have been disclosed; (ii) discovery from your opponent's expert witnesses has been completed or is scheduled to be completed; and (iii) you can comply with the provision for the disclosure and completion of discovery of expert witnesses 60 days prior to trial.

> (b) In cases going into litigation, serve interrogatories pursuant to Supreme Court Rule 220 as early as possible in order to assure that you are protected insofar as your opponent's disclosure of expert witnesses is concerned.

(7) **Discovery.** After disclosure, the expert is subject to discovery. The Rule contemplates discovery by interrogatory to the party (220(c)), but depositions of the expert are also commonly taken. Unlike interrogatories pursuant to Supreme Court Rule 213, Rule 220 interrogatories must be supplemented as additional information becomes known to the party or to his counsel concerning expert witnesses without receipt of a supplemental interrogatory. Rule 220(c)(3).

(8) **Interrogatories Pursuant to Supreme Court Rule 220—Form.** A sample Rule 220 interrogatory follows. The interrogatory seeks disclosure of both the identity of the opposition's experts and the substance of their opinions. The early request for disclosure attempts to both make a record of the request, and to set a time framework for disclosure well in advance of the 60 day deadline.

ILLINOIS S. CT. RULES   S. Ct. Rule 220

IN THE CIRCUIT COURT OF COOK COUNTY, ILLINOIS
COUNTY DEPARTMENT—DOMESTIC RELATIONS DIVISION

IN RE THE MARRIAGE OF)
)
ROSA ROUNCEWELL,)
      Petitioner and)
      Counter-Respondent,)
)
and) No. ____ D _____
)
WATT ROUNCEWELL,)
      Respondent and)
      Counter-Petitioner.)

INTERROGATORIES PURSUANT TO SUPREME COURT RULE 220

TO: Joseph Blowers

    Blowers & Associates, Ltd.

    Address

Respondent and Counter–Petitioner, WATT ROUNCEWELL, by his attorneys, Samuel Kenge of Kenge and Carboy, pursuant to Rule 220 of the Illinois Supreme Court, propounds the following Interrogatories to Petitioner and Counter–Respondent, ROSA ROUNCEWELL, to be answered under oath within 28 days after services hereof.

DEMAND TO SUPPLEMENT: In accord with Supreme Court Rule 220 (c)(3), the party answering these interrogatories is hereby requested to seasonably supplement all answers to these interrogatories as additional information becomes known to the party or the party's attorneys.

DEFINITIONS: The terms "expert witness" and "consulting expert" as used herein shall have the meaning defined in Supreme Court Rule 220 (a) and shall include but not be limited to (1) a party, (2) an employee of a party, (3) former employees of a party, and (4) independent contractors.

INTERROGATORY NO. 1

State the full name(s), address(es), telephone number(s), and occupation(s) or profession(s) of each expert (other than consulting experts) who may be called at the trial of this cause to testify to opinions within his or her expertise on behalf of the party answering these interrogatories.

ANSWER TO INTERROGATORY NO. 1

INTERROGATORY NO. 2

With regard to each expert witness disclosed above, state the following:

(a) The subject matter upon which the expert is expected to testify;

(b) Each and every opinion and conclusion upon which the expert is expected to testify;

(c) Each and every basis of the opinions and conclusions disclosed in answer to No. 2(b);

(d) The expert's qualifications, including but not limited to his educational background, practical experience in the area he is expected to testify in, any articles or papers he has written, any and all seminars or post-graduate training he has received, his experience, if any, as a teacher or lecturer and his professional appointments and associations. (In lieu of answering No. 2(d), a complete curriculum vitae of the expert may be attached to the answers to interrogatories.)

(e) Response to Interrogatory No. 2 may be made by submitting the signed report of the expert containing the required information. Any required information not included in the report shall be presented as an additional response to Interrogatory No. 2.

ANSWER TO INTERROGATORY NO. 2

INTERROGATORY NO. 3

State whether the party answering these interrogatories or anyone on his/her behalf has engaged the services of a consulting expert.

ANSWER TO INTERROGATORY NO. 3

INTERROGATORY NO. 4

If the answer to No. 3 is yes, identify all documents, objects and other tangible items which are or were in the possession of the consulting expert, and which do not contain the opinions of the consulting expert. Identify the dates each such item was acquired and/or prepared.

ANSWER TO INTERROGATORY NO. 4

ILLINOIS S. CT. RULES   S. Ct. Rule 220

PLEASE TAKE NOTICE that a copy of the answers to these Interrogatories should be served upon the undersigned within 28 days after the service of these Interrogatories.

By_____
Samuel Kenge
Attorney for WATT ROUNCEWELL

Samuel Kenge
Kenge and Carboy
Address
Telephone number

CERTIFICATE OF DELIVERY

The undersigned hereby certifies under penalties of perjury as provided by law pursuant to Section 1-109 of the Code of Civil Procedure, that the above 220 Interrogatories were [ ]placed in the U.S. Mail properly addressed and mailed with first class postage prepaid, [ ]sent via messenger, [ ]sent via facsimile (___ pages, from the office of _____, sender's facsimile number _____, to recipient's facsimile number _____), to the party at the address set forth above on the ___ day of _____, 199__, before the hour of 5:00 p.m.

_____   _____
(Signature)   (Print Name)

(9) **Rule 220 Disclosure Statement—Form.** A sample Rule 220 disclosure statement follows. It should be used where no interrogatory has been propounded. It is important to make a timely record of the disclosure of expert witnesses, whether or not an interrogatory has been served.

IN THE CIRCUIT COURT OF COOK COUNTY, ILLINOIS
COUNTY DEPARTMENT—DOMESTIC RELATIONS DIVISION

IN RE THE MARRIAGE OF	)
	)
ROSA ROUNCEWELL,	)
Petitioner and	)
Counter-Respondent,	)
	)
and	) No. ___ D _____
	)
WATT ROUNCEWELL,	)
Respondent and	)
Counter-Petitioner.	)

S. Ct. Rule 220   PROCEDURE

RULE 220 DISCLOSURE STATEMENT

TO: Samuel Kenge
     Kenge and Carboy
     Address

This Disclosure Statement is hereby served upon you pursuant to Supreme Court Rule 220(b). The following are the identities of the expert witnesses acting on behalf of Petitioner and Counter-Respondent, ROSA ROUNCEWELL:

1. Joshua Smallweed
   Smallweed & Smallweed, Accountants
   Address

2. Morgan Snagsby
   Address

3. Dr. Prince Turveydrop
   Address

                                            Joseph Blowers
                                            Attorney for ROSA ROUNCEWELL

Joseph Blowers
Blowers & Associates, Ltd.
Address
Telephone number

CERTIFICATE OF DELIVERY

The undersigned hereby certifies under penalties of perjury as provided by law pursuant to Section 1-109 of the Code of Civil Procedure, that the above Rule 220 Disclosure Statement was [ ]placed in the U.S. Mail properly addressed and mailed with first class postage prepaid, [ ]sent via messenger, [ ]sent via facsimile (___ pages, from the office of _____, sender's facsimile number _____, to recipient's facsimile number _____), to the party at the address set forth above on the ___ day of _____, 199__, before the hour of 5:00 p.m.

_____   _____
(Signature)   (Print Name)

(10) **Experts, consulting experts, and occurrence witnesses.** A party is obliged to disclose expert witnesses who may be expected to testify within their expertise at trial. 220(a)(1). See, e.g., In re Marriage of Olson, 223 Ill.App.3d 636, 166 Ill.Dec. 60, 585 N.E.2d 1082 (2d Dist.), *appeal denied*, 145 Ill.2d 636, 173 Ill.Dec. 6, 596 N.E.2d 630 (1992) (witness retained by wife qualified as an expert witness; witness was a trained CPA, and his limited experience in valuation of closely held corporations went to the weight, not admissibility, of his testimony).

An expert can be a party, an employee of a party, or an independent contractor. If a party herself is going to testify in the capacity of an expert witness, she must be identified as such. Karr v. Noel, 212 Ill.App.3d 575, 156 Ill.Dec. 684, 571 N.E.2d 271 (5th Dist.), *appeal denied*, 141 Ill.2d 542, 162 Ill.Dec. 490, 580 N.E.2d 116 (1991) (defendant physician was an expert witness for purposes of the provisions of Rule 220 governing disclosure and discovery of expert witnesses was "subject to discovery by deposition only [220(c)(4)], and the scope of his testimony at trial [could] not exceed that of his deposition testimony"). But see Hill v. Ben Franklin Sav. & Loan Ass'n, 177 Ill.App.3d 51, 126 Ill.Dec. 462, 531 N.E.2d 1089 (2d Dist.1988) (landowner testifying to the value of his own land was not an expert under Supreme Court Rule 220; landowner should have been permitted to testify although not disclosed as an expert witness).

It is not necessary to disclose a consulting expert who has been retained in connection with the litigation, but who is not going to testify within his area of expertise at the trial. 220(b)(2). Information concerning consulting experts is discoverable pursuant to 220(c)(5) only upon a showing of exceptional circumstances under which it is impracticable for the parties seeking discovery to obtain the information by other means, or where there are documents and other tangible things in the possession of the consulting expert that do not contain his opinions.

It is also not necessary to disclose occurrence witnesses, such as treating physicians, who may be experts and may testify as to opinions obtained during their participation in the occurrence.

> An expert who acquires information because he was an actor or viewer with respect to transactions or occurrences that are part of the subject matter of the lawsuit rather than acquiring information because a lawsuit is contemplated or is pending should be treated as an ordinary witness; thus, Rule 220 disclosure and discovery provisions do not apply....

Jessee v. Amoco Oil Co., 230 Ill.App.3d 337, 344, 171 Ill.Dec. 690, 695, 594 N.E.2d 1210, 1215 (1st Dist.1992). Similarly, the Illinois Supreme Court stated that

> the question of whether a witness must be disclosed as an expert under Rule 220 depends upon the expert's relationship with the case. If the expert is intimately involved in the underlying facts giving rise to the litigation and he would reasonably be expected to form an opinion through that involvement, then disclosure is not required. On the other hand, where the expert's contact with the case is slight, or where the opinion rendered is unrelated to the expert's involvement in the case, then disclosure is required.

Wakeford v. Rodehouse Restaurants of Missouri, Inc., 154 Ill.2d 543, 548, 182 Ill.Dec. 653, 656, 610 N.E.2d 77, 80 (1992).

(11) **Other remedies.** Courts have repeatedly interpreted the provisions of Supreme Court Rule 220 strictly and disqualified expert witnesses from testifying who have not been disclosed in a timely manner. Disqualification, however, is not the only sanction available, and in many circumstances disqualification may not advance the fairness that Supreme Court Rule was enacted to promote. See Vallejo v. Mercado, 220 Ill.App.3d 1, 162 Ill.Dec. 692, 580 N.E.2d 655 (2d Dist.1991) (sanctions under Rule 220 are "not to punish but to insure fair discovery and a trial on the merits"). Disqualification may be particularly inappropriate where the trial court does not enter an order scheduling the disclosure of expert witnesses. Other remedies available to the court include disregarding the 60 day limitation, permission to disclose and discover after the 60 day time limit, continuance of the trial date, or even adjournment of a trial in progress to allow the taking of a deposition of an expert witness not

S. Ct. Rule 220 PROCEDURE

previously disclosed. See Sohaey v. Van Cura, 158 Ill.2d 375, 199 Ill.Dec. 654, 634 N.E.2d 707 (1994) ("in order for Rule 220 to serve the purpose [of avoiding surprise testimony that prejudices the opposing party] trial courts must have the discretion to impose sanctions other than outright disqualification for technical violations"). See also Kosinski v. Inland Steel Co., 192 Ill.App.3d 1017, 140 Ill.Dec. 133, 549 N.E.2d 784 (1st Dist.1989) (trial court did not abuse its discretion by refusing to bar testimony of expert witness not seasonably identified; opposing party had not shown any interest in deposing witness who had been identified, and trial court allowed opposing party to depose expert witness before he testified); Dietrich v. Jones, 172 Ill.App.3d 201, 122 Ill.Dec. 191, 526 N.E.2d 450 (1st Dist.), *appeal denied*, 122 Ill.2d 572, 125 Ill.Dec. 215, 530 N.E.2d 243 (1988) (trial court did not abuse its discretion by allowing plaintiff's expert witness to testify; defendant waived objection to untimely disclosure of expert witness when defendant refused plaintiff's offer to continue the trial so defendant could depose plaintiff's expert).

The factors that the court should consider in determining the severity of discovery sanctions include

(1) the surprise to the adverse party; (2) the prejudicial effect of the expert's testimony; (3) the nature of the expert's testimony; (4) the diligence of the adverse party; (5) whether objection to the expert's testimony was timely; and (6) the good faith of the party calling the witness.

Sohaey v. Van Cura, 240 Ill.App.3d 266, 286, 180 Ill.Dec. 359, 375, 607 N.E.2d 253, 269 (2d Dist.1992), *aff'd, remanded*, 158 Ill.2d 375, 199 Ill.Dec. 654, 634 N.E.2d 707 (1994) (citations omitted).

(12) **Motion to Allow Testimony of Experts, or, in Alternative, to Set Discovery Schedule, or to Continue Trial—Form.** There follows a sample motion seeking remedies other than disqualification for untimely disclosure of expert witnesses.

IN THE CIRCUIT COURT OF COOK COUNTY, ILLINOIS
COUNTY DEPARTMENT—DOMESTIC RELATIONS DIVISION

IN RE THE MARRIAGE OF)
)
ROSA ROUNCEWELL,)
    Petitioner and)
    Counter-Respondent,)
)
and) No. ___ D _____
)
WATT ROUNCEWELL,)
    Respondent and)
    Counter-Petitioner.)

MOTION TO ALLOW TESTIMONY OF EXPERTS, OR, IN ALTERNATIVE, TO SET DISCOVERY SCHEDULE, OR TO CONTINUE TRIAL

WATT ROUNCEWELL ("WATT"), through his attorneys, Kenge and Carboy, in support of his Motion to Allow Testimony of Experts, or, in Alternative, to Set Discovery Schedule, or to Continue Trial, alleges:

ILLINOIS S. CT. RULES   S. Ct. Rule 220

1. This matter is set for trial commencing December 10, 1994 pursuant to an Order entered on April 14, 1994.

2. On April 21, 1993, WATT served his Interrogatories requesting disclosure and discovery of experts pursuant to Illinois Supreme Court Rule 220 on counsel for ROSA ROUNCEWELL ("ROSA").

3. On May 11, 1994, ROSA served her Interrogatories requesting disclosure and discovery of experts pursuant to Illinois Supreme Court Rule 220 on counsel for WATT.

4. On October 29, 1994, WATT filed his Answer to ROSA's Rule 220 Interrogatories which detailed a list of three (3) experts to be called by WATT at the trial of this cause.

5. WATT's counsel spoke with ROSA's counsel on November 3, 1994 regarding his disclosure of experts. ROSA's counsel stated in a letter dated November 5, 1994 that she would seek to bar any experts WATT would offer at trial of this cause because of failure to disclose the experts 60 days prior to the trial date.

6. To date, ROSA has not responded to WATT's Rule 220 Interrogatories, nor made any disclosure of experts to WATT.

7. This Court has never entered an Order scheduling the dates upon which the parties' shall disclose their expert witnesses or rebuttal expert witnesses.

8. The instant case involves complex questions regarding the acquisition of property, the characterization of property as non-marital or marital, the valuation of property, and the amounts and sources of income available to WATT. It is imperative that experts testify on these topics to assist the court in evaluating the issues presented to it.

9. Supreme Court Rule 220(b)(1) provides:

Expert Witness. Where the testimony of experts is reasonably contemplated, the parties will act in good faith to reasonably:

(i) ascertain the identity of such witnesses, and

(ii) obtain from them the opinions upon which they may be requested to testify.

In order to insure fair and equitable preparation for trial by all parties the identity of an expert who is retained to render an opinion at trial on behalf of a party must be disclosed by that party either within 90 days after the substance of the expert's opinion first becomes known to that party or his counsel or, if the substance of the expert's opinion is then known, at the first pretrial conference in the case, whichever is later. **In any event, as to all expert witnesses not previously disclosed, the trial court, on its own motion, or on the motion of any party after the first pretrial conference, shall enter an order scheduling the dates upon which all expert witnesses, including rebuttal experts, shall be disclosed. The schedule established by the trial** court will sequence the disclosure of expert witnesses in accordance with the complexities of the issues involved and the burdens of proof of the respective parties as to those issues. *All dates set by the trial court shall be chosen to insure that discovery regarding such expert witnesses will be completed not later than 60 days before the date on which the trial court reasonably anticipates the trial will commence.* Upon disclosure, the expert's opinion may be the subject of discovery as provided in paragraph (c) hereof. Failure to make the disclosure required by this rule or to comply with the discovery contemplated herein will result in disqualification of the expert as a witness.

(Emphasis added.)

10. The purpose of Rule 220 governing pretrial disclosure of expert witnesses is to ensure fair discovery in a trial on the merits and to prevent trial by ambush.

11. Although WATT has fully disclosed his expert witnesses as required by Rule 220, ROSA has refused to depose WATT's experts. Further, ROSA has not brought any motion to bar WATT's experts, but has only stated in a letter that she would seek to bar them at a later date.

12. The Appellate Court in *Kosinski v. Inland Steel Co.*, 192 Ill.App.3d 1017, 140 Ill.Dec. 133, 549 N.E.2d 784 (1st Dist.1989) held that although the plaintiff had violated the 60–day provision of Rule 220, disqualification of the plaintiff's expert was not the only sanction available and that, unless late disclosure materially prejudices a party-opponent's ability to respond with rebuttal expert testimony, the trial court has the discretion to ignore the disclosure provisions of section (b) of the rule.

13. The Appellate Court in *Marshall v. Osborn*, 213 Ill.App.3d 134, 156 Ill.Dec. 708, 571 N.E.2d 492 (3d Dist.1991) held that disqualification of a previously undisclosed expert witness on the eve of trial was not the only sanction available to the court, and, under some circumstances, allowing the offended party the opportunity to depose the expert may be an appropriate response.

14. WATT disclosed his expert witnesses to ROSA on October 29, 1994, forty-two (42) days prior to trial. Forty-two days is more than ample time to allow ROSA to be fully informed of the opinions of WATT's experts and the bases thereof. ROSA's refusal to pursue discovery of the disclosed experts, preferring instead to seek their disqualification, is an attempt to keep important evidence from the court, and will not advance the fairness of the trial that Supreme Court Rule 220 was enacted to promote.

15. In light of the fact that full compliance with outstanding discovery requests is still being sought by both parties as of the filing of this motion, WATT's disclosure of experts 18 days after the 60–day limit set by Rule 220, with 42 days remaining, does not amount to trial by ambush.

16. Even a strict interpretation of Supreme Court Rule 220 does not preclude a continuance of trial in order to obtain full compliance with the disclosure and discovery provisions of the Rule.

17. In *Vallejo v. Mercado*, 220 Ill.App.3d 1, 162 Ill.Dec. 692, 580 N.E.2d 655 (2d Dist.1991), the Appellate Court held the 60–day rule mandatory, but found that the trial court had abused its discretion when it refused to continue the trial date to avoid, in essence, strict compliance with Rule 220(b).

18. This Court has the discretion to continue trial in this cause to ensure strict compliance with Rule 220, as well as to ensure that both parties are adequately prepared for trial.

WHEREFORE, Respondent and Counter–Petitioner, WATT ROUNCEWELL, prays as follows:

A. The Court enter an Order directing that WATT's expert witnesses may testify at trial.

B. The Court enter an Order setting a discovery schedule for disclosure of ROSA's rebuttal experts, if any, as well as a deposition schedule for completion of all expert depositions.

C. In the alternative, the Court enter an Order continuing the trial in this cause to ensure compliance with the disclosure deadlines contained in Illinois Supreme Court Rule 220(b).

D. For such other and further relief as may be appropriate under the evidence and circumstances.

WATT ROUNCEWELL

BY: Samuel Kenge, One of his Attorneys

Samuel Kenge
Kenge and Carboy
Address
Telephone number

(13) **Scope of testimony.** The Courts have strictly interpreted Supreme Court Rule 220(d) in confining expert witnesses to testimony that is not inconsistent with and which does not go beyond the scope of facts and opinions disclosed during discovery, providing that appropriate inquiry was made.

> Supreme Court Rule 220(d) ... safeguards against an expert witness ... testifying during direct examination in a manner inconsistent with the facts known or the opinions disclosed during discovery. The rule also prevents the expert from going beyond the fair scope of the opinions or facts given at the deposition.... As a result, any opinion expressed by an expert in addition to the opinion expressed in his deposition must be excluded.

Lee v. Ingalls Memorial Hosp., 238 Ill.App.3d 154, 159, 179 Ill.Dec. 328, 332, 606 N.E.2d 160, 164 (1st Dist.1992) (expert could not testify that use of certain drug during delivery caused presiding physician to apply excess force to the child when during deposition expert stated that the drug had no relationship to the injury). See also Stennis v. Rekkas, 233 Ill.App.3d 813, 175 Ill.Dec. 45, 599 N.E.2d 1059 (1st Dist.1992) *appeal denied*, 148 Ill.2d 654, 183 Ill.Dec. 32, 610 N.E.2d 1276 (1993) (expert witness could give opinions at trial on topics not covered in his prior deposition).

It is therefore crucial that upon appropriate inquiry an expert witness disclose all that he will testify to at trial, in order that he not be precluded from presenting subject matter at trial that he failed to divulge during discovery. Similarly, the questioner during discovery should make comprehensive inquiry, so that if new or inconsistent subject matter is introduced during the trial, he will have preserved his objection.

Rule 231. Motions for continuance

(a) Absence of material evidence. If either party applies for a continuance of a cause on account of the absence of material evidence, the motion shall be supported by the affidavit of the party so applying or his authorized agent. The affidavit shall show (1) that due diligence has been used to obtain the evidence, or the want of time to obtain it; (2) of what particular fact or facts the evidence consists; (3) if the evidence consists of the testimony of a witness, his place of residence, or if his place of residence is not known, that due diligence has been used to ascertain it; and (4) that if further time is given the evidence can be procured.

(b) When continuance will be denied. If the court is satisfied that the evidence would not be material, or if the other party will admit the affidavit in evidence as proof only of what the absent witness would testify to if present, the continuance shall be denied unless the court, for the furtherance of justice, shall consider a continuance necessary.

(c) Other causes for continuance. It is sufficient cause for the continuance of any action: (1) that in time of war or insurrection, a party whose presence is necessary for the full and fair prosecution or defense of the action is in the military service of the United States or of this State and that his military service materially impairs his ability to prosecute or defend the action; or (2) that the party applying therefor or his attorney is a member of either house of the General Assembly during the time the General Assembly is in session, if the presence of that party is necessary for the full and fair trial of the action, and in the case of the attorney, if the attorney was retained by the party prior to the time the cause was set for trial.

(d) Amendment as cause. No amendment is cause for continuance unless the party affected thereby, or his agent or attorney, shall make affidavit that, in consequence thereof, he is unprepared to proceed to or with the trial. If the cause thereof is the want of material evidence, a continuance shall be granted only on a further showing as may be required for continuance for that cause.

(e) Court's own motion. The court may on its own motion, or with the consent of the adverse party, continue a cause for trial to a later day.

(f) Time for motion. No motion for the continuance of a cause made after the cause has been reached for trial shall be heard, unless a sufficient excuse is shown for the delay.

(g) Taxing of costs. When a continuance is granted upon payment of costs, the costs may be taxed summarily by the court, and on being taxed shall be paid on demand of the party, his agent, or his attorney, and, if not so paid, on affidavit of the fact, the continuance may be vacated, or the court may enforce the payment with the accruing costs, by contempt proceedings.

Author's Notes

Analysis

1. Other causes.
2. Continuance subpoenas.

(1) **Other causes.** The causes for granting a continuance set forth in Supreme Court Rule 231 are not exclusive. See, e.g., Stern v. Stern 179 Ill.App.3d 313, 128 Ill.Dec. 351, 534 N.E.2d 533 (1st Dist.), *appeal denied*, 126 Ill.2d 566, 133 Ill.Dec. 677, 541 N.E.2d 1115 (1989) (wife set forth sufficient grounds for granting her a continuance; she was emotionally unable to attend the trial, she had shown due diligence in proceeding with the litigation, and husband's failure to comply with discovery requests forced wife to call former counsel to testify concerning important financial matters, and former counsel was unable to appear until a later date); People ex rel. Schejbal v. Kanner, 54 Ill.App.2d 208, 203 N.E.2d 759 (1st Dist.1964) (court abused its discretion in refusing to grant defendant's motion for continuance after plaintiff terminated agreement between the parties to postpone discovery on the day before the trial was scheduled to begin).

(2) **Continuance subpoenas.** Orders that continue trial dates should include provisions that all previously served subpoenas and 237 Notices compelling appearance of witnesses are continued to the new trial date, in order to obviate the necessity of reserving those documents. The witnesses of course should be notified, preferably by sending them a copy of the order.

Rule 236. Admission of business records in evidence.

(a) Any writing or record, whether in the form of any entry in a book or otherwise, made as a memorandum or record of any act, transaction, occurrence, or event, shall be admissible as evidence of the act, transaction, occurrence, or event, if made in the regular course of any business, and if it was the regular course of the business to make such a memorandum or record at the time of such an act, transaction, occurrence, or event or within a reasonable time thereafter. All other circumstances of the making of the writing or record, including lack of personal knowledge by the entrant or maker, may be shown to affect its weight, but shall not affect its admissibility. The term "business," as used in this rule, includes business, profession, occupation, and calling of every kind.

(b) Although police accident reports may otherwise be admissible in evidence under the law, subsection (a) of this rule does not allow such

S. Ct. Rule 236   PROCEDURE

writings to be admitted as a record or memorandum made in the regular course of business.

Author's Notes

Analysis

1. Hearsay exception.
2. Foundation.
3. Medical records.
4. Police reports.

(1) **Hearsay exception.** Business records are admissible in evidence after a proper foundation has been made as an exception to the hearsay rule pursuant to Supreme Court Rule 236.

(2) **Foundation.** The proper foundation is made by the testimony of the custodian of the records, under whose supervision and control the business records have been made. The custodian must identify the records and testify that the records were made by a person within the business with personal knowledge, under his supervision and control, in the regular course of business, either at the time of the act or transaction or within a reasonable time thereafter. Michael H. Graham, *Cleary & Graham's Handbook of Illinois Evidence* § 803.10 (6th ed. 1994).

(3) **Medical records.** The Supreme Court amended Supreme Court Rule 236(b) to eliminate the medical records exclusion, thereby making medical records admissible in civil proceedings as business records, effective August 1, 1992. See Michael H. Graham, *Cleary & Graham's Handbook of Illinois Evidence* § 803.11 (6th ed. 1994).

(4) **Police reports.** Police reports are not admissible under the business records exception to the hearsay rule in civil cases. Michael H. Graham, *Cleary & Graham's Handbook of Illinois Evidence* § 803.13 (6th ed. 1994).

Rule 237. Compelling appearance of witnesses at trial

(a) Service of subpoenas. Any witness shall respond to any lawful subpoena of which he has actual knowledge, if payment of the fee and mileage has been tendered. Service of a subpoena by mail may be proved prima facie by a return receipt showing delivery to the witness or his authorized agent by certified or registered mail at least 7 days before the date on which appearance is required and an affidavit showing that the mailing was prepaid and was addressed to the witness, restricted delivery, with a check or money order for the fee and mileage enclosed.

(b) Notice to parties, et al. The appearance at the trial of a party or a person who at the time of trial is an officer, director, or employee of a party may be required by serving the party with a notice designating the person who is required to appear. The notice also may require the production at the trial of documents or tangible things. If the party or person is a nonresident of the county, the court may order any terms and conditions in connection with his appearance at the trial that are just, including payment of his reasonable expenses. Upon a failure to comply with the notice, the court may addressed and mailed with first class postage prepaid, [ ]sent via messenger, [ ]sent via facsimile (__ pages, from the office of _____, sender's facsimile number _____, to recipient's facsimile number _____), to the party at the address set forth above on the __ day of _____, 199__, before the hour of 5:00 p.m.

_____   _____
(Signature)   (Print Name)

Richard Vholes
Address
Telephone Number

Rule 238. Impeachment of witnesses—Hostile witnesses

(a) The credibility of a witness may be attacked by any party, including the party calling him.

(b) If the court determines that a witness is hostile or unwilling, he may be examined by the party calling him as if under cross-examination.

Author's Notes

Analysis

1. Voucher rule.
2. § 1102 of the Civil Practice Act.

(1) **Voucher rule.** Pursuant to the common law voucher rule a party vouched for the truthfulness of a witness she called, and she could not impeach him. Amended Supreme Court Rule 238 (effective April 1, 1982) abolished the common law voucher rule and permits impeachment of a witness by the party calling him. Rule 238(a). Whether surprise and affirmative damage to the party calling the witness is required before prior inconsistent statements can be introduced to impeach a party's own witness is still not clearly decided. Michael H. Graham, *Cleary & Graham's Handbook of Illinois Evidence* § 607.4 (6th ed. 1994).

(2) **§ 1102 of the Civil Practice Act.** 735 ILCS 5/2–1102 permits examination as if under cross-examination and impeachment by prior inconsistent statements of adverse parties who are called as witnesses. Pursuant to Supreme Court Rule 238(b) the court must first determine that a witness is hostile or unwilling before he may be examined as if under cross-examination.

Rule 272. When judgment is entered

If at the time of announcing final judgment the judge requires the submission of a form of written judgment to be signed by the judge or if a circuit court rule requires the prevailing party to submit a draft order, the clerk shall make a notation to that effect and the judgment becomes final only when the signed judgment is filed. If no such signed written judgment is to be filed, the judge or clerk shall forthwith make a notation of judgment and enter the judgment of record promptly, and the judgment is entered at the time it is entered of record.

Rule 296. Enforcement of order for support

(a) Scope of rule. This rule applies to any proceeding in which a temporary, final, or modified order of support is entered as provided by law. No provision of this rule affects the enforcement provisions of section 706.1 of the Illinois Marriage and Dissolution of Marriage Act (Ill.Rev.Stat. 1987, ch. 40, par. 706.1).

(b) Definitions. For the purposes of this rule:

(1) "Order for Support" means any order of the court which provides for the periodic payment of funds for the support of a child, maintenance of a spouse, or combination thereof, whether temporary, final, or modified;

(2) "Obligor" means the individual who owes a duty to make payments under an Order for Support;

(3) "Obligee" means the individual to whom a duty of support is owed or the individual's legal representative;

(4) "Payor" means any payor of income to an obligor.

(c) Payments to the clerk. All payments required under all Orders for Support must be made to the clerk of the circuit court in the county in which the Order for Support was entered, or the clerk of the circuit court of any other county to which the payment obligation may be transferred, as provided by law. This requirement may not be waived by the court or parties.

(d) Order for support. Whenever an Order for Support is to be entered or modified, the court, in addition to any other requirements of law, shall forthwith enter an Order for Support in quadruplicate, in substantially the form set forth in paragraph (o). The prevailing party must complete the form order and present it to the court for the judge's signature.

(e) Notice of financial aid. The parties and counsel in any proceeding involving support must advise the court at the time of entry or modification of the order whether either the obligor or obligee or their children are receiving a grant of financial aid or support services under articles III through VII, or section 10-1, of the Illinois Public Aid Code, as amended (Ill.Rev.Stat. 1987, ch. 23, par. 3-1 et seq.; par. 10-1), and the court must enter its findings of record.

(f) Petition for abatement. Upon written petition of the obligor, and after due notice to obligee (and the Department of Public Aid, if the obligee is receiving public aid), and upon hearing by the court, the court may temporarily reduce or totally abate the payments of support, subject to the understanding that those payments will continue to accrue as they come due, to be paid at a later time. The reduction or abatement may not exceed a period of six months except that, upon further written petition of the obligor, notice to the obligee, and hearing, the reduction or abatement may be continued for an additional period not to exceed six months.

(g) Clerk's fund, records and disbursements. The clerks of the circuit courts receiving payments pursuant to orders for support under paragraph (c) of this rule shall maintain records of:

   (1) all such monies received and disbursed, and

   (2) any delinquencies on such payments as required by law and by administrative order of the Supreme Court of Illinois.

Such records are admissible as evidence of payments received and disbursed. After receiving a payment pursuant to an Order for Support, the clerk shall promptly deposit that payment and issue a check drawn on an account of the circuit clerk to the obligee or other person or agency entitled thereto under the terms of the Order for Support. All payments shall be disbursed within seven days after receipt thereof by the clerk of the circuit court.

(h) Method of payment to the clerk of the circuit court. When local circuit court rules allow payment of Orders for Support by personal check and the obligor submits a personal check which is not honored by the institution upon which it is drawn, the clerk of the circuit court may direct that all future payments be made by certified check, money order, United States currency, or credit card (with statutory fee), unless otherwise ordered by the court, and the court may order obligor to pay $50 to defray the cost of processing the dishonored check, to be paid within a time period to be determined by the court. Notice of future nonacceptance of personal checks shall be sent by the clerk of the circuit court to the obligor or payor by regular mail at the obligor's or payor's last known mailing address. The clerk's proof of mailing shall be spread of record. If a personal check used in payment of an Order for Support is not honored at the institution upon which it is drawn, the clerk of the circuit court shall forthwith notify the State's Attorney of the county, the Attorney General, if that office has the duty of enforcing the Order for Support on which the check was written, or the attorney appointed pursuant to section (k) of this rule.

(i) Clerk's notice of delinquency. Whenever an obligor is 14 days delinquent in payments pursuant to an Order for Support, the clerk of the circuit court shall, within 72 hours thereof, transmit a notice of delinquency directed to the obligor at the obligor's last known mailing address, by regular U.S. mail, postage prepaid, specifying that the delinquency will be referred for enforcement unless the payments due and owing, together with all subsequently accruing payments, are paid within seven days thereafter. The court may waive this notice requirement on a case-by-case basis, and direct that immediate enforcement commence against the obligor.

(j) Referral for enforcement. If the delinquency and all subsequent accrued obligations are not paid within the time period as specified in paragraph (i) of this rule, the clerk of the circuit court shall promptly refer the matter for enforcement by reporting the delinquency to the State's Attorney of the county, the Title IV–D enforcement attorney, or the attorney appointed by the court pursuant to paragraph (k) of this rule. The clerk of the circuit court may complete, sign, and verify the petition for contempt and appropriate notices, under the supervision of the enforcement counsel, but is not required to provide investigative services unless otherwise required by local circuit court rules.

(k) Enforcement counsel.

(1) Enforcement counsel for those receiving a grant of financial aid under article IV of the Illinois Public Aid Code and parties who apply and qualify for support services pursuant to section 10-1 of such code shall be as designated by an agreement made between the State of Illinois and United States government under 42 U.S. C. Title IV, part D.

(2) The State's Attorney of each county may prosecute any criminal contempt or civil contempt brought for the enforcement of an Order for Support if not in conflict with the agreement described above between the State of Illinois and the United States government.

(3) When the presiding judge of the county or of the domestic relations division of Orders for Support under this rule, the presiding judge shall appoint counsel, to be known as support enforcement counsel, on a contract basis. The fees and expenses of the support enforcement counsel shall be paid by the county. The court may assess attorney fees against an obligor found in contempt.

(4) If the counsel responsible for enforcement under the Illinois Department of Public Aid or the State's Attorney of a county does not commence enforcement within 30 days after referral by the clerk of the circuit court, the court shall refer the matter to the support enforcement counsel of the county for further proceedings.

(5) Representation by counsel under this rule shall be limited to enforcement of Orders for Support and shall not include matters of visitation, custody, or property.

(6) A person entitled to monies under an Order for Support may institute independent enforcement proceedings. However, if enforcement proceedings under paragraph (k) of this rule are pending, then independent enforcement proceedings may be brought only by leave of court.

(*l*) Contempt proceedings for enforcement of orders for support. A failure to comply with payment obligations under an Order for Support may be enforced by contempt in the following manner:

(1) Petition for adjudication of contempt. The proceeding shall be initiated by the filing of a petition for adjudication of contempt in an action where an Order for Support was entered or as otherwise provided by law. The petition shall be verified pursuant to section 1-109 of the Code of Civil Procedure, as amended (Ill.Rev.Stat. 1987, ch. 110, par. 1-109), and specify in both its caption and body whether the relief sought is for indirect criminal contempt, indirect civil contempt, or both. The petition shall identify the relevant terms of the Order for Support being enforced, the court, and date of its entry, the last payment made under its

provisions, the delinquency, and an allegation that the respondent obligor's failure to comply with the provision of the Order for Support constitutes willful indirect civil contempt, indirect criminal contempt, or both. A petition for adjudication of indirect civil contempt and indirect criminal contempt shall be filed in the same cause of action out of which the contempt arose.

(2) Notice of hearing. A petition for adjudication of civil contempt may be presented *ex parte* to the court, which, if satisfied that *prima facie* evidence of civil contempt exists, may order the respondent to show cause why he should not be held in contempt, or may instead set the petition itself for hearing and order that notice be given to the respondent. Notice of hearing on a petition for indirect civil contempt may be served by regular mail, postage prepaid, to the respondent's last known mailing address, or by any method provided in Rule 105(b)(1) or (b)(2) (107 Ill. 2d Rules 105(b)(1), (b)(2)), as the court may direct. Notice by personal service shall be served not less than seven days prior to hearing, and notice by mail not less than 10 days prior to hearing. Upon petition for adjudication of indirect criminal contempt being presented to the court, the court shall set the matter for arraignment and order summons to issue for respondent.

(A) Body attachment. If a respondent fails to appear after receiving notice, or if the petition for adjudication of contempt alleges facts to show that the respondent will not respond to a notice, will flee the jurisdiction of the court, or will attempt to conceal himself from service, the court may issue a body attachment on the respondent, addressed to all law enforcement officers in the State or, in proceedings for indirect criminal contempt, for the arrest of the respondent.

(B) Bond. The court may fix bond on the body attachment order or warrant of arrest, as the case may be.

(3) Contempt hearing. If the petition prays that respondent be held in indirect criminal contempt, or both indirect criminal contempt and indirect civil contempt, the hearing shall be conducted according to the applicable rules of the criminal law. However, if the court at the time of respondent's first appearance notifies the respondent that, if found to be in indirect criminal contempt, he will not be incarcerated for more than six months, fined a sum up to $500, or both, then respondent will not be entitled to a trial by jury. At the contempt hearing, a certified copy of the records of the clerk of the circuit court shall be received in evidence to show the amounts paid to the clerk, the dates of such payments, and the dates and amounts of disbursals. In indirect civil contempt cases the respondent has the burden of proving that such failure to pay was not wilful and that he does not have the present means to comply with any purge order the court may impose. The burden of proof shall be by a preponderance of the evidence in a civil contempt proceeding and beyond

a reasonable doubt in a criminal contempt proceeding. After hearing, the court may:

>(A) find in favor of the respondent and dismiss the petition or discharge the rule, as the case may be;

>(B) continue the hearing under such terms as the court deems appropriate, including an order to seek work, if unemployed;

>(C) find in favor of the petitioner and impose sanctions specifically including, but not limited to, the following:

>>(i) a direction to seek employment, if unemployed, and to participate in job search, training and work programs as provided by law;

>>(ii) keep a detailed accounting of all income and expenditures and submit same to the court until further order;

>>(iii) impose a sentence of imprisonment or periodic imprisonment with an appropriate purge order;

>>(iv) assess a fine;

>>(v) assess attorney fees and costs;

>>(vi) initiate immediate wage withholding; or

>>(vii) such other sanctions as the court deems appropriate.

(m) Supervision by the Administrative Office of the Illinois Courts. The Administrative Office of the Illinois Courts shall exercise supervision over the operation of this rule and shall submit an annual report to the Supreme Court together with its recommendation for any modification or amendment thereto. Oversight shall include, but not be limited to, promulgating forms necessary to carry out the intent and purpose of this rule, initiating administrative procedures and standards for the effective operation of the rule, providing liaison between the various agencies of State and Federal government concerning enforcement of Orders for Support and between the various branches of State government, and such other duties as may be directed by the Supreme Court from time to time hereafter.

(n) Effective date. The Supreme Court will authorize experimental sites to operate pursuant to this rule, in counties in which both the chief circuit judge and the clerk of the circuit court have agreed to undertake the experimental use of the procedures contained herein, and have jointly sought the Court's permission to do so, by filing a petition with the Administrative Director.

(o) Order for support form. The Order for Support shall be in substantially the following form:

ILLINOIS S. CT. RULES   S. Ct. Rule 296

In The Circuit Court of the _____ Judicial Circuit
_____ County, Illinois

In re the Marriage of

Petitioner

CASE NO. _____

and

SUPPORT ACCOUNT NO.

Respondent _____

UNIFORM ORDER FOR SUPPORT

File Stamp Here

IT IS HEREBY ORDERED that the Obligor make support payments in the gross sum of $_____ commencing on _____ and a like sum payable [ ] weekly, [ ] bi-weekly, [ ] monthly, [ ] semi-monthly, or [ ] annually thereafter until further order of the court and transmit such payments to the clerk of the circuit court at the following address:

The clerk of the circuit court is directed to deposit all payments received and forward payment to the Obligee or Agency within 7 days.

*Note: If an Order of Protection prohibits disclosure of the address and telephone number of an Obligee, the information then must be kept separate from the Order for Support.

OBLIGOR

FIRST NAME	M.I.	LAST NAME		
RESIDENCE	APT. NO	CITY	STATE	ZIP
BIRTHDATE	SOCIAL SECURITY #	HOME TELEPHONE NUMBER	DRIVER'S LICENSE NUMBER	
PLACE OF EMPLOYMENT (PAYOR)	ADDRESS		PHONE NUMBER	

OBLIGEE

FIRST NAME*	M.I.	LAST NAME		
RESIDENCE	APT. NO	CITY	STATE	ZIP
BIRTHDATE	SOCIAL SECURITY #	HOME TELEPHONE NUMBER		
PLACE OF EMPLOYMENT	ADDRESS		PHONE NUMBER	

PAYMENT

COMPLETE THIS SECTION ONLY IF PAYMENTS ARE TO BE MADE TO A PARTY OTHER THAN THE OBLIGEE

NAME				
ADDRESS		CITY	STATE	ZIP

IDENTIFICATION NO. (If Any)   [G19022]

S. Ct. Rule 296 PROCEDURE

ENFORCEMENT AUTHORITY

☐ Attorney General of Illinois
☐ Illinois Department of Public Aid
☐ State's Attorney _____ County
☐ Private Attorney: _____
☐ Other: _____

Reviewed and approved as to form

Clerk's Support Division

DATE: _____

Page 2 - Order for Support Form

Support Account Number: _____   Case Number: _____

DEFINITIONS: "FREQUENCY"—"Weekly" means every week on the same day (52 or 53 times per year); "Bi-weekly" means every other week on the same day (26 times a year); "Semi-monthly" means two different days of the month 15 days apart (24 times a year); "Monthly" means once each month on the same day (12 times a year); "Annually" means once each year on the same date (1 time a year). "UNALLOCATED SUPPORT" means a total amount for maintenance and child support and not a specific amount for either item. "OBLIGOR" means the party who has the obligation to pay the support or maintenance. "OBLIGEE" means the party who receives the support or maintenance. "PAYOR" means the employer (or bank, trust, etc.) of the Obligor who pays a salary or other monies to the Obligor.

☐	UNALLOCATED SUPPORT Whether support is allocated or unallocated, you must complete the shaded areas	Amount	Start Date	End Date

CHILDREN

First Name	Birth Date	Amount	Start Date	End Date
First Name	Birth Date	Amount	Start Date	End Date
First Name	Birth Date	Amount	Start Date	End Date
First Name	Birth Date	Amount	Start Date	End Date
First Name	Birth Date	Amount	Start Date	End Date

It is further ordered that the Obligor shall:

1) Obey this Order for Support until further order of the court or until modified in writing by the court;

2) Make all payments in the amounts and at the times specified herein;

3) Make all payments to the clerk of the circuit court at the address noted herein. Payments made to any other person may be regarded as a gift and not credited against the amounts due under the Order for Support;

4) Pay the clerk of the circuit court by certified check, personal check, money order, United States currency, or credit card (with statutory fee), unless otherwise ordered by the court. U.S. currency should not be sent through the mail.

5) Notify the clerk of the circuit court in writing of any change of name, address, employment status or daytime telephone number within 2 weeks of such change.

[G19023]

FAILURE TO OBEY ANY OF THE PROVISIONS OF THIS ORDER FOR SUPPORT, OR MAKING A PAYMENT BY PERSONAL CHECK WHICH IS NOT HONORED BY THE INSTITUTION ON WHICH IT IS WRITTEN, MAY SUBJECT OBLIGOR TO CONTEMPT OF COURT AND A POSSIBLE JAIL SENTENCE.

NOTICE TO OBLIGEE: You are directed to notify the clerk of the circuit court in writing of any change of name or address within 2 weeks thereof.

NOTICE TO OBLIGOR: If there is a major change of conditions and you are unable to make a payment in the amount and time required, you may petition the court for modification of this order for support or you may petition the court for temporary abatement of the payments, setting forth the reasons in the petition. The petition will be set for hearing and you and the obligee will be given notice by mail. If the support payments are temporarily abated, the amount will continue to accrue and you will be required to repay those amounts at some future date.

Enter: _____   _____
            Date   Judge

Clerk's Certificate of Mailing/Delivery

I, the clerk of the circuit court, certify that I: mailed a copy of this Order for Support to [ ] Obligor, [ ] Obligee [ ] Illinois Department of Public Aid by enclosing the same in an envelope addressed to said addressees with postage prepaid and deposited said envelope in a U.S. Postal Service Mail Box on the _____ day of _____, 19___
           date   month   year
or I hand delivered a true copy to [ ] Obligor on the _____ day of _____, 19___
and/or I delivered a true copy to [ ] Obligee on the _____ day of _____, 19___

[G19024]

Author's Notes

Analysis

1. Separate system.
2. Counties of operation.
3. Cross reference.

(1) **Separate system.** Supreme Court Rule 296 is separate from other support enforcement programs, such as Supreme Court Rules 100.1 et seq. The key difference is that the clerk of the court pursuant to Supreme Court Rule 296(i) and (j) initiates the enforcement action and prepares the petition for contempt, rather than the State's Attorney as in other enforcement programs.

(2) **Counties of operation.** The enforcement program under Supreme Court Rule 296 is currently operating in only four downstate counties.

(3) **Cross reference.** See also Expedited child support rules, Supreme Court Rule 100.1 et seq. and accompanying Author's Notes, and 750 ILCS 20/1 Author's Note (4) for a list of statutes pursuant to which support can be enforced.

Rule 301. Method of review

Every final judgment of a circuit court in a civil case is appealable as of right. The appeal is initiated by filing a notice of appeal. No other step is jurisdictional. An appeal is a continuation of the proceeding.

Author's Notes

Analysis

1. Jurisdiction of trial and appellate courts upon notice of appeal.
2. Notice of appeal.

3. Cross reference.
4. Finality.

(1) **Jurisdiction of trial and appellate courts upon notice of appeal.** Only the filing of the notice of appeal is jurisdictional. After the notice of appeal is filed, the trial court loses jurisdiction over the issues in the notice of appeal, and the appellate court gains jurisdiction to consider the issues contained in the notice of appeal.

> When a notice of appeal is perfected the trial court loses jurisdiction as to the judgment or part thereof from which the appeal is taken and, as to such matter, the case thereafter proceeds in the appellate court not as a new case but as a continuation of the case in the trial court.... [A] notice of appeal confers jurisdiction on a court of review to consider only the judgments or part thereof specified in the notice of appeal.

Burtell v. First Charter Serv. Corp., 76 Ill.2d 427, 433, 31 Ill.Dec. 178, 180, 394 N.E.2d 380, 382 (1979) (citations omitted).

Once a notice of appeal has been filed and the trial court loses jurisdiction over those matters raised in the notice of appeal, the trial court can act only on those matters that are independent of or collateral to the issues on appeal, or which arise subsequent to entry of the judgment from which the appeal has been taken and which do not have the effect of interfering with review of the judgment. See Dear v. Locke, 128 Ill.App.2d 356, 262 N.E.2d 27 (4th Dist.1970) (allowing trial court to determine visitation where order on appeal concerned custody; visitation was independent of and collateral to the issue of custody); In re Marriage of Giammerino, 94 Ill.App.3d 1058, 50 Ill.Dec. 490, 419 N.E.2d 598 (1st Dist.1981) (trial court had jurisdiction to award prospective attorney's fees to defend pending appeal; such fees necessarily involved an issue that arose after the notice of appeal was filed).

The trial court can enforce the judgment from which the appeal is taken in the absence of the filing of a supersedeas bond, or a stay granted by the trial or appellate court. See In re Marriage of Hilkovitch, 124 Ill.App.3d 401, 425, 79 Ill.Dec. 891, 906, 464 N.E.2d 795, 810 (1st Dist.1984) ("The mere filing of a notice of appeal does not automatically stay the trial judge's jurisdiction over proceedings to enforce the judgment.") (citing Graff v. Graff, 71 Ill.App.3d 496, 503, 27 Ill.Dec. 798, 803, 389 N.E.2d 1206, 1211 (1st Dist.1979)). See also Supreme Court Rule 305.

(2) **Notices of appeal.** See Supreme Court Rule 303 for the contents and form of the Notice of Appeal and the ability to amend a notice of appeal.

(3) **Cross reference.** See 750 ILCS 5/504(c) for maintenance pending appeal, and 750 ILCS 5/508(a)(3) for attorney's fees for the defense of an appeal.

(4) **Finality.** See Supreme Court Rule 272 for the time when a written or oral judgment becomes final. See Supreme Court Rule 304 for appeals from final judgments that dispose of fewer than all of the claims or are judgments for fewer than all of the parties.

Rule 303. Appeals from final judgments of the circuit courts in civil cases

(a) Time; Filing; Transmission of copy.

(1) Except as provided in paragraph (b) below, the notice of appeal must be filed with the clerk of the circuit court within 30 days after the entry of the final judgment appealed from, or, if a timely post-trial motion

directed against the judgment is filed, whether in a jury or a nonjury case, within 30 days after the entry of the order disposing of the last pending post-judgment motion.

(2) When a timely post-judgment motion has been filed by any party, whether in a jury case or a nonjury case, a notice of appeal filed before the entry of the order disposing of the last pending post-judgment motion shall have no effect and shall be withdrawn by the party who filed it, by moving for dismissal pursuant to Rule 309. This is so whether the timely post-judgment motion was filed before or after the date on which the notice of appeal was filed. A new notice of appeal must be filed within the prescribed time measured from the entry of the order disposing of the post-judgment motion, as provided in subparagraph (a)(1) of this rule. No request for reconsideration of a ruling on a post-judgment motion will toll the running of the time within which a notice of appeal must be filed under this rule. A party who filed a premature notice of appeal will not be required to pay a filing fee for a future appeal in the same case if, at the time of filing the future appeal, the party presents the receipt for the fee paid for filing the premature notice of appeal and a copy of the circuit court order dismissing the premature appeal.

(3) If a timely notice of appeal is filed and served by a party, any other party, within 10 days after service upon him or her, or within 30 days from the entry of the judgment or order being appealed, or within 30 days of the entry of the order disposing of the last pending post-trial motion, whichever is later, may join in the appeal, appeal separately, or cross-appeal by filing a notice of appeal, indicating which type of appeal is being taken.

(4) Within five days after the filing of a notice of appeal, or an amendment of a notice of appeal filed in the circuit court pursuant to subparagraph (c)(4) of this rule, the clerk of the circuit court shall transmit to the clerk of the court to which the appeal is being taken a copy of the notice of appeal or of the amendment.

(b) Form and contents of notice of appeal.

(1) The notice of appeal shall be captioned as follows:

(i) At the top shall appear the statement "Appeal to the _____," naming the court to which the appeal is taken, and below this shall be the statement "From the Circuit Court of _____," naming the court from which the appeal is taken.

(ii) It shall bear the title of the case, naming and designating the parties in the same manner as in the circuit court and adding the further designation "appellant" or "appellee," e.g., "Plaintiff–Appellee."

(iii) It shall be designated "Notice of Appeal," "Joining Prior Appeal," "Separate Appeal," or "Cross–Appeal," as appropriate.

(2) It shall specify the judgment or part thereof or other orders appealed from and the relief sought from the reviewing court.

(3) It shall contain the signature and address of each appellant or appellant's attorney.

(4) The notice of appeal may be amended without leave of court within the original 30 day period to file the notice as set forth in paragraph (a) above. Thereafter it may be amended only on motion, in the reviewing court, pursuant to paragraph (d) of this rule. Amendments relate back to the time of the filing of the notice of appeal.

(c) *Service of notice of appeal.* The party filing the notice of appeal or an amendment as of right, shall, within 7 days, file a notice of filing with the reviewing court and serve a copy of the notice of appeal upon every other party and upon any other person or officer entitled by law to notice. Proof of service, as provided by Rule 12, shall be filed with the notice.

(d) *Extension of time in certain circumstances.* On motion supported by a showing of reasonable excuse for failure to file a notice of appeal on time, accompanied by the proposed notice of appeal and the filing fee, filed in the reviewing court within 30 days after expiration of the time for filing a notice of appeal, the reviewing court may grant leave to appeal and order the clerk to transmit the notice of appeal to the trial court for filing.

(e) *Docketing.* Upon receipt of the copy of the notice of appeal transmitted to the reviewing court pursuant to paragraph (a) of this rule, or receipt of a motion for leave to appeal under paragraph (d) of this rule, the clerk of the reviewing court shall enter the appeal upon the docket.

Rule 304. Appeals from final judgments that do not dispose of an entire proceeding

(a) Judgments as to fewer than all parties or claims—Necessity for special finding. If multiple parties or multiple claims for relief are involved in an action, an appeal may be taken from a final judgment as to one or more but fewer than all of the parties or claims only if the trial court has made an express written finding that there is no just reason for delaying either enforcement or appeal or both. Such a finding may be made at the time of the entry of the judgment or thereafter on the court's own motion or on motion of any party. The time for filing the notice of appeal shall be as provided in Rule 303. In computing the time provided in Rule 303 for filing the notice of appeal, the entry of the required finding shall be treated as the date of the entry of final judgment. In the absence of such a finding, any judgment that adjudicates fewer than all the claims or the rights and liabilities of fewer than all the parties is not enforceable or appealable and is subject to revision at any time before the entry of a judgment adjudicating all the claims, rights, and liabilities of all the parties.

(b) Judgments and orders appealable without special finding. The following judgments and orders are appealable without the finding required for appeals under paragraph (a) of this rule:

(1) A judgment or order entered in the administration of an estate, guardianship, or similar proceeding which finally determines a right or status of a party.

(2) A judgment or order entered in the administration of a receivership, rehabilitation, liquidation, or other similar proceeding which finally determines a right or status of a party and which is not appealable under Rule 307(a).

(3) A judgment or order granting or denying any of the relief prayed in a petition under section 2-1401 of the Code of Civil Procedure.

(4) A final judgment or order entered in a proceeding under section 2-1402 of the Code of Civil Procedure.

(5) An order finding a person in contempt of court which imposes a monetary or other penalty.

Author's Notes

Analysis

1. Final judgment.
2. Examples.
3. Cross reference.
4. Appeal of finding of contempt.

(1) **Final judgment.** Generally, judgments that do not decide all of the issues of a case are not final, and therefore are not appealable. "A judgment is final for appeal purposes if it determines the litigation on the merits or some definite part thereof so that, if affirmed, the only thing remaining is to proceed with the execution of the judgment." In re Marriage of Verdung, 126 Ill.2d 542, 553, 129 Ill.Dec. 53, 58, 535 N.E.2d 818, 823 (1989) (citations omitted).

Except as otherwise provided in the Supreme Court Rules, a final judgment as to less than all of the claims or as to fewer than all of the parties is made appealable only by a Rule 304(a) finding that there is no just reason for delaying enforcement or appeal. A valid finding of finality requires substance rather than form: "the trial court cannot make a nonfinal order final and appealable simply by including in its order the requisite 304(a) language." In re Marriage of Young, 244 Ill.App.3d 313, 316, 185 Ill.Dec. 289, 291, 614 N.E.2d 423, 425 (1st Dist.1993).

(2) **Examples.** Judgments are not final and appealable until the court has decided all claims in the dissolution proceeding. The interdependence of issues involved in a dissolution of marriage necessitates concurrent resolution. In re Marriage of Leopando, 96 Ill.2d 114, 70 Ill.Dec. 263, 449 N.E.2d 137 (1983). See, e.g., In re Marriage of Koch, 119 Ill.App.3d 388, 74 Ill.Dec. 923, 456 N.E.2d 644 (2d Dist.1983) (judgment failing to resolve support and maintenance, property distribution and attorney's fees not appealable). See 750 ILCS 5/401 Author's Note (10).

(a) Attorney's fees. Frequently a court adjudicates the dissolution of marriage issues, and reserves a claim for attorney's fees against the party opponent for hearing after the entry of judgment. Such a judgement is not appealable because the issue of attorney's fees is intertwined with other issues in the dissolution proceeding, such as the most equitable property distribution and the need for support. See, e.g., In re Marriage of Derning, 117 Ill.App.3d 620, 72 Ill.Dec. 785, 453 N.E.2d 90 (2d Dist.1983) (judgment reserving question of attorney's fees not appealable).

(b) Temporary orders of support. Temporary orders of support are not appealable.

> A temporary support or maintenance order is nonappealable because it does not constitute a separate claim and is inextricably interrelated to the single claim of dissolution of marriage. Any inequity in a temporary order could be addressed in the trial court either at the hearing for permanent maintenance and division of marital property and debts or on any appeal of the entire case when it is final.... The fact that an order is enforceable ... does not necessarily make it appealable.

In re Marriage of Ryan, 188 Ill.App.3d 679, 136 Ill.Dec. 1, 3, 544 N.E.2d 454, 456 (2d Dist.1989) (citations omitted). See 750 ILCS 5/501 Author's Note (2).

(c) Retirement plans. The Illinois courts have split over the issue of whether a judgment reserving the division of retirement plans is appealable. See, e.g., In re Marriage of Rosenow, 123 Ill.App.3d 546, 78 Ill.Dec. 933, 462 N.E.2d 1287 (4th Dist.1984) (judgment in dissolution reserving apportionment of pension benefits not appealable); but see In re Marriage of Britton, 141 Ill.App.3d 588, 592, 96 Ill.Dec. 43, 45, 490 N.E.2d 1079, 1081 (5th Dist.1986) ("Such a result is unacceptable because it means a judgment might not be appealable for many years if the court decides to reserve the issue until the employee spouse retires.").

(d) Declaratory judgements. Section 2–701(a) of the Code of Civil Procedure, 735 ILCS 5/2–701(a), provides, *inter alia*,

> The court may, in cases of actual controversy, make binding declarations of rights, having the force of *final judgments*, whether or not any consequential relief is or could be claimed, including the determination, at the instance of anyone interested in the controversy, of the construction of any statute, ... or of any ... contract or other written instrument, and a declaration of the rights of the parties interested. (Emphasis supplied.)

Courts have differed over whether the entry of a declaratory judgment that does not dispose of the entire controversy is actually final and appealable. See In re Marriage of Richardson, 237 Ill.App.3d 1067, 179 Ill.Dec. 224, 606 N.E.2d 56 (1st Dist.1992), *appeal denied* sub nom. Richardson v. Richardson, 149 Ill.2d 660, 183 Ill.Dec. 871, 612 N.E.2d 523 (1993) (reviewing declaratory judgment concerning validity of prenuptial agreement which husband alleged was dispositive of all property, maintenance, child custody and support issues in dissolution action). But *Cf.* Lindsey v. Chicago Park District, 134 Ill.App. 3d 744, 89 Ill.Dec. 706, 481 N.E.2d 58 (1st Dist.1985) (declaratory judgment that adjudicated liability but not damages was not appealable even though it contained 304(a) language).

(3) **Cross reference.** See 750 ILCS 5/413 and accompanying Author's Notes for appealability of dissolution judgments.

(4) **Appeal of finding of contempt.** Subsection (b)(5) of Supreme Court Rule 304 allows an appeal of an order finding a person in contempt of court which imposes a monetary or other penalty without a Rule 304(a) special finding. Rule 304(b)(5) became effective February 1, 1994.

Rule 305. Stay of judgments pending appeal

(a) *Stay of enforcement of money judgments.* The enforcement of a judgment for money only, or any portion of a judgment which is for money, is stayed only if a timely notice of appeal is filed and an appeal bond is presented, approved, and filed within the time for filing the notice of appeal or within any extension of time granted under paragraph (c) of this rule. Notice of the presentment of the bond shall be given to the appellee. The bond shall be in an amount sufficient to cover the amount of the judgment, interest and costs.

(b) *Other stays of enforcements of judgments and appealable orders.* On notice and motion, and an opportunity for opposing parties to be heard, the court may stay the enforcement of any judgment, or the enforcement, force and effect of interlocutory orders or any other judicial or administrative order. The stay shall be conditioned upon such terms as are just. A bond may be required in any case, and shall be required in money judgments or to protect an appellee's interest in property.

(c) *Extensions of time.* On motion made within the time for filing the notice of appeal or within any extension granted pursuant to this paragraph, the time for the filing and approval of the bond may be extended by the trial court or by the reviewing court or a judge thereof, but the extensions of time granted by the trial court may not aggregate more than 45 days unless the parties stipulate otherwise. A motion in the reviewing court for any extension of time for the filing and approval of the bond in the trial court must be supported by affidavit and accompanied by a supporting record (Rule 328), if the record on appeal has not been filed.

(d) *Stays by the reviewing court.* Application for a stay ordinarily must be made in the first instance to the trial court. A motion for a stay may be made to the reviewing court, or to a judge thereof, but such a motion must show that application to the trial court is not practical, or that the trial court has denied an application or has failed to afford the relief that the applicant has requested, and must be accompanied by suggestions in support of the motion and a supporting record (Rule 328), if the record on appeal has not been filed. If a stay is granted by the reviewing court or a judge thereof, the clerk shall notify the parties and transmit to the clerk of the trial court or administrative agency a certified copy of the order granting the stay.

(e) *When notice of appeal is amended.* If a notice of appeal is amended to specify parts of the judgment not specified in the original notice of appeal, the stay of the judgment described in the original notice of appeal does not extend to any added part of the judgment, but a stay of the added part may be obtained under the same conditions and by the same procedure set forth in paragraphs (a) and (b) of this rule.

(f) *Condition of the bond.* If an appeal is from a judgment for money, the condition of the bond shall be for the prosecution of the appeal and the payment of the judgment, interest, damages, and costs in case the judgment is affirmed or the appeal dismissed, except that the bond of an executor or administrator shall be conditioned upon payment in due course of administration and that the bond of a guardian for a minor or a person under legal disability shall be conditioned on payment as he has funds therefor. In all other cases, the condition shall be fixed with reference to the character of the judgment.

(g) Changing the amount, terms, and security of the bond after the appeal is docketed. After the case is docketed in the reviewing court, that court or a judge thereof upon motion may change the amount, terms, or security of the bond, whether fixed by it or by the trial court, and failure to comply with the order of the reviewing court or judge shall terminate the stay.

(h) Appeals by public agencies. If an appeal is prosecuted by a public, municipal, governmental, or quasi-municipal corporation, or by a public officer in his official capacity for the benefit of the public, the trial court, or the reviewing court or a judge thereof, may stay the judgment pending appeal without requiring that any bond be given.

(i) Insurance policy as bond. The filing of an insurance policy pursuant to section 392.1 of the Illinois Insurance Code (215 ILCS 5/392.1 (West 1992)) shall be considered the filing of a bond for purposes of this rule.

(j) Failure to obtain stay; Effect on interests in property. If a stay is not perfected within the time for filing the notice of appeal, or within any extension of time granted under subparagraph (c) of this rule, the reversal or modification of the judgment does not affect the right, title, or interest of any person who is not a party to the action in or to any real or personal property that is acquired after the judgment becomes final and before the judgment is stayed; nor shall the reversal or modification affect any right of any person who is not a party to the action under or by virtue of any certificate of sale issued pursuant to a sale based on the judgment and before the judgment is stayed. This paragraph applies even if the appellant is a minor or a person under legal disability or under duress at the time the judgment becomes final.

(k) Land trust bond. The filing of a bond by a beneficiary under a land trust where the land trust is a party shall be considered filing of a bond for purposes of this rule.

Rule 306. Appeals from orders of the circuit court granting new trials and granting or denying certain motions

(a) Orders appealable by petition. A party may petition for leave to appeal to the Appellate Court from the following orders of the trial court:

* * *

(5) from interlocutory orders affecting the care and custody of unemancipated minors, if the appeal of such orders is not otherwise specifically provided for elsewhere in these rules....

* * *

(b) Petition. The petition shall contain a statement of the facts of the case, supported by reference to the supporting record, and of the grounds for the appeal. An original and three copies of the petition (or original and five copies in workers' compensation cases) arising under Rule 22(g) shall be filed in the Appellate Court in accordance with the requirements for briefs within 30 days after the entry of the order. A supporting record conforming to the requirements of Rule 328 shall be filed with the petition.

(c) Answer. Any other party may file an original and three copies of an answer (or original and five copies in workers' compensation cases) arising under Rule 22(g) within 21 days of the filing of the petition, together with a supplementary supporting record conforming to Rule 328 consisting of any additional parts of the record the party desires to have considered by the Appellate Court. No reply will be received except by leave of court or a judge thereof.

(d) Appendix to petition; Abstract. The petition shall include, as an appendix, a copy of the order appealed from, and of any opinion, memorandum, or findings of fact entered by the trial judge, and a table of contents of the record on appeal in the form provided in Rule 342(a). If the Appellate Court orders that an abstract of the record be filed, it shall be in the form set forth in Rule 342(b) and shall be filed within the time fixed in the order.

(e) Extensions of time. The above time limits may be extended by the reviewing court of a judge thereof upon notice and motion, accompanied by an affidavit showing good cause, filed before expiration of the original or extended time.

(f) Stay; Notice of allowance of petition. If the petition is granted, the proceedings in the trial court are stayed. Upon good cause shown, the Appellate Court or a judge thereof may require the petitioner to file an appropriate bond. Within 48 hours after the granting of the petition, the clerk shall send notice thereof to the clerk of the circuit court.

(g) Additional record. If leave to appeal is allowed, any party to the appeal may request that additional portions of the record on appeal be prepared as provided in Rule 321 et seq., or the court may order the appellant to file the record, which shall be filed within 35 days of the date on which such leave was allowed. The filing of an additional record shall not affect the time for filing briefs under this rule.

(h) Briefs. A party may allow his or her petition or answer to stand as his or her brief or may file a further brief in lieu of or in addition thereto. If a party elects to allow a petition or answer to stand as a brief, he or she must notify the other parties and the Clerk of the Appellate Court on or before the due date of the brief and supply the court with the requisite number of briefs required by Rule 344. If the appellant elects to file a further brief, it must be filed within 35 days from the date on which leave to appeal was granted. The appellant's brief, and other briefs if filed, shall conform to the schedule and requirements as provided in Rules 341 through 344. Oral argument may be requested as provided in Rule 352(a).

Rule 307. Interlocutory appeals as of right

(a) *Orders appealable; Time.* An appeal may be taken to the Appellate Court from an interlocutory order of court

   (1) granting, modifying, refusing, dissolving, or refusing to dissolve or modify an injunction;

   (2) appointing or refusing to appoint a receiver or sequestrator;

   (3) giving or refusing to give other or further powers or property to a receiver or sequestrator already appointed;

* * *

   (6) terminating parental rights or granting, denying or revoking temporary commitment in adoption cases;

* * *

Except as provided in paragraph (b), the appeal must be perfected within 30 days from the entry of the interlocutory order by filing a notice of appeal designated "Notice of Interlocutory Appeal" conforming substantially to the notice of appeal in other cases. The record must be filed in the Appellate Court within the same 30 days unless the time for filing the record is extended by the Appellate Court or any judge thereof.

(b) *Motion to vacate.* If an interlocutory order is entered on *ex parte* application, the party intending to take an appeal therefrom shall first present, on notice, a motion to the trial court to vacate the order. An appeal may be taken if the motion is denied, or if the court does not act thereon within 7 days after its presentation. The 30 days allowed for taking an appeal and filing the record begins to run from the day the motion is denied or from the last day for action thereon.

(c) *Time for briefs and abstract if an abstract is required.* Unless the Appellate Court orders a different schedule or orders that no briefs be filed, the schedule for filing briefs shall be as follows: The brief of appellant shall be filed in the Appellate Court, with proof of service, within 7 days from the filing of the record on appeal. Within 7 days from the date appellant's brief is filed, the appellee shall file his brief in the Appellate Court with proof of service. Within 7 days from the date appellee's brief is filed, appellant may serve and file a reply brief. The briefs shall otherwise conform to the requirements of Rules 341 through 344. If the Appellate Court so orders, an abstract shall be prepared and filed as provided in Rule 342.

(d) *Appeals of temporary restraining orders; Time; Memoranda.*

   (1) *Petition; Service; Record.* Unless another form is ordered by the Appellate Court, review of the granting or denial of a temporary restraining order as authorized in paragraph (a) shall be by petition filed in the Appellate Court, but notice of interlocutory appeal as provided in paragraph (a) shall also be filed, within the same time for filing the petition. The petition shall be in writing, state the relief requested and

the grounds for the relief requested, and shall be filed in the Appellate Court, with proof of personal service, within two days of the entry or denial of the temporary restraining order from which review is being sought. An appropriate supporting record shall accompany the petition, which shall include the notice of interlocutory appeal, the temporary restraining order or the proposed temporary restraining order, the complaint, the motion requesting the granting of the temporary restraining order, and any supporting documents or matters of record necessary to the petition. The supporting record must be authenticated by the certificate of the clerk of the trial court or by the affidavit of the attorney or party filing it.

(2) Legal memoranda. The petitioner may file a memorandum supporting the petition which shall not exceed 15 typewritten pages and which must also be filed within two days of the entry or denial of the temporary restraining order. The respondent shall file, with proof of personal service, any responding memorandum within two days following the filing of the petition, supporting record, and any memorandum which must be personally served upon the respondent. The respondent's memorandum may not exceed 15 typewritten pages and must also be personally served upon the petitioner.

(3) Replies; Extensions of time. Except by order of court, no replies will be allowed and no extension of time will be allowed.

(4) Time for decision; Oral argument. After the petitioner has filed the petition, supporting record, and any memorandum and the time for filing any responding memorandum has expired, the Appellate Court shall consider and decide the petition within two days thereafter. Oral argument on the petition will not be heard.

(5) Variations by order of court. The Appellate Court may, if it deems it appropriate, order a different schedule, or order that no memoranda be filed, or order the other materials need not be filed.

(e) Appeals from denials of waiver of parental notice under the parental notice of Abortion Act of 1983.

(1) Petition; Service; Record. Unless another form is ordered by the Appellate Court, review of the denial of a waiver of parental notice as authorized in paragraph (a) shall be by petition filed in the Appellate Court, but notice of interlocutory appeal as provided in paragraph (a) shall also be filed, within the same time for filing the petition. The petition shall be prepared and filed in accordance with the provision of subparagraph (d)(1). An appropriate supporting record shall accompany the petition which shall include the notice of interlocutory appeal; the pleadings filed in the circuit court, if any; the decision of the circuit court including the specific findings of facts and legal conclusions supporting the decision; and any supporting documents of record the petition may offer. The supporting record may be authenticated by the certificate of

the clerk of the trial court or by the affidavit of an attorney or party filing it.

(2) Statement of facts and memoranda of law. The minor or incompetent petitioner may file a brief statement of facts and a short memorandum of law supporting her petition which may be filed win lieu of a brief and abstract and shall be filed within two days of the denial of the waiver of parental notice. Any respondent that desires to do so may file, with proof of personal service, any responding memorandum within two days following the filing of the petition, supporting record, and any memorandum which the minor or incompetent petitioner files and serves on respondent of record. Respondent's memorandum may not exceed 15 typewritten pages and must also be personally served upon the petitioner.

(3) Replies; Extensions of time. Except by order of court, no replies will be allowed and no extension of time will be allowed.

(4) Time for decision; Oral argument. After the petitioner has filed the petition, supporting record, and any memorandum and the time for filing any responding memorandum has expired, the Appellate Court shall consider and decide the petition within two days thereafter. Oral argument on the petition will not be heard.

(5) Variations by order of court. The Appellate Court may, if it deems it appropriate, order a different schedule, or order that no memoranda be filed, or order the other materials need not be filed.

(6) The minor or incompetent petitioner may appear, file her notice of appeal and her petition using only her initials or pseudonym. However, if she does not use her own name, she shall provide the Clerk of the Appellate Court with a name, telephone number and address where she can be reached to be informed of the time and place of any hearings and the decision of the court.

(7) The Appellate Court shall appoint counsel to assist the minor or incompetent petitioner if she so requests or the Appellate Court deems it appropriate or necessary.

(8) All Appellate Court records pursuant to this appeal shall be sealed as confidential. Inspection and copying of any court records relating to these proceedings and the minor who is subject of any proceedings shall not be available to the public and shall be restricted to the following:

(i) the minor who is the subject of the record, her counsel and/or guardian ad litem, and

(ii) judges, social workers or other individuals whom the court may find necessary to assist in this appeal.

(9) Any further appeals may be taken in a manner similar to that provided herein and in accordance with Supreme Court Rules 315, 316 or 317, and 318.

Rule 308. Interlocutory appeals by permission

(a) Requests. When the trial court, in making an interlocutory order not otherwise appealable, finds that the order involves a question of law as to which there is substantial ground for difference of opinion and that an immediate appeal from the order may materially advance the ultimate termination of the litigation, the court shall so state in writing, identifying the question of law involved. Such a statement may be made at the time of the entry of the order or thereafter on the court's own motion or on motion of any party. The Appellate Court may thereupon in its discretion allow an appeal from the order.

(b) How sought. The appeal will be sought by filing an application for leave to appeal with the clerk of the Appellate Court within 14 days after the entry of the order in the trial court or the making of the prescribed statement by the trial court, whichever is later. An original and 3 copies of the application shall be filed.

(c) Application; Answer. The application shall contain a statement of the facts necessary to an understanding of the question of law determined by the order of the trial court; a statement of the question itself; and a statement of the reasons why a substantial basis exists for a difference of opinion on the question and why an immediate appeal may materially advance the termination of the litigation. The application shall be accompanied by an original supporting record (Rule 328), containing the order appealed from and of the other parts of the trial court record necessary for the determination of the application for permission to appeal. Within 14 days after the due date of the application, an adverse party may file an answer in opposition, with copies in the number required for the application, together with an original of a supplementary supporting record containing any additional parts of the record the adverse party desires to have considered by the Appellate Court. The application and answer shall be submitted without oral argument unless otherwise ordered.

(d) Record; Briefs. If leave to appeal is allowed, any party may request that an additional record on appeal be prepared as provided in Rule 321 et seq., or the court may order the appellant to file the record, which shall be filed within 35 days of the date on which such leave was allowed. The appellant shall file a brief in the reviewing court within the same 35 days. Otherwise the schedule and requirements for briefs shall be as provided in Rules 341 through 344. If the reviewing court so orders, an abstract shall be prepared and filed as provided in Rule 342.

(e) Stay. The application for permission to appeal or the granting thereof shall not stay proceedings in the trial court unless the trial court or the Appellate Court or a judge thereof shall so order.

Rule 311. Accelerated docket

Any time after the docketing statement is filed in the reviewing court, the court, on its own motion, or on the motion of any party, for good cause shown,

S. Ct. Rule 311   PROCEDURE

may place the case on an accelerated docket. The motion shall be supported by an affidavit stating reasons why the appeal should be expedited. If warranted by the circumstances, the court may enter an order accepting a supporting record prepared pursuant to Rule 328, consisting of those lower court pleadings, reports of proceedings or other materials that will fully present the issues. In its discretion the court may accept memoranda in lieu of formal briefs. The court may then enter an order setting forth an expedited schedule for the disposition of the appeal.

Rule 312. Docketing statement

(a) Appellant's docketing statement. All appellants, including cross-appellants and separate appellants, whether as a matter of right or as a matter of the court's discretion, shall file a docketing statement with the clerk of the reviewing court. In the case of an appeal as of right, the appellant shall file the statement within 14 days after filing the notice of appeal or petition for review of an administrative order or the date upon which a motion to file late notice of appeal is allowed. In the case of a discretionary appeal pursuant to Rule 306 or Rule 308, the statement shall be due at the time that the appellant files his or her Rule 306 petition or Rule 308 application. In cases of appeal pursuant to Rule 307(a), the docketing statement shall be filed within 7 days from the filing of the notice of appeal. The docketing statement shall be accompanied by the required reviewing court filing fee if it has not been previously paid. The docketing statement shall be accompanied by any written requests to the circuit clerk or court reporter for preparation of their respective portions of the record on appeal and be served on all parties to the case with proof of service attached. Within 7 days thereafter, appellee, if it is deemed necessary, may file a short responsive statement with the clerk of the reviewing court with proof of service on all parties.

The form and contents of the docketing statement shall be as follows:

Docket Number in the Reviewing Court

Case Title (Complete)) Appeal from _____ County
) Circuit Number _____
) Trial Judge _____
) Date of Notice of Appeal _____
) Date of Judgment _____
) Date of Post–Judgment Motion Order

DOCKETING STATEMENT
(Civil)

1. Is this a cross-appeal, separate appeal, joining in a prior appeal, or related to another appeal which is currently pending or which has been disposed of by this court? _____

If so, state the docket number(s) of the other appeal(s): _____

2. If any party is a corporation or association, identify any affiliate, subsidiary, or parent group: _____

3. Full name of appellant(s) filing this statement:

_____

Counsel on Appeal
For appellant(s) filing this statement
    Name: _____
    Address: _____
    Telephone: _____
    Fax: _____
Trial counsel, if different
    Name: _____
    Address: _____
    Telephone: _____

4. Counsel on Appeal
For appellee(s) (if there are multiple appellees represented by different counsel, identify separately)
    Name: _____
    Address: _____
    Telephone: _____
    Fax: _____
Trial counsel, if different
    Name: _____
    Address: _____
    Telephone: _____

5. Court reporter(s) (if more space is needed, use other side)
    Name: _____
    Address: _____
    Telephone: _____

Approximate Duration of trial court proceedings to be transcribed _____

Can this appeal be accelerated? _____

S. Ct. Rule 312   PROCEDURE

6. Briefly state the supreme court rule, or other law, which confers jurisdiction upon the reviewing court; the facts of the case which bring it within this rule or other law; and the date that the order being appealed was entered and any other facts which are necessary to demonstrate that the appeal is timely:

7. Nature of case:

Administrative Review	_____	Domestic Relations	_____
Contract	_____	Child Custody or	
Estates	_____	Support	_____
Personal Injury	_____	Product Liability	_____
Tort	_____	Forcible Detainer	_____
Juvenile	_____	Other	_____

8. Briefly describe the nature of the case and the result in the trial court, and set forth any reasons for an expedited schedule:

9. State the general issues proposed to be raised (failure to include an issue in this statement will not result in the waiver of the issue on appeal):

I, as attorney for the appellant, hereby certify that on _____ (Date) I (asked/made a written request to) the clerk of the circuit court (Indicate which)

to prepare the record, and on (Date) _____ I made a written request to the court reporter(s) to prepare the transcript(s).

Date _____   _____
                                                    Appellant's Attorney

In lieu of a reporter's signature I have attached the written request to the court reporter(s) to prepare the transcript(s).

Date _____   _____
                                                    Appellant's Attorney

I hereby acknowledge receipt of an order for the preparation of a report of proceedings.

Date _____   _____
                                              Court Reporter or Supervisor

Rule 366. Powers of reviewing court—Scope of review and procedure—Lien of judgment

* * *

(b) Scope of review

(3) Scope and procedure on review in nonjury cases. In nonjury cases the following rules govern:

(i) Special findings and motions unnecessary. No special findings of fact, certificate of evidence, propositions of law, motion for a finding, or demurrer to the evidence is necessary to support the judgment or as a basis for review. The sufficiency of the evidence to support the judgment is subject to review without formal action to preserve the question.

(ii) Post-trial motions. Neither the filing of nor the failure to file a post-trial motion limits the scope of review.

* * *

Author's Notes

(1) **Post-trial motions to preserve issues for appeal.** As a general rule, issues that have not been raised in the trial court are not subject to review in the Appellate Court. See, e.g., In re Marriage of Monken, 255 Ill.App.3d 1044, 194 Ill.Dec. 422, 627 N.E.2d 759 (5th Dist.1994) (wife could not raise claim that judgment was void because of failure to file a written waiver of the two-year waiting period for a no-fault dissolution for the first time on appeal). Post-trial motions are therefore occasionally used to make sure that issues have been presented to the trial court. However, there are cases holding that issues raised for the first time in post-trial motions are raised too late in the trial Court to be subject to review by the Appellate Court. See In re Marriage of McKeever, 117 Ill.App.3d 905, 73 Ill.Dec. 164, 453 N.E.2d 1153 (3d Dist.1983) (wife could not raise issue of ineffective counsel for the first time on appeal; language in post-trial motion was insufficient to raise the issue); Mendelson v. Lillard, 83 Ill.App.3d 1088, 39 Ill.Dec. 373, 404 N.E.2d 964 (1st Dist.1980) (defense alluded to in petition to vacate void judgment would not be considered by reviewing court).

*

DIVISION E. FEDERAL LAWS

26 U.S.C.A.
INTERNAL REVENUE CODE

(Selected Provisions)

Sec.
71.	Alimony and separate maintenance payments.
215.	Alimony, etc., payments.
414(p).	Qualified domestic relations order defined.
408(d)(6).	Transfer of account incident to divorce.
3405(c).	Eligible rollover distributions.
682.	Income of an estate or trust in case of divorce, etc.
1041.	Transfers of property between spouses or incident to divorce.
1034.	Rollover of gain on sale of principal residence.
121.	One-time exclusion of gain from sale of principal residence by individual who has attained age 55.
151.	Allowance of deductions for personal exemptions.
152.	Dependent defined.
262.	Personal, living, and family expenses.
2(b).	Definitions and special rules.
7703.	Determination of marital status.
6013.	Joint returns of income tax by husband and wife.

WESTLAW Electronic Research

See WESTLAW Electronic Research Guide preceding the Summary of Contents.

---

26 U.S.C.A. § 71

§ 71. Alimony and separate maintenance payments

(a) General rule. Gross income includes amounts received as alimony or separate maintenance payments.

(b) Alimony or separate maintenance payments defined. For purposes of this section—

(1) In general. The term "alimony or separate maintenance payment" means any payment in cash if—

(A) such payment is received by (or on behalf of) a spouse under a divorce or separation instrument,

(B) the divorce or separation instrument does not designate such payment as a payment which is not includible in gross income under this section and not allowable as a deduction under section 215,

(C) in the case of an individual legally separated from his spouse under a decree of divorce or of separate maintenance, the payee spouse and the payor spouse are not members of the same household at the time such payment is made, and

(D) there is no liability to make any such payment for any period after the death of the payee spouse and there is no liability to make any payment (in cash or property) as a substitute for such payments after the death of the payee spouse.

(2) Divorce or separation instrument. The term "divorce or separation instrument" means—

(A) a decree of divorce or separate maintenance or a written instrument incident to such a decree,

(B) a written separation agreement, or

(C) a decree (not described in subparagraph (A)) requiring a spouse to make payments for the support or maintenance of the other spouse.

(c) Payments to support children.

(1) In general. Subsection (a) shall not apply to that part of any payment which the terms of the divorce or separation instrument fix (in terms of an amount of money or a part of the payment) as a sum which is payable for the support of children of the payor spouse.

(2) Treatment of certain reductions related to contingencies involving child. For purposes of paragraph (1), if any amount specified in the instrument will be reduced—

(A) on the happening of a contingency specified in the instrument relating to a child (such as attaining a specified age, marrying, dying, leaving school, or a similar contingency), or

(B) at a time which can clearly be associated with a contingency of a kind specified in subparagraph (A), an amount equal to the amount of such reduction will be treated as an amount fixed as payable for the support of children of the payor spouse.

(3) Special rule where payment is less than amount specified in instrument. For purposes of this subsection, if any payment is less than the amount specified in the instrument, then so much of such payment as does not exceed the sum payable for support shall be considered a payment for such support.

(d) Spouse. For purposes of this section, the term "spouse" includes a former spouse.

(e) Exception for joint returns. This section and section 215 shall not apply if the spouses make a joint return with each other.

(f) Recomputation where excess front-loading of alimony payments.

(1) In general. If there are excess alimony payments—

(A) the payor spouse shall include the amount of such excess payments in gross income for the payor spouse's taxable year beginning in the 3rd post-separation years, and

(B) the payee spouse shall be allowed a deduction in computing adjusted gross income for the amount of such excess payments for the payee's taxable year beginning in the 3rd post-separation year.

(2) Excess alimony payments. For purposes of this subsection, the term "excess alimony payments" mean the sum of—

(A) the excess payments for the 1st post-separation year, and

(B) the excess payments for the 2nd post-separation year.

(3) Excess payments for 1st post-separation year. For purposes of this subsection, the amount of the excess payments for the 1st post-separation year is the excess (if any) of—

(A) the amount of the alimony or separate maintenance payments paid by the payor spouse during the 1st post-separation year, over

(B) the sum of—

(i) the average of—

(I) the alimony or separate maintenance payments paid by the payor spouse during the 2nd post-separation year, reduced by the excess payments for the 2nd post-separation year, and

(II) the alimony or separate maintenance payments paid by the payor spouse during the 3rd post-separation year, plus

(ii) $15,000.

(4) Excess payments for 2nd post-separation year. For purposes of this subsection, the amount of the excess payments for the 2nd post-separation year is the excess (if any) of—

(A) the amount of the alimony or separate maintenance payments paid by the payor spouse during the 2nd post-separation year, over

(B) the sum of—

(i) the amount of the alimony or separate maintenance payments paid by the payor spouse during the 3rd post-separation year, plus

(ii) $15,000.

(5) Exceptions.

(A) Where payment ceases by reason of death or remarriage. Paragraph (1) shall not apply if—

(i) either spouse dies before the close of the 3rd post-separation year, or the payee spouse remarries before the close of the 3rd post-separation year, and

(ii) the alimony or separation maintenance payments cease by reason of such death or remarriage.

(B) Support payments. For purposes of this subsection, the term "alimony or separate maintenance payment" shall not include any payment received under a decree described in subsection (b)(2)(C).

(C) Fluctuating payments not within control of payor spouse. For purposes of this subsection, the term "alimony or separate maintenance payment" shall not include any payment to the extent it is made pursuant to a continuing liability (over a period of not less than 3 years) to pay a fixed portion or portions of the income from a business or property or from compensation for employment or self-employment.

(6) Post-separation years. For purposes of this subsection, the term "1st post-separation years" means the 1st calendar year in which the payor spouse paid to the payee spouse alimony or separate maintenance payments to which this section applies. The 2nd and 3rd post-separation years shall be the 1st and 2nd succeeding calendar years, respectively.

(g) Cross references.

(1) For deduction of alimony or separate maintenance payments, see section 215.

(2) For taxable status of income of an estate or trust in the case of divorce, etc., see section 682.

[Author's Notes follow § 215.]

26 U.S.C.A. § 215

§ 215. Alimony, etc., payments

(a) General rule. In the case of an individual, there shall be allowed as a deduction an amount equal to the alimony or separate maintenance payments paid during such individual's taxable year.

(b) Alimony or separate maintenance payments defined. For purposes of this section, the term "alimony or separate maintenance payment" means any alimony or separate maintenance payment (as defined in section 71(b)) which is includible in the gross income of the recipient under section 71.

(c) Requirement of identification number. The Secretary may prescribe regulations under which—

(1) any individual receiving alimony or separate maintenance payments is required to furnish such individual's taxpayer identification number to the individual making such payments, and

(2) the individual making such payments is required to include such taxpayer identification number on such individual's return for the taxable year in which such payments are made.

(d) Coordination with section 682. No deduction shall be allowed under this section with respect to any payment if, by reason of section 682 (relating to income of alimony trusts), the amount thereof is not includible in such individual's gross income.

Author's Notes to §§ 71, 215

Analysis

1. Nomenclature.
2. Use of deductible alimony.
3. Requirements for deductible/taxable.
4. Children's support.
5. Unallocated.
6. Deductible children's support.
7. Recapture.
8. Recapture not apply.
9. Attorney's fees.
10. More than $15,000.
11. Three calendar years.
12. Mortgage and taxes.
13. Payments to third parties.
14. Payments by third parties.
15. Adjusted gross income.
16. Property payments.
17. Interest.
18. Tax ramifications.
19. IRS rejection.
20. Cross reference—Form.
21. Neither deductible nor taxable.
22. Use of non-taxable.
23. Additional use of non-taxable.
24. Cross reference—Form.
25. Life insurance on payor.
26. Life insurance on payee.
27. Social Security number.
28. Net amounts.
29. Net amounts table.
30. Approximate calculations.
31. Federal tax tables.
32. Illinois tax.
33. Standard deduction.
34. IRS Publication 504.

(1) **Nomenclature.** Spousal support is called "maintenance" in § 504 of the Illinois Marriage and Dissolution of Marriage Act and "alimony or separate maintenance" in §§ 71 and 215 of the Internal Revenue Code, in actions to obtain a "dissolution" under the Illinois Dissolution Act and a "divorce" in the Internal

Revenue Code. The Internal Revenue Code is sometimes herein referred to as IRC, and the Internal Revenue Service is sometimes referred to as IRS. The Illinois Marriage and Dissolution of Marriage Act, 750 ILCS 5/101 et seq. is sometimes referred to as IMDMA.

(2) **Use of deductible alimony.** Despite the mixed terms, alimony may have become a more useful way of paying money in divorces after 1993. The reason is that the increase in the marginal rate to 39.6% on taxable incomes over $250,000 increases the possibility that for high income payors the payor will be in a higher tax bracket than will the payee, and therefore, because of the deductibility/taxation of alimony, the Treasury in effect makes part of the payment.

(3) **Requirements for deductible/taxable.** Alimony and separate maintenance payments are deductible by the payor pursuant to § 215 of the Internal Revenue Code, and taxable to the payee pursuant to § 71 of the Internal Revenue Code, provided that the payments meet certain requirements set forth in § 71 of the Internal Revenue Code.

A. The payments must be in cash.

B. The payments must be made pursuant to a divorce or separation instrument. These instruments include a decree of divorce or separate maintenance, a written separation agreement, and temporary support orders.

C. The spouses must be living in separate households when the alimony is pursuant to a decree of divorce or a decree of separate maintenance, but not where the payments are made under a written separation agreement or a temporary support order.

D. The payments must terminate at the payee's death.

E. The payments cannot be fixed for children's support.

F. The parties must not have opted out of deductible/taxable alimony by designating their payments as ones that are not includible in the gross income of the payee pursuant to § 71 and not allowable as a deduction of the payor under § 215.

(4) **Children's support.** The general rule is that children's support, unlike most alimony, is neither deductible to the payor nor taxable to the payee.

(5) **Unallocated.** It was formerly possible under Commissioner of Internal Revenue v. Lester, 366 U.S. 299, 81 S.Ct. 1343, 6 L.Ed.2d 306 (1961) to pay children's support as alimony (called unallocated alimony and children's support) in order to gain the deduction for the children's support for the payor. Section 71(c)(2) of the Internal Revenue Code was rewritten in order to substantially reduce the opportunity to treat child support as alimony. Under the current § 71(c)(2), if alimony payments are reduced because of a contingency relating to a child, such as attaining a specified age, marrying, dying, leaving school, or a similar contingency, or if there is a reduction at a time which can be clearly associated with such a contingency, the alimony payment is fixed as child support, and there can be no deduction for the payor, and, conversely, the payment is not taxable to the payee.

(6) **Deductible children's support.** There are still some ways by which children's support can be made deductible. The children's support will be deductible (and taxable to the recipient) by paying alimony that includes children's support which terminates at a period of time that is not related to a child contingency. For example, if the children are only two and three years old, alimony that includes children's

support could be paid for a period of five years, after which it would terminate (at a period of time not related to a child contingency). Thereafter the parties could agree or the Court could fix regular children's support. In this fashion, a deduction for children's support can be obtained for at least a period of time.

(7) **Recapture.** In some situations pursuant to § 71(f) where there is reduction in the maintenance payments of more than $15,000 in the first three years of payment, there can be a recapture of some of the payments that have been deducted by the payor back into the income of the payor in the third year. The result of this recomputation is that some of the alimony payments that the payor previously deducted become taxable income to him, and some of the payments that were previously taxable to the payee are no longer taxable, and a refund should result to the payee. The recomputation rules do not apply to level alimony or separate maintenance payments, annual payments of less than $15,000, or to payments that increase over the three-year period. Payments may decline over the three-year period without any recomputation if the highest year is not more than $15,000 more than the lowest year.

(8) **Recapture not apply.** Even where there is a reduction of more than $15,000 during the first three years, there are three circumstances in which the recomputation rules do not take effect.

   A. If either spouse dies or the payee spouse remarries and the alimony payments cease for one of those reasons. (The exception does not appear to include the statutory termination of maintenance in Illinois upon cohabitation, IMDMA § 510(c).)

   B. Temporary support payments are not subject to the recomputation rules.

   C. Recomputation does not apply to payments where the payor's liability is to pay a percentage of the income from his business or property or from compensation, if the liability to pay continues for at least three full years.

(9) **Attorney's fees.** The recapture provisions were presumably designed to prevent the payment of attorney's fees as alimony, thereby gaining a deduction for portions of attorney's fees that would not otherwise be deductible. As is the rule for the Internal Revenue Service, the provisions, designed to cure a simple ill, produced a convoluted recomputation formula and loopholes. Attorney's fees can be paid as part of a temporary support order, which is not subject to the recomputation rules. Also, there is a safe harbor of $15,000 that can be used for attorney's fees. The Worksheets for Recapture of Alimony are set forth at pages 10 and 15 of Internal Revenue Service Publication 504 "Tax Information for Divorced or Separated Individuals, For use in preparing 1993 Returns," which is reproduced following the Author's Note (34) of this Section.

(10) **More than $15,000.** Internal Revenue Service Publication 504 at page 10 limits the possibility of recapture to the situation where the payments in either the second or third year decrease by more than $15,000 from the prior year. Because of the complexity of the formula, however, where the payments decline by more than $15,000 in the first three years in any fashion, and the payments do not fit one of the three exceptions, it is advisable to run through the recomputation formula to make sure that recapture does not result. When recapture is the result, it may be possible to tinker with the payments and level them out in such a manner as to avoid the recapture.

26 U.S.C.A. § 215   **FEDERAL LAWS**

(11) **Three calendar years.** *Nota bene*, the three years that are counted in recomputation are the first three calendar years in which alimony is paid. (IRC¶71(f)(6)). If a decree is entered near the end of the first year, say November, an amount can be paid as alimony, even to include attorney's fees, and it may not exceed the annual amounts paid in the second and third years, because you are paying support for 12 months in the second and third years, and only for 2 months in the first year. You can therefore take advantage of the first 10 months of the first calendar year, when support does not have to be paid, to include deductible payments for other purposes.

The three post-separation calendar years concept probably does not apply to the requirement that there must be a liability for three years (36 months) for the percentage payment exception to the recomputation rules. Marjorie A. O'Connell, *Divorce Taxation*, ¶3602 (1989).

(12) **Mortgage and taxes.** Deductible/taxable alimony can be used to good effect in an agreement where the husband is to pay the mortgage interest and taxes for a house that he does not own, in which his wife is living, and which does not qualify as a residence for which he can deduct mortgage interest. The sum of the mortgage interest and taxes is paid by the husband as alimony, and is therefore deductible to him, and received by the wife as taxable alimony, but she itemizes the mortgage interest and taxes as deductions, and it is therefore a wash to her, with one exception. The exception to the wash is that the wife cannot take the deductions on her Illinois return.

(13) **Payments to third parties.** Payments to third parties by the payor can qualify as alimony received on behalf of the payee spouse. The common forms of such payments include life insurance premiums, mortgage installments and real estate taxes, and medical bills. The payments should be pursuant to a judgment or separation agreement, or written request and consent, and must satisfy the qualifications for alimony. The payments are then taxable to the payee spouse and deductible by the payor spouse. The taxation/deduction of mortgage payments, however, depends upon ownership of the property, e.g. in joint tenancy, half the mortgage payments by the payor are taxable to the payee as alimony and half of the payments are deductible to the payor. Marjorie A. O'Connell, *Divorce Taxation*, ¶3102 (1989).

(14) **Payments by third parties.** Payments on behalf of a payor by a third party to the payee spouse may partially qualify as alimony. Such payments that qualify as alimony will be included in the gross income of the payee spouse and be taxable to her, but the deduction allowed under § 215 of the Internal Revenue Code is in most cases not allowed or not completely allowed to the obligor, or to the third party trust, or other person who may pay the alimony obligation of the obligor spouse. Therefore the matching of income and deduction is lost for third party payments. One exception is for payments by an estate, which may deduct the payments both on the estate tax return and on the decedent's income tax return. When the third party is the obligor's employer under a withholding order, the third party is paying the alimony with the obligor's money, and the obligor retains the deduction. Marjorie A. O'Connell, *Divorce Taxation*, ¶3103 (1990).

(15) **Adjusted gross income.** Alimony is a deduction on line 29 of the 1993 1040 U.S. Individual Income Tax Return in order to arrive at adjusted gross income, not an itemized deduction. Alimony can therefore be taken as a deduction in addition to the standard deduction. Alimony is also not subject to the 3% reduction in itemized deductions for high income taxpayers (Internal Revenue Code § 68). Because the

Illinois Form 1040 starts with adjusted gross income, deductible alimony payments are also free from Illinois tax.

(16) **Property payments.** Installment property payments can be made deductible to the payor and taxable to the payee if they otherwise qualify as alimony. The payments must terminate on the payee's death, however, a contingency that is not usually a part of the property settlements. See Author's Note (26) below for possible ways to solve the problem of termination on the payee's death.

(17) **Interest.** Provision is frequently made for property settlement payments to be made in installments over a period of time. When such an agreement includes the payment of interest on the unpaid balance of the property settlement payments, a problem arises in regard to the tax treatment of the interest portion of the settlement. The interest will ordinarily be taxable to the payee, but not deductible to the payor, since the deductibility of personal interest payments has been eliminated in most instances. One solution to this problem is to pay the interest payments as deductible/taxable alimony. The only drawback is that the interest payments in order to qualify as deductible/taxable alimony must terminate on the payee's death. See, however, Author's Note (26) below.

(18) **Tax ramifications.** It is always wise to set out in any property settlement agreement the tax ramifications that are contemplated for any particular set of provisions.

(19) **IRS rejection.** When it is contemplated that alimony be both deductible to the payor and taxable to the payee, there are at least four possible ways of providing a mechanism for resolution in the event the IRS does not accept the contemplated result. (1) The parties may agree to try and resolve the problem themselves, or, failing, refer the matter to the Court. This is the simplest paragraph, and it is particularly useful in smaller cases. (2) The payee can be required to pay back to the payor the amount of the payee's tax benefit that results from the payee not being required to pay tax on the alimony payments. The payee will in that instance come out even, because she will be able to obtain a refund of the tax that she has paid on the alimony payments, but if the payor is in a higher tax bracket, he may suffer. (3) The payee can be required to pay back to the payor the amount of the detriment that the payor suffers from not being able to deduct the alimony payments. The payee may have less net income here, if the payor is in a tax bracket higher than that of the payee, but the payor will be even. (4) The payee may be required to pay back to the payor the average between the tax detriment suffered by the payor and the tax benefit gained by the payee. Here whatever burden results from disallowance is shared by the parties. Because of the complex mechanics of recapture, it is necessary to treat recapture specifically.

(20) **Cross reference—Form.** See 750 ILCS 5/502 Author's Note (11) para. 2(d) for a sample paragraph requiring that the parties or the court resolve the issue when the IRS does not accept the contemplated maintenance tax result.

(21) **Neither deductible nor taxable.** If they so choose, either the parties or the Court can make the designation pursuant to IRC § 71(b)(1)(B) that payments that would otherwise qualify as deductible/taxable alimony be neither deductible nor taxable. Such a designation can be made and later changed. Moreover, the designation can be made for only a part of the alimony payments, making one stream deductible/taxable, and the other neither. The two streams might also terminate at different times. Marjorie A. O'Connell, *Divorce Taxation*, ¶3501 (1989); D. Mahoney, A. Koritzinsky & T. Forkin, *Tax Strategies in Divorce*, ¶8 p. 79 (1990).

(22) **Use of non-taxable.** The introduction of § 71(b)(1)(B), which in a backhanded way allows alimony payments to be designated as neither deductible to the payor nor taxable to the payee, has provided a useful tool. Payments that are designated as neither deductible nor taxable do not qualify as alimony under the Code, and therefore they are not subject to the recapture rules of § 71(f). The lawyer does not have to worry about variations in payments in the first three years. The same reasoning applies to the anti-Lester rules in § 71(c)(2). In the unusual case where the parties want percentage children's support to be paid, which was prohibited in Illinois, IMDMA § 505(a)(5), In re Marriage of Ferguson, f/k/a Hoferle v. Hoferle, 207 Ill. App.3d 649, 152 Ill.Dec. 648, 566 N.E.2d 335 (1st Dist.1990), they might agree to pay the percentage children's support as non-deductible and non-taxable alimony.

(23) **Additional use of non-taxable.** Non-deductible and non-taxable alimony is also frequently useful in negotiations, particularly where a net amount is being sought by the payee and the deduction is not important to the payor, for example, where the payor has other ways to shelter his income from tax and he would pay a lower amount in non-taxable alimony.

(24) **Cross reference—Form.** See 750 ILCS 5/502 Author's Note (11) para. 2(e) for a sample paragraph that designates alimony as neither deductible nor taxable.

(25) **Life insurance on payor.** Life insurance on the life of the payor of alimony and children's support is a common device used to secure the payee spouse should the payor spouse die before his obligation to make payments terminates. Generally if the payor spouse owns the policy, the premiums are not deductible by him or taxable to the payee; conversely, where the payee spouse owns the policy and the payor spouse pays the premiums on her behalf, the premiums may be deductible to the payor and taxable to the payee. Even though the death proceeds of the insurance are used to guarantee alimony, they are not taxable to the payee when paid. Marjorie A. O'Connell, *Divorce Taxation*, ¶9004 (1990). The insurance proceeds are ordinarily includible in the decedent's estate when the payor decedent is the owner of the policy. The insurance payment to the payee is ordinarily deductible to the decedent's estate as a debt. It may not, however, be deductible as a claim against the estate, unless the settlement agreement is drafted to specify that the obligation of the payor is to pay a specific sum of money to the payee upon his death, so that, if the insurance company does not make the payment, the payor would be personally liable. Marjorie A. O'Connell, *Divorce Taxation*, ¶13,106 (1987). See 750 ILCS 5/502 Author's Note (11) para. 7(a) for model life insurance paragraph. See also IRC § 682 and accompanying Author's Notes for the tax ramifications of securing alimony with trusts and estates.

(26) **Life insurance on payee.** Section 71 of the Internal Revenue Code requires that for payments to qualify as alimony they must terminate on the death of the payee, and there cannot be any substitute payments. The question is whether life insurance owned and paid for by the payor on the life of the payee is a substitute payment? Although the House Committee Report states that life insurance on the payee's life is not a substitute payment, this resolution of the issue may not have been accepted by the Internal Revenue Service, and it is not yet settled. O'Connell suggests that the way to avoid the problem is to have the alimony payments increased, and thereby allow the payee to purchase her own insurance on her own life. In that way, the payor is not paying the premiums and the proceeds would not be treated as a substitute payment. Marjorie A. O'Connell, *Divorce Taxation*, ¶9106 (1987).

(27) **Social Security number.** The payor of alimony is required on line 29 of the 1993 1040 tax return to report the alimony payee's social security number. It is

therefore prudent to include a blank for the payee's social security number in all settlement agreements that include the payment of alimony, with the blank to be filled in at the time of the signing of the settlement agreement. In that way the payor will have the tax identification number when he prepares his tax return. See 750 ILCS 5/502 Author's Note (11) para. 5(d) for sample.

(28) **Net amounts.** A common miscalculation, particularly in the press of court hearings or negotiations, is to arrive at a figure or a percentage for maintenance and children's support, without taking into account the tax consequences to the payor and the payee. Maintenance is ordinarily deductible to the payor, thereby reducing his tax, and taxable to the payee, thereby increasing her tax. Children's support is neither deductible nor taxable. Consequently, a determination that 50% of the husband's income will be paid for a wife and two children will produce different results depending upon whether the percentage is applied to the: (1) payor's gross income, (2) gross income minus his current annualized tax payments, (3) gross income minus his projected annualized tax computed after deducting his maintenance payments, or (4) the percentage is calculated by utilizing the aggregate net after tax incomes of the payor and the payee after calculating the deductibility of the maintenance to the payor and the tax paid by each of the parties. Method (4) will produce the truest picture of the net income and percentages to each of the parties. Children's support calculated under the guidelines of IMDMA § 505 should also utilize a Federal income tax figure calculated after deducting maintenance payments to determine the net income for § 505(a)(3).

(29) **Net amounts table.** The following is a table that can be used to make approximate calculations. Explanatory notes keyed to the line numbers follow the table. The assumption is a husband supporting a wife and two children, and the wife has no outside income.

Payor and Payee's net incomes:

Payor		Sample figures	Your figures
Tax calculation			
(1) Gross income of payor		$100,000	$_____
(2) Maintenance paid	−	25,000	− _____
(3) Adjusted gross income of payor		75,000	_____
(4) Dependency exemption (one)	−	2,450	− _____
(5) Standard deduction	−	3,800	− _____
(6) Taxable income of payor		68,750	_____
(7) Approximate Federal and State Tax percentage of gross income		19 %	_____%
(8) Federal and State tax paid		18,952	_____
Net income calculation			
(9) Gross income		100,000	_____
(10) Maintenance paid	−	25,000	− _____
(11) Children's support paid (25% of $100,000 − 18,952 tax)	−	20,262	− _____
(12) Federal and State tax paid	−	18,952	− _____
(13) Payor's net income		$ 35,786	$_____

26 U.S.C.A. § 215 **FEDERAL LAWS**

Payee

Tax calculation
(14)	Adjusted gross income of payee (maintenance and other if exist)	$ 25,000	$_____
(15)	Dependency exemptions (three)	− 7,350	− _____
(16)	Standard deduction	− 5,600	− _____
(17)	Taxable income of payee	12,050	_____
(18)	Approximate Federal and State Tax percentage of adjusted gross income	10 %	_____ %
(19)	Federal and State tax paid	2,558	_____

Net income calculation
(20)	Taxable income of payee (maintenance and other if exist)	$ 25,000	$_____
(21)	Non-taxable income of payee (children's support and other if exist)	+ 20,262	+ _____
(22)	Gross income of payee	45,262	_____
(23)	Federal and State tax paid	− 2,558	− _____
(24)	Payee's net income	$ 42,704	$_____

Payee's percentage of aggregate net incomes:
(25)	Payor's net income	$ 35,763	$_____
(26)	Payee's net income	+ 42,704	+ _____
(27)	Aggregate net incomes	78,467	_____
(28)	Payee's net income 42,704 = Aggregate net incomes 78,467	54% =	_____ %

Notes

(4)(15) The dependency exemptions in (4) and (15) are for 1994 as calculated by CCH. *1994 United States Master Tax Guide,* (CCH) ¶133 (1994). *Nota bene* that the exemptions are subject to a phase out for higher income tax payers. See IRS § 151(d)(3) Author's Note (4).

(5)(16) The standard deduction is as calculated by CCH for 1994 in (5) for single filers and in (16) for head of household filers. *1994 United States Master Tax Guide,* (CCH) ¶126 (1994). See Author's Note (33), this Section.

(7)(18) The percentages in lines (7) and (18) may be approximated, or the actual tax calculated in lines (8) and (19) can be used for the calculation.

(8) The Federal rate is for a 1994 single taxpayer. The Illinois rate is 3% of the Federal adjusted gross income. See Author's Note (31), this Section.

(11) The children's support in line (11) is calculated from the guidelines in IMDMA § 505(a)(1) for two children.

(14) It is assumed that the payee will have no deductions from gross income, and therefore gross income and adjusted gross income would be the same.

FEDERAL LAWS 26 U.S.C.A. § 215

(19)   The Federal rate is for a 1994 head of household taxpayer. The Illinois rate is 3% of the Federal adjusted gross income. See Author's Note (31), this Section.

(28)   The resulting percentage is the payee's net income as a percentage of the total net income of the parties.

(30) **Approximate calculations.** The table is designed to make preliminary approximate calculations in a complex area. The table does not contain many elements that are necessary to make a refined calculation. Missing elements include: itemized deductions, Illinois dependent exemptions, Illinois adjustments to the Federal adjusted gross income, FICA, Medicare, other family obligations, such as college tuitions and medical expenses, and the like. These elements can make a significant difference. Before a final commitment is made, it is advisable to run more precise calculations. There are computer programs available that include the elements not included in the rapid calculation table.

(31) **Federal tax tables.** There follows 1993 and 1994 tax tables for single unmarried, married filing jointly, married filing separately, and head of household taxpayers. The source for the tables is *1994 United States Master Tax Guide*, (CCH) ¶¶5–13 (1994).

SCHEDULE X: Single Individuals

1993

Taxable Income Over	But Not Over	Pay	+	% on Excess	of the amount over—
$ 0	$ 22,100	$ 0		15 %	$ 0
22,100	53,500	3,315		28	22,100
53,500	115,000	12,107		31	53,500
115,000	250,000	31,172		36	115,000
250,000	......	79,772		39.6	250,000

1994

Taxable Income Over	But Not Over	Pay	+	% on Excess	of the amount over—
$ 0	$ 22,750	$ 0		15 %	$ 0
22,750	55,100	3,412.50		28	22,750
55,100	115,000	12,470.50		31	55,100
115,000	250,000	31,039.50		36	115,000
250,000	......	79,639.50		39.6	250,000

SCHEDULE Y-1: Married Individuals Filing Jointly and Surviving Spouses

1993

Taxable Income Over	But Not Over	Pay	+	% on Excess	of the amount over—
$ 0	$ 36,900	$ 0		15 %	$ 0
36,900	89,150	5,535		28	36,900
89,150	140,000	20,165		31	89,150
140,000	250,000	35,928.50		36	140,000
250,000	......	75,528.50		39.6	250,000

1994

Taxable Income Over	But Not Over	Pay	+	% on Excess	of the amount over—
$ 0	$ 38,000	$ 0		15 %	$ 0
38,000	91,850	5,700		28	38,000
91,850	140,000	20,778		31	91,850
140,000	250,000	35,704.50		36	140,000
250,000	......	75,304.50		39.6	250,000

[G19025]

SCHEDULE Y-2: Separate Returns, Married Persons

1993

Taxable Income Over	But Not Over	Pay	+ % on Excess	of the amount over—
$ 0—	$ 18,450	$ 0	15 %	$ 0
18,450—	44,575	2,767.50	28	18,450
44,575—	70,000	10,082.50	31	44,575
70,000—	125,000	17,964.25	36	70,000
125,000—	....	37,764.25	39.6	125,000

1994

Taxable Income Over	But Not Over	Pay	+ % on Excess	of the amount over—
$ 0—	$ 19,000	$ 0	15 %	$ 0
19,000—	45,925	2,850	28	19,000
45,925—	70,000	10,389	31	45,925
70,000—	125,000	17,825.25	36	70,000
125,000—	....	37,652.25	39.6	125,000

SCHEDULE Z: Heads of Households

1993

Taxable Income Over	But Not Over	Pay	+ % on Excess	of the amount over—
$ 0—	$ 29,600	$ 0	15 %	$ 0
29,600—	76,400	4,440	28	29,600
76,400—	127,500	17,544	31	76,400
127,500—	250,000	33,385	36	127,500
250,000—	....	77,485	39.6	250,000

1994

Taxable Income Over	But Not Over	Pay	+ % on Excess	of the amount over—
$ 0—	$ 30,500	$ 0	15 %	$ 0
30,500—	78,700	4,575	28	30,500
78,700—	127,500	18,071	31	78,700
127,500—	250,000	33,199	36	127,500
250,000—	....	77,299	39.6	250,000

[G19026]

(32) **Illinois tax.** Because alimony is part of the Federal adjusted gross income of the recipient, it is subject to Illinois tax. The current Illinois rate is 3% of the

26 U.S.C.A. § 215   **FEDERAL LAWS**

Federal adjusted gross income as adjusted on the Illinois return. 35 ILCS 5/201 et seq. Since maintenance is a deduction on the Federal tax return of the payor before adjusted gross income, maintenance is also a deduction to the payor for purposes of Illinois tax.

(33) **Standard deduction.** There follows the 1993 and 1994 standard deductions for various tax payers who are neither over 65 or blind as calculated by Commerce Clearing House. *1994 United States Master Tax Guide*, (CCH) ¶126 (1994).

Filing status	1993 standard deduction amount
Married filing jointly and surviving spouses	$6,200
Married filing separately	3,100
Head of household filers	5,450
Single filers	3,700

Filing status	1994 standard deduction amount
Married filing jointly and surviving spouses	$6,350
Married filing separately	3,175
Head of household filers	5,600
Single filers	3,800

[G19027]

(34) **IRS Publication 504.** There follows Publication 504 issued by the Internal Revenue Service to assist divorced or separated persons in preparing their 1993 tax returns.

FEDERAL LAWS   26 U.S.C.A. § 215

Department of the Treasury

Internal Revenue Service

Publication 504
Cat. No. 15006I

Divorced or Separated Individuals

For use in preparing
1993 Returns

Contents

Introduction	1
Filing Status	2
Joint Return	2
Separate Returns	2
Head of Household	3
Exemptions	4
Exemption for Your Spouse	4
Exemptions for Dependents	4
Dependency Tests	4
Children of Divorced or Separated Parents	5
Multiple Support Agreement	7
Phaseout of Exemptions	7
Alimony	7
General Rules	8
Instruments Executed After 1984	8
Instruments Executed Before 1985	10
Qualified Domestic Relations Order	11
Individual Retirement Arrangements	12
Property Settlements	12
Transfer Between Spouses	12
Gift Tax on Property Settlements	13
Sale of Jointly-Owned Property	14
Costs of Getting a Divorce	14
Tax Withholding and Estimated Tax	14
Community Property	14
Community Income	15
Alimony (Community Income)	16
Worksheet for Recapture of Alimony	15
Index	17

Important Reminders

Change of address. If you change your mailing address, be sure to notify the Internal Revenue Service using **Form 8822**, *Change of Address.* Mail it to the Internal Revenue Service Center for your old address (addresses for the Service Centers are on the back of the form).

Change of name. If you change your name, be sure to notify the Social Security Administration using **Form SS–5**, *Application for a Social Security Card.*

Introduction

This publication explains tax rules that apply if you are divorced or separated from your spouse. The first part covers general filing information. It can help you choose your filing status whether you are separated or divorced. It also can help you decide which exemptions

[G19028]

you are entitled to claim, including dependency exemptions.

The next part of the publication discusses payments and transfers of property that often occur as a result of divorce and whether you can deduct them on your tax return. Examples include alimony, child support, other court-ordered payments, property settlements, and transfers of individual retirement arrangements. This part also explains deductions allowed for some of the costs of obtaining a divorce.

The last part of the publication explains special rules that may apply to persons who live in community property states.

Useful Items
You may want to see:

Publications

☐ 501 Exemptions, Standard Deduction, and Filing Information

☐ 544 Sales and Other Dispositions of Assets

☐ 555 Federal Tax Information on Community Property

☐ 590 Individual Retirement Arrangements (IRAs)

Ordering publications and forms. To order free publications and forms, call our toll-free telephone number 1–800–TAX–FORM (1–800–829–3676). You can also write to the IRS Forms Distribution Center nearest you. Check your income tax package for the address.

Filing Status

Your filing status is used in determining your filing requirement, standard deduction, and correct tax. It may also determine whether you can claim certain deductions and credits. The filing status you may choose depends partly on your marital status on the last day of your tax year.

Marital status. If you are considered unmarried, your filing status is single or, if you meet certain requirements, head of household. If you are considered married, your filing status is either married filing a joint return or married filing a separate return. If both you and your spouse have income, you should usually figure your tax on both a joint return and separate returns to see which gives you the lower tax.

Considered unmarried. You are considered unmarried for the whole year if either of the following applies.

1) You have obtained a final *decree of divorce or separate maintenance* by the last day of your tax year. You must follow your state law to determine if you are divorced or legally separated. *Exception*: If you and your spouse obtain a divorce in one year for the sole purpose of filing tax returns as unmarried individuals, and at the time of divorce you intend to remarry each other and do so in the next tax year, you and your spouse must file as married individuals.

2) You have obtained a *decree of annulment*, which holds that no valid marriage ever existed. You also must file amended returns claiming unmarried status for all tax years affected by the annulment that are not closed by the statute of limitations. The statute of limitations generally does not end until 3 years after the due date of your original return.

Considered married. You are considered married for the whole year if you are separated but you have not obtained a final decree of divorce or separate maintenance by the last day of your tax year. An interlocutory decree is not a final decree.

Exception. If you live apart from your spouse, under certain circumstances you may be considered unmarried and can file as head of household. See *Head of Household*, later.

Joint Return

If you are married, you and your spouse can choose to file a joint return. If you file jointly, you both must include all your income, exemptions, deductions, and credits on that return. You can file a joint return even if one of you had no income or deductions.

To file a joint return, at least one of you must be a U.S. citizen or resident at the end of the tax year. However, if either of you was a nonresident alien at any time during the tax year, you can file a joint return only if you agree to treat the nonresident spouse as a resident of the United States. This means that your combined worldwide incomes are subject to U.S. income tax. Get Publication 519, *U.S. Tax Guide for Aliens*.

Signing a joint return. Both you and your spouse must sign the return, or it will not be considered a joint return.

Joint and individual liability. Both you and your spouse are responsible, jointly and individually, for the tax and any interest or penalty due on your joint return. This means that one spouse may be held liable for all the tax due even if all the income was earned by the other spouse.

Divorced taxpayers. If you are divorced, you are still jointly and individually responsible for any tax, interest, and penalties due on a joint return filed before your divorce. This responsibility applies even if your divorce decree states that your former spouse will be responsible for any amounts due on previously filed joint returns.

Innocent spouse exception. You may not have to pay the additional tax, interest, and penalties if the tax on your joint return was understated by more than $500 because your spouse either:

1) Omitted an item of his or her gross income, or

2) Claimed a deduction, credit, or property basis for which there was no basis in fact or law.

To determine whose gross income was omitted (other than income from property), do not apply community property rules.

To qualify under this exception, you must meet both of the following requirements.

1) You must establish that you did not know, and had no reason to know, about the tax understatement.

2) It must be unfair, under all the facts and circumstances, to hold you liable for the additional tax, interest, and penalties.

A factor in determining that it is unfair to hold you liable is the absence of any significant benefit to you, either direct or indirect, from the understatement of tax. Your receipt of property from your spouse may be a significant benefit, even if it is received several years after the year of the tax understatement. Normal support is not a significant benefit.

In addition, if the tax understatement resulted from claiming a deduction, credit, or basis, the exception applies only if the additional tax, interest, and penalties are more than:

1) 10% of your adjusted gross income (AGI) for the preadjustment year, if your AGI was $20,000 or less, or

2) 25% of your AGI for the preadjustment year, if your AGI was more than $20,000.

Your preadjustment year is your most recent tax year ending before a deficiency notice was mailed. If you were married to a different person at the end of the preadjustment year, your AGI includes your new spouse's income, whether or not you filed a joint return for that year.

Tax refund applied to debts. If you are due a refund but have not paid certain debts, all or part of your refund may be used to pay the past-due amount. Amounts may be paid from your refund to repay state child support agencies and federal agencies for debts such as student loans and overpayments of social security benefits.

Separate Returns

If you and your spouse file separate returns, you should each report only your own income, exemptions, deductions, and credits on your individual return. You can also file a separate return if only one of you had income. For information on exemptions you can claim on your separate return, see *Exemptions*, later.

Community or separate income. If you live in a community property state and file a separate return, your income may be separate income or community income for income tax purposes. For more information, see *Community Income*, later.

Itemized deductions. If you and your spouse file separate returns and one of you itemizes deductions, the other spouse will not qualify for the standard deduction and should also itemize deductions.

[G19029]

FEDERAL LAWS 26 U.S.C.A. § 215

Dividing itemized deductions. You may be able to claim itemized deductions on a separate return for certain expenses that you paid separately or jointly with your spouse. The rules that follow apply only if you do not live in a community property state.

If you paid the medical expenses of a qualifying person with funds deposited in a joint checking account in which you and your spouse have an equal interest, you and your spouse are presumed to have paid the medical expenses equally for purposes of computing the medical expense deduction on your separate returns. You can rebut this presumption if you can show that you alone paid the expenses.

If both you and your spouse paid property tax or mortgage interest on property held as tenants by the entirety, you can deduct on your separate return the amount of property tax or qualifying interest that you alone actually paid.

If you file a separate state income tax return, you can deduct on your separate federal return the amount of state income tax you paid during the year.

If you file a joint state income tax return, and you and your spouse are jointly and individually liable for the full amount of the state income tax, you can deduct on your separate federal return the amount of state income tax you alone paid during the year. But if you are liable for only your own share of the state income tax, your deduction is limited to the smaller of:

1) The state income tax you alone paid during the year, or
2) The total state income tax you and your spouse paid during the year multiplied by a fraction, the numerator of which is the amount of your gross income and the denominator of which is your combined gross income.

If you sustain a casualty loss on a residence you own as tenants by the entirety, you can report half of the loss on your separate return. Neither spouse may report the total casualty loss.

Separate liability. If you and your spouse file separately, you each are responsible only for the tax due on your own return.

Separate returns may give you a higher tax. Some married couples file separate returns because each wants to be responsible only for his or her own tax. But in almost all instances, if you file separate returns, you will pay more combined federal tax than you would with a joint return. This is because the tax rate is higher for married persons filing separately. The following rules also apply if you file a separate return.

1) You cannot take the credit for child and dependent care expenses in most cases.
2) You cannot take the earned income credit.

3) You cannot exclude the interest from Series EE savings bonds that you used for higher education expenses.
4) If you lived with your spouse at any time during the tax year—
   a) You cannot claim the credit for the elderly or the disabled, and
   b) You will have to include in income one-half of any social security or equivalent railroad retirement benefits you received.
5) You will become subject to the limit on itemized deductions and the phaseout of the deduction for personal exemptions at income levels that are half those for a joint return.

Joint return after separate returns. If you or your spouse, or both, file separate returns, you can change to a joint return any time within 3 years from the due date (not including extensions) of the separate returns. This applies even if the separate returns were filed as head of household. Use Form 1040X, *Amended U.S. Individual Income Tax Return.*

If the tax on your joint return is more than the total paid on your separate returns, you must pay the additional tax when you file Form 1040X.

Separate returns after joint return. After the due date of your return, you and your spouse *cannot* file separate returns if you previously filed a joint return.

Head of Household

You may be eligible to file as head of household if you meet the requirements discussed later. Filing as head of household has the following advantages.

1) You can claim the standard deduction even if your spouse itemizes deductions on a separate return.
2) Your standard deduction is higher than that allowed on a single or married filing separate return.
3) Your tax rate may be lower than that on a single or married filing separate return.
4) You may be able to claim certain credits you cannot claim on a married filing separate return.
5) You will become subject to the limit on itemized deductions at an income level that is twice that for a married filing separate return.
6) You will become subject to the phaseout of the deduction for personal exemptions at a higher income level than those for a single or a married filing separate return.

Requirements. You can file as head of household only if you were unmarried or were considered unmarried on the last day of the year. You also must have paid more than half the cost of keeping up a home that was the main home for more than half the year (except for temporary absences, such as for school) for you and any of the following:

1) ***Your unmarried child***, grandchild, stepchild, foster child, or adopted child. This child (except foster child) does not have to be your dependent. A foster child must qualify as your dependent.
2) ***Your married child***, grandchild, stepchild, foster child, or adopted child whom you can claim as your dependent, or whom you could claim as your dependent except that:
   a) By your written declaration you allow the noncustodial parent to claim the dependent, or
   b) The noncustodial parent provided at least $600 for the support of the dependent and claims the dependent under a pre-1985 agreement.
3) ***Any other relative*** whom you can claim as a dependent. However, your dependent parent does not have to live with you (see *Father or mother*, later). For persons who qualify as a relative, see *Test 1—Relationship* under *Dependency Tests*, later.

Your married child or other relative will not qualify you as a head of household if you claim that person as a dependent under a multiple support agreement (discussed later).

Father or mother. If your dependent parent does not live with you, you can file as head of household if you paid more than half the cost of keeping up a home that was your parent's main home for the *whole year*. Keeping up the main home for your dependent parent includes paying more than half the cost of keeping your parent in a rest home or home for the elderly.

Considered unmarried. If you are married, you will be considered unmarried if you meet all of the following tests.

1) You file a separate return.
2) You paid more than half the cost of keeping up your home for the tax year.
3) Your spouse did not live in your home during the last 6 months of the tax year.
4) Your home was, for more than half the year, the main home of your child, stepchild, adopted child, or foster child whom you can claim as a dependent, or whom you could claim as your dependent except that:
   a) By your written declaration you allow the noncustodial parent to claim the dependent, or
   b) The noncustodial parent provided at least $600 for the support of the dependent and claims the dependent under a pre-1985 agreement.

Nonresident alien spouse. If your spouse was a nonresident alien at any time during the tax year, and you have not chosen to treat your spouse as a resident alien, you are considered unmarried for head of household purposes. However, your spouse does not qualify as a relative. You must have another qualifying relative and meet the other requirements to file as head of household.

3
[G19030]

26 U.S.C.A. § 215 **FEDERAL LAWS**

Keeping up a home. You are keeping up a home only if you pay more than half the cost of its upkeep. This includes such costs as rent, mortgage interest, taxes, insurance on the home, repairs, utilities, and food eaten in the home. This does not include the cost of clothing, education, medical treatment, or transportation for any member of the household.

For more information on filing as head of household, get Publication 501, *Exemptions, Standard Deduction, and Filing Information.*

Exemptions

For 1993 you are allowed a $2,350 deduction for each exemption you can claim. However, see *Phaseout of Exemptions*, later. You can claim your exemptions whether or not you itemize deductions.

You can claim your own exemption unless someone else can claim you as a dependent. If you are married, you may be able to take an exemption for your spouse. You can take an exemption for each person who qualifies as your dependent under the dependency tests discussed later.

Exemption for Your Spouse

Your spouse is never considered your dependent. You can take an exemption for your spouse only because you are married.

Joint return. If you and your spouse file a joint return, you can claim an exemption for each of you.

Separate return. If you file a separate return, you can take an exemption for your spouse only if your spouse had no gross income and was not the dependent of someone else. This is true even if your spouse is a nonresident alien.

Alimony paid. If you paid alimony to your spouse and deduct it on your separate return, you cannot take an exemption for your spouse. This is because alimony is gross income to the spouse who received it.

Former spouse. You cannot take an exemption for your former spouse for the year in which you were divorced or legally separated under a final decree. This rule applies even if you paid all your former spouse's support that year.

Exemptions for Dependents

You can take an exemption for each person who is your dependent. A dependent is any person who meets all five of the dependency tests discussed below.

Note. If you can claim an exemption for your dependent, the dependent cannot claim his or her own exemption on his or her own tax return. This is true even if you do not claim the dependent's exemption or the exemption will be reduced or eliminated under the phaseout rule for high-income individuals.

Social security numbers for dependents. If you claim a dependent who is at least **one year old** by the end of your tax year, you must list the dependent's social security number (SSN) on your Form 1040 or Form 1040A. If you do not list the dependent's SSN when required or if you list an incorrect SSN, you may be subject to a $50 penalty.

Birth or death of dependent. You can take an exemption for a dependent who was born or who died during the year if he or she met the dependency tests while alive. This means that a child who lived only for a moment can be claimed as a dependent. Whether a child was born alive depends on state or local law. There must be proof of a live birth shown by an official document, such as a birth certificate. You cannot claim an exemption for a stillborn child.

Dependency Tests

A dependent must meet *all* the following tests:

1) Relationship,
2) Married person,
3) Citizen or resident,
4) Income, and
5) Support.

Test 1—Relationship

The dependent must either:

Be related to you, or

Have been a member of your household.

Related. If the dependent is not a member of your household, he or she must be related to you (or your spouse if you are filing a joint return) in one of the following ways:

Child	Great grand-child, etc.	Brother-in-law
Stepchild		Sister-in-law
Mother	Half-brother	Son-in-law
Father	Half-sister	Daughter-in-law
Grandparent	Stepbrother	If related by
Great Grand-parent, etc.	Stepsister	blood:
	Stepmother	Uncle
Brother	Stepfather	Aunt
Sister	Mother-in-law	Nephew
Grandchild	Father-in-law	Niece

Any relationships that have been established by marriage are not considered ended by death or divorce.

Child. Your child is:

1) Your son, daughter, stepson, stepdaughter, or adopted son or daughter,

2) A child who lived in your home as a member of your family, if placed with you by an authorized placement agency for legal adoption, or

3) A foster child (any child who lived in your home as a member of your family for the whole year, for whom you did not receive qualified foster care payments).

Member of household. If the dependent is not related to you, he or she must have lived in your home as a member of your household for the whole year (except for temporary absences, such as for vacation or school). A person is not a member of your household if at any time during your tax year the relationship between you and that person violates local law.

Test 2—Married Person

The dependent cannot have filed a joint return for 1993. However, this test does not have to be met if neither the dependent nor the dependent's spouse is required to file, but they file a joint return to get a refund of all tax withheld.

Test 3—Citizen or Resident

To meet the citizen or resident test, a person must be a U.S. citizen or resident, or a resident of Canada or Mexico for some part of the calendar year in which your tax year begins.

Children usually are citizens or residents of the country of their parents.

If you were a U.S. citizen when your child was born, the child may be a U.S. citizen although the other parent was a nonresident alien and the child was born in a foreign country. If so, and the other dependency tests are met, the child is your dependent and you may take the exemption. It does not matter if the child lives abroad with the nonresident alien parent.

If you are a U.S. citizen living abroad who has legally adopted a child who is not a U.S. citizen or resident, and the other dependency tests are met, the child is your dependent and you may take the exemption if your home is the child's main home and the child is a member of your household for your entire tax year.

Test 4—Income

The dependent must have received less than $2,350 of gross income in 1993. Gross income does not include nontaxable income, such as welfare benefits or nontaxable social security benefits.

Special rules for your dependent child. The income test does not apply if your child:

1) Was under age 19 at the end of 1993, or

2) Was a student during 1993 and was under age 24 at the end of 1993.

Child. See Test 1—*Relationship*, earlier, for the definition of "child."

Student. To qualify as a student, your child must have been, during some part of each of 5 calendar months (not necessarily consecutive) during 1993:

1) A full-time student at a school that has a regular teaching staff and course of study, and a regularly enrolled body of students in attendance, or

2) A student taking a full-time, on-farm training course given by a school described in (1) above or a state, county, or local government.

A *full-time student* is one who was enrolled for the number of hours or courses the school considers to be full-time attendance.

The term "school" includes elementary schools, junior and senior high schools, colleges, universities, and technical, trade, and mechanical schools. It does not include on-the-job training courses, correspondence schools, or night schools.

Test 5—Support

In general, you must have given over half the dependent's support in 1993. If you file a joint return, the support could have come from you or your spouse. Even if you did not give over half the dependent's support, you will be treated as having given over half the support if you meet the tests explained later under *Multiple Support Agreement*.

If you are divorced or separated and you or the other parent, or both together, gave over half your child's support in 1993, the support test for your child may be based on a special rule. See *Children of Divorced or Separated Parents*, later.

In figuring total support, you must include money the dependent used for his or her own support, even if this money was not taxable (for example, gifts, savings, and welfare benefits). If your child was a student, do not include amounts he or she received as scholarships.

Support includes items such as food, a place to live, clothes, medical and dental care, recreation, and education. In figuring support, use the actual cost of these items. However, the cost of a place to live is figured at its fair rental value.

Do not include in support items such as income tax and social security and Medicare taxes paid by persons from their own income, premiums for life insurance, or funeral expenses.

Joint ownership of home. If your dependent lives with you in a home that is jointly owned by you and your spouse or former spouse, and each of you has the right to use and live in the home, each of you is considered to provide half your dependent's lodging. However, if your decree of divorce gives only you the right to use and live in the home, you are considered to provide your dependent's entire lodging, even though legal title to the home remains in the names of both you and your former spouse.

Capital items. You must include capital items such as a car or furniture in figuring support, but only if they were actually given to, or bought by, the dependent for his or her use or benefit. Do not include the cost of a capital item for the household or for use by persons other than the dependent. For example, include in support a bicycle purchased by and used solely by the dependent for transportation; do not include a lawn mower you purchase that is occasionally used by the dependent.

Children of Divorced or Separated Parents

In general, a dependent must meet the support test explained earlier under *Test 5—Support*. However, the support test for a child of divorced or separated parents is based on a special rule (explained under *Custodial Parent* and *Noncustodial Parent*, later) if certain requirements are met.

Special-Rule Requirements

In determining whether the support test for a child of divorced or separated parents has been met, the special rule applies only if the parents meet all of the following three requirements.

1) The parents were divorced or legally separated under a decree of divorce or separate maintenance, were separated under a written separation agreement, or lived apart at all times during the last 6 months of the calendar year.

2) One or both parents provided more than half the child's total support for the calendar year.

3) One or both parents had custody of the child for more than half the calendar year.

Child is defined earlier under *Test 1—Relationship*.

Support provided by parents. Support given to a child of a divorced or separated parent by a relative or friend is not included as support given by that parent.

Example. You are divorced. During the whole year, you and your child lived with your mother in a house she owns. You must include the fair rental value of the home provided by your mother for your child in figuring total support but not as part of the support provided by you.

Remarried parent. If you remarried, the support your new spouse gave is treated as given by you.

Example. You have two children from a former marriage who lived with you. You remarried and lived in a home owned by your present spouse. The fair rental value of the home provided to the children by your present spouse is treated as provided by you.

Exceptions. This discussion does not apply in any of the following situations.

1) A third party, such as a relative or friend, gave half or more of the child's support.
2) The child was in the custody of someone other than the parents for half the year or more.
3) The child's support is determined under a multiple support agreement.
4) The parents were separated under a written separation agreement, or lived apart, but they file a joint return for the tax year.

In these situations, support is determined under the regular method discussed earlier under *Test 5—Support*.

Custodial Parent

Under the special rule, the parent who had custody of the child for the greater part of the year (the custodial parent) is generally treated as the parent who provided more than half the child's support. This parent is usually allowed to claim the exemption for the child, if the other dependency tests are met. However, see *Noncustodial Parent*, later.

Custody. Custody is usually determined by the most recent decree of divorce or separate maintenance, or a later custody decree. If there is no decree, use the written separation agreement.

If neither a decree nor an agreement establishes custody, then the parent who had physical custody of the child for the greater part of the year is considered the custodial parent. This also applies if a decree or agreement calls for "split" custody, or if the validity of a decree or agreement awarding custody is uncertain because of legal proceedings pending on the last day of the calendar year.

If the parents were divorced or separated during the year after having had joint custody of the child before the separation, the parent who had custody for the greater part of the rest of the year is considered the custodial parent for the tax year.

Example 1. Under your divorce decree, you have custody of your child for 10 months of the year. Your former spouse has custody for the other 2 months. You and your former spouse provided the child's total support. You are considered to have given more than half the child's support.

Example 2. You and your former spouse provided your child's total support for 1993. You had custody of your child under your 1990 divorce decree, but on October 15, 1993, a new custody decree granted custody to your former spouse. Because you had custody for the greater part of the year, you are considered to have provided more than half the child's support.

Example 3. You were separated on June 1. Your child's support for the year was $1,200, of which you gave $500, your spouse $400, and the child's grandparents $300. No multiple support agreement was entered into. (See *Multiple Support Agreement*, later.) Before the separation, you and your spouse had joint custody of your child. Your spouse had custody from June through September and you had custody from October through December. Because your spouse had custody for 4 of the 7 months following the separation, your spouse was the custodial parent for the year and is treated as having given more than half the child's support for the year.

Noncustodial Parent

Under the special rule, the parent who did not have custody, or who had it for the shorter time, is treated as the parent who gave more than half the child's support if:

1) The custodial parent signs a statement agreeing not to claim the child's exemption, and the noncustodial parent attaches this statement to his or her return (see *Form 8332*, later), or

2) A decree or written agreement **made before 1985** provides that the noncustodial parent can take the exemption and

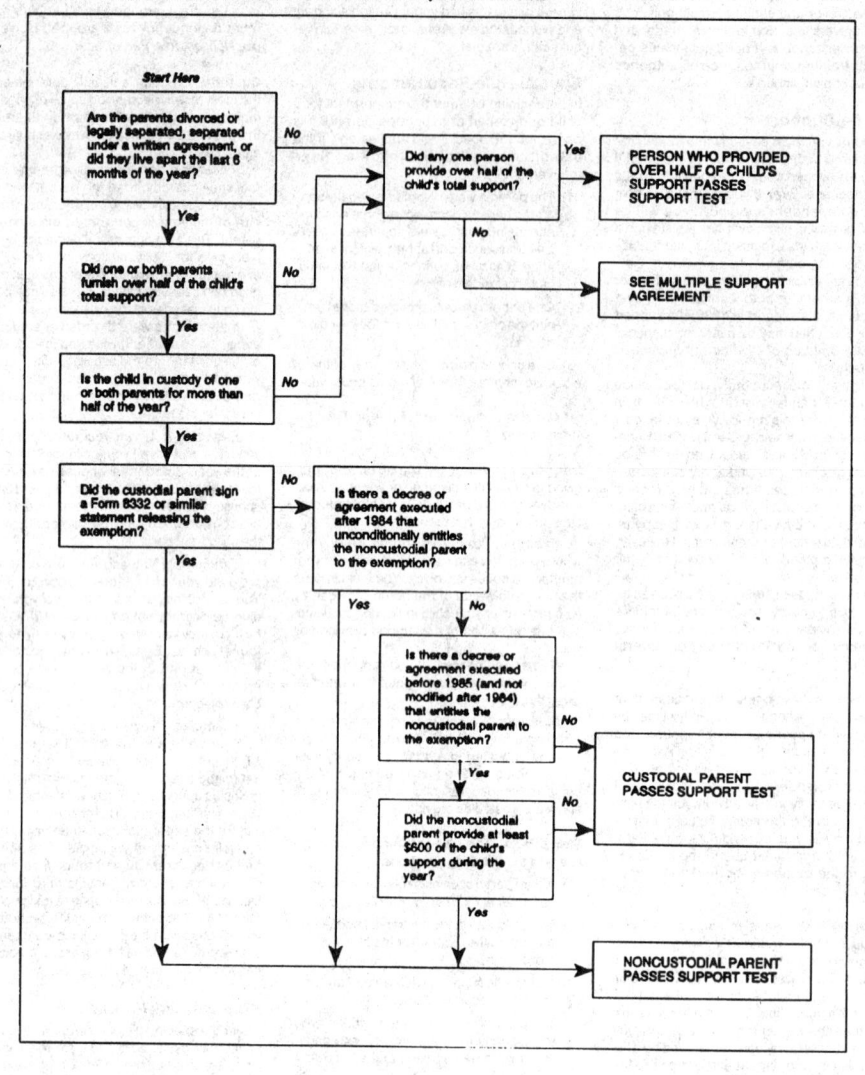

Figure 1. Support Test for Children of Divorced or Separated Parents

[Flowchart:

Start Here

Are the parents divorced or legally separated, separated under a written agreement, or did they live apart the last 6 months of the year?
- No → Did any one person provide over half of the child's total support?
  - Yes → PERSON WHO PROVIDED OVER HALF OF CHILD'S SUPPORT PASSES SUPPORT TEST
  - No → SEE MULTIPLE SUPPORT AGREEMENT
- Yes → Did one or both parents furnish over half of the child's total support?
  - No → (to Did any one person provide over half...)
  - Yes → Is the child in custody of one or both parents for more than half of the year?
    - No → (to Did any one person provide over half...)
    - Yes → Did the custodial parent sign a Form 8332 or similar statement releasing the exemption?
      - Yes → NONCUSTODIAL PARENT PASSES SUPPORT TEST
      - No → Is there a decree or agreement executed after 1984 that unconditionally entitles the noncustodial parent to the exemption?
        - Yes → (to NONCUSTODIAL PARENT PASSES SUPPORT TEST)
        - No → Is there a decree or agreement executed before 1985 (and not modified after 1984) that entitles the noncustodial parent to the exemption?
          - No → CUSTODIAL PARENT PASSES SUPPORT TEST
          - Yes → Did the noncustodial parent provide at least $600 of the child's support during the year?
            - No → CUSTODIAL PARENT PASSES SUPPORT TEST
            - Yes → NONCUSTODIAL PARENT PASSES SUPPORT TEST]

he or she gave at least $600 for the child's support during the year, unless the pre-1985 decree or agreement was modified after 1984 to specify that this provision will not apply.

Example 1. Under your 1983 divorce decree, your former spouse has custody of your child. The decree states that you can claim the child's exemption. You gave $1,000 of your child's support during the year and your spouse gave the rest. You are considered to have given over half the child's support, even if your former spouse gave more than $1,000.

Example 2. You and your spouse provided all of your child's support. Under your 1988 written separation agreement, your spouse has custody of your child. The agreement conditionally states that you can claim the child's exemption. Because the agreement was made after 1984, you are considered to have given over half the child's support only if your spouse agrees not to claim the child's exemption on Form 8332 or a similar statement.

Example 3. You and your former spouse provided all of your child's support. Your divorce decree gives custody of your child to your former spouse. It does not say who can claim the child's exemption. Your former spouse is considered to have given over half the child's support, unless he or she agrees not to claim the child's exemption on Form 8332 or a similar statement.

Form 8332. The custodial parent can sign Form 8332, *Release of Claim to Exemption for Child of Divorced or Separated Parents,* or a similar statement, agreeing not to claim the child's exemption. The exemption may be released for a single year, for a number of specified years (for example, alternate years), or for all future years.

If you are the noncustodial parent, you must attach the release to your return. If the exemption is released for more than one year, you must attach the original release to your return the first year and a copy each following year.

Similar statement. If your divorce decree or separation agreement made after 1984 *unconditionally* states that you can claim the child as your dependent, you can attach to your return copies of the following pages from the decree or agreement instead of Form 8332:

1) The cover page (write the other parent's social security number on this page),
2) The page that unconditionally states you can claim the child as your dependent, and
3) The signature page showing the date of the agreement.

Agreements made before 1985. If you are a noncustodial parent who claims a child's exemption under a decree or agreement made before 1985, you must give at least $600 for that child's support. Check the box on line 6d of your Form 1040 or line 6d of your Form 1040A.

Child support. Child support payments received from the noncustodial parent are considered used for the child's support, even if actually spent on things other than support.

Example. Your 1982 divorce decree requires you to pay child support to the custodial parent and states that you can claim your child's exemption. The custodial parent paid for all support items and put the $1,000 child support you paid during the year into a savings account for the child. Because your payments are considered used for support, you are considered to have given over half the child's support.

Back child support. Even if you owed child support for an earlier year, your payments are considered support for the year paid, up to the amount of your required child support for that year. If you paid back child support by paying more than the amount required for the year paid, the back child support is not considered support for either the year paid or the earlier year.

Example. You and your former spouse provide all your child's support. Your 1981 divorce decree requires you to pay $800 child support each year to the custodial parent and allows you to claim your child's exemption. Last year you paid only $500, but you made up the $300 you owed by paying $1,100 this year. Because you did not pay at least $600 last year, you cannot take the exemption unless the custodial parent signs a Form 8332 or similar statement. The $300 back child support you paid this year is not considered support for last year or for this year.

Medical Expenses
A child of divorced or separated parents whose support test is based on the special rule described in this section is treated as a dependent of both parents for the medical expense deduction. Thus, a parent can deduct medical expenses he or she paid for the child even if an exemption for the child is claimed by the other parent.

Multiple Support Agreement
Sometimes two or more people together pay over half a dependent's support, but no one alone pays over half. One of those people can claim an exemption for the dependent if all the following requirements are met.

1) The person paid over 10% of the dependent's support.
2) If not for the support test, the person could claim the dependent's exemption.
3) The person attaches to his or her tax return a signed **Form 2120**, *Multiple Support Declaration,* from every other person who meets the previous two requirements. This form states that the person who signs it will not claim the dependent's exemption for that year.

Phaseout of Exemptions
The amount you can claim as a deduction for exemptions is phased out if your adjusted gross income (AGI) falls within the bracket shown below for your filing status.

Filing Status	AGI
Single	$108,450 – $230,950
Married filing jointly or qualifying widow(er)	$162,700 – $285,200
Married filing separately	$ 81,350 – $142,600
Head of household	$135,600 – $258,100

If your AGI is more than the highest amount in the bracket for your filing status, your deduction for exemptions is zero. If your AGI falls within the bracket, use the worksheet in the instructions for Form 1040 to figure your deduction.

Alimony
Alimony is a payment to or for a spouse or former spouse under a divorce or separation instrument. It does not include voluntary payments that are not made pursuant to a divorce or separation instrument.

Alimony is deductible by the payer and must be included in the spouse's or former spouse's income. Although this discussion is generally written for the payer of the alimony, the recipient can use the information to determine whether an amount received is alimony.

To be alimony, a payment must meet certain requirements. Different requirements apply to payments under instruments executed after 1984 and to payments under instruments executed before 1985. These requirements are discussed later.

Spouse or former spouse. Unless otherwise stated in the following discussions about alimony, the term "spouse" includes former spouse.

Divorce or separation instrument. The term "divorce or separation instrument" means:

1) A decree of divorce or separate maintenance or a written instrument incident to that decree,
2) A written separation agreement, or
3) A decree or any type of court order requiring a spouse to make payments for the support or maintenance of the other spouse, including a temporary decree, an interlocutory (not final) decree, and a decree of alimony *pendente lite* (while awaiting action on the final decree or agreement).

Invalid decree. Payments under a divorce decree can be alimony even if the decree's validity is in question. A divorce decree is valid for tax purposes until a court having proper jurisdiction holds it invalid.

Amended instrument. An amendment to a divorce decree may change the nature of your payments. Amendments are not ordinarily retroactive for federal tax purposes. However, a retroactive amendment to a divorce decree correcting a clerical error to reflect the original intent of the court will generally be effective retroactively for federal tax purposes.

Example 1. A court order retroactively corrected a mathematical error under your divorce decree to express the original intent to spread the payments over more than 10 years. This change also is effective retroactively for federal tax purposes.

Example 2. Your original divorce decree did not fix any part of the payment as child support. To reflect the true intention of the court, a court order retroactively corrected the error by designating a part of the payment as child support. The amended order is effective retroactively for federal tax purposes.

26 U.S.C.A. § 215   FEDERAL LAWS

Deducting alimony paid. You can deduct alimony you paid, whether or not you itemize deductions on your return. Enter the alimony on line 29 of Form 1040. You cannot use Form 1040A or Form 1040EZ.

In the space on line 29, enter your spouse's or former spouse's social security number. If you do not, you may have to pay a $50 penalty and your deduction may be disallowed.

If you paid alimony to more than one person, enter the social security number of one of the recipients. Show the social security number and amount paid for each recipient on an attached statement. Enter your total payments on line 29.

Reporting alimony received. Report alimony you received on line 11 of Form 1040. You cannot use Form 1040A or Form 1040EZ.

You must give the person who paid the alimony your social security number. If you do not, you may have to pay a $50 penalty.

Withholding on nonresident aliens. If you are a U.S. citizen or resident and you pay alimony to a nonresident alien spouse or former spouse, you must withhold income tax at a rate of 30% (or lower treaty rate) on each payment. For more information, get Publication 515, *Withholding of Tax on Nonresident Aliens and Foreign Corporations.*

General Rules

The following rules apply to alimony regardless of when the divorce or separation instrument was executed.

Payments not alimony. Not all payments under a divorce or separation instrument are alimony. Alimony does not include:

1) Child support,
2) Noncash property settlements,
3) Payments that are your spouse's part of community income, as explained later under *Community Property*,
4) Use of property, or
5) Payments to keep up the payer's property.

Example. Under your written separation agreement, your spouse lives rent-free in a home you own and you must pay the mortgage, real estate taxes, insurance, repairs, and utilities for the home. Because you own the home and the debts are yours, your payments for the mortgage, real estate taxes, insurance, and repairs are not alimony. Neither is the value of your spouse's use of the home.

If they otherwise qualify, you can deduct the payments for utilities as alimony. Your spouse must report them as income. If you itemize deductions, you can deduct the real estate taxes and, if the home is a qualified residence, you can also include the interest on the mortgage in figuring your deductible interest.

Child support. To determine whether a payment is child support, see the separate discussions under *Instruments Executed After 1984* or *Instruments Executed Before 1985*, later.

Underpayment. If both alimony and child support payments are called for by your divorce or separation instrument, and you pay less than the total required, the payments apply first to child support and then to alimony.

Example. Your divorce decree calls for you to pay your former spouse $200 a month as child support and $150 a month as alimony. If you pay the full amount of $4,200 during the year, you can deduct $1,800 as alimony and your former spouse must report $1,800 as alimony received. If you pay only $3,600 during the year, $2,400 is child support. You can deduct only $1,200 as alimony and your former spouse must report $1,200 as alimony received.

Payments to a third party. Payments to a third party on behalf of your spouse under the terms of your divorce or separation instrument may be alimony, if they otherwise qualify. This includes payments for your spouse's medical expenses, housing costs (rent, utilities, etc.), taxes, tuition, etc. The payments are treated as received by your spouse and then paid to the third party.

Example 1. Under your divorce decree, you must pay your former spouse's medical and dental expenses. If the payments otherwise qualify, you can deduct them as alimony on your return. Your former spouse must report them as alimony received and can include them in figuring deductible medical expenses.

Example 2. Under your separation agreement, you must pay the real estate taxes, mortgage payments, and insurance premiums on a home owned by your spouse. If they otherwise qualify, you can deduct the payments as alimony on your return, and your spouse must report them as alimony received. If itemizing deductions, your spouse can deduct the real estate taxes and, if the home is a qualified residence, also include the interest on the mortgage in figuring deductible interest.

Life insurance premiums. Premiums you must pay under your divorce or separation instrument for insurance on your life qualify as alimony to the extent your spouse owns the policy.

Payments for jointly-owned home. If your divorce or separation instrument states that you must pay expenses for a home owned by you and your spouse, some of your payments may be alimony.

Mortgage payments. If you must make all the mortgage payments (principal and interest) on a jointly-owned home, and they otherwise qualify, you can deduct one-half of the total payments as alimony. If you itemize deductions and the home is a qualified residence, you can include the other half of the interest in figuring your deductible interest. Your spouse must report one-half of the payments as alimony received and, if itemizing deductions and the home is a qualified residence, can include one-half of the interest on the mortgage in figuring deductible interest.

Taxes and insurance. If you must pay all the real estate taxes or insurance on a home held as **tenants in common**, you can deduct one-half of these payments as alimony. Your spouse must report one-half of these payments as alimony received. If you and your spouse itemize deductions, you can each deduct one-half of the real estate taxes.

If your home is held as **tenants by the entirety** or **joint tenants** (with the right of survivorship), none of your payments for taxes or insurance are alimony. But if you itemize deductions, you can deduct all of the real estate taxes.

Instruments Executed After 1984

The following rules for alimony apply to payments under divorce or separation instruments executed after 1984. They also apply to payments under earlier instruments that have been modified to:

1) Specify that these rules will apply, or
2) Change the amount or period of payment or add or delete any contingency or condition.

The rules in this section do not apply to divorce or separation instruments executed after 1984 if the terms for alimony are unchanged from an instrument executed before 1985. For the rules for alimony payments under other pre-1985 instruments, see *Instruments Executed Before 1985*, later.

Example 1. In November 1984, you and your former spouse executed a written separation agreement. In February 1985, a decree of divorce was substituted for the written separation agreement. The decree of divorce did not change the terms for the alimony you pay your former spouse. The decree of divorce is treated as executed before 1985. Therefore, alimony payments under the decree are not subject to the rules for payments under instruments executed after 1984.

Example 2. Assume the same facts as in Example 1 except that the decree of divorce changed the amount of the alimony. In this example, the decree of divorce is not treated as executed before 1985. Therefore, the alimony payments are subject to the rules for payments under instruments executed after 1984.

Alimony Requirements

A payment to or for a spouse under a divorce or separation instrument is alimony if the spouses do not file a joint return with each other and all the following requirements are met.

1) The payment is in cash.
2) The instrument does not designate the payment as not alimony.
3) The spouses are not members of the same household (if separated under a decree of divorce or separate maintenance).
4) There is no liability to make any payment (in cash or property) after the death of the recipient spouse.

[G19035]

FEDERAL LAWS   26 U.S.C.A. § 215

5) The payment is not treated as child support.

Each of these requirements is discussed below.

Payment must be in cash. Only cash payments, including checks and money orders, qualify as alimony. Transfers of services or property (including a debt instrument of a third party or an annuity contract), execution of a debt instrument, or the use of property do not qualify as alimony.

Payments to a third party. Cash payments to a third party under the terms of your divorce or separation instrument can qualify as a cash payment to your spouse. See *Payments to a third party* under *General Rules*, earlier.

Also, cash payments made to a third party at the written request of your spouse qualify as alimony if all the following requirements are met.

1) The payments are in lieu of payments of alimony directly to your spouse.
2) The written request states that both spouses intend the payments to be treated as alimony.
3) You receive the written request from your spouse before you file your return for the year you made the payments.

Payments designated as not alimony. You and your spouse may designate that otherwise qualifying payments are not alimony by including a provision in your divorce or separation instrument that the payments are not deductible by you and are excludable from your spouse's income. For this purpose, any writing signed by both of you that makes this designation and that refers to a previous written separation agreement is treated as a written separation agreement. If you are subject to temporary support orders, the designation must be made in the original or a subsequent temporary support order.

To exclude the payments from income, your spouse must attach a copy of the instrument designating them as not alimony to his or her return for each year the designation applies.

Spouses cannot be members of the same household. Payments to your spouse while you are members of the same household are not alimony if you are separated under a decree of divorce or separate maintenance. A home you formerly shared is considered one household, even if you physically separate yourselves in the home.

You are not treated as members of the same household if one of you is preparing to leave the household and does leave not more than one month after the date of the payment.

Exception. If you are not legally separated under a decree of divorce or separate maintenance, a payment under a written separation agreement, support decree or other court order may qualify as alimony even if you are members of the same household when the payment is made.

Liability for payments after death of recipient spouse. If you must continue to make payments for any period after your spouse's death, none of the payments made before or after the death are alimony.

The divorce or separation instrument does not have to expressly state that the payments cease upon the death of your spouse if, for example, the liability for continued payments would end under state law.

Example. You must pay your former spouse $10,000 in cash each year for 10 years. Your divorce decree states that the payments will end upon your former spouse's death. You must also pay your former spouse or your former spouse's estate $20,000 in cash each year for 10 years. The death of your spouse would not terminate the payments under state law.

The $10,000 annual payments are alimony. But because the $20,000 annual payments will not end upon your former spouse's death, they are not alimony.

Substitute payments. If you must make any payments in cash or property after your spouse's death as a substitute for continuing otherwise qualifying payments, the otherwise qualifying payments are not alimony. Substitute payments can also include, depending on the facts and circumstances, payments to the extent they increase in amount or begin or accelerate as a result of your spouse's death.

Example 1. Under your divorce decree, you must pay your former spouse $30,000 annually. The payments will stop at the end of 6 years or upon your former spouse's death, if earlier.

Your former spouse has custody of your minor children. The decree provides that if any child is still a minor at your spouse's death, you must pay $10,000 annually to a trust until the youngest child reaches the age of majority. The trust income and corpus (principal) are to be used for your children's benefit.

These facts indicate that the payments to be made after your former spouse's death are a substitute for $10,000 of the $30,000 annual payments. Therefore, $10,000 of each of the $30,000 annual payments is not alimony.

Example 2. Under your divorce decree, you must pay your former spouse $30,000 annually. The payments will stop at the end of 15 years or upon your former spouse's death, if earlier. The decree provides that if your former spouse dies before the end of the 15-year period, you must pay the estate the difference between $450,000 ($30,000 × 15) and the total amount paid up to that time. For example, if your spouse dies at the end of the tenth year, you must pay the estate $150,000 ($450,000 − $300,000).

These facts indicate that the lump-sum payment to be made after your former spouse's death is a substitute for the full amount of the $30,000 annual payments. Therefore, none of the annual payments are alimony. The result would be the same if the payment required at death were to be discounted by an appropriate interest factor to account for the prepayment.

Child support. A payment that is specifically designated as child support or treated as specifically designated as child support under your divorce or separation instrument is not alimony. The designated amount or part may vary from time to time. Child support payments are neither deductible by the payer, nor taxable to the payee.

A payment will be **treated as specifically designated** as child support to the extent that the payment is reduced either:

1) On the happening of a contingency relating to your child, or
2) At a time that can be clearly associated with the contingency.

A payment may be treated as specifically designated as child support even if other separate payments are specifically designated as child support.

Contingency relating to your child. A contingency relates to your child if it depends on any event relating to that child. It does not matter whether the event is certain or likely to occur. Events relating to your child include the child's:

Reaching a specified age or income level,

Dying,

Marrying,

Leaving school,

Leaving the household, or

Becoming employed.

Clearly associated with a contingency. Payments are presumed to be reduced at a time clearly associated with the happening of a contingency relating to your child only in the following situations.

1) The payments are to be reduced not more than 6 months before or after the date the child will reach 18, 21, or local age of majority.
2) The payments are to be reduced on two or more occasions that occur not more than one year before or after a different child reaches a certain age from 18 to 24. This certain age must be the same for each child, but need not be a whole number of years.

In all other situations, reductions in payments are not treated as clearly associated with the happening of a contingency relating to your child.

Either you or the IRS may overcome the presumption in the two situations above. This is done by showing that the time at which the payments are to be reduced was determined independently of any contingencies relating to your children. For example, if you can show that the period of alimony payments is customary in the local jurisdiction, such as a period equal to one-half of the duration of the marriage, you can treat the amount as alimony.

26 U.S.C.A. § 215 FEDERAL LAWS

Table 1. **Worksheet for Recapture of Alimony** (For instruments executed after 1986)

Note: Do not enter less than zero on any line.

1.	Alimony paid in **2nd year**	*$40,000*
2.	Alimony paid in **3rd year**	*$20,000*
3.	Floor	$15,000
4.	Add lines 2 and 3	*35,000*
5.	Subtract line 4 from line 1	*$5,000*
6.	Alimony paid in **1st year**	*60,000*
7.	Adjusted alimony paid in **2nd year** (line 1 less line 5)	*35,000*
8.	Alimony paid in **3rd year**	*30,000*
9.	Add lines 7 and 8	*55,000*
10.	Divide line 9 by 2	*27,500*
11.	Floor	$15,000
12.	Add lines 10 and 11	*42,500*
13.	Subtract line 12 from line 6	*17,500*
14.	**Recaptured alimony.** Add lines 5 and 13	*$22,500*

* If you deducted alimony paid, report this amount as income on line 11, Form 1040.
If you reported alimony received, deduct this amount on line 29, Form 1040.

Recapture of Alimony

If your alimony payments decrease or terminate during the first 3 calendar years, you may be subject to the recapture rule. If you are subject to this rule, you have to include in income in 1993 part of the alimony payments you deducted in 1991 and 1992. Your spouse can deduct in 1993 part of the alimony payments included in income in those previous years.

The 3-year period starts with the first calendar year you make a payment qualifying as alimony under a decree of divorce or separate maintenance, or a written separation agreement. Do not include any time in which payments were being made under temporary support orders. The second and third years are the next 2 calendar years, whether or not payments are made during those years.

The reasons for a reduction or termination of alimony payments can include:

A failure to make timely payments,

A change in your instrument,

A reduction in your spouse's support needs, or

A reduction in your ability to provide support.

Subject to recapture for 1993. You are subject to the recapture rule for 1993, if you answer "Yes" to the following questions.

1) Was 1991 the first year in which you made alimony payments to this spouse under a decree of divorce or separate maintenance, or a written separation agreement?

2) Did your total payments in 1992 or 1993 decrease by more than $15,000 from the prior year?

In answering the above questions, do not include payments required over a period of at least 3 calendar years of a fixed part of your income from a business or property, or from compensation for employment or self-employment. These payments are not subject to the recapture rule.

Exception. You are not subject to recapture if your payments were reduced because of the death of either spouse or the remarriage of the spouse receiving the payments.

Including the recapture in income. If you must include a recapture amount in income, show it on Form 1040, line 11 ("Alimony received"). Cross out "received" and write "recapture." On the dotted line next to the amount, enter your spouse's last name and social security number.

Deducting the recapture. If you can deduct a recapture amount, show it on Form 1040, line 29 ("Alimony paid"). Cross out "paid" and write "recapture." In the space provided, enter your spouse's social security number.

Figuring the recapture. Both you and your spouse can use *Table 2* at the end of this publication to figure recaptured alimony.

Example. Myrna pays Phil the following amounts of alimony under their 1991 divorce decree.

Year	Amount
1991	$60,000
1992	40,000
1993	20,000

The recaptured alimony is $22,500, as shown in *Table 1*.

Myrna shows $22,500 as income on line 11 of her 1993 Form 1040. Phil deducts $22,500 on line 29 of his 1993 Form 1040.

Instruments Executed Before 1985

The following rules for alimony apply to payments under divorce or separation instruments executed before 1985. However, if an earlier instrument has been modified to specify that the rules for instruments executed after 1984 apply, or to change the terms regarding the amount or period of payment or other contingency or condition, follow the rules under *Instruments Executed After 1984*, earlier.

Alimony Requirements

A payment to or for a spouse under a divorce or separation instrument is alimony if the spouses do not file a joint return and the payment meets all of the following requirements.

1) It is periodic instead of a lump sum.

2) It is based on the marital or family relationship.

[G19037]

FEDERAL LAWS 26 U.S.C.A. § 215

3) It is not child support.

In addition, the spouses must be separated and living apart for a payment under a separation agreement or court order to qualify as alimony.

Periodic payments. Periodic payments are payments of:

1) A fixed amount for an indefinite period (for example, $400 a month for life),
2) An indefinite amount for either a fixed or an indefinite period (for example, 10% of a salary that changes from year to year to be paid for 6 years), or
3) A fixed amount for a fixed period of more than 10 years, subject to a limit.

Indefinite period. Payments are for an indefinite period if they are to end or change in amount on the happening of one or more of the following contingencies.

1) Your or your spouse's death,
2) Your spouse's remarriage, or
3) A change in your or your spouse's economic status.

The contingency may be either specified in your instrument or imposed by local law.

Example. Under your 1984 divorce decree, you must pay your former spouse $24,000. You are to pay this amount in installments of $200 a month for 120 months. The payments will stop if your former spouse dies or remarries. Because the payments are subject to those contingencies, they are periodic.

More than 10 years. If you must pay a fixed amount for a fixed period of more than 10 years, the amount of each annual payment considered periodic is limited to 10% of the total you will pay over the entire period. The 10% limit applies to payments made in advance, but not to payments for an earlier period.

Example 1. Your 1984 divorce decree states that you must pay your former spouse $150,000 in installments of $20,000 a year for 6 years and $5,000 a year for the following 6 years. The payments are not subject to any contingencies. For the first 6 years, only $15,000 (10% of $150,000) of each year's payment is considered periodic. The entire $5,000 you will pay in each of the last 6 years is considered periodic.

Example 2. Your 1984 divorce decree states that you must pay your former spouse $150,000 in installments of $10,000 for 15 years. The payments are not subject to any contingencies. You paid $10,000 each year through 1991, but you made no payment in 1992. In 1993 you paid $30,000, consisting of $10,000 for 1992, $10,000 for 1993, and a $10,000 advance payment for 1994.

Only $25,000 of your $30,000 payment is considered periodic. This is the $10,000 payment for 1992 and $15,000 (10% of $150,000) of the payments for 1993 and 1994.

Marital or family relationship. To be alimony, your payments must be based on your obligation, because of the marital or family relationship, to continue supporting your spouse. Any payment that does not arise out of that support obligation, such as the repayment of a loan, is not alimony.

Property settlement. Payments are not based on your obligation to continue support if they are a settlement of property rights. However, even if a state court describes payments made under a divorce decree as payments for property rights, they are alimony if they are made to fulfill a legal support obligation and they otherwise qualify.

Child support. A payment that is specifically designated as child support under your divorce or separation instrument is not alimony. If the instrument calls for payments that otherwise qualify as alimony and does not separately designate an amount as child support, all the payments are alimony. This is true even if the payments are subject to a contingency relating to your child.

Example. Your divorce decree states that you must pay your former spouse $400 a month for life for the support of your former spouse and your child. The payment is to be reduced to $300 upon the first of the following to happen: the child's death, the child's 22nd birthday, or the child's marriage. Despite these contingencies, no amount of child support is fixed by the decree. Therefore, the entire payment is alimony.

Alimony Trusts, Annuities, and Endowment Contracts

If you transferred property to a trust or bought or transferred an annuity or endowment contract to pay the alimony you owe, the trust income or other proceeds that would ordinarily be includible in your income must be included in your former spouse's income as alimony received. You do not include the payments in your income, nor can you deduct them as alimony paid. This rule applies whether the proceeds are from the earnings or the principal of the transferred property. It does not apply to any trust income that is fixed for child support.

Example. You are required to make monthly alimony payments of $500. You bought your former spouse a commercial annuity contract paying $500 a month. Your former spouse must include the full amount received under the contract in income, as alimony. It does not matter whether the amount is paid out of principal or interest. You do not include any part of the payment in your income, nor can you deduct any part.

Annuity and endowment contracts. Proceeds from annuity and endowment contracts bought for or transferred to a spouse after July 18, 1984, cannot be treated as alimony. However, this does not apply to contracts bought or transferred to pay alimony under a divorce or separation instrument executed on or before July 18, 1984, unless both spouses choose to have it apply. For information on how to make this choice, see *Section 1041 election* under *Property Settlements*, later.

Proceeds not alimony. If the proceeds from an annuity or endowment contract cannot be treated as alimony, the amount received is reduced by the cost of the contract. Get Publication 575, *Pension and Annuity Income (Including Simplified General Rule)*, for information on reporting annuities, and Publication 525, *Taxable and Nontaxable Income*, for information on reporting endowment proceeds.

If the proceeds from a trust cannot be treated as alimony, see the rules for reporting trust income in Publication 525.

Qualified Domestic Relations Order

A qualified domestic relations order (QDRO) is a judgment, decree, or court order (including an approved property settlement agreement) issued under a domestic relations law. A QDRO relates to the rights of someone other than a participant to receive benefits from a qualified retirement plan (such as most pension and profit-sharing plans) or a tax-sheltered annuity. It specifies the amount or portion of the participant's benefits to be paid to the participant's spouse, former spouse, child, or dependent.

Benefits paid to a child or dependent. Benefits paid under a QDRO to the plan participant's child or dependent are treated as paid to the participant. For information about the tax treatment of benefits from retirement plans, see Publication 575, *Pension and Annuity Income (Including Simplified General Rule)*.

Benefits paid to a spouse or former spouse. Benefits paid under a QDRO to the plan participant's spouse or former spouse generally must be included in the spouse's or former spouse's income. If the participant contributed to the retirement plan, a prorated share of the participant's cost (investment in the contract) is used to figure the taxable amount.

The spouse or former spouse can use the special rules for lump-sum distributions (special averaging method or capital gain treatment) if, had the participant received the benefits, they would have been treated as a lump-sum distribution. For this purpose, consider only the balance to the spouse's or former spouse's credit in determining whether the distribution is a total distribution. See *Lump-Sum Distributions* in Publication 575 for information about the special rules.

Rollovers. If you receive an eligible rollover distribution under a QDRO as the plan participant's spouse or former spouse, you can generally roll it over tax free into an individual retirement arrangement (IRA) or an other qualified retirement plan. This applies to taxable distributions other than required distributions (generally, distributions that must begin once you reach age 70½) and certain long-term periodic payments.

You can choose to have the distribution paid directly to the new plan. If any part of the taxable distribution is paid to you, 20% will be

26 U.S.C.A. § 215   FEDERAL LAWS

withheld for federal income tax. You can still make a tax-free rollover to another plan or an IRA within 60 days, but for a complete rollover you must add funds from another source equal to the tax withheld.

If you roll over only part of the taxable distribution, you cannot use the special lump-sum distribution rules to figure the tax on the part you keep. If you are under age 59½, any taxable distribution you keep may be subject to an additional 10% tax on early distributions.

For more information on the tax treatment of eligible rollover distributions, see Publication 575, *Pension and Annuity Income*.

Individual Retirement Arrangements

The following discussions explain some of the effects of divorce or separation on individual retirement arrangements (IRAs).

Spousal IRA. If you get a final decree of divorce or separate maintenance by the end of your tax year, you cannot deduct contributions you make to your former spouse's IRA. You can deduct only contributions to your own IRA. For information on IRAs, get Publication 590, *Individual Retirement Arrangements (IRAs)*.

IRA transferred as a result of divorce. The transfer of all or part of your interest in an IRA to your spouse or former spouse, under a decree of divorce or separate maintenance or a written instrument incident to the decree, is not considered a taxable transfer. Starting from the date of the transfer, the IRA interest transferred is treated as your spouse's or former spouse's IRA.

IRA contribution and deduction limit. All taxable alimony you receive under a decree of divorce or separate maintenance is treated as compensation for the IRA contribution and deduction limit. Your contributions to your IRA are limited to the smaller of:

- $2,000, or
- 100% of your compensation.

If you are covered by an employer retirement plan, your deduction for contributions to your IRA may be reduced or eliminated. For more information, see Chapter 4 of Publication 590.

Property Settlements

You do not recognize a gain or loss on the transfer of property between spouses, or former spouses if the transfer is because of a divorce. You may, however, have to report the transaction on a gift tax return. See *Gift Tax on Property Settlements*, later. If you sell property that you owned jointly in order to split the proceeds as part of your property settlement, you each must report your share of the gain or loss on the sale. See *Sale of Jointly-Owned Property*, later.

Transfer Between Spouses

No gain or loss is recognized on a transfer of property from you to (or in trust for the benefit of):

- Your spouse, or
- Your former spouse, but only if the transfer is incident to your divorce.

This rule applies even if the transfer was in exchange for cash, the release of marital rights, the assumption of liabilities, or other considerations.

However, this rule does not apply if your spouse or former spouse is a nonresident alien. Nor does it apply to certain transfers covered under *Transfers in trust*, later.

The term "property" includes all property whether real or personal, tangible or intangible, or separate or community. It includes property acquired after the end of your marriage and transferred to your former spouse. It does not include services.

Incident to divorce. A property transfer is incident to your divorce if the transfer:

- Occurs within one year after the date your marriage ends, or
- Is related to the ending of your marriage.

A divorce, for this purpose, includes the ending of your marriage by annulment or due to violations of state laws.

Related to the ending of marriage. A property transfer is related to the ending of your marriage if both the following conditions apply.

1) The transfer is made under your original or modified divorce or separation instrument.

2) The transfer occurs within 6 years after the date your marriage ends.

Unless these conditions are met, the transfer is presumed not to be related to the ending of your marriage. However, this presumption will not apply if you can show that the transfer was made to carry out the division of property owned by you and your spouse at the time your marriage ended. For example, the presumption will not apply if you can show that the transfer was made more than 6 years after the end of your marriage because of business or legal factors which prevented earlier transfer of the property.

Transfers to third parties. If you transfer property to a third party on behalf of your spouse (or former spouse, if incident to your divorce), the transfer is treated as two transfers:

1) A transfer of the property from you to your spouse or former spouse, and

2) An immediate transfer of the property from your spouse or former spouse to the third party.

You do not recognize gain or loss on the first deemed transfer. Instead, your spouse or former spouse may have to recognize gain or loss on the second deemed transfer.

For this treatment to apply, the transfer from you to the third party must be one of the following:

1) Required by your divorce or separation instrument,

2) Requested in writing by your spouse or former spouse, or

3) Consented to in writing by your spouse or former spouse. The consent must state that both you and your spouse or former spouse intend the transfer to be treated as a transfer from you to your spouse or former spouse subject to the rules of section 1041 of the Internal Revenue Code. You must receive the consent before filing your tax return for the year you transfer the property.

Transfers in trust. If you make a transfer in trust for the benefit of your spouse (or former spouse, if incident to your divorce), you must recognize gain or loss in certain situations. You generally must recognize gain or loss if you transfer an installment obligation to a trust. However, this does not apply if the deferred profit portion of the installment obligation will revert to you or your spouse. For information on the disposition of an installment obligation, see Publication 537, *Installment Sales*.

On other transfers in trust, you must recognize gain to the extent that the liabilities assumed by the trust, plus the liabilities to which the property is subject, exceed the total of your adjusted basis in the property transferred.

Example. You own property with a fair market value of $10,000 and an adjusted basis of $1,000. The trust did not assume any liabilities. The property is subject to a $5,000 liability. Your recognized gain on the transfer of the property in trust for the benefit of your spouse is $4,000 ($5,000 − $1,000).

Reporting income from property. If you transfer income-producing property (for example, an interest in a business, rental property, stocks, or bonds), include on your tax return any profit or loss, rental income or loss, dividends, or interest generated or derived from the property during the year up to the date of transfer. Your spouse or former spouse who receives the property must report any income or loss generated or derived from the property after the date of transfer.

U.S. savings bond interest. If you transfer a U.S. savings bond, include in income all interest on the bond that has been earned up to the date of transfer but not previously reported. Your spouse or former spouse who receives the bond will be taxed on interest earned after the transfer, but can usually defer reporting the interest until the bond is cashed or matures. Get Publication 550, *Investment Income and Expenses*, for more information.

Unused passive activity losses. If you transfer an interest in a passive activity to your

[G19039]

FEDERAL LAWS   26 U.S.C.A. § 215

spouse, or former spouse if incident to divorce, you cannot deduct your accumulated unused passive activity losses allocable to the interest. Instead, the adjusted basis of the transferred interest is increased by the amount of the unused losses. For information on passive activity losses, get Publication 925, *Passive Activity and At-Risk Rules*.

Investment credit recapture. If you transfer property for which you claimed an investment credit in an earlier year to your spouse (or former spouse if incident to divorce) you do not have to recapture any part of the credit. Instead, your spouse or former spouse may have to recapture part of the credit if he or she disposes of the property or changes its use before the end of the recapture period. For more information, see the instructions for Form 4255, *Recapture of Investment Credit*.

Record requirements. When you transfer property under these rules, you must give the recipient sufficient records to determine the adjusted basis and holding period of the property on the date of the transfer. If the recipient could be subject to recapture of investment credit, you also must provide sufficient records to determine the amount and period of the recapture.

Tax treatment of property received. Property you receive from your spouse (or former spouse if the transfer is incident to divorce) is treated as acquired by gift for income tax purposes. Therefore, its value is not taxable to you.

Basis of property received. Your basis in property received from your spouse (or former spouse if incident to divorce) is the same as the transferor's adjusted basis. This applies for determining either gain or loss when you later dispose of the property. It applies whether the property's adjusted basis is less than, equal to, or greater than either its value at the time of the transfer or any consideration you paid. It also applies even if the property's liabilities are more than its adjusted basis.

Note. If you received property before July 19, 1984, in exchange for your release of marital rights (see *Release of marital rights* under *Gift Tax on Property Settlements*, later) your basis in the property is its fair market value at the time of receipt. However, if you made a section 1041 election to apply the post-July 18, 1984 rules, your basis is the same as the transferor's adjusted basis, as explained above. See *Section 1041 election*, later.

Property transferred in trust. If the transferor recognizes gain on property transferred in trust, as described earlier under *Transfers in trust*, the trust's basis in the property is increased by the recognized gain.

Example. Your spouse transfers property in trust, recognizing a $4,000 gain. Your spouse's adjusted basis in the property was $1,000. The trust's basis in the property is $5,000 ($1,000 + $4,000).

U.S. savings bonds. The basis of U.S. savings bonds you receive is increased by the interest included in the transferor's income, as described earlier under *U.S. savings bond interest*.

Section 1041 election. These rules generally apply to all transfers after July 18, 1984. However, these rules do not apply to transfers after that date made under an instrument in effect on or before July 18, 1984, unless both parties choose to have them apply. If you make this choice, these rules will apply to all property transferred under the instrument.

To make this choice, both spouses or former spouses must sign and include their social security numbers on a statement specifying they are making the choice. This statement must be attached to the first income tax return filed by the transferor for the tax year the first transfer occurs. A copy of the signed statement must be kept by both parties, and a copy must be attached to the transferor's return for each later tax year in which a transfer is made under the election.

Sample election. The following is an example of an acceptable statement.

Section 1041 Election

The undersigned hereby elect to have the provisions of section 1041 of the Internal Revenue Code apply to all qualifying transfers of property after July 18, 1984, under any instrument in effect on or before July 18, 1984. The undersigned understand that section 1041 applies to all property transferred between spouses, or former spouses incident to divorce. The parties further understand that the effects for federal income tax purposes of having section 1041 apply are that (1) no gain or loss is recognized by the transferor spouse or former spouse as a result of this transfer; and (2) the basis of the transferred property in the hands of the transferee is the adjusted basis of the property in the hands of the transferor immediately before the transfer, whether or not the adjusted basis of the transferred property is less than, equal to, or greater than its fair market value at the time of the transfer. The undersigned understand that if the transferee spouse or former spouse disposes of the property in a transaction in which gain is recognized, the amount of gain which is taxable may be larger than it would have been if this election had not been made.

Gift Tax on Property Settlements

If you transfer property to your spouse or former spouse in exchange for the release of marital rights, and you do not qualify for an exception (explained later), you generally must report the transfer on a gift tax return for the calendar year the transfer was made. Get Publication 448, *Federal Estate and Gift Taxes*, for more information.

Release of marital rights. This is the giving up by your spouse or former spouse of dower, curtesy, or other marital rights in your property or estate. This does not include the release of spousal or child support rights. The transfer of property in exchange for support rights is not subject to gift tax.

If you transfer property in exchange for the release of both marital and support rights, the reportable amount is the value of the property less the value of the support rights given up.

Exceptions

Your transfer of property in exchange for the release of marital rights is not subject to gift tax if it meets any of the following exceptions.

1) It qualifies for the annual exclusion.
2) It is for qualified tuition or medical care.
3) It qualifies for the marital deduction.
4) It is required by a divorce decree.
5) It is made under a written agreement, and you are divorced within a specified period.

Annual exclusion. The first $10,000 of gifts of present interests to any person during the calendar year is not subject to gift tax. The annual exclusion is $100,000 for transfers to a spouse who is not a U.S. citizen that would qualify for the marital deduction if the donee were a U.S. citizen.

Tuition and medical care. Amounts you pay as tuition to a qualifying educational organization for the benefit of your spouse or former spouse and amounts you pay to provide medical care for your spouse or former spouse are not subject to gift tax.

Marital deduction. A transfer of property to a spouse before receiving a final decree of divorce or separate maintenance is not subject to gift tax. However, this rule does not apply to:

Transfers of certain terminable interests, or

Transfers to a spouse who is not a U.S. citizen.

Get the instructions for Form 709 for more information.

Transfer under divorce decree. A transfer of property under the decree of a divorce court having the power to prescribe a property settlement is not subject to gift tax. This rule also applies to a property settlement agreed on before the divorce if it was made part of or approved by the decree.

Transfer under written agreement. A transfer of property under a written agreement in exchange for the release of marital rights or to provide a reasonable child support allowance is not subject to gift tax if you are divorced within the 3-year period beginning 1 year before and ending 2 years after the date of the agreement. This applies whether or not the agreement is part of or approved by the divorce decree.

26 U.S.C.A. § 215   FEDERAL LAWS

Form 709
Report a transfer of property subject to gift tax on Form 709, *United States Gift (and Generation-Skipping Transfer) Tax Return*. Generally, Form 709 is due April 15 following the year of the transfer.

Transfer under written agreement. If a property transfer would be subject to gift tax except that it is made under a written agreement, and you do not receive a final decree of divorce by the due date for filing the gift tax return, you must report the transfer on Form 709 and attach a copy of your written agreement. The transfer will be treated as not subject to the gift tax until the final decree of divorce is granted, but no longer than 2 years after the effective date of the written agreement.

Within 60 days after you receive a final decree of divorce, send a certified copy of the decree to the IRS office where you filed Form 709.

Sale of Jointly-Owned Property

If you sell property that you and your spouse own jointly, you must report your share of the gain or loss on your income tax return for the year of the sale. Your share of the gain or loss is determined by your state law governing ownership of property. For information on reporting gain or loss, get Publication 544, *Sales and Other Dispositions of Assets*.

Sale of home. If you sell your main home and buy or build a new one, you may be able to postpone paying the tax on some or all of any gain from the sale. If you and your spouse have agreed to live apart and sell your jointly-owned home, the rules for postponing tax apply separately to the gain realized by each of you. For information on these rules, and on the rules for excluding gain if you are 55 or older when you sell your home, get Publication 523, *Selling Your Home*.

If you are divorced after filing a joint return on which you postponed tax on the gain on the sale of your home, but you do not buy or build a new home in the time required (and your former spouse does), you must file an amended joint return to report the tax on your share of the gain. If your former spouse refuses to sign the amended joint return, attach a letter explaining why your former spouse's signature is missing.

Costs of Getting a Divorce

You cannot deduct legal fees and court costs for getting a divorce. But you may be able to deduct legal fees paid for tax advice in connection with a divorce and legal fees to get alimony that you must include in gross income. In addition, you may be able to deduct fees you pay to appraisers, actuaries, and accountants for services in determining your correct tax or in helping to get alimony.

Fees you pay may include charges that are deductible and charges that are not deductible. You should request a breakdown showing the amount charged for each service performed.

You can claim deductible fees only if you itemize deductions on Schedule A (Form 1040). Claim them as miscellaneous deductions subject to the 2% of adjusted gross income limit. For more information, get Publication 529, *Miscellaneous Deductions*.

Fees for tax advice. You can deduct fees for advice on federal, state, and local taxes of all types, including income, estate, gift, inheritance, and property taxes.

If a fee is also for other services, you must determine and prove the expense for tax advice. The following examples show how you can meet this requirement.

Example 1. The lawyer handling your divorce consults another law firm, which handles only tax matters, to get information on how the divorce will affect your taxes. You can deduct the part of the fee paid over to the second firm and separately stated on your bill, subject to the 2% limit.

Example 2. The lawyer handling your divorce uses the firm's tax department for tax matters related to your divorce. Your statement from the firm shows the part of the total fee for tax matters. This is based on the time used, the difficulty of the tax questions, and the amount of tax involved. You can deduct this part of your bill, subject to the 2% limit.

Example 3. The lawyer handling your divorce also works on the tax matters. The fee for tax advice and the fees for other services are shown on the lawyer's statement. They are based on such things as the time spent on each service and the fees charged locally for similar services. You can deduct the fee charged for tax advice, subject to the 2% limit.

Fees for getting alimony. Because you must include alimony you receive in your gross income, you can deduct fees you pay to get or collect alimony.

Example. You pay your attorney a fee for handling your divorce and an additional fee that is for services in getting and collecting alimony. You can deduct the fee for getting and collecting alimony, subject to the 2% limit, if it is separately stated on your attorney's bill.

Nondeductible expenses. You cannot deduct the costs of personal advice, counseling, or legal action in a divorce. These costs are not deductible, even if they are paid, in part, to arrive at a financial settlement or to protect income-producing property.

However, you can add certain legal fees you pay specifically for a property settlement to the basis of the property you receive. For example, you can add the cost of preparing and filing a deed to put title to your house in your name alone to the basis of the house.

You cannot deduct fees you pay for your spouse or former spouse, unless your payments qualify as alimony. (See *Payments to a third party* in the earlier discussion of the general rules for alimony.) If you have no legal responsibility arising from the divorce settlement or decree to pay your spouse's legal fees, your payments are gifts and may be subject to the gift tax.

Tax Withholding and Estimated Tax

When you become divorced or separated, you will usually have to file a new **Form W-4**, *Employee's Withholding Allowance Certificate*, with your employer to claim your proper withholding allowances. If you receive alimony, you may have to make estimated tax payments.

If you do not pay enough tax either through withholding or by making estimated tax payments, you will have an underpayment of estimated tax and you may have to pay a penalty. If you do not pay enough tax by the due date of each payment, you may have to pay a penalty even if you are due a refund when you file your tax return.

For more information, get Publication 505, *Tax Withholding and Estimated Tax*.

Joint estimated tax payments. If you and your spouse made joint estimated tax payments for 1993 but file separate returns, either of you can claim all of your payments, or you may divide them in any way you agree on. If you cannot agree, you must divide the payments in proportion to your individual tax amounts as shown on your separate returns for 1993.

If you claim any of the payments on your tax return, enter your spouse's or former spouse's social security number in the block provided on the front of Form 1040 or Form 1040A. If you were divorced and remarried in 1993, enter your present spouse's social security number in that block and write your former spouse's social security number, followed by "DIV," to the left of line 55, Form 1040, or line 28b, Form 1040A.

Community Property

If you are married and your domicile (permanent legal home) is in a community property state, special rules determine your income. Some of these rules are explained in the following discussions. For more information, get Publication 555, *Federal Tax Information on Community Property*.

Community property states. The following are community property states:

Arizona,
California,
Idaho,
Louisiana,
Nevada,
New Mexico,
Texas,

[G19041]

FEDERAL LAWS   26 U.S.C.A. § 215

Table 2. **Worksheet for Recapture of Alimony** (For instruments executed after 1986)

Note: Do not enter less than zero on any line.

1. Alimony paid in **2nd year** .... _____
2. Alimony paid in **3rd year** .... _____
3. Floor $15,000

4. Add lines 2 and 3 .... _____
5. Subtract line 4 from line 1 .... _____
6. Alimony paid in **1st year** .... _____
7. Adjusted alimony paid in **2nd year** (line 1 less line 5) .... _____
8. Alimony paid in **3rd year** .... _____
9. Add lines 7 and 8 .... _____
10. Divide line 9 by 2 .... _____
11. Floor $15,000

12. Add lines 10 and 11 .... _____
13. Subtract line 12 from line 6 .... _____
14. **Recaptured alimony.** Add lines 5 and 13 .... *

* If you deducted alimony paid, report this amount as income on line 11, Form 1040.
If you reported alimony received, deduct this amount on line 29, Form 1040.

Washington, and Wisconsin.

Community Income

If your domicile is in a community property state during any part of your tax year, you may have community income. Your state law determines whether your income is separate or community income. If you and your spouse file separate returns, you must report half of any income described by state law as community income, and your spouse must report the other half. Each of you can claim credit for half the income tax withheld from community income.

Spousal agreements. In some states a husband and wife may enter into an agreement that affects the status of property or income as community or separate property. Check your state law to determine how it affects you.

Spouses Living Apart All Year

Special rules apply if all the following conditions exist.

1) You and your spouse live apart all year.
2) You and your spouse do not file a joint return for a tax year beginning or ending in the calendar year.
3) You or your spouse has earned income for the calendar year that is community income.
4) You and your spouse have not transferred, directly or indirectly, any of the earned income in (3) between yourselves before the end of the year. Do not take into account transfers satisfying child support obligations or transfers of very small amounts or value.

If all of these conditions exist, you and your spouse must report your *community* income as explained in the following discussions.

Earned income. Treat earned income that is not trade or business or partnership income as the income of the spouse who performed the services to earn the income. Earned income is wages, salaries, professional fees, and other compensation for personal services.

Earned income does not include amounts paid by a corporation that are a distribution of earnings and profits rather than a reasonable allowance for personal services rendered.

Trade or business income. Treat income and related deductions from a trade or business that is not a partnership as those of the spouse carrying on the trade or business.

If capital investment and personal services both produce business income, treat all of the income as trade or business income.

Partnership income or loss. Treat income or loss from a trade or business carried on by a partnership as the income or loss of the spouse who is the partner.

Separate property income. Treat income from the separate property of one spouse as the income of that spouse.

Social security benefits. Treat social security and equivalent railroad retirement benefits as the income of the spouse who receives the benefits.

Other income. Treat all other community income, such as dividends, interest, rents, royalties, or gains, as provided under your state's community property law.

Example. George and Sharon were married throughout the year but did not live together at any time during the year. Both domiciles were in a community property state. They did not file a joint return or transfer any of their earned income between themselves. During the year their incomes were as follows:

	George	Sharon
Wages	$20,000	$22,000
Consulting business	5,000	
Partnership		10,000
Dividends from separate property	1,000	2,000
Interest from community property	500	500
Totals	$26,500	$34,500

Under the community property law of their state, all the income is considered community income. (Some states treat income from separate property as separate income—check your

Page 15
[G19042]

26 U.S.C.A. § 215 FEDERAL LAWS

state law.) Sharon did not take part in George's consulting business.

Ordinarily, they would each report $30,500, half the total community income, on their separate returns. But because they meet the four conditions discussed earlier, they must disregard community property law in reporting all their income except the interest income from community property. They each report on their returns only their own earnings and other income, and their share of the interest income from community property. George reports $26,500 and Sharon reports $34,500.

Ending the Community

When the marital community ends, the community assets (money and property) are divided between the spouses. Income received before the community ended is treated according to the rules explained earlier. Income received after the community ended is separate income, taxable only to the spouse to whom it belongs.

An **absolute decree of divorce or annulment** ends the community in all community property states. A decree of annulment, even though it holds that no valid marriage ever existed, usually does not nullify community property rights arising during the "marriage." However, you should check your state law for exceptions.

A **decree of legal separation or of separate maintenance** may or may not end the community. The court issuing the decree may terminate the community and divide the property between the spouses.

A **separation agreement** may divide the community property between you and your spouse. It may provide that this property, along with future earnings and property acquired, will be separate property. Such an agreement may end the community.

In some states, the community ends when the spouses permanently separate, even if there is no formal agreement. Check your state law.

Alimony (Community Income)

Payments that may otherwise qualify as alimony are not deductible by the payer if they are the recipient spouse's part of community income. They are deductible as alimony only to the extent they are more than that spouse's part of community income.

Example. You live in a community property state. You are separated and your spouse has no income. Under a written agreement, you pay your spouse $12,000 of your $20,000 total yearly community income. Under your state law, earnings of a spouse living separately and apart from the other spouse continue as community property.

On your separate returns, each of you must report $10,000 gross income (half of the total community income). In addition, your spouse must report $2,000 as alimony received on line 11 of Form 1040. You can deduct $2,000 as alimony paid on line 29 of Form 1040.

Index

A
Address, change of 1
Alimony 7
  Community income 16
  Fees for getting 14
  Instruments executed after
    1984 8
  Instruments executed before
    1985 10
  Recapture 10
  Withholding, nonresident alien ... 8
Alimony trusts 11
Annuities 11
Annulment decree 2

C
Child 3, 4
Child support 7, 8, 9, 11
Citizen or resident test for
  dependents 4
Community property 14
  Alimony paid 16
  Income 15
Custodial parent, dependency
  exemption 5

D
Dependency tests 4
Divorce decree 2, 7
  Amended 7
  Costs of getting 14
  Invalid 7

E
Endowment contracts 11
Estimated tax 14
Exemptions 4
  Dependents 4
  Phaseout 7
  Spouse 4

F
Filing status 2
  Head of household 3
  Joint return 2
  Separate returns 2
Form:
  2120 7
  709 14
  8332 7
  8822 1
  W–4 14

G
Gift tax on property settlements 13

H
Head of household 3
Home owned jointly 5, 8
  Sale of 14

I
Income test for dependents 4
Individual retirement
  arrangements 12
Innocent spouse 2

J
Joint return 2

L
Life insurance premiums 8

M
Married person test for
  dependents 4
Medical expenses, child of divorced
  or separated parents 7
Multiple support agreement 7

N
Name, change of 1
Noncustodial parent, dependency
  exemption 5
Nonresident alien, withholding on
  alimony 8

P
Phaseout of exemptions 7
Property settlements 12

Q
Qualified domestic relations
  order 11

R
Recapture of alimony 10
Relationship test for dependents 4

S
Sale of jointly-owned property 14
Savings bonds 12
Section 1041 election 13
Separate maintenance decree 2, 7
Separate returns 2
Separation agreement 7
Social security numbers for
  dependents 4
Support test for dependents 5
  Children of divorced or separated
    parents 5
  Multiple support agreement 7

T
Tax advice, fees for 14
Tax withholding 14

G (cont.)
Gift tax 13
Jointly-owned property, sale
  of 14

853

26 U.S.C.A. § 215   **FEDERAL LAWS**

[Page 18 of Publication 504 is blank.]

FEDERAL LAWS   26 U.S.C.A. § 215

List of Tax Publications for Individuals

General Guides
- 1 — Your Rights as a Taxpayer
- 17 — Your Federal Income Tax
- 225 — Farmer's Tax Guide
- 334 — Tax Guide for Small Business
- 509 — Tax Calendars for 1994
- 553 — Highlights of 1993 Tax Changes
- 595 — Tax Guide for Commercial Fishermen
- 910 — Guide to Free Tax Services (Includes a list of publications)

Specialized Publications
- 3 — Tax Information for Military Personnel (Including Reservists Called to Active Duty)
- 4 — Student's Guide to Federal Income Tax
- 54 — Tax Guide for U.S. Citizens and Resident Aliens Abroad
- 378 — Fuel Tax Credits and Refunds
- 448 — Federal Estate and Gift Taxes
- 463 — Travel, Entertainment, and Gift Expenses
- 501 — Exemptions, Standard Deduction, and Filing Information
- 502 — Medical and Dental Expenses
- 503 — Child and Dependent Care Expenses
- 504 — Divorced or Separated Individuals
- 505 — Tax Withholding and Estimated Tax
- 508 — Educational Expenses
- 513 — Tax Information for Visitors to the United States
- 514 — Foreign Tax Credit for Individuals
- 516 — Tax Information for U.S. Government Civilian Employees Stationed Abroad
- 517 — Social Security and Other Information for Members of the Clergy and Religious Workers
- 519 — U.S. Tax Guide for Aliens
- 520 — Scholarships and Fellowships
- 521 — Moving Expenses
- 523 — Selling Your Home
- 524 — Credit for the Elderly or the Disabled
- 525 — Taxable and Nontaxable Income
- 526 — Charitable Contributions
- 527 — Residential Rental Property
- 529 — Miscellaneous Deductions
- 530 — Tax Information for First-Time Homeowners
- 531 — Reporting Tip Income
- 533 — Self-Employment Tax
- 534 — Depreciation
- 537 — Installment Sales
- 541 — Tax Information on Partnerships
- 544 — Sales and Other Dispositions of Assets
- 547 — Nonbusiness Disasters, Casualties, and Thefts
- 550 — Investment Income and Expenses
- 551 — Basis of Assets
- 552 — Recordkeeping for Individuals
- 554 — Tax Information for Older Americans
- 555 — Federal Tax Information on Community Property
- 556 — Examination of Returns, Appeal Rights, and Claims for Refund
- 559 — Survivors, Executors, and Administrators
- 560 — Retirement Plans for the Self-Employed
- 561 — Determining the Value of Donated Property
- 564 — Mutual Fund Distributions
- 570 — Tax Guide for Individuals with Income from U.S. Possessions
- 571 — Tax-Sheltered Annuity Programs for Employees of Public Schools and Certain Tax-Exempt Organizations
- 575 — Pension and Annuity Income (Including Simplified General Rule)
- 584 — Nonbusiness Disaster, Casualty, and Theft Loss Workbook
- 587 — Business Use of Your Home
- 590 — Individual Retirement Arrangements (IRAs)
- 593 — Tax Highlights for U.S. Citizens and Residents Going Abroad
- 594 — Understanding The Collection Process
- 596 — Earned Income Credit
- 597 — Information on the United States-Canada Income Tax Treaty
- 721 — Tax Guide to U.S. Civil Service Retirement Benefits
- 901 — U.S. Tax Treaties
- 907 — Information for Persons with Disabilities
- 908 — Bankruptcy and Other Debt Cancellation
- 909 — Alternative Minimum Tax for Individuals
- 911 — Tax Information for Direct Sellers
- 915 — Social Security Benefits and Equivalent Railroad Retirement Benefits
- 917 — Business Use of a Car
- 919 — Is My Withholding Correct for 1994?
- 925 — Passive Activity and At-Risk Rules
- 926 — Employment Taxes for Household Employers
- 929 — Tax Rules for Children and Dependents
- 936 — Home Mortgage Interest Deduction
- 938 — Real Estate Mortgage Investment Conduits (REMICs) Reporting Information
- 945 — Tax Information for Those Affected by Operation Desert Storm
- 946 — How To Begin Depreciating Your Property
- 947 — Practice Before the IRS and Power of Attorney
- 1244 — Employee's Daily Record of Tips and Report to Employers
- 1544 — Reporting Cash Payments of Over $10,000
- 1546 — How to use the Problem Resolution Program of the IRS

Spanish Language Publications
- 1SP — Derechos del Contribuyente
- 556SP — Revisión de las Declaraciones de Impuesto, Derecho de Apelación y Reclamaciones de Reembolsos
- 579SP — Cómo Preparar la Declaración de Impuesto Federal
- 594SP — Comprendiendo el Proceso de Cobro
- 596SP — Crédito por Ingreso del Trabajo
- 850 — English–Spanish Glossary of Words and Phrases Used in Publications Issued by the Internal Revenue Service

Tax forms, publications and instructions listed on the order blank

You can get the following forms, schedules, and instructions at participating banks, post offices, or libraries.

Form 1040
Instructions for Form 1040 & Schedules
Schedule A for itemized deductions
Schedule B for interest and dividend income if over $400; and for answering the foreign accounts or foreign trusts questions

Schedule EIC for the earned income credit
Form 1040A
Instructions for Form 1040A & Schedules
Schedule 1 for Form 1040A filers to report interest and dividend income

Schedule 2 for Form 1040A filers to report child and dependent care expenses
Form 1040EZ
Instructions for Form 1040EZ

You can photocopy the items listed below (as well as those listed above) at participating libraries or order them from the IRS.

Schedule 3, Credit for the Elderly or the Disabled for Form 1040A Filers
Schedule C, Profit or Loss From Business
Schedule C-EZ, Net Profit From Business
Schedule D, Capital Gains and Losses
Schedule E, Supplemental Income and Loss
Schedule F, Profit or Loss From Farming
Schedule R, Credit for the Elderly or the Disabled
Schedule SE, Self-Employment Tax
Form 1040-ES, Estimated Tax for Individuals
Form 1040X, Amended U.S. Individual Income Tax Return
Form 2106, Employee Business Expenses
Form 2119, Sale of Your Home
Form 2210, Underpayment of Estimated Tax by Individuals and Fiduciaries
Form 2441, Child and Dependent Care Expenses
Form 3903, Moving Expenses
Form 4562, Depreciation and Amortization
Form 4868, Application for Automatic Extension of Time To File U.S. Individual Income Tax Return
Form 5329, Return for Additional Taxes Attributable to Qualified Retirement Plans, Annuities, and Modified Endowment Contracts
Form 8283, Noncash Charitable Contributions
Form 8582, Passive Activity Loss Limitations
Form 8606, Nondeductible IRA Contributions, IRA Basis, and Nontaxable IRA Distributions
Form 8822, Change of Address
Form 8829, Expenses for Business Use of Your Home

26 U.S.C.A. § 414(p)   FEDERAL LAWS

How to Get IRS Forms and Publications

You can visit your local IRS office or order tax forms and publications from the IRS Forms Distribution Center listed for your state at the address below. Or, if you prefer, you can photocopy tax forms from reproducible copies kept at participating public libraries. In addition, many of these libraries have reference sets of IRS publications that you can read or copy.

If you are located in:	Send to "Forms Distribution Center" for your state
Alaska, Arizona, California, Colorado, Hawaii, Idaho, Kansas, Montana, Nevada, New Mexico, Oklahoma, Oregon, Utah, Washington, Wyoming, Guam, Northern Marianas, American Samoa	**Western Area Distribution Center** Rancho Cordova, CA 95743-0001
Alabama, Arkansas, Illinois, Indiana, Iowa, Kentucky, Louisiana, Michigan, Minnesota, Mississippi, Missouri, Nebraska, North Dakota, Ohio, South Dakota, Tennessee, Texas, Wisconsin	**Central Area Distribution Center** P.O. Box 8903 Bloomington, IL 61702-8903
Connecticut, Delaware, District of Columbia, Florida, Georgia, Maine, Maryland, Massachusetts, New Hampshire, New Jersey, New York, North Carolina, Pennsylvania, Rhode Island, South Carolina, Vermont, Virginia, West Virginia	**Eastern Area Distribution Center** P.O. Box 85074 Richmond, VA 23261-5074

Foreign Addresses—Taxpayers with mailing addresses in foreign countries should send their requests for forms and publications to:
Eastern Area Distribution Center
P.O. Box 85074
Richmond, VA 23261-5074
or
Western Area Distribution Center
Rancho Cordova, CA 95743-0001,
whichever is closer.

Puerto Rico
Eastern Area Distribution Center
P.O. Box 85074
Richmond, VA 23261-5074

Virgin Islands
V.I. Bureau of Internal Revenue
Lockharts Garden, No. 1A
Charlotte Amalie, St. Thomas
VI 00802

Detach at This Line

Order Blank

We will send you 2 copies of each form and 1 copy of each publication or set of instructions you circle. Please cut the order blank on the dotted line above and **be sure to print or type your name and address accurately on the bottom portion.**

Enclose this order blank in your own envelope and address your envelope to the IRS address shown above for your state.

To help reduce waste, please order only the forms, instructions, and publications you think you will need to prepare your return.

Use the blank spaces to order items not listed. If you need more space, attach a separate sheet of paper listing the additional forms and publications you may need.

You should either receive your order or notification of the status of your order within 7-15 work days after we receive your request.

1040	Schedule F (1040)	1040EZ	3903 & instructions	8829 & Instructions	Pub. 508	Pub. 575
Instructions for 1040 & Schedules	Schedule R (1040) & instructions	Instructions for 1040EZ	4562 & instructions	Pub. 1	Pub. 521	Pub. 590
Schedules A&B (1040)	Schedule SE (1040)	1040-ES (1994) & Instructions	4868 & Instructions	Pub. 17	Pub. 523	Pub. 596
Schedule C (1040)	1040A	1040X & Instructions	5329 & Instructions	Pub. 334	Pub. 525	Pub. 910
Schedule C-EZ (1040)	Instructions for 1040A & Schedules	2106 & Instructions	8283 & Instructions	Pub. 463	Pub. 527	Pub. 917
Schedule D (1040)	Schedule 1 (1040A)	2119 & Instructions	8582 & Instructions	Pub. 501	Pub. 529	Pub. 929
Schedule E (1040)	Schedule 2 (1040A)	2210 & Instructions	8606 & Instructions	Pub. 502	Pub. 550	Pub. 936
Schedule EIC (1040A or 1040)	Schedule 3 (1040A) & Instructions	2441 & Instructions	8822 & Instructions.	Pub. 505	Pub. 554	

Name

Number and street

City or town   State   ZIP code

20   [G19047]

26 U.S.C.A. § 414(p)

§ 414(p). Qualified domestic relations order defined

For purposes of this subsection and section 401(a)(13)—

(1) In general.

(A) Qualified domestic relations order. The term "qualified domestic relations order" means a domestic relations order—

(i) which creates or recognizes the existence of an alternate payee's right to, or assigns to an alternate payee the right to, receive all or a portion of the benefits payable with respect to a participant under a plan, and

(ii) with respect to which the requirements of paragraphs (2) and (3) are met.

(B) Domestic relations order. The term "domestic relations order" means any judgment, decree, or order (including approval of a property settlement agreement) which-

(i) relates to the provision of child support, alimony payments, or marital property rights to a spouse, former spouse, child, or other dependent of a participant, and

(ii) is made pursuant to a State domestic relations law (including a community property law).

(2) Order must clearly specify certain facts. A domestic relations order meets the requirements of this paragraph only if such order clearly specifies—

(A) the name and the last known mailing address (if any) of the participant and the name and mailing address of each alternate payee covered by the order,

(B) the amount or percentage of the participant's benefits to be paid by the plan to each such alternate payee, or the manner in which such amount or percentage is to be determined,

(C) the number of payments or period to which such order applies, and

(D) each plan to which such order applies.

(3) Order may not alter amount, form, etc., of benefits. A domestic relations order meets the requirements of this paragraph only if such order—

(A) does not require a plan to provide any type or form of benefit, or any option, not otherwise provided under the plan,

(B) does not require the plan to provide increased benefits (determined on the basis of actuarial value), and

(C) does not require the payment of benefits to an alternate payee which are required to be paid to another alternate payee under another order previously determined to be a qualified domestic relations order.

(4) Exception for certain payments made after earliest retirement age.

(A) In general. A domestic relations order shall not be treated as failing to meet the requirements of subparagraph (A) of paragraph (3) solely because such order requires that payment of benefits be made to an alternate payee—

> (i) in the case of any payment before a participant has separated from service, on or after the date on which the participant attains (or would have attained) the earliest retirement age,
>
> (ii) as if the participant had retired on the date on which such payment is to begin under such order (but taking into account only the present value of the benefits actually accrued and not taking into account the present value of any employer subsidy for early retirement), and
>
> (iii) in any form in which such benefits may be paid under the plan to the participant (other than in the form of a joint and survivor annuity with respect to the alternate payee and his or her subsequent spouse).

For purposes of clause (ii), the interest rate assumption used in determining the present value shall be the interest rate specified in the plan or, if no rate is specified, 5 percent.

> (B) Earliest retirement age. For purposes of this paragraph, the term "earliest retirement age" means the earlier of—
>
> (i) the date on which the participant is entitled to a distribution under the plan, or
>
> (ii) the later of—
>
> > (I) the date the participant attains age 50, or
> >
> > (II) the earliest date on which the participant could begin receiving benefits under the plan if the participant separated from service.

(5) Treatment of former spouse as surviving spouse for purposes of determining survivor benefits. To the extent provided in any qualified domestic relations order—

> (A) the former spouse of a participant shall be treated as a surviving spouse of such participant for purposes of sections 401(a)(11) and 417 (and any spouse of the participant shall not be treated as a spouse of the participant for such purposes), and
>
> (B) if married for at least 1 year, the surviving former spouse shall be treated as meeting the requirements of section 417(d).

(6) Plan procedures with respect to orders.

> (A) Notice and determination by administrator. In the case of any domestic relations order received by a plan—
>
> (i) the plan administrator shall promptly notify the participant and each alternate payee of the receipt of such order and the plan's procedures for determining the qualified status of domestic relations orders, and

(ii) within a reasonable period after receipt of such order, the plan administrator shall determine whether such order is a qualified domestic relations order and notify the participant and each alternate payee of such determination.

(B) Plan to establish reasonable procedures. Each plan shall establish reasonable procedures to determine the qualified status of domestic relations orders and to administer distributions under such qualified orders.

(7) Procedures for period during which determination is being made.

(A) In general. During any period in which the issue of whether a domestic relations order is a qualified domestic relations order is being determined (by the plan administrator, by a court of competent jurisdiction, or otherwise), the plan administrator shall separately account for the amounts (hereinafter in this paragraph referred to as the "segregated amounts") which would have been payable to the alternate payee during such period if the order had been determined to be a qualified domestic relations order.

(B) Payment to alternate payee if order determined to be qualified domestic relations order. If within the 18–month period described in subparagraph (E) the order (or modification thereof) is determined to be a qualified domestic relations order, the plan administrator shall pay the segregated amounts (including any interest thereon) to the person or persons entitled thereto.

(C) Payment to plan participant in certain cases. If within the 18–month period described in subparagraph (E)—

(i) it is determined that the order is not a qualified domestic relations order, or

(ii) the issue as to whether such order is a qualified domestic relations order is not resolved, then the plan administrator shall pay the segregated amounts (including any interest thereon) to the person or persons who would have been entitled to such amounts if there had been no order.

(D) Subsequent determination or order to be applied prospectively only. Any determination that an order is a qualified domestic relations order which is made after the close of the 18–month period described in subparagraph (E) shall be applied prospectively only.

(E) Determination of 18–month period. For purposes of this paragraph, the 18–month period described in this subparagraph is the 18–month period beginning with the date on which the first payment would be required to be made under the domestic relations order.

(8) Alternate payee defined. The term "alternate payee" means any spouse, former spouse, child or other dependent of a participant who is

26 U.S.C.A. § 414(p)   FEDERAL LAWS

recognized by a domestic relations order as having a right to receive all, or a portion of, the benefits payable under a plan with respect to such participant.

(9) Subsection not to apply to plans to which section 401(a)(13) does not apply. This subsection shall not apply to any plan to which section 401(a)(13) does not apply. For purposes of this title, except as provided in regulations, any distribution from an annuity contract under section 403(b) pursuant to a qualified domestic relations order shall be treated in the same manner as a distribution from a plan to which section 401(a)(13) applies.

(10) Waiver of certain distribution requirements. With respect to the requirements of subsections (a) and (k) of section 401, section 403(b), and section 409(d), a plan shall not be treated as failing to meet such requirements solely by reason of payments to an alternative payee pursuant to a qualified domestic relations order.

(11) Application of rules to governmental and church plans. For purposes of this title, a distribution or payment from a governmental plan (as defined in subsection (d)) or a church plan (as described in subsection (e)) shall be treated as made pursuant to a qualified domestic relations order if it is made pursuant to a domestic relations order which meets the requirement of clause (i) of paragraph (1)(A).

(12) Consultation with the secretary. In prescribing regulations under this subsection and section 401(a)(13), the Secretary of Labor shall consult with the Secretary.

Author's Notes

Analysis

1. Types of plans.
2. Transfer of cash or securities.
3. Other allocations.
4. Defined benefit plans.
5. QDRO.
6. QDRO—Form.
7. Additional provisions.
8. Cross references.

(1) **Types of plans.** There are two principal types of qualified retirement plans. A defined benefit plan is one where the benefit to be received at retirement is stated. A defined contribution plan is one in which the contributions to the plan are fixed, but the future benefit is uncertain, because the future benefit depends upon the performance of the investment of the contributions. A defined contribution plan will have an individual account balance; a defined benefit plan usually does not have an individual account balance. See also 750 ILCS 5/503 Author's Notes (29) and (30).

(2) **Transfer of cash or securities.** The simplest allocation is the transfer of cash or securities out of the qualified contribution plan of one spouse into an IRA of the other spouse. It is this transfer that is in the model QDRO in Author's Note (6) in this Section and it is the same transfer that is contemplated in the Settlement Agreement at 750 ILCS 5/502 Author's Note (11) para. 6(*l*)(i). As a result of this

allocation each spouse owns his or her own portion of the original plan, and can invest it and draw from it as he or she desires. The transfer from the retirement plan into an IRA can also be made in cash without tax consequences, inasmuch as securities in a qualified plan can be sold without paying capital gains tax. A transfer in cash obviates valuations and bases problems. There are, however, other more complex possibilities.

(3) **Other allocations.** Retirement plans can be valued at the time of the divorce, and one spouse can keep the entire plan while the other spouse receives a set off comprised of other assets. Alternatively, the retirement plan benefits can be allocated at the time they are actually paid. In the latter case, jurisdiction of the court should be expressly reserved in case disputes arise over the future allocation. See IRC § 408(d)(6) and accompanying Author's Notes for a transfer of an Individual Retirement Account from one spouse to another.

(4) **Defined benefit plans.** Particularly when defined benefit plans are involved, valuation, allocation, options, such as survivor benefits, and the QDROs themselves can be very complex. It is therefore almost always advisable to retain an expert in the field to read the plan and assist in the allocation.

(5) **QDRO.** A Qualified Domestic Relations Order (QDRO) is required in order to have a valid and enforceable assignment of all or part of a tax-qualified retirement plan.

(6) **QDRO—Form.** There follows a typical Qualified Domestic Relations Order for the transfer of cash from the qualified plan of one spouse into the IRA of the other spouse. After drafting a QDRO, the order should be submitted to the plan administrator for approval.

FIRM #_____

IN THE CIRCUIT COURT OF COOK COUNTY, ILLINOIS
COUNTY DEPARTMENT—DOMESTIC RELATIONS DIVISION

IN RE THE MARRIAGE OF)
)
SUSAN JELLYBY,)
)
           Petitioner,)
)
and) No. ____ D _____
)
ARTHUR JELLYBY,)
)
           Respondent.)

QUALIFIED DOMESTIC RELATIONS ORDER

THIS MATTER COMING ON TO BE HEARD for the purpose of entry of a Qualified Domestic Relations Order as defined in 26 U.S.C.A. Section 414(p) and any amendments thereto; the Court on _____, 199__, having entered a Judgment of Dissolution of Marriage of this Court pertaining, inter alia, to a division of Petitioner's interest in the Bleak House Retirement Plan between Petitioner and Respondent; due notice having been given; the Court having

26 U.S.C.A. § 414(p)   FEDERAL LAWS

jurisdiction of the parties and of the subject matter; and the Court being fully advised in the premises:

IT IS HEREBY ORDERED as follows:

(a) For the purposes of this Order, the term "Participant" means Respondent, ARTHUR JELLYBY, and the "Alternate Payee" means Petitioner, SUSAN JELLYBY.

(b) On _____, 199__, this Court entered a Judgment pursuant to the Illinois Marriage and Dissolution of Marriage Act. The Judgment, inter alia, assigned to SUSAN JELLYBY the right to receive a benefit derived from the Bleak House Retirement Plan. ARTHUR JELLYBY is a participant in the Bleak House Retirement Plan to which this Order applies.

(c) The name and last known mailing address of the Participant is: ARTHUR JELLYBY, _____, _____, Illinois _____.

(d) The name and last known mailing address of the Alternate Payee covered by this Order is: SUSAN JELLYBY, _____, _____, Illinois _____.

(e) The Judgment contains, in pertinent part, the following provisions of the parties' settlement agreement which are incorporated herein and which relate to the right of SUSAN JELLYBY to receive benefits otherwise payable to ARTHUR JELLYBY pursuant to the Plan:

6(*l*)(i). ARTHUR has a vested interest in the Bleak House Retirement Plan (hereinafter referred to as the "Retirement Plan"). ARTHUR agrees that on the effective date of this Agreement he will cause to be paid by certified check the sum of TWO HUNDRED THOUSAND DOLLARS ($200,000.00) from the Retirement Plan to an IRA in the name of SUSAN at _____ Bank, known as Account No. _____. The $200,000.00 shall be the sole property of SUSAN, free of any right, title or interest in ARTHUR. The transfer from ARTHUR's Retirement Plan to SUSAN's IRA rather than directly to SUSAN is in order to avoid the necessity of withholding. The remaining balance of the Retirement Plan after the aforedescribed payment to SUSAN shall be owned by ARTHUR as his sole property, free of any right, title or interest of SUSAN. The parties shall cooperate to draft a Qualified Domestic Relations Order (QDRO) acceptable to the Administrator of the Retirement Plan to effectuate this provision. A copy of the QDRO is attached hereto and made a part hereof as Exhibit E. The parties intend that the distribution from the Retirement Plan to SUSAN's IRA will not result in any tax consequences to SUSAN until such time as she begins to make withdrawals from her IRA, and the parties agree to prepare their income tax returns accordingly. The parties shall and hereby do ask the Court to retain jurisdiction to enter any order(s) that may be necessary to bring such order(s) within the definition of a Qualified Domestic Relations Order as defined in Section 414(p) of the Internal Revenue Code of 1986, and amendments thereto, to resolve any tax issues in a manner consistent with this Agreement, to amend this paragraph 6(l)(i), if necessary, consistent with the parties' intentions, and to adjudicate consistent with this Agreement other issues that may arise concerning this paragraph 6(l)(i). The parties shall also execute all documents, including but not limited to releases, election forms, and consent forms, that are necessary to effectuate the provisions of this paragraph 6(l)(i).

(f) The parties have agreed to transfer the funds (or securities) directly to SUSAN JELLYBY's IRA because such a transfer is not subject to withholding tax.

(g) Nothing in this Order requires and the Order shall not be construed to require:

　　1. The Bleak House Retirement Plan to provide any type or form of benefit or any option not otherwise provided under the Plan.

　　2. The payment of benefits to SUSAN JELLYBY, the Alternate Payee, which are required to be paid to another alternate payee under another Order previously determined to be a Qualified Domestic Relations Order.

　　3. The Plan to provide increased benefits.

(h) It is intended by the parties that this Order will qualify as a Qualified Domestic Relations Order pursuant to the Internal Revenue Code of 1954 and the Employees Retirement Income Security Act of 1974, both as amended by the Retirement Equity Act of 1984, and subsequent amendments, and that it will be interpreted and administered as such.

(i) The Court retains jurisdiction to amend this Order for the purpose of establishing or maintaining this Order as a Qualified Domestic Relations Order; and, further, the Court may amend this Order to revise or conform its terms so as to effect the expressed provisions of the Order, the parties' Settlement Agreement dated _____, 199__, and the Judgment of Dissolution of Marriage, as well as to modify this Order to comply with the requirements of Section 414(p) of the Internal Revenue Code as it relates to Qualified Domestic Relations Orders.

SUSAN JELLYBY

Samuel Kenge
Attorney for SUSAN JELLYBY

ARTHUR JELLYBY

Joseph Blowers
Attorney for ARTHUR JELLYBY

ENTER:

JUDGE

26 U.S.C.A. § 414(p)   FEDERAL LAWS

Samuel Kenge
Kenge and Carboy
Address
Telephone number

(7) **Additional provisions.** The provisions in the settlement agreement or judgment authorizing the Qualified Domestic Relations Order can be as simple as those incorporated in paragraph (e) of the Qualified Domestic Relations Order, or they can be more elaborate. See 750 ILCS 5/502 Author's Note (11) para. 6(l)(i) for settlement agreement paragraph. Retirement plans are a specialized and complex area of the law and care is required in dealing with them. Ideally, the attorney for the transferee will examine the plan or have an expert so do, particularly in the case of defined benefit plans. When the attorney for the transferee has not examined the plan or obtained an expert opinion concerning the transferee's expectations about the plan and the contemplated tax results, appropriate warranties and indemnifications should be sought from the transferor or even from the plan administrator. At a minimum, the anticipated tax results should be stated, and what will happen if they do not materialize. General provisions concerning the tax ramifications of a transfer of cash from a defined contribution retirement plan to an IRA are set forth in 750 ILCS 5/502 Author's Note (11) paras. 6(l)(i) and 6(o).

(8) **Cross references.** See IRC § 3405(c) and accompanying Author's Note for income tax withholding provisions for retirement plan transfers. See 750 ILCS 5/503 Author's Note (29) et seq. for discussion of retirement benefits as part of the marital estate.

26 U.S.C.A. § 408(d)(6)

§ 408(d)(6). Transfer of account incident to divorce

The transfer of an individual's interest in an individual retirement account or an individual retirement annuity to his spouse or former spouse under a divorce or separation instrument described in subparagraph (A) of section 71(b)(2) is not to be considered a taxable transfer made by such individual notwithstanding any other provision of this subtitle, and such interest at the time of the transfer is to be treated as an individual retirement account of such spouse, and not of such individual. Thereafter such account or annuity for purposes of this subtitle is to be treated as maintained for the benefit of such spouse.

Author's Notes

Analysis

1. Transfers of IRAs.
2. Cross reference—Form.
3. Tax implications.

(1) **Transfers of IRAs.** Transfers of IRAs from one spouse to another are not accomplished by Qualified Domestic Relations Orders, because they are not tax-qualified plans.

(2) **Cross reference—Form.** A settlement agreement or judgment sample paragraph for an IRA transfer is at 750 ILCS 5/502 Author's Note (11) para. 6(l)(ii). As is provided in the model, transfers of a portion of an IRA from one spouse to another are accomplished by the transferor creating a new IRA, to which he transfers a portion of his existing IRA, after which he assigns the new IRA to the transferee.

(3) **Tax implications.** The IRA transfer from one spouse to another should set forth the contemplated tax consequences. See 750 ILCS 5/502 Author's Note (11) paras. 6(l)(ii) and 6(o).

26 U.S.C.A. § 3405(c)

§ 3405(c). Eligible rollover distributions

(1) In general. In the case of any designated distribution which is an eligible rollover distribution—

(A) subsections (a) and (b) shall not apply, and

(B) the payor of such distribution shall withhold from such distribution an amount equal to 20 percent of such distribution.

(2) Exception. Paragraph (1)(B) shall not apply to any distribution if the distributee elects under section 401(a)(31)(A) to have such distribution paid directly to an eligible retirement plan.

(3) Eligible rollover distribution. For purposes of this subsection, the term "eligible rollover distribution" has the meaning given such term by section 402(f)(2)(A) (or in the case of an annuity contract under section 403(b)), a distribution from such contract described in section 402(f)(2)(A).

Author's Notes

(1) **Withholding provisions.** Congress has enacted withholding provisions at the rate of 20% on any retirement plan distribution after 1992 that is transferred directly to an eligible transferee, such as a former spouse. This withholding can be avoided by making the transfer directly to the former spouse's own IRA or other plan, rather than to the former spouse himself. If the transfer is directly to the former spouse, and he subsequently transfers it into his IRA within the time allotted for tax free transfers, he can obtain a refund of the withholding, but he will not then be able to deposit the refund into his plan because the time period will have expired, and he will have to pay tax on the amount of the refund.

26 U.S.C.A. § 682

§ 682. Income of an estate or trust in case of divorce, etc.

(a) Inclusion in gross income of wife. There shall be included in the gross income of a wife who is divorced or legally separated under a decree of divorce or of separate maintenance (or who is separated from her husband under a written separation agreement) the amount of the income of any trust which such wife is entitled to receive and which, except for this section, would be includible in the gross income of her husband, and such amount shall not, despite any other provision of this subtitle, be includible in the gross income of such husband. This subsection shall not apply to that part of any such income of the trust which the terms of the decree, written separation agreement, or trust instrument fix, in terms of an amount of money or a portion of such income, as a sum which is payable for the support of minor children of such husband. In case such income is less than the amount specified in the decree, agreement, or instrument, for the purpose of applying the preceding sentence, such income, to the extent of such sum payable for such support, shall be considered a payment for such support.

(b) Wife considered a beneficiary. For purposes of computing the taxable income of the estate or trust and the taxable income of a wife to whom subsection (a) applies, such wife shall be considered as the beneficiary specified in this part.

Author's Notes

Analysis

1. Insurance trust.
2. § 682 governs.
3. Alimony trust.
4. Estate.
5. § 71 governs.
6. Non-taxable alimony.

(1) **Insurance trust.** When life insurance proceeds are paid into an insurance trust upon the decedent's death, the insurance trust is governed by Internal Revenue Code § 682. Marjorie A. O'Connell, *Divorce Taxation*, ¶5201 (1989). A § 682 Trust may be used to provide for post-death payments to the payee. Marjorie A. O'Connell, *Divorce Taxation*, ¶5207 (1987).

(2) **§ 682 governs.** Section 71 of the Internal Revenue Code is eliminated and the taxation rules for the payee of the insurance trust are governed by § 682 of the Internal Revenue Code. Marjorie A. O'Connell, *Divorce Taxation*, ¶5201 (1989). The payee of the insurance trust is taxed on distributions to the extent of the trust's distributable net income, which in most cases means that the payee is taxed on the income distributed to her from the insurance trust and is not taxed on principal distributed to her from the insurance trust, regardless of the amount of the alimony obligation. Marjorie A. O'Connell, *Divorce Taxation*, ¶¶5201, 5203 (1989, 1987). Conversely, the deductions for the insurance trust are those in effect for any other trust. In simple trusts income that is required to be distributed can be deducted, limited by the trust's distributable net income. Marjorie A. O'Connell, *Divorce Taxation*, ¶5305 (1987).

(3) **Alimony trust.** Although as a practical matter the use is of limited utility because of the reluctance of payors to transfer assets, a § 682 Trust can also be used as a collateral trust to secure alimony or as an alimony trust. Marjorie A. O'Connell, *Divorce Taxation*, ¶5201 (1989). Because § 682 now supplants § 71 of the Internal Revenue Code in regard to an alimony trust, an alimony trust can be used to make payments that are prohibited by § 71. For example, payments after the payee's death. Marjorie A. O'Connell, *Divorce Taxation*, ¶¶3402, 5205 (1989, 1987). Section 682 Trusts can also be used to avoid the recapture provisions under § 71 of the Internal Revenue Code, and to pay unallocated alimony and children's support, which is

otherwise prohibited by the anti-Lester rules IRC § 71(c)(2). Marjorie A. O'Connell, *Divorce Taxation*, ¶5205 (1987).

(4) **Estate.** The payor can also use his estate as security for the payment of alimony owing to the payee. The payments made by the payor's estate after the payor's death in order to carry out the payor's alimony obligation are deductible to the estate. Marjorie A. O'Connell, *Divorce Taxation*, ¶¶2411 through 2413 (1988). The amount of the claim is usually established by actuarial calculations as of the date of death. Marjorie A. O'Connell, *Divorce Taxation*, ¶13,102 (1987).

(5) **§ 71 governs.** The payee of the alimony payments from the payor's estate is fully taxed on the alimony payments pursuant to § 71 of the Internal Revenue Code, regardless of the amount of the income and principal comprising the alimony payment distributed to the payee. Marjorie A. O'Connell, *Divorce Taxation*, ¶13,202 (1990). This rule appears to apply whether the estate is obligated to continue making periodic payments or whether the estate commutes the periodic payments to a present value. Marjorie A. O'Connell, *Divorce Taxation*, ¶13,202 (1990).

(6) **Non-taxable alimony.** Since § 71 of the Internal Revenue Code governs, where payments to the payee from the payor's estate are designated as not taxable pursuant to § 71(b)(1)(B), that Section should control.

26 U.S.C.A. § 1041

§ 1041. Transfers of property between spouses or incident to divorce

(a) General rule. No gain or loss shall be recognized on a transfer of property from an individual to (or in trust for the benefit of)—

(1) a spouse, or

(2) a former spouse, but only if the transfer is incident to the divorce

(b) Transfer treated as gift; transferee has transferor's basis. In the case of any transfer of property described in subsection (a)—

(1) for purposes of this subtitle, the property shall be treated as acquired by the transferee by gift, and

(2) the basis of the transferee in the property shall be the adjusted basis of the transferor.

(c) Incident to divorce. For purposes of subsection (a)(2), a transfer of property is incident to the divorce if such transfer—

(1) occurs within 1 year after the date on which the marriage ceases, or

(2) is related to the cessation of the marriage.

(d) Special rule where spouse is nonresident alien. Subsection (a) shall not apply if the spouse (or former spouse) of the individual making the transfer is a nonresident alien.

(e) Transfers in trust where liability exceeds basis. Subsection (a) shall not apply to the transfer of property in trust to the extent that—

(1) the sum of the amount of the liabilities assumed, plus the amount of the liabilities to which the property is subject, exceeds

(2) the total of the adjusted basis of the property transferred.

Proper adjustment shall be made under subsection (b) in the basis of the transferee in such property to take into account gain recognized by reason of the preceding sentence.

Author's Notes

Analysis

1. Non-recognition rule.
2. Transfer incident to the divorce.
3. Capital gains tax.
4. Previous law.
5. Present law under § 1041.
6. Basis.
7. Cross reference—Form.
8. § 1401 requirements.
9. Effective date.

(1) **Non-recognition rule.** Section 1041 of the Internal Revenue Code provides that no gain or loss shall be recognized on almost all transfers of property between spouses during marriage, or between former spouses, provided that the transfer between former spouses is incident to their divorce. Two exceptions to the non-recognition rule are that § 1041 does not apply to non-resident aliens, nor to transfers into trust of property with liabilities that exceed the property's adjusted basis. Otherwise transfers into trust for the benefit of a spouse or a former spouse incident to a divorce qualify for non-recognition treatment.

(2) **Transfer incident to the divorce.** Section 1041 defines a transfer "incident to the divorce" as a transfer that occurs within one year after the date on which the marriage terminates, or is related to the cessation of the marriage. If the transfer is not to occur within one year after the date of the entry of the dissolution of marriage judgment, it is important to show in the settlement agreement or judgment how the transfer is related to the termination of the marriage.

The temporary regulations provide that property transfers will be treated as related to the cessation of the marriage if the transfer is (a) made pursuant to a divorce or separation agreement, and (b) the transfer is not made more than six years after the marriage is terminated. A transfer that fails both tests (one year after the marriage termination, or six years under the regulations provision) can still be related to the cessation of the marriage, but it must be demonstrated by the parties. Marjorie A. O'Connell, *Divorce Taxation*, ¶6004 (1989).

(3) **Capital gains tax.** There is no capital gains tax assessed on the appreciation of property that qualifies for § 1041 treatment. The property is treated as acquired by the spouse or the former spouse as a gift. The basis in the hands of the transferee is the carry-over basis from the transferor.

(4) **Previous law.** Section 1041 represents a change in the prior law of property exchanges in divorces as it was enunciated in Davis v. U.S., 370 U.S. 65, 82 S.Ct. 1190, 8 L.Ed.2d 335 (1962). Under *Davis*, the transferor spouse paid a capital gains tax on

the difference between the basis of the transferred property and its fair market value at the time of the transfer, and the transferee spouse received the property with its basis increased to the fair market value of the property.

The former rule generally benefited women. To take a simple example, if the marital home was in the sole name of the husband, and, pursuant to a divorce settlement, the wife received the marital home, the husband would pay a capital gains tax on the gain in the value of the marital home. The wife would receive the marital home with its basis increased to the fair market value of the home. When the wife subsequently sold the marital home, she would have no, or at least a greatly diminished, capital gains tax to pay. Husbands, however, complained, because it was necessary for them to pay a capital gains tax on a divorce transfer to the wife, which, although the transfer was treated as a sale, produced no proceeds from which the husband could pay the tax.

(5) **Present law under § 1041.** Section 1041 eliminates the requirement that the husband pay a tax at the time of the transfer to the wife, but, conversely, former wives receive appreciated property without bases increased to the fair market value of the property. This creates a time bomb for the former wife when she sells the marital home, or other asset of increased value. At the time of her sale, she may be required to pay a tax greater than she anticipated. Lawyers representing transferees of appreciated property should therefore be careful to advise their clients that they are taking the transferor's basis and there may be a large tax down the road.

(6) **Basis.** Basis is obviously very important in any marital settlement agreement or judgment that involves appreciated property, and basis needs to be analyzed as carefully as are values. For example, if a marital estate of appreciated property is divided equally between the spouses in terms of current market values, the supposed equal division can be distorted if one spouse receives more high basis property than does the other spouse. The equal division is distorted because the spouse receiving the low basis property will pay a greater capital gains tax upon sale to a third party than will the spouse who receives a majority of the high basis property. It is therefore critical to determine the bases of property to be allocated, and to agree upon a fair distribution of bases in the same way that an agreement is reached as to the allocation of current market values of the property. In the courtroom, the judge must be made aware of the bases of property in the same manner as evidence is introduced concerning the values of property.

(7) **Cross reference—Form.** As in other places in the marital settlement agreement, where there are tax ramifications, it is wise to set forth what tax results are contemplated, and what is to happen if, for some unanticipated reasons, the tax results are different. A suggested paragraph can be found at 750 ILCS 5/502 Author's Note (11) para. 6(*o*).

(8) **§ 1041 requirements.** The Internal Revenue Service has established requirements for parties who make transfers under § 1041. The transferor is required to give the transferee records concerning the adjusted basis of the property, the holding period of the property, and the investment tax credit recapture, where applicable. The transferee is required to maintain the records for the Internal Revenue Service. Marjorie A. O'Connell, *Divorce Taxation*, ¶6009 (1990).

(9) **Effective date.** Section 1041 became effective on July 18, 1984, and it applies to all transfers under instruments that are executed after July 18, 1984. Marjorie A. O'Connell, *Divorce Taxation*, ¶6010 (1990).

26 U.S.C.A. § 1034

§ 1034. Rollover of gain on sale of principal residence

(a) Nonrecognition of gain. If property (in this section called "old residence") used by the taxpayer as his principal residence is sold by him and, within a period beginning 2 years before the date of such sale and ending 2 years after such date, property (in this section called "new residence") is purchased and used by the taxpayer as his principal residence, gain (if any) from such sale shall be recognized only to the extent that the taxpayer's adjusted sales price (as defined in subsection (b)) of the old residence exceeds the taxpayer's cost of purchasing the new residence.

(b) Adjusted sales price defined.

(1) In general. For purposes of this section, the term "adjusted sales price" means the amount realized, reduced by the aggregate of the expenses for work performed on the old residence in order to assist in its sale.

(2) Limitations. The reduction provided in paragraph (1) applies only to expenses—

(A) for work performed during the 90-day period ending on the day on which the contract to sell the old residence is entered into;

(B) which are paid on or before the 30th day after the date of the sale of the old residence; and

(C) which are—

(i) not allowable as deductions in computing taxable income under section 63 (defining taxable income), and

(ii) not taken into account in computing the amount realized from the sale of the old residence.

(c) Rules for application of section. For purposes of this section:

(1) An exchange by the taxpayer of his residence for other property shall be treated as a sale of such residence, and the acquisition of a residence on the exchange of property shall be treated as a purchase of such residence.

(2) A residence any part of which was constructed or reconstructed by the taxpayer shall be treated as purchased by the taxpayer. In determining the taxpayer's cost of purchasing a residence, there shall be included only so much of his cost as is attributable to the acquisition, construction, reconstruction, and improvements made which are properly chargeable to capital account, during the period specified in subsection (a).

(3) If a residence is purchased by the taxpayer before the date of his sale of the old residence, the purchased residence shall not be treated as his new residence if sold or otherwise disposed of by him before the date of the sale of the old residence.

(4) If the taxpayer, during the period described in subsection (a), purchases more than one residence which is used by him as his principal residence at some time within 2 years after the date of the sale of the old residence, only the last of such residences so used by him after the date of such sale shall constitute the new residence. If a principal residence is sold in a sale to which subsection (d)(2) applies within 2 years after the sale of the old residence, for purposes of applying the preceding sentence with respect to the old residence, the principal residence so sold shall be treated as the last residence used during such 2-year period.

(d) Limitation

(1) In general. Subsection (a) shall not apply with respect to the sale of the taxpayer's residence if within 2 years before the date of such sale the taxpayer sold at a gain other property used by him as his principal residence, and any part of such gain was not recognized by reason of subsection (a).

(2) Subsequent sale connected with commencing work at new place. Paragraph (1) shall not apply with respect to the sale of the taxpayer's residence if—

(A) such sale was in connection with the commencement of work by the taxpayer as an employee or as a self-employed individual at a new principal place of work, and

(B) if the residence so sold is treated as the former residence for purposes of section 217 (relating to moving expenses), the taxpayer would satisfy the conditions of subsection (c) of section 217 (as modified by the other subsections of such section).

(e) Basis of new residence. Where the purchase of a new residence results, under subsection (a) or under section 112 (n) of the Internal Revenue Code of 1939, in the nonrecognition of gain on the sale of an old residence, in determining the adjusted basis of the new residence as of any time following the sale of the old residence, the adjustments to basis shall include a reduction by an amount equal to the amount of the again not so recognized on the sale of the old residence. For this purpose, the amount of the gain not so recognized on the sale of the old residence includes only so much of such gain as is not recognized by reason of the cost, up to such time, of purchasing the new residence.

(f) Tenant-stockholder in a cooperative housing corporation. For purposes of this section, section 1016 (relating to adjustments to basis), and section 1223 (relating to holding period), references to property used by the taxpayer as his principal residence, and references to the residence of a taxpayer, shall include stock held by a tenant-stockholder (as defined in section 216, relating to deduction for amounts representing taxes and interest paid to a cooperative housing corporation) in a cooperative housing corporation (as defined in such section) if—

(1) in the case of stock sold, the house or apartment which the taxpayer was entitled to occupy as such stockholder was used by him as his principal residence, and

(2) in the case of stock purchased, the taxpayer used as his principal residence the house or apartment which he was entitled to occupy as such stockholder.

(g) *Husband and wife.* If the taxpayer and his spouse, in accordance with regulations which shall be prescribed by the Secretary pursuant to this subsection, consent to the application of paragraph (2) of this subsection, then—

(1) for purposes of this section—

(A) the taxpayer's adjusted sales price of the old residence is the adjusted sales price (of the taxpayer, or of the taxpayer and his spouse) of the old residence, and

(B) the taxpayer's cost of purchasing the new residence is the cost (to the taxpayer, his spouse, or both) of purchasing the new residence (whether held by the taxpayer, his spouse, or the taxpayer and his spouse); and

(2) so much of the gain on the sale of the old residence as is not recognized solely by reason of this subsection, and so much of the adjustment under subsection (e) to the basis of the new residence as results solely from this subsection shall be allocated between the taxpayer and his spouse as provided in such regulations.

This subsection shall apply only if the old residence and the new residence are each used by the taxpayer and his spouse as their principal residence. In case the taxpayer and his spouse do not consent to the application of paragraph (2) of this subsection then the recognition of gain on the sale of the old residence shall be determined under this section without regard to the rules provided in this subsection. For purposes of this subsection, except to the extent provided in regulations, in the case of an individual who dies after the date of the sale of the old residence and is married on the date of death, consent to the application of paragraph (2) by such individual's spouse and use of the new residence as the principal residence of such spouse shall be treated as consent and use by such individual.

(h) *Members of armed forces.*

(1) *In general.* The running of any period of time specified in subsection (a) or (c) (other than the 2 years referred to in subsection (c)(4)) shall be suspended during any time that the taxpayer (or his spouse if the old residence and the new residence are each used by the taxpayer and his spouse as their principal residence) serves on extended active duty with the Armed Forces of the United States after the date of the sale of the old residence, except that any such period of time as so suspended shall not extend beyond the date 4 years after the date of the sale of the old residence.

(2) **Members stationed outside the united states or required to reside in government quarters.** In the case of any taxpayer who, during any period of time the running of which is suspended by paragraph (1)—

(A) is stationed outside of the United States, or

(B) after returning from a tour of duty outside of the United States and pursuant to a determination by the Secretary of Defense that adequate off-base housing is not available at a remote base site, is required to reside in on-base Government quarters, any such period of time as so suspended shall not expire before the day which is 1 year after the last day described in subparagraph (A) or (B), as the case may be, except that any such period of time as so suspended shall not extend beyond the date which is 8 years after the date of the sale of the old residence.

(3) **Extended active duty defined.** For purposes of this subsection, the term "extended active duty" means any period of active duty pursuant to a call or order to such duty for a period in excess of 90 days or for an indefinite period.

(i) **Special rule for condemnation.** In the case of the seizure, requisition, or condemnation of a residence, or the sale or exchange of a residence under threat or imminence thereof, the provisions of this section, in lieu of section 1033 (relating to involuntary conversions), shall be applicable if the taxpayer so elects. If such election is made, such seizure, requisition, or condemnation shall be treated as the sale of the residence. Such election shall be made at such time and in such manner as the Secretary shall prescribe by regulations.

(j) **Statute of limitations.** If the taxpayer during a taxable year sells at a gain property used by him as his principal residence, then—

(1) the statutory period for the assessment of any deficiency attributable to any part of such gain shall not expire before the expiration of 3 years from the date the Secretary is notified by the taxpayer (in such manner as the Secretary may by regulations prescribe) of—

(A) the taxpayer's cost of purchasing the new residence which the taxpayer claims results in nonrecognition of any part of such gain,

(B) the taxpayer's intention not to purchase a new residence within the period specified in subsection (a), or

(C) a failure to make such purchase within such period; and

(2) such deficiency may be assessed before the expiration of such 3-year period notwithstanding the provisions of any other law or rule of law which would otherwise prevent such assessment.

(k) **Individual whose tax home is outside the united states.** The running of any period of time specified in subsection (a) or (c) (other than the 2 years referred to in subsection (c)(4)) shall be suspended during any time that the taxpayer (or his spouse if the old residence and the new residence are each used by the taxpayer and his spouse as their principal residence) has a tax home (as defined in section 911(d)(3)) outside the United States after the date of the sale of the old residence; except that any such period of time as so suspended shall not extend beyond the date 4 years after the date of the sale of the old residence.

(*l*) Cross reference. For one-time exclusion from gross income of gain from sale of principal residence by individual who has attained age 55, see section 121.

Author's Notes

Analysis

1. Time.
2. Price.
3. Reduced basis.
4. Principal residence.
5. Joint ownership.
6. Reporting.

(1) **Time.** Section 1034 of the Internal Revenue Code allows the rollover of gain from the sale of a principal residence into a new principal residence if the new principal residence is bought within a period of time beginning two years before the date of the sale of the old principal residence and ending two years after the date of the sale of the old principal residence.

(2) **Price.** In order to completely roll over the gain from the old principal residence into the new principal residence, the new principal residence must cost at least as much as the sale price of the old principal residence. Gain is recognized to the extent that the adjusted sales price of the old principal residence exceeds the cost of the new principal residence. The adjusted sales price of the old principal residence is the amount realized less any expenses for work performed on the old residence to assist in its sale.

(3) **Reduced basis.** The gain that is not recognized on the old principal residence, but is rolled over into the new principal residence, reduces the basis of the new principal residence. The gain is therefore not eliminated, but is only deferred until such time as a principal residence is sold and no new principal residence is purchased, or a less costly principal residence is purchased. There are two exceptions to the eventual recognition of gain. Section 121 of the Internal Revenue Code permits a one time exclusion of $125,000 in gain for taxpayers who have attained the age of 55. See IRC § 121 and accompanying Author's Notes. A second exception is where the gain is deferred by roll over until the taxpayer's death, in which case the capital gains tax on the deferred gain is never paid, although an estate tax may be due on the fair market value of the house.

(4) **Principal residence.** A taxpayer's principal residence is his primary place of abode. This criterion can present problems in a marital dissolution where one of the spouses leaves the principal residence. The IRS may take the position that it is no longer his principal residence, and therefore he is not entitled to the rollover of gain pursuant to § 1034. The test is whether the taxpayer has abandoned the residence. Legislation is pending in Congress as of this writing to clarify the principal residence rule in dissolution of marriage situations. Marjorie A. O'Connell, *Divorce Taxation*,

(3) Child defined. For purposes of paragraph (1)(B), the term "child" means an individual who (within the meaning of section 152) is a son, stepson, daughter, or stepdaughter of the taxpayer.

(4) Student defined. For purposes of paragraph (1)(B)(ii), the term "student" means an individual who during each of 5 calendar months during the calendar year in which the taxable year of the taxpayer begins—

(A) is a full-time student at an educational organization described in section 170(b)(1)(A)(ii); or

(B) is pursuing a full-time course of institutional on-farm training under the supervision of an accredited agent of an educational organization described in section 170(b)(1)(A)(ii) or of a State or political subdivision of a State.

(5) Certain income of handicapped dependents not taken into account.

(A) In general. For purposes of paragraph (1)(A), the gross income of an individual who is permanently and totally disabled shall not include income attributable to services performed by the individual at a sheltered workshop if—

(i) the availability of medical care at such workshop is the principal reason for his presence there, and

(ii) the income arises solely from activities at such workshop which are incident to such medical care.

(B) Sheltered workshop defined. For purposes of subparagraph (A), the term "sheltered workshop" means a school—

(i) which provides special instruction or training designed to alleviate the disability of the individual, and

(ii) which is operated by—

(I) an organization described in section 501(c)(3) and exempt from tax under section 501(a), or

(II) a State, a possession of the United States, any political subdivision of any of the foregoing, the United States, or the District of Columbia.

(C) Permanent and total disability defined. An individual shall be treated as permanently and totally disabled for purposes of this paragraph if such individual would be so treated under paragraph (3) of section 22(e).

(d) Exemption amount. For purposes of this section—

(1) In general. Except as otherwise provided in this subsection, the term "exemption amount" means $2,000.

(2) Exemption amount disallowed in case of certain dependents. In the case of an individual with respect to whom a deduction under this section is allowable to another taxpayer for a taxable year beginning in the calendar year in which the individual's taxable year begins, the exemption amount applicable to such individual for such individual's taxable year shall be zero.

(3) Phaseout.

(A) In general. In the case of any taxpayer whose adjusted gross income for the taxable year exceeds the threshold amount, the exemption amount shall be reduced by the applicable percentage.

(B) Applicable percentage. For purposes of subparagraph (A), the term "applicable percentage" means 2 percentage points for each $2,500 (or fraction thereof) by which the taxpayer's adjusted gross income for the taxable year exceeds the threshold amount. In the case of a married individual filing a separate return, the preceding sentence shall be applied by substituting "$1,250" for "$2,500". In no event shall the applicable percentage exceed 100 percent.

(C) Threshold amount. For purposes of this paragraph, the term "threshold amount" means—

(i) $150,000 in the case of a joint of a [sic] return or a surviving spouse (as defined in section 2(a)),

(ii) $125,000 in the case of a head of a household (as defined in section 2(b)),

(iii) $100,000 in the case of an individual who is not married and who is not a surviving spouse or head of a household, and

(iv) $75,000 in the case of a married individual filing a separate return.

For purposes of this paragraph, marital status shall be determined under section 7703.

(D) Coordination with other provisions. The provisions of this paragraph shall not apply for purposes of determining whether a deduction under this section with respect to any individual is allowable to another taxpayer for any taxable year.

(4) Inflation adjustments.

(A) Adjustment to basic amount of exemption. In the case of any taxable year beginning in a calendar year after 1989, the dollar amount contained in paragraph (1) shall be increased by an amount equal to—

(i) such dollar amount, multiplied by

(ii) the cost-of-living adjustment determined under section 1(f)(3) for the calendar year in which the taxable year begins, by substituting "calendar year 1988" for "calendar year 1992" in subparagraph (B) thereof.

(B) Adjustment to threshold amounts for years after 1991. In the case of any taxable year beginning in a calendar year after 1991, each dollar amount contained in paragraph (3)(C) shall be increased by an amount equal to—

(i) such dollar amount, multiplied by

(ii) the cost-of-living adjustment determined under section 1(f)(3) for the calendar year in which the taxable year begins, by substituting "calendar year 1990" for "calendar year 1992" in subparagraph (B) thereof.

26 U.S.C.A. § 152

§ 152. Dependent defined

(a) General definition. For purposes of this subtitle, the term "dependent" means any of the following individuals over half of whose support, for the calendar year in which the taxable year of the taxpayer begins, was received from the taxpayer (or is treated under subsection (c) or (e) as received from the taxpayer):

(1) A son or daughter of the taxpayer, or a descendant of either,

(2) A stepson or stepdaughter of the taxpayer,

(3) A brother, sister, stepbrother, or stepsister of the taxpayer,

(4) The father or mother of the taxpayer, or an ancestor of either,

(5) A stepfather or stepmother of the taxpayer,

(6) A son or daughter of a brother or sister of the taxpayer,

(7) A brother or sister of the father or mother of the taxpayer,

(8) A son-in-law, daughter-in-law, father-in-law, mother-in-law, brother-in-law, or sister-in-law of the taxpayer, or

(9) An individual (other than an individual who at any time during the taxable year was the spouse, determined without regard to section 7703, of the taxpayer) who, for the taxable year of the taxpayer, has as his principal place of abode the home of the taxpayer and is a member of the taxpayer's household.

(b) Rules relating to general definition. For purposes of this section—

(1) The terms "brother" and "sister" include a brother or sister by the halfblood.

(2) In determining whether any of the relationships specified in subsection (a) or paragraph (1) of this subsection exists, a legally adopted child of an individual (and a child who is a member of an individual's household, if placed with such individual by an authorized placement agency for legal adoption by such individual), or a foster child of an

individual (if such child satisfies the requirements of subsection (a)(9) with respect to such individual), shall be treated as a child of such individual by blood.

(3) The term "dependent" does not include any individual who is not a citizen or national of the United States unless such individual is a resident of the United States or of a country contiguous to the United States. The preceding sentence shall not exclude from the definition of "dependent" any child of the taxpayer legally adopted by him, if, for the taxable year of the taxpayer, the child has as his principal place of abode the home of the taxpayer and is a member of the taxpayer's household, and if the taxpayer is a citizen or national of the United States.

(4) A payment to a wife which is includible in the gross income of the wife under section 71 or 682 shall not be treated as a payment by her husband for the support of any dependent.

(5) An individual is not a member of the taxpayer's household if at any time during the taxable year of the taxpayer the relationship between such individual and the taxpayer is in violation of local law.

(c) Multiple support agreements. For purposes of subsection (a), over half of the support of an individual for a calendar year shall be treated as received from the taxpayer if—

(1) no one person contributed over half of such support;

(2) over half of such support was received from persons each of whom, but for the fact that he did not contribute over half of such support, would have been entitled to claim such individual as a dependent for a taxable year beginning in such calendar year;

(3) the taxpayer contributed over 10 percent of such support; and

(4) each person described in paragraph (2) (other than the taxpayer) who contributed over 10 percent of such support files a written declaration (in such manner and form as the Secretary may by regulations prescribe) that he will not claim such individual as a dependent for any taxable year beginning in such calendar year.

(d) Special support test in case of students. For purposes of subsection (a), in the case of any individual who is—

(1) a son, stepson, daughter, or stepdaughter of the taxpayer (within the meaning of this section), and

(2) a student (within the meaning of section 151(c)(4)), amounts received as scholarships for study at an educational organization described in section 170(b)(1)(A)(ii) shall not be taken into account in determining whether such individual received more than half of his support from the taxpayer.

(e) Support test in case of child of divorced parents, etc.

(1) Custodial parent gets exemption. Except as otherwise provided in this subsection, if—

(A) a child (as defined in section 151(c)(3)) receives over half of his support during the calendar year from his parents—

(i) who are divorced or legally separated under a decree of divorce or separate maintenance,

(ii) who are separated under a written separation agreement, or

(iii) who live apart at all times during the last 6 months of the calendar year, and

(B) such child is in the custody of one or both of his parents for more than one-half of the calendar year, such child shall be treated, for purposes of subsection (a), as receiving over half of his support during the calendar year from the parent having custody for a greater portion of the calendar year (hereinafter in this subsection referred to as the "custodial parent").

(2) Exception where custodial parent releases claim to exemption for the year. A child of parents described in paragraph (1) shall be treated as having received over half of his support during a calendar year from the noncustodial parent if—

(A) the custodial parent signs a written declaration (in such manner and form as the Secretary may by regulations prescribe) that such custodial parent will not claim such child as a dependent for any taxable year beginning in such calendar year, and

(B) the noncustodial parent attaches such written declaration to the noncustodial parent's return for the taxable year beginning during such calendar year.

For purposes of this subsection, the term "noncustodial parent" means the parent who is not the custodial parent.

(3) Exception for multiple-support agreement. This subsection shall not apply in any case where over half of the support of the child is treated as having been received from a taxpayer under the provisions of subsection (c).

(4) Exception for certain pre–1985 instruments.

(A) In general. A child of parents described in paragraph (1) shall be treated as having received over half his support during a calendar year from the noncustodial parent if—

(i) a qualified pre–1985 instrument between the parents applicable to the taxable year beginning in such calendar year provides that the noncustodial parent shall be entitled to any deduction allowable under section 151 for such child, and

(ii) the noncustodial parent provides at least $600 for the support of such child during such calendar year.

For purposes of this subparagraph, amounts expended for the support of a child or children shall be treated as received from the noncustodial parent to the extent that such parent provided amounts for such support.

(B) Qualified pre–1985 instrument. For purposes of this paragraph, the term "qualified pre–1985 instrument" means any decree of divorce or separate maintenance or written agreement—

(i) which is executed before January 1, 1985,

(ii) which on such date contains the provision described in subparagraph (A)(i), and

(iii) which is not modified on or after such date in a modification which expressly provides that this paragraph shall not apply to such decree or agreement.

(5) Special rule for support received from new spouse of parent. For purposes of this subsection, in the case of the remarriage of a parent, support of a child received from the parent's spouse shall be treated as received from the parent.

(6) Cross reference. For provision treating child as dependent of both parents for purposes of medical expense deduction, see section 213(d)(5).

Author's Notes

Analysis

1. Dependency exemptions.
2. Common situations.
3. Release of Claim to Exemption for Child of Divorced or Separated Parents—Form.
4. Amount.

(1) **Dependency exemptions.** The rules for dependency exemptions in dissolution of marriages are complicated, but legislation is pending to simplify them. Marjorie A. O'Connell, *Divorce Taxation*, Report Bulletin ¶6.1 (June 11, 1993). See IRC § 71 Author's Note (34) p. 4 of IRS Publication 504 for the Internal Revenue Service's explanation of exemptions.

(2) **Common situations.** In the most common situation, the spouse who provides over half of the support for a son or daughter during a calendar year is entitled to the dependency exemption, and a divorced spouse who has custody of the child for the greater portion of the year is treated as supplying over half of his support. Therefore that spouse is entitled to the dependency exemption. In order to reverse the result, and give the dependency exemption to the non-custodial parent, the custodial parent must sign a written release, and the non-custodial parent must attach the release to his tax return. In order for the custodial or non-custodial parent to have the dependency exemption, as described above, the child must be in the custody of one or both of the parents for more than one-half of the calendar year.

FEDERAL LAWS　　　　26 U.S.C.A. § 152

(3) **Release of Claim to Exemption for Child of Divorced or Separated Parents—Form.** The form of release of dependency exemption from the Internal Revenue Service follows (form 8332).

Form **8332** (Rev. December 1987)
Department of the Treasury
Internal Revenue Service

Release of Claim to Exemption for Child of Divorced or Separated Parents
▶ Attach to Tax Return of Parent Claiming Exemption

OMB No. 1545-0915
Expires 10-31-90
Attachment Sequence No. **51**

Name(s) of parent claiming exemption as shown on tax return　　　Social security number

Part I　Release of Claim to Exemption for Current Year

I agree not to claim an exemption for _____
　　　　　　　　　　　　　　　　　　　　Name(s) of child (or children)

for the calendar year 19 ____ .

Signature of parent releasing claim to exemption　　Social security number　　Date

If you choose not to claim an exemption for this child (or children) for future tax years, complete Part II, as explained in the instructions below.

Part II　Release of Claim to Exemption for Future Years

I agree not to claim an exemption for _____
　　　　　　　　　　　　　　　　　　　　Name(s) of child (or children)

for tax year(s) _____
　　　　　　　　(Specify. See instructions.)

Signature of parent releasing claim to exemption　　Social security number　　Date

---

Paperwork Reduction Act Notice.— We ask for this information to carry out the Internal Revenue laws of the United States. We need it to ensure that taxpayers are complying with these laws and to allow us to figure and collect the right amount of tax. You are required to give us this information.

Purpose of Form.— This form may be used to release the claim to a child's exemption by a parent who has custody of his or her child and might have been entitled to claim the exemption for this child. This form is completed by the parent who has custody of the child and is given to the parent who will claim the exemption. The parent who will claim the child's exemption must attach this form, or a similar statement, to his or her tax return. See **How To File Form 8332**, below.

Exemption for Child of Divorced or Separated Parents.— In general, the parent who has custody of the child (or children) for the greater part of the year is treated as having provided over half of the child's support for purposes of the dependency exemption for the child if:

1. The child receives over half of his or her support from both of the parents; AND

2. The child was in the custody of one or both of his or her parents for more than half of the year.

This general rule applies to parents who are divorced or legally separated under a decree of divorce or separate maintenance, separated under a written separation agreement, or who lived apart at all times during the last 6 months of the calendar year.

This general rule does not apply if **any** of the following apply:

(a) The parent having custody signs a written statement agreeing not to claim the child's exemption and the parent not having custody attaches this statement to his or her tax return for the tax year. (See **Parent Who Releases Claim to Exemption,** below.)

(b) The child is treated as having received over half of his or her support from a person under a multiple support agreement (**Form 2120,** Multiple Support Declaration).

(c) A qualified divorce decree or written agreement was in effect before January 1, 1985, and provides that the noncustodial parent can claim the exemption for the child, and the noncustodial parent provides at least $600 for the support of the child during the year.

Note: *If items (b) or (c) above do not apply, the noncustodial parent must attach a completed Form 8332, or similar statement, to his or her tax return for each year in which the noncustodial parent claims the child's exemption.*

Parent Who Releases Claim to Exemption.— A parent who might be entitled to claim the child's (or children's) exemption because of having custody of the child for a greater part of the calendar year may agree to release claim to the child's exemption for the current calendar year or for future years, or both. The release can be made by completing Form 8332 or a similar statement.

Part I should be completed by the parent who chooses to release claim to the child's (or children's) exemption for the current calendar year.

Part II should be completed by the parent who chooses to release claim to the child's (or children's) exemption for a specified number of future years, or for all future years. If the parent is releasing claim for all future years, "all future years" should be written in the space provided for in Part II.

How To File Form 8332.— The noncustodial parent must attach Form 8332, or a similar statement, to his or her tax return for the tax year in which the noncustodial parent claims the child's exemption. If the parent having custody of the child completes Part II of Form 8332, the noncustodial parent must attach a copy of this form to his or her tax return for each succeeding year in which the noncustodial parent claims the exemption

The parent who receives the release of claim to the child's exemption may claim the exemption **only** if the other tests in the Form 1040 or 1040A Instructions for dependency exemptions are met.

For more information, get **Publication 504,** Tax Information for Divorced or Separated Individuals.

Form **8332** (Rev. 12-87)
[G19048]

885

26 U.S.C.A. § 152

(4) **Amount.** The amount of the dependency exemption for 1994 is $2,450.00 per dependent, as calculated by Commerce Clearing House. *1994 United States Master Tax Guide*, (CCH) ¶133 (1994). However, the dependency exemption is subject to a phase out for high income taxpayers. The exemption for a taxpayer whose adjusted gross income exceeds a threshold amount is reduced by 2% for each $2,500 ($1,250 for a married person filing separately) or fraction thereof of the excess. The threshold amounts for the phase outs for 1994 as calculated by Commerce Clearing House are: $167,700 (joint returns), $139,750 (heads of households), $111,800 (single taxpayers), and $83,850 (married filing separately). *1994 United States Master Tax Guide*, (CCH) ¶133 (1994). Where one spouse obtains no benefit from the dependency exemption, it is good tax planning to assign the dependency exemption to the other spouse by agreement.

26 U.S.C.A. § 262

§ 262. Personal, living, and family expenses

(a) General rule. Except as otherwise expressly provided in this chapter, no deduction shall be allowed for personal, living, or family expenses.

(b) Treatment of certain phone expenses. For purposes of subsection (a), in the case of an individual, any charge (including taxes thereon) for basic local telephone service with respect to the 1st telephone line provided to any residence of the taxpayer shall be treated as a personal expense.

Author's Notes

Analysis

1. Children's support not deductible.
2. Children's support not taxable.
3. Cross reference.

(1) **Children's support not deductible.** Children's support is not deductible. Children's support is treated as a family expense under § 262 of the Internal Revenue Code of 1986. Marjorie A. O'Connell, *Divorce Taxation*, ¶4002 (1987).

(2) **Children's support not taxable.** Children's support is not taxable to the recipient pursuant to § 71(c) of the Internal Revenue Code.

(3) **Cross reference.** See IRC § 71(c) Author's Notes (5) and (6) for a discussion of the anti-Lester rules that have attempted to prevent, but have not completely succeeded in preventing, the payment of children's support as unallocated alimony, thereby making it deductible to the payor and taxable to the recipient.

26 U.S.C.A. § 2(b)

§ 2(b). Definitions and special rules

(b) Definition of head of household.

(1) In general. For purposes of this subtitle, an individual shall be considered a head of a household if, and only if, such individual is not married at the close of his taxable year, is not a surviving spouse (as defined in subsection (a)), and either—

(A) maintains as his home a household which constitutes for more than one-half of such taxable year the principal place of abode, as a member of such household, of—

(i) a son, stepson, daughter, or stepdaughter of the taxpayer, or a descendant of a son or daughter of the taxpayer, but if such son, stepson, daughter, stepdaughter, or descendant is married at the close of the taxpayer's taxable year, only if the taxpayer is entitled to a deduction for the taxable year for such person under section 151 (or would be so entitled but for paragraph (2) or (4) of section 152(e)), or

(ii) any other person who is a dependent of the taxpayer, if the taxpayer is entitled to a deduction for the taxable year for such person under section 151, or

(B) maintains a household which constitutes for such taxable year the principal place of abode of the father or mother of the taxpayer, if the taxpayer is entitled to a deduction for the taxable year for such father or mother under section 151.

For purposes of this paragraph, an individual shall be considered as maintaining a household only if over half of the cost of maintaining the household during the taxable year is furnished by such individual.

(2) Determination of status. For purposes of this subsection—

(A) a legally adopted child of a person shall be considered a child of such person by blood;

(B) an individual who is legally separated from his spouse under a decree of divorce or of separate maintenance shall not be considered as married;

(C) a taxpayer shall be considered as not married at the close of his taxable year if at any time during the taxable year his spouse is a nonresident alien; and

(D) a taxpayer shall be considered as married at the close of his taxable year if his spouse (other than a spouse described in subparagraph (C)) died during the taxable year.

(3) Limitations. Notwithstanding paragraph (1), for purposes of this subtitle a taxpayer shall not be considered to be a head of a household—

(A) if at any time during the taxable year he is a nonresident alien; or

(B) by reason of an individual who would not be a dependent for the taxable year but for—

(i) paragraph (9) of section 152(a), or

(ii) subsection (c) of section 152.

26 U.S.C.A. § 7703

§ 7703. Determination of marital status

(a) General rule. For purposes of part V of subchapter B of chapter 1 and those provisions of this title which refer to this subsection—

(1) the determination of whether an individual is married shall be made as of the close of his taxable year; except that if his spouse dies during his taxable year such determination shall be made as of the time of such death; and

(2) an individual legally separated from his spouse under a decree of divorce or of separate maintenance shall not be considered as married.

(b) Certain married individuals living apart. For purposes of those provisions of this title which refer to this subsection, if—

(1) an individual who is married (within the meaning of subsection (a)) and who files a separate return maintains as his home a household which constitutes for more than one-half of the taxable year the principal place of abode of a child (within the meaning of section 151(c)(3)) with respect to whom such individual is entitled to a deduction for the taxable year under section 151 (or would be so entitled but for paragraph (2) or (4) of section 152(e)),

(2) such individual furnishes over one-half of the cost of maintaining such household during the taxable year, and

(3) during the last 6 months of the taxable year, such individual's spouse is not a member of such household, such individual shall not be considered as married.

Author's Notes

Analysis

1. Head of household.
2. Qualification.
3. One-half cost.
4. Unmarried persons.
5. Dependency exemption.
6. Medical expenses.

(1) **Head of household.** The head of household tax rates are less than those for single taxpayers, but higher than those for joint returns. See IRC § 71 Author's Note (31) to compare rates.

(2) **Qualification.** One or both of the parents can qualify for head of household treatment after they are divorced if either or both provide for more than half of the cost for the household that for the taxable calendar year is the home of a child of the taxpayer.

(3) **One-half cost.** The requirement that the taxpayer pay over half of the cost of the maintenance of a household includes only half of the actual household expenses, such as property taxes, mortgage interest, rent, utility charges, upkeep and repairs,

property insurance, and food consumed on the premises. Marjorie A. O'Connell, *Divorce Taxation*, ¶18,201 (1987).

(4) **Unmarried persons.** In order to claim a head of household tax rate, the taxpayer cannot be married at the close of the taxable year. Marital status is determined by Code § 7703. Unmarried persons include, as well as divorced couples, an individual legally separated from his spouse under a decree of separate maintenance. Section 7703 also includes provisions designed to protect abandoned spouses who are left with children. A person cannot qualify for the head of household tax rates when the parties are separated pursuant to temporary separation orders.

(5) **Dependency exemption.** If the child living with the taxpayer who is claiming a head of household tax rates is unmarried, then the child does not have to qualify as the taxpayer's dependent in order for the taxpayer to qualify for head of household filing status. *1994 United States Master Tax Guide*, (CCH) ¶173 (1994).

(6) **Medical expenses.** It is also true that for medical expenses for a dependent child where the dependency exemption is determined pursuant to IRC § 152(e), IRC § 213 allows either parent who actually pays for the medical expenses of a dependent child to a limited deduction regardless of which parent is entitled to the dependency exemption for the child. Marjorie A. O'Connell, *Divorce Taxation*, ¶4401 (1987).

26 U.S.C.A. § 6013

§ 6013. Joint returns of income tax by husband and wife

(a) Joint returns. A husband and wife may make a single return jointly of income taxes under subtitle A, even though one of the spouses has neither gross income nor deductions, except as provided below:

(1) no joint return shall be made if either the husband or wife at any time during the taxable year is a nonresident alien;

(2) no joint return shall be made if the husband and wife have different taxable years; except that if such taxable years begin on the same day and end on different days because of the death of either or both, then the joint return may be made with respect to the taxable year of each. The above exception shall not apply if the surviving spouse remarries before the close of his taxable year, nor if the taxable year of either spouse is a fractional part of a year under section 443(a)(1);

(3) in the case of death of one spouse or both spouses the joint return with respect to the decedent may be made only by his executor or administrator; except that in the case of the death of one spouse the joint return may be made by the surviving spouse with respect to both himself and the decedent if no return for the taxable year has been made by the decedent, no executor or administrator has been appointed, and no executor or administrator is appointed before the last day prescribed by law for filing the return of the surviving spouse. If an executor or administrator of the decedent is appointed after the making of the joint return by the surviving spouse, the executor or administrator may disaffirm such joint return by making, within 1 year after the last day prescribed by law for filing the return of the surviving spouse, a separate return for the taxable year of the decedent with respect to which the joint

return was made, in which case the return made by the survivor shall constitute his separate return.

(b) Joint return after filing separate return.

(1) In general. Except as provided in paragraph (2), if an individual has filed a separate return for a taxable year for which a joint return could have been made by him and his spouse under subsection (a) and the time prescribed by law for filing the return for such taxable year has expired, such individual and his spouse may nevertheless make a joint return for such taxable year. A joint return filed by the husband and wife under this subsection shall constitute the return of the husband and wife for such taxable year, and all payments, credits, refunds, or other repayments made or allowed with respect to the separate return of either spouse for such taxable year shall be taken into account in determining the extent to which the tax based upon the joint return has been paid. If a joint return is made under this subsection, any election (other than the election to file a separate return) made by either spouse in his separate return for such taxable year with respect to the treatment of any income, deduction, or credit of such spouse shall not be changed in the making of the joint return where such election would have been irrevocable if the joint return had not been made. If a joint return is made under this subsection after the death of either spouse, such return with respect to the decedent can be made only by his executor or administrator.

(2) Limitations for making of election. The election provided for in paragraph (1) may not be made—

(A) unless there is paid in full at or before the time of the filing of the joint return the amount shown as tax upon such joint return; or

(B) after the expiration of 3 years from the last date prescribed by law for filing the return for such taxable year (determined without regard to any extension of time granted to either spouse); or

(C) after there has been mailed to either spouse, with respect to such taxable year, a notice of deficiency under section 6212, if the spouse, as to such notice, files a petition with the Tax Court within the time prescribed in section 6213; or

(D) after either spouse has commenced a suit in any court for the recovery of any part of the tax for such taxable year; or

(E) after either spouse has entered into a closing agreement under section 7121 with respect to such taxable year, or after any civil or criminal case arising against either spouse with respect to such taxable year has been compromised under section 7122.

(3) When return deemed filed.

(A) Assessment and collection. For purposes of section 6501 (relating to periods of limitations on assessment and collection), and for purposes of section 6651 (relating to delinquent returns), a joint return made under this subsection shall be deemed to have been filed—

    (i) Where both spouses filed separate returns prior to making the joint return—on the date the last separate return was filed (but not earlier than the last date prescribed by law for filing the return of either spouse);

    (ii) Where only one spouse filed a separate return prior to the making of the joint return, and the other spouse had less than the exemption amount of gross income for such taxable year—on the date of the filing of such separate return (but not earlier than the last date prescribed by law for the filing of such separate return); or

    (iii) Where only one spouse filed a separate return prior to the making of the joint return, and the other spouse had gross income of the exemption amount or more for such taxable year— on the date of the filing of such joint return.

For purposes of this subparagraph, the term "exemption amount" has the meaning given to such term by section 151(d). For purposes of clauses (ii) and (iii), if the spouse whose gross income is being compared to the exemption amount is 65 or over, such clauses shall be applied by substituting "the sum of the exemption amount and the additional standard deduction under section 63(c)(2) by reason of section 63(f)(1)(A)" for "the exemption amount".

    (B) Credit or refund. For purposes of section 6511, a joint return made under this subsection shall be deemed to have been filed on the last date prescribed by law for filing the return for such taxable year (determined without regard to any extension of time granted to either spouse).

  (4) Additional time for assessment. If a joint return is made under this subsection, the periods of limitations provided in sections 6501 and 6502 on the making of assessments and the beginning of levy or a proceeding in court for collection shall with respect to such return include one year immediately after the date of the filing of such joint return (computed without regard to the provisions of paragraph (3)).

  (5) Additions to the tax and penalties.

    (A) Coordination with part II of subchapter a of chapter 68. For purposes of part II of subchapter A of chapter 68, where the sum of the amounts shown as tax on the separate returns of each spouse is less than the amount shown as tax on the joint return made under this subsection—

        (i) such sum shall be treated as the amount shown on the joint return,

(ii) any negligence (or disregard of rules or regulations) on either separate return shall be treated as negligence (or such disregard) on the joint return, and

(iii) any fraud on either separate return shall be treated as fraud on the joint return.

(B) Criminal penalty. For purposes of section 7206(1) and (2) and section 7207 (relating to criminal penalties in the case of fraudulent returns) the term "return" includes a separate return filed by a spouse with respect to a taxable year for which a joint return is made under this subsection after the filing of such separate return.

(c) Treatment of joint return after death of either spouse. For purposes of sections 15, 443, and 7851(a)(1)(A), where the husband and wife have different taxable years because of the death of either spouse, the joint return shall be treated as if the taxable years of both spouses ended on the date of the closing of the surviving spouse's taxable year.

(d) Special rules. For purposes of this section—

(1) the status as husband and wife of two individuals having taxable years beginning on the same day shall be determined—

(A) if both have the same taxable year—as of the close of such year; or

(B) if one dies before the close of the taxable year of the other—as of the time of such death;

(2) an individual who is legally separated from his spouse under a decree of divorce or of separate maintenance shall not be considered as married; and

(3) if a joint return is made, the tax shall be computed on the aggregate income and the liability with respect to the tax shall be joint and several.

(e) Spouse relieved of liability in certain cases.

(1) In general. Under regulations prescribed by the Secretary, if—

(A) a joint return has been made under this section for a taxable year,

(B) on such return there is a substantial understatement of tax attributable to grossly erroneous items of one spouse,

(C) the other spouse establishes that in signing the return he or she did not know, and had no reason to know, that there was such substantial understatement, and

(D) taking into account all the facts and circumstances, it is inequitable to hold the other spouse liable for the deficiency in tax for such taxable year attributable to such substantial understatement, then the other spouse shall be relieved of liability for tax (including interest, penalties, and other amounts) for such taxable year to the extent such liability is attributable to such substantial understatement.

(2) Grossly erroneous items. For purposes of this subsection, the term "grossly erroneous items" means, with respect to any spouse—

(A) any item of gross income attributable to such spouse which is omitted from gross income, and

(B) any claim of a deduction, credit, or basis by such spouse in an amount for which there is no basis in fact or law.

(3) Substantial understatement. For purposes of this subsection, the term "substantial understatement" means any understatement (as defined in section 6662(d)(2)(A)) which exceeds $500.

(4) Understatement must exceed specified percentage of spouse's income.

(A) Adjusted gross income of $20,000 or less. If the spouse's adjusted gross income for the preadjustment year is $20,000 or less, this subsection shall apply only if the liability described in paragraph (1) is greater than 10 percent of such adjusted gross income.

(B) Adjusted gross income of more than $20,000. If the spouse's adjusted gross income for the preadjustment year is more than $20,000, subparagraph (A) shall be applied by substituting "25 percent" for "10 percent".

(C) Preadjustment year. For purposes of this paragraph, the term "preadjustment year" means the most recent taxable year of the spouse ending before the date the deficiency notice is mailed.

(D) Computation of spouse's adjusted gross income. If the spouse is married to another spouse at the close of the preadjustment year, the spouse's adjusted gross income shall include the income of the new spouse (whether or not they file a joint return).

(E) Exception for omissions from gross income. This paragraph shall not apply to any liability attributable to the omission of an item from gross income.

(5) Special rule for community property income. For purposes of this subsection, the determination of the spouse to whom items of gross income (other than gross income from property) are attributable shall be made without regard to community property laws.

(f) Joint return where individual is in missing status. For purposes of this section and subtitle A—

(1) Election by spouse. If—

(A) an individual is in a missing status (within the meaning of paragraph (3)) as a result of service in a combat zone (as determined for purposes of section 112), and

(B) the spouse of such individual is otherwise entitled to file a joint return for any taxable year which begins on or before the day which is 2 years after the date designated under section 112 as the date of termination of combatant activities in such zone, then such spouse may elect under subsection (a) to file a joint return for such taxable year. With respect to service in the combat zone designated for purposes of the Vietnam conflict, such election may be made for any taxable year while an individual is in missing status.

(2) Effect of election. If the spouse of an individual described in paragraph (1)(A) elects to file a joint return under subsection (a) for a taxable year, then, until such election is revoked—

(A) such election shall be valid even if such individual died before the beginning of such year, and

(B) except for purposes of section 692 (relating to income taxes of members of the Armed Forces on death), the income tax liability of such individual, his spouse, and his estate shall be determined as if he were alive throughout the taxable year.

(3) Missing status. For purposes of this subsection—

(A) Uniformed services. A member of a uniformed service (within the meaning of section 101(3) of title 37 of the United States Code) is in a missing status for any period for which he is entitled to pay and allowances under section 552 of such title 37.

(B) Civilian employees. An employee (within the meaning of section 5561(2) of title 5 of the United States Code) is in a missing status for any period for which he is entitled to pay and allowances under section 5562 of such title 5.

(4) Making of election; Revocation. An election described in this subsection with respect to any taxable year may be made by filing a joint return in accordance with subsection (a) and under such regulations as may be prescribed by the Secretary. Such an election may be revoked by either spouse on or before the due date (including extensions) for such taxable year, and, in the case of an executor or administrator, may be revoked by disaffirming as provided in the last sentence of subsection (a)(3).

(g) Election to treat nonresident alien individual as resident of the united states.

(1) In general. A nonresident alien individual with respect to whom this subsection is in effect for the taxable year shall be treated as a resident of the United States—

(A) for purposes of chapters 1 and 5 for all of such taxable year, and

(B) for purposes of chapter 24 (relating to wage withholding) for payments of wages made during such taxable year.

(2) Individuals with respect to whom this subsection is in effect. This subsection shall be in effect with respect to any individual who, at the close of the taxable year for which an election under this subsection was made, was a nonresident alien individual married to a citizen or resident of the United States, if both of them made such election to have the benefits of this subsection apply to them.

(3) Duration of election. An election under this subsection shall apply to the taxable year for which made and to all subsequent taxable years until terminated under paragraph (4) or (5); except that any such election shall not apply for any taxable year if neither spouse is a citizen or resident of the United States at any time during such year.

(4) Termination of election. An election under this subsection shall terminate at the earliest of the following times:

(A) Revocation by taxpayers. If either taxpayer revokes the election, as of the first taxable year for which the last day prescribed by law for filing the return of tax under chapter 1 has not yet occurred.

(B) Death. In the case of the death of either spouse, as of the beginning of the first taxable year of the spouse who survives following the taxable year in which such death occurred; except that if the spouse who survives is a citizen or resident of the United States who is a surviving spouse entitled to the benefits of section 2, the time provided by this subparagraph shall be as of the close of the last taxable year for which such individual is entitled to the benefits of section 2.

(C) Legal separation. In the case of the legal separation of the couple under a decree of divorce or of separate maintenance, as of the beginning of the taxable year in which such legal separation occurs.

(D) Termination by secretary. At the time provided in paragraph (5).

(5) Termination by secretary. The Secretary may terminate any election under this subsection for any taxable year if he determines that either spouse has failed—

(A) to keep such books and records,

(B) to grant such access to such books and records, or

(C) to supply such other information, as may be reasonably necessary to ascertain the amount of liability for taxes under chapters 1 and 5 of either spouse for such taxable year.

(6) Only one election. If any election under this subsection for any two individuals is terminated under paragraph (4) or (5) for any taxable year, such two individuals shall be ineligible to make an election under this subsection for any subsequent taxable year.

26 U.S.C.A. § 6013 **FEDERAL LAWS**

(h) Joint return, etc., For year in which nonresident alien becomes resident of United States.

(1) In general. If—

(A) any individual is a nonresident alien individual at the beginning of any taxable year but is a resident of the United States at the close of such taxable year,

(B) at the close of such taxable year, such individual is married to a citizen or resident of the United States, and

(C) both individuals elect the benefits of this subsection at the time and in the manner prescribed by the Secretary by regulation,

then the individual referred to in subparagraph (A) shall be treated as a resident of the United States for purposes of chapters 1 and 5 for all of such taxable year, and for purposes of chapter 24 (relating to wage withholding) for payments of wages made during such taxable year.

(2) Only one election. If any election under this subsection applies for any 2 individuals for any taxable year, such 2 individuals shall be ineligible to make an election under this subsection for any subsequent taxable year.

Author's Notes

Analysis

1. Less tax.
2. December 31.
3. Joint Tax Return Indemnity—Form.

(1) **Less tax.** It is generally advisable for spouses during dissolution proceedings to file joint returns, inasmuch as the tax is usually less than if the spouses file as married individuals filing separate returns. See IRC § 71 Author's Note (31) to compare rates. If a spouse refuses to sign a joint return, and a greater tax is incurred, a dissipation claim should result. Interestingly enough, the 1993 tax revisions have in many situations where both married spouses earn income caused them to pay more tax than they would if they were single filing separate returns.

(2) **December 31.** To qualify to file a joint return, the parties must be married on December 31 of their tax year. They will, however, not qualify to file a joint return if they are legally separated pursuant to a decree of separate maintenance. Temporary orders do not qualify as final orders of divorce or separate maintenance. Marjorie A. O'Connell, *Divorce Taxation*, ¶18,002 (1993).

(3) **Joint Tax Return Indemnity—Form.** Where divorcing spouses are in a contest over income, and where one or both of the parties should be indemnified against tax liability, an appropriate agreement should be signed at the time of the signing of the joint tax returns. The following sample agreement is for the situation where one of the spouses has a monopoly of the financial information, causes the income tax returns to be prepared, and pays all of the tax. The agreement can be appropriately modified to fit other situations.

FEDERAL LAWS   26 U.S.C.A. § 6013

April _____, 199__

JOINT TAX RETURN INDEMNITY

John Jarndyce (John) has requested that Ellen Jarndyce (Ellen) execute the parties' 199__ Federal and State Joint Tax Returns. Ellen states and John acknowledges, that Ellen has no knowledge or information whatever about the facts and figures appearing on the 199__ Joint Returns which John has prepared and submitted to Ellen for her signature. John agrees that Ellen shall not be bound by any facts or figures appearing on the 199__ Joint Returns prepared by John, and that Ellen's execution of these Joint Returns will not estop or preclude her from challenging the accuracy or validity of any of the facts or figures appearing on the Returns, if it becomes necessary so to do.

Ellen agrees to execute the parties' 199__ Federal and State Joint Income Tax Returns with John. John agrees to pay the income tax to the Internal Revenue Service and to the Illinois Department of Revenue due under such 199__ Joint Income Tax Returns, and to indemnify and hold harmless Ellen, her heirs, executors, administrators, and personal representatives, of and from any and all claims and demands of and obligations and liabilities to or assessments by the Internal Revenue Service (including the Director of Internal Revenue) or the Illinois Department of Revenue, and costs and expenses in connection with the parties' 199__ Joint Returns or proceedings for the year 199__.

_____
John Jarndyce

_____
Ellen Jarndyce

Frederick Tulkinghorn
Attorney for John Jarndyce
Address
Telephone number

29 U.S.C.A.
EMPLOYEE RETIREMENT INCOME SECURITY PROGRAM

Analysis

Sec.
1169. Additional standards for group health plans.

WESTLAW Electronic Research

See WESTLAW Electronic Research Guide preceding the Summary of Contents.

29 U.S.C.A. § 1169

§ 1169. Additional standards for group health plans

ERISA § 609. [Act Sec. 4301(a) amended Part 6 of Subtitle B of title I of ERISA by adding new ERISA Sec. 609 to read as below.]

(a) Group health plan coverage pursuant to medical child support orders.

(1) In general. Each group health plan shall provide benefits in accordance with the applicable requirements of any qualified medical child support order.

(2) Definitions. For purposes of this subsection—

(A) Qualified medical support order. The term "qualified medical child support order" means a medical child support order—

(i) which creates or recognizes the existence of an alternate recipient's right to, or assigns to an alternate recipient the right to, receive benefits for which a participant or beneficiary is eligible under a group health plan, and

(ii) with respect to which the requirements of paragraphs (3) and (4) are met.

(B) Medical child support order. The term "medical child support order" means any judgment, decree, or order (including approval of a settlement agreement) issued by a court of competent jurisdiction which—

(i) provides for child support with respect to a child of a participant under a group health plan or provides for health benefit coverage to such a child, is made pursuant to a State domestic relations law (including a community property law), and relates to benefits under such plan, or

(ii) enforces a law relating to medical child support described in section 1908 of the Social Security Act (as added by section 13822 of the Omnibus Budget Reconciliation Act of 1993) with respect to a group health plan.

(C) Alternate recipient. The term "Alternate recipient" means any child of a participant who is recognized under a medical child support order as having a right to enrollment under a group health plan with respect to such participant.

(3) Information to be included in qualified order. A medical child support order meets the requirements of this paragraph only if such an order clearly specified—

(A) the name and last known mailing address (if any) of the participant and the name and mailing address of each alternate recipient covered by the order.

(B) a reasonable description of the type of coverage to be provided by the plan to each such alternate recipient, or the manner in which such type of coverage is to be determined,

(C) the period to which such order applies, and

(D) each plan to which such order applies.

(4) Restriction of new types or forms of benefits. A medical child support order meets the requirements of this paragraph only if such order does not require a plan to provide any type or form of benefit, or any option, not otherwise provided under the plan, except to the extent necessary to meet the requirements of a law relating to medical child support described in section 1908 of the Social Security Act (as added by section 13822 of the Omnibus Budget Reconciliation Act of 1993).

(5) Procedural requirements.

(A) Timely notifications and determinations. In the case of any medical child support order received by a group health plan—

(i) the plan administrator shall promptly notify the participant and each alternate recipient of the receipt of such order and the plan's procedures for determining whether medical child support orders are qualified medical child support orders, and

(ii) within a reasonable period after receipt of such order, the plan administrator shall determine whether such order is a medical child support order and notify the participant and each alternate recipient of such determination.

(B) Establishment of procedures for determining qualified status of orders. Each group health plan shall establish reasonable procedures to determine whether medical child support orders are qualified medical child support orders and to administer the provision of benefits under such qualified orders. Such procedures—

(i) shall be in writing,

(ii) shall provide for the notification of each person specified in a medical child support order as eligible to receive benefits under the plan (at the address included in the medical child support order) of such procedures promptly upon receipt by the plan of the medical child support order, and

(iii) shall permit an alternate recipient to designate a representative for receipt of copies of notices that are sent to the alternate recipient with respect to a medical child support order.

(6) Actions taken by fiduciaries. If a plan fiduciary acts in accordance with part 4 of this subtitle in treating a medical child support order as being (or not being) a qualified medical child support order, then the plan's obligation to the participant and each alternate recipient shall be discharged to the extent of any payment made pursuant to such act of the fiduciary.

(7) Treatment of alternate recipients.

(A) Treatment as beneficiary generally. A person who is an alternate recipient under a qualified medical child support order shall be considered a beneficiary under the plan for purposes of any provision of this Act.

(B) Treatment as participant for purposes of reporting and disclosure requirements. A person who is an alternate recipient under any medical child support order shall be considered a participant under the plan for purposes of the reporting and disclosure requirements of part 1.

(8) Direct provision of benefits provided to alternate recipients. Any payment for benefits made by a group health plan pursuant to a medical child support order in reimbursement for expenses paid by an alternate recipient or an alternate recipient's custodial parent or legal guardian shall be made to the alternate recipient or the alternate recipient's custodial parent or legal guardian.

(b) Rights of states with respect to group health plans where participants or beneficiaries thereunder are eligible for Medicaid benefits.

(1) Compliance by plans with assignment of rights. A group health plan shall provide that payment for benefits with respect to a participant under the plan will be made in accordance with any assignment of rights made by or on behalf of such participant or a beneficiary of the participant as required by a State plan for medical assistance provided under title XIX of the Social Security Act pursuant to section 1912(a)(1)(A) of such Act (as in effect on the date of the enactment of the Omnibus Budget Reconciliation Act of 1993).

(2) Enrollment and provision of benefits without regard to Medicaid eligibility. A group health plan shall provide that, in enrolling an individual as a participant or beneficiary or in determining or making any payments for benefits of an individual as a participant or beneficiary, the fact that the individual is eligible for or is provided medical assistance under a State plan for medical assistance approved under title XIX of the Social Security Act will not be taken into account.

(3) Acquisition by states of rights of third parties. A groups health plan shall provide that, to the extent that payment has been made under a State plan for medical assistance approved under title XIX of the Social Security Act in any case in which a group health plan has a legal liability to make payment for items or services constituting such assistance, payment for benefits under the plan will be made in accordance with any State law which provides that the State has acquired the rights with respect to a participant to such payment for such items or services.

(c) Group health plan coverage of dependent children in cases of adoption.

(1) Coverage effective upon placement for adoption. In any case in which a group health plan provides coverage for dependent children of participants or beneficiaries, such plan shall provide benefits to dependent children placed with participants or beneficiaries for adoption under the same terms and conditions as apply in the case of dependent children who are natural children of participants or beneficiaries under the plan, irrespective of whether the adoption has become final.

(2) Restrictions based on preexisting conditions at time of placement for adoption prohibited. A group health plan may not restrict coverage under the plan of any dependent child adopted by a participant or beneficiary, or placed with a participant or beneficiary for adoption, solely on the basis of a preexisting condition of such child at the time that such child would otherwise become eligible for coverage under the plan, if the adoption of placement for adoption occurs while the participant or beneficiary is eligible for coverage under the plan.

(3) Definitions. For purposes of this subsection—

(A) Child. The term child means, in connection with any adoption, or placement for adoption, of a child, an individual who has not attained age 18 as of the date of such adoption or placement for adoption.

(B) Placement for adoption. The term placement, or being placed for adoption, in connection with any placement for adoption of a child with any person, means the assumption and retention by such person of a legal obligation for total or partial support of such child in anticipation of adoption of such child. The child's placement with such person terminates upon the termination of such legal obligation.

(d) Continued coverage of costs of a pediatric vaccine under group health plans. A group health plan may not reduce its coverage of the costs of pediatric vaccines (as defined under section 1928(h)(6) of the Social Security Act as amended by section 13830 of the Omnibus Budget Reconciliation Act of 1993) below the coverage it provided as of May 1, 1993.

(e) Regulations. Any regulations prescribed under the section shall be prescribed by the Secretary of Labor, in consultation with the Secretary of Health and Human Services.

Author's Notes

Analysis

1. Purpose.
2. Prior practice.
3. Times when entered.
4. QMCSO advantages.
5. Procedure.
6. QMCSO—Form.

29 U.S.C.A. § 1169   **FEDERAL LAWS**

(1) **Purpose.** Qualified Medical Child Support Orders are similar in operation to Qualified Domestic Relations Orders. The purpose of Qualified Medical Child Support Orders is to provide group health insurance coverage to children of participants in group health insurance plans.

(2) **Prior practice.** Prior to the enactment of the new ERISA § 609 (29 U.S.C.A. § 1169), effective August 10, 1993, the common practice was to make one of the parents responsible for covering the children of the parties with medical insurance. These provisions are enforceable by contempt proceedings, but the serious illness of a child occurring during a period when there is a failure of coverage can result in enormous uninsured costs.

(3) **Times when entered.** Qualified Medical Child Support Orders can be entered at any time (at decree, pre- or post-decree) when: (1) child support is ordered under IMDMA, and a parent is a participant in a group health plan; (2) when an order provides for medical benefit coverage to a child pursuant to IMDMA; or (3) when state law relating to medical child support described in § 1908 of the Social Security Act is enforced. See 750 ILCS 5/505.2 (health insurance).

(4) **QMCSO advantages.** The principal advantage of a Qualified Medical Child Support Order (QMCSO) is that it obligates the group health insurance plan to cover the children of the participant parent, not just the parent. Coverage is therefore more secure. A secondary advantage is that through the use of a QMCSO payments can be required to be made to the custodial parent, thereby eliminating the complexity of medical reimbursement being paid to the non-custodial participant parent, when the underlying medical costs have been paid by the custodial parent.

(5) **Procedure.** The best procedure, as in the past, is to continue to require one of the parents to cover the children with medical insurance, to continue to provide for the payment of ordinary and extraordinary medical expenses that are not covered by medical insurance by one or both of the parents, but now also to add the security of a QMCSO. See 750 ILCS 5/502 Author's Note (11) paras. 4(e)(i) and 4(e)(ii) for sample paragraphs.

(6) **QMCSO—Form.** There follows a sample QMCSO taken from Appendix P of Canan & Mitchell, *Employee Fringe and Welfare Benefit Plans*, West Publishing Co. (1994 ed.) as presented by the ABA Section of Family Law in its "Qualified Medical Child Support Orders" seminar of April 8, 1994, and somewhat modified. After the QMCSO is drafted, it is necessary to submit it to the medical plan administrator for approval.

Firm #_____

IN THE CIRCUIT COURT OF COOK COUNTY, ILLINOIS
COUNTY DEPARTMENT—DOMESTIC RELATIONS DIVISION

IN RE THE MARRIAGE OF)
)
SUSAN JELLYBY,)
)
        Petitioner,)
)
and) No. ___ D _____
)
ARTHUR JELLYBY,)
)
        Respondent.)

FEDERAL LAWS   29 U.S.C.A. § 1169

QUALIFIED MEDICAL CHILD SUPPORT ORDER

This court having entered a judgment of dissolution of marriage on the same date as the entry of this Order, the judgment having incorporated by reference the provisions of this Order so that the Order became a part of, but not merged into, the judgment of dissolution, and the court being otherwise fully advised in the premises;

IT IS HEREBY ORDERED AND ADJUDGED:

1. This Order is intended to serve as a Qualified Medical Child Support Order ("QMCSO") which orders the Medical Plan specified below to provide medical benefits to the children of Petitioner, SUSAN JELLYBY, and Respondent, ARTHUR JELLYBY ("Participant"), who are named below ("Alternate Recipients"), pursuant to a Judgment of Dissolution of even date herewith, and in accordance with Section 609 and other relevant sections of the Employee Retirement Income Security Act of 1974, as amended ("ERISA"), and Section 505.2 of the Illinois Marriage and Dissolution of Marriage Act.

2. The Medical Plan subject to this Order is as follows:

   "Medical Plan for the Employees of _____,"

   or successor plans

   Plan Administrator:

   a. Name: _____

   b. Address: _____

3. The Participant is the Respondent, ARTHUR JELLYBY, whose last known address, Social Security Number, and date of birth are:

   a. Last Known Address: _____

   b. Social Security Number: _____

   c. Date of Birth: _____

4. The Petitioner is SUSAN JELLYBY whose last known address, Social Security Number, and date of birth are:

   a. Last Known Address: _____

   b. Social Security Number: _____

   c. Date of Birth: _____

5. The Alternate Recipients, their last known addresses, Social Security Numbers, dates of birth, and custodial parent(s) are:

   I. Caddy Jellyby

   a. Last Known Address: _____

   b. Social Security Number: _____

29 U.S.C.A. § 1169   **FEDERAL LAWS**

      c. Date of Birth: _____
      d. Custodial Parent: _____

II. Peepy Jellyby

      a. Last Known Address: _____
      b. Social Security Number: _____
      c. Date of Birth: _____
      d. Custodial Parent: _____

6. The Petitioner and the Respondent were married on _____ and their marriage was dissolved on the date of this Order.

7. The Alternate Recipients shall receive the following benefits under the Medical Plan:

[Family medical and dental coverage/family medical coverage/medical coverage under the _____ option presently available under the Medical Plan/coverage in the HMO] Other: _____

If the Medical Plan is changed so that the Medical Benefits specified in this paragraph are no longer available, the medical benefits provided shall be the family medical coverage (taking into account the extent of coverage, coinsurance amount, and deductible (if applicable)) that is most similar to the coverage specified; however, such benefits shall be benefits that are permitted under the Medical Plan, or its successor.

8. The period to which this Order applies shall be from the date of the entry of this Order to the first to occur of the youngest surviving alternate recipient completing his or her education or reaching his or her 23rd birthday.

9. The Petitioner, SUSAN JELLYBY, having been awarded residential custody of each of the Alternate Recipients, the Petitioner, SUSAN JELLYBY, pursuant to ERISA § 609, is deemed to have been appointed by each of the Alternate Recipients to receive copies of notices sent to each Alternate Recipient with respect to this Order.

10. Any payment of medical benefits made pursuant to this Order in reimbursement of expenses paid by an Alternate Recipient or an Alternate Recipient's custodial parent shall be made to the Alternate Recipient or the Alternate Recipient's residential custodial parent, SUSAN JELLYBY, as applicable.

11. This Order does not require the Medical Plan to provide any type or form of benefit, or any option, not otherwise provided under the Medical Plan.

12(i). It is intended by the parties that this Order will qualify as a Qualified Medical Child Support Order pursuant to ERISA Section 609 (29 U.S.C.A. § 1169), and subsequent amendments, and that it will be interpreted and administered as such.

12(ii). The Court retains jurisdiction to amend this Order for the purpose of establishing or maintaining this Order as a Qualified Medical Child

Support Order; and, further, the Court may amend this Order to revise or conform its terms so as to effect the expressed provisions of the Order, the parties' Settlement Agreement dated _____, 199__, and the Judgment of Dissolution of Marriage, as well as to enforce this Order against successor medical insurance plans, to provide coverage for a child who moves out of the service area, or to modify this Order to comply with the requirements of ERISA Section 609 (29 U.S.C.A. § 1169).

SUSAN JELLYBY

ARTHUR JELLYBY

Samuel Kenge
Attorney for SUSAN JELLYBY

Joseph Blowers
Attorney for ARTHUR JELLYBY

ENTER:

JUDGE

Samuel Kenge
Kenge and Carboy
Address
Telephone number

11 U.S.C.A.
UNITED STATES BANKRUPTCY CODE

Analysis

Sec.
523. Exceptions to discharge.

WESTLAW Electronic Research

See WESTLAW Electronic Research Guide preceding the Summary of Contents.

---

11 U.S.C.A. § 523

§ 523. **Exceptions to discharge**

(a) A discharge [in bankruptcy under] this title does not discharge an individual debtor from any debt—

* * *

(5) to a spouse, former spouse, or child of the debtor, for alimony to, maintenance for, or support of such spouse or child, in connection with a

separation agreement, divorce decree or other order of a court of record, determination made in accordance with State or territorial law by a governmental unit, or property settlement agreement, but not to the extent that—

> (A) such debt is assigned to another entity, voluntarily, by operation of law, or otherwise (other than debts assigned pursuant to section 402(a)(26) of the Social Security Act, or any such debt which has been assigned to the Federal Government or to a State or any political subdivision of such State); or
>
> (B) such debt includes a liability designated as alimony, maintenance, or support, unless such liability is actually in the nature of alimony, maintenance, or support;

* * *

Author's Notes

Analysis

1. Discharge property but not support.
2. Maintenance.
3. Attorney's fees.
4. 1994 amendment.

(1) **Discharge property but not support.** As a general matter, discharges in bankruptcy will discharge dissolution of marriage property indebtednesses, but will not discharge maintenance or children's support obligations. 11 U.S.C.A. § 523(a)(5)(B).

(2) **Maintenance.** The Bankruptcy Court, however, can determine independently whether what is designated as maintenance is actually for support, and therefore is not dischargeable, or is actually in the nature of property, and therefore is dischargeable. In determining whether an obligation is a liability for support, the court is directed to examine the substance of the obligation, not just the labels imposed by state law. In re Maitlen, 658 F.2d 466, 468 (7th Cir.1981). Furthermore,

> Bankruptcy law, not state law, is controlling when determining what constitutes alimony, maintenance or support.... Observance of bankruptcy law does not, however, preclude an examination of state law. State law should be considered ... [T]he Bankruptcy Court should examine the totality of the circumstances, which includes state law, to determine the divorce Court's purpose in making the awards and whether the essential elements of maintenance and support are present in the award.

In re Calisoff, 92 B.R. 346 (Bkrtcy.N.D.Ill.1988).

The court should consider, *inter alia,*

> 1) the language and substance of the agreement in the context of surrounding circumstances; 2) the function served by the obligation; 3) the relative incomes and financial circumstances; 4) the nature and duration of the payments; 5) the comparative ages, employability and educational levels; and 6) other factors bearing on the spouse's need for support at the time the order was entered.

In re Hansel, 1992 WL 280799 at *3, *4 (Bkrtcy. N.D.Ill.1992) (citing In re Woods, 561 F.2d 27 (7th Cir.1977)). In other words, if maintenance is appreciably higher than is necessary for support, or if maintenance is really a property settlement, but has been denominated maintenance in order to achieve deductibility, the Bankruptcy Court can declare that portion of the maintenance that is not for support to be discharged in bankruptcy. See also In re Haas, 129 B.R. 531 (Bkrtcy.N.D.Ill.1989) (award of marital residence to wife was in the nature of support and therefore not dischargeable).

(3) **Attorney's fees.** Under the Federal Bankruptcy Act, a debtor can generally discharge a marital property obligation, but he cannot discharge a debt "for alimony to, maintenance for, or support of" a spouse, former spouse, or child of the debtor. 11 U.S.C.A. § 523(a)(5). The issue, therefore, is whether attorney's fees qualify as support or property.

> State law should be considered to determine what prompted the state court to award the fees.... An award of maintenance and support is meant to provide an ex-spouse with necessary goods or services which he or she would otherwise not be able to purchase.... As such, attorney fees awarded to a spouse in an Illinois divorce action are generally considered in the nature of maintenance and support.

In re Calisoff, 92 B.R. 346, 352–53 (Bkrtcy. N.D.Ill.1988). The court concluded: "If the award tends to balance the income of the parties, then the award is in the nature of support." *Id.* at 353.

(4) **1994 amendment.** The Bankruptcy Reform Act of 1994, P.L. 103–394, amends 11 U.S.C.A. § 523(a), adding § 523(a)(15), which provides that a debtor cannot discharge a debt

> (15) not of the kind described in paragraph (5) that is incurred by the debtor in the course of a divorce or separation or in connection with a separation agreement, divorce decree or other order of a court of record, a determination made in accordance with State or territorial law by a governmental unit unless—
>
> (A) the debtor does not have the ability to pay such debt from income or property of the debtor not reasonably necessary to be expended for the maintenance or support of the debtor or a dependent of the debtor and, if the debtor is engaged in a business, for the payment of expenditures necessary for the continuation, preservation, and operation of such business; or
>
> (B) discharging such debt would result in a benefit to the debtor that outweighs the detrimental consequences to a spouse, former spouse, or child of the debtor....

As explained by the House Committee on the Judiciary Report, the section

> adds a new exception to discharge for some debts arising out of a divorce decree or separation agreement that are not in the nature of alimony, maintenance or support. In some instances, divorcing spouses have agreed to make payments of marital debts, holding the other spouse harmless from those debts, in exchange for a reduction in alimony payments. In other cases, spouses have agreed to lower alimony based on a larger property settlement. If such "hold harmless" and property settlement obligations are not found to be in the nature of alimony, maintenance, or support, they are dischargeable under current law. The nondebtor spouse may be saddled with substantial debt and little or no alimony or support. This subsection will make such obligations nondischargeable in cases where the debtor has the ability to pay them and the detriment to the nondebtor spouse from their nonpayment outweighs the benefit to the debtor of discharging such debts. In other words, the debt will remain dischargeable if paying the debt

would reduce the debtor's income below that necessary for the support of the debtor and the debtor's dependents. The Committee believes that payment of support needs must take precedence over property settlement debts. The debt will also be discharged if the benefit to the debtor of discharging it outweighs the harm to the obligee. For example, if a nondebtor spouse would suffer little detriment from the debtor's nonpayment of an obligation required to be paid under a hold harmless agreement (perhaps because it could not be collected from the nondebtor spouse or because the nondebtor spouse could easily pay it) the obligation would be discharged. The benefits of the debtor's discharge should be sacrificed only if there would be substantial detriment to the nondebtor spouse that outweighs the debtor's need for a fresh start.

140 Cong. Rec. H10770 (daily ed. October 4, 1994); American Bar Association, Section of Family Law, *Practice Alert* (October 10, 1994).

42 U.S.C.A.
THE INTERNATIONAL CHILD ABDUCTION REMEDIES ACT (THE HAGUE CONVENTION)

Analysis

Sec.
11601. Findings and declarations.
11602. Definitions.
11603. Judicial remedies.
11604. Provisional remedies.
11605. Admissibility of documents.
11606. United States Central Authority.
11607. Costs and fees.
11608. Collection, maintenance, and dissemination of information.
11609. Interagency coordinating group.
11610. Authorization of appropriations.
Text of Hague Convention.
State Department Analysis of Hague Convention.

WESTLAW Electronic Research

See WESTLAW Electronic Research Guide preceding the Summary of Contents.

---

42 U.S.C.A. § 11601

§ 11601. Findings and declarations

(a) Findings. The Congress makes the following findings:

(1) The international abduction or wrongful retention of children is harmful to their well-being.

(2) Persons should not be permitted to obtain custody of children by virtue of their wrongful removal or retention.

(3) International abductions and retentions of children are increasing, and only concerted cooperation pursuant to an international agreement can effectively combat this problem.

(4) The Convention on the Civil Aspects of International Child Abduction, done at The Hague on October 25, 1980, establishes legal rights and procedures for the prompt return of children who have been wrongfully removed or retained, as well as for securing the exercise of visitation rights. Children who are wrongfully removed or retained within the meaning of the Convention are to be promptly returned unless one of the narrow exceptions set forth in the Convention applies. The Convention provides a sound treaty framework to help resolve the problem of international abduction and retention of children and will deter such wrongful removals and retentions.

(b) Declarations. The Congress makes the following declarations:

(1) It is the purpose of this chapter to establish procedures for the implementation of the Convention in the United States.

(2) The provisions of this chapter are in addition to and not in lieu of the provisions of the Convention.

(3) In enacting this chapter the Congress recognizes—

(A) the international character of the Convention; and

(B) the need for uniform international interpretation of the Convention.

(4) The Convention and this chapter empower courts in the United States to determine only rights under the Convention and not the merits of any underlying child custody claims.

42 U.S.C.A. § 11602

§ 11602. Definitions

For the purposes of this chapter—

(1) the term "applicant" means any person who, pursuant to the Convention, files an application with the United States Central Authority or a Central Authority of any other party to the Convention for the return of a child alleged to have been wrongfully removed or retained or for arrangements for organizing or securing the effective exercise of rights of access pursuant to the Convention;

(2) the term "Convention" means the Convention on the Civil Aspects of International Child Abduction, done at The Hague on October 25, 1980;

(3) the term "Parent Locator Service" means the service established by the Secretary of Health and Human Services under section 653 of this title;

(4) the term "petitioner" means any person who, in accordance with this chapter, files a petition in court seeking relief under the Convention;

(5) the term "person" includes any individual, institution, or other legal entity or body;

(6) the term "respondent" means any person against whose interests a petition is filed in court, in accordance with this chapter, which seeks relief under the Convention;

(7) the term "rights of access" means visitation rights;

(8) the term "State" means any of the several States, the District of Columbia, and any commonwealth, territory, or possession of the United States; and

(9) the term "United States Central Authority" means the agency of the Federal Government designated by the President under section 11606(a) of this title.

42 U.S.C.A. § 11603

§ 11603. Judicial remedies

(a) Jurisdiction of courts. The courts of the States and the United States district courts shall have concurrent original jurisdiction of actions arising under the Convention.

(b) Petitions. Any person seeking to initiate judicial proceedings under the Convention for the return of a child or for arrangements for organizing or securing the effective exercise of rights of access to a child may do so by commencing a civil action by filing a petition for the relief sought in any court which has jurisdiction of such action and which is authorized to exercise its jurisdiction in the place where the child is located at the time the petition is filed.

(c) Notice. Notice of an action brought under subsection (b) of this section shall be given in accordance with the applicable law governing notice in interstate child custody proceedings.

(d) Determination of case. The court in which an action is brought under subsection (b) of this section shall decide the case in accordance with the Convention.

(e) Burdens of proof.

(1) A petitioner in an action brought under subsection (b) of this section shall establish by a preponderance of the evidence—

(A) in the case of an action for the return of a child, that the child has been wrongfully removed or retained within the meaning of the Convention; and

(B) in the case of an action for arrangements for organizing or securing the effective exercise of rights of access, that the petitioner has such rights.

(2) In the case of an action for the return of a child, a respondent who opposes the return of the child has the burden of establishing—

(A) by clear and convincing evidence that one of the exceptions set forth in article 13b or 20 of the Convention applies; and

(B) by a preponderance of the evidence that any other exception set forth in article 12 or 13 of the Convention applies.

(f) Application of Convention. For purposes of any action brought under this chapter—

(1) the term "authorities", as used in article 15 of the Convention to refer to the authorities of the state of the habitual residence of a child, includes courts and appropriate government agencies;

(2) the terms "wrongful removal or retention" and "wrongfully removed or retained", as used in the Convention, include a removal or retention of a child before the entry of a custody order regarding that child; and

(3) the term "commencement of proceedings", as used in article 12 of the Convention, means, with respect to the return of a child located in the United States, the filing of a petition in accordance with subsection (b) of this section.

(g) Full faith and credit. Full faith and credit shall be accorded by the courts of the States and the courts of the United States to the judgment of any other such court ordering or denying the return of a child, pursuant to the Convention, in an action brought under this chapter.

(h) Remedies under Convention not exclusive. The remedies established by the Convention and this chapter shall be in addition to remedies available under other laws or international agreements.

42 U.S.C.A. § 11604

§ 11604. Provisional remedies

(a) Authority of courts. In furtherance of the objectives of article 7(b) and other provisions of the Convention, and subject to the provisions of subsection (b) of this section, any court exercising jurisdiction of an action brought under section 11603(b) of this title may take or cause to be taken measures under Federal or State law, as appropriate, to protect the well-being of the child involved or to prevent the child's further removal or concealment before the final disposition of the petition.

(b) Limitation on authority. No court exercising jurisdiction of an action brought under section 11603(b) of this title may, under subsection (a) of this section, order a child removed from a person having physical control of the child unless the applicable requirements of State law are satisfied.

42 U.S.C.A. § 11605

§ 11605. Admissibility of documents

With respect to any application to the United States Central Authority, or any petition to a court under section 11603 of this title, which seeks relief under the Convention, or any other documents or information included with such application or petition or provided after such submission which relates to the application or petition, as the case may be, no authentication of such application, petition, document, or information shall be required in order for the application, petition, document, or information to be admissible in court.

42 U.S.C.A. § 11606
§ 11606. United States Central Authority

(a) Designation. The President shall designate a Federal agency to serve as the Central Authority for the United States under the Convention.

(b) Functions. The functions of the United States Central Authority are those ascribed to the Central Authority by the Convention and this chapter.

(c) Regulatory authority. The United States Central Authority is authorized to issue such regulations as may be necessary to carry out its functions under the Convention and this chapter.

(d) Obtaining information from Parent Locator Service. The United States Central Authority may, to the extent authorized by the Social Security Act (42 U.S.C. 301 et seq.), obtain information from the Parent Locator Service.

42 U.S.C.A. § 11607
§ 11607. Costs and fees

(a) Administrative costs. No department, agency, or instrumentality of the Federal Government or of any State or local government may impose on an applicant any fee in relation to the administrative processing of applications submitted under the Convention.

(b) Costs incurred in civil actions.

(1) Petitioners may be required to bear the costs of legal counsel or advisors, court costs incurred in connection with their petitions, and travel costs for the return of the child involved and any accompanying persons, except as provided in paragraphs (2) and (3).

(2) Subject to paragraph (3), legal fees or court costs incurred in connection with an action brought under section 11603 of this title shall be borne by the petitioner unless they are covered by payments from Federal, State, or local legal assistance or other programs.

(3) Any court ordering the return of a child pursuant to an action brought under section 11603 of this title shall order the respondent to pay necessary expenses incurred by or on behalf of the petitioner, including court costs, legal fees, foster home or other care during the course of proceedings in the action, and transportation costs related to the return of the child, unless the respondent establishes that such order would be clearly inappropriate.

42 U.S.C.A. § 11608
§ 11608. Collection, maintenance, and dissemination of information

(a) In general. In performing its functions under the Convention, the United States Central Authority may, under such conditions as the Central

Authority prescribes by regulation, but subject to subsection (c) of this section, receive from or transmit to any department, agency, or instrumentality of the Federal Government or of any State or foreign government, and receive from or transmit to any applicant, petitioner, or respondent, information necessary to locate a child or for the purpose of otherwise implementing the Convention with respect to a child, except that the United States Central Authority—

    (1) may receive such information from a Federal or State department, agency, or instrumentality only pursuant to applicable Federal and State statutes; and

    (2) may transmit any information received under this subsection notwithstanding any provision of law other than this chapter.

(b) Requests for information. Requests for information under this section shall be submitted in such manner and form as the United States Central Authority may prescribe by regulation and shall be accompanied or supported by such documents as the United States Central Authority may require.

(c) Responsibility of government entities. Whenever any department, agency, or instrumentality of the United States or of any State receives a request from the United States Central Authority for information authorized to be provided to such Central Authority under subsection (a) of this section, the head of such department, agency, or instrumentality shall promptly cause a search to be made of the files and records maintained by such department, agency, or instrumentality in order to determine whether the information requested is contained in any such files or records. If such search discloses the information requested, the head of such department, agency, or instrumentality shall immediately transmit such information to the United States Central authority, except that any such information the disclosure of which—

    (1) would adversely affect the national security interests of the United States or the law enforcement interests of the United States or of any State; or

    (2) would be prohibited by section 9 of title 13; shall not be transmitted to the Central Authority. The head of such department, agency, or instrumentality shall, immediately upon completion of the requested search, notify the Central Authority of the results of the search, and whether an exception set forth in paragraph (1) or (2) applies. In the event that the United States Central Authority receives information and the appropriate Federal or State department, agency, or instrumentality thereafter notifies the Central Authority that an exception set forth in paragraph (1) or (2) applies to that information, the Central Authority may not disclose that information under subsection (a) of this section.

(d) Information available from Parent Locator Service. To the extent that information which the United States Central Authority is authorized to obtain under the provisions of subsection (c) of this section can be obtained through the Parent Locator Service, the United States Central Authority shall

42 U.S.C.A. § 11608   FEDERAL LAWS

first seek to obtain such information from the Parent Locator Service, before requesting such information directly under the provisions of subsection (c) of this section.

(e) Recordkeeping. The United States Central Authority shall maintain appropriate records concerning its activities and the disposition of cases brought to its attention.

42 U.S.C.A. § 11609

§ 11609. Interagency coordinating group

The Secretary of State, the Secretary of Health and Human Services, and the Attorney General shall designate Federal employees and may, from time to time, designate private citizens to serve on an interagency coordinating group to monitor the operation of the Convention and to provide advice on its implementation to the United States Central Authority and other Federal agencies.

This group shall meet from time to time at the request of the United States Central Authority. The agency in which the United States Central Authority is located is authorized to reimburse such private citizens for travel and other expenses incurred in participating at meetings of the interagency coordinating group at rates not to exceed those authorized under subchapter I of chapter 57 of title 5 for employees of agencies.

42 U.S.C.A. § 11610

§ 11610. Authorization of appropriations

There are authorized to be appropriated for each fiscal year such sums as may be necessary to carry out the purposes of the Convention and this chapter.

Text of Hague Convention

CONVENTION ON THE CIVIL ASPECTS OF
INTERNATIONAL CHILD ABDUCTION

The States signatory to the present Convention,

Firmly convinced that the interests of children are of paramount importance in matters relating to their custody,

Desiring to protect children internationally from the harmful effects of their wrongful removal or retention and to establish procedures to ensure their prompt return to the State of their habitual residence, as well as to secure protection for rights of access,

Have resolved to conclude a Convention to this effect, and have agreed upon the following provisions:

CHAPTER I—SCOPE OF THE CONVENTION

Article 1

The objects of the present Convention are—

TEXT OF HAGUE CONVENTION

(a) to secure the prompt return of children wrongfully removed to or retained in any Contracting State; and

(b) to ensure that rights of custody and of access under the law of one Contracting State are effectively respected in the other Contracting States.

Article 2

Contracting States shall take all appropriate measures to secure within their territories the implementation of the objects of the Convention. For this purpose they shall use the most expeditious procedures available.

Article 3

The removal or the retention of a child is to be considered wrongful where—

(a) it is in breach of rights of custody attributed to a person, an institution or any other body, either jointly or alone, under the law of the State in which the child was habitually resident immediately before the removal or retention; and

(b) at the time of removal or retention those rights were actually exercised, either jointly or alone, or would have been so exercised but for the removal or retention. The rights of custody mentioned in sub-paragraph (a) above, may arise in particular by operation of law or by reason of a judicial or administrative decision, or by reason of an agreement having legal effect under the law of that State.

Article 4

The Convention shall apply to any child who was habitually resident in a Contracting State immediately before any breach of custody or access rights. The Convention shall cease to apply when the child attains the age of 16 years.

Article 5

For the purposes of this Convention—

(a) "rights of custody" shall include rights relating to the care of the person of the child and, in particular, the right to determine the child's place of residence;

(b) "rights of access" shall include the right to take a child for a limited period of time to a place other than the child's habitual residence.

CHAPTER II—CENTRAL AUTHORITIES

Article 6

A Contracting State shall designate a Central Authority to discharge the duties which are imposed by the Convention upon such authorities.

Federal States, States with more than one system of law or States having autonomous territorial organizations shall be free to appoint more than one Central Authority and to specify the territorial extent of their powers. Where a State has appointed more than one Central Authority, it shall designate the Central Authority to which applications may be addressed for transmission to the appropriate Central Authority within that State.

Article 7

Central Authorities shall co-operate with each other and promote co-operation amongst the competent authorities in their respective States to secure the prompt return of children and to achieve the other objects of this Convention.

In particular, either directly or through any intermediary, they shall take all appropriate measures—

(a) to discover the whereabouts of a child who has been wrongfully removed or retained;

(b) to prevent further harm to the child or prejudice to interested parties by taking or causing to be taken provisional measures;

(c) to secure the voluntary return of the child or to bring about an amicable resolution of the issues;

(d) to exchange, where desirable, information relating to the social background of the child;

(e) to provide information of a general character as to the law of their State in connection with the application of the Convention;

(f) to initiate or facilitate the institution of judicial or administrative proceedings with a view to obtaining the return of the child and, in a proper case, to make arrangements for organizing or securing the effective exercise of rights of access;

(g) where the circumstances so require, to provide or facilitate the provision of legal aid and advice, including the participation of legal counsel and advisers;

(h) to provide such administrative arrangements as may be necessary and appropriate to secure the safe return of the child;

(i) to keep each other informed with respect to the operation of this Convention and, as far as possible, to eliminate any obstacles to its application.

CHAPTER III—RETURN OF CHILDREN

Article 8

Any person, institution or other body claiming that a child has been removed or retained in breach of custody rights may apply either to the Central Authority of the child's habitual residence or to the Central Authority of any other Contracting State for assistance in securing the return of the child.

The application shall contain—

(a) information concerning the identity of the applicant, of the child and of the person alleged to have removed or retained the child;

(b) where available, the date of birth of the child;

(c) the grounds on which the applicant's claim for return of the child is based;

(d) all available information relating to the whereabouts of the child and the identity of the person with whom the child is presumed to be.

The application may be accompanied or supplemented by—

(e) an authenticated copy of any relevant decision or agreement;

(f) a certificate or an affidavit emanating from a Central Authority, or other competent authority of the State of the child's habitual residence, or from a qualified person, concerning the relevant law of that State;

(g) any other relevant document.

Article 9

If the Central Authority which receives an application referred to in Article 8 has reason to believe that the child is in another Contracting State, it shall directly and without delay transmit the application to the Central Authority of that Contracting State and inform the requesting Central Authority, or the applicant, as the case may be.

Article 10

The Central Authority of the State where the child is shall take or cause to be taken all appropriate measures in order to obtain the voluntary return of the child.

Article 11

The judicial or administrative authorities of Contracting States shall act expeditiously in proceedings for the return of children.

If the judicial or administrative authority concerned has not reached a decision within six weeks from the date of commencement of the proceedings, the applicant or the Central Authority of the requested State, on its own initiative or if asked by the Central Authority of the requesting State, shall have the right to request a statement of the reasons for the delay. If a reply is received by the Central Authority of the requested State, that Authority shall transmit the reply to the Central Authority of the requesting State, or to the applicant, as the case may be.

Article 12

Where a child has been wrongfully removed or retained in terms of Article 3 and, at the date of the commencement of the proceedings before the judicial or administrative authority of the Contracting State where the child is, a period of less than one year has elapsed from the date of the wrongful removal or retention, the authority concerned shall order the return of the child forthwith.

The judicial or administrative authority, even where the proceedings have been commenced after the expiration of the period of one year referred to in the preceding paragraph, shall also order the return of the child, unless it is demonstrated that the child is now settled in its new environment.

Where the judicial or administrative authority in the requested State has reason to believe that the child has been taken to another State, it may stay the proceedings or dismiss the application for the return of the child.

Article 13

Notwithstanding the provisions of the preceding Article, the judicial or administrative authority of the requested State is not bound to order the return of the child if the person, institution or other body which opposes its return establishes that—

(a) the person, institution or other body having the care of the person of the child was not actually exercising the custody rights at the time of removal or retention, or had consented to or subsequently acquiesced in the removal or retention; or

(b) there is a grave risk that his or her return would expose the child to physical or psychological harm or otherwise place the child in an intolerable situation.

The judicial or administrative authority may also refuse to order the return of the child if it finds that the child objects to being returned and has attained an age and degree of maturity at which it is appropriate to take account of its views.

In considering the circumstances referred to in this Article, the judicial and administrative authorities shall take into account the information relating to the social background of the child provided by the Central Authority or other competent authority of the child's habitual residence.

Article 14

In ascertaining whether there has been a wrongful removal or retention within the meaning of Article 3, the judicial or administrative authorities of the requested State may take notice directly of the law of, and of judicial or administrative decisions, formally recognized or not in the State of the habitual residence of the child, without recourse to the specific procedures for the proof of that law or for the recognition of foreign decisions which would otherwise be applicable.

TEXT OF HAGUE CONVENTION

Article 15

The judicial or administrative authorities of a Contracting State may, prior to the making of an order for the return of the child, request that the applicant obtain from the authorities of the State of the habitual residence of the child a decision or other determination that the removal or retention was wrongful within the meaning of Article 3 of the Convention, where such a decision or determination may be obtained in that State. The Central Authorities of the Contracting States shall so far as practicable assist applicants to obtain such a decision or determination.

Article 16

After receiving notice of a wrongful removal or retention of a child in the sense of Article 3, the judicial or administrative authorities of the Contracting State to which the child has been removed or in which it has been retained shall not decide on the merits of rights of custody until it has been determined that the child is not to be returned under this Convention or unless an application under this Convention is not lodged within a reasonable time following receipt of the notice.

Article 17

The sole fact that a decision relating to custody has been given in or is entitled to recognition in the requested State shall not be a ground for refusing to return a child under this Convention, but the judicial or administrative authorities of the requested State may take account of the reasons for that decision in applying this Convention.

Article 18

The provisions of this Chapter do not limit the power of a judicial or administrative authority to order the return of the child at any time.

Article 19

A decision under this Convention concerning the return of the child shall not be taken to be a determination on the merits of any custody issue.

Article 20

The return of the child under the provisions of Article 12 may be refused if this would not be permitted by the fundamental principles of the requested State relating to the protection of human rights and fundamental freedoms.

CHAPTER IV—RIGHTS OF ACCESS

Article 21

An application to make arrangements for organizing or securing the effective exercise of rights of access may be presented to the Central Authorities of the Contracting States in the same way as an application for the return of a child.

The Central Authorities are bound by the obligations of co-operation which are set forth in Article 7 to promote the peaceful enjoyment of access rights and the fulfilment of any conditions to which the exercise of those rights may be subject. The Central Authorities shall take steps to remove, as far as possible, all obstacles to the exercise of such rights. The Central Authorities, either directly or through intermediaries, may initiate or assist in the institution of proceedings with a view to organizing or protecting these rights and securing respect for the conditions to which the exercise of these rights may be subject.

CHAPTER V—GENERAL PROVISIONS

Article 22

No security, bond or deposit, however described, shall be required to guarantee the payment of costs and expenses in the judicial or administrative proceedings falling within the scope of this Convention.

Article 23

No legalization or similar formality may be required in the context of this Convention.

Article 24

Any application, communication or other document sent to the Central Authority of the requested State shall be in the original language, and shall be accompanied by a translation into the official language or one of the official languages of the requested State or, where that is not feasible, a translation into French or English.

However, a Contracting State may, by making a reservation in accordance with Article 42, object to the use of either French or English, but not both, in any application, communication or other document sent to its Central Authority.

Article 25

Nationals of the Contracting States and persons who are habitually resident within those States shall be entitled in matters concerned with the application of this Convention to legal aid and advice in any other Contracting State on the same conditions as if they themselves were nationals of and habitually resident in that State.

Article 26

Each Central Authority shall bear its own costs in applying this Convention.

Central Authorities and other public services of Contracting States shall not impose any charges in relation to applications submitted under this Convention. In particular, they may not require any payment from the applicant towards the costs and expenses of the proceedings or, where applicable, those arising from the participation of legal counsel or advisers. However, they may, require the payment of the expenses incurred or to be incurred in implementing the return of the child.

However, a Contracting State may, by making a reservation in accordance with Article 42 declare that it shall not be bound to assume any costs referred to in the preceding paragraph resulting from the participation of legal counsel or advisers or from court proceedings, except insofar as those costs may be covered by its system of legal aid and advice.

Upon ordering the return of a child or issuing an order concerning rights of access under this Convention, the judicial or administrative authorities may, where appropriate, direct the person who removed or retained the child, or who prevented the exercise of rights of access, to pay necessary expenses incurred by or on behalf of the applicant, including travel expenses, any costs incurred or payments made for locating the child, the costs of legal representation of the applicant, and those of returning the child.

Article 27

When it is manifest that the requirements of this Convention are not fulfilled or that the application is otherwise not well founded, a Central Authority is not bound to accept the application. In that case, the Central Authority shall forthwith inform the applicant or the Central Authority through which the application was submitted, as the case may be, of its reasons.

Article 28

A Central Authority may require that the application be accompanied by a written authorization empowering it to act on behalf of the applicant, or to designate a representative so to act.

Article 29

This Convention shall not preclude any person, institution or body who claims that there has been a breach of custody or access rights within the meaning of Article 3 or 21 from applying directly to the judicial or administrative authorities of a Contracting State, whether or not under the provisions of this Convention.

Article 30

Any application submitted to the Central Authorities or directly to the judicial or administrative authorities of a Contracting State in accordance with the terms of this Convention, together with documents and any other information appended thereto or provided by a Central Authority, shall be admissible in the courts or administrative authorities of the Contracting States.

Article 31

In relation to a State which in matters of custody of children has two or more systems of law applicable in different territorial units—

(a) any reference to habitual residence in that State shall be construed as referring to habitual residence in a territorial unit of that State;

(b) any reference to the law of the State of habitual residence shall be construed as referring to the law of the territorial unit in that State where the child habitually resides.

Article 32

In relation to a State which in matters of custody of children has two or more systems of law applicable to different categories of persons, any reference to the law of that State shall be construed as referring to the legal system specified by the law of that State.

Article 33

A State within which different territorial units have their own rules of law in respect of custody of children shall not be bound to apply this Convention where it State with a unified system of law would not be bound to do so.

Article 34

This Convention shall take priority in matters within its scope over the *Convention of 5 October 1961 concerning the powers of authorities and the law applicable in respect of the protection of minors,* as between Parties to both Conventions. Otherwise the present Convention shall not restrict the application of an international instrument in force between the State of origin and the State addressed or other law of the State addressed for the purposes of obtaining the return of a child who has been wrongfully removed or retained or of organizing access rights.

Article 35

This Convention shall apply as between Contracting States only to wrongful removals or retentions occurring after its entry into force in those States.

Where a declaration has been made under Article 39 or 40, the reference in the preceding paragraph to a Contracting State shall be taken to refer to the territorial unit or units in relation to which this Convention applies.

Article 36

Nothing in this Convention shall prevent two or more Contracting States, in order to limit the restrictions to which the return of the child may be subject, from agreeing among themselves to derogate from any provisions of this Convention which may imply such a restriction.

TEXT OF HAGUE CONVENTION

CHAPTER VI—FINAL CLAUSES

Article 37

The Convention shall be open for signature by the States which were Members of the Hague Conference on Private International Law at the time of its Fourteenth Session.

It shall be ratified, accepted or approved and the instruments of ratification, acceptance or approval shall be deposited with the Ministry of Foreign Affairs of the Kingdom of the Netherlands.

Article 38

Any other State may accede to the Convention.

The instrument of accession shall be deposited with the Ministry of Foreign Affairs of the Kingdom of the Netherlands.

The Convention shall enter into force for a State acceding to it on the first day of the third calendar month after the deposit of its instrument of accession.

The accession will have effect only as regards the relations between the acceding State and such Contracting States as will have declared their acceptance of the accession. Such a declaration will also have to be made by any Member State ratifying, accepting or approving the Convention after an accession. Such declaration shall be deposited at the Ministry of Foreign Affairs of the Kingdom of the Netherlands; this Ministry shall forward, through diplomatic channels, a certified copy to each of the Contracting States.

The Convention will enter into force as between the acceding State and the State that has declared its acceptance of the accession on the first day of the third calendar month after the deposit of the declaration of acceptance.

Article 39

Any State may at the time of signature, ratification, acceptance, approval or accession, declare that the Convention shall extend to all the territories for the international relations of which it is responsible, or to one or more of them. Such a declaration shall take effect at the time the Convention enters into force for that State.

Such declaration, as well as any subsequent extension, shall be notified to the Ministry of Foreign Affairs of the Kingdom of the Netherlands.

Article 40

If a Contracting State has two or more territorial units in which different systems of law are applicable in relation to matters dealt with in this Convention, it may at the time of signature, ratification, acceptance, approval or accession declare that this Convention shall extend to all its territorial units or only to one or more of them and may modify this declaration by submitting another declaration at any time.

Any such declaration shall be notified to the Ministry of Foreign Affairs of the Kingdom of the Netherlands and shall state expressly the territorial units to which the Convention applies.

Article 41

Where a Contracting State has a system of government under which executive, judicial and legislative powers are distributed between central and other authorities within that State, its signature or ratification, acceptance or approval of, or accession to this Convention, or its making of any declaration in terms of Article 40 shall carry no implication as to the internal distribution of powers within that State.

Article 42

Any State may, not later than the time of ratification, acceptance, approval or accession, or at the time of making a declaration in terms of Article 39 or 40, make one or both of the reservations provided for in Article 24 and Article 26, third paragraph. No other reservation shall be permitted.

Any State may at any time withdraw a reservation it has made. The withdrawal shall be notified to the Ministry of Foreign Affairs of the Kingdom of the Netherlands.

The reservation shall cease to have effect on the first day of the third calendar month after the notification referred to in the preceding paragraph.

Article 43

The Convention shall enter into force on the first day of the third calendar month after the deposit of the third instrument of ratification, acceptance, approval or accession referred to in Articles 37 and 38.

Thereafter the Convention shall enter into force—

(1) for each State ratifying, accepting, approving or acceding to it subsequently, on the first day of the third calendar month after the deposit of its instrument of ratification, acceptance, approval or accession,

(2) for any territory or territorial unit to which the Convention has been extended in conformity with Article 39 or 40, on the first day of the third calendar month after the notification referred to in that Article.

Article 44

The Convention shall remain in force for five years from the date of its entry into force in accordance with the first paragraph of Article 43 even for States which subsequently have ratified, accepted, approved it or acceded to it.

If there has been no denunciation, it shall be renewed tacitly every five years.

TEXT OF HAGUE CONVENTION

Any denunciation shall be notified to the Ministry of Foreign Affairs of the Kingdom of the Netherlands at least six months before the expiry of the five year period. It may be limited to certain of the territories or territorial units to which the Convention applies.

The denunciation shall have effect only as regards the State which has notified it. The Convention shall remain in force for the other Contracting States.

Article 45

The Ministry of Foreign Affairs of the Kingdom of the Netherlands shall notify the States Members of the Conference, and the States which have acceded in accordance with Article 38, of the following—

(1) the signatures and ratifications, acceptances and approvals referred to in Article 37;

(2) the accessions referred to in Article 38;

(3) the date on which the Convention enters into force in accordance with Article 43;

(4) the extensions referred to in Article 39;

(5) the declarations referred to in Articles 38 and 40;

(6) the reservations referred to in Article 24 and Article 26, third paragraph, and the withdrawals referred to in Article 42;

(7) the denunciations referred to in Article 44.

In witness whereof the undersigned, being duly authorized thereto, have signed this Convention.

Done at The Hague, on the 25th day of October, 1980, in the English and French languages, both texts being equally authentic, in a single copy which shall be deposited in the archives of the Government of the Kingdom of the Netherlands, and of which a certified copy shall be sent, through diplomatic channels, to each of the States Members of the Hague Conference on Private International Law at the date of its Fourteenth Session.

FEDERAL LAWS

ANALYSIS OF HAGUE CONVENTION
(prepared by State Department)

Legal Analysis of the Hague Convention on the Civil Aspects of International Child Abduction

Introduction

The Hague Convention on the Civil Aspects of International Child Abduction consists of six chapters containing forty-five articles. While not formally incorporated into the Convention, a model form was prepared when the Convention was adopted by the Hague Conference on Private International Law and was recommended for use in making application for the return of wrongfully removed or retained children. A copy of that form is annexed to this Legal Analysis. (The form to be used for the return of children from the United States may seek additional information.)

Table of Contents

To facilitate understanding of the Convention by the Senate and the use and interpretation of the Convention by parents, judges, lawyers and public and private agency personnel, the articles are analyzed and discussed in the following categories:

I. Children Protected by the Convention
(Preamble, Article 1)

A. Age (Articles 4, 36, 18, 29, 34, 13)
B. Residence (Article 4)
C. Timing/cases covered (Article 35)
D. Effect of custody order concerning the child
  1. Existing custody orders (Articles 17, 3)
  2. Pre-decree removals or retentions (Article 3)

II. Conduct Actionable Under the Convention

A. International "child abduction" not criminal: Hague Convention distinguished from extradition treaties (Article 12)
B. "Wrongful removal or retention" (Articles 1, 3, 5(a))
  1. Holders of rights protected by the Convention (*i.e.*, with respect to whom the removal or retention is wrongful)
    (a) "Person, institution or other body" (Article 3(a), (b))
    (b) "Jointly or alone" (Article 3(a), (b))
  2. Defined
    (a) Breach of "custody rights" (Articles 3(a), 5(a))
    (b) "Custody rights" determined by law of child's habitual residence (Articles 3(a), 31, 32, 33)
    (c) Sources of "Custody rights" (Article 3, last paragraph)
      i. Operation of law (Articles 3, 15)
      ii. Judicial or administrative decision (Article 3)
      iii. Agreement having legal effect (Article 3)

(d) "Actually exercised" (Articles 3(b), 5, 8(c), 13)

III Judicial Proceedings for Return of the Child

A. Right to seek return (Articles 29, 12, 34, 8)
B. Legal advice and costs (Articles 25, 26, 42)
C. Pleading requirements (Articles 8, 24)
D. Admissibility of evidence (Articles 30, 23)
E. Judicial promptitude/status report (Article 11)
F. Judicial notice (Article 14)
G. Court determination of "wrongfulness" (Articles 15, 3, 11, 12, 14)
H. Constraints upon courts in requested states in making substantive custody decisions (Article 16)
I. Duty to return not absolute
  1. Temporal qualifications
    (a) Article 4
    (b) Article 35
    (c) Article 12
  2. Article 13 limitations on return obligation
    (a) Legislative history (Articles 13, 20)
    (b) Non-exercise of custody rights (Articles 13(a), 3(b))
    (c) Grave risk of harm/intolerable situation (Article 13(b))
    (d) Child's preference (Article 13)
    (e) Role of social studies
  3. Article 20
  4. Custody order no defense to return (Article 17)
J. Return of the child (Article 12)
  1. Return order not on custody merits (Article 19)
  2. Costs, fees and expenses shifted to abductor (Article 26)

IV. Central Authority
(Articles 1, 10, 21)

A. Establishment of Central Authority (Article 6)
B. Duties (Article 7)
C. Other Tasks (Articles 8, 9, 10, 11, 15, 21, 26, 27, 28)
  1. Processing applications (Articles 8, 9, 27, 28)
  2. Assistance in connection with judicial proceedings
    (a) Request for status report (Article 11)
    (b) Social studies/background reports (Article 13)
    (c) Determination of "wrongfulness" (Article 15)
    (d) Costs (Article 26), reservation (Articles 42, 22)

V. Access Rights—Article 21

A. Remedies for breach (Articles 21, 12)
B. Defined (Article 5(b))
C. Procedure for obtaining relief (Articles 21, 8, 7)
D. Alternative remedies (Articles 18, 29, 34)

VI. Miscellaneous and Final Clauses

A. Article 36
B. Articles 37 and 38
C. Articles 42, 43 and 44
D. Articles 39 and 40

E. Article 41
F. Article 45

Annexes
—Recommended Return Application Form
—Bibliography

Guide to Terminology Used in the Legal Analysis

"Abduction" as used in the Convention title is not intended in a criminal sense. That term is shorthand for the phrase "wrongful removal or retention" which appears throughout the text, beginning with the preambular language and Article 1. Generally speaking, "wrongful removal" refers to the taking of a child from the person who was actually exercising custody of the child. "Wrongful retention" refers to the act of keeping the child without the consent of the person who was actually exercising custody. The archetype of this conduct is the refusal by the noncustodial parent to return a child at the end of an authorized visitation period. "Wrongful retention" is not intended by this Convention to cover refusal by the custodial parent to permit visitation by the other parent. Such obstruction of visitation may be redressed in accordance with Article 21.

The term "abductor" as used in this analysis refers to the person alleged to have wrongfully removed or retained a child. This person is also referred to as the "alleged wrongdoer" or the "respondent."

The term "person" as used in this analysis includes the person, institution or other body who (or which) actually exercised custody prior to the abduction and is seeking the child's return. The "person" seeking the child's return is also referred to as "applicant" and "petitioner."

The terms "court" and "judicial authority" are used throughout the analysis to mean both judicial and administrative bodies empowered to make decisions on petitions made pursuant to this Convention. "Judicial decree" and "court order" likewise include decisions made by courts or administrative bodies.

"Country of origin" and "requesting country" refer to the child's country ("State") of habitual residence prior to the wrongful removal or retention. "Country addressed" refers to the country ("State") where the child is located or the country to which the child is believed to have been taken. It is in

ANALYSIS OF HAGUE CONVENTION

that country that a judicial or administrative proceeding for return would be brought.

"Access rights" correspond to "visitation rights."

References to the "reporter" are to Elisa Perez-Vera, the official Hague Conference reporter for the Convention. Her explanatory report is recognized by the Conference as the official history and commentary on the Convention and is a source of background on the meaning of the provisions of the Convention available to all States becoming parties to it. It is referred to herein as the "Perez-Vera Report." The Perez-Vera Report appears in *Actes et documents de la Quatorzieme Session (1980), Volume III, Child Abduction,* edited by the Permanent Bureau of the Hague Conference on Private International Law, The Hague, Netherlands. (The volume may be ordered from the Netherlands Government Printing and Publishing Office, 1 Christoffel Plantijnstraat, Postbox 20014, 2500 EA The Hague, Netherlands.)

I. Children Protected by the Convention

A fundamental purpose of the Hague Convention is to protect children from wrongful international removals or retentions by persons bent on obtaining their physical and/or legal custody. Children who are wrongfully moved from country to country are deprived of the stable relationships which the Convention is designed promptly to restore. Contracting States are obliged by Article 2 to take all appropriate measures to implement the objectives of the Convention as set forth in Article 1: (1) To secure the prompt return of children wrongfully removed to or retained in any Contracting State; and (2) to ensure that rights of custody and of access under the law of one Contracting State are effectively respected in other Contracting States. While these objectives are universal in their appeal, the Convention does not cover all children who might be victims of wrongful takings or retentions. A threshold inquiry, therefore, is whether the child who has been abducted or retained is subject to the Convention's provisions. Only if the child falls within the scope of the Convention will the administrative and judicial mechanisms of the Convention apply.

A. Age

The Convention applies only to children under the age of sixteen (16). Even if a child is under sixteen at the time of the wrongful removal or retention as well as when the Convention is invoked, the Convention ceases to apply when the child reaches sixteen. Article 4.

Absent action by governments to expand coverage of the Convention to children aged sixteen and above pursuant to Article 36, the Convention itself is unavailable as the legal vehicle for securing return of a child sixteen or older. However, it does not bar return of such child by other means.

Articles 18, 29 and 34 make clear that the Convention is a nonexclusive remedy in cases of international child abduction. Article 18 provides that the Convention does not limit the power of a judicial authority to order return of a child at any time, presumably under other laws, procedures or comity, irrespective of the child's age. Article 29 permits the person who claims a breach of custody or access rights, as defined by Articles 3 and 21, to bypass the Convention completely by invoking any applicable laws or procedures to secure the child's return. Likewise, Article 34 provides that the Convention shall not restrict the application of any law in the State addressed for purposes of obtaining the child's return or for organizing visitation rights. Assuming such laws are not restricted to children under sixteen, a child sixteen or over may be returned pursuant to their provisions.

Notwithstanding the general application of the Convention to children under sixteen, it should be noted that the wishes of mature children regarding their return are not ignored by the Convention. Article 13 permits, but does not require, the judicial authority to refuse to order the child returned if the child "objects to being returned and has attained an age and degree of maturity at which it is appropriate to take account of its views." The role of the child's preference in return proceedings is discussed further at III.I(2)(d), *infra*.

B. Residence

In order for the Convention to apply the child must have been "habitually resident in a Contracting State immediately before any breach of custody or access rights." Article 4. In practical terms, the Convention may be invoked only where the child was habitually resident in a Contracting State and taken to or retained in another Contracting State. Accordingly, child abduction and retention cases are actionable under the Convention if they are international in nature (as opposed to interstate), and provided the Convention has entered into force for both countries involved. *See* discussion of Article 38, VI.B, *infra*.

To illustrate, take the case of a child abducted to California from his home in New York. The Convention could not be invoked to secure the return of such child. This is true even if one of the child's parents is an American citizen and the other a foreign national. The Uniform Child Custody Jurisdiction Act (UCCJA) and/or the Parental Kidnapping Prevention Act (PKPA), domestic state and federal law, respectively, would govern the return of the child in question. If the same child were removed from New York to Canada, application under the Convention could be made to secure the child's return provided the Convention had entered into force both for the United States and the Canadian province to which the child was taken. An alternative remedy might also lie under other Canadian law. If the child had been removed from Canada and taken to the United States, the aggrieved custodial parent in Canada could seek to secure the child's return by petitioning for enforcement of a Canadian custody order pursuant to the UCCJA, or by invoking the Convention, or both.

C. Timing/Cases Covered

Article 35 states that the Convention shall apply as between Contracting States only to wrongful removals or retentions occurring after its entry into force in those States. Following a strict interpretation of that Article, the Convention will not apply to a child who is wrongfully shifted from one Contracting State to another if the wrongful removal or retention occurred before the Convention's entry into force in those States. However, under a liberal interpretation Article 35 could be construed to cover wrongful removal or retention cases which began before the Convention took effect but which continued and were ongoing after its entry into force.

D. Effect of Custody Order Concerning the Child

1. Existing Custody Orders

Children who otherwise fall within the scope of the Convention are not automatically removed from its protections by virtue of a judicial decision awarding custody to the alleged wrongdoer. This is true whether the decision as to custody was made, or is entitled to recognition, in the State to which the child has been taken. Under Article 17 that State cannot refuse to return a child solely on the basis of a court order awarding custody to the alleged wrongdoer made by one of its own courts or by the courts of another country. This provision is intended to ensure, *inter alia*, that the Convention takes precedence over decrees made in favor of abductors before the court had notice of the wrongful removal or retention.

Thus, under Article 17 the person who wrongfully removes or retains the child in a Contracting State cannot insulate the child from the Convention's return provisions merely by obtaining a custody order in the country of new residence, or by seeking there to enforce another country's order. Nor may the alleged wrongdoer rely upon a stale decree awarding him or her custody, the provisions of which have been derogated from subsequently by agreement or acquiescence of the parties, to prevent the child's return under the Convention. Article 3.

It should be noted that Article 17 does permit a court to take into account the reasons underlying an existing custody decree when it applies the Convention.

II. Pre-Decree Removals or Retentions

Children who are wrongfully removed or retained prior to the entry of a custody order are protected by the Convention. There need not be a custody order in effect in order to invoke the Convention's return provisions. Accordingly, under the Convention a child will be ordered returned to the person with whom he or she was habitually resident in pre-decree abduction cases as well as in cases involving violations of existing custody orders.

Application of the Convention to pre-decree cases comes to grips with the reality that many children are abducted or retained long before custody actions have been initiated. In this manner a child is not prejudiced by the legal inaction of his or her physical custodian, who may not have anticipated the abduction, and the abductor is denied any legal advantage since the child is subject to the return provisions of the Convention.

The Convention's treatment of pre-decree abduction cases is distinguishable from the Council of Europe's Convention on Recognition and Enforcement of Decisions Relating to the Custody of Children, adopted in Strasbourg, France in November 1979 ("Strasbourg Convention"), and from domestic law in the United States, specifically the UCCJA and the PKPA, all of which provide for enforcement of custody decrees. Although the UCCJA and PKPA permit enforcement of a decree obtained by a parent in the home state after the child has been removed from that state, in the absence of such decree the enforcement provisions of those laws are inoperative. In contrast to the restoration of the *legal* status quo ante brought about by application of the UCCJA, the PKPA, and the Strasbourg Convention, the Hague Convention seeks restoration of the *factual* status quo ante and is not contingent on the existence of a custody decree. The Convention is premised upon the notion that the child should be promptly restored to his or her country of habitual residence so that a court there can examine the merits of the custody dispute and award custody in the child's best interests.

Pre-decree abductions are discussed in greater detail in the section dealing with actionable conduct. *See* II.B(2)(c)(i).

II. Conduct Actionable Under the Convention

A. "International Child Abduction" not Criminal: Hague Convention Distinguished From Extradition Treaties

Despite the use of the term "abduction" in its title, the Hague Convention is not an extradition treaty. The conduct made actionable by the Convention—the wrongful removal or retention of children—is wrongful not in a criminal sense but in a civil sense.

The Hague Convention establishes civil procedures to secure the return of so-called "abducted" children. Article 12. In this manner the Hague Convention seeks to satisfy the overriding concern of the aggrieved parent. The Convention is not concerned with the question of whether the person found to have wrongfully removed or retained the child returns to the child's country of habitual residence once the child has been returned pursuant to the Convention. This is in contrast to the criminal extradition process which is designed to secure the return of the fugitive wrong-doer. Indeed, when the fugitive-parent is extradited for trial or to serve a criminal sentence, there is no guarantee that the abducted child will also be returned.

While it is uncertain whether criminal extradition treaties will be routinely invoked in international custody cases between countries for which the Hague Convention is in force, nothing in the Convention bars their application or use.

B. Wrongful Removal or Retention

The Convention's first stated objective is to secure the prompt return of children who are wrongfully removed from or retained in any Contracting State. Article 1(a). (The second stated objective, i.e., to ensure that rights of custody and of access under the law of one Contracting State are effectively exercised in other Contracting States (Article 1(b)), is discussed under the heading "Access Rights," V., *infra*.) The removal or retention must be wrongful within the meaning of Article 3, as further clarified by Article 5(a), in order to trigger the return procedures established by the Convention. Article 3 provides that the removal or retention of a child is to be considered wrongful where:

(a) it is in breach of custody rights attributed to a person, an institution or another body, either jointly or alone, under the law of the State in which the child was habitually resident immediately before the removal or retention; and (b) at the time of the removal or retention those rights were actually exercised, either jointly or alone, or would have been so exercised but for the removal or retention.

This Article is a cornerstone of the Convention. It is analyzed by examining two questions:

1. Who holds rights protected by the Convention (or, with respect to whom is the removal or retention deemed to be wrongful?); and

2. What are the factual and legal elements of a wrongful removal or retention?

1. Holders of Rights Protected by the Convention

(a) *"Person, institution or other body"*. While the child is the ultimate beneficiary of the Convention's judicial and administrative machinery, the child's role under the Convention is passive. In contrast, it is up to the "person, institution or other body" (hereinafter referred to simply as "the person") who "actually exercised" custody of the child prior to the abduction, or who would have exercised custody but for the abduction, to invoke the Convention to secure the child's return. Article 3 (a), (b). It is this person who holds the rights protected by the Convention and who has the right to seek relief pursuant to its terms.

Since the vast majority of abduction cases arises in the context of divorce or separation, the person envisioned by Article 3(a) most often will be the child's parent. The typical scenario would involve one parent taking a child from one Contracting State to another Contracting State over objections of the parent with whom the child had been living.

However, there may be situations in which a person other than a biological parent has actually been exercising custody of the child and is therefore eligible to seek the child's return pursuant to the Convention. An example would be a grandparent who has had

ANALYSIS OF HAGUE CONVENTION

physical custody of a child following the death of the parent with whom the child had been residing. If the child is subsequently removed from the custody of the grandparent by the surviving parent, the aggrieved grandparent could invoke the Convention to secure the child's return. In another situation, the child may be in the care of foster parents. If custody rights exercised by the foster parents are breached, for instance, by abduction of the child by its biological parent, the foster parents could invoke the Convention to secure the child's return.

In the two foregoing examples (not intended to be exhaustive) a family relationship existed between the victim-child and the person who had the right to seek the child's return. However, institutions such as public or private child care agencies also may have custody rights the breach of which would be remediable under the Convention. If a natural parent relinquishes parental rights to a child and the child is subsequently placed in the care of an adoption agency, that agency may invoke the Convention to recover the child if the child is abducted by its parent(s).

(b) *"Jointly or alone"*. Article 3 (a) and (b) recognize that custody rights may be held either jointly or alone. Two persons, typically mother and father, can exercise joint custody, either by court order following a custody adjudication, or by operation of law prior to the entry of a decree. The Convention does not distinguish between these two situations, as the commentary of the Convention reporter indicates:

Now, from the Convention's standpoint, the removal of a child by one of the joint holders without the consent of the other, is wrongful, and this wrongfulness derives in this particular case, not from some action in breach of a particular law, but from the fact that such action has disregarded the rights of the other parent which are also protected by law, and has interfered with their normal exercise. The Convention's true nature is revealed most clearly in these situations: it is not concerned with establishing the person to whom custody of the child will belong at some point in the future, nor with the situations in which it may prove necessary to modify a decision awarding joint custody on the basis of facts which have subsequently changed. It seeks, more simply, to prevent a later decision on the matter being influenced by a change of circumstances brought about through unilateral action by one of the parties. Perez-Vera Report, paragraph 71 at 447-448.

Article 3(a) ensures the application of the Convention to pre-decree abductions, since it protects the rights of a parent who was exercising custody of the child jointly with the abductor at the time of the abduction, before the issuance of a custody decree.

2. "Wrongful Removal or Retention" Defined

The obligation to return an abducted child to the person entitled to custody arises only if the removal or the retention is wrongful within the meaning of the Convention. To be considered wrongful, certain factual and legal elements must be present.

(a) *Breach of "custody rights"*. The removal or retention must be in breach of "custody rights," defined in Article 5(a) as "rights relating to the care of the person of the child and, in particular, the right to determine the child's place of residence."

Accordingly, a parent who sends his or her child to live with a caretaker has not relinquished custody rights but rather has exercised them within the meaning of the Convention. Likewise, a parent hospitalized for a protracted period who places the child with grandparents or other relatives for the duration of the illness has effectively exercised custody.

(b) *"Custody rights" determined by law of child's habitual residence*. In addition to including the right to determine the child's residence (Article 5(a)), the term "custody rights" covers a collection of rights which take on more specific meaning by reference to the law of the country in which the child was habitually resident immediately before the removal or retention. Article 3(a). Nothing in the Convention limits this "law" to the internal law of the State of the child's habitual residence. Consequently, it could include the laws of another State if the choice of law rules in the State of habitual residence so indicate.

If a country has more than one territorial unit, the habitual residence refers to the particular territorial unit in which the child was resident, and the applicable laws are those in effect in that territorial unit. Article 31. In the United States, the law in force in the state in which a child was habitually resident (as possibly preempted by federal legislation enacted in connection with U.S. ratification of the Convention) would be applicable for the determination as to whether a removal or retention is wrongful.

Articles 32 and 33 also control, respectively, how and whether the Convention applies in States with more than one legal system. Perez-Vera Report, paragraphs 141 and 142 at 470.

(c) *Sources of "custody rights"*. Although the Convention does not exhaustively list all possible sources from which custody rights may derive, it does identify three sources. According to the final paragraph of Article 3, custody rights may arise: (1) by operation of law; (2) by reason of a judicial or administrative decision; or (3) by reason of an agreement having legal effect under the law of that State.

i. *Custody rights arising by operation of law*. Custody rights which arise by operation of law in the State of habitual residence are protected; they need not be conferred by court order to fall within the scope of the Convention. Article 3. Thus, a person whose child is abducted prior to the entry of a custody order is not required to obtain a custody order in the State of the child's habitual residence as a prerequisite to invoking the Convention's return provisions.

In the United States, as a general proposition both parents have equal rights of custody of their children prior to the issuance of a court order allocating rights between them. If one parent interferes with the other's equal rights by unilaterally removing or retaining the child abroad without consent of the other parent, such interference could constitute wrongful conduct within the meaning of the Convention. (See excerpts from Perez-Vera Report quoted at II.B.1(b), *supra*.) Thus, a parent left in the United States after a pre-decree abduction could seek return of a child from a Contracting State abroad pursuant to the Convention. In cases involving children wrongfully brought to or retained in the United States from a Contracting State abroad prior to the entry of a decree, in the absence of an agreement between the parties the question of wrongfulness would be resolved by looking to the law of the child's country of habitual residence.

Although a custody decree is not needed to invoke the Convention, there are two situations in which the aggrieved parent may nevertheless benefit by securing a custody order, assuming the courts can hear swiftly a petition for custody. First, to the extent that an award of custody to the left-behind parent (or other person) is based in part upon an express finding by the court that the child's removal or retention was wrongful within the meaning of Article 3, the applicant anticipates a possible request by the judicial authority applying the Convention, pursuant to Article 15, for a court determination of wrongfulness. This may accelerate disposition of a return petition under the Convention. Second, a person outside the United States who obtains a custody decree from a foreign court subsequent to the child's abduction, after notice and opportunity to be heard have been accorded to the absconding parent, may be able to invoke either the Convention or the UCCJA, or both, to secure the child's return from the United States. The UCCJA may be preferable inasmuch as its enforcement provisions are not subject to the exceptions contained in the Convention.

ii. *Custody rights arising by reason of judicial or administrative decision.* Custody rights embodied in judicial or administrative decisions fall within the Convention's scope. While custody determinations in the United States are made by state courts, in some Contracting States, notably the Scandinavian countries, administrative bodies are empowered to decide matters relating to child custody including the allocation of custody and visitation rights. Hence the reference to "administrative decisions" in Article 3.

The language used in this part of the Convention can be misleading. Even when custody rights are conferred by court decree, technically speaking the Convention does not mandate recognition and enforcement of that decree. Instead, it seeks only to restore the factual custody arrangements that existed prior to the wrongful removal or retention (which incidentally in many cases will be the same as those specified by court order).

Finally, the court order need not have been made by a court in the State of the child's habitual residence. It could be one originating from a third country. As the reporter points out, when custody rights were exercised in the State of the child's habitual residence on the basis of a foreign decree, the Convention does not require that the decree have been formally recognized. Perez-Vera Report, paragraph 69 at 447.

iii. *Custody rights arising by reason of agreement having legal effect.* Parties who enter into a private agreement concerning a child's custody have recourse under the Convention if those custody rights are breached. Article 3. The only limitation is that the agreement have legal effect under the law of the child's habitual residence.

Comments of the United States with respect to language contained in an earlier draft of the Convention (*i.e.,* that the agreement "have the force of law") shed some light on the meaning of the expression "an agreement having legal effect". In the U.S. view, the provision should be interpreted expansively to cover more than only those agreements that have been incorporated in or referred to in a custody judgment. *Actes et documents de la Quatorzieme Session, (1980) Volume III. Child*

Abduction, Comments of Governments at 240. The reporter's observations affirm a broad interpretation of this provision:

As regards the definition of an agreement which has "legal effect" in terms of a particular law, it seems that there must be included within it any sort of agreement which is not prohibited by such a law and which may provide a basis for presenting a legal claim to the competent authorities. Perez-Vera Report, paragraph 70 at 447.

(d) *"Actually exercised".* The most predictable fact pattern under the Convention will involve the abduction of a child directly from the parent who was actually exercising physical custody at the time of the abduction.

To invoke the Convention, the holder of custody rights must allege that he or she actually exercised those rights at the time of the breach or would have exercised them but for the breach. Article 3(b). Under Article 5, custody rights are defined to include the right to determine the child's place of residence. Thus, if a child is abducted from the physical custody of the person in whose care the child has been entrusted by the custodial parent who was "actually exercising" custody, it is the parent who placed the child who may make application under the Convention for the child's return.

Very little is required of the applicant in support of the allegation that custody rights have actually been or would have been exercised. The applicant need only provide some preliminary evidence that he or she actually exercised custody of the child, for instance, took physical care of the child. Perez-Vera Report, paragraph 73 at 448. The Report points out the informal nature of the pleading and proof requirements; Article 8(c) merely requires a statement in the application to the Central Authority as to "the grounds on which the applicant's claim for return of the child is based." *Id.*

In the scheme of the Convention it is presumed that the person who has custody actually exercised it. Article 13 places on the alleged abductor the burden of proving the nonexercise of custody rights by the applicant as an exception to the return obligation. Here, again, the reporter's comments are insightful:

Thus, we may conclude that the Convention, taken as a whole, is built upon the tacit presumption that the person who has care of the child actually exercises custody over it. This idea has to be overcome by discharging the burden of proof which has shifted, as is normal with any presumption (*i.e.* discharged by the "abductor" if he wishes to prevent the return of the child.) Perez-Vera Report paragraph 73 at 449.

III. Judicial Proceedings for Return of Child

A. *Right To Seek Return*

When a person's custody rights have been breached by the wrongful removal or retention of the child by another, he or she can seek return of the child pursuant to the Convention. This right of return is the core of the Convention. The Convention establishes two means by which the child may be returned. One is through direct application by the aggrieved person to a court in the Contracting State to which the child has been taken or in which the child is being kept. Articles 12, 29. The other is through application to the Central Authority to be established by every Contracting State. Article 8. These remedies are not mutually exclusive; the aggrieved person may invoke either or both of them. Moreover, the aggrieved person may also pursue remedies outside the Convention. Articles 18, 29 and 34. This part of the report describes the Convention's judicial remedy in detail. The administrative remedy is discussed in IV, *infra.*

Articles 12 and 29 authorize any person who claims a breach of custody rights within the meaning of Article 3 to apply for the child's return directly to the judicial authorities of the Contracting State where the child is located.

A petition for return pursuant to the Convention may be filed any time after the child has been removed or retained up until the child reaches sixteen. While the window of time for filing may be wide in a particular case without threat of technically losing rights under the Convention, there are numerous reasons to commence a return proceeding promptly if the likelihood of a voluntary return is remote. The two most crucial reasons are to preclude adjudication of custody on the merits in a country other than the child's habitual residence (see discussion of Article 16, *infra*) and to maximize the chances for the child's return by reducing the alleged abductor's opportunity to establish that the child is settled in a new environment (see discussion of Article 12, *infra*).

A petition for return would be made directly to the appropriate court in the Contracting State where the child is located. If the return proceedings are commenced less than one year from the date of the wrongful removal or retention, Article 12 requires the court to order the return of the child forthwith. If the return proceedings are commenced a year or more after the alleged wrongful removal or retention, the court remains

ANALYSIS OF HAGUE CONVENTION

obligated by Article 12 to order the child returned unless it is demonstrated that the child is settled in its new environment.

Under Article 29 a person is not precluded from seeking judicially-ordered return of a child pursuant to laws and procedures other than the Convention. Indeed, Articles 18 and 34 make clear that nothing in the Convention limits the power of a court to return a child at any time by applying other laws and procedures conducive to that end.

Accordingly, a parent seeking return of a child from the United States could petition for return pursuant to the Convention, or in the alternative or additionally, for enforcement of a foreign court order pursuant to the UCCJA. For instance, an English father could petition courts in New York either for return of his child under the Convention and/or for recognition and enforcement of his British custody decree pursuant to the UCCJA. If he prevailed in either situation, the respective court could order the child returned to him in England. The father in this illustration may find the UCCJA remedy swifter than invoking the Convention for the child's return because it is not subject to the exceptions set forth in the Convention, discussed at III.I., *infra*.

B. Legal Advice and Costs

Article 25 provides for the extension of legal aid and advice to foreign applicants on the same basis and subject only to the same eligibility requirements as for nationals of the country in which that aid is sought.

Article 26 prohibits Central Authorities from charging applicants for the cost and expenses of the proceedings or, where applicable, those arising from the participation of legal counsel or advisers. This provision will be of no help to an applicant, however, if the Contracting State in question has made a reservation in accordance with Articles 26 and 42 declaring that it shall not be bound to assume any costs resulting from the participation of legal counsel or advisers or from court proceedings, except insofar as those costs may be covered by its system of legal aid and advice.

It is expected that the United States will enter a reservation in accordance with Articles 26 and 42. This will place at least the initial burden of paying for counsel and legal proceedings on the applicant rather than on the federal government. Because the reservation is nonreciprocal, use of it will not automatically operate to deny applicants from the United States free legal services and judicial proceedings in other Contracting States. However, if the Contracting State in which the child is located has itself made use of the reservation in question, the U.S. applicant will not be eligible for cost-free legal representation and court proceedings. For more information on costs, including the possibility that the petitioner's costs may be levied on the abductor if the child is ordered returned, see III.J 2 and IV.C (d) of this analysis.

C. Pleading Requirements

The Convention does not expressly set forth pleading requirements that must be satisfied by an applicant who commences a judicial return proceeding. In contrast, Article 8 sets forth the basic requirements for an application placed before a Central Authority (discussed IV.C(1), *infra*) for the return of the child. Since the objective is identical—the child's return—whether relief is sought through the courts or through intercession of the Central Authority, it follows that a court should be provided with at least as much information as a Central Authority is to be provided in a return application filed in compliance with Article 8. To ensure that all necessary information is provided, the applicant may wish to append to the petition to the court a completed copy of the recommended model form for return of a child (see Annex A to this analysis).

In addition to providing the information set forth in Article 8, the petition for return should allege that the child was wrongfully removed or retained by the defendant in violation of custody rights that were actually being exercised by the petitioner. The petition should state the source of the custody rights, the date of the wrongful conduct, and the child's age at that time. In the prayer for relief, the petitioner should request the child's return and an order for payment by the abducting or retaining parent of all fees and expenses incurred to secure the child's return.

Any return petition filed in a court in the United States pursuant to the Convention must be in English. Any person in the United States who seeks return of a child from a foreign court must likewise follow the requirements of the foreign state regarding translation of legal documents. See Perez-Vera Report, paragraph 132 at page 467.

D. Admissibility of Evidence

Under Article 30, any application submitted to the Central Authority or petition submitted to the judicial authorities of a Contracting State, and any documents or information appended thereto, are admissible in the courts of the State. Moreover, under Article 23, no legalization or similar formalities may be required. However, authentication of private documents may be required. According to the official report, "any requirement of the internal law of the authorities in question that copies or private documents be authenticated remains outside the scope of this provision." Perez-Vera Report, paragraph 131 at page 467.

E. Judicial Promptitude/Status Report

Once an application for return has been filed, the court is required by Article 11 "to act expeditiously in proceedings for the return of children." To keep matters on the fast track, Article 11 gives the applicant or the Central Authority of the requested State the right to request a statement from the court of the reasons for delay if a decision on the application has not been made within six weeks from the commencement of the proceedings.

F. Judicial Notice

In ascertaining whether there has been a wrongful removal or retention of a child within the meaning of Article 3, Article 14 empowers the court of the requested State to take notice directly of the law and decisions in the State of the child's habitual residence. Standard procedures for the proof of foreign law and for recognition of foreign decisions would not need to be followed and compliance with such procedures is not to be required.

G. Court Determination of "Wrongfulness"

Prior to ordering a child returned pursuant to Article 12, Article 15 permits the court to request the applicant to obtain from the authorities of the child's State of habitual residence a decision or other determination that the alleged removal or retention was wrongful within the meaning of Article 3. Article 15 does not specify which "authorities" may render such a determination. It therefore could include agencies of government (*e.g.*, state attorneys general) and courts. Central Authorities shall assist applicants to obtain such a decision or determination. This request may only be made where such a decision or determination is obtainable in that State.

This latter point is particularly important because in some countries the absence of the defendant-abductor and child from the forum makes it legally impossible to proceed with an action for custody brought by the left-behind parent. If an adjudication in such an action were a prerequisite to obtaining a determination of wrongfulness, it would be impossible for the petitioner to comply with an Article 15 request. For this reason a request for a decision or determination on wrongfulness can not be made in such circumstances consistent with the limitation in Article 15. Even if local law permits an adjudication of custody in the absence of the child and defendant (*i.e.*, post-abduction) or would otherwise allow a petitioner to obtain a determination of wrongfulness, the provisions of Article 15 will probably not be resorted to routinely. That is so because doing so would convert the purpose of the Convention from seeking to restore the *factual* status quo prior to an abduction to emphasizing substantive legal relationships.

A further consideration in deciding whether to request an applicant to comply with Article 15 is the length of time it will take to obtain the determination. In countries where such a determination can be made only by a court, if judicial dockets are seriously backlogged, compliance with an Article 15 order could significantly prolong disposition of the return petition, which in turn would extend the time that the child is kept in a state of legal and emotional limbo. If "wrongfulness" can be established some other way, for instance by taking judicial notice of the law of the child's habitual residence as permitted by Article 14, the objective of Article 15 can be satisfied without further prejudice to the child's welfare or undue delay of the return proceeding. This would also be consistent with the Convention's desire for expeditious judicial proceedings as evidenced by Article 11.

In the United States, a left-behind parent or other claimant can petition for custody after the child has been removed from the forum. The right of action is conferred by the UCCJA, which in many states also directs courts to hear such petitions expeditiously. The result of such proceeding is a temporary or permanent custody determination allocating custody and visitation rights, or joint custody rights, between the parties. However, a custody determination on the merits that makes no reference to the Convention may not by itself satisfy an Article 15 request by a foreign court for a determination as to the wrongfulness of the conduct within the meaning of Article 3. Therefore, to ensure compliance with a possible Article 15 request the parent in the United States would be well-advised to request an explicit finding as to the wrongfulness of the alleged removal or retention within the meaning of Article 3 in addition to seeking custody.

H. Constraints Upon Courts in Requested States in Making Substantive Custody Decisions

Article 16 bars a court in the country to which the child has been taken or in which the child has been retained from considering the merits of custody claims once it has received notice of the removal or retention of the child. The constraints continue either until it is determined that the child is not to be returned under the Convention, or it becomes evident that an application under the Convention will not be forthcoming within a reasonable time following receipt of the notice.

A court may get notice of a wrongful removal or retention in some manner other than the filing of a petition for return, for instance by communication from a Central Authority, from the aggrieved party (either directly or through counsel), or from a court in a Contracting State which has stayed or dismissed return proceedings upon removal of the child from that State. No matter how notice may be given, once the tribunal has received notice, a formal application for the child's return pursuant to the Convention will normally be filed promptly to avoid a decision on the merits from being made. If circumstances warrant a delay in filing a return petition, for instance pending the outcome of private negotiations for the child's return or interventions toward that end by the Central Authority, or pending determination of the location of the child and alleged abductor, the aggrieved party may nevertheless wish to notify the court as to the reason(s) for the delay so that inaction is not viewed as a failure to proceed under the Convention.

I. Duty To Return not Absolute

The judicial duty to order return of a wrongfully removed or retained child is not absolute. Temporal qualifications on this duty are set forth in Articles 12, 4 and 35. Additionally, Articles 13 and 20 set forth grounds upon which return may be denied.

1. Temporal Qualifications

Articles 4, 35 and 12 place time limitations on the return obligation.

(a) *Article 4.* Pursuant to Article 4, the Convention ceases to apply once the child reaches age sixteen. This is true regardless of when return proceedings were commenced and irrespective of their status at the time of the child's sixteenth birthday. *See* I.A., *supra.*

(b) *Article 35.* Article 35 limits application of the Convention to wrongful removals or retentions occurring after its entry into force between the two relevant Contracting States. *But see* I.C., *supra.*

(c) *Article 12.* Under Article 12, the court is not obligated to return a child when return proceedings pursuant to the Convention are commenced a year or more after the alleged removal or retention *and* it is demonstrated that the child is settled in its new environment. The reporter indicates that "(T)he provision does not state how this fact is to be proved, but it would seem logical to regard such a task as falling upon the abductor or upon the person who opposes the return of the child . . ." Perez-Vera Report, paragraph 109 at page 459.

If the Convention is to succeed in deterring abductions, the alleged abductor must not be accorded preferential treatment by courts in his or her country of origin, which, in the absence of the Convention, might be prone to favor "home forum" litigants. To this end, nothing less than substantial evidence of the child's significant connections to the new country is intended to suffice to meet the respondent's burden of proof. Moreover, any claims made by the person resisting the child's return will be considered in light of evidence presented by the applicant concerning the child's contacts with and ties to his or her State of habitual residence. The reason for the passage of time, which may have made it possible for the child to form ties to the new country, is also relevant to the ultimate disposition of the return petition. If the alleged wrongdoer concealed the child's whereabouts from the custodian necessitating a long search for the child and thereby delayed the commencement of a return proceeding by the applicant, it is highly questionable whether the respondent should be permitted to benefit from such conduct absent strong countervailing considerations.

2. Article 13 Limitations on the Return Obligation

(a) *Legislative history.* In drafting Articles 13 and 20, the representatives of countries participating in negotiations on the Convention were aware that any exceptions had to be drawn very narrowly lest their application undermine the express purposes of the Convention—to effect the prompt return of abducted children. Further, it was generally believed that courts would understand and fulfill the objectives of the Convention by narrowly interpreting the exceptions and allowing their use only in clearly meritorious cases, and only when the person opposing return had met the burden of proof.

ANALYSIS OF HAGUE CONVENTION

Importantly, a finding that one or more of the exceptions provided by Articles 13 and 20 are applicable does not make refusal of a return order mandatory. The courts retain the discretion to order the child returned even if they consider that one or more of the exceptions applies. Finally, the wording of each exception represents a compromise to accommodate the different legal systems and tenets of family law in effect in the countries negotiating the Convention, the basic purpose in each case being to provide for an exception that is narrowly construed.

(b) *Non-exercise of custody rights.* Under Article 13(a), the judicial authority may deny an application for the return of a child if the person having the care of the child was not actually exercising the custody rights at the time of the removal or retention, or had consented to or acquiesced in the removal or retention. This exception derives from Article 3(b) which makes the Convention applicable to the breach of custody rights that were actually exercised at the time of the removal or retention, or which would have been exercised but for the removal or retention.

The person opposing return has the burden of proving that custody rights were not actually exercised at the time of the removal or retention, or that the applicant had consented to or acquiesced in the removal or retention. The reporter points out that proof that custody was not actually exercised does not form an exception to the duty to return if the dispossessed guardian was unable to exercise his rights precisely because of the action of the abductor. Perez-Vera Report, paragraph 115 at page 461.

The applicant seeking return need only allege that he or she was actually exercising custody rights conferred by the law of the country in which the child was habitually resident immediately before the removal or retention. The statement would normally include a recitation of the circumstances under which physical custody had been exercised, *i.e.*, whether by the holder of these rights, or by a third person on behalf of the actual holder of the custody rights. The applicant would append copies of any relevant legal documents or court orders to the return application. *See* III. C., *supra*, and Article 8.

(c) *Grave risk of harm/intolerable situation.* Under Article 13(b), a court in its discretion need not order a child returned if there is a grave risk that return would expose the child to physical harm or otherwise place the child in an intolerable situation.

This provision was not intended to be used by defendants as a vehicle to litigate (or relitigate) the child's best interests. Only evidence directly establishing the existence of a grave risk that would expose the child to physical or emotional harm or otherwise place the child in an intolerable situation is material to the court's determination. The person opposing the child's return must show that the risk to the child is grave, not merely serious.

A review of deliberations on the Convention reveals that "intolerable situation" was not intended to encompass return to a home where money is in short supply, or where educational or other opportunities are more limited than in the requested State. An example of an "intolerable situation" is one in which a custodial parent sexually abuses the child. If the other parent removes or retains the child to safeguard it against further victimization, and the abusive parent then petitions for the child's return under the Convention, the court may deny the petition. Such action would protect the child from being returned to an "intolerable situation" and subjected to a grave risk of psychological harm.

(d) *Child's preference.* The third, unlettered paragraph of Article 13 permits the court to decline to order the child returned if the child objects to being returned and has attained an age and degree of maturity at which it is appropriate to take account of the child's views. As with the other Article 13 exceptions to the return obligation, the application of this exception is not mandatory. This discretionery aspect of Article 13 is especially important because of the potential for brainwashing of the child by the alleged abductor. A child's objection to being returned may be accorded little if any weight if the court believes that the child's preference is the product of the abductor parent's undue influence over the child.

(e) *Role of social studies.* The final paragraph of Article 13 requires the court, in considering a respondent's assertion that the child should not be returned, to take into account information relating to the child's social background provided by the Central Authority or other competent authority in the child's State of habitual residence. This provision has the dual purpose of ensuring that the court has a balanced record upon which to determine whether the child is to be returned, and preventing the abductor from obtaining an unfair advantage through his or her own forum selection with resulting ready access to evidence of the child's living conditions in that forum.

3. Article 20

Article 20 limits the return obligation of Article 12. It states: "The return of the child under the provisions of Article 12 may be refused if this would not be permitted by the fundamental principles of the requested State relating to the protection of human rights and fundamental freedoms."

The best explanation for this unique formulation is that the Convention might never have been adopted without it. The negotiating countries were divided on the inclusion of a public policy exception in the Convention. Those favoring a public policy exception believed that under some extreme circumstances not covered by the exceptions of Article 13 a court should be excused from returning a child to the country of habitual residence. In contrast, opponents of a public policy exception felt that such an exception could be interpreted so broadly as to undermine the fabric of the entire Convention.

A public policy clause was nevertheless adopted at one point by a margin of one vote. That clause provided: "Contracting States may reserve the right not to return the child when such return would be manifestly incompatible with the fundamental principles of the law relating to the family and children in the State addressed." To prevent imminent collapse of the negotiating process engendered by the adoption of this clause, there was a swift and determined move to devise a different provision that could be invoked on the rare occasion that return of a child would utterly shock the conscience of the court or offend all notions of due process.

The resulting language of Article 20 has no known precedent in other international agreements to serve as a guide in its interpretation. However, it should be emphasized that this exception, like the others, was intended to be restrictively interpreted and applied, and is not to be used, for example, as a vehicle for litigating custody on the merits or for passing judgment on the political system of the country from which the child was removed. Two characterizations of the effect to be given Article 20 are recited below for illumination.

The following explanation of Article 20 is excerpted from paragraph 118 of the Perez-Vera Report at pages 461-2:

> It is significant that the possibility, acknowledged in *article 20*, that the child may not be returned when its return 'would not be permitted by the fundamental principles of the requested State relating to the protection of human rights and

FEDERAL LAWS

fundamental freedoms' has been placed in the last article of the chapter; it was thus intended to emphasize the always clearly exceptional nature of this provision's application. As for the substance of this provision, two comments only are required. Firstly, even if its literal meaning is strongly reminiscent of the terminology used in international texts concerning the protection of human rights, this particular rule is not directed at developments which have occurred on the international level, but is concerned only with the principles accepted by the law of the requested State, either through general international law and treaty law, or through internal legislation. Consequently, so as to be able to refuse to return a child on the basis of this article, it will be necessary to show that the fundamental principles of the requested State concerning the subject-matter of the Convention do not permit it; it will not be sufficient to show merely that its return would be incompatible, even manifestly incompatible, with these principles. Secondly, such principles must not be invoked any more frequently, nor must their invocation be more readily admissible than they would be in their application to purely internal matters. Otherwise, the provision would be discriminatory in itself, and opposed to one of the most widely recognized fundamental principles in internal laws. A study of the case law of different countries shows that the application by ordinary judges of the laws on human rights and fundamental freedoms is undertaken with a care which one must expect to see maintained in the international situations which the Convention has in view.

A.E. Anton, Chairman of the Commission on the Hague Conference on Private International Law that drafted the Convention, explained Article 20 in his article, "The Hague Convention on International Child Abduction," 30 I.C.L.Q. 537, 551-2 (July, 1981), as follows:

Its acceptance may in part have been due to the fact that it states a rule whch many States would have been bound to apply in any event, for example, by reason of the terms of their constitutions. The reference in this provision to "the fundamental principles of the requested State" make it clear that the reference is not one to international conventions or declarations concerned with the protection of human rights and fundamental freedoms which have been ratified or accepted by Contracting States. It is rather to the fundamental provisions of the law of the requested State in such matters
. . . If the United Kingdom decides to ratify Hague Covention, it will, of course, be for th. mplementing legislation or the courts to specify what provisions of United kingdom law come within the scope of Article 20. The Article, however, is merely permissive and it is to be hoped that States will exercise restraint in availing themselves of it.

4. Custody Order no Defense to Return

See I.D.1, supra, for discussion of Article 17.

J. Return of the Child

Assuming the court has determined that the removal or retention of the child was wrongful within the meaning of the Convention and that no exceptions to the return obligation have been satisfactorily established by the respondent, Article 12 provides that "the authority concerned shall order the return of the child forthwith." The Convention does not technically require that the child be returned to his or her State of habitual residence, although in the classic abduction case this will occur. If the petitioner has moved from the child's State of habitual residence the child will be returned to the petitioner, not the State of habitual residence.

1. Return Order not on Custody merits

Under Article 19, a decision under the Convention concerning the return of the child shall not be taken to be a determination on the merits of any custody issue. It follows that once the factual status quo ante has been restored, litigation concerning custody or visitation issues could proceed. Typically this will occur in the child's State of habitual residence.

2. Costs, Fees and Expenses Shifted to Abductor

In connection with the return order, Article 26 permits the court to direct the person who removed or retained the child to pay necessary expenses incurred by or on behalf of the applicant to secure the child's return, including expenses, costs incurred or payments made for locating the child, costs of legal representation of the applicant, and those of returing the child. The purposes underlying Article 26 are to restore the applicant to the financial position he or she would have been in had there been no removal or retention, as well as to deter such conduct from happening in the first place. This fee shifting provision has counterparts in the UCCJA (sections 7(g), 8(c), 15(b)) and the PKPA (28 U.S.C. 1738A note).

IV. Central Authority

In addition to creating a judicial remedy for cases of wrongful removal and retention, the Convention requires each Contracting State to establish a Centeral Authority (hereinafter "CA") with the broad mandate of assisting applicants to secure the return of their children or the effective excercise of their visitation rights. Articles 1, 10, 21. The CA is expressly directed by Article 10 to take all appropriate measures to obtain the voluntary return of children. The role of the CA with respect to visitation rights is discussed in V., *infra*.

A. Establishment of Central Authoirty

Article 6 requires each Contracting State to designate a Central Authority to discharge the duties enumerated in Articles 7, 9, 10, 11, 15, 21, 26, 27, and 28.

In France, the Central Authority is located within the Ministry of Justice. Switzerland has designated its Federal Justice Office as CA, and Canada has designated its Department of Justice. However, each Canadian province and territory in which the Convention has come into force has directed its Attorney General to serve as local CA for cases involving that jurisdiction.

In the United States it is very unlikely that the volume of cases will warrant the establishment of a new agency or office to fulfill Convention responsibilities. Rather, the duties of the CA will be carried out by an existing agency of the federal government with experience in dealing with authorities of other countries.

The Department of State's Office of Citizens Consular Services (CCS) within its Bureau of Consular Affairs will most likely serve as CA under the Hague Convention. CCS presently assists parents here and abroad with child custody-related problems within the framework of existing laws and procedures. The Convention should systematize and expedite CCS handling of requests from abroad for assistance in securing the return of children wrongfully abducted to or retained in the United States, and will provide additional tools with which CCS can help parents in the United States who are seeking return of their children from abroad.

The establishment of an interagency coordinating body is envisioned to assist the State Department in executing its functions as CA. This body is to include representatives of the Departments of State, Justice, and Health and Human Services.

In addition to the mandatory establishment of a CA in the national government, Contracting States are free to appoint similar entities in political subdivisions throughout the country. Rather than mandating the establishment of a CA in every state, it is expected that state governments in the United States will be requested on a case-by-case basis to render specified assistance, consistent with the Convention, aimed at resolving international custody and visitation disputes with regard to children located within their jurisdiction.

B. Duties

Article 7 enumerates the majority of the tasks to be carried out either directly by the CA or through an intermediary.

ANALYSIS OF HAGUE CONVENTION

The CA is to take "all appropriate measures" to execute these responsibilities. Although they are free to do so, the Convention does not obligate Contracting States to amend their internal laws to discharge Convention tasks more efficaciously. See Perez-Vera Report, paragraph 63 at page 444.

The following paragraphs of subsections of Article 7 of the Convention are couched in terms of the tasks and functions of the United States CA. The corresponding tasks and functions of the CA's in other States party to the Convention will be carried out somewhat differently in the context of each country's legal system.

Article 7(a). When the CA in the United States is asked to locate a child abducted from a foreign contracting State to this country, it would utilize all existing tools for determining the whereabouts of missing persons. Federal resources available for locating missing persons include the FBI-operated National Crime Information Center (NCIC) computer (pursuant to Pub. L. No. 97-292, the Missing Children Act), the Federal Parent Locator Service (pursuant to section 9 of Pub. L. No. 96-611, the Parental Kidnapping Prevention Act) and the National Center for Missing and Exploited Children. If the abductor's location is known or suspected, the relevant state's Parent Locator Service or Motor Vehicle Bureau and the Internal Revenue Service, Attorney General and Secretary of Education may be requested to conduct field and/or record searches. Also at the state level, public or private welfare agencies can be called upon to verify discreetly any address information about the abductor that may be discovered.

Article 7(b). To prevent further harm to the child, the CA would normally call upon the state welfare agency to take whatever protective measures are appropriate and available consistent with that state's child abuse and neglect laws. The CA, either directly or with the help of state authorities, may seek a written agreement from the abductor (and possibly from the applicant as well) not to remove the child from the jurisdiction pending procedures aimed at return of the child. Bonds or other forms of security may be required.

Article 7(c). The CA, either directly or through local public or private mediators, attorneys, social workers, or other professionals, would attempt to develop an agreement for the child's voluntary return and/or resolution of other outstanding issues. The obligation of the CA to take or cause to be taken all appropriate measures to obtain the voluntary return of the child is so fundamental a purpose of this Convention that it is restated in Article 10. However, overtures to secure the voluntary return of a child may not be advisable if advance awareness by the abductor that the Convention has been invoked is likely to prompt further flight and concealment of the child. If the CA and state authorities are successful in facilitating a voluntary agreement between the parties, the applicant would have no need to invoke or pursue the Convention's judicial remedy.

Article 7(d). The CA in the United States would rely upon court personnel or social service agencies in the child's state of habitual residence to compile information on the child's social background for the use of courts considering exceptions to a return petition in another country in which an abducted or retained child is located. See Article 13.

Article 7(e). The CA in the United States would call upon U.S. state authorities to prepare (or have prepared) general statements about the law of the state of the child's habitual residence for purposes of application of the Convention in the country where the child is located, *i.e.*, to determine whether a removal or retention was wrongful.

Articles 7 (f) and (g). In the United States the federal CA will not act as legal advocate for the applicant. Rather, in concert with state authorities and interested family law attorneys, the CA, through state or local bodies, will assist the applicant in identifying competent private legal counsel or, if eligible, in securing representation by a Legal Aid or Legal Services lawyer. In some states, however, the Attorney General or local District Attorney may be empowered under state law to intervene on behalf of the applicant-parent to secure the child's return.

In some foreign Contracting States, the CA may act as the legal representative of the applicant for all purposes under the Convention.

Article 28 permits the CA to require written authorization empowering it to act on behalf of the applicant, or to designate a representative to act in such capacity.

Article 7(h). Travel arrangements for the return of a child from the United States would be made by the CA or by state authorities closest to the case in cooperation with the petitioner and/or interested foreign authorities. If it is necessary to provide short-term care for the child pending his or her return, the CA presumably will arrange for the temporary placement of the child in the care of the person designated for that purpose by the applicant, or, failing that, request local authorities to appoint a guardian, foster parent, etc. The costs of transporting the child are borne by the applicant unless the court, pursuant to Article 26, orders the wrongdoer to pay.

Article 7(i). The CA will monitor all cases in which its assistance has been sought. It will maintain files on the procedures followed in each case and the ultimate disposition thereof. Complete records will aid in determining how frequently the Convention is invoked and how well it is working.

C. Other Tasks

1. Processing Applications

Article 8 sets forth the required contents of a return application submitted to a CA, all of which are incorporated into the model form recommended for use when seeking a child's return pursuant to the Convention (see Annex A of this analysis). Article 8 further provides that an application for assistance in securing the return of a child may be submitted to a CA either in the country of the child's habitual residence or in any other Contracting State. If a CA receives an application with respect to a child whom it believes to be located in another Contracting State, pursuant to Article 9 it is to transmit the application directly to the appropriate CA and inform the requesting CA or applicant of the transmittal.

It is likely that an applicant who knows the child's whereabouts can expedite the return process by electing to file a return application with the CA in the country in which the child is located. The applicant who pursues this course of action may also choose to file a duplicate copy of the application for information purposes with the CA in his or her own country. Of course, the applicant may prefer to apply directly to the CA in his or her own country even when the abductor's location is known, and rely upon the CA to transfer documents and communicate with the foreign CA on his or her behalf. An applicant who does not know the whereabouts of the child will most likely file the return application with the CA in the child's State of habitual residence.

Under Article 27, a CA may reject an application if "it is manifest that the requirements of the Convention are not fulfilled or that the application is otherwise not well founded." The CA must promptly inform the CA in the requesting State, or the applicant directly, of its reasons for such rejection. Consistent with the spirit of the

FEDERAL LAWS

Convention and in the absence of any prohibition on doing so, the applicant should be allowed to correct the defects and refile the application.

Under Article 28, a CA may require the applicant to furnish a written authorization empowering it to act on behalf of the applicant, or designating a representative so to act.

2. Assistance in Connection With Judicial Proceedings

(a) *Request for status report.* When an action has been commenced in court for the return of a child and no decision has been reached by the end of six weeks, Article 11 authorizes the applicant or the CA of the requested State to ask the judge for a statement of the reasons for the delay. The CA in the country where the child is located may make such a request on its own initiative, or upon request of the CA of another Contracting State. Replies received by the CA in the requested State are to be transmitted to the CA in the requesting State or directly to the applicant, depending upon who initiated the request.

(b) *Social studies/background reports.* Information relating to the child's social background collected by the CA in the child's State of habitual residence pursuant to Article 7(d) may be submitted for consideration by the court in connection with a judicial return proceeding. Under the last paragraph of Article 13, the court must consider home studies and other social background reports provided by the CA or other competent authorities in the child's State of habitual residence.

(c) *Determination of "wrongfulness".* If a court requests an applicant to obtain a determination from the authorities of the child's State of habitual residence that the removal or retention was wrongful, Central Authorities are to assist applicants, so far as practicable, to obtain such a determination. Article 15.

(d) *Costs.* Under Article 26, each CA bears its own costs in applying the Convention. The actual operating expenses under the Convention will vary from one Contracting State to the next depending upon the volume of incoming and outgoing requests and the number and nature of the procedures available under internal law to carry out specified Convention tasks.

Subject to limited exceptions noted in the next paragraph, the Central Authority and other public services are prohibited from imposing any charges in relation to applications submitted under the Convention. Neither the applicant nor the CA in the requesting State may be required to pay for the services rendered directly or indirectly by the CA of the requested State.

The exceptions relate to transportation and legal expenses to secure the child's return. With respect to transportation, the CA in the requested State is under no obligation to pay for the child's return. The applicant can therefore be required to pay the costs of transporting the child. With respect to legal expenses, if the requested State enters a reservation in accordance with Articles 26 and 42, the applicant can be required to pay all costs and expenses of the legal proceedings, and those arising from the participation of legal counsel or advisers. However, see III. J 2 of this analysis discussing the possibility that the court ordering the child's return will levy these and other costs upon the abductor. Even if the reservation under Articles 26 and 42 is entered, under Article 22 no security, bond or deposit can be required to guarantee the payment of costs and expenses of the judicial or administrative proceedings falling within the Convention.

Under the last paragraph of Article 26 the CA may be able to recover some of its expenses from the person who engaged in the wrongful conduct. For instance, a court that orders a child returned may also order the person who removed or retained the child to pay the expenses incurred by or on behalf of the petitioner, including costs of court proceedings and legal fees of the petitioner. Likewise, a court that issues an order concerning visitation may direct the person who prevented the exercise of visitation rights to pay necessary expenses incurred by or on behalf of the petitioner. In such cases, the petitioner could recover his or her expenses, and the CA could recover its outlays on behalf of the petitioner, including costs associated with, or payments made for, locating the child and the legal representation of the petitioner.

V. Access Rights—Article 21

A. *Remedies for Breach*

Up to this point this analysis has focussed on judicial and administrative remedies for the removal or retention of children in breach of custody rights. "Access rights," which are synonymous with "visitation rights", are also protected by the Convention, but to a lesser extent than custody rights. While the Convention preamble and Article 1(b) articulate the Convention objective of ensuring that rights of access under the law of one state are respected in other Contracting States, the remedies for breach of access rights are those enunciated in Article 21 and do not include the return remedy provided by Article 12.

B. *Defined*

Article 5(b) defines "access rights" as including "the right to take a child for a limited period of time to a place other than the child's habitual residence."

A parent who takes a child from the country of its habitual residence to another country party to the Convention for a summer visit pursuant to either a tacit agreement between the parents or a court order is thus exercising his or her access rights. Should that parent fail to return the child at the end of the agreed upon visitation period, the retention would be wrongful and could give rise to a petition for return under Article 12. If, on the other hand, a custodial parent resists permitting the child to travel abroad to visit the noncustodial parent, perhaps out of fear that the child will not be returned at the end of the visit, this interference with access rights does not constitute a wrongful retention within the meaning of Article 3 of the Convention. The parent whose access rights have been infringed is not entitled under the Convention to the child's "return," but may request the Central Authority to assist in securing the exercise of his or her access rights pursuant to Article 21.

Article 21 may also be invoked as a precautionary measure by a custodial parent who anticipates a problem in getting the child back at the end of a visit abroad. That parent may apply to the CA of the country where the child is to visit the noncustodial parent for steps to ensure the return of the child at the end of the visit—for example, through appropriate imposition of a performance bond or other security.

C. *Procedure for Obtaining Relief*

Procedurally Article 21 authorizes a person complaining of, or seeking to prevent, a breach of access rights to apply to the CA of a Contracting State in the same way as a person seeking return of the child. The application would contain the information described in Article 8, except that information provided under paragraph (c) would be the grounds upon which the claim is made for assistance in organizing or securing the effective exercise of rights of access.

Once the CA receives such application, it is to take all appropriate measures pursuant to Article 7 to promote the peaceful enjoyment of access rights and the fulfillment of any conditions to which the exercise of those rights is subject. This includes initiating or facilitating the institution of proceedings, either directly or through intermediaries, to organize or protect access rights and to secure respect for conditions to which these rights are subject.

If legal proceedings are instituted in the Contracting State in which the noncustodial parent resides, Article 21 may not be used by the noncustodial

ANALYSIS OF HAGUE CONVENTION

parent to evade the jurisdiction of the courts of the child's habitual residence, which retain authority to define and/or condition the exercise of visitation rights. A parent who has a child abroad for a visit is not to be allowed to exploit the presence of the child as a means for securing from the CA (or court) in that country more liberal visitation rights than those set forth in a court order agreed upon in advance of the visit. Such result would be tantamount to sanctioning forum-shopping contrary to the intent of the Convention. Any such application should be denied and the parent directed back to the appropriate authorities in the State of the child's habitual residence for consideration of the desired modification. Pending any such modification, once the lawful visitation period has expired, the custodial parent would have the right to seek the child's return under Article 3.

The Perez-Vera Report gives some limited guidance as to how CA's are to cooperate to secure the exercise of access rights:

> ... it would be advisable that the child's name not appear on the passport of the holder of the right of access, whilst in 'transfrontier' access cases it would be sensible for the holder of the access rights to give an undertaking to the Central Authority of the child's habitual residence to return the child on a particular date and to indicate also the places where he intends to stay with the child. A copy of such an undertaking would then be sent to the Central Authority of the habitual residence of the holder of the access rights, as well as to the Central Authority of the State in which he has stated his intention of staying with the child. This would enable the authorities to know the whereabouts of the child at any time and to set in motion proceedings for bringing about its return, as soon as the stated time-limit has expired. Of course, none of the measures could by itself ensure that access rights are exercised properly, but in any event we believe that this Report can go no further: the specific measures which the Central Authorities concerned are able to take will depend on the circumstances of each case and on the capacity to act enjoyed by each Central Authority. Perez-Vera Report, paragraph 128 at page 466.

D. Alternative Remedies

In addition to or in lieu of invoking Article 21 to resolve visitation-related problems, under Articles 18, 29 and 34 an aggrieved parent whose access rights have been violated may bypass the CA and the Convention and apply directly to the judicial authorities of a Contracting State for relief under other applicable laws.

In at least one case it is foreseeable that a parent abroad will opt in favor of local U.S. law instead of the Convention. A noncustodial parent abroad whose visitation rights are being thwarted by the custodial parent resident in the United States could invoke the UCCJA to seek enforcement of an existing foreign court order conferring visitation rights. Pursuant to section 23 of the UCCJA, a state court in the United States could order the custodial parent to comply with the prescribed visitation period by sending the child to the parent outside the United States. This remedy is potentially broader and more meaningful than the Convention remedy, since the latter does not include the right of return when a custodial parent obstructs the noncustodial parent's visitation rights, *i.e.*, by refusing to allow the other parent to exercise those rights. It is possible that a parent in the United States seeking to exercise access rights with regard to a child habitually resident abroad may similarly find greater relief under foreign law than under the Convention.

VI. Miscellaneous and Final Clauses

A. Article 36

Article 36 permits Contracting States to limit the restrictions to which a child's return may be subject under the Convention, *i.e.*, expand the return obligation or cases to which the Convention will apply. For instance, two or more countries may agree to extend coverage of the Convention to children beyond their sixteenth birthdays, thus expanding upon Article 4. Or, countries may agree to apply the Convention retroactively to wrongful removal and retention cases arising prior to its entry into force for those countries. Such agreement would remove any ambiguity concerning the scope of Article 35. The Department of State is not proposing that the United States make use of this Article.

B. Articles 37 and 38

Chapter VI of the Hague Convention consists of nine final clauses concerned with procedural aspects of the treaty, most of which are self-explanatory. Article 37 provides that states which were members of the Hague Conference on Private International Law at the time of the Fourteenth Session (October 1980) may sign and become parties to the Convention by ratification, acceptance or approval. Significantly, under Article 38 the Convention is open to accession by non-member States, but enters into force only between those States and member Contracting States which specifically accept their accession to the Convention. Article 38.

C. Articles 43 and 44

In Article 43 the Convention provides that it enters into force on the first day of the third calendar month after the third country has deposited its instrument of ratification, acceptance, approval or accession. For countries that become parties to the Convention subsequently, the Convention enters into force on the first day of the third calendar month following the deposit of the instrument of ratification. Pursuant to Article 43, the Convention entered into force on December 1, 1983 among France, Portugal and five provinces of Canada, and on January 1, 1984 for Switzerland. As of January, 1986 it is in force for all provinces and territories of Canada with the exception of Alberta, the Northwest Territories, Prince Edward Island and Sasketchewan.

The Convention enters into force in ratifying countries subject to such declarations or reservations pursuant to Articles 39, 40, 24 and 26 (third paragraph) as may be made by each ratifying country in accordance with Article 42.

The Convention remains in force for five years from the date it first entered into force (*i.e.*, December 1, 1983), and is renewed tacitly every five years absent denunciations notified in accordance with Article 44.

D. Articles 39 and 40

Article 39 authorizes a Contracting State to declare that the Convention extends to some or all of the territories for the conduct of whose international relations it is responsible.

Under Article 40, countries with two or more territorial units having different systems of law relative to custody and visitation rights may declare that the Convention extends to all or some of them. This federal state clause was included at the request of Canada to take account of Canada's special constitutional situation. The Department of State is not proposing that the United States make use of this provision. Thus, if the United States ratifies the Convention, it would come into force throughout the United States as the supreme law of the land in every state and other jurisdiction.

E. Article 41

Article 41 is another provision inserted at the request of one country, and is best understood by reciting the reporter's explanatory comments:

> Finally a word should be said on Article 41, since it contains a wholly novel provision in Hague Conventions. It also appears in the other Conventions adopted at the Fourteenth Session, *i.e.* the *Convention on International Access to Justice*, at the express request of the Australian delegation.
>
> This article seeks to make it clear that ratification of the Convention by a State will carry no implication as to the internal distribution of executive, judicial and legislative powers in that State.

FEDERAL LAWS

This may seem self-evident, and this is the point which the head of the Canadian delegation made during the debates of the Fourth Commission where it was decided to insert such a provision in both Conventions (see P.-v. No. 4 of the Plenary Session). The Canadian delegation, openly expressing the opinion of a large number of delegations, regarded the insertion of this article in the two Conventions as unnecessary. Nevertheless, Article 41 was adopted, largely to satisfy the Australian delegation, for which the absence of such a provision would apparently have created insuperable constitutional difficulties. Perez-Vera Report, paragraph 149 at page 472.

F. Article 45

Article 45 vests the Ministry of Foreign Affairs of the Kingdom of the Netherlands, as depository for the Convention, with the responsibility to notify Hague Conference member States and other States party to the Convention of all actions material to the operation of the Convention.

Annex A

The following model form was recommended by the Fourteenth Session of the Hague Conference on Private International Law (1980) for use in making applications pursuant to the 1980 Hague Convention on the Civil Aspects of International Child Abduction for the return of wrongfully removed or retained children. The version of the form to be used for requesting the return of such children from the United States will probably seek additional information, in particular to help authorities in the United States in efforts to find a child whose whereabouts are not known to the applicant.

Request for Return

Hague Convention of 25 October 1980 on the Civil Aspects of International Child Abduction.

Requesting Central Authority or Applicant ....

Requested Authority ....
Concerns the following child: ....
who will attain the age of 16 on ....
19—.

Note.—The following particulars should be completed insofar as possible.

I—Identity of the Child and its Parents
1 Child
Name and first names ....
Date and place of birth ....
Passport or identity card No., if any ....
Description and photo, if possible (see annexes) ....
2 Parents
2.1 Mother:
Name and first names ....
Date and place of birth ....
Nationality ....
Occupation ....
Habitual residence ....
Passport or identity card No., if any ....
2.2 Father:

Name and first names ....
Date and place of birth ....
Nationality ....
Occupation ....
Habitual residence ....
Passport or identity card No., if any ....
2.3 Date and place of marriage ....
II—Requesting Individual or Institution (who actually exercised custody before the removal or retention)
3 Name and first names
Nationality of individual applicant ....
Occupation of individual applicant ....
Address ....
Passport or identity card No., if any ....
Relation to the child ....
Name and address of legal adviser, if any ....
III—Place Where the Child Is Thought To Be
4.1 Information concerning the person alleged to have removed or retained the child
Name and first names ....
Date and place of birth, if known ....
Nationality, if known ....
Occupation ....
Last known address ....
Passport or identity card No., if any ....
Description and photo, if possible (see annexes) ....
4.2 Address of the child ....
4.3 Other persons who might be able to supply additional information relating to the whereabouts of the child ....
IV—Time, Place, Date and Circumstances of the Wrongful Removal or Retention
....
V—Factual or Legal Grounds Justifying the Request
....
VI—Civil Proceedings in Progress
....
VII—Child Is To Be Returned To:
a. Name and first names ....
Date and place of birth ....
Address ....
Telephone number ....
b. Proposed arrangements for return of the child ....
VIII—Other Remarks
....
IX—List of Documents Attached*
....
Date ....
Place ....
Signature and/or stamp of the requesting Central Authority or applicant
....

Annex B.—Bibliography

Explanatory Report by E. Perez-Vera, Hague Conference on Private International Law, Actes et documents de la Quatorzieme session, vol. III, 1980, p. 426.

Anton, A.E.—The Hague Convention on International Child Abduction; 30 Int'l & Comp. L.Q. (1981), p. 537.

Bodenheimer, B.—The Hague Convention on International Child Abduction; XIV Fam. L.Q. (1980), p. 99.

Chatin, L.—Les conflicts relatifs a la garde des enfants et au droit de visite en droit international prive; Travaux du Comite francais de droit international prive, Seance du 12 mai 1982, Publication du Ministere de la Justice.

Crouch, R.E.—Effective Measures Against International Child Snatching; 131 New L.J. (1981), p. 592.

Deschenaux, D.—La Convention de La Haye sur les aspects civils de l'enlevement international d'enfants, du 25 octobre 1980; XXXVII Schweizerisches Jahrbuch fur internationales Recht (1981), p. 119.

Dyer, A.—International child abduction by parents; 168 Recueil des Cours de l'Academie de droit international de La Haye (1980), p. 231.

Eekelaar, J.M.—The Hague Convention on the Civil Aspects of International Child Abduction; Explanatory Documentation prepared for Commonwealth Jurisdictions, Commonwealth Secretariat, 1981.

Farquhar, K.B.—The Hague Convention on International Child Abduction Comes to Canada; 4 Can. J. Fam. L. (1983), p. 5.

Frank, R.J.—American and International Responses to International Child Abductions, 16 N.Y.U. J. Int'l L. & Pol. (Winter 1984), p. 415.

Hoff, P., Schulman, J. and Volenik, A.—Interstate Child Custody Disputes and Parental Kidnapping: Policy, Practice and Law, Legal Services Corporation—American Bar Association, 1982.

Huesstege, R.—Internationale Kindesentfuehrungen und Landesverfassungsrecht; IPRax (1982), p. 95—Der Uniform Child Custody Jurisdiction Act—Rechtsvergleichende Betrachtungen zu Internationalen Kindesentfuehrengen, Verlag fur Standesamtswesen, Frankfurt am Main, 1982.

Morgenstern, B.R.—The Hague Convention on the Civil Aspects of International Child Abduction: The Need for Ratification; 10 N.C.J. Int'l L. & Com. Reg. (1985), p. 463.

Reymond, P.H.—Convention de La Haye et Convention de Strasbourg. Aspects comparatifs des conventions concernant l'enlevement d'un enfant par l'un de ses parents; Revue de droit suisse 1981, p. 329.

Schulman, J.—cf. Hoff, P.

Vink, E.L.M.—Enkele civielrechtelijke aspecten van de internationale ontvoeringen van kinderen door een van de ouders; Leiden, mai 1981.

Volenik, A.—cf. Hoff, P.

Westbrook, G.R.—Law and Treaty Responses to International Child Abductions; 20 Va. J. Int'l L. (1980), p. 669.

[FR Doc. 86-6495 Filed 3-25-86; 8:45 am]

---

*E.g. Certified copy of relevant decision or agreement concerning custody or a court certificate or affidavit as to the applicable law, information relating to the social background of the child, authorization empowering the Central Authority to act on behalf of applicant.

ANALYSIS OF HAGUE CONVENTION

Author's Notes

Analysis

1. Return of child from one country to another.
2. Current contracting states.
3. State Department analysis.
4. Central authority.
5. Location of judicial proceedings.
6. Request for return—Form.
7. Custody order not required.
8. "Wrongful."
9. Application to age 16.

(1) **Return of child from one country to another.** The Hague Convention is a mechanism for the return of a child who is wrongfully removed from one contracting country to another contracting country. (Referred to in the text of the Convention as a "state.")

(2) **Current contracting states.** As of October 1, 1994, the following states are signatories to the Hague Child Abduction Convention: Argentina, Australia, Austria, Bahamas, Belgium, Belize, Burkina Faso, Canada, Chile, Czech Republic, Denmark, Ecuador, Finland, France, Germany, Greece, Honduras, Hungary, Ireland, Israel, Italy, Luxembourg, Mauritius, Mexico, Monaco, Netherlands, New Zealand, Norway, Panama, Poland, Portugal, Romania, Slovak Republic, Slovenia, Spain, St. Kitts & Nevis, Sweden, Switzerland, United Kingdom, United States, and Yugoslavia (Croatia, Bosnia & Herzegovina, and Macedonia continue to be bound).

(3) **State Department analysis.** The text of the Convention and the procedures to obtain the return of a wrongfully removed child are well explicated by the analysis of the Convention prepared by the State Department, which follows the text of the Convention.

(4) **Central authority.** When a child has been wrongfully removed from one contracting state to another contracting state, the petitioner seeking the return of the child can either apply directly to the Central Authority or the courts of the state in which the child is located, or can apply to the Central Authority of the state in which the petitioner is located for assistance. Each contracting state is required to establish its own Central Authority. The United States Central Authority is the Department of State's Office of Citizens' Counsellor Services within the Bureau of Counsellor Affairs. The American Central Authority may be contacted at Room 4811, CA/OCS/CI, Department of State, Washington, DC 20520; telephone (202) 647-2688.

(5) **Location of judicial proceedings.** Any judicial proceedings necessary to return the child take place in the state where the wrongfully removed child is located. For example, if a child has been wrongfully removed from her mother in Great Britain to Chicago, Illinois, the petitioning mother would contact the Central Authority in Great Britain, which would contact the U.S. State Department, which in turn will contact a lawyer in Chicago to institute proceedings in the Cook County Circuit Court for the return of the child under the Hague Convention to the petitioner in Great Britain. The converse would be true for a child removed from Chicago to Great Britain.

FEDERAL LAWS

(6) **Request for Return—Form.** A model "Request for Return" follows the analysis by the State Department. For a child wrongfully removed from Chicago, the Request for Return should be filed with the United States Central Authority, which would then transmit the Request for Return to the Central Authority in the state where the wrongfully removed child has been taken. Where the petitioner applies directly to the courts in the state where the wrongfully removed child is located, rather than seeking the intercession of the Central Authorities of the home state and the state where the wrongfully removed child is located, the petitioner in his petition should supply the court with at least as much information as is sought in the Request for Return, which would otherwise be filed with the Central Authorities.

(7) **Custody order not required.** In order to proceed under the Hague Convention, the child must have been "wrongfully" removed from one country to another, or "wrongfully" retained in a country. It is most significant that for a wrongful removal or retention to take place: it is not necessary that there be a judicial order of custody. It is only necessary that there be a breach of custody rights under the law of the state in which the child is habitually resident. Custody rights under the Hague Convention can arise: (1) by operation of law, e.g., in the United States, in the absence of a court order, both parents have equal rights of custody, and therefore a removal by one parent that unilaterally interferes with the equal rights of custody of the other parent could constitute a wrongful removal under the Hague Convention (for Illinois, see 755 ILCS 5/11–7); (2) by reason of a judicial or administrative decision; or (3) by reason of an agreement having legal effect; but these three sources do not rule out other potential sources. The three identified sources are analyzed in Section IIB2(c) of the State Department's analysis. Conversely, custody orders are not definitive. There can be a return of a child under the Hague Convention in situations where the child has been wrongfully removed from one state to another, and the person who has accomplished the wrongful removal obtains a custody order in the state where he has taken the child.

(8) **"Wrongful."** The critical showing in order to trigger the return procedures established by the Hague Convention is that the removal or retention of the child out of the home state is "wrongful." Removal or retention is wrongful if it is in breach of custody rights of the law of the state in which the child is habitually resident, and those rights are actually being exercised. The analysis of wrongful removal or retention is contained in Section IIB of the State Department's analysis.

(9) **Application to age 16.** The Hague Convention ceases to apply when a child reaches his 16th birthday.

DIVISION F. SELECTED NOTES AND STATUTES

Analysis

Hearsay.
Objection: Not responsive.
Offers of proof.
State and federal eavesdropping statutes (720 ILCS 5/14–1 et seq.; 18 U.S.C.A. § 2510 et seq.).
Federal and state constitutional right against self-incrimination (U.S. Const. amend. V; Ill. Const. art. I, § 10).
Perjury.
Conflicts of interest.

WESTLAW Electronic Research

See WESTLAW Electronic Research Guide preceding the Summary of Contents.

HEARSAY

Author's Notes

Analysis

1. Definition.
2. Simple formulation.
3. Example: Hearsay.
4. Example: Not hearsay.
5. Exceptions.
6. Cross reference: Domestic violence, child abuse.
7. Wilson v. Clark.
8. Statement outside presence of opposite party.

(1) **Definition.** There is more confusion in courtrooms about what is and what is not hearsay, than there is confusion about whether the hearsay, once established, is or is not admissible under an exception to the hearsay rule. Cleary defines hearsay as

> testimony in court or written evidence, of a statement made out of court, such statement being offered as an assertion to show the truth of matters asserted therein, and thus resting for its value upon the credibility of the out-of-court asserter.

Michael H. Graham, *Cleary & Graham's Handbook of Illinois Evidence*, § 801.1 (6th ed. 1994).

(2) **Simple formulation.** The definition is so abstract and tries to cover so many bases as to be of little use in the courtroom. It is easier to remember that not every out-of-court statement to which a witness testifies is hearsay. When an out-of-court statement (oral or written) is offered, the simple reflex can be: is the out-of-

SELECTED NOTES AND STATUTES

court statement offered to prove the truth of what is asserted in it? If yes, it is hearsay and may be admitted only under an exception.

(3) **Example: Hearsay.** Clothing the definition with the most common examples illustrates the application of the definition. Every lawyer's mother told him the date on which he was born. Suppose the lawyer is a witness and testifies that his mother told him that his birthday was April 23, 1935: pure hearsay, offered for the purpose of proving the truth of what is contained in the mother's out-of-court statement; namely, the date of the witness's birth. All the problems of hearsay are present: the mother made the statement to her son outside of the courtroom; the mother was not under oath; and the mother is not present in the courtroom to be cross-examined concerning her credibility and the reliability of her report. Furthermore, although the son was present, he could hardly have had first hand knowledge of the event of his birth. To be admissible, an exception to the hearsay rule must be found for the son's testimony about what his mother told him.

(4) **Example: Not hearsay.** Conversely, suppose the witness testifies that his mother told him to come to her house on Saturday for a birthday party. The out-of-court statement by the mother is not reporting anything, it is not offered to prove the truth of anything asserted in the statement. The mother's out-of-court statement to which the son testifies is not hearsay, and it does not need a hearsay exception to be admitted. The birthday invitation to the son by the mother is merely notice to him of a party. A witness can always testify to something said to him, provided that what he heard is not offered to prove what is asserted in the statement, in the same way that a witness can always testify to what he saw. The difference is between: testimony about an out-of-court statement offered to prove just the fact the statement was made (not hearsay), as opposed to testimony offered to prove not only that the statement was made, but also the truth of what is asserted in the statement (hearsay).

(5) **Exceptions.** When an attorney anticipates that it will be necessary to offer or object to hearsay evidence at trial, the attorney should always prepare the argument supporting the admissibility of or objection to the evidence prior to the trial.

The principal categories of hearsay exceptions identified by *Cleary* are:

Admission of a party opponent

Excited utterance

Mental or emotional state

Statements for the purpose of medical treatment

Past recollection recorded

Business records, medical records, public records, and various other records (See Supreme Court Rule 236)

Reputation

Child abuse

Former testimony

Dying Declaration

Declaration against interest

Michael H. Graham, *Cleary and Graham's Handbook of Illinois Evidence*, Article VIII, (6th ed. 1994).

HEARSAY

(6) **Cross reference: Domestic violence, child abuse.** For special hearsay exceptions in Domestic Violence actions, see 750 ILCS 60/213.1. For hearsay exceptions in child abuse cases, see 735 ILCS 5/8–2601.

(7) **Wilson v. Clark.** The greatest relaxation of the hearsay rule occurred in Wilson v. Clark, 84 Ill.2d 186, 49 Ill.Dec. 308, 417 N.E.2d 1322 (1981). Wilson v. Clark adopted Federal Rules of Evidence 703, which provides that experts may base their opinions on nonadmissible out-of-court hearsay if it is of a type reasonably relied upon by experts in the particular field in forming opinions or inferences upon the subject; and FRE 705, which provides that experts may give opinion testimony without disclosing the facts underlying the opinion. For example, a doctor testifying to his medical opinion may base his opinion on information on which experts in the medical field would reasonably rely, such as medical records of other doctors, and out-of-court conclusions by technicians and nurses. See, e.g., Melecosky v. McCarthy Bros. Co., 115 Ill.2d 209, 104 Ill.Dec. 798, 503 N.E.2d 355 (1986) (court erred in excluding doctor's testimony based on patient's subjective statements and symptoms; experts in their own practice normally rely on such statements). See also In re Marriage of Hazard, 167 Ill.App.3d 61, 117 Ill.Dec. 770, 520 N.E.2d 1121 (1st Dist.1988) (psychiatric testimony recommending custody should be granted to the husband was properly stricken; psychiatric witness never interviewed the children, contrary to the standards of the psychiatric profession). Surveys may also be used by expert witnesses if the methods utilized to conduct the survey are generally accepted in the scientific community to produce statistically accurate results. See Galindo v. Riddell, Inc., 107 Ill.App.3d 139, 62 Ill.Dec. 849, 437 N.E.2d 376 (3d Dist.1982) (expert testimony including results of survey made by the expert should not have been permitted; no foundation was laid regarding the methodology of the survey); Antry v. Illinois Educational Labor Relations Bd., 195 Ill.App.3d 221, 141 Ill.Dec. 945, 552 N.E.2d 313 (1990) (surveys were properly admitted; "surveys are generally deemed admissible ... [if the surveyor] adhere[s] to generally accepted survey principles and utiliz[es] the results in a statistically correct manner"). See also Michael H. Graham, *Cleary and Graham's Handbook of Illinois Evidence*, § 703.1 (6th ed. 1994).

Although Wilson v. Clark does not require that the hearsay foundation supporting the expert's opinion be introduced into evidence, such supporting data may be exposed on cross-examination to challenge the reliability of the expert's opinion.

Illinois also follows the test from Frye v. United States, 293 Fed. 1013 (1923), which excludes expert testimony based on a scientific technique unless the technique is "generally accepted" as reliable in the relevant scientific community. See, e.g., People v. Eyler, 133 Ill.2d 173, 139 Ill.Dec. 756, 549 N.E.2d 268 (1989), *cert. denied*, 498 U.S. 881, 111 S.Ct. 215, 112 L.Ed.2d 174 (1990). However, in Daubert v. Merrell Dow Pharmaceuticals, Inc., ___ U.S. ___, 113 S.Ct. 2786, 125 L.Ed.2d 469 (1993), the Supreme Court held that the general acceptance test in *Frye* had been superseded by the Federal Rules of Evidence. Therefore, the *Frye* test is no longer valid in Federal court. The Illinois courts have not yet addressed whether Illinois will adopt the abandonment of *Frye* in *Daubert* as they adopted the underlying Federal Rules. See also Michael H. Graham, *Cleary and Graham's Handbook of Illinois Evidence*, § 702.4 (6th ed. 1994) ("many theoretical and practical arguments support Illinois retaining adherence to *Frye*, at least until the impact of *Daubert* is fully understood").

(8) **Statement outside presence of opposite party.** The frequently heard hearsay objection that a statement was made outside the presence of a party opponent is not a proper objection except where an admission by silence is claimed, and it has no

bearing on the determination of the admissibility of hearsay evidence. Michael H. Graham, *Cleary & Graham's Handbook of Illinois Evidence*, § 801.7 (6th ed. 1994).

OBJECTION: NOT RESPONSIVE

Author's Notes

(1) **Questioner only.** The objection that an answer to a question is not responsive to the question asked lies only with the questioner; it cannot be properly raised by the opposing party. See People v. Gardner, 47 Ill.App.3d 529, 5 Ill.Dec. 701, 362 N.E.2d 14 (5th Dist.1977) ("the party who is not conducting the examination of the witness may not complain that an answer is not responsive to the question propounded unless the answer volunteers testimony that is incompetent or otherwise inadmissible"); Hester v. Goldsbury, 64 Ill.App.2d 66, 212 N.E.2d 316 (1st Dist.1965) ("An attorney who is not conducting the examination may not have the unresponsive testimony stricken unless it is incompetent.")

OFFERS OF PROOF

Author's Notes

(1) **Preserving issue for appeal.** When an objection to testimony is sustained, in order to preserve the question of the admissibility of the evidence for review on appeal, it is necessary to make an offer of proof. People v. Andrews, 146 Ill.2d 413, 167 Ill.Dec. 996, 588 N.E.2d 1126 (1992) (citing Michael H. Graham, *Cleary & Graham's Handbook of Illinois Evidence*, § 103.7 (5th ed. 1990)).

> The classic method of making an offer is actually to place the witness on the stand, ask the question, and, upon the sustaining of an objection, permit the witness to state with particularity what the witness would answer if permitted to do so.... An offer is sufficient if counsel makes known to the court, outside the hearing of the jury, with particularity, the substance of the witness's anticipated answer even if the witness is not actually produced, provided no question is raised as to her ability to produce the witness who would so testify.... A statement by counsel that the witness would contradict certain testimony is also sufficient.... Conversely an offer of proof by counsel that merely summarizes the witness's testimony in a conclusory manner is insufficient.

Michael H. Graham, *Cleary & Graham's Handbook of Illinois Evidence*, § 103.7 (6th ed. 1994) (citations omitted). It is not necessary to make an offer of proof when the admissibility of a document is denied, because the document that is not admitted into evidence can itself go up with the record on appeal. *Id.* The court does not have a right to forbid the making of an offer of proof. In re Marriage of Strauss, 183 Ill.App.3d 424, 132 Ill.Dec. 245, 539 N.E.2d 808 (1989) (if an offer of proof is necessary, it is error for the trial court to refuse counsel opportunity to state what he or she proposed to prove through the evidence).

STATE AND FEDERAL EAVESDROPPING STATUTES

CHAPTER 720

CRIMINAL OFFENSES

ACT 5. CRIMINAL CODE OF 1961
ARTICLE XIV. EAVESDROPPING

Analysis

Sec.
14–1. Definition.
14–2. Elements of the offense; Affirmative defense.
14–3. Exemptions.
14–4. Sentence.
14–5. Evidence inadmissible.
14–6. Civil remedies to injured parties.
14–7. Common carrier to aid in detection.
14–8. Discovery of eavesdropping device by an individual, common carrier, private investigative agency or non-governmental corporation.
14–9.1 Discovery of eavesdropping device by common carrier by wire—Disclosure to subscriber.

WESTLAW Electronic Research

See WESTLAW Electronic Research Guide preceding the Summary of Contents.

---

720 ILCS 5/14–1

§ 14–1. Definition

(a) Eavesdropping device.

An eavesdropping device is any device capable of being used to hear or record oral conversation whether such conversation is conducted in person, by telephone, or by any other means; Provided, however, that this definition shall not include devices used for the restoration of the deaf or hard-of-hearing to normal or partial hearing.

(b) Eavesdropper.

An eavesdropper is any person, including law enforcement officers, who operates or participates in the operation of any eavesdropping device contrary to the provisions of this Article.

720 ILCS 5/14–1 SELECTED NOTES AND STATUTES

(c) Principal.

A principal is any person who:

(1) Knowingly employs another who illegally uses an eavesdropping device in the course of such employment; or

(2) Knowingly derives any benefit or information from the illegal use of an eavesdropping device by another; or

(3) Directs another to use an eavesdropping device illegally on his behalf.

720 ILCS 5/14–2

§ 14–2. Elements of the offense; Affirmative defense

A person commits eavesdropping when he:

(a) Uses an eavesdropping device to hear or record all or any part of any conversation unless he does so (1) with the consent of all of the parties to such conversation or (2) in accordance with Article 108A or Article 108B of the "Code of Criminal Procedure of 1963", approved August 14, 1963, as amended; or

(b) Uses or divulges, except as authorized by this Article or by Article 108A or 108B of the "Code of Criminal Procedure of 1963", approved August 14, 1963, as amended, any information which he knows or reasonably should know was obtained through the use of an eavesdropping device.

(c) It is an affirmative defense to a charge brought under this Article relating to the interception of a privileged communication that the person charged:

1. was a law enforcement officer acting pursuant to an order of interception, entered pursuant to Section 108A–1 or 108B–5 of the Code of Criminal Procedure of 1963; and

2. at the time the communication was intercepted, the officer was unaware that the communication was privileged; and

3. stopped the interception within a reasonable time after discovering that the communication was privileged; and

4. did not disclose the contents of the communication.

720 ILCS 5/14–3

§ 14–3. Exemptions

The following activities shall be exempt from the provisions of this Article:

(a) Listening to radio, wireless and television communications of any sort where the same are publicly made;

(b) Hearing conversation when heard by employees of any common carrier by wire incidental to the normal course of their employment in the operation, maintenance or repair of the equipment of such common carrier by wire so long as no information obtained thereby is used or divulged by the hearer;

(c) Any broadcast by radio, television or otherwise whether it be a broadcast or recorded for the purpose of later broadcasts of any function where the public is in attendance and the conversations are overheard incidental to the main purpose for which such broadcasts are then being made;

(d) Recording or listening with the aid of any device to any emergency communication made in the normal course of operations by any federal, state or local law enforcement agency or institutions dealing in emergency services, including, but not limited to, hospitals, clinics, ambulance services, fire fighting agencies, any public utility, emergency repair facility, civilian defense establishment or military installation;

(e) Recording the proceedings of any meeting required to be open by the Open Meetings Act, as amended; and

(f) Recording or listening with the aid of any device to incoming telephone calls of phone lines publicly listed or advertised as consumer "hotlines" by manufacturers or retailers of food and drug products. Such recordings must be destroyed, erased or turned over to local law enforcement authorities within 24 hours from the time of such recording and shall not be otherwise disseminated. Failure on the part of the individual or business operating any such recording or listening device to comply with the requirements of this subsection shall eliminate any civil or criminal immunity conferred upon that individual or business by the operation of this Section.

720 ILCS 5/14-4
§ 14-4. Sentence

Eavesdropping, for a first offense, is a Class 4 felony, and, for a second or subsequent offense, is a Class 3 felony.

720 ILCS 5/14-5
§ 14-5. Evidence inadmissible

Any evidence obtained in violation of this Article is not admissible in any civil or criminal trial, or any administrative or legislative inquiry or proceeding, nor in any grand jury proceedings; provided, however, that so much of the contents of an alleged unlawfully intercepted, overheard or recorded conversation as is clearly relevant, as determined as a matter of law by the court in chambers, to the proof of such allegation may be admitted into evidence in any criminal trial or grand jury proceeding brought against any person charged with violating any provision of this Article.

720 ILCS 5/14-6
§ 14-6. Civil remedies to injured parties

(1) Any or all parties to any conversation upon which eavesdropping is practiced contrary to this Article shall be entitled to the following remedies:

720 ILCS 5/14-6 SELECTED NOTES AND STATUTES

(a) To an injunction by the circuit court prohibiting further eavesdropping by the eavesdropper and by or on behalf of his principal, or either;

(b) To all actual damages against the eavesdropper or his principal or both;

(c) To any punitive damages which may be awarded by the court or by a jury;

(d) To all actual damages against any landlord, owner or building operator, or any common carrier by wire who aids, abets, or knowingly permits the eavesdropping concerned;

(e) To any punitive damages which may be awarded by the court or by a jury against any landlord, owner or building operator, or common carrier by wire who aids, abets, or knowingly permits the eavesdropping concerned.

(2) No cause of action shall lie in any court against any common carrier by wire or its officers, agents or employees for providing information, assistance or facilities in accordance with the terms of a court order entered under Article 108A of the Code of Criminal Procedure of 1963.

720 ILCS 5/14-7

§ 14-7. Common carrier to aid in detection

Subject to regulation by the Illinois Commerce Commission, any common carrier by wire shall, upon request of any subscriber and upon responsible offer to pay the reasonable cost thereof, furnish whatever services may be within its command for the purpose of detecting any eavesdropping involving its wires which are used by said subscriber. All such requests by subscribers shall be kept confidential unless divulgence is authorized in writing by the requesting subscriber.

720 ILCS 5/14-8

§ 14-8. Discovery of eavesdropping device by an individual, common carrier, private investigative agency or non-governmental corporation

Any agent, officer or employee of a private investigative agency or non-governmental corporation, or of a common carrier by wire, or any individual, who discovers any physical evidence of an eavesdropping device being used which such person does not know to be a legal eavesdropping device shall, within a reasonable time after such discovery disclose the existence of such eavesdropping device to the State's Attorney of the county where such device was found. The State's Attorney shall within a reasonable time notify the person or persons apparently being eavesdropped upon of the existence of that device if the device is illegal. A violation of this Section is a Business Offense for which a fine shall be imposed not to exceed $500.

720 ILCS 5/14-9.1

§ 14-9.1 Discovery of eavesdropping device by common carrier by wire—Disclosure to subscriber

Any agent, officer or employee of any common carrier by wire who discovers any physical evidence of an eavesdropping device which such person does not know to be a legal eavesdropping device shall, within a reasonable time after such discovery, disclose the existence of the eavesdropping device to the State's Attorney of the County where such device was found. The State's Attorney shall within a reasonable time notify the person or persons apparently being eavesdropped upon of the existence of that device if the device is illegal. A violation of this Section is a Business Offense for which a fine shall be imposed not to exceed $500.

[*Author's Notes follow 18 U.S.C.A. § 2521.*]

18 U.S.C.A.
TITLE III OF THE OMNIBUS CRIME CONTROL AND SAFE STREETS ACT OF 1968

Analysis

Sec.
2510. Definitions.
2511. Interception and disclosure of wire, oral, or electronic communications prohibited.
2515. Prohibition of use as evidence of intercepted wire or oral communications.
2520. Recovery of civil damages authorized.
2521. Injunction against illegal interception.

WESTLAW Electronic Research

See WESTLAW Electronic Research Guide preceding the Summary of Contents.

---

18 U.S.C.A. § 2510

§ 2510. Definitions

As used in this chapter—

(1) "wire communication" means any aural transfer made in whole or in part through the use of facilities for the transmission of communications by the aid of wire, cable, or other like connection between the point of origin and the point of reception (including the use of such connection in a switching station) furnished or operated by any person engaged in providing or operating such facilities for the transmission of interstate or foreign communications or communications affecting interstate or foreign commerce and such term includes any electronic storage of such communication, but such term does not include the radio portion of a cordless telephone communication that is transmitted between the cordless telephone handset and the base unit;

(2) "oral communication" means any oral communication uttered by a person exhibiting an expectation that such communication is not subject to interception under circumstances justifying such expectation, but such term does not include any electronic communication;

(3) "State" means any State of the United States, the District of Columbia, the Commonwealth of Puerto Rico, and any territory or possession of the United States;

(4) "intercept" means the aural or other acquisition of the contents of any wire, electronic, or oral communication through the use of any electronic, mechanical, or other device.

(5) "electronic, mechanical, or other device" means any device or apparatus which can be used to intercept a wire, oral, or electronic communication other than—

(a) any telephone or telegraph instrument, equipment or facility, or any component thereof, (i) furnished to the subscriber or user by a provider of wire or electronic communication service in the ordinary course of its business and being used by the subscriber or user in the ordinary course of its business or furnished by such subscriber or user for connection to the facilities of such service and used in the ordinary course of its business; or (ii) being used by a provider of wire or electronic communication service in the ordinary course of its business, or by an investigative or law enforcement officer in the ordinary course of his duties;

(b) a hearing aid or similar device being used to correct subnormal hearing to not better than normal;

(6) "person" means any employee, or agent of the United States or any State or political subdivision thereof, and any individual, partnership, association, joint stock company, trust, or corporation;

(7) "Investigative or law enforcement officer" means any officer of the United States or of a State or political subdivision thereof, who is empowered by law to conduct investigations of or to make arrests for offenses enumerated in this chapter, and any attorney authorized by law to prosecute or participate in the prosecution of such offenses;

(8) "contents", when used with respect to any wire, oral, or electronic communication, includes any information concerning the substance, purport, or meaning of that communication;

(9) "Judge of competent jurisdiction" means—

(a) a judge of a United States district court or a United States court of appeals; and

(b) a judge of any court of general criminal jurisdiction of a State who is authorized by a statute of that State to enter orders authorizing interceptions of wire, oral, or electronic communications;

(10) "communication common carrier" shall have the same meaning which is given the term "common carrier" by section 153(h) of title 47 of the United States Code;

(11) "aggrieved person" means a person who was a party to any intercepted wire, oral, or electronic communication or a person against whom the interception was directed;

(12) "electronic communication" means any transfer of signs, signals, writing, images, sounds, data, or intelligence of any nature transmitted in whole or in part by a wire, radio, electromagnetic, photoelectronic or photooptical system that affects interstate or foreign commerce, but does not include—

18 U.S.C.A. § 2510 SELECTED NOTES AND STATUTES

(A) the radio portion of a cordless telephone communication that is transmitted between the cordless telephone handset and the base unit;

(B) any wire or oral communication;

(C) any communication made through a tone-only paging device; or

(D) any communication from a tracking device (as defined in section 3117 of this title);

(13) "user" means any person or entity who—

(A) uses an electronic communication service; and

(B) is duly authorized by the provider of such service to engage in such use;

(14) "electronic communications system" means any wire, radio, electromagnetic, photooptical or photoelectronic facilities for the transmission of electronic communications, and any computer facilities or related electronic equipment for the electronic storage of such communications;

(15) "electronic communication service" means any service which provides to users thereof the ability to send or receive wire or electronic communications;

(16) "readily accessible to the general public" means, with respect to a radio communication, that such communication is not—

(A) scrambled or encrypted;

(B) transmitted using modulation techniques whose essential parameters have been withheld from the public with the intention of preserving the privacy of such communication;

(C) carried on a subcarrier or other signal subsidiary to a radio transmission;

(D) transmitted over a communication system provided by a common carrier, unless the communication is a tone only paging system communication; or

(E) transmitted on frequencies allocated under part 25, subpart D, E, or F of part 74, or part 94 of the Rules of the Federal Communications Commission, unless, in the case of a communication transmitted on a frequency allocated under part 74 that is not exclusively allocated to broadcast auxiliary services, the communication is a two-way voice communication by radio;

(17) "electronic storage" means—

(A) any temporary, intermediate storage of a wire or electronic communication incidental to the electronic transmission thereof; and

(B) any storage of such communication by an electronic communication service for purposes of backup protection of such communication; and

(18) "aural transfer" means a transfer containing the human voice at any point between and including the point of origin and the point of reception.

18 U.S.C.A. § 2511

§ 2511. Interception and disclosure of wire, oral, or electronic communications prohibited

(1) Except as otherwise specifically provided in this chapter any person who—

(a) intentionally intercepts, endeavors to intercept, or procures any other person to intercept or endeavor to intercept, any wire, oral, or electronic communication;

(b) intentionally uses, endeavors to use, or procures any other person to use or endeavor to use any electronic, mechanical, or other device to intercept any oral communication when—

(i) such device is affixed to, or otherwise transmits a signal through, a wire, cable, or other like connection used in wire communication; or

(ii) such device transmits communications by radio, or interferes with the transmission of such communication; or

(iii) such person knows, or has reason to know, that such device or any component thereof has been sent through the mail or transported in interstate or foreign commerce; or

(iv) such use or endeavor to use (A) takes place on the premises of any business or other commercial establishment the operations of which affect interstate or foreign commerce; or (B) obtains or is for the purpose of obtaining information relating to the operations of any business or other commercial establishment the operations of which affect interstate or foreign commerce; or

(v) such person acts in the District of Columbia, the Commonwealth of Puerto Rico, or any territory or possession of the United States;

(c) intentionally discloses, or endeavors to disclose, to any other person the contents of any wire, oral, or electronic communication, knowing or having reason to know that the information was obtained through the interception of a wire, oral, or electronic communication in violation of this subsection; or

(d) intentionally uses, or endeavors to use, the contents of any wire, oral, or electronic communication, knowing or having reason to know that the information was obtained through the interception of a wire, oral, or electronic communication in violation of this subsection; shall be punished as provided in subsection (4) or shall be subject to suit as provided in subsection (5).

(2)(a)(i) It shall not be unlawful under this chapter for an operator of a switchboard, or an officer, employee, or agent of a provider of wire or electronic communication service, whose facilities are used in the transmission of a wire communication, to intercept, disclose, or use that communication in the normal course of his employment while engaged in any activity which is a necessary incident to the rendition of his service or to the protection of the rights or property of the provider of that service, except that a provider of wire communication service to the public shall not utilize service observing or random monitoring except for mechanical or service quality control checks.

(ii) Notwithstanding any other law, providers of wire or electronic communication service, their officers, employees, and agents, landlords, custodians, or other persons, are authorized to provide information, facilities, or technical assistance to persons authorized by law to intercept wire, oral, or electronic communications or to conduct electronic surveillance, as defined in section 101 of the Foreign Intelligence Surveillance Act of 1978, if such provider, its officers, employees, or agents, landlord, custodian, or other specified person, has been provided with—

(A) a court order directing such assistance signed by the authorizing judge, or

(B) a certification in writing by a person specified in section 2518(7) of this title or the Attorney General of the United States that no warrant or court order is required by law, that all statutory requirements have been met, and that the specified assistance is required, setting forth the period of time during which the provision of the information, facilities, or technical assistance is authorized and specifying the information, facilities, or technical assistance required. No provider of wire or electronic communication service, officer, employee, or agent thereof, or landlord, custodian, or other specified person shall disclose the existence of any interception or surveillance or the device used to accomplish the interception or surveillance with respect to which the person has been furnished a court order or certification under this chapter, except as may otherwise be required by legal process and then only after prior notification to the Attorney General or to the principal prosecuting attorney of a State or any political subdivision of a State, as may be appropriate. Any such disclosure, shall render such person liable for the civil damages provided for in section 2520. No cause of action shall lie in any court against any provider of wire or electronic communication service, its officers, employees, or agents, landlord, custodian, or other specified person for providing information, facilities, or assistance in accordance with the terms of a court order or certification under this chapter.

(b) It shall not be unlawful under this chapter for an officer, employee, or agent of the Federal Communications Commission, in the normal course of his employment and in discharge of the monitoring responsibilities exercised by the Commission in the enforcement of chapter 5 of title 47 of the United States Code, to intercept a wire or electronic communication, or oral communication transmitted by radio, or to disclose or use the information thereby obtained.

(c) It shall not be unlawful under this chapter for a person acting under color of law to intercept a wire, oral, or electronic communication, where such person is a party to the communication or one of the parties to the communication has given prior consent to such interception.

(d) It shall not be unlawful under this chapter for a person not acting under color of law to intercept a wire, oral, or electronic communication where such person is a party to the communication or where one of the parties to the communication has given prior consent to such interception unless such communication is intercepted for the purpose of committing any criminal or tortious act in violation of the Constitution or laws of the United States or of any State.

(e) Notwithstanding any other provision of this title or section 705 or 706 of the Communications Act of 1934, it shall not be unlawful for an officer, employee, or agent of the United States in the normal course of his official duty to conduct electronic surveillance, as defined in section 101 of the Foreign Intelligence Surveillance Act of 1978, as authorized by that Act.

(f) Nothing contained in this chapter or chapter 121, or section 705 of the Communications Act of 1934, shall be deemed to affect the acquisition by the United States Government of foreign intelligence information from international or foreign communications, or foreign intelligence activities conducted in accordance with otherwise applicable Federal law involving a foreign electronic communications system, utilizing a means other than electronic surveillance as defined in section 101 of the Foreign Intelligence Surveillance Act of 1978, and procedures in this chapter or chapter 121 and the Foreign Intelligence Surveillance Act of 1978 shall be the exclusive means by which electronic surveillance, as defined in section 101 of such Act, and the interception of domestic wire and oral communications may be conducted.

(g) It shall not be unlawful under this chapter or chapter 121 of this title for any person—

(i) to intercept or access an electronic communication made through an electronic communication system that is configured so that such electronic communication is readily accessible to the general public;

(ii) to intercept any radio communication which is transmitted—

(I) by any station for the use of the general public, or that relates to ships, aircraft, vehicles, or persons in distress;

(II) by any governmental, law enforcement, civil defense, private land mobile, or public safety communications system, including police and fire, readily accessible to the general public;

(III) by a station operating on an authorized frequency within the bands allocated to the amateur, citizens band, or general mobile radio services; or

(IV) by any marine or aeronautical communications system;

(iii) to engage in any conduct which—

(I) is prohibited by section 633 of the Communications Act of 1934; or

(II) is excepted from the application of section 705(a) of the Communications Act of 1934 by section 705(b) of that Act;

(iv) to intercept any wire or electronic communication the transmission of which is causing harmful interference to any lawfully operating station or consumer electronic equipment, to the extent necessary to identify the source of such interference; or

(v) for other users of the same frequency to intercept any radio communication made through a system that utilizes frequencies monitored by individuals engaged in the provision or the use of such system, if such communication is not scrambled or encrypted.

(h) It shall not be unlawful under this chapter—

(i) to use a pen register or a trap and trace device (as those terms are defined for the purposes of chapter 206 (relating to pen registers and trap and trace devices) of this title); or

(ii) for a provider of electronic communication service to record the fact that a wire or electronic communication was initiated or completed in order to protect such provider, another provider furnishing service toward the completion of the wire or electronic communication, or a user of that service, from fraudulent, unlawful or abusive use of such service.

(3)(a) Except as provided in paragraph (b) of this subsection, a person or entity providing an electronic communication service to the public shall not intentionally divulge the contents of any communication (other than one to such person or entity, or an agent thereof) while in transmission on that service to any person or entity other than an addressee or intended recipient of such communication or an agent of such addressee or intended recipient.

(b) A person or entity providing electronic communication service to the public may divulge the contents of any such communication—

(i) as otherwise authorized in section 2511(2)(a) or 2517 of this title;

(ii) with the lawful consent of the originator or any addressee or intended recipient of such communication;

(iii) to a person employed or authorized, or whose facilities are used, to forward such communication to its destination; or

(iv) which were inadvertently obtained by the service provider and which appear to pertain to the commission of a crime, if such divulgence is made to a law enforcement agency.

(4)(a) Except as provided in paragraph (b) of this subsection or in subsection (5), whoever violates subsection (1) of this section shall be fined under this title or imprisoned not more than five years, or both.

(b) If the offense is a first offense under paragraph (a) of this subsection and is not for a tortious or illegal purpose or for purposes of direct or indirect commercial advantage or private commercial gain, and the wire or electronic communication with respect to which the offense under paragraph (a) is a radio communication that is not scrambled or encrypted, then—

(i) if the communication is not the radio portion of a cellular telephone communication, a public land mobile radio service communication or a paging service communication, and the conduct is not that described in subsection (5), the offender shall be fined under this title or imprisoned not more than one year, or both; and

(ii) if the communication is the radio portion of a cellular telephone communication, a public land mobile radio service communication or a paging service communication, the offender shall be fined not more than $500.

(c) Conduct otherwise an offense under this subsection that consists of or relates to the interception of a satellite transmission that is not encrypted or scrambled and that is transmitted—

(i) to a broadcasting station for purposes of retransmission to the general public; or

(ii) as an audio subcarrier intended for redistribution to facilities open to the public, but not including data transmissions or telephone calls, is not an offense under this subsection unless the conduct is for the purposes of direct or indirect commercial advantage or private financial gain.

(5)(a)(i) If the communication is—

(A) a private satellite video communication that is not scrambled or encrypted and the conduct in violation of this

18 U.S.C.A. § 2511 SELECTED NOTES AND STATUTES

chapter is the private viewing of that communication and is not for a tortious or illegal purpose or for purposes of direct or indirect commercial advantage or private commercial gain; or

(B) a radio communication that is transmitted on frequencies allocated under subpart D of part 74 of the rules of the Federal Communications Commission that is not scrambled or encrypted and the conduct in violation of this chapter is not for a tortious or illegal purpose or for purposes of direct or indirect commercial advantage or private commercial gain, then the person who engages in such conduct shall be subject to suit by the Federal Government in a court of competent jurisdiction.

(ii) In an action under this subsection—

(A) if the violation of this chapter is a first offense for the person under paragraph (a) of subsection (4) and such person has not been found liable in a civil action under section 2520 of this title, the Federal Government shall be entitled to appropriate injunctive relief; and

(B) if the violation of this chapter is a second or subsequent offense under paragraph (a) of subsection (4) or such person has been found liable in any prior civil action under section 2520, the person shall be subject to a mandatory $500 civil fine.

(b) The court may use any means within its authority to enforce an injunction issued under paragraph (ii)(A), and shall impose a civil fine of not less than $500 for each violation of such an injunction.

18 U.S.C.A. § 2515

§ 2515. Prohibition of use as evidence of intercepted wire or oral communications

Whenever any wire or oral communication has been intercepted, no part of the contents of such communication and no evidence derived therefrom may be received in evidence in any trial, hearing, or other proceeding in or before any court, grand jury, department, officer, agency, regulatory body, legislative committee, or other authority of the United States, a State, or a political subdivision thereof if the disclosure of that information would be in violation of this chapter.

18 U.S.C.A. § 2520

§ 2520. Recovery of civil damages authorized

(a) In general.

Except as provided in section 2511(2)(a)(ii), any person whose wire, oral, or electronic communication is intercepted, disclosed, or intentionally used in violation of this chapter may in a civil action recover from the person or entity which engaged in that violation such relief as may be appropriate.

(b) Relief.

In an action under this section, appropriate relief includes—

(1) such preliminary and other equitable or declaratory relief as may be appropriate;

(2) damages under subsection (c) and punitive damages in appropriate cases; and

(3) a reasonable attorney's fee and other litigation costs reasonably incurred.

(c) Computation of damages.

(1) In an action under this section, if the conduct in violation of this chapter is the private viewing of a private satellite video communication that is not scrambled or encrypted or if the communication is a radio communication that is transmitted on frequencies allocated under subpart D of part 74 of the rules of the Federal Communications Commission that is not scrambled or encrypted and the conduct is not for a tortious or illegal purpose or for purposes of direct or indirect commercial advantage or private commercial gain, then the court shall assess damages as follows:

(A) If the person who engaged in that conduct has not previously been enjoined under section 2511(5) and has not been found liable in a prior civil action under this section, the court shall assess the greater of the sum of actual damages suffered by the plaintiff, or statutory damages of not less than $50 and not more than $500.

(B) If, on one prior occasion, the person who engaged in that conduct has been enjoined under section 2511(5) or has been found liable in a civil action under this section, the court shall assess the greater of the sum of actual damages suffered by the plaintiff, or statutory damages of not less than $100 and not more than $1000.

(2) In any other action under this section, the court may assess as damages whichever is the greater of—

(A) the sum of the actual damages suffered by the plaintiff and any profits made by the violator as a result of the violation; or

(B) statutory damages of whichever is the greater of $100 a day for each day of violation or $10,000.

(d) Defense.

A good faith reliance on—

(1) a court warrant or order, a grand jury subpoena, a legislative authorization, or a statutory authorization;

(2) a request of an investigative or law enforcement officer under section 2518(7) of this title; or

(3) a good faith determination that section 2511(3) of this title permitted the conduct complained of; is a complete defense against any civil or criminal action brought under this chapter or any other law.

(e) Limitation.

A civil action under this section may not be commenced later than two years after the date upon which the claimant first has a reasonable opportunity to discover the violation.

18 U.S.C.A. § 2521

§ 2521. Injunction against illegal interception

Whenever it shall appear that any person is engaged or is about to engage in any act which constitutes or will constitute a felony violation of this chapter, the Attorney General may initiate a civil action in a district court of the United States to enjoin such violation. The court shall proceed as soon as practicable to the hearing and determination of such an action, and may, at any time before final determination, enter such a restraining order or prohibition, or take such other action, as is warranted to prevent a continuing and substantial injury to the United States or to any person or class of persons for whose protection the action is brought. A proceeding under this section is governed by the Federal Rules of Civil Procedure, except that, if an indictment has been returned against the respondent, discovery is governed by the Federal Rules of Criminal Procedure.

Author's Notes to State and Federal Eavesdropping Statutes

Analysis

1. Sanctions.
2. Liberal interpretation.
3. Answering machines.

(1) **Sanctions.** Violation of either the Illinois eavesdropping statute or the Federal eavesdropping statute is a criminal offense. 720 ILCS 5/14–4, 18 U.S.C.A. § 2511(4). In addition, both statutes authorize civil actions. 720 ILCS 5/14–6, 18 U.S.C.A. § 2520.

(2) **Liberal interpretation.** The language of the Illinois eavesdropping statute permits recording a conversation with consent of all of the parties to the conversation. The courts' interpretation of the statute, however, has been much more liberal. In People v. Beardsley, 115 Ill.2d 47, 104 Ill.Dec. 789, 503 N.E.2d 346 (1986), the Illinois Supreme Court held that in order for the recording of a conversation to be illegal, the parties to the conversation had to intend that their conversation be private. In *Beardsley*, two police officers conversed in the front seat of the car, and the conversation was recorded by the defendant who was in the back seat of the car. Both police officers testified that they did not consent to the recording by the defendant. The Illinois Supreme Court held that the recording did not violate the Eavesdropping Statute, because, if the police officers had intended their conversation to be private, they would not have had it in the presence of the defendant who was in the back seat. In People v. Jansen, 203 Ill.App.3d 985, 149 Ill.Dec. 34, 561 N.E.2d 312 (5th

Dist.1990), the Appellate Court held that a telephone conversation could be recorded if only one party to the conversation consented and the other did not. In other words, the recording of a telephone conversation by a party to the conversation, even without the consent of the other party to the telephone conversation, is not prohibited by the Illinois Eavesdropping Statute. In both the *Beardsley* and the *Jansen* situations the person who made the recording could himself have testified to the content of the recorded conversations.

The same is true under 18 U.S.C.A. § 2511(2)(d), which allows a "person not acting under color of law" to tape a conversation "where such person is a party to the communication or where one of the parties to the communication has given prior consent to such interception unless such communication is intercepted for the purpose of committing any criminal or tortious act in violation of the Constitution or laws of the United States or of any State." The interception cannot be made for an unlawful purpose. See, e.g., United States v. Zarnes, 33 F.3d 1454 (7th Cir.1994) (rejecting defendant's argument that tape of conversation was made for the purpose of blackmailing him and therefore inadmissible; defendant failed to meet his burden of proof by a preponderance of the evidence). See Thompson v. Dulaney, 970 F.2d 744 (10th Cir.1992) (adopting "majority rule" that no interspousal exception exists to liability under Title III). Accord, Heggy v. Heggy, 944 F.2d 1537 (10th Cir.1991), *cert. denied,* — U.S. —, 112 S.Ct. 1514, 117 L.Ed.2d 651 (1992), Platt v. Platt, 951 F.2d 159 (8th Cir.1989). The minority rule is found in Anonymous v. Anonymous, 558 F.2d 677 (2d Cir.1977) (interspousal wiretaps are a "mere marital disput[e]; a matter left to the states," rather than criminal conduct covered by the federal wiretap statutes).

Compare, however, the recording of a telephone conversation by a detective through a wire tap where neither party has consented to the recording, which is prohibited under the Federal and State Eavesdropping Statutes.

(3) **Answering machines.** Tape recordings of telephone conversations are now frequently received in evidence where the recording has been made on a telephone answering machine. Such recordings should not be prohibited by the Federal or State Eavesdropping Statutes, and should be admissible in evidence, inasmuch as the calling party when he hears the answering machine obviously knows that his conversation is being recorded, and he consents by proceeding to leave a message.

FEDERAL AND STATE CONSTITUTIONAL RIGHTS AGAINST SELF–INCRIMINATION

U.S. Const. amend. V

No person shall be held to answer for a capital, or otherwise infamous crime, unless on a presentment or indictment of a Grand Jury, except in cases arising in the land or naval forces, or in the Militia, when in actual service in time of War or public danger; nor shall any person be subject for the same offence to be twice put in jeopardy of life or limb; nor shall be compelled in any criminal case to be a witness against himself, nor be deprived of life, liberty, or property, without due process of law; nor shall private property be taken for public use, without just compensation.

Ill. Const. art. I, § 10

§ 10. Self-incrimination and double jeopardy

No person shall be compelled in a criminal case to give evidence against himself nor be twice put in jeopardy for the same offense.

Author's Notes

Analysis

1. Applicability to dissolution proceedings.
2. Conclusion can be drawn.
3. Expert criminal advice.
4. Tax prosecutions.

(1) **Applicability to dissolution proceedings.** In dissolution proceedings, a party may invoke the right to not testify against herself or himself which arises under the Fifth Amendment of the United States Constitution and Article I, § 10 of the Illinois Constitution where the party is in jeopardy of being prosecuted for a crime concerning which his testimony is sought.

> Although a party may claim the fifth amendment privilege in any proceeding, whether civil or criminal ... the propriety of invoking the privilege must be determined by the court when the question is presented to it in an appropriate fashion.... In making that determination the court should be aware that "in the deviousness of crime and its detection, incrimination may be approached and achieved by obscure and unlikely lines of inquiry...." Thus, it must be perfectly clear under all of the circumstances that the answers cannot possibly have a tendency to incriminate the party claiming the privilege.

People ex rel. Mathis v. Brown, 44 Ill.App.3d 783, 784, 3 Ill.Dec. 475,, 358 N.E.2d 1160, 1161(1st Dist.1976). The issue of whether to rely on the Fifth Amendment in order to refuse to testify frequently arises in dissolution cases. For example, a party may assert his or her Fifth Amendment rights in order to avoid testifying about situations involving abuse, the sale of drugs where cash is received but not reported as taxable income, or the personal use of business funds or assets, such as art or boats.

(2) **Conclusion can be drawn.** Unlike criminal proceedings, however, in civil dissolution proceedings, the judge is permitted to draw a conclusion from a witness's refusal to testify under the protection of the Fifth Amendment. Shea v. Civil Serv. Comm'n, 224 Ill.App.3d 282, 166 Ill.Dec. 554, 586 N.E.2d 512 (1st Dist.1991) *appeal denied*, 144 Ill.2d 643, 169 Ill.Dec. 151, 591 N.E.2d 31 (1992). For example, when a spouse refuses to testify concerning the alleged receipt of cash in his business that he did not report on his income tax returns, although he cannot be required to testify and incriminate himself, the dissolution judge can conclude from his failure to testify that the cash was in fact received.

(3) **Expert criminal advice.** Many criminal prosecutions arise from divorce cases. Private matters become public as a result of the litigation. Wrongdoing may be highlighted, because it is always in the interest of the non-income earning spouse to show that the income earning spouse has high cash receipts, whether reported or not, and whether earned legitimately or not. When criminal elements are involved in dissolution actions, it is a good precaution to obtain expert advice in determining legal strategy such as whether to rely on the Fifth Amendment.

CONFLICTS OF INTEREST

(4) **Tax prosecutions.** Particularly in tax prosecutions involving joint returns, it is important to remember that both spouses may be held liable for any irregularities, even though only one actively participated in the crime. See Marjorie A. O'Connell, *Divorce Taxation*, ¶18,101 et seq. (1993).

PERJURY

Author's Notes

Analysis

1. Lawyer's obligations.
2. Application in practice.

(1) **Lawyer's obligations.** It is a crime for a lawyer to suborn perjury. 720 ILCS 5/32-3. A lawyer is an officer of the court, and therefore limits are imposed by the interests of justice on the representation of his client. If a lawyer knows his client intends to perjure himself in testimony or other evidence, the lawyer is obligated to try to persuade the client to present the truth. If the client refuses to present the truth, the obligation of the lawyer is to withdraw from the representation. See Rule of Professional Conduct 3.3(a)(4) (a lawyer shall not "offer evidence that the lawyer knows to be false"); Rule of Professional Conduct 3.3(c) ("A lawyer may refuse to offer evidence that the lawyer reasonably believes is false."). If a client commits perjury, known to the lawyer, while the lawyer is representing him, it is the obligation of the lawyer to advise the court that perjury has been committed. Rule of Professional Conduct 3.3(a)(4) ("If a lawyer has offered material evidence and comes to know of its falsity, the lawyer shall take reasonable remedial measures...."). For the best discussion of these rules, see Nix v. Whiteside, 475 U.S. 157, 106 S.Ct. 988, 89 L.Ed.2d 123 (1986) (criminal defendant's 6th Amendment right to effective counsel was not violated when attorney refused to cooperate in presenting perjured testimony).

(2) **Application in practice.** While the rules are fairly easy to state, they are often difficult to apply. Frequently, a lawyer does not know if his client is telling the truth. But even as an advocate, there are times when it is apparent that a client is untruthful and the obligation of the lawyer is clear. Other times the circumstances are more ambiguous, and the obligation of the lawyer is to press the inquiry so as to insure that he presents a true story to the court.

CONFLICTS OF INTEREST

Author's Notes

Analysis

1. Rule of Professional Conduct.
2. Conflict of interest when parties seek same firm.
3. Waiver.
4. Consent to waive conflict of interest—Form.

(1) **Rule of Professional Conduct.** Rule 1.9 of the Illinois Rules of Professional Conduct provides in pertinent part:

SELECTED NOTES AND STATUTES

(a) A lawyer who has formerly represented a client in a matter shall not thereafter:

(1) Represent another person in the same or a substantially related matter in which that person's interests are materially adverse to the interest of the former client, unless the former client consents after disclosure; ...

(2) **Conflict of interest when parties seek same firm.** There are a myriad possible conflicts of interest. The most common situation in dissolution cases is for one party to a dissolution proceeding to interview a law firm, and then decide to be represented by a second law firm. His spouse may then request the first law firm to represent her. The initial interview by the husband is sufficient to disqualify the first law firm from representing the wife, unless both parties consent to the representation of the wife by the first firm. See, e.g., In re Marriage of Gordon, 233 Ill.App.3d 617, 175 Ill.Dec. 137, 599 N.E.2d 1151 (1st Dist.), *appeal denied*, 147 Ill.2d 626, 180 Ill.Dec. 149, 606 N.E.2d 1226 (1992); King v. King, 52 Ill.App.3d 749, 10 Ill.Dec. 592, 367 N.E.2d 1358 (4th Dist.1977).

Another possibility is that each spouse will interview a different member of the same firm, thereby requiring consents by both spouses for the firm to represent either spouse. The latter situation can be prevented in most instances by firms maintaining a good conflicts of interest system that is regularly checked prior to client interviews.

A conflict can also arise after representation has been completed. For example, a conflict exists when the first wife who is owed money by her husband from her divorce is represented by the same firm from whom the second wife of the same husband now seeks representation. Both the first and second spouses will be seeking the same money from the same husband, and, without a waiver, the firm's duty is not to jeopardize their first client by representing the second.

(3) **Waiver.** Conflicts can be waived. There must first be complete disclosure of the conflict. After full disclosure, the best consent is in writing. The consent, after full disclosure, can be express, Lavaja v. Carter, 153 Ill.App.3d 317, 106 Ill.Dec. 147, 505 N.E.2d 694 (2d Dist.), *appeal denied*, 116 Ill.2d 560, 113 Ill.Dec. 301, 515 N.E.2d 110 (1987); Nandorf, Inc. v. CNA Ins. Co., 134 Ill.App.3d 134, 88 Ill.Dec. 968, 479 N.E.2d 988 (1st Dist.1985), or the consent can be implied by failure of the former client to make a timely objection, Tanner v. Board of Trustees, 121 Ill.App.3d 139, 76 Ill.Dec. 687, 459 N.E.2d 324 (4th Dist.1984); Roth v. Roth, 84 Ill.App.3d 240, 39 Ill.Dec. 872, 405 N.E.2d 851 (3d Dist.1980). Relying on an implied waiver, however, is not recommended. A consent in writing should be obtained.

(4) **Consent to waive conflict of interest—Form.** There follows a sample consent.

BLOWERS & ASSOCIATES, LTD.

April ___, 199_

Frederick Tulkinghorn
Attorney for John Jarndyce
Address

RE: THE MARRIAGE OF JARNDYCE

Dear Frederick:

CONFLICTS OF INTEREST

As you know, John Jarndyce briefly consulted me in regard to representing him in the marital litigation between him and Ellen Jarndyce. I conducted a preliminary interview with Mr. Jarndyce and obtained from him the basic family and financial facts concerning his marriage. I understand that, subsequent to my interview with John Jarndyce, he has engaged you to represent him.

Ellen Jarndyce has now inquired of my availability to represent her in the same proceeding.

Either party may object to the conflict. Therefore, before we undertake the representation of Ellen Jarndyce, it is necessary that we determine whether John Jarndyce has an objection to our representation of Ellen. We would therefore be appreciative if you would inquire of John Jarndyce, now your client, whether, because of our initial interview with him, he objects to me or to our law firm taking on the representation of Ellen Jarndyce. If he does not, he should sign a copy of this letter to expressly waive any objection to the representation of Ellen Jarndyce by me and by our firm. I will also request of Ellen Jarndyce that she sign this letter as well in order to acknowledge that she is aware of our initial interview with John Jarndyce, and, despite such knowledge, she desires me and our law firm to represent her.

Thank you for your cooperation.

Sincerely yours,

Joseph Blowers

JB/xx

Having read and understood the above, and, after consulting with counsel, I waive any objection to Joseph Blowers and Blowers and Associates, Ltd. representing Ellen Jarndyce.

_____   _____
Ellen Jarndyce   John Jarndyce

*

TABLE OF CASES

Abbott v. Abbott, 52 Ill.App.3d 728, 10 Ill.Dec. 464, 367 N.E.2d 1073 (Ill.App. 3 Dist.1977)—**750 ILCS 5/411, n. 2.**
Adams, In re Marriage of, 183 Ill.App.3d 296, 131 Ill.Dec. 730, 538 N.E.2d 1286 (Ill.App. 4 Dist.1989)—**750 ILCS 5/503, n. 18.**
Adoption of Baby Girls Mandell, In re, 213 Ill.App.3d 670, 157 Ill.Dec. 290, 572 N.E.2d 359 (Ill.App. 2 Dist.1991)—**750 ILCS 50/0.01, n. 14.**
Adoption of Kindgren, In re, 184 Ill.App.3d 661, 132 Ill.Dec. 745, 540 N.E.2d 485 (Ill.App. 2 Dist.1989)—**750 ILCS 50/0.01, n. 14.**
Agazim, In re Marriage of, 147 Ill.App.3d 646, 101 Ill.Dec. 418, 498 N.E.2d 742 (Ill.App. 2 Dist.1986)—**750 ILCS 5/503, n. 3.**
Agustsson, In re Marriage of, 223 Ill.App.3d 510, 165 Ill.Dec. 811, 585 N.E.2d 207 (Ill.App. 2 Dist.1992)—**750 ILCS 5/502, n. 4.**
Albiani, In re Marriage of, 159 Ill.App.3d 519, 111 Ill.Dec. 126, 512 N.E.2d 30 (Ill.App. 1 Dist.1987)—**750 ILCS 5/513, n. 2.**
Allen, In re Marriage of, 81 Ill.App.3d 517, 36 Ill.Dec. 767, 401 N.E.2d 608 (Ill.App. 3 Dist.1980)—**750 ILCS 5/602, n. 2.**
Allott v. American Strawboard Co., 237 Ill. 55, 86 N.E. 685 (Ill.1908)—**750 ILCS 5/501, n. 11.**
Alush, In re Marriage of, 172 Ill.App.3d 646, 122 Ill.Dec. 694, 527 N.E.2d 66 (Ill.App. 2 Dist.1988)—**750 ILCS 35/17, n.1.**
Andersen, In re Marriage of, 236 Ill.App.3d 679, 177 Ill.Dec. 289, 603 N.E.2d 70 (Ill.App. 2 Dist.1992)—**750 ILCS 5/602, n. 2.**
Andrew, In re Marriage of, 258 Ill.App.3d 924, 194 Ill.Dec. 724, 628 N.E.2d 221 (Ill.App. 1 Dist.1993)—**750 ILCS 5/503, n. 33.**
Andrews, People v., 146 Ill.2d 413, 167 Ill.Dec. 996, 588 N.E.2d 1126 (Ill.1992)—**p. 944, n. 1.**
Anonymous v. Anonymous, 558 F.2d 677 (2nd Cir.1977)—**p. 961, n.2.**
Antonich, In re Marriage of, 148 Ill.App.3d 575, 102 Ill.Dec. 97, 499 N.E.2d 654 (Ill.App. 2 Dist.1986)—**750 ILCS 5/510, n. 16.**
Antry v. Illinois Educational Labor Relations Bd., 195 Ill.App.3d 221, 141 Ill.Dec. 945, 552 N.E.2d 313 (Ill.App. 4 Dist.1990)—**p. 943, n. 7.**
Arvin, In re Marriage of, 184 Ill.App.3d 644, 133 Ill.Dec. 53, 540 N.E.2d 919 (Ill.App. 2 Dist.1989)—**750 ILCS 5/510, n. 11, 16.**
Ashby, In re Marriage of, 193 Ill.App.3d 366, 140 Ill.Dec. 272, 549 N.E.2d 923 (Ill.App. 5 Dist.1990)—**750 ILCS 5/607, n. 1.**
Atkinson v. Atkinson, 87 Ill.2d 174, 57 Ill.Dec. 567, 429 N.E.2d 465 (Ill.1981)—**750 ILCS 5/503, n. 5, 21.**
Azotea, In re Marriage of, 200 Ill.App.3d 182, 146 Ill.Dec. 587, 558 N.E.2d 550 (Ill.App. 4 Dist.1990)—**750 ILCS 5/511, n. 10.**

Baker v. Baker, 193 Ill.App.3d 294, 140 Ill.Dec. 303, 549 N.E.2d 954 (Ill.App. 4 Dist.1990)—**750 ILCS 5/505, n. 15, 16; 750 ILCS 5/511, n. 10.**
Baltzer, In re Marriage of, 150 Ill.App.3d 890, 104 Ill.Dec. 196, 502 N.E.2d 459 (Ill.App. 2 Dist.1986)—**750 ILCS 5/508, n. 6.**
Balzell, In re Marriage of, 207 Ill.App.3d 310, 152 Ill.Dec. 492, 566 N.E.2d 20 (Ill.App. 3 Dist.1991)—**750 ILCS 5/602, n. 2; 750 ILCS 5/604, n. 1; 750 ILCS 5/607, n. 3.**
Baptist, In re Marriage of, 232 Ill.App.3d 906, 174 Ill.Dec. 81, 598 N.E.2d 278 (Ill.App. 4 Dist.1992)—**750 ILCS 5/505, n. 6, 8, 10; 750 ILCS 5/510, n. 4.**
Bashwiner v. Bashwiner, 126 Ill.App.3d 365, 81 Ill.Dec. 359, 466 N.E.2d 1161 (Ill.App. 1 Dist.1984)—**750 ILCS 5/501, n. 12.**
Bass, In re Marriage of, 176 Ill.App.3d 249, 125 Ill.Dec. 559, 530 N.E.2d 717 (Ill.App. 3 Dist.1988)—**750 ILCS 35/4, n. 4, 7.**

TABLE OF CASES

Bates, In re Marriage of, 141 Ill.App.3d 566, 95 Ill.Dec. 922, 490 N.E.2d 1014 (Ill.App. 2 Dist.1986)—**750 ILCS 5/401, n. 4.**
Beardsley, People v., 115 Ill.2d 47, 104 Ill.Dec. 789, 503 N.E.2d 346 (Ill.1986)—**p. 960, n. 2.**
Bellow v. Bellow, 94 Ill.App.3d 361, 50 Ill.Dec. 656, 419 N.E.2d 924 (Ill.App. 1 Dist.1981)—**750 ILCS 5/508, n. 4.**
Bellow v. Bellow, 40 Ill.App.3d 442, 352 N.E.2d 427 (Ill.App. 1 Dist.1976)—**750 ILCS 5/502, n. 4, 5.**
Benkendorf, In re Marriage of, 252 Ill.App.3d 429, 191 Ill.Dec. 863, 624 N.E.2d 1241 (Ill.App. 1 Dist.1993)—**750 ILCS 5/503, n. 21, 28.**
Berk, In re Marriage of, 215 Ill.App.3d 459, 158 Ill.Dec. 971, 574 N.E.2d 1364 (Ill.App. 2 Dist.1991)—**750 ILCS 5/609, n. 2.**
Betts, In re Marriage of, 200 Ill.App.3d 26, 146 Ill.Dec. 441, 558 N.E.2d 404 (Ill.App. 4 Dist.1990)—**750 ILCS 5/511, n. 5.**
Bielby v. Bielby, 333 Ill. 478, 165 N.E. 231 (Ill.1929)—**750 ILCS 5/301, n. 2.**
Birt, In re Marriage of, 157 Ill.App.3d 363, 109 Ill.Dec. 691, 510 N.E.2d 559 (Ill.App. 2 Dist.1987)—**750 ILCS 5/2-1001, n. 2.**
Black, In re Marriage of, 155 Ill.App.3d 52, 107 Ill.Dec. 790, 507 N.E.2d 943 (Ill.App. 3 Dist.1987)—**750 ILCS 5/401, n. 11.**
Black, In re Marriage of, 133 Ill.App.3d 59, 87 Ill.Dec. 831, 477 N.E.2d 1359 (Ill.App. 2 Dist.1985)—**750 ILCS 5/502, n. 1.**
Bland v. Department of Children & Family Services, 141 Ill.App.3d 818, 96 Ill.Dec. 122, 490 N.E.2d 1327 (Ill.App. 3 Dist.1986)—**740 ILCS 110/10, n. 2.**
Blisset, In re Marriage of, 144 Ill.App.3d 1088, 99 Ill.Dec. 161, 495 N.E.2d 608 (Ill.App. 4 Dist.1986)—**750 ILCS 5/502, n. 2.**
Blisset v. Blisset, 123 Ill.2d 161, 121 Ill.Dec. 931, 526 N.E.2d 125 (Ill.1988)—**750 ILCS 5/505, n. 17; 750 ILCS 5/510, n. 1; 750 ILCS 5/511, n. 10.**
Bramson, In re Marriage of, 83 Ill.App.3d 657, 39 Ill.Dec. 85, 404 N.E.2d 469 (Ill.App. 1 Dist.1980)—**750 ILCS 5/510, n. 16.**
Brandon v. Caisse, 172 Ill.App.3d 841, 122 Ill.Dec. 746, 527 N.E.2d 118 (Ill.App. 2 Dist.1988)—**750 ILCS 5/401, n. 11.**
Brandt v. John S. Tilley Ladders Co., 145 Ill.App.3d 304, 99 Ill.Dec. 534, 495 N.E.2d 1269 (Ill.App. 1 Dist.1986)—**S.Ct. Rule 201, n. 5.**
Brenner, In re Marriage of, 235 Ill.App.3d 840, 176 Ill.Dec. 572, 601 N.E.2d 1270 (Ill.App. 1 Dist.1992)—**750 ILCS 5/503, n. 25, 28.**
Brenner, In re Marriage of, 95 Ill.App.3d 100, 50 Ill.Dec. 292, 419 N.E.2d 400 (Ill.App. 1 Dist.1981)—**750 ILCS 5/503, n. 21.**
Breyley, In re Marriage of, 247 Ill.App.3d 486, 187 Ill.Dec. 215, 617 N.E.2d 423 (Ill.App. 3 Dist.1993)—**750 ILCS 5/2-1401, n. 2; 750 ILCS 35/8, n. 1; 750 ILCS 35/9, n. 1.**
Britton, In re Marriage of, 141 Ill.App.3d 588, 96 Ill.Dec. 43, 490 N.E.2d 1079 (Ill.App. 5 Dist.1986)—**S.Ct. Rule 304, n. 2; 750 ILCS 5/401, n. 10.**
Brooks, In re Marriage of, 138 Ill.App.3d 252, 93 Ill.Dec. 166, 486 N.E.2d 267 (Ill.App. 1 Dist.1985)—**750 ILCS 5/503, n. 7, 20.**
Brown v. Farkas, 158 Ill.App.3d 772, 110 Ill.Dec. 823, 511 N.E.2d 1143 (Ill.App. 1 Dist.1986)—**750 ILCS 5/4, n. 2.**
Brown, People ex rel. Mathis v., 44 Ill.App.3d 783, 3 Ill.Dec. 475, 358 N.E.2d 1160 (Ill.App. 1 Dist.1976)—**p. 962, n. 1.**
Bueche, In re Marriage of, 193 Ill.App.3d 594, 140 Ill.Dec. 566, 550 N.E.2d 48 (Ill.App. 2 Dist.1990)—**750 ILCS 35/4, n. 1, 7.**
Bullard v. Bullard, 66 Ill.App.3d 132, 22 Ill.Dec. 876, 383 N.E.2d 684 (Ill.App. 5 Dist.1978)—**750 ILCS 5/11-102, n. 4.**
Burch, In re Marriage of, 205 Ill.App.3d 1082, 150 Ill.Dec. 922, 563 N.E.2d 1049 (Ill.App. 1 Dist.1990)—**750 ILCS 5/502, n. 4, 5.**
Burgess, In re Marriage of, 123 Ill.App.3d 487, 78 Ill.Dec. 345, 462 N.E.2d 203 (Ill.App. 3 Dist.1984)—**750 ILCS 5/503, n. 9.**
Burtell v. First Charter Service Corp., 76 Ill.2d 427, 31 Ill.Dec. 178, 394 N.E.2d 380 (Ill.1979)—**S.Ct. Rule 301, n. 1.**
Bush, In re Marriage of, 209 Ill.App.3d 671, 153 Ill.Dec. 851, 567 N.E.2d 1078 (Ill.App. 1 Dist.1991)—**750 ILCS 5/501, n. 14; 750 ILCS 5/503, n. 21.**
Bush, In re Marriage of, 191 Ill.App.3d 249, 138 Ill.Dec. 423, 547 N.E.2d 590 (Ill.App. 4 Dist.1989)—**750 ILCS 5/505, n. 6; 750 ILCS 5/602, n. 9; 750 ILCS 5/602.1, n. 3.**
Bush v. Turner, 129 Ill.2d 561, 140 Ill.Dec. 668, 550 N.E.2d 553 (Ill.1990)—**750 ILCS 5/505, n. 6.**

TABLE OF CASES

Bussey, In re Marriage of, 108 Ill.2d 286, 91 Ill.Dec. 594, 483 N.E.2d 1229 (Ill.1985)—**750 ILCS 5/510, n. 4.**
Butler, In re Marriage of, 106 Ill.App.3d 831, 62 Ill.Dec. 535, 436 N.E.2d 561 (Ill.App. 1 Dist.1982)—**750 ILCS 5/505, n. 2, 12.**
Byrne, In re Marriage of, 179 Ill.App.3d 944, 128 Ill.Dec. 800, 535 N.E.2d 14 (Ill.App. 1 Dist.1989)—**750 ILCS 5/503, n. 21; 750 ILCS 5/2-701, n. 1.**

Calisoff, In re, 92 B.R. 346 (Bkrtcy.N.D.Ill.1988)—**750 ILCS 5/508, n. 7; 11 U.S.C.A. § 523, n. 2, 3.**
Calisoff, In re Marriage of, 176 Ill.App.3d 721, 126 Ill.Dec. 183, 531 N.E.2d 810 (Ill.App. 1 Dist.1988)—**750 ILCS 5/513, n. 1.**
Caradonna, In re Marriage of, 197 Ill.App.3d 155, 143 Ill.Dec. 175, 553 N.E.2d 1161 (Ill.App. 2 Dist.1990)—**750 ILCS 5/510, n. 16.**
Carlisle v. Harp, 200 Ill.App.3d 908, 146 Ill.Dec. 355, 558 N.E.2d 318 (Ill.App. 5 Dist.1990)—**S.Ct. Rule 201, n. 4.**
Carlson, In re Marriage of, 186 Ill.App.3d 635, 134 Ill.Dec. 414, 542 N.E.2d 760 (Ill.App. 1 Dist.1989)—**750 ILCS 5/502, n. 6, 7.**
Carlson, In re Marriage of, 101 Ill.App.3d 924, 57 Ill.Dec. 325, 428 N.E.2d 1005 (Ill.App. 1 Dist.1981)—**750 ILCS 5/502, n. 3.**
Carlson v. Healey, 69 Ill.App.2d 236, 215 N.E.2d 831 (Ill.App.1966)—**S.Ct. Rule 206, n. 1.**
Carpel, In re Marriage of, 232 Ill.App.3d 806, 173 Ill.Dec. 873, 597 N.E.2d 847 (Ill.App. 4 Dist.1992)—**750 ILCS 5/504, n. 3; 750 ILCS 5/505, n. 12; 750 ILCS 5/510, n. 7.**
Carr, In re Marriage of, 221 Ill.App.3d 609, 164 Ill.Dec. 189, 582 N.E.2d 752 (Ill.App. 5 Dist.1991)—**750 ILCS 5/508, n. 3.**
Cecil, In re Marriage of, 202 Ill.App.3d 783, 148 Ill.Dec. 72, 560 N.E.2d 374 (Ill.App. 3 Dist.1990)—**750 ILCS 5/503, n. 1, 5, 7, 21; 750 ILCS 5/504, n. 4.**
Chaney v. Civil Service Commission, 82 Ill.2d 289, 45 Ill.Dec. 146, 412 N.E.2d 497 (Ill.1980)—**750 ILCS 5/21-101, n. 1.**
Cheger, In re Marriage of, 213 Ill.App.3d 371, 157 Ill.Dec. 116, 571 N.E.2d 1135 (Ill.App. 4 Dist.1991)—**750 ILCS 5/504, n. 1.**
Chenoweth, In re Marriage of, 134 Ill.App.3d 1015, 89 Ill.Dec. 922, 481 N.E.2d 765 (Ill.App. 5 Dist.1985)—**750 ILCS 5/510, n. 4.**
Chodzko v. Chodzko, 66 Ill.2d 28, 4 Ill.Dec. 313, 360 N.E.2d 60 (Ill.1976)—**750 ILCS 5/607, n. 3.**
Cierny, In re Marriage of, 187 Ill.App.3d 334, 134 Ill.Dec. 918, 543 N.E.2d 201 (Ill.App. 1 Dist.1989)—**750 ILCS 5/502, n. 1.**
Cohn, In re Marriage of, 94 Ill.App.3d 732, 50 Ill.Dec. 621, 419 N.E.2d 729 (Ill.App. 2 Dist.1981)—**750 ILCS 5/401, n. 10.**
Colombo, In re Marriage of, 197 Ill.App.3d 767, 144 Ill.Dec. 159, 555 N.E.2d 56 (Ill.App. 2 Dist.1990)—**750 ILCS 5/510, n. 5.**
Comiskey v. Comiskey, 48 Ill.App.3d 17, 8 Ill.Dec. 925, 366 N.E.2d 87 (Ill.App. 1 Dist.1977)—**750 ILCS 5/509, n .1.**
Commissioner v. _____ (see opposing party)
Conley v. McNamara, 334 Ill.App. 396, 79 N.E.2d 645 (Ill.App.1948)—**750 ILCS 5/2-203, n. 2.**
Cook, In re Marriage of, 117 Ill.App.3d 844, 73 Ill.Dec. 222, 453 N.E.2d 1357 (Ill.App. 1 Dist.1983)—**750 ILCS 5/503, n. 1, 11.**
Coons v. Wilder, 93 Ill.App.3d 127, 48 Ill.Dec. 512, 416 N.E.2d 785 (Ill.App. 2 Dist.1981)—**750 ILCS 5/510, n. 4.**
Couri v. Korn, 202 Ill.App.3d 848, 148 Ill.Dec. 77, 560 N.E.2d 379 (Ill.App. 3 Dist.1990)—**S.Ct. Rule 137, n. 1.**
Courtright, In re Marriage of, 229 Ill.App.3d 1089, 172 Ill.Dec. 258, 595 N.E.2d 619 (Ill.App. 3 Dist.1992)—**750 ILCS 5/504, n. 5; 750 ILCS 5/510, n. 7.**
Crawford v. Crawford, 39 Ill.App.3d 457, 350 N.E.2d 103 (Ill.App. 1 Dist.1976)—**750 ILCS 5/502, n. 6.**
Cross v. Cross, 5 Ill.2d 456, 125 N.E.2d 488 (Ill.1955)—**750 ILCS 5/503, n. 4.**
Cumbo v. Cumbo, 9 Ill.App.3d 1056, 293 N.E.2d 694 (Ill.App. 1 Dist.1973)—**750 ILCS 5/2-203, n. 2.**
Custody of Bozarth, In re, 182 Ill.App.3d 345, 131 Ill.Dec. 410, 538 N.E.2d 785 (Ill.App. 2 Dist.1989)—**750 ILCS 35/4, n. 3, 5.**
Custody of Carter, In re, 137 Ill.App.3d 439, 92 Ill.Dec. 320, 484 N.E.2d 1175 (Ill.App. 2 Dist.1985)—**750 ILCS 5/610, n. 1.**

TABLE OF CASES

Custody of Gonzalez, In re, 204 Ill.App.3d 28, 149 Ill.Dec. 580, 561 N.E.2d 1276 (Ill.App. 3 Dist.1990)—**750 ILCS 5/601, n. 1; 750 ILCS 5/602, n. 7.**

Custody of Peterson, In re, 112 Ill.2d 48, 96 Ill.Dec. 690, 491 N.E.2d 1150 (Ill.1986)—**750 ILCS 5/601, n. 1.**

Custody of Townsend, In re, 86 Ill.2d 502, 56 Ill.Dec. 685, 427 N.E.2d 1231 (Ill.1981)—**750 ILCS 5/601, n. 2.**

Custody of Williams, In re, 104 Ill.App.3d 16, 59 Ill.Dec. 791, 432 N.E.2d 375 (Ill.App. 3 Dist.1982)—**750 ILCS 5/602, n. 7.**

Dagher v. Dagher, 145 Ill.App.3d 379, 99 Ill.Dec. 269, 495 N.E.2d 1004 (Ill.App. 1 Dist.1986)—**750 ILCS 35/2, n. 1.**

Dall, In re Marriage of, 212 Ill.App.3d 85, 155 Ill.Dec. 520, 569 N.E.2d 1131 (Ill.App. 5 Dist.1991)—**750 ILCS 5/510, n. 4; 750 ILCS 5/511, n. 10.**

Dall, In re Marriage of, 191 Ill.App.3d 652, 138 Ill.Dec. 879, 548 N.E.2d 109 (Ill.App. 5 Dist.1989)—**750 ILCS 5/602, n. 9.**

Daubert v. Merrell Dow Pharmaceuticals, Inc., ___ U.S. ___, 113 S.Ct. 2786, 125 L.Ed.2d 469 (1993)—**p. 943, n. 7.**

Davis, In re Marriage of, 215 Ill.App.3d 763, 159 Ill.Dec. 375, 576 N.E.2d 44 (Ill.App. 1 Dist.1991)—**750 ILCS 5/503, n. 1, 2, 5, 15, 16, 21, 30.**

Davis v. United States, 370 U.S. 65, 82 S.Ct. 1190, 8 L.Ed.2d 335 (1962)—**26 U.S.C.A. § 1041, n. 4.**

Deahl v. Deahl, 13 Ill.App.3d 150, 300 N.E.2d 497 (Ill.App. 1 Dist.1973)—**750 ILCS 5/2-1401, n. 2.**

Dear v. Locke, 128 Ill.App.2d 356, 262 N.E.2d 27 (Ill.App.1970)—**S.Ct. Rule 301, n. 1.**

Debrey v. Debrey, 132 Ill.App.2d 1072, 270 N.E.2d 43 (Ill.App.1971)—**750 ILCS 5/503, n. 21.**

De Franco v. De Franco, 67 Ill.App.3d 760, 24 Ill.Dec. 130, 384 N.E.2d 997 (Ill.App. 1 Dist.1978)—**750 ILCS 5/602, n. 1.**

Deisenroth v. Dodge, 350 Ill.App. 20, 111 N.E.2d 575 (Ill.App.1953)—**750 ILCS 5/501, n. 8; 750 ILCS 5/11-102, n. 5.**

Derning, In re Marriage of, 117 Ill.App.3d 620, 72 Ill.Dec. 785, 453 N.E.2d 90 (Ill.App. 2 Dist.1983)—**S.Ct. Rule 304, n. 2; 750 ILCS 5/401, n. 10.**

De Rosa, In re Marriage of, 115 Ill.App.3d 774, 71 Ill.Dec. 525, 451 N.E.2d 13 (Ill.App. 1 Dist.1983)—**750 ILCS 5/501, n. 7.**

DeYoung v. DeYoung, 62 Ill.App.3d 837, 19 Ill.Dec. 732, 379 N.E.2d 396 (Ill.App. 3 Dist.1978)—**750 ILCS 5/604, n. 1.**

Diehl, In re Marriage of, 221 Ill.App.3d 410, 164 Ill.Dec. 73, 582 N.E.2d 281 (Ill.App. 2 Dist.1991)—**750 ILCS 5/602, n. 7.**

Dietrich v. Jones, 172 Ill.App.3d 201, 122 Ill.Dec. 191, 526 N.E.2d 450 (Ill.App. 1 Dist.1988)—**S.Ct. Rule 220, n. 11.**

Dile, In re Marriage of, 248 Ill.App.3d 683, 188 Ill.Dec. 595, 618 N.E.2d 1165 (Ill.App. 5 Dist.1993)—**750 ILCS 5/601, n. 1.**

Divarco, In re Marriage of, 167 Ill.App.3d 1014, 118 Ill.Dec. 949, 522 N.E.2d 619 (Ill.App. 1 Dist.1988)—**750 ILCS 5/502, n. 2.**

Dobkowski v. Lowe's, Inc., 20 Ill.App.3d 275, 314 N.E.2d 623 (Ill.App. 5 Dist.1974)—**S.Ct. Rule 212, n. 1.**

Dodds, In re Marriage of, 222 Ill.App.3d 99, 164 Ill.Dec. 692, 583 N.E.2d 608 (Ill.App. 2 Dist.1991)—**750 ILCS 5/505, n. 8.**

Doehner, In re Marriage of, 215 Ill.App.3d 570, 158 Ill.Dec. 987, 574 N.E.2d 1380 (Ill.App. 3 Dist.1991)—**750 ILCS 35/4, n. 3; 750 ILCS 35/8, n. 1.**

Dowd, In re Marriage of, 214 Ill.App.3d 156, 157 Ill.Dec. 894, 573 N.E.2d 312 (Ill.App. 2 Dist.1991)—**750 ILCS 5/401, n. 6.**

Drummond, In re Marriage of, 156 Ill.App.3d 672, 109 Ill.Dec. 46, 509 N.E.2d 707 (Ill.App. 4 Dist.1987)—**750 ILCS 5/503, n. 21.**

Druss, In re Marriage of, 226 Ill.App.3d 470, 168 Ill.Dec. 474, 589 N.E.2d 874 (Ill.App. 1 Dist.1992)—**750 ILCS 5/502, n. 4.**

Duncan v. Duncan, 94 Ill.App.3d 868, 50 Ill.Dec. 592, 419 N.E.2d 700 (Ill.App. 3 Dist.1981)—**750 ILCS 5/2-209, n. 1.**

Durante, In re Marriage of, 201 Ill.App.3d 376, 147 Ill.Dec. 56, 559 N.E.2d 56 (Ill.App. 1 Dist.1990)—**750 ILCS 5/503, n. 5, 16, 21; 750 ILCS 5/504, n. 3.**

TABLE OF CASES

Eckert, In re Marriage of, 119 Ill.2d 316, 116 Ill.Dec. 220, 518 N.E.2d 1041 (Ill.1988)—**750 ILCS 5/609, n. 2.**
Eddy, In re Marriage of, 210 Ill.App.3d 450, 155 Ill.Dec. 174, 569 N.E.2d 174 (Ill.App. 1 Dist.1991)—**750 ILCS 5/503, n. 1, 10, 21.**
Ehr v. Ehr, 77 Ill.App.3d 540, 33 Ill.Dec. 11, 396 N.E.2d 87 (Ill.App. 2 Dist.1979)—**750 ILCS 5/610, n. 1.**
Eldert, In re Marriage of, 158 Ill.App.3d 798, 110 Ill.Dec. 768, 511 N.E.2d 945 (Ill.App. 3 Dist.1987)—**750 ILCS 5/610, n. 1.**
Eleopoulos, In re Marriage of, 186 Ill.App.3d 374, 134 Ill.Dec. 326, 542 N.E.2d 505 (Ill.App. 4 Dist.1989)—**750 ILCS 5/610, n. 1.**
Emery, In re Marriage of, 179 Ill.App.3d 744, 128 Ill.Dec. 569, 534 N.E.2d 1014 (Ill.App. 4 Dist.1989)—**750 ILCS 5/504, n. 3.**
Erickson, In re Marriage of, 136 Ill.App.3d 907, 91 Ill.Dec. 346, 483 N.E.2d 692 (Ill.App. 2 Dist.1985)—**750 ILCS 5/510, n. 15.**
Evers v. Edward Hosp. Ass'n, 247 Ill.App.3d 717, 187 Ill.Dec. 490, 617 N.E.2d 1211 (Ill.App. 2 Dist.1993)—**S.Ct. Rule 201, n. 1.**
Eyler, People v., 133 Ill.2d 173, 139 Ill.Dec. 756, 549 N.E.2d 268 (Ill.1989)—**p. 943, n. 7.**

Fahy, In re Marriage of, 208 Ill.App.3d 677, 153 Ill.Dec. 594, 567 N.E.2d 552 (Ill.App. 1 Dist.1991)—**750 ILCS 5/602, n. 1.**
Falat, In re Marriage of, 201 Ill.App.3d 320, 147 Ill.Dec. 33, 559 N.E.2d 33 (Ill.App. 1 Dist.1990)—**750 ILCS 5/502, n. 1, 2, 16.**
Faris v. Faris, 142 Ill.App.3d 987, 97 Ill.Dec. 209, 492 N.E.2d 645 (Ill.App. 2 Dist.1986)—**750 ILCS 5/510, n. 5.**
Fazioli, In re Marriage of, 202 Ill.App.3d 245, 147 Ill.Dec. 495, 559 N.E.2d 835 (Ill.App. 1 Dist.1990)—**750 ILCS 5/510, n. 4, 5.**
Ferguson, In re Marriage of, 207 Ill.App.3d 649, 152 Ill.Dec. 648, 566 N.E.2d 335 (Ill.App. 1 Dist.1990)—**26 U.S.C.A. § 215, n. 22.**
Ferraro, In re Marriage of, 211 Ill.App.3d 797, 156 Ill.Dec. 160, 570 N.E.2d 636 (Ill.App. 1 Dist.1991)—**750 ILCS 5/505, n. 17; 750 ILCS 5/510, n. 17.**
Filko v. Filko, 127 Ill.App.2d 10, 262 N.E.2d 88 (Ill.App.1970)—**750 ILCS 5/502, n. 6.**
Finley v. Finley, 81 Ill.2d 317, 43 Ill.Dec. 12, 410 N.E.2d 12 (Ill.1980)—**750 ILCS 5/510, n. 17.**
Fiore v. City of Highland Park, 93 Ill.App.2d 24, 235 N.E.2d 23 (Ill.App.1968)—**750 ILCS 35/4, n. 2.**
Fischer, In re Marriage of, 228 Ill.App.3d 482, 170 Ill.Dec. 168, 592 N.E.2d 604 (Ill.App. 4 Dist.1992)—**750 ILCS 60/224, n. 2.**
Flemming, In re Marriage of, 143 Ill.App.3d 592, 97 Ill.Dec. 859, 493 N.E.2d 666 (Ill.App. 3 Dist.1986)—**750 ILCS 5/503, n. 21.**
Flynn v. Flynn, 232 Ill.App.3d 394, 173 Ill.Dec. 735, 597 N.E.2d 709 (Ill.App. 1 Dist.1992)—**750 ILCS 5/502, n. 1, 3.**
Forbes, In re Marriage of, 251 Ill.App.3d 133, 190 Ill.Dec. 543, 621 N.E.2d 996 (Ill.App. 4 Dist.1993)—**750 ILCS 5/503, n. 21.**
Ford, In re Marriage of, 91 Ill.App.3d 1066, 47 Ill.Dec. 541, 415 N.E.2d 546 (Ill.App. 1 Dist.1980)—**750 ILCS 5/602, n. 4.**
Foster, In re Marriage of, 115 Ill.App.3d 969, 71 Ill.Dec. 761, 451 N.E.2d 915 (Ill.App. 5 Dist.1983)—**750 ILCS 5/502, n. 3.**
Frazier, In re Marriage of, 205 Ill.App.3d 621, 151 Ill.Dec. 130, 563 N.E.2d 1236 (Ill.App. 3 Dist.1990)—**750 ILCS 5/505, n. 6.**
Frazier, In re Marriage of, 203 Ill.App.3d 847, 148 Ill.Dec. 854, 561 N.E.2d 160 (Ill.App. 5 Dist.1990)—**750 ILCS 5/2-1401, n. 1, 3.**
Frederick, In re Marriage of, 218 Ill.App.3d 533, 161 Ill.Dec. 254, 578 N.E.2d 612 (Ill.App. 2 Dist.1991)—**750 ILCS 5/504, n. 3.**
Freeman, In re Marriage of, 106 Ill.2d 290, 88 Ill.Dec. 11, 478 N.E.2d 326 (Ill.1985)—**750 ILCS 5/510, n. 1; 750 ILCS 5/510, n. 11, 12.**
Frus, In re Marriage of, 202 Ill.App.3d 844, 148 Ill.Dec. 240, 560 N.E.2d 638 (Ill.App. 3 Dist.1990)—**750 ILCS 5/510, n. 6, 7.**
Frye v. United States, 293 F. 1013 (D.C.Cir.1923)—**p. 943, n. 7.**
Fuesting, In re Marriage of, 228 Ill.App.3d 339, 169 Ill.Dec. 456, 591 N.E.2d 960 (Ill.App. 5 Dist.1992)—**750 ILCS 5/610, n. 1.**

Gainey v. Gainey, 237 Ill.App.3d 868, 178 Ill.Dec. 427, 604 N.E.2d 950 (Ill.App. 3 Dist.1992)—**750 ILCS 35/4, n. 5.**

TABLE OF CASES

Galindo v. Riddell, Inc., 107 Ill.App.3d 139, 62 Ill.Dec. 849, 437 N.E.2d 376 (Ill.App. 3 Dist. 1982)—**p. 943, n. 7.**

Galvin, In re Marriage of, 94 Ill.App.3d 1032, 50 Ill.Dec. 309, 419 N.E.2d 417 (Ill.App. 1 Dist.1981)—**750 ILCS 5/508, n. 1, 2.**

Gardner, People v., 47 Ill.App.3d 529, 5 Ill.Dec. 701, 362 N.E.2d 14 (Ill.App. 5 Dist.1977)—**p. 944, n. 1.**

Garlinski, In re Marriage of, 99 Ill.App.3d 107, 54 Ill.Dec. 510, 425 N.E.2d 22 (Ill.App. 2 Dist.1981)—**750 ILCS 5/401, n. 11.**

Garrison v. Garrison, 107 Ill.App.2d 311, 246 N.E.2d 9 (Ill.App.1969)—**750 ILCS 5/401, n. 1.**

Gasperini v. Gasperini, 57 Ill.App.3d 578, 15 Ill.Dec. 230, 373 N.E.2d 576 (Ill.App. 1 Dist.1978)—**750 ILCS 5/508, n. 4.**

Geis, In re Marriage of, 159 Ill.App.3d 975, 111 Ill.Dec. 717, 512 N.E.2d 1354 (Ill.App. 1 Dist.1987)—**750 ILCS 5/510, n. 4.**

Giammerino, In re Marriage of, 94 Ill.App.3d 1058, 50 Ill.Dec. 490, 419 N.E.2d 598 (Ill.App. 1 Dist.1981)—**S.Ct. Rule 301, n. 1.**

Gigele, In re Estate of, 64 Ill.App.3d 136, 20 Ill.Dec. 935, 380 N.E.2d 1144 (Ill.App. 1 Dist.1978)—**750 ILCS 10/7, n. 5.**

Girrulat, In re Marriage of, 219 Ill.App.3d 164, 161 Ill.Dec. 734, 578 N.E.2d 1380 (Ill.App. 5 Dist.1991)—**750 ILCS 5/508, n. 4.**

Glater v. Fabianich, 252 Ill.App.3d 372, 192 Ill.Dec. 136, 625 N.E.2d 96 (Ill.App. 1 Dist.1993)—**750 ILCS 60/221, n. 4.**

Glessner, In re Marriage of, 119 Ill.App.3d 306, 74 Ill.Dec. 809, 456 N.E.2d 311 (Ill.App. 1 Dist.1983)—**750 ILCS 5/503, n. 36; 750 ILCS 5/504, n. 2; 750 ILCS 5/514, n. 3.**

Glickman, In re Marriage of, 211 Ill.App.3d 792, 156 Ill.Dec. 162, 570 N.E.2d 638 (Ill.App. 1 Dist.1991)—**750 ILCS 5/502, n. 2, 16; 750 ILCS 5/510, n. 1, 4.**

Gocal, In re Marriage of, 216 Ill.App.3d 221, 159 Ill.Dec. 1023, 576 N.E.2d 946 (Ill.App. 1 Dist.1991)—**750 ILCS 5/607, n. 1.**

Goldman, In re Marriage of, 196 Ill.App.3d 785, 143 Ill.Dec. 944, 554 N.E.2d 1016 (Ill.App. 1 Dist.1990)—**750 ILCS 5/603, n. 1.**

Gordon, In re Marriage of, 233 Ill.App.3d 617, 175 Ill.Dec. 137, 599 N.E.2d 1151 (Ill.App. 1 Dist.1992)—**p. 964, n. 2.**

Gorsich, In re Marriage of, 208 Ill.App.3d 852, 153 Ill.Dec. 643, 567 N.E.2d 601 (Ill.App. 2 Dist.1991)—**S.Ct. Rule 220, n. 4.**

Gottemoller v. Gottemoller, 37 Ill.App.3d 689, 346 N.E.2d 393 (Ill.App. 3 Dist.1976)—**740 ILCS 110/10, n. 1.**

Graff v. Graff, 71 Ill.App.3d 496, 27 Ill.Dec. 798, 389 N.E.2d 1206 (Ill.App. 1 Dist.1979)—**750 ILCS 5/301, n. 1.**

Graham v. Graham, 44 Ill.App.3d 519, 3 Ill.Dec. 141, 358 N.E.2d 308 (Ill.App. 5 Dist.1976)—**750 ILCS 5/401, n. 3; 750 ILCS 5/402, n. 1.**

Gratz, In re Marriage of, 193 Ill.App.3d 142, 139 Ill.Dec. 611, 548 N.E.2d 1325 (Ill.App. 2 Dist.1989)—**750 ILCS 5/609, n. 1, 2, 3.**

Grauer, In re Marriage of, 133 Ill.App.3d 1019, 88 Ill.Dec. 962, 479 N.E.2d 982 (Ill.App. 1 Dist.1985)—**750 ILCS 5/501, n. 7.**

Gray v. Gray, 57 Ill.App.3d 1, 14 Ill.Dec. 630, 372 N.E.2d 909 (Ill.App. 1 Dist.1978)—**750 ILCS 5/609, n. 3.**

Greiman v. Friedman, 90 Ill.App.3d 941, 46 Ill.Dec. 355, 414 N.E.2d 77 (Ill.App. 1 Dist.1980)—**750 ILCS 5/513, n. 1.**

Guerra, In re Marriage of, 153 Ill.App.3d 550, 106 Ill.Dec. 201, 505 N.E.2d 748 (Ill.App. 2 Dist.1987)—**750 ILCS 5/503, n. 16.**

Gunn, In re Marriage of, 233 Ill.App.3d 165, 174 Ill.Dec. 381, 598 N.E.2d 1013 (Ill.App. 5 Dist.1992)—**750 ILCS 5/504, n. 3; 750 ILCS 5/510, n. 7.**

Guntren, In re Marriage of, 141 Ill.App.3d 1, 95 Ill.Dec. 392, 489 N.E.2d 1120 (Ill.App. 4 Dist.1986)—**750 ILCS 5/503, n. 15, 21, 32.**

Gurin, In re Marriage of, 212 Ill.App.3d 806, 156 Ill.Dec. 877, 571 N.E.2d 857 (Ill.App. 1 Dist.1991)—**750 ILCS 5/502, n. 2, 4; 750 ILCS 10/7, n. 6.**

Gustafson, In re Marriage of, 187 Ill.App.3d 551, 135 Ill.Dec. 192, 543 N.E.2d 575 (Ill.App. 4 Dist.1989)—**750 ILCS 5/602, n. 12.**

Haas, In re, 129 B.R. 531 (Bkrtcy.N.D.Ill.1989)—**11 U.S.C.A. § 523, n. 2.**

TABLE OF CASES

Haas, In re Marriage of, 215 Ill.App.3d 959, 158 Ill.Dec. 983, 574 N.E.2d 1376 (Ill.App. 3 Dist.1991)—**750 ILCS 5/504, n. 1, 3, 5; 750 ILCS 5/508, n. 3.**

Hacker, In re Marriage of, 239 Ill.App.3d 658, 179 Ill.Dec. 816, 606 N.E.2d 648 (Ill.App. 4 Dist.1992)—**750 ILCS 5/602.1, n. 3.**

Hagshenas, In re Marriage of, 234 Ill.App.3d 178, 175 Ill.Dec. 506, 600 N.E.2d 437 (Ill.App. 2 Dist.1992)—**750 ILCS 5/503, n. 18, 21.**

Halas, In re Marriage of, 173 Ill.App.3d 218, 123 Ill.Dec. 11, 527 N.E.2d 474 (Ill.App. 1 Dist.1988)—**750 ILCS 5/2-1401, n. 2, 3.**

Hansel, In re, 1992 WL 280799 (N.D.Ill.1992)—**11 U.S.C.A. 523, n. 2.**

Harding, In re Marriage of, 189 Ill.App.3d 663, 136 Ill.Dec. 935, 545 N.E.2d 459 (Ill.App. 1 Dist.1989)—**750 ILCS 5/503, n. 21.**

Harding v. Harding, 180 Ill. 481, 54 N.E. 587 (Ill.1899)—**750 ILCS 5/508, n. 1.**

Haring v. Haring, 125 Ill.App.2d 116, 260 N.E.2d 396 (Ill.App.1970)—**750 ILCS 5/403, n. 2.**

Harlow, In re Marriage of, 251 Ill.App.3d 152, 190 Ill.Dec. 476, 621 N.E.2d 929 (Ill.App. 4 Dist.1993)—**750 ILCS 5/504, n. 3.**

Harmon, In re Marriage of, 210 Ill.App.3d 92, 154 Ill.Dec. 727, 568 N.E.2d 948 (Ill.App. 2 Dist.1991)—**750 ILCS 5/505, n. 8.**

Harner v. Harner, 105 Ill.App.3d 430, 61 Ill.Dec. 312, 434 N.E.2d 465 (Ill.App. 1 Dist.1982)—**750 ILCS 5/510, n. 4.**

Harris, In re Marriage of, 203 Ill.App.3d 241, 148 Ill.Dec. 541, 560 N.E.2d 1138 (Ill.App. 1 Dist.1990)—**750 ILCS 5/510, n. 15.**

Harris v. Minardi, 74 Ill.App.2d 262, 220 N.E.2d 39 (Ill.App.1966)—**S.Ct. Rule 215, n. 3.**

Hart, In re Marriage of, 194 Ill.App.3d 839, 141 Ill.Dec. 550, 551 N.E.2d 737 (Ill.App. 4 Dist.1990)—**750 ILCS 5/505, n. 9.**

Hartian, In re Marriage of, 222 Ill.App.3d 566, 165 Ill.Dec. 66, 584 N.E.2d 245 (Ill.App. 1 Dist.1991)—**750 ILCS 5/511, n. 10; 750 ILCS 5/2-1001, n. 2.**

Hartman v. Hartman, 89 Ill.App.3d 969, 45 Ill.Dec. 360, 412 N.E.2d 711 (Ill.App. 4 Dist.1980)—**750 ILCS 5/506, n. 1.**

Harvey, In re Marriage of, 136 Ill.App.3d 116, 91 Ill.Dec. 115, 483 N.E.2d 397 (Ill.App. 3 Dist.1985)—**750 ILCS 5/505, n. 14.**

Harwell v. Harwell, 233 Ga. 89, 209 S.E.2d 625 (Ga.1974)—**750 ILCS 5/401, n. 4.**

Havens, In re Marriage of, 213 Ill.App.3d 151, 156 Ill.Dec. 737, 571 N.E.2d 521 (Ill.App. 3 Dist.1991)—**750 ILCS 5/511, n. 3, 5.**

Hawking, In re Marriage of, 240 Ill.App.3d 419, 181 Ill.Dec. 254, 608 N.E.2d 327 (Ill.App. 1 Dist.1992)—**750 ILCS 5/510, n. 1.**

Hawkins v. Hawkins, 102 Ill.App.3d 1037, 58 Ill.Dec. 620, 430 N.E.2d 652 (Ill.App. 3 Dist.1981)—**750 ILCS 5/607, n. 3.**

Hazard, In re Marriage of, 167 Ill.App.3d 61, 117 Ill.Dec. 770, 520 N.E.2d 1121 (Ill.App. 1 Dist.1988)—**750 ILCS 5/605, n. 1; p. 943, n. 7.**

Hazel, In re Marriage of, 219 Ill.App.3d 920, 162 Ill.Dec. 451, 579 N.E.2d 1265 (Ill.App. 5 Dist.1991)—**750 ILCS 5/503, n. 21.**

Head v. Head, 168 Ill.App.3d 697, 119 Ill.Dec. 549, 523 N.E.2d 17 (Ill.App. 1 Dist.1988)—**750 ILCS 5/503, n. 21.**

Heady, In re Marriage of, 115 Ill.App.3d 126, 71 Ill.Dec. 27, 450 N.E.2d 462 (Ill.App. 5 Dist.1983)—**750 ILCS 5/104, n. 3.**

Healy, In re Marriage of, 263 Ill.App.3d 596, 200 Ill.Dec. 327, 635 N.E.2d 666 (Ill.App. 1 Dist.1994)—**750 ILCS 60/221, n. 4.**

Heggy v. Heggy, 944 F.2d 1537 (10th Cir.1991)—**p. 961, n. 2.**

Heil, In re Marriage of, 233 Ill.App.3d 888, 174 Ill.Dec. 622, 599 N.E.2d 168 (Ill.App. 5 Dist.1992)—**750 ILCS 5/510, n. 1, 3, 4.**

Hellwig v. Hellwig, 100 Ill.App.3d 452, 55 Ill.Dec. 762, 426 N.E.2d 1087 (Ill.App. 1 Dist.1981)—**750 ILCS 5/2-1501, n. 1.**

Henry, In re Marriage of, 156 Ill.2d 541, 190 Ill.Dec. 773, 622 N.E.2d 803 (Ill.1993)—**750 ILCS 5/510, n. 17.**

Hensley, In re Marriage of, 210 Ill.App.3d 1043, 155 Ill.Dec. 486, 569 N.E.2d 1097 (Ill.App. 4 Dist.1991)—**750 ILCS 5/504, n. 3.**

Henzler, In re Marriage of, 134 Ill.App.3d 318, 89 Ill.Dec. 261, 480 N.E.2d 147 (Ill.App. 4 Dist.1985)—**750 ILCS 5/510, n. 7.**

Herkert, In re Marriage of, 245 Ill.App.3d 1068, 186 Ill.Dec. 29, 615 N.E.2d 833 (Ill.App. 4 Dist.1993)—**750 ILCS 5/511, n. 3.**

TABLE OF CASES

Herrin, In re Marriage of, 262 Ill.App.3d 573, 199 Ill.Dec. 814, 634 N.E.2d 1168 (Ill.App. 4 Dist.1994)—**750 ILCS 5/510, n. 16.**
Hess v. Hess, 87 Ill.App.3d 947, 42 Ill.Dec. 882, 409 N.E.2d 497 (Ill.App. 3 Dist.1980)—**750 ILCS 5/607, n. 4.**
Hester v. Goldsbury, 64 Ill.App.2d 66, 212 N.E.2d 316 (Ill.App.1965)—**p. 944, n. 1.**
Hewitt v. Hewitt, 77 Ill.2d 49, 31 Ill.Dec. 827, 394 N.E.2d 1204 (Ill.1979)—**750 ILCS 5/214, n. 1.**
Heyman v. Heyman, 548 F.Supp. 1041 (D.C.Ill.1982)—**750 ILCS 65/1, n. 1.**
Hilkovitch, In re Marriage of, 124 Ill.App.3d 401, 79 Ill.Dec. 891, 464 N.E.2d 795 (Ill.App. 1 Dist.1984)—**S.Ct. Rule 301, n. 1; 750 ILCS 5/505, n. 14; 750 ILCS 5/511, n. 5.**
Hill v. Ben Franklin Sav. & Loan Ass'n, 177 Ill.App.3d 51, 126 Ill.Dec. 462, 531 N.E.2d 1089 (Ill.App. 2 Dist.1988)—**S.Ct. Rule 220, n. 10.**
Hilliard, In re Marriage of, 178 Ill.App.3d 620, 127 Ill.Dec. 671, 533 N.E.2d 543 (Ill.App. 3 Dist.1989)—**750 ILCS 35/8, n. 1.**
Hindenburg, In re Marriage of, 227 Ill.App.3d 228, 169 Ill.Dec. 187, 591 N.E.2d 67 (Ill.App. 2 Dist.1992)—**750 ILCS 5/604, n. 1.**
Hobson, In re Marriage of, 220 Ill.App.3d 1006, 163 Ill.Dec. 437, 581 N.E.2d 388 (Ill.App. 4 Dist.1991)—**750 ILCS 5/503, n. 33.**
Hoffman v. City of Evanston, 101 Ill.App.2d 440, 243 N.E.2d 478 (Ill.App.1968)—**750 ILCS 5/11-106, n. 1.**
Hofstetter, In re Marriage of, 102 Ill.App.3d 392, 58 Ill.Dec. 137, 430 N.E.2d 79 (Ill.App. 1 Dist.1981)—**750 ILCS 5/701, n. 1.**
Hollo v. Hollo, 131 Ill.App.3d 119, 85 Ill.Dec. 867, 474 N.E.2d 827 (Ill.App. 5 Dist.1985)—**750 ILCS 35/4, n. 3, 4, 5.**
Hunter, In re Marriage of, 223 Ill.App.3d 947, 166 Ill.Dec. 242, 585 N.E.2d 1264 (Ill.App. 2 Dist.1992)—**750 ILCS 5/503, n. 5.**
Hutchinson v. Bambas, 249 Ill. 624, 94 N.E. 987 (Ill.1911)—**S.Ct. Rule 211, n. 1.**

Ingram, In re Marriage of, 185 Ill.App.3d 395, 133 Ill.Dec. 520, 541 N.E.2d 731 (Ill.App. 5 Dist.1989)—**750 ILCS 5/510, n. 5.**
Ingrassia, In re Marriage of, 140 Ill.App.3d 826, 95 Ill.Dec. 165, 489 N.E.2d 386 (Ill.App. 2 Dist.1986)—**750 ILCS 5/505, n. 3.**
In Interest of Armell, 194 Ill.App.3d 31, 141 Ill.Dec. 14, 550 N.E.2d 1060 (Ill.App. 1 Dist.1990)—**750 ILCS 50/0.01, n. 4.**
In Interest of Austin, 61 Ill.App.3d 344, 19 Ill.Dec. 37, 378 N.E.2d 538 (Ill.App. 1 Dist.1978)—**750 ILCS 50/0.01, n. 3.**
In re (see name of party)
Interstate Bank of Oak Forest v. Cardona, 167 Ill.App.3d 214, 118 Ill.Dec. 72, 521 N.E.2d 140 (Ill.App. 3 Dist.1988)—**750 ILCS 5/703, n. 1.**
Irvine, In re Marriage of, 215 Ill.App.3d 629, 160 Ill.Dec. 332, 577 N.E.2d 462 (Ill.App. 4 Dist.1991)—**750 ILCS 5/508, n. 9.**

Jacks, In re Marriage of, 200 Ill.App.3d 112, 146 Ill.Dec. 143, 558 N.E.2d 106 (Ill.App. 2 Dist.1990)—**750 ILCS 5/503, n. 6, 21.**
Jansen, People v., 203 Ill.App.3d 985, 149 Ill.Dec. 34, 561 N.E.2d 312 (Ill.App. 5 Dist.1990)—**p. 960, n. 2.**
Jaster, In re Marriage of, 222 Ill.App.3d 122, 164 Ill.Dec. 743, 583 N.E.2d 659 (Ill.App. 2 Dist.1991)—**750 ILCS 5/501, n. 6.**
Jelinek, In re Marriage of, 244 Ill.App.3d 496, 184 Ill.Dec. 692, 613 N.E.2d 1284 (Ill.App. 1 Dist.1993)—**750 ILCS 5/503, n. 7.**
Jessee v. Amoco Oil Co., 230 Ill.App.3d 337, 171 Ill.Dec. 690, 594 N.E.2d 1210 (Ill.App. 1 Dist.1992)—**S.Ct. Rule 220, n. 10.**
Joerger, In re Marriage of, 221 Ill.App.3d 400, 163 Ill.Dec. 796, 581 N.E.2d 1219 (Ill.App. 4 Dist.1991)—**750 ILCS 5/501, n. 7, 8, 10.**
Johnson, In re Marriage of, 215 Ill.App.3d 174, 158 Ill.Dec. 742, 574 N.E.2d 855 (Ill.App. 4 Dist.1991)—**750 ILCS 5/510, n. 16.**
Johnson, In re Marriage of, 209 Ill.App.3d 1025, 154 Ill.Dec. 706, 568 N.E.2d 927 (Ill.App. 3 Dist.1991)—**750 ILCS 5/510, n. 4.**
Johnson v. Frontier Ford, Inc., 68 Ill.App.3d 315, 24 Ill.Dec. 908, 386 N.E.2d 112 (Ill.App. 2 Dist.1979)—**S.Ct. Rule 201, n. 1; 750 ILCS 5/404, n. 1.**
Johnson v. La Grange State Bank, 73 Ill.2d 342, 22 Ill.Dec. 709, 383 N.E.2d 185 (Ill.1978)—**750 ILCS 10/1, n. 1.**

TABLE OF CASES

Jones, In re Marriage of, 187 Ill.App.3d 206, 134 Ill.Dec. 836, 543 N.E.2d 119 (Ill.App. 1 Dist.1989)—**750 ILCS 5/504, n. 2; 750 ILCS 5/508, n. 4.**

Jones, In re Marriage of, 104 Ill.App.3d 490, 60 Ill.Dec. 214, 432 N.E.2d 1113 (Ill.App. 1 Dist.1982)—**750 ILCS 5/104, n. 2.**

Kaiser, People v., 239 Ill.App.3d 295, 179 Ill.Dec. 863, 606 N.E.2d 695 (Ill.App. 2 Dist.1992)—**740 ILCS 110/10, n. 4.**

Kamp, In re Marriage of, 199 Ill.App.3d 1080, 146 Ill.Dec. 57, 557 N.E.2d 999 (Ill.App. 3 Dist.1990)—**750 ILCS 5/503, n. 10.**

Kanner, People ex rel. Schejbal v., 54 Ill.App.2d 208, 203 N.E.2d 759 (Ill.App.1964)—**S.Ct. Rule 231, n. 1.**

Kaplan v. Kaplan, 25 Ill.2d 181, 182 N.E.2d 706 (Ill.1962)—**750 ILCS 10/7, n. 5.**

Kapp v. Alexander, 218 Ill.App.3d 412, 161 Ill.Dec. 158, 578 N.E.2d 285 (Ill.App. 3 Dist.1991)—**750 ILCS 5/601, n. 3.**

Karr v. Noel, 212 Ill.App.3d 575, 156 Ill.Dec. 684, 571 N.E.2d 271 (Ill.App. 5 Dist.1991)—**S.Ct. Rule 220, n. 10.**

Keating v. Dominick's Finer Foods, Inc., 224 Ill.App.3d 981, 167 Ill.Dec. 175, 587 N.E.2d 57 (Ill.App. 2 Dist.1992)—**S.Ct. Rule 220, n. 1.**

Kehres, In re Marriage of, 164 Ill.App.3d 148, 115 Ill.Dec. 206, 517 N.E.2d 617 (Ill.App. 5 Dist.1987)—**750 ILCS 35/4, n. 6.**

Kelly v. Warner, 119 Ill.App.3d 217, 77 Ill.Dec. 273, 460 N.E.2d 329 (Ill.App. 3 Dist.1983)—**750 ILCS 35/4, n. 2.**

Kenik, In re Marriage of, 181 Ill.App.3d 266, 129 Ill.Dec. 932, 536 N.E.2d 982 (Ill.App. 1 Dist.1989)—**750 ILCS 5/401, n. 6, 10.**

Kennedy, In re Marriage of, 214 Ill.App.3d 849, 158 Ill.Dec. 172, 573 N.E.2d 1357 (Ill.App. 1 Dist.1991)—**750 ILCS 5/508, n. 1.**

Kennedy, In re Marriage of, 170 Ill.App.3d 726, 121 Ill.Dec. 362, 525 N.E.2d 168 (Ill.App. 5 Dist.1988)—**750 ILCS 5/513, n. 1.**

Kennedy, In re Marriage of, 94 Ill.App.3d 537, 49 Ill.Dec. 927, 418 N.E.2d 947 (Ill.App. 1 Dist.1981)—**750 ILCS 5/602, n. 9.**

Keown, In re Marriage of, 225 Ill.App.3d 808, 167 Ill.Dec. 375, 587 N.E.2d 644 (Ill.App. 4 Dist.1992)—**750 ILCS 5/505, n. 6.**

Kerber, In re Marriage of, 215 Ill.App.3d 248, 158 Ill.Dec. 717, 574 N.E.2d 830 (Ill.App. 4 Dist.1991)—**750 ILCS 5/504, n. 1, 3.**

Kern, In re Marriage of, 245 Ill.App.3d 575, 185 Ill.Dec. 843, 615 N.E.2d 402 (Ill.App. 4 Dist.1993)—**750 ILCS 5/510, n. 4.**

Kessler, In re Marriage of, 110 Ill.App.3d 61, 65 Ill.Dec. 707, 441 N.E.2d 1221 (Ill.App. 1 Dist.1982)—**750 ILCS 5/510, n. 1, 4.**

King v. King, 52 Ill.App.3d 749, 10 Ill.Dec. 592, 367 N.E.2d 1358 (Ill.App. 4 Dist.1977)—**p. 964, n. 2.**

Kirkwood v. Checker Taxi Co., 12 Ill.App.3d 129, 298 N.E.2d 233 (Ill.App. 1 Dist.1973)—**S.Ct. Rule 213, n. 2.**

Klein, In re Marriage of, 231 Ill.App.3d 901, 173 Ill.Dec. 335, 596 N.E.2d 1214 (Ill.App. 4 Dist.1992)—**750 ILCS 5/504, n. 3; 750 ILCS 5/510, n. 16.**

Kocal v. Holt, 229 Ill.App.3d 1023, 172 Ill.Dec. 106, 595 N.E.2d 169 (Ill.App. 3 Dist.1992)—**750 ILCS 5/602.1, n. 3.**

Koch, In re Marriage of, 119 Ill.App.3d 388, 74 Ill.Dec. 923, 456 N.E.2d 644 (Ill.App. 2 Dist.1983)—**S.Ct. Rule 304, n. 2; 750 ILCS 5/401, n. 10.**

Kolb v. Kolb, 99 Ill.App.3d 895, 55 Ill.Dec. 128, 425 N.E.2d 1301 (Ill.App. 1 Dist.1981)—**750 ILCS 5/510, n. 15.**

Kopec, In re Marriage of, 106 Ill.App.3d 1060, 62 Ill.Dec. 658, 436 N.E.2d 684 (Ill.App. 1 Dist.1982)—**750 ILCS 5/405, n. 2.**

Korte, In re Marriage of, 193 Ill.App.3d 243, 140 Ill.Dec. 255, 549 N.E.2d 906 (Ill.App. 4 Dist.1990)—**750 ILCS 5/513, n. 2.**

Kosinski v. Inland Steel Co., 192 Ill.App.3d 1017, 140 Ill.Dec. 133, 549 N.E.2d 784 (Ill.App. 1 Dist.1989)—**S.Ct. Rule 220, n. 11.**

Kosterka, In re Marriage of, 174 Ill.App.3d 954, 124 Ill.Dec. 295, 529 N.E.2d 12 (Ill.App. 2 Dist.1988)—**750 ILCS 5/508, n. 4.**

Kruse, In re Marriage of, 92 Ill.App.3d 335, 48 Ill.Dec. 145, 416 N.E.2d 40 (Ill.App. 1 Dist.1980)—**750 ILCS 5/508, n. 4.**

Kuhn, In re Marriage of, 221 Ill.App.3d 1, 163 Ill.Dec. 429, 581 N.E.2d 380 (Ill.App. 2 Dist.1991)—**750 ILCS 5/513, n. 2.**

TABLE OF CASES

Kujawinski v. Kujawinski, 71 Ill.2d 563, 17 Ill.Dec. 801, 376 N.E.2d 1382 (Ill.1978)—**750 ILCS 5/503, n. 22.**

Kush, In re Marriage of, 106 Ill.App.3d 233, 62 Ill.Dec. 123, 435 N.E.2d 921 (Ill.App. 3 Dist.1982)—**750 ILCS 5/514, n. 2.**

Kusper, In re Marriage of, 195 Ill.App.3d 494, 142 Ill.Dec. 282, 552 N.E.2d 1023 (Ill.App. 1 Dist.1990)—**750 ILCS 5/504, n. 3.**

Lambdin, In re Marriage of, 245 Ill.App.3d 797, 184 Ill.Dec. 789, 613 N.E.2d 1381 (Ill.App. 4 Dist.1993)—**750 ILCS 5/510, n. 16.**

Landfield, In re Marriage of, 209 Ill.App.3d 678, 153 Ill.Dec. 834, 567 N.E.2d 1061 (Ill.App. 1 Dist.1991)—**750 ILCS 5/503, n. 10, 15, 21; 750 ILCS 5/508, n. 4.**

Landwehr, In re Marriage of, 225 Ill.App.3d 149, 167 Ill.Dec. 260, 587 N.E.2d 529 (Ill.App. 1 Dist.1992)—**750 ILCS 5/503, n. 21.**

Larsen v. Larsen, 126 Ill.App.3d 1072, 82 Ill.Dec. 103, 468 N.E.2d 165 (Ill.App. 3 Dist.1984)—**750 ILCS 5/513, n. 3.**

Lasota, In re Marriage of, 125 Ill.App.3d 37, 80 Ill.Dec. 537, 465 N.E.2d 649 (Ill.App. 1 Dist.1984)—**750 ILCS 5/510, n. 3.**

Lavaja v. Carter, 153 Ill.App.3d 317, 106 Ill.Dec. 147, 505 N.E.2d 694 (Ill.App. 2 Dist.1987)—**p. 964, n. 3; S.Ct. Rule 201, n. 5.**

Lavelle, In re Marriage of, 206 Ill.App.3d 607, 152 Ill.Dec. 49, 565 N.E.2d 291 (Ill.App. 5 Dist.1990)—**750 ILCS 5/511, n. 3, 9.**

Lee v. Ingalls Memorial Hosp., 238 Ill.App.3d 154, 179 Ill.Dec. 328, 606 N.E.2d 160 (Ill.App. 1 Dist.1992)—**S.Ct. Rule 220, n. 12.**

Lees, In re Marriage of, 224 Ill.App.3d 691, 167 Ill.Dec. 135, 587 N.E.2d 17 (Ill.App. 3 Dist.1992)—**750 ILCS 5/503, n. 19, 31.**

Leff, In re Marriage of, 148 Ill.App.3d 792, 102 Ill.Dec. 262, 499 N.E.2d 1042 (Ill.App. 2 Dist.1986)—**750 ILCS 5/402, n. 4.**

Legan v. Legan, 69 Ill.App.3d 304, 25 Ill.Dec. 757, 387 N.E.2d 413 (Ill.App. 3 Dist.1979)—**750 ILCS 5/510, n. 3, 4.**

Lehr, In re Marriage of, 217 Ill.App.3d 929, 160 Ill.Dec. 840, 578 N.E.2d 19 (Ill.App. 1 Dist.1991)—**750 ILCS 5/508, n. 3; 750 ILCS 5/510, n. 5.**

Leisner, In re Marriage of, 219 Ill.App.3d 752, 162 Ill.Dec. 277, 579 N.E.2d 1091 (Ill.App. 1 Dist.1991)—**750 ILCS 5/503, n. 6, 10, 16.**

Lenkner, In re Marriage of, 241 Ill.App.3d 15, 181 Ill.Dec. 646, 608 N.E.2d 897 (Ill.App. 4 Dist.1993)—**750 ILCS 5/504, n. 2.**

Lentz, In re Marriage of, 73 Ill.App.3d 93, 29 Ill.Dec. 319, 391 N.E.2d 582 (Ill.App. 4 Dist.1979)—**750 ILCS 5/413, n. 1.**

Leopando, In re Marriage of, 96 Ill.2d 114, 70 Ill.Dec. 263, 449 N.E.2d 137 (Ill.1983)—**S.Ct. Rule 304, n. 2; 750 ILCS 5/401, n. 10.**

Lester, Commissioner v., 366 U.S. 299, 81 S.Ct. 1343, 6 L.Ed.2d 306 (1961)—**26 U.S.C.A. § 215, n. 5.**

Levy v. Levy, 105 Ill.App.3d 355, 61 Ill.Dec. 247, 434 N.E.2d 400 (Ill.App. 1 Dist.1982)—**750 ILCS 35/2, n. 1; 750 ILCS 35/4, n. 1, 4.**

Levy v. Levy, 388 Ill. 179, 57 N.E.2d 366 (Ill.1944)—**750 ILCS 5/403, n. 2.**

Lewis, In re Marriage of, 188 Ill.App.3d 142, 135 Ill.Dec. 667, 544 N.E.2d 24 (Ill.App. 5 Dist.1989)—**750 ILCS 5/610, n. 3.**

Lewis v. Canty, 115 Ill.App.3d 306, 71 Ill.Dec. 176, 450 N.E.2d 864 (Ill.App. 1 Dist.1983)—**750 ILCS 35/4, n. 5.**

Lewis v. West Side Trust & Savings Bank, 286 Ill.App. 130, 2 N.E.2d 976 (Ill.App.1936)—**750 ILCS 5/2-203, n. 2.**

Lewy v. Koeckritz Intern., Inc., 211 Ill.App.3d 330, 155 Ill.Dec. 848, 570 N.E.2d 361 (Ill.App. 1 Dist.1991)—**S.Ct. Rule 137, n. 1.**

Lindsey, In re Marriage of, 158 Ill.App.3d 769, 110 Ill.Dec. 363, 511 N.E.2d 198 (Ill.App. 4 Dist.1987)—**750 ILCS 5/607, n. 3.**

Lindsey v. Chicago Park Dist., 134 Ill.App.3d 744, 89 Ill.Dec. 706, 481 N.E.2d 58 (Ill.App. 1 Dist.1985)—**S.Ct. Rule 304, n. 2.**

Lingwall v. Hoener, 108 Ill.2d 206, 91 Ill.Dec. 166, 483 N.E.2d 512 (Ill.1985)—**750 ILCS 5/607, n. 3.**

Lipkin, In re Marriage of, 163 Ill.App.3d 1033, 115 Ill.Dec. 76, 517 N.E.2d 41 (Ill.App. 4 Dist.1987)—**750 ILCS 5/402, n. 4.**

TABLE OF CASES

Liss (Karen), n/k/a Fox (Karen), Liss (Allen), In re Marriage of 1994 WL 700385 (Ill.App. 1 Dist.1994)—**750 ILCS 5/505, n. 13.**

Loffredi, In re Marriage of, 232 Ill.App.3d 709, 173 Ill.Dec. 933, 597 N.E.2d 907 (Ill.App. 3 Dist.1992)—**750 ILCS 5/510, n. 1.**

Lombaer, In re Marriage of, 200 Ill.App.3d 712, 146 Ill.Dec. 425, 558 N.E.2d 388 (Ill.App. 1 Dist.1990)—**750 ILCS 5/603, n. 1; 750 ILCS 5/607, n. 2; 750 ILCS 5/701, n. 1; 740 ILCS 110/1, n. 2; 740 ILCS 110/10, n. 1, 2, 4.**

Lorton, In re Marriage of, 203 Ill.App.3d 823, 148 Ill.Dec. 850, 561 N.E.2d 156 (Ill.App. 5 Dist.1990)—**750 ILCS 5/502, n. 6, 7, 14.**

Los, In re Marriage of, 229 Ill.App.3d 357, 170 Ill.Dec. 584, 593 N.E.2d 126 (Ill.App. 2 Dist.1992)—**750 ILCS 35/4, n. 1.**

Louis v. Louis, 124 Ill.App.2d 325, 260 N.E.2d 469 (Ill.App.1970)—**750 ILCS 5/301, n. 2.**

Lovejoy, In re Marriage of, 84 Ill.App.3d 53, 39 Ill.Dec. 501, 404 N.E.2d 1092 (Ill.App. 3 Dist.1980)—**750 ILCS 5/602, n. 4.**

L.R., In re Marriage of, 202 Ill.App.3d 69, 147 Ill.Dec. 439, 559 N.E.2d 779 (Ill.App. 1 Dist.1990)—**750 ILCS 5/506, n. 1; 750 ILCS 5/607, n. 1.**

Lynch v. Mullenix, 48 Ill.App.3d 963, 6 Ill.Dec. 831, 363 N.E.2d 645 (Ill.App. 3 Dist.1977)—**S.Ct. Rule 206, n. 1.**

Lyons v. Lyons, 228 Ill.App.3d 407, 169 Ill.Dec. 502, 591 N.E.2d 1006 (Ill.App. 5 Dist.1992)—**750 ILCS 5/607, n. 1.**

Madoch, In re Marriage of, 212 Ill.App.3d 1007, 157 Ill.Dec. 10, 571 N.E.2d 1029 (Ill.App. 1 Dist.1991)—**S.Ct. Rule 218, n. 2.**

Maher, In re Marriage of, 95 Ill.App.3d 1039, 51 Ill.Dec. 586, 420 N.E.2d 1144 (Ill.App. 2 Dist.1981)—**750 ILCS 5/502, n. 2.**

Maitlen, In re, 658 F.2d 466 (7th Cir.1981)—**11 U.S.C.A. § 523, n. 2.**

Malec, In re Marriage of, 205 Ill.App.3d 273, 150 Ill.Dec. 207, 562 N.E.2d 1010 (Ill.App. 1 Dist.1990)—**750 ILCS 5/508, n. 4.**

Malters, In re Marriage of, 133 Ill.App.3d 168, 88 Ill.Dec. 460, 478 N.E.2d 1068 (Ill.App. 1 Dist.1985)—**750 ILCS 5/503, n. 6, 21.**

Mantei, In re Marriage of, 222 Ill.App.3d 933, 164 Ill.Dec. 870, 583 N.E.2d 1192 (Ill.App. 4 Dist.1991)—**750 ILCS 5/504, n. 1, 3; 750 ILCS 5/508, n. 1, 3.**

Marcello, In re Marriage of, 247 Ill.App.3d 304, 187 Ill.Dec. 81, 617 N.E.2d 289 (Ill.App. 1 Dist.1993)—**S.Ct. Rule 218, n. 2; 750 ILCS 5/504, n. 3.**

Markey, In re Marriage of, 223 Ill.App.3d 1055, 166 Ill.Dec. 392, 586 N.E.2d 350 (Ill.App. 1 Dist.1991)—**740 ILCS 110/4, n. 1.**

Marriage of (see name of party)

Marshall v. Osborn, 213 Ill.App.3d 134, 156 Ill.Dec. 708, 571 N.E.2d 492 (Ill.App. 3 Dist.1991)—**S.Ct. Rule 220, n. 12.**

Marthens, In re Marriage of, 215 Ill.App.3d 590, 159 Ill.Dec. 3, 575 N.E.2d 3 (Ill.App. 3 Dist.1991)—**750 ILCS 5/503, n. 20; 750 ILCS 5/504, n. 1, 3.**

Martin, In re Marriage of, 223 Ill.App.3d 855, 166 Ill.Dec. 136, 585 N.E.2d 1158 (Ill.App. 4 Dist.1992)—**750 ILCS 5/504, n. 3, 5.**

Martin v. Martin, 327 Ill.App. 552, 64 N.E.2d 379 (Ill.App.1946)—**750 ILCS 5/403, n. 2.**

Martino, In re Marriage of, 166 Ill.App.3d 692, 117 Ill.Dec. 788, 520 N.E.2d 1139 (Ill.App. 2 Dist.1988)—**750 ILCS 5/510, n. 1, 5.**

Martino v. Family Service Agency of Adams County, 112 Ill.App.3d 593, 67 Ill.Dec. 714, 445 N.E.2d 6 (Ill.App. 4 Dist.1982)—**740 ILCS 110/10, n. 2.**

Mathis, People ex rel. v. Brown, 44 Ill.App.3d 783, 3 Ill.Dec. 475, 358 N.E.2d 1160 (Ill.App. 1 Dist.1976)—**p. 962, n. 1.**

Matter of (see name of party)

Mattson, In re, 240 Ill.App.3d 993, 181 Ill.Dec. 810, 608 N.E.2d 1284 (Ill.App. 2 Dist.1993)—**750 ILCS 5/21-101, n. 2.**

McBride, In re Marriage of, 166 Ill.App.3d 504, 116 Ill.Dec. 880, 519 N.E.2d 1095 (Ill.App. 1 Dist.1988)—**750 ILCS 5/505, n. 9; 750 ILCS 5/510, n. 4.**

McClelland v. McClelland, 231 Ill.App.3d 214, 172 Ill.Dec. 461, 595 N.E.2d 1131 (Ill.App. 1 Dist.1992)—**750 ILCS 5/506, n. 6.**

McCoy, In re Marriage of, 253 Ill.App.3d 958, 192 Ill.Dec. 728, 625 N.E.2d 883 (Ill.App. 4 Dist.1993)—**750 ILCS 60/221, n. 4.**

McCoy, In re Marriage of, 225 Ill.App.3d 966, 168 Ill.Dec. 27, 589 N.E.2d 141 (Ill.App. 3 Dist.1992)—**750 ILCS 5/503, n. 5, 17, 18.**

TABLE OF CASES

McGaughy v. McGaughy, 410 Ill. 596, 102 N.E.2d 806 (Ill.1951)—**750 ILCS 5/403, n. 3.**

McGory, In re Marriage of, 185 Ill.App.3d 517, 133 Ill.Dec. 590, 541 N.E.2d 801 (Ill.App. 3 Dist.1989)—**750 ILCS 5/510, n. 6, 7; 750 ILCS 5/513, n. 3.**

McKeever, In re Marriage of, 117 Ill.App.3d 905, 73 Ill.Dec. 164, 453 N.E.2d 1153 (Ill.App. 3 Dist.1983)—**S.Ct. Rule 366, n. 1; 750 ILCS 5/602, n. 1.**

McVey v. Fredrickson, 226 Ill.App.3d 1082, 169 Ill.Dec. 77, 590 N.E.2d 996 (Ill.App. 3 Dist. 1992)—**750 ILCS 5/607, n. 3.**

Melecosky v. McCarthy Bros. Co., 115 Ill.2d 209, 104 Ill.Dec. 798, 503 N.E.2d 355 (Ill.1986)—**p. 943, n. 7.**

Mendelson v. Feingold, 69 Ill.App.3d 227, 25 Ill.Dec. 707, 387 N.E.2d 363 (Ill.App. 2 Dist.1979)— **S.Ct. Rule 204, n. 6.**

Mendelson v. Lillard, 83 Ill.App.3d 1088, 39 Ill.Dec. 373, 404 N.E.2d 964 (Ill.App. 1 Dist.1980)— **S.Ct. Rule 366, n. 1.**

Messenger v. Edgar, 157 Ill.2d 162, 191 Ill.Dec. 65, 623 N.E.2d 310 (Ill.1993)—**750 ILCS 5/501.1, n. 1.**

Meyer, In re Marriage of, 146 Ill.App.3d 83, 100 Ill.Dec. 128, 496 N.E.2d 1193 (Ill.App. 1 Dist.1986)—**750 ILCS 5/11-106, n. 1.**

Meyer v. Meyer, 222 Ill.App.3d 357, 164 Ill.Dec. 800, 583 N.E.2d 716 (Ill.App. 5 Dist.1991)—**750 ILCS 5/510, n. 17.**

Meyer, People ex rel. v. Nein, 209 Ill.App.3d 1087, 154 Ill.Dec. 436, 568 N.E.2d 436 (Ill.App. 4 Dist.1991)—**750 ILCS 5/510, n. 4.**

Miche, In re Marriage of, 131 Ill.App.3d 1029, 87 Ill.Dec. 72, 476 N.E.2d 774 (Ill.App. 2 Dist.1985)—**750 ILCS 35/4, n. 3, 4.**

Miller, In re Marriage of, 231 Ill.App.3d 480, 172 Ill.Dec. 679, 595 N.E.2d 1349 (Ill.App. 3 Dist.1992)—**750 ILCS 5/504, n. 3.**

Miller v. Miller, 163 Ill.App.3d 602, 114 Ill.Dec. 682, 516 N.E.2d 837 (Ill.App. 1 Dist.1987)—**750 ILCS 5/513, n. 5.**

Miller v. Miller, 160 Ill.App.3d 354, 112 Ill.Dec. 191, 513 N.E.2d 605 (Ill.App. 3 Dist.1987)—**750 ILCS 5/513, n. 5.**

Miroballi, In re Marriage of, 225 Ill.App.3d 1094, 168 Ill.Dec. 165, 589 N.E.2d 565 (Ill.App. 1 Dist.1991)—**750 ILCS 5/609, n. 2.**

M.M., In re, 156 Ill.2d 53, 189 Ill.Dec. 1, 619 N.E.2d 702 (Ill.1993)—**750 ILCS 50/0.01, n. 17.**

Mobley, In re Marriage of, 210 Ill.App.3d 936, 155 Ill.Dec. 323, 569 N.E.2d 323 (Ill.App. 5 Dist.1991)—**750 ILCS 35/4, n. 1.**

Moll, In re Marriage of, 232 Ill.App.3d 746, 174 Ill.Dec. 18, 597 N.E.2d 1230 (Ill.App. 2 Dist.1992)—**750 ILCS 5/503, n. 32.**

Monier v. Chamberlain, 35 Ill.2d 351, 221 N.E.2d 410 (Ill.1966)—**S.Ct. Rule 201, n. 1.**

Monken, In re Marriage of, 255 Ill.App.3d 1044, 194 Ill.Dec. 422, 627 N.E.2d 759 (Ill.App. 5 Dist.1994)—**S.Ct. Rule 366, n. 1.**

Montgomery v. Roudez, 156 Ill.App.3d 262, 108 Ill.Dec. 803, 509 N.E.2d 499 (Ill.App. 1 Dist. 1987)—**750 ILCS 5/601, n. 1, 2; 750 ILCS 5/602, n. 1.**

Moran, In re Marriage of, 136 Ill.App.3d 331, 91 Ill.Dec. 234, 483 N.E.2d 580 (Ill.App. 1 Dist.1985)—**750 ILCS 5/502, n. 4.**

Morgan, People v., 28 Ill.2d 55, 190 N.E.2d 755 (Ill.1963)—**S.Ct. Rule 212, n. 2.**

Morrical, In re Marriage of, 216 Ill.App.3d 643, 159 Ill.Dec. 796, 576 N.E.2d 465 (Ill.App. 3 Dist.1991)—**750 ILCS 5/503, n. 21.**

Morris, In re Marriage of, 147 Ill.App.3d 380, 100 Ill.Dec. 811, 497 N.E.2d 1173 (Ill.App. 1 Dist.1986)—**750 ILCS 5/502, n. 4.**

Morse, In re Marriage of, 240 Ill.App.3d 296, 180 Ill.Dec. 563, 607 N.E.2d 632 (Ill.App. 2 Dist.1993)—**750 ILCS 5/511, n. 5.**

Morse, In re Marriage of, 143 Ill.App.3d 849, 98 Ill.Dec. 67, 493 N.E.2d 1088 (Ill.App. 5 Dist.1986)—**750 ILCS 5/508, n. 4.**

Mosher, In re Marriage of, 243 Ill.App.3d 97, 183 Ill.Dec. 911, 612 N.E.2d 838 (Ill.App. 3 Dist.1993)—**750 ILCS 5/214, n. 3.**

Mullins, In re Marriage of, 135 Ill.App.3d 279, 89 Ill.Dec. 771, 481 N.E.2d 322 (Ill.App. 4 Dist.1985)—**750 ILCS 5/511, n. 2.**

Myer v. Alvarado, 100 Ill.App.3d 27, 55 Ill.Dec. 358, 426 N.E.2d 333 (Ill.App. 4 Dist.1981)—**750 ILCS 5/601, n. 3.**

Myers v. Myers, 51 Ill.App.3d 830, 9 Ill.Dec. 603, 366 N.E.2d 1114 (Ill.App. 3 Dist.1977)—**750 ILCS 5/413, n. 2.**

Nadler, In re, 91 Ill.2d 326, 63 Ill.Dec. 460, 438 N.E.2d 198 (Ill.1982)—**750 ILCS 50/0.01, n. 14.**

TABLE OF CASES

Naguit, In re Marriage of, 104 Ill.App.3d 709, 60 Ill.Dec. 499, 433 N.E.2d 296 (Ill.App. 5 Dist.1982)—**750 ILCS 5/301, n. 2.**
Nandorf, Inc. v. CNA Ins. Companies, 134 Ill.App.3d 134, 88 Ill.Dec. 968, 479 N.E.2d 988 (Ill.App. 1 Dist.1985)—**p. 964, n. 3.**
Nein, People ex rel. Meyer v., 209 Ill.App.3d 1087, 154 Ill.Dec. 436, 568 N.E.2d 436 (Ill.App. 4 Dist.1991)—**750 ILCS 5/510, n. 4.**
Nicks, In re Marriage of, 177 Ill.App.3d 76, 126 Ill.Dec. 442, 531 N.E.2d 1069 (Ill.App. 4 Dist.1988)—**750 ILCS 5/503, n. 5, 12.**
Nilsson, In re Marriage of, 81 Ill.App.3d 580, 37 Ill.Dec. 394, 402 N.E.2d 284 (Ill.App. 3 Dist.1980)—**750 ILCS 5/413, n. 2.**
Nix v. Whiteside, 475 U.S. 157, 106 S.Ct. 988, 89 L.Ed.2d 123 (1986)—**p. 963, n. 1.**
Noble, In re Marriage of, 192 Ill.App.3d 501, 139 Ill.Dec. 133, 548 N.E.2d 518 (Ill.App. 2 Dist.1989)—**750 ILCS 5/605, n. 1.**
Nolte v. Nolte, 241 Ill.App.3d 320, 182 Ill.Dec. 78, 609 N.E.2d 381 (Ill.App. 3 Dist.1993)—**750 ILCS 5/602, n. 7; 750 ILCS 5/610, n. 2.**

Oakes v. Oakes, 45 Ill.App.2d 387, 195 N.E.2d 840 (Ill.App.1964)—**750 ILCS 5/604, n. 1.**
O'Brien, In re Marriage of, 235 Ill.App.3d 520, 176 Ill.Dec. 529, 601 N.E.2d 1227 (Ill.App. 1 Dist.1992)—**750 ILCS 5/402, n. 4; 750 ILCS 5/504, n. 3.**
Oertel, In re Marriage of, 216 Ill.App.3d 806, 159 Ill.Dec. 766, 576 N.E.2d 435 (Ill.App. 2 Dist.1991)—**750 ILCS 5/607, n. 1.**
Ohrt, In re Marriage of, 154 Ill.App.3d 738, 107 Ill.Dec. 496, 507 N.E.2d 160 (Ill.App. 3 Dist.1987)—**750 ILCS 5/503, n. 6.**
Oliver, In re Marriage of, 155 Ill.App.3d 181, 107 Ill.Dec. 929, 507 N.E.2d 1298 (Ill.App. 5 Dist.1987)—**750 ILCS 5/610, n. 5.**
Olsen, In re Marriage of, 229 Ill.App.3d 107, 171 Ill.Dec. 39, 593 N.E.2d 859 (Ill.App. 1 Dist.1992)—**750 ILCS 5/510, n. 3, 4.**
Olson, In re Marriage of, 223 Ill.App.3d 636, 166 Ill.Dec. 60, 585 N.E.2d 1082 (Ill.App. 2 Dist.1992)—**S.Ct. Rule 220, n. 10; 750 ILCS 5/503, n. 5; 750 ILCS 5/513, n. 2.**
Olson, In re Marriage of, 98 Ill.App.3d 316, 53 Ill.Dec. 751, 424 N.E.2d 386 (Ill.App. 3 Dist.1981)—**750 ILCS 5/610, n. 1.**
O'Neill, In re Marriage of, 138 Ill.2d 487, 150 Ill.Dec. 607, 563 N.E.2d 494 (Ill.1990)—**750 ILCS 5/503, n. 21.**
Orlando, In re Marriage of, 218 Ill.App.3d 312, 160 Ill.Dec. 763, 577 N.E.2d 1334 (Ill.App. 1 Dist.1991)—**750 ILCS 5/503, n. 5, 20; 750 ILCS 5/508, n. 3.**
Oros, In re Marriage of, 256 Ill.App.3d 167, 194 Ill.Dec. 604, 627 N.E.2d 1246 (Ill.App. 4 Dist.1994)—**750 ILCS 5/602.1, n. 3.**
Orr v. Orr, 228 Ill.App.3d 234, 170 Ill.Dec. 117, 592 N.E.2d 553 (Ill.App. 1 Dist.1992)—**750 ILCS 5/513, n. 5.**
Osborn, In re Marriage of, 206 Ill.App.3d 588, 151 Ill.Dec. 663, 564 N.E.2d 1325 (Ill.App. 5 Dist.1990)—**750 ILCS 5/505, n. 6; 750 ILCS 5/510, n. 4.**

Pagano, In re Marriage of, 181 Ill.App.3d 547, 130 Ill.Dec. 331, 537 N.E.2d 398 (Ill.App. 2 Dist.1989)—**750 ILCS 5/508, n. 2.**
Palmisano v. Connell, 179 Ill.App.3d 1089, 128 Ill.Dec. 638, 534 N.E.2d 1243 (Ill.App. 2 Dist.1989)—**750 ILCS 5/2-1001, n. 2.**
Partney, In re Marriage of, 212 Ill.App.3d 586, 156 Ill.Dec. 679, 571 N.E.2d 266 (Ill.App. 5 Dist.1991)—**750 ILCS 5/505, n. 9.**
Partyka, In re Marriage of, 158 Ill.App.3d 545, 110 Ill.Dec. 499, 511 N.E.2d 676 (Ill.App. 1 Dist.1987)—**750 ILCS 5/503, n. 21.**
Paschen Contractors, Inc. v. Illinois State Toll Highway Authority, 225 Ill.App.3d 930, 168 Ill.Dec. 902, 590 N.E.2d 539 (Ill.App. 2 Dist.1992)—**750 ILCS 5/2-1001, n. 2.**
Passiales, In re Marriage of, 144 Ill.App.3d 629, 98 Ill.Dec. 419, 494 N.E.2d 541 (Ill.App. 1 Dist.1986)—**750 ILCS 5/2-209, n. 1.**
Pavelcik, In re Marriage of, 138 Ill.App.3d 1060, 93 Ill.Dec. 589, 487 N.E.2d 33 (Ill.App. 1 Dist.1985)—**750 ILCS 35/8, n. 1.**
Pearson, In re Marriage of, 236 Ill.App.3d 337, 177 Ill.Dec. 650, 603 N.E.2d 720 (Ill.App. 1 Dist.1992)—**750 ILCS 5/503, n. 21; 750 ILCS 5/504, n. 1, 2.**
Pease, In re Marriage of, 106 Ill.App.3d 617, 62 Ill.Dec. 389, 435 N.E.2d 1361 (Ill.App. 2 Dist.1982)—**750 ILCS 5/610, n.1.**
Peirce v. Peirce, 379 Ill. 185, 39 N.E.2d 990 (Ill.1942)—**750 ILCS 5/214, n. 3.**
People v. _____ (see opposing party)

TABLE OF CASES

People ex rel. v. _____ (see opposing party and relator)

Peoples Gas Light and Coke Co. v. Illinois Commerce Com'n, 222 Ill.App.3d 738, 165 Ill.Dec. 162, 584 N.E.2d 341 (Ill.App. 1 Dist.1991)—**750 ILCS 65/15, n. 1.**

Perlmutter, In re Marriage of, 225 Ill.App.3d 362, 167 Ill.Dec. 340, 587 N.E.2d 609 (Ill.App. 2 Dist.1992)—**750 ILCS 5/503, n. 10, 11, 15, 16.**

Perry, In re Marriage of, 96 Ill.App.3d 370, 51 Ill.Dec. 766, 421 N.E.2d 274 (Ill.App. 1 Dist.1981)—**750 ILCS 5/502, n. 6.**

Philips, In re Marriage of, 200 Ill.App.3d 395, 146 Ill.Dec. 191, 558 N.E.2d 154 (Ill.App. 1 Dist.1990)—**750 ILCS 5/503, n. 6.**

Phillips, In re Marriage of, 244 Ill.App.3d 577, 186 Ill.Dec. 108, 615 N.E.2d 1165 (Ill.App. 4 Dist.1993)—**750 ILCS 5/504, n. 1.**

Phillips, In re Marriage of, 229 Ill.App.3d 809, 171 Ill.Dec. 501, 594 N.E.2d 353 (Ill.App. 2 Dist.1992)—**750 ILCS 5/503, n. 15, 21.**

Pick, In re Marriage of, 167 Ill.App.3d 294, 118 Ill.Dec. 53, 521 N.E.2d 121 (Ill.App. 2 Dist.1988)—**750 ILCS 5/508, n. 8.**

Pick, In re Marriage of, 119 Ill.App.3d 1061, 75 Ill.Dec. 865, 458 N.E.2d 33 (Ill.App. 2 Dist.1983)—**750 ILCS 5/501, n. 12.**

Pieper, In re Marriage of, 79 Ill.App.3d 835, 34 Ill.Dec. 877, 398 N.E.2d 868 (Ill.App. 1 Dist.1979)—**750 ILCS 5/503, n. 36; 750 ILCS 5/514, n. 3.**

Pierce v. Pierce, 69 Ill.App.3d 42, 25 Ill.Dec. 511, 386 N.E.2d 1175 (Ill.App. 5 Dist.1979)—**750 ILCS 5/510, n. 5.**

Pittman, In re Marriage of, 213 Ill.App.3d 60, 157 Ill.Dec. 177, 571 N.E.2d 1196 (Ill.App. 5 Dist.1991)—**750 ILCS 5/508, n. 1.**

Pittman, In re Marriage of, 212 Ill.App.3d 99, 155 Ill.Dec. 667, 569 N.E.2d 1278 (Ill.App. 5 Dist.1991)—**750 ILCS 5/503, n. 10, 16.**

Platt v. Platt, 951 F.2d 159 (8th Cir.1989)—**p. 961, n. 2.**

Plotz, In re Marriage of, 229 Ill.App.3d 389, 171 Ill.Dec. 514, 594 N.E.2d 366 (Ill.App. 3 Dist.1992)—**750 ILCS 5/510, n. 3, 4.**

Plymale, In re Marriage of, 172 Ill.App.3d 455, 122 Ill.Dec. 489, 526 N.E.2d 882 (Ill.App. 2 Dist.1988)—**750 ILCS 5/304, n. 1.**

Ponsart, In re Marriage of, 118 Ill.App.3d 664, 74 Ill.Dec. 241, 455 N.E.2d 271 (Ill.App. 1 Dist.1983)—**750 ILCS 5/511, n. 2.**

Pope v. Pope, 12 Ill.App.3d 800, 299 N.E.2d 161 (Ill.App. 1 Dist.1973)—**750 ILCS 5/403, n. 3.**

Potocki v. Potocki, 98 Ill.App.3d 501, 53 Ill.Dec. 923, 424 N.E.2d 714 (Ill.App. 1 Dist.1981)—**750 ILCS 5/510, n. 17.**

Powers, In re Marriage of, 252 Ill.App.3d 506, 191 Ill.Dec. 541, 624 N.E.2d 390 (Ill.App. 2 Dist.1993)—**750 ILCS 5/508, n. 4.**

Presson, In re Marriage of, 102 Ill.2d 303, 80 Ill.Dec. 294, 465 N.E.2d 85 (Ill.1984)—**750 ILCS 5/21-101, n. 2.**

Pribble and Wagenblast, In re Marriage of, 239 Ill.App.3d 761, 180 Ill.Dec. 455, 607 N.E.2d 349 (Ill.App. 5 Dist.1993)—**750 ILCS 5/609, n. 2.**

Radae, In re Marriage of, 208 Ill.App.3d 1027, 153 Ill.Dec. 802, 567 N.E.2d 760 (Ill.App. 5 Dist.1991)—**750 ILCS 5/602, n. 1, 7.**

Rai, In re Marriage of, 189 Ill.App.3d 559, 136 Ill.Dec. 922, 545 N.E.2d 446 (Ill.App. 1 Dist.1989)—**750 ILCS 5/503, n. 21; 750 ILCS 5/505, n. 2.**

Randall, In re Marriage of, 157 Ill.App.3d 892, 110 Ill.Dec. 122, 510 N.E.2d 1153 (Ill.App. 1 Dist.1987)—**750 ILCS 5/503, n. 27.**

Rasgaitis v. Rasgaitis, 347 Ill.App. 477, 107 N.E.2d 273 (Ill.App.1952)—**750 ILCS 5/403, n. 3.**

Rayfield, In re Marriage of, 221 Ill.App.3d 763, 164 Ill.Dec. 469, 583 N.E.2d 23 (Ill.App. 1 Dist.1991)—**750 ILCS 5/501, n. 11.**

Reddig v. Reddig, 12 Ill.App.3d 1009, 299 N.E.2d 353 (Ill.App. 3 Dist.1973)—**750 ILCS 5/609, n. 3.**

Reed, In re Marriage of, 100 Ill.App.3d 873, 56 Ill.Dec. 202, 427 N.E.2d 282 (Ill.App. 5 Dist.1981)—**750 ILCS 5/505, n. 2.**

Reib, In re Marriage of, 114 Ill.App.3d 993, 70 Ill.Dec. 572, 449 N.E.2d 919 (Ill.App. 1 Dist.1983)—**750 ILCS 5/413, n. 4.**

Renzi v. Morrison, 249 Ill.App.3d 5, 188 Ill.Dec. 224, 618 N.E.2d 794 (Ill.App. 1 Dist.1993)—**740 ILCS 110/15, n. 1.**

Richardson, In re Marriage of, 237 Ill.App.3d 1067, 179 Ill.Dec. 224, 606 N.E.2d 56 (Ill.App. 1 Dist.1992)—**S.Ct. Rule 304, n. 2; 750 ILCS 5/502, n. 3; 750 ILCS 10/7, n. 6.**

TABLE OF CASES

Richheimer v. Richheimer, 59 Ill.App.2d 354, 208 N.E.2d 346 (Ill.App.1965)—**750 ILCS 5/508, n. 4.**

Rink, In re Marriage of, 136 Ill.App.3d 252, 91 Ill.Dec. 34, 483 N.E.2d 316 (Ill.App. 1 Dist.1985)—**750 ILCS 5/504, n. 3.**

Riordan v. Riordan, 47 Ill.App.3d 1019, 8 Ill.Dec. 254, 365 N.E.2d 492 (Ill.App. 1 Dist.1977)—**750 ILCS 5/104, n. 3.**

Rizza, In re Marriage of, 237 Ill.App.3d 83, 177 Ill.Dec. 353, 603 N.E.2d 134 (Ill.App. 2 Dist.1992)—**750 ILCS 35/8, n. 1; 750 ILCS 35/9, n. 1.**

Rizzo v. Rizzo, 95 Ill.App.3d 636, 51 Ill.Dec. 141, 420 N.E.2d 555 (Ill.App. 1 Dist.1981)—**750 ILCS 5/602, n. 12.**

Roach, In re Marriage of, 245 Ill.App.3d 742, 185 Ill.Dec. 735, 615 N.E.2d 30 (Ill.App. 4 Dist.1993)—**750 ILCS 5/2-1001, n. 1, 2.**

Robin v. Robin, 45 Ill.App.3d 365, 3 Ill.Dec. 950, 359 N.E.2d 809 (Ill.App. 1 Dist.1977)—**750 ILCS 5/510, n. 4.**

Robinson, In re Marriage of, 225 Ill.App.3d 1037, 167 Ill.Dec. 1113, 588 N.E.2d 1243 (Ill.App. 3 Dist.1992)—**750 ILCS 5/401, n. 5.**

Robinson v. Robinson, 146 Ill.App.3d 474, 100 Ill.Dec. 260, 497 N.E.2d 140 (Ill.App. 3 Dist. 1986)—**750 ILCS 5/503, n. 30.**

Rogers, In re Marriage of, 141 Ill.App.3d 561, 95 Ill.Dec. 908, 490 N.E.2d 1000 (Ill.App. 5 Dist.1986)—**750 ILCS 35/4, n. 2.**

Rogliano, In re Marriage of, 198 Ill.App.3d 404, 144 Ill.Dec. 595, 555 N.E.2d 1114 (Ill.App. 5 Dist.1990)—**750 ILCS 5/505, n. 2.**

Rosche v. Rosche, 163 Ill.App.3d 308, 114 Ill.Dec. 846, 516 N.E.2d 1001 (Ill.App. 5 Dist.1987)—**750 ILCS 5/513, n. 1.**

Rosen, In re Marriage of, 126 Ill.App.3d 766, 81 Ill.Dec. 840, 467 N.E.2d 962 (Ill.App. 1 Dist.1984)—**750 ILCS 5/503, n. 3, 27.**

Rosenow, In re Marriage of, 123 Ill.App.3d 546, 78 Ill.Dec. 933, 462 N.E.2d 1287 (Ill.App. 4 Dist.1984)—**S.Ct. Rule 304, n. 2; 750 ILCS 5/401, n. 10.**

Rosenshine v. Rosenshine, 60 Ill.App.3d 514, 17 Ill.Dec. 942, 377 N.E.2d 132 (Ill.App. 1 Dist.1978)—**750 ILCS 5/401, n. 1.**

Roth v. Roth, 84 Ill.App.3d 240, 39 Ill.Dec. 872, 405 N.E.2d 851 (Ill.App. 3 Dist.1980)—**p. 964, n. 3.**

Rubinstein, In re Marriage of, 145 Ill.App.3d 31, 99 Ill.Dec. 212, 495 N.E.2d 659 (Ill.App. 2 Dist.1986)—**750 ILCS 5/504, n. 3.**

Ryan, In re Marriage of, 188 Ill.App.3d 679, 136 Ill.Dec. 1, 544 N.E.2d 454 (Ill.App. 2 Dist.1989)—**S.Ct. Rule 304, n. 2; 750 ILCS 5/501, n. 2.**

Sales, In re Marriage of, 106 Ill.App.3d 378, 62 Ill.Dec. 441, 436 N.E.2d 23 (Ill.App. 1 Dist.1982)—**750 ILCS 5/503, n. 23.**

Sanchez v. Randall, 31 Ill.App.2d 41, 175 N.E.2d 645 (Ill.App.1961)—**750 ILCS 5/2-203, n. 2.**

Sanda, In re Marriage of, 245 Ill.App.3d 314, 184 Ill.Dec. 186, 612 N.E.2d 1346 (Ill.App. 2 Dist.1993)—**750 ILCS 5/508, n. 4.**

Sanders v. Shephard, 258 Ill.App.3d 626, 196 Ill.Dec. 845, 630 N.E.2d 1010 (Ill.App. 1 Dist. 1994)—**750 ILCS 5/511, n. 5.**

Sappington, In re Marriage of, 106 Ill.2d 456, 88 Ill.Dec. 61, 478 N.E.2d 376 (Ill.1985)—**750 ILCS 5/510, n. 16.**

Scafuri, In re Marriage of, 203 Ill.App.3d 385, 149 Ill.Dec. 124, 561 N.E.2d 402 (Ill.App. 2 Dist.1990)—**750 ILCS 5/505, n. 3, 6; 750 ILCS 5/510, n. 4.**

Schejbal, People ex rel. v. Kanner, 54 Ill.App.2d 208, 203 N.E.2d 759 (Ill.App.1964)—**S.Ct. Rule 231, n. 1.**

Schlenz v. Castle, 132 Ill.App.3d 993, 87 Ill.Dec. 571, 477 N.E.2d 697 (Ill.App. 2 Dist.1985)—**750 ILCS 5/2-1001, n. 2.**

Schmidt, In re Marriage of, 242 Ill.App.3d 961, 182 Ill.Dec. 804, 610 N.E.2d 673 (Ill.App. 4 Dist.1993)—**750 ILCS 5/503, n. 2.**

Schmidt, In re Marriage of, 118 Ill.App.3d 467, 74 Ill.Dec. 93, 455 N.E.2d 123 (Ill.App. 1 Dist.1983)—**750 ILCS 5/501, n. 10, 11, 12.**

Schneider v. Schneider, 312 Ill.App. 59, 37 N.E.2d 911 (Ill.App.1941)—**750 ILCS 5/703, n. 1.**

Schoenhard v. Schoenhard, 74 Ill.App.3d 296, 30 Ill.Dec. 109, 392 N.E.2d 764 (Ill.App. 2 Dist.1979)—**750 ILCS 5/510, n. 1.**

Schroeder, In re Marriage of, 215 Ill.App.3d 156, 158 Ill.Dec. 721, 574 N.E.2d 834 (Ill.App. 4 Dist.1991)—**750 ILCS 5/501, n. 14; 750 ILCS 5/504, n. 3; 750 ILCS 5/505, n. 3, 12.**

TABLE OF CASES

Schuham, In re Marriage of, 120 Ill.App.3d 339, 76 Ill.Dec. 159, 458 N.E.2d 559 (Ill.App. 1 Dist.1983)—**750 ILCS 35/4, n. 1.**
Schuster, In re Marriage of, 224 Ill.App.3d 958, 167 Ill.Dec. 73, 586 N.E.2d 1345 (Ill.App. 2 Dist.1992)—**750 ILCS 5/505, n. 2.**
Scordo, In re Marriage of, 176 Ill.App.3d 269, 125 Ill.Dec. 761, 530 N.E.2d 1170 (Ill.App. 3 Dist.1988)—**750 ILCS 5/511, n. 4.**
Scott, In re Marriage of, 205 Ill.App.3d 561, 150 Ill.Dec. 868, 563 N.E.2d 995 (Ill.App. 4 Dist.1990)—**750 ILCS 5/502, n. 16.**
Seagram Distillers Co. v. Foremost Sales Promotions, Inc., 13 Ill.App.3d 166, 300 N.E.2d 490 (Ill.App. 1 Dist.1973)—**750 ILCS 5/11-102, n. 5.**
Sechrest, In re Marriage of, 202 Ill.App.3d 865, 148 Ill.Dec. 615, 560 N.E.2d 1212 (Ill.App. 4 Dist.1990)—**750 ILCS 5/601, n. 1.**
Security Sav. & Loan Ass'n v. Hofmann, 181 Ill.App.3d 419, 130 Ill.Dec. 197, 537 N.E.2d 18 (Ill.App. 3 Dist.1989)—**750 ILCS 5/2-1901, n. 2.**
Seymour, In re Marriage of, 206 Ill.App.3d 506, 152 Ill.Dec. 27, 565 N.E.2d 269 (Ill.App. 2 Dist.1990)—**750 ILCS 5/602, n. 2, 4.**
Shea v. Civil Service Com'n, 224 Ill.App.3d 282, 166 Ill.Dec. 554, 586 N.E.2d 512 (Ill.App. 1 Dist.1991)—**p. 962, n. 2.**
Sheber, In re Marriage of, 121 Ill.App.3d 328, 76 Ill.Dec. 921, 459 N.E.2d 1056 (Ill.App. 1 Dist.1984)—**750 ILCS 5/405, n. 1.**
Sherrick, In re Marriage of, 214 Ill.App.3d 92, 157 Ill.Dec. 917, 573 N.E.2d 335 (Ill.App. 4 Dist.1991)—**750 ILCS 5/502, n. 6.**
Sherwin, In re Marriage of, 123 Ill.App.3d 748, 79 Ill.Dec. 201, 463 N.E.2d 755 (Ill.App. 1 Dist.1984)—**750 ILCS 5/501, n. 8.**
Shields, In re Marriage of, 167 Ill.App.3d 205, 118 Ill.Dec. 50, 521 N.E.2d 118 (Ill.App. 4 Dist.1988)—**750 ILCS 5/504, n. 3.**
Shoff, In re Marriage of, 179 Ill.App.3d 178, 128 Ill.Dec. 280, 534 N.E.2d 462 (Ill.App. 5 Dist.1989)—**750 ILCS 5/602, n. 2.**
Siddens, In re Marriage of, 225 Ill.App.3d 496, 167 Ill.Dec. 680, 588 N.E.2d 321 (Ill.App. 5 Dist.1992)—**750 ILCS 5/503, n. 5, 7, 21; 750 ILCS 5/508, n. 4.**
Siegel, In re Marriage of, 123 Ill.App.3d 710, 79 Ill.Dec. 219, 463 N.E.2d 773 (Ill.App. 1 Dist.1984)—**750 ILCS 5/602, n. 10.**
Siegel v. Siegel, 84 Ill.2d 212, 49 Ill.Dec. 298, 417 N.E.2d 1312 (Ill.1981)—**750 ILCS 35/8, n. 1.**
Siegel v. Siegel, 80 Ill.App.3d 583, 35 Ill.Dec. 869, 400 N.E.2d 6 (Ill.App. 1 Dist.1979)—**750 ILCS 5/509, n. 1.**
Siklossy, In re Marriage of, 87 Ill.App.3d 124, 42 Ill.Dec. 534, 409 N.E.2d 29 (Ill.App. 1 Dist.1980)—**750 ILCS 5/609, n. 2.**
Silber, In re Marriage of, 176 Ill.App.3d 853, 126 Ill.Dec. 283, 531 N.E.2d 910 (Ill.App. 1 Dist.1988)—**750 ILCS 5/510, n. 5.**
Silvestri–Gagliardoni, In re Marriage of, 186 Ill.App.3d 46, 134 Ill.Dec. 106, 542 N.E.2d 106 (Ill.App. 1 Dist.1989)—**750 ILCS 35/24, n. 1.**
Simmons, In re Marriage of, 221 Ill.App.3d 89, 163 Ill.Dec. 562, 581 N.E.2d 716 (Ill.App. 5 Dist.1991)—**750 ILCS 5/501, n. 14; 750 ILCS 5/503, n. 3.**
Sisul, In re Marriage of, 234 Ill.App.3d 1038, 175 Ill.Dec. 463, 600 N.E.2d 86 (Ill.App. 3 Dist.1992)—**750 ILCS 5/504, n. 3.**
Slavenas, In re Marriage of, 139 Ill.App.3d 581, 93 Ill.Dec. 914, 487 N.E.2d 739 (Ill.App. 2 Dist.1985)—**750 ILCS 5/604, n. 1.**
Smith, In re Marriage of, 164 Ill.App.3d 1011, 115 Ill.Dec. 925, 518 N.E.2d 450 (Ill.App. 1 Dist.1987)—**750 ILCS 5/502, n. 4.**
Smith, In re Marriage of, 128 Ill.App.3d 1017, 84 Ill.Dec. 242, 471 N.E.2d 1008 (Ill.App. 2 Dist.1984)—**750 ILCS 5/508, n. 3.**
Smoller, In re Marriage of, 218 Ill.App.3d 340, 161 Ill.Dec. 129, 578 N.E.2d 256 (Ill.App. 1 Dist.1991)—**750 ILCS 5/401, n. 3.**
Sobo, In re Marriage of, 205 Ill.App.3d 357, 150 Ill.Dec. 280, 562 N.E.2d 1083 (Ill.App. 1 Dist.1990)—**750 ILCS 5/503, n. 21.**
Sohaey v. Van Cura, 158 Ill.2d 375, 199 Ill.Dec. 654, 634 N.E.2d 707 (Ill.1994)—**S.Ct. Rule 220, n. 11.**
Sohaey v. Van Cura, 240 Ill.App.3d 266, 180 Ill.Dec. 359, 607 N.E.2d 253 (Ill.App. 2 Dist.1992)—**S.Ct. Rule 220, n. 11.**
Sokolowski, In re Marriage of, 232 Ill.App.3d 535, 173 Ill.Dec. 701, 597 N.E.2d 675 (Ill.App. 1 Dist.1992)—**750 ILCS 5/503, n. 17.**

TABLE OF CASES

Solomon, In re Marriage of, 84 Ill.App.3d 901, 40 Ill.Dec. 197, 405 N.E.2d 1289 (Ill.App. 1 Dist.1980)—**750 ILCS 5/602, n. 13; 750 ILCS 5/607, n. 2.**

Soraparu, In re Marriage of, 147 Ill.App.3d 857, 101 Ill.Dec. 241, 498 N.E.2d 565 (Ill.App. 1 Dist.1986)—**750 ILCS 5/506, n. 6; 750 ILCS 5/602, n. 1.**

Spengler v. Spengler, 53 Ill.App.3d 620, 11 Ill.Dec. 432, 368 N.E.2d 1040 (Ill.App. 2 Dist.1977)—**750 ILCS 5/2-1401, n. 2; 750 ILCS 5/2-1401, n. 3.**

Spomer, In re Marriage of, 123 Ill.App.3d 31, 78 Ill.Dec. 605, 462 N.E.2d 724 (Ill.App. 5 Dist.1984)—**750 ILCS 5/607, n. 3.**

Stacke v. Bates, 200 Ill.App.3d 85, 146 Ill.Dec. 118, 557 N.E.2d 1305 (Ill.App. 2 Dist.1990)—**750 ILCS 5/503, n. 7.**

Stallings v. Stallings, 75 Ill.App.3d 96, 30 Ill.Dec. 718, 393 N.E.2d 1065 (Ill.App. 5 Dist.1979)—**750 ILCS 5/503, n. 6, 20, 21.**

Stam, In re Marriage of, 260 Ill.App.3d 754, 198 Ill.Dec. 467, 632 N.E.2d 1078 (Ill.App. 3 Dist.1994)—**750 ILCS 5/504, n. 3.**

Steele, In re Marriage of, 212 Ill.App.3d 425, 156 Ill.Dec. 649, 571 N.E.2d 236 (Ill.App. 5 Dist.1991)—**750 ILCS 5/503, n. 7, 20.**

Steffen, In re Marriage of, 253 Ill.App.3d 966, 192 Ill.Dec. 709, 625 N.E.2d 864 (Ill.App. 4 Dist.1993)—**750 ILCS 5/503, n. 33.**

Steichen, In re Marriage of, 163 Ill.App.3d 1074, 115 Ill.Dec. 234, 517 N.E.2d 645 (Ill.App. 2 Dist.1987)—**750 ILCS 5/502, n. 4.**

Stennis v. Rekkas, 233 Ill.App.3d 813, 175 Ill.Dec. 45, 599 N.E.2d 1059 (Ill.App. 1 Dist.1992)—**S.Ct. Rule 220, n. 13.**

Stephenson, In re Marriage of, 121 Ill.App.3d 698, 77 Ill.Dec. 142, 460 N.E.2d 1 (Ill.App. 5 Dist.1983)—**750 ILCS 5/503, n. 21.**

Stern v. Stern, 179 Ill.App.3d 313, 128 Ill.Dec. 351, 534 N.E.2d 533 (Ill.App. 1 Dist.1989)—**S.Ct. Rule 231, n. 1.**

Stern v. Stern, 105 Ill.App.3d 805, 61 Ill.Dec. 567, 434 N.E.2d 1164 (Ill.App. 2 Dist.1982)—**750 ILCS 5/502, n. 4.**

Stevenson's Estate, In re, 44 Ill.2d 525, 256 N.E.2d 766 (Ill.1970)—**S.Ct. Rule 215, n. 2.**

Stiarwalt, In re, 190 Ill.App.3d 547, 137 Ill.Dec. 420, 546 N.E.2d 44 (Ill.App. 2 Dist.1989)—**750 ILCS 50/0.01, n. 4.**

Stockton, In re Marriage of, 169 Ill.App.3d 318, 119 Ill.Dec. 817, 523 N.E.2d 573 (Ill.App. 4 Dist.1988)—**750 ILCS 5/508, n. 3; 750 ILCS 5/513, n. 2.**

Stone, In re Marriage of, 191 Ill.App.3d 172, 138 Ill.Dec. 547, 547 N.E.2d 714 (Ill.App. 4 Dist.1989)—**750 ILCS 5/505, n. 8.**

Strauss, In re Marriage of, 183 Ill.App.3d 424, 132 Ill.Dec. 245, 539 N.E.2d 808 (Ill.App. 2 Dist.1989)—**p. 944, n. 1.**

Support of Pearson, In re, 111 Ill.2d 545, 96 Ill.Dec. 69, 490 N.E.2d 1274 (Ill.1986)—**750 ILCS 5/513, n. 1.**

Sutton, In re Marriage of, 178 Ill.App.3d 928, 128 Ill.Dec. 37, 533 N.E.2d 1125 (Ill.App. 3 Dist.1989)—**750 ILCS 5/502, n. 16.**

Swigers, In re Marriage of, 176 Ill.App.3d 795, 126 Ill.Dec. 231, 531 N.E.2d 858 (Ill.App. 1 Dist.1988)—**750 ILCS 5/503, n. 21.**

Szesny v. Szesny, 197 Ill.App.3d 966, 145 Ill.Dec. 452, 557 N.E.2d 222 (Ill.App. 1 Dist.1990)—**750 ILCS 5/503, n. 21, 32.**

Talty, In re Marriage of, 252 Ill.App.3d 80, 191 Ill.Dec. 451, 623 N.E.2d 1041 (Ill.App. 3 Dist.1993)—**750 ILCS 5/503, n. 7, 25.**

Tanner v. Board of Trustees of University of Illinois, 121 Ill.App.3d 139, 76 Ill.Dec. 687, 459 N.E.2d 324 (Ill.App. 4 Dist.1984)—**p. 964, n. 3.**

Tatham, In re Marriage of, 173 Ill.App.3d 1072, 123 Ill.Dec. 576, 527 N.E.2d 1351 (Ill.App. 5 Dist.1988)—**750 ILCS 5/503, n. 10, 21; 750 ILCS 5/505, n. 8.**

Taylor, In re Marriage of, 202 Ill.App.3d 740, 147 Ill.Dec. 810, 559 N.E.2d 1150 (Ill.App. 3 Dist.1990)—**750 ILCS 5/609, n. 2.**

Thacker, In re Marriage of, 185 Ill.App.3d 465, 133 Ill.Dec. 573, 541 N.E.2d 784 (Ill.App. 5 Dist.1989)—**750 ILCS 5/503, n. 18.**

Theis, In re Marriage of, 121 Ill.App.3d 1092, 77 Ill.Dec. 608, 460 N.E.2d 912 (Ill.App. 3 Dist.1984)—**750 ILCS 5/605, n. 1.**

Thomas, In re Marriage of, 239 Ill.App.3d 992, 181 Ill.Dec. 512, 608 N.E.2d 585 (Ill.App. 3 Dist.1993)—**750 ILCS 5/503, n. 23.**

Thomas v. Thomas, 100 Ill.App.3d 1080, 56 Ill.Dec. 604, 427 N.E.2d 1009 (Ill.App. 1 Dist.1981)—**750 ILCS 5/21-101, n. 1.**

TABLE OF CASES

Thompson v. Dulaney, 970 F.2d 744 (10th Cir.1992)—**p. 961, n. 2.**

Thompson v. Thompson, 484 U.S. 174, 108 S.Ct. 513, 98 L.Ed.2d 512 (1988)—**750 ILCS 35/2, n. 1, 2.**

Thornton, In re Marriage of, 138 Ill.App.3d 906, 93 Ill.Dec. 453, 486 N.E.2d 1288 (Ill.App. 1 Dist.1985)—**750 ILCS 5/503, n. 10.**

Thornton, In re Marriage of, 89 Ill.App.3d 1078, 45 Ill.Dec. 612, 412 N.E.2d 1336 (Ill.App. 1 Dist.1980)—**750 ILCS 5/503, n. 21.**

Tisckos, In re Marriage of, 161 Ill.App.3d 302, 112 Ill.Dec. 860, 514 N.E.2d 523 (Ill.App. 4 Dist.1987)—**750 ILCS 5/607, n. 2.**

Toth, In re Marriage of, 224 Ill.App.3d 43, 166 Ill.Dec. 478, 586 N.E.2d 436 (Ill.App. 1 Dist.1991)—**750 ILCS 5/504, n. 3.**

Treacy v. Treacy, 204 Ill.App.3d 282, 149 Ill.Dec. 802, 562 N.E.2d 266 (Ill.App. 1 Dist.1990)—**750 ILCS 5/510, n. 20.**

Tucker, In re Marriage of, 223 Ill.App.3d 671, 166 Ill.Dec. 83, 585 N.E.2d 1105 (Ill.App. 3 Dist.1992)—**750 ILCS 5/502, n. 16.**

United States v. _____ (see opposing party)

Vallejo v. Mercado, 220 Ill.App.3d 1, 162 Ill.Dec. 692, 580 N.E.2d 655 (Ill.App. 2 Dist.1991)—**S.Ct. Rule 220, n. 11.**

Valter, In re Marriage of, 191 Ill.App.3d 584, 138 Ill.Dec. 799, 548 N.E.2d 29 (Ill.App. 5 Dist.1989)—**750 ILCS 5/610, n. 11.**

Van Zuidam, In re Marriage of, 162 Ill.App.3d 942, 114 Ill.Dec. 176, 516 N.E.2d 331 (Ill.App. 1 Dist.1987)—**750 ILCS 5/401, n. 3; 750 ILCS 5/502, n. 3.**

Varap v. Varap, 76 Ill.App.2d 402, 222 N.E.2d 77 (Ill.App.1966)—**750 ILCS 5/703, n. 1.**

Vella, In re Marriage of, 237 Ill.App.3d 194, 177 Ill.Dec. 328, 603 N.E.2d 109 (Ill.App. 2 Dist.1992)—**750 ILCS 5/502, n. 4; 750 ILCS 5/503, n. 9.**

Vendredi v. Vendredi, 230 Ill.App.3d 1061, 174 Ill.Dec. 329, 598 N.E.2d 961 (Ill.App. 1 Dist. 1992)—**750 ILCS 5/504, n. 3.**

Verdung, In re Marriage of, 126 Ill.2d 542, 129 Ill.Dec. 53, 535 N.E.2d 818 (Ill.1989)—**S.Ct. Rule 304, n. 1; 750 ILCS 5/501, n. 2.**

Vernon, In re Marriage of, 253 Ill.App.3d 783, 192 Ill.Dec. 668, 625 N.E.2d 823 (Ill.App. 4 Dist.1993)—**750 ILCS 5/504, n. 10.**

Vollmer v. Mattox, 137 Ill.App.3d 1, 91 Ill.Dec. 752, 484 N.E.2d 311 (Ill.App. 5 Dist.1985)—**750 ILCS 5/610, n. 1.**

Vucic, In re Marriage of, 216 Ill.App.3d 692, 159 Ill.Dec. 737, 576 N.E.2d 406 (Ill.App. 2 Dist.1991)—**750 ILCS 5/503, n. 27, 33.**

Wakeford v. Rodehouse Restaurants of Missouri, Inc., 154 Ill.2d 543, 182 Ill.Dec. 653, 610 N.E.2d 77 (Ill.1992)—**S.Ct. Rule 220, n. 10.**

Walker, In re Marriage of, 203 Ill.App.3d 632, 149 Ill.Dec. 112, 561 N.E.2d 390 (Ill.App. 4 Dist.1990)—**750 ILCS 5/503, n. 1, 3.**

Walton, In re Marriage of, 28 Cal.App.3d 108, 104 Cal.Rptr. 472 (Cal.App. 4 Dist.1972)—**750 ILCS 5/401, n. 4.**

Warren v. Warren, 169 Ill.App.3d 226, 119 Ill.Dec. 924, 523 N.E.2d 680 (Ill.App. 5 Dist.1988)—**750 ILCS 10/7, n. 7.**

Wartell v. Formusa, 34 Ill.2d 57, 213 N.E.2d 544 (Ill.1966)—**750 ILCS 65/1, n. 1.**

Watson v. Watson, 5 Ill.2d 526, 126 N.E.2d 220 (Ill.1955)—**750 ILCS 10/7, n. 7.**

Webber, In re Marriage of, 191 Ill.App.3d 327, 138 Ill.Dec. 582, 547 N.E.2d 749 (Ill.App. 4 Dist.1989)—**750 ILCS 5/510, n. 4.**

Wehmeier v. UNR Industries, Inc., 213 Ill.App.3d 6, 157 Ill.Dec. 251, 572 N.E.2d 320 (Ill.App. 4 Dist.1991)—**S.Ct. Rule 215, n. 2.**

Weiler, In re Marriage of, 258 Ill.App.3d 454, 196 Ill.Dec. 372, 629 N.E.2d 1216 (Ill.App. 5 Dist.1994)—**750 ILCS 5/503, n. 2, 5.**

Weiss, In re Marriage of, 129 Ill.App.3d 166, 84 Ill.Dec. 378, 472 N.E.2d 128 (Ill.App. 1 Dist.1984)—**S.Ct. Rule 219, n. 3.**

Weiss, In re Marriage of, 87 Ill.App.3d 643, 42 Ill.Dec. 714, 409 N.E.2d 329 (Ill.App. 1 Dist.1980)—**750 ILCS 5/401, n. 2.**

Wentink, In re Marriage of, 132 Ill.App.3d 71, 87 Ill.Dec. 117, 476 N.E.2d 1109 (Ill.App. 1 Dist.1984)—**750 ILCS 5/508, n. 8.**

Werries, In re Marriage of, 247 Ill.App.3d 639, 186 Ill.Dec. 747, 616 N.E.2d 1379 (Ill.App. 4 Dist.1993)—**750 ILCS 5/503, n. 2, 21, 32.**

TABLE OF CASES

Wettstein, In re Marriage of, 160 Ill.App.3d 554, 113 Ill.Dec. 1, 514 N.E.2d 783 (Ill.App. 4 Dist.1987)—**750 ILCS 5/510, n. 17.**
Weybright v. Puckett, 262 Ill.App.3d 605, 200 Ill.Dec. 18, 635 N.E.2d 119 (Ill.App. 4 Dist.1994)—**750 ILCS 5/607, n. 3.**
Wheeler v. Fox, 16 Ill.App.3d 1089, 307 N.E.2d 633 (Ill.App. 4 Dist.1974)—**740 ILCS 5/7, n. 1.**
White, In re Marriage of, 204 Ill.App.3d 579, 149 Ill.Dec. 691, 561 N.E.2d 1387 (Ill.App. 4 Dist.1990)—**750 ILCS 5/510, n. 4.**
Whiting, In re Marriage of, 179 Ill.App.3d 187, 128 Ill.Dec. 286, 534 N.E.2d 468 (Ill.App. 5 Dist.1989)—**750 ILCS 5/510, n. 5.**
Wier v. Isenberg, 95 Ill.App.3d 839, 51 Ill.Dec. 376, 420 N.E.2d 790 (Ill.App. 2 Dist.1981)—**750 ILCS 5/2-1001, n. 2.**
Wiley, In re Marriage of, 199 Ill.App.3d 169, 145 Ill.Dec. 191, 556 N.E.2d 809 (Ill.App. 4 Dist.1990)—**750 ILCS 5/503, n. 21.**
Wiley, In re Marriage of, 199 Ill.App.3d 223, 145 Ill.Dec. 170, 556 N.E.2d 788 (Ill.App. 4 Dist.1990)—**750 ILCS 5/510, n. 5.**
Willis, In re Marriage of, 234 Ill.App.3d 156, 174 Ill.Dec. 633, 599 N.E.2d 179 (Ill.App. 3 Dist.1992)—**750 ILCS 5/604, n. 1.**
Wilson v. Clark, 84 Ill.2d 186, 49 Ill.Dec. 308, 417 N.E.2d 1322 (Ill.1981)—**p. 943, n. 7.**
Wilson v. Smart, 324 Ill. 276, 155 N.E. 288 (Ill.1927)—**750 ILCS 5/703, n. 1; 750 ILCS 5/2 -209, n. 1.**
Winton, In re Marriage of, 216 Ill.App.3d 1084, 159 Ill.Dec. 933, 576 N.E.2d 856 (Ill.App. 2 Dist.1991)—**750 ILCS 5/508, n. 1.**
Wisniewski, In re Marriage of, 107 Ill.App.3d 711, 63 Ill.Dec. 378, 437 N.E.2d 1300 (Ill.App. 4 Dist.1982)—**750 ILCS 5/503, n. 30.**
Wittenauer, In re Marriage of, 103 Ill.App.3d 53, 58 Ill.Dec. 593, 430 N.E.2d 625 (Ill.App. 5 Dist.1981)—**750 ILCS 5/503, n. 5.**
Woods, In re, 561 F.2d 27 (7th Cir.1977)—**11 U.S.C.A. § 523, n. 2.**

Yakubec, In re Marriage of, 154 Ill.App.3d 540, 107 Ill.Dec. 453, 507 N.E.2d 117 (Ill.App. 1 Dist.1987)—**750 ILCS 5/511, n. 10.**
Young, In re Marriage of, 244 Ill.App.3d 313, 185 Ill.Dec. 289, 614 N.E.2d 423 (Ill.App. 1 Dist.1993)—**S.Ct. Rule 304, n. 1; 750 ILCS 5/501, n. 2.**

Zamarripa-Gesundheit, In re Marriage of, 175 Ill.App.3d 184, 124 Ill.Dec. 799, 529 N.E.2d 780 (Ill.App. 1 Dist.1988)—**750 ILCS 5/609, n. 3.**
Zarnes, United States v. (7th Cir.1994)—**p. 961, n. 2.**
Zells, In re Marriage of, 143 Ill.2d 251, 157 Ill.Dec. 480, 572 N.E.2d 944 (Ill.1991)—**S.Ct. Rule 218, n. 2; 750 ILCS 5/503, n. 25.**
Zeman, In re Marriage of, 198 Ill.App.3d 722, 145 Ill.Dec. 149, 556 N.E.2d 767 (Ill.App. 2 Dist.1990)—**750 ILCS 5/510, n. 3, 5.**
Zieske v. Zieske, 41 Ill.App.3d 746, 354 N.E.2d 513 (Ill.App. 1 Dist.1976)—**750 ILCS 5/2-1401, n. 2.**
Zito v. Zito, 196 Ill.App.3d 1031, 143 Ill.Dec. 606, 554 N.E.2d 541 (Ill.App. 1 Dist.1990)—**750 ILCS 5/503, n. 21.**
Zwart, In re Marriage of, 245 Ill.App.3d 567, 185 Ill.Dec. 443, 614 N.E.2d 884 (Ill.App. 2 Dist.1993)—**750 ILCS 5/503, n. 21.**
Zymali, In re Marriage of, 94 Ill.App.3d 1145, 50 Ill.Dec. 379, 419 N.E.2d 487 (Ill.App. 1 Dist.1981)—**750 ILCS 5/501, n. 2.**

*

TABLE OF STATUTES

To find the statute cited in the left-hand side of each column, see the author's note following the statute rule, or page number cited in the right-hand side of each column.

ILLINOIS COMPILED STATUTES

ILCS	This Work
215 ILCS 5/356(d)	750 ILCS 5/502, n. 11
215 ILCS 5/367.2	750 ILCS 5/502, n. 11
325 ILCS 5/1 et seq.	740 ILCS 110/10, n. 5
325 ILCS 5/4.02	325 ILCS 5/4, n. 1
325 ILCS 5/7	325 ILCS 5/4, n. 2
705 ILCS 405/1 et seq.	750 ILCS 5/601, n. 1
	750 ILCS 5/601, n. 2
720 ILCS 5/5–1 et seq.	750 ILCS 60/216, n. 1
720 ILCS 5/10–5.5	750 ILCS 5/607.1, n. 3
720 ILCS 5/12–30	750 ILCS 60/223.1, n. 1
	750 ILCS 60/301, n. 2
720 ILCS 5/14–4	18 U.S.C.A. § 2521, n. 1
720 ILCS 5/14–6	18 U.S.C.A. § 2521, n. 1
720 ILCS 5/32–3	p. 963, n. 1
720 ILCS 525/1 et seq.	750 ILCS 50/0.01, n. 22
720 ILCS 525/4	750 ILCS 50/0.01, n. 14
720 ILCS 525/4.1	750 ILCS 50/0.01, n. 14
735 ILCS 5/1–109	735 ILCS 5/2–620, n. 1
	750 ILCS 5/403, n. 1
	S. Ct. R. 219, n. 3
735 ILCS 5/2–103	750 ILCS 5/510, n. 9
735 ILCS 5/2–104	750 ILCS 5/104, n. 1
	750 ILCS 5/402, n. 2
	750 ILCS 5/512, n. 1
	750 ILCS 5/601, n. 4

ILLINOIS COMPILED STATUTES

ILCS	This Work
735 ILCS 5/2–104—2–107	750 ILCS 5/104, n. 1
735 ILCS 5/2–203	750 ILCS 60/210.1, n. 2
735 ILCS 5/2–203(a)	735 ILCS 5/2–203, n. 2
735 ILCS 5/2–208	735 ILCS 5/2–209, n. 2
735 ILCS 5/2–209(5)	735 ILCS 5/2–209, n. 1
735 ILCS 5/2–701(a)	S. Ct. R. 304, n. 2
735 ILCS 5/2–1001	750 ILCS 5/104, n. 1
735 ILCS 5/2–1001.5	735 ILCS 5/2–1001, n. 1
	750 ILCS 5/104, n. 1
735 ILCS 5/2–1102	S. Ct. R. 238, n. 2
735 ILCS 5/2–1203	750 ILCS 5/413, n. 7
735 ILCS 5/2–1401	750 ILCS 5/413, n. 7
	750 ILCS 5/413, n. 12
	750 ILCS 5/502, n. 8
	750 ILCS 5/502, n. 16
	750 ILCS 5/510, n. 9
735 ILCS 5/2–1901 et seq.	750 ILCS 5/514, n. 5
735 ILCS 5/8–801	750 ILCS 65/1, n. 2
735 ILCS 5/8–2601	p. 943, n. 6
735 ILCS 5/11–101	750 ILCS 5/501, n. 12
	750 ILCS 60/220, n. 3
735 ILCS 5/11–101 to 11–110	750 ILCS 5/501, n. 15
735 ILCS 5/11–101 et seq.	735 ILCS 5/11–102, n. 1
	750 ILCS 5/501, n. 1
	750 ILCS 5/501, n. 9

TABLE OF STATUTES

ILLINOIS COMPILED STATUTES

ILCS	This Work
735 ILCS 5/11–101 et seq.	750 ILCS 60/201, n. 3
	750 ILCS 60/214, n. 1
	750 ILCS 60/215, n. 1
735 ILCS 5/11–102	750 ILCS 60/220, n. 3
735 ILCS 5/12–107	740 ILCS 115/7, n. 1
735 ILCS 5/12–650 et seq.	750 ILCS 5/511, n. 2
	750 ILCS 20/1, n. 4
735 ILCS 5/12–652	750 ILCS 20/1, n. 5
735 ILCS 5/12–901 et seq.	750 ILCS 65/9, n. 1
735 ILCS 5/15–1503	735 ILCS 5/2–1901, n. 1
735 ILCS 5/17–101 et seq.	750 ILCS 5/514, n. 1
735 ILCS 5/21–101 et seq.	735 ILCS 5/21–101, n. 1
740 ILCS 5/101 et seq.	26 U.S.C.A. § 215, n. 1
740 ILCS 65/11	750 ILCS 5/703, n. 4
740 ILCS 80/1	750 ILCS 5/502, n. 6
750 ILCS 5/104	735 ILCS 5/2–104, n. 1
750 ILCS 5/401	735 ILCS 5/2–209, n. 1
750 ILCS 5/403(a)	S. Ct. R. 137, n. 3
750 ILCS 5/413	S. Ct. R. 304, n. 3
750 ILCS 5/413(c)	735 ILCS 5/21–101, n. 1
750 ILCS 5, Pt. V	750 ILCS 20/1, n. 4
750 ILCS 5/501	735 ILCS 5/11–102, n. 1
	750 ILCS 60/201, n. 3
	750 ILCS 60/214, n. 1
	750 ILCS 60/215, n. 1
	750 ILCS 60/220, n. 3
750 ILCS 5/504(c)	S. Ct. R. 301, n. 3
750 ILCS 5/505	750 ILCS 60/201, n. 3
750 ILCS 5/505.2	29 U.S.C.A. § 1169, n. 3

ILLINOIS COMPILED STATUTES

ILCS	This Work
750 ILCS 5/508(a)(3)	S. Ct. R. 301, n. 3
750 ILCS 5/510	750 ILCS 20/1, n. 5
750 ILCS 5/601 et seq.	750 ILCS 60/201, n. 3
750 ILCS 5/604(b)	S. Ct. R. 215, n. 5
750 ILCS 5/605(b)	740 ILCS 110/4, n. 1
750 ILCS 5, Pt. VII	750 ILCS 20/1, n. 4
750 ILCS 5/701	750 ILCS 60/214, n. 1
750 ILCS 5/703	735 ILCS 5/2–209, n. 1
	740 ILCS 65/11, n. 1
750 ILCS 5/705	S. Ct. R. 100.1, n. 6
750 ILCS 5/706.1	750 ILCS 20/26.1, n. 1
750 ILCS 5/709—712	S. Ct. R. 100.1, n. 6
750 ILCS 10/1 et seq.	750 ILCS 5/503, n. 21
750 ILCS 15/1 et seq.	750 ILCS 5/214, n. 1
	750 ILCS 5/304, n. 2
	750 ILCS 20/1, n. 4
750 ILCS 20/1 et seq.	750 ILCS 20/1, n. 4
	S. Ct. R. 100.1, n. 2
750 ILCS 20/35 et seq.	750 ILCS 20/1, n. 4
750 ILCS 22/100 et seq.	750 ILCS 20/1, n. 3
	750 ILCS 20/1, n. 4
750 ILCS 22/611	750 ILCS 20/1, n. 5
	750 ILCS 20/24, n. 1
750 ILCS 22/950	750 ILCS 20/1, n. 5
750 ILCS 22/999	750 ILCS 20/1, n. 5
750 ILCS 25/1 et seq.	750 ILCS 5/709, n. 2
750 ILCS 25/4(a)(1)	750 ILCS 25/2, n. 1
750 ILCS 25/4(d)	750 ILCS 25/2, n. 1
750 ILCS 25/6	750 ILCS 25/2, n. 1

TABLE OF STATUTES

ILLINOIS ADOPTION ACT

Sec.	This Work
20a	750 ILCS 50/0.01, n. 2
21	750 ILCS 50/0.01, n. 22

ILLINOIS DOMESTIC VIOLENCE ACT OF 1986

Sec.	This Work
103	750 ILCS 60/201, n. 1
103(1)	750 ILCS 60/103, n. 2
103(3)	750 ILCS 60/103, n. 2
103(5)	750 ILCS 60/103, n. 4
103(6)	750 ILCS 60/103, n. 5
103(7)	750 ILCS 60/103, n. 2
103(8)	750 ILCS 60/103, n. 4
103(11)	750 ILCS 60/103, n. 6
103(14)	750 ILCS 60/103, n. 2
201	750 ILCS 60/103, n. 3
201(b)	735 ILCS 5/11-102, n. 2; 750 ILCS 60/201, n. 2; 750 ILCS 60/214, n. 1
202(a)	750 ILCS 60/202, n. 1
202(a)(3)	750 ILCS 60/202, n. 1
202(c)	750 ILCS 60/202, n. 1
208	750 ILCS 60/217, n. 1; 750 ILCS 60/218, n. 1; 750 ILCS 60/219, n. 1
210	750 ILCS 60/210.1, n. 1; 750 ILCS 60/217, n. 1; 750 ILCS 60/218, n. 1; 750 ILCS 60/219, n. 1
210(a)	750 ILCS 60/210.1, n. 2

ILLINOIS DOMESTIC VIOLENCE ACT OF 1986

Sec.	This Work
210(a) (Cont'd)	750 ILCS 60/210.1, n. 3
210(a)(2)	750 ILCS 60/210.1, n. 4
210(d)	750 ILCS 60/210.1, n. 4
210(e)	750 ILCS 60/210.1, n. 4
210(f)	750 ILCS 60/210.1, n. 4
210.1	750 ILCS 60/210.1, n. 2; 750 ILCS 60/210.1, n. 4; 750 ILCS 60/210.1, n. 5
210.1(a)	750 ILCS 60/210.1, n. 2
210.1(b)	750 ILCS 60/210.1, n. 5
210.1(c)	750 ILCS 60/210.1, n. 6
211	750 ILCS 60/217, n. 1; 750 ILCS 60/218, n. 1; 750 ILCS 60/219, n. 1
213.1	750 ILCS 60/213.1, n. 1
214	735 ILCS 5/11-102, n. 2; 750 ILCS 60/201, n. 3; 750 ILCS 60/214, n. 1; 750 ILCS 60/214, n. 2; 750 ILCS 60/217, n. 1; 750 ILCS 60/218, n. 1; 750 ILCS 60/219, n. 1
214(b)(1)	750 ILCS 60/223.1, n. 1
214(b)(1)—(b)(6)	750 ILCS 60/214, n. 3
214(b)(2)	750 ILCS 60/223.1, n. 1
214(b)(3)	750 ILCS 60/223.1, n. 1
214(b)(5)	750 ILCS 60/223.1, n. 1
214(b)(6)	750 ILCS 60/223.1, n. 1
214(b)(8)	750 ILCS 60/223.1, n. 1

TABLE OF STATUTES

ILLINOIS DOMESTIC VIOLENCE ACT OF 1986

Sec.	This Work
214(b)(14)	750 ILCS 60/223.1, n. 1
214(b)(17)	750 ILCS 60/214, n. 3
214(c)	750 ILCS 60/214, n. 3
	750 ILCS 60/221, n. 2
214(d)	750 ILCS 60/214, n. 3
	750 ILCS 60/221, n. 2
214(e)	750 ILCS 60/214, n. 3
215	750 ILCS 60/215, n. 1
216	750 ILCS 60/220, n. 1
217	750 ILCS 60/210.1, n. 2
	750 ILCS 60/214, n. 2
	750 ILCS 60/217, n. 1
217(a)(3)	750 ILCS 60/217, n. 2
217(b)	750 ILCS 60/219, n. 2
218	750 ILCS 60/214, n. 2
	750 ILCS 60/217, n. 1
	750 ILCS 60/219, n. 2
	750 ILCS 60/220, n. 1
218(b)	750 ILCS 60/219, n. 2
219	750 ILCS 60/214, n. 2
	750 ILCS 60/217, n. 1
	750 ILCS 60/219, n. 2
	750 ILCS 60/220, n. 2
220(b)(1)(ii)	750 ILCS 60/220, n. 3
221	750 ILCS 60/221, n. 1
221(a)(2)	750 ILCS 60/221, n. 2
221(b)(2)	750 ILCS 60/221, n. 2
221(b)(5)	750 ILCS 60/221, n. 3

ILLINOIS DOMESTIC VIOLENCE ACT OF 1986

Sec.	This Work
222	750 ILCS 60/222, n. 1
222(c)	750 ILCS 60/210.1, n. 2
223(a)	750 ILCS 60/223.1, n. 1
223(b)	750 ILCS 60/223.1, n. 2
223(b)(1)	750 ILCS 60/223.1, n. 2
223(c)	750 ILCS 60/223.1, n. 3
223(d)	750 ILCS 60/223.1, n. 4
223(g)(3)(ii)	750 ILCS 60/223.1, n. 5
224	750 ILCS 60/225, n. 1
224(c)	750 ILCS 60/210.1, n. 6
224(d)	750 ILCS 60/210.1, n. 6
	750 ILCS 60/225, n. 1
226	750 ILCS 60/226, n. 1

ILLINOIS MARRIAGE AND DISSOLUTION OF MARRIAGE ACT

Sec.	This Work
102(6)	750 ILCS 5/102, n. 1
104	735 ILCS 5/2-104, n. 1
	750 ILCS 5/104, n. 1
	750 ILCS 5/402, n. 2
	750 ILCS 5/512, n. 1
	750 ILCS 5/601, n. 4
212	750 ILCS 5/301, n. 3
212(c)	750 ILCS 5/214, n. 1
304	750 ILCS 5/304, n. 1
401	735 ILCS 5/2-209, n. 1
	750 ILCS 5/457, n. 2
401(a)	750 ILCS 5/104, n. 1
401(a)(1)	750 ILCS 5/102, n. 1
	750 ILCS 5/406, n. 1

TABLE OF STATUTES

ILLINOIS MARRIAGE AND DISSOLUTION OF MARRIAGE ACT

Sec.	This Work
401(a)(2)	750 ILCS 5/408, n. 1
401(b)	750 ILCS 5/401, n. 10
	750 ILCS 5/403, n. 4
	750 ILCS 5/504, n. 3
402	750 ILCS 5/402, n. 1
402(a)	750 ILCS 5/102, n. 1
	750 ILCS 5/406, n. 1
402(b)	750 ILCS 5/104, n. 1
	750 ILCS 5/402, n. 2
403	750 ILCS 5/403, n. 1
403(a)	S. Ct. R. 137, n. 3
403(c)	750 ILCS 5/403, n. 3
	750 ILCS 5/406, n. 1
403(e)	750 ILCS 5/403, n. 4
404	750 ILCS 5/404.1, n. 1
404.1	750 ILCS 5/404.1, n. 1
405	750 ILCS 5/403, n. 5
406	750 ILCS 5/406, n. 1
407	750 ILCS 5/408, n. 1
408	750 ILCS 5/408, n. 1
411(b)	750 ILCS 5/411, n. 7
411(d)	750 ILCS 5/411, n. 7
413(a)	750 ILCS 5/413, n. 1
413(c)	735 ILCS 5/21-101, n. 1
	750 ILCS 5/413, n. 5
413(d)	750 ILCS 5/413, n. 6
451—457	750 ILCS 5/457, n. 1
Art. V	750 ILCS 60/223.1, n. 3
501	735 ILCS 5/11-102, n. 1

ILLINOIS MARRIAGE AND DISSOLUTION OF MARRIAGE ACT

Sec.	This Work
501 (Cont'd)	735 ILCS 5/11-102, n. 2
	750 ILCS 5/501, n. 1
	750 ILCS 5/501, n. 9
	750 ILCS 5/501, n. 12
	750 ILCS 5/501, n. 15
	750 ILCS 5/505, n. 1
501(a)(1)	750 ILCS 5/402, n. 3
	750 ILCS 5/501, n. 2
	750 ILCS 5/501, n. 3
	750 ILCS 5/504, n. 1
501(a)(2)	735 ILCS 5/11-102, n. 1
	750 ILCS 5/501, n. 11
501(a)(2)(i)	750 ILCS 5/501, n. 7
501(a)(3)	750 ILCS 5/501, n. 1
	750 ILCS 60/214, n. 2
501(b)	750 ILCS 5/501, n. 12
501(c)	750 ILCS 5/501, n. 12
	750 ILCS 5/501, n. 13
501(d)(1)	750 ILCS 5/501, n. 2
	750 ILCS 5/501, n. 14
501(d)(2)	750 ILCS 5/501, n. 14
501(d)(3)	750 ILCS 5/501, n. 14
501.1	750 ILCS 5/501.1, n. 1
	750 ILCS 5/501.1, n. 2
502	750 ILCS 5/413, n. 8
	750 ILCS 5/502, n. 4
	750 ILCS 5/503, n. 21
502(a)	750 ILCS 5/502, n. 6
502(b)	750 ILCS 5/502, n. 2

993

TABLE OF STATUTES

ILLINOIS MARRIAGE AND DISSOLUTION OF MARRIAGE ACT

Sec.	This Work
502(d)	750 ILCS 5/502, n. 9
	750 ILCS 5/502, n. 10
502(e)	750 ILCS 5/502, n. 14
502(f)	750 ILCS 5/413, n. 8
	750 ILCS 5/502, n. 11
	750 ILCS 5/502, n. 16
	750 ILCS 5/510, n. 1
	750 ILCS 5/510, n. 2
	750 ILCS 5/510, n. 9
	750 ILCS 10/11, n. 2
503	750 ILCS 5/214, n. 1
	750 ILCS 5/503, n. 21
503(a)	750 ILCS 5/503, n. 1
	750 ILCS 5/503, n. 3
	750 ILCS 5/503, n. 4
	750 ILCS 5/503, n. 6
	750 ILCS 5/503, n. 19
	750 ILCS 10/1, n. 2
503(a)(1)	750 ILCS 5/503, n. 2
503(a)(2)	750 ILCS 5/503, n. 7
503(a)(3)	750 ILCS 5/402, n. 3
	750 ILCS 5/503, n. 8
503(a)(4)	750 ILCS 5/502, n. 4
	750 ILCS 5/503, n. 9
	750 ILCS 5/503, n. 21
	750 ILCS 10/11, n. 2
503(a)(5)	750 ILCS 5/503, n. 9
503(a)(6)	750 ILCS 5/503, n. 2
503(a)(7)	750 ILCS 5/503, n. 10

ILLINOIS MARRIAGE AND DISSOLUTION OF MARRIAGE ACT

Sec.	This Work
503(a)(8)	750 ILCS 5/503, n. 11
	750 ILCS 10/1, n. 2
503(b)	750 ILCS 5/503, n. 1
	750 ILCS 5/503, n. 3
	750 ILCS 5/503, n. 4
	750 ILCS 5/503, n. 5
	750 ILCS 5/503, n. 6
	750 ILCS 5/503, n. 8
503(c)	750 ILCS 5/503, n. 10
	750 ILCS 5/503, n. 12
	750 ILCS 5/503, n. 16
503(c)(1)	750 ILCS 5/503, n. 13
	750 ILCS 5/503, n. 14
	750 ILCS 5/503, n. 16
503(c)(2)	750 ILCS 5/503, n. 13
	750 ILCS 5/503, n. 15
	750 ILCS 5/503, n. 16
	750 ILCS 5/503, n. 17
	750 ILCS 5/503, n. 18
	750 ILCS 5/503, n. 19
503(d)	750 ILCS 5/503, n. 19
	750 ILCS 5/503, n. 20
	750 ILCS 5/503, n. 21
	750 ILCS 5/503, n. 23
503(d)(1)	750 ILCS 5/102, n. 1
	750 ILCS 5/503, n. 5
	750 ILCS 5/503, n. 8
	750 ILCS 5/503, n. 21
	750 ILCS 5/503, n. 28

TABLE OF STATUTES

ILLINOIS MARRIAGE AND DISSOLUTION OF MARRIAGE ACT

Sec.	This Work
503(d)(1)—503(d)(12)	750 ILCS 5/503, n. 21
503(d)(2)	750 ILCS 5/503, n. 21
503(d)(3)	750 ILCS 5/503, n. 21
	750 ILCS 5/503, n. 21
503(d)(4)	750 ILCS 5/503, n. 21
503(d)(5)	750 ILCS 5/503, n. 21
503(d)(6)	750 ILCS 5/503, n. 21
503(d)(7)	750 ILCS 5/503, n. 21
503(d)(8)	750 ILCS 5/503, n. 21
503(d)(9)	750 ILCS 5/503, n. 21
503(d)(10)	750 ILCS 5/503, n. 21
503(d)(11)	750 ILCS 5/503, n. 21
503(d)(12)	750 ILCS 5/503, n. 21
503(e)	750 ILCS 5/503, n. 22
503(f)	750 ILCS 5/503, n. 28
503(g)	750 ILCS 5/503, n. 33
	750 ILCS 5/503, n. 34
503(h)	750 ILCS 5/503, n. 35
503(i)	750 ILCS 5/503, n. 36
504	750 ILCS 5/214, n. 1
	750 ILCS 5/503, n. 21
	750 ILCS 5/504, n. 1
	750 ILCS 5/504, n. 2
	750 ILCS 5/504, n. 3
	750 ILCS 10/1, n. 6
	750 ILCS 10/7, n. 1
	26 U.S.C.A. § 215, n. 1
504(a)	750 ILCS 5/703, n. 1
	750 ILCS 5/703, n. 4

ILLINOIS MARRIAGE AND DISSOLUTION OF MARRIAGE ACT

Sec.	This Work
504(a) (Cont'd)	750 ILCS 5/503, n. 19
	750 ILCS 5/504, n. 1
	750 ILCS 5/504, n. 3
	750 ILCS 5/504, n. 7
	750 ILCS 5/505, n. 12
504(a)(1)	750 ILCS 5/503, n. 11
	750 ILCS 5/504, n. 3
504(a)(2)	750 ILCS 5/504, n. 3
504(a)(3)	750 ILCS 5/504, n. 3
504(a)(4)	750 ILCS 5/504, n. 3
504(a)(5)	750 ILCS 5/504, n. 3
504(a)(6)	750 ILCS 5/504, n. 3
504(a)(7)	750 ILCS 5/504, n. 3
504(a)(8)	750 ILCS 5/504, n. 3
504(a)(9)	750 ILCS 5/504, n. 3
504(a)(10)	750 ILCS 5/102, n. 1
	750 ILCS 5/503, n. 21
	750 ILCS 5/504, n. 3
504(a)(11)	750 ILCS 5/504, n. 3
504(a)(12)	750 ILCS 5/504, n. 3
504(c)	750 ILCS 5/504, n. 9
505	750 ILCS 5/505, n. 1
	750 ILCS 5/505, n. 6
	750 ILCS 5/505, n. 12
	750 ILCS 5/510, n. 4
	750 ILCS 10/1, n. 6
	26 U.S.C.A. § 215, n. 28
505(a)	750 ILCS 5/214, n. 1
	750 ILCS 5/304, n. 2

TABLE OF STATUTES

ILLINOIS MARRIAGE AND DISSOLUTION OF MARRIAGE ACT

Sec.	This Work
505(a) (Cont'd)	750 ILCS 5/505, n. 1
	750 ILCS 5/505, n. 2
	750 ILCS 5/505, n. 3
505(a)(1)	750 ILCS 5/413, n. 8
	750 ILCS 5/502, n. 11
	750 ILCS 5/505, n. 4
	750 ILCS 5/505, n. 8
	750 ILCS 5/505.2, n. 3
	750 ILCS 5/510, n. 3
	26 U.S.C.A. § 215, n. 29
505(a)(2)	750 ILCS 5/413, n. 8
	750 ILCS 5/505, n. 5
	750 ILCS 5/505, n. 6
505(a)(2)(d)	750 ILCS 5/505, n. 6
505(a)(3)	750 ILCS 5/503, n. 11
	750 ILCS 5/505, n. 4
	26 U.S.C.A. § 215, n. 28
505(a)(3)(a)—(a)(3)(h)	750 ILCS 5/505, n. 8
505(a)(3)(h)	750 ILCS 5/505, n. 9
	750 ILCS 5/505, n. 10
505(a)(4)	750 ILCS 5/505, n. 11
	750 ILCS 5/505.2, n. 3
505(a)(5)	750 ILCS 5/503, n. 19
	750 ILCS 5/505, n. 12
	750 ILCS 5/505, n. 13
	26 U.S.C.A. § 215, n. 22
505(b)	750 ILCS 5/505, n. 6
	750 ILCS 5/505, n. 14
505(c)	750 ILCS 5/505, n. 15

ILLINOIS MARRIAGE AND DISSOLUTION OF MARRIAGE ACT

Sec.	This Work
505(d)	750 ILCS 5/505, n. 16
505(e)	750 ILCS 5/505, n. 6
505(g)	750 ILCS 5/505, n. 17
505.1	750 ILCS 5/505.1, n. 1
505.2	750 ILCS 5/505, n. 11
	750 ILCS 5/505.2, n. 1
	750 ILCS 5/510, n. 6
	750 ILCS 5/706.1, n. 6
	29 U.S.C.A. § 1169, n. 6
505.2(b)	750 ILCS 5/505.2, n. 1
505.2(c)(2)	750 ILCS 5/505.2, n. 2
505.2(d)	750 ILCS 5/505.2, n. 3
	750 ILCS 5/510, n. 1
506	750 ILCS 5/506, n. 6
	750 ILCS 5/602, n. 11
	750 ILCS 5/604, n. 2
507	750 ILCS 5/502, n. 11
	750 ILCS 5/705, n. 2
508	750 ILCS 5/501, n. 1
	750 ILCS 5/506, n. 6
	750 ILCS 5/508, n. 1
	750 ILCS 5/508, n. 4
	750 ILCS 5/508, n. 8
508(a)	750 ILCS 5/508, n. 2
508(a)(1)—(a)(5)	750 ILCS 5/508, n. 8
508(a)(3)	750 ILCS 5/508, n. 8
508(b)	750 ILCS 5/508, n. 9
	750 ILCS 5/511, n. 6
509	750 ILCS 5/509, n. 1

TABLE OF STATUTES

ILLINOIS MARRIAGE AND DISSOLUTION OF MARRIAGE ACT

Sec.	This Work
509 (Cont'd)	750 ILCS 5/607, n. 4
510	750 ILCS 5/504, n. 6
	750 ILCS 5/505, n. 1
	750 ILCS 5/505, n. 17
	750 ILCS 5/510, n. 1
	750 ILCS 5/510, n. 7
	750 ILCS 5/510, n. 15
	750 ILCS 5/510, n. 17
	750 ILCS 20/1, n. 5
510(a)	750 ILCS 5/502, n. 11
	750 ILCS 5/510, n. 1
	750 ILCS 5/510, n. 2
	750 ILCS 5/510, n. 3
	750 ILCS 5/510, n. 6
510(a)(1)	750 ILCS 5/510, n. 3
510(b)	750 ILCS 5/413, n. 8
	750 ILCS 5/502, n. 16
	750 ILCS 5/510, n. 9
	750 ILCS 5/510, n. 10
	750 ILCS 10/11, n. 2
510(c)	750 ILCS 5/214, n. 1
	750 ILCS 5/504, n. 1
	750 ILCS 5/510, n. 6
	750 ILCS 5/510, n. 11
	750 ILCS 5/510, n. 12
	750 ILCS 5/510, n. 15
	750 ILCS 5/510, n. 16
	26 U.S.C.A. § 215, n. 8
510(d)	750 ILCS 5/502, n. 11

ILLINOIS MARRIAGE AND DISSOLUTION OF MARRIAGE ACT

Sec.	This Work
510(d) (Cont'd)	750 ILCS 5/505, n. 17
	750 ILCS 5/510, n. 6
	750 ILCS 5/510, n. 17
	750 ILCS 5/510, n. 19
	750 ILCS 5/510, n. 20
510(e)	750 ILCS 5/502, n. 11
	750 ILCS 5/510, n. 20
	750 ILCS 5/513, n. 6
511	750 ILCS 5/511, n. 1
	750 ILCS 5/511, n. 9
	750 ILCS 5/512, n. 1
511(c)	750 ILCS 5/511, n. 1
512	750 ILCS 5/104, n. 1
	750 ILCS 5/511, n. 9
	750 ILCS 5/512, n. 1
512(d)	750 ILCS 5/512, n. 1
513	750 ILCS 5/502, n. 11
	750 ILCS 5/510, n. 6
	750 ILCS 5/510, n. 18
	750 ILCS 5/513, n. 1
	750 ILCS 5/513, n. 5
	750 ILCS 5/513, n. 6
513(b)	750 ILCS 5/513, n. 3
514	750 ILCS 5/514, n. 4
601	750 ILCS 5/505, n. 1
	750 ILCS 5/601, n. 2
601(b)	750 ILCS 5/104, n. 1
	750 ILCS 5/214, n. 1
	750 ILCS 5/304, n. 2

997

TABLE OF STATUTES

ILLINOIS MARRIAGE AND DISSOLUTION OF MARRIAGE ACT

Sec.	This Work
601(b) (Cont'd)	750 ILCS 5/601, n. 4
601(c)	750 ILCS 5/601, n. 4
	750 ILCS 5/610, n. 4
601(d)	750 ILCS 5/601, n. 5
	750 ILCS 5/610, n. 4
602	750 ILCS 5/602, n. 1
602(a)	750 ILCS 5/602, n. 1
602(a)(2)	750 ILCS 5/604, n. 1
602(a)(6)	750 ILCS 5/602, n. 7
602(a)(7)	750 ILCS 5/602, n. 7
602(b)	750 ILCS 5/602, n. 7
602(c)	750 ILCS 5/602, n. 8
602.1	750 ILCS 5/602, n. 8
602.1(b)	750 ILCS 5/602.1, n. 3
603	750 ILCS 5/501, n. 1
	750 ILCS 5/501, n. 2
	750 ILCS 5/601, n. 5
	750 ILCS 5/603, n. 1
	750 ILCS 5/603, n. 2
604	750 ILCS 5/602, n. 3
604(b)	750 ILCS 5/602, n. 11
	750 ILCS 5/602.1, n. 3
	750 ILCS 5/604, n. 2
605	740 ILCS 110/10, n. 1
	750 ILCS 5/605, n. 1
605(c)	750 ILCS 5/605, n. 2
607	750 ILCS 5/607, n. 1
607(b)	750 ILCS 5/607, n. 3
607(c)	750 ILCS 5/607, n. 2

ILLINOIS MARRIAGE AND DISSOLUTION OF MARRIAGE ACT

Sec.	This Work
607(d)	750 ILCS 5/607, n. 3
607.1	750 ILCS 5/607, n. 4
	750 ILCS 5/607.1, n. 3
607.1(g)	750 ILCS 5/607.1, n. 3
608(a)	750 ILCS 5/608, n. 1
610	750 ILCS 5/603, n. 1
610(b)	750 ILCS 5/610, n. 5
610(c)	750 ILCS 5/610, n. 3
611	750 ILCS 60/223.1, n. 3
Art. VII	750 ILCS 60/223.1, n. 3
701	750 ILCS 5/701, n. 1
	750 ILCS 5/701, n. 2
	750 ILCS 5/701, n. 3
702	750 ILCS 5/304, n. 3
703	735 ILCS 5/2–209, n. 1
	750 ILCS 5/703, n. 1
	750 ILCS 5/703, n. 4
	750 ILCS 5/504, n. 8
705	750 ILCS 5/705, n. 1
	750 ILCS 5/705, n. 2
	750 ILCS 5/709, n. 1
	S. Ct. R. 100.1, n. 6
706.1	750 ILCS 5/505.2, n. 2
	750 ILCS 5/706.1, n. 1
	750 ILCS 5/706.1, n. 2
	750 ILCS 15/4.1, n. 1
	750 ILCS 20/26.1, n. 1
706.1(A)(1)	750 ILCS 5/706.1, n. 1
706.1(A)(7)	750 ILCS 5/706.1, n. 2

TABLE OF STATUTES

ILLINOIS MARRIAGE AND DISSOLUTION OF MARRIAGE ACT

Sec.	This Work
706.1(B)	750 ILCS 5/413, n. 8
	750 ILCS 5/502, n. 11
706.1(B)(1)	750 ILCS 5/706.1, n. 3
706.1(B)(5)	750 ILCS 5/706.1, n. 3
706.1(B)(7)	750 ILCS 5/706.1, n. 5
706.1(B)(8)	750 ILCS 5/706.1, n. 4
	750 ILCS 5/706.1, n. 9
706.1(C)	750 ILCS 5/706.1, n. 5
	750 ILCS 5/706.1, n. 9
706.1(D)	750 ILCS 5/706.1, n. 5
706.1(E)	750 ILCS 5/706.1, n. 5
706.1(F)	750 ILCS 5/706.1, n. 5
706.1(F)(3)	750 ILCS 5/706.1, n. 5
706.1(G)	750 ILCS 5/706.1, n. 6
706.1(G)(1)	750 ILCS 5/706.1, n. 6
706.1(H)(1)	750 ILCS 5/706.1, n. 5
706.1(H)(2)	750 ILCS 5/706.1, n. 7
706.1(J)	750 ILCS 5/706.1, n. 6
	750 ILCS 5/706.1, n. 8
706.1(K)	750 ILCS 5/706.1, n. 9
709—712	750 ILCS 5/705, n. 1
	750 ILCS 5/705, n. 2
	750 ILCS 5/709, n. 1
	750 ILCS 5/709, n. 2
	750 ILCS 25/2, n. 2
	S. Ct. R. 100.1, n. 6
713	750 ILCS 5/511, n. 8
	750 ILCS 5/713, n. 1
713(a)	750 ILCS 5/713, n. 1

ILLINOIS MARRIAGE AND DISSOLUTION OF MARRIAGE ACT

Sec.	This Work
713(b)	750 ILCS 5/713, n. 1

ILLINOIS MENTAL HEALTH AND DEVELOPMENTAL DISABILITIES CONFIDENTIALITY ACT

Sec.	This Work
2	740 ILCS 110/3, n. 1
	740 ILCS 110/10, n. 1
3	740 ILCS 110/3, n. 1
	740 ILCS 110/10, n. 2
4	740 ILCS 110/10, n. 1
4(a)(1)	740 ILCS 110/4, n. 1
4(a)(2)	740 ILCS 110/4, n. 1
5	740 ILCS 110/5, n. 1
10	740 ILCS 110/10, n. 1
10(a)	740 ILCS 110/5, n. 1
	740 ILCS 110/10, n. 3
10(a)(1)	740 ILCS 110/10, n. 2
10(b)	740 ILCS 110/10, n. 3
10(d)	740 ILCS 110/10, n. 1

ILLINOIS NON-SUPPORT OF SPOUSE AND CHILDREN ACT

Sec.	This Work
3	750 ILCS 15/1, n. 1
4	750 ILCS 15/1, n. 1

ILLINOIS REVISED UNIFORM RECIPROCAL ENFORCEMENT OF SUPPORT ACT

Sec.	This Work
2(b)	750 ILCS 20/7, n. 1
Pt. III	750 ILCS 20/1, n. 4

TABLE OF STATUTES

ILLINOIS REVISED UNIFORM RECIPROCAL ENFORCEMENT OF SUPPORT ACT

Sec.	This Work
Pt. III (Cont'd)	750 ILCS 20/1, n. 5
	750 ILCS 20/39, n. 1
Pt. IV	750 ILCS 20/1, n. 4
	750 ILCS 20/1, n. 5
	750 ILCS 20/39, n. 1
18	750 ILCS 20/12, n. 1
24	750 ILCS 20/1, n. 3
24(3)	750 ILCS 20/1, n. 5
26	750 ILCS 20/24, n. 1
26.1	750 ILCS 20/26.1, n. 1
40(a)	750 ILCS 20/1, n. 5

ILLINOIS RIGHTS OF MARRIED PERSONS ACT

Sec.	This Work
5	750 ILCS 65/15, n. 1
15	750 ILCS 65/5, n. 1
	750 ILCS 65/15, n. 1

ILLINOIS UNIFORM CHILD CUSTODY JURISDICTION ACT

Sec.	This Work
2(a)(5)	750 ILCS 35/9, n. 1
3.04	750 ILCS 35/4, n. 2
4	750 ILCS 35/9, n. 1
4(a)	750 ILCS 35/2, n. 1
	750 ILCS 35/4, n. 2
	750 ILCS 35/8, n. 1
4(a)(1)(ii)	750 ILCS 35/4, n. 3
4(a)(2)	750 ILCS 35/4, n. 4

ILLINOIS UNIFORM CHILD CUSTODY JURISDICTION ACT

Sec.	This Work
4(b)	750 ILCS 35/4, n. 2
	750 ILCS 35/4, n. 7
	750 ILCS 35/15, n. 1
4(c)	750 ILCS 35/4, n. 5
8	750 ILCS 35/4, n. 2
8(f)	750 ILCS 35/8, n. 2
8(g)	750 ILCS 35/8, n. 3
8(h)	750 ILCS 35/8, n. 1
9	750 ILCS 35/8, n. 1
14	750 ILCS 35/17, n. 1
15	750 ILCS 35/4, n. 7
	750 ILCS 35/15, n. 1
16	750 ILCS 35/17, n. 1
19	750 ILCS 35/20, n. 1
21	750 ILCS 35/20, n. 1

ILLINOIS UNIFORM ENFORCEMENT OF FOREIGN JUDGMENTS ACT

Sec.	This Work
12–652	750 ILCS 20/1, n. 5

ILLINOIS UNIFORM INTERSTATE FAMILY SUPPORT ACT

Sec.	This Work
611	750 ILCS 20/1, n. 5
	750 ILCS 20/24, n. 1
950	750 ILCS 20/1, n. 5

ILLINOIS UNIFORM PREMARITAL AGREEMENT ACT

Sec.	This Work
7	750 ILCS 10/7, n. 1

TABLE OF STATUTES

ILLINOIS UNIFORM PREMARITAL AGREEMENT ACT

Sec.	This Work
7 (Cont'd)	750 ILCS 10/7, n. 2
7(a)(2)(ii)	750 ILCS 10/7, n. 8
7(a)(2)(iii)	750 ILCS 10/7, n. 7
7(b)	750 ILCS 10/7, n. 9
7(c)	750 ILCS 10/7, n. 10

UNITED STATES

UNITED STATES CONSTITUTION

Sec.	This Work
5	p. 962, n. 1
	p. 962, n. 2
	p. 962, n. 3

UNITED STATES CODE ANNOTATED

11 U.S.C.A.—Bankruptcy

Sec.	This Work
235(a)(15)	11 U.S.C.A. § 523, n. 4
523	750 ILCS 5/508, n. 7
	750 ILCS 5/510, n. 2
	750 ILCS 5/510, n. 9
523(a)	11 U.S.C.A. § 523, n. 4
523(a)(5)	750 ILCS 5/508, n. 7
	750 ILCS 5/510, n. 2
	750 ILCS 5/510, n. 9
	11 U.S.C.A. § 523, n. 3
523(a)(5)(B)	11 U.S.C.A. § 523, n.1

15 U.S.C.A.—Commerce and Trade

Sec.	This Work
1681s–1	S. Ct. R. 100.13, n. 1

UNITED STATES CODE ANNOTATED
18 U.S.C.A.—Crimes and Criminal Procedure

Sec.	This Work
228	S. Ct. R. 100.13, n. 1
2511(2)(d)	18 U.S.C.A. § 2521, n. 2
2511(4)	18 U.S.C.A. § 2521, n. 1
2520	18 U.S.C.A. § 2521, n. 1

25 U.S.C.A.—Indians

Sec.	This Work
1901—1923	750 ILCS 35/2, n. 2
1901 et seq.	750 ILCS 50/0.01, n. 4

26 U.S.C.A.—Internal Revenue Code

Sec.	This Work
68	26 U.S.C.A. § 215, n. 15
71	750 ILCS 5/402, n. 3
	750 ILCS 5/502, n. 11
	750 ILCS 5/504, n. 6
	750 ILCS 5/504, n. 12
	750 ILCS 5/510, n. 12
	26 U.S.C.A. § 215, n. 1
	26 U.S.C.A. § 215, n. 3
	26 U.S.C.A. § 215, n. 26
	26 U.S.C.A. § 682, n. 2
	26 U.S.C.A. § 682, n. 3
	26 U.S.C.A. § 682, n. 5
	26 U.S.C.A. § 682, n. 6
71(a)	750 ILCS 5/502, n. 11
71(b)	750 ILCS 5/502, n. 11
71(b)(1)(B)	750 ILCS 5/502, n. 11
	26 U.S.C.A. § 215, n. 21

TABLE OF STATUTES

UNITED STATES CODE ANNOTATED
26 U.S.C.A.—Internal Revenue Code

Sec.	This Work
71(b)(1)(B) (Cont'd)	26 U.S.C.A. § 215, n. 22
	26 U.S.C.A. § 682, n. 6
71(c)	26 U.S.C.A. § 262, n. 2
71(c)(2)	26 U.S.C.A. § 215, n. 5
	26 U.S.C.A. § 215, n. 22
	26 U.S.C.A. § 682, n. 3
71(f)	26 U.S.C.A. § 215, n. 7
	26 U.S.C.A. § 215, n. 22
71(f)(6)	26 U.S.C.A. § 215, n. 11
121	26 U.S.C.A. § 1034, n. 3
121(a)	750 ILCS 5/503, n. 21
152(e)	26 U.S.C.A. § 7703, n. 6
213	26 U.S.C.A. § 7703, n. 6
215	750 ILCS 5/402, n. 3
	750 ILCS 5/502, n. 11
	750 ILCS 5/504, n. 6
	750 ILCS 5/504, n. 12
	750 ILCS 5/510, n. 12
408(d)(6)	750 ILCS 5/502, n. 11
	750 ILCS 5/503, n. 21
	750 ILCS 5/503, n. 30
	750 ILCS 5/503, n. 31
	26 U.S.C.A. § 414(p), n. 3
414(p)	750 ILCS 5/502, n. 11
	750 ILCS 5/503, n. 21
	750 ILCS 5/503, n. 30
	750 ILCS 5/503, n. 31
417	750 ILCS 10/11, n. 1
	750 ILCS 10/11, n. 2

UNITED STATES CODE ANNOTATED
26 U.S.C.A.—Internal Revenue Code

Sec.	This Work
417(a)	750 ILCS 10/11, n. 2
417(a)(2)(A)(i)	750 ILCS 10/11, n. 1
682	750 ILCS 5/504, n. 12
	26 U.S.C.A. § 215, n. 25
1034	750 ILCS 5/503, n. 21
	26 U.S.C.A. § 121, n. 4
1041	750 ILCS 5/502, n. 11
	750 ILCS 5/503, n. 21
	750 ILCS 5/503, n. 31
3405(c)	750 ILCS 5/503, n. 21
	750 ILCS 5/503, n. 31
	26 U.S.C.A. § 414(p), n. 8

28 U.S.C.A.—Judiciary and Judicial Procedure

Sec.	This Work
1738A et seq.	750 ILCS 35/2, n. 2

29 U.S.C.A.—Labor

Sec.	This Work
1169	750 ILCS 5/502, n. 11
	750 ILCS 5/505.2, n. 4

42 U.S.C.A.—The Public Health and Welfare

Sec.	This Work
651 et seq.	750 ILCS 5/709, n. 2
	S. Ct. R. 100.13, n. 1
659	S. Ct. R. 100.13, n. 1
666	S. Ct. R. 100.13, n. 1
11601	750 ILCS 35/14, n. 1
11601 et seq.	750 ILCS 35/2, n. 2

TABLE OF STATUTES

UNITED STATES CODE ANNOTATED
42 U.S.C.A.—The Public Health and Welfare

Sec.	This Work
11601 et seq. (Cont'd)	750 ILCS 35/24, n. 1

43 U.S.C.A.—Public Lands

Sec.	This Work
1606	750 ILCS 50/0.01, n. 4

STATUTES AT LARGE

Year	This Work
1986, Apr. 7, P.L. 99–272, 100 Stat. 82	750 ILCS 5/502, n. 11

EMPLOYEE RETIREMENT INCOME SECURITY ACT

Sec.	This Work
609	750 ILCS 5/502, n. 11
	29 U.S.C.A. § 1169, n. 2
	29 U.S.C.A. § 1169, n. 6

SOCIAL SECURITY ACT

Sec.	This Work
Tit. IV–D	750 ILCS 5/709, n. 2
1908	29 U.S.C.A. § 1169, n. 3

TABLE OF RULES AND REVENUE RULINGS

To find the rule or regulation cited in the left-hand side of each column,
see the author's note following the rule, statute or page number
cited in the right-hand side of each column.

ILLINOIS SUPREME COURT RULES	
Rule	This Work
11	735 ILCS 5/2-620, n. 2
	750 ILCS 60/210.1, n. 6
12	735 ILCS 5/2-620, n. 1
	750 ILCS 60/210.1, n. 6
100.1—100.13	750 ILCS 5/709, n. 2
	750 ILCS 5/709, n. 3
100.1 et seq.	750 ILCS 20/1, n. 4
	750 ILCS 25/2, n. 2
	S. Ct. R. 296, n. 1
	S. Ct. R. 296, n. 3
101(d)	750 ILCS 60/210.1, n. 3
104(a)	735 ILCS 5/2-203, n. 1
105	735 ILCS 5/2-1401, n. 1
105(b)	750 ILCS 5/511, n. 4
106	735 ILCS 5/2-1401, n. 1
137	750 ILCS 60/226, n. 1
	S. Ct. R. 137, n. 1
	S. Ct. R. 137, n. 2
201 et seq.	S. Ct. R. 204, n. 5
201(b)(1)	S. Ct. R. 201, n. 6
	S. Ct. R. 213, n. 2
	S. Ct. R. 213, n. 4
201(b)(2)	S. Ct. R. 201, n. 1
201(c)	S. Ct. R. 201, n. 3
201(f)	S. Ct. R. 201, n. 4

ILLINOIS SUPREME COURT RULES	
Rule	This Work
201(k)	S. Ct. R. 219, n. 2
204(a)(3)	S. Ct. R. 204, n. 5
204(b)	S. Ct. R. 204, n. 7
206(a)	S. Ct. R. 204, n. 5
206(e)	S. Ct. R. 206, n. 1
210	S. Ct. R. 213, n. 8
211	S. Ct. R. 206, n. 1
211(c)	S. Ct. R. 211, n. 1
211(c)(4)	S. Ct. R. 211, n. 2
211(d)	S. Ct. R. 211, n. 2
212	S. Ct. R. 211, n. 1
213	S. Ct. R. 204, n. 6
	S. Ct. R. 215, n. 8
	S. Ct. R. 220, n. 7
213(e)	S. Ct. R. 201, n. 4
	S. Ct. R. 201, n. 6
	S. Ct. R. 213, n. 2
	S. Ct. R. 213, n. 4
	S. Ct. R. 213, n. 6
214	S. Ct. R. 204, n. 5
	S. Ct. R. 219, n. 3
215	740 ILCS 110/10, n. 1
	750 ILCS 5/602, n. 11
	750 ILCS 5/602.1, n. 3
	750 ILCS 5/604, n. 2

TABLE OF RULES AND REVENUE RULINGS

ILLINOIS SUPREME COURT RULES

Rule	This Work
215(a)	S. Ct. R. 215, n. 1
	S. Ct. R. 215, n. 2
	S. Ct. R. 215, n. 4
	S. Ct. R. 215, n. 6
215(c)	S. Ct. R. 215, n. 3
215(d)(1)	S. Ct. R. 215, n. 1
	S. Ct. R. 215, n. 4
215(d)(3)	S. Ct. R. 215, n. 4
216(d)	S. Ct. R. 216, n. 1
219	S. Ct. R. 206, n. 1
	S. Ct. R. 211, n. 2
219(c)	S. Ct. R. 219, n. 1
220	S. Ct. R. 213, n. 7
220(a)	S. Ct. R. 220, n. 8
220(a)(1)	S. Ct. R. 220, n. 10
220(b)	S. Ct. R. 220, n. 1
	S. Ct. R. 220, n. 2
	S. Ct. R. 220, n. 3
	S. Ct. R. 220, n. 9
	S. Ct. R. 220, n. 12
220(b)(1)	S. Ct. R. 220, n. 12
220(b)(2)	S. Ct. R. 220, n. 10
220(c)	S. Ct. R. 220, n. 2
	S. Ct. R. 220, n. 7
220(c)(3)	S. Ct. R. 220, n. 7
	S. Ct. R. 220, n. 8
220(c)(4)	S. Ct. R. 220, n. 10
220(c)(5)	S. Ct. R. 220, n. 10
220(d)	S. Ct. R. 220, n. 13
231	S. Ct. R. 235, n. 1

ILLINOIS SUPREME COURT RULES

Rule	This Work
236	S. Ct. R. 216, n. 2
236(b)	S. Ct. R. 236, n. 3
238	735 ILCS 5/2-1102, n. 1
	S. Ct. R. 238, n. 1
238(a)	S. Ct. R. 238, n. 1
238(b)	S. Ct. R. 238, n. 2
272	750 ILCS 5/413, n. 7
	S. Ct. R. 301, n. 4
296	750 ILCS 20/1, n. 4
	S. Ct. R. 100.1, n.6
296(i)	S. Ct. R. 296, n. 1
296(j)	S. Ct. R. 296, n. 1
303	750 ILCS 5/413, n. 2
	750 ILCS 5/413, n. 7
	S. Ct. R. 301, n. 2
303(a)	735 ILCS 5/2-1203, n. 1
304	750 ILCS 5/413, n. 2
	750 ILCS 5/413, n. 7
	S. Ct. R. 301, n. 4
304(a)	735 ILCS 5/2-701, n.1
	750 ILCS 5/501, n. 2
	S. Ct. R. 304, n. 1
	S. Ct. R. 304, n. 2
	S. Ct. R. 304, n. 4
304(b)(5)	S. Ct. R. 304, n. 4
305	S. Ct. R. 301, n. 1
307	735 ILCS 5/11-102, n. 7
	750 ILCS 60/221, n. 4
366(b)(3)(i)	735 ILCS 5/2-1203, n. 1
366(b)(3)(ii)	735 ILCS 5/2-1203, n. 1

TABLE OF RULES AND REVENUE RULINGS

COOK COUNTY LOCAL RULES

Rule	This Work
6.1(a)	750 ILCS 5/511, n. 4
10.7	750 ILCS 50/0.01, n. 14
13.4(h)	S. Ct. R. 201, n. 4
13.9	750 ILCS 5/404.1, n. 1

ILLINOIS RULES OF PROFESSIONAL CONDUCT

Rule	This Work
1.5(d)(1)	750 ILCS 5/508, n. 4

ILLINOIS RULES OF PROFESSIONAL CONDUCT

Rule	This Work
3.3(a)(4)	p. 963, n. 1
3.3(c)	p. 963, n. 1
3.6	750 ILCS 10/1, n. 1

FEDERAL RULES OF EVIDENCE

Rule	This Work
703	p. 943, n. 7

REVENUE RULINGS

Rev. Rule	This Work
59–60	750 ILCS 5/503, n. 24

TABLE OF AUTHORITIES

American Bar Association, Section of Family Law, *Practice Alert* (October 10, 1994)--11 U.S.C.A. § 523, n. 2.
Angst, Gerald L. and Dennis M. Coghlan, Substitution of Judges: Recent Statute Codifies and Modifies Existing Law, 82 Ill.B.J. 240 (1994)--735 ILCS 5/2-1001, n. 1.

Canan & Mitchell, *Employee Fringe and Welfare Benefit Plans*, West Publishing Co. (1994 ed.)--29 U.S.C.A. § 1169, n. 6.
Chicago Law Bulletin, August 17, 1994, p. 1--750 ILCS 5/404.1, n. 3.

Dickens, Charles, *Bleak House, A Norton Critical Edition*, (George Ford & Sylvere Monod, eds., 1977)--750 ILCS 5/401, n. 7.

Graham, Michael H., *Cleary & Graham's Handbook of Illinois Evidence* § 103.7 (6th ed.1994)--p. 944, n. 1.
§ 607.4 (6th ed.1994)--S.Ct. Rule 238, n. 1.
§§ 613.3, 607.2 (6th ed.1994)--S.Ct. Rule 212, n. 2.
§§ 614.1, 706.1 (6th ed.1994)--750 ILCS 5/604, n. 2.
§ 702.4 (6th ed.1994)--p. 943, n. 7.
§ 703.1 (6th ed.1994)--p. 943, n. 7.
Art. VIII (6th ed.1994)--p. 942, n. 5.
§ 801.1 (6th ed.1994)--p. 941, n. 1.
§ 801.7 (6th ed.1994)--p. 944, n. 8.
§ 803.10 (6th ed.1994)--S.Ct. Rule 236, n. 2.
§ 803.11 (6th ed.1994)--S.Ct. Rule 236, n. 3.
§ 803.12 (6th ed.1994)--S.Ct. Rule 216, n. 1.
§ 803.13 (6th ed.1994)--S.Ct. Rule 236, n. 4.

Hammond, Celeste M. and Ronald L. Otto, The Illusion of Reform: Illinois Statutory Tenancy by the Entirety, 78 Ill.B.J. 198 (1990)--750 ILCS 65/22, n. 1.
House Committee on the Judiciary Report, 140 Cong. Rec. H10770 (daily ed. October 4, 1994)--11 U.S.C.A. § 523, n. 2.

Mahoney, D., A. Koritzinsky & T. Forkin, *Tax Strategies in Divorce*, para. 8, p. 79 (1990)--26 U.S.C.A. § 215, n. 21.

1994 United States Master Tax Guide, (CCH) paras. 5-13 (1994)--26 U.S.C.A. § 215, n. 31.
1994 United States Master Tax Guide, (CCH) para. 126 (1994)--26 U.S.C.A. § 215, n. 29, 33.
1994 United States Master Tax Guide, (CCH) para. 133 (1994)--26 U.S.C.A. § 152, n. 4; 26 U.S.C.A. § 215, n. 29.
1994 United States Master Tax Guide, (CCH) para. 173 (1994)--26 U.S.C.A. § 7703, n. 5.

O'Connell, Marjorie A., *Divorce Taxation*, paras. 2411-2413 (1988)--26 U.S.C.A. § 682, n. 4.
para. 3102 (1989)--26 U.S.C.A. § 215, n. 13.
para. 3103 (1989)--26 U.S.C.A. § 215, n. 14.
para. 3402 (1989)--26 U.S.C.A. § 682, n. 3.
para. 3501 (1989)--26 U.S.C.A. § 215, n. 21.
para. 3602 (1989)--26 U.S.C.A. § 215, n. 11.
para. 4002 (1990)--26 U.S.C.A. § 262, n. 1.
para. 4401 (1990)--26 U.S.C.A. § 7703, n. 6.

TABLE OF AUTHORITIES

para. 5201 (1989)--26 U.S.C.A. § 682, n. 1, 2, 3.
para. 5203 (1987)--26 U.S.C.A. § 682, n. 2.
para. 5205 (1987)--26 U.S.C.A. § 682, n. 3.
para. 5207 (1987)--26 U.S.C.A. § 682, n. 1.
para. 5305 (1987)--26 U.S.C.A. § 682, n. 2.
para. 6004 (1989)--26 U.S.C.A. § 1041, n. 2.
para. 6009 (1990)--26 U.S.C.A. § 1041, n. 8.
para. 6010 (1990)--26 U.S.C.A. § 1041, n. 9.
para. 8004 (1990)--26 U.S.C.A. § 1034, n. 4, 5.
para. 8005 (1990)--26 U.S.C.A. § 121, n. 2.
para. 9004 (1989)--26 U.S.C.A. § 215, n. 25.
para. 9106 (1989)--26 U.S.C.A. § 215, n. 26.
para. 13102 (1987)--26 U.S.C.A. § 682, n. 4.
para. 13106 (1989)--26 U.S.C.A. § 215, n. 25.
para. 13202 (1990)--26 U.S.C.A. § 682, n. 5.
para. 18002 (1990)--26 U.S.C.A. § 6013, n. 2.
para. 18101 et seq. (1990)--p. 963, n. 4.
para. 18201 (1990)--26 U.S.C.A. § 7703, n. 3.
Report Bulletins para. 1.1 (Jan. 29, 1993)--26 U.S.C.A. § 1034, n. 4.
Report Bulletins para. 4.1 (April 6, 1993)--26 U.S.C.A. § 1034, n. 4.
Report Bulletins para. 6.1 (April 6, 1993)--26 U.S.C.A. § 152, n. 1.
Report Bulletin para. 11.2 (Nov. 16, 1993)--750 ILCS 10/11, n. 1.
Report Bulletins para. 17.1 (May 20, 1994)--26 U.S.C.A. § 1034, n. 4, 5.
Report Bulletins para. 19.1 (July 15, 1994)--26 U.S.C.A. § 1034, n. 4.

Philip, Alex J. & Lawrence Gadd, *Who's Who in Dickens* (1992)--750 ILCS 5/401, n. 7.

Schatz, Barry A. & Jacalyn Birnbaum, New Statute Promotes Homemakers' Rights, 80 Ill. B.J. 610 (1992)--750 ILCS 5/504, n. 2.

INDEX

ABANDONMENT OF CHILD
Adoption, unfit person, 750 ILCS 50/1
Crimes and offenses, 750 ILCS 15/1 et seq.
  Continuing offense, 750 ILCS 15/9; 750 ILCS 15/10
Fines, 750 ILCS 15/4
Orders of support, 750 ILCS 15/3; 750 ILCS 15/5
Proceedings, 750 ILCS 15/2
Release on probation, 750 ILCS 15/4
Time of action, 750 ILCS 15/8; 750 ILCS 15/9
Witnesses, husband and wife, 750 ILCS 15/7

ABANDONMENT OF SPOUSE
Generally, 750 ILCS 15/1 et seq.; 750 ILCS 65/3; 750 ILCS 65/11; 750 ILCS 65/16
Children, custody of, 750 ILCS 65/16
Deserted party, assumed rights of others, 750 ILCS 65/11; 750 ILCS 65/12
Continuing offense, 750 ILCS 15/10
Dissolution of marriage, 750 ILCS 5/401
Evidence, 750 ILCS 15/6
Fines and penalties, 750 ILCS 15/1 et seq.
Indictment, 750 ILCS 15/2
Order for support, 750 ILCS 15/3; 750 ILCS 15/5
Proceedings, 750 ILCS 15/2
Property rights, 750 ILCS 65/11 et seq.
Release on probation, 750 ILCS 15/4
Sales, 750 ILCS 65/11
  Setting aside, 750 ILCS 65/13
  Validity, 750 ILCS 65/12
Time of action, 750 ILCS 15/8; 750 ILCS 15/9
Uniform Desertion and Nonsupport Act, 750 ILCS 15/1 et seq.
Wife Abandonment Act, 750 ILCS 15/1 et seq.
Witnesses,
  Husband or wife, 750 ILCS 15/7

ABDUCTION
Child Abduction, generally, this index

ABORTION
Children and minors,
  Expense payment, nonconsenting parent, 750 ILCS 65/15
Consent,
  Parental consent,
    Expense payments, nonconsenting parent, 750 ILCS 65/15
Expenses, payment by spouse, 750 ILCS 65/15
Fathers, opposition, injunctions, 735 ILCS 5/11-107.1
Injunctions, fathers, 735 ILCS 5/11-107.1
Minors,
  Expense payment, nonconsenting parent, 750 ILCS 65/15
Nonconsenting parent, childrens abortion, payment of expenses, 750 ILCS 65/15
Parental consultation,
  Expense payments, nonconsenting parent, 750 ILCS 65/15

ABSENCE AND ABSENTEES
Child support, expedited hearings, parties, S.Ct.Rule 100.8

ABUSE
Aged Persons, this index
Alcoholics and Intoxicated Persons, generally, this index
Children and Minors, this index
Criminal sexual abuse. Sexual Abuse, generally, this index
Defined,
  Domestic violence, 750 ILCS 60/103
Domestic Violence, generally, this index
Mentally Ill Persons, this index
Sexual Abuse, generally, this index

ABUSED ADULTS
Domestic Violence, generally, this index
Protection Orders, generally. Domestic Violence, this index

ABUSED AND NEGLECTED CHILD REPORTING ACT
Generally, 325 ILCS 5/1 et seq.
Dissolution of marriage, custody, application of law, 750 ILCS 5/606

ABUSED AND NEGLECTED CHILDREN
Children and Minors, this index

ACCESS
Abused or neglected children, records, 325 ILCS 5/11.1

ACCIDENT AND HEALTH INSURANCE
Dissolution of marriage, support obligation, 750 ILCS 5/505; 750 ILCS 5/505.2
Support, this index

ACCOMPLICES AND ACCESSORIES
Child abduction, 720 ILCS 5/10-7

ACKNOWLEDGMENTS
Adoption of children, consent, 750 ILCS 50/10
Consent and surrender, adoption proceedings, 750 ILCS 50/10
Foreign marriage, proof, 750 ILCS 5/409
Parentage, expedited child support hearings, S.Ct.Rule 100.4

ACQUIRED IMMUNE DEFICIENCY SYNDROME
AIDS, generally, this index

ACT
Defined,
  Expedited child support proceedings, S.Ct.Rule 100.13

ACTED
Defined, adoption of children,
  Property rights, construction of instruments, 760 ILCS 30/1

ACTIONS AND PROCEEDINGS
Abortion, this index
Administrative Law and Procedure, generally, this index
Adoption of Adults, generally, this index
Adoption of Children, generally, this index
Appeal and Review, generally, this index
Attachment, generally, this index
Attorneys Fees, generally, this index
Breach of Marriage Promise, generally, this index
Child custody proceedings, simultaneous proceeding in other state, 750 ILCS 35/7
Child support, expedited rules, S.Ct. Rule 100.3
Children and Minors, this index
Commencement of actions,
  Dissolution of marriage proceedings, 750 ILCS 5/411
  Limitation of Actions, generally, this index
Contempt, generally, this index
Continuance, generally, this index
Costs, generally, this index
Counterclaims. Set-off and Counterclaim, generally, this index

ACTIONS

ACTIONS AND PROCEEDINGS
—Cont'd
Counties, this index
Damages, generally, this index
Depositions, generally, this index
Dismissal of Actions, generally, this index
Drugs and Medicine, this index
Evidence, generally, this index
Garnishment, generally, this index
Guardian Ad Litem, generally, this index
Guardians and Guardianship, generally, this index
Husband and wife, rights of married persons, 750 ILCS 65/0.01 et seq.
Immunities. Privileges and Immunities, generally, this index
Infants. Children and Minors, generally, this index
Injunctions, generally, this index
Joinder of actions,
 Children and minors, emancipation of mature minors, 750 ILCS 30/10
 Emancipation of mature minors, 750 ILCS 30/10
 Paternity proceedings, 750 ILCS 45/9
Judgments, generally, this index
Jurisdiction, generally, this index
Limitation of Actions, generally, this index
Mandamus, generally, this index
Married persons, rights, 750 ILCS 65/0.01 et seq.
Minors. Children and Minors, generally, this index
Municipalities, this index
Non-family expenses, creditors claims against spouses or former spouses, 750 ILCS 65/15
Nonsupport, Uniform Reciprocal Enforcement of Support Act, 750 ILCS 20/1 et seq.
Parental Responsibility Law, 740 ILCS 115/1 et seq.
Parties, generally, this index
Partition, generally, this index
Paternity. Children Born Out of Wedlock, this index
Pending Actions, generally, this index
Place of trial. Venue, generally, this index
Pleadings, generally, this index
Political Subdivisions, this index
Presumptions, generally. Evidence, this index
Privileges and Immunities, generally, this index
Probate Proceedings, generally, this index
Process, generally, this index
Rules of Court, generally, this index
Set-off and Counterclaim, generally, this index
Social Services, this index
Supersedeas or Stay, generally, this index
Support, generally, this index
Third Parties, generally, this index

ACTIONS AND PROCEEDINGS
—Cont'd
Torts, generally, this index
Transcripts of Record, generally, this index
Trial, generally, this index
Uniform Reciprocal Enforcement of Support Act, 750 ILCS 20/1 et seq.
Venue, generally, this index

ACTS
Statutes, generally, this index

ADDICT
Alcoholics and Intoxicated Persons, generally, this index
Drug Addicts, generally, this index

ADMINISTRATION OF ESTATES
Probate Proceedings, generally, this index

ADMINISTRATIVE EXPENSES
Defined, expedited child support, 750 ILCS 25/3

ADMINISTRATIVE HEARING OFFICERS
Child support, expedited rules, S.Ct. Rule 100.2 et seq.
Defined,
 Expedited child support proceedings, 750 ILCS 25/3: S.Ct. Rule 100.13
Rules of Court, this index

ADMINISTRATIVE LAW AND PROCEDURE
Abused or neglected children, reports, witnesses, 325 ILCS 5/10
Witnesses, child abuse reports, 325 ILCS 5/10

ADMISSIBILITY OF EVIDENCE
Evidence, generally, this index

ADMISSIONS
Children and minors, custody actions, marital privilege, 735 ILCS 5/8–801
Husband and wife, privileged communications, 735 ILCS 5/8–801
Privileged communications, 735 ILCS 5/8–801 et seq.
Spouse, privileged communications, 735 ILCS 5/8–801
Wife, privileged communications, 735 ILCS 5/8–801

ADOPTION
Termination of rights of putative father,
 Putative father registry, 750 ILCS 50/12.1

ADOPTION ACT
Generally, 750 ILCS 50/0.01 et seq.

ADOPTION COMPENSATION PROHIBITION ACT
Generally, 720 ILCS 525/0.01 et seq.

ADOPTION DISRUPTION
Defined,
 Adoption of children, 750 ILCS 50/1

ADOPTION OF ADULTS
Appeal, 750 ILCS 50/20
Certificate of adoption, 750 ILCS 50/19
Civil Practice Law, application, 750 ILCS 50/20
Consents, 750 ILCS 50/8 et seq.
Construction of law, liberal construction, 750 ILCS 50/20
Effective date of law, 750 ILCS 50/24
Interim order, 750 ILCS 50/13
Investigation, 750 ILCS 50/6
Judgment of adoption, 750 ILCS 50/14
Jurisdiction and venue, 750 ILCS 50/4
 Judgment attacked on ground of lack of, 750 ILCS 50/20
 Order attacked on ground of lack of, 750 ILCS 50/20
Liberal construction of law, 750 ILCS 50/20
Order for adoption, 750 ILCS 50/14
 Setting aside, 750 ILCS 50/20
Partial invalidity, 750 ILCS 50/22
Persons who may be adopted, 750 ILCS 50/3
Pleadings, waiver of defect, 750 ILCS 50/20
Supreme court rules, applicability, 750 ILCS 50/20
Venue, 750 ILCS 50/4
Waiver, defense in pleadings, 750 ILCS 50/20

ADOPTION OF CHILDREN
Abused child, defined, 750 ILCS 50/1
Acknowledgment of consent, 750 ILCS 50/10 et seq.
Affidavits,
 Fees, 750 ILCS 50/14
 Identification, biological father, 750 ILCS 50/11
 Location of defendants, 750 ILCS 50/7
Affirmative defenses, unfit persons, intent to forgo parental rights, 750 ILCS 50/1
Age, eligibility to adopt, 750 ILCS 50/2
Agency. Child welfare agency, generally, post
Aliens, 750 ILCS 50/4.1
Guardians, 750 ILCS 50/13
Investigation, 750 ILCS 50/6
Petitions, 750 ILCS 50/5
Placement in United States, 750 ILCS 50/4.1
Reports, investigations, 750 ILCS 50/6
Appeal and review, 750 ILCS 50/20
 Appellate court, jurisdiction, 750 ILCS 50/20
Father, failure of notice, 750 ILCS 55/1
Identification, parties, 750 ILCS 50/18

ADOPTION

ADOPTION OF CHILDREN
—Cont'd
Appeal and review—Cont'd
  Notice, failure to give father, 750 ILCS 55/1
  Time, relief from final judgment or order, 750 ILCS 50/20b
Armed forces members, 750 ILCS 50/2
Attorneys fees,
  Affidavits, 750 ILCS 50/14
  Permitted compensation, 720 ILCS 525/4.1
Birth records, disclosure, jurisdiction, 750 ILCS 50/14
Bonds (officers and fiduciaries), child placing agencies, 750 ILCS 50/4.1
Born out of wedlock, etc., not to be used in proceeding, 750 ILCS 50/18
Certificate, 750 ILCS 50/19
Certificate of evidence, necessity, 750 ILCS 50/14
Certified copies of papers and records, order of court, 750 ILCS 50/18
Child, defined, 750 ILCS 50/1
Child placing agencies, licenses, 750 ILCS 50/4.1
Child welfare agency,
  Commitment of child to by interim order, 750 ILCS 50/13
  Consent, form, etc., 750 ILCS 50/10
  Defined, 750 ILCS 50/1
  Discretion of court to adopt report of investigation by, 750 ILCS 50/6
  Expenses, affidavits, issuance of judgments, 750 ILCS 50/14
  Fees for placing, 720 ILCS 525/0.01 et seq.; 750 ILCS 50/21
  Investigations, 750 ILCS 50/6
  Residence requirement, 750 ILCS 50/2
Circuit Court Clerks, this index
Civil Practice Act, applicability, 750 ILCS 50/20
Compacts, 750 ILCS 50/2.1
  Interstate compact on placement of children, generally, post
Compensation for placing, 720 ILCS 525/0.01 et seq.; 750 ILCS 50/21
Compliance with designated existing law, 750 ILCS 50/4.1
Confidential intermediary, obtaining psychological or health and medical information from biological parents or siblings, 750 ILCS 50/18.3a
Confidential records, 750 ILCS 50/18
  Jurisdiction, disclosure, 750 ILCS 50/14
  Report of investigation, 750 ILCS 50/6
Consents, 750 ILCS 50/8 et seq.
  Affidavit of identification, biological father, 750 ILCS 50/11
  Child, 750 ILCS 50/12
  Exemptions, 750 ILCS 50/8
  Forms, 750 ILCS 50/10

ADOPTION OF CHILDREN
—Cont'd
Consents—Cont'd
  Guardian ad litem, mentally ill parents, 750 ILCS 50/8
  Identifying information, exchange, 750 ILCS 50/18.1 et seq.
  Irrevocability, 750 ILCS 50/11
  Minor parent, validity, 750 ILCS 50/11
  Parent of illegitimate child, 750 ILCS 50/8
  Persons authorized to consent, 750 ILCS 50/8
  Revocation of consent, 750 ILCS 50/9
  Saving provision, 750 ILCS 50/23
  Time for taking consent, 750 ILCS 50/9
  Unborn child, form, 750 ILCS 50/10
  Waiver, putative father registry, 750 ILCS 50/12.1
Construction of instruments, 760 ILCS 30/1
Construction of law, 750 ILCS 50/2.1
  Liberal construction, 750 ILCS 50/20
Contest, failure to give notice to father, 750 ILCS 55/1
Cook County of Department of Public Aid, courts services division, investigations, 750 ILCS 50/6
Costs,
  Investigations and investigators, Petition, determination whether charge to petitioner, 750 ILCS 50/6
Court file, inspection, 750 ILCS 50/18
Crimes and offenses, placing out children, receipt of compensation, 720 ILCS 525/5
Criminal background checks, 750 ILCS 50/5; 750 ILCS 50/6; 750 ILCS 50/15.1
Custody, vacating order or denying petition, 750 ILCS 50/20
Death,
  Availability for adoption, 750 ILCS 50/1
  Before final judgment, 750 ILCS 50/14a
  Consent, 750 ILCS 50/12
  Estates of decedents, 750 ILCS 50/14a
  Parents, visitation rights of grandparents, 755 ILCS 5/11–7.1
  Probate proceedings, 750 ILCS 50/14a
Declaration of paternity, putative father,
  Filing, effect, 750 ILCS 50/12a
Default, 750 ILCS 50/7
Definitions, 750 ILCS 50/1
Disclaimer of paternity, putative father,
  Effect, 750 ILCS 50/12a

ADOPTION OF CHILDREN
—Cont'd
Disclosure,
  Confidential intermediaries, identity of biological parents or siblings without consent, damages and fines, 750 ILCS 50/18.3a
  Jurisdiction, court files and birth records, 750 ILCS 50/14
Dismissal of action, death of child, 750 ILCS 50/14a
Duress, limitation of actions, 750 ILCS 50/11
Effective date of law, 750 ILCS 50/24
Evidence,
  Putative father registry, termination of parental rights, 750 ILCS 50/12.1
Expenses,
  Affidavits, issuance of judgments, 750 ILCS 50/14
  Reasonable living expenses, biological parents, payment by petitioners, 720 ILCS 525/4.1
Father, failure to give notice, 750 ILCS 55/1
Fees,
  Placing, 750 ILCS 50/21
Female as included in term male, 750 ILCS 50/1
Final judgment, death of child, 750 ILCS 50/14a
Fines and penalties, disclosure of information about biological parents or siblings without consent, confidential intermediaries or physicians, 750 ILCS 50/18.3a
Fingerprints, criminal background checks, 750 ILCS 50/5; 750 ILCS 50/6; 750 ILCS 50/15.1
Foreign countries,
  Aliens, generally, ante
Forms,
  Adoption notice, 750 ILCS 50/7
  Affidavit of identification, biological father, 750 ILCS 50/11
  Consent and surrender, etc., 750 ILCS 50/10
  Service of process by publication, 750 ILCS 50/7
Foster parents, adoption of foster children, preference, 750 ILCS 50/15.1
Fraud, limitation of actions, 750 ILCS 50/11
Grandparents, visitation rights, 750 ILCS 5/607
  Death of parents, 755 ILCS 5/11–7.1
Guardian ad litem,
  Appointment, 750 ILCS 50/13
  Consent, 750 ILCS 50/8
  Unborn children, appointments, 720 ILCS 525/4.1
Guardianship or conservatorship,
  Consent, 750 ILCS 50/10
  Foster parents, preference, 750 ILCS 50/15.1

ADOPTION

ADOPTION OF CHILDREN
—Cont'd
Health information,
　Confidential intermediaries, obtaining from biological parents or siblings, 750 ILCS 50/18.3a
　Release, 750 ILCS 50/18.4a
Hearing, 750 ILCS 50/13
　Report of facts of investigation not considered, exception, 750 ILCS 50/6
Identifying information,
　Appeal and review, 750 ILCS 50/18
　Exchange, 750 ILCS 50/18.1 et seq.
　Parties, 750 ILCS 50/18
Illegitimate, etc., not to be used in proceedings, 750 ILCS 50/18
Impounding file relating to proceedings, order of court, 750 ILCS 50/18
In need of mental treatment defined, 750 ILCS 50/1
　Psychological, health or medical information, confidential intermediaries, obtaining from biological parents or siblings, 750 ILCS 50/18.3a
Information,
　Furnished by petitioners to clerk of court, 750 ILCS 50/5
　Release, 750 ILCS 50/18.4a
Instruments, construction, property rights, 760 ILCS 30/1
Interim order, 750 ILCS 50/13
Interstate compact on placement of children,
　Foreign children, 750 ILCS 50/4.1
Investigations and investigators,
　Criminal background checks, 750 ILCS 50/5; 750 ILCS 50/6; 750 ILCS 50/15.1
　Petition, 750 ILCS 50/6
Judgments, 750 ILCS 50/14; 750 ILCS 50/15
　Death of children, 750 ILCS 50/14a
　Setting aside, 750 ILCS 50/20
　Waiver of waiting period, 750 ILCS 50/16
Jurisdiction, 750 ILCS 50/4
　Disclosure of birth records, 750 ILCS 50/14
　Lack of jurisdiction,
　Attacking order, 750 ILCS 50/20
Juvenile Delinquents and Dependents, this index
Liberal construction of law, 750 ILCS 50/20
Licensed child placement agency, investigations, 750 ILCS 50/6
Limitation of actions, 750 ILCS 50/11
Male as including female, 750 ILCS 50/1
Medical information,
　Confidential intermediaries, obtaining from biological parents or siblings, 750 ILCS 50/18.3a
　Release, 750 ILCS 50/18.4a

ADOPTION OF CHILDREN
—Cont'd
Mentally ill persons,
　Children, consent, 750 ILCS 50/12
　Defined, 750 ILCS 50/1
Mentally retarded, defined, 750 ILCS 50/1
Minor parents, consent, validity, 750 ILCS 50/11
Natural parents,
　Death, visitation rights of grandparents, 755 ILCS 5/11-7.1
　Termination of rights, 750 ILCS 50/17
Neglected child, defined, 750 ILCS 50/1
Notices, 750 ILCS 50/7
　Application for decree for adoption, 750 ILCS 50/14
　Failure to give father, appeal, 750 ILCS 55/1
　Putative father, 750 ILCS 50/12a
　Waiver, putative father registry, 750 ILCS 50/12.1
Orders, 750 ILCS 50/14
　Determination by interim order, 750 ILCS 50/13
　Setting aside, extent, 750 ILCS 50/20
　Vacating, custody hearings, 750 ILCS 50/20
Parent, defined, 750 ILCS 50/1
Parental rights, effect of order terminating, 750 ILCS 50/17
Partial invalidity, 750 ILCS 50/22
Parties to proceeding, 750 ILCS 50/7
　Identification, 750 ILCS 50/18
Paternity. Children Born Out of Wedlock, this index
Persons who may adopt, 750 ILCS 50/2
Persons who may be adopted, 750 ILCS 50/3
Petition, 750 ILCS 50/5
　Confidential intermediaries, obtaining psychological, health or medical information from biological parents or siblings, 750 ILCS 50/18.3a
　Denial, custody hearings 750 ILCS 50/20
　Final judgment after death of child, 750 ILCS 50/14a
　Verification, consent, 750 ILCS 50/8
Placing out children, receipt of compensation, crimes and offenses, 720 ILCS 525/5
Pleadings, waiver of defect, 750 ILCS 50/20
Plural as including singular and vice versa, 750 ILCS 50/1
Policemen, compensation for, 720 ILCS 525/0.01 et seq.
Preference, foster parents, 750 ILCS 50/15.1
Presumptions,
　Biological father, affidavit of identification, 750 ILCS 50/11
　Probation officer, investigation, 750 ILCS 50/6
Process, 750 ILCS 50/7

ADOPTION OF CHILDREN
—Cont'd
Property rights, construction of instruments, 760 ILCS 30/1
Psychological information, confidential intermediaries, obtaining from biological parents or siblings, 750 ILCS 50/18.3a
Publication, service of process, 750 ILCS 50/7
Putative father,
　Defined, 750 ILCS 50/1
　Notice, 750 ILCS 50/12a
Putative father registry, 750 ILCS 50/12.1
Record of proceedings, report of investigation of petition, 750 ILCS 50/6
　Confidential, 750 ILCS 50/18
　Court files, 750 ILCS 50/18
　Proceedings, report of investigation of petition, 750 ILCS 50/6
Refusal to identify biological father, 750 ILCS 50/11
Registry, putative fathers, 750 ILCS 50/12.1
Related child,
　Defined, 750 ILCS 50/1
　Investigation, 750 ILCS 50/6
　Order, 750 ILCS 50/14
　Petition, 750 ILCS 50/5
Relatives, visitation rights, 755 ILCS 5/11-7.1
Religious beliefs, consideration by court, 750 ILCS 50/15
Report on investigation of petitioner, 750 ILCS 50/6
Reports,
　Criminal background checks, 750 ILCS 50/5; 750 ILCS 50/6; 750 ILCS 50/15.1
　Investigation of petitioner, 750 ILCS 50/6
Residence qualifications, persons who may adopt, 750 ILCS 50/2
Revocation, consent or surrender, 750 ILCS 50/9
Saving provisions, 750 ILCS 50/23
Service of process by publication, 750 ILCS 50/7
Singular as including plural and vice versa, 750 ILCS 50/1
Special findings of fact, necessity, 750 ILCS 50/14
Subject to involuntary admission, defined, 750 ILCS 50/1
Support, failure to pay, consent exemption, 750 ILCS 50/8
Support petitions, filing, Uniform Reciprocal Enforcement of Support Act, 750 ILCS 20/11
Supreme court rules, applicability, 750 ILCS 50/20
Surrender, 750 ILCS 50/9; 750 ILCS 50/10
　Acknowledgment, form, etc., 750 ILCS 50/10
　Consent or surrender, 750 ILCS 50/9
　　Minority of parent, voidability of consent, 750 ILCS 50/11
　Exemptions, 750 ILCS 50/8

ADOPTION OF CHILDREN
—Cont'd
Surrender—Cont'd
Persons authorized to, 750 ILCS 50/8
Revocation of surrender, 750 ILCS 50/9
Time for taking, 750 ILCS 50/9
Surrendered children, information exchanges, 750 ILCS 50/18.1 et seq.
Termination of rights of putative father, 750 ILCS 50/12a
Time,
Consent or surrender of child, 750 ILCS 50/9
Relief from final judgment or order, 750 ILCS 50/20b
Unborn child, consent to adoption, form, 750 ILCS 50/10
Unfit person,
Consent, 750 ILCS 50/8
Defined, 750 ILCS 50/1
Venue, 750 ILCS 50/4
Verification, petition, 750 ILCS 50/5
Visitation,
Failure to visit, consent exemption, 750 ILCS 50/8
Grandparents, 750 ILCS 5/607
Death of parents, 755 ILCS 5/11–7.1
Relatives, death of parents, 755 ILCS 5/11–7.1
Waiver,
Defense in pleadings, 750 ILCS 50/20
Putative father registry, notice and consent, 750 ILCS 50/12.1
Service of process, parties, 750 ILCS 50/7
Waiting period, discretion of court, 750 ILCS 50/16
Welfare of child prime consideration, 750 ILCS 50/15

ADOPTIVE HOME
Child Care Facilities, generally, this index

ADULT
Legal age, 755 ILCS 5/11–1

ADULTERY
Dissolution of marriage, 750 ILCS 5/401
Paternity proceedings, admissibility of evidence, 750 ILCS 45/6

ADULTS WITH DISABILITIES
Defined,
Domestic violence, 750 ILCS 60/103

ADVOCATES
Domestic abuse advocates, participation in proceedings, 750 ILCS 60/205
Domestic violence,
Confidential or privileged information, 750 ILCS 60/227; 750 ILCS 60/227.1
Participation in proceedings, 750 ILCS 60/205

AFFIDAVITS
Adoption of children,
Fees, costs, etc., 750 ILCS 50/14
Location of defendants, 750 ILCS 50/7
Certification, verification by certification, 735 ILCS 5/1–109
Change of name, 735 ILCS 5/21–102
Change of venue, 735 ILCS 5/2–1001.5
Child Custody Jurisdiction Act, proof of service, 750 ILCS 35/6
Child custody proceedings,
Information from parties, 750 ILCS 35/10
Proof of service, Uniform Child Custody Jurisdiction Act, 750 ILCS 35/6
Dissolution of marriage, joint simplified procedure, 750 ILCS 5/454
False,
Paternity proceedings, attorneys fees and costs, 750 ILCS 45/7
Injunctions, this index
Judgments,
Relief petition, 735 ILCS 5/2–1401
Juvenile Delinquents and Dependents, this index
Marriage, minors, affidavits, 750 ILCS 5/203
Orders of court, relief petition, 735 ILCS 5/2–1401
Paternity proceedings, false, attorneys fees and costs, 750 ILCS 45/7
Petition,
Change of name, 735 ILCS 5/21–102
Preliminary injunctions, denial, 735 ILCS 5/11–102
Summons, individual service, 735 ILCS 5/2–203; 735 ILCS 5/2–203.1
Support,
Income withholding, 750 ILCS 5/706.1; 750 ILCS 15/4.1; 750 ILCS 20/26.1
Temporary restraining orders, Denial, 735 ILCS 5/11–101
Uniform Child Custody Jurisdiction Act, information from parties, 750 ILCS 35/10
Venue,
Change of venue, 735 ILCS 5/2–1001.5
Transfer of causes, motions, 735 ILCS 5/2–104
Verification, generally, this index

AFFINITY
Relatives, generally, this index

AFFIRMATIONS
Oaths and Affirmations, generally, this index

AFFIRMATIVE DEFENSES
Adoption, unfit parents, intent to forgo parental rights, 750 ILCS 50/1
Child abduction, offenses, 720 ILCS 5/10–5

AFFIRMATIVE RELIEF
Judgments, 735 ILCS 5/2–1301

AGE
Adults, legal age, 755 ILCS 5/11–1
Children and Minors, this index
Emancipation of Mature Minors Act, 750 ILCS 30/1 et seq.
Guardians and conservators, person acting as, 755 ILCS 5/11–3
Marriage license, 750 ILCS 5/208
Minors. Children and Minors, this index
Process, private person, 735 ILCS 5/2–202

AGED PERSONS
Assault and battery,
Domestic Violence, generally, this index
Cousins, marriage, 750 ILCS 5/212
Crimes and offenses,
Protection orders, generally. Domestic Violence, this index
Domestic Violence, generally, this index
Income taxes, principal residence, sale, one-time exclusion, 26 U.S.C.A. § 121
Marriage, cousins, 750 ILCS 5/212
Not for profit agencies, conservators, 755 ILCS 5/11–3
Protection orders, generally. Domestic Violence, this index
Social Services, generally, this index

AGENCIES
Defined,
Adoption of children, 750 ILCS 50/1
Law Enforcement Agencies, generally, this index

AGENTS
Defined,
Mental Health and Developmental Disabilities Confidentiality Act, 740 ILCS 110/2
Examination, 735 ILCS 5/2–1102
Power of Attorney, generally, this index

AGGRAVATED DAMAGES
Alienation of affections, 740 ILCS 5/3

AGGRAVATED KIDNAPPING
Kidnapping, generally, this index

AIDS
Abused and neglected children, tests, 325 ILCS 5/5
Disclosure,
Tests, identity,
Abused or neglected children, temporary caretakers, 325 ILCS 5/5
Marriage, medical information brochure, 750 ILCS 5/204
Medical information brochure, marriage license applicants and others, 750 ILCS 5/204

AIDS

AIDS—Cont'd
Tests and testing,
Abused and neglected children, 325 ILCS 5/5
Disclosure,
Temporary caretakers, abused or neglected children, 325 ILCS 5/5

ALCOHOLICS AND INTOXICATED PERSONS
Cause for dissolution of marriage, 750 ILCS 5/401
Dissolution of marriage, ground, 750 ILCS 5/401
Domestic violence, protective orders, 750 ILCS 60/208
Protection orders, domestic violence, 750 ILCS 60/214

ALIENATION OF AFFECTIONS ACT
Generally, 740 ILCS 5/0.01 et seq.

ALIENS
Adoption of Children, this index
Marriage, 750 ILCS 5/216 et seq.
Dissolution, support order, information, 750 ILCS 5/706.1
Paternity proceedings, support orders, 750 ILCS 45/20
Support, 750 ILCS 15/4.1; 750 ILCS 20/26.1
Dissolution of marriage, 750 ILCS 5/706.1
Withholding, 750 ILCS 5/706.1
Children born out of wedlock 750 ILCS 45/20
Uniform enforcement of support, 750 ILCS 20/26.1

ALIMONY
See, also, Maintenance; Support, generally, this index
Income taxes, 26 U.S.C.A. § 71
Deductions, 26 U.S.C.A. § 215

AMBULATORY SURGICAL TREATMENT CENTERS
Abortion, generally, this index

ANNUITIES
Withholding, eligible rollover distributions, 26 U.S.C.A. § 3405(c)

ANNULMENT OF MARRIAGE
Marriage, this index

ANSWER
See, also, Pleadings, generally, this index
Certification, verification by certification, 735 ILCS 5/1-109
Injunctions, dissolution motions, affidavits, 735 ILCS 5/11-109
Judgment for plaintiff, defendant answer or otherwise plead, 735 ILCS 5/2-1301
Summons, form, S.Ct.Rule 101
Verification by certification, 735 ILCS 5/1-109

APPEAL AND REVIEW
Abolishment, bills of review, 735 ILCS 5/2-1401
Adoption of Children, this index
Bills of review, abolishment, 735 ILCS 5/2-1401
Children and Minors, this index
Emancipation of mature minors, 750 ILCS 30/11
Rules of Court, this index
Support,
Expedited child support hearings, 750 ILCS 25/8; 750 ILCS 25/9

APPEARANCE
Child custody proceedings,
Order for appearance, 750 ILCS 35/12
Ordering appearance, 750 ILCS 35/20
Child support, expedited proceedings, S.Ct.Rule 100.4
Default judgments, failure to appear, 735 ILCS 5/2-1301
Failure to appear, default judgment, 735 ILCS 5/2-1301
Injunctions, temporary injunctions, dissolution of modification, 735 ILCS 5/11-101
Summons, form, S.Ct.Rule 101
Temporary restraining order, dissolution and modification, 735 ILCS 5/11-101
Uniform Child Custody Jurisdiction Act, court order, 750 ILCS 35/12

APPELLATE COURT
Courts of Appeals, generally, this index

ARMED FORCES
Military Forces, generally, this index

ARRAIGNMENT
Temporary order for support or maintenance of wife or children of defendant, 750 ILCS 15/3

ARREARAGE
Defined,
Expedited child support, 750 ILCS 25/3
Paternity proceedings, withholding of income, 750 ILCS 45/20
Support, 750 ILCS 5/706.1; 750 ILCS 15/4.1; 750 ILCS 20/26.1

ARREST
Bail, generally, this index
Domestic violence, protection orders, 750 ILCS 60/301.1
Habeas Corpus, generally, this index
Juvenile Delinquents and Dependents, this index
Protection orders, domestic violence, 750 ILCS 60/301.1
Support proceedings,
Interstate enforcement, 750 ILCS 22/305

ARREST—Cont'd
Support proceedings—Cont'd
Uniform Reciprocal Enforcement of Support Act, 750 ILCS 20/16
Without warrant,
Domestic violence, 750 ILCS 60/301

ARTIFICIAL INSEMINATION
Husband and wife, 750 ILCS 40/1 et seq.

ASSAULT AND BATTERY
Domestic Violence, generally, this index

ASSESSMENTS
Injunctions, damages, 735 ILCS 5/11-110

ASSIGNMENTS
Confession of judgment, consumer transactions, void, 735 ILCS 5/2-1301
Consumers,
Confession of judgment, void, 735 ILCS 5/2-1301
Paternity proceedings, wages, 750 ILCS 45/20
Support, this index
Wage assignments. Compensation and Salaries, this index

ASSOCIATIONS AND SOCIETIES
Nonprofit Corporations, generally, this index
Religious Organizations and Societies, generally, this index

ATTACHMENT
See, also, Garnishment, generally, this index
Child support obligor, 750 ILCS 5/713
Husband and wife, rights of married persons, 750 ILCS 65/1
Rights of married persons, 750 ILCS 65/0.01 et seq.
Support,
Interstate enforcement, 750 ILCS 22/305
Writs, abolishment, 735 ILCS 5/2-1501

ATTORNEY FEES
Attorneys Fees, generally, this index

ATTORNEY GENERAL
Support, dependents,
Appeal of support orders, Uniform Reciprocal Enforcement of Support Act, 750 ILCS 20/34
Duties, 750 ILCS 15/1b; 750 ILCS 15/3
Enforcement agencies, powers and duties, 750 ILCS 22/308
Enforcement proceedings, 750 ILCS 15/1b
Petitioners representation, 750 ILCS 20/12; 750 ILCS 20/18

ATTORNEY IN FACT
Power of Attorney, generally, this index

ATTORNEYS
Compensation and salaries, Attorneys Fees, generally, this index
Conflicts of interest, p. 963
Dissolution of marriage,
  Joint simplified procedure, 750 ILCS 5/457
  Reconciliation conferences, presence, 750 ILCS 5/404
Domestic abuse advocates, participation in proceedings, 750 ILCS 60/205
Domestic violence, high-risk adults with disabilities, protection orders, 750 ILCS 60/213.3
Fees. Attorneys Fees, generally, this index
Illegitimate children, paternity proceedings, right to counsel, 750 ILCS 45/18
Judges, generally, this index
Paternity proceedings, right to counsel, 750 ILCS 45/18
Right to counsel,
  Paternity proceedings, 750 ILCS 45/18
Support, interstate enforcement, 750 ILCS 22/309

ATTORNEYS FEES
Adoption of children,
  Affidavits, 750 ILCS 50/14
  Permitted compensation, 720 ILCS 525/4.1
Child support proceedings, 750 ILCS 5/508
Children and minors,
  Custody visitation, enforcement actions, 750 ILCS 5/607.1
  Uniform Child Custody Jurisdiction Act, this index
Creditors claims for non-family expenses, spouses or former spouses, 750 ILCS 65/15
Dissolution of marriage proceedings, 750 ILCS 5/508
Domestic violence, protection orders, enforcement, 750 ILCS 60/223
Husband and wife, creditors claims for non-family expenses, 750 ILCS 65/15
Paternity proceedings, 750 ILCS 45/17
  False affidavits, 750 ILCS 45/7
Process, false statements, 735 ILCS 5/2–203
Summons, false statements, 735 ILCS 5/2–203
Support proceedings, 750 ILCS 5/508
Uniform Child Custody Jurisdiction Act, this index
Venue, transfer of causes, 735 ILCS 5/2–107

AUNTS
Marriages, 750 ILCS 5/212

AUTOMOBILES
Motor Vehicles, generally, this index

BACKGROUND INVESTIGATIONS
Criminal History Record Information, generally, this index

BAIL
Bonds,
  Domestic violence, protection orders violations, 750 ILCS 60/223
  Support proceedings, arrested support obligor, 750 ILCS 20/16
Drivers' licenses. Motor Vehicles, this index
Performance bond. Bonds, generally, ante
Support proceedings, 750 ILCS 20/16

BANK–OFFERED SPOT RATE
Defined, foreign money claims, 735 ILCS 5/12–655

BANKRUPTCY
Discharge, exceptions, 11 U.S.C.A. § 523
Lis pendens, 735 ILCS 5/2–1901

BATTERED WOMEN
Domestic Violence, generally, this index

BATTERY
Assault and Battery, generally, this index

BENEVOLENT ASSOCIATIONS OR CORPORATIONS
Nonprofit Corporations, generally, this index

BEQUESTS AND LEGACIES
Probate Proceedings, generally, this index
Wills, generally, this index

BIAS OR PREJUDICE
Change of venue, 735 ILCS 5/2–1001.5
Discrimination, generally, this index
Substitution of judge, 735 ILCS 5/2–1001

BIGAMY
Dissolution of marriage, 750 ILCS 5/401
Maintenance in case of, 750 ILCS 5/702

BILL OF SALE
Guardianship or conservatorship, authority of conservator to execute and deliver bill, 755 ILCS 5/11–13

BILLS OF REVIEW
Abolishment, 735 ILCS 5/2–1401

BIOLOGICAL PARENTS
Adoption, identifying information, exchange, 750 ILCS 50/18.1 et seq.

BIOLOGICAL PARENTS—Cont'd
Confidential intermediaries, obtaining psychological, medical or health information, 750 ILCS 50/18.3a

BIOLOGICAL SIBLINGS
Adoption, identifying information, exchange, 750 ILCS 50/18.1 et seq.
Confidential intermediaries, obtaining psychological, medical or health information, 750 ILCS 50/18.3a

BLOOD TESTS
Child support, expedited proceedings, S.Ct.Rule 100.5
Marriage, generally, this index
Paternity. Children Born Out of Wedlock, this index

BOARDING HOMES FOR CHILDREN
Child Care Facilities, generally, this index

BODY
Attachment, body of child support obligor, 750 ILCS 5/713

BONDS (OFFICERS AND FIDUCIARIES)
See, also, Security, generally, this index
Bail, this index
Child placing agencies, adoption of children, 750 ILCS 50/4.1
Children and minors,
  Return to state, condition of removal by parent having custody, 750 ILCS 5/609
Guardians and Guardianship, this index
Injunctions, this index
Paternity. Children Born Out of Wedlock, this index
Recognizance, generally, this index
Support, this index
Testamentary guardians,
  Estate of minor, 755 ILCS 5/11–5
Uniform Reciprocal Enforcement of Support Act, arrested support obligor, 750 ILCS 20/16

BREACH OF MARRIAGE PROMISE
Generally, 740 ILCS 15/0.01 et seq.
Application of law relating to action for, 740 ILCS 15/7
Construction of act relating to action, 740 ILCS 15/9
Criminal law, effect of relating to, 740 ILCS 15/8
Damages,
  Actual damages recoverable, 740 ILCS 15/2
  Exemplary, punitive, etc., damages precluded, 740 ILCS 15/3
Dismissal of action for, failure to give notice, 740 ILCS 15/5

BREACH

BREACH OF MARRIAGE PROMISE—Cont'd
Effective date of act relating to, 740 ILCS 15/10
Notice of intent to bring action for, 740 ILCS 15/4
 Dismissal for failure to give, 740 ILCS 15/5
Public policy, declaration of, 740 ILCS 15/1
Repeals, criminal law, 740 ILCS 15/8
Time of commencing action for, 740 ILCS 15/6

BREACH OF PROMISE ACT
Generally, 740 ILCS 15/0.01 et seq.

BRITAIN
Support, convention country designation, reciprocal enforcement, 750 ILCS 20/4.1

BROTHERS AND SISTERS
Incestuous marriages, 750 ILCS 5/212

BUILDINGS
Abandoned,
 Process, service by publication, removal, 735 ILCS 5/2-206
Children and minors, luring into, abduction, 720 ILCS 5/10-5
Crimes and offenses,
 Child abduction, luring into, 720 ILCS 5/10-5
Dwellings, generally, this index

BURDEN OF PROOF
Evidence, this index

CALENDAR
Uniform Child Custody Jurisdiction Act, priority, 750 ILCS 35/25

CARS
Motor Vehicles, generally, this index

CERTIFICATES AND CERTIFICATION
Artificial insemination, consent, 750 ILCS 40/3
Marriage, this index
Orders of court, 735 ILCS 5/2-1501
Summons, individual service, 735 ILCS 5/2-203
Venue, transfer of causes, 735 ILCS 5/2-106
Verification by certification, 735 ILCS 5/1-109

CERTIFIED COPIES
Adoption proceeding records and papers, order of court, 750 ILCS 50/18
Custody judgments, Uniform Child Custody Jurisdiction Act, 750 ILCS 35/18; 750 ILCS 35/20

CHANGE OF ADDRESS
Support, mandatory payments, 750 ILCS 5/709

CHANGE OF NAME
Names, this index

CHARITIES
Nonprofit Corporations, generally, this index

CHEMICAL DEPENDENCY
Alcoholics and Intoxicated Persons, generally, this index
Drug Addicts, generally, this index

CHILD
Children and Minors, generally, this index
Defined,
 Abduction of children, 720 ILCS 5/10-5
 Adoption of children, 750 ILCS 50/1
 Support, interstate enforcement, 750 ILCS 22/101

CHILD ABDUCTION
Generally, 720 ILCS 5/10-5
Aiding and abetting, 720 ILCS 5/10-7
International Child Abduction Remedies Act, generally, this index
Uniform Child Custody Jurisdiction Act, this index

CHILD ABUSE
Children and Minors, this index

CHILD CARE ACT
Adoption of children, construction, 750 ILCS 50/2.1

CHILD CARE FACILITIES
Abused and neglected children,
 Records, access, 325 ILCS 5/11.1
 Reports, 325 ILCS 5/4
Foster family homes, generally. Social Services, this index
Records and recordation,
 Noncustodial parent, access, 750 ILCS 5/602.1

CHILD PLACING AGENCIES
Adoption of children, licenses, 750 ILCS 50/4.1

CHILD PROTECTIVE SERVICE UNIT
Abused or neglected children, reports, 325 ILCS 5/7 et seq.
Defined, abused or neglected children, reports, 325 ILCS 5/3

CHILD SUPPORT
Support, generally, this index

CHILD SUPPORT ENFORCEMENT PROGRAM
Generally, 750 ILCS 5/710 et seq.

CHILD SUPPORT ORDER
Defined, interstate enforcement, 750 ILCS 22/101

CHILDREN AND FAMILY SERVICES, DEPARTMENT OF
Abused and neglected children, reports, 325 ILCS 5/1 et seq.

CHILDREN AND FAMILY SERVICES, DEPARTMENT OF—Cont'd
Adoption,
 Identifying information, exchange, 750 ILCS 50/18.1 et seq.
 Background investigations, access to records, 325 ILCS 5/11.1
Child abduction, offenses, 720 ILCS 5/10-5
Child protective service unit, abused or neglected children, reports, 325 ILCS 5/7 et seq.
Contracts,
 Background investigations, child abuse reports, access to records, 325 ILCS 5/11.1
Guardianship administrator, aids tests, immunity from liability, 325 ILCS 5/5
Intercounty adoption coordinator, 750 ILCS 50/4.1
Reports,
 Family preservation services, abused and neglected children, 325 ILCS 5/8.2
Social Services, generally, this index

CHILDREN AND MINORS
Abandonment of Child, generally, this index
Abduction. Child Abduction, generally, this index
Abortion, generally, this index
Abused and neglected children,
 See, also,
  Juvenile Delinquents and Dependents, generally, this index
  Sexual Crimes Against Children, generally, this index
 Abduction, offenses, 720 ILCS 5/10-5
 AIDS test results, temporary caretakers, 325 ILCS 5/5
 Best interest of child, referrals, 325 ILCS 5/8.1
 Child Care Facilities, this index
 Child protective service unit, reports, 325 ILCS 5/7
 Confidential or privileged information, reports, 325 ILCS 5/4; 325 ILCS 5/10; 325 ILCS 5/11
 Defined,
  Adoption, 750 ILCS 50/1
  Reports, 325 ILCS 5/3
 Dissolution of marriage, custody proceedings, prior statements, 750 ILCS 5/606
 Domestic Violence, generally, this index
 Employment discrimination, persons making abuse reports, 325 ILCS 5/9.1
 False reports, 325 ILCS 5/4
 Guardian ad litem, abuse reports, copies, 325 ILCS 5/11.1
 Guardians,
  Prior statements, evidence of abuse, 755 ILCS 5/11-5

CHILDREN

CHILDREN AND MINORS—Cont'd
Abused and neglected children
—Cont'd
Medical care and treatment, quality, investigations, access to records, 325 ILCS 5/11.1
Mentally or developmentally disabled persons, disclosure of confidential information, 740 ILCS 110/11
Records and recordation,
Access, 325 ILCS 5/11.1
Referrals, department of alcoholism and substance abuse, best interest of child, 325 ILCS 5/8.1
Reports, 325 ILCS 5/1 et seq.; 325 ILCS 5/7.14
Confidential or privileged information, 325 ILCS 5/4; 325 ILCS 5/10; 325 ILCS 5/11
Employment discrimination, persons making reports, 325 ILCS 5/9.1
Guardian ad litem, copies, 325 ILCS 5/11.1
Referrals, best interest of child, 325 ILCS 5/8.1
School Officers and Employees, this index
Schoolteachers, this index
Sexual abuse, generally, post
Sexual Crimes Against Children, generally, this index
Unfounded reports, retention, 325 ILCS 5/7.7
Witnesses, administrative hearings, 325 ILCS 5/10
Actions and proceedings,
Dismissal of actions, generally, post
Parental Responsibility Law, 740 ILCS 115/1 et seq.
Adoption of Children, generally, this index
Age,
Emancipation of Mature Minors Act, 750 ILCS 30/1 et seq.
Legal age, 755 ILCS 5/11–1
AIDS, notice,
Tests, children taken into protective custody, 325 ILCS 5/5
Appeal and review,
Emancipation of mature minors, 750 ILCS 30/11
Applications,
Change of name, notice, 735 ILCS 5/21–103
Notice, application for change of name, 735 ILCS 5/21–101
Artificial insemination, legitimacy of child, 750 ILCS 40/1 et seq.
Attorneys Fees, this index
Battered children. Abused and neglected children, generally, ante
Care facilities. Child Care Facilities, generally, this index
Child abuse. Abused and neglected children, generally, ante
Child Care Facilities, generally, this index
Child care records, noncustodial parent, access, 750 ILCS 5/602.1

CHILDREN AND MINORS—Cont'd
Child protective service unit, abused or neglected children, reports, 325 ILCS 5/7 et seq.
Children Born Out of Wedlock, generally, this index
Class 4 felonies. Crimes and offenses, post
Class A misdemeanors. Crimes and offenses, generally, post
Common law marriage, offspring from, legitimate, 750 ILCS 5/212
Compensation and salaries,
Placing out children, receipt of compensation, crimes and offenses, 720 ILCS 525/5
Concealment, protection orders, 750 ILCS 60/214
Confidential or privileged information,
Abused or neglected children, reports, 325 ILCS 5/5; 325 ILCS 5/10; 325 ILCS 5/11
Consent,
Artificial insemination, 750 ILCS 40/1 et seq.
Contracts,
Emancipation of mature minors, 750 ILCS 30/1 et seq.
Contributing to delinquency and neglect, generally. Juvenile Delinquents and Dependents, this index
Court liability, parental responsibility law, 740 ILCS 115/1 et seq.
Crimes and offenses,
Abduction, 720 ILCS 5/10–5
Child abduction, 720 ILCS 5/10–5
Harboring runaways, 720 ILCS 5/10–6
Interference with visitation, contempt, 750 ILCS 5/607.1
Placing out, receipt of compensation, 720 ILCS 525/5
Sexual Crimes Against Children, generally, this index
Visitation, interference, 720 ILCS 5/10–5.5
Custody and care, 750 ILCS 5/601 et seq.; 755 ILCS 5/11–7
Abduction. Child Abduction, generally, this index
Abortion, expense payment by nonconsenting parent, 750 ILCS 65/15
Abused or neglected children, 325 ILCS 5/5
Witnesses, prior statements, 750 ILCS 5/606
AIDS test results, abused or neglected children, 325 ILCS 5/5
As between husband and wife, 750 ILCS 65/16
Dissolution of marriage proceedings, 750 ILCS 5/601 et seq.
Child support, expedited proceedings, S.Ct.Rule 100.9
Contempt of court, visitation, 750 ILCS 5/607.1
Dissolution of marriage proceedings, 750 ILCS 5/601 et seq.

CHILDREN AND MINORS—Cont'd
Custody and care—Cont'd
Dissolution of marriage proceedings—Cont'd
Bifurcated proceedings, 750 ILCS 5/401
Judgment, reserved questions, 750 ILCS 5/401
Foreign parties, actions, 750 ILCS 5/601
Guardianship, rights of parents, 755 ILCS 5/11–7
Husband and wife, 750 ILCS 65/16
Dissolution of marriage proceedings, 750 ILCS 5/601 et seq.
Joint custody, modification, 750 ILCS 5/610
Marital privilege, 735 ILCS 5/8–801
Modification, 750 ILCS 5/610
Notice, petition for visitation enforcement, 750 ILCS 5/607.1
Prior statements, abused or neglected children, 750 ILCS 5/606
Protection orders,
Temporary legal custody, 750 ILCS 60/214
Violation, 750 ILCS 60/223
Removal of child from state, 750 ILCS 5/609
Rights of parents, 755 ILCS 5/11–7
Siblings, visitation, 750 ILCS 5/607
Temporary custody, protection orders, 750 ILCS 60/214
Temporary orders, 750 ILCS 5/603
Temporary removal of child from state, 750 ILCS 5/609
Uniform Child Custody Jurisdiction Act, generally, this index
Visitation, enforcement, attorney fees, 750 ILCS 5/607.1
Damages,
Willful and malicious acts, Parental Responsibility Law, 740 ILCS 115/1 et seq.
Day care facilities. Child Care Facilities, generally, this index
Death,
Abuse or neglect, reports, 325 ILCS 5/4.1
Parents, visitation rights of grandparents, 755 ILCS 5/11–7.1
Defined, 755 ILCS 5/11–1
Abused and neglected children, reports, 325 ILCS 5/3
Child abduction, 720 ILCS 5/10–5
Legal guardian, Parental Responsibility Law, 740 ILCS 115/2
Parental Responsibility Law, 740 ILCS 115/2
Probate proceedings, 755 ILCS 5/11–1
Delinquent children. Juvenile Delinquents and Dependents, generally, this index
Dependent children. Juvenile Delinquents and Dependents, generally, this index

CHILDREN

CHILDREN AND MINORS—Cont'd
Depositions, perpetuating testimony, S.Ct.Rule 217
Custody proceedings, taking in other states, 750 ILCS 35/19
Developmentally disabled persons. Mentally Retarded and Developmentally Disabled Persons, this index
Dismissal of actions,
Custody proceedings, inconvenient forum, 750 ILCS 35/8
Dissolution of marriage. Marriage, this index
Domestic Violence, generally, this index
Education,
Parental rights, 755 ILCS 5/11-7
Schools and School Districts, generally, this index
Emancipation of Mature Minors Act, 750 ILCS 30/1 et seq.
Evidence,
Out-of-court statements, sexual acts or abuse, admissibility, 735 ILCS 5/8-2601
Foster family homes, generally. Social Services, this index
Grandparents and Grandchildren, generally, this index,
Death of parents, 755 ILCS 5/11-7.1
Guardian Ad Litem, generally, this index
Guardians and Guardianship, generally, this index
Guardians for Minors, generally, this index
Harboring runaways, crimes, 720 ILCS 5/10-6
Hearings,
Emancipation of mature minors, 750 ILCS 30/9
Heterologous artificial insemination, legitimacy of child, 750 ILCS 40/1 et seq.
Hospitals, this index
Husband and wife, removal from state by parent granted custody, security, 750 ILCS 5/609
Illegitimate children. Children Born Out of Wedlock, generally, this index
Incest, generally, this index
Injuries,
Abused and neglected children, reports, 325 ILCS 5/1 et seq.
Caused by child's willful or malicious acts, Parental Responsibility Law, 740 ILCS 115/1 et seq.
Reports, 325 ILCS 5/1 et seq.
Instructions to jury, sexual acts, out-of-court statements, 735 ILCS 5/8-2601
Interference, custody,
Contempt, 750 ILCS 5/607.1
Visitation, 720 ILCS 5/10-5.5
International Child Abduction Remedies Act, 42 U.S.C.A. § 11601 et seq.
Joinder, emancipation of mature minors, 750 ILCS 30/10

CHILDREN AND MINORS—Cont'd
Joint custody, marriage dissolution, separation, etc., 750 ILCS 5/602.1
Jurisdiction,
Removal from state by parent in custody, 750 ILCS 5/609
Uniform Child Custody Jurisdiction Act, generally, this index
Juvenile Delinquents and Dependents, generally, this index
Kidnapping, generally, this index
Legal age, 755 ILCS 5/11-1
Legitimacy, heterologous artificial insemination, 750 ILCS 40/1 et seq.
Legitimation of illegal marriage, 750 ILCS 5/303
Lewdness or Obscenity, this index
Limitation of actions,
Liability from Willful Act, Parental Responsibility Law, 740 ILCS 115/5
Malicious injury caused by minor, Parental Responsibility Law, 740 ILCS 115/1 et seq.
Marital privilege, custody actions, 735 ILCS 5/8-801
Marriage, this index
Mature minors, emancipation, 750 ILCS 30/1 et seq.
Medical care and treatment,
Abused and neglected children, quality of care, investigations, access to records, 325 ILCS 5/11.1
Emergency care, temporary protective custody, 325 ILCS 5/5
Mental injuries, reports, 325 ILCS 5/1 et seq.
Mentally Ill Persons, this index
Mentally Retarded and Developmentally Disabled Persons, this index
Missing persons,
Abductions. Child Abduction, generally, this index
Abused and neglected children, records, access, intergovernmental missing child recovery, 325 ILCS 5/11.1
Motor Vehicles, this index
Natural parents, death, visitation rights of grandparents, 755 ILCS 5/11-7.1
Neglected or abused children. Abused and neglected children, generally, ante
Negligence, Parental Responsibility Law, 740 ILCS 115/1 et seq.
Notice,
Abused or neglected children, false reports, 325 ILCS 5/7; 325 ILCS 5/7.6
Application for change of name, 735 ILCS 5/21-103
Emancipation of mature minors, 750 ILCS 30/8
Sexual acts, out-of-court statements, intent to offer into evidence, 735 ILCS 5/8-2601

CHILDREN AND MINORS—Cont'd
Nurses,
Abuse or neglect, reports, 325 ILCS 5/4
Offenses. Crimes and offenses, generally, ante
Orders,
Custody of children,
Appearance, parties and child, 750 ILCS 35/12; 750 ILCS 35/20
Emancipation of mature minors, 750 ILCS 30/6
Protection orders, generally. Juvenile Delinquents and Dependents, this index
Termination of parental rights, effect, 750 ILCS 50/17
Out-of-court statements, unlawful sexual acts, admissibility, 735 ILCS 5/8-2601
Parentage Act, 750 ILCS 40/1 et seq.
Parental Responsibility Law, 740 ILCS 115/1 et seq.
Parental right to custody, 755 ILCS 5/11-7
Parental rights, termination,
Effect of order, 750 ILCS 50/17
Paternity. Children Born Out of Wedlock, generally, this index
Pay. Compensation and salaries, generally, ante
Petitions, emancipation of mature minors, 750 ILCS 30/7
Physical injuries. Injuries, generally, ante
Placing out children, crimes and offenses, receipt of compensation, 720 ILCS 525/5
Pornography. Lewdness or Obscenity, this index
Probate Proceedings, this index
Protection orders,
Domestic Violence, this index
Rape,
Sexual Crimes Against Children, generally, this index
Records,
Medical records, noncustodial parent, access, 750 ILCS 5/602.1
Related child, residence requirements, 750 ILCS 50/2
Relatives, visitation rights, 755 ILCS 5/11-7.1
Removal,
Dissolution of marriage proceedings, 750 ILCS 5/609
Protection orders, 750 ILCS 60/214
Reports,
Sexual abuse, 325 ILCS 5/7.14
Salaries. Compensation and salaries, generally, ante
School records,
Noncustodial parent, access, 750 ILCS 5/602.1
Security, removal of child from state by parent granted custody, 750 ILCS 5/609
Sexual abuse,
See, also, Abused and neglected children, generally, ante

CHILDREN

CHILDREN AND MINORS—Cont'd
Sexual abuse—Cont'd
  Hearsay, admissibility, civil proceedings, 735 ILCS 5/8–2601
  Reports, 325 ILCS 5/7.14
  Retention, 325 ILCS 5/7.14
Sexual acts, out-of-court statements, admissibility, 735 ILCS 5/8–2601
Sexual Crimes Against Children, generally, this index
Shelter Care Homes, generally, this index
Social Services, this index
Statements, out-of-court declarations, unlawful sexual acts, 735 ILCS 5/8–2601
Support, generally, this index
Telecommunications, this index
Termination of parental rights, effect of order, authority, 750 ILCS 50/17
Unfounded report, abuse or neglect, retention, 325 ILCS 5/7.7
Uniform Child Custody Jurisdiction Act, generally, this index
Vandalism, Parental Responsibility Law, 740 ILCS 115/1 et seq.
Visitation, 750 ILCS 5/607
  Abuse, 750 ILCS 5/607.1
  Enforcement, 750 ILCS 5/607.1
  Grandparents, 750 ILCS 5/607
    Death of parents, 755 ILCS 5/11–7.1
  Interference, 720 ILCS 5/10–5.5
    Contempt, 750 ILCS 5/607.1
  Protection orders, 750 ILCS 60/214
Wages. Compensation and salaries, generally, ante
Witnesses,
  Custody, marital privilege, 735 ILCS 5/8–801

CHILDREN BORN OUT OF WEDLOCK
Acknowledgments, parentage, expedited child support proceedings, S.Ct.Rule 100.4
Actions and proceedings. Paternity, post
Adoption,
  Affidavit of identification, biological father, 750 ILCS 50/11
  Paternity proceedings, 750 ILCS 45/4
  Putative father registry, 750 ILCS 50/12.1
Attorneys fees. Paternity, post
Blood tests,
  Expedited child support proceedings, rules, S.Ct.Rule 100.5
  Paternity, post
  Chain of custody, tests, 750 ILCS 45/11
Child support, expedited proceedings, rules, S.Ct.Rule 100.1 et seq.
Childbirth expenses, parentage judgments, 750 ILCS 45/8
Costs. Paternity, post
Custody, presumptions, 750 ILCS 45/14

CHILDREN BORN OUT OF WEDLOCK—Cont'd
Declaration of invalidity of marriage affecting legitimacy, 750 ILCS 5/303
Declaratory judgments,
  Father and child relationship, 750 ILCS 45/7
  Mother and child relationship, 750 ILCS 45/19
Evidence. Paternity, post
Grandparents, visitation, 750 ILCS 5/607
Guardian and ward. Paternity, post
Hearings,
  Child support, expedited proceedings, transfers, S.Ct.Rule 100.9
Indigent persons. Paternity, post
Judgments. Paternity, post
Limitation of actions,
  Parentage proceedings, 750 ILCS 45/8
Marriage, 750 ILCS 5/212
  Issue of illegal marriage legitimated, 750 ILCS 5/303
  License to issue when woman has given birth to illegitimate child, irrespective of venereal diseases, 750 ILCS 5/205
Notice. Paternity, post
Parentage,
  Natural father relationship, father's parental rights forgone, limitation of actions, 750 ILCS 45/8
  Natural parent, relationship, Limitation of actions, 750 ILCS 45/8
  Social services,
    Reimbursement, child support orders, 750 ILCS 45/8
Paternity,
  Actions and proceedings,
    Father and child relation, 750 ILCS 45/7 et seq.
    Juries, 750 ILCS 45/13
    Jurisdiction, 750 ILCS 45/9
    Limitation of actions, 750 ILCS 45/8
    Mother and child relationships, establishment, 750 ILCS 45/19
    Parties, 750 ILCS 45/7
    Pretrial proceedings, 750 ILCS 45/10; 750 ILCS 45/12
    Venue, 750 ILCS 45/9
  Adoption of children,
    Affidavit of identification, biological father, 750 ILCS 50/11
    Parental relationship, 750 ILCS 45/4
    Putative father registry, 750 ILCS 50/12.1
  Adultery, evidence, admissibility, 750 ILCS 45/6
  Affidavits, false, attorneys fees and costs, 750 ILCS 45/7
  Age, judgments, reserve provisions, 750 ILCS 45/14

CHILDREN BORN OUT OF WEDLOCK—Cont'd
Paternity—Cont'd
  Aliens, support orders, 750 ILCS 45/20
  Alternative procedures, withholding order, 750 ILCS 45/20
  Appeal and review, 750 ILCS 45/18
    Payment of costs, 750 ILCS 45/17
  Application of law, 750 ILCS 45/25
  Arrearages, withholding order, 750 ILCS 45/20
  Assignments, wages, 750 ILCS 45/20
  Attorneys,
    Public defenders, appointment, 750 ILCS 45/18
    Right to counsel, 750 ILCS 45/18
  Attorneys fees,
    False affidavits, 750 ILCS 45/7
  Blood tests, 750 ILCS 45/11
    Prebirth actions, 750 ILCS 45/7
  Bonds (officers and fiduciaries), judgments, reserve provisions, 750 ILCS 45/14
  Chain of custody, blood test results, 750 ILCS 45/11
  Child abduction, concealing or removing child after service of process in paternity action, 720 ILCS 5/10–5
  Childbirth expenses, judgments, reserve provisions, 750 ILCS 45/14
  Circuit courts, jurisdiction and venue, 750 ILCS 45/9
  Compensation and salaries, Withholding, delinquent support payments, 750 ILCS 45/20
    Witnesses, blood tests, 750 ILCS 45/11
  Complaint, actions, 750 ILCS 45/7
  Compromise and settlement,
    Orders, 750 ILCS 45/12.1
    Pretrial recommendations, 750 ILCS 45/12
  Conferences, pretrial proceedings, 750 ILCS 45/10
  Consent,
    Nonconsenting fathers, orders, settlement, 750 ILCS 45/12.1
    Parental relationship, establishment, 750 ILCS 45/6
    Pretrial recommendations, 750 ILCS 45/12
  Consumer Credit Protection Act, withholding, allowance, 750 ILCS 45/20
  Contempt of court, failure to comply with court orders, 750 ILCS 45/15
  Continuance, representation for visitation and other matters, 750 ILCS 45/18
  Contracts, actions, terms, 750 ILCS 45/7
  Copies, support orders, 750 ILCS 45/20

CHILDREN

CHILDREN BORN OUT OF WED-LOCK—Cont'd
Paternity—Cont'd
  Costs,
    Blood tests, 750 ILCS 45/11
    Expert witnesses, compensation, 750 ILCS 45/11
    False affidavits, 750 ILCS 45/7
    Orders, 750 ILCS 45/17
    Tests, 750 ILCS 45/11
  Counties, actions, venue, 750 ILCS 45/9
  Counties of less than 3,000,000, orders, support, 750 ILCS 45/21
  Crimes and offenses, evidence, admissibility, 750 ILCS 45/6
  Custody, modification, 750 ILCS 45/16
  Declaratory judgments,
    Father and child relationship, 750 ILCS 45/7
    Mother and child relationship, 750 ILCS 45/19
  Default judgments, 750 ILCS 45/14
  Delinquent payments, support, withholding orders, 750 ILCS 45/20
  Demands, jury trials, 750 ILCS 45/13
  Depositions, prebirth actions, 750 ILCS 45/7
  Disabled persons, judgments, reserve provisions, 750 ILCS 45/14
  Dismissal of actions, limitations, 750 ILCS 45/8
  DNA testing, 750 ILCS 45/11
  Evidence,
    Adoptive parents, relationship, 750 ILCS 45/4
    Blood tests, 750 ILCS 45/11
    Criminal proceedings, admissibility, 750 ILCS 45/6
    Delinquent payments, admissibility, 750 ILCS 45/20
    Tests, 750 ILCS 45/11
  Expenses, blood tests, 750 ILCS 45/11
  Expert witnesses, tests, 750 ILCS 45/11
  Father and child relationship, determination, 750 ILCS 45/7 et seq.
    Contempt of court, 750 ILCS 45/15
    Support orders, violations, 750 ILCS 45/20
  Fornication, evidence, admissibility, 750 ILCS 45/6
  Guardian and ward,
    Actions, appointment, 750 ILCS 45/7
    Judgments, reserve provisions, 750 ILCS 45/14
    Parental relationships, petitions, 750 ILCS 45/6
  Indigent persons,
    Appeals, transcripts, 750 ILCS 45/18
    Blood tests, 750 ILCS 45/11
    Tests, 750 ILCS 45/11

CHILDREN BORN OUT OF WED-LOCK—Cont'd
Paternity—Cont'd
  Indigent persons—Cont'd
    Transcripts, furnishing, orders, 750 ILCS 45/18
  Joinder of actions, 750 ILCS 45/9
  Judgments,
    Custody, presumptions, 750 ILCS 45/14
    Default judgments, 750 ILCS 45/14
    Enforcement, 750 ILCS 45/15
    Modification, 750 ILCS 45/16
    Pretrial recommendations, 750 ILCS 45/12
    Reserve provisions, 750 ILCS 45/14
    Support orders, failure to pay, penalties, 750 ILCS 45/20
  Jurisdiction, actions, 735 ILCS 5/2–209; 750 ILCS 45/9
  Limitation of actions, 750 ILCS 45/8
  Maintenance obligations, minority of parent, 750 ILCS 45/3.1
  Marital status, parent and child relationship, 750 ILCS 45/3
  Marriage, presumptions, parental relationship, 750 ILCS 45/5
  Notice to presumed father, other petitioners, 750 ILCS 45/9.1
  Minority of parent, support, 750 ILCS 45/3.1
  Modification, judgments, 750 ILCS 45/16
  Mother and child relationships, establishment, actions, 750 ILCS 45/19
  Natural parent, relationship, 750 ILCS 45/4
  Nonexistence of parent-child relationship, actions, 750 ILCS 45/7
  Non-United States citizens, support orders, 750 ILCS 45/20
  Notice,
    Blood tests, independent blood tests, 750 ILCS 45/11
    Delinquent support payments, 750 ILCS 45/20
    Presumed fathers, other petitioners, 750 ILCS 45/9.1
    Public aid department, payments received, 750 ILCS 45/23
  Orders,
    Blood tests, 750 ILCS 45/11
    Counties of less than 3,000,000, 750 ILCS 45/21
    Delinquent payments, stays, 750 ILCS 45/20
    Enforcement, 750 ILCS 45/15
    Modification petitions, 750 ILCS 45/20
    Tests, 750 ILCS 45/11
    Withholding, delinquent support payments, 750 ILCS 45/20
  Parent and child relationship, 750 ILCS 45/2 et seq.
  Parties, costs, apportionment, 750 ILCS 45/17

CHILDREN BORN OUT OF WED-LOCK—Cont'd
Paternity—Cont'd
  Payments, support, designated counties, 750 ILCS 45/21
  Petitions, 750 ILCS 45/20
    Parental relationship, establishment, 750 ILCS 45/6
  Prebirth actions, 750 ILCS 45/7
  Pregnancy,
    Actions, parties, 750 ILCS 45/7
    Expenses, judgments, reserve provisions, 750 ILCS 45/14
  Presumptions, 750 ILCS 45/5
    Actions, parties, 750 ILCS 45/7
    Blood tests, evidentiary standards, 750 ILCS 45/11
    Father, notice of petition by other petitioner, 750 ILCS 45/9.1
    Petitions, parental relationship, establishment, 750 ILCS 45/6
    Tests, evidentiary standards, 750 ILCS 45/11
  Pretrial proceedings, 750 ILCS 45/10
    Settlement orders, nonconsenting fathers, 750 ILCS 45/12.1
  Pretrial recommendation, 750 ILCS 45/12
  Priorities,
    Application of law, 750 ILCS 45/20
    Withholding orders, delinquent payments, 750 ILCS 45/20
  Protection orders, status, 750 ILCS 45/15.2
  Public aid department, support, collection fees, 750 ILCS 45/22
  Public policy, 750 ILCS 45/1; 750 ILCS 45/1.1
  Refusal of blood test, 750 ILCS 45/11
  Refusal to test, 750 ILCS 45/11
  Reports, blood tests, expert opinion, 750 ILCS 45/11
  Restitution, failure to pay support orders, 750 ILCS 45/20
  Right to counsel, 750 ILCS 45/18
  Service of process,
    Delinquent support papers, notice, 750 ILCS 45/20
    Long arm jurisdiction, 735 ILCS 5/2–209
    Prebirth actions, 750 ILCS 45/7
    Social service agencies, petitions, 750 ILCS 45/6
  Settlement,
    Orders, 750 ILCS 45/12.1
    Pretrial recommendations, 750 ILCS 45/12
  Sexual abuse, evidence, admissibility, 750 ILCS 45/6
  Signatures, petitions, parental relationship, 750 ILCS 45/6
  Social services,
    Actions, parties, 750 ILCS 45/7
    Collection fees, actions instituted by public aid department, 750 ILCS 45/22

CHILDREN BORN OUT OF WEDLOCK—Cont'd
Paternity—Cont'd
Social services—Cont'd
Delinquent support orders, records, 750 ILCS 45/20
Department of public aid, parties, 750 ILCS 45/18
Guardians, actions, appointments, 750 ILCS 45/7
Judgments, reserve provisions, 750 ILCS 45/14
Petitions, parental relationships, service, 750 ILCS 45/6
States attorneys,
Mothers, representation, 750 ILCS 45/18
Stay of proceedings, prebirth actions, 750 ILCS 45/7
Summons, actions, contents, 750 ILCS 45/9
Support,
Adjudication of issue, 750 ILCS 20/27
Default judgments, 750 ILCS 45/14
Interstate enforcement, parentage proceedings, 750 ILCS 22/701
Judgments,
Modification, 750 ILCS 45/16
Reserve provisions, 750 ILCS 45/14
Minority of parent, 750 ILCS 45/3.1
Minors, 750 ILCS 45/3.1
Orders,
Aliens, 750 ILCS 45/20
Delinquent payments, 750 ILCS 45/20
Modification, 750 ILCS 45/16
Public aid department, collection fees, 750 ILCS 45/22
Public policy, 750 ILCS 45/1
Series of judgments, 750 ILCS 45/14
State's attorneys, representation, 750 ILCS 45/18
Time, limitation of actions, 750 ILCS 45/8
Transcripts, appeal, 750 ILCS 45/18
Trial, juries, 750 ILCS 45/13
Venue, actions, 750 ILCS 45/9
Visitation,
Judgments,
Modification, 750 ILCS 45/16
Reserve provisions, 750 ILCS 45/14
State's attorney, scope of representation, 750 ILCS 45/18
Vital statistics,
Adoptive parents, proof of relationship, 750 ILCS 45/4
Judgments, reserve provisions, 750 ILCS 45/14
Postbirth marriages, parental relationship, presumptions, 750 ILCS 45/5
Witnesses,
Expert testimony,
Blood tests, 750 ILCS 45/11
Fees, 750 ILCS 45/17

CHILDREN BORN OUT OF WEDLOCK—Cont'd
Paternity—Cont'd
Witnesses—Cont'd
Expert testimony—Cont'd
Tests, 750 ILCS 45/11
Petitions. Paternity, ante
Pregnancy,
Expenses, parentage judgments, 750 ILCS 45/8
Presumptions,
Custody, 750 ILCS 45/14
Paternity, ante
Process. Paternity, ante
Protection orders, status of previous orders, 750 ILCS 45/15.2
Putative father registry, 750 ILCS 50/12.1
Registry, putative fathers, 750 ILCS 50/12.1
Social services,
Limitation of actions, 750 ILCS 45/8
Paternity, ante
Support. Paternity, ante
Visitation, grandparents, 750 ILCS 5/607
Vital statistics. Paternity, ante

CHIROPODISTS
Podiatrists, generally, this index

CHIROPRACTORS
See, also, Physicians and Surgeons, generally, this index
Children, abuse or neglect, reports, 325 ILCS 5/4

CHRISTIAN SCIENCE
Practitioners and readers,
Children, abuse or neglect, reports, 325 ILCS 5/4
Willful or malicious injury, parental responsibility, expenses, 740 ILCS 115/5

CHURCHES
Religious Organizations and Societies, generally, this index

CIRCUIT COURT
Circuit Courts, generally, this index

CIRCUIT COURT CLERKS
Acknowledgments, generally, this index
Adoption of children,
Certificate of adoption, fees, 750 ILCS 50/19
Information furnished to clerk by petitioners, 750 ILCS 50/5
Attachment, generally, this index
Child support payment, 750 ILCS 5/507
Costs, generally, this index
Depositions, generally, this index
Fees,
Adoption certificate, preparation, etc., 750 ILCS 50/19
Records and recordation,
Child support payments, 750 ILCS 5/507
Registry of foreign support orders, maintenance, 750 ILCS 20/37

CIRCUIT COURT CLERKS—Cont'd
Support, this index

CIRCUIT COURTS
Administrative aides, dissolution of marriage, 750 ILCS 5/106
Adoption of Children, generally, this index
Appeal and Review, generally, this index
Child custody, determination, jurisdiction, Uniform Child Custody Jurisdiction Act, 750 ILCS 35/4
Child support, expedited rules, S.Ct. Rule 100.1 et seq.
Clerks. Circuit Court Clerks, generally, this index
Compensation and salaries,
Administrative aides in dissolution of marriage proceedings, etc., 750 ILCS 5/106
Costs, generally, this index
Custody Jurisdiction Act. Uniform Child Custody Jurisdiction Act, generally, this index
Implementation plans, expedited child support rules, S.Ct.Rule 100.1 et seq.
Judges,
Compensation and salaries,
Administrative assistants, dissolutions of marriage proceedings, 750 ILCS 5/106
Judgments, generally, this index
Jurisdiction,
Adoption of children, 750 ILCS 50/4
Child custody, determination, 750 ILCS 35/4
Custody. Uniform Child Custody Jurisdiction Act, generally, this index
Names, proceedings to change, 735 ILCS 5/21-101
Jury, generally, this index
Juvenile Delinquents and Dependents, generally, this index
Paternity proceedings, 750 ILCS 45/6
Rules of courts, S.Ct.Rule 1 et seq.
See, also, Rules of Courts, generally, this index
Terms of office,
Administrative aides in dissolution of marriage proceedings, etc., 750 ILCS 5/106
Uniform Child Custody Jurisdiction Act, generally, this index

CIRCUMSTANTIAL EVIDENCE
Dissolution of marriage, foreign marriage, 750 ILCS 5/409

CITIES, VILLAGES AND INCORPORATED TOWNS
Municipalities, generally, this index

CITY, VILLAGE AND TOWN COURTS
Circuit Courts, generally, this index

CIVIL PENALTIES
Fines and Penalties, generally, this index

CIVIL

CIVIL PRACTICE AND PROCEDURE RULES
Rules of Court, generally, this index

CLERKS
Circuit Court Clerks, generally, this index
County Clerks, generally, this index

CLERKS OF COURT
Circuit Court Clerks, generally, this index
Support, this index

CLOSE RELATIVE
Defined, adoption, visitation, 755 ILCS 5/11-7.1

COERCION
Duress or Coercion, generally, this index

COHABITATION
Foreign marriage, evidence, 750 ILCS 5/409
Maintenance termination, 750 ILCS 5/510

COLLECTIONS
Dissolution of marriages,
Support, fees, 750 ILCS 5/516
Enforcement of support collection fees, 750 ILCS 20/15a
Support,
Fees, 750 ILCS 15/11
Court fees, 750 ILCS 5/705
Dissolution of marriages, 750 ILCS 5/516
Reciprocal enforcement, 750 ILCS 20/15a
Uniform Reciprocal Enforcement of Support Act, fees, 750 ILCS 20/15a

COLLEGES AND UNIVERSITIES
Community colleges and districts, Judgments, interest computation, 735 ILCS 5/2-1303
Judgments, interest computation, 735 ILCS 5/2-1303

COLLUSION
Dissolution of marriage, 750 ILCS 5/408

COMMENCEMENT OF ACTIONS
Actions and Proceedings, this index

COMMISSIONS AND COMMISSIONERS
Boards and Commissions, generally, this index

COMMON LAW MARRIAGE
Validity, 750 ILCS 5/214

COMMON OWNERSHIP
Dissolution of marriage, property, pending proceeding, 750 ILCS 5/503

COMMUNICATIONS
Defined, Mental Health and Developmental Disabilities Confidentiality Act, 740 ILCS 110/2

COMPACTS
Adoption of Children, this index
Placement of children,
Foreign children, 750 ILCS 50/4.1
Interstate compact on, 750 ILCS 50/2.1

COMPENSATION AND SALARIES
Administrative aides, dissolution of marriage proceedings, 750 ILCS 5/106
Adoption of children, 750 ILCS 50/21
Assignments,
Support, this index
Wife or children, 750 ILCS 15/4
Attorneys Fees, generally, this index
Children and Minors, this index
Circuit Courts, this index
Crimes and offenses,
Class 3 felony, placing out children, receipt of compensation, 720 ILCS 525/5
Class 4 felonies, placing out children for adoption, receipt of compensation, 720 ILCS 525/5
Placing out children, receipt of compensation, 720 ILCS 525/5
Dissolutions of marriage, administrative aides to courts, 750 ILCS 5/106
Garnishment, generally, this index
Husband and wife, right to earnings, 750 ILCS 65/7
Juvenile Delinquents and Dependents, this index
Minors. Children and Minors, this index
Offenses. Crimes and offenses, generally, ante
Paternity proceedings,
Expert witnesses, blood tests, 750 ILCS 45/11
Wage assignment, withholding, 750 ILCS 45/20
Retirement and Pensions, generally, this index
Spouse, right to earnings, 750 ILCS 65/7
Summons, mileage outside county, 735 ILCS 5/2-202
Support of wife or children, compelling assignment of wages, 750 ILCS 5/706.1; 750 ILCS 15/4.1; 750 ILCS 20/26.1
Temporary order of support, 750 ILCS 15/3
Trade organizations, support, income withholding, 750 ILCS 5/706.1; 750 ILCS 15/4.1; 750 ILCS 20/26.1
Trade unions, support, income withholding, 750 ILCS 5/706.1; 750 ILCS 15/4.1; 750 ILCS 20/26.1
Venue, transfer of causes, 735 ILCS 5/2-107
Wife, right to earnings, 750 ILCS 65/7
Withholding,
Support enforcement, 750 ILCS 5/706.1; 750 ILCS 15/4.1; 750 ILCS 20/26.1
Workers' Compensation, generally, this index

COMPLAINT
See, also, Pleadings, generally, this index
Certification, verification by certification, 735 ILCS 5/1-109
Declaration of rights, 735 ILCS 5/2-701
Injunctions, this index
Judgments, setting aside, 735 ILCS 5/2-1301
Paternity proceedings, 750 ILCS 45/7
Preliminary injunctions, denial, 735 ILCS 5/11-102
Temporary restraining order, denial, 735 ILCS 5/11-101

COMPUTERS
Electronic Data Processing, generally, this index

CONCEALMENT
Child abduction, offenses, 720 ILCS 5/10-5
Judgments, relief, tolling, 735 ILCS 5/2-1401
Orders of court, relief, tolling, 735 ILCS 5/2-1401
Process, publication, 735 ILCS 5/2-206

CONFESSION OF JUDGMENT
Generally, 735 ILCS 5/2-1301
Process, 735 ILCS 5/2-1301
Venue, wrong venue, 735 ILCS 5/2-104

CONFIDENTIAL OR PRIVILEGED INFORMATION
Abused or neglected children, Reports, 325 ILCS 5/4; 325 ILCS 5/10; 325 ILCS 5/11
Adoption records, 750 ILCS 50/18
Identifying information, exchange, 750 ILCS 50/18.1 et seq.
Artificial insemination, 750 ILCS 40/3
Children and Minors, this index
Crimes and offenses,
Child abuse and neglect reports, dissemination of information, 325 ILCS 5/11
Defined,
Mental Health and Developmental Disabilities Confidentiality Act, 740 ILCS 110/2
Domestic violence, counselors and victims, 750 ILCS 60/227.1
Husband and wife, 750 ILCS 15/7
Support proceedings,
Interstate enforcement, 750 ILCS 22/316
Support proceedings, competency to testify, 750 ILCS 20/22
Juvenile Delinquents and Dependents, this index
Medical Records, generally, this index
Mentally Retarded and Developmentally Disabled Persons, this index

CONFIDENTIAL OR PRIVILEGED INFORMATION—Cont'd

Neglected or abused children, reports, 325 ILCS 5/10; 325 ILCS 5/11
Putative father registry, 750 ILCS 50/12.1
Support,
Interstate enforcement, addresses and identities, 750 ILCS 22/312
Spousal and other communications, interstate enforcement, 750 ILCS 22/316

CONFLICT OF INTEREST
Attorneys, p. 963

CONFLICT OF LAWS
Dissolution of marriage, joint simplified procedure, 750 ILCS 5/451

CONSENT
Abortion, this index
Adoption of Children, this index
Artificial insemination, husband and wife, 750 ILCS 40/1 et seq.
Change of venue, 735 ILCS 5/2–1001.5
Children and Minors, this index
Marriage, minors, parents, 750 ILCS 5/203

CONSERVATORS AND CONSERVATORSHIP
Guardians and Guardianship, generally, this index

CONSTITUTION OF ILLINOIS
Self-incrimination and double jeopardy, p. 962

CONSTITUTION OF UNITED STATES
Self-incrimination, p. 961

CONSTITUTIONAL CONVENTIONS
Declaratory judgments, 735 ILCS 5/2–701

CONSUMER INSTALLMENT LOANS
Confession of judgment, 735 ILCS 5/2–1301

CONTEMPT
Children and minors,
Custody and care, visitation enforcement, 750 ILCS 5/607.1
Domestic violence, protection orders, violation, 750 ILCS 60/223
Enforcement of judgments, 750 ILCS 5/511
Judges, character or conduct impugned, substitution, 735 ILCS 5/2–1001
Juvenile Delinquents and Dependents, this index
Process,
False statements, 735 ILCS 5/2–203
Neglect or refusal, 735 ILCS 5/2–202
Substitution of judge. 735 ILCS 5/2–1001

CONTEMPT—Cont'd
Summons, false statements, 735 ILCS 5/2–203
Support, this index
Uniform Reciprocal Enforcement of Support Act, enforcing duties of support, 750 ILCS 20/9
Visitation, interference with, 720 ILCS 5/10–5.5

CONTEST OF ADOPTIONS ACT
Generally, 750 ILCS 55/0.01; 750 ILCS 55/1

CONTESTANTS
Defined, Uniform Child Custody Jurisdiction Act, 750 ILCS 35/3.01

CONTINUANCE
See, also, Rules of Court, generally, this index
Children born out of wedlock, paternity actions, representation for visitation and other matters, 750 ILCS 45/18
Support,
Payees, representation for other matters, 750 ILCS 5/710
Uniform Reciprocal Enforcement of Support Act, 750 ILCS 20/20

CONTRACTORS
See, also, Contracts, generally, this index
Independent Contractors, generally, this index

CONTRACTS
Children and Minors, this index
Construction,
Declaratory judgments, 735 ILCS 5/2–701
Declaratory judgments, construction, 735 ILCS 5/2–701
Dissolution of marriage proceedings, 750 ILCS 5/502
Emancipation of Mature Minors Act, 750 ILCS 30/1 et seq.
Guardians and Guardianship, this index
Husband and/or wife, 750 ILCS 65/6; 750 ILCS 65/12
Married persons, 750 ILCS 65/6
Minors. Children and Minors, this index
Premarital agreements, 750 ILCS 10/1 et seq.
Process, 735 ILCS 5/2–209
Reformation or rescission, 735 ILCS 5/2–206
Spouse, 750 ILCS 65/6

CONTROLLED SUBSTANCES
Drug Addicts, generally, this index

COOK COUNTY
See, also, Counties, generally, this index
Adoption of children, investigation, 750 ILCS 50/6
County departments of public aid. Public aid, department of, generally, post

COOK COUNTY—Cont'd
Court services division of Cook County department of public aid, adoption of children, investigations, 750 ILCS 50/6
Dissolution of marriage, support payments, 750 ILCS 5/705
Public aid, department of,
Adoption of children, court services division to investigate, 750 ILCS 50/6
Fines and penalties, nonsupport of wife or children receiving public aid, 750 ILCS 15/4
Support or maintenance payments for wife or children, 750 ILCS 5/705; 750 ILCS 15/2.1 et seq.

CORAM NOBIS AND CORAM VOBIS
Abolishment, 735 ILCS 5/2–1401

CORONERS
Abused and neglected children, Reports, 325 ILCS 5/4
Children and minors, abuse or neglect, reports, 325 ILCS 5/4
Mentally ill persons, investigation of death, confidential or privileged information, 740 ILCS 110/10
Process, 735 ILCS 5/2–202
Fees for service of process, taxing as costs, 735 ILCS 5/2–202

CORPORATIONS NOT FOR PROFIT
Nonprofit Corporations, generally, this index

COSTS
Adoption of children,
Affidavits, 750 ILCS 50/14
Change of venue, 735 ILCS 5/2–1001.5
Child custody and visitation, vexatious enforcement actions, 750 ILCS 5/607.1
Conservators,
Proceeding for appointment of conservator, 755 ILCS 5/11–11
Declaratory judgments, 735 ILCS 5/2–701
Dissolution of marriage, support payments, receiving and disbursing agents, 750 ILCS 5/705
Injunctions, 735 ILCS 5/11–103
Service of process, fees for service, taxing as costs, 735 ILCS 5/2–202
Support,
Proceedings to enforce liability, Uniform Reciprocal Enforcement of Support Act, 750 ILCS 20/15
Venue,
Change of, 735 ILCS 5/2–1001.5
Transfer of causes, 735 ILCS 5/2–107

COUNSEL
Attorneys, generally, this index

COUNSELING 1026

COUNSELING AND COUNSELORS
Defined, family preservation services, abused and neglected children, 325 ILCS 5/8.2
Dissolution of marriage, period of separation, 750 ILCS 5/401
Domestic violence,
  Confidential or privileged information, 750 ILCS 60/227; 750 ILCS 60/227.1
  Protection orders, 750 ILCS 60/214
Juvenile Delinquents and Dependents, this index

COUNTERCLAIMS
Set-Off and Counterclaim, generally, this index

COUNTIES
Actions and proceedings,
  Parental Responsibility Law, 740 ILCS 115/1 et seq.
  Support proceedings, Uniform Reciprocal Enforcement of Support Act, 750 ILCS 20/8
Attorneys. State's Attorneys, generally, this index
Children and minors,
  Parental Responsibility Law, action by county, 740 ILCS 115/1 et seq.
Circuit Courts, generally, this index
Clerks. County Clerks, generally, this index
Dissolution of marriage, administrative aides to courts, 750 ILCS 5/106
Expedited child support system, 750 ILCS 25/4
Parental Responsibility Law, action by county, 740 ILCS 115/1 et seq.
Paternity proceedings, support, 750 ILCS 45/21
Social Services, generally, this index
State's Attorneys, generally, this index
Support, enforcement, withholding of income, 750 ILCS 5/706.1; 750 ILCS 15/4.1; 750 ILCS 20/26.1
Withholding income, support enforcement, 750 ILCS 5/706.1; 750 ILCS 15/4.1; 750 ILCS 20/26.1

COUNTY ATTORNEY
State's Attorneys, generally, this index

COUNTY CLERKS
Electronic data processing,
  Marriage certificates, registration, 750 ILCS 35/9
Records and recordation,
  Marriage certificates, 750 ILCS 5/210
Reports,
  Marriages, 750 ILCS 5/211
Return, marriages, 750 ILCS 5/210

COUNTY COURTS
Circuit Courts, generally, this index

COUNTY DEPARTMENTS OF PUBLIC AID
Counties over 3,000,000,
  Fines and penalties, nonsupport for wife and children receiving public aid, 750 ILCS 15/4
  Support payments under court order, disposition, 750 ILCS 15/2.1 et seq.
Legal separation payments, wife and children receiving aid, 750 ILCS 5/705
Payments under court order, receipt and deposit, 750 ILCS 15/2.1 et seq.
Social Services, generally, this index
Support, representing dependents, Uniform Reciprocal Enforcement of Support Act, 750 ILCS 20/12

COUNTY OFFICERS AND EMPLOYEES
Clerks. County Clerks, generally, this index
Medical examiners. Coroners, generally, this index
State's Attorneys, generally, this index

COUNTY TRUANT OFFICERS
School Officers and Employees, this index

COURT COSTS
Costs, generally, this index

COURT ORDERS
Orders, generally, this index

COURT RULES
Rules of Court, generally, this index

COURT SUPPORTIVE SERVICES
Adoption, identifying information, exchange, 750 ILCS 50/18.1 et seq.

COURTS
Administrative office of Illinois courts,
  Support orders, enforcement, supervision, S.Ct.Rule 296
Appeal and Review, generally, this index
Circuit Courts, generally, this index
Courts of Appeals, generally, this index
Defined,
  Uniform Reciprocal Enforcement of Support Act, 750 ILCS 20/2
Judges, generally, this index
Orders, generally, this index
Seal, summons, S.Ct.Rule 101
Supreme Court, generally, this index

COURTS OF APPEALS
See, also, Appeal and Review, generally, this index
Adoption proceedings, jurisdiction of appeals, 750 ILCS 50/20

COUSINS
Aged persons, marriages, 750 ILCS 5/212
Marriages, 750 ILCS 5/212

CREDITORS AND DEBTORS
Debtors and Creditors, generally, this index

CRIMES AND OFFENSES
See, also, Fines and Penalties, generally, this index
Abandonment of Child, this index
Abduction, generally, this index
Abettors. Accomplices and Accessories, generally, this index
Abortion, generally, this index
Abuse,
  Domestic Violence, generally, this index
  Sexual Abuse, generally, this index
Accomplices and Accessories, generally, this index
Adultery, generally, this index
Aged Persons, this index
Aggravated criminal sexual assault, generally. Sexual Assault, this index
Aggravated kidnapping, generally. Kidnapping, this index
Aiders and abettors. Accomplices and Accessories, generally, this index
Arraignment, generally, this index
Arrest, generally, this index
Assault and Battery, generally, this index
Background investigations. Criminal History Record Information, generally, this index
Bail, generally, this index
Battery. Assault and Battery, generally, this index
Child Abduction, generally, this index
Children and Minors, this index
Class 2 felonies,
  Abortion, this index
Class 3 felonies,
  Placing out children, receipt of compensation, 720 ILCS 525/5
  Verification by certification, 735 ILCS 5/1–109
Class 4 felonies,
  Child abduction, 720 ILCS 5/10–5; 720 ILCS 5/10–7
  Placing out children for adoption, receipt of compensation, 720 ILCS 525/5
Class A misdemeanors,
  Abused or neglected children,
    False reports or failure to report, 325 ILCS 5/4
  Child abuse or neglect, 325 ILCS 5/4.02; 325 ILCS 5/11.1
  Harboring runaways, 720 ILCS 5/10–6
  Non-support of spouse or children, 750 ILCS 15/1
  Runaways, harboring, 720 ILCS 5/10–6

CRIMES AND OFFENSES—Cont'd

Community service,
    Defacement of property, 705 ILCS 405/5–19, 705 ILCS 405/5–23
Compensation and Salaries, this index
Confidential or Privileged Information, this index
Controlled Substances, generally, this index
Conviction,
    Criminal History Record Information, generally, this index
    Dissolution of marriage, 750 ILCS 5/401
Damages,
    Restitution, generally, this index
Defenses,
    Insanity,
        Confidential or privileged communications, 740 ILCS 110/10
Deviate sexual conduct. Sexual Abuse, generally, this index
Discrimination, generally, this index
Dissolution of marriage,
    Grounds, 750 ILCS 5/401
Domestic Violence, generally, this index
False reports,
    Abused or neglected children, 325 ILCS 5/4
Family,
    Domestic Violence, generally, this index
Fines and Penalties, generally, this index
Fornication, generally, this index
Fraud, generally, this index
Habeas Corpus, generally, this index
Harboring runaways, 720 ILCS 5/10–6
Homicide, generally, this index
Immunity,
    Reports of abuse of children, 325 ILCS 5/9
Incest, generally, this index
Indecency. Lewdness or Obscenity, generally, this index
Indictment and Information, generally, this index
Infamous Crimes, generally, this index
Information,
    Indictment and Information, generally, this index
Injuries, child abduction, aggravating factors, 720 ILCS 5/10–5
Insanity defense,
    Confidential or privileged communications, 740 ILCS 110/10
Jury, generally, this index
Juvenile Delinquents and Dependents, generally, this index
Kidnapping, generally, this index
Lewdness or Obscenity, generally, this index
Malicious Mischief, generally, this index
Marriage, this index
Minors. Children and Minors, this index

CRIMES AND OFFENSES—Cont'd

Mobilehomes and Mobilehome Parks, this index
Murder, generally. Homicide, this index
Narcotics. Controlled Substances, generally, this index
Nonsupport of spouse or children, 750 ILCS 15/1
Obscenity. Lewdness or Obscenity, generally, this index
Orders,
    Protective orders,
        Domestic Violence, this index
Paternity proceedings, admissibility of evidence, 750 ILCS 45/6
Perjury, generally, this index
Placing out children, receipt of compensation, 720 ILCS 525/5
Probation, generally, this index
Protection orders, generally. Domestic Violence, this index
Putative father registry, 750 ILCS 50/12.1
Rape. Sexual Assault, generally, this index
Reports,
    Disclosure,
        Child abuse reports, unauthorized information releases, class A misdemeanor, 325 ILCS 5/11.1
        Juveniles, serious habitual offenders, 325 ILCS 5/11.1
Restitution, generally, this index
Runaways, harboring runaways, 720 ILCS 5/10–6
Sex Offenses, generally, this index
Sexual Abuse, generally, this index
Sexual Crimes Against Children, generally, this index
Threats, generally, this index
Trial, generally, this index
Vandalism, generally, this index
Verification by certification, 735 ILCS 5/1–109
Victims,
    Protection orders, generally. Domestic Violence, this index
    Sexual Assault, generally, this index
Weapons, generally, this index
Wife. Husband and Wife, this index

CRIMINAL HISTORY RECORD INFORMATION

Adoption of children, 750 ILCS 50/5; 750 ILCS 50/6; 750 ILCS 50/15.1

CRIMINAL PROCEDURE CODE OF 1963

Crimes and Offenses, generally, this index

CRIMINAL SEXUAL ABUSE

Sexual Abuse, generally, this index

CRIMINAL SEXUAL ASSAULT

Sexual Assault, generally, this index

CRISIS SERVICES

Abused or neglected children, reports, 325 ILCS 5/4

CROSS–EXAMINATION

Witnesses, this index

CRUELTY

Dissolution of marriage, 750 ILCS 5/401

CURTESY

Mentally deficient or mentally ill spouse, 750 ILCS 65/17

CUSTODY

Child abduction, offenses, 720 ILCS 5/10–5
Children and Minors, this index
Dissolution of marriage proceedings, 750 ILCS 5/601 et seq., 1033
Guardianship or conservatorship, custody of ward, 755 ILCS 5/11–13
Juvenile Delinquents and Dependents, this index
Protective custody, abused or neglected children, 325 ILCS 5/5
Uniform Child Custody Jurisdiction Act, generally, this index

CUSTODY DETERMINATION

Defined, Uniform Child Custody Jurisdiction Act, 750 ILCS 35/3.02

CUSTODY JUDGMENT

Defined, Uniform Child Custody Jurisdiction Act, 750 ILCS 35/3.06

CUSTODY PROCEEDINGS

Defined, Uniform Child Custody Jurisdiction Act, 750 ILCS 35/3.03

CUSTOMERS

Defined,
    Plastic dies and molds, ownership transfers, 750 ILCS 5/202

DAMAGES

Adoption of children,
    Confidential intermediaries, disclosure of identity of biological parents or siblings, without consent, 750 ILCS 50/18.3a
Alienation of affections, limiting damages, 740 ILCS 5/0.01 et seq.
Breach of marriage promise, 740 ILCS 15/1; 740 ILCS 15/2
Children and Minors, this index
Exemplary damages. Punitive Damages, generally, this index
Guardian, Parental Responsibility Law, 740 ILCS 115/1 et seq.
Injunctions, this index
Limitations,
    Parental Responsibility Law, 740 ILCS 115/1 et seq.
Malicious acts of minors, Parental Responsibility Law, 740 ILCS 115/1 et seq.
Parental Responsibility Law, 740 ILCS 115/1 et seq.
Process, false statements, 735 ILCS 5/2–203
Punitive Damages, generally, this index

DAMAGES

DAMAGES—Cont'd
Restitution, generally, this index
Summons, false statements, 735 ILCS 5/2-203
Torts, this index
Wilful acts of minors, Parental Responsibility Law, 740 ILCS 115/1 et seq.
Wire or oral communications, interception, 18 U.S.C.A. § 2520

DATA PROCESSING
Electronic Data Processing, generally, this index

DAY CARE FACILITIES
Child Care Facilities, generally, this index

DEADLY WEAPONS
Weapons, generally, this index

DEATH
Abused or neglected children, reports, 325 ILCS 5/4.1
Adoption of Children, this index
Children and Minors, this index
Coroners, generally, this index
Homicide, generally, this index
Minors. Children and Minors, this index
Natural parents, visitation rights of grandparents, 755 ILCS 5/11-7.1
Neglected or abused children, reports, 325 ILCS 5/4.1
Parents, visitation rights of grandparents, 755 ILCS 5/11-7.1
Registration. Vital Statistics, this index
Support, death of parent, modification or termination, 750 ILCS 5/510

DEBTORS AND CREDITORS
Attachment, generally, this index
Confession of judgment, 735 ILCS 5/2-1301
Enforcement of Judgments, generally, this index
Garnishment, generally, this index
Husband and wife, claims against, 750 ILCS 65/15
Judgments,
  Enforcement of Judgments, generally, this index
  Interest computation, 735 ILCS 5/2-1303
Judicial Sales, generally, this index
Support, multiple orders, payments, interstate enforcement, 750 ILCS 22/209

DECEDENTS' ESTATES
Descent and Distribution, generally, this index
Probate Proceedings, generally, this index

DECEIT
Fraud, generally, this index

DECLARATION OF INVALIDITY
Marriage, this index

DECLARATION OF RIGHTS
Generally, 735 ILCS 5/2-701

DECLARATORY JUDGMENTS
Generally, 735 ILCS 5/2-701
Illegitimate children,
  Father and child relationship, 750 ILCS 45/7
  Paternity, mother and child relationship, 750 ILCS 45/19

DECREES
Judgments, generally, this index

DEEDS AND CONVEYANCES
Construction of,
  Declaratory judgments, 735 ILCS 5/2-701
Declaratory judgments, construction, 735 ILCS 5/2-701
Guardians and Guardianship, this index
Husband and Wife, this index
Lis pendens,
  Authorizing conveyance of real estate, 735 ILCS 5/2-1901
Married persons, 750 ILCS 65/9
Process, 735 ILCS 5/2-206

DEFAULT JUDGMENTS
Entry, 735 ILCS 5/2-1301
Notice, 735 ILCS 5/2-1302
Mail and mailing, entry notice, 735 ILCS 5/2-1302
Notice,
  Entry, 735 ILCS 5/2-1302
Orders of court,
  Notice, 735 ILCS 5/2-1302
Process,
  Personal service outside state, 735 ILCS 5/2-208
  Publication, 735 ILCS 5/2-207
Vacating or setting aside, 735 ILCS 5/2-1301
Want of prosecution, notice, 735 ILCS 5/2-1302

DEFENDANTS
Parties, generally, this index

DEFENSES
Child abduction, offenses, 720 ILCS 5/10-5
Injunctions, 735 ILCS 5/11-107
Judgments, defendant answer or otherwise plead, 735 ILCS 5/2-1301
Support,
  Nonparentage, interstate enforcement, 750 ILCS 22/315
  Registration, foreign orders, 750 ILCS 22/607

DEFINITIONS
Words and Phrases, generally, this index

DELINQUENCY
Defined,
  Paternity proceedings, withholding of income, 750 ILCS 45/20
  Support, 750 ILCS 5/706.1; 750 ILCS 15/4.1; 750 ILCS 20/26.1

DELINQUENT CHILDREN
Juvenile Delinquents and Dependents, generally, this index

DEMOLITION OF BUILDINGS
Process, service by publication, 735 ILCS 5/2-206

DEMONSTRATION PROJECTS
Expedited child support, 750 ILCS 25/4

DENTAL HYGIENISTS
Abused or neglected children, reports, 325 ILCS 5/4

DENTISTS AND DENTISTRY
Abused or neglected children, reports, 325 ILCS 5/4
Children and minors,
  Abuse or neglect, reports, 325 ILCS 5/4
  Records, noncustodial parents, access, 750 ILCS 5/602.1
Records and recordation,
  Children, noncustodial parent, access, 750 ILCS 5/602.1

DEPARTMENT
Defined,
  Abused and neglected children, reports, 325 ILCS 5/3
State Departments, generally, this index

DEPENDENT CHILDREN
Juvenile Delinquents and Dependents, generally, this index

DEPENDENTS
Income taxes, personal exemptions, 26 U.S.C.A. § 151
Defined, income taxes, 26 U.S.C.A. § 152
Residence, obligor, as affecting duties of support, 750 ILCS 20/4
Support, generally, this index

DEPOSITIONS
Children and Minors, this index
Rules of Court, this index
Support,
  Evidence of duty of support, Uniform Reciprocal Enforcement of Support Act, 750 ILCS 20/20
  Interstate enforcement, 750 ILCS 22/316
  Uniform Child Custody Jurisdiction Act, taking in other state, 750 ILCS 35/19

DESCENT AND DISTRIBUTION
Children and minors, artificial insemination, legitimacy, 750 ILCS 40/1 et seq.

DESERTION
Abandonment of Spouse, generally, this index
Dissolution of marriage, 750 ILCS 5/401

DETAINS
Defined, child abduction, 720 ILCS 5/10-5

DETECTIVES AND DETECTIVE AGENCIES
Process, service of process, 735 ILCS 5/2-202
Service of process, 735 ILCS 5/2-202

DETENTION
Juvenile Delinquents and Dependents, this index

DETENTION CENTERS
Juvenile Delinquents and Dependents, this index

DEVELOPMENTALLY DISABLED PERSONS
Mentally Retarded and Developmentally Disabled Persons, generally, this index

DEVIATE SEXUAL CONDUCT
Sexual Abuse, generally, this index

DIRECTORS
Examinations, 735 ILCS 5/2-1102

DISABILITY ASSISTANCE
Social Services, generally, this index

DISABILITY INSURANCE
Accident and Health Insurance, generally, this index

DISABLED PERSONS
Handicapped Persons, generally, this index

DISASTERS
Emergency Medical Services (EMS) Systems, generally, this index

DISBURSEMENTS
Guardianship, funds of ward, 755 ILCS 5/11-13

DISCLOSURE
Adoption, identifying information, exchange, 750 ILCS 50/18.1 et seq.
AIDS, this index
Domestic Violence, this index
Husband and wife, premarital agreements, 750 ILCS 10/9
Juvenile Delinquents and Dependents, this index
Putative father registry, 750 ILCS 50/12.1
Support,
Income withholding, 750 ILCS 5/706.1; 750 ILCS 15/4.1; 750 ILCS 20/26.1

DISCOVERY
Admissions, generally, this index
Depositions, generally, this index
Developmentally disabled persons, Psychological test material, 740 ILCS 110/3
Therapists personal notes, 740 ILCS 110/3

DISCOVERY—Cont'd
Mentally disabled persons,
Psychological test material, 740 ILCS 110/3
Therapists personal notes, 740 ILCS 110/3
Rules of Court, this index
Support, interstate enforcement, 750 ILCS 22/202; 750 ILCS 22/206; 750 ILCS 22/318
Therapists, mentally or developmentally disabled persons,
Personal notes, 740 ILCS 110/3
Psychological test material, 740 ILCS 110/3

DISCRIMINATION
Employment,
Child abuse, reports, 325 ILCS 5/9.1

DISEASES
AIDS, generally, this index
Hospitals, generally, this index
Inherited metabolic diseases, medical information brochure, 750 ILCS 5/204
Marriage, medical information brochure, 750 ILCS 5/204

DISMISSAL OF ACTIONS
Adoption of children, death of child, 750 ILCS 50/14a
Breach of marriage promise, action, 740 ILCS 15/5
Child custody proceedings, inconvenient forum, 750 ILCS 35/8
Entry, notice, 735 ILCS 5/2-1302
Mail and mailing, entry notice, 735 ILCS 5/2-1302
Marriage, breach of marriage promise, 740 ILCS 15/5
Notice,
Entry, 735 ILCS 5/2-1302
Orders,
Notice, 735 ILCS 5/2-1302
Want of prosecution, notice, 735 ILCS 5/2-1302

DISSOLUTION OF MARRIAGE
Marriage, this index

DISTRIBUTION OF DECEDENTS ESTATES
Descent and Distribution, generally, this index

DISTRICTS
Schools and School Districts, generally, this index

DIVISION OF CHILD SUPPORT ENFORCEMENT
Generally, 750 ILCS 5/712

DIVORCE
Dissolution of marriage, generally. Marriage, this index

DNA TESTING
Paternity proceedings, 750 ILCS 45/11

DOCKETS
Change of venue, 735 ILCS 5/2-1001.5
Venue, change of venue, 735 ILCS 5/2-1001.5

DOCTORS
Physicians and Surgeons, generally, this index

DOMESTIC VIOLENCE
Generally, 750 ILCS 60/101 et seq.
Abuse, protection orders, 750 ILCS 60/214
Accountability for actions of others, protection orders, 750 ILCS 60/216
Actual knowledge, protection order violations, 750 ILCS 60/223
Address nondisclosure, protection order petitions, 750 ILCS 60/203
Advocates,
Confidential or privileged information, 750 ILCS 60/227; 750 ILCS 60/227.1
Domestic abuse advocates, participation in proceedings, 750 ILCS 60/205
Alcoholics or intoxicated persons, protection orders, 750 ILCS 60/214
Appearance orders, 750 ILCS 60/214
Applications of law, 750 ILCS 60/201
Arrest, protection orders, 750 ILCS 60/301.1
Arrest without warrants, 750 ILCS 60/301
Assistance by law enforcement officers, 750 ILCS 60/304
Attorneys, high-risk adults with disabilities, protection orders, 750 ILCS 60/213.3
Attorneys fees, protection orders, enforcement, 750 ILCS 60/223
Available services, information, liability, 750 ILCS 60/401
Bail violation, warrantless arrest, 750 ILCS 60/301
Balance of hardships, protection orders, 750 ILCS 60/214
Civil procedure rules, application, protection orders, 750 ILCS 60/205
Concealment of child, prohibition, 750 ILCS 60/214
Confidential or privileged information,
Domestic violence counselors and victims, 750 ILCS 60/227; 750 ILCS 60/227.1
Schools, protection orders, 750 ILCS 60/222
Consolidation, protection order petitions, 750 ILCS 60/202
Constructive service of process, remedies allowing, 750 ILCS 60/210
Contempt, protection orders, violation, 750 ILCS 60/223
Continuances, 750 ILCS 60/213
Correlative orders of protection, 750 ILCS 60/215

DOMESTIC

DOMESTIC VIOLENCE—Cont'd
Counselors and counseling, 750 ILCS 60/214
  Confidential or privileged information, 750 ILCS 60/227; 750 ILCS 60/227.1
Court rules, application, protection orders, 750 ILCS 60/205
Definitions, 750 ILCS 60/103
  Counselors, confidential or privileged information, 750 ILCS 60/227
Denial of remedies, 750 ILCS 60/214
Disabled persons. High-risk adults with disabilities, generally, post
Disclosures,
  Civil immunity, 750 ILCS 60/225
  Confidential or privileged information, generally, ante
Dismissal, protection order petitions, 750 ILCS 60/202
Duration, protection orders, 750 ILCS 60/220
Elder abuse, disclosure of information, civil immunity, 750 ILCS 60/225
Emergency orders. Protection orders, post
Evidence,
  High-risk adults with disabilities,
    Hearsay exception, 750 ILCS 60/213.1
    Waiver of privilege, 750 ILCS 60/213.2
  Venue, 750 ILCS 60/209[40 § 2312-9]
Exploitation, defined, 750 ILCS 60/103
Extensions, protection orders, 750 ILCS 60/220; 750 ILCS 60/222
Fees,
  Service of process, 750 ILCS 60/210
  Filing fees, protection order petitions, 750 ILCS 60/202
Fines and penalties,
  Protection order violations, 750 ILCS 60/223
Guardians and guardianship,
  Appointment proceedings, protection orders in conjunction with, 755 ILCS 5/11-9
  Temporary substitute guardian, high-risk adults with disabilities, protection orders, 750 ILCS 60/213.3
Health care providers, information regarding services available, 750 ILCS 60/401
Hearings, 750 ILCS 60/212
  Notice, service, 750 ILCS 60/211
Hearsay exception, high-risk adults with disabilities, protection orders, 750 ILCS 60/213.1
High-risk adults with disabilities,
  Application of law, 750 ILCS 60/102
  Defined, 750 ILCS 60/103
  Good faith reporters of abuse, etc., privileges and immunities, 750 ILCS 60/225

DOMESTIC VIOLENCE—Cont'd
High-risk adults with disabilities—Cont'd
  Law enforcement officers, referrals to service agencies, 750 ILCS 60/304
  Protection orders, 750 ILCS 60/201 et seq.
    Access to agencies or organizations, obstruction, 750 ILCS 60/201.1
    Hearsay exception, 750 ILCS 60/213.1
    Independent counsel, 750 ILCS 60/213.3
    Remedies, 750 ILCS 60/214
    Temporary substitute guardian, 750 ILCS 60/213.3
    Waiver of privilege, evidence, 750 ILCS 60/213.2
Inconvenient forum, protection orders, venue, 750 ILCS 60/209
Independent counsel, protection orders, high-risk adults with disabilities, 750 ILCS 60/213.3
Injunction, 750 ILCS 60/214
Interim orders. Protection orders, post
Investigations, law enforcement officers, reports, 750 ILCS 60/303
Jurisdiction,
  Protection orders, 750 ILCS 60/207; 750 ILCS 60/208
Jury trial,
  Protection orders, 750 ILCS 60/206
Law enforcement agencies, records, extension of protection orders, 750 ILCS 60/220
Law enforcement responsibilities, 750 ILCS 60/301 et seq.
Liability, health care providers, information regarding services available, 750 ILCS 60/401
Limited liability, law enforcement officers, 750 ILCS 60/305
Losses, orders for payment, 750 ILCS 60/214
Medical care and treatment, assistance by law enforcement officers, 750 ILCS 60/304
Modification, protection orders, 750 ILCS 60/222; 750 ILCS 60/224
Mutual orders of protection, 750 ILCS 60/215
Neglect, defined, 750 ILCS 60/103
Nondisclosure of address, protection order petitions, 750 ILCS 60/203
Notice,
  Hearings, service, 750 ILCS 60/211
Protection orders, post
Objections, venue, protection orders, 750 ILCS 60/209
Orders of protection. Protection orders, generally, post
Past abuse, protection orders, 750 ILCS 60/214
Personal jurisdiction, protection orders, 750 ILCS 60/208
Personal property possession, 750 ILCS 60/214

DOMESTIC VIOLENCE—Cont'd
Personal service of process, remedies requiring, 750 ILCS 60/210
Physical care of children, 750 ILCS 60/214
Pleadings. Protection orders, generally, post
Plenary orders. Protection orders, post
Privileged information. Confidential or privileged information, generally, ante
Privileges and immunities,
  Good faith reporters, abuse, neglect, or exploitation, high-risk adults with disabilities, 750 ILCS 60/225
  High-risk adults with disabilities, protection orders, waiver of privilege, 750 ILCS 60/213.2
  Law enforcement officers, 750 ILCS 60/305
  Protection orders, 750 ILCS 60/225
Pro se petitions, protection orders, 750 ILCS 60/202
Process, 750 ILCS 60/210 et seq.
Protection of property, 750 ILCS 60/214
Protection orders, 750 ILCS 60/201 et seq.
  Abuse prohibition, 750 ILCS 60/214
  Accountability for others actions, 750 ILCS 60/216
  Actual knowledge of violations, 750 ILCS 60/223
  Address disclosure, 750 ILCS 60/203
  Alcoholics or intoxicated persons, 750 ILCS 60/214
  Appearance orders, 750 ILCS 60/214
  Arrest, 750 ILCS 60/301.1
  Assistance by law enforcement officers, 750 ILCS 60/304
  Attorneys fees, enforcement, 750 ILCS 60/223
  Balance of hardships, 750 ILCS 60/214
  Civil procedure rules, application, 750 ILCS 60/205
  Commencement of action, 750 ILCS 60/202
  Concealment of child, 750 ILCS 60/214
  Confidential or privileged information,
    Counselors and victims, 750 ILCS 60/227; 750 ILCS 60/227.1
  Conjunction with other proceedings, filing, 750 ILCS 60/202
  Consolidation of petitions, 750 ILCS 60/202
  Contempt of court, violations, 750 ILCS 60/223
  Contents, 750 ILCS 60/221
  Continuances, 750 ILCS 60/213
  Correlative separate orders, 750 ILCS 60/215
  Counseling, 750 ILCS 60/214

DOMESTIC VIOLENCE—Cont'd
Protection orders—Cont'd
  Court rules, application, 750 ILCS 60/205
  Crimes and offenses, 750 ILCS 60/223
  Defined, 750 ILCS 60/103
  Denial of remedies, 750 ILCS 60/214
  Dismissal of petitions, 750 ILCS 60/202
  Duration, 750 ILCS 60/220
  Emergency orders, 750 ILCS 60/217
    Continuances, 750 ILCS 60/213
    Duration, 750 ILCS 60/220
    Venue, 750 ILCS 60/209
  Expedited proceedings, hearings, 750 ILCS 60/212
  Extension, 750 ILCS 60/220; 750 ILCS 60/222
  Filing fees, 750 ILCS 60/202
  Fines and penalties, 750 ILCS 60/223
  Guardianship appointments, proceedings in conjunction with, 755 ILCS 5/11-9
  High-risk adults with disabilities, ante
  Inconvenient forum, venue, 750 ILCS 60/209
  Injunctions, 750 ILCS 60/214
  Interim orders, 750 ILCS 60/218
    Continuances, 750 ILCS 60/213
    Duration, 750 ILCS 60/220
  Jurisdiction, 750 ILCS 60/207; 750 ILCS 60/208
  Jury trials, 750 ILCS 60/206
  Losses, orders for payment of, 750 ILCS 60/214
  Modification, 750 ILCS 60/222; 750 ILCS 60/224
  Mutual orders, 750 ILCS 60/215
  Notice, 750 ILCS 60/222
    Pending civil cases, in conjunction with orders, 750 ILCS 60/210.1
  Objection to venue, 750 ILCS 60/209
  Personal jurisdiction, 750 ILCS 60/208
  Personal property possession, 750 ILCS 60/214
  Petitions, 750 ILCS 60/201 et seq.
    Address, disclosure, 750 ILCS 60/203
    Dismissal, 750 ILCS 60/202
    Filing fees, 750 ILCS 60/202
    Pleading, 750 ILCS 60/203
  Physical care of child, 750 ILCS 60/214
  Physical evidence of abuse, necessity, 750 ILCS 60/214; 750 ILCS 60/223
  Plenary orders, 750 ILCS 60/203; 750 ILCS 60/219
    Continuances, 750 ILCS 60/213
    Duration, 750 ILCS 60/220
    Filing fees, 750 ILCS 60/202
  Previous orders, status, 750 ILCS 60/223.1

DOMESTIC VIOLENCE—Cont'd
Protection orders—Cont'd
  Previous orders, status—Cont'd
    Dissolution of marriage, 750 ILCS 5/107
  Privileges and immunities, 750 ILCS 60/225
  Pro se petitions, 750 ILCS 60/202
  Process, 750 ILCS 60/210 et seq.
  Prohibition of entry, respondents under the influence of alcohol or drugs, 750 ILCS 60/214
  Property protection, 750 ILCS 60/214
  Records and recordation,
    Access prohibited, 750 ILCS 60/214
    Law enforcement agencies, 750 ILCS 60/302
  Removal of child, prohibition, 750 ILCS 60/214
  Restitution, enforcement, 750 ILCS 60/223
  Revocation, 750 ILCS 60/222
  Schools and school districts, Notice, 750 ILCS 60/222
  Service of process, 750 ILCS 60/210 et seq.
  Shelter services, payment of expenses, 750 ILCS 60/214
  Standard of proof, 750 ILCS 60/205
  Status,
    Previous orders, 750 ILCS 60/223.1
      Dissolution of marriage, 750 ILCS 5/107
  Stay away orders, 750 ILCS 60/214
  Support payments, 750 ILCS 60/214
  Temporary legal custody, 750 ILCS 60/214
  Time, duration or extension, 750 ILCS 60/220
  Title to property, 750 ILCS 60/214
  Transfer of contested matters, 750 ILCS 60/212
  Untrue statements, 750 ILCS 60/226
  Venue, 750 ILCS 60/209
  Victims assistance, law enforcement officers, 750 ILCS 60/304
  Violation, 750 ILCS 60/223
  Visitation, 750 ILCS 60/214
  Warning, consequences of disobedience, 750 ILCS 60/221
Records and recordation,
  Access prohibited, protection orders, 750 ILCS 60/214
  Law enforcement agencies, protection orders, 750 ILCS 60/302
Relevant factors, protection orders, 750 ILCS 60/214
Removal of child, prohibition, 750 ILCS 60/214
Reopening, protection orders, 750 ILCS 60/214; 750 ILCS 60/224
Reports,
  Abused or neglected children, 325 ILCS 5/4

DOMESTIC VIOLENCE—Cont'd
Reports—Cont'd
  Law enforcement officers investigations, 750 ILCS 60/303
Reserving judgment, transfer of contested matters, 750 ILCS 60/212
Residence, exclusive possession, protection orders, 750 ILCS 60/214
Restitution, protection orders, enforcement, 750 ILCS 60/223
Revocations, protection orders, 750 ILCS 60/222
Schools and School Districts, this index
Service of process, 750 ILCS 60/210 et seq.
Social services, assistance by law enforcement officers, 750 ILCS 60/304
Stalking, protection orders, 750 ILCS 60/214
Standard of proof, protection orders, 750 ILCS 60/205
Stay away orders, protection orders, 750 ILCS 60/214
Support orders, 750 ILCS 60/214
Temporary legal custody, protection orders, 750 ILCS 60/214
Temporary substitute guardian, high-risk adults with disabilities, protection orders, 750 ILCS 60/213.3
Time, protection orders, duration or extension, 750 ILCS 60/220
Title to property, protection order effect, 750 ILCS 60/214
Torts, spouses, 750 ILCS 65/1
Training and curriculum task force, 750 ILCS 60/306
Transfer of contested matters, 750 ILCS 60/212
Untrue statements, protection orders, 750 ILCS 60/226
Venue, protection orders, 750 ILCS 60/209
Visitation, protection orders, 750 ILCS 60/214
Waiver,
  Objections to venue, protection orders, 750 ILCS 60/209
  Privilege, protection orders for high-risk adults with disabilities, 750 ILCS 60/213.2

DOMICILE AND RESIDENCE
Adoption of children, qualification of person who may adopt, 750 ILCS 50/2
Dissolution of marriage, 750 ILCS 5/401
  Jurisdiction over parties, 735 ILCS 5/2-209
Guardian of the estate, resident qualified to act as, 755 ILCS 5/11-3
Nonresidents, generally, this index
Support obligees, effect on duties of support obligors, 750 ILCS 20/4

DOMICILE

DOMICILE AND RESIDENCE
—Cont'd
Venue, generally, this index

DRUG ADDICTS
Dissolution of marriage, grounds, 750 ILCS 5/401

DRUGGISTS
Pharmacists, generally, this index

DRUGS AND MEDICINE
Addicts. Drug Addicts, generally, this index
Domestic violence, protective orders, 750 ILCS 60/208
Drug Addicts, generally, this index

DURESS OR COERCION
See, also, Threats, generally, this index
Adoption of children, limitation of actions, 750 ILCS 50/11
Judgments, relief, tolling, 735 ILCS 5/2–1401
Orders of court, relief, tolling, 735 ILCS 5/2–1401
Premarital agreements, 750 ILCS 10/7

DUTY OF SUPPORT
Defined,
Interstate enforcement, 750 ILCS 22/101
Reciprocal Enforcement of Support Act, 750 ILCS 20/2

DWELLINGS
Crimes and offenses,
Child abduction, luring into, 720 ILCS 5/10–5
Homesteads, generally, this index

EARNINGS
Compensation and Salaries, generally, this index

EAVESDROPPING
Wiretapping and Eavesdropping, generally, this index

EDUCATION
Children and Minors, this index
Colleges and Universities, generally, this index
Expenses, 750 ILCS 65/15
Schools and School Districts, generally, this index
Support, this index

ELDER ADULT WITH DISABILITIES
Defined, domestic violence, 750 ILCS 60/103

ELDERLY PERSONS
Aged Persons, generally, this index

ELECTIONS
State officers and employees, declaratory judgments, 735 ILCS 5/2–701

ELECTRONIC DATA PROCESSING
Marriage certificates, registration, 750 ILCS 5/210

EMANCIPATION OF MATURE MINORS ACT
Generally, 750 ILCS 30/1 et seq.

EMERGENCY ASSISTANCE AND ADVOCACY
Defined, family preservation services, abused and neglected children, 325 ILCS 5/8.2

EMERGENCY MEDICAL SERVICES (EMS) SYSTEMS
Abused or neglected children, reports, 325 ILCS 5/4
Children, abuse or neglect, reports, 325 ILCS 5/4

EMERGENCY TREATMENT
Children and minors, temporary protective custody, 325 ILCS 5/5

EMINENT DOMAIN
Lis pendens, 735 ILCS 5/2–1901
Venue,
Change of venue,
Records, 735 ILCS 5/2–1001.5

EMPLOYEE RETIREMENT INCOME SECURITY PROGRAM
Group health plans, additional standards, 29 U.S.C.A. § 1169

EMPLOYMENT
Labor and Employment, generally, this index

ENCUMBRANCES
Liens and Incumbrances, generally, this index

ENDORSEMENTS
Process, 735 ILCS 5/2–202

ENFORCEMENT OF JUDGMENTS
See, also, Support, Enforcement, this index
Books and papers, personal property, exemptions,
Certification, 735 ILCS 5/2–1501
Dissolution of marriage proceedings, 750 ILCS 5/511
Paternity proceedings, 750 ILCS 45/15

ENHANCED PENALTIES
Child abduction, offenses, 720 ILCS 5/10–5

ESCAPE
Developmentally disabled persons,
Confidential information released, 740 ILCS 110/12.2

ESTATES
Deeds and Conveyances, generally, this index
Descent and Distribution, generally, this index
Income, taxation, divorce or separation, 26 U.S.C.A. § 682
Partition, generally, this index

ESTATES OF DECEDENTS
Probate Proceedings, generally, this index

ESTOPPEL
Premarital agreements, enforcement, 750 ILCS 10/9

EVICTION
Dissolution of marriage proceedings, marital home, 750 ILCS 5/701

EVIDENCE
Abandonment of wife or child, marriage, 750 ILCS 15/6; 750 ILCS 15/7
Abuse of children,
Proceedings resulting from reports, 325 ILCS 5/10
Admissions, generally, this index
Adverse party or agent, rebuttal or impeachment, 735 ILCS 5/2–1102
Burden of proof,
Children and minors, removal from state, dissolution of marriage, 750 ILCS 5/609
Dissolution of marriage, removal of children from state, 750 ILCS 5/609
Children and minors,
Custody actions, marital privilege, 735 ILCS 5/8–801
Sexual crimes,
Hearsay exception, 735 ILCS 5/8–2601
Default judgments, 735 ILCS 5/2–1301
Depositions, generally, this index
Foreign marriage, dissolution of marriage, 750 ILCS 5/409
Guardians for minors, abused and neglected minors, admissibility of prior statements, 755 ILCS 5/11–5
Hearsay, generally, this index
Husband and wife,
Privileged communications, 735 ILCS 5/8–801
Support proceedings, competency, Uniform Reciprocal Enforcement of Support Act, 750 ILCS 20/22
Impeachment, adverse party or agent, 735 ILCS 5/2–1102
Juvenile Delinquents and Dependents, this index
Proceedings resulting from reports, 325 ILCS 5/10
Objections, answer not responsive, p. 944
Offers of proof, p. 944
Parentage of child, 750 ILCS 15/7
Paternity. Children Born Out of Wedlock, this index
Perjury, p. 963
Presumptions,
Child abduction, offenses, 720 ILCS 5/10–5
Support,
Interstate enforcement, delays, hearings, 750 ILCS 22/313
Presence of support obligor in responding state, Uniform Reciprocal Enforcement of Support Act, 750 ILCS 20/7
Uniform Reciprocal Enforcement of Support Act, presence of support obligor in responding state, 750 ILCS 20/7

FOREIGN

EVIDENCE—Cont'd
Presumptions—Cont'd
Weapons,
    Mentally ill persons, disclosures, firearm owners identification cards, 740 ILCS 110/12
Prima facie evidence,
    Torts, marriage dissolution proceedings, testimony, 750 ILCS 65/1
Prior inconsistent statements, impeachment, 735 ILCS 5/2-1102
Privileged communications, 735 ILCS 5/8-801 et seq.
Rebuttal, adverse party or agent, 735 ILCS 5/2-1102
Records and Recordation, this index
Rules of Court, this index
Self-incrimination,
    Constitution of Illinois, p. 962
    Constitution of United States, p. 961
Sexual Crimes Against Children, this index
Spouse, privileged communications, 735 ILCS 5/8-801
Support, this index
Wife, privileged communications, 735 ILCS 5/8-801
Wire and oral communications, interception, 18 U.S.C.A. § 2515
Witnesses, generally, this index

EXEMPLARY DAMAGES
Punitive Damages, generally, this index

EXPEDITED CHILD SUPPORT ACT
Generally, 750 ILCS 25/1 et seq.

EXPEDITED CHILD SUPPORT HEARING
Defined, 750 ILCS 25/3
    Expedited child support proceedings, S.Ct.Rule 100.13

EXPERTS
Witnesses, this index

EXPLOITATION
Defined,
    Domestic violence, 750 ILCS 60/103

EXTRADITION
Relief from extradition, Uniform Reciprocal Enforcement of Support Act, 750 ILCS 20/6
Support of dependents,
    Interstate enforcement, 750 ILCS 22/801; 750 ILCS 22/802
    Uniform Reciprocal Enforcement of Support Act, 750 ILCS 20/5; 750 ILCS 20/6

FACILITIES
Patient information, therapists, disclosure, 740 ILCS 110/9

FALSE EVIDENCE
Perjury, generally, this index

FALSE REPRESENTATIONS
Fraud, generally, this index

FALSE SWEARING
Perjury, generally, this index

FAMILY EXPENSE LAW
Generally, 750 ILCS 65/15

FAMILY OR HOUSEHOLD MEMBERS
Defined,
    Domestic violence, 750 ILCS 60/103

FAMILY PRESERVATION SERVICES
Defined, abused and neglected children, 325 ILCS 5/8.2

FEDERAL GOVERNMENT
United States, generally, this index

FEDERAL TIME FRAMES
Defined, expedited child support, 750 ILCS 25/3

FELONY
Crimes and Offenses, generally, this index

FEMALES
Women, generally, this index

FIDUCIARIES
Bonds (Officers and Fiduciaries), generally, this index
Guardian Ad Litem, generally, this index
Jurisdiction, 735 ILCS 5/2-209
Official bonds. Bonds (Officers and Fiduciaries), generally, this index
Process, 735 ILCS 5/2-209
Trusts and Trustees, generally, this index

FINANCIAL ASSISTANCE
Social Services, generally, this index

FINES AND PENALTIES
Adoption of children,
    Confidential intermediaries, disclosure of identity without permission, 750 ILCS 50/18.3a
Domestic violence, protection orders, violations, 750 ILCS 60/223
Husband and wife, support, failure to, disposition, 750 ILCS 15/4
Marriages, 750 ILCS 5/215
Process,
    Return violations, 735 ILCS 5/2-202
Social Services, this index
Support, this index
Writs, abolishment, 735 ILCS 5/2-1501

FINGERPRINTS
Adoption of children, criminal background checks and reports, 750 ILCS 50/6

FINGERPRINTS—Cont'd
Support proceedings, identification of obligor, Uniform Reciprocal Enforcement of Support Act, 750 ILCS 20/11

FIREARMS
Weapons, generally, this index

FORCIBLE ENTRY AND DETAINER
Writs, abolishment, 735 ILCS 5/2-1501

FOREIGN COUNTRIES
Convention country designation, uniform reciprocal enforcement of support, 750 ILCS 20/4.1
International Child Abduction Remedies Act, 42 U.S.C.A. § 11601 et seq.
Support,
    Convention country designation, reciprocal enforcement, 750 ILCS 20/4.1

FOREIGN JUDGMENTS
Action to enforce judgment, optional procedure, 735 ILCS 5/12-656
Child support, expedited proceedings, S.Ct.Rule 100.4
Defined, enforcement, 735 ILCS 5/12-651
Fees, enforcement proceedings, 735 ILCS 5/12-655
Filing, 735 ILCS 5/12-652
    Notice, 735 ILCS 5/12-653
Mail and mailing, notice of filing, 735 ILCS 5/12-653
Notice,
    Filing, 735 ILCS 5/12-653
Optional procedure, action to enforce judgments, 735 ILCS 5/12-656
Status, 735 ILCS 5/12-652
Supersedeas or stay,
    Enforcement, 735 ILCS 5/12-654
Uniformity of interpretation, 735 ILCS 5/12-657

FOREIGN MARRIAGE
Proof, 750 ILCS 5/409

FOREIGN MONEY CLAIMS
Generally, 735 ILCS 5/12-654 et seq.

FOREIGN NATIONS
Foreign Countries, generally, this index

FOREIGN PLACING AGENCIES
Defined, adoption of children, 750 ILCS 50/1

FOREIGN STATES
Child abduction, 720 ILCS 5/10-5
Child custody actions, parties, 750 ILCS 5/601
Compacts, generally, this index
Extradition, generally, this index
Process, personal service, 735 ILCS 5/2-208
Support,
    Uniform interstate family support, 750 ILCS 22/100 et seq.

FOREIGN

FOREIGN STATES—Cont'd
Support—Cont'd
Uniform Reciprocal Enforcement of Support Act, 750 ILCS 20/1 et seq.
Uniform Child Custody Jurisdiction Act, generally, this index
Uniform Reciprocal Enforcement of Support Act, 750 ILCS 20/1 et seq.

FOREIGN SUPPORT ORDERS
Registration, Uniform Reciprocal Enforcement of Support Act, 750 ILCS 20/35

FOREIGNERS
Aliens, generally, this index

FOREMAN
Examinations, 735 ILCS 5/2-1102

FORMS
See, also, Table of Forms
Adoption,
Consent and surrender, 750 ILCS 50/10
Identifying information, exchange, 750 ILCS 50/18.1 et seq.
Casts, dies and molds, plastics, ownership transfer, 750 ILCS 5/201 et seq.
Dissolution of marriage, joint simplified procedure, 750 ILCS 5/456
Juvenile Delinquents and Dependents, this index
Marriage, this index
Motions, 735 ILCS 5/2-620
Pharmaceutical assistance, senior citizens and disabled persons, claims, 320 ILCS 25/5
Plastics, dies and molds, ownership transfer, 750 ILCS 5/201 et seq.
Property tax relief, senior citizens and disabled persons, claims, 320 ILCS 25/5
Rules of Court, this index
Senior Citizens and Disabled Persons Property Tax Relief Act, claims, 320 ILCS 25/5
Summons. Process, this index
Support, this index

FORNICATION
Paternity proceedings, admissibility of evidence, 750 ILCS 45/6

FOSTER FAMILY HOMES
Social Services, this index

FOSTER PARENTS
Adoption of foster child, preference, 750 ILCS 50/15.1

FRAUD
Adoption of children, limitation of actions, 750 ILCS 50/11
Aged Persons, this index
Judgments, relief, tolling, 735 ILCS 5/2-1401
Orders of court, relief, tolling, 735 ILCS 5/2-1401
Verification by certification, 735 ILCS 5/1-109

FRAUDULENT REPRESENTATIONS
Fraud, generally, this index

GARNISHMENT
See, also, Attachment, generally, this index
Paternity proceedings, 750 ILCS 45/20

GENERAL ASSISTANCE
Social Services, this index

GENERAL ASSISTANCE FUND
Support, public aid recipients, mandatory payments, 750 ILCS 5/709

GOOD FAITH
Firearm owners identification cards, mental health disclosures, immunity, 740 ILCS 110/12
Venue, transfer of causes, 735 ILCS 5/2-107

GOODS, WARES AND MERCHANDISE
Consumer transactions, confession of judgments, 735 ILCS 5/2-1301

GOVERNMENT
State, generally, this index

GOVERNMENTAL AGENCIES
Public Agencies, generally, this index

GOVERNMENTAL CORPORATIONS
Declaratory judgments, 735 ILCS 5/2-701
Judgments, interest computation, 735 ILCS 5/2-1303

GOVERNOR
Defined,
Uniform Reciprocal Enforcement of Support Act, 750 ILCS 20/2
Extradition, generally, this index

GRAND JURY
Indictment and Information, generally, this index

GRANDPARENTS AND GRANDCHILDREN
Adopted children, death of parents, visitation rights, 755 ILCS 5/11-7.1
Death of parents, visitation rights, 755 ILCS 5/11-7.1
Descent and Distribution, generally, this index
Marriages, 750 ILCS 5/212
Parents, death, children, visitation rights, 755 ILCS 5/11-7.1
Visitation rights, 750 ILCS 5/607
Death of parents, 755 ILCS 5/11-7.1

GROUP CARE HOME
Child Care Facilities, generally, this index

GUARDIAN AD LITEM
See, also, Next Friend, generally, this index
Abuse and neglect reports, copies, 325 ILCS 5/11.1
Adoption of Children, this index
Appointment,
Uniform Child Custody Jurisdiction Act, 750 ILCS 35/12
Juvenile Delinquents and Dependents, this index
Marital dissolutions, 750 ILCS 5/506
Support proceedings, 750 ILCS 20/13
Uniform Child Custody Jurisdiction Act, appointment, 750 ILCS 35/12

GUARDIANS AND GUARDIANSHIP
Adoption of Children, this index
Appointments, S.Ct.Rule 61
Successor guardian, 755 ILCS 5/11-18
Bonds (officers and fiduciaries),
Next friend of minor, of proceedings, 755 ILCS 5/11-13
Children Born Out of Wedlock, this index
Contracts,
Performance of contracts of wards, 755 ILCS 5/11-13
Conveyances. Deeds and conveyances, generally, post
Death, appointment of successor guardian, 755 ILCS 5/11-18
Deeds and conveyances,
Authority of conservator to execute and deliver deeds, 755 ILCS 5/11-13
Defined,
Parental Responsibility Law, 740 ILCS 115/2
Domestic violence, protection order petitions,
Filing in conjunction with guardianship petition, 750 ILCS 60/202
High-risk adults with disabilities, temporary substitute guardian, 750 ILCS 60/213.3
Issuance in conjunction with proceedings, 755 ILCS 5/11-9
Emancipation of Mature Minors Act, 750 ILCS 30/1 et seq.
Guardians for Minors, generally, this index
Juvenile Delinquents and Dependents, this index
Mental Health and Developmental Disabilities Confidentiality Act, 740 ILCS 110/2
Protection orders, domestic violence,
Filing in conjunction with support, 750 ILCS 60/202
Issuance, 755 ILCS 5/11-9
Qualifications, 755 ILCS 5/11-3
Removal,
Appointment of successor guardian, 755 ILCS 5/11-18
Successor guardian, appointment, 755 ILCS 5/11-18

HEALTH

GUARDIANS AND GUARDIAN-SHIP—Cont'd
Veterans' administration,
 Benefits paid to estate, notice,
  Application to invest or expend funds of wards estate, 755 ILCS 5/11-13

GUARDIANS FOR MINORS
Abused or neglected minors,
 Prior statements, admissibility of evidence, 755 ILCS 5/11-5
Actions, representative of estate of ward, appearing for and representing ward, 755 ILCS 5/11-13
Adults, legal age, 755 ILCS 5/11-1
Age,
 Children and minors, legal age, 755 ILCS 5/11-1
 Legal age, 755 ILCS 5/11-1
 Persons acting as guardians, 755 ILCS 5/11-3
Appointments, 755 ILCS 5/11-5
 Persons causing or contributing to neglect or abuse, 755 ILCS 5/11-5
 Persons who may act as guardians, 755 ILCS 5/11-3
 Petition, 755 ILCS 5/11-8
 Procedure, 755 ILCS 5/11-10.1
 Testamentary guardian of estate of minor, 755 ILCS 5/11-5
Bill of sale, power of guardian to execute and deliver, 755 ILCS 5/11-13
Bonds (officers and fiduciaries),
 Next friend of minor, commencement and prosecution of proceedings, 755 ILCS 5/11-13
 Testamentary guardian of estate of minor, 755 ILCS 5/11-5
Care, wards of state, 755 ILCS 5/11-13
Contracts, performance of contracts of ward, 755 ILCS 5/11-13
Costs, appointment of guardian, proceeding, 755 ILCS 5/11-11
Custody of ward, 755 ILCS 5/11-13
 Parental right, 755 ILCS 5/11-7
Definitions, Probate Act of 1975, 755 ILCS 5/11-1
Disbursements, funds of ward, 755 ILCS 5/11-13
Divorce of minors' parents, award of custody and education of minor, 755 ILCS 5/11-7
Domicile and residence, 755 ILCS 5/11-3
Duties of guardian, 755 ILCS 5/11-13
Education of ward,
 Expenditures by representative, 755 ILCS 5/11-13
 Parental rights, 755 ILCS 5/11-7
Estate of ward, 755 ILCS 5/11-3
 Care, management and investment, 755 ILCS 5/11-13
Expenditures of representative, 755 ILCS 5/11-13
Funds of ward, disbursements, 755 ILCS 5/11-13
Guardian ad litem, appointment, 755 ILCS 5/11-10.1

GUARDIANS FOR MINORS—Cont'd
Hearings, appointment procedure, 755 ILCS 5/11-10.1
Husband and wife, custody and education of children of ward, 755 ILCS 5/11-13
Investments,
 Estate of ward, 755 ILCS 5/11-13
Legal age, Probate Act of 1975, 755 ILCS 5/11-1
Management, estate of ward, 755 ILCS 5/11-13
Mentally deficient or mentally ill persons, qualifications, 755 ILCS 5/11-3
Next friend, appointment, 755 ILCS 5/11-13
Nomination, guardian, minor age 14 years or more, 755 ILCS 5/11-5
Nonresidents, appointment, venue, 755 ILCS 5/11-6
Notices,
 Appointment procedure, 755 ILCS 5/11-10.1
 Veterans benefits paid directly to estate of ward, application to invest or expend funds, 755 ILCS 5/11-13
Parental right to custody, 755 ILCS 5/11-3; 755 ILCS 5/11-7
Patient, state institution or mental hospital, 755 ILCS 5/11-3
 Costs, appointment of guardian, procedure, 755 ILCS 5/11-11
 Persons who may act as guardians, 755 ILCS 5/11-3
 Petitions, 755 ILCS 5/11-8
 Appointment, 755 ILCS 5/11-5
 Procedure for appointment, 755 ILCS 5/11-10.1
 Qualifications, 755 ILCS 5/11-3
Representative of ward,
 Appointment, 755 ILCS 5/11-5
 Petition for, 755 ILCS 5/11-8
 Duties, 755 ILCS 5/11-13
 Qualifications, 755 ILCS 5/11-3
Residence,
 Guardian of estate, resident qualified to act as, 755 ILCS 5/11-3
 Venue, 755 ILCS 5/11-6
Revocation, letters of office, minor reaching age of majority, 755 ILCS 5/11-14.1
Separation, parents of minor, award of custody and education of minor, 755 ILCS 5/11-7
Spouse of ward, custody and education of children of ward, 755 ILCS 5/11-13
State mental hospitals, appointment of guardian, procedure, costs, 755 ILCS 5/11-11
Support, visitation by person providing support of ward, 755 ILCS 5/11-13
Termination, minor reaching age of majority, 755 ILCS 5/11-14.1
Testamentary guardian of estate of minor, appointment and bond, 755 ILCS 5/11-5

GUARDIANS FOR MINORS—Cont'd
Venue, proceeding for appointment, 755 ILCS 5/11-6
Veterans administration,
 Appointment of guardian, procedure, costs, 755 ILCS 5/11-11
 Benefits paid to estate, notice, application to invest or expend funds of estate of ward, 755 ILCS 5/11-13
Wills, appointment of guardian by parent of unmarried minor, 755 ILCS 5/11-5

GUNS
Weapons, generally, this index

HABEAS CORPUS
Support petition, filing, Uniform Reciprocal Enforcement of Support Act, 750 ILCS 20/11
Writs, abolishment, 735 ILCS 5/2-1501

HABITUAL CRIMINALS
Child abduction, aggravating factors, 720 ILCS 5/10-5

HABITUAL JUVENILE OFFENDERS
Generally, 705 ILCS 405/5-35

HAGUE CONVENTION
International Child Abduction Remedies Act, generally, this index

HANDICAPPED PERSONS
Judgments, relief, tolling, 735 ILCS 5/2-1401
Mentally Retarded and Developmentally Disabled Persons, generally, this index
Orders of court, relief, tolling, 735 ILCS 5/2-1401
Support, enforcement, withholding of income from benefits, 750 ILCS 5/706.1; 750 ILCS 15/4.1; 750 ILCS 20/26.1
Withholding of income, support enforcement, disability benefits, 750 ILCS 5/706.1; 750 ILCS 15/4.1; 750 ILCS 20/26.1

HARASSMENT
Defined,
 Domestic violence, 750 ILCS 60/103
Domestic Violence, generally, this index

HARBORING RUNAWAYS
Crimes, 720 ILCS 5/10-6

HEAD OF HOUSEHOLD
Defined, income taxes, 26 U.S.C.A. § 2(b)

HEALTH AND SANITATION
AIDS, generally, this index
Diseases, generally, this index
Hospitals, generally, this index

HEALTH

HEALTH AND SANITATION
—Cont'd
Registration of births and deaths, generally. Vital Statistics, this index

HEALTH CARE AND TREATMENT
Medical Care and Treatment, generally, this index

HEALTH CARE FACILITIES
Abused or neglected children,
  Records, access, 325 ILCS 5/11.1
Children and minors,
  Quality of care, investigations, access to records, 325 ILCS 5/11.1
Hospitals, generally, this index

HEALTH CARE PROFESSIONALS
Dentists and Dentistry, generally, this index
Nurses, generally, this index
Physicians and Surgeons, generally, this index

HEALTH CARE PROVIDERS
Domestic violence,
  Information regarding services available, liability, 750 ILCS 60/401
Liability, domestic violence, information regarding services available, 750 ILCS 60/401
Victims of abuse, information regarding services available, liability, 750 ILCS 60/401

HEALTH DEPARTMENTS
Public Health, Department of, generally, this index

HEALTH INSURANCE
Accident and Health Insurance, generally, this index

HEARSAY
Generally, p. 941
Children and minors, sexual crimes, 735 ILCS 5/8-2601
High-risk adults with disabilities, domestic violence, protection orders, 750 ILCS 60/213.1
Sexual assault or abuse,
  Child under thirteen, admissibility, civil proceedings, 735 ILCS 5/8-2601

HEIRS
Descent and Distribution, generally, this index
Judgments,
  Setting aside, petition, 735 ILCS 5/2-1301
Wills, generally, this index

HEMOPHILIA
Medical information brochure, marriage license applicants and others, 750 ILCS 5/204

HIGHER EDUCATION
Colleges and Universities, generally, this index

HIGH-RISK ADULT WITH DISABILITIES
Defined, domestic violence, 750 ILCS 60/103

HIV
AIDS, generally, this index

HOLIDAYS
Injunctions, 735 ILCS 5/11-106

HOME STATE
Defined,
  Support, interstate enforcement, 750 ILCS 22/101
  Uniform Child Custody Jurisdiction Act, 750 ILCS 35/3.04

HOMEMAKER
Defined, family preservation services, abused and neglected children, 325 ILCS 5/8.2

HOMESTEADS
Income taxes,
  Principal residence, rollover of gain on sale, 26 U.S.C.A. § 1034
  Sale, one-time exclusion, 26 U.S.C.A. § 121
Removal from without consent of husband or wife, 750 ILCS 65/16
Tenancy by entirety,
  Husband and wife, 750 ILCS 65/22

HOMICIDE
Attempts to commit,
  Dissolution of marriage, 750 ILCS 5/401
Disclosure, mentally deficient and mentally ill persons, 740 ILCS 110/10
Mentally deficient and mentally ill persons,
  Disclosure, 740 ILCS 110/10

HOSPITALS
Abused and neglected children,
  Quality of care, investigations, access to records, 325 ILCS 5/11.1
  Records, access, 325 ILCS 5/11.1
  Reports, 325 ILCS 5/1 et seq.
Administrators,
  Abused or neglected children, reports, 325 ILCS 5/4
Children and minors,
  Abuse, reports, 325 ILCS 5/1 et seq.
Definitions,
  Mental Health and Developmental Disabilities Confidentiality Act, 740 ILCS 110/12
Emergency Medical Services (EMS) Systems, generally, this index
Injuries,
  Children, reports, 325 ILCS 5/1 et seq.
Investigations,
  Abused or neglected children, quality of care, records, access, 325 ILCS 5/11.1

HOSPITALS—Cont'd
Mentally Ill Persons, generally, this index
Neglect of children, reports, 325 ILCS 5/1 et seq.
Perinatal care,
  Coordinator, appointment, 325 ILCS 5/7.3a
Physical abuse of children, reports, 325 ILCS 5/1 et seq.
Reports,
  Abuse of children, 325 ILCS 5/1 et seq.

HOUSEHOLD GOODS
Confession of judgment, void, 735 ILCS 5/2-1301

HOUSING
See, also, Dwellings, generally, this index
Homesteads, generally, this index
Mortgages, generally, this index

HUMAN IMMUNODEFICIENCY VIRUS
AIDS, generally, this index

HUSBAND AND WIFE
Generally, 750 ILCS 65/0.01 et seq.
Abandonment of Spouse, generally, this index
Abortions, opposed fathers, injunctions, 735 ILCS 5/11-107.1
Abuse. Domestic Violence, generally, this index
Actions, 750 ILCS 65/0.01 et seq.
Adoption of Children, generally, this index
Adultery, generally, this index
Annulment of marriage, generally. Marriage, this index
Artificial insemination, legitimacy of child, 750 ILCS 40/1 et seq.
Assault and battery. Domestic Violence, generally, this index
Attachment, 750 ILCS 65/1
Attorney, appointment for each other, revocation, 750 ILCS 65/14
Attorneys fees, creditors claims for non-family expenses, 750 ILCS 65/15
Bigamy, generally, this index
Certification, consent to artificial insemination, 750 ILCS 40/3
Chattels, may be owned separately, 750 ILCS 65/9
Child abduction, offenses, 720 ILCS 5/10-5
Children,
  Removal from state by parent having custody, 750 ILCS 5/609
Compensation and salaries,
  Freedom from interference, 750 ILCS 65/7
Consent, artificial insemination, 750 ILCS 40/1 et seq.
Contracts, 750 ILCS 65/6
  Abandoned spouse, 750 ILCS 65/12

HUSBAND AND WIFE—Cont'd

Conveyances. Deeds and conveyances, generally, post
Creditors claims for non-family expenses, 750 ILCS 65/15
Crimes and offenses,
  Sale of property by abandoned spouse, 750 ILCS 65/11 et seq.
Custody of children, abandonment, 750 ILCS 65/16
Damages, recovery, 750 ILCS 65/4
Debts,
  Neither liable for other's, 750 ILCS 65/5
  Non-family expenses, creditors claims, 750 ILCS 65/15
Deeds and conveyances, 750 ILCS 65/9
  Mentally deficient or mentally ill, 750 ILCS 65/17 et seq.
Destitute wife or children, neglect to provide for, 750 ILCS 15/1 et seq.
Disclosure,
  Property or financial obligations, premarital agreements, 750 ILCS 10/7
Domestic Violence, generally, this index
Donor of semen, artificial insemination, 750 ILCS 40/3
Earnings, freedom from interference, 750 ILCS 65/7
Estoppel, premarital agreements, enforcement, 750 ILCS 10/9
Eviction of spouse, 750 ILCS 5/701
Evidence, this index
Expenses of family, liability for, 750 ILCS 65/15
Fine for neglect to support, 750 ILCS 15/4
Guardianship or conservatorship,
  Custody and education of children of ward, 755 ILCS 5/11-13
Heterologous artificial insemination, legitimacy of child, 750 ILCS 40/1 et seq.
Homesteads, generally, this index
Imprisonment of either, effect of, 750 ILCS 65/11 et seq.
Income taxes, joint returns, 26 U.S.C.A. § 6013
Injunctions, abortion, opposed fathers, 735 ILCS 5/11-107.1
Jointly sued, effects, 750 ILCS 65/2
Judgments, sale of real estate, insane spouse, 750 ILCS 65/19
Laches, premarital agreements, enforcement, 750 ILCS 10/9
Legitimacy of child, artificial insemination, 750 ILCS 40/1 et seq.
Life insurance,
  Premarital agreements, 750 ILCS 10/4
Limitation of actions, premarital agreements, 750 ILCS 10/9
Mentally ill persons, 750 ILCS 65/17 et seq.
  Conveyance of property, effect, 750 ILCS 65/17 et seq.

HUSBAND AND WIFE—Cont'd

Mortgages, mentally deficient or mentally ill, 750 ILCS 65/17 et seq.
Neglect to provide for destitute wife or child, 750 ILCS 15/1 et seq.
Nonsupport Act, 750 ILCS 15/1 et seq.
Notice,
  Real estate, sales, persons under legal disability, 750 ILCS 65/18
Offenses. Crimes and offenses, generally, ante
Order for support, 750 ILCS 15/3
Parentage Act, 750 ILCS 40/1 et seq.
Paternity proceedings, 750 ILCS 45/5
Persons under legal disability, conveyances, 750 ILCS 65/17 et seq.
Petitions, persons under legal disability, real estate sales, 750 ILCS 65/17; 750 ILCS 65/18
Premarital agreements, 750 ILCS 10/1 et seq.
Privileged communications, 735 ILCS 5/8-801
Support proceedings, interstate enforcement, 750 ILCS 22/316
Probation, neglect to support, 750 ILCS 15/4
Protection orders, generally. Domestic Violence, this index
Real estate may be owned separately, 750 ILCS 65/9
Rights of married persons, 750 ILCS 65/0.01 et seq.
Sale of property by deserted spouse, 750 ILCS 65/11
Setting aside, 750 ILCS 65/13
Security, return of children to state, 750 ILCS 5/609
Support, generally, this index
Surviving spouse,
  Descent and Distribution, generally, this index
  Premarital agreements, property, 750 ILCS 10/4
Torts, rights of married persons, 750 ILCS 65/0.01 et seq.
Trusts and trustees,
  Premarital agreements, 750 ILCS 10/4
Uniform Desertion and Nonsupport Act, 750 ILCS 15/1 et seq.
Unlawfully obtaining property of the other, 750 ILCS 65/10
Widows and widowers. Surviving spouse, generally, ante
Wife Abandonment Act, 750 ILCS 15/1 et seq.
Wills,
  Premarital agreements, 750 ILCS 10/4
Witnesses,
  Privileged communications, 735 ILCS 5/8-801
  Prosecution for neglect to support, 750 ILCS 15/7
  Support proceedings, competency of spouses, 750 ILCS 20/22

INCOME

IDENTITY AND IDENTIFICATION

Adoption, identifying information, exchange, 750 ILCS 50/18.1 et seq.
Cards. Identification Cards, generally, this index
Juvenile Delinquents and Dependents, this index
Masks, generally, this index
Support, obligor,
  Aliens, 750 ILCS 5/706.1; 750 ILCS 15/4.1; 750 ILCS 20/26.1
  Uniform Reciprocal Enforcement of Support Act, 750 ILCS 20/11

ILLEGITIMATE CHILDREN

Children Born Out of Wedlock, generally, this index

ILLINOIS PARENTAGE ACT

Generally, 750 ILCS 40/1 et seq.

ILLNESS

Diseases, generally, this index

IMMEDIATE RELATIVES

Defined,
  Adoption of children, 750 ILCS 50/1

IMMUNITIES

Privileges and Immunities, generally, this index

IMPEACHMENT

Adverse party or agent, examination, 735 ILCS 5/2-1102

IMPOTENCE

Dissolution of marriage, 750 ILCS 5/401

IMPOUNDING

Adoption proceeding papers on order of court, 750 ILCS 50/18

IN NEED OF MENTAL TREATMENT

Defined, adoption of person, 750 ILCS 50/1

INCEST

Generally, 750 ILCS 5/212
Aunts and nephews, 750 ILCS 5/212
Cousins, 750 ILCS 5/212
Grandparents and grandchildren, 750 ILCS 5/212
Parents and children, 750 ILCS 5/212
Uncles and nieces, 750 ILCS 5/212
Void, 750 ILCS 5/212

INCOME

Compensation and Salaries, generally, this index
Defined,
  Support, 750 ILCS 5/706.1; 750 ILCS 15/4.1; 750 ILCS 20/26.1

INCOME

INCOME TAXES
Alimony, 26 U.S.C.A. § 71
Deductions, 26 U.S.C.A. § 215
Dependents,
  Defined, 26 U.S.C.A. § 152
  Personal exemptions, 26 U.S.C.A. § 151
Estates, income, divorce or separation, 26 U.S.C.A. § 682
Expenses and expenditures, personal, living and family expenses, disallowance of deductions, 26 U.S.C.A. § 262
Head of household, defined, 26 U.S.C.A. § 2(b)
Homesteads, sale, one-time exclusion, 26 U.S.C.A. § 121
Individual retirement accounts, transfer of account incident to divorce, 26 U.S.C.A. § 408(d)(6)
Joint returns, husband and wife, 26 U.S.C.A. § 6013
Interstate enforcement, 750 ILCS 22/101
Marital status, determination, 26 U.S.C.A. § 7703
Personal exemptions, 26 U.S.C.A. § 151
Personal, living or family expenses, deductions, disallowance, 26 U.S.C.A. § 262
Principal residence,
  Rollover of gain on sale, 26 U.S.C.A. § 1034
  Sale, one-time exclusion, 26 U.S.C.A. § 121
Qualified domestic relations order, defined, 26 U.S.C.A. § 414(p)
Real estate, principal residence, rollover of gain on sale, 26 U.S.C.A. § 1034
Separate maintenance, 26 U.S.C.A. § 71
Transfers of property between spouses or incident to divorce, 26 U.S.C.A. § 1041
Trusts, income, divorce or separation, 26 U.S.C.A. § 682
Withholding, eligible rollover distributions, pensions, annuities and certain other deferred income, 26 U.S.C.A. § 3405(c)

INCOME–WITHHOLDING ORDER
Defined, support, interstate enforcement, 750 ILCS 22/101

INCOMPETENT PERSONS
Mentally Ill Persons, generally, this index

INCONVENIENT FORUM
Child Custody Jurisdiction Act, 750 ILCS 35/8

INCRIMINATION
Self-Incrimination, generally, this index

INCUMBRANCES
Liens and Incumbrances, generally, this index

INDECENCY
Lewdness or Obscenity, generally, this index

INDEMNITY BONDS
Bonds (Officers and Fiduciaries), generally, this index

INDEPENDENT CONTRACTORS
Support, enforcement, withholding of income, 750 ILCS 5/706.1; 750 ILCS 15/4.1; 750 ILCS 20/26.1

INDICATED REPORT
Defined, abused or neglected children, reports, 325 ILCS 5/3

INDICTMENT AND INFORMATION
Abandonment of spouse, 750 ILCS 15/2

INDIGENT PERSONS
Paternity. Children Born Out of Wedlock, this index
Social Services, generally, this index

INDIVIDUAL RETIREMENT ACCOUNTS
Transfer of account incident to divorce, 26 U.S.C.A. § 408(d)(6)

INDUSTRIAL COMMISSION
Workers' Compensation, generally, this index

INFAMOUS CRIMES
Dissolution of marriage, grounds, 750 ILCS 5/401

INFANTS
Children and Minors, generally, this index

INFECTIOUS DISEASES
Diseases, generally, this index

INHERITANCE
Descent and Distribution, generally, this index

INITIAL JUDGMENT
Defined, Uniform Child Custody Jurisdiction Act, 750 ILCS 35/3.05

INITIATING COURT
Defined, Uniform Reciprocal Enforcement of Support Act, 750 ILCS 20/2

INITIATING STATE
Defined,
  Support, interstate enforcement, 750 ILCS 22/101
  Uniform Reciprocal Enforcement of Support Act, 750 ILCS 20/2

INITIATING TRIBUNAL
Defined, support, interstate enforcement, 750 ILCS 22/101

INJUNCTIONS
Generally, 735 ILCS 5/11–101 et seq.

INJUNCTIONS—Cont'd
Abortion, opposed fathers, 735 ILCS 5/11–107.1
Affidavits,
  Dissolution, motion, 735 ILCS 5/11–109
  Holidays, Saturdays or Sundays, 735 ILCS 5/11–106
  Preliminary injunctions, denial, 735 ILCS 5/11–102
  Temporary restraining order, denial, 735 ILCS 5/11–101
Amendments, pleadings, 735 ILCS 5/11–107
Answer, dissolution motion, affidavits, 735 ILCS 5/11–109
Appearance, dissolution of modification, temporary restraining order, 735 ILCS 5/11–101
Assessments,
  Damages, 735 ILCS 5/11–110
  Bonds (officers and fiduciaries), 735 ILCS 5/11–103 et seq.
Complaint,
  Dissolution motion, affidavits, 735 ILCS 5/11–109
  Holidays, Saturday or Sunday, 735 ILCS 5/11–106
  Preliminary injunctions, denial, 735 ILCS 5/11–102
  Temporary restraining order, denial, 735 ILCS 5/11–101
  Third party complaints, 735 ILCS 5/11–107
Costs, 735 ILCS 5/11–103
Counterclaims, 735 ILCS 5/11–107
Damages,
  Assessments, 735 ILCS 5/11–110
  Bonds (officers and fiduciaries), 735 ILCS 5/11–103
Defenses, 735 ILCS 5/11–107
Denial,
  Preliminary injunctions, 735 ILCS 5/11–102
  Temporary restraining order, 735 ILCS 5/11–101
Dissolution, 735 ILCS 5/11–108 et seq.
Dissolution of marriage proceedings, Eviction, 750 ILCS 5/701
Temporary motions, 750 ILCS 5/501
Temporary restraining order, 735 ILCS 5/11–101
Domestic violence,
  Protection orders, 750 ILCS 60/214
Emergencies, holidays, Saturdays or Sundays, 735 ILCS 5/11–106
Filing,
  Bonds (officers and fiduciaries), 735 ILCS 5/11–105
  Damage assessment, petition, 735 ILCS 5/11–110
  Dissolution motions, affidavits, 735 ILCS 5/11–109
  Temporary restraining order, 735 ILCS 5/11–101
Holidays, 735 ILCS 5/11–106
Indorsement, temporary restraining orders, 735 ILCS 5/11–101
Judgments, damage assessments, 735 ILCS 5/11–110
Jury trial, 735 ILCS 5/11–107

JUDGES

INJUNCTIONS—Cont'd
Modification or change, temporary restraining order, 735 ILCS 5/11-101
Motions,
  Bonds (officers and fiduciaries), 735 ILCS 5/11-103
  Dissolution, 735 ILCS 5/11-108
  Preliminary injunctions, 735 ILCS 5/11-101
  Wrong remedies, 735 ILCS 5/11-107
Notice,
  Preliminary injunctions, 735 ILCS 5/11-102
  Temporary restraining order, 735 ILCS 5/11-101
Oaths and affirmation, damages, assessments, 735 ILCS 5/11-110
Petitions,
  Damage assessment, filing, 735 ILCS 5/11-110
Pleadings, wrong remedies, 735 ILCS 5/11-107
Preliminary injunctions, 735 ILCS 5/11-102
  Motions, 735 ILCS 5/11-101
  Temporary restraining orders, generally, post
Saturday, 735 ILCS 5/11-106
Service, holidays, Saturdays or Sundays, 735 ILCS 5/11-106
Set-off and counterclaim, 735 ILCS 5/11-107
Summary judgments, wrong remedy, 735 ILCS 5/11-107
Sunday, 735 ILCS 5/11-106
Temporary eviction of spouse, 750 ILCS 5/701
Temporary restraining orders, 735 ILCS 5/11-101
Third-party procedure, 735 ILCS 5/11-107
Time,
  Dissolution, motion, 735 ILCS 5/11-108
  Temporary restraining orders, 735 ILCS 5/11-101
Wire or oral communications, interception, 18 U.S.C.A. § 2521
Writs, abolishment, 735 ILCS 5/2-1501
Wrong remedy, 735 ILCS 5/11-107

INJURIES
Personal Injuries, generally, this index

INSANE PERSONS
Mentally Ill Persons, generally, this index

INSTITUTES
Patient information, therapists, disclosure, 740 ILCS 110/9

INSTRUCTIONS TO JURY
Children and minors, sexual acts, out-of-court statements, 735 ILCS 5/8-2601

INSTRUMENTS REGARDING ADOPTED CHILDREN ACT
Generally, 760 ILCS 30/0.01; 760 ILCS 30/1

INSURANCE
Accident and Health Insurance, generally, this index
Developmentally disabled persons, consent, disclosure of confidential information, 740 ILCS 110/5
Health insurance. Accident and Health Insurance, generally, this index
Life Insurance, generally, this index
Medical insurance. Accident and Health Insurance, generally, this index
Mentally deficient and mentally ill persons,
  Consent, disclosures of confidential information, 740 ILCS 110/5
Workers' compensation insurance. Workers' Compensation, generally, this index

INTERCOUNTY ADOPTION
Defined,
  Adoption of children, 750 ILCS 50/1

INTERCOUNTY ADOPTION COUNTY COORDINATOR
Department of children and family services, 750 ILCS 50/4.1

INTERNATIONAL CHILD ABDUCTION REMEDIES ACT
Generally, 42 U.S.C.A. § 11601 et seq.
Actions and proceedings, 42 U.S.C.A. §§ 11603, 11604
Analysis of Hague Convention, p. 926
Appropriations, authorization, 42 U.S.C.A. § 11610
Costs, 42 U.S.C.A. § 11607
Definitions, 42 U.S.C.A. § 11602
Documents, admissibility, 42 U.S.C.A. § 11605
Fees, 42 U.S.C.A. § 11607
Findings and declarations, 42 U.S.C.A. § 11601
Information, collection, maintenance and dissemination, 42 U.S.C.A. § 11608
Interagency coordinating group, 42 U.S.C.A. § 11609
United States central authority, 42 U.S.C.A. § 11606

INTERROGATORIES
Certification, verification by certification, 735 ILCS 5/1-109
Rules of Court, this index
Verification by certification, 735 ILCS 5/1-109

INTERSTATE COMPACT ON THE PLACEMENT OF CHILDREN
Defined,
  Adoption of children, 750 ILCS 50/1

INTERSTATE COMPACTS
Compacts, generally, this index

INTERSTATE RENDITION
Uniform Reciprocal Enforcement of Support Act, 750 ILCS 20/5; 750 ILCS 20/6

INTESTACY
Descent and Distribution, generally, this index

INTIMIDATION OF A DEPENDENT
Defined,
  Domestic violence, 750 ILCS 60/103

INTOXICATED PERSONS
Alcoholics and Intoxicated Persons, generally, this index

ISSUES
Declaration of rights, 735 ILCS 5/2-701

ISSUING STATE
Defined, support, interstate enforcement, 750 ILCS 22/101

ISSUING TRIBUNAL
Defined, support, interstate enforcement, 750 ILCS 22/101

IV-D PROGRAM
Defined,
  Expedited child support proceedings, S.Ct.Rule 100.13; 750 ILCS 25/3

JOB TRAINING PROGRAMS
Unemployed persons with support obligations, orders to seek employment, 750 ILCS 5/505.1; 750 ILCS 15/12; 750 ILCS 20/24.1

JOBS
Labor and Employment, generally, this index

JOINDER OF ACTIONS
Actions and Proceedings, this index

JOINT CUSTODY
Dissolution of marriage, 750 ILCS 5/602.1

JOINT TENANTS
Marital property, distribution, dissolution of marriage, 750 ILCS 5/503
Partition, generally, this index

JUDGES
Circuit Courts, this index
Contempt,
  Judge impugned, 735 ILCS 5/2-1001

JUDGES

JUDGES—Cont'd
Contempt—Cont'd
  Proceedings, substitution, 735 ILCS 5/2-1001
Interested party,
  Change of venue, 735 ILCS 5/2-1001.5
  Substitution, 735 ILCS 5/2-1001
Marriage,
  Celebration by, 750 ILCS 5/209
  Solemnization by retired judges, effect, 750 ILCS 5/209
Prejudice, substitution, 735 ILCS 5/2-1001
Substitution, motion for, 735 ILCS 5/2-1001

JUDGMENT CREDITORS
Attachment, generally, this index

JUDGMENT DEBTORS
Attachment, generally, this index

JUDGMENTS
Generally, 735 ILCS 5/2-1301 et seq.
Adoption of Children, this index
Affidavits,
  Relief petition, 735 ILCS 5/2-1401
Affirmative relief, 735 ILCS 5/2-1301
Alteration, 735 ILCS 5/2-1301
Amendments, 735 ILCS 5/2-1301
Attachment, generally, this index
Child support, expedited proceedings, registration, S.Ct.Rule 100.4
Colleges and universities, interest computation, 735 ILCS 5/2-1303
Community colleges, interest computation, 735 ILCS 5/2-1303
Complaint, setting aside judgment, 735 ILCS 5/2-1301
Computation, interest, 735 ILCS 5/2-1303
Concealment,
  Relief, tolling, 735 ILCS 5/2-1401
Conditions, setting aside, 735 ILCS 5/2-1301
Counties,
  Interest computation, 735 ILCS 5/2-1303
Declaratory Judgments, generally, this index
Default Judgments, generally, this index
Defined,
  Uniform Child Custody Jurisdiction Act, 750 ILCS 35/3.06
Disability, relief, tolling, 735 ILCS 5/2-1401
Dismissal of Actions, generally, this index
Dissolution of marriage, generally. Marriage, this index
Duress or coercion, relief, tolling, 735 ILCS 5/2-1401
Enforcement of Judgments, generally, this index
Fees,
  Foreign judgments, enforcement proceedings, 735 ILCS 5/12-655

JUDGMENTS—Cont'd
Filing,
  Foreign judgments, 735 ILCS 5/12-652
  Notice, 735 ILCS 5/12-653
  Relief petition, 735 ILCS 5/2-1401
Foreign Judgments, generally, this index
Forms, 735 ILCS 5/2-1301
Fraud,
  Relief, tolling, 735 ILCS 5/2-1401
Governmental corporations, interest computations, 735 ILCS 5/2-1303
Husband and wife,
  Rights of married persons, 750 ILCS 65/0.01 et seq.
  Sale of real estate of insane spouse, 750 ILCS 65/19
Injunctions, damage assessments, 735 ILCS 5/11-110
Interest, 735 ILCS 5/2-1303
Joint, setting aside, 735 ILCS 5/2-1301
Judicial Sales, generally, this index
Legatees, setting aside, petition, 735 ILCS 5/2-1301
Levy. Enforcement of Judgments, generally, this index
Local governments,
  Interest, computation, 735 ILCS 5/2-1303
Mail and mailing, foreign judgments, notice of filing, 735 ILCS 5/12-653
Maintenance,
  Bigamy, 750 ILCS 5/702
Marriage, this index
Modification,
  Interest, 735 ILCS 5/2-1303
  Motions, 735 ILCS 5/2-1203
  Relief petition, 735 ILCS 5/2-1401
  Venue, transcript, 735 ILCS 5/2-1001.5
Motions,
  After judgment, 735 ILCS 5/2-1203
  Reimbursement, satisfied party, 735 ILCS 5/2-1301
  Setting aside, 735 ILCS 5/2-1301
Multiple judgments, 735 ILCS 5/2-1301
Municipal corporations, interest computation, 735 ILCS 5/2-1303
Notice,
  Foreign judgments, filing, 735 ILCS 5/12-653
  Reimbursement, satisfied parties, 735 ILCS 5/2-1301
  Relief petition, 735 ILCS 5/2-1401
  Vacating or setting aside, 735 ILCS 5/2-1301
Optional procedure, action to enforce foreign judgments, 735 ILCS 5/12-656
Orders, generally, this index
Paternity. Children Born Out of Wedlock, this index
Perishable property, sales,
  Relief petition, 735 ILCS 5/2-1401
Petitions,
  Relief, 735 ILCS 5/2-1401

JUDGMENTS—Cont'd
Petitions—Cont'd
  Vacating or setting aside, 735 ILCS 5/2-1301
Post-judgment proceedings, relief, 735 ILCS 5/2-1401
Publication, service, setting aside judgment, 735 ILCS 5/2-1301
Rates and charges,
  Interest, 735 ILCS 5/2-1303
Real estate,
  Relief petition, 735 ILCS 5/2-1401
Reimbursements, satisfied parties, 735 ILCS 5/2-1301
Relief, 735 ILCS 5/2-1401
Revival,
  Plaintiffs judgment, defendant, answer or otherwise plead, 735 ILCS 5/2-1301
Rights of married persons, 750 ILCS 65/0.01 et seq.
Sales,
  Judicial Sales, generally, this index
  Relief petition, 735 ILCS 5/2-1401
  Vacating or setting aside, 735 ILCS 5/2-1301
Satisfaction,
  Reimbursements, 735 ILCS 5/2-1301
Status, foreign judgments, 735 ILCS 5/12-652
Stay. Supersedeas or Stay, generally, this index
Summary Judgments, generally, this index
Supersedeas or Stay, generally, this index
Support, this index
Suspension, relief petition, 735 ILCS 5/2-1401
Tender, payments, interest, 735 ILCS 5/2-1303
Time,
  Interest,
    Computation, 735 ILCS 5/2-1303
  Relief, 735 ILCS 5/2-1401
  Vacating or setting aside, 735 ILCS 5/2-1301
Title to property, relief petition, 735 ILCS 5/2-1401
Tolling, relief, time, 735 ILCS 5/2-1401
Uniform Child Custody Jurisdiction Act, this index
Vacating or setting aside, 735 ILCS 5/2-1301
  Interest, 735 ILCS 5/2-1303
  Motions, 735 ILCS 5/2-1203
  Relief petition, 735 ILCS 5/2-1401
Venue, change of venue, transcripts, 735 ILCS 5/2-1001.5
Void judgments, relief petition, 735 ILCS 5/2-1401

JUDICIAL REVIEW
Appeal and Review, generally, this index

JUDICIAL SALES
Dissolution of marriage,
Proceedings, satisfaction of order, 750 ILCS 5/703
Enforcement of Judgments, generally, this index
Maintenance orders, 750 ILCS 5/703

JURISDICTION
Acts submitting to jurisdiction, 735 ILCS 5/2-209
Adoption of children or adults, 750 ILCS 50/4
Children and minors,
Emancipation of mature minors, 750 ILCS 30/4; 750 ILCS 30/6
Uniform Child Custody Jurisdiction Act, generally, this index
Circuit Courts, this index
Crimes and offenses,
Domestic violence, protection orders, 750 ILCS 60/207; 750 ILCS 60/208
Custody of children. Uniform Child Custody Jurisdiction Act, generally, this index
Dissolution of marriage, 750 ILCS 5/104; 750 ILCS 5/401
Domestic violence, protection orders, 750 ILCS 60/207; 750 ILCS 60/208
Emancipation, mature minors, 750 ILCS 30/4; 750 ILCS 30/6
Infants, emancipation of mature minors, 750 ILCS 30/4; 750 ILCS 30/6
Long arm jurisdiction, 735 ILCS 5/2-209
Partition,
Dissolution of marriage proceedings, 750 ILCS 5/514
Paternity, 735 ILCS 5/2-209
Protection orders, domestic violence, 750 ILCS 60/207; 750 ILCS 60/208
Submission to jurisdiction, acts, 735 ILCS 5/2-209
Summons, wrongful form, S.Ct.Rule 101
Support, this index
Trusts and trustees, 735 ILCS 5/2-209
Uniform Child Custody Jurisdiction Act, generally, this index
Uniform Reciprocal Enforcement of Support Act, 750 ILCS 20/10; 750 ILCS 20/32

JURY
See, also, Trial, generally, this index
Declaration of rights, 735 ILCS 5/2-701
Dissolution of marriage, 750 ILCS 5/103
Domestic violence,
Protection orders, 750 ILCS 60/206
Injunctions, demand, 735 ILCS 5/11-107
Instructions to Jury, generally, this index

JURY—Cont'd
Paternity proceedings, 750 ILCS 45/13

JUVENILE COURT ACT
Adoption of children, construction, 750 ILCS 50/2.1
Dissolution of marriage, abused and neglected children, application of law, 750 ILCS 5/606

JUVENILE COURTS
Circuit Courts, generally, this index
Juvenile Delinquents and Dependents, generally, this index

JUVENILE DELINQUENTS AND DEPENDENTS
Absence and absentees,
Non-emergency authorized absence, habitual juvenile offenders, 705 ILCS 405/5-35
Abused and neglected children,
Domestic Violence, generally, this index
Reports, 325 ILCS 5/1 et seq.
Child protective service unit, abused or neglected children, reports, 325 ILCS 5/7 et seq.
Commitment,
Habitual juvenile offenders, 705 ILCS 405/5-35
Continuance under supervision,
Habitual juvenile offenders, 705 ILCS 405/5-35
Credit,
Good conduct credit, habitual juvenile offenders, 705 ILCS 405/5-35
Defacement of property, community service, 705 ILCS 405/5-19; 705 ILCS 405/5-23
Definitions,
Habitual juvenile offender, 705 ILCS 405/5-35
Dispositional hearings,
Habitual juvenile offenders, 705 ILCS 405/5-35
Emancipated minors,
Mature minors, 750 ILCS 30/1 et seq.
Evidence,
Habitual juvenile offender proceedings, 705 ILCS 405/5-35
Furloughs, habitual juvenile offenders, 705 ILCS 405/5-35
Good conduct credit, habitual juvenile offenders, 705 ILCS 405/5-35
Guardians and guardianship,
Guardian ad litem, generally, ante
Habitual juvenile offender, 705 ILCS 405/5-35
Reports or records, access, 325 ILCS 5/11.1
Jury, habitual juvenile offender trial, 705 ILCS 405/5-35
Neglected children, reports, 325 ILCS 5/1 et seq.
Nonemergency authorized absence, habitual juvenile offenders, 705 ILCS 405/5-35

JUVENILE DELINQUENTS AND DEPENDENTS—Cont'd
Parole,
Habitual juvenile offenders, 705 ILCS 405/5-35
Petitions,
Habitual juvenile offender adjudication, 705 ILCS 405/5-35
Probation,
Records, access, abused or neglected children, 325 ILCS 5/11.1
Reports,
Abused and neglected children, 325 ILCS 5/1 et seq.
Revocation,
Good conduct credit, habitual juvenile offenders, 705 ILCS 405/5-35
Service of process,
Notice,
Habitual juvenile offender adjudication petition, 705 ILCS 405/5-35
Time,
Habitual juvenile offenders, duration of commitment, 705 ILCS 405/5-35
Trial, habitual juvenile offender petition, 705 ILCS 405/5-35
Violence. Domestic Violence, generally, this index

KIDNAPPING CHILD
See, also, Abduction, generally, this index
International Child Abduction Remedies Act, 42 U.S.C.A. § 11601 et seq.

KNOWLEDGE
Marriage, persons prohibited, issuing license or celebrating, 750 ILCS 5/219

LABOR AND EMPLOYMENT
Administrative aides to courts, dissolution of marriage, 750 ILCS 5/106
Circuit courts, administrative aides, dissolution of marriage, 750 ILCS 5/106
Compensation and Salaries, generally, this index
Courts, administrative aides, dissolution of marriage, 750 ILCS 5/106
Dissolution of marriage, administrative aides to courts, 750 ILCS 5/106
Domestic violence, protection orders, 750 ILCS 60/214
Job Training Programs, generally, this index
Labor organizations, support, income withholding, 750 ILCS 5/706.1; 750 ILCS 15/4.1; 750 ILCS 20/26.1
Protection orders, domestic violence, 750 ILCS 60/214
Salaries. Compensation and Salaries, generally, this index

LABOR

LABOR AND EMPLOYMENT
—Cont'd
Support, orders to seek employment, interstate enforcement, 750 ILCS 22/305
Trade organizations, support, income withholding, 750 ILCS 5/706.1; 750 ILCS 15/4.1; 750 ILCS 20/26.1
Wages. Compensation and Salaries, generally, this index
Workers' Compensation, generally, this index

LABOR ORGANIZATIONS
Support, enforcement, withholding of income, 750 ILCS 5/706.1; 750 ILCS 15/4.1; 750 ILCS 20/26.1

LAND
Real Estate, generally, this index

LAND TITLES
Deeds and Conveyances, generally, this index

LAW
Defined,
Uniform Reciprocal Enforcement of Support Act, 750 ILCS 20/2
Statutes, generally, this index

LAW ENFORCEMENT, DEPARTMENT OF
State Police, Department of, generally, this index

LAW ENFORCEMENT AGENCIES
Bail violations, warrantless arrest, domestic violence, 750 ILCS 60/301
Defined,
Mental health and developmental disability confidentiality, 740 ILCS 110/12.2
Domestic violence, responsibilities, 750 ILCS 60/301 et seq.
Mentally deficient or developmentally disabled persons, confidential information, release, 740 ILCS 110/12.2
Privileges and immunities, mentally or developmentally disabled persons, confidential information, release, 740 ILCS 110/12
Records and recordation,
Domestic violence protection orders, extension, 750 ILCS 60/220

LAW ENFORCEMENT OFFICERS
See, also, Peace Officers, generally, this index
Peace Officers, generally, this index
Police, generally, this index
Sheriffs, generally, this index

LAW ENFORCEMENT TRAINING STANDARDS BOARD
Domestic violence training and curriculum task force, 750 ILCS 60/306

LAWFUL CUSTODIAN
Defined, child abduction, 720 ILCS 5/10–5

LAWS
Statutes, generally, this index

LAWSUITS
Actions and Proceedings, generally, this index

LAWYERS
Attorneys, generally, this index

LEASES
Confession of judgment, consumer transactions, void, 735 ILCS 5/2–1301
Consumers, confession of judgment, void, 735 ILCS 5/2–1301
Lis pendens, authorizing conveyance, 735 ILCS 5/2–1901

LEGACIES
Probate Proceedings, generally, this index
Wills, generally, this index

LEGAL SEPARATION
Marriage, this index
Process, 735 ILCS 5/2–209

LEGATEES
Judgments, setting aside, petition, 735 ILCS 5/2–1301

LEGISLATURE
General Assembly, generally, this index

LEGITIMATING ACT
Generally, 750 ILCS 5/303
Common law marriage issue, 750 ILCS 5/212

LEWDNESS OR OBSCENITY
Children and minors,
Records, access, intergovernmental missing child recovery, 325 ILCS 5/11.1
Class A misdemeanors, 720 ILCS 5/11–20

LICENSES AND PERMITS
Child placing agencies,
Adoption of children, 750 ILCS 50/4.1
Marriage, this index

LIENS AND INCUMBRANCES
Dissolution of marriage orders, 750 ILCS 5/503; 750 ILCS 5/703
Mortgages, generally, this index
Support,
Interstate enforcement, 750 ILCS 22/305

LIFE INSURANCE
Husband and wife, premarital agreements, 750 ILCS 10/4

LIMITATION OF ACTIONS
Adoption of children, 750 ILCS 50/11
Breach of marriage promise, 740 ILCS 15/6

LIMITATION OF ACTIONS—Cont'd
Marriage, breach of promise, 740 ILCS 15/6
Paternity proceedings, 750 ILCS 45/8
Premarital agreements, 750 ILCS 10/9
Support, arrearages, interstate enforcement, 750 ILCS 22/604

LIMITATION OF LIABILITY
Parental Responsibility Law, 740 ILCS 115/5

LIS PENDENS
Generally, 735 ILCS 5/2–1901 et seq.

LOANS
Confession of judgment, consumer transactions, void, 735 ILCS 5/2–1301
Mortgages, generally, this index

LOCAL GOVERNMENT
See, also, Political Subdivisions, generally, this index
Judgments, interest computation, 735 ILCS 5/2–1303

LOCAL LAW ENFORCEMENT AGENCIES
Defined,
Abused and neglected children, reports, 325 ILCS 5/3

LOCAL SUBDIVISIONS
Political Subdivisions, generally, this index

LONG ARM STATUTE
Process, 735 ILCS 5/2–209
Support, 750 ILCS 22/201

LOW INCOME FAMILIES
Indigent Persons, generally, this index

MAIL AND MAILING
Child Custody Jurisdiction Act, service of process, 750 ILCS 35/6
Default judgments, entry notice, 735 ILCS 5/2–1302
Dismissal, entry notice, 735 ILCS 5/2–1302
Foreign judgments, notice of filing, 735 ILCS 5/12–653
Notice,
Breach of marriage promise, 740 ILCS 15/4

MAINTENANCE
Generally, 750 ILCS 5/504
Bigamy, 750 ILCS 5/702
Costs,
Receiving and disbursing agents, 750 ILCS 5/507
Marriage, this index
Modification of judgment, 750 ILCS 5/510
Receiving and disbursing agents, 750 ILCS 5/507

MARRIAGE

MALES
Includes female, adoption of children, 750 ILCS 50/1

MALICIOUS MISCHIEF
Parental Responsibility Law, 740 ILCS 115/1 et seq.

MANAGING AGENTS
Examinations, 735 ILCS 5/2-1102

MANDAMUS
Abolishment, 735 ILCS 5/2-1501

MARITAL PROPERTY
Defined, dissolution of marriage, 750 ILCS 5/503

MARRIAGE
Generally, 750 ILCS 5/101 et seq.
Abuse. Domestic Violence, generally, this index
Affidavits, minors, consent, 750 ILCS 5/203
Age, 750 ILCS 5/208
Alimony. Maintenance, generally, post
Annulment of marriage,
 Declaration of invalidity, generally, post
Bigamy, generally, this index
Blood tests,
 Venereal disease,
  Exceptions, 750 ILCS 5/205
Breach of Marriage Promise, generally, this index
Celebrating, 750 ILCS 5/209
 Persons authorized, 750 ILCS 5/209
Certificate of examination, venereal disease,
 Exception, 750 ILCS 5/205
Certificate of marriage,
 Issuance, 750 ILCS 5/203
 Registration, 750 ILCS 5/210
Child abduction, removing or concealing child, 720 ILCS 5/10-5
Children and minors,
 Age for contracting, 750 ILCS 5/208
 Common law marriage, offspring as legitimate, 750 ILCS 5/212
 Court order for issuance of license, 750 ILCS 5/208
 Dissolution of marriage, post
 Joint custody, 750 ILCS 5/602.1
 Pregnancy, 750 ILCS 5/208
Children Born Out of Wedlock, generally, this index
Class B misdemeanors, 750 ILCS 5/215
Common law, validity, 750 ILCS 5/214
Consent, minors, affidavits, 750 ILCS 5/203
Contracting prohibited marriage in another state, 750 ILCS 5/216 et seq.
Contracts. Premarital agreements, generally, post
Counseling and counselors,
 Period of separation, 750 ILCS 5/401

MARRIAGE—Cont'd
County clerks. Licenses and permits, post
Crimes and offenses,
 Bigamy, generally, this index
 Illegal celebration, 750 ILCS 5/219
 Solemnizing illegal marriage, petty offenses, 750 ILCS 5/219
Custody of children. Dissolution of marriage, post
Debts, non-family expenses, creditors claims, 750 ILCS 65/15
Declaration of invalidity, 750 ILCS 5/301 et seq.
 Certificate to be filed with department of public health, 750 ILCS 5/707
 Commencement of action, 750 ILCS 5/306
 Grounds, 750 ILCS 5/301
 Judges, inspection, certificate, 750 ILCS 5/707
 Legitimacy of children, 750 ILCS 5/303
 Persons seeking, 750 ILCS 5/302
 Putative spouse, 750 ILCS 5/305
 Retroactivity, 750 ILCS 5/304
 Time for commencement, 750 ILCS 5/302
Diseases,
 Medical information brochure, 750 ILCS 5/204
Dissolution of marriage, 750 ILCS 5/101 et seq.; 750 ILCS 5/401 et seq.
 Abused or neglected children, custody proceedings, prior statements, 750 ILCS 5/606
 Accident and health insurance, support obligations, 750 ILCS 5/505; 750 ILCS 5/505.2
 Acknowledgment of parties, proof of foreign marriage, 750 ILCS 5/409
 Address, custodian, disclosure for visitation purposes, 750 ILCS 5/708
 Administrative aides to assist courts, 750 ILCS 5/106
 Admissibility of evidence, 750 ILCS 5/407
 Adultery,
  Grounds, 750 ILCS 5/401
 Affidavits, joint simplified procedure, 750 ILCS 5/454
 Agreements,
  Joint simplified procedure, 750 ILCS 5/451 et seq.
  Reserved questions, judgment, 750 ILCS 5/401
 Alcohol addiction, 750 ILCS 5/401
 Alimony, income taxes, 26 U.S.C.A. § 71
 Alimony. Maintenance, generally, post
 Appeal and review, marital property, proceedings on remand, 750 ILCS 5/503
 Appearance of parties, joint simplified procedure, 750 ILCS 5/453

MARRIAGE—Cont'd
Dissolution of marriage—Cont'd
 Application of law,
  Joint simplified procedure, 750 ILCS 5/451
 Assessments, marital property, proceedings on remand, 750 ILCS 5/503
 Assignment of wages, 750 ILCS 15/2.1 et seq.
  Child support, 750 ILCS 15/2.1 et seq.
 Attempt, homicide of spouse, grounds, 750 ILCS 5/401
 Attorney fees, 750 ILCS 5/508
 Attorneys,
  Joint simplified procedure, 750 ILCS 5/457
  Reconciliation conferences, presence, 750 ILCS 5/404
 Best interest of child, determination, 750 ILCS 5/602
 Bifurcated trial, 750 ILCS 5/403
 Bigamy,
  Grounds, 750 ILCS 5/401
  Maintenance, 750 ILCS 5/702
 Brochures, joint simplified procedure, 750 ILCS 5/457
 Burden of proof, removal of children from state, 750 ILCS 5/609
 Causes, 750 ILCS 5/401
 Certificate, filing with department of public health, 750 ILCS 5/707
 Children and minors,
  Abduction, offenses, 720 ILCS 5/10-5
  Custody, 750 ILCS 5/601 et seq.
   Joint custody, 750 ILCS 5/602.1
   Jurisdiction, retention, 750 ILCS 35/8
   Orders, enforcement, 750 ILCS 5/611
  Custody of children,
   Hearings, transfers, expedited child support proceedings, S.Ct.Rule 100.9
   Educational program on effects, 750 ILCS 5/404.1
   Grandparents, visitation, 750 ILCS 5/607
   Guardian-ad-litem, 750 ILCS 5/506
   Joint simplified procedure, 750 ILCS 5/452
   Legitimacy of children, 750 ILCS 5/303
   Orders,
    Educational program on effects, 750 ILCS 5/404.1
    Removal of child from jurisdiction, enforcement, 750 ILCS 5/611
   Records, noncustodial parent, access, 750 ILCS 5/602.1
   Removal from state, security, guarantying return, 750 ILCS 5/609
   Representation, 750 ILCS 5/506
   Siblings, visitation, 750 ILCS 5/607

MARRIAGE

MARRIAGE—Cont'd
Dissolution of marriage—Cont'd
  Children and minors—Cont'd
    Support, 750 ILCS 5/505; 750 ILCS 5/510
      Assignment of wages, 750 ILCS 15/2.1 et seq.
      Expedited rules, S.Ct.Rule 100.1 et seq.
      Non-minor children, educational expenses, 750 ILCS 5/513
    Visitation, 750 ILCS 5/607
      Disclosure of custodians address, 750 ILCS 5/708
  Circuit courts,
    Administrative aides to assist, 750 ILCS 5/106
    Rules, 750 ILCS 5/802
  Circumstantial evidence, proof of foreign marriage, 750 ILCS 5/409
  Civil Practice Law, application, 750 ILCS 5/105
  Cohabitation, proof of foreign marriage, 750 ILCS 5/409
  Collection fee, support, 750 ILCS 5/516
  Collusion, 750 ILCS 5/408
    Admission of respondent, 750 ILCS 5/407
    Both parties guilty, 750 ILCS 5/408
  Commencement of proceedings, 750 ILCS 5/411
  Commingled property, 750 ILCS 5/503
  Common ownership, pending proceedings, 750 ILCS 5/503
  Complaint, 750 ILCS 5/411
    Default of defendant, 750 ILCS 5/405
    Filing, 750 ILCS 5/411
  Conduct of petitioner, pleading, 750 ILCS 5/406
  Conflict of laws, joint simplified procedure, 750 ILCS 5/451
  Conviction of crime, grounds, 750 ILCS 5/401
  Copies,
    Joint simplified procedure, judgments, 750 ILCS 5/455
  Counseling,
    Reconciliation conferences, 750 ILCS 5/404
  Counties, administrative aides, assisting courts, 750 ILCS 5/106
  Courts, administrative aides to assist, 750 ILCS 5/106
  Crimes and offenses,
    Cause for dissolution, 750 ILCS 5/401
  Cruelty, grounds, 750 ILCS 5/401
  Custody of children, 750 ILCS 5/601 et seq.
    Bifurcated proceedings, 750 ILCS 5/401
    Joint custody, 750 ILCS 5/602.1
    Records and recordation, non-custodial parent, access, 750 ILCS 5/602.1
    Retention of jurisdiction, 750 ILCS 35/8

MARRIAGE—Cont'd
Dissolution of marriage—Cont'd
  Debts, non-family expenses, creditors claims, 750 ILCS 65/15
  Default, 750 ILCS 5/405
  Defenses abolished, 750 ILCS 5/403
  Desertion, grounds, 750 ILCS 5/401
  Disposition of property, 750 ILCS 5/503
    Judgments, reserved questions, 750 ILCS 5/401
  Domestic Violence, generally, this index
  Domicile, jurisdiction over parties, 735 ILCS 5/2-209
  Drug addiction, grounds, 750 ILCS 5/401
  Drunkenness, 750 ILCS 5/401
  Educational program on effects on children, 750 ILCS 5/404.1
  Effective date of law, 750 ILCS 5/801
  Employment, administrative aides to courts, 750 ILCS 5/106
  Eviction of spouse, 750 ILCS 5/701
    Torts, 750 ILCS 65/1
  Existing defenses abolished, 750 ILCS 5/403
  Expenses,
    Administrative aides to courts, appropriations, 750 ILCS 5/106
    Non-family expenses, creditors claims, 750 ILCS 65/15
  Family expenses, 750 ILCS 65/15
  Fault or conduct of petitioner, 750 ILCS 5/406
  Fees, 750 ILCS 5/411
    Collection fees, 750 ILCS 5/516
    Filing, commencement of proceeding, 750 ILCS 5/411
  Felony conviction, grounds, 750 ILCS 5/401
  Filing fees, 750 ILCS 5/411
  Filing of petition,
    Cases requiring service by publication, 750 ILCS 5/412
    Service by publication, 750 ILCS 5/412
  Foreign marriage, proof, 750 ILCS 5/409
  Foreign states, custody proceedings, parties, 750 ILCS 5/601
  Forms, joint simplified procedure, 750 ILCS 5/456
  Fraud, admission of respondent, 750 ILCS 5/407
  Grandparents, visitation of children, 750 ILCS 5/607
  Grounds, 750 ILCS 5/401
  Guidelines, support, maintenance and property disposition, 750 ILCS 5/504; 750 ILCS 5/505
  Habitual drunkenness, grounds, 750 ILCS 5/401
  Hearings,
    Child custody, 750 ILCS 5/606
    Joint simplified procedure, 750 ILCS 5/453

MARRIAGE—Cont'd
Dissolution of marriage—Cont'd
  Homicide, attempt to commit, grounds, 750 ILCS 5/401
  Impotency, grounds, 750 ILCS 5/401
  Income, estates or trusts, taxation, 26 U.S.C.A. § 682
  Independence of provisions of judgment for temporary order, 750 ILCS 5/509
  Individual retirement accounts, transfer incident to divorce, 26 U.S.C.A. § 408(d)(6)
  Infamous crime, grounds, 750 ILCS 5/401
  Injunction,
    Eviction, 750 ILCS 5/701
    Investigations, child custody, 750 ILCS 5/605
  Irretrievable breakdown, grounds, 750 ILCS 5/401
    Joint simplified procedure, 750 ILCS 5/452
  Joint custody, children, 750 ILCS 5/602.1
  Joint simplified procedure, 750 ILCS 5/451 et seq.
  Judges, inspection, certificate filed with public health department, 750 ILCS 5/707
  Judgments, 750 ILCS 5/413
    Joint simplified procedure, 750 ILCS 5/453
    Copies, 750 ILCS 5/455
    Liens, sales, 750 ILCS 5/703
    Marital property, enforcement, 750 ILCS 5/503
    Modification, 750 ILCS 5/510
    Refusal, 750 ILCS 5/405
    Removal of children from court jurisdiction, 750 ILCS 5/611
    Reserved questions, subsequent proceedings, 750 ILCS 5/401
  Jurisdiction,
    Retention, Uniform Child Custody Jurisdiction Act, 750 ILCS 35/8
  Jury trial, 750 ILCS 5/103
  Legal separation, generally, post
  Liens, 750 ILCS 5/503
    Orders, 750 ILCS 5/703
  Living apart and separate, grounds, 750 ILCS 5/401
  Maintenance, generally, post
  Marital property,
    Disposition, judgments, 750 ILCS 5/503
    Joint simplified procedure, 750 ILCS 5/452
    Proceedings on rematch, 750 ILCS 5/503
  Marital residence, order granting possession to spouse, 750 ILCS 5/701
  Mediation, 750 ILCS 5/404
  Mental cruelty, grounds, 750 ILCS 5/401
  Modification of custody orders, 750 ILCS 5/601; 750 ILCS 5/610

MARRIAGE

MARRIAGE—Cont'd
Dissolution of marriage—Cont'd
Modification of decree, support, maintenance, and property disposition, 750 ILCS 5/504; 750 ILCS 5/510
Motions, reserved questions, subsequent proceedings, 750 ILCS 5/401
Nonjudicial duties, administrative aides to courts, 750 ILCS 5/106
Non-marital property, proceedings on remand, 750 ILCS 5/503
Notice,
  Partition of real property, 750 ILCS 5/514; 750 ILCS 5/515
Orders,
  Educational program on effects on children, 750 ILCS 5/404.1
  Joint custody, 750 ILCS 5/602.1
  Support, increases, 750 ILCS 5/510
  Temporary relief, 750 ILCS 5/501
Partition, 750 ILCS 5/514; 750 ILCS 5/515
Pendency of action, 750 ILCS 5/801
  Law governing, 750 ILCS 5/801
Petitions,
  Contents, 750 ILCS 5/403
  Joint simplified procedure, 750 ILCS 5/452
Physical cruelty, grounds, 750 ILCS 5/401
Pleadings, 750 ILCS 5/403
Poisons, attempted homicide, grounds, 750 ILCS 5/401
Post-judgment venue, 750 ILCS 5/511; 750 ILCS 5/512
Practice and procedure, law governing, 750 ILCS 5/801; 750 ILCS 5/802
Praecipe,
  Summons, 750 ILCS 5/411
Procedure, 750 ILCS 5/403
Process, 735 ILCS 5/2–209; 750 ILCS 5/410
  Practice and proceeding, 750 ILCS 5/410
Promotion, joint simplified procedure, 750 ILCS 5/457
Proof of foreign marriage, 750 ILCS 5/409
Property,
  Disposition, 750 ILCS 5/503
  Joint simplified procedure, 750 ILCS 5/452
  Premarital agreements, 750 ILCS 10/4
Protection orders, generally. Domestic Violence, this index
Public aid, 750 ILCS 5/704
Publication,
  Filing of petition, 750 ILCS 5/412
  Process, 750 ILCS 5/410
Purposes of act, 750 ILCS 5/102
Reconciliation conference, 750 ILCS 5/404

MARRIAGE—Cont'd
Dissolution of marriage—Cont'd
Removal of children from state, 750 ILCS 5/609
Reports,
  Custody investigation, 750 ILCS 5/605
Representation of child, 750 ILCS 5/506
Reserved questions, judgments, subsequent proceedings, 750 ILCS 5/401
Residence, 750 ILCS 5/401
  Joint simplified procedure, 750 ILCS 5/452
  Jurisdiction over parties, 735 ILCS 5/2–209
Rules of construction, 750 ILCS 5/102
Rules of court, 750 ILCS 5/802
  Civil Practice Law, 750 ILCS 5/105
  Process, practice and procedure, 750 ILCS 5/410
Sales, realty under decree, 750 ILCS 5/703
Security,
  Removal of children from state, 750 ILCS 5/609
Separate living period,
  Joint simplified procedure, 750 ILCS 5/452
  Time periods, computation, 750 ILCS 5/401
  Waiver, 750 ILCS 5/401
Separate maintenance. Legal separation, generally, post
Separation agreements, 750 ILCS 5/502
Simplified joint procedure, 750 ILCS 5/451 et seq.
Stays, 750 ILCS 5/501.1
Support,
  Aliens, information, 750 ILCS 5/706.1
  Children, 750 ILCS 5/505
  Bifurcated proceedings, 750 ILCS 5/401
  Collection fees, 750 ILCS 5/516
  Expedited hearing, rule, S.Ct. Rule 100.1 et seq.
  Income withholding, enforcement, 750 ILCS 5/706.1
  Increases, 750 ILCS 5/510
  Joint simplified procedure, waiver, 750 ILCS 5/452
  Judgments, reserved questions, 750 ILCS 5/401
  Petition filing, Uniform Reciprocal Enforcement of Support Act, 750 ILCS 20/11
  Withholding of income, enforcement, 750 ILCS 5/706.1
Supreme court, rules, 750 ILCS 5/802
Taxation, property disposition, 750 ILCS 5/503
Temporary custody orders, 750 ILCS 5/603
Temporary relief, 750 ILCS 5/501
  Eviction of spouse, 750 ILCS 5/701

MARRIAGE—Cont'd
Dissolution of marriage—Cont'd
Temporary removal of child from state, 750 ILCS 5/609
Termination of provisions for maintenance, support or property disposition, 750 ILCS 5/510
Terms of office, administrative aides to courts, 750 ILCS 5/106
Time,
  Actions pending, computation of desertion period, 750 ILCS 5/401
  Joint simplified procedure, 750 ILCS 5/452
  Residence, 750 ILCS 5/401
  Separate living period, 750 ILCS 5/401
Transfers of property between spouses or incident to divorce, 26 U.S.C.A. § 1041
Trial by jury, 750 ILCS 5/103
Trusts,
  Property disposition, 750 ILCS 5/503
Uniform Child Custody Jurisdiction Act, retention of jurisdiction over marriage, 750 ILCS 35/8
Validation, judgments, 750 ILCS 5/401
Value, marital property, proceedings on remand, 750 ILCS 5/503
Venereal diseases, infecting spouse, grounds, 750 ILCS 5/401
Venue, 750 ILCS 5/104
  Post judgment, 750 ILCS 5/512
Visitation of children, 750 ILCS 5/607
  Expedited child support hearings, transfers, S.Ct.Rule 100.9
Waiver, living apart and separate, grounds, 750 ILCS 5/401
Witnesses, abused or neglected children, prior statements, 750 ILCS 5/606
Divorce. Dissolution of marriage, generally, ante
Domestic Violence, generally, this index
Domicile, dissolution of marriage, jurisdiction over parties, 735 ILCS 5/2–209
Evasion, 750 ILCS 5/216 et seq.
Evidence,
  Proof of marriage, generally, post
Examinations,
  Syphilis,
    Exceptions, 750 ILCS 5/205
Fines and penalties, 750 ILCS 5/215
Formalities, 750 ILCS 5/201
Forms,
  Return to department of public health, 750 ILCS 5/210
Grandparents, dissolution of marriage, visitation of children, 750 ILCS 5/607

MARRIAGE

MARRIAGE—Cont'd
Hemophilia, medical information brochure, 750 ILCS 5/204
Income taxes,
 Determination of marital status, 26 U.S.C.A. § 7703
 Joint returns, 26 U.S.C.A. § 6013
Income withholding, support enforcement, 750 ILCS 5/706.1
Irretrievable breakdown, grounds for dissolution, 750 ILCS 5/401
Issue of illegal, legitimated, 750 ILCS 5/303
Joint custody, children, 750 ILCS 5/602.1
Joint parenting agreement, 750 ILCS 5/602.1
Joint simplified dissolution procedure, 750 ILCS 5/451 et seq.
Judges, this index
Judgments,
 Dissolution of marriage, ante
 Married persons, rights, 750 ILCS 65/0.01 et seq.
Judicial approval of underage marriages, 750 ILCS 5/208
Legal separation, 750 ILCS 5/402
 Administrative aides to assist in administration of proceedings, 750 ILCS 5/106
 Child support and maintenance payments, 750 ILCS 5/705
 Commencement of action, 750 ILCS 5/411
 Computation of time, 750 ILCS 5/401
 Desertion by spouse, computation of desertion period, 750 ILCS 5/401
 Grounds for dissolution, 750 ILCS 5/401
 Income taxes, 26 U.S.C.A. § 71
 Process, 750 ILCS 5/410
Legitimation of issue of illegal marriage, 750 ILCS 5/303
Licenses and permits, 750 ILCS 5/202 et seq.; 750 ILCS 5/218
 Age of applicant, 750 ILCS 5/208
 AIDS, medical information brochure, 750 ILCS 5/204
 Application, 750 ILCS 5/202
 County clerks,
  Duties, 750 ILCS 5/218
  Medical information brochure, 750 ILCS 5/204
  Penalty for wrongful issue, 750 ILCS 5/219
  Report to department of public health, 750 ILCS 5/211
  Underage applicants, 750 ILCS 5/208
 Duty of officer issuing, 750 ILCS 5/218
 Effective date, 750 ILCS 5/207
 Examinations,
  AIDS, 750 ILCS 5/204
  Hemophilia, medical information brochure, 750 ILCS 5/204
  Information on application, 750 ILCS 5/202
  Medical examination required, 750 ILCS 5/205
   Exceptions, 750 ILCS 5/205

MARRIAGE—Cont'd
Licenses and permits—Cont'd
 Medical information brochure, 750 ILCS 5/204
 Penalty for issuing illegally, 750 ILCS 5/219
 Proof of age, 750 ILCS 5/203
 Tay-Sachs disease, medical information brochure, 750 ILCS 5/204
 Underage applicants, 750 ILCS 5/208
Maintenance, 750 ILCS 5/504
 Bigamy, 750 ILCS 5/702
 Costs, receiving and disbursing agents, 750 ILCS 5/507
 Counties of 1,000,000 or less, payment through clerk of court, 750 ILCS 5/505
 Income taxes, 26 U.S.C.A. § 71
  Deductions, 26 U.S.C.A. § 215
 Job search, training or work programs, 750 ILCS 5/505.1; 750 ILCS 15/12; 750 ILCS 20/24.1
 Judgments,
  Dissolution of marriage, reserved questions, 750 ILCS 5/401
  Enforcement and lien, 750 ILCS 5/703
  Legal separation, 750 ILCS 5/402
  Modification, 750 ILCS 5/504; 750 ILCS 5/510
  Payments, 750 ILCS 5/705
 Permanent maintenance, 750 ILCS 5/504
 Temporary maintenance, 750 ILCS 5/504
 Temporary relief, 750 ILCS 5/501
 Termination, 750 ILCS 5/510
Minors, consent, affidavits, 750 ILCS 5/203
Nonresidents, 750 ILCS 5/217
Notice,
 Dissolution of marriage, ante
Offenses. Crimes and offenses, generally, ante
Permanent maintenance, 750 ILCS 5/504
Persons authorized to celebrate, 750 ILCS 5/209
Premarital agreements, 750 ILCS 10/1 et seq.; 750 ILCS 10/4
 Amendment, 750 ILCS 10/6
 Application and construction, 750 ILCS 10/10
 Consideration, 750 ILCS 10/3
 Definitions, 750 ILCS 10/2
 Effect of marriage, 750 ILCS 10/5
 Enforcement, 750 ILCS 10/7; 750 ILCS 10/8
 Formalities, 750 ILCS 10/3
 Limitation of actions, 750 ILCS 10/9
 Revocation, 750 ILCS 10/6
 Time of taking effect, 750 ILCS 10/11
Process, dissolution, 735 ILCS 5/2–209
Prohibited marriages, 750 ILCS 5/212; 750 ILCS 5/216 et seq.

MARRIAGE—Cont'd
Proof of marriage,
 Abandonment of wife, 750 ILCS 15/6; 750 ILCS 15/7
 Foreign marriage, 750 ILCS 5/409
Property, premarital agreements, 750 ILCS 10/1 et seq.
Protection orders, generally. Domestic Violence, this index
Putative spouse, 750 ILCS 5/305
Records and recordation, 750 ILCS 5/206
 Children and minors, noncustodial parent, access, 750 ILCS 5/602.1
 Declaration of invalidity, ante
 Public health, department of, 750 ILCS 5/206
Religious societies, 750 ILCS 5/209
Report, county clerk to department of public health, 750 ILCS 5/211
Retired judges, solemnization, 750 ILCS 5/209
Rules of court. Dissolution of marriage, ante
Separation. Legal separation, generally, ante
Siblings, dissolution of marriage, visitation, 750 ILCS 5/607
Signatures, premarital agreements, 750 ILCS 10/3
 Amendment or revocation, 750 ILCS 10/6
Solemnization, 750 ILCS 5/209
 Illegal marriage, petty offenses, 750 ILCS 5/219
Support, generally, this index
Taxation, dissolution of marriage, property disposition, 750 ILCS 5/503
Tay-Sachs disease, 750 ILCS 5/204
Temporary maintenance, 750 ILCS 5/504
Tests,
 Syphilis,
  Exceptions, 750 ILCS 5/205
Transfers of property between spouses or incident to divorce, income taxes, 26 U.S.C.A. § 1041
Validity, 750 ILCS 5/201; 750 ILCS 5/213
Venue. Dissolution of marriage, ante
Visitation of children, disclosure of custodians address, 750 ILCS 5/708
Waiver, dissolution of marriage, living apart and separate, grounds, 750 ILCS 5/401
Withholding income, support enforcement, 750 ILCS 5/706.1

MARRIAGE EVASION ACT
Generally, 750 ILCS 5/216 et seq.

MATURE MINOR
Defined, emancipation, 750 ILCS 30/3–2

MEDICAL CARE AND TREATMENT
Abortion, generally, this index

MEDICAL CARE AND TREATMENT—Cont'd

Abused or neglected children,
Quality of care, records, access, 325 ILCS 5/11.1
AIDS, generally, this index
Child support, expedited rules, S.Ct. Rule 100.1 et seq.
Children and Minors, this index
Domestic violence, assistance by law enforcement officers, 750 ILCS 60/304
Emergency Medical Services (EMS) Systems, generally, this index
Employee retirement income security program, group health plans, additional standards, 29 U.S.C.A. § 1169
Insurance,
Accident and Health Insurance, generally, this index
Investigations,
Abused or neglected children, quality of care, records, access, 325 ILCS 5/11.1
Mentally Ill Persons, generally, this index
Quality of care,
Abused or neglected children, records, access, 325 ILCS 5/11.1
Records. Medical Records, generally, this index

MEDICAL EXAMINERS

Coroners, generally, this index

MEDICAL INSURANCE

Accident and Health Insurance, generally, this index

MEDICAL RECORDS

Abused or neglected children, quality of care, access, 325 ILCS 5/11.1
Adoption, genetic medical problems, confidential intermediary, 750 ILCS 50/18.3a
Artificial insemination, 750 ILCS 40/3
Children and minors, noncustodial parent, records, 750 ILCS 5/602.1

MEDICAL SUPPORT

Defined, expedited child support, 750 ILCS 25/3

MENTAL ANGUISH

Alienation of affections, damages, 740 ILCS 5/4
Dissolution of marriage, grounds, 750 ILCS 5/401

MENTAL HEALTH AND DEVELOPMENTAL DISABILITIES, DEPARTMENT OF

Collections, disclosure of information relating to abused children, 740 ILCS 110/11
Disclosure, recipients record or communications, 740 ILCS 110/9.1
Records and recordation,
Communications of recipients, disclosure, 740 ILCS 110/9.1

MENTAL HEALTH AND DEVELOPMENTAL DISABILITIES CONFIDENTIALITY ACT

Generally, 740 ILCS 110/1 et seq.

MENTAL HEALTH AND DEVELOPMENTAL DISABILITIES SERVICES

Defined, Mental Health and Developmental Disabilities Confidentiality Act, 740 ILCS 110/2

MENTAL HEALTH FACILITIES

Mentally Ill Persons, generally, this index

MENTAL INSTITUTIONS

Mentally Ill Persons, generally, this index

MENTALLY HANDICAPPED CHILDREN

Children and minors, generally.
Mentally Retarded and Developmentally Disabled Persons, this index

MENTALLY ILL PERSONS

Abuse,
Children,
Disclosure of confidential information, 740 ILCS 110/11
Children, reports, 325 ILCS 5/1 et seq.
Access, records, 740 ILCS 110/4
Adoption of Children, this index
Agencies, reviews of agencies, limited disclosure of confidential information, 740 ILCS 110/7; 740 ILCS 110/8
Agents, defined, Mental Health and Developmental Disabilities Confidentiality Act, 740 ILCS 110/2
Audits and auditors,
United States department of justice, compliance review, 740 ILCS 110/7
Blanket consent, disclosures of information, invalidity, 740 ILCS 110/5
Confidential or privileged information, 740 ILCS 110/1 et seq.
Crimes and offenses,
Investigations, 740 ILCS 110/12.1
Definitions, 740 ILCS 110/2
Disclosure, 740 ILCS 110/5; 740 ILCS 110/6
Without consent, 740 ILCS 110/6; 740 ILCS 110/9.1
Inspections, authorized persons, 740 ILCS 110/4
Interagency disclosures, 740 ILCS 110/7.1
Limitations, interagency disclosures, 740 ILCS 110/7.1; 740 ILCS 110/9.2
Release to authorities upon escape, 740 ILCS 110/12.2
Review, therapists or agency, limited disclosures, 740 ILCS 110/7; 740 ILCS 110/8
Secret service, disclosure, 740 ILCS 110/12

MENTALLY ILL PERSONS—Cont'd

Confidential or privileged information—Cont'd
State police, department of, disclosures, 740 ILCS 110/12
Therapists,
Disclosure without consent, 740 ILCS 110/9
Personal notes, 740 ILCS 110/3; 740 ILCS 110/4
Psychological test material, 740 ILCS 110/3
Consent,
Disclosure of confidential information, without consent, 740 ILCS 110/6
Insurance companies, disclosure of confidential information, 740 ILCS 110/5
Records of communications, disclosure, 740 ILCS 110/5
Conveyances by husband or wife, relinquishment of rights, 750 ILCS 65/17 et seq.
Coroners investigation of death, confidential or privileged information, 740 ILCS 110/10
Crimes and offenses,
Confidential or privileged information,
Insanity defense, 740 ILCS 110/10
Investigations, 740 ILCS 110/12.1
Defenses, insanity, confidential or privileged information, 740 ILCS 110/10
Disclosure, homicide, 740 ILCS 110/10
Homicide, disclosure, 740 ILCS 110/10
Insanity defense, confidential or privileged information, 740 ILCS 110/10
Death,
Confidential records and communications, 740 ILCS 110/5
Coroners investigation, 740 ILCS 110/10
Definitions,
Adoption of children, 750 ILCS 50/1
Mental Health and Developmental Disabilities Confidentiality Act, 740 ILCS 110/2
Disclosure,
Confidential information, 740 ILCS 110/5
Without consent, 740 ILCS 110/6
Firearm owners identification cards, immunity, 740 ILCS 110/12
Homicide, 740 ILCS 110/10
Escape,
Release of confidential information, 740 ILCS 110/12.2
General consents, insurance companies, confidential information, 740 ILCS 110/5
Guardian Ad Litem, generally, this index

MENTALLY

MENTALLY ILL PERSONS—Cont'd
Homicide,
  Disclosures, 740 ILCS 110/10
Husband and Wife, this index
Insanity defense,
  Confidential or privileged information, 740 ILCS 110/10
Inspection and inspectors,
  Authorized persons, 740 ILCS 110/4
Insurance,
  Confidential communications and records, general consents to disclosure, 740 ILCS 110/5
Interagency disclosures, 740 ILCS 110/7.1
Investigations,
  Crimes and offenses, confidential or privileged information, 740 ILCS 110/12.1
Law enforcement agencies, confidential information, release, 740 ILCS 110/12.2
Neglect,
  Children, reports, 325 ILCS 5/1 et seq.
Privileges and immunities,
  Law enforcement agencies, providing information, 740 ILCS 110/12.2
  Secret service, state police, providing information, 740 ILCS 110/12
Records and recordation,
  Disclosure, 740 ILCS 110/5; 740 ILCS 110/9.1
  Inspection,
    Authorized persons, 740 ILCS 110/4
  Interpretation assistance, 740 ILCS 110/4
State mental hospitals, appointment of guardian procedure, costs, 755 ILCS 5/11–11
State police, department of, disclosures of confidential information, 740 ILCS 110/12
Subpoenas,
  Confidential or privileged information, 740 ILCS 110/10
Therapists,
  Abuse of children, disclosure of confidential information, 740 ILCS 110/11
  Confidential information, disclosure, 740 ILCS 110/9; 740 ILCS 110/10
  Personal notes, confidentiality, 740 ILCS 110/3
  Privilege, disclosure of confidential information, 740 ILCS 110/10
  Psychological test material, disclosure, 740 ILCS 110/3
  Reviews, confidential records, disclosures, 740 ILCS 110/7; 740 ILCS 110/8
Transportation,
  Confidential information, peace officers, 740 ILCS 110/12
Weapons,
  Disclosures, firearm owners identification cards, 740 ILCS 110/12

MENTALLY RETARDED AND DEVELOPMENTALLY DISABLED PERSONS
See, also, Mentally Ill Persons, generally, this index
Abuse,
  Children, disclosure of confidential information, 740 ILCS 110/11
Access, records, 740 ILCS 110/4
Agencies,
  Reviews of agencies, limited disclosures of confidential information, 740 ILCS 110/7; 740 ILCS 110/8
Audits and auditors,
  United States department of justice, compliance review, 740 ILCS 110/7
Blanket consent, disclosures of information invalidity, 740 ILCS 110/5
Children and minors,
  Abused and neglected children, reports, 325 ILCS 5/1 et seq.
  Neglected children, reports, 325 ILCS 5/1 et seq.
Reports,
  Abused and neglected children, 325 ILCS 5/1 et seq.
Communications,
  Disclosures, 740 ILCS 110/5
Confidential or privileged information, 740 ILCS 110/1 et seq.
  Access, records, 740 ILCS 110/4
  Copying, 740 ILCS 110/8.1
  Criminal investigation, 740 ILCS 110/12.1
  Definitions, 740 ILCS 110/2
  Disclosure, 740 ILCS 110/5; 740 ILCS 110/8.1
    Consent, 740 ILCS 110/5
    Without consent, 740 ILCS 110/6; 740 ILCS 110/9.1
  Inspections, 740 ILCS 110/4
  Interagency disclosures, 740 ILCS 110/7.1
  Limitations, interagency disclosures, 740 ILCS 110/7.1; 740 ILCS 110/9.2
  Release of information upon escape, 740 ILCS 110/12.2
  Review of therapist or agency, limited disclosures, 740 ILCS 110/7; 740 ILCS 110/8
  Secret service, disclosures, 740 ILCS 110/12
  State police, department of, disclosures, 740 ILCS 110/12
  Therapists,
    Disclosure without consent, 740 ILCS 110/9
    Personal notes, 740 ILCS 110/4
Consent,
  Confidential information, without consent, 740 ILCS 110/6
Disclosure, records of communications, 740 ILCS 110/5
Insurance companies, disclosure of confidential information, 740 ILCS 110/5
Copies,
  Records, 740 ILCS 110/8.1

MENTALLY RETARDED AND DEVELOPMENTALLY DISABLED PERSONS—Cont'd
Crimes and offenses,
  Confidential information, investigations, 740 ILCS 110/12.1
Custody and transport,
  Confidential information, peace officers, 740 ILCS 110/12
Death,
  Confidential records and communications, 740 ILCS 110/5
Definitions,
  Adoption, 750 ILCS 50/1
  Mental Health and Developmental Disabilities Confidentiality Act, 740 ILCS 110/2
Escapes,
  Confidential information released, 740 ILCS 110/12.2
Forensic recipient,
  Confidential information, release, 740 ILCS 110/12.2
General consent, insurance companies, disclosures of confidential information, 740 ILCS 110/5
High-risk adults with disabilities, generally. Domestic Violence, this index
Inspection and inspectors,
  Records, 740 ILCS 110/8.1
  Authorized persons, 740 ILCS 110/4
Insurance companies, confidential communications and records, general consents to disclosure, 740 ILCS 110/5
Interagency disclosures, 740 ILCS 110/7.1
Investigations,
  Criminal investigations, confidential information, 740 ILCS 110/12.1
Law enforcement, department of, disclosures of confidential information, 740 ILCS 110/12
Law enforcement agencies,
  Confidential information, release, 740 ILCS 110/12.2
Mentally Ill Persons, generally, this index
Notice,
  Records,
    Inspection, 740 ILCS 110/8.1
Privileges and immunities,
  Law enforcement agencies, providing information, 740 ILCS 110/12.2
  Secret service, state police, providing information, 740 ILCS 110/12
Records and recordation,
  Confidential or privileged information, generally, ante
  Copying, 740 ILCS 110/8.1
  Disclosure, 740 ILCS 110/5; 740 ILCS 110/9.1
  Inspection, 740 ILCS 110/8.1
    Authorized persons, 740 ILCS 110/4
  Interpretation assistance, 740 ILCS 110/4

MENTALLY RETARDED AND DEVELOPMENTALLY DISABLED PERSONS—Cont'd

Secret service, disclosure of confidential information, 740 ILCS 110/12

Subpoenas,
Confidential or privileged information, 740 ILCS 110/10

Therapists,
Abuse of children, disclosure of confidential information, 740 ILCS 110/11
Confidential information, disclosure without consent, 740 ILCS 110/9
Personal notes, confidentiality, 740 ILCS 110/3
Privileges, refusal to disclosure, confidential information, 740 ILCS 110/10
Psychological test material, confidentiality, 740 ILCS 110/3
Reviews of therapists, limited disclosures of confidential information, 740 ILCS 110/7; 740 ILCS 110/8

MILITARY FORCES

Adoption of children, 750 ILCS 50/2
Veterans' Administration, generally, this index

MINORS

Children and Minors, generally, this index
Defined,
Emancipation of Mature Minors Act, 750 ILCS 30/3–1

MISDEMEANORS

Crimes and Offenses, generally, this index

MISREPRESENTATION

Fraud, generally, this index

MISSING PERSONS

Children and Minors, this index
Mentally deficient or developmentally disabled persons, law enforcement agencies, confidential information, 740 ILCS 110/12.2

MOBILEHOMES AND MOBILEHOME PARKS

Crimes and offenses,
Child abduction, luring into, 720 ILCS 5/10–5

MODIFICATION

Dissolution of marriage, 750 ILCS 5/501; 750 ILCS 5/510
Injunctions, temporary restraining order, 735 ILCS 5/11–101
Orders of court, relief petition, 735 ILCS 5/2–1401
Temporary restraining order, 735 ILCS 5/11–101

MODIFICATION JUDGMENT

Defined, Uniform Child Custody Jurisdiction Act, 750 ILCS 35/3.07

MORTALITY

Death, generally, this index

MORTGAGES

Default,
Foreclosures, notice, 735 ILCS 5/2–1302
Default judgments,
Notice, 735 ILCS 5/2–1302
Foreclosures,
Default judgments, notice, 735 ILCS 5/2–1302
Notice,
Default judgments, 735 ILCS 5/2–1302
Husband and wife, persons under legal disability, 750 ILCS 65/17 et seq.
Lis pendens, authorizing mortgages, 735 ILCS 5/2–1901
Notice,
Entry of order of default, Foreclosures, 735 ILCS 5/2–1302

MOTIONS

After judgment motions, 735 ILCS 5/2–1203
Dissolution of marriage, 750 ILCS 5/501
Forms, 735 ILCS 5/2–620
Hearings, 735 ILCS 5/2–620
Injunctions, this index
Modification or change, judgment, 735 ILCS 5/2–1203
Non-jury cases, 735 ILCS 5/2–1203
Preliminary injunctions, 735 ILCS 5/11–101
Process, private persons, 735 ILCS 5/2–202
Rehearing, after judgment, 735 ILCS 5/2–1203
Retrial, after judgment, motion, 735 ILCS 5/2–1203
Rules and regulations, 735 ILCS 5/2–620
Rules of Court, this index
Setting aside,
Judgments, 735 ILCS 5/2–1203; 735 ILCS 5/2–1301
Substitution of judge, 735 ILCS 5/2–1001
Time,
After judgment, 735 ILCS 5/2–1203
Vacating or setting aside,
Judgments, 735 ILCS 5/2–1203; 735 ILCS 5/2–1301
Venue, transfer of causes, 735 ILCS 5/2–104 et seq.

MOTOR VEHICLES

Children and minors,
Luring into, abduction, crimes, 720 ILCS 5/10–5

MULTIPLE JUDGMENTS

Generally, 735 ILCS 5/2–1301

MUNICIPAL CORPORATIONS

Municipalities, generally, this index

MUNICIPAL COURTS

Circuit Courts, generally, this index

MUNICIPALITIES

Actions and proceedings,
Court proceedings,
Uniform Reciprocal Enforcement of Support Act, 750 ILCS 20/8
Parental Responsibility Law, 740 ILCS 115/1 et seq.
Support proceedings, Uniform Reciprocal Enforcement of Support Act, 750 ILCS 20/8
Children,
Parental Responsibility Law, action by municipality, 740 ILCS 115/1 et seq.
Declaratory judgments, ordinances, 735 ILCS 5/2–701
Judgments,
Interest computation, 735 ILCS 5/2–1303
Licenses and Permits, generally, this index
Parental Responsibility Law, action by municipality, 740 ILCS 115/1 et seq.
Police, generally, this index
Proceedings. Actions and proceedings, generally, ante
Social Services, generally, this index
Support, enforcement, withholding of income, 750 ILCS 5/706.1; 750 ILCS 15/4.1; 750 ILCS 20/26.1
Taxation, generally, this index
Withholding of income, support enforcement, 750 ILCS 5/706.1; 750 ILCS 15/4.1; 750 ILCS 20/26.1

MUNICIPALITIES OF 500,000 OR MORE

Process, vehicles, parking or standing violations, 735 ILCS 5/2–203; 735 ILCS 5/2–203.1

MURDER

Homicide, generally, this index

NAMES

Change of name,
Affidavit to petition, 735 ILCS 5/21–102
Best interest of child, 735 ILCS 5/21–101
Children and minors,
Publication, 735 ILCS 5/21–101
Notice, 735 ILCS 5/21–103
Petition, 735 ILCS 5/21–101
Proceedings in the circuit court, 735 ILCS 5/21–101
Process, service, 735 ILCS 5/21–104
Service of process, 735 ILCS 5/21–104
Pardons and reprieves, changes, time, 735 ILCS 5/21–101
Process, change of name, service, 735 ILCS 5/21–104

NATURAL PARENTS

Adoption, identifying information, exchange, 750 ILCS 50/18.1 et seq.

NEGLECT

NEGLECT
Defined,
  Domestic violence, 750 ILCS 60/103
  Mentally Ill Persons, this index

NEGLECTED AND DELINQUENT CHILDREN
Juvenile Delinquents and Dependents, generally, this index

NEGLECTED CHILD
Defined,
  Abused and neglected children, reports, 325 ILCS 5/3
  Adoption, 750 ILCS 50/1

NEGOTIABLE INSTRUMENTS
Confession of judgment, 735 ILCS 5/2-1301

NEPHEWS
Marriages, 750 ILCS 5/212

NET INCOME
Defined,
  Support, 750 ILCS 45/14

NEWSPAPERS
Process, publication, 735 ILCS 5/2-206
Publication, generally, this index

NEXT FRIEND
See, also, Guardian Ad Litem, generally, this index
Guardianship or conservatorship, Appointment, 755 ILCS 5/11-13
Minors, commencement and prosecution of actions, 755 ILCS 5/11-13

NEXT OF KIN
Relatives, generally, this index

NIECES
Marriages, 750 ILCS 5/212

NOMINATIONS
Guardian, minor 14 years of age or more, 755 ILCS 5/11-5

NON COMPOS MENTIS
Mentally Ill Persons, generally, this index

NONCOMPACT STATE
Defined,
  Adoption of children, 750 ILCS 50/1

NONMARITAL PROPERTY
Defined, dissolution of marriage, 750 ILCS 5/503

NONPROFIT CORPORATIONS
Conservator, mentally retarded individuals, 755 ILCS 5/11-3
Mentally retarded or developmentally disabled persons,
  Corporation acting as conservator of person, 755 ILCS 5/11-3
Religious Organizations and Societies, generally, this index

NONRESIDENTS
See, also, Domicile and Residence, generally, this index
Aliens, generally, this index
Guardianship or conservatorship, appointment, venue, 755 ILCS 5/11-6
Marriage, 750 ILCS 5/216 et seq.
Service of process,
  Products liability, service on secretary of state, 735 ILCS 5/2-209
Support, 750 ILCS 22/201
Support, personal jurisdiction, 750 ILCS 22/201; 750 ILCS 22/202
Venue,
  Guardianship or conservatorship, appointment, 755 ILCS 5/11-6

NONSUIT
Dismissal of Actions, generally, this index

NONSUPPORT
Generally, 750 ILCS 15/1 et seq.
Support, generally, this index

NOTICE
Adoption of Children, this index
Change of name. Names, this index
Child abuse false reports, 325 ILCS 5/7; 325 ILCS 5/7.6
Child Custody Jurisdiction Act, prejudgment, notice, 750 ILCS 35/5 et seq.
Child support, expedited hearings, absence parties, S.Ct.Rule 100.8
Children and Minors, this index
Dissolution of Marriage. Marriage, this index
Domestic Violence, this index
Emancipation of mature minors, 750 ILCS 30/8
Foreign judgments, filing, 735 ILCS 5/12-653
Foreign support orders, registration, 750 ILCS 20/39
Injunctions, this index
Mentally Retarded and Developmentally Disabled Persons, this index
Minors. Children and Minors, this index
Partition, dissolution of marriage proceedings, 750 ILCS 5/515
Paternity. Children Born Out of Wedlock, this index
Process, this index
Registration, foreign support orders, 750 ILCS 20/39
Rules of Court, this index
Support, this index
Uniform Child Custody Jurisdiction Act, dismissal or stay, informing foreign court, 750 ILCS 35/8

NOTICE DATE
Defined, adoption of children,
  Property rights, construction of instruments, 760 ILCS 30/1

NURSERY SCHOOLS
Abused or neglected children, reports, 325 ILCS 5/4

NURSES
Abused or neglected children, Reports, 325 ILCS 5/4

OATHS AND AFFIRMATIONS
Affidavits, generally, this index
Certification, verification by certification, 735 ILCS 5/1-109
Child custody proceedings, information, 750 ILCS 35/10
Perjury, generally, this index
Uniform Child Custody Jurisdiction Act, parties, information, 750 ILCS 35/10
Verification by certification, 735 ILCS 5/1-109

OBLIGEE
Defined,
  Enforcement of support orders, S.Ct.Rule 296
  Expedited child support, 750 ILCS 25/3
  Paternity proceedings, withholding of income, 750 ILCS 45/20
  Support, 750 ILCS 5/706.1; 750 ILCS 15/4.1; 750 ILCS 20/26.1
  Health insurance, 750 ILCS 5/505.2
  Interstate enforcement, 750 ILCS 22/101
  Uniform Reciprocal Enforcement of Support Act, 750 ILCS 20/2

OBLIGOR
Defined,
  Expedited child support, 750 ILCS 25/3
  Paternity proceedings, withholding of income, 750 ILCS 45/20
  Support, 750 ILCS 5/706.1; 750 ILCS 15/4.1; 750 ILCS 20/26.1
  Health insurance, 750 ILCS 5/505.2
  Interstate enforcement, 750 ILCS 22/101
  Uniform Reciprocal Enforcement of Support Act, 750 ILCS 20/2

OBSCENITY
Lewdness or Obscenity, generally, this index

OFFENSES
Crimes and Offenses, generally, this index

OFFICERS AND EMPLOYEES
Bonds (Officers and Fiduciaries), generally, this index
Compensation and Salaries, generally, this index
Examinations, 735 ILCS 5/2-1102
Labor and Employment, generally, this index

OFFICIAL BONDS
Bonds (Officers and Fiduciaries), generally, this index

OLD AGE
Aged Persons, generally, this index

OMNIBUS CRIME CONTROL AND SAFE STREETS ACT OF 1968
Wire and oral communications, interception, 18 U.S.C.A. § 2511
Damages, recovery, 18 U.S.C.A. § 2520
Definitions, 18 U.S.C.A. § 2510
Evidence, prohibition, 18 U.S.C.A. § 2515
Injunction, 18 U.S.C.A. § 2521

ORDER FOR SUPPORT
Defined, 750 ILCS 5/706.1; 750 ILCS 15/4.1; 750 ILCS 20/26.1
Enforcement of support orders, S.Ct.Rule 296

ORDERS
Adoption of Children, this index
Affidavits, relief petitions, 735 ILCS 5/2-1401
Certificates and certification, 735 ILCS 5/2-1501
Change of venue, 735 ILCS 5/2-1001.5
Child abduction, offenses, 720 ILCS 5/10-5
Children and Minors, this index
Concealment, relief, tolling, 735 ILCS 5/2-1401
Conditions, setting aside, 735 ILCS 5/2-1301
Custody of children, appearance, parties and child, 750 ILCS 35/12; 750 ILCS 35/20
Declaratory judgments, 735 ILCS 5/2-701
Disability, relief, tolling, 735 ILCS 5/2-1401
Dismissal,
Notice, 735 ILCS 5/2-1302
Dissolution of marriage, maintenance, 750 ILCS 5/504
Emancipation of mature minors, 750 ILCS 30/6
Filing, relief, petition, 735 ILCS 5/2-1401
Foreign support orders, registration, Uniform Reciprocal Enforcement of Support Act, 750 ILCS 20/35
Fraud, relief, tolling, 735 ILCS 5/2-1401
Invalid marriages, maintenance, 750 ILCS 5/504
Joint orders, setting aside, 735 ILCS 5/2-1301
Minors. Children and Minors, this index
Modification or change,
Relief petitions, 735 ILCS 5/2-1401
Motions,
Setting aside, 735 ILCS 5/2-1301
Neglect to support wife or child, 750 ILCS 15/3; 750 ILCS 15/5
Notice, relief petition, 735 ILCS 5/2-1401
Paternity. Children Born Out of Wedlock, this index
Personal property,
Relief petitions, 735 ILCS 5/2-1401

ORDERS—Cont'd
Petitions, relief, 735 ILCS 5/2-1401
Process, private persons, service, 735 ILCS 5/2-202
Protection orders, generally. Domestic Violence, this index
Relief, 735 ILCS 5/2-1401
Rules of Court, this index
Sales, relief petition, 735 ILCS 5/2-1401
Separation, husband and wife, maintenance, 750 ILCS 5/504
Setting aside, 735 ILCS 5/2-1301
Support, this index
Suspension, relief petition, 735 ILCS 5/2-1401
Time,
Relief, 735 ILCS 5/2-1401
Tolling, relief, 735 ILCS 5/2-1401
Uniform Child Custody Jurisdiction Act, appearance, parties and child, 750 ILCS 35/12; 750 ILCS 35/20
Venue,
Change, 735 ILCS 5/2-1001.5
Transfers of causes, cost and expenses, 735 ILCS 5/2-107
Void orders, relief petition, 735 ILCS 5/2-1401

ORDINANCES
Declaratory judgments, 735 ILCS 5/2-701

OSTEOPATHS
See, also, Physicians and Surgeons, generally, this index
Abused or neglected children, reports, 325 ILCS 5/4
Children and minors, abuse or neglect, reports, 325 ILCS 5/4

OTHER STATES
Foreign States, generally, this index

PARDONS AND REPRIEVES
Names, changes, time, 735 ILCS 5/21-101

PARENT AND CHILD
Children and Minors, generally, this index

PARENTAGE
Generally, 750 ILCS 40/1 et seq.; 750 ILCS 45/1 et seq.
Paternity, generally. Children Born Out of Wedlock, this index

PARENTAL RESPONSIBILITY LAW
Generally, 740 ILCS 115/1 et seq.

PARTIES
Adoption proceedings, 750 ILCS 50/7
Adverse parties,
Examination, 735 ILCS 5/2-1102
Appearance, generally, this index
Buildings, petitions for demolition or repair,
Process, service by publication, 735 ILCS 5/2-206
Costs, generally, this index

PEACE

PARTIES—Cont'd
Declaration of rights, 735 ILCS 5/2-701
Default judgments, notice, 735 ILCS 5/2-1302
Depositions, generally, this index
Dismissal of actions,
Notice, 735 ILCS 5/2-1302
Dissolution of marriage, custody proceedings, foreign states, 750 ILCS 5/601
Examination, adverse parties, 735 ILCS 5/2-1102
Guardian ad Litem, generally, this index
Judgments, answer or otherwise plead, 735 ILCS 5/2-1301
Notice,
Default or dismissal, 735 ILCS 5/2-1302
Paternity proceedings, 750 ILCS 45/7
Process, 735 ILCS 5/2-202
Buildings, petitions for demolition or repair, service by publication, 735 ILCS 5/2-206
Rights, declaration, 735 ILCS 5/2-701
Third Parties, generally, this index
Uniform Child Custody Jurisdiction Act, this index
Unknown parties,
Process, 735 ILCS 5/2-206
Publication, 735 ILCS 5/2-206
Venue, generally, this index

PARTITION
Dissolution of marriage proceedings, 750 ILCS 5/514; 750 ILCS 5/515
Jurisdiction,
Dissolution of marriage proceedings, 750 ILCS 5/514

PARTNERSHIP
Spouses, power to contract, 750 ILCS 65/6

PATERNITY
Child abduction, offenses, 720 ILCS 5/10-5
Children Born Out of Wedlock, this index

PATIENTS
Defined,
Mental Health and Developmental Disabilities Confidentiality Act, 740 ILCS 110/12

PAYOR
Defined,
Enforcement of support orders, S.Ct.Rule 296
Paternity proceedings, withholding of income, 750 ILCS 45/20
Support, 750 ILCS 5/706.1; 750 ILCS 15/4.1; 750 ILCS 20/26.1

PEACE OFFICERS
See, also, Law Enforcement Officers, generally, this index

PEACE

PEACE OFFICERS—Cont'd
Abused or neglected children, reports, 325 ILCS 5/4
Arrest, generally, this index
Children and minors, abuse or neglect, reports, 325 ILCS 5/4
Domestic violence,
 Responsibilities, 750 ILCS 60/301 et seq.
 Training and curriculum, 750 ILCS 60/306
Police, generally, this index
Privileges and immunities, domestic violence, 750 ILCS 60/305
Sheriffs, generally, this index

PENALTIES
Fines and Penalties, generally, this index

PENDING ACTIONS
Support proceedings, pendente lite support orders, Uniform Reciprocal Enforcement of Support Act, 750 ILCS 20/30

PENSIONS
Retirement and Pensions, generally, this index

PERFORMANCE BONDS
Bonds (Officers and Fiduciaries), generally, this index

PERJURY
Generally, p. 963
Adoption of children, affidavits, costs, expenses, etc., 750 ILCS 50/14
Support proceedings, Uniform Reciprocal Enforcement of Support Act, 750 ILCS 20/21
Verification by certification, 735 ILCS 5/1–109

PERMITS
Licenses and Permits, generally, this index

PERSON
Defined,
 Foreign money claims, 735 ILCS 5/12–655

PERSON ACTING AS PARENT
Defined, Uniform Child Custody Jurisdiction Act, 750 ILCS 35/3.09

PERSON RESPONSIBLE FOR THE CHILD'S WELFARE
Defined, abused or neglected children, reports, 325 ILCS 5/3

PERSONAL INJURIES
Abused and neglected children, reports, 325 ILCS 5/1 et seq.
Crimes and offenses, child abduction, aggravating factors, 720 ILCS 5/10–5
Neglected children, reports, 325 ILCS 5/1 et seq.

PERSONAL INJURIES—Cont'd
Reports,
 Abused and neglected children, 325 ILCS 5/1 et seq.
Restitution, generally, this index

PERSONAL NOTES
Defined, Mental Health and Developmental Disabilities Confidentiality Act, 740 ILCS 110/2

PERSONAL PROPERTY
Attachment, generally, this index
Confession of judgment, void, 735 ILCS 5/2–1301
Domestic violence, possession orders, 750 ILCS 60/214
Orders of court,
 Relief petition, 735 ILCS 5/2–1401
Recovery of possession, summons, S.Ct.Rule 101

PETIT JURORS
Jury, generally, this index

PETITIONER
Defined,
 Domestic violence, 750 ILCS 60/103

PHOTOGRAPHY AND PICTURES
Abused and neglected children, Investigations, 325 ILCS 5/6
Support obligor, Uniform Reciprocal Enforcement of Support Act, 750 ILCS 20/11

PHYSICAL ABUSE
Defined,
 Domestic violence, 750 ILCS 60/103
Dissolution of marriage, grounds, 750 ILCS 5/401

PHYSICAL CUSTODY
Defined, Uniform Child Custody Jurisdiction Act, 750 ILCS 35/3.08

PHYSICALLY HANDICAPPED PERSONS
Handicapped Persons, generally, this index

PHYSICIANS AND SURGEONS
Abused or neglected children, Reports, 325 ILCS 5/1 et seq.
Child abuse or neglect, wilful failure to report, disciplinary action, 325 ILCS 5/4.02
Disciplinary proceedings,
 Child abuse or neglect, willful failure to report, 325 ILCS 5/4.02
Emergency medical care,
 Children and minors,
  Temporary protective custody, immunity, 325 ILCS 5/5
Neglected children, reports, 325 ILCS 5/1 et seq.
Reports,
 Abused or neglected children, 325 ILCS 5/1 et seq.

PHYSICIANS AND SURGEONS—Cont'd
Reports—Cont'd
 Child abuse or neglect, willful failure to report, disciplinary action, 325 ILCS 5/4.02
 Neglected children, 325 ILCS 5/1 et seq.

PICTURES
Photography and Pictures, generally, this index

PLACING OUT
Defined, adoption of children, 720 ILCS 525/3

PLAINTIFFS
Parties, generally, this index
Third Parties, generally, this index
Venue, generally, this index

PLANS AND SPECIFICATIONS
Child support, expedited rules, S.Ct. Rule 100.1 et seq.
Defined,
 Expedited child support, 750 ILCS 25/3; S.Ct.Rule 100.13
 Expedited child support system, 750 ILCS 25/4

PLEADINGS
Answer, generally, this index
Certification, verification by certification, 735 ILCS 5/1–109
Complaint, generally, this index
Counterclaim. Set-off and Counterclaim, generally, this index
Declaration of rights, 735 ILCS 5/2–701
Default judgments, failure to plead, 735 ILCS 5/2–1301
Dissolution of marriage, 750 ILCS 5/403
 Fault or conduct of petitioner, 750 ILCS 5/406
Failure to plead, default judgment, 735 ILCS 5/2–1301
Habeas Corpus, generally, this index
Injunctions, wrong remedies, 735 ILCS 5/11–107
Judgments,
 Plaintiff, defendant answer or otherwise plead, 735 ILCS 5/2–1301
Motions, generally, this index
Rules of Court, this index
Set-off and Counterclaim, generally, this index
Third Parties, generally, this index
Verification,
 Verification by certification, 735 ILCS 5/1–109

PLURAL
Singular as including,
 Adoption of children, 750 ILCS 50/1

PODIATRISTS
Abused or neglected children, reports, 325 ILCS 5/4

POISONS
Dissolution of marriage for attempt to poison, 750 ILCS 5/401

POLICE
See, also, Peace Officers, generally, this index
Abused or neglected children, reports, 325 ILCS 5/4
Children and minors,
Abuse or neglect, reports, 325 ILCS 5/4
Custody, abused or neglected children, 325 ILCS 5/5
Limited liability, domestic violence, 750 ILCS 60/305
Privileges and immunities,
Domestic violence, 750 ILCS 60/305
Reports,
Domestic crime, investigations, 750 ILCS 60/303

POLITICAL QUESTION
Declaratory judgments, 735 ILCS 5/2–701

POLITICAL SUBDIVISIONS
See, also, Local Government, generally, this index
Actions and proceedings,
Parental Responsibility Law, 740 ILCS 115/1 et seq.
Support proceedings, Uniform Reciprocal Enforcement of Support Act, 750 ILCS 20/8
Children and minors, Parental Responsibility Law, action by political subdivision, 740 ILCS 115/1 et seq.
Counties, generally, this index
Municipalities, generally, this index
Parental Responsibility Law, action by political subdivision, 740 ILCS 115/1 et seq.
Support, enforcement, withholding of income, 750 ILCS 5/706.1; 750 ILCS 15/4.1; 750 ILCS 20/26.1
Withholding of income, support enforcement, 750 ILCS 5/706.1; 750 ILCS 15/4.1; 750 ILCS 20/26.1

POOR PERSONS
Indigent Persons, generally, this index

POPULAR NAME LAWS
Abused and Neglected Child Reporting Act, 325 ILCS 5/1 et seq.
Adoption Act, 750 ILCS 50/0.01 et seq.
Adoption Compensation Prohibition Act, 720 ILCS 525/0.01 et seq.
Breach of Marriage Promise Act, 740 ILCS 15/0.01 et seq.
Child Custody Jurisdiction Act, 750 ILCS 35/1 et seq.
Contest of Adoptions Act, 750 ILCS 55/0.01; 750 ILCS 55/1
Domestic Violence Act of 1986, 750 ILCS 60/101 et seq.
Emancipation of Mature Minors Act, 750 ILCS 30/1

POPULAR NAME LAWS—Cont'd
Expedited Child Support Act, 750 ILCS 25/1 et seq.
Family Expense Law, 750 ILCS 65/15
Instruments Regarding Adopted Children Act, 760 ILCS 30/0.01; 760 ILCS 30/1
International Child Abduction Remedies Act, 42 U.S.C.A. § 11601 et seq.
Marriage and Dissolution of Marriage Act, 750 ILCS 5/101 et seq.
Name Change Act, 735 ILCS 5/21–101 et seq.
Parentage Act, 750 ILCS 40/1 et seq.
Parentage Act of 1984, 750 ILCS 45/1 et seq.
Parental Responsibility Law, 740 ILCS 115/1 et seq.
Rights of Married Persons Act, 750 ILCS 65/0.01 et seq.
Uniform Child Custody Jurisdiction Act, 750 ILCS 35/1 et seq.
Uniform Interstate Family Support Act, 750 ILCS 22/100 et seq.
Uniform Premarital Agreement Act, 750 ILCS 10/2 et seq.
Uniform Reciprocal Enforcement of Support Act, 750 ILCS 20/1 et seq.

PORNOGRAPHY
Lewdness or Obscenity, generally, this index

POST–JUDGMENT PROCEEDINGS
Relief, 735 ILCS 5/2–1401

POWER OF ATTORNEY
Husband or wife, acting for the other, 750 ILCS 65/14

PRACTICE RULES
Rules of Courts, generally, this index

PRAYER FOR RELIEF
Judgments, 735 ILCS 5/2–1401
Orders of court, 735 ILCS 5/2–1401

PRAYERS
Treatment of sickness or disease, abused or neglected children, 325 ILCS 5/4

PREADOPTION REQUIREMENTS
Defined,
Adoption of children, 750 ILCS 50/1

PREFERENCES
Priorities and Preferences, generally, this index

PREGNANCY
Abortion, generally, this index
Children born out of wedlock, parentage judgments, pregnancy and delivery expenses, 750 ILCS 45/14

PREGNANCY—Cont'd
Marriage license,
Issuance when woman is pregnant irrespective of venereal diseases, 750 ILCS 5/205
Minor, 750 ILCS 5/208

PRE–HEARING MOTIONS
Defined, expedited child support, 750 ILCS 25/3

PREJUDICE
Discrimination, generally, this index

PRELIMINARY INJUNCTIONS
Injunctions, this index

PREMARITAL AGREEMENT
Defined, 750 ILCS 10/2

PREMIUMS
Defined,
Support, income withholding, health insurance,
Marriage and Dissolution Act, 750 ILCS 5/706.1
Non-Support of Spouse and Children Act, 750 ILCS 15/4.1
Parentage Act, 750 ILCS 45/20
Uniform Reciprocal Enforcement of Support Act, 750 ILCS 20/26.1

PRESUMPTIONS
Children Born Out of Wedlock, this index
Evidence, this index

PRETRIAL CONFERENCES
Paternity proceedings, 750 ILCS 45/12

PRETRIAL RELEASE
Bail, generally, this index

PRIMA FACIE EVIDENCE
Evidence, generally, this index

PRINCIPAL AND ACCESSORY
Accomplices and Accessories, generally, this index

PRIOR INCONSISTENT STATEMENTS
Impeachment, 735 ILCS 5/2–1102

PRIORITIES AND PREFERENCES
Paternity proceedings, 750 ILCS 45/20
Support orders, Uniform Reciprocal Enforcement of Support Act, 750 ILCS 20/31
Uniform Child Custody Jurisdiction Act, 750 ILCS 35/25

PRIVATE RESIDENTIAL AGENCIES
Children and minors, abuse or neglect, reports, 325 ILCS 5/2

PRIVILEGED COMMUNICATIONS
Evidence, this index

PRIVILEGED

PRIVILEGED INFORMATION
Confidential or Privileged Information, generally, this index

PRIVILEGES AND IMMUNITIES
Abused or neglected children,
  Removal from custody, 325 ILCS 5/5
  Reporting, criminal or civil liability, 325 ILCS 5/9
Adopted children, information exchanges, involved personnel, 750 ILCS 50/18.5
Domestic Violence, this index
Firearm owners identification cards, mental health disclosures, 740 ILCS 110/12
High-risk adults with disabilities, protection orders, waiver of privilege, 750 ILCS 60/213.2
Juvenile Delinquents and Dependents, this index
Law enforcement agencies, mentally or developmentally disabled persons, confidential information, release, 740 ILCS 110/12
Law enforcement officers, domestic violence, 750 ILCS 60/305
Medical care,
  Emergency,
    Children under temporary protective custody, 325 ILCS 5/5
Mentally retarded or developmentally disabled persons, confidential information, disclosure to law enforcement agencies, 740 ILCS 110/12
Support, this index
Surrendered child, information exchanges, state agencies and others, 750 ILCS 50/18.5
Therapists, mentally or developmentally disabled persons, disclosure, confidential information, 740 ILCS 110/10

PROBATE COURT
Circuit Courts, generally, this index
Probate Proceedings, generally, this index

PROBATE PROCEEDINGS
Adoption of children,
  Death of child to be adopted, 750 ILCS 50/14a
Children and minors,
  Artificial insemination, legitimacy, 750 ILCS 40/1 et seq.
Conservatorship. Guardians and Guardianship, generally, this index
Descent and Distribution, generally, this index
Guardians and Guardianship, generally, this index
Legitimacy of children, artificial insemination, 750 ILCS 40/1 et seq.
Personal representatives,
  Judgments,
    Setting aside, petition, 735 ILCS 5/2–1301

PROBATE PROCEEDINGS
—Cont'd
Personal representatives—Cont'd
  Process, personal service, 735 ILCS 5/2–209
Trusts and Trustees, generally, this index
Wills, generally, this index

PROBATION
Revocation or modification,
  Domestic violence, protection order violations, 750 ILCS 60/223

PROBATION OFFICERS
Support or maintenance, wife or children, payments to, 750 ILCS 15/2.1; 750 ILCS 15/4

PROCEEDINGS
Actions and Proceedings, generally, this index

PROCESS
Adoption of children, 750 ILCS 50/7
Affidavits,
  Individual service, 735 ILCS 5/2–203; 735 ILCS 5/2–203.1
  Outside state, personal service, 735 ILCS 5/2–208
  Private person, 735 ILCS 5/2–202
  Publication, service by, 735 ILCS 5/2–206
Age, private person, 735 ILCS 5/2–202
Agents, 735 ILCS 5/2–209
Attachment, generally, this index
Attorneys fees, false statements, 735 ILCS 5/2–203
Buildings,
  Demolition or repair, service by publication, 735 ILCS 5/2–206
Certificates and certification,
  Individual service, 735 ILCS 5/2–203
  Publication notice, copies, 735 ILCS 5/2–206
  Return or proof of service, verification by certification, 735 ILCS 5/1–109
Certified or registered mail,
  Children and minors, emancipation of mature minors, 750 ILCS 30/8
Complaint, generally, this index
Concealment,
  Publication, 735 ILCS 5/2–206
Confession of judgment, 735 ILCS 5/2–1301
Constructive service, 735 ILCS 5/2–209 et seq.
Contempt,
  False statements, 735 ILCS 5/2–203
  Neglect or refusal, 735 ILCS 5/2–202
Contracts, 735 ILCS 5/2–209
  Reformation or rescission, publication, 735 ILCS 5/2–206
Conveyances, service by publication, 735 ILCS 5/2–206

PROCESS—Cont'd
Copies, publication notice, 735 ILCS 5/2–206
Costs,
  Fees for service of process, taxing as costs, 735 ILCS 5/2–202
Damages, false statements, 735 ILCS 5/2–203
Deeds and conveyances, 735 ILCS 5/2–206
Detectives and detective agencies, service of process, 735 ILCS 5/2–202
Dissolution,
  Marriage, 735 ILCS 5/2–209; 750 ILCS 5/410
Domestic violence, 750 ILCS 60/210 et seq.
Endorsement, 735 ILCS 5/2–202
False statements, contempt, 735 ILCS 5/2–203
Family, leaving copy with, 735 ILCS 5/2–202
Fees,
  Service of process, taxing as costs, 735 ILCS 5/2–202
Fiduciaries, 735 ILCS 5/2–209
Fines and penalties,
  Return violations, 735 ILCS 5/2–202
Foreign counties, mail, 735 ILCS 5/2–202
Foreign states, personal service, 735 ILCS 5/2–208
Habeas Corpus, generally, this index
Individuals, 735 ILCS 5/2–203; 735 ILCS 5/2–203.1
  Outside state, 735 ILCS 5/2–208
Injunctions, generally, this index
Jurisdiction, acts submitting to, 735 ILCS 5/2–209
Legal separation, 735 ILCS 5/2–209
Long arm statute, 735 ILCS 5/2–209
Marriage, dissolution or legal separation, 735 ILCS 5/2–209
Motions, private persons, 735 ILCS 5/2–202
Neglect, 735 ILCS 5/2–202
Notice,
  Change of names, 735 ILCS 5/21–104
  Return order, 735 ILCS 5/2–202
Orders of court, private persons, service, 735 ILCS 5/2–202
Outside state, personal service, 735 ILCS 5/2–208; 735 ILCS 5/2–209
Personal representatives, 735 ILCS 5/2–209
Personal service, outside state, 735 ILCS 5/2–208; 735 ILCS 5/2–209
Petitions,
  Return order, 735 ILCS 5/2–202
Private persons, 735 ILCS 5/2–202
Proof of service,
  Names, change, 735 ILCS 5/21–104
  Verification by certification, 735 ILCS 5/1–109
Publication, 735 ILCS 5/2–206
  Defaults, 735 ILCS 5/2–207

PROCESS—Cont'd
Publication—Cont'd
Judgments, setting aside, 735 ILCS 5/2-1301
Service of process, post Time, 735 ILCS 5/2-207
Real estate, 735 ILCS 5/2-209
Records, individual service, 735 ILCS 5/2-203
Reformation, contracts, service by publication, 735 ILCS 5/2-206
Refusal, 735 ILCS 5/2-202
Rescission, contracts, service by publication, 735 ILCS 5/2-206
Returns, 735 ILCS 5/2-202
Verification by certification, 735 ILCS 5/1-109
Rules of Court, this index
Service of process, 735 ILCS 5/2-202
Adoption of children, service by publication, 750 ILCS 50/7
Buildings, demolition or repair, service by publication, 735 ILCS 5/2-206
Certification, verification by certification, return or proof of service, 735 ILCS 5/1-109
Child Custody Jurisdiction Act, 750 ILCS 35/6
Child support expedited proceedings, absence parties, S.Ct. Rule 100.8
Children and minors, emancipation of mature minors, 750 ILCS 30/8
Coroners, 735 ILCS 5/2-202
Demolition or repair, buildings, service by publication, 735 ILCS 5/2-206
Emancipation of mature minors, 750 ILCS 30/8
Fees,
Taxing as costs, 735 ILCS 5/2-202
Infants, emancipation of mature minors, 750 ILCS 30/8
Mail and mailing,
Foreign counties, 735 ILCS 5/2-202
Publication notice, 735 ILCS 5/2-206
Proof of service,
Verification by certification, 735 ILCS 5/1-109
Publication,
Adoption of children, notices, 750 ILCS 50/7
Repair or demolition, buildings, service by publication, 735 ILCS 5/2-206
Return of service,
Verification by certification, 735 ILCS 5/1-109
Rules of Court, this index
Support,
Nonresidents, 750 ILCS 22/201
Uniform Child Custody Jurisdiction Act, 750 ILCS 35/6
Verification by certification, return or proof of service, 735 ILCS 5/1-109

PROCESS—Cont'd
Sexual intercourse within state, act submitting to jurisdiction, parentage actions, 735 ILCS 5/2-209
Show cause rule, return violations, 735 ILCS 5/2-202
Specific performance, publication, 735 ILCS 5/2-206
Summons,
Affidavits,
Individual service, 735 ILCS 5/2-203; 735 ILCS 5/2-203.1
Outside state, personal service, 735 ILCS 5/2-208
Answer, form, S.Ct.Rule 101
Appearance required, S.Ct.Rule 101
Attorneys fees, false statements, 735 ILCS 5/2-203
Certificates and certification, individual service, 735 ILCS 5/2-203
Compensation, fees and salaries, mileage outside county, 735 ILCS 5/2-202
Contempt, false statements, 735 ILCS 5/2-203
Copies,
Individual, 735 ILCS 5/2-203
Damages, false statements, 735 ILCS 5/2-203
Date, S.Ct.Rule 101
Dissolutions of marriage, 750 ILCS 5/411
False statements, contempt, 735 ILCS 5/2-203
Fees, mileage outside county, 735 ILCS 5/2-202
Forms, S.Ct.Rule 101
Individuals, 735 ILCS 5/2-203; 735 ILCS 5/2-203.1
Outside state, 735 ILCS 5/2-208
Issuance, S.Ct.Rule 101
Mail and mailing,
Individuals, 735 ILCS 5/2-203
Municipal corporations,
Parking or standing violations, 735 ILCS 5/2-203
Municipalities of 500,000 or more, parking or standing violations, 735 ILCS 5/2-203; 735 ILCS 5/2-203.1
Name of clerk, S.Ct.Rule 101
Outside state, personal service, 735 ILCS 5/2-208
Paternity proceedings, 750 ILCS 45/9
Personal service, outside state, 735 ILCS 5/2-208
Seal of court, S.Ct.Rule 101
Wrong form, jurisdiction, S.Ct. Rule 101
Support, 735 ILCS 5/2-209
Nonresidents, 750 ILCS 22/201
Time, 735 ILCS 5/2-202
Publication notice, 735 ILCS 5/2-207
Torts, 735 ILCS 5/2-209
Vacating or setting aside, judgments, 735 ILCS 5/2-1301

PROCESS—Cont'd
Verification by certification, return or proof of service, 735 ILCS 5/1-109
Written instrument, return, notice, 735 ILCS 5/2-202

PRODUCTS LIABILITY
Process, nonresidents, service on secretary of state, 735 ILCS 5/2-209

PROFESSIONAL ASSOCIATIONS
Nonprofit Corporations, generally, this index

PROOF
Evidence, generally, this index

PROPERTY
Attachment, generally, this index
Defined,
Premarital agreements, 750 ILCS 10/2
Dissolution of marriage proceedings, disposition, 750 ILCS 5/503
Garnishment, generally, this index
Marriage, premarital agreements, 750 ILCS 10/1 et seq.
Personal Property, generally, this index
Real Estate, generally, this index
Taxation, generally, this index

PROPERTY TAXATION
Taxation, generally, this index

PROSECUTING ATTORNEYS
Defined, Uniform Reciprocal Enforcement of Support Act, 750 ILCS 20/2
State's Attorneys, generally, this index

PROTECTION ORDERS
Domestic Violence, this index
Support, this index

PROTECTIVE CUSTODY
Abused or neglected children, 325 ILCS 5/5

PRURIENT MATERIAL
Lewdness or Obscenity, generally, this index

PSYCHIATRISTS AND PSYCHIATRY
Abused or neglected children, reports, 325 ILCS 5/4
Children and minors,
Abuse or neglect, reports, 325 ILCS 5/4

PSYCHOLOGISTS
Abused or neglected children, reports, 325 ILCS 5/4

PUBLIC AGENCIES
Children, abuse or neglect, reports, 325 ILCS 5/2

PUBLIC AID, DEPARTMENT OF
Paternity proceedings, support orders, collection, 750 ILCS 45/22

PUBLIC

PUBLIC AID, DEPARTMENT OF
—Cont'd
Payments under court order,
   Dependent receiving public aid, 750 ILCS 15/2.1 et seq.
   Receipt and deposit, 750 ILCS 15/2.1 et seq.
Perinatal coordinator, 325 ILCS 5/7.3a
Social Services, generally, this index
State information agency,
   Support, interstate enforcement, 750 ILCS 22/310
Uniform Reciprocal Enforcement of Support Act, 750 ILCS 20/17
Support, interstate enforcement, state information agency, 750 ILCS 22/310

PUBLIC ASSISTANCE
Social Services, generally, this index

PUBLIC ASSISTANCE RECOVERIES TRUST FUND
Support,
   Public aid recipients, mandatory payments, 750 ILCS 5/709

PUBLIC HEALTH
Health and Sanitation, generally, this index

PUBLIC HEALTH, DEPARTMENT OF
Abused or neglected children,
   Investigations, medical care and treatment, quality, 325 ILCS 5/11.1
   Medical care and treatment, quality, investigations, 325 ILCS 5/11.1
Adoption, identifying information, exchange, 750 ILCS 50/18.1 et seq.
Investigations,
   Abused or neglected children, medical care and treatment, quality, records, access, 325 ILCS 5/11.1
Vital Statistics, generally, this index

PUBLIC OFFICE
Defined,
   Paternity proceedings, withholding of income, 750 ILCS 45/20
   Support, 750 ILCS 5/706.1; 750 ILCS 15/4.1; 750 ILCS 20/26.1
      Health insurance, 750 ILCS 5/505.2

PUBLIC OFFICIALS
Defined,
   Mental Health and Developmental Disabilities Confidentiality Act, 740 ILCS 110/12

PUBLIC POLICY
Breach of marriage promise actions, 740 ILCS 15/1
Expedited child support, 750 ILCS 25/2

PUBLIC POLICY—Cont'd
Support, expedited child support, 750 ILCS 25/2

PUBLIC RECORDS
Records and Recordation, generally, this index

PUBLIC SCHOOLS
Schools and School Districts, generally, this index

PUBLIC SERVICES
Social Services, generally, this index

PUBLIC UTILITIES
Telecommunications, generally, this index

PUBLIC WELFARE
Social Services, generally, this index

PUBLIC WELFARE, DEPARTMENT OF
Public Aid, Department of, generally, this index

PUBLICATION
Application for,
   Change of name, 735 ILCS 5/21-103
Change of name, 735 ILCS 5/21-103
Service of process. Process, this index

PUNISHMENT
Crimes and Offenses, generally, this index

PUNITIVE DAMAGES
Alienation of affections, recovery prohibited, 740 ILCS 5/3
Breach of marriage promise, recovery precluded, 740 ILCS 15/3

PUPILS
Schools and School Districts, generally, this index

PUTATIVE FATHER
Defined, adoption of children, 750 ILCS 50/1

PUTATIVE FATHER REGISTRY
Generally, 750 ILCS 50/12.1

QUALIFIED DOMESTIC RELATIONS ORDER
Defined, 26 U.S.C.A. § 414(p)
Qualified Medical Child Support Order, 29 U.S.C.A. 1169

RATE OF EXCHANGE
Defined, foreign money claims, 735 ILCS 5/12-655

REAL ESTATE
Deeds and Conveyances, generally, this index
Descent and Distribution, generally, this index
Dissolution of marriage, orders, sale under, 750 ILCS 5/703
Eminent Domain, generally, this index
Enforcement of Judgments, generally, this index

REAL ESTATE—Cont'd
Homesteads, generally, this index
Liens and Incumbrances, generally, this index
Lis pendens, 735 ILCS 5/2-1901
Married persons may own separately, 750 ILCS 65/9
Mortgages, generally, this index
Orders of court,
   Relief petition, 735 ILCS 5/2-1401
Partition, generally, this index
Probate Proceedings, this index
Process, 735 ILCS 5/2-209
Sales,
   Dissolution of marriage order, 750 ILCS 5/703
Taxation, generally, this index
Title to Property, generally, this index
Writs, possession, abolishment, 735 ILCS 5/2-1501

REASONABLE LIVING EXPENSES
Defined, adoption, biological parents, payment by petitioners, 720 ILCS 525/4.1

REBUTTAL
Adverse party or agent, examination, 735 ILCS 5/2-1102

RECIPIENT
Defined,
   Mental Health and Developmental Disabilities Confidentiality Act, 740 ILCS 110/2

RECIPROCITY
Support, uniform interstate family support, 750 ILCS 22/100 et seq.

RECOGNIZANCE
Husband and wife, neglect to support, 750 ILCS 15/4; 750 ILCS 15/5
Forfeiture, 750 ILCS 15/5
Support proceedings, arrested support obligor, giving, 750 ILCS 20/16

RECOMMENDATIONS
Defined, expedited child support, 750 ILCS 25/3

RECONCILIATION
Dissolution of marriage, attempt, conference, 750 ILCS 5/404

RECORD CUSTODIAN
Defined, Mental Health and Developmental Disabilities Confidentiality Act, 740 ILCS 110/2

RECORDATION
Records and Recordation, generally, this index

RECORDERS
Notice,
   Partition in dissolution of marriage proceedings, 750 ILCS 5/515

RECORDERS—Cont'd
Partition in dissolution of marriage proceedings, filing notice, 750 ILCS 5/515

RECORDS AND RECORDATION
Abused or neglected children, access, 325 ILCS 5/11.1
Access,
  Abused or neglected children, 325 ILCS 5/11.1
  Juveniles, serious habitual offenders, 325 ILCS 5/11.1
Adoption of Children, this index
Change of venue, 735 ILCS 5/2–1001.5
Child Care Facilities, this index
Child support payments, 750 ILCS 5/507
Confidential or Privileged Information, generally, this index
Criminal History Record Information, generally, this index
Defined,
  Mental Health Developmental Disabilities Confidentiality Act, 740 ILCS 110/2
Domestic Violence, this index
Intergovernmental missing child recovery, access to records, 325 ILCS 5/11.1
Juvenile Delinquents and Dependents, this index
Law Enforcement Agencies, this index
Marriage, this index
Medical Records, generally, this index
Process, individual service, 735 ILCS 5/2–203
Support payments,
  Income withholding, 750 ILCS 5/706.1; 750 ILCS 15/4.1; 750 ILCS 20/26.1
  Receiving and disbursing agents, 750 ILCS 5/507
Taxation,
  Tax relief, senior citizens and disabled persons, 320 ILCS 25/8
Transcripts of Record, generally, this index
Venue, change of venue, 735 ILCS 5/2–1001.5
Vital Statistics, generally, this index

REDEMPTION
Default judgments, notice, 735 ILCS 5/2–1302
Judgment creditors,
  Vacating or setting aside, 735 ILCS 5/2–1301
Notices, default judgments, 735 ILCS 5/2–1302
Trust deeds,
  Foreclosures, notices, 735 ILCS 5/2–1302

REFORMATION
Contracts, process, 735 ILCS 5/2–206

REGISTER
Defined, support, interstate enforcement, 750 ILCS 22/101

REGISTERED NURSES
Nurses, generally, this index

REGISTERING COURT
Defined, Uniform Reciprocal Enforcement of Support Act, 750 ILCS 20/2

REGISTERING TRIBUNAL
Defined, support, interstate enforcement, 750 ILCS 22/101

REGISTERS
Defined,
  Uniform Reciprocal Enforcement of Support Act, 750 ILCS 20/2

REGISTRATION
Adoption, identifying information, exchange, 750 ILCS 50/18.1 et seq.
Foreign support order, Reciprocal Enforcement of Support Act, 750 ILCS 20/35
Marriages,
  Certificates, 750 ILCS 5/210
Support, foreign orders, 750 ILCS 22/601 et seq.

REGISTRY
Putative father registry, 750 ILCS 50/12.1
Uniform Child Custody Jurisdiction Act, out-of-state custody judgments and proceedings, 750 ILCS 35/17

REGISTRY OF FOREIGN SUPPORT ORDERS
Maintenance, Uniform Reciprocal Enforcement of Support Act, 750 ILCS 20/37
Support, interstate enforcement, 750 ILCS 22/101

REIMBURSEMENT
Judgments, satisfied, 735 ILCS 5/2–1301
Paternity proceedings, 750 ILCS 45/20

RELATED CHILD
Adoption of Children, this index
Defined, adoption of children, 750 ILCS 50/1

RELATIVES
Abuse. Domestic Violence, generally, this index
Adopted children, death of parents, visitation rights, 755 ILCS 5/11–7.1
Children, death of parents, visitations rights, 755 ILCS 5/11–7.1
Descent and Distribution, generally, this index
Domestic Violence, generally, this index
Incestuous marriages, 750 ILCS 5/212

RELATIVES—Cont'd
Intestate succession. Descent and Distribution, generally, this index
Marriage, 750 ILCS 5/212
Minors, death of parents, visitation rights, 755 ILCS 5/11–7.1
Process, leaving copy with, 735 ILCS 5/2–203
Protection orders, generally. Domestic Violence, this index
Visitation rights, children, death of parents, 755 ILCS 5/11–7.1

RELEASE
Support proceedings, arrested support obligor, 750 ILCS 20/16
Uniform Reciprocal Enforcement of Support Act, arrested support obligor, 750 ILCS 20/16

RELIGION
Adoption of children, consideration, 750 ILCS 50/15

RELIGIOUS ORGANIZATIONS AND SOCIETIES
Marriages, 750 ILCS 5/209

RENDERING STATE
Defined, Uniform Reciprocal Enforcement of Support Act, 750 ILCS 20/2

RENT
Husband and wife, liability for separate debts of either, 750 ILCS 65/5
Leases, generally, this index

REPLEVIN
Writs, abolishment, 735 ILCS 5/2–1501

REPLY
Certification, verification by certification, 735 ILCS 5/1–109
Verification by certification, 735 ILCS 5/1–109

REPORTS
Abused and neglected children, 325 ILCS 5/1 et seq.
Adoption of child,
  Criminal background checks, 750 ILCS 50/5; 750 ILCS 50/6; 750 ILCS 50/15.1
Child support, expedited rules, S.Ct. Rule 100.1
Children and Minors, this index
Crimes and Offenses, this index
Domestic Violence, this index
Expedited child support, 750 ILCS 25/4
False reports, abused or neglected children, 325 ILCS 5/4
Marriages,
  County clerk to department of public health, 750 ILCS 5/211
Neglect,
  Neglected and abused children, 325 ILCS 5/1 et seq.
Offenses. Crimes and Offenses, this index

REPORTS

REPORTS—Cont'd
Private residential agencies, abused or neglected children, 325 ILCS 5/2
Public agencies, abused or neglected children, 325 ILCS 5/2
Revenue department, pharmaceutical assistance, integration with federal law, 320 ILCS 25/9.1
Support, expedited child support, 750 ILCS 25/4

RES JUDICATA
Uniform Child Custody Jurisdiction Act, judgments, 750 ILCS 35/13

RESIDENCE
Domicile and Residence, generally, this index

RESPONDING COURT
Defined, Uniform Reciprocal Enforcement of Support Act, 750 ILCS 20/2

RESPONDING STATE
Defined,
Support, interstate enforcement, 750 ILCS 22/101
Uniform Reciprocal Enforcement of Support Act, 750 ILCS 20/2

RESPONDING TRIBUNAL
Defined, support, interstate enforcement, 750 ILCS 22/101

RESTITUTION
Domestic violence, protection orders, enforcement, 750 ILCS 60/223
Writs, abolishment, 735 ILCS 5/2–1501

RESTRAINING ORDERS
Injunctions, generally, this index

RETARDED PERSONS
Mentally Retarded and Developmentally Disabled Persons, generally, this index

RETIREMENT AND PENSIONS
Employee retirement income security program, group health plans, additional standards, 29 U.S.C.A. § 1169
IRA transfers, 26 U.S.C.A. § 408(d)(6)
Qualified domestic relations order, 26 U.S.C.A. 4146
Support, enforcement, withholding of income, 750 ILCS 5/706.1; 750 ILCS 15/4.1; 750 ILCS 20/26.1
Withholding,
Eligible rollover distributions, 26 U.S.C.A. § 3405(c)
Support enforcement, 750 ILCS 5/706.1; 750 ILCS 15/4.1; 750 ILCS 20/26.1

RETRIAL
Motions, non-jury cases, 735 ILCS 5/2–1203

RETURNS
Marriage, department of public health, 750 ILCS 5/210

REVENUE, DEPARTMENT OF
Aged persons, pharmaceutical assistance, reports, 320 ILCS 25/9.1

REVIEW
Appeal and Review, generally, this index

REVISED UNIFORM RECIPROCAL ENFORCEMENT OF SUPPORT ACT
Generally, 750 ILCS 20/1 et seq.

RIGHTS OF MARRIED PERSONS ACT
Generally, 750 ILCS 65/0.01 et seq.

RULES OF COURT
Accelerated dockets, appeals, S.Ct. Rule 311
Administrative hearing officers, support, S.Ct.Rule 100.2
Authority, S.Ct.Rule 100.4
Submission of recommendations, S.Ct.Rule 100.10
Admissions,
Refusal, expenses, S.Ct.Rule 216
Request for admission of facts or genuineness of documents, S.Ct.Rule 216
Affidavits, income and expenses, support, S.Ct.Rule 100.6
Appeal and review, S.Ct.Rules 1, 306 et seq.
Accelerated dockets, S.Ct.Rule 311
Circuit courts, S.Ct.Rule 301 et seq.
Docketing statements, S.Ct.Rule 312
Final judgments, S.Ct.Rule 303
Interlocutory appeals, S.Ct.Rules 307, 308
Lien of judgment, reviewing court, S.Ct.Rule 366
Multiple parties or multiple claims, S.Ct.Rule 304
Orders, S.Ct.Rule 306
Powers of reviewing court, S.Ct. Rule 366
Scope of review, S.Ct.Rule 366
Stay of judgments pending appeal, S.Ct.Rule 305
Support, recommended orders, S.Ct.Rule 100.11
Without special finding, S.Ct.Rule 304
Appearances, S.Ct.Rules 13, 237
Form of summons, S.Ct.Rule 101
Attorney fees,
Depositions, failure to attend or proceed, S.Ct.Rule 209
Refusal to admit genuineness of documents or truth of matters, S.Ct.Rule 216
Attorneys, appearance and withdrawal, S.Ct.Rule 13
Blood tests, support, S.Ct.Rule 100.5
Bonds (officers and fiduciaries), stay pending appeal, S.Ct.Rule 305
Business records, evidence, S.Ct. Rule 236

RULES OF COURT—Cont'd
Certificates and certification, depositions, S.Ct.Rule 207
Child support. Support, generally, post
Circuit courts, appeal and review, S.Ct.Rule 301 et seq.
Complaints, delivery, S.Ct.Rule 104
Conferences, pretrial conferences, S.Ct.Rule 218
Contempt, orders for support, enforcement, S.Ct.Rule 296
Continuance, motions, S.Ct.Rule 231
Costs, depositions, S.Ct.Rule 208
Definitions,
Expert witnesses, S.Ct.Rule 220
Support, S.Ct.Rule 100.13
Depositions, S.Ct.Rule 201 et seq.
Discovery, S.Ct.Rules 201, 212
Errors and irregularities, S.Ct. Rule 211
Evidence depositions, S.Ct.Rule 212
Expenses, failure to attend or proceed, S.Ct.Rule 209
Failure to attend or proceed, S.Ct. Rule 209
Fees, S.Ct.Rule 208
Objections, S.Ct.Rule 211
Oral examination, S.Ct.Rule 206
Place of deposition, S.Ct.Rule 203
Purposes, S.Ct.Rules 202, 212
Refusal to answer, S.Ct.Rule 219
Signing and filing, S.Ct.Rule 207
Subpoenas, S.Ct.Rule 204
Written questions, S.Ct.Rule 210
Discovery, S.Ct.Rule 201
Depositions, S.Ct.Rule 212
Documents, objects and tangible things, S.Ct.Rule 214
Expert witnesses, S.Ct.Rule 220
Mental examinations, S.Ct.Rule 215
Physical examinations, S.Ct.Rule 215
Real estate, inspection, S.Ct.Rule 214
Refusal to comply, S.Ct.Rule 219
Dismissal for lack of diligence, service of process, S.Ct.Rule 103
Dissolution of marriage, 750 ILCS 5/105; 750 ILCS 5/410
Docketing statements, appeals, S.Ct. Rule 312
Dockets, accelerated dockets, appeals, S.Ct.Rule 311
Documents,
Discovery, S.Ct.Rules 201, 214
Request for admission of genuineness, S.Ct.Rule 216
Request for production of documents, failure to comply, S.Ct.Rule 219
Enforcement counsel, support, S.Ct. Rule 296
Enforcement of support orders, S.Ct.Rule 296
Evidence,
Absence of material evidence, motion for continuance, S.Ct. Rule 231
Business records, S.Ct.Rule 236
Discovery, S.Ct.Rule 201

RULES

RULES OF COURT—Cont'd
Evidence—Cont'd
  Support, hearings, S.Ct.Rule 100.7
Evidence depositions, S.Ct.Rule 212
Expert witnesses, S.Ct.Rule 220
Facsimile transmissions, service,
  Effective date, S.Ct.Rule 12
  Papers other than process and complaints, S.Ct.Rule 11
Fees, depositions, S.Ct.Rule 208
Filing, S.Ct.Rule 21
Forms,
  Docketing statement, appeals, S.Ct.Rule 312
  Order for support, S.Ct.Rule 296
  Summons, S.Ct.Rule 101
Hearings, support,
  Absence of party, S.Ct.Rule 100.8
  Evidence and conduct of hearing, S.Ct.Rule 100.7
  Recommended orders, S.Ct.Rule 100.10
  Scheduling, S.Ct.Rule 100.6
Hostile witnesses, S.Ct.Rule 238
Impeachment, witnesses, S.Ct.Rule 238
Inspections, real estate, discovery, S.Ct.Rule 214
  Interlocutory appeals, S.Ct.Rules 307, 308
  Support, enforcement, S.Ct.Rule 296
Interrogatories, S.Ct.Rule 213
  Discovery, S.Ct.Rule 201
  Failure to answer, S.Ct.Rule 219
Judges, support, authority, S.Ct. Rule 100.11
Judgments and decrees, S.Ct.Rule 272
  Final judgments, appeal and review, S.Ct.Rule 303
Judicial hearings, support and parentage matters, S.Ct.Rules 100.11, 100.12
  Transfers, S.Ct.Rule 100.9
Liens and incumbrances, reviewing court, final judgment, S.Ct.Rule 366
Mail and mailing, service, effective date, S.Ct.Rule 12
Mental examinations, discovery, S.Ct.Rules 201, 215
Motions,
  Continuance, S.Ct.Rule 231
  Discovery, S.Ct.Rule 201
  Signing, S.Ct.Rule 137
Multiple parties or attorneys, service, papers other than process and complaints, S.Ct.Rule 11
Notice,
  Additional relief, S.Ct.Rule 105
  Appeal and review, form and contents, S.Ct.Rule 303
  Depositions, written questions, S.Ct.Rule 210
  Depositions on oral examination, S.Ct.Rule 206
  Hearings, support, S.Ct.Rule 100.6
  Officers and employees of party, service, S.Ct.Rule 237

RULES OF COURT—Cont'd
Notice—Cont'd
  Petitions filed for relief from or revival of judgments, S.Ct. Rule 106
Order for support, enforcement, S.Ct.Rule 296
Orders of court,
  Appeal and review, S.Ct.Rule 306
  Interlocutory appeals, S.Ct.Rules 307, 308
  Support, enforcement, S.Ct.Rule 296
Parentage,
  Blood tests, S.Ct.Rule 100.5
  Support, S.Ct.Rule 100.1 et seq.
Payments, order for support, enforcement, S.Ct.Rule 296
Petitions, orders, appeals, S.Ct.Rule 306
Petitions, support, abatement, S.Ct. Rule 296
Physical examinations, discovery, S.Ct.Rules 201, 215
Physicians and surgeons,
  Depositions, S.Ct.Rule 204
  Examinations, discovery, S.Ct. Rule 215
Pleadings,
  Delivery or service, S.Ct.Rule 104
  New or amended pleadings, notice, S.Ct.Rule 105
  Signing, S.Ct.Rule 137
Pretrial procedure, S.Ct.Rule 218
Process, S.Ct.Rule 101
  Complaints, delivery, S.Ct.Rule 104
  Dismissal for lack of diligence, service, S.Ct.Rule 103
  New or additional relief, notice, S.Ct.Rule 105
  New or amended pleadings, notice, S.Ct.Rule 105
  Service, generally, post
  Summons, service, S.Ct.Rule 101
Proof of service, return, S.Ct.Rule 101
Real estate, inspection,
  Discovery, S.Ct.Rule 214
  Requests, failure to comply, S.Ct. Rule 219
Records and recordation, business records, S.Ct.Rule 236
Request for admission of fact or genuineness of document, S.Ct. Rule 216
Service,
  Notice, additional relief, S.Ct.Rule 105
  Notice of appeal, S.Ct.Rule 303
  Papers other than process and complaint, S.Ct.Rule 11
  Pleadings and other papers, S.Ct. Rule 104
  Proof, S.Ct.Rule 12
  Pleadings subsequent to complaint, S.Ct.Rule 104
  Subpoenas, depositions, S.Ct.Rule 204
  Summons, S.Ct.Rule 101
  Witnesses, subpoenas, S.Ct.Rule 237

RULES OF COURT—Cont'd
Signatures,
  Depositions, S.Ct.Rule 207
  Pleadings, S.Ct.Rule 137
Stay of judgments pending appeal, S.Ct.Rule 305
Subpoenas,
  Depositions, S.Ct.Rule 204
  Hearings, support, S.Ct.Rule 100.6
  Witnesses, S.Ct.Rule 237
Summons, S.Ct.Rule 101
  Additional parties, S.Ct.Rule 103
  Alias summons, S.Ct.Rule 103
  Form, S.Ct.Rule 101
Supplemental interrogatories, S.Ct. Rule 213
Support, S.Ct.Rule 100.1 et seq.
  Absence of party, hearing, S.Ct. Rule 100.8
  Actions subject to hearings, S.Ct. Rule 100.3
  Administrative hearing officers, S.Ct.Rule 100.2
  Authority, S.Ct.Rule 100.4
  Submission of recommendations, S.Ct.Rule 100.10
  Appeal and review, recommended orders, S.Ct.Rule 100.11
  Blood tests, S.Ct.Rule 100.5
  Definitions, S.Ct.Rule 100.13
  Enforcement of order, S.Ct.Rule 296
  Hearings,
    Absence of party, S.Ct.Rule 100.8
    Evidence and conduct of hearing, S.Ct.Rule 100.7
    Recommended orders, S.Ct. Rule 100.10
    Scheduling, S.Ct.Rule 100.6
    Transfers for judicial hearings, S.Ct.Rule 100.9
  Judges, authority, S.Ct.Rule 100.11
  Judicial hearings, S.Ct.Rule 100.12
  Plan of implementation, S.Ct.Rule 100.1
  Transfers for judicial hearings, S.Ct.Rule 100.9
Transfers for judicial hearings, support and parentage matters, S.Ct.Rule 100.9
Videotaped depositions, S.Ct.Rule 206
Waiver, depositions, errors and irregularities, S.Ct.Rule 211
Withdrawal of attorneys, S.Ct.Rule 13
Witnesses,
  Expert witnesses, S.Ct.Rule 220
  Impeachment, S.Ct.Rule 238
  Subpoenas, S.Ct.Rule 237
  Written interrogatories, S.Ct.Rule 213
  Discovery, S.Ct.Rule 201

RULES TO SHOW CAUSE
Declaration of rights, 735 ILCS 5/2–701
Process, return violations, 735 ILCS 5/2–202

RUNAWAYS

RUNAWAYS
Harboring, crimes, 720 ILCS 5/10–6

SAILORS
Military Forces, generally, this index

SALARIES
Compensation and Salaries, generally, this index

SALES
Confession of judgment, consumer transactions, void, 735 ILCS 5/2–1301
Consumers,
  Confession of judgment, void, 735 ILCS 5/2–1301
Dissolution of marriage orders, sale of realty under, 750 ILCS 5/703
Judicial Sales, generally, this index
Orders of court, relief petition, 735 ILCS 5/2–1401

SANITATION
Health and Sanitation, generally, this index

SATURDAYS
Injunctions, 735 ILCS 5/11–106

SCHOOL DISTRICTS
Schools and School Districts, generally, this index

SCHOOL OFFICERS AND EMPLOYEES
Abuse of children,
  Investigations, 325 ILCS 5/7.4
  Notice, unfounded reports, 325 ILCS 5/7.4
  Reports, 325 ILCS 5/4
County truant officers,
  Abused or neglected children, reports, 325 ILCS 5/4
  Children and minors, abuse or neglect, reports, 325 ILCS 5/4
Notice,
  Abuse or neglect, investigations, erroneous report, 325 ILCS 5/7.4
Principals. School Principals, generally, this index
Schoolteachers, generally, this index
Sexual crimes against children,
  Investigations, 325 ILCS 5/7.4
Teachers. Schoolteachers, generally, this index
Truant officers,
  County truant officers, generally, ante

SCHOOLS AND SCHOOL DISTRICTS
Abuse and neglect of children,
  Reports, 325 ILCS 5/4
Child Care Facilities, generally, this index
Confidential or privileged information,
  Protection orders, domestic violence, 750 ILCS 60/214
County truant officers, generally.
  School Officers and Employees, this index

SCHOOLS AND SCHOOL DISTRICTS—Cont'd
Disclosure, protection orders, domestic violence, 750 ILCS 60/222
Domestic violence,
  Protection orders, 750 ILCS 60/214
  Notice, 750 ILCS 60/222
Educational advocate, abused or neglected children, reports, 325 ILCS 5/4
Employees. School Officers and Employees, generally, this index
Judgments,
  Interest computation, 735 ILCS 5/2–1303
Notice,
  Domestic violence, protection orders, 750 ILCS 60/222
  Protection orders, domestic violence, 750 ILCS 60/222
Officers. School Officers and Employees, generally, this index
Orders,
  Protection orders, generally, post
Privileged information. Confidential or privileged information, generally, ante
Protection orders,
  Domestic violence, 750 ILCS 60/214
  Notice, 750 ILCS 60/222
Records and recordation,
  Domestic violence protection orders, inspection of records by person prohibited contact with child, 750 ILCS 60/214
  Noncustodial parent, access, 750 ILCS 5/602.1
School Officers and Employees, generally, this index
Schoolteachers, generally, this index
Support, enforcement, withholding of income, 750 ILCS 5/706.1; 750 ILCS 15/4.1; 750 ILCS 20/26.1
Teachers. Schoolteachers, generally, this index
Truant children,
  Abuse or neglect, not attending school considered as, 325 ILCS 5/3; 325 ILCS 5/4; 325 ILCS 5/7.4
  Notice, educational service region superintendent, 325 ILCS 5/7.4
Withholding compensation by salary deductions,
  Support enforcement, 750 ILCS 5/706.1; 750 ILCS 15/4.1; 750 ILCS 20/26.1

SCHOOLTEACHERS
Abused or neglected children, reports, 325 ILCS 5/4
Investigations, 325 ILCS 5/7.4
Notice, unfounded reports, 325 ILCS 5/7.4
Infants, abused or neglected infants, Reports, 325 ILCS 5/4

SCHOOLTEACHERS—Cont'd
Notice,
  Abuse of children, investigations, notice of erroneous report, 325 ILCS 5/7.4

SEALS
Court, summons, S.Ct.Rule 101

SECRECY
Confidential or Privileged Information, generally, this index

SECRET SERVICES
Mentally or developmentally disabled persons, disclosures, confidential information, 740 ILCS 110/12; 740 ILCS 110/12.2

SECRETARY OF STATE
Process,
  Agent for service of process, Products liability, 735 ILCS 5/2–209

SECURITY
See, also, Bonds (Officers and Fiduciaries), generally, this index
Dissolution of marriage proceedings, removal of children from state, 750 ILCS 5/609
Return of children removed from Illinois, parent having custody, 750 ILCS 5/609

SEDUCTION
Breach of promise action, 740 ILCS 15/1

SELF-INCRIMINATION
Support proceeding,
  Refusal to answer, interstate enforcement, 750 ILCS 22/316
  Uniform Reciprocal Enforcement of Support Act, 750 ILCS 20/21

SENIOR CITIZENS
Aged Persons, generally, this index

SENTENCE AND PUNISHMENT
Crimes and Offenses, generally, this index

SEPARATE MAINTENANCE
Legal separation, generally. Marriage, this index

SEQUESTRATION
Writs, abolishment, 735 ILCS 5/2–1501

SERVICE OF PROCESS
Process, this index

SET-OFF AND COUNTERCLAIM
Declaration of rights, 735 ILCS 5/2–701
Injunctions, 735 ILCS 5/11–107

SEVERANCE
Venue, transfer of causes, 735 ILCS 5/2–106

SEX OFFENSES
Abuse. Sexual Abuse, generally, this index
Adultery, generally, this index
Children and minors. Sexual Crimes Against Children, generally, this index
Deviant sexual conduct. Sexual Abuse, generally, this index
Fornication, generally, this index
Incest, generally, this index
Lewdness or Obscenity, generally, this index
Mentally or developmentally disabled persons, disclosures, confidential information, 740 ILCS 110/12.2
Protection orders,
  Domestic violence, filing petition in conjunction with proceedings, 750 ILCS 60/202
Sexual Abuse, generally, this index
Sexual Crimes Against Children, generally, this index

SEXUAL ABUSE
Children and Minors, this index
Domestic Violence, generally, this index
Paternity proceedings, admissibility of evidence, 750 ILCS 45/6

SEXUAL CRIMES AGAINST CHILDREN
Abuse,
  Neglected children, reports, 325 ILCS 5/7
  Out-of-court statements, admissibility and civil proceedings, 735 ILCS 5/8–2601
  Reports, 325 ILCS 5/1 et seq.
Child protective services unit, reports, 325 ILCS 5/7
Evidence, hearsay, admissibility in civil proceedings, 735 ILCS 5/8–2601
Protection orders, generally. Juvenile Delinquents and Dependents, this index
Public identification, 325 ILCS 5/11.3
School Officers and Employees, this index
Visitation, noncustodial parents and relatives, parole and release, 750 ILCS 5/607

SEXUAL INTERCOURSE
Adultery, generally, this index
Fornication, generally, this index

SEXUALLY DANGEROUS PERSONS
Sexual Crimes Against Children, generally, this index

SEXUALLY TRANSMITTED DISEASES
AIDS, generally, this index

SHERIFFS
Arrest, generally, this index
Attachment, generally, this index
Enforcement of Judgments, generally, this index

SHERIFFS—Cont'd
Judicial Sales, generally, this index
Service of process,
  Counties less than 1,000,000, service by civilians, 735 ILCS 5/2–202
  Fees, taxing as costs, 735 ILCS 5/2–202

SICKLE CELL ANEMIA
Marriage, medical information brochure, 750 ILCS 5/204

SICKNESS
Diseases, generally, this index
Hospitals, generally, this index
Medical Care and Treatment, generally, this index

SIGNATURES
Premarital agreements, 750 ILCS 10/3
  Amendment or revocation, 750 ILCS 10/6

SINGULAR NUMBER
Plural included,
  Adoption of children, 750 ILCS 50/1

SISTERS AND BROTHERS
Relatives, generally, this index

SOCIAL ORGANIZATIONS
Nonprofit Corporations, generally, this index

SOCIAL SECURITY
Numbers and numbering,
  Support proceedings,
    Disclosure, income withholding, Dissolution of marriage, paternity, 750 ILCS 5/706.1; 750 ILCS 15/4.1; 750 ILCS 20/26.1; 750 ILCS 45/20
    Identification of obligor, Uniform Reciprocal Enforcement of Support Act, 750 ILCS 20/11

SOCIAL SERVICES
Abused and neglected children, Reports, 325 ILCS 5/1 et seq.
Actions and proceedings,
  Support responsibility of relatives, generally, post
Attorney general,
  Proceedings to enforce support of wife and children, 750 ILCS 15/1b
Automated data processing system, support, transmittal to department, 750 ILCS 5/705 et seq.
Child protective service unit, abused or neglected children, reports, 325 ILCS 5/7 et seq.
Charge, delinquent payments,
  Dissolution of marriage, paternity, 750 ILCS 5/505; 750 ILCS 15/3 et seq.; 750 ILCS 20/24

SOCIAL

SOCIAL SERVICES—Cont'd
Child protective service unit, abused or neglected children, reports —Cont'd
  Delinquent payments, charge,
    Dissolution of marriage, paternity, 750 ILCS 5/505; 750 ILCS 15/3 et seq.; 750 ILCS 20/24
  Expedited rules, S.Ct.Rule 100.1 et seq.
    Actions, S.Ct.Rule 100.3
  Job search, training or work programs, 750 ILCS 5/505.1; 750 ILCS 15/12; 750 ILCS 20/24.1; 750 ILCS 45/15.1
  Payments,
    Recipients of aid,
      Receiving and disbursing agents, 750 ILCS 5/705
      Transmittal to department, 750 ILCS 5/705 et seq.
Computation and payment of aid,
  Payments under court order, 750 ILCS 15/2.1 et seq.
  Dependent receiving public aid, 750 ILCS 15/2.1 et seq.
  Receipt and deposit, 750 ILCS 15/2.1 et seq.
Domestic violence, assistance by law enforcement officers, 750 ILCS 60/304
Fines and penalties,
  Nonsupport, wife or children receiving public aid, 750 ILCS 15/4
Foster family homes,
  Abused or neglected children, reports, 325 ILCS 5/4
Crimes and offenses,
  Placing out children, receipt of compensation, 720 ILCS 525/5
General assistance,
  Reports,
    Child abuse, 325 ILCS 5/4
Job search, training and work programs,
  Child support, dissolution of marriage, paternity, 750 ILCS 5/505.1; 750 ILCS 15/12; 750 ILCS 20/24.1; 750 ILCS 45/15.1
Judgments and decrees,
  Support orders, dissolution of marriage, 750 ILCS 5/505; 750 ILCS 5/4; 750 ILCS 20/24; 750 ILCS 45/14
Legal separation payments, wife and children receiving aid, 750 ILCS 5/705
Local governmental units,
  Fine for nonsupport of wife or children receiving aid, 750 ILCS 15/4
Legal separation payments, wife or children receiving aid, 750 ILCS 5/705
Payments under court order, 750 ILCS 15/2.1 et seq.
  Dependent receiving public aid, 750 ILCS 15/2.1 et seq.

SOCIAL

SOCIAL SERVICES—Cont'd
Local governmental units—Cont'd
Payments under court order
—Cont'd
Receipt and deposit, 750 ILCS 15/2.1 et seq.
Neglected and abused children, reporting, 325 ILCS 5/1 et seq.
Perinatal care, coordinator, appointment, 325 ILCS 5/7.3a
Reports,
Abused or neglected children, 325 ILCS 5/1 et seq.
Support,
Payments, transmittal to department, 750 ILCS 5/705 et seq.
Public aid recipients,
Payments, transmittal to department, 750 ILCS 5/705 et seq.
Receiving and disbursing agents, 750 ILCS 5/705
Support responsibility of relatives, 750 ILCS 15/1
Bonds (officers and fiduciaries), posting security, 750 ILCS 5/706.2
Charge, overdue payment,
Dissolution of marriage, paternity, 750 ILCS 5/505; 750 ILCS 15/3 et seq.; 750 ILCS 20/24; 750 ILCS 45/14
Delinquencies, charge, dissolution of marriage, paternity, 750 ILCS 5/505; 750 ILCS 15/3 et seq.; 750 ILCS 20/24; 750 ILCS 45/14
Dissolution of marriage, 750 ILCS 15/1
Judgments, 750 ILCS 5/505; 750 ILCS 15/4; 750 ILCS 20/24; 750 ILCS 45/14
Posting security, 750 ILCS 5/706.2
Security, posting, 750 ILCS 5/706.2
Work programs. Job search, training and work programs, generally, ante

SOCIAL WORKERS
Abused or neglected children, reports, 325 ILCS 5/4

SOCIETIES
Associations and Societies, generally, this index

SPECIFIC PERFORMANCE
Process, publications, service by, 735 ILCS 5/2-206

SPECIFICATIONS
Plans and Specifications, generally, this index

SPOUSAL-SUPPORT ORDER
Defined, uniform interstate family support, 750 ILCS 22/101

SPOUSES
Husband and Wife, generally, this index

STALKING
Protection orders, domestic violence, 750 ILCS 60/214

STATE
Actions and proceedings,
Support proceedings, Uniform Reciprocal Enforcement of Support Act, 750 ILCS 20/8
Defined,
Support, interstate enforcement, 750 ILCS 22/101
Uniform Child Custody Jurisdiction Act, 750 ILCS 35/3.10
Uniform Reciprocal Enforcement of Support Act, 750 ILCS 20/2
Support, enforcement, withholding of income, 750 ILCS 5/706.1; 750 ILCS 15/4.1; 750 ILCS 20/26.1
Withholding of income, support enforcement, 750 ILCS 5/706.1; 750 ILCS 15/4.1; 750 ILCS 20/26.1

STATE ATTORNEYS
State's Attorneys, generally, this index

STATE BOARDS
Boards and Commissions, generally, this index

STATE DEPARTMENTS
Confidential or privileged information,
Therapists, patients information, 740 ILCS 110/9
Disclosure,
Therapists, 740 ILCS 110/9
Parental Responsibility Law, actions in state's behalf, 740 ILCS 115/1 et seq.
Therapists, patient information, disclosure, 740 ILCS 110/9

STATE GOVERNMENT
State, generally, this index

STATE INFORMATION AGENCY
Designation, support proceedings, Uniform Reciprocal Enforcement of Support Act, 750 ILCS 20/17

STATE LEGISLATURE
General Assembly, generally, this index

STATE OFFICERS AND EMPLOYEES
Declaratory judgments, elections, 735 ILCS 5/2-701
Elections, declaratory judgments, 735 ILCS 5/2-701

STATE PARENTAGE ACT
Generally, 750 ILCS 40/1 et seq.

STATE POLICE, DEPARTMENT OF
Developmentally disabled persons, disclosures of confidential information, 740 ILCS 110/12

STATE POLICE, DEPARTMENT OF—Cont'd
Mentally ill persons, disclosures of confidential information, 740 ILCS 110/12
Mentally or developmentally disabled persons, confidential information, disclosure, 740 ILCS 110/12
Records and recordation,
Contempt, child visitation enforcement, 750 ILCS 5/607.1

STATE'S ATTORNEYS
Motion before trial for temporary order for support or maintenance of wife or children of defendant, 750 ILCS 15/3
Support, this index

STATE-WIDE CITIZENS COMMITTEE ON CHILD ABUSE AND NEGLECT
Appointments, 325 ILCS 5/11.7

STATUTES
Construction of statutes,
Adoption of persons, 750 ILCS 50/2.1
Declaratory judgments, 735 ILCS 5/2-701
Uniform Child Custody Jurisdiction Act, 750 ILCS 35/2
Uniform Enforcement of Foreign Judgments Act, 735 ILCS 5/12-657
Declaratory judgments, construction, 735 ILCS 5/2-701

STAY
Supersedeas or Stay, generally, this index

STIPULATIONS
Declaratory judgments, cost, 735 ILCS 5/2-701

STUDENTS
Schools and School Districts, generally, this index

STUDIES
Child custody proceedings, requesting from foreign courts, 750 ILCS 35/20
Uniform Child Custody Jurisdiction Act, requesting from foreign court, 750 ILCS 35/20

SUBDIVISIONS
Political Subdivisions, generally, this index

SUBJECT OF REPORT
Defined, abused or neglected children, reports, 325 ILCS 5/3

SUBPOENAS
Rules of Court, this index

SUBSTANCE ABUSE
Alcoholics and Intoxicated Persons, generally, this index

SUBSTITUTION
Judges, 735 ILCS 5/2–1001

SUCCESSION
Descent and Distribution, generally, this index

SUITS
Actions and Proceedings, generally, this index

SUMMARY JUDGMENTS
Injunctions, wrong remedies, 735 ILCS 5/11–107

SUMMONS
Process, this index
Rules of Court, this index

SUNDAY
Injunctions, 735 ILCS 5/11–106

SUPERSEDEAS OR STAY
Child custody proceedings, simultaneous proceeding in other state, 750 ILCS 35/7
Dissolution of marriage, 750 ILCS 5/501.1
Support proceedings or support order enforcement, 750 ILCS 20/30
Registered foreign support orders, enforcement, 750 ILCS 20/40

SUPERVISOR OF GENERAL ASSISTANCE
Support, representing dependents, Uniform Reciprocal Enforcement of Support Act, 750 ILCS 20/12

SUPPORT
See, also, Maintenance, generally, this index
Generally, 750 ILCS 5/505; 750 ILCS 15/1 et seq.; 750 ILCS 22/100 et seq.
Accident and health insurance, Income withholding,
Marriage and dissolution, 750 ILCS 5/706.1
Non-support of spouse and children, 750 ILCS 15/4.1
Parentage, 750 ILCS 45/20
Uniform Reciprocal Enforcement of Support Act, 750 ILCS 20/26.1
Orders, 750 ILCS 5/505.2
Acknowledgments, parentage, expedited hearings, S.Ct.Rule 100.4
Actions and proceedings, interstate enforcement, 750 ILCS 22/301 et seq.
Address, change, mandatory payments, 750 ILCS 5/709
Adjournment of hearing, paternity issue adjudication, 750 ILCS 20/27
Administrative enforcement, Foreign orders lacking registration, 750 ILCS 22/502
Administrative office of Illinois courts, supervision, enforcement, S.Ct.Rule 296

SUPPORT—Cont'd
Adoption of children, failure to pay, consent exemption, 750 ILCS 50/8
Adult children, educational expenses, dissolution of marriage, 750 ILCS 5/513
Advance moneys, mandatory payment program, preparations, 750 ILCS 5/712
Affidavits,
Immediate withholding of income, 750 ILCS 5/706.1; 750 ILCS 15/4.1; 750 ILCS 20/26.1; 750 ILCS 45/20
Order of withholding, 750 ILCS 5/706.1; 750 ILCS 15/4.1; 750 ILCS 20/26.1
Aliens, this index
Alternative procedures, withholding order, 750 ILCS 5/706.1; 750 ILCS 15/4.1; 750 ILCS 20/26.1
Amendment, order, etc., mandatory payments, 750 ILCS 5/709
Appeals,
Expedited child support hearings, 750 ILCS 25/8; 750 ILCS 25/9
Orders of support, 750 ILCS 20/34
Appearance, expedited child support hearings, 750 ILCS 25/10
Application of law, interstate enforcement, 750 ILCS 22/202; 750 ILCS 22/301; 750 ILCS 22/303; 750 ILCS 22/901
Applications of payments made under support orders, 750 ILCS 20/31
Arrearages,
Duty of payment, enforcement, 750 ILCS 20/9
Withholding, order, 750 ILCS 5/706.1; 750 ILCS 15/4.1; 750 ILCS 20/26.1
Arrest,
Obligors, interstate enforcement, 750 ILCS 22/305
Support obligor, 750 ILCS 20/16
Assignments, wages, 750 ILCS 5/706.1; 750 ILCS 15/4.1; 750 ILCS 20/26.1
Attachment,
Body of obligor, 750 ILCS 5/713
Interstate enforcement, 750 ILCS 22/305
Attorneys,
Enforcement counsel, S.Ct.Rule 296
Interstate enforcement, 750 ILCS 22/309
Attorneys fees,
Child support, proceedings, 750 ILCS 5/508
Interstate enforcement, 750 ILCS 22/305; 750 ILCS 22/313
Bonds (officers and fiduciaries),
Assurance of support payment, 750 ILCS 20/26
Pending proceedings, prompt prosecution, 750 ILCS 20/30
Posting security, 750 ILCS 5/706.2
Securing payment, 750 ILCS 5/706.2

SUPPORT—Cont'd
Bonds (officers and fiduciaries)—Cont'd
Support obligor, 750 ILCS 20/16
Cash deposits, assurance of support payment, 750 ILCS 20/26
Change of address,
Mandatory payments, 750 ILCS 5/709
Notice, 750 ILCS 5/706.1; 750 ILCS 15/4.1; 750 ILCS 20/26.1
Charge, delinquency,
Dissolution of marriage, paternity, 750 ILCS 5/505; 750 ILCS 15/3 et seq.; 750 ILCS 20/24; 750 ILCS 45/14
Child, defined, interstate enforcement, 750 ILCS 22/101
Child support, 750 ILCS 5/505
Child support order, defined, interstate enforcement, 750 ILCS 22/101
Circuit court clerks,
Fees, 750 ILCS 15/2.1 et seq.
Payment, department of public aid, transmittal,
Dissolution of marriage, 750 ILCS 5/705; 750 ILCS 5/709; 750 ILCS 15/2.1; 750 ILCS 20/29B
Public aid, department of, payment, transmittal,
Dissolution of marriage, 750 ILCS 5/705; 750 ILCS 5/709; 750 ILCS 15/2.1; 750 ILCS 20/29B
Civil enforcement of Uniform Reciprocal Enforcement of Support Act, 750 ILCS 20/7 et seq.
Clerks of court,
Mandatory payments, S.Ct.Rule 296; 750 ILCS 5/709
Notice of payment,
Uniform Reciprocal Enforcement of Support Act, 750 ILCS 20/29A
Payment, department of public aid, transmittal,
Dissolution of marriage, 750 ILCS 5/705; 750 ILCS 5/709; 750 ILCS 15/2.1; 750 ILCS 20/29B
Records and recordation, disbursements, S.Ct.Rule 296
Commencement of action,
Enforcement proceedings, 750 ILCS 5/710
Payments, 750 ILCS 45/14
Confidential or privileged information,
Addresses and identities, interstate enforcement, 750 ILCS 22/312
Spousal and other communications, 750 ILCS 22/316
Confirmation, registered foreign orders, 750 ILCS 22/608
Conflict of laws,
Duties of support, 750 ILCS 20/7
Interstate enforcement, 750 ILCS 22/202; 750 ILCS 22/303; 750 ILCS 22/910
Multiple child support orders, 750 ILCS 22/207; 750 ILCS 22/208

SUPPORT 1064

SUPPORT—Cont'd
Conflict of laws—Cont'd
Payments and arrearages, interstate enforcement, 750 ILCS 22/604
Construction of law, interstate enforcement, 750 ILCS 22/901
Consumer credit protection, withholding, allowances, 750 ILCS 5/706.1; 750 ILCS 15/4.1; 750 ILCS 20/26.1
Contempt, S.Ct.Rule 296
Default proceedings, 750 ILCS 5/710
Fines and penalties, 750 ILCS 5/505
Hearings, S.Ct.Rule 296
Interstate enforcement, 750 ILCS 22/305
Order for support, wife or child, 750 ILCS 15/3
Penalties, 750 ILCS 5/505
Support duties, enforcement, Uniform Reciprocal Enforcement of Support Act, 750 ILCS 20/9
Support order violations, 750 ILCS 20/26
Support proceedings, Uniform Reciprocal Enforcement of Support Act, 750 ILCS 20/26
Continuance of proceedings, 750 ILCS 20/20
Payees, representation for other matters, 750 ILCS 5/710
Continuing jurisdiction, interstate enforcement, 750 ILCS 22/205
Convention country, designation, uniform reciprocal enforcement, 750 ILCS 20/4.1
Copies,
Petition for support and certificates, sending to responding court, 750 ILCS 20/14
Support orders,
Evidence of duty of support, 750 ILCS 20/23
Sending to initiating court, 750 ILCS 20/25
Costs,
Interstate enforcement, 750 ILCS 22/305; 750 ILCS 22/313
Receiving and disbursing agents, 750 ILCS 5/507; 750 ILCS 5/705
Support proceedings, 750 ILCS 20/15
Counties, expedited child support system, 750 ILCS 25/4
Court fees, 750 ILCS 5/705
Credit, multiple orders, payments, interstate enforcement, 750 ILCS 22/209
Crimes and offenses, class A misdemeanors, nonsupport of spouse or children, 750 ILCS 15/1
Criminal enforcement, 750 ILCS 20/5; 750 ILCS 20/6
Death of parents, modification or termination, 750 ILCS 5/510

SUPPORT—Cont'd
Declaration of invalidity of marriage, support petitions, filing, 750 ILCS 20/11
Deduction, withholding income by payor, 750 ILCS 5/706.1; 750 ILCS 15/4.1; 750 ILCS 20/26.1
Defenses,
Nonparentage, interstate enforcement, 750 ILCS 22/315
Proceedings for support enforcement, 750 ILCS 20/9
Registration, foreign orders, 750 ILCS 22/607
Definitions, 750 ILCS 20/2
Expedited child support, 750 ILCS 25/3
Net income, 750 ILCS 45/14
Delays, hearings, interstate enforcement, costs and attorneys fees, 750 ILCS 22/313
Delinquent payments, 750 ILCS 5/710
Charge, dissolution of marriage, paternity, 750 ILCS 5/505; 750 ILCS 15/3 et seq.; 750 ILCS 20/24; 750 ILCS 45/14
Interstate enforcement, 750 ILCS 22/305
Limitation of actions, interstate enforcement, 750 ILCS 22/604
Notice, service, 750 ILCS 5/706.1; 750 ILCS 15/4.1; 750 ILCS 20/26.1
Demonstration program, expedited child support, 750 ILCS 25/4
Depositions,
Duty of support, evidence, 750 ILCS 20/20
Interstate enforcement, 750 ILCS 22/316
Deposits of cash, assurance of support payments, 750 ILCS 20/26
Direct enforcement, foreign orders lacking registration, 750 ILCS 22/501; 750 ILCS 22/502
Disclosure,
Addresses and identities, interstate enforcement, 750 ILCS 22/312
Social security number, income withholding, dissolution of marriage, paternity, 750 ILCS 5/706.1; 750 ILCS 15/4.1; 750 ILCS 20/26.1; 750 ILCS 45/20
Discovery, interstate enforcement, 750 ILCS 22/202; 750 ILCS 22/206; 750 ILCS 22/318
Dissolution of marriage proceedings,
Bifurcated proceedings, 750 ILCS 5/401
Collection fees, 750 ILCS 5/516
Judgments, reserved questions, 750 ILCS 5/401
Modification of judgment, 750 ILCS 5/510
Postjudgment proceedings, venue, 750 ILCS 5/511
Reserved issues, subsequent proceedings, 750 ILCS 5/401
Temporary relief, 750 ILCS 5/501
Termination, 750 ILCS 5/510

SUPPORT—Cont'd
Division of child support enforcement, creation, 750 ILCS 5/712
Documentary evidence, interstate enforcement, 750 ILCS 22/316
Domestic violence, protection orders, 750 ILCS 60/214
Filing in conjunction with support proceedings, 750 ILCS 60/202
Duties of support, 750 ILCS 20/4
Defined, interstate enforcement, 750 ILCS 22/101
Education of children, 750 ILCS 65/15
Dissolution of marriage proceedings, 750 ILCS 5/505; 750 ILCS 5/513
Modification or termination, 750 ILCS 5/510
Educational expenses, non-minor children, 750 ILCS 5/513
Endorsements, name of recipient, mandatory payments, 750 ILCS 5/709
Enforcement, 750 ILCS 5/511; 750 ILCS 5/710 et seq.
See also, Expedited Child Support Act; Foreign Judgment; Foreign States, this index
Attorneys, enforcement counsel, S.Ct.Rule 296
Civil enforcement, 750 ILCS 5/706.1; 750 ILCS 15/4.1; 750 ILCS 20/7 et seq.
Contempt, generally, ante
Criminal enforcement, 750 ILCS 20/5; 750 ILCS 20/6
Foreign support and income-withholding orders, registration, 750 ILCS 22/601 et seq.
Judgments,
Dissolution of marriage, 750 ILCS 5/505; 750 ILCS 15/3 et seq.; 750 ILCS 20/24; 750 ILCS 45/14
Orders of support, S.Ct.Rule 296
Referral to prosecuting authorities, S.Ct.Rule 296
Evidence, 750 ILCS 15/6
Certified copy of support order, evidence of duty of support, 750 ILCS 20/23
Delays, hearings, interstate enforcement, 750 ILCS 22/313
Delinquent payment, 750 ILCS 5/710
Duty of support, 750 ILCS 20/20
Expedited child support hearings, 750 ILCS 25/7
Foreign states, interstate enforcement, 750 ILCS 22/202; 750 ILCS 22/206
Husband and wife, competency as witnesses, 750 ILCS 20/22
Interstate enforcement, 750 ILCS 22/316
Rules of evidence, 750 ILCS 20/23
Uniform Reciprocal Enforcement of Support Act, 750 ILCS 20/20 et seq.
Exclusive jurisdiction, interstate enforcement, 750 ILCS 22/205
Expedited child support, 750 ILCS 25/1 et seq.
Rules, S.Ct.Rule 100.1 et seq.
Expenses of family, 750 ILCS 65/15

SUPPORT

SUPPORT—Cont'd
Extent of duties of support, 750 ILCS 20/4
Extradition,
  Interstate enforcement, 750 ILCS 22/801; 750 ILCS 22/802
  Uniform Reciprocal Enforcement of Support Act, 750 ILCS 20/5; 750 ILCS 20/6
Failure to appear, expedited child support hearings, 750 ILCS 25/10
Fees,
  Collection fees,
    Dissolution of marriage, paternity, 750 ILCS 5/516; 750 ILCS 15/11; 750 ILCS 20/15a
    Withholding income by payor, 750 ILCS 5/706.1; 750 ILCS 15/4.1; 750 ILCS 20/26.1
  Court fees, 750 ILCS 5/705
  Default, 750 ILCS 5/710
  Interstate enforcement, 750 ILCS 22/313
  Support proceedings, 750 ILCS 20/15
Filing, petition for support, 750 ILCS 20/11
Fines and penalties, 750 ILCS 15/4
  Contempt, 750 ILCS 5/505
  Default, 750 ILCS 5/710
  Income withholding, 750 ILCS 5/706.1; 750 ILCS 15/4.1; 750 ILCS 20/26.1
Fingerprint identification, support obligor, support proceedings, 750 ILCS 20/11
Foreign countries,
  Convention country designation, reciprocal enforcement, 750 ILCS 20/4.1
Foreign states,
  Uniform interstate family support, 750 ILCS 22/100 et seq.
  Uniform Reciprocal Enforcement of Support Act, 750 ILCS 20/1 et seq.
Foreign support orders, registration, 750 ILCS 20/35 et seq.
Forms,
  Income withholding, 750 ILCS 5/706.1; 750 ILCS 15/4.1; 750 ILCS 20/26.1
  Petition for support, 750 ILCS 20/1; 750 ILCS 20/11
  Uniform orders for support, S.Ct. Rule 296
Garnishment, wages assigned to secure support order, 750 ILCS 15/3
Guardian ad litem, necessity, proceedings for minor, 750 ILCS 20/13
Guardians and guardianship,
  Nonresidents, personal jurisdiction, 750 ILCS 22/201; 750 ILCS 22/202
  Visitation by person providing support of ward, 755 ILCS 5/11–13

SUPPORT—Cont'd
Guidelines,
  Child support, 750 ILCS 5/505
  Orders, civil enforcement, 750 ILCS 20/24
  Responding tribunals, interstate enforcement, 750 ILCS 22/303
Health insurance. Accident and Health Insurance, generally, ante
Hearings,
  Adjournment, paternity issue adjudication, 750 ILCS 20/27
  Contempt, enforcement, S.Ct.Rule 296
  Expedited child support, 750 ILCS 25/7; S.Ct.Rule 100.6 et seq.
  Actions subject to, 750 ILCS 25/5
  Blood tests, parentage, officers authority to order, 750 ILCS 45/11
  Failure to appear, 750 ILCS 25/10
  Officers, authority, 750 ILCS 25/6
  Tests, parentage, orders, 750 ILCS 45/11
  Immunity from criminal prosecution, 750 ILCS 20/21
  Judicial hearings, expedited procedures, S.Ct.Rule 100.12
  Registered foreign support orders, Contesting validity or enforcement, 750 ILCS 22/606
  Enforcement, 750 ILCS 20/40
  Rules of evidence, 750 ILCS 20/23
  Self-incrimination, immunity from criminal prosecution, obligor, 750 ILCS 20/21
  Uniform Reciprocal Enforcement of Support Act, 750 ILCS 20/20
Home state, defined, interstate enforcement, 750 ILCS 22/101
Identification, support obligor, support proceedings, 750 ILCS 20/11
  Aliens, 750 ILCS 5/706.1; 750 ILCS 15/4.1; 750 ILCS 20/26.1
  Immediate withholding of income, 750 ILCS 5/706.1; 750 ILCS 15/4.1; 750 ILCS 20/26.1; 750 ILCS 45/20
Immunity from criminal prosecution, testimony, 750 ILCS 20/21
Immunity from suit, party relationships, defense availability, 750 ILCS 20/9
Inappropriate tribunals, interstate enforcement, 750 ILCS 22/306
Income, defined, interstate enforcement, 750 ILCS 22/101
Income taxes, 26 U.S.C.A. § 71
Income withholding,
  Civil enforcement, 750 ILCS 5/706.1; 750 ILCS 15/4.1; 750 ILCS 20/26.1
  Foreign orders lacking registration, 750 ILCS 22/501; 750 ILCS 22/502
  Interstate enforcement, 750 ILCS 22/305

SUPPORT—Cont'd
Income withholding—Cont'd
  Marriage and dissolution, 750 ILCS 5/706.1
  Non-support of spouse and children, 750 ILCS 15/4.1
  Notice, registration, foreign orders, 750 ILCS 22/605
  Parentage, 750 ILCS 45/20
  Registration, interstate enforcement, 750 ILCS 22/601 et seq.
  Uniform Reciprocal Enforcement of Support Act, 750 ILCS 20/26.1
Income-withholding order, defined, interstate enforcement, 750 ILCS 22/101
Initiating court,
  Duties, 750 ILCS 20/14; 750 ILCS 20/29
  Fees, 750 ILCS 20/15
  Support orders, 750 ILCS 20/25
Initiating state, defined, interstate enforcement, 750 ILCS 22/101
Initiating tribunals,
  Defined, interstate enforcement, 750 ILCS 22/101
  Enforcement or modification, orders, 750 ILCS 22/206
  Forwarding proceedings to another state, 750 ILCS 22/203
  Parentage proceedings, interstate enforcement, 750 ILCS 22/701
  Powers and duties, 750 ILCS 22/304
Interest, invested moneys, mandatory payments, 750 ILCS 5/709
Interstate rendition, 750 ILCS 20/5
  Relief from extradition, 750 ILCS 20/6
Intrastate application of Uniform Reciprocal Enforcement of Support Act, 750 ILCS 20/33
Investments, mandatory payments, 750 ILCS 5/709
Issuing state, defined, interstate enforcement, 750 ILCS 22/101
Issuing tribunal, defined, interstate enforcement, 750 ILCS 22/101
Job search, training or work programs,
  Dissolution of marriage, paternity, 750 ILCS 5/505.1; 750 ILCS 15/12; 750 ILCS 45/15.1
Judgments, dissolution of marriage, 750 ILCS 5/505; 750 ILCS 15/4; 750 ILCS 20/24; 750 ILCS 45/14
Jurisdiction, 735 ILCS 5/2–209
  Continuing and exclusive jurisdiction, 750 ILCS 22/205
  Enforcement actions, 750 ILCS 20/10
  Immunity, personal jurisdiction, interstate enforcement, 750 ILCS 22/314
  Nonresidents, 750 ILCS 22/201; 750 ILCS 22/202

SUPPORT

SUPPORT—Cont'd
Jurisdiction—Cont'd
  Participation in support proceedings conferring jurisdiction in other proceedings, 750 ILCS 20/32
  Simultaneous foreign proceedings, 750 ILCS 22/204
Labor and employment, orders to seek employment, interstate enforcement, 750 ILCS 22/305
Labor organizations, income withholding, 750 ILCS 5/706.1; 750 ILCS 15/4.1; 750 ILCS 20/26.1
Laws governing duties of support, 750 ILCS 20/7
Legal separation, 750 ILCS 5/402
Long arm statute, 750 ILCS 22/201
Liens and incumbrances, interstate enforcement, 750 ILCS 22/305
Limitation of actions, arrearages, interstate enforcement, 750 ILCS 22/604
Maintenance, see Maintenance, this index
Mandatory payments, 750 ILCS 5/709 et seq.
Medical insurance. Accident and Health Insurance, generally, ante
Minimum order, 750 ILCS 45/14
Minor parents, interstate enforcement proceedings, 750 ILCS 22/302
Modifications,
  Foreign orders, 750 ILCS 22/609 et seq.
  Interstate enforcement, 750 ILCS 22/205; 750 ILCS 22/206
  Judgment, 750 ILCS 5/510
  Orders of withholding, 750 ILCS 5/706.1; 750 ILCS 15/4.1; 750 ILCS 20/26.1
Multiple child support orders, interstate enforcement, 750 ILCS 22/207 et seq.
Names, endorsement, mandatory payments, 750 ILCS 5/709
Neglect to support, 750 ILCS 15/1 et seq.
Nonparentage, defense, interstate enforcement, 750 ILCS 22/315
Nonresidents, personal jurisdiction, 750 ILCS 22/201; 750 ILCS 22/202
Nonsupport of spouse and children, withholding of income, 750 ILCS 15/4.1
Non-United States citizens, 750 ILCS 5/706.1; 750 ILCS 15/4.1; 750 ILCS 20/26.1
Notice,
  Expedited child support hearings, recommendations, 750 ILCS 25/7
  Financial aid, enforcement of support orders, S.Ct.Rule 296
  Immediate withholding of income, 750 ILCS 5/706.1; 750 ILCS 15/4.1; 750 ILCS 20/26.1; 750 ILCS 45/20
  Inappropriate tribunals, interstate enforcement, 750 ILCS 22/306

SUPPORT—Cont'd
Notice—Cont'd
  Income withholding, 750 ILCS 5/706.1; 750 ILCS 15/4.1; 750 ILCS 20/26.1
  Foreign orders, registration, 750 ILCS 22/605
  Mandatory payments, 750 ILCS 5/709; 750 ILCS 5/710
  Payment, clerk of court,
  Uniform Reciprocal Enforcement of Support Act, 750 ILCS 20/29A
  Petitions for support, interstate enforcement, 750 ILCS 22/306
  Registration of foreign support orders, 750 ILCS 20/39; 750 ILCS 22/605
  Sufficiency, obligors last known address, 750 ILCS 5/709
Objections, nonappearing parties, expedited proceedings, S.Ct. Rule 100.8
Obligee, defined, interstate enforcement, 750 ILCS 22/101
Obligor,
  Defined, interstate enforcement, 750 ILCS 22/101
  Locating obligor, state information agency, 750 ILCS 22/310
  Presence or residence of as affecting duties of support, 750 ILCS 20/4
Orders of support, 750 ILCS 15/3; 750 ILCS 15/4; 750 ILCS 20/24
  Administrative enforcement, foreign orders lacking registration, 750 ILCS 22/502
  Appeals, 750 ILCS 20/34
  Certified copies, evidence of duty of support, 750 ILCS 20/23
  Confirmation, registered foreign orders, 750 ILCS 22/608
  Confirmation by operation of law, registered foreign orders, 750 ILCS 22/606
  Contempt, penalties, 750 ILCS 5/505
  Copies, sending to initiating court, 750 ILCS 20/25
  Counties of 1,000,000 or less, payment through clerk of court, 750 ILCS 5/405
  Crediting payments under other support orders, 750 ILCS 20/31
  Defined, Uniform Reciprocal Enforcement of Support Act, 750 ILCS 20/2
  Direct enforcement, foreign orders lacking registration, 750 ILCS 22/501; 750 ILCS 22/502
  Enforcement, S.Ct.Rule 296
  Establishment, interstate enforcement, 750 ILCS 22/401
  Expedited child support hearings, 750 ILCS 25/7
  Foreign orders,
    Modification, 750 ILCS 22/609 et seq.

SUPPORT—Cont'd
Orders of support—Cont'd
  Foreign support orders, registration, 750 ILCS 20/35 et seq.; 750 ILCS 22/601 et seq.
  Form, S.Ct.Rule 296
  Health insurance, 750 ILCS 5/505.2
  Immediate withholding of income, 750 ILCS 5/706.1; 750 ILCS 15/4.1; 750 ILCS 20/26.1; 750 ILCS 45/20
  Initiating court, 750 ILCS 20/25
  Interstate enforcement, responding tribunals, 750 ILCS 22/305
  Jurisdiction, continuing and exclusive, 750 ILCS 22/205
  Mandatory payments, 750 ILCS 5/709
  Minimum amount, 750 ILCS 45/14
  Modification, jurisdiction, interstate enforcement, 750 ILCS 22/205
  Multiple child support orders, interstate enforcement, 750 ILCS 22/207 et seq.
  Notice, registration, foreign orders, 750 ILCS 22/605
  Nullification of other support orders, 750 ILCS 20/31
  Payment,
    Department of public aid or local governmental unit, 750 ILCS 15/2.1 et seq.
  Prior orders, subsequent petitions, filing, 750 ILCS 20/11
  Priorities, 750 ILCS 20/31
  Reconciliation with orders of other states, 750 ILCS 22/207 et seq.
  Registration,
    Foreign support orders, stay of enforcement, 750 ILCS 20/40
    Simultaneous foreign proceedings, 750 ILCS 22/204
    Registration, foreign orders, 750 ILCS 22/601 et seq.
  Stay of enforcement, 750 ILCS 20/30
  Temporary support,
    Dissolution of marriages, 750 ILCS 5/50
    Jurisdiction, interstate enforcement, 750 ILCS 22/205
  Temporary orders, interstate enforcement, 750 ILCS 22/401
  Violation of order, 750 ILCS 15/5
  Wife or child, 750 ILCS 15/3
  Withholding income, 750 ILCS 5/706.1; 750 ILCS 15/4.1; 750 ILCS 20/26.1
Participation in support proceedings, jurisdiction over parties and other proceedings, 750 ILCS 20/32
Paternity. Children Born Out of Wedlock, this index
Payments,
  Clerks of court, 750 ILCS 5/705
  Dependent receiving public aid, 750 ILCS 15/2.1 et seq.
  Mandatory payments, 750 ILCS 5/709 et seq.

SUPPORT—Cont'd
Payments—Cont'd
Clerks of court—Cont'd
Public aid, department of, transmittal, 750 ILCS 5/705 et seq.
Conflict of law, interstate enforcement, 750 ILCS 22/604
Credit, multiple orders, interstate enforcement, 750 ILCS 22/209
Crediting payments under other support orders, 750 ILCS 20/31
Defined, mandatory payments, 750 ILCS 5/709
Delinquent payments, 750 ILCS 5/710
Disbursement, interstate enforcement, 750 ILCS 22/319
Mandatory payments, 750 ILCS 5/709 et seq.
Notice, clerk of court,
Uniform reciprocal enforcement of support, 750 ILCS 20/29A
Receipt, interstate enforcement, 750 ILCS 22/319
Reception and disbursement by initiating court, 750 ILCS 20/29
Records, mandatory support, 750 ILCS 5/709
Support order,
Complying with, 750 ILCS 20/26
Transmission of payments to initiating court, 750 ILCS 20/28
Penalties. Fines and penalties, generally, ante
Perjury, 750 ILCS 20/21
Personal jurisdiction,
Interstate enforcement,
Limited immunity, 750 ILCS 22/314
Nonresidents, 750 ILCS 22/201; 750 ILCS 22/202
Petition for support, 750 ILCS 20/11
Abatement, S.Ct.Rule 296
Expedited child support hearings, 750 ILCS 25/5
Filing fees, 750 ILCS 20/15
Initiating court, duties, 750 ILCS 20/14
Initiating tribunals, interstate enforcement, copies, 750 ILCS 22/304
Minors, filing on behalf of, 750 ILCS 20/13
Simultaneous foreign proceedings, 750 ILCS 22/204
Responding tribunals, interstate enforcement, 750 ILCS 22/305
Uniform Reciprocal Enforcement of Support Act, 750 ILCS 20/11
Minor, 750 ILCS 20/13
Verification, interstate enforcement, 750 ILCS 22/311
Petitions to vacate registration of foreign support orders, 750 ILCS 20/40
Photographs, support obligor identification, support proceedings, 750 ILCS 20/11

SUPPORT—Cont'd
Plan, expedited child support system, 750 ILCS 25/4
Political subdivision furnishing support, reimbursement, 750 ILCS 20/8
Posting security, guaranteeing payment, 750 ILCS 5/706.2
Premarital agreements, 750 ILCS 10/4; 750 ILCS 10/7
Presumptions,
Delays, hearings, interstate enforcement, 750 ILCS 22/313
Respondents presence in responding state, 750 ILCS 20/7
Priorities and preferences,
Orders of support, 750 ILCS 20/31
Withholding of income, 750 ILCS 5/706.1; 750 ILCS 15/4.1; 750 ILCS 20/26.1
Privileges and immunities,
Husband and wife, competency to testify, 750 ILCS 20/22
Immunity from criminal prosecution, obligor testifying, 750 ILCS 20/21
Interstate enforcement, 750 ILCS 22/314
Spousal and other communications, interstate enforcement, 750 ILCS 22/316
Probation, neglect to support, 750 ILCS 15/4
Process, 735 ILCS 5/2–209
Nonresidents, 750 ILCS 22/201
Protection orders,
Domestic violence, filing in conjunction with support, 750 ILCS 60/202
Violations, 750 ILCS 60/223
Previous orders, status, 750 ILCS 15/12.1
Public aid, department of, state information agency, interstate enforcement, 750 ILCS 22/310
Public aid recipients,
Circuit court clerks, transmittal to department, 750 ILCS 5/705 et seq.
Court orders, 750 ILCS 15/2.1 et seq.
Mandatory payments, 750 ILCS 5/709
Public policy, expedited child support, 750 ILCS 25/2
Receipt and disbursement of payments, interstate enforcement, 750 ILCS 22/319
Receiving and disbursing agents, 750 ILCS 5/507; 750 ILCS 5/705
Receiving public aid, fine for nonsupport, 750 ILCS 15/4
Reciprocity, uniform interstate family support, 750 ILCS 22/100 et seq.
Recognizance, arrested support obligor giving, release, 750 ILCS 20/16
Recommendations, administrative hearing officers, submission, S.Ct.Rule 100.10
Record,
Clerks of court, S.Ct.Rule 296

SUPPORT—Cont'd
Record—Cont'd
Expedited child support hearings, 750 ILCS 25/7
Income withholding, 750 ILCS 5/706.1; 750 ILCS 15/4.1; 750 ILCS 20/26.1
Mandatory payments, 750 ILCS 5/710
Register, defined, interstate enforcement, 750 ILCS 22/101
Registering tribunal, defined, interstate enforcement, 750 ILCS 22/101
Registration of foreign support orders, 750 ILCS 20/35 et seq.; 750 ILCS 22/601 et seq.
Enforcement without, income-withholding orders, 750 ILCS 22/501; 750 ILCS 22/502
Notice, 750 ILCS 22/605
Registry of foreign support orders, 750 ILCS 20/37; 750 ILCS 22/101
Reimbursement,
Costs of enforcement, 750 ILCS 5/711
State assistance, 750 ILCS 5/712
State or political subdivisions furnishing support, 750 ILCS 20/8
Release, arrested support obligor, 750 ILCS 20/16
Remedies for support, 750 ILCS 20/3
Additional remedies, 750 ILCS 20/3; 750 ILCS 20/35
Interstate enforcement, cumulative remedies, 750 ILCS 22/103
State or political subdivisions furnishing support, 750 ILCS 20/8
Reports, expedited child support, 750 ILCS 25/4
Representation,
Petitioner for support, 750 ILCS 20/18
Support obligees, 750 ILCS 20/12
Residence of support of obligee, effect on duties of support obligor, 750 ILCS 20/4
Responding court,
Duties, 750 ILCS 20/18; 750 ILCS 20/28
Powers, 750 ILCS 20/26
Responding state,
Defined, interstate enforcement, 750 ILCS 22/101
Duties of court and officials, 750 ILCS 20/19
Responding tribunals,
Choice of law and support guidelines, 750 ILCS 22/303
Defined, interstate enforcement, 750 ILCS 22/101
Enforcement or modification, orders, 750 ILCS 22/206
Orders of support, establishment, 750 ILCS 22/401
Parentage proceedings, interstate enforcement, 750 ILCS 22/701

SUPPORT

SUPPORT—Cont'd
Responding tribunals—Cont'd
Powers and duties, 750 ILCS 22/305
Proceedings initiated in another state, 750 ILCS 22/203
Revised Uniform Reciprocal Enforcement of Support Act, 750 ILCS 20/1 et seq.
Rules of Court, this index
Rules of evidence, 750 ILCS 20/23
Scope of duties, 750 ILCS 20/4
Security, payment, posting, 750 ILCS 5/706.2
Self-incrimination,
Obligor testifying, immunity from prosecution, 750 ILCS 20/21
Refusal to answer, interstate enforcement, 750 ILCS 22/316
Separated spouses, 750 ILCS 5/402
Service of process,
Nonresidents, 750 ILCS 22/201
Withholding of income order, 750 ILCS 5/706.1; 750 ILCS 15/4.1; 750 ILCS 20/26.1
Simultaneous proceedings in another state, 750 ILCS 22/204
Social security number,
Disclosure, income withholding,
Dissolution of marriage, paternity, 750 ILCS 5/706.1; 750 ILCS 15/4.1; 750 ILCS 20/26.1; 750 ILCS 45/20
Support obligor identification, support proceedings, 750 ILCS 20/11
Social Services, this index
Special fund, enforcement costs, mandatory payments, 750 ILCS 5/711
Spousal-support order, defined, interstate enforcement, 750 ILCS 22/101
State information agency, duties, 750 ILCS 20/17; 750 ILCS 22/310
Statements of payments, responding toward furnishing to initiating court, 750 ILCS 20/28
State's attorneys, representation, Enforcement proceedings, 750 ILCS 5/710
Support obligees, 750 ILCS 20/12
Support petitioner, 750 ILCS 20/12; 750 ILCS 20/18
Stay of proceedings, 750 ILCS 20/30
Registered foreign support orders, enforcement, 750 ILCS 20/40
Stay of service, order for withholding, 750 ILCS 5/706.1; 750 ILCS 15/4.1; 750 ILCS 20/26.1
Supervisor of general assistance, representation of support obligees, 750 ILCS 20/12
Support enforcement agency,
Defined, interstate enforcement, 750 ILCS 22/101
Duties, interstate enforcement, 750 ILCS 22/307
Neglect, 750 ILCS 22/308
Support order, defined, interstate enforcement, 750 ILCS 22/101

SUPPORT—Cont'd
Supreme court, expedited child support system plan, approval, 750 ILCS 25/4
Suspension, orders of withholding, 750 ILCS 5/706.1; 750 ILCS 15/4.1; 750 ILCS 20/26.1
Temporary order, 750 ILCS 15/3
Expedited child support hearings, 750 ILCS 25/5
Interstate enforcement, 750 ILCS 22/401
Jurisdiction, interstate enforcement, 750 ILCS 22/205
Termination,
Judgment, 750 ILCS 5/510
Orders of withholding, 750 ILCS 5/706.1; 750 ILCS 15/4.1; 750 ILCS 20/26.1
Testimony,
Immunity from criminal prosecution, 750 ILCS 20/21
Interstate enforcement proceedings, 750 ILCS 22/316
Time,
Action, 750 ILCS 15/8
Mandatory payments, 750 ILCS 5/709; 750 ILCS 5/710
Registered foreign orders, contesting validity or enforcement, 750 ILCS 22/606
Trade organizations, income withholding, 750 ILCS 5/706.1; 750 ILCS 15/4.1; 750 ILCS 20/26.1
Tribunals, interstate enforcement, 750 ILCS 22/102
Communications between, 750 ILCS 22/317
Defined, 750 ILCS 22/101
Discovery, 750 ILCS 22/318
Uniform Desertion and Nonsupport Act, 750 ILCS 15/1 et seq.
Uniform Interstate Family Support Act, 750 ILCS 22/100 et seq.
Uniform orders, form, S.Ct.Rule 296
Uniform Reciprocal Enforcement of Support Act, 750 ILCS 20/1 et seq.
United Kingdom, convention country designation, 750 ILCS 20/4.1
Vacation of registration of foreign support orders, petition, 750 ILCS 20/40
Venue,
Petitions, filing, 750 ILCS 20/11
Postjudgment proceedings, 750 ILCS 5/511
Visitation, support order conditioned upon, interstate enforcement, 750 ILCS 22/305
Verification, pleadings and documents, interstate enforcement, 750 ILCS 22/311
Withholding of income. Income withholding, generally, ante
Witnesses,
Husband and wife, competency, 750 ILCS 20/22
Interstate enforcement proceedings, 750 ILCS 22/316

SUPPORT ENFORCEMENT AGENCY
Defined, support, interstate enforcement, 750 ILCS 22/101

SUPPORT ORDER
Defined, interstate enforcement, 750 ILCS 22/101

SUPREME COURT
Adoption of persons, rules of court, applicability, 750 ILCS 50/20
Appeal and Review, generally, this index
Dissolution of marriage proceedings, rules, 750 ILCS 5/802
Expedited child support system plan, approval, 750 ILCS 25/4
Habeas Corpus, generally, this index
Review. Appeal and Review, generally, this index
Rules of Court, generally, this index

SUPREME COURT RULES
Rules of Courts, generally, this index

SURETY BONDS
Bonds (Officers and Fiduciaries), generally, this index

SURGEONS
Physicians and Surgeons, generally, this index

SURRENDERED CHILD
Defined, adoption, 750 ILCS 50/18.1

SURVIVING SPOUSE
Husband and Wife, this index

SWEARING
Oaths and Affirmations, generally, this index

SYSTEM
Defined, expedited child support, 750 ILCS 25/3; S.Ct.Rule 100.13

TANGIBLE PERSONAL PROPERTY
Personal Property, generally, this index

TASK FORCES
Domestic violence training and curriculum task force, 750 ILCS 60/306

TAXATION
Dissolution of marriage, property disposition, 750 ILCS 5/503
Income Taxes, generally, this index
Marriages, dissolution, property disposition, 750 ILCS 5/503

TAY–SACHS DISEASE
Medical information brochure, marriage license applicants and others, 750 ILCS 5/204

TEACHERS
Schoolteachers, generally, this index

TELECOMMUNICATIONS
Children and minors,
  Abused or neglected children, reports, toll free telephone numbers, 325 ILCS 5/7
Eavesdropping. Wiretapping and Eavesdropping, generally, this index
Interception, 18 U.S.C.A. § 2511
  Damages, 18 U.S.C.A. § 2520
  Evidence, 18 U.S.C.A. § 2515
  Injunctions, 18 U.S.C.A. § 2521
Toll-free telephone numbers,
  Child abuse reports, 325 ILCS 5/7
Wiretapping and Eavesdropping, generally, this index

TEMPORARY PROTECTIVE CUSTODY
Defined, abused or neglected children, reports, 325 ILCS 5/3
Medical emergencies, children, 325 ILCS 5/5

TEMPORARY RESTRAINING ORDERS
Injunctions, this index

TEMPORARY SUPPORT AND MAINTENANCE
Dissolution of marriage proceedings, 750 ILCS 5/501

TENANCY BY ENTIRETIES
Homesteads, husband and wife, 750 ILCS 65/22

TENDER
Judgments, payments, interest, 735 ILCS 5/2-1303

TESTAMENTS
Wills, generally, this index

TESTIMONY
Depositions, generally, this index
Evidence, generally, this index
Witnesses, generally, this index

TESTS
AIDS, this index
Blood tests, prevention of prenatal syphilis. Venereal Diseases, generally, this index

THERAPISTS
Counseling and Counselors, generally, this index
Defined, Mental Health and Developmental Disabilities Confidentiality Act, 740 ILCS 110/2

THIRD PARTIES
Injunctions, 735 ILCS 5/11-107

THREATS
  See, also, Duress or Coercion, generally, this index
Child abduction, offenses, 720 ILCS 5/10-5

TIME
Adoption proceedings, consent or surrender, 750 ILCS 50/9

TIME—Cont'd
Breach of marriage promise, commencement of action for, 740 ILCS 15/6
Change of venue, 735 ILCS 5/2-1001.5
Child support, expedited rules, S.Ct. **Rule 100.1 et seq.**
Desertion of spouse, computation of desertion period, dissolution of marriage, or legal separation, 750 ILCS 5/401
Dissolution of marriage. Marriage, this index
Injunctions, temporary restraining orders, 735 ILCS 5/11-101
Orders of court,
  Relief, 735 ILCS 5/2-1401
Paternity proceedings, 750 ILCS 45/8
Process, 735 ILCS 5/2-202
  Publication notice, 735 ILCS 5/2-207
Temporary restraining orders, 735 ILCS 5/11-101
Venue,
  Change, of, 735 ILCS 5/2-1001.5
  Objections, 735 ILCS 5/2-104

TITLE TO PROPERTY
Deeds and Conveyances, generally, this index
Domestic violence, protection orders, 750 ILCS 60/214
Judgments,
  Relief petition, 735 ILCS 5/2-1401
  Orders of court, relief petition, 735 ILCS 5/2-1401
Partition, generally, this index

TOLL-FREE TELEPHONE NUMBERS
Telecommunications, this index

TOLLING
Judgments, relief, 735 ILCS 5/2-1401
Orders of court, relief, 735 ILCS 5/2-1401

TORTS
Children and minors, Parental Responsibility Law, 740 ILCS 115/1 et seq.
Damages,
  Recovery, spouse, 750 ILCS 65/4
Dissolution of marriage, evidence, 750 ILCS 65/1
Husband and wife, actions, 750 ILCS 65/0.01 et seq.
Parental Responsibility Law, 740 ILCS 115/1 et seq.
Process, 735 ILCS 5/2-209
Rights of married persons, 750 ILCS 65/0.01 et seq.
Spouses, 750 ILCS 65/1

TOWNS
Municipalities, generally, this index

TOWNSHIPS
  See, also, Municipalities, generally, this index

TOWNSHIPS—Cont'd
Actions and proceedings,
  Parental Responsibility Law, 740 ILCS 115/1 et seq.
  Uniform Reciprocal Enforcement of Support Act, 750 ILCS 20/8
Children and minors,
  Parental Responsibility Law, action by township, 740 ILCS 115/1 et seq.

TRADE ORGANIZATIONS
Support, income withholding, 750 ILCS 5/706.1; 750 ILCS 15/4.1; 750 ILCS 20/26.1

TRAFFIC RULES AND REGULATIONS
Abandoned vehicles,
  Summons, municipalities of 500,000 or more, 735 ILCS 5/2-203; 735 ILCS 5/2-203.1
Parking,
  Summons, municipalities of 500,000 or more, 735 ILCS 5/2-203; 735 ILCS 5/2-203.1
Process,
  Parking or standing, summons, 735 ILCS 5/2-203; 735 ILCS 5/2-203.1
Summons,
  Parked or standing vehicles, 735 ILCS 5/2-203; 735 ILCS 5/2-203.1

TRANSCRIPTS OF RECORD
Change of venue, 735 ILCS 5/2-1001.5
Child custody proceedings, certified copies, foreign courts, 750 ILCS 35/20
Venue, change of venue, 735 ILCS 5/2-1001.5

TRAVELING EXPENSES
Child custody proceedings. Uniform Child Custody Jurisdiction Act, this index
Process, outside county, 735 ILCS 5/2-202
Uniform Child Custody Jurisdiction Act, this index

TRIAL
Generally, 735 ILCS 5/2-1301 et seq.
Burden of proof, generally. Evidence, this index
Dismissal of Actions, generally, this index
Dissolution of marriage, jury, 750 ILCS 5/103
Evidence, generally, this index
Instructions to Jury, generally, this index
Judgments, generally, this index
Jury, generally, this index
Motions, generally, this index
Pleadings, generally, this index
Rehearing, motion, 735 ILCS 5/2-1203
Summary Judgments, generally, this index

TRIAL

TRIAL—Cont'd
Transcripts of Record, generally, this index
Venue, generally, this index
Witnesses, generally, this index

TRIBUNAL
Defined, support, interstate enforcement, 750 ILCS 22/101

TRUST DEEDS
Default,
 Notice, foreclosure judgments, 735 ILCS 5/2–1302
Foreclosures,
 Default judgments, notice, 735 ILCS 5/2–1302
Notice,
 Default judgments, foreclosure, 735 ILCS 5/2–1302
Redemptions, foreclosure notices, 735 ILCS 5/2–1302

TRUSTS AND TRUSTEES
Dissolution in marriage, property disposition, 750 ILCS 5/503
Husband and wife, premarital agreements, 750 ILCS 10/4
Income, taxation, divorce or separation, 26 U.S.C.A. § 682
Jurisdiction, 735 ILCS 5/2–209
Marriage, dissolution, property disposition, 750 ILCS 5/503

UNCLES
Marriages, 750 ILCS 5/212

UNDETERMINED REPORT
Defined,
 Abused or neglected children, reports, 325 ILCS 5/3

UNDUE INFLUENCE
Change of venue, 735 ILCS 5/2–1001.5

UNFIT PERSONS
Defined, adoption of children, 750 ILCS 50/1

UNFOUNDED REPORT
Defined, abused or neglected children, reports, 325 ILCS 5/3

UNIFORM CHILD CUSTODY JURISDICTION ACT
Generally, 750 ILCS 35/1 et seq.
Abduction, 750 ILCS 35/15
 Decline of jurisdiction, 750 ILCS 35/9
 Foreign judgments, registration, communications or documents, 750 ILCS 35/17
 Judgments, entry, 750 ILCS 35/15
Actions, simultaneous proceedings in foreign states, exercise of jurisdiction, 750 ILCS 35/7
Affidavits,
 Information from parties, 750 ILCS 35/10
 Proof of service, 750 ILCS 35/6
Appearance,
 Court order, 750 ILCS 35/21

UNIFORM CHILD CUSTODY JURISDICTION ACT—Cont'd
Appearance—Cont'd
 Parties and child, court order, 750 ILCS 35/12; 750 ILCS 35/20
Application of law, international application, 750 ILCS 35/24
Assistance, courts of other states, 750 ILCS 35/21
Attorneys fees,
 Guardian ad litem, assessment, 750 ILCS 35/12
 Inconvenient forum, 750 ILCS 35/8
 Judgment violations, 750 ILCS 35/16
 Jurisdiction declined, wrongful conduct, 750 ILCS 35/9
Calendar priority, jurisdiction questions, 750 ILCS 35/25
Certified copies,
 Custody judgments, 750 ILCS 35/18
 Foreign custody judgments, filing, 750 ILCS 35/16
 Transcripts, foreign court, 750 ILCS 35/20
Circuit courts, determination of jurisdiction, 750 ILCS 35/4
Construction, 750 ILCS 35/2
Costs,
 Charging petitioner inconvenient forum, 750 ILCS 35/8
 Documents and proceedings, foreign courts, 750 ILCS 35/20
 Judgment violations, 750 ILCS 35/16
 Jurisdiction declined, wrongful conduct, 750 ILCS 35/9
Court orders,
 Appearance,
  Foreign state, 750 ILCS 35/20; 750 ILCS 35/21
  Parties and child, 750 ILCS 35/12
Custodian, additional party, joinder, 750 ILCS 35/11
Decline of jurisdiction, 750 ILCS 35/9
Decrees. Judgments and decrees, generally, post
Definitions, 750 ILCS 35/3 et seq.
Depositions, taking in other state, 750 ILCS 35/19
Dismissal of proceedings, inconvenient forum, 750 ILCS 35/8
Dissolution of marriage, retention or jurisdiction over proceeding, 750 ILCS 35/8
Documents, preservation, 750 ILCS 35/22
Duty of parties, information regarding other proceedings, 750 ILCS 35/10
Expenses and expenditures,
 Inconvenient forum, 750 ILCS 35/8
 Judgment violations, 750 ILCS 35/16
 Jurisdiction declined, wrongful conduct, 750 ILCS 35/9
 Order to appear in foreign state, 750 ILCS 35/21

UNIFORM CHILD CUSTODY JURISDICTION ACT—Cont'd
Fee,
 Certified copies, judgments, 750 ILCS 35/18
 Registration of out-of-state judgments, communications or documents, 750 ILCS 35/17
Foreign countries, international application of law, 750 ILCS 35/24
Guardian ad litem, appointment, 750 ILCS 35/12
Hearings, foreign courts, 750 ILCS 35/20
Home state, residence of child, determination of jurisdiction, 750 ILCS 35/4
Inconvenient forum, 750 ILCS 35/8
Joinder, additional parties, 750 ILCS 35/11
Judgments and decrees,
 Certified copies, 750 ILCS 35/18
 Filing and enforcement, 750 ILCS 35/16
 Modification, foreign state judgments, 750 ILCS 35/15
 Out-of-state custody judgments, Recognition, 750 ILCS 35/14
 Registry, 750 ILCS 35/17
 Registry, out-of-state custody judgments, 750 ILCS 35/17
 Res judicata effect, 750 ILCS 35/13
Mail and mailing, service process, nonresidence, 750 ILCS 35/6
Marriage, dissolution, retention of jurisdiction, 750 ILCS 35/8
Modification, judgments, foreign states, 750 ILCS 35/15
Motions, inconvenient forum, 750 ILCS 35/8
Notice,
 Dismissal or stay, informing foreign court, 750 ILCS 35/8
 Prejudgment notice, contestants, parents or custodians, 750 ILCS 35/5
Oaths and affirmations, information from party, 750 ILCS 35/10
Orders. Court orders, generally, ante
Parties,
 Additional parties, joinder, 750 ILCS 35/11
 Court order, appearance, 750 ILCS 35/12; 750 ILCS 35/20
 Duty, informing court of other proceedings, 750 ILCS 35/10
 Informing court of other proceedings, 750 ILCS 35/10
Petitioner, wrongful conduct, decline of jurisdiction, 750 ILCS 35/9
Physical presence of child, jurisdiction determination, 750 ILCS 35/4
Preservation, documents, 750 ILCS 35/22
Priority, jurisdiction questions, 750 ILCS 35/25
Process, notice, nonresidents, 750 ILCS 35/6
Proof of service, 750 ILCS 35/6
Purposes, 750 ILCS 35/2

UNIFORM CHILD CUSTODY JURISDICTION ACT—Cont'd

Reciprocity, recognition and enforcement of out-of-state custody judgments, 750 ILCS 35/14
Records, preservation, 750 ILCS 35/22; 750 ILCS 35/23
Registry, out-of-state custody judgments and proceedings, 750 ILCS 35/17
Res judicata, effect of judgment, 750 ILCS 35/13
Residence, home state determination, 750 ILCS 35/4
Service of process, nonresidents, 750 ILCS 35/6
Simultaneous proceedings in other states, exercise of jurisdiction, 750 ILCS 35/7
Stay of proceedings, simultaneous proceedings in foreign state, 750 ILCS 35/7
Studies, foreign courts, 750 ILCS 35/20; 750 ILCS 35/21
Supersedeas or stay, simultaneous proceeding in other state, 750 ILCS 35/7
Testimony, deposition in other state, 750 ILCS 35/19
Transcripts, 750 ILCS 35/23
  Certified copies from foreign courts, 750 ILCS 35/20
  Foreign courts, 750 ILCS 35/20
Traveling expenses,
  Appearance, parties and child, 750 ILCS 35/12; 750 ILCS 35/20
  Court order to appear in other state, 750 ILCS 35/21
Inconvenient forum, 750 ILCS 35/8
Judgment violations, 750 ILCS 35/16
Jurisdiction declined, wrongful conduct, 750 ILCS 35/9
Wrongful conduct, decline of jurisdiction, 750 ILCS 35/9

UNIFORM DESERTION AND NONSUPPORT ACT
Generally, 750 ILCS 15/1 et seq.

UNIFORM ENFORCEMENT OF FOREIGN JUDGMENTS ACT
Generally, 735 ILCS 5/12–650 et seq.

UNIFORM INTERSTATE FAMILY SUPPORT ACT
Generally, 750 ILCS 22/100 et seq.

UNIFORM LAWS
Child Custody Jurisdiction Act, 750 ILCS 35/1 et seq.
Declaratory Judgments Act, 735 ILCS 5/2–701
Desertion and Nonsupport Act, 750 ILCS 15/1 et seq.
Enforcement of Foreign Judgments Act, 735 ILCS 5/12–651 et seq.
Foreign Money Claims Act, 735 ILCS 5/12–654 et seq.
Marriage and Dissolution of Marriage Act, 750 ILCS 5/101 et seq.

UNIFORM LAWS—Cont'd
Parentage Act, 750 ILCS 45/1 et seq.
Premarital agreement Act, 750 ILCS 10/1 et seq.
Reciprocal Enforcement of Support Act, 750 ILCS 20/1 et seq.
Support, uniform interstate family support, 750 ILCS 22/100 et seq.

UNIFORM PREMARITAL AGREEMENT ACT
Generally, 750 ILCS 10/1 et seq.

UNIFORM RECIPROCAL ENFORCEMENT OF SUPPORT ACT
Generally, 750 ILCS 20/1 et seq.
Support, generally, this index

UNITED KINGDOM
State, designation as convention country, 750 ILCS 20/4.1

UNITED STATES
Support, enforcement, withholding of income, 750 ILCS 5/706.1; 750 ILCS 15/4.1; 750 ILCS 20/26.1

UNITED STATES SECRET SERVICE
Mentally or developmentally disabled persons, disclosures, confidential information, 740 ILCS 110/12; 740 ILCS 110/12.2

UNJUST ENRICHMENT
Breach of marriage promise, actions, 740 ILCS 15/1

VACATING OR SETTING ASIDE
Default judgments, 735 ILCS 5/2–1301
  Personal service outside state, 735 ILCS 5/2–208
Orders of court, 735 ILCS 5/2–1301
  Relief, petition, 735 ILCS 5/2–1401
Relief petition, 735 ILCS 5/2–1401

VANDALISM
Parental Responsibility Law, 740 ILCS 115/1 et seq.

VEHICLES
Motor Vehicles, generally, this index

VENEREAL DISEASES
AIDS, generally, this index
Dissolution of marriage, grounds, 750 ILCS 5/401
Medical information brochure, marriage license applicants and others, 750 ILCS 5/204

VENUE
Adoption of children, 750 ILCS 50/4
Affidavits, transfer of causes, motions, 735 ILCS 5/2–104
Attorneys fees, transfer of causes, 735 ILCS 5/2–107
Certificates and certification, transfer of causes, 735 ILCS 5/2–106

VENUE—Cont'd
Change of venue, 735 ILCS 5/2–1001.5
  Affidavits, 735 ILCS 5/2–1001.5
  Application, 735 ILCS 5/2–1001.5
  Bias or prejudice, 735 ILCS 5/2–1001.5
  Causes, 735 ILCS 5/2–1001.5
  Conditions, 735 ILCS 5/2–1001.5
  Consent, 735 ILCS 5/2–1001.5
  Costs, 735 ILCS 5/2–1001.5
  Court, 735 ILCS 5/2–1001.5
  Docketing, 735 ILCS 5/2–1001.5
  Eminent domain, records, 735 ILCS 5/2–1001.5
  Expenses and expenditures, 735 ILCS 5/2–1001.5
  Irregularities, waiver, 735 ILCS 5/2–1001.5
  Judgments, transcript, 735 ILCS 5/2–1001.5
  Notice, 735 ILCS 5/2–1001.5
  Orders of court, 735 ILCS 5/2–1001.5
  Petitions, 735 ILCS 5/2–1001.5
  Prejudice, 735 ILCS 5/2–1001.5
  Records, 735 ILCS 5/2–1001.5
  Time, 735 ILCS 5/2–1001.5
  Transcripts, 735 ILCS 5/2–1001.5
  Undue influence, 735 ILCS 5/2–1001.5
  Verdict, waiver of irregularities, 735 ILCS 5/2–1001.5
  Waiver, irregularities, 735 ILCS 5/2–1001.5
Confession of judgment, 735 ILCS 5/2–1301
  Wrong venue, 735 ILCS 5/2–104
Costs, transfer of causes, 735 ILCS 5/2–107
Dissolution of marriage, 750 ILCS 5/104
  Post judgment venue, 750 ILCS 5/512
Domestic violence, protection orders, 750 ILCS 60/209
Expenses and expenditures, transfer of causes, 735 ILCS 5/2–107
Filing, transfer of causes, 735 ILCS 5/2–106
Guardianship or conservatorship, Proceedings for appointment, 755 ILCS 5/11–6
Improper, 735 ILCS 5/2–104
Juvenile Delinquents and Dependents, this index
Motions, transfer of causes, 735 ILCS 5/2–104 et seq.
Nonresidents, this index
Objections and exceptions, improper venue, 735 ILCS 5/2–104
Orders of court, transfer of causes, cost and expenses, 735 ILCS 5/2–107
Paternity proceedings, 750 ILCS 45/9
Severance, transfer of causes, 735 ILCS 5/2–106
Support petitions, filing, Uniform Reciprocal Enforcement of Support Act, 750 ILCS 20/11
Time, objections, 735 ILCS 5/2–104

VENUE

VENUE—Cont'd
Transfer of causes, 735 ILCS 5/2-106; 735 ILCS 5/2-107
Improper venue, 735 ILCS 5/2-104
Waiver, improper venue, 735 ILCS 5/2-104
Wrong venue, 735 ILCS 5/2-104
  Transfer of causes, 735 ILCS 5/2-106; 735 ILCS 5/2-107

VERDICTS
Change of venue, waiver, irregularities, 735 ILCS 5/2-1001.5

VERIFICATION
Adoption of children, petition, 750 ILCS 50/8
Affidavit, verification by certification, 735 ILCS 5/1-109
Answer to,
  Verification by certification, 735 ILCS 5/1-109
Bill of particulars,
  Verification by certification, 735 ILCS 5/1-109
Certification, verification by certification, 735 ILCS 5/1-109
Change of venue, petition, 735 ILCS 5/2-1001.5
Complaints,
  Verification by certification, 735 ILCS 5/1-109
Documents, verification by certification, 735 ILCS 5/1-109
Oaths and affirmations, verification by certification, 735 ILCS 5/1-109
Petition,
  Verification by certification, 735 ILCS 5/1-109
Petition, adoption, 750 ILCS 50/5
Pleadings,
  Verification by certification, 735 ILCS 5/1-109
Process, service, verification by certification, 735 ILCS 5/1-109
Support, interstate enforcement, pleadings and documents, 750 ILCS 22/311
Venue, change of venue, petition, 735 ILCS 5/2-1001.5
Verification by certification, 735 ILCS 5/1-109

VETERANS ADMINISTRATION
Appointment of guardian procedure, costs, 755 ILCS 5/11-11

VILLAGES
Municipalities, generally, this index

VIOLENCE
Domestic Violence, generally, this index

VISITATION
Adopted children, death of parents, 755 ILCS 5/11-7.1
Children and minors,
  Abuse and enforcement, 750 ILCS 5/607.1

VISITATION—Cont'd
Children and minors—Cont'd
  Death of parents, visitation rights of grandparents, 755 ILCS 5/11-7.1
  Interference, 720 ILCS 5/10-5.5
  Contempt, 750 ILCS 5/607.1
Crimes and offenses, interference with visitation, 720 ILCS 5/10-5.5
Dissolution of marriages, 750 ILCS 5/607
Grandparents, children, death of parents, 755 ILCS 5/11-7.1
Interference, 720 ILCS 5/10-5.5
  Contempt, 750 ILCS 5/607.1
Juvenile Delinquents and Dependents, this index
Paternity. Children Born Out of Wedlock, this index
Relatives, children, death of parents, 755 ILCS 5/11-7.1
Support, conditioned upon, interstate enforcement, 750 ILCS 22/305

VITAL STATISTICS
Registration of births and deaths, Certificate,
  Adoption, 750 ILCS 50/19

WAGE ASSIGNMENTS
Compensation and Salaries, this index

WAGES
Compensation and Salaries, generally, this index

WAIVER
Adoption of Children, this index
Appeal and Review, this index
Change of venue, verdict, 735 ILCS 5/2-1001.5
Juvenile Delinquents and Dependents, this index
Marriages, dissolution, living apart and separate, grounds, 750 ILCS 5/401
Venue, improper venue, 735 ILCS 5/2-104

WEAPONS
Child abduction, aggravating factors, 720 ILCS 5/10-5
Disclosures,
  Firearm owners identification cards, immunity, 740 ILCS 110/12
Evidence,
  Presumptions, disclosures, firearm owners identification cards, 740 ILCS 110/12
Mentally ill persons,
  Disclosures, firearm owners identification cards, 740 ILCS 110/12
Presumptions,
  Mentally ill persons, disclosures, firearm owners identification cards, 740 ILCS 110/12
Privileges and immunities,
  Mental health disclosures, firearm owners identification cards, 740 ILCS 110/12

WELFARE
Social Services, generally, this index

WIDOWS AND WIDOWERS
Descent and Distribution, generally, this index

WIFE
Husband and Wife, generally, this index

WIFE ABANDONMENT ACT
Generally, 750 ILCS 15/1 et seq.

WILLFUL DEPRIVATION
Defined, domestic violence, 750 ILCS 60/103

WILLS
Children and minors,
  Guardian, parent of unmarried minor nominated by will, 755 ILCS 5/11-5
  Legitimacy, artificially inseminated children, 750 ILCS 40/1 et seq.
Construction, declaratory judgments, 735 ILCS 5/2-701
Declaratory judgments, construction, 735 ILCS 5/2-701
Dissolution of marriage, 755 ILCS 5/4-7
Future Interests, generally, this index
Guardian of minor, parent of unmarried minor nominated by will, 755 ILCS 5/11-5
Premarital agreements, 750 ILCS 10/4
Probate Proceedings, generally, this index

WIRETAPPING AND EAVESDROPPING
Generally, 720 ILCS 5/14-1 et seq; 18 U.S.C.A. § 2510 et seq.
Interception, 18 U.S.C.A. § 2511
Damages, 18 U.S.C.A. § 2520
Evidence, 18 U.S.C.A. § 2515
Injunctions, 18 U.S.C.A. § 2521

WITHHOLDING
Compensation and Salaries, this index
Paternity proceedings, income, 750 ILCS 45/20

WITNESSES
Adverse parties or agent,
  Examination, 735 ILCS 5/2-1102
Agents,
  Examination, 735 ILCS 5/2-1102
Children and Minors, this index
Communications,
  Privileged communications, 735 ILCS 5/8-801 et seq.
Cross-examination,
  Adverse parties, 735 ILCS 5/2-1102
Depositions, generally, this index
Evidence, generally, this index
Experts, S.Ct.Rule 220
  Paternity proceedings,
    Blood tests, 750 ILCS 45/11
    Tests, 750 ILCS 45/11
Husband and Wife, this index

WORDS

WITNESSES—Cont'd
Impeachment,
Adverse party or agent, examination, 735 ILCS 5/2-1102
Paternity proceedings, expert testimony,
Blood tests, 750 ILCS 45/11
Tests, 750 ILCS 45/11
Perjury, generally, this index
Prior inconsistent statements, 735 ILCS 5/2-1102
Privileged communications, 735 ILCS 5/8-801 et seq.
Rules of Court, this index
Spouse, privileged communications, 735 ILCS 5/8-801
Support, interstate enforcement proceedings, 750 ILCS 22/316
Wife. Husband and Wife, this index

WOMEN
Abuse. Domestic Violence, generally, this index
Domestic Violence, generally, this index
Included in term male, adoption of children, 750 ILCS 50/1
Pregnancy, generally, this index
Protection Orders, generally. Domestic Violence, this index
Sexual Assault, generally, this index
Violence. Domestic Violence, generally, this index

WORDS AND PHRASES
Ability of the parents to cooperate, joint custody of children, 750 ILCS 5/602.1
Abuse,
Domestic violence, 750 ILCS 60/103
Abused child,
Adoption, 750 ILCS 50/1
Reports, 325 ILCS 5/3
Act,
Expedited child support, S.Ct. Rule 100.13
Acted, adoption of children,
Property rights, construction of instruments, 760 ILCS 30/1
Administrative expense,
Expedited child support, 750 ILCS 25/3
Administrative hearing officer, expedited child support, 750 ILCS 25/3; S.Ct.Rule 100.13
Adoption disruption,
Adoption of children, 750 ILCS 50/1
Adult with disabilities,
Domestic violence, 750 ILCS 60/103
Agency,
Adoption of children, 750 ILCS 50/1
Agent,
Mental health and Developmental Disabilities Confidentiality Act, 740 ILCS 110/2
Arrearage,
Paternity proceedings, withholding of income, 750 ILCS 45/20

WORDS AND PHRASES—Cont'd
Arrearage—Cont'd
Support, 750 ILCS 5/706.1; 750 ILCS 15/4.1; 750 ILCS 20/26.1
Expedited, 750 ILCS 25/3
Child,
Abduction, 720 ILCS 5/10-5
Abused and neglected children, reports, 325 ILCS 5/3
Adoption of children, 750 ILCS 50/1
Support, interstate enforcement, 750 ILCS 22/101
Child protective service unit, abused or neglected children, reports, 325 ILCS 5/3
Child support order, interstate enforcement, 750 ILCS 22/101
Child support payment, mandatory payments, 750 ILCS 5/709
Close relative adoption, visitation, 755 ILCS 5/11-7.1
Communications, Mental Health and Developmental Disabilities Confidentiality Act, 740 ILCS 110/2
Confidential communication,
Domestic violence counselors, 750 ILCS 60/227
Mental Health and Developmental Disabilities Confidentiality Act, 740 ILCS 110/2
Contestant, Uniform Child Custody Jurisdiction Act, 750 ILCS 35/3.01
Conversion,
Foreign money claims, 735 ILCS 5/12-655
Conversion date, foreign money claims, 735 ILCS 5/12-655
Counseling, family preservation services, abused and neglected children, 325 ILCS 5/8.2
Court,
Uniform Reciprocal Enforcement of Support Act, 750 ILCS 20/2
Custody determination, Uniform Child Custody Jurisdiction Act, 750 ILCS 35/3.02
Custody judgment, Uniform Child Custody Jurisdiction Act, 750 ILCS 35/3.06
Custody proceedings, Uniform Child Custody Jurisdiction Act, 750 ILCS 35/3.03
Customer,
Plastic dies and molds ownership transfers, 750 ILCS 5/202
Day care, family preservation services, abused and neglected children, 325 ILCS 5/8.2
Delinquency,
Paternity proceedings, withholding of income, 750 ILCS 45/20
Support, 750 ILCS 5/706.1; 750 ILCS 15/4.1; 750 ILCS 20/26.1
Department,
Abused and neglected children, reports, 325 ILCS 5/3
Dependent, income taxes, 26 U.S.C.A. § 152

WORDS AND PHRASES—Cont'd
Developmental disabilities,
Records, 740 ILCS 110/8.1
Domestic violence, 750 ILCS 60/103
Confidential or privileged information, 750 ILCS 60/227
Domestic violence advocate or counselor, confidential or privileged information, 750 ILCS 60/227
Domestic violence victim, advocates and counselors, confidential or privileged information, 750 ILCS 60/227
Duty of support,
Interstate enforcement, 750 ILCS 22/101
Uniform Reciprocal Enforcement of Support Act, 750 ILCS 20/2
Elder adult with disabilities, domestic violence, 750 ILCS 60/103
Emergency assistance and advocacy, family preservation services, abused and neglected children, 325 ILCS 5/8.2
Expedited child support hearing, 750 ILCS 25/3
Expedited child support, S.Ct. Rule 100.13
Exploitation,
Domestic violence victims, 720 ILCS 5/45-1; 750 ILCS 60/103
Failure to make reasonable progress toward the return of the child to the parents, adoption, 750 ILCS 50/1
Family members,
Domestic violence, 750 ILCS 60/103
Family preservation services, abused and neglected children, 325 ILCS 5/8.2
Federal time frames, expedited child support, 750 ILCS 25/3
Foreign judgment,
Enforcement, 735 ILCS 5/12-651
Forensic recipient,
Mental health and developmental disability confidentiality, 740 ILCS 110/12.2
Governor,
Uniform Reciprocal Enforcement of Support Act, 750 ILCS 20/2
Guardian,
Emancipation of Mature Minors Act, 750 ILCS 30/3-4
Mental Health and Developmental Disabilities Confidentiality Act, 740 ILCS 110/2
Harassment,
Domestic violence, 750 ILCS 60/103
Head of household, income taxes, 26 U.S.C.A. § 2(b)
High-risk adult with disabilities, domestic violence, 720 ILCS 5/45-1; 750 ILCS 60/103
Home state,
Support, interstate enforcement, 750 ILCS 22/101
Uniform Child Custody Jurisdiction Act, 750 ILCS 35/3.04

WORDS

WORDS AND PHRASES—Cont'd
Homemaker, family preservation services, abused and neglected children, 325 ILCS 5/8.2
Hospital,
  Mental Health and Developmental Disabilities Confidentiality Act, 740 ILCS 110/12
Identifying information, mental health and developmental disability confidentiality, 740 ILCS 110/12.2
Immediate relatives, adoption of children, 750 ILCS 50/1
In need of mental treatment, adoption of persons, 750 ILCS 50/1
Income,
  Paternity proceedings, withholding of income, 750 ILCS 45/20
  Support, 750 ILCS 5/706.1; 750 ILCS 15/4.1; 750 ILCS 20/26.1
  Interstate enforcement, 750 ILCS 22/101
Income-withholding order, support, interstate enforcement, 750 ILCS 22/101
Initial judgment, Uniform Child Custody Jurisdiction Act, 750 ILCS 35/3.05
Initiating court, Uniform Reciprocal Enforcement of Support Act, 750 ILCS 20/2
Initiating state,
  Support, interstate enforcement, 750 ILCS 22/101
  Uniform Reciprocal Enforcement of Support Act, 750 ILCS 20/2
Initiating tribunal, support, interstate enforcement, 750 ILCS 22/101
Intercounty adoption,
  Adoption of children, 750 ILCS 50/1
Intercounty adoption coordinator,
  Adoption of children, 750 ILCS 50/1
Interference with personal liberty,
  Domestic violence, 750 ILCS 60/103
Interstate compact on the placement of children,
  Adoption of children, 750 ILCS 50/1
Intimidation of a dependent,
  Domestic violence, 750 ILCS 60/103
Issuing state, support, interstate enforcement, 750 ILCS 22/101
Issuing tribunal, support, interstate enforcement, 750 ILCS 22/101
IV-D program, expedited child support, 750 ILCS 25/3; S.Ct.Rule 100.13
Judge,
  Uniform Child Custody Jurisdiction Act, 750 ILCS 35/3.06
Judgment,
  Uniform Child Custody Jurisdiction Act, 750 ILCS 35/3.06
Law,
  Uniform Reciprocal Enforcement of Support Act, 750 ILCS 20/2

WORDS AND PHRASES—Cont'd
Law enforcement agency,
  Mental health and developmental disability confidentiality, 740 ILCS 110/12.2
Legal guardian,
  Parental Responsibility Law, 740 ILCS 115/2
Local law enforcement agency,
  Abused and neglected children, reports, 325 ILCS 5/3
Marital property, dissolution of marriage, 750 ILCS 5/503
Mature minor, emancipation, 750 ILCS 30/3-2
Medical support, expedited child support, 750 ILCS 25/3
Mental health or developmental disability services,
  Confidential communications, 740 ILCS 110/2
Mentally deficient,
  Adoption of children, 750 ILCS 50/1
Mentally ill,
  Adoption of children, 750 ILCS 50/1
Mentally retarded,
  Adoption of persons, 750 ILCS 50/1
Minors, 755 ILCS 5/11-1
  Emancipation of Mature Minors Act, 750 ILCS 30/3-1
  Parental Responsibility Law, 740 ILCS 115/2
  Probate Act of 1975, 755 ILCS 5/11-1
Modification judgment, Uniform Child Custody Jurisdiction Act, 750 ILCS 35/3.07
Molder, plastic dies and molds ownership transfers, 750 ILCS 5/202
Neglect,
  Domestic violence, 750 ILCS 60/103
Neglected child,
  Adoption, 750 ILCS 50/1
  Reports, 325 ILCS 5/3
Net income,
  Support, 750 ILCS 5/505; 750 ILCS 45/14
Non-compact state,
  Adoption of children, 750 ILCS 50/1
Nonmarital property, dissolution of marriage, 750 ILCS 5/503
Notice date, adoption of children,
  Property rights, construction of instruments, 760 ILCS 30/1
Obligee,
  Enforcement of support orders, S.Ct.Rule 296
  Paternity proceedings, withholding of income, 750 ILCS 45/20
  Support, 750 ILCS 5/706.1; 750 ILCS 15/4.1; 750 ILCS 20/26.1
  Expedited, 750 ILCS 25/3
  Health insurance, 750 ILCS 5/505.2
  Interstate enforcement, 750 ILCS 22/101

WORDS AND PHRASES—Cont'd
Obligee—Cont'd
  Uniform Reciprocal Enforcement of Support Act, 750 ILCS 20/2
Obligor,
  Enforcement of support orders, S.Ct.Rule 296
  Paternity proceedings, withholding of income, 750 ILCS 45/20
  Support, 750 ILCS 5/706.1; 750 ILCS 15/4.1; 750 ILCS 20/26.1
  Expedited, 750 ILCS 25/3
  Health insurance, 750 ILCS 5/505.2
  Interstate enforcement, 750 ILCS 22/101
  Uniform Reciprocal Enforcement of Support Act, 750 ILCS 20/2
Order for support, 750 ILCS 5/706.1; 750 ILCS 15/4.1; 750 ILCS 20/26.1
  Enforcement of support orders, S.Ct.Rule 296
  Paternity proceedings, withholding of income, 750 ILCS 45/20
Order of protection,
  Domestic violence, 750 ILCS 60/103
Parent,
  Adoption of children, 750 ILCS 50/1
  Emancipation of Mature Minors Act, 750 ILCS 30/3-3
  Mental Health and Developmental Disabilities Confidentiality Act, 740 ILCS 110/2
Patient,
  Mental Health and Developmental Disabilities Confidentiality Act, 740 ILCS 110/12
Payments,
  Mandatory child support payments, 750 ILCS 5/709
Payor,
  Enforcement of support orders, S.Ct.Rule 296
  Paternity proceedings, withholding of income, 750 ILCS 45/20
  Support, 750 ILCS 5/706.1; 750 ILCS 15/4.1; 750 ILCS 20/26.1
Perpetrator, abused and neglected children, reports, 325 ILCS 5/3
Person acting as parent, Uniform Child Custody Jurisdiction Act, 750 ILCS 35/3.09
Person responsible for the child's welfare,
  Abused or neglected children, reports, 325 ILCS 5/3
Personal notes, Mental Health and Developmental Disabilities Confidentiality Act, 740 ILCS 110/2
Petition,
  Emancipation of Mature Minors Act, 750 ILCS 30/3-5
Petitioner,
  Domestic violence, 750 ILCS 60/103
Physical abuse,
  Domestic violence, 750 ILCS 60/103

X-RAY

WORDS AND PHRASES—Cont'd
Physical custody, Uniform Child Custody Jurisdiction Act, 750 ILCS 35/3.08

Plan,
  Expedited child support, 750 ILCS 25/3; S.Ct.Rule 100.13

Preadoption,
  Adoption of children, 750 ILCS 50/1

Pre-hearing motions, expedited child support, 750 ILCS 25/3

Premarital agreements, 750 ILCS 10/2

Premiums,
  Support,
    Income withholding, health insurance,
      Marriage and dissolution, 750 ILCS 5/706.1
      NonSupport of spouse and children, 750 ILCS 15/4.1
      Parentage, 750 ILCS 45/20
    Uniform reciprocal enforcement of support, 750 ILCS 20/26.1

Property,
  Premarital agreements, 750 ILCS 10/2

Prosecuting attorney, Uniform Reciprocal Enforcement of Support Act, 750 ILCS 20/2

Public office,
  Paternity proceedings, withholding of income, 750 ILCS 45/20
  Support, 750 ILCS 5/706.1; 750 ILCS 15/4.1; 750 ILCS 20/26.1
    Health insurance, 750 ILCS 5/505.2

Public official,
  Mental Health and Developmental Disability Confidentiality Act, 740 ILCS 110/12

Qualified domestic relations order, 26 U.S.C.A. § 414(p)

Putative father, adoption of children, 750 ILCS 50/1

Reasonable living expenses, adoption, biological parents, payment by petitioners, 720 ILCS 525/4.1

Recipient,
  Mental Health and Developmental Disabilities Confidentiality Act, 740 ILCS 110/2

Recommendations, expedited child support, 750 ILCS 25/3

WORDS AND PHRASES—Cont'd
Record,
  Mental Health and Developmental Disabilities Confidentiality Act, 740 ILCS 110/2

Record custodian, Mental Health and Developmental Disabilities Confidentiality Act, 740 ILCS 110/2

Register,
  Support, interstate enforcement, 750 ILCS 22/101
  Uniform Reciprocal Enforcement of Support Act, 750 ILCS 20/2

Registering court, Uniform Reciprocal Enforcement of Support Act, 750 ILCS 20/2

Registering tribunal, support, interstate enforcement, 750 ILCS 22/101

Related child, adoption of children, 750 ILCS 50/1

Rendering state, Uniform Reciprocal Enforcement of Support Act, 750 ILCS 20/2

Requirements,
  Adoption of children, 750 ILCS 50/1

Responding court, Uniform Reciprocal Enforcement of Support Act, 750 ILCS 20/2

Responding state,
  Support, interstate enforcement, 750 ILCS 22/101
  Uniform Reciprocal Enforcement of Support Act, 750 ILCS 20/2

Responding tribunal, support, interstate enforcement, 750 ILCS 22/101

Services,
  Mental Health and Developmental Disabilities Confidentiality Act, 740 ILCS 110/2

Spousal-support order, interstate enforcement, 750 ILCS 22/101

State,
  Support, interstate enforcement, 750 ILCS 22/101
  Uniform Child Custody Jurisdiction Act, 750 ILCS 35/3.10
  Uniform Reciprocal Enforcement of Support Act, 750 ILCS 20/2

Subject of report, abused or neglected children, reports, 325 ILCS 5/3

Subject to involuntary admission, Adoption of children, 750 ILCS 50/1

WORDS AND PHRASES—Cont'd
Support enforcement agency, support, interstate enforcement, 750 ILCS 22/101

Support order,
  Interstate enforcement, 750 ILCS 22/101
  Uniform Reciprocal Enforcement of Support Act, 750 ILCS 20/2

Surrendered child, adoption, 750 ILCS 50/18.1

System,
  Expedited child support, 750 ILCS 25/3; S.Ct.Rule 100.13

Temporary protective custody,
  Abused or neglected children, reports, 325 ILCS 5/3

Therapist, Mental Health and Developmental Disabilities Confidentiality Act, 740 ILCS 110/2

Tribunal, support, interstate enforcement, 750 ILCS 22/101

Unfit person, adoption of children, 750 ILCS 50/1

Uniform Reciprocal Enforcement of Support Act, 750 ILCS 20/2

Willful deprivation,
  Domestic violence, 750 ILCS 60/103

WORK
Labor and Employment, generally, this index

WORKERS' COMPENSATION
Support, enforcement, withholding of income, 750 ILCS 5/706.1; 750 ILCS 15/4.1; 750 ILCS 20/26.1
Withholding of income, support enforcement, 750 ILCS 5/706.1; 750 ILCS 15/4.1; 750 ILCS 20/26.1

WRITS
Abolishment, 735 ILCS 5/2–1501
  Coram nobis and coram nobis, 735 ILCS 5/2–1401
Attachment, generally, this index
Execution. Enforcement of Judgments, generally, this index
Garnishment, generally, this index
Injunctions, generally, this index

WRITTEN INSTRUMENTS
Construction, declaratory judgments, 735 ILCS 5/2–701
Declaratory judgments, construction, 735 ILCS 5/2–701
Process, return, notice, 735 ILCS 5/2–202

X-RAY
Abused or neglected children, investigations, 325 ILCS 5/6
Juvenile Delinquents and Dependents, this index